ECONOMICS

THIRD EDITION

WILLIAM BOYES

Arizona State University

MICHAEL MELVIN

Arizona State University

HOUGHTON MIFFLIN COMPANY   BOSTON   TORONTO
Geneva, Illinois   Palo Alto   Princeton, New Jersey

To our families

W.B.

M.M.

Sponsoring Editor: Bonnie Binkert
Basic Book Editor: Karla Paschkis
Senior Project Editor: Susan Westendorf
Senior Production/Design Coordinator: Carol Merrigan
Senior Manufacturing Coordinator: Marie Barnes

CREDITS

Cover designer: Harold Burch, Harold Burch Design, New York City.
Cover image: illustration by Ken McMillan

Chapter photos: p. 3 © Bob Daemmrich/The Image Works; p. 8 © Robert Frerck/ Odyssey/Chicago; p. 31 © David Butow/Black Star; p. 42 © Cameramann/The Image Works; p. 49 © Enrique Marti/Impact Visuals; p. 50 © Ron McMillan/Gamma-Liaison; p. 50 © David R. Frazier Photolibrary; p. 66 © Robert Frerck/Odyssey/Chicago; p. 81 © Lisa Quinones/Black Star; p. 95 © Paul Chesley/Tony Stone Images; p. 107 © Cameramann International, Ltd.; p. 109 © Porter Gifford/Liaison *(continued on p. C-1)*

Printed in the U.S.A.

Library of Congress Catalog Card Number: 95-76926

ISBN: 0-395-74432-6

EXAMINATION COPY ISBN: 0-395-74657-4

INTERNATIONAL EDITION ISBN: 0-395-77716-X

456789-VH-99 98 97

Preface

When we started work on the first edition of this book we were keenly aware that economics students were not being prepared for the world they would enter upon graduation. Looking at the traditional principles texts and the information our students would need, we saw a gap: the current economic world is vastly different from the one described in most textbooks. Thus, we set out to close that gap by writing a textbook that would give students the tools they would need to understand the world of the present—and the future. In the first edition we integrated the global perspective within the traditional economics principles as much as we believed possible at the time. Events since then have made this approach even more imperative. The Soviet Union has disintegrated, newly independent nations have emerged, and markets have been established where none had existed before. Events in both the developed world and the less-developed world have drawn the United States ever more into the global economy. As a result, both students and instructors embrace the idea that economies are interrelated and that this should be made clear in the study of economics. *Economics* gives students the tools they need to make connections between the economic principles they learn and the world they live in.

From the outset, too, we acknowledged the importance of keeping students interested in what they were reading by making the material accessible and relevant. To this end, we have kept in mind that this text had to:

- Stress the fundamental concepts and carry them through all topics.
- Connect students to the real world through applications and examples.
- Note and explain the deviations and departures from the outcomes predicted in models.
- Provide a framework for understanding and critiquing rather than a prescription for answers.

- Motivate students to engage in further observation and critical thinking.

We feel we've succeeded in this respect when current users of *Economics* report that their students find the book "very interesting," "really easy to understand," and "easy to learn from." We have also discovered that this book has well served students from many different backgrounds and with varying future plans—from those who major in business, psychology, education, engineering, and English, as well as other fields, to those who choose to pursue economics.

Now, in the third edition, we continue to refine and improve the text as a teaching and learning instrument while capitalizing on its international base by updating and adding examples related to global economics throughout.

CHANGES TO THE THIRD EDITION

The third edition of *Economics* has been thoroughly updated, polished, and refined. However, the structure of the text remains the same. The first part of the book covers the price system, including Chapter 5 on the role of government in the market system. Macroeconomic content follows in the next fourteen chapters, followed by microeconomic theory and applications. The last four chapters of the book address issues in international trade and finance. Thanks to many comments from reviewers and users of the text we have been able to make many changes which we feel can only strengthen the book's student appeal. A broad outline of these revisions follows, but we urge you to read the Transition Guide in the IRM for a more detailed accounting of all the changes made in each chapter.

Revised Introductory Material

Although the structure of the first five chapters remains the same, we've rewritten many of the introductions and examples in accordance with reviewers who told us that we needed to work on grabbing students' interest from page 1. For instance, Chapter 3 now begins with a questionnaire which leads into the discussion of the price allocation mechanism and then into markets. A new figure on price allocation is also included in this chapter. Examples focus even more frequently than in previous editions on student-oriented products.

Revised Macroeconomic Coverage

The macroeconomic chapters have been updated to include the latest available economic statistics, in most instances, up through 1994. In many chapters, numerical examples have been revised to provide greater clarity in the graphical presentations. These chapters stress one model—aggregate demand and aggregate supply. The Keynesian aggregate expenditures material is available and thoroughly covered in Chapters 10 and 11 and then is integrated into the aggregate demand model at the end of Chapter 11. Real GDP replaces national income in the macro models and discussion throughout the macro chapters. In addition, Chapter 6 introduces the new U.S. Department of Commerce method for calculating the growth of real GDP which has replaced the old method of calculating a "constant dollar" real GDP. Data on the new "chain-type" real GDP series are included inside the front cover.

Revised Microeconomic Coverage

The microeconomic material includes further refinements toward the objective of enabling students to see the forest while wandering around the trees. A well-known and effective teaching method is to inform your students what you are going to discuss, discuss it, and then review what was discussed. This technique is used to make the difficult material of costs and market structures as accessible to students as possible. Because many reviewers pointed out their preference to cover elasticity directly after supply and demand, Chapters 20 and 21 now appear in reverse order. The new chapter on elasticity includes a clarified discussion of close substitutes and new material on customer loyalty and brand names. The discussion of utility and diminishing marginal utility has been expanded and clarified in the new Chapter 21, with a new section on utility maximization and consumer behavior which raises questions about the implications of utility maximization and discusses current research on how consumers make decisions. Chapter 23 introduces all of the market structures and compares and contrasts firm

behavior in each. Chapters 24–26 present each market structure in detail. A new chapter, Chapter 27, *Product Market Applications* uses the product market material (market structures and costs) to explain real-world business practices. In-depth case studies in this chapter help students review what they have learned about product markets in a lively and exciting way.

Modern Topics and Features Throughout

Modern topics continue to be the emphasis of the text. The economics of personnel, strategic behavior, and the economics of information are maintained but are restructured and reemphasized. The economics of information is included with the chapter on oligopoly and monopolistic competition, thus ensuring that students realize that what they are studying is indeed real-world oriented.

Each chapter contains approximately fifteen exercises that challenge students, test their retention and understanding of the material, and extend the student's knowledge. A new "cooperative learning exercise" has been added to this set of questions for each chapter. The cooperative learning exercise allows those instructors so inclined to include group projects, assignments, and discussions as part of the learning process.

Reviewers and users of the second edition have passed along high praise for the *Economically Speaking* boxes included at the end of each chapter. Part of their appeal is their currency, and we have replaced 34 of 40 boxes in this edition in order to keep them up to date. The articles included come from a wider range of regional newspapers, with topics as diverse as efforts to privatize the Internet, the growth of Ben and Jerry's ice cream, trade squabbles between Japan and the U.S., and increasing consumer preferences for brand names in China. Commentaries have also been updated to help students make the connections between reality and economic theory.

Reduced Price/Loose-leaf Form/Early Publication

Everyone associated with college textbooks realizes how expensive these books are. While those of us supplying the texts might argue that the value per dollar is even higher when you add up the cost of color printing, photos, computer software, and all the other ancillaries, no one can deny that book prices are high. One consequence of high prices is that many students who would benefit from textbooks aren't buying them. Thus, to remain consistent with our goal of responding to student and faculty desires, we have decided to reduce the price by nearly one-half over the second edition by offering the text in loose-leaf form. *Economics* is the only economics text offered in loose-leaf form and the only full-color text with photographs offered at such a low price. The loose-leaf form has an added advantage in that students are no longer obliged to carry around a ten-pound text, but can instead choose to carry just those pages of interest or those chapters to be read that day—perhaps adding chapters from the Study Guide and/or classroom handouts and newspaper articles—to make one centralized learning package. Faculty, too, benefit from the flexibility that a loose-leaf format provides.

Because we felt this pricing change was so important and because updating is constantly needed in today's world, we decided to bring the third edition out a year early—only two years after the second edition—rather than wait the usual three years.

SUCCESSFUL FEATURES RETAINED FROM THE SECOND EDITION

In addition to the considerable updating and revising we've done for the third edition, there are several unique features preserved from the second edition which we think instructors will find interesting.

Enhanced Student Relevance

With all the demands on today's students, it's no wonder that they resist spending time on a subject unless they see how the material relates to them and how they will benefit from mastering it. We worked hard to incorporate features throughout the text that would show economics as the relevant and necessary subject we know it to be.

Real-world Examples. Students are rarely intrigued by a large manufacturer or a service company. Our text talks about people and firms that students recognize. We describe business decisions made by McDonald's and Pizza Hut, by Kodak and Fuji, by the local video store or café. We discuss the policies of Bill Clinton, Boris Yeltsin, John Major, and other world leaders. These examples grab students' interest. Reviewers have repeatedly praised the use of novel examples to convey economic concepts.

Economic Insight Boxes. These brief boxes bring in contemporary material from current periodicals and journals to illustrate or extend the discussion in the chapter. By reserving interesting but more technical sidelights for boxes, we lessen the likelihood that students will be confused or distracted by issues that are not critical to understanding the chapter. By including excerpts from articles we help students learn to move from theory to real-world example. And by including plenty of contemporary issues, we guarantee that students will see how economics relates to their own lives.

Economically Speaking Boxes. The objective of the principles course is to teach students how to translate the predictions that come out of economic models to the real world and to translate real-world events into an economic model in order to analyze and understand what lies behind the events. The *Economically Speaking* boxes, over 30 of them new to this edition, present students with a model of this kind of analysis. Students read an article which appears on the left-hand page of a two-page spread at the end of each chapter. The commentary on the right-hand page shows how the facts and events in the article translate into a specific economic model or idea, thereby moving the student from reality back to theory.

An Effective and Proven System of Teaching and Learning Aids

This text is designed to make teaching easier by enhancing student learning. Tested pedagogy motivates students, emphasizes clarity, reinforces relationships, simplifies review, and fosters critical thinking. And, as we have discovered from reviewer and user feedback, this pedagogy works.

In-text Referencing System. Sections are numbered for easy reference and to reinforce hierarchies of ideas. The numbering of sections serves as an outline of the chapter, allowing instructors flexibility in assigning reading, and making it easy for students to find topics to review. The key term list and summary at the end of the chapter refer students back to the appropriate *section's number*.

The section numbering system appears throughout the Boyes/Melvin ancillary package; the *Test Banks, Study Guides,* and *Instructor's Resource Manual* are organized according to the same system.

Fundamental Questions. These questions help to organize the chapter and highlight those issues that are critical to understanding. Students can preview chapters with these questions in mind, reading actively for understanding and retention. The Fundamental

Questions reappear in the margin by the text discussion that helps students to answer the question. Fundamental Questions also serve to organize the chapter summaries. Brief paragraphs answering each of these questions are found in the *Study Guides* available as supplements to this text. They also serve as one of several criteria used to categorize questions in the *Test Banks*.

Preview. This motivating lead-in sets the stage for the chapter. Much more than a road map, it helps students identify real issues that relate to the concepts that will be presented. In this third edition, many previews have been rewritten to better capture students' interest.

Recaps. Briefly listing the main points covered, a recap appears at the end of each major section within a chapter. Students are able to quickly review what they have just read before going on to the next section.

Summary. The summary at the end of each chapter is organized along two dimensions. The primary organizational device is the list of Fundamental Questions. A brief synopsis of the discussion that helps students to answer those questions is arranged by section below each of the questions. Students are encouraged to create their own links among topics as they keep in mind the connections between the "big picture" and the details that comprise it.

Reminders. Found in the text margins, these hints and comments highlight especially important concepts, point out common mistakes, and warn students of common pitfalls. They alert students to parts of the discussion that they should read with particular care.

Key Terms. Key terms appear in bold type in the text. They also appear with their definition in the margin and are listed at the end of the chapter for easy review. All key terms are included in the glossary at the end of the text.

Exercises

End-of-chapter exercises provide excellent self-checks for students and a homework assignment option for instructors. An average of 15 exercises appears at the end of every chapter. New to this edition are cooperative learning exercises—one per chapter—which provide opportunities for active learning and teamwork.

All of the end-of-chapter exercises ask students to work with the ideas presented in the chapter: Do they know how to apply the concepts? Can they perform necessary computations? Can they draw conclusions about the real world based on the theories presented?

Friendly Appearance

Economics can be intimidating, which is why we've striven to keep *Economics* looking friendly and inviting. The one column design and ample white space in this text provide an accessible backdrop. Over 300 figures rely on well-developed pedagogy and consistent use of color to reinforce understanding. Striking colors were chosen to enhance readability and provide visual interest. Specific curves were assigned specific colors, and families of curves assigned related colors.

Annotations on the art point out areas of particular concern or importance. Students can see exactly what parts of a graph illustrate a shortage or a surplus, a change in consumption or consumer surplus. Tables that provide data from which graphs are plotted are paired with their graphs. Where appropriate, color is used to show correlations between the art and the table, and captions clearly explain what is shown in the figures, linking them to the text discussion.

The color photographs not only provide visual images but make the text appear more human. These vibrant photos tell stories as well as illustrate concepts, and lengthy captions explain what is in the photo—again to draw connections between the images and the text discussion.

Thoroughly International Coverage

Students understand that they live in a global economy—they can hardly shop, watch the news, or read a newspaper without understanding this basic fact. International examples are presented in every chapter but are not merely "added on" as is the case with other texts. By introducing international effects on demand in Chapter 3, and then describing, in a descriptive and nontechnical manner, the basics of the foreign exchange market and the balance of payments in Chapter 7, we are able to incorporate the international sector into the economic models and applications wherever appropriate thereafter. Because the international content is incorporated from the beginning, students develop a far more realistic picture of the economy; as a result they won't have to alter their thinking to allow for international factors later on. The four chapters which focus on international topics at the end of the text allow those instructors who desire to delve much more deeply into international issues to do so.

The fact that we live in a global world is also

emphasized through osmosis: *using traditional economic concepts to explain international economic events and using international events to illustrate economic concepts that have traditionally been illustrated with domestic examples.* Instructors need not know the international institutions to introduce international examples since the topics through which they are addressed are familiar, for example, price ceilings, price discrimination, expenditures on resources, marginal productivity theory, and others.

Uniquely international elements of the macroeconomic coverage include

- Treatment of the international sector as one of the economic participants and inclusion of net exports as early as Chapter 4.
- Early description of the foreign exchange market and the balance of payments in Chapter 7.
- Inclusion of international elements in the development of Aggregate Demand and Supply.
- Extended treatment of macroeconomic links between countries in Chapter 17.

Unique international elements of microeconomic coverage include

- Introduction of exchange rates as a determinant of demand in Chapter 3.
- Extensive analyses of the effects of trade barriers, tariffs, and quotas.
- Examination of strategic trade.
- Examination of dumping as a special case of price discrimination.
- Identification of problems faced by multinational firms.
- Comparison of behavior, results, and institutions among nations with respect to consumption, production, firm size, government policies toward business, labor markets, health care, income distribution, environmental policy, and other issues.

Modern Macroeconomic Organization and Content

Macroeconomics is changing and textbooks must reflect that change. We begin with the basics—GDP, unemployment, and inflation. These are the ongoing concerns of any economy, for they have a significant influence on how people feel. These are the issues that don't go away. Added to these core basics is an easy-to-understand, descriptive introduction to the foreign exchange market and the balance of payments. We provide a critical alternative for those instructors who

believe that it is no longer reasonable to relegate this material to the final chapters, where coverage may be rushed.

Armed with these basics, students are ready to delve into the richness of macroeconomic thought. Macro models and approaches have evolved over the years, and they continue to invite exciting theoretical and policy debates. The majority of instructors we asked voiced frustration with the challenge of pulling this rich and varied material together in class and stressed that a coherent picture of the aggregate demand and supply model was critical. We have structured the macro portion to allow for many teaching preferences while assuring a clear delineation of the aggregate demand/aggregate supply model.

To help instructors successfully present a single coherent model, we present aggregate demand and aggregate supply first, in Chapter 9, immediately following the chapter on inflation and unemployment. This sequence allows for the smooth transition from business cycle fluctuations to aggregate demand/aggregate supply (AD/AS). The Keynesian income and expenditures model is presented in full in Chapters 10 and 11, where it is presented as the fixed price version of the AD/AS model (with a horizontal aggregate supply curve). Those who want to use the AD/AS model exclusively will have no problem moving from the Chapter 9 presentation of it to the fiscal policy material in Chapter 12. The policy chapters rely on the AD/AS model for analysis.

The macroeconomic policy chapters begin with a thorough presentation of fiscal policy, money and banking, and monetary policy—with international elements included. Chapter 15 covers contemporary policy issues, and various schools of thought are treated in Chapter 16, when students are ready to appreciate the differences and can benefit from a discussion of new Keynesian and new classical models as well as of their precursors. Chapter 17 develops macroeconomic links between countries. This chapter helps students understand why economies cannot function in isolation from each other and clearly demonstrates why policy actions undertaken by one government affect not only that government's own citizens but citizens and businesses in other countries as well.

Part IV, Economic Growth and Development, brings together the concepts and issues presented in the core macro chapters to explain how economies grow and what factors encourage or discourage growth. Most of the world's population live in poor countries. Growth and development are critical to them. The material in these chapters also addresses issues of importance to industrial countries, such as the slowdown of productivity growth in the United States.

Modern Microeconomic Content and Organization

All too often microeconomics is presented as a succession of facts, graphs, and theories whose connections are not easily grasped or appreciated. Because students don't see the big picture, they find microeconomics difficult and unrelated to their lives. We give students a context for organizing and understanding the material covered and point out how it relates to their everyday experience. We also draw students' interest by extending the application of economic principles to important social issues of the day—families, aging, health care, college and occupational choice, and discrimination.

Part V presents basic concepts such as elasticity, consumer behavior, and costs of production. Parts VI and VII both begin with overview chapters (Chapter 23 on product markets and Chapter 29 on resource markets). These overviews give students a chance to look at the big picture before delving into details they often find confusing. Chapter 23, for instance, gives students an intuitive overview to the market structures before they explore each type of structure in more detail in succeeding chapters. Chapter 23 lightens the load that the more detailed chapters have to bear, easing students into the market structure material. The traditional topics are covered in the separate market structure chapters, Chapter 24–26 but the coverage is also modern, including such topics as strategic behavior, price discrimination, nonprice competition, and the economics of information. Having fought their way first through the cost curves and then the market structures, students often complain that they do not see the relevance of that material and see no real world applications of the material. The intuitive overview chapter alleviates some of that frustration. And, a new chapter entitled "Product Market Applications" shows how the product market material can be used to better understand business decisions and to design business strategies. The chapter uses real-world cases to illustrate the topics discussed. In test trials, students have found that the chapter enables them to better understand what the market structure and cost material is all about.

Part VIII extends microeconomics to issues that are of high interest to students and which includes both public and private sectors. Chapter 33 offers an analysis of the problems of an aging population—families, health care, and social security. *Economics* continues

to be the only text that treats the issues of aging and health care so carefully. Chapter 34 lays out the tension between equity and efficiency as it examines the distribution of income and poverty, and Chapter 35 delves into environmental issues.

Throughout *Economics,* students are able to connect their experiences to what they are learning about microeconomics.

A COMPLETE TEACHING AND LEARNING PACKAGE

In today's market no book is complete without a full complement of ancillaries. Our package provides the breadth and depth of support for both instructors and students that is second to none. Throughout its development, we have kept today's economics instructor in mind. Those instructors who face huge classes find good transparencies (acetates) to be critical instructional tools. Others may find that computer simulations and tutorials are invaluable. *Economics* meets both challenges. And to foster the development of consistent teaching and study strategies, the ancillaries pick up pedagogical features of the text—like the fundamental questions—wherever appropriate.

Transparencies. Available to adopters are over 100 color acetates showing the most important figures in the text. Over 10 percent of these figures have one to three overlays, which in addition to adding clarity and flexibility to the discussion, allow instructors to visually demonstrate the dynamic nature of economics.

Instructor's Resource Manual. Stuart Glosser has produced a manual that will streamline preparation for both new and experienced faculty. Preliminary sections cover class administration, alternative syllabi, and a guide to the use of cooperative learning in teaching principles of economics.

The IRM also contains a detailed chapter-by-chapter review of all the changes made in the third edition. This Transition Guide should help instructors more easily move from the use of the second edition to this new edition.

Each chapter of the IRM contains

■ Teaching Objectives *that address (1) critical points to cover if your students are to succeed with later chapters; (2) concepts traditionally difficult for students to master; and (3) the unique features of the chapter.*

- listing of Fundamental Questions.
- Key Terms
- Lecture Outline with **Teaching Strategies**—general techniques and guidelines, essay topics, and other hints to enliven your classes.
- Opportunities for Discussion.
- Answers to End-of-Chapter Questions. Every exercise in the text is answered here.
- Answers to Study Guide homework questions.

Study Guides. Janet L. Wolcutt and James E. Clark of the Center for Economic Education at Wichita State University have revised the *Macroeconomics* and *Microeconomics* Study Guides to give students the practice they need to master this course. Initially received by students and instructors with great enthusiasm, the guides maintain their warm and lively style to keep students on the right track. In each chapter:

- Fundamental Questions are answered in one or several paragraphs. For students who have trouble formulating their own answers to these questions after reading the text, the study guides provide an invaluable model.
- Key terms are listed.
- Quick Check Quiz is organized by section, so any wrong answers send the student directly to the relevant material in the text.
- Practice Questions and Problems, which is also organized by section, includes a variety of question formats—multiple choice, true/false, matching, and fill-in-the-blank. They test understanding of the concepts and ask students to construct or perform computations.
- Thinking About and Applying . . . use newspaper headlines or some other real-life applications to test students' ability to reason in economic terms.
- A Homework page at the end of each chapter contains 5 (2 factual, 2 applied, and 1 synthesis/analysis) questions which can be answered on the sheet and turned in for grading. Answers are included in the IRM.
- Sample Tests. These tests appear at the end of each Study Guide part and consist of 25 to 50 questions similar to test bank questions. Taking the sample tests will help students determine whether or not they've really prepared for exams.
- Answers are provided to all but Homework questions. Students are referred back to relevant pages in the main text.

Test Banks. Test Banks for both *Macroeconomics* and *Microeconomics* are available. Over 7,000 test items, 1,400 of them new to this edition, provide a wealth of material for classroom testing. Features include

- Multiple choice, true/false, and essay questions in every chapter.
- Over 1,400 questions new to this edition, marked for easy identification.
- An increased number of analytical, applied, and graphical questions appear in this edition.
- Identification of all test items according to topic, question type (factual, interpretive, or applied), level of difficulty, and applicable fundamental question.
- Study Guide section of test which includes five test items taken directly from the Study Guide and five test items that parallel Study Guide questions, for the instructor who is interested in rewarding students for working through the Study Guide.

ESA TEST II for IBM and Macintosh Machines

This innovative test-assembly program, revised for this edition, renders precise, preprogrammed graphs on the computer quickly, easily, and accurately. You can select from among more than 7,000 questions, edit nongraphic items, peruse items in order, add your own questions to customize tests, and print out alternate versions using a number of variables. Individual items or tests in their entirety can be previewed before printing. The sophisticated data retrieval capabilities of the computerized test bank allow instructors to generate multiple versions of a test automatically and assure compatability of tests consisting of different test items. This program also allows importation of files from ASCII, WordStar, and WordPerfect. Available for IBM-PC®, PS/2, and compatible microcomputers.

Laserdisc: Graphs!

Our laserdisc offers instructors the capability to show graphs and their movements in a dynamic way. Each graph is introduced and motivated by interesting, brief video clips. Instructors can choose from a collection of key economic graphs. Each graph is easily accessed and controlled to provide optimal lecture support. Also available in VHS format for video projection.

Boyes/Melvin Economics Courseware. The Boyes/ Melvin Economics Courseware provides the opportunity for students to review and apply the most important concepts covered in the text. It consists of two major components—Tutorial and Simulation—either of which can be used for independent study and practice, small group work in a computer lab, or as part of a classroom demonstration. The instructor could also assign specific modules as homework, since students can print the graphs they generate.

■ Tutorial. The tutorial portion of the program consists of modules tied to the major topics of the text (e.g., "Supply and Demand," "Consumer Theory and Utility," "The Role of Government," and "Monetary Policy"). Each module is broken up into several major sections, with a self-test offered at the end of each section to reinforce what has been covered.

Working at their own pace, students experiment with the curves by entering and changing values of discrete variables in order to see the results played out in the corresponding graph window. Narrating text prompts the student to make changes to variables and, with reinforcing explanation, encourages the student to reflect on what has happened in the graph window. A View menu allows students to view the graphs with or without a background grid (in a variety of styles) or with thin or thick curves. (This feature is also handy for classroom demonstrations.) An extensive Help menu enables students to access the Boyes/Melvin glossary whenever they need to refresh their memories on the meaning of a particular term.

■ Simulation. In the Simulation component of the Courseware, the structured sequence of the tutorial is replaced by more open-ended problem-solving. Students begin by choosing one of several scenarios, which range from "Effects of a Tariff" to "A Pollution Policy for Denver." But, instead of being presented with graphs linked to text screens, the student is encouraged to pull up their own graphs or tables from a rich library of data, choose a relevant time period, and thereby construct a meaningful graph or table. Here the student not only must choose and assemble the data but also begin the process of interpretation. With over 20 complete sets of data which include such information as Nominal GDP, Inflation Rate, and Unemployment Rate, the possibilities for analysis of data are almost endless. All data is provided in both annual and quarterly figures from 1930 to 1994 where those years are available.

The simulation scenarios also offer a kind of exploration that is not possible in other software

programs. When the student is interested in doing some independent exploring, the screen is cleared, and all the micro and macro data sets become accessible. Students can plot up to three data series against time, or choose from among the data series to plot variables against each other. This is an ideal vehicle around which professors can build substantive student assignments.

Electronic Lecture Manager. This Windows-based software developed by Houghton Mifflin allows instructors to create customized lecture presentations that can be displayed on computer-based projection systems. The software makes available the figures and key tables from the text and also allows for access to laser disc sequences and screens from other Windows-based software. With the Electronic Lecture Manager, instructors can quickly and easily integrate all these components—and create their own screens as well—to prepare a seamless classroom presentation with minimal in-class tinkering.

ACKNOWLEDGMENTS

Writing a text of this scope is a challenge that requires the expertise and efforts of many. We are grateful to our friends and colleagues who have so generously given their time, creativity, and insight to help us create a text that best meets the needs of today's classroom.

We'd like to thank the many reviewers who provided us with feedback on the second edition and careful reading of the third edition manuscript. Calvin Hoy of County College of Morris, Peter B. Lund of California State University at Sacramento, Alana Orrison of Saddleback College, Theodore C. Kariotis of the University of Maryland, University College at College Park, Fatma Wahdan Antar of Manchester Community Technical College, David C. Black of the University of Toledo, Richard L. Hannah of Middle Tennessee State University, David Jaques of California Polytechnic University, Nicholas Karatjas of Indiana University of Pennsylvania, Charles Knapp of Waubonsee Community College, Charles W. Martie of Quinnipiac College, Carl Pearl of Cypress College, Mitchell H. Redlo of Monroe Community College, and Nan Wilson of Johnson County Community College all deserve our thanks for their suggestions in helping to revise this edition. Special thanks go to Robert Reinke of the University of South Dakota for his candor and diligence in pointing out problems and offering solutions at several stages of manuscript development. Unsolicited feedback from current users has also been greatly appreciated. We'd like to thank Peter Lund of California State University, Sacramento, Bob Kirk of Indiana University/Purdue University at Indianapolis, and Marian Schoen at Rockland Community College for their very useful feedback.

Special thanks go to Richard Donovan of Arizona State University for his hard work on the *Test Banks* for this edition. The important contributions of Bettina Peiers and Karen Thomas-Brandt of Arizona State University on the second edition *Test Bank* and Michael Couvillion of Plymouth State College on the first edition *Test Bank* must also be acknowledged. Thanks, too, go to Paul S. Estenson of Gustavus Adolphus College and Edward T. Merkel of Troy State University for their tremendous contribution in preparing the second edition *Instructor's Resource Manual.*

We want to thank the many people at Houghton Mifflin Company who devoted countless hours to making this text the best it could be, including Bonnie Binkert, Ann West, Susan Westendorf, Gabrielle Stone, Carol Merrigan, and Ann Schroeder. We are grateful for their enthusiasm, expertise, and energy.

Finally, we wish to thank our families and friends. The inspiration they provided through the conception and development of this book cannot be measured, but certainly was essential.

Our students at Arizona State University continue to help us improve the text through each edition; their many questions have given us invaluable insight into how best to present this intriguing subject. It is our hope that this textbook will bring a clear understanding of economic thought to many other students as well. We welcome any feedback for improvements.

W.B.
M.M.

REVIEWERS WHO HELPED SET THE
STAGE FOR SUCCESSFUL FIRST AND SECOND EDITIONS:

Shahid Alam
Northeastern University

Lori Alden
California State University,
Sacramento

John Atkins
Pensacola Junior College

Kevin Baird
Montgomery County Community
College

Maurice Ballabon
City University of New York—
Baruch College

James T. Bennett
George Mason University

Mark Berger
University of Kentucky

Donna Bialik
Indiana—Purdue University

Mary Bone
Pensacola Junior College

Bradley Braun
University of Central Florida

Jacqueline Brux
University of Wisconsin

Joan Buccino
Florida Southern College

Conrad Caligaris
Northeastern University

Cindy Cannon
North Harris College

Michael Couvillion
Plymouth State College

Andy Dane
Angelo State University

Elynor Davis
Georgia Southern College

Gary Dymski
University of Southern California

Ana Eapen
William Paterson College

Duane Eberhardt
Missouri Southern State College

John Eckalbar
California State University, Chico

Mary Edwards
Saint Cloud State University

Paul Estenson
Gustavus Adolphus College

Paul Fahy
Eastern Illinois University

Joel Feiner
State University of New York at Old
Westbury

John F. Ficks
College of DuPage

Martha Field
Greenfield Community College

Peter Garlick
State University of New York at New
Paltz

John Gemello
San Francisco State University

George Greenwade
Sam Houston State University

Morton Hirsch
Kingsboro Community College

Beth Ingram
University of Iowa

David Jobson
Keystone Junior College

Marcia Jones
Georgia Southern University

John Kane
State University of New York at
Oswego

George Kelley
Worcester State College

Dick Kennedy
Odessa College

Barbara Killen
University of Minnesota

Michael Klein
Clark University

Keith Leeseberg
Manatee Community College

Thomas Maloy
Nukegon Community College

Yousef Mansur
Oklahoma City Community College

James Marchand
Radford University

James Mason
San Diego Mesa College

Edward Merkel
Troy State University

Irving Morrissett
University of Colorado

Denny Myers
Oklahoma City College

Joseph Nieb
Embry-Riddle Aeronautical
University

Thomas Oberhofer
Eckerd College

Gerard O'Boyle
St. John's University

Erin O'Brien
San Diego Mesa College

Albert Okunade
Memphis State University

Bettina Peirs
Arizona State University

Paul Reali
Bryant & Stratton Business Institute

Robert Reinke
University of South Dakota

James Rigterink
Polk Community College

Nancy Roberts
Arizona State University

Randell Routt
Elizabethtown Community College

Gerald Sazama
University of Connecticut

Ted Scheinman
Mount Hood Community College

Paul Schmitt
St. Clair County Community College

Carole Scott
West Georgia College

William Doyle Smith
University of Texas at El Paso

W.R. Smith
Georgia Southern College

Todd Steen
Hope College

Andrew Stern
California State University, Long Beach

Thomas Tacker
Embry-Riddle Aeronautical University

Eugenia Toma
University of Kentucky

William Trumbull
West Virginia University

Thomas Watkins
Eastern Kentucky University

Louise Wolitz
University of Texas at Austin

Marc Zagara
Community College of the Finger Lakes

Brief Contents

Contents

Contents

Contents

xxv

.

Macroeconomic Emphasis

1 Economics: The World Around You
2 Choice, Opportunity Costs, and Specialization
3 Markets, Demand and Supply, and the Price System
4 The Market System and the Private Sector
5 The Public Sector
6 National Income Accounting
7 An Introduction to the Foreign Exchange Market and the Balance of Payments
8 Unemployment and Inflation
9 Macroeconomic Equilibrium: Aggregate Demand and Supply
10 Aggregate Expenditures
11 Income and Expenditures Equilibrium
12 Fiscal Policy
13 Money and Banking
14 Monetary Policy
15 Macroeconomic Policy: Trade-offs, Expectations, Credibility, and Sources of Business Cycles
16 Macroeconomic Viewpoints: New Keynesian, Monetarist, and New Classical
17 Macroeconomic Links Between Countries
18 Economic Growth
19 Development Economics
39 Exchange-Rate Systems and Practices
40 The Transition from Socialism to Capitalism

Microeconomic Emphasis

1 Economics: The World Around You
2 Choice, Opportunity Costs, and Specialization
3 Markets, Demand and Supply, and the Price System
4 The Market System and the Private Sector
5 The Public Sector
20 Elasticity: Demand and Supply
21 Consumer Choice
22 Supply: The Costs of Doing Business
23 An Overview of Product Markets and Profit Maximization
24 Perfect Competition
25 Monopoly
26 Monopolistic Competition and Oligopoly
27 Product Market Applications
28 Government Policy Toward Business
29 An Overview of Resource Markets
30 The Labor Market: Wage Differentials and Personnel Practices
31 Wage Differentials: Race, Gender, Age and Unionization
32 Capital, Land, and Entrepreneurial Ability
33 The Economics of Aging and Health Care
34 Income Distribution, Poverty, and Government Policy
35 Market Failure and Environmental Policy
36 Government and Public Choice
37 World Trade Equilibrium
38 Commercial Policy

Balanced Micro-Macro

1 Economics: The World Around You
2 Choice, Opportunity Costs, and Specialization
3 Markets, Demand and Supply, and the Price System
4 The Market System and the Private Sector
5 The Public Sector
6 National Income Accounting
8 Unemployment and Inflation
9 Macroeconomic Equilibrium: Aggregate Demand and Supply
12 Fiscal Policy
13 Money and Banking
14 Monetary Policy
20 Elasticity: Demand and Supply
21 Consumer Choice
22 Supply: The Costs of Doing Business
23 An Overview of Product Markets and Profit Maximization
29 An Overview of Resource Markets
30 The Labor Market: Wage Differentials and Personnel Practices
31 Wage Differentials: Race, Gender, Age, and Unionization
32 Capital, Land, and Entrepreneurial Ability
33 The Economics of Aging and Health Care
34 Income Distribution, Poverty, and Government Policy
35 Market Failure and Environmental Policy
36 Government and Public Choice
37 World Trade Equilibrium
38 Commercial Policy
39 Exchange-Rate Systems and Practices
40 The Transition from Socialism to Capitalism

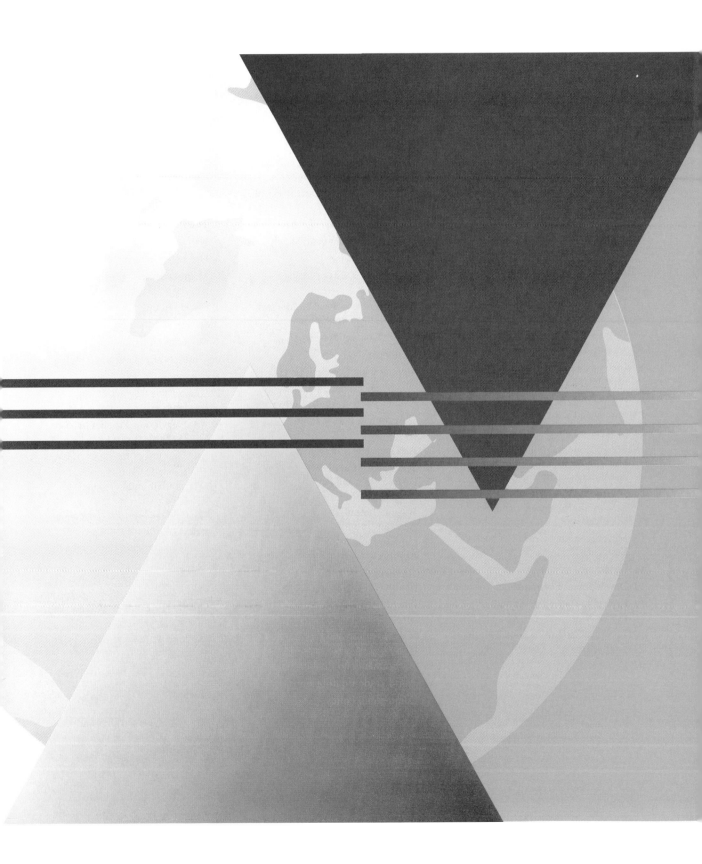

I

Introduction
to the Price System

1

Economics: The World Around You

FUNDAMENTAL
QUESTIONS

1. What is economics?
2. What are the principles of economics?
3. What is the economic way of thinking?

You are a member of a very select group: you are attending college. Only about 19 percent of the American population has a college degree (bachelor's or associate's), and about 45% of people between the ages of 18 and 22 are currently attending college.

Why aren't more people attending college? Part of the reason may be the increased costs of college; during the 1980s and 1990s, the direct expenses associated with college rose much more rapidly than average income. Yet, attending college and acquiring an education is more valuable today than it was during the 1970s and early 1980s. Technological change and increased international trade have placed a premium on a college education; more and more jobs require the skills acquired in college. As a result, the wage disparity between college-educated and non-college-educated workers is rising fairly rapidly. A college-educated person earns nearly twice as much as the person without a college degree.

Why are you attending college? Perhaps you've never really given it a great deal of thought—your family always just assumed that college was a necessary step after high school; perhaps you analyzed the situation and decided that college was better than the alternatives. Whichever approach you took, you were practicing economics. You, or your family, were examining alternatives and making choices. This is what economics is about.

The objective of economics is to understand why the real world is what it is. This is not an easy proposition, for the real world is very complex. After all, what happens in the real world is the result of human behavior, and humans are not simple creatures. Nonetheless, there are some fundamental regularities of human behavior that can help to explain the world we observe.

One such regularity is that people behave in ways that make themselves and those they care about better off and happier. Even without knowing that having a college education means your income will be higher than if you do not earn a college degree, you and your family knew or suspected that the college degree would mean a better lifestyle and a more secure or more prestigious job for you. However, what makes one person happy may not make others happy.

Knowing that it is the person without a college degree who is first laid off or unemployed during a recession, that the riskier jobs are held by those without a college degree, and that a person without a college degree is six times more likely to fall into poverty than a person with a college degree, we might be inclined to argue that the 75 percent of young people not attending college are making the wrong choice. But we can't say that. We don't know their circumstances; we don't know what makes them and their families happy. We only know that they do not believe the benefits of college outweigh the costs; otherwise they would be in college.

Knowing that most people behave in ways that make themselves better off and that most people compare costs and benefits in coming to a decision is powerful stuff. It allows us to explain much of the real world and to predict how that world might change if certain events occur.

This knowledge of human behavior is the subject matter of economics. To study economics is to seek answers not only for why people choose to go to college but also for why economies go through cycles, at times expanding and creating new jobs and at other times dipping into recessions; for why some people are thrown out of jobs to join the ranks of the unemployed while others are drawn out of the ranks of the unemployed into new jobs; for why some people live on welfare; for why some nations are richer than others; for why the illegal drug trade is so difficult to stop; for why health care is so expensive; or, in general, for why the world is what it is.

This chapter is the introduction to our study of economics. In it we present some of the terminology commonly used in economics and outline what the study of economics is.

What is economics?

I. THE DEFINITION OF ECONOMICS

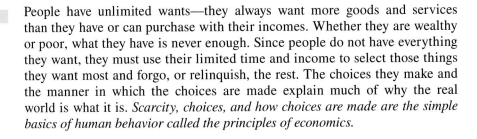

What are the principles of economics?

People have unlimited wants—they always want more goods and services than they have or can purchase with their incomes. Whether they are wealthy or poor, what they have is never enough. Since people do not have everything they want, they must use their limited time and income to select those things they want most and forgo, or relinquish, the rest. The choices they make and the manner in which the choices are made explain much of why the real world is what it is. *Scarcity, choices, and how choices are made are the simple basics of human behavior called the principles of economics.*

I.a. Scarcity

scarcity:
when less of something is available than is wanted at a zero price

economic good:
any item that is scarce

free good:
a good for which there is no scarcity

Neither the poor nor the wealthy have unlimited time, income, or wealth, and both must make choices to use these limited items in a way that best satisfies their wants. Because wants are unlimited and incomes, time, and other items are not, scarcity exists everywhere. **Scarcity** of something means that there is not enough of that item to satisfy everyone who wants it; it means that at a zero price the amount of an item that people want is greater than the amount that is available. Anything for which this condition holds is called an **economic good**. An economic good refers to *goods and services*—where goods are physical products, such as books or food, and services are nonphysical products, such as haircuts or golf lessons.

If there is enough of an item to satisfy wants, even at a zero price, the item is said to be a **free good**. It is difficult to think of examples of free goods. At one time people referred to air as free, but with air pollution control devices and other costly activities directed toward the maintenance of air quality

"Free" Air?

Although air might be what we describe as a free good, quality, breathable air is not free in many places in the world. One of the most successful new business ventures in Mexico City, in fact, is providing clean, breathable air. In this city of 19 million people and 3 million cars, dust, lead, and chemicals make the air unsafe to breathe more than 300 days a year. Private companies are now operating oxygen booths in local parks and malls. Breathable air, which costs more than $1.60 per minute, has become a popular product.

No city in the United States has resorted to oxygen boutiques, but there are large costs for air pollution abatement in many cities. It has been estimated that the cost of meeting federal air quality standards in Los Angeles will soon exceed $1,200 per year for every resident of the Los Angeles metropolitan area.

Sources: "Breathable Air for Swap or Sale," Peter Passell, *New York Times*, Jan. 30, 1992, p. D2; "Best Things in Life Aren't Always Free," Matt Moffett, *The Wall Street Journal*, May 8, 1992, p. A1.

economic bad:
any item for which we would pay to have less

resources, factors of production, or inputs:
goods used to produce other goods, i.e., land, labor, capital, entrepreneurial ability

land:
all natural resources, such as minerals, timber, and water, as well as the land itself

labor:
the physical and intellectual services of people, including the training, education, and abilities of the individuals in a society

capital:
products such as machinery and equipment that are used in production

entrepreneurial ability:
the ability to recognize a profitable opportunity and the willingness and ability to organize land, labor, and capital and assume the risk associated with the opportunity

standards, "clean" air, at least, is not a free good, as noted in the Economic Insight "'Free' Air?"

If people would pay to have less of an item, that item is called an **economic bad**. It is not so hard to think of examples of bads: pollution, garbage, and disease fit the description.

Some goods are used to produce other goods. For instance, to make chocolate chip cookies we need flour, sugar, chocolate chips, butter, our own labor, and an oven. To distinguish between the ingredients of a good and the good itself, we call the ingredients **resources**. (Resources are also called **factors of production** and **inputs**; the terms are interchangeable.) The ingredients of the cookies are the resources, and the cookies are the goods.

As illustrated in Figure 1(a), economists have classified resources into four categories: land, labor, capital, and entrepreneurial ability.

1. **Land** includes all natural resources, such as minerals, timber, and water, as well as the land itself.

2. **Labor** refers to the physical and intellectual services of people and includes the training, education, and abilities of the individuals in a society.

3. **Capital** refers to products such as machinery and equipment that are used in production. Capital is a manufactured or created product used solely for the production of the goods and services that are consumed by individuals. You will often hear the term *capital* used to describe the financial backing for some project or the stocks and bonds used to finance some business. This common usage is not incorrect but should be distinguished from the physical entity—the machinery and equipment and the buildings, warehouses, and factories. Thus we refer to the stocks and bonds as *financial capital* and to the physical entity as capital.

4. **Entrepreneurial ability** refers to the ability to recognize a profitable opportunity and the willingness and ability to organize the other resources and undertake the risk associated with the opportunity. It is

Figure 1
Flow of Resources and Income
Four types of resources are used to produce goods and services: land, labor, capital, and entrepreneurial ability. See 1(a). The owners of resources are provided income for selling their services. Landowners are paid rent; laborers receive wages; capital receives interest; and entrepreneurs acquire profit. See 1(b). Figure 1(c) links Figures 1(a) and 1(b). People use their resources to acquire income with which they purchase the goods they want. Producers use the money received from selling the goods to pay for the use of the resources in making goods. Resources and income flow between certain firms and certain resource owners as people allocate their scarce resources to best satisfy their wants.

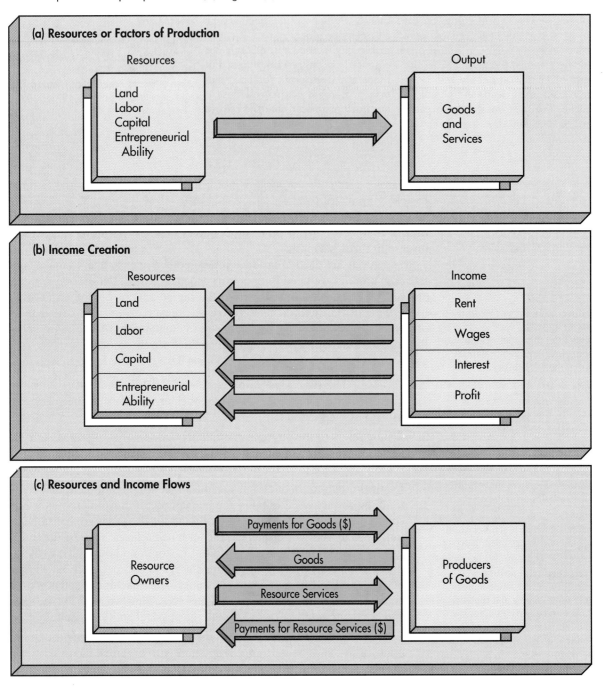

Part I/Introduction to the Price System

a special talent few individuals have, and it plays such an important role in the economy that it is considered to be a resource on its own rather than just grouped together with labor. People who demonstrate entrepreneurial abilities are called **entrepreneurs**.

entrepreneur:
an individual with entrepreneurial ability

People obtain income by selling their resources or the use of their resources, as illustrated in Figure 1(b). Owners of land receive *rent*; when people provide labor services they are paid *wages*; owners of capital receive *interest*; and people with entrepreneurial ability receive the *profits* from starting, running, and operating businesses.

Figures 1(a) and 1(b) are linked because the income that resource owners acquire from selling the use of their resources provides them the ability to buy goods and services. And producers use the money received from selling their goods to pay for the resource services. In Figure 1(c), the flows of money are indicated along the outside arrows, and the flows of goods or resource services are indicated along the inside arrows. The resource services flow from resource owners to producers of goods in return for income; the flows of goods go from the producers of the goods to resource owners in return for the money payment for these goods.

I.b. Choices

Scarcity means that people have to make choices. People don't have everything they want; they do not have the time or the money to purchase everything they want. When people choose some things, they have to give up, or forgo, other things. *Economics is the study of how people choose to use their scarce resources to attempt to satisfy their unlimited wants.*

I.c. Rational Self-Interest

rational self-interest:
how people choose the options that give them the greatest amount of satisfaction

Rational self-interest is the term economists use to describe how people make choices. It means that people will make the choices that, at the time and with the information they have at their disposal, will give them the greatest amount of satisfaction.

You chose to attend college although 75 percent of those in your age group chose not to attend. All of you made rational choices based on what you perceived was in your best interest. How could it be in your best interest to do one thing and in another person's best interest to do exactly the opposite? Each person has unique goals and attitudes and faces different costs. Although your weighing of the alternatives came down on the side of attending college, another person weighed similar alternatives and came down on the side of not attending college. Both decisions were rational because in both cases the individual compared alternatives and selected the option that the *individual* thought was in his or her best interest.

It is important to note that rational self-interest depends on the information at hand and the individual's perception of what is in his or her best interest. People will make different choices even when facing the same information. Even though the probability of death in an accident is nearly 20 percent less if seat belts are worn, many people choose not to use them. Are these people rational? The answer is yes. Perhaps they do not want their clothes wrinkled or perhaps seat belts are just too inconvenient or perhaps they think the odds

Having only a few minutes before his economics class begins, and having to reach the building located on the lower peninsula, the student grabs his hang glider and prepares to jump off the cliff. The student knows that instead of attending class, he might continue hang gliding, hike in the Guatemalan mountains, or sail in the beautiful waters. However, he has compared benefits and costs of attending class versus not attending; he decided to attend class.

of getting in an accident are just too small to worry about. Whatever the reason, these people are choosing the option that at the time gives them the greatest satisfaction. *This is rational self-interest.* Economists sometimes use the term *bounded rationality* to emphasize the point that people do not have perfect knowledge or perfect insight. In this book we simply use the term *rational* to refer to the comparison of costs and benefits.

If we told those people choosing not to wear seat belts that they definitely would have an accident and would suffer very serious injuries unless they wore the seat belts, their choice would probably be different. But because *we* think wearing seat belts is smart does not mean that others who choose not to wear seat belts are irrational or any less smart. Similarly, the expense of college and the commitment of four or more years of time might not make college seem like such a good choice to many people. Because some people choose not to attend college does not make them irrational. They are rational because they are comparing alternatives in order to select the option that *they* think will make them better off.

Economists think that most of the time most human beings are weighing alternatives, looking at costs and benefits, and making decisions in a way that they believe makes them better off. This is not to say that economists look upon human beings as androids lacking feelings and able only to carry out complex calculations like a computer. Rather, economists believe that the feelings and attitudes of human beings enter into people's comparisons of alternatives and help determine how people decide something is in their best interest.

Economists believe that human beings are self-interested, *not selfish*. People do contribute to charitable organizations and help others; people do make individual sacrifices because those sacrifices benefit their families or people they care about; soldiers do risk their lives to defend their country. All these acts are made in the name of rational self-interest.

Relying on the idea that most people, most of the time, are rationally self-interested allows economists to explain many real-world observations that otherwise might be inexplicable. Why, for instance, has the number of driver deaths from automobile accidents declined while the number of pedestrian deaths risen since the introduction of safety devices such as seat belts, air bags, antilock brakes, and reinforced passenger cages? One possible explanation, based on self-interest, is that because they now feel safer, drivers have become more reckless. They drive faster, run more red lights, and take more chances. In fact, research has shown that since the introduction of these safety devices there have been more accidents but fewer driver deaths per accident, and more pedestrians have been killed. As we will see throughout the book, rational self-interest provides a valuable first step in analyzing issues and answering questions.

RECAP

1. Scarcity exists when people want more of an item than exists at a zero price.
2. Goods are produced with resources (also called factors of production and inputs). Economists have classified resources into four categories: land, labor, capital, and entrepreneurial ability.
3. Choices have to be made because of scarcity. People cannot have or do everything they desire all the time. Economics is the study of how people choose to use their scarce resources in an attempt to satisfy their wants.
4. People make choices in a manner known as rational self-interest; people make the choices that at the time and with the information they have at their disposal will give them the greatest satisfaction.

2. THE ECONOMIC APPROACH

What is the economic way of thinking?

Economists often refer to the "economic approach" or to "economic thinking." By this, they mean that the principles of scarcity, choice, and rational self-interest are used in a specific way to search out answers to questions about the real world. The specific way is to focus on positive analysis and apply the scientific method. The value of economic thinking is that it provides a way to understand human behavior and to use that understanding to make predictions that aid in economic decision making. In this section we will examine economic thinking.

2.a. Positive and Normative Analysis

positive analysis: analysis of what is

In applying the principles of economics to questions about the real world, it is important to avoid imposing your opinions or value judgments on others. Analysis that does not impose the value judgments of one individual on the decisions of others is called **positive analysis**. If you demonstrate that unemployment in the automobile industry in the United States rises when people purchase cars produced in other countries instead of cars produced in the

United States, you are undertaking positive analysis. However, if you claim that there ought to be a law to stop people from buying foreign-made cars, you are imposing your value judgments on the decisions and desires of others. That is not positive analysis. It is, instead, **normative analysis**. *Normative means "what ought to be"; positive means "what is."* If you demonstrate that the probability of death in an automobile accident is 20 percent higher if seat belts are not worn, you are using positive analysis. If you argue that there should be a law requiring seat belts to be worn, you are using normative analysis.

Economics involves mostly positive analysis because normative analysis does not explain the real world or lead to predictions about it. Normative analysis does, however, play a role in economic policy formation. Typically, policymakers discuss some aspects of human behavior and then make a proposal to change that behavior. For instance, many politicians believe that the United States consumes too much gasoline. They argue that a high tax should be placed on gasoline in order to change people's behavior. This is a normative approach; it is someone's opinion that too much gasoline is consumed.

The problem with normative analysis is that everything depends on the norm being used. For instance, suppose society decides to evaluate policies like the gas-tax proposal using the norm that if more people are helped than are hurt by a program then the program is beneficial. A program of taxing gas at the pump might meet this norm, but—and this is the key point—if the norm is changed, the result could change. Suppose the norm used to evaluate a program is that at least one person must be made better off by the program without harming anyone else. Then the gas-tax program would fail, since someone or some group—those who drive the most—would be made worse off by the tax scheme. The point here is that the outcome of normative analysis depends on the norms or value judgments being applied. Positive analysis is free of value judgments, so its outcome does not vary as norms change.

2.b. Scientific Method

As stated before, economists want to understand the real world and to be able to predict the results of certain events. These goals are hardly unique to economics—they are the same goals most scientists strive toward. A chemist may want to predict the results of combining certain chemicals, and an astronomer may want to predict the results of black holes on galaxy behavior. Similarly, an economist may want to predict the result of an increase in the tuition and fees of college or the result of an increase in taxes. The economist uses much the same methodology as the chemist and astronomer to examine the real world—the **scientific method**. There are five steps in the scientific method, as noted in Figure 2: (1) recognize the problem or issue, (2) cut away unnecessary detail by making assumptions, (3) develop a model or story of the problem or issue, (4) make predictions, and (5) test the model.

The first step in the scientific method, the recognition of the problem, means that an issue is identified—rise in unemployment, accelerated inflation, failure of a business, growth of social security taxes, increased cocaine addiction, the AIDS epidemic, the purchase of one cereal over another, the choice of one job over another, and on and on. Once the issue is identified, the next step is to explain it. This step may seem simple enough, but often it

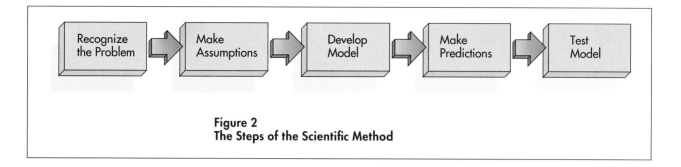

Figure 2
The Steps of the Scientific Method

is not. Each problem in economics is so complex that the task of explaining it seems impossible. Thousands, even hundreds of thousands, of details are involved in something as apparently straightforward as deciding why people choose one college over another. The location of the college relative to the home, the appearance of the college, the friendliness of the admissions officers, the reputation of the football team, the occupations of parents, whether friends are attending college, the weather during the day the college was visited, and whether the student was feeling well the day applications were submitted are all details involved in the decision. Economists, like sociologists, political scientists, and paleontologists, cannot often take into account all the details surrounding an event they want to study. They have to reduce the complexity of the real world to manageable proportions using models and assumptions.

A **theory**, or **model**, is merely a simplification, or abstraction, of the real world that enables scientists to organize their thoughts. A paper airplane is a model of a real airplane; a computer simulation of space is a model of the galaxies. Each model can illustrate certain aspects of the real world but is not intended to capture every aspect of the real world. Good economic models are those that explain or predict well; poor models are those that do not explain or predict well.

An economic model uses assumptions to simplify the problem at hand. **Assumptions** are statements taken for granted or accepted as true without proof. One of the most commonly used assumptions is *everything else held constant*, referred to quite often in its Latin form, **ceteris paribus**. We might say that fewer people attend college as the tuition of college rises, *ceteris paribus*. This means that if only the tuition and number of people attending college are allowed to change, then a higher tuition means fewer people attend college. If we did not make the assumption of everything else held constant, then the statement could be grossly in error. If, for instance, incomes quadrupled while tuition rose a mere 5 percent, we could observe more people attending college even as the tuition rose. Similarly, if the income-earning potential of those with a college degree increased significantly, we might observe that more people attended college even as the tuition rose. Assumptions allow us to focus on the relationship between the variables in which we are interested, in this case tuition and the number of people attending college.

An economic model (or theory) is a tool used in the attempt to understand the real world. As with any theory, it must undergo a **test** to see whether it is consistent with the facts—whether it can be used to make accurate predictions.

theory or model:
a simplification or abstraction of the real world that enables scientists to organize their thoughts

assumptions:
statements accepted as true without proof

ceteris paribus:
other things being equal, or everything else held constant

tests:
trials or measurements used to determine whether a theory is consistent with the facts

Puzzles and Mysteries

Pricing goods at $2.99 rather than $3 first started in the early nineteenth century. Some attribute its beginning to J.C. Penney. One interesting explanation for its use is that it was originally intended as a means of reducing employee theft. Handing a sales clerk three one-dollar bills for a $2.99 item, the customer, expecting change, would ensure that the clerk would ring up the sale and withdraw the correct change from the cash register. The problem with this explanation is that in today's world, sales taxes offset the price, and scanners in checkouts minimize sales clerk errors. As a result, the pricing scheme remains a puzzle. There are many such mysteries in economics. Consider, for instance, why it is common to see products endorsed by celebrities who have no particular expertise. Well-known actors and actresses tell us about the benefits of health clubs and exercise equipment. Basketball players endorse tires. How can it be rational to choose tires on the basis of endorsements? Another puzzle that has caught the attention of economists is why people leave tips at restaurants they do not plan on visiting again. It is easy to try to explain these behaviors as ignorance or stupidity on the part of some individuals. But, if we wouldn't behave ignorantly or stupidly, why would we attribute such behavior to others? The economic way of thinking is to offer an explanation based on rational self-interest. Can you provide answers to these mysteries? If so, please send the explanations to us.

2.c. Common Mistakes

Why are so many items sold for $2.99 rather than $3? Most people attribute this practice to ignorance on the part of others: "People look at the first number and round to it—they see $2.99 but think $2." Although this reasoning may be correct, no one admits to such behavior when asked. As discussed in the Economic Insight "Puzzles and Mysteries," a common error in the attempt to understand human behavior is to argue that other people do not understand something or are stupid. Instead of relying on rational self-interest to explain human behavior, ignorance or stupidity is called on.

fallacy of composition:
the mistaken assumption that what applies in the case of one applies to the case of many

Another common mistake in economic analysis, called the **fallacy of composition,** is the error of attributing what applies in the case of one to the case of many. If one person in a theater realizes a fire has begun and races to the exit, that one person is better off. If we assume that a thousand people in a crowded theater would be better off behaving exactly like the single individual, we would be committing the mistake known as the fallacy of composition.

association as causation:
the mistaken assumption that because two events seem to occur together, one causes the other

The mistaken interpretation of **association as causation** occurs when unrelated or coincidental events that occur at about the same time are believed to have a cause-and-effect relationship. For example, the result of the football Super Bowl game is sometimes said to predict how the stock market will perform. According to this "theory," if the NFC team wins, the stock market will rise in the new year, but if the AFC team wins, the market will fall. This bit of folklore is a clear example of confusion between causation and association. Simply because two events seem to occur together does not mean that one causes the other. Clearly, a football game cannot cause the stock market to rise or fall.

Economics is the study of how people choose to allocate their scarce resources among their unlimited wants and involves the application of certain principles—scarcity, choice, rational self-interest—in a consistent manner using the scientific method. The study of economics is usually separated into two general areas, microeconomics and macroeconomics. **Microeconomics** is the study of economics at the level of the individual economic entity: the individual firm, the individual consumer, and the individual worker. In **macroeconomics**, rather than analyzing the behavior of an individual consumer, we look at the sum of the behaviors of all consumers, which is called the consumer sector, or household sector. Similarly, instead of examining the behavior of an individual firm, in macroeconomics we examine the sum of the behaviors of all firms, called the business sector.

microeconomics:
the study of economics at the level of the individual

macroeconomics:
the study of the economy as a whole

RECAP

1. The objective of economics is to understand why the real world is what it is.

2. Positive analysis refers to what is, while normative economics refers to what ought to be.

3. The scientific method consists of five steps: recognition of the problem, assumptions, model, predictions, and tests of the model.

4. Assumptions are a means of simplifying the analysis; they are statements accepted as true without proof.

5. Assuming that others are ignorant, the fallacy of composition, and interpreting association as causation are three commonly made errors in economic analysis.

6. The study of economics is typically divided into two parts, macroeconomics and microeconomics.

SUMMARY

▲▼ *What is economics?*

1. The objective of economics is to understand why the real world is what it is. Preview

2. The resources that go into the production of goods are land, labor, capital, and entrepreneurial ability. §1.a

3. Economics is the study of how people choose to allocate scarce resources to satisfy their unlimited wants. §1.b

▲▼ *What are the principles of economics?*

4. Scarcity is universal; it applies to anything people would like more of than is available at a zero price. Because of scarcity, choices must be made, and choices are made in a way that is in the decision-maker's rational self-interest. §1.a, 1.b, 1.c

5. People make choices that, at the time and with the information at hand, will give them the greatest satisfaction. §1.c

▲▼ *What is the economic way of thinking?*

6. Positive analysis is analysis of what is; normative analysis is analysis of what ought to be. §2.a

7. The scientific method consists of five steps: recognition of the problem, assumptions, model, predictions, and tests of the model. §2.b

8. Assumptions are a means of simplifying the analysis. §2.b

9. Assuming that others are ignorant, the fallacy of composition, and interpreting association as causation are three commonly made errors in economic analysis. §2.c

10. The study of economics is typically divided into two parts, macroeconomics and micro-economics. §2.d

KEY TERMS

scarcity §1.a

economic good §1.a

free good §1.a

economic bad §1.a

resources, factors of production, or inputs §1.a

land §1.a

labor §1.a

capital §1.a

entrepreneurial ability §1.a

entrepreneur §1.a

rational self-interest §1.c

positive analysis §2.a

normative analysis §2.a

scientific method §2.b

theory or model §2.b

assumptions §2.b

ceteris paribus §2.b

test §2.b

fallacy of composition §2.c

association as causation §2.c

microeconomics §2.d

macroeconomics §2.d

EXERCISES

1. Which of the following are economic goods? Explain why each is or is not an economic good.

   a. Steaks

   b. Houses

   c. Cars

   d. Garbage

   e. T-shirts

2. Many people go to a medical doctor every time they are ill; others never visit a doctor. Explain how a "model" of human behavior can include such opposite behaviors.

3. Erin has purchased a $35 ticket to a "Grateful Dead" concert. She is invited to a sendoff party for a friend who is moving to another part of the country. The party is scheduled for the same day as the concert. If she had known about the party before she bought the concert ticket, she would have chosen to attend the party. However, having purchased the ticket, Erin will choose to attend the concert. Evaluate this problem.

4. It is well documented in scientific research that smoking is harmful to our health. Smokers have higher incidences of coronary disease, cancer, and other catastrophic ill-nesses. Knowing this, about 30 percent of young people begin smoking and about 25 percent of the U.S. population smokes. Are the people who choose to smoke irrational? What do you think of the argument that we should ban smoking in order to protect these people from themselves?

5. Indicate which of the following statements is true or false. If the statement is false, change it to make it true.

   a. Positive analysis imposes the value judg-ments of one individual on the decisions of others.

b. *Ceteris paribus* is Latin for "let the buyer beware."

c. Rational self-interest is the same thing as selfishness.

d. An economic good is scarce if it has a positive price.

e. An economic bad is an item that has a positive price.

f. A resource is the ingredient used to make factors of production.

6. Are the following statements normative or positive? If a statement is normative, change it to a positive statement.

a. The government should provide free tuition to all college students.

b. An effective way to increase the skills of the work force is to provide free tuition to all college students.

c. The government must provide job training if we are to compete with other countries.

7. In the *New York Times Magazine* in 1970, Milton Friedman, a Nobel Prize–winning economist, argued that "the social responsibility of business is to increase profits." How would Friedman's argument fit with the basic economic model that people behave in ways they believe are in their best self-interest?

8. Two economists crossed the street one day when one spied a twenty-dollar bill on the sidewalk. The first economist pointed out to the second economist that there was a twenty-dollar bill on the sidewalk. The second said, "No, there isn't a twenty-dollar bill there. If it were a twenty-dollar bill, somebody would have picked it up." In what sense does this joke describe the scientific methodology used by economists?

9. Use economics to explain why men's and women's restrooms tend to be located near each other in airports and other public buildings.

10. Use economics to explain why diamonds are more expensive than water, when water is necessary for survival and diamonds are not.

11. Use economics to explain why people leave tips in the following two cases: (a) at a restaurant they visit often; (b) at a restaurant they visit only once.

12. Use economics to explain why people contribute to charities.

13. Use economics to explain this statement: "Increasing the speed limit has, to some degree, compromised highway safety on interstate roads but enhanced safety on non-interstate roads."

COOPERATIVE LEARNING EXERCISE

Divide students into groups of five to eight. Within each group, have students number off. Then all number 1s form a discussion group, as do number 2s, 3s, and so on. Assign each group an economic riddle and ask it to devise an explanation based on economic reasoning. Once a solution is agreed on, the groups disperse to their original group and proceed to explain the problem and solution to that group. Some riddles to discuss include:

1. Why do people leave tips at restaurants they do not plan to visit again?

2. Why are tall men more successful in business than average or short men?

3. Why do firms hire athletes to endorse products having nothing to do with athletics?

4. Why do some students copy answers from an exam being taken by someone they do not know and whose quality of answers they cannot be sure of?

5. Why do people vote when their single vote will never be that important?

Pumped Up Over Cheap Gas

Two women duked it out. Two men crashed their cars. Another woman wrote a letter to her grandmother, read 150 pages in a paperback and sat for 3 and one-half hours. Why? Cheap gas.

Circle K sold 49-cent gas for two hours Saturday at two new stores at Priest Drive and Elliot Road in south Tempe and Chandler Boulevard and Desert Foothills Parkway in Phoenix.

The stores are Circle K's first to open in the Valley in five years, an event the corporation celebrated by dropping gasoline prices lower than they've been since Gerald Ford was president.

"I remember when I was little going with my mom when there were gasoline wars. That's what it reminds me of," said Ann Vry, spokeswoman for Circle K. "People would get very excited about filling up their tanks." Whitney Hamilton of Gilbert knows the feeling. She got in the Tempe line at 6:30 a.m.; the special began at 10. "I was in line before there was a line," said Hamilton, who read and wrote her grandmother. "I've never seen them (gas prices) this low. I don't think I'll ever see them this low again."

Vera Lujan drove the 15 or so miles from her central Phoenix home to Tempe, arriving at 8 a.m. Seven cars were ahead of her. "I was already on empty, so I put in $1 and drove over," Lujan said. "I know. It's weird."

About 300 cars were in line at the Tempe store when the cheap gas began. Crowds were lighter in Phoenix, where only about 25 cars waited at any given time.

Circle K officials estimated that they filled up at least 12 cars every five minutes. A 15-gallon limit on the fill-ups was enforced.

"I think I burned more gas than I'm going to get," Ben Valdez of Tempe said as he approached the pumps after waiting 90 minutes.

Some of those waiting could have used a lesson in patience.

"There've been a few little temper raises," Tempe police Officer Dick Steely said, including a fistfight that broke out when one woman tried to cut in front of another.

John Fecther of Tempe came for the gas but saw the long lines and tried to make a U-turn away from the area. He was hit by another vehicle.

"I was going to get the heck out of here," he said as he filled out a police report. "People are crazy. What are you going to save? $4 or $5? I guess to some people that's a lot of money."

Source: "Pumped Up Over Cheap Gas," *The Arizona Republic*, January 22, 1995, p. B1. Used with permission. Permission does not imply endorsement.

Commentary

Economics is the study of human behavior. How then does economics explain the rush to purchase cheap gas? Economists claim that decisions are the process of comparing costs and benefits. In this article, people have chosen to drive to the Circle K store and spend time in line in order to purchase 15 gallons of gasoline at a price of $.49. Thus, people looked at their costs of driving to the station and spending time in line and decided that these costs were less than the benefits they derived from the cheap gas. So let's look at this decision.

The usual price for gasoline at this time in this market was $1.09 a gallon. Thus, each gallon purchased at the cheap price, $.49, means a savings of $.60. Since 15 gallons could be purchased, the most one could save on the gas purchase would be $9.00.

Did the savings outweigh the costs?

At one station, 300 cars were in line. Since 12 cars each five minutes were served, the wait at that station was about 2 hours and 5 minutes. If one gallon of gas was consumed waiting in line and another gallon driving to and from the station, then the savings would be 13 gallons at $.60 or $7.80. Thus, it would seem that those people choosing to purchase the gas believed that more than 2 hours of their time was worth less than $7.80.

However, the time waiting was not the only possible cost of purchasing the gas. The story indicates that some people got into fights and another was in an accident. The possibility of a mishap could also be considered a cost. In addition, the wear and tear on the car from starting and stopping or idling could be considered. The frustration of waiting and in observing other people attempting to crowd or cheat in line could also be a cost. And, whatever else a person could have been doing for that 2 to 3 hours is a cost.

There might be benefits we haven't considered yet. For some people, the joy of being in a large group might be a benefit. These same people might drive anywhere that large groups form. For other people, the demonstration of how important cheap gas is, is the important point, not the money savings. These people are price shoppers—always on the lookout for the best price. For still others, getting out of the house with a good excuse and having some time for reading or reflection might be a benefit.

Whatever factors go into the calculation of costs and benefits, it seems that for many people, the benefits of the cheap gas outweighed the costs. John Fecther said that he was attempting to get out of there after seeing the long lines. John had made a comparison of costs and benefits, apparently assuming that there would be shorter lines. Once he altered his calculation of costs, he changed his mind. He said, "People are crazy. What are you going to save—$4 or $5? I guess that's a lot of money for some people." Is Mr. Fecther right? Was it the $4 or $5 savings that enticed people? Would Mr. Fecther have driven to another appliance store a mile or two away if he was shopping for a dishwasher and learned that he could save $4 or $5 at the other store? Probably not. Why then did he decide to go purchase the cheap gas, even thinking the lines would be shorter?

Working with Graphs

According to the old saying, one picture is worth a thousand words. If that maxim is correct, and, in addition, if producing a thousand words takes more time and effort than producing one picture, it is no wonder that economists rely so extensively on pictures. The pictures that economists use to explain concepts are called *graphs*. The purpose of this appendix is to explain how graphs are constructed and how to interpret them.

I. READING GRAPHS

The three kinds of graphs used by economists are shown in Figures 1, 2, and 3. Figure 1 is a *line graph*. It is the most commonly used type of graph in eco-

Figure 1
Ratio of Median Incomes of College- to High School-Educated Workers
Figure 1 is a line graph showing the ratio of the median income of people who have completed four or more years of college to the median income of those who completed four years of high school. The line shows the income premium for educational attainment, or the value of a college education in terms of income from year to year. The rise in the line since about 1979 shows that the premium for completing college has risen.
Source: *Statistical Abstract of the United States, 1994* (Washington, D.C.: U.S. Government Printing Office).

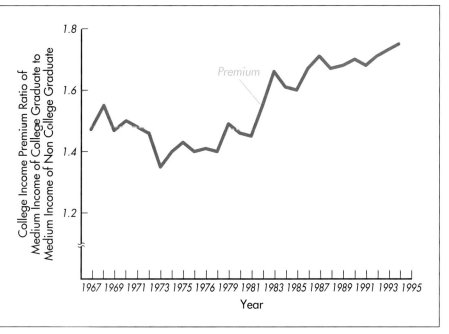

Figure 2
Unemployment and Education
Figure 2 is a bar graph indicating the unemployment rate by educational attainment. The blue refers to high school dropouts, the red refers to those with four years of high school, and the green refers to those with four or more years of college. One set of bars is presented for males and one set for females. The bars are arranged in order, with the highest incidence of unemployment shown first, the next highest second, and the lowest located third. This arrangement is made only for ease in reading and interpretation. The bars could be arranged in any order. Sources: *Economic Report of the President, 1995. Statistical Abstract of the United States, 1995* (Washington, D.C.: U.S. Government Printing Office).

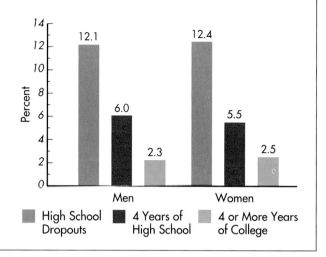

nomics. Figure 2 is a *bar graph*. It is probably used more often in popular magazines than any other kind of graph. Figure 3 is a *pie graph*, or *pie chart*. Although it is less popular than the bar and line graphs, it appears often enough that you need to be familiar with it.

1.a. Relationships Between Variables

Figure 1 is a line graph showing the ratio of the median income of people who have completed four or more years of college to the median income of those who have completed just four years of high school. The line shows the value of a college education in terms of the additional income earned relative to the income earned without a college degree on a year-to-year basis. You can see that the premium for completing college has risen in recent years.

Figure 2 is a bar graph indicating the unemployment rate by educational attainment. The blue refers to high school dropouts, the red refers to those with four years of high school, and the green refers to those with four or more years of college. One set of bars is presented for males and one set for females. The bars are arranged in order, with the highest incidence of unemployment depicted first, the next highest second, and the lowest located third. This arrangement is made only for ease in reading and interpretation. The bars could be arranged in any order. The graph illustrates that unemployment strikes those with less education more than it does those with more education.

Figure 3 is a pie chart showing the percentage of the U.S. population completing various years of schooling. Unlike line and bar graphs, a pie chart is not actually a picture of a relationship between two variables. Instead, the pie represents the whole, 100 percent of the U.S. population, and the pieces of the pie represent parts of the whole—the percentage of the population completing one to four years of elementary school only, five to seven years of elementary school, and so on up to four or more years of college.

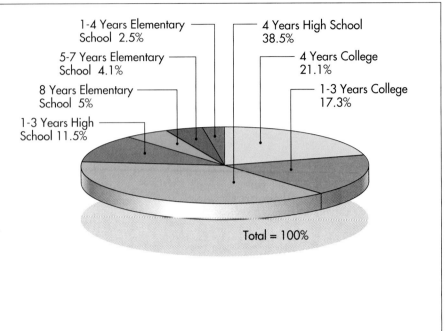

Figure 3
Educational Attainment
Figure 3 is a pie chart showing the percentage of the U.S. population completing various years of schooling. Unlike line and bar graphs, a pie chart is not actually a picture of a relationship between two variables. Instead, the pie represents the whole, 100 percent of the U.S. population, and the pieces of the pie represent parts of the whole—the percentage of the population completing one to four years of elementary school only, five to seven years of elementary school, and so on up to four or more years of college. Source: *Statistical Abstract of the United States, 1994* (Washington, D.C.: U.S. Government Printing Office).

1-4 Years Elementary School 2.5%
5-7 Years Elementary School 4.1%
8 Years Elementary School 5%
1-3 Years High School 11.5%
4 Years High School 38.5%
4 Years College 21.1%
1-3 Years College 17.3%
Total = 100%

Because a pie chart does not show the relationship between variables, it is not as useful for explaining economic concepts as line and bar graphs. Line graphs are used more often than bar graphs to explain economic concepts.

1.b. Independent and Dependent Variables

independent variable:
the variable whose value does not depend on the value of other variables

dependent variable:
the variable whose value depends on the value of the independent variable

Most line and bar graphs involve just two variables, an **independent variable** and a **dependent variable**. An independent variable is one whose value does not depend on the values of other variables; a dependent variable, on the other hand, is one whose value does depend on the values of other variables. The value of the dependent variable is determined after the value of the independent variable is determined.

In Figure 2, the *independent* variable is the educational status of the man or woman, and the *dependent* variable is the incidence of unemployment (percentage of group that is unemployed). The incidence of unemployment depends on the educational attainment of the man or woman.

1.c. Direct and Inverse Relationships

direct or positive relationship:
the relationship that exists when the values of related variables move in the same direction

inverse or negative relationship:
the relationship that exists when the values of related variables move in opposite directions

If the value of the dependent variable increases as the value of the independent variable increases, the relationship between the two types of variables is called a **direct**, or **positive**, **relationship**. If the value of the dependent variable decreases as the value of the independent variable increases, the relationship between the two types of variables is called an **inverse**, or **negative**, **relationship**.

In Figure 2, unemployment and educational attainment are inversely, or negatively, related: as people acquire more education, they are less likely to be unemployed.

2. CONSTRUCTING A GRAPH

Let's now construct a graph. We will begin with a consideration of the horizontal and vertical axes, or lines, and then we will put the axes together. We are going to construct a *straight-line curve*. This sounds contradictory, but it is common terminology. Economists often refer to the demand or supply *curve*, and that curve may be a straight line.

2.a. The Axes

It is important to understand how the *axes* (the horizontal and vertical lines) are used and what they measure. Let's begin with the horizontal axis, the line running across the page in a horizontal direction. Notice in Figure 4(a) that the line is divided into equal segments. Each point on the line represents a quantity, or the value of the variables being measured. For example, each segment could represent one year or 10,000 pounds of diamonds or some other value. Whatever is measured, the value increases from left to right, beginning with negative values, going on to zero, which is called the *origin*, and then moving on to positive numbers.

Figure 4
The Axes, the Coordinate System, and the Positive Quadrant

Figure 4(a) shows the vertical and horizontal axes. The horizontal axis has an origin, measured as zero, in the middle. Negative numbers are to the left of zero, positive numbers to the right. The vertical axis also has an origin in the middle. Positive numbers are above the origin, negative numbers below. The horizontal and verti-cal axes together show the entire coordinate system. Positive numbers are in quadrant I, negative numbers in quadrant III, and combinations of negative and positive numbers in quadrants II and IV.

Figure 4(b) shows only the positive quadrant. Because most economic data are positive, often only the upper right quadrant, the positive quadrant, of the coordinate system is used.

(a) The Coordinate System

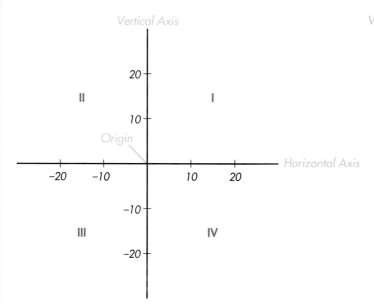

(b) The Positive Quadrant

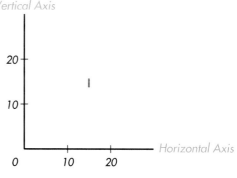

A number line in the vertical direction can be constructed as well, also shown in Figure 4(a). Zero is the origin, and the numbers increase from bottom to top. Like the horizontal axis, the vertical axis is divided into equal segments; the distance between 0 and 10 is the same as the distance between 0 and –10, between 10 and 20, and so on.

In most cases, the variable measured along the horizontal axis is the independent variable. This isn't always true in economics, however. Economists often measure the independent variable on the vertical axis. Do not assume that the variable on the horizontal axis is independent and the variable on the vertical axis is dependent.

Putting the horizontal and vertical lines together lets us express relationships between two variables graphically. The axes cross, or intersect, at their origins, as shown in Figure 4(a). From the common origin, movements to the right and up, in the area—called a quadrant—marked I, are combinations of positive numbers; movements to the left and down, in quadrant III, are combinations of negative numbers; movements to the right and down, in quadrant IV, are negative values on the vertical axis and positive values on the horizontal axis; and movements to the left and up, in quadrant II, are positive values on the vertical axis and negative values on the horizontal axis.

Economic data are typically positive numbers: the unemployment rate, the inflation rate, the price of something, the quantity of something produced or sold, and so on. Because economic data are usually positive numbers, the only part of the coordinate system that usually comes into play in economics is the upper right portion, quadrant I. That is why economists may simply sketch a vertical line down to the origin and then extend a horizontal line out to the right, as shown in Figure 4(b). Once in a while, economic data are negative—for instance, profit is negative when costs exceed revenues. When data are negative, quadrants II, III, and IV of the coordinate system could be used.

2.b. Constructing a Graph from a Table

Now that you are familiar with the axes, that is, the coordinate system, you are ready to construct a graph using the data in the table in Figure 5. The table lists a series of possible price levels for a personal computer (PC) and the corresponding number of PCs people choose to purchase. The data are only hypothetical; they are not drawn from actual cases.

The information given in the table is graphed in Figure 5. We begin by marking off and labeling the axes. The vertical axis is the list of possible price levels. We begin at zero and move up the axis at equal increments of $1,000. The horizontal axis is the number of PCs sold. We begin at zero and move out the axis at equal increments of 1,000 PCs. According to the information presented in the table, if the price is $10,000, no one buys a PC. The combination of $10,000 and 0 PCs is point A on the graph. To plot this point, find the quantity zero on the horizontal axis (it is at the origin), and then move up the vertical axis from zero to a price level of $10,000. (Note that we have measured the units in the table and on the graph in thousands.) At a price of $9,000, there are 1,000 PCs purchased. To plot the combination of $9,000 and 1,000 PCs, find 1,000 units on the horizontal axis and then measure up from there to a price of $9,000. This is point B. Point C represents a

Figure 5
Personal Computer Prices and Purchases

The information given in the table is graphed in Figure 5. We begin by marking off and labeling the axes. The vertical axis is the list of possible price levels. The horizontal axis is the number of PCs purchased. Beginning at zero, the axes are marked at equal increments of 1,000. According to the information presented in the table, if the price level is $10,000, no PCs are purchased. The combination of $10,000 and 0 PCs is point A on the graph. At a price of $9,000, there are 1,000 PCs purchased. This is point B. The final step in constructing a line graph is to connect the points that are plotted. When the points are connected, the straight line slanting downward shows the relationship between the price of PCs and the number of PCs purchased.

Point	Price per PC (thousands)	Number of PCs Purchased (thousands)
A	$10	0
B	9	1
C	8	2
D	7	3
E	6	4
F	5	5
G	4	6
H	3	7
I	2	8
J	1	9
K	0	10

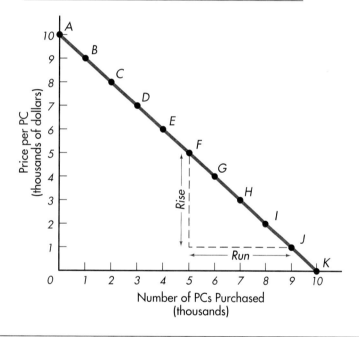

price of $8,000 and 2,000 PCs. Point D represents a price of $7,000 and 3,000 PCs. Each combination of price and PCs purchased listed in the table is plotted in Figure 5.

The final step in constructing a line graph is to connect the points that are plotted. When the points are connected, the straight line slanting downward from left to right in Figure 5 is obtained. It shows the relationship between the price of PCs and the number of PCs purchased.

2.c. Interpreting Points on a Graph

Let's use Figure 5 to demonstrate how points on a graph may be interpreted. Suppose the current price of a PC is $6,000. Are you able to tell how many PCs are being purchased at this price? By tracing that price level from the vertical axis over to the curve and then down to the horizontal axis, you find that 4,000 PCs are purchased. You can also find what happens to the number purchased if the price falls from $6,000 to $5,000. By tracing the price from $5,000 to the curve and then down to the horizontal axis, you discover that 5,000 PCs are purchased. Thus, according to the graph, a decrease in the price from $6,000 to $5,000 results in an increase in the number of PCs purchased.

2.d. Shifts of Curves

Graphs can be used to illustrate the effects of a change in a variable not represented on the graph. For instance, the curve drawn in Figure 5 shows the relationship between the price of PCs and the number of PCs purchased. When this curve was drawn, the only two variables that were allowed to change were the price and the number of computers. However, it is likely that people's incomes determine their reaction to the price of computers as well. An increase in income would enable more people to purchase computers. Thus, at every price more computers would be purchased. How would this be represented? As an outward shift of the curve, from points *A, B, C,* etc. to *A', B', C',* etc. as shown in Figure 6.

Following the shift of the curve, we can see that more PCs are purchased at each price than was the case prior to the income increase. For instance, at a price of $8,000 the increased income allows 4,000 PCs to be purchased rather than 2,000. The important point to note is that if some variable that

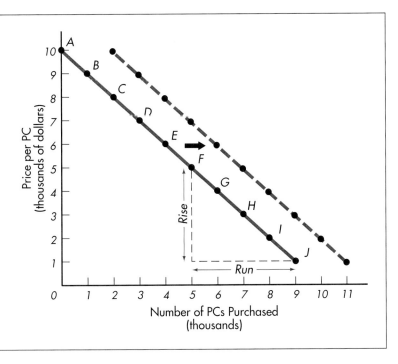

Figure 6
Shift of Curve
An increase in income allows more people to purchase PCs at each price. At a price of $8,000, for instance, 4,000 PCs are purchased rather than 2,000.

Part I / Introduction to the Price System

influences the relationship shown in a curve or line graph changes, then the entire curve or line changes—that is, it shifts.

3. SLOPES

A curve may represent an inverse, or negative, relationship or a direct, or positive, relationship. The slope of the curve reveals the kind of relationship that exists between two variables.

3.a. Positive and Negative Slopes

slope:
the steepness of a curve, measured as the ratio of the rise to the run

The **slope** of a curve is its steepness, the rate at which the value of a variable measured on the vertical axis changes with respect to a given change in the value of the variable measured on the horizontal axis. If the value of a variable measured on one axis goes up when the value of the variable measured on the other axis goes down, the variables have an inverse (or negative) relationship. If the values of the variables rise or fall together, the variables have a direct (or positive) relationship. Inverse relationships are represented by curves that run downward from left to right; direct relationships by curves that run upward from left to right.

Slope is calculated by measuring the amount by which the variable on the vertical axis changes and dividing that figure by the amount by which the variable on the horizontal axis changes. The vertical change is called the *rise*, and the horizontal change is called the *run*. Slope is referred to as the *rise over the run*:

$$\text{Slope} = \frac{\text{rise}}{\text{run}}$$

The slope of any inverse relationship is negative. The slope of any direct relationship is positive.

Let's calculate the slope of the curve in Figure 5. Price (P) is measured on the vertical axis, and quantity of PCs purchased (Q) is measured on the horizontal axis. The rise is the change in price (ΔP), the change in the value of the variable measured on the vertical axis. The run is the change in quantity of PCs purchased (ΔQ), the change in the value of the variable measured on the horizontal axis. The symbol Δ means "change in"; it is the Greek letter delta, so ΔP means "change in P" and ΔQ means "change in Q." Remember that slope equals the rise over the run. Thus the equation for the slope of the straight-line curve running downward from left to right in Figure 5 is

$$\text{Slope} = \frac{\Delta P}{\Delta Q}$$

As the price (P) declines, the number of PCs purchased (Q) increases. The rise is negative, and the run is positive. Thus, the slope is a negative value.

The slope is the same anywhere along a straight line. Thus, it does not matter where we calculate the changes along the vertical and horizontal axes. For instance, from 0 to 9,000 on the horizontal axis—a change of 9,000—the vertical change is a negative $9,000 (from $10,000 down to $1,000). Thus, the rise over the run is –9,000/9,000, or –1. Similarly, from 5,000 to 9,000 in the horizontal direction, the corresponding rise is $5,000 to $1,000, or –$4,000, so that the rise over the run is –4,000/4,000, or –1.

Remember that direct, or positive, relationships between variables are represented by lines that run upward from left to right. These lines have positive slopes. Figure 7 is a graph showing the number of PCs that producers offer for sale at various price levels. The curve represents the relationship between the two variables, number of PCs offered for sale and price. It shows that as price rises, so does the number of PCs offered for sale. The slope of the curve is positive. The change in the rise (the vertical direction) that comes with an increase in the run (the horizontal direction) is positive. Because the graph is a straight line, you can measure the rise and run using any two points along the curve and the slope will be the same. We find the slope by calculating the rise that accompanies the run. Moving from 0 to 4,000 PCs gives us a run of 4,000. Looking at the curve, we see that the corresponding rise is 2,000. Thus, the rise over the run is 2,000/4,000, or .50.

3.b. Equations

Graphs and equations can be used to illustrate the same topics. Some people prefer to use equations rather than graphs, or both equations and graphs, to explain a concept. Since a few equations are used in this book, we need to briefly discuss how they demonstrate the same things as a graph.

The general equation of a straight line has the form: $Y = a + bX$, where Y is the dependent variable, X is the independent variable, a defines the intercept (the value of Y when $X = 0$), and b is the slope. If b is negative, the line slopes downward. If b is positive, the line slopes upward. In the case of Figure 5, the price, P, is the independent variable, and the number of PCs purchased, Q, is the dependent variable. The number of PCs purchased depends on the price. In equation form, substituting Q for Y and P for X, the relationship between

Figure 7
Personal Computers Offered for Sale and Price
Figure 7 is a graph showing the number of PCs offered for sale at various price levels. The curve shows that as price rises, so does the number of PCs purchased. We move from 0 to 4,000, giving us a run of 4,000. The corresponding rise is 2,000. Thus, the rise over the run is 2,000/4,000 or .50.

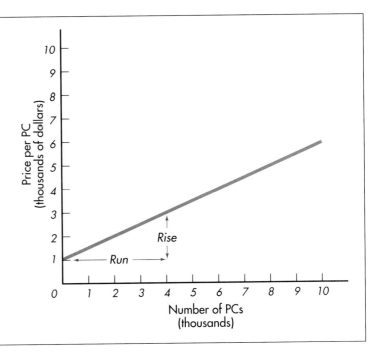

Part I/Introduction to the Price System

price and PCs purchased is $Q = a + bP$. We already know that the slope, b, is negative. For each $1,000 decline in price, 1,000 more PCs are purchased. The slope, b, is -1. The value of a represents the value of Q when P is zero. When the price is zero, 10,000 PCs are purchased. Thus, $a = 10,000$. The equation of Figure 5 is $Q = 10,000 - 1P$.

The equation can be used to tell us how many PCs will be purchased at any given price. Suppose the price is $P = \$4,000$. Substituting $4,000 for P in the equation yields:

$$Q = 10,000 - 1(4,000)$$
$$= 6,000$$

SUMMARY

1. There are three commonly used types of graphs: the line graph, the bar graph, and the pie chart. §1

2. An independent variable is a variable whose value does not depend on the values of other variables. The values of a dependent variable do depend on the values of other variables. §1.b

3. A direct, or positive, relationship occurs when the value of the dependent variable increases as the value of the independent variable increases. An indirect, or negative, relationship occurs when the value of the dependent variable decreases as the value of the independent variable increases. §1.c

4. Most economic data are positive numbers, so often only the upper right quadrant of the

coordinate system is used in economics. §2.a

5. A curve shifts when a variable that affects the dependent variable and is not measured on the axes changes.

6. The slope of a curve is the rise over the run: the change in the variable measured on the vertical axis that corresponds to a change in the variable measured on the horizontal axis. §3.a

7. The slope of a straight-line curve is the same at all points along the curve. §3.a

8. The equation of a straight line has the general form: $Y = a + bX$, where Y is the dependent variable, X the independent variable, a the value of Y when X equals zero, and b the slope. §3.b

KEY TERMS

independent variable §1.b

dependent variable §1.b

direct or positive relationship §1.c

inverse or negative relationship §1.c

slope §3.a

EXERCISES

1. Listed below are two sets of figures: the total quantity of Mexican pesos (new pesos) in circulation (the total amount of Mexican money available) and the peso price of a dollar (how many pesos are needed to purchase one dol-

lar). Values are given for the years 1987 through 1993 for each variable.

a. Plot each variable by measuring time (years) on the horizontal axis and, in the first graph, pesos in circulation on the vertical axis and, in the second graph, peso price of a dollar on the vertical axis.

b. Plot the combinations of variables by measuring pesos in circulation on the horizontal axis and peso prices of a dollar on the vertical axis.

c. In each of the graphs in parts a and b, what are the dependent and independent variables?

d. In each of the graphs in parts a and b, indicate whether the relationship between the dependent and independent variables is direct or inverse.

Year	Pesos in Circulation (billions)	Peso Price of a Dollar
1987	12,627	1.3782
1988	21,191	2.2731
1989	29,087	2.4615
1990	47,439	2.8126
1991	106,227	3.0184
1992	122,220	3.0949
1993	143,902	3.1156

2. Plot the data listed in the following table.

a. Use price as the vertical axis and quantity as the horizontal axis and plot the first two columns.

Price	Quantity Sold	Total Revenue
$1,000	200	200,000
900	400	360,000
800	600	480,000
700	800	560,000
600	1,000	600,000
500	1,200	600,000
400	1,400	560,000
300	1,600	480,000
200	1,800	360,000
100	2,000	200,000

b. Show what quantity is sold when the price is $550.

c. Directly below the graph in part a, plot the data in columns 2 and 3. Use quantity as the horizontal axis and total revenue as the vertical axis.

d. What is total revenue when the price is $550? Will total revenue increase or decrease when the price is lowered?

2

Choice, Opportunity Costs, and Specialization

FUNDAMENTAL
QUESTIONS

1. What are opportunity costs? Are they part of the economic way of thinking?
2. What is a production possibilities curve?
3. How are specialization and opportunity costs related?
4. Why does specialization occur?
5. What are the benefits of trade?

I n the previous chapter we learned that scarcity forces people to make choices. This occurs whether we are speaking of individuals or of societies. Individuals must allocate their scarce resources to attempt to satisfy their unlimited wants, and societies also have scarce resources that must somehow be allocated.

There are costs involved in any choice. As the old saying goes, "There is no free lunch." In every choice, alternatives are forgone, or sacrificed. Having nearly 4 million people in the armed forces, as the United States did in 1969, meant that these 4 million people were not employed in producing automobiles, health care, or other nondefense-related items. The nondefense goods and services not produced—forgone—during that period are part of the costs of choosing to focus on military activities. However, reducing the numbers employed in the military and in military-related activities, as occurred in the early 1990s, is not free either. The equipment and the skills people had acquired that were useful in the production of military goods sometimes had little value in other industries.

PREVIEW

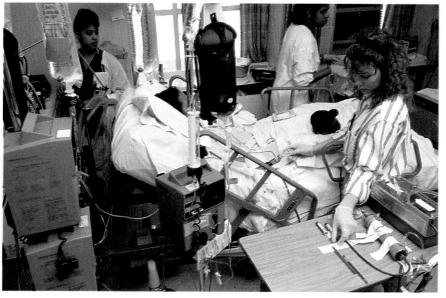

All choices, then, have both costs and benefits. This chapter explains how to calculate these costs and benefits from the perspective of both the individual and society as a whole.

I. OPPORTUNITY COSTS

A choice is simply a comparison of alternatives: to attend college or not to attend college, to change jobs or not to change jobs, to purchase a new car or to keep the old one. An individual compares the costs and benefits of each option and chooses the option expected to provide the most happiness or net benefit. Of course, when one option is chosen, the benefits of the alternatives are forgone. You choose not to attend college and you forgo the benefits of attending college; you buy a new car and forgo the benefits of having the money to use in other ways. *Economists refer to the forgone opportunities or forgone benefits of the next best alternative as* **opportunity costs**—the highest-valued alternative that must be forgone when a choice is made.

Opportunity costs are part of every decision and activity. Your opportunity costs of reading this book are whatever else you could be doing—perhaps watching TV, talking with friends, working, or listening to music. Your opportunity costs of attending college are whatever else you could be doing—perhaps working full time or traveling around the world. Each choice means giving up something else. Waiting in line to be seated at a restaurant or waiting to be seen by a doctor also involve opportunity costs. Many businesses have taken this into account by considering "time utility" when marketing

What are opportunity costs? Are they part of the economic way of thinking?

opportunity costs:
the highest-valued alternative that must be forgone when a choice is made

The cost of any item or activity includes the opportunity cost involved in its purchase.

Chapter 2 / Choice, Opportunity Costs, and Specialization

The Opportunity Cost of Waiting

Standing in line has never been a popular activity, but today it seems that Americans are even more impatient about waiting in line. According to a recent survey, Americans' leisure time has shrunk by 37 percent in the last two decades.

Businesses recognize that people choose products on the basis of the full opportunity cost, not just the price of the good or service. For example, people choose one establishment over another because of shorter waits. As a result, businesses are focusing their marketing efforts on what marketers call time utility—providing products and services in ways that do not consume valuable time or providing values to offset the time losses. When the multiple-line approach—customers line up behind the teller or clerk of their choice—is used in banks and stores, people get frustrated because they often find themselves

in the slowest line. Single lines, where customers wait in one line that allows the first person in line to go to the next available server, do not move any quicker, but they reduce the variance of the wait and thus reduce frustration. As a result, most types of businesses in which several service people handle customers have switched to the single-server line.

Firms have tried several other approaches to dealing with lines. Chemical Bank began a program where any customer who had to wait in a teller line for more than seven minutes was given $5. Hospital emergency rooms in Los Gatos, California, now offer a "no waiting" guarantee: if you wait longer than five minutes for emergency-room care, the billing department knocks 25 percent off your bill. The Manhattan Savings Bank offers live entertainment during noontime banking hours. Some hotels and office buildings have

mirrors on their elevator doors in an attempt to distract people while waiting.

Sometimes just telling people how long they have to wait cheers them up. Disneyland has had to learn to comfort those in line, since a popular attraction like Star Tours can attract as many as 1,800 people in a line. Like many amusement parks, Disneyland provides entertainment for those standing in line, but it also gives people updates, in the form of signs noting "From this point on the wait is 30 minutes."

Sources: "Companies Try a Trick or Two to Conquer Those Killer Queues," N. R. Kleinfield, *New York Times,* Sept. 25, 1988, p. F-11. "It'll Only Hurt for a Very Little While," *Business Week,* Feb. 8, 1988, p. 34; "Profiling the Recreational Shopper," Danny N. Bellenger and Pradeep K. Korganokar, *Journal of Retailing,* Vol. 56 (Fall 1980), pp. 77–92.

their products, as described in the Economic Insight "The Opportunity Cost of Waiting." Let's look at opportunity costs a little more closely.

1.a. The Opportunity Cost of Going to College

Suppose you decided to attend a college where the tuition and other expenses add up to $4,290 per year. Are these your total costs of attending college? If you answer yes, you are ignoring opportunity costs. Remember that you must account for forgone opportunities. If instead of going to college you could have worked full time, then the benefits of full-time employment are your opportunity costs. If you could have obtained a position with an annual income of $20,800, the actual cost of college is the $4,290 of direct expenses plus the $20,800 of forgone salary, or $25,090. This calculation assumes you would not work part-time or during the summer.

1.b. Tradeoffs and Decisions at the Margin

Life is a continuous sequence of decisions, and every single decision involves choosing one thing over another or trading off something for something else.

tradeoff:
the giving up of one good or activity in order to obtain some other good or activity

marginal cost:
additional cost

marginal benefit:
additional benefit

A **tradeoff**, then, means giving up one good or activity in order to obtain some other good or activity. Each term you must decide whether to register for college or not. You could work full time and not attend college, attend college and not work, or work part time and attend college. The time you devote to college will decrease as you devote more time to work. You trade off hours spent at work for hours spent in college; in other words, you compare the benefits you think you will get from going to college this term with the costs of college this term. Once you decide to go to college, you must constantly decide how much to study. Once you sit down and begin studying, you are constantly deciding whether to continue studying or to do something else. Economists say that making choices involves comparing the **marginal costs** and the **marginal benefits**. *Marginal* means "change," so a decision involves the comparison of a change in benefits and a change in costs.

I.c. The Production Possibilities Curve

What is a production possibilities curve?

production possibilities curve (PPC):
a graphical representation showing the maximum quantity of goods and services that can be produced using limited resources to the fullest extent possible

Societies, like individuals, face scarcities and must make choices. And societies, like individuals, forgo opportunities each time they make a particular choice and must compare the marginal costs and marginal benefits of each alternative.

The tradeoffs facing a society can be illustrated in a graph known as the **production possibilities curve (PPC)**. The production possibilities curve shows the maximum quantity of goods and services that can be produced using limited resources to the fullest extent possible. Figure 1 shows a production possibilities curve based on the information (see table) about the production of defense goods and services and nondefense goods and services by a nation such as the United States. Defense goods and services include guns, ships, bombs, personnel, and so forth, that are used for national defense. Nondefense goods and services include education, housing, and food that are not used for national defense. All societies allocate their scarce resources in order to produce some combination of defense and nondefense goods and services. Because resources are scarce, a nation cannot produce as much of everything as it wants. When it produces more health care, it must forgo the production of education or automobiles; when it devotes more of its resources to the military area, fewer are available to devote to health care.

If we could draw or even visualize many dimensions, we could draw a PPC that has a specific good measured along the axis in each dimension. Since we can't, we typically just draw a two-dimensional graph and thus can have just two classes of goods. In Figure 1 the two classes are defense-type goods and nondefense-type goods. But we could just as easily draw a PPC for health care and all other goods or for education and all other goods. These PPCs would look like Figure 1 except that the axes would measure units of health care and other goods or units of education and other goods.

A production possibilities curve shows that more of one type of good can be produced only by reducing the quantity of other types of goods that are produced; it shows that a society has scarce resources; and it shows what the marginal costs and marginal benefits of alternative decisions are. In what way does the PPC show these things? We can answer that question by looking more carefully at Figure 1. In this figure, units of defense goods and services are measured on the vertical axis; units of nondefense goods and services on the horizontal axis. If all resources are allocated to producing defense goods and services, then 200 million units can be produced, but the

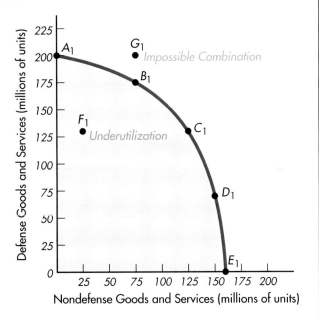

Combination	Defense Goods and Services (millions of units)	Nondefense Goods and Services (millions of units)
A_1	200	0
B_1	175	75
C_1	130	125
D_1	70	150
E_1	0	160
F_1	130	25
G_1	200	75

Figure 1
The Production Possibilities Curve
With a limited amount of resources, only certain combinations of defense and nondefense goods and services can be produced. The maximum amounts that can be produced, given various tradeoffs, are represented by points A_1 through E_1. Point F_1 lies inside the curve and represents the underutilization of resources. More of one type of goods and less of another could be produced, or more of both types could be produced. Point G_1 represents an impossible combination. There are insufficient resources to produce quantities lying beyond the curve.

The production possibilities curve represents the maximum, or the outer limit, of what can be produced.

production of nondefense goods and services will cease. The combination of 200 million units of defense goods and services and 0 units of nondefense goods and services is point A_1, a point on the vertical axis. At 175 million units of defense goods and services, 75 million units of nondefense goods and services can be produced (point B_1). Point C_1 represents 125 million units of nondefense goods and services and 130 million units of defense goods. Point D_1 represents 150 million units of nondefense goods and services and 70 million units of defense goods and services. Point E_1, a point on the horizontal axis, shows the combination of no production of defense goods and services and total production of nondefense goods and services.

The production possibilities curve shows the *maximum* output that can be produced with a limited quantity and quality of resources. The PPC is a picture of the tradeoffs facing society. Only one combination of goods and services can be produced at any one time. All other combinations are forgone.

1.c.1. Points Inside the Production Possibilities Curve Suppose a nation produces 130 million units of defense goods and services and 25 million units of nondefense goods and services. That combination, Point F_1 in Figure 1, lies inside the production possibilities curve. A point lying inside the production possibilities curve indicates that resources are not being fully or efficiently used. If the existing work force is employed only 20 hours per week, it is not being fully used. If two workers are used when one would be sufficient—say, two people in each Domino's Pizza delivery car—then resources are not being used efficiently. If there are resources available for use, society can move from point F_1 to a point on the PPC, such as point C_1. The move would gain 100 million units of nondefense goods and services with no loss of defense goods and services.

1.c.2. Points Outside the Production Possibilities Curve

Point G_1 in Figure 1 represents the production of 200 million units of defense goods and services and 75 units of nondefense goods and services. Point G_1, however, represents the use of more resources than are available—it lies outside the production possibilities curve. Unless more resources can be obtained and/or the quality of resources improved so that the nation can produce more with the same quantity of resources, there is no way the society can currently produce 200 million units of defense goods and 75 million units of nondefense goods.

1.c.3. Shifts of the Production Possibilities Curve

If a nation obtains more resources, points outside its current production possibilities curve become attainable. Suppose a country discovers new sources of oil within its borders and is able to greatly increase its production of oil. Greater oil supplies would enable the country to increase production of all types of goods and services.

Figure 2 shows the production possibilities curve before (PPC_1) and after (PPC_2) the discovery of oil. PPC_1 is based on the data given in Figure 1. PPC_2 is based on the data given in Figure 2 (see table), which shows the increase in production of goods and services that results from the increase in oil supplies. The first combination of goods and services on PPC_2, point A_2, is 220 million units of defense goods and 0 units of nondefense goods. The second point, B_2, is a combination of 200 million units of defense goods and 75 million units of nondefense goods. C_2 through F_2 are the combinations shown in the table of Figure 2. Connecting these points yields the bowed-out curve, PPC_2. Because of the availability of new supplies of oil, the nation is able to increase production of all goods, as shown by the *shift* from PPC_1 to PPC_2. A comparison of the two curves shows that more goods and services for both defense and nondefense are possible along PPC_2 than along PPC_1.

The outward shift of the PPC can be the result of an increase in the quantity of resources, but it also can occur because the quality of resources improves. For instance, a technological breakthrough could conceivably improve the way that communication occurs, thereby requiring fewer people and machines and less time to produce the same quantity and quality of goods. The work force could become more literate, thereby requiring less time to produce the same quantity and quality of goods. Each of these quality improvements in resources could lead to an outward shift of the PPC.

The outward shift of the PPC illustrates that the capacity, or potential, of the economy has grown. However, being able to produce more of all goods doesn't mean that a society will do that. A society might produce at a point on the PPC, inside the PPC, or even attempt to produce at a point outside the PPC. In the early 1990s, for example, the United States was producing at a point inside its PPC. Resources were not being used fully and efficiently. Resources became more fully and efficiently utilized in 1992, and the United States moved out toward its PPC. Conversely, there are times when a society tries to produce a combination of goods and services that are beyond its capacity—a point outside its current PPC. The result can be similar to that when individuals attempt to carry out physical exertion that is beyond their capabilities. They become overheated and can damage internal organs. Such

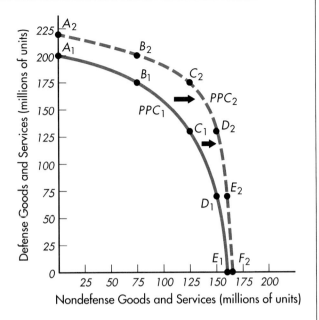

Combination	Defense Goods and Services (millions of units)	Nondefense Goods and Services (millions of units)
A_2	220	0
B_2	200	75
C_2	175	125
D_2	130	150
E_2	70	160
F_2	0	165

Figure 2
A Shift of the Production Possibilities Curve
Whenever everything else is not constant, the curve shifts. In this case, an increase in the quantity of a resource enables the society to produce more of both types of goods. The curve shifts out, away from the origin.

was the case for the United States in the late 1960s when it attempted to pay for the Vietnam War and to increase expenditures on social programs.

Knowing that the opportunity costs include the entire PPC plus the forgone production of those resources not fully or efficiently used, why would a society produce at a point inside the PPC? Almost as puzzling is why a society might try to produce beyond its capacity, something it cannot sustain, when the opportunity costs include not only the entire PPC but the possible damage to the society's "internal organs." The answers to these questions are far from straightforward; in fact, a significant part of macroeconomics is devoted to answering them.

RECAP

1. Opportunity costs are the benefits that are forgone due to a choice. When you choose one thing you must give up—forgo—others.
2. Opportunity cost is an individual concept but can be used to demonstrate scarcity and choice for a society as a whole.
3. The production possibilities curve represents all combinations of goods and services that can be produced using limited resources efficiently to their full capabilities.
4. Points inside the production possibilities curve represent the underutilization or inefficient use of resources—more goods and services could

be produced by using the limited resources more fully or efficiently.

5. Points outside the production possibilities curve represent combinations of goods and services that are unattainable given the limitation of resources. More resources would have to be obtained, or a more efficient means of production through the development of technology or innovative management techniques would have to be discovered, to produce quantities of goods and services outside the current production possibilities curve.

2. SPECIALIZATION AND TRADE

No matter which combination of goods and services a society chooses to produce, other combinations of goods are forgone. The PPC illustrates what these forgone combinations are. The PPC also illustrates how easily a society can transfer resources from one activity to another. If someone is equally productive making either rocket launchers or medical equipment, total output will not change as that person moves from producing one type of product to producing the other type. However, a specialist in the design of rocket launchers might not be very good at designing medical equipment. By taking that specialist from the production of defense goods and placing her into the health-care industry, many rocket launchers may have to be forgone with little additional production in the health-care industry. We describe how specialization affects the shape of the PPC curve in the following section.

2.a. Marginal Opportunity Cost

marginal opportunity cost:
the amount of one good or service that must be given up to obtain one additional unit of another good or service, no matter how many units are being produced

The shape of the PPC illustrates the ease with which resources can be transferred from one activity to another. If it becomes increasingly more difficult or costly to move resources from one activity to another, the PPC will have the bowed-out shape of Figure 1. With each successive increase in the production of nondefense goods, we see that some amount of defense goods has to be given up. The incremental amounts of defense production given up with each increase in the production of nondefense goods are known as marginal opportunity costs. **Marginal opportunity cost** is the amount of one good or service that must be given up to obtain one additional unit of another good or service, no matter how many units are being produced.

The bowed-out shape shows that for each additional nondefense good, more and more defense goods have to be forgone. According to the table and graph in Figure 3, we see that moving from point A to point B on the PPC means increasing nondefense production from 0 to 25 million units and decreasing defense production from 200 million to 195 million units, resulting in a marginal opportunity cost of 5 million units of defense goods and services for each 25 million units of nondefense goods and services. Moving from point B to point C means increasing nondefense production from 25 to 50 million units, decreasing defense production from 195 to 188 million units and creating a marginal opportunity cost of 7 million units. Moving from point C to point D causes nondefense production to increase from 50 to 75 million units, a decrease in defense production from 188 million to 175 million units and a marginal opportunity cost of 13 million units. As you can see from the table for Figure 3, marginal opportunity costs increase with

Figure 3
The Production Possibilities Curve and Marginal Opportunity Costs

With a limited amount of resources, only certain combinations of defense and nondefense goods and services can be produced. The maximum amounts that can be produced are represented by points A through H. With each increase of nondefense production, marginal opportunity costs increase. This occurs as a result of specialization. The first resources switched from defense to nondefense production are those that are least specialized in the production of defense goods. But as more and more nondefense goods are produced, the more specialized resources have to be switched as well. This means higher opportunity costs; increasing amounts of defense goods have to be forgone.

Combination	Defense Goods and Services (millions of units)	Marginal Opportunity Costs (defense units forgone per 25 units of nondefense units gained)	Nondefense Goods and Services (millions of units)
A	200		0
		5	
B	195		25
		7	
C	188		50
		13	
D	175		75
		20	
E	155		100
		30	
F	125		125
		50	
G	75		150
		75	
H	0		160

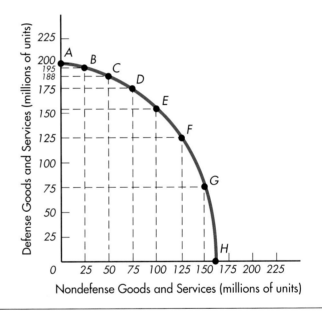

each successive increase of nondefense production. In other words, it gets more and more costly to produce nondefense goods. The increased marginal opportunity costs occur as a result of specialization. The first resources switched from defense to nondefense production are those that are least specialized in the production of defense goods. Switching these resources is less costly (less has to be given up) than switching the specialists. An accountant can do accounting in either defense- or nondefense-related industries equally well; an expert rocket physicist cannot work as efficiently in health care as in the defense area. But as more and more nondefense goods are produced, the more specialized resources have to be switched as well. This means higher opportunity costs, and increasing amounts of defense goods have to be forgone.

2.b. Specialize Where Opportunity Costs Are Lowest

How are specialization and opportunity costs related?

Why does specialization occur?

Individuals, firms, and nations select the option with the lowest opportunity cost.

Why does specialization occur? Every coach, every band director, and every manager of a firm knows the answer to this question. Each has a limited number of talented people and must decide where to position each person in order to create the best team, band, or firm. A band director doesn't expect one person to play the clarinet, trumpet, and drums, even if that person has the ability to play all three instruments, because that would not result in the best band. A coach doesn't expect one person to play every position, and a manager doesn't expect one worker to do every task. Each of these leaders must allocate the scarce resources to best perform the job.

We also have to decide how to use our own scarce resources. We must choose where to devote our energies. Few of us are jacks-of-all-trades. Nations, similarly, have limited amounts of resources and must choose where to devote those resources.

How do we decide where to devote our energies? The answer is to *specialize in those activities that require us to give up the smallest amount of other things*. A plumber does plumbing and leaves teaching to the teachers. The teacher teaches and leaves electrical work to the electrician. A country such as Grenada, which has abundant rich land suitable for the cultivation and production of nutmeg and other spices, specializes in spice production. If we specialize, however, how do we get the other things we want? The answer is that we trade, or exchange goods and services.

2.b.1. Trade By specializing in activities in which opportunity costs are lowest and then trading, each country or individual will end up with more than if each tried to produce everything. Consider a simple hypothetical example, as given in Figure 4, which concerns two countries, Haiti and the Dominican Republic, that share an island. Assume Haiti and the Dominican Republic must decide how to allocate their resources between food production and health care. Haiti's daily production possibilities curve is plotted using the data in columns 2 and 3 of the table. If Haiti devotes all of its resources to health care, then it would be able to provide 1,000 people adequate care each day but would have no resources with which to produce food. If it devotes half of its available resources to each activity, then it would provide 500 people adequate health care and produce 7 tons of food. Devoting all of its resources to food production would mean that Haiti could produce 10 tons of food but would have no health care. The Dominican Republic's production possibilities curve is plotted using the data in columns 4 and 5 of the table. If the Dominican Republic devotes all of its resources to health care, it could provide adequate care to 500 people daily but would be unable to produce any food. If it devotes half of its resources to each activity then it could provide 300 people health care and produce 5 tons of food; and if it devotes all of its resources to food production, it could produce 10 tons of food but no health care.

Suppose that Haiti and the Dominican Republic each want 500 people per day provided adequate health care. By itself, the Dominican Republic would be unable to grow any food if it devoted resources to health care for 500 people. However, if the Dominican Republic and Haiti could agree to some type of exchange, perhaps the Dominican Republic could get some food and give the 500 people the health care. But who produces what? The answer depends

Figure 4
The Benefits of Trade
The trade point of providing health care to 500 people and 2 tons of food is beyond the Dominican Republic's PPC; similarly, the trade point of providing health care to 500 people and 8 tons of food is beyond Haiti's PPC. However, through specialization and trade, these points are achieved by the two nations.

	Haiti		Dominican Republic	
Allocation of Resources to Health Care	Health Care (no. of people provided care)	Food (tons)	Health Care (no. of people provided care)	Food (tons)
100%	1,000	0	500	0
50	500	7	300	5
0	0	10	0	10

(a) Haiti

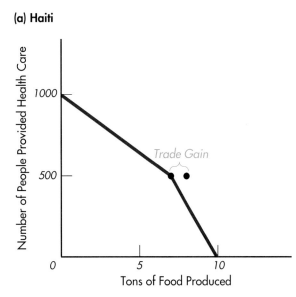

(b) Dominican Republic

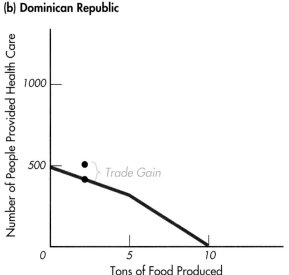

on opportunity costs. If the Dominican Republic decides to provide health care to 500 people, it must forgo 10 tons of food; Haiti, on the other hand, must forgo only 3 tons of food if it decides to provide health care to 500 people. Haiti's opportunity cost for devoting its resources to providing 500 people health care, 3 tons of food, is lower than the Dominican Republic's, 10 tons. Conversely, if the Dominican Republic produces 10 tons of food, it forgoes providing health care for only 500 people while Haiti forgoes health care for 1,000 people. Clearly, the Dominican Republic's opportunity costs of producing food are lower than Haiti's.

Given the differences in opportunity costs, it would make sense for Haiti to devote its resources to health care and for the Dominican Republic to devote its resources to food production. In this case, Haiti would provide 1,000 people health care and produce no food and the Dominican Republic would produce 10 tons of food but no health care. The two nations would then trade. The Dominican Republic might give 8 tons of food to Haiti in exchange for health care for 500 people. Under this scheme, where each country gets health care for 500 people, the Dominican Republic would be better off by the 2 tons of food it would also get, while Haiti would be better off by the 8 rather than 7 tons of food it would get if it provided the 500 people health care using its own resources. Each is made better off by specialization and trade.

Specialization and trade enable nations to acquire combinations of goods that lie beyond their own resource capabilities. This is shown in Figure 4: the trade point of 500 people being provided health care and 2 tons of food is beyond the Dominican Republic's PPC. Similarly, the trade point of 500 people being provided health care and 8 tons of food is beyond Haiti's PPC. The same result applies to individuals and firms. Even though one person, one firm, or one nation is limited to the combinations of goods it can produce using its own resources along or inside its own PPC, through specialization and trade more goods can be acquired. This is why people, firms, and nations trade; this is why there are buyers and sellers.

2.c. Comparative Advantage

comparative advantage:
the ability to produce a good or service at a lower opportunity cost than someone else

We have seen that the choice of which area or activity to specialize in is made on the basis of opportunity costs. Economists refer to the ability of one person or nation to do something with a lower opportunity cost than another as **comparative advantage**. In the example shown in Figure 4, the Dominican Republic had a comparative advantage in food production and Haiti had a comparative advantage in health-care provision. Devoting all resources to health care, Haiti can provide 1,000 people health care while the Dominican Republic can provide only 500 people health care. Devoting all resources to food production, both Haiti and the Dominican Republic can produce 10 tons of food. Clearly, Haiti is better at health care and no worse at food production. Yet, each country has a comparative advantage. Haiti's comparative advantage is in producing health care—it gives up three tons of food for providing 500 people health care while the Dominican Republic gives up ten tons of food for providing 500 people health care. Conversely, the Dominican Republic has a comparative advantage in food production. It gives up providing 500 people health care if it produces ten tons of food while Haiti gives up providing 1,000 people health care if it produces ten tons of food. Haiti has a *comparative advantage* in health care and the Dominican Republic has a *comparative advantage* in food production. It is the relative amount given up not the absolute amount that can be produced that determines comparative advantage. Even if Haiti could produce eleven tons of food while the Dominican Republic could produce only ten, the Dominican Republic's comparative advantage would be in food production.

Comparative advantage applies to every case of trade or exchange. You may be better at both computer programming and literature than your roommate, but you may be much better at computer programming and only slightly better at literature. You, then, have a comparative advantage in computers. Your roommate has a comparative advantage as well, in literature. Remember, comparative advantage depends on opportunity costs. Just because you are better than your roommate at both activities, you do not have the same opportunity costs in both. Like Haiti and the Dominican Republic, you and your roommate are better off specializing and then trading (helping each other) than if both of you do all the studying all by yourselves. You both get better grades and have more time to devote to other activities.

The fruit of the prickly pear cactus is popular in salads and drinks. Recently, the extract from the cactus leaves has been found to relieve some of the symptoms of diabetes. Physicians in Mexico and Japan prescribe the extract as a substitute for insulin in some cases and as an enhancement to insulin in others. Though the prickly pear cactus grows in southwestern United States as well, the harvesting of the cacti occurs mainly in Mexico because most of the prickly pear cactus forests are in Mexico, and the labor-intensive harvesting process is less costly in Mexico than it would be in the United States. Mexico has a comparative advantage in the harvesting of the cacti.

2.d. Specialization and Trade Occur Everywhere

What are the benefits of trade?

Individuals specialize in the activity in which their opportunity costs are lowest.

Each of us will specialize in some activity, earn an income, and then trade our output (or income) for other goods and services we want. Specialization and trade ensure that we are better off than doing everything ourselves. A firm, a team, or a band can be thought of as an organization in which people specialize according to their comparative advantage and then trade or exchange their output. This ensures that the organization gets the greatest output at the lowest cost. Nations also are better off if they devote resources to the production of goods and services in which they have a comparative advantage and then exchange those goods and services. *Specialization according to comparative advantage followed by trade allows everyone to acquire more of the goods they want.*

We have now explored the basics of economics. We know that scarcity means that choices must be made. We have learned that choices are made according to rational self-interest. And we just discovered that specialization according to comparative advantage followed by trade ensures that people are as well off as they can possibly be. Trade usually refers to the exchange of goods and services by nations, but trade is also what we do when we purchase goods and services. We trade money for goods and services. We acquired money as a payment for the resource services we provided—working, owning land, providing funds for capital, or being an entrepreneur. Thus, we are, in essence, trading our resource services for the goods and services others provide.

1. Marginal opportunity cost is the amount of one good or service that must be given up to obtain one additional unit of another good or service.

2. The rule of specialization is: the individual (firm, region, or nation) will specialize in the production of the good or service that has the lowest opportunity cost.

3. Comparative advantage exists whenever one person (firm, nation) can do something with fewer opportunity costs than some other individual (firm, nation) can.

4. Specialization and trade enable individuals, firms, and nations to get more than they could without specialization and trade.

SUMMARY

▲▼ *What are opportunity costs? Are they part of the economic way of thinking?*

1. Opportunity costs are the forgone opportunities of the next best alternative. Choice means both gaining something and giving up something. When you choose one option you forgo all others. The benefits of the next best alternative are the opportunity costs of your choice. §1

▲▼ *What is a production possibilities curve?*

2. A production possibilities curve represents the tradeoffs involved in the allocation of scarce resources. It shows the maximum quantity of goods and services that can be produced using limited resources to the fullest extent possible. §1.c

3. The bowed-out shape of the PPC occurs because of specialization and increasing marginal opportunity costs. §2.a

▲▼ *How are specialization and opportunity costs related?*

4. Comparative advantage is when one person (one firm, one nation) can perform an activity or produce a good with fewer opportunity costs than someone else. §2.c

▲▼ *Why does specialization occur?*

5. Comparative advantage accounts for specialization. We specialize in the activities in which we have the lowest opportunity costs, that is, in which we have a comparative advantage. §2.c

▲▼ *What are the benefits of trade?*

6. Specialization and trade enable those involved to acquire more than they could by not specializing and engaging in trade. §2.d

KEY TERMS

opportunity costs §1

tradeoff §1.b

marginal §1.b

marginal cost §1.b

marginal benefit §1.b

production possibilities curve (PPC) §1.c

marginal opportunity cost §2.a

comparative advantage §2.c

EXERCISES

1. In the 1992 presidential campaign, critics of the Bill Clinton/Al Gore team argued that it would be impossible for them to fulfill their promises. Clinton and Gore promised more and better health care, a better environment, only minor reductions in defense, better education, and a better and improved system of roads, bridges, sewer systems, water systems, and so on. Accepting the promises as facts, what economic concept were the critics claiming that Clinton and Gore ignored?

2. Janine is an accountant who makes $30,000 a year. Robert is a college student who makes $8,000 a year. All other things being equal, who is more likely to stand in a long line to get a concert ticket?

3. Back in the 1960s, President Lyndon Johnson passed legislation that increased expenditures for both the Vietnam War and social problems in the United States. Since the U.S. economy was operating at its full employment level when President Johnson did this, he appeared to be ignoring what economic concept?

4. The following numbers measure the tradeoff between grades and income.

Total Hours	Hours Studying	GPA	Hours Working	Income
60	60	4.0	0	$ 0
60	40	3.0	20	100
60	30	2.0	30	150
60	10	1.0	50	250
60	0	0.0	60	300

a. Calculate the opportunity cost of an increase in the number of hours spent studying in order to earn a 3.0 grade point average (GPA) rather than a 2.0 GPA.

b. Is the opportunity cost the same for a move from a 0.0 GPA to a 1.0 GPA as it is for a move from a 1.0 GPA to a 2.0 GPA?

c. What is the opportunity cost of an increase in salary from $100 to $150?

5. Suppose a second individual has the following tradeoffs between income and grades:

Total Hours	Hours Studying	GPA	Hours Working	Income
60	50	4.0	10	$ 60
60	40	3.0	20	120
60	20	2.0	40	240
60	10	1.0	50	300
60	0	0.0	60	360

a. Define comparative advantage.

b. Does either individual (the one in question 4 or the one in question 5) have a comparative advantage in both activities?

c. Who should specialize in studying and who should specialize in working?

6. A doctor earns $250,000 per year while a professor earns $40,000. They play tennis against each other each Saturday morning, each giving up a morning of relaxing, reading the paper, and playing with their children. They could each decide to work a few extra hours on Saturday and earn more income. But they choose to play tennis or to relax around the house. Are their opportunity costs of playing tennis different?

7. Plot the PPC given by the following data.

Combination	Health Care	All Other Goods
A	0	100
B	25	90
C	50	70
D	75	40
E	100	0

a. Calculate the marginal opportunity cost of each combination.

b. What is the opportunity cost of combination C?

c. Suppose a second nation has the following PPC. Plot the PPC and then determine which nation has the comparative advantage in which activity. Show whether the two nations can gain from specialization and trade.

Combination	Health Care	All Other Goods
A	0	50
B	20	40
C	40	25
D	60	5
E	65	0

8. A doctor earns $200 per hour, a plumber $40 per hour, and a professor $20 per hour. Everything else the same, which one will devote more hours to negotiating the price of a new car?

9. Perhaps you've heard of the old saying "There is no such thing as a free lunch." What does it mean? If someone invites you to a lunch and offers to pay for it, is it free to you?

10. You have waited 30 minutes in a line for the Star Tours ride at Disneyland. You see a sign that says, "From this point on your wait is 45 minutes." You must decide whether to continue in line or to move elsewhere. On what basis do you make the decision? Do the 30 minutes you've already stood in line come into play?

11. The university is deciding between two meal plans. One plan charges a fixed fee of $600 per semester and allows students to eat as much as they want. The other plan charges a fee based on the quantity of food consumed. Under which plan will students eat the most?

12. Evaluate this statement: "You are a natural athlete, an attractive person who learns easily and communicates well. Clearly, you can do everything better than your friends and acquaintances. As a result, the term *specialization* has no meaning for you. Specialization would cost you rather than benefit you."

13. During China's Cultural Revolution in the late 1960s and early 1970s, many people with a high school or college education were forced to move to farms and work in the fields. Some were common laborers for eight or more years. What does this policy say about specialization and the PPC? Would you predict that the policy would lead to an increase in output?

14. In elementary school and through middle school most students have the same teacher throughout the day and for the entire school year. Then, beginning in high school different subjects are taught by different teachers. In college, the same subject is often taught at different levels, freshman, sophomore, junior-senior, or graduate, by different faculty. Is education taking advantage of specialization only from high school on? Comment on the differences between elementary school and college and the use of specialization.

15. The top officials in federal government and high-ranking officers of large corporations often have chauffeurs to drive them around the city or from meeting to meeting. Is this simply one of the perquisites of their position, or is the use of chauffeurs justifiable on the basis of comparative advantage?

COOPERATIVE LEARNING EXERCISE

Students count off to form groups (1 through 4 for a four-person group). Students in each group then take a few minutes to develop an answer to one of the following questions. Then a number is drawn to identify students to answer the questions. Questions could include:

1. Explain how opportunity costs differ from out-of-pocket expenses in the case of a purchase of (a) a meal at a restaurant, (b) a portable CD player, (c) books for class.

2. How does the PPC illustrate the concepts of opportunity cost, scarcity, tradeoffs, and the necessity for allocating scarce goods and resources?

As Year Ends, Deregulation Still Starting

Deregulation appears to remain in an early stage in Japan as 1994 draws to a close. The government of Prime Minister Tomiichi Murayama plans to put forward a five year deregulation plan in March, but no national consensus appears to have developed yet as to how far Japan should go.

Proponents insist that deregulation would expand business opportunity, intensify competition, improve productivity and thereby move Japanese consumer prices close to international standards.

Opponents argue that deregulation could jeopardize jobs and push down not only prices but also wages. They say Japan's extremely low unemployment rate, 3% or less, is the result of regulation and high consumer prices. They point to how the U.S. aviation industry has been disrupted by deregulation.

Keidanren, the nation's most influential business lobby, has pressed for deregulation partly because of the yen's rapid appreciation, which has pushed up domestic costs and undermined the global competitiveness of Japan-based manufacturers.

"This is an unstoppable move because Japan is at a historic turning point," Uchida said. "Industrial policy tailored by the government no longer works and companies should act on their own."

Source: "As Year Ends, Deregulation Still Starting," *The Nikkei Weekly*, December 26, 1994 and January 2, 1995. Reprinted by permission.

The Nikkei Weekly/December 26, 1994 and January 2, 1995

Commentary

Japan has come under increasing pressure to open up its market—to allow firms from other nations to sell more products to the Japanese consumers. The article focuses on this process, called deregulation. Historically Japan has been an economy whose business is tightly controlled. The initial business organizations in the late 1860s were called zaibatsus, powerful family-based groups that dominated the economy. During the American occupation following World War II, zaibatsus were blamed for helping start the war and were broken up. But they formed again into keiretsus. Today there are two main kinds of keiretsus: groups of companies involved in many different industries but centered around a large bank, and companies grouped around a major manufacturer. In addition to the keiretsus, the government played a large role in determining which businesses would be growth businesses. The government's Ministry of International Trade and Industry or MITI dictated which firms would receive support from the government in the form of government restrictions on foreign competition. MITI's policies were referred to as industrial policy.

During the 1970s and 1980s, the industrial policy was given the credit for Japan's economic success. But, the recession in Japan in the early 1990s has forced Japan to reconsider its approach. The Japanese consumers are beginning to demand more access to goods produced in other counties and are beginning to rebel at the high prices they pay on Japanese goods.

The main question the article raises is whether deregulation will resolve Japan's economic problems. Let's see if what we've learned in this chapter can provide some answers.

First, will deregulation be beneficial?

The article points out that the opponents to the deregulation policies argue that the trade restrictions (regulation) means that consumers pay higher prices which keeps unemployment low. We learned in the chapter that nations could gain by specializing where their opportunity costs are lowest and then trading. Trade allows a society to acquire goods and services beyond its own PPC. Suppose that the figure below represents Japan's PPC. With trade, Japan could gain some amount, say A to B. Not allowing trade means that consumers can consume less than they could with trade. They are restricted to the nation's own PPC—represented by point A or any point on or inside the PPC. Japanese consumers have an opportunity cost of amount A to B; they forgo the additional amount of goods and services. Trade will benefit Japanese consumers.

By not allowing its citizens the opportunity to purchase more goods produced in other countries, Japan is forcing the demand for Japanese produced goods to be higher than it otherwise would be. A report in the February 6, 1995 issue of *Fortune* magazine indicated that in 1989 Japanese consumers paid nearly 4 percent of Japan's GDP for higher priced goods because of the trade restrictions. This indeed increased employment at the expense of higher prices for the Japanese consumer. The *Fortune* report indicated that Japanese consumers effectively paid upwards of $600,000 for each job protected by trade barriers.

Restrictions on trade have benefitted Japanese businesses and some employees who might otherwise not have been employed.

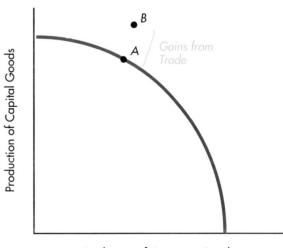

Production of Consumer Goods

3

Markets, Demand and Supply, and the Price System

FUNDAMENTAL
QUESTIONS

1. What is a market?
2. What is demand?
3. What is supply?
4. How is price determined by demand and supply?
5. What causes price to change?
6. What happens when price is not allowed to change with market forces?

W e are going to begin this chapter with a questionnaire. Please select one of the following responses for each of the eight following scenarios:

a. Completely fair
b. Acceptable
c. Unfair
d. Very unfair
e. Totally unacceptable

PREVIEW

At a sightseeing point, reachable only after a strenuous hike, a well has been tapped. The water is sold to thirsty hikers in six-ounce bottles. The price is $1 per bottle. The well provides enough for only 100 bottles per day. On a particularly hot day, 200 hikers want to buy a bottle. Indicate what you think of each of the following means of distributing the water to the hikers.

1. Increasing the price until only 100 hikers buy a bottle.

2. Selling the water for $1 per bottle on a first-come, first-served basis.

3. Having the local authority (government) buy the water for $1 per bottle and distribute it according to its own judgment.

4. Selling the water at $1 per bottle following a random selection procedure or lottery.

A physician has been providing medical services at a fee of $100 per patient and can take care of only 30 patients per day. One day the flu bug has been so vicious that the number of patients attempting to visit the physician exceeds 60. Indicate what you think of each of the following means of distributing the physician's services to the sick patients.

5. Raising the price until only 30 patients purchase the doctor's services.

6. Selling the services at $100 per patient on a first-come, first-served basis.

7. The local authority (government) pays the physician $100 per patient and chooses who is to receive the services according to its own judgment.

8. Selling the physician's services for $100 per patient following a random selection procedure or lottery.

Why is it necessary to choose a way to allocate the bottled water or the physician's services? The reason is scarcity; more people want the water or the physician's services than can be provided for. Since scarcity exists almost everywhere, it is necessary to define a way to allocate the scarce goods and resources. Although this allocation process might seem straightforward initially, it isn't; there are many possible ways to allocate scarce goods and resources. Four of the more commonly used ways are prices, a first-come, first-served rule, government dictate, and lottery (random).

What did you think of the various allocation schemes? A questionnaire like the one you just did but longer has been completed by many people in different settings during the past few years. Some results are shown in Figure 1. Figure 1(a) shows the evaluation of allocation schemes for non-health-related items like the bottled water by three groups: students in principles of economics courses, MBA students, and students in an advanced economics course who are economics majors. Figure 1(b) shows the evaluation by these same groups for health-related items like physicians' services. You can see that students in the principles courses thought the government allocation scheme the fairest and had the greatest distaste for the price allocation scheme. The economics majors, on the other hand, thought price most fair. All groups reduced their taste for the price mechanism when the scarce good involved health-related items.

Why don't people think that allocation using prices is fair? Why are people more willing to rely on prices for non-health-related items than for health-related items? We will discuss many of these questions in later portions of the book. For now, we focus on the price allocation mechanism, since it is the primary allocation device used today. Although we observe many goods and services allocated by government, lotteries, and first-come, first-served rules, the price mechanism is relied on far more than the others. Where does the price on a good or service come from? It is determined in a market. Thus, we begin our examination of price by discussing markets.

A market arises when buyers and sellers exchange a well-defined good or service. In stock markets, buyers and sellers exchange their "goods," or stocks, solely through electronic connections. Shoppers at a fish market can examine the day's catch and make their choices.

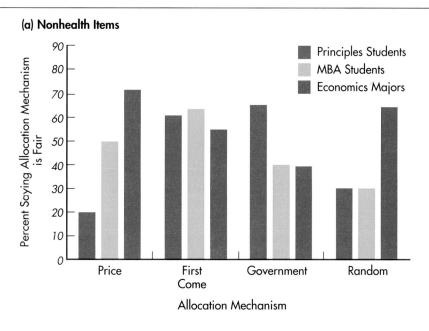

(a) Nonhealth Items

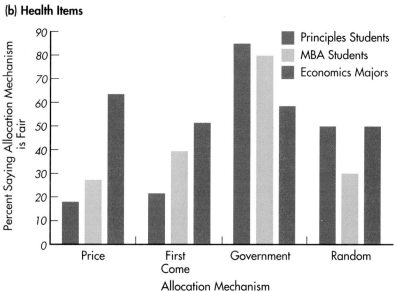

(b) Health Items

Figure 1
Allocation Mechanisms
The bar graphs show the results of a questionnaire asking people to evaluate four alternative allocation mechanisms—price, government, first-come, first-served, and random. Figure 1(a) shows the evaluation of allocation schemes for the non-health-related items by three groups: students in principles of economics courses, MBA students, and students in an advanced economics course. Figure 1(b) shows the evaluation by these same groups for health-related items. You can see that students in the principles courses thought the government allocation scheme the fairest and had the greatest distaste for the price allocation scheme. The advanced economics students, on the other hand, thought price most fair. All groups reduced their taste for the price mechanism when the scarce good involved health-related items.

I. MARKETS

What is a market?

The supermarket, the stock market, the market for foreign exchange, and all other markets are similar in that well-defined goods and services are exchanged. A market may be a specific location, such as the supermarket or the stock market, or it may be the exchange of particular goods or services at many different locations, such as the foreign exchange market.

I.a. Market Definition

market:
a place or service that enables buyers and sellers to exchange goods and services

A **market** makes possible the exchange of goods and services between buyers and sellers. Buyers and sellers communicate with each other about the quantity and quality of a product, what the buyers are willing and able to pay, and what the sellers must receive. Food, shares of stock, and various national monies are bought and sold in, respectively, the supermarket, the stock market, and the foreign exchange market.

Markets may be general or specialized, large or small, localized or global; they may consist of one or many buyers and sellers, but a well-defined commodity is always traded. A market may be a formally organized exchange, such as the New York Stock Exchange, or it may be loosely organized like the market for used bicycles or automobiles. A market may be confined to one location, as in the case of a supermarket or the stock market, or it may encompass a city, a state, a country, or the entire world. The market for agricultural products, for instance, is international, but the market for labor services is mostly local or national.

I.b. Barter and Money Exchanges

barter:
the direct exchange of goods and services without the use of money

The purpose of markets is to facilitate the exchange of goods and services between buyers and sellers. In some cases money changes hands; in others only goods and services are exchanged. The exchange of goods and services directly, without money, is called **barter**. Barter occurs when a plumber fixes a leaky pipe for a lawyer in exchange for the lawyer's work on a will, and when a Chinese citizen provides fresh vegetables to an American visitor in exchange for a pack of American cigarettes.

double coincidence of wants:
the situation that exists when A has what B wants and B has what A wants

transaction costs:
the cost involved in making an exchange

Most markets involve money because goods and services can be exchanged more easily with money than without it. When IBM purchases microchips from Yakamoto of Japan, IBM and Yakamoto don't exchange goods directly. Neither firm may have what the other wants. Barter requires a **double coincidence of wants**: IBM must have what Yakamoto wants, and Yakamoto must have what IBM wants. The **transaction costs** (the costs associated with making an exchange) of finding a double coincidence of wants for barter transactions are typically very high. Money reduces these transaction costs. To obtain the microchips, all IBM has to do is provide dollars to Yakamoto. Yakamoto is willing to accept the money since it can spend it to obtain the goods that it wants.

I.c. Relative Price

relative price:
the price of one good expressed in terms of the price of another good

When people agree to trade or exchange, they must agree on the rate of exchange, or the price. The price of an exchange is a **relative price**—the price of one good expressed in terms of the price of another good. In a barter exchange a relative price is established between the goods traded. When the lawyer exchanges 2 hours of work for 1 hour of the plumber's work, the relative price established is 2/1. In a money exchange the relative price is more implicit. You pay a money price of $1 for a carton of milk. But, with that purchase you are forgoing everything else you could get for that dollar. Thus, the carton of milk is worth 1/3 of a $3 box of Quaker Oats 100% Natural cereal, 1/200 of a $200 used Diamond Back mountain bike, 20 sticks of $.05/stick Trident gum, and so on. These are the relative prices of the milk. Relative prices are a measure of what you must give up to get one unit of a good or service and are, therefore, a measure of opportunity costs. Since opportunity costs are what decisions are based on, when economists refer to the price of something, it is the relative price they have in mind.

The relative price is the price that affects economic decision making.

RECAP

1. A market is not necessarily a specific location or store. Instead, the term *market* refers to buyers and sellers communicating with each other regarding the quality and quantity of a well-defined product, what buyers are willing and able to pay for a product, and what sellers must receive in order to produce and sell a product.
2. Barter refers to exchanges made without the use of money.
3. Money makes it easier and less expensive to exchange goods and services.
4. The price of a good or service is a measure of what you must give up to get one unit of that good or service.

2. DEMAND

What is demand?

demand:
the amount of a product that people are willing and able to purchase at every possible price

quantity demanded:
the amount of a product that people are willing and able to purchase at a specific price

Demand and supply determine the price of any good or service. To understand how a price level is determined and why a price rises or falls, it is necessary to know how demand and supply function. We begin by considering demand alone, then supply, and then we put the two together. Before we begin, we discuss some economic terminology that is often confusing.

Economists distinguish between the terms **demand** and **quantity demanded**. When they refer to the *quantity demanded* they are talking about the amount of a product that people are willing and able to purchase at a *specific* price. When they refer to *demand* they are talking about the amount that people would be willing and able to purchase at *every possible* price. Demand is the quantities demanded at every price. Thus, the statement that "the demand for U.S. white wine rose after a 300 percent tariff was applied to French white wine" means that at each price for U.S. white wine, more people were willing and able to purchase U.S. white wine. And the statement that "the quantity demanded of white wine fell as the price of white wine rose" means that people were willing and able to purchase less white wine because the price of the wine rose.

2.a. **The Law of Demand**

Consumers and merchants know that if you lower the price of a good or service without altering its quality or quantity, people will beat a path to your doorway. This simple truth is referred to as the **law of demand**.

According to the law of demand, people purchase more of something when the price of that item falls. More formally, the law of demand states that the quantity of some item that people are willing and able to purchase, during a particular period of time, decreases as the price rises, and vice versa.

The more formal definition of the law of demand can be broken down into five phrases:

1. the quantity of a well-defined good or service that
2. people are willing and able to purchase
3. during a particular period of time
4. decreases as the price of that good or service rises and increases as the price falls
5. everything else held constant

The first phrase ensures that we are referring to the same item, that we are not mixing different goods. A watch is a commodity defined and distinguished from other goods by several characteristics: quality, color, and design of the watch face, to name a few. The law of demand applies to the well-defined good, in this case, a watch. If one of the characteristics should change, the good would no longer be well-defined—in fact, it would be a different good. A Rolex watch is different from a Timex watch; Polo brand golf shirts are different goods than generic brand golf shirts; Mercedes-Benz automobiles are different goods than Yugo automobiles.

The second phrase indicates that people must not only *want* to purchase some good, they must be *able* to purchase that good in order for their wants to be counted as part of demand. For example, Sue would love to buy a membership to the Paradise Valley Country Club, but because the membership costs $35,000, she is not able to purchase the membership. Though willing, she is not able. At a price of $5,000, however, she is willing and able to purchase the membership.

The third phrase points out that the demand for any good is defined for a specific period of time. Without reference to a time period, a demand relationship would not make any sense. For instance, the statement that "at a price of $3 per Happy Meal, 13 million Happy Meals are demanded" provides no useful information. Are the 13 million meals sold in one week or one year? Think of demand as a rate of purchase at each possible price over a period of time—2 per month, 1 per day, and so on.

The fourth phrase points out that price and quantity demanded move in opposite directions; that is, as the price rises, the quantity demanded falls, and as the price falls, the quantity demanded rises.

Demand is a measure of the relationship between the price and quantity demanded of a particular good or service, when the determinants of demand do not change. The **determinants of demand** are income, tastes, prices of related goods and services, expectations, and the number of buyers. If any one of these items changes, demand changes. The final phrase, everything else held constant, ensures that the determinants of demand do not change.

2.b. The Demand Schedule

A **demand schedule** is a table or list of the prices and the corresponding quantities demanded of a particular good or service. The table in Figure 2 is a demand schedule for video rentals (movies). It shows the number of videos

Figure 2
Bob's Demand Schedule and Demand Curve for Videos
The number of videos that Bob is willing and able to rent at each price during the year is listed in the table, or demand schedule. The demand curve is derived from the combinations given in the demand schedule. The price-quantity combination of $5 per video and 10 videos is point A. The combination of $4 per video and 20 videos is point B. Each combination is plotted, and the points are connected to form the demand curve.

Combination	Price per Video (constant-quality units)	Quantity Demanded per Year (constant-quality units)
A	$5	10
B	4	20
C	3	30
D	2	40
E	1	50

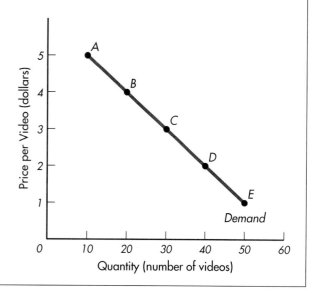

demand schedule:
a table or list of the prices and the corresponding quantities demanded of a particular good or service

that a consumer named Bob would be willing and able to rent at each price during the year, everything else held constant. As the rental price of the videos gets higher relative to the prices of other goods, Bob would be willing and able to rent fewer videos.

At the high price of $5 per video, Bob indicates that he will rent only 10 videos during the year. At a price of $4 per video, Bob tells us that he will rent 20 videos during the year. As the price drops from $5 to $4 to $3 to $2 and to $1, Bob is willing and able to rent more videos. At a price of $1, Bob would rent 50 videos during the year, nearly 1 per week.

2.c. The Demand Curve

demand curve:
a graph of a demand schedule that measures price on the vertical axis and quantity demanded on the horizontal axis

A **demand curve** is a graph of the demand schedule. The demand curve shown in Figure 2 is plotted from the information given in the demand schedule. Price is measured on the vertical axis, quantity per unit of time on the horizontal axis. The demand curve slopes downward because of the inverse relationship between the rental price of the videos and the quantity an individual is willing and able to purchase (rent). Point *A* in Figure 2 corresponds to combination A in the table: a price of $5 and 10 videos demanded. Similarly, points *B, C, D,* and *E* in Figure 2 represent the corresponding combinations in the table. The line connecting these points is Bob's demand curve for videos.

All demand curves slope down because of the law of demand: as price falls, quantity demanded increases. The demand curves for bread, electricity, automobiles, colleges, labor services, and any other good or service you can think of slope down. You might be saying to yourself, "That's not true. What about the demand for Mercedes-Benz cars or Gucci bags? As their price goes up, they become more prestigious and the quantity demanded actually rises." To avoid confusion in such circumstances, we say "everything else held constant." With this statement we are assuming that tastes don't change and that, therefore, the goods *cannot* become more prestigious as the price changes. Similarly, we do not allow the quality or the brand name of a product to change as we define the demand schedule or demand curve. We concentrate on the one quality or the one brand; so when we say that the price of a good has risen, we are talking about a good that is identical at all prices.

2.d. From Individual Demand Curves to a Market Curve

Bob's demand curve for video rentals is plotted in Figure 2. Unless Bob is the only renter of the videos, his demand curve is not the total, or market demand, curve. Market demand is the sum of all individual demands. To derive the market demand curve, then, the individual demand curves of all consumers in the market must be added together. The table in Figure 3 lists the demand schedules of three individuals, Bob, Helen, and Art. Because in this example the market consists only of Bob, Helen, and Art, their individual demands are added together to derive the market demand. The market demand is the last column of the table.

Bob's, Helen's, and Art's demand schedules are plotted as individual demand curves in Figure 3(a). In Figure 3(b) their individual demand curves have been added together to obtain the market demand curve. (Notice that we add in a horizontal direction—that is, we add quantities at each price, not the prices at each quantity.) At a price of $5, we add the quantity Bob would buy, 10, to the quantity Helen would buy, 5, to the quantity Art would buy, 15, to get the market demand of 30. At a price of $4, we add the quantities each of the consumers is willing and able to buy to get the total quantity demanded of 48. At all prices, then, we add the quantities demanded by each individual consumer to get the total, or market quantity, demanded.

2.e. Changes in Demand and Changes in Quantity Demanded

When one of the determinants of demand—income, tastes, prices of related goods, expectations, or number of buyers—is allowed to change, the demand for a good or service changes as well. What does it mean to say that demand changes? Demand is the entire demand schedule, or demand curve. When we say that demand changes, we are referring to a change in the quantities demanded at each and every price.

For example, if Bob's income rises, then his demand for video rentals rises. At each and every price, the number of videos Bob is willing and able to rent each year rises. This increase is shown in the last column of the table in Figure 4. A change in demand is represented by a shift of the demand curve, as shown in Figure 4(a). The shift to the right, from D_1 to D_2, indicates that Bob is willing and able to rent more videos at every price.

When the price of a good or service is the only factor that changes, the quantity demanded changes but the demand curve does not shift. Instead, as the price of the rentals is decreased (increased), everything else held constant, the quantity that people are willing and able to purchase increases (decreases). This change is merely a movement from one point on the demand curve to another point on the same demand curve, not a shift of the demand curve. *Change in the quantity demanded* is the phrase economists use

Figure 3
The Market Demand Schedule and Curve for Videos

The market is defined to consist of three individuals: Bob, Helen, and Art. Their demand schedules are listed in the table and plotted as the individual demand curves shown in Figure 3(a). By adding the quantities that each demands at every price, we obtain the market demand curve shown in Figure 3(b). At a price of $1 we add Bob's quantity demanded of 50 to Helen's quantity demanded of 25 to Art's quantity demanded of 27 to obtain the market quantity demanded of 102. At a price of $2 we add Bob's 40 to Helen's 20 to Art's 24 to obtain the market quantity demanded of 84. To obtain the market demand curve, for every price we sum the quantities demanded by each market participant.

Price per Video						Quantities Demanded per Year by		Market Demand
	Bob		Helen		Art		=	
$5	10	+	5	+	15		=	30
4	20		10		18			48
3	30		15		21			66
2	40		20		24			84
1	50		25		27			102

(a) Individual Demand Curves

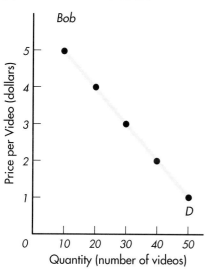
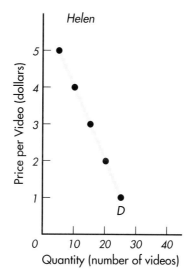
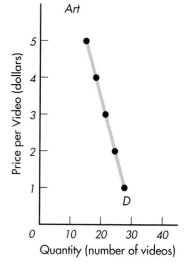

(b) Market Demand Curve

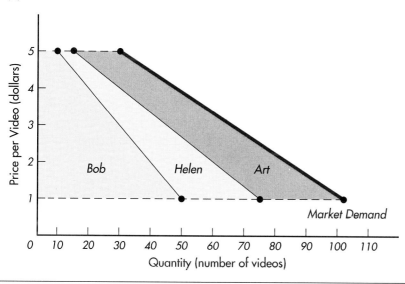

Figure 4
A Change in Demand and a Change in the Quantity Demanded
According to the table, Bob's demand for videos has increased by 5 videos at each price level. In Figure 4(a), this change is shown as a shift of the demand curve from D_1 to D_2. Figure 4(b) shows a change in the quantity demanded. The change is an increase in the quantity that consumers are willing and able to purchase at a lower price. It is shown as a movement along the demand curve from point A to point B.

Price per Video	Quantity Demanded per Year	
	Before	After
$5	10	15
4	20	25
3	30	35
2	40	45
1	50	55

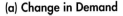
(a) Change in Demand

(b) Change in Quantity Demanded

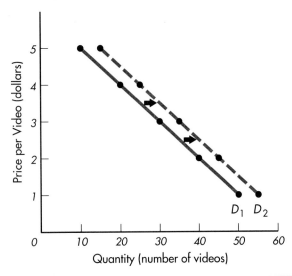

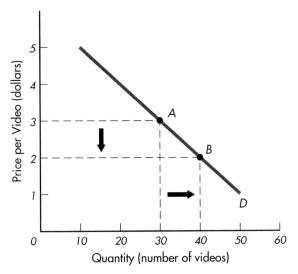

to describe the change in the quantities of a particular good or service that people are willing and able to purchase as the price of that good or service changes. A change in the quantity demanded, from point A to point B on the demand curve, is shown in Figure 4(b).

The demand curve shifts when income, tastes, prices of related goods, expectations, or the number of buyers changes. Let's consider how each of these determinants of demand affects the demand curve.

Income The demand for any good or service depends on income. The higher someone's income is, the more goods and services that person can purchase at any given price. The increase in Bob's income causes his demand to increase. This change is shown in Figure 4(a) by the shift to the right from the curve labeled D_1 to the curve labeled D_2. Increased income means a greater ability to purchase goods and services. At every price, more videos are demanded along curve D_2 than along curve D_1.

Tastes The demand for any good or service depends on individuals' tastes and preferences. For decades, the destination of choice for college students in the East and Midwest during spring break was Fort Lauderdale, Florida. In the early 1990s, many students decided that Mexico offered a more exciting destination than Fort Lauderdale. Regardless of the prices of the Fort Lauderdale and Mexican vacations, tastes changed so that more students went to Mexico. The demand curve for the Mexican vacation shifted to the right while that for the Fort Lauderdale vacation shifted to the left.

Prices of Related Goods and Services   Goods and services may be related in two ways. **Substitute goods** can be used for each other, so that as the price of one rises, the demand for the other rises. Bread and crackers, BMWs and Acuras, video rentals and theater movies, universities and community colleges, electricity and natural gas are, more or less, pairs of substitutes. As the price of cassette tapes rises, everything else held constant, the demand for CDs will rise and the demand curve for CDs will shift to the right. As the price of theater movies increases, the demand for video rentals will rise and the demand curve for the videos will shift to the right.

substitute goods:
goods that can be used in place of each other; as the price of one rises, the demand for the other rises

   Complementary goods are used together, and as the price of one rises, the demand for the other falls. Bread and margarine, beer and peanuts, cameras and film, shoes and socks, CDs and CD players, video rentals and VCRs are examples of pairs of complementary goods. As the price of cameras rises, people tend to purchase fewer cameras, but they also tend to purchase less film. As the price of VCRs rises, people tend to purchase fewer VCRs, but they also demand fewer video rentals. The demand curve for a complementary good shifts to the left when the price of the related good increases.

complementary goods:
goods that are used together; as the price of one rises, the demand for the other falls

A change in demand is represented by a shift of the demand curve.

Expectations   Expectations about future events can have an effect on demand today. People make purchases today because they expect their income level to be a certain amount in the future, or they expect the price of certain items to be higher in the future. A change in expected income or expected prices can have an effect on today's expenditures. For instance, you might be planning to purchase a car, some furniture, or a house today thinking that your income will be a certain amount next year. If for some reason you change your expectation of next year's income, you may also change your current expenditures. In November 1992, the United States threatened to impose a 300 percent tariff on French white wine beginning in December 1992. The tariff would have increased white wine prices in the United States from about $8 a bottle to $24. Expecting the higher prices in December, U.S. consumers immediately went out and stockpiled French white wine. The effect of changed expectations on demand is represented by a shift of the demand curve. The demand for a good or service may rise (fall) and the demand curve may shift to the right (left) because of a change in expectations.

Number of Buyers   Market demand consists of the sum of the demands of all individuals. The more individuals there are with income to spend, the greater the market demand is likely to be. For example, the populations of Florida and Arizona are much larger during the winter than they are during the summer. The demand for any particular good or service in Arizona and Florida rises (the demand curve shifts to the right) during the winter and falls (the demand curve shifts to the left) during the summer.

2.f. International Effects

The law of demand says the amount of a good or service that people are willing and able to purchase during a particular period of time falls as the price rises and rises as the price falls. It does not indicate whether those people are

The Foreign Exchange Market

Most countries have their own national currency. Germany has the deutsche mark, France the franc, England the pound sterling, Japan the yen, the United States the dollar, and so on. The citizens of each country use their national currency to carry out transactions. For transactions among nations to occur, however, some exchange of foreign currencies is necessary.

Americans buy Toyotas and Nissans from Japan, while American computer companies sell pocket calculators to businesses in Mexico. Some Americans open bank accounts in Switzerland, while American real estate companies sell property to citizens in England. These transactions require the acquisition of a foreign currency. An English businessman who wants to buy property in the United States will have to exchange his money, pounds sterling, for dollars. An American car distributor who imports Toyotas will have to exchange dollars for yen in order to pay the Toyota manufacturer.

The exchange of currency and the determination of the value of national currencies occur in the foreign exchange market. This is not a tightly organized market operating in a building in New York. Usually, the term *foreign exchange market* refers to the trading that occurs among large international banks. Such trading is global and is done largely through telephone and computer communication systems. If, for example, a foreign exchange trader at First Chicago Bank calls a trader at Bank of Tokyo to buy $1 million worth of Japanese yen, that is a foreign exchange market transaction. Banks buy and sell currencies according to the needs and demands of their customers. Business firms and individuals rely largely on banks to buy and sell foreign exchange for them.

The price of one currency expressed in terms of another currency is called a *foreign exchange rate*, or just *exchange rate*. You can think of an exchange rate as the number of dollars it costs to purchase one unit of another country's currency. For instance, how many dollars does it take to purchase one unit of Japan's currency, the yen? One yen (¥) costs about $.008, or eight-tenths of a cent. The list that follows shows the number of U.S. dollars it took to purchase one unit of several different nations' currencies in April 1995.

Number of U.S. Dollars Needed to Purchase One

Australian dollar	.7430
Belgian franc	.03522
Canadian dollar	.7189
French franc	.20896
German mark	.7263
Italian lira	.0005884
Japanese yen	.011951
Dutch guilder	.6491
Spanish peseta	.008043
Swedish krona	.1360
Swiss franc	.8856
United Kingdom pound	1.6155

exchange rate:
the rate at which monies of different countries are exchanged

residents of the United States or some other country. The demand for a product that is available to residents of other countries as well as to residents of the United States will consist of the sum of the demands by U.S. and foreign residents. However, because nations use different monies or currencies, the demand will be affected by the rate at which the different currencies are exchanged. As pointed out in the Economic Insight "The Foreign Exchange Market," an **exchange rate** is the rate at which monies of different countries are exchanged. If the exchange rate changes, then the foreign price of a good produced in the United States will change. To illustrate this, let's consider an example using Levi's blue jeans sold to both U.S. and Japanese customers. The Japanese currency is the yen (¥). In November 1992, it took 124 yen to purchase one dollar. Suppose that a pair of Levi's blue jeans is priced at $20 in the United States. That dollar price in terms of yen is ¥2,480. The exchange rate between the yen and the dollar means that ¥2,480 converts to $20; ¥2,480 = $20 × 124¥/$. When in April of 1995 the exchange rate changed to ¥83 per dollar and nothing else changed, the U.S. price of the blue jeans remained at $20, while in Japan, the yen value of the blue jeans fell to $20 × ¥83/$ = ¥1,660. Since the blue jeans were now less expensive in Japan because of the exchange rate change, even though the U.S. price of blue jeans did not change, the demand for U.S. blue jeans rose. Thus, changes in exchange rates can affect the demand for goods. At constant U.S. prices, demand curves for U.S. goods will shift around as exchange rates change and foreign purchases fluctuate.

RECAP

1. According to the law of demand, as the price of any good or service rises (falls), the quantity demanded of that good or service falls (rises), during a specific period of time, everything else held constant.

2. A demand schedule is a listing of the quantity demanded at each price.

3. The demand curve is a downward-sloping line plotted using the values of the demand schedule.

4. Market demand is the sum of all individual demands.

5. Demand changes when one of the determinants of demand changes. A demand change is a shift of the demand curve.

6. The quantity demanded changes when the price of the good or service changes. This is a change from one point on the demand curve to another point on the same demand curve.

7. The determinants of demand are income, tastes, prices of related goods and services, expectations, and number of buyers.

8. The exchange rate also is a determinant of demand when a good is sold in both the United States and other countries.

3. SUPPLY

Why is the price of hotel accommodations higher in Phoenix in the winter than in the summer? Demand AND supply. Why is the price of beef higher in Japan than in the United States? Demand AND supply. Why did the price of the dollar in terms of the Japanese yen fall in 1995? Demand AND supply. Both demand and supply determine price; neither demand nor supply alone determine price. We now discuss supply.

3.a. The Law of Supply

What is supply?

supply:
the amount of a good or service that producers are willing and able to offer for sale at each possible price during a period of time, everything else held constant

Just as demand is the relation between the price and the quantity demanded of a good or service, supply is the relation between price and quantity supplied. **Supply** is the amount of the good or service producers are willing and able to offer for sale at each possible price during a period of time, everything else held constant. **Quantity supplied** is the amount of the good or service producers are willing and able to offer for sale at a *specific* price, during a period of time, everything else held constant. According to the **law of supply**, as the price of a good or service rises, the quantity supplied rises, and vice versa.

quantity supplied:
the amount sellers are willing to offer at a given price, during a particular period of time, everything else held constant

law of supply:
as the price of a good or service that producers are willing and able to offer for sale at each possible price during a particular period of time rises (falls), the quantity of that good or service rises (falls), everything else held constant

The formal statement of the law of supply consists of five phrases:

1. the quantity of a well-defined good or service that
2. producers are willing and able to offer for sale
3. during a particular period of time
4. increases as the price of the good or service increases and decreases as the price decreases
5. everything else held constant

The first phrase is the same as the first phrase in the law of demand. The second phrase indicates that producers must not only *want* to offer the product for sale but must be *able* to offer the product. The third phrase points out that the quantities producers will offer for sale depend on the period of time being considered. For instance, the prices at which producers of personal computers would sell their products in January 1995 may be significantly different than in January 1998. The fourth phrase points out that more will be supplied at higher than at lower prices. The final phrase ensures that the **determinants of supply** do not change. The determinants of supply are those factors that influence the willingness and ability of producers to offer their goods and services for sale other than the price of the good or service—the prices of resources used to produce the product, technology and productivity, expectations of producers, the number of producers in the market, and the prices of related goods and services. If any one of these should change, supply changes.

determinants of supply:
factors other than the price of the good that influence supply—prices of resources, technology and productivity, expectations of producers, number of producers, and the prices of related good and services

3.b. The Supply Schedule and Supply Curve

supply schedule:
a table or list of prices and corresponding quantities supplied of a particular good or service

supply curve:
a graph of a supply schedule that measures price on the vertical axis and quantity supplied on the horizontal axis

A **supply schedule** is a table or list of the prices and the corresponding quantities supplied of a good or service. The table in Figure 5 presents MGA's supply schedule of videos. The schedule lists the quantities that MGA is willing and able to supply at each price, everything else held constant. As the price increases, MGA is willing and able to offer more videos for rent.

A **supply curve** is a graph of the supply schedule. Figure 5 shows MGA's supply curve of videos. The price and quantity combinations given in the supply schedule correspond to the points on the curve. For instance, combination A in the table corresponds to point *A* on the curve; combination B in the table corresponds to point *B* on the curve, and so on for each price-quantity combination.

MGA's supply curve slopes upward. This means that MGA is willing and able to supply more at higher prices than it is at lower prices. Recall from Chapter 2 that as society puts more and more resources into the production of any specific item, the opportunity cost of each additional unit of production rises because more specialized resources are transferred to activities in which they are relatively less productive. MGA, too, finds that as it increases production, the opportunity costs of additional production rise. Hence, the only way that MGA, or any producer, is willing and able to produce more is if the price rises sufficiently to cover these increasing opportunity costs.

3.c. From Individual Supply Curves to the Market Supply

To derive market supply, the quantities that each producer supplies at each price are added together, just as the quantities demanded by each consumer

Figure 5
MGA's Supply Schedule and Supply Curve for Videos
The quantity that MGA is willing and able to offer for sale at each price is listed in the supply schedule and shown on the supply curve. At point *A*, the price is $5 per video and the quantity supplied is 60 videos. The combination of $4 per video and 50 videos is point *B*. Each price-quantity combination is plotted, and the points are connected to form the supply curve.

Combination	Price per Video (constant-quality units)	Quantity Supplied per Year (constant-quality units)
A	$5	60
B	4	50
C	3	40
D	2	30
E	1	20

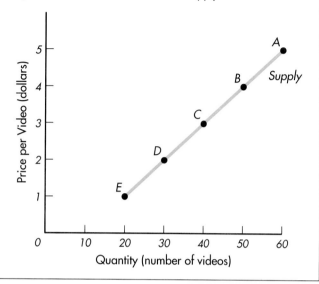

are added together to get market demand. The table in Figure 6 lists the supply schedules of three video rental stores: MGA, Motown, and Blockmaster. For our example, we assume that these three are the only video rental stores. (We are also assuming that the brand names are not associated with quality or any other differences.)

The supply schedule of each producer is plotted in Figure 6(a). Then in Figure 6(b) the individual supply curves have been added together to obtain the market supply curve. At a price of $5, the quantity supplied by MGA is 60, the quantity supplied by Motown is 30, and the quantity supplied by Blockmaster is 12. This means a total quantity supplied in the market of 102. At a price of $4, the quantities supplied are 50 by MGA, 25 by Motown, and 9 by Blockmaster for a total market quantity supplied of 84. The market supply schedule is the last column in the table. The plot of the price and quantity combinations listed in this column is the market supply curve. The market supply curve slopes up because each of the individual supply curves has a positive slope. The market supply curve tells us that the quantity supplied in the market increases as the price rises.

3.d. Changes in Supply and Changes in Quantity Supplied

A change in the quantity supplied is a movement along the supply curve. A change in the supply is a shift of the supply curve.

When we draw the supply curve, we allow only the price and quantity supplied of the good or service we are discussing to change. Everything else that might affect supply is assumed not to change. If any of the determinants of supply—the prices of resources used to produce the product, technology and productivity, expectations of producers, the number of producers in the market, and the prices of related goods and services—changes, the supply schedule changes and the supply curve shifts.

Figure 6
The Market Supply Schedule and Curve for Videos

The market supply is derived by summing the quantities that each producer is willing and able to offer for sale at each price. In this example, there are three producers: MGA, Motown, and Blockmaster. The supply schedules of each are listed in the table and plotted as the individual supply curves shown in Figure 6(a). By adding the quantities supplied at each price, we obtain the market supply curve shown in Figure 6(b). For instance, at a price of $5, MGA offers 60 units, Motown 30 units, and Blockmaster 12 units, for a market supply quantity of 102. The market supply curve reflects the quantities that each producer is able and willing to supply at each price.

Price per Video	Quantities Supplied per Year by			Market Supply
	MGA	Motown	Blockmaster	
$5	60 +	30 +	12 =	102
4	50	25	9	84
3	40	20	6	66
2	30	15	3	48
1	20	10	0	30

(a) Individual Supply Curves

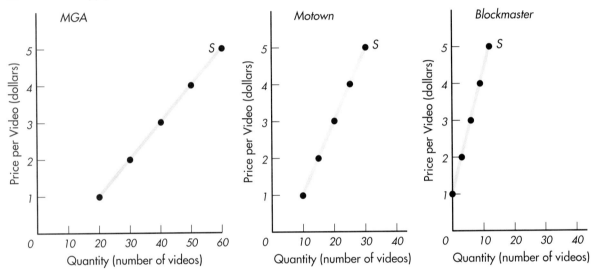

(b) Market Supply Curve

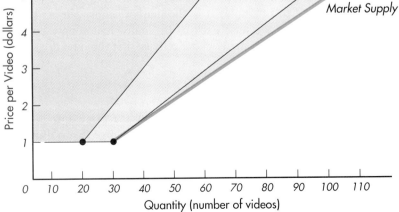

Part I/Introduction to the Price System

Figure 7
A Shift of the Supply Curve

Figure 7(a) shows a decrease in supply and the shift of the supply curve to the left, from S_1 to S_2. The decrease is caused by a change in one of the determinants of video supply—an increase in the price of labor. Because of the increased price of labor, producers are willing and able to offer fewer videos for rent at each price than they were before the price of labor rose. Supply curve S_2 shows that at a price of $3 per video, suppliers will offer 57 videos. That is 9 units less than the 66 videos at $3 per video indicated by supply curve S_1. Conversely, to offer a given quantity, producers must receive a higher price per video than they previously were getting: $3.50 per video for 66 videos (on supply curve S_2) instead of $3 per video (on supply curve S_1).

Figure 7(b) shows an increase in supply. A technological improvement or an increase in productivity causes the supply curve to shift to the right, from S_1 to S_2. At each price, a higher quantity is offered for sale. At a price of $3, 66 units were offered, but with the shift of the supply curve, the quantity of units for sale at $3 apiece increases to 84. Conversely, producers can reduce prices for a given quantity—for example, charging $2 per video for 66 units.

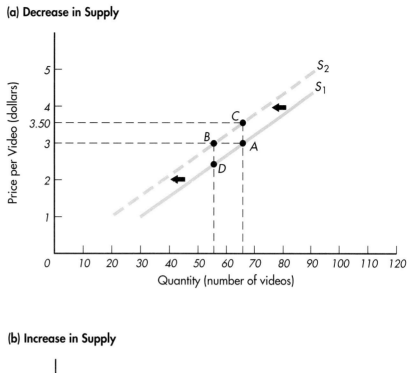

(a) Decrease in Supply

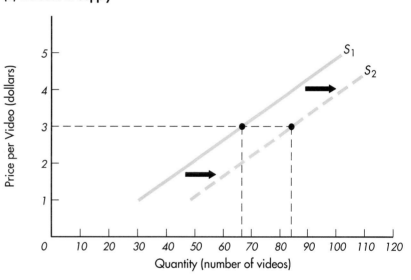

(b) Increase in Supply

Prices of Resources   If labor costs—one of the resources used to produce video rentals—rise, higher rental prices will be necessary to induce each store to offer as many videos as it did before the cost of the resource rose. The higher cost of resources causes a decrease in supply, meaning a leftward shift of the supply curve, from S_1 to S_2 in Figure 7(a).

Two interpretations of a leftward shift of the supply curve are possible. One comes from comparing the old and new curves in a horizontal direction; the other comes from comparing the curves in a vertical direction. In the vertical direction, the decrease in supply informs us that sellers want a higher price to produce any given quantity. Compare, for example, point A on curve

S_1 with C on curve S_2. A and C represent the same quantity but different prices. Sellers will offer 66 videos at a price of $3 per video according to supply curve S_1. But if the supply curve shifts to the left, then the sellers want more ($3.50) for 66 units.

In the horizontal direction, the decrease in supply means that sellers will offer less for sale at any given price. This can be seen by comparing point B on curve S_2 with A on curve S_1. Both points correspond to a price of $3, but along curve S_1, sellers are willing to offer 66 units for rent, while curve S_2 indicates that sellers will offer only 57 videos for rent.

If resource prices declined, then supply would increase. That combination would be illustrated by a rightward shift of the supply curve. If a firm purchases supplies from other nations, exchange rate changes can affect the firm's costs and thus, its supply curve. For instance, suppose a U.S. firm purchases lumber from Canada. At an exchange rate of 1 Canadian dollar per 1 U.S. dollar, 1,000 Canadian dollars worth of supplies costs 1,000 U.S. dollars. In 1995, with the Canadian dollar worth only .7129 U.S. dollars, the supplies worth 1,000 Canadian dollars cost only 713.90 U.S. dollars. Since the cost of supplies has declined for the U.S. firm, its supply curve shifts out.

Technology and Productivity If resources are used more efficiently in the production of a good or service, more of that good or service can be produced for the same cost, or the original quantity can be produced for a lower cost. As a result, the supply curve shifts to the right, as in Figure 7(b).

The move from horse-drawn plows to tractors or from mainframe computers to personal computers meant that each worker was able to produce more. The increase in output produced by each unit of a resource is called a *productivity increase*. **Productivity** is defined as the quantity of output produced per unit of resource. Improvements in technology cause productivity increases, which lead to an increase in supply.

Expectations of Producers Sellers may choose to alter the quantity offered for sale today because of a change in expectations regarding the determinants

productivity:
the quantity of output produced per unit of resource

Before computers and x-ray fluorescence equipment were invented, curators of museums and authenticators of art had to destroy portions of art to determine the age and components of the art. Now, as shown in the Prada Museum in Madrid, the hi-tech equipment is used to study the inorganic pigments in paint and determine when, where, and how the art was created, all without damaging any aspect of the art.

of supply. A supply curve illustrates the quantities that suppliers are willing and able to supply at every possible price level. If suppliers expect something to occur to resource supplies or technology, then suppliers may alter the quantities they are willing and able to supply at every possible price. The key point is that the supply curve will shift if producers expect something to occur that will alter the anticipated profits at every possible price level, not just a change in one price. For instance, the expectation that demand will decline in the future does not lead to a shift of the supply curve; it leads instead to a decline in quantity supplied as the new demand curve intersects the supply curve at a lower level of prices and output.

Number of Producers When more people decide to produce a good or service, the market supply increases. More is offered for sale at each and every price, causing a rightward shift of the supply curve.

Prices of Related Goods or Services The opportunity cost of producing and selling any good or service is the forgone opportunity to produce any other good or service. If the price of an alternative good changes, then the opportunity cost of producing a particular good changes. This could cause the supply curve to change. For instance, if the video store can offer videos or arcade games with equal ease, an increase in the price of the arcade games could induce the store owner to offer more arcade games and fewer videos. The supply curve of videos would then shift to the left.

A *change in supply* occurs when the quantity supplied at each and every price changes or there is a shift in the supply curve—like the shift from S_1 to S_2 in Figure 8(a). A change in one of the determinants of supply brings about a change in supply.

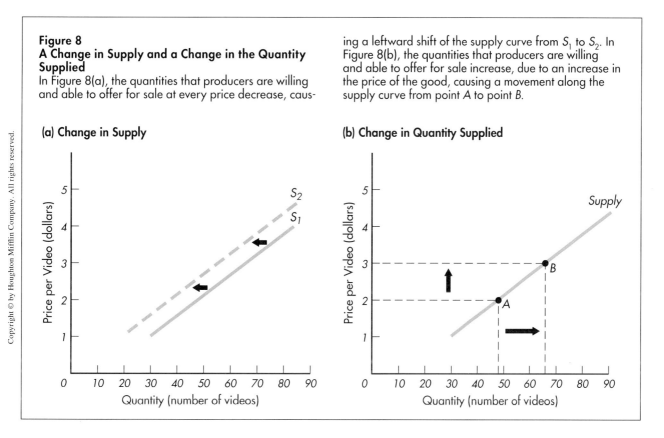

Figure 8
A Change in Supply and a Change in the Quantity Supplied
In Figure 8(a), the quantities that producers are willing and able to offer for sale at every price decrease, caus-ing a leftward shift of the supply curve from S_1 to S_2. In Figure 8(b), the quantities that producers are willing and able to offer for sale increase, due to an increase in the price of the good, causing a movement along the supply curve from point A to point B.

(a) Change in Supply

(b) Change in Quantity Supplied

When only the price changes, a greater or smaller quantity is supplied. This is shown as a movement along the supply curve, not as a shift of the curve. A change in price is said to cause a *change in the quantity supplied*. An increase in quantity supplied is shown in the move from point *A* to point *B* on the supply curve of Figure 8(b).

RECAP

1. According to the law of supply, the quantity supplied of any good or service is directly related to the price of the good or service, during a specific period of time, everything else held constant.
2. Market supply is found by adding together the quantities supplied at each price by every producer in the market.
3. Supply changes if the prices of relevant resources change, if technology or productivity changes, if producers' expectations change, if the number of producers changes, or if the prices of related goods and services change.
4. Changes in supply are reflected in shifts of the supply curve. Changes in the quantity supplied are reflected in movements along the supply curve.

4. EQUILIBRIUM: PUTTING DEMAND AND SUPPLY TOGETHER

equilibrium:
the price and quantity at which quantity demanded and quantity supplied are equal

The demand curve shows the quantity of a good or service that buyers are willing and able to purchase at each price. The supply curve shows the quantity that producers are willing and able to offer for sale at each price. Only where the two curves intersect is the quantity supplied equal to the quantity demanded. This intersection is the point of **equilibrium**.

4.a. Determination of Equilibrium

How is price determined by demand and supply?

disequilibrium:
a point at which quantity demanded and quantity supplied are not equal at a particular price

surplus:
a quantity supplied that is larger than the quantity demanded at a given price; it occurs whenever the price is greater than the equilibrium price

shortage:
a quantity supplied that is smaller than the quantity demanded at a given price; it occurs whenever the price is less than the equilibrium price

Figure 9 brings together the market demand and market supply curves for video rentals. The supply and demand schedules are listed in the table and the curves are plotted in the graph in Figure 9. Notice that the curves intersect at only one point, labeled *e*, a price of $3 and a quantity of 66. The intersection point is the equilibrium price, the only price at which the quantity demanded and quantity supplied are the same. You can see that at any other price the quantity demanded and quantity supplied are not the same. These are called **disequilibrium** points.

Whenever the price is greater than the equilibrium price, a **surplus** arises. For example, at $4, the quantity of videos demanded is 48 and the quantity supplied is 84. Thus, at $4 per video there is a surplus of 36 videos—that is, 36 videos are not rented. Conversely, whenever the price is below the equilibrium price, the quantity demanded is greater than the quantity supplied and there is a **shortage**. For instance, if the price is $2 per video, consumers will want and be able to pay for more videos than are available. As shown in the table in Figure 9, the quantity demanded at a price of $2 is 84 but the quantity supplied is only 48. There is a shortage of 36 videos at the price of $2.

Neither a surplus nor a shortage exists for long if the price of the product is free to change. Producers who are stuck with videos sitting on the shelves getting brittle and out of style will lower the price and reduce the quantities

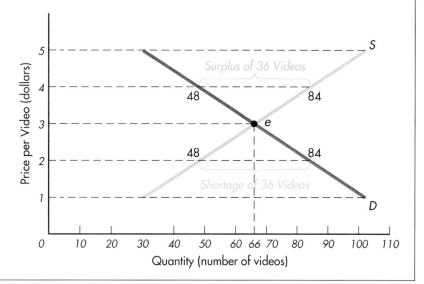

Figure 9
Equilibrium
Equilibrium is established at the point where the quantity that suppliers are willing and able to offer for sale is the same as the quantity that buyers are willing and able to purchase. Here, equilibrium occurs at the price of $3 per video and the quantity of 66 videos. It is shown as point e at the intersection of the demand and supply curves. At prices above $3, the quantity supplied is greater than the quantity demanded, and the result is a surplus. At prices below $3, the quantity supplied is less than the quantity demanded, and the result is a shortage. The area shaded brown shows all prices at which there is a surplus—where quantity supplied is greater than the quantity demanded. The surplus is measured in horizontal direction at each price. The area shaded blue represents all prices at which a shortage exists—where the quantity demanded is greater than the quantity supplied. The shortage is measured in a horizontal direction at each price.

Price per Video	Quantity Demanded per Year	Quantity Supplied per Year	Status
$5	30	102	Surplus of 72
4	48	84	Surplus of 36
3	66	66	Equilibrium
2	84	48	Shortage of 36
1	102	30	Shortage of 72

they are offering for rent in order to eliminate a surplus. Conversely, producers whose shelves are empty even as consumers demand videos will acquire more videos and raise the rental price to eliminate a shortage. Surpluses lead to decreases in the price and the quantity supplied and increases in the quantity demanded. Shortages lead to increases in the price and the quantity supplied and decreases in the quantity demanded.

Note that a shortage is not the same thing as scarcity. A shortage exists only when the quantity that people are willing and able to purchase at a particular price is more than the quantity supplied *at that price.* Scarcity occurs when more is wanted at a zero price than is available.

4.b. Changes in the Equilibrium Price: Demand Shifts

What causes price to change?

Equilibrium is the combination of price and quantity at which the quantities demanded and supplied are the same. Once an equilibrium is achieved, there is no incentive for producers or consumers to move away from it. An equilibrium price changes only when demand and/or supply changes—that is, when the determinants of demand or determinants of supply change.

Let's consider a change in demand and what it means for the equilibrium price. Suppose that experiments on rats show that watching videos causes brain damage. As a result, a large segment of the human population decides not to rent videos. Stores find that the demand for videos has decreased, as

Figure 10
The Effects of a Shift of the Demand Curve
The initial equilibrium price ($3 per video) and quantity (66 videos) are established at point e_1, where the initial demand and supply curves intersect. A change in the tastes for videos causes demand to decrease, and the demand curve shifts to the left. At $3 per video, the initial quantity supplied, 66 videos, is now greater than the quantity demanded, 48 videos. The surplus of 18 units causes producers to reduce production and lower the price. The market reaches a new equilibrium, at point e_2, $2.50 per video and 57 videos.

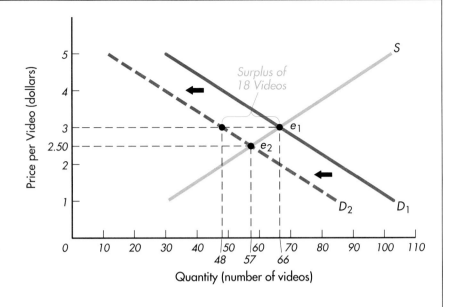

shown in Figure 10 by a leftward shift of the demand curve, from curve D_1 to curve D_2.

Once the demand curve has shifted, the original equilibrium price of $3 per video at point e_1 is no longer equilibrium. At a price of $3, the quantity supplied is still 66, but the quantity demanded has declined to 48 (look at the demand curve D_2 at a price of $3). There is, therefore, a surplus of 18 videos at the price of $3.

With a surplus comes downward pressure on the price. This downward pressure occurs because producers acquire fewer videos to offer for rent and reduce the rental price in an attempt to rent the videos sitting on the shelves. Producers continue reducing the price and the quantity available until consumers rent all copies of the videos that the sellers have available, or until a new equilibrium is established. That new equilibrium occurs at point e_2 with a price of $2.50 and a quantity of 57.

The decrease in demand is represented by the leftward shift of the demand curve. A decrease in demand results in a lower equilibrium price and a lower equilibrium quantity as long as there is no change in supply. Conversely, an increase in demand would be represented as a rightward shift of the demand curve and would result in a higher equilibrium price and a higher equilibrium quantity as long as there is no change in supply.

4.c. Changes in Equilibrium Price: Supply Shifts

The equilibrium price and quantity may be altered by a change in supply as well. If the price of relevant resources, technology and productivity, expectations of producers, the number of producers, or the price of related products change, supply changes.

Let's consider an example. Petroleum is a key ingredient in videotapes. Suppose the quantity of oil available is reduced by 40 percent, causing the price of oil to rise. Every video manufacturer has to pay more for oil, which

Figure 11
The Effects of a Shift of the Supply Curve
The initial equilibrium price and quantity are $3 and 66 units, at point e_1. When the price of labor increases, suppliers are willing and able to offer fewer videos for rent at each price. The result is a leftward (upward) shift of the supply curve, from S_1 to S_2. At the old price of $3, the quantity demanded is still 66, but the quantity supplied falls to 48. The shortage is 18 videos. The shortage causes suppliers to acquire more videos to offer for rent and to raise the rental price. The new equilibrium, e_2, the intersection between curves S_2 and D, is $3.50 per video and 57 videos.

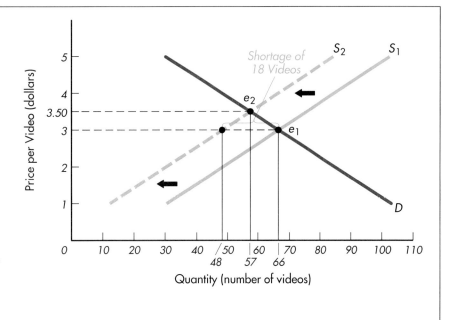

means that the rental stores must pay more for each videotape. To purchase the videos and offer them for rent, the rental stores must receive a higher rental price in order to cover their higher costs. This is represented by a leftward shift of the supply curve in Figure 11.

The leftward shift of the supply curve, from curve S_1 to curve S_2, leads to a new equilibrium price and quantity. At the original equilibrium price of $3 at point e_1, 66 videos are supplied. After the shift in the supply curve, 48 videos are offered for rent at a price of $3 apiece, and there is a shortage of 18 videos. The shortage puts upward pressure on price. As the price rises, consumers decrease the quantities that they are willing and able to rent, and sellers increase the quantities that they are willing and able to supply. Eventually, a new equilibrium price and quantity is established at $3.50 and 57 videos at point e_2.

The decrease in supply is represented by the leftward shift of the supply curve. A decrease in supply with no change in demand results in a higher price and a lower quantity. Conversely, an increase in supply would be represented as a rightward shift of the supply curve. An increase in supply with no change in demand would result in a lower price and a higher quantity.

4.d. Equilibrium in Reality

What happens when price is not allowed to change with market forces?

We have examined a hypothetical (imaginary) market for video rentals in order to represent what goes on in real markets. We have established that the price of a good or service is defined by equilibrium between demand and supply. We noted that an equilibrium could be disturbed by a change in demand or a change in supply and the equilibrium could also be disturbed by simultaneous changes in demand and supply. The important point of this discussion is to demonstrate that when not in equilibrium, the price and the quantities demanded and/or supplied change until equilibrium is established. The market is always attempting to reach equilibrium.

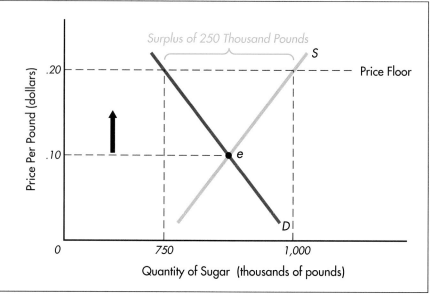

Figure 12
A Price Floor
The equilibrium price of sugar is $.10 a pound, but because the government has set a price floor of $.20 a pound, as shown by the solid yellow line, the price is not allowed to move to its equilibrium level. A surplus of 250,000 pounds of sugar results from the price floor. Sugar growers produce 1 million pounds of sugar and consumers purchase 750,000 pounds of sugar.

Looking at last year's sweaters piled up on the sale racks, waiting over an hour for a table at a restaurant, finding that the VCR rental store never has a copy of the movie you want to rent in stock, or hearing that 5 or 6 percent of people willing and able to work are unemployed may make you wonder whether equilibrium is ever established. In fact, it is not uncommon to observe situations where quantities demanded and supplied are not equal. But this observation does not cast doubt on the usefulness of the equilibrium concept. Even if all markets do not clear, or reach equilibrium, all the time, we can be reasonably assured that market forces are operating so that the market is moving toward an equilibrium. The market forces exist even when the price is not allowed to change, as illustrated in the following section.

price floor:
a situation where the price is not allowed to decrease below a certain level

4.d.1. **Price Ceilings and Price Floors** A **price floor** is the situation where the price is not allowed to decrease below a certain level. Consider Figure 12 representing the market for sugar. The equilibrium price of sugar is $.10 a pound, but because the government has set a price floor of $.20 a pound, as shown by the solid yellow line, the price is not allowed to move to its equilibrium level. A surplus of 250,000 pounds of sugar results from the price floor. Sugar growers produce 1 million pounds of sugar and consumers purchase 750,000 pounds of sugar.

We saw previously that whenever the price is above the equilibrium price, market forces work to decrease the price. The price floor interferes with the functioning of the market; a surplus exists because the government will not allow the price to drop. How does the government ensure that the price floor remains in force? It has to purchase the excess sugar. The government must purchase the surplus so that its price floor of $.20 per pound remains in force.

What would occur if the government had set the price floor at $.09 a pound? Since at $.09 a pound a shortage of sugar would result, the price would rise. A price floor only keeps the price from falling, not rising. So the price rises to its equilibrium level of $.10. Only if the price floor is set above the equilibrium price is it an effective price floor.

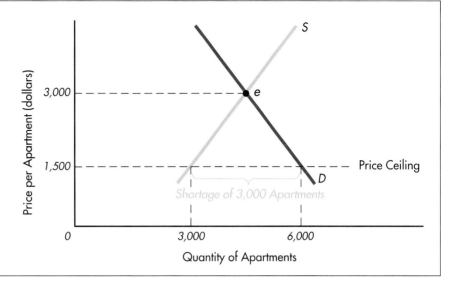

Figure 13
Rent Controls
A demand and supply graph representing the market for apartments in New York City is shown. The equilibrium price is $3,000 a month. The government has set a price of $1,500 a month. The government's price ceiling is shown by the solid yellow line. At the government's price, 3,000 apartments are available but consumers want 6,000. There is a shortage of 3,000 apartments.

price ceiling:
a situation where the price is not allowed to rise above a certain level

A **price ceiling** is the situation where a price is not allowed to rise to its equilibrium level. Los Angeles, San Francisco, and New York are among over 125 U.S. cities that have *rent controls*. A rent control law places a ceiling on the rents that landlords can charge for apartments. Figure 13 is a demand and supply graph representing the market for apartments in New York. The equilibrium price is $3,000 a month. The government has set a price of $1,500 a month as the maximum that can be charged. The price ceiling is shown by the solid yellow line. At the rent control price of $1,500 per month, 3,000 apartments are available but consumers want 6,000 apartments. There is a shortage of 3,000 apartments.

The shortage means that not everyone willing and able to purchase the apartment will be allowed to. Since the price is not allowed to ration the apartments, something else will have to. It may be that those willing and able to stand in line the longest get the apartments. Perhaps bribing an important official might be the way to get an apartment. Perhaps relatives of officials or important citizens will get the apartments. Whenever a price ceiling exists, a shortage results and some rationing device other than price will arise.

Had the government set the rent control price at $4,000 per month, the price ceiling would not have had an effect. Since the equilibrium is $3,000 a month, the price would not have risen to $4,000. Only if the price ceiling is below the equilibrium price will it be an effective price ceiling.

Price ceilings are not uncommon features in the United States or in other economies. China had a severe housing shortage for thirty years because the price of housing was kept below equilibrium. Faced with unhappy citizens and realizing the cause of the shortage, officials began to lift the restrictions on housing prices in 1985. The shortage has diminished. In the former Soviet Union, prices on all goods and services were defined by the government. For most consumer items, the price was set below equilibrium; shortages existed. The long lines of people waiting to purchase food or clothing were the result of the price ceilings on all goods and services. In the United States, price ceilings on all goods and services have been imposed at times. During the first and second world wars and during the Nixon administration of the early

1970s, wage and price controls were imposed. These were price ceilings on all goods and services. As a result of the ceilings, people were unable to purchase many of the products they desired. The Organization of Petroleum Exporting Countries (OPEC) restricted the quantity of oil in the early 1970s and drove its price up considerably. The United States government responded by placing a price ceiling on gasoline. The result was long lines at gas stations—shortages of gasoline.

Price floors are quite common features in economies as well. The agricultural policies of most of the developed nations are founded on price floors—the government guarantees that the price of an agricultural product will not fall below some level. Price floors result in surpluses, and this has been the case with agricultural products as well. The surpluses in agricultural products in the United States have resulted in cases where dairy farmers dumped milk in the river, where grain was given to other nations at taxpayer expense, and where citrus ranchers picked and then discarded thousands of tons of citrus, all to reduce huge surpluses.

There are many reasons other than price ceilings and price floors why we observe excess supplies or demands in the real world. In most cases, the excess demands or supplies are due to the difficulty of changing prices rapidly or to the desires of either the demanders or suppliers not to have prices change rapidly. We shall consider many such cases in the text. The important part of the discussion in this chapter is to keep in mind that unless the price is not allowed to change, surpluses and shortages will put pressure on the price to move to its equilibrium level.

RECAP

1. Equilibrium occurs when quantity demanded and quantity supplied are equal: it is the price-quantity combination where the demand and supply curves intersect.

2. A price that is above the equilibrium price creates a surplus. Producers are willing and able to offer more for sale than buyers are willing and able to purchase.

3. A price that is below the equilibrium price leads to a shortage, because buyers are willing and able to purchase more than producers are willing and able to offer for sale.

4. When demand changes, price and quantity change in the same direction—both rise as demand increases and both fall as demand decreases.

5. When supply changes, price and quantity change but not in the same direction. When supply increases, price falls and quantity rises. When supply decreases, price rises and quantity falls.

6. When both demand and supply change, the direction of the change in price and quantity depends on the relative sizes of the changes of demand and supply.

7. A price floor is a situation where a price is set above the equilibrium price. This creates a surplus.

8. A price ceiling is a case where a price is set below the equilibrium price. This creates a shortage.

SUMMARY

▲▼ **What is a market?**

1. A market is where buyers and sellers trade a well-defined good or service. §1

▲▼ **What is demand?**

2. Demand is the quantities that buyers are willing and able to buy at alternative prices. §2

3. The quantity demanded is a specific amount at one price. §2

4. The law of demand states that as the price of a well-defined commodity rises (falls), the quantity demanded during a given period of time will fall (rise), everything else held constant. §2.a

5. Demand will change when one of the determinants of demand changes, that is, when income, tastes, prices of related goods and services, expectations, or number of buyers change. In addition, the demand may change when exchange rates change. A demand change is illustrated as a shift of the demand curve. §2.e, 2.f

▲▼ **What is supply?**

6. Supply is the quantities that sellers will offer for sale at alternative prices. §3.a

7. The quantity supplied is the amount sellers offer for sale at one price. §3.a

8. The law of supply states that as the price of a well-defined commodity rises (falls), the quantity supplied during a given period of time will rise (fall), everything else held constant. §3.a

9. Supply changes when one of the determinants of supply changes, that is, when prices of resources, technology and productivity, expectations of producers, the number of producers, or the prices of related goods or services change. A supply change is illustrated as a shift of the supply curve. §3.d

▲▼ **How is price determined by demand and supply?**

10. Together, demand and supply determine the equilibrium price and quantity. §4

▲▼ **What causes price to change?**

11. A price that is above equilibrium creates a surplus, which leads to a lower price. A price that is below equilibrium creates a shortage, which leads to a higher price. §4.a

12. A change in demand or a change in supply (a shift of either curve) will cause the equilibrium price and quantity to change. §4.b, 4.c

13. Markets are not always in equilibrium, but forces work to move them toward equilibrium. §4.d

▲▼ **What happens when price is not allowed to change with market forces?**

14. A price floor is a situation where a price is not allowed to decrease below a certain level—it is set above the equilibrium price. This creates a surplus. A price ceiling is a case where a price is not allowed to rise—it is set below the equilibrium price. This creates a shortage. §4.d

KEY TERMS

market §1.a

barter §1.b

double coincidence of wants §1.b

transaction costs §1.b

relative price §1.c

demand §2

quantity demanded §2

law of demand §2.a

determinants of demand §2.a

demand schedule §2.b

demand curve §2.c

substitute goods §2.e

complementary goods §2.e

exchange rate §2.f

supply §3.a

quantity supplied §3.a

law of supply §3.a
determinants of supply §3.a
supply schedule §3.b
supply curve §3.b
productivity §3.d
equilibrium §4

disequilibrium, §4.a
surplus §4.a
shortage §4.a
price floor §4.d
price ceiling §4.d

EXERCISES

1. Illustrate each of the following events using a demand and supply diagram for bananas.

   a. Reports surface that imported bananas are infected with a deadly virus.

   b. Consumers' incomes drop.

   c. The price of bananas rises.

   d. The price of oranges falls.

   e. Consumers expect the price of bananas to decrease in the future.

2. Answer true or false and if the statement is false, change it to make it true. Illustrate your answers on a demand and supply graph.

   a. An increase in demand is represented by a movement up the demand curve.

   b. An increase in supply is represented by a movement up the supply curve.

   c. An increase in demand without any changes in supply will cause the price to rise.

   d. An increase in supply without any changes in demand will cause the price to rise.

3. Using the following schedule, define the equilibrium price and quantity. Describe the situation at a price of $10. What will occur? Describe the situation at a price of $2. What will occur?

Price	Quantity Demanded	Quantity Supplied
$ 1	500	100
2	400	120
3	350	150
4	320	200
5	300	300
6	275	410
7	260	500
8	230	650
9	200	800
10	150	975

4. Suppose the government imposed a minimum price of $7 in the schedule of question 3. What would occur? Illustrate.

5. In question 3, indicate what the price would have to be to represent an effective price ceiling. Point out the surplus or shortage that results. Illustrate a price floor and provide an example of a price floor.

6. A common feature of skiing is waiting in lift lines. Does the existence of lift lines mean that the price is not working to allocate the scarce resource? If so, what should be done about it?

7. Why don't we observe barter systems as often as we observe the use of currency?

8. A severe drought in California has resulted in a nearly 30 percent reduction in the quantity of citrus grown and produced in California. Explain what effect this event might have on the Florida citrus market.

9. According to a 1993/94 laws, all automobiles produced after 1996 must withstand side impacts of 30 miles per hour. Explain what this law could mean for autos in 1995.

10. The prices of the Ralph Lauren "Polo" line of clothing are considerably higher than comparable quality lines. Yet, it sells more than a J.C. Penney brand line of clothing. Does this violate the law of demand?

11. In December, the price of Christmas trees rises and the quantity of trees sold rises. Is this a violation of the law of demand?

12. In recent years, the price of artificial Christmas trees has fallen while the quality has risen. What impact has this event had on the price of cut Christmas trees?

13. Many restaurants don't take reservations. You simply arrive and wait your turn. If you arrive at 7:30 in the evening, you have at least an

hour wait. Notwithstanding that fact, a few people arrive, speak quietly with the maitre d', hand him some money, and are promptly seated. At some restaurants that do take reservations, there is a month wait for a Saturday evening, three weeks for a Friday evening, two weeks for Tuesday through Thursday, and virtually no wait for Sunday or Monday evening. How do you explain these events using demand and supply?

14. Evaluate the following statement: "The demand for U.S. oranges has increased because the quantity of U.S. oranges demanded in Japan has risen."

15. In December 1992, the federal government began requiring that all foods display information about fat content and other ingredients on food packages. The displays had to be verified by independent laboratories. The price of an evaluation of a food product could run as much as $20,000. What impact do you think this law had on the market for meat?

16. Draw a PPC. Which combination shown by the PPC will be produced? Does the combination that is produced depend on how goods and services are allocated?

COOPERATIVE LEARNING EXERCISE

With the class divided into groups, assign each group an allocation mechanism: price, government, first-come, first-served, and random. Each group is to come up with an answer to each of the following questions. Once the groups have defined answers, a spokesperson for each group should be selected to present the results to the rest of the class.

1. What incentives are created if everything is allocated according to the allocation mechanism you have been assigned? For instance, will you work? Will you want to earn the most income? Will you go to college?

2. If everything is allocated according to the mechanism you have been assigned, who will be the winners and who the losers? Consider the following individuals: (a) a very large, strong person, (b) a person requiring a wheelchair, (c) a government official, (c) a college graduate, (d) a member of a minority group.

Panel Denies Rent Hike Request Because of Complaints on Upkeep

CANYON COUNTRY—Managers of a mobile-home park were denied the rent increase they requested because residents complained about the park's upkeep.

The Manufactured Home Rent Stabilization Panel, the city commission that oversees rent at mobile home parks, approved a 4 percent rent increase at the Soledad Trailer Lodge, rather than the 13.7 percent hike the manager proposed.

The higher increase was rejected because the management had failed to take good care of the park, panel member Leslee Bowman said.

"It's a slum," she said. "The roads are cracking, the septic tanks are leaking. The wiring appears to be inadequate." . . .

The park deserved the bigger hike because management had not raised rents since 1989, and maintenance costs have increased, park manager William Reed said.

Over the past couple of years, many improvements have been made to the 30-home park, including repainting the laundry room and upgrading the sewage system, he said.

"I don't think management has been unresponsive," Reed said. "When we have a problem, we try to fix it."

But several park residents said the park has deteriorated.

Parts of the roof on the newly painted laundry room, for example, have dry-rotted, said Don Johnson, president of the Soledad Trailer Lodge Mobile Home Owners Association.

Also, the park has had two large sewage spills in the past two years, he said.

"There's been a lack of it [maintenance] throughout many years," said Johnson, standing astride cracks in the park's driveway. . . .

The city sent an inspector to the park in late September after receiving a complaint from a resident, said code enforcement officer Kyle Lan-caster. Inspectors found the property littered with debris and broken cars, according to a letter sent to the state dated Oct. 1. Park management later addressed many of the concerns, Lancaster said.

The state regulates mobile-home parks and is responsible for code enforcement, Lancaster added.

City code permits annual rate hikes up to 6 percent or the consumer price index increase, whichever is lower. Bigger raises are permitted in "extraordinary circumstances," said Kevin Michel, city senior planner.

Park residents pay an average of $250 a month. The Canyon Country park has operated for more than 30 years.

Source: "Panel Denies Rent Hike Request Because of Complaints on Upkeep," Marc Ballon, *Daily News*, Dec. 17, 1992, p. SC1. Reprinted by permission.

Commentary

Rent control—the attempt to make housing available to more people by controlling its cost—is among the most hotly contested local political issues in America. Since 1960, the number of jurisdictions with rent-control ordinances has swelled to more than 125, and the decision to adopt such laws is being debated in still more communities.

Rent controls, at their simplest, can be represented as a price ceiling (see figure, below left). A rent control could be represented as a maximum, or ceiling price, of P_m, which is less than the equilibrium price P_1. This price ceiling creates a shortage: At the rent-control price P_m, the quantity of housing units demanded is Q_d while the quantity of housing units supplied is only Q_s. The difference, $Q_d - Q_s$, is the number of families willing and able to rent a house at price P_m but for whom there are no homes available.

How is this excess demand resolved? Two things occur. One is that something other than price serves as the allocater. Common replacements for price are: first-come, first-served; preferences of the landlord; or black market or under-the-table payoffs. The second is that the landlord decreases the maintenance on the existing rentals, and new rental units are not brought to the market. As the landlord experiences a lower return on the rental housing, he or she has a lower incentive to devote resources to the upkeep of the unit. As a result, the quality of the housing deteriorates.

This is what occurred at the Soledad Trailer Lodge. Unable to secure what it considered a fair return, the management of the park let it deteriorate. When the landlord asked for a 13.7 percent rent hike in order to increase the quality of the park, the city commission said no because the park had deteriorated. The landlord will not receive increased compensation until the maintenance and upkeep are improved, but the landlord has no incentive to make improvements at the low, rent-controlled price.

Not only does rent control lead to deterioration but the lower return on the rental housing means that some landlords may convert their units to condominiums or to commercial properties and sell them. Over time, the supply of rental housing declines. The supply curve shifts in, to S_2 in the Figure, below right, creating greater excess demand.

If rent control provides the same return as the free market would, there is no rent control. If the law provides a lower return, then the benefits to tenants rise, but the incentives for deterioration of the housing market also rise.

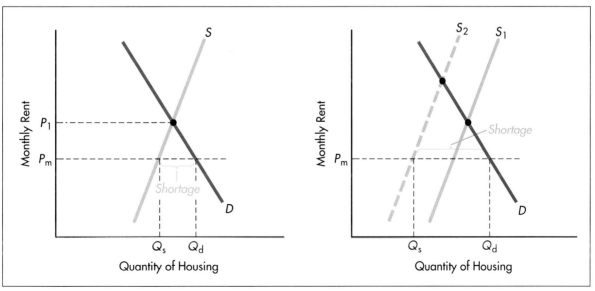

4

The Market System and the Private Sector

FUNDAMENTAL QUESTIONS

1. In a market system, who decides what goods and services are produced and how they are produced, and who obtains the goods and services that are produced?
2. What is a household, and what is household income and spending?
3. What is a business firm, and what is business spending?
4. How does the international sector affect the economy?
5. How do the three private sectors—households, businesses, and the international sector—interact in the economy?

You decide to buy a new Toyota, so you go to a Toyota dealer and exchange money for the car. The Toyota dealer has rented land and buildings and hired workers in order to make cars available to you and other members of the public. The employees earn incomes paid by the Toyota dealer and then use their incomes to buy food from the grocery store. This transaction generates revenue for the grocery store, which hires workers and pays them incomes that they then use to buy groceries and Toyotas. Your expenditure for the Toyota is part of a circular flow. Revenue is received by the Toyota dealer, who pays employees, who, in turn, buy goods and services.

Of course, the story is complicated by the fact that the Toyota is originally manufactured and purchased in Japan and then shipped to the United States before it can be sold by the local Toyota dealer. Your purchase of the Toyota creates revenue for the local dealer as well as for the manufacturer in Japan, who pays Japanese autoworkers to produce Toyotas. Furthermore, when you buy your Toyota, you must pay a tax to the government, which uses tax revenues to pay for police protection, national defense, the legal system, and other services. Many people in different areas of the economy are involved.

PREVIEW

An economy is made up of individual buyers and sellers. Economists could discuss the neighborhood economy that surrounds your university, the economy of the city of Chicago, or the economy of the state of Massachusetts. But typically it is the national economy, the economy of the United States, that is the center of their attention. To clarify the operation of the national economy, economists usually group individual buyers and sellers into three sectors: households, businesses, and government. Omitted from this grouping, however, is an important source of activity, the international sector. Since the U.S. economy affects, and is affected by, the rest of the world, to understand how the economy functions we must include the international sector.

We begin this chapter by examining the way that buyers and sellers interact in a market system. The impersonal forces of supply and demand operate to answer the following questions: Who determines what is produced and how they are produced? Who gets the output that is produced? The answers are given by the market system and involve the private-sector participants: households, business firms, and the international sector. Government also plays a major role in answering these questions, but we leave government and its role for the next chapter.

Following the discussion of the market system, we examine basic data and information on each individual sector with the objective of answering some general questions: What is a household, and how do households spend their

---

In a market system, who decides what goods and services are produced and how they are produced, and who obtains the goods and services that are produced?

---

incomes? What is a business firm, and how does a corporation differ from a partnership? What does it mean if the United States has a trade deficit?

After describing the three sectors that make up the private sector of the national economy, we present a simple economic model to illustrate the interrelationships linking all the individual sectors into the national economy.

1. THE MARKET SYSTEM

As we learned in Chapter 2, the production possibilities curve represents all possible combinations of goods and services that a society can produce if its resources are used fully and efficiently. Which combination, that is, which point on the PPC, will society choose? In a price or market system, the answer is given by demand and supply.

1.a. Consumer Sovereignty

This year, for the first time, time-starved Americans will spend as much time eating out as they do eating at home.[1] In the 1950s and 1960s, this trend was just beginning. Consumers wanted more and more restaurants and fast-food outlets. As a result, McDonald's, Wendy's, Big Boy, White Castle, Pizza Hut, Godfather's Pizza, and other fast-food outlets flourished. The trend toward eating away from home reached fever pitch in the late 1970s, when the average number of meals per person eaten out (excluding brown-bag lunches and other meals prepared at home but eaten elsewhere) exceeded one per day.

In the 1980s, people wanted the fast food but didn't want to go get it. By emphasizing delivery, Domino's Pizza and a few other fast-food outlets became very successful. In the 1990s, the takeout taxi business—where restaurant food is delivered to homes—grew ten percent per year. However, the star of this story is not Domino's, Pizza Hut, or other restaurants. It is the consumer. In a market system, if consumers are willing and able to pay for more restaurant meals, more restaurants appear. If consumers are willing and able to pay for food delivered to their homes, food is delivered to their homes.

Why does the consumer wield such power? The name of the game for business is profit, and the only way business can make a profit is by satisfying consumer wants. The consumer, not the politician or the business firm, ultimately determines what is to be produced. A firm that produces something that no consumers want will not remain in business very long. **Consumer sovereignty**—the authority of consumers to determine what is produced through their purchases of goods and services—dictates what goods and services will be produced. Supermarkets and grocery stores are responding to the consumer as well, by putting fast-food restaurants, like Pizza Hut and Taco Bell, inside their stores.

consumer sovereignty: the authority of consumers to determine what is produced through their purchases of goods and services

1.b. Profit and the Allocation of Resources

When a good or service seems to have the potential to generate a profit, someone with entrepreneurial ability will put together the resources needed

---

[1]"Too Busy to Cook," by Ellen Neuborne, *USA Today*, October 1994, p. 1B.

Competitive firms produce in the manner that minimizes costs and maximizes profits.

to produce that good or service. An individual with entrepreneurial ability aims to earn a profit by renting land, hiring labor, and using capital to produce a good or service that can be sold for more than the sum of rent, wages, and interest. If the potential profit turns into a loss, the entrepreneur may stop buying resources and turn to some other occupation or project. The resources used in the losing operation would then be available for use in an activity where they would be more highly valued.

Ownership of resources determines who gets what goods and services in a market system.

To illustrate how resources get allocated in the market system, let's look at the market for fast foods. Figure 1 shows a change in demand for meals eaten in restaurants. The initial demand curve, D_1, and supply curve, S, are shown in Figure 1(a). With these demand and supply curves, the equilibrium price (P_1) is \$8, and the equilibrium quantity (Q_1) is 100 units (meals). At this price-quantity combination, the number of meals demanded equals the number of meals sold; equilibrium is reached, so we say the market clears (there is no shortage or surplus).

The second part of the figure shows what happened when consumer tastes changed, and people preferred to have food delivered to their homes. This change in tastes caused the demand for restaurants to decline and is represented by a leftward shift of the demand curve, from D_1 to D_2, in Figure 1(b). The demand curve shifted to the left because fewer in-restaurant meals were demanded at each price. Consumer tastes, not the price of in-restaurant meals, changed first. (A price change would have led to a change in the quantity demanded and would be represented by a move *along* demand curve D_1.)

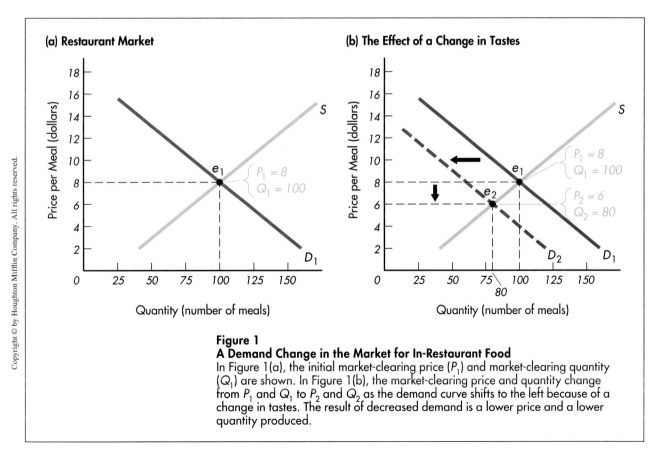

Figure 1
A Demand Change in the Market for In-Restaurant Food
In Figure 1(a), the initial market-clearing price (P_1) and market-clearing quantity (Q_1) are shown. In Figure 1(b), the market-clearing price and quantity change from P_1 and Q_1 to P_2 and Q_2 as the demand curve shifts to the left because of a change in tastes. The result of decreased demand is a lower price and a lower quantity produced.

The change in tastes caused a change in demand and a leftward shift of the demand curve. The shift from D_1 to D_2 created a new equilibrium point. The equilibrium price (P_2) decreased to $6, and the equilibrium quantity (Q_2) decreased to 80 units (meals).

While the market for in-restaurant food was changing, so was the market for delivered food. People substituted meals delivered to their homes for meals eaten in restaurants. Figure 2(a) shows the original demand for food delivered to the home. Figure 2(b) shows a rightward shift of the demand curve, from D_1 to D_2, representing increased demand for home delivery. This demand change resulted in a higher market-clearing price for food delivered to the home, from $10 to $12.

The changing profit potential of the two markets induced existing firms to switch from in-restaurant service to home delivery and for new firms to offer delivery from the start. Domino's Pizza, which is a delivery-only firm, grew from a one-store operation to become the second largest pizza chain in the United States, with sales exceeding $2 billion per year. Little Caesar's, another takeout chain, grew from $63.6 million in sales in 1980 to nearly $1 billion in 1987. Pizza Hut, which at first did not offer home delivery, had to play catch-up; and by 1992, about two-thirds of Pizza Hut's more than 5,000 restaurants were delivering pizza. In 1994, many non-fast-food restaurants began offering delivery.

As the market-clearing price of in-restaurant fast food fell (from $8 to $6 in Figure 1), the quantity of in-restaurant meals sold also declined (from 100 to 80) because the decreased demand, lower price, and resulting lower profit induced some firms to decrease production. In the delivery business, the

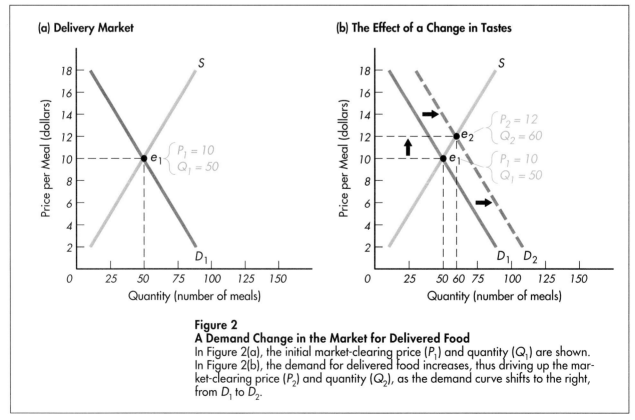

Figure 2
A Demand Change in the Market for Delivered Food
In Figure 2(a), the initial market-clearing price (P_1) and quantity (Q_1) are shown. In Figure 2(b), the demand for delivered food increases, thus driving up the market-clearing price (P_2) and quantity (Q_2), as the demand curve shifts to the right, from D_1 to D_2.

Part I/Introduction to the Price System

opposite occurred. As the market-clearing price rose (from $10 to $12 in Figure 2[b]), the number of meals delivered also rose (from 50 to 60). The increased demand, higher price, and resulting higher profit induced firms to increase production.

Why did the production of delivered foods increase while the production of meals at restaurants decreased? Not because of government decree. Not because of the desires of the business sector, especially the owners of restaurants. The consumer—consumer sovereignty—made all this happen. Businesses that failed to respond to consumer desires and failed to provide the desired good at the lowest price failed to survive.

I.c. The Flow of Resources

After demand shifted to home-delivered food, the resources that had been used in the restaurants were available for use elsewhere. A few former waiters, waitresses, and cooks were able to get jobs in the delivery firms. Some of the equipment used in eat-in restaurants—ovens, pots, and pans—was purchased by the delivery firms; and some of the ingredients that previously would have gone to the eat-in restaurants were bought by the delivery firms. A few former employees of the eat-in restaurants became employed at department stores, at local pubs, and at hotels. Some of the equipment was sold as scrap; other equipment was sold to other restaurants. In other words, the resources moved from an activity where their value was relatively low to an activity where they were more highly valued. No one commanded the resources to move. They moved because they could earn more in some other activity.

Adam Smith described this phenomenon in his 1776 treatise *The Wealth of Nations*, saying it was as if an invisible hand reached out and guided the resources to their most-valued use. That invisible hand is the self-interest that drives firms to provide what consumers want to buy, leads consumers to use their limited incomes to buy the goods and services that bring them the greatest satisfaction, and induces resource owners to supply resource services where they are most highly valued. (There is more about Smith in the Economic Insight "Adam Smith.")

Firms produce the goods and services and use the resources that enable them to generate the highest profits. If one firm does this better than others, then that firm earns a greater profit than others. Seeing that success, other firms copy or mimic the first firm. If a firm cannot be as profitable as the others, it will eventually go out of business or move to another line of business where it can be successful. In the process of firms always seeking to lower costs and make higher profits, society finds that the goods and services buyers want are produced in the least costly manner. Consumers not only get the goods and services they want and will pay for, but they get these products at the lowest possible price.

I.d. The Determination of Income

Consumer demands dictate *what* is produced, and the search for profit defines *how* goods and services are produced. *For whom* are the goods and services produced, that is, who gets the goods and services? In a price or market system, those who have the ability to pay for the products get the products. Your income determines your ability to pay, but where does income come from? Income is obtained by selling the services of resources.

Adam Smith

Adam Smith was born in 1723 and reared in Kirkcaldy, Scotland, near Edinburgh. He went to the University of Glasgow when he was fourteen, and three years later began studies at Oxford, where he stayed for six years. In 1751, Smith became professor of logic and then moral philosophy at Glasgow. From 1764 to 1766, he tutored the future duke of Buccleuch in France, and then he was given a pension for the remainder of his life. Between 1766 and 1776, Smith completed *The Wealth of Nations*. He became commissioner of customs for Scotland and spent his remaining years in Edinburgh. He died in 1790.

Economists date the beginning of their discipline from the publication of *The Wealth of Nations* in 1776. In this major treatise, Smith emphasizes the role of self-interest in the functioning of markets, specialization, and division of labor.

According to Smith, the funda-mental explanation of human behavior is found in the rational pursuit of self-interest. Smith uses it to explain how men choose occupations, how farmers till their lands, and how leaders of the American Revolution were led by it to rebellion. Smith did not equate self-interest with selfishness but broadened the definition of self-interest, believing that a person is interested "in the fortune of others and renders their happiness necessary to him, though he derives nothing from it, except the pleasure of seeing it." On the basis of self-interest, Smith constructed a theory of how markets work: how goods, once produced, are sold to the highest bidders, and how the quantities of the goods that are produced are governed by their costs and selling prices. But Smith's insight showed that this self-interest resulted in the best situation for society as a whole. In a cele-brated and often-quoted passage from the treatise Smith says:

> But man has almost constant occasion for the help of his brethren, and it is in vain for him to expect it from their benevolence only. He will be more likely to prevail if he can interest their self-love in his favour, and show them that it is for their own advantage to do for him what he requires of them. . . . It is not from the benevolence of the butcher, the brewer, or the baker, that we can expect our dinner, but from their regard to their own inter-est.

Source: *An Inquiry into the Nature and Causes of the Wealth of Nations,* edited and with an introduction, notes, mar-ginal summary, and index by Edwin Cannan, with a preface by George J. Stigler (Chicago: University of Chicago Press, 1976). Reprinted by permission of the publisher.

When you sell your labor services, your money income reflects your wage rate or salary level. When you sell the services of the capital you own, you receive interest; and when you sell the services of the land you own, you receive rent. A person with entrepreneurial ability earns profit as a payment for services. Thus, we see that buyers and sellers of goods and services and resource owners are linked together in an economy: the more one buys, the more income or revenue the other receives. In the remainder of this chapter, we learn more about the linkages among the sectors of the economy. We classify the buyers and the resource owners into the household sector; the sellers or business firms are the business sector; households and firms in other countries, who may also be buyers and sellers of this country's goods and services, are the international sector. These three sectors—households, business firms, and the international sector—constitute the **private sector** of the economy. In this chapter we focus on the interaction among the compo-nents of the private sector. In the next chapter we focus on the **public sector**, government, and examine its role in the economy.

private sector:
households, businesses, and the international sector

public sector:
the government

1. In a market system, consumers are sovereign and decide by means of their purchases what goods and services will be produced.

2. In a market system, firms decide how to produce the goods and services that consumers want. In order to earn maximum profits, firms use the least-cost combinations of resources.

3. Income and prices determine who gets what in a market system. Income is determined by the ownership of resources.

2. HOUSEHOLDS

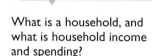

What is a household, and what is household income and spending?

household:
one or more persons who occupy a unit of housing

A **household** consists of one or more persons who occupy a unit of housing. The unit of housing may be a house, an apartment, or even a single room, as long as it constitutes separate living quarters. A household may consist of related family members, like a father, mother, and children, or it may comprise unrelated individuals, like three college students sharing an apartment. The person in whose name the house or apartment is owned or rented is called the *householder*.

2.a. Number of Households and Household Income

In 1994, there were more than 95 million households in the United States. The breakdown of households by age of householder is shown in Figure 3. Householders between 35 and 44 years old make up the largest number of households. Householders between 45 and 54 years old have the largest median income. The *median* is the middle value—half of the households in an age group have an income higher than the median and half have an income lower than the median. Figure 3 shows that households in which the householder is between 45 and 54 years old have a median income of about

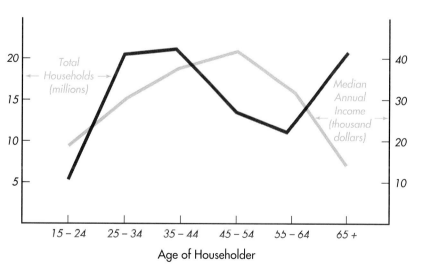

Figure 3
Age of Householder, Number of Households, and Median Household Income in the United States
The graph reveals that householders aged 35 to 44 make up the largest number of households, and householders aged 45 to 54 earn the highest median annual income. Source: U.S. Department of Commerce, *Statistical Abstract of the United States, 1994* (Washington, D.C.: U.S. Government Printing Office, 1994), p. 466.

$42,000, substantially higher than the median incomes of other age groups. Typically, workers in this age group are at the peak of their earning power. Younger households are gaining experience and training; older households include retired workers.

The size distribution of households in the United States is shown in Figure 4. Thirty-two percent of all households, or 30,200,000, are two-person households. The stereotypical household of husband, wife, and two children accounts for only 16 percent of all households. There are relatively few large households in the United States. Of the more than 93 million households in the country, only 1,500,000 (2 percent) have seven or more persons.

2.b. Household Spending

consumption:
household spending

Household spending is called **consumption**. Householders consume housing, transportation, food, entertainment, and other goods and services. Household spending (also called *consumer spending*) per year in the United States between 1959 and 1994 is shown in Figure 5, along with household income. The pattern is one of steady increase. Spending by the household sector is the largest component of total spending in the economy—rising to over $4 trillion in 1994.

RECAP

1. A household consists of one or more persons who occupy a unit of housing.
2. An apartment or house is rented or owned by a householder.
3. As a group, householders between the ages of 45 and 54 have the highest median incomes.
4. Household spending is called *consumption*.

Figure 4
Size Distribution of Households in the United States
As the pie chart illustrates, two-person households make up a larger percentage of the total number of households than any other group, a total of 32 percent. Large households with seven or more persons are becoming a rarity, accounting for only 2 percent of the total number of households. Source: *Statistical Abstract of the United States, 1994* (Washington, D.C.: U.S. Government Printing Office, 1994).

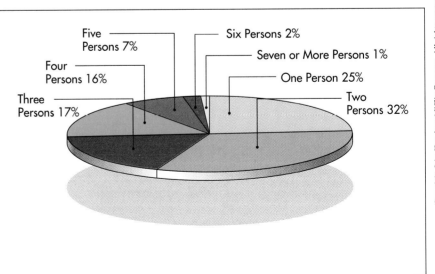

Five Persons 7%
Six Persons 2%
Seven or More Persons 1%
Four Persons 16%
One Person 25%
Three Persons 17%
Two Persons 32%

Part I/Introduction to the Price System

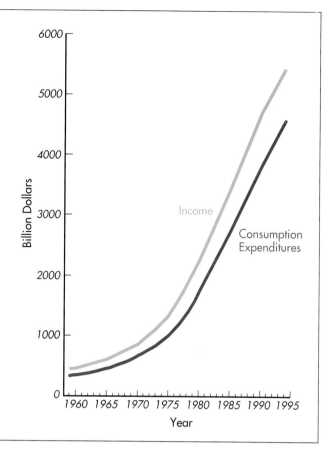

Figure 5
Household Spending and Income
Household spending (consumption) and income each year from 1959 to 1994 are shown. Both show a pattern of steady income.

3. BUSINESS FIRMS

What is a business firm, and what is business spending?

A **business firm** is a business organization controlled by a single management. The firm's business may be conducted at more than one location. The terms *company*, *enterprise*, and *business* are used interchangeably with *firm*.

3.a. Forms of Business Organizations

business firm:
a business organization controlled by a single management

sole proprietorship:
a business owned by one person who receives all the profits and is responsible for all the debts incurred by the business

partnership:
a business with two or more owners who share the firm's profits and losses

Firms are organized as sole proprietorships, partnerships, or corporations. A **sole proprietorship** is a business owned by one person. This type of firm may be a one-person operation or a large enterprise with many employees. In either case, the owner receives all the profits and is responsible for all the debts incurred by the business.

A **partnership** is a business owned by two or more partners who share both the profits of the business and responsibility for the firm's losses. The partners could be individuals, estates, or other businesses.

A **corporation** is a business whose identity in the eyes of the law is distinct from the identity of its owners. State law allows the formation of corporations. A corporation is an economic entity that, like a person, can own property and borrow money in its own name. The owners of a corporation are shareholders. If a corporation cannot pay its debts, creditors cannot seek payment from the shareholders' personal wealth. The corporation itself is

corporation:
a legal entity owned by shareholders whose liability for the firm's losses is limited to the value of the stock they own

multinational business:
a firm that owns and operates producing units in foreign countries

responsible for all its actions. The shareholders' liability is limited to the value of the stock they own.

Many firms are global in their operations even though they may have been founded and may be owned by residents of a single country. Firms typically first enter the international market by selling products to foreign countries. As revenues from these sales increase, the firms realize advantages by locating subsidiaries in foreign countries. A **multinational business** is a firm that owns and operates producing units in foreign countries. The best-known U.S. corporations are multinational firms. Ford, IBM, PepsiCo, and McDonald's all own operating units in many different countries. Ford Motor Company, for instance, is the parent firm of sales organizations and assembly plants located around the world. As transportation and communication technologies progress, multinational business activity will grow.

Figure 6
Number and Revenue of Business Firms

As Figure 6(a) illustrates, most sole proprietorships and partnerships are small firms, with nearly 70 percent of all proprietorships falling into the less-than-$25,000 revenue category, and over 60 percent of all partnerships falling into the same lowest revenue category. Corporations are more likely to be larger—17 percent have revenues exceeding $1 million. Figure 6(b) shows that most sole proprietorship revenues are earned by the larger proprietorships, those in the $100,000 to $499,000 category. By contrast, the small number of partnerships in the top revenue category is enough to account for 79 percent of all partnership revenues. Source: *Statistical Abstract of the United States, 1994* (Washington, D.C.: U.S. Government Printing Office, 1994).

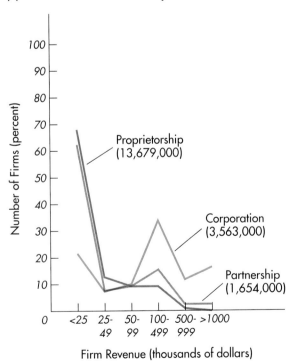

(a) Number of Business Firms by Revenue Amount

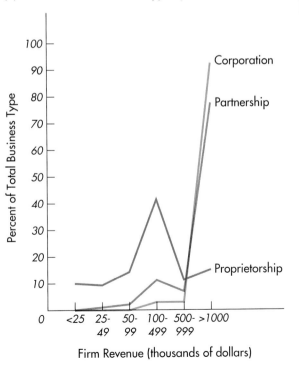

(b) Percent of Total Business Type by Revenue Amount

3.b. Business Statistics

Figure 6(a) shows that in the United States there are far more sole proprietorships than partnerships or corporations. Figure 6(a) also compares the revenues earned by each type of business. The great majority of sole proprietorships are small businesses, with revenues under $25,000 a year. Similarly, over half of all partnerships also have revenues under $25,000 a year, but only 22 percent of the corporations are in this category.

Figure 6(b) shows that the 69 percent of sole proprietorships that earn less than $25,000 a year account for only 10 percent of the revenue earned by proprietorships. The 0.3 percent of proprietorships with revenue of $1 million or more account for 15 percent. Even more striking are the figures for partnerships and corporations. The 64 percent of partnerships with the smallest revenue account for only 0.5 percent of the total revenue earned by partnerships. At the other extreme, the 3.3 percent of partnerships with the largest revenue account for 79 percent of total partnership revenue. The 22 percent of corporations in the smallest range account for only 0.1 percent of total corporate revenue, while the 17 percent of corporations in the largest range account for 93 percent of corporate revenue.

The message of Figure 6 is that big business is important in the United States. There are many small firms, but large firms and corporations account for the greatest share of business revenue. Although there are only about one-third as many corporations as sole proprietorships, corporations have more than fifteen times the revenue of sole proprietorships.

3.c. Firms Around the World

Big business is a dominant force in the United States. Many people believe that because the United States is the world's largest economy, U.S. firms are the largest in the world. Figure 7 shows that this is not true. Of the ten largest

Figure 7
The World's Ten Largest Public Companies
As shown in the chart, large firms are not just an American phenomenon. Source: *Forbes*, July 18, 1994, p. 223.

Rank	Firm (country)	Sales (millions)
1	Mitsui & Co. (Japan)	$163,529
2	Mitsubishi (Japan)	160,184
3	Sumimoto (Japan)	157,624
4	Itochu (Japan)	155,229
5	Marubeni (Japan)	144,570
6	General Motors (U.S.)	138,220
7	Ford Motor Co. (U.S.)	108,521
8	Exxon (U.S.)	97,825
9	Nissho Iwai (Japan)	95,507
10	Royal Dutch/Shell Group (Netherlands)	95,153

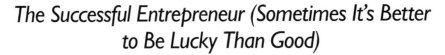
The Successful Entrepreneur (Sometimes It's Better to Be Lucky Than Good)

Entrepreneurs do not always develop an abstract idea into reality when starting a new firm. Sometimes people stumble onto a good thing by accident and then are clever enough and willing to take the necessary risk to turn their lucky find into a commercial success.

In 1875, a Philadelphia pharmacist on his honeymoon tasted tea made from an innkeeper's old family recipe. The tea, made from sixteen wild roots and berries, was so delicious that the pharmacist asked the innkeeper's wife for the recipe. When he returned to his pharmacy, he created a solid concentrate of the drink that could be sold for home consumption.

The pharmacist was Charles Hires, a devout Quaker, who intended to sell "Hires Herb Tea" to hard-drinking Pennsylvania coal miners as a nonalcoholic alternative to beer and whiskey. A friend of Hires suggested that miners would not drink anything called "tea" and recommended that he call his drink "root beer."

The initial response to Hires Root Beer was so enthusiastic that Hires soon began nationwide distribution. The yellow box of root beer extract was a familiar sight in homes and drugstore fountains across America. By 1895, Hires, who started with a $3,000 loan, was operating a business valued at half a million dollars (a lot of money in 1895) and bottling ready-to-drink root beer across the country.

Hires, of course, is not the only entrepreneur clever enough to turn a lucky discovery into a business success. In 1894, in Battle Creek, Michigan, a sanitarium handyman named Will Kellogg was helping his older brother prepare wheat meal to serve to patients in the sanitarium's dining room. The two men would boil wheat dough and then run it through rollers to produce thin sheets of meal. One day they left a batch of the dough out overnight. The next day, when the dough was run through the rollers, it broke up into flakes instead of forming a sheet.

By letting the dough stand overnight, the Kelloggs had allowed moisture to be distributed evenly to each individual wheat berry. When the dough went through the rollers, the berries formed separate flakes instead of binding together. The Kelloggs toasted the wheat flakes and served them to the patients. They were an immediate success. In fact, the brothers had to start a mail-order flaked-cereal business because patients wanted flaked cereal for their households.

Kellogg saw the market potential for the discovery and started his own cereal company (his brother refused to join him in the business). He was a great promoter who used innovations like four-color magazine ads and free-sample promotions. In New York City, he offered a free box of corn flakes to every woman who winked at her grocer on a specified day. The promotion was considered risqué, but Kellogg's sales in New York increased from two railroad cars of cereal a month to one car a day.

Will Kellogg, a poorly paid sanitarium worker in his mid-forties, became a daring entrepreneur after his mistake with wheat flour led to the discovery of a way to produce flaked cereal. He became one of the richest men in America because of his entrepreneurial ability.

Source: Based on Joseph J. Fucini and Suzy Fucini, *Entrepreneurs* (Boston: Hall and Co., 1985).

corporations in the world (measured by sales), six are Japanese. Big business is not just an American phenomenon.

3.d. Entrepreneurial Ability

The emphasis on bigness should not hide the fact that many new firms are started each year. Businesses are typically begun as small sole proprietorships. Many of them are forced to go out of business within a year or two. Businesses survive in the long run only if they provide a good or service that

Figure 8
U.S. Investment Spending, 1959–1994
Business expenditures on capital goods have been increasing erratically since 1959. Source: *Economic Report of the President, 1995* (Washington, D.C.: U.S. Government Printing Office, 1995). Table B-1.

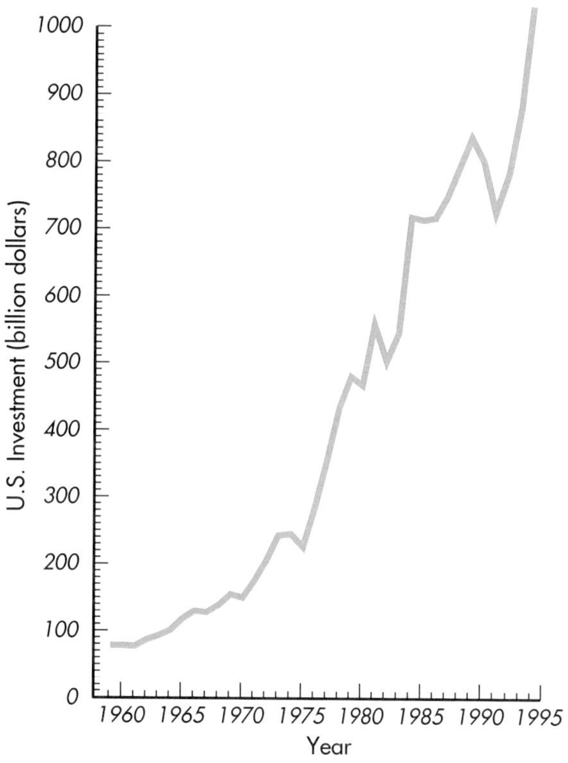

people want enough to yield a profit for the entrepreneur. Although there are fabulous success stories, the failure rate among new firms is high. Thorough research of the market and careful planning play a large part in determining whether or not a new business succeeds but so can luck, as the Economic Insight "The Successful Entrepreneur" confirms.

That many new businesses fail is a fact of economic life. In the U.S. economy, anyone with an idea and sufficient resources has the freedom to open a business. However, if buyers do not respond to the new offering, the business fails. Only firms that satisfy this "market test" survive. Entrepreneurs thus try to ensure that as wants change, goods and services are produced to satisfy those wants.

3.e. Business Spending

investment:
spending on capital goods to be used in producing goods and services

Investment is the expenditure by business firms for capital goods—machines, tools, and buildings—that will be used to produce goods and services. The economic meaning of *investment* is different from the everyday meaning, "a financial transaction such as buying bonds or stocks." In economics, the term *investment* refers to business spending for capital goods.

Investment spending in 1993 was $892 billion, an amount equal to roughly one-fifth of consumption, or household spending. Investment spending between 1959 and 1993 is shown in Figure 8. Compare Figures 5 and 8 and

Figure 9
World Economic Development
The colors on the map identify low-income, middle-income, and high-income economies. Countries have been placed in each group on the basis of GNP per capita and, in some instances, other distinguishing economic characteristics. Source: From *World Development Report, 1991* by The World Bank. Copyright © 1991 by The International Bank for Reconstruction and Development/The World Bank. Reprinted by permission of Oxford University Press, Inc.

Low-income economies
Middle-income economies
High-income economies
Countries where data are not available

notice the different patterns of spending. Investment increases unevenly, actually falling at times and then rising very rapidly. Even though investment spending is much smaller than consumption, the wide swings in investment spending mean that business expenditures are an important factor in determining the economic health of the nation.

RECAP

1. Business firms may be organized as sole proprietorships, partnerships, or corporations.
2. Large corporations account for the largest fraction of total business revenue.
3. Many new firms are started each year, but the failure rate is high.
4. Business investment spending fluctuates widely over time.

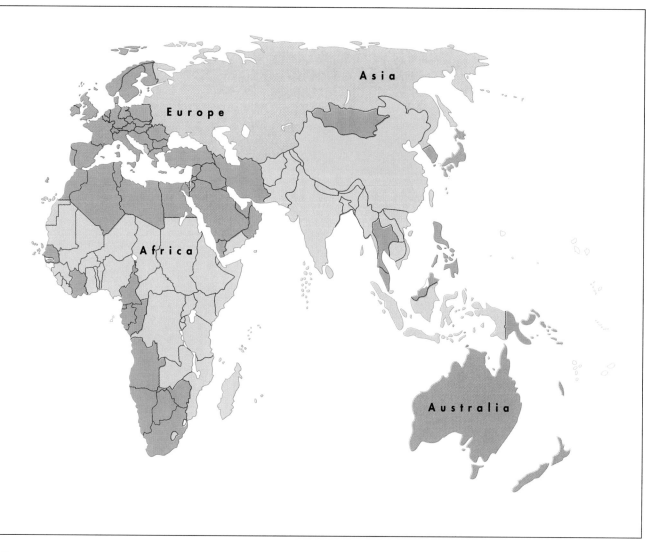

4. THE INTERNATIONAL SECTOR

How does the international sector affect the economy?

4.a. Types of Countries

Today, foreign buyers and sellers have a significant effect on economic conditions in the United States, and developments in the rest of the world often influence U.S. buyers and sellers. We saw in Chapter 3, for instance, how exchange rate changes can affect the demand for U.S. goods and services.

The nations of the world may be divided into two categories: industrial countries and developing countries. Developing countries greatly outnumber industrial countries (see Figure 9). The World Bank (an international organization that makes loans to developing countries) groups countries according to per capita income (income per person). Low-income economies are those with per capita incomes of $675 or less. Middle-income economies have per capita incomes of $675–$8,355. High-income economies—oil exporters and industrial market economies—are distinguished from the middle-income

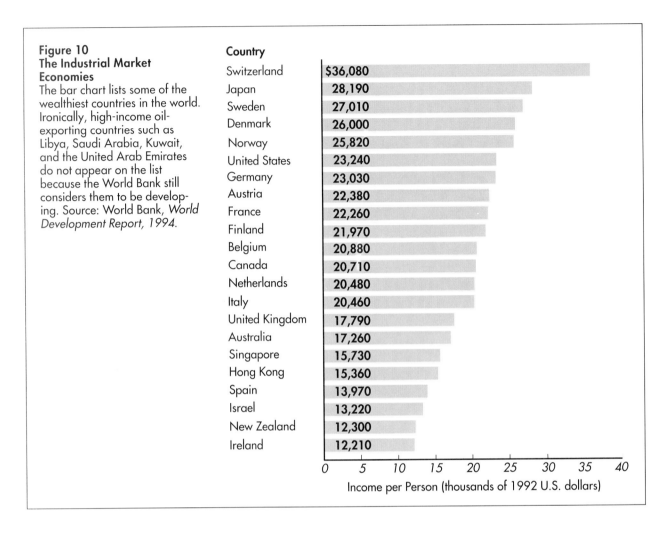

Figure 10
The Industrial Market Economies
The bar chart lists some of the wealthiest countries in the world. Ironically, high-income oil-exporting countries such as Libya, Saudi Arabia, Kuwait, and the United Arab Emirates do not appear on the list because the World Bank still considers them to be developing. Source: World Bank, *World Development Report, 1994.*

Country

Country	Income
Switzerland	$36,080
Japan	28,190
Sweden	27,010
Denmark	26,000
Norway	25,820
United States	23,240
Germany	23,030
Austria	22,380
France	22,260
Finland	21,970
Belgium	20,880
Canada	20,710
Netherlands	20,480
Italy	20,460
United Kingdom	17,790
Australia	17,260
Singapore	15,730
Hong Kong	15,360
Spain	13,970
Israel	13,220
New Zealand	12,300
Ireland	12,210

Income per Person (thousands of 1992 U.S. dollars)

economies and have per capita incomes of greater than $8,355. Some countries are not members of the World Bank and so are not categorized, and information about a few small countries is so limited that the World Bank is unable to classify them.

It is readily apparent from Figure 9 that low-income economies are heavily concentrated in Africa and Asia. Countries in these regions have a low profile in U.S. trade, although they may receive aid from the United States. U.S. trade is concentrated with its neighbors Canada and Mexico, along with the major industrial powers. Nations in each group present different economic challenges to the United States.

4.a.1. The Industrial Countries The World Bank uses per capita income to classify twenty-two countries as "industrial market economies." They are listed in the bar chart in Figure 10. The twenty-two countries listed in Figure 10 are among the wealthiest countries in the world. Not appearing on the list are the high-income oil-exporting nations like Libya, Saudi Arabia, Kuwait, and the United Arab Emirates. The World Bank considers those countries to be "still developing."

Part I/Introduction to the Price System

The economies of the industrial nations are highly interdependent. As conditions change in one nation, business firms and individuals looking for the best return or interest rate on their funds may shift large sums of money between countries. As the funds flow from one country to another, economic conditions in one country spread to other countries. As a result, the industrial countries, particularly the major economic powers like the United States, Germany, and Japan, are forced to pay close attention to each other's economic policies.

4.a.2. The Developing Countries The developing countries (sometimes referred to as *less developed countries*, or *LDCs*) provide a different set of problems for the United States than do the industrial countries. In the 1980s, the debts of the developing countries to the developed nations reached tremendous heights. For instance, at the end of 1989, Brazil owed foreign creditors $111.3 billion, Mexico owed $95.6 billion, and Argentina owed $64.7 billion. In each case, the amounts owed were more than several times the annual sales of goods and services by those countries to the rest of the world. The United States had to arrange loans at special terms and establish special trade arrangements in order for those countries to be able to buy U.S. goods.

The United States tends to buy, or *import*, primary products such as agricultural produce and minerals from the developing countries. Products that a country buys from another country are called **imports**. The United States tends to sell, or *export*, manufactured goods to developing countries.

imports:
products that a country buys from other countries

Trade between the United States and the Asian nations has been growing for several years even though some of the Asian nations attempt to restrict the sale of foreign goods in their country or to otherwise limit trade. In the photos shown here, it is clear that Coca Cola has been able to enter the Korean market, dominating its soft drink industry. In contrast, the United States has been relatively open to foreign goods. Although threatening trade sanctions against Japan or China at times, citizens of the United States clamor for the goods made in other nations. Here, seamstresses in Korea prepare clothes for major distributors in the United States.

exports:
products that a country sells to other countries

Products that a country sells to another country are called **exports**. The United States is the largest producer and exporter of grains and other agricultural output in the world. The efficiency of U.S. farming relative to farming in much of the rest of the world gives the United States a comparative advantage in many agricultural products.

4.b. International Sector Spending

U.S. economic activity with the rest of the world includes U.S. spending on foreign goods and foreign spending on U.S. goods. Figure 11 shows how U.S. exports and imports are spread over different countries. Notice that two countries, Canada and Japan, account for roughly one-third of U.S. exports and more than one-third of U.S. imports. Trade with the industrial countries is approximately twice as large as trade with the developing countries, and U.S. trade with Eastern Europe is trivial.

trade surplus:
the situation that exists when imports are less than exports

trade deficit:
the situation that exists when imports exceed exports

net exports:
the difference between the value of exports and the value of imports

When exports exceed imports, a **trade surplus** exists. When imports exceed exports, a **trade deficit** exists. Figure 11 shows that the United States is importing much more than it exports.

The term **net exports** refers to the difference between the value of exports and the value of imports: net exports equals exports minus imports. Figure 12 traces U.S. net exports for the period 1959 to 1994. Positive net exports represent trade surpluses; negative net exports represent trade deficits. The trade deficits (indicated by negative net exports) of the 1980s were unprecedented. Reasons for this pattern of international trade are discussed in later chapters.

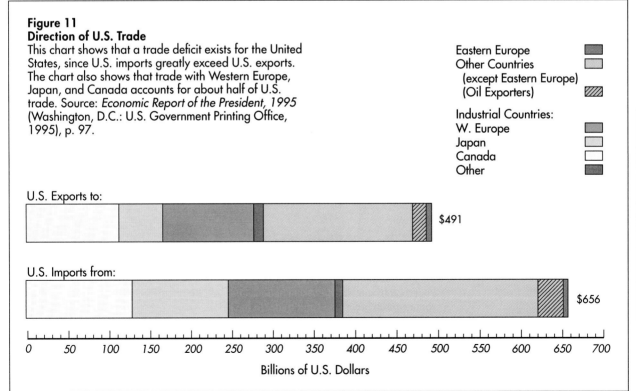

Figure 11
Direction of U.S. Trade
This chart shows that a trade deficit exists for the United States, since U.S. imports greatly exceed U.S. exports. The chart also shows that trade with Western Europe, Japan, and Canada accounts for about half of U.S. trade. Source: *Economic Report of the President, 1995* (Washington, D.C.: U.S. Government Printing Office, 1995), p. 97.

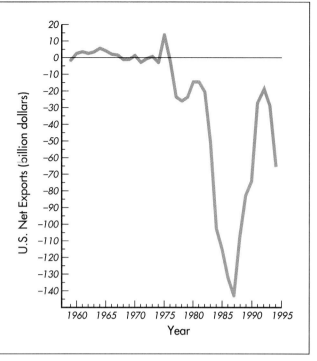

Figure 12
U.S. Net Exports, 1959–1994
Prior to the late 1960s, the United States generally exported more than it imported and had a trade surplus. Since 1976, net exports have been negative, and the United States has had a trade deficit. Source: *Economic Report of the President, 1994* (Washington, D.C.: U.S. Government Printing Office, 1994), p. 268.

RECAP

1. The majority of U.S. trade is with the industrial market economies.
2. Exports are products sold to foreign countries; imports are products bought from foreign countries.
3. Exports minus imports equals net exports.
4. Positive net exports signal a trade surplus; negative net exports signal a trade deficit.

5. LINKING THE SECTORS

Now that we have an idea of the size and structure of each of the private sectors—households, businesses, and international—let's discuss how the sectors interact.

5.a. Households and Firms

How do the three private sectors—households, businesses, international—interact in the economy?

Households own all the basic resources, or factors of production, in the economy. Household members own land and provide labor, and they are the entrepreneurs, stockholders, proprietors, and partners who own business firms.

Households and businesses interact with each other by means of buying and selling. Businesses employ the services of resources in order to produce goods and services. Business firms pay households for their services of resources.

Households sell their resource services to businesses in exchange for money payments. The flow of resource services from households to businesses is shown by the blue-green line at the bottom of Figure 13. The flow of money payments from firms to households is shown by the gold line at the bottom of Figure 13. Households use the money payments to buy goods and services from firms. These money payments are the firms' revenues. The flow of money payments from households to firms is shown by the gold line at the top of the diagram. The flow of goods and services from firms to households is shown by the blue-green line at the top of Figure 13. There is, therefore, a flow of money and goods and services from one sector to the other. The payments made by one sector are the receipts taken in by the other sector. Money, goods, and services flow from households to firms and back to households in a circular flow.

Households do not spend all of the money they receive. They save some fraction of their income. In Figure 13, we see that household saving is deposited in **financial intermediaries** like banks, credit unions, and saving

financial intermediaries: institutions that accept deposits from savers and make loans to borrowers

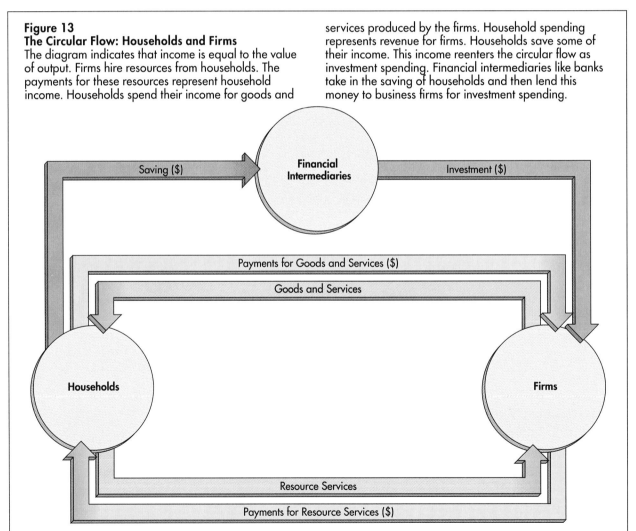

Figure 13
The Circular Flow: Households and Firms
The diagram indicates that income is equal to the value of output. Firms hire resources from households. The payments for these resources represent household income. Households spend their income for goods and services produced by the firms. Household spending represents revenue for firms. Households save some of their income. This income reenters the circular flow as investment spending. Financial intermediaries like banks take in the saving of households and then lend this money to business firms for investment spending.

and loan firms. A financial intermediary accepts deposits from savers and makes loans to borrowers. The money that is saved by the households reenters the economy in the form of investment spending as business firms borrow for expansion of their productive capacity.

circular flow diagram:
a model showing the flow of output and income from one sector of the economy to another

The **circular flow diagram** represented in Figure 13 indicates that income is equal to the value of output. Money flows to the household sector are the sum of the payments to the resource owners, including the payments to entrepreneurs. Money flows to firms are the revenue that firms receive when they sell the goods and services they produce. Revenue minus the costs of land, labor, and capital is profit. Profit represents the payment to entrepreneurs and other owners of corporations, partnerships, and sole proprietorships. In this simple economy, household income is equal to business revenue—the value of goods and services produced.

5.b. Households, Firms, and the International Sector

Figure 14 includes foreign countries in the circular flow. To simplify the circular flow diagram, let's assume that households are not directly engaged in international trade and that only business firms are buying and selling goods and services across international borders. This assumption is not far from the truth for the industrial countries and for many developing countries. We typically buy a foreign-made product from a local business firm rather than directly from the foreign producer.

A line labeled "net exports" connects firms and foreign countries in Figure 14, as well as a line labeled "payments for net exports." Notice that neither line has an arrow indicating the direction of flow as do the other lines in the diagram. The reason is that net exports of the home country may be either positive (a trade surplus) or negative (a trade deficit). When net exports are positive, there is a net flow of goods from the firms of the home country to foreign countries and a net flow of money from foreign countries to the firms of the home country. When net exports are negative, the opposite occurs. A trade deficit involves net flows of goods from foreign countries to the firms of the home country and net money flows from the domestic firms to the foreign countries. If exports and imports are equal, net exports are zero because the value of exports is offset by the value of imports.

Figure 14 shows the circular flow linking the private sectors of the economy. This model is a simplified view of the world, but it highlights the important interrelationships. The value of output equals income, as always; but spending may be for foreign as well as domestic goods. Domestic firms may produce for foreign as well as domestic consumption.

RECAP

1. The circular flow diagram illustrates how the main sectors of the economy fit together.

2. The circular flow diagram shows that the value of output is equal to income.

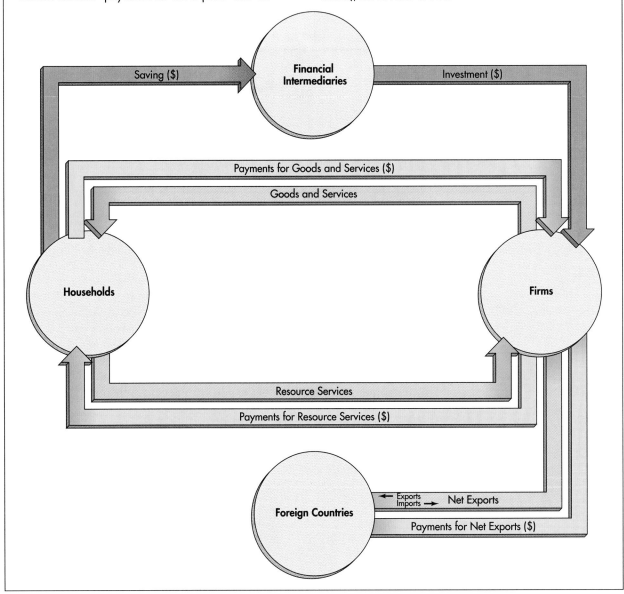

Figure 14
The Circular Flow: Households, Firms, and Foreign Countries
The diagram assumes that households are not directly engaged in international trade. The flow of goods and services between countries is represented by the line labeled "net exports." Neither the net exports line nor the line labeled "payments for net exports" has an arrow indicating the direction of the flow because the flow can go from the home country to foreign countries or vice versa. When the domestic economy has positive net exports (a trade surplus), goods and services flow out of the domestic firms toward foreign countries and money payments flow from the foreign countries to the domestic firms. With negative net exports (a trade deficit), the reverse is true.

SUMMARY

▲▼ *In a market system, who decides what goods and services are produced?*

1. In a market system, consumers are sovereign and decide by means of their purchases what goods and services will be produced. §1.a

▲▼ How are goods and services produced?

2. In a market system, firms decide how to produce the goods and services that consumers want. In order to earn maximum profits, firms use the least-cost combinations of resources. §1.c

▲▼ Who obtains the goods and services that are produced?

3. Income and prices determine who gets what in a market system. Income is determined by the ownership of resources. §1.d

▲▼ What is a household, and what is household income and spending?

4. A household consists of one or more persons who occupy a unit of housing. §2

5. Household spending is called *consumption* and is the largest component of spending in the economy. §2.b

▲▼ What is a business firm, and what is business spending?

6. A business firm is a business organization controlled by a single management. §3

7. Businesses may be organized as sole proprietorships, partnerships, or corporations. §3.a

8. Business investment spending—the expenditure by business firms for capital goods—fluctuates a great deal over time. §3.e

▲▼ How does the international sector affect the economy?

9. The international trade of the United States occurs predominantly with the other industrial economies. §4.a

10. Exports are products sold to the rest of the world. Imports are products bought from the rest of the world. §4.a.2

11. Exports minus imports equals net exports. Positive net exports mean that exports are greater than imports and a trade surplus exists. Negative net exports mean that imports exceed exports and a trade deficit exists. §4.b

▲▼ How do the three private sectors—households, businesses, and the international sector—interact in the economy?

12. The resources combined to produce goods and services are also known as factors of production. They consist of land, labor, capital, and entrepreneurial ability. §5.a

13. The total value of output produced by the factors of production is equal to the income received by the owners of the factors of production. §5.a

KEY TERMS

consumer sovereignty §1.a

private sector §1.d

public sector §1.d

household §2

consumption §2.b

business firm §3

sole proprietorship §3.a

partnership §3.a

corporation §3.a

multinational business §3.a

investment §3.e

imports §4.a.2

exports §4.a.2

trade surplus §4.b

trade deficit §4.b

net exports §4.b

financial intermediaries §5.a

circular flow diagram §5.a

EXERCISES

1. What is consumer sovereignty? What does it have to do with determining what goods and services are produced? Who determines how goods and services are produced? Who receives the goods and services in a market system?

2. Is a family a household? Is a household a family?

3. What is the median value of the following series?
   4, 6, 8, 3, 9, 10, 10, 1, 5, 7, 12

4. Which sector (households, business, or international) spends the most? Which sector spends the least? Which sector, because of volatility, has importance greater than is warranted by its size?

5. What does it mean if net exports are negative?

6. Why does the value of output always equal the income received by the resources that produced the output?

7. Total spending in the economy is equal to consumption plus investment plus government spending plus net exports. If households want to save and thus do not use all of their income for consumption, what will happen to total spending? Because total spending in the economy is equal to total income and output, what will happen to the output of goods and services if households want to save more?

8. People sometimes argue that imports should be limited by government policy. Suppose a government quota on the quantity of imports causes net exports to rise. Using the circular flow diagram as a guide, explain why total expenditures and national output may rise after the quota is imposed. Who is likely to benefit from the quota? Who will be hurt?

9. Draw the circular flow diagram linking households, business firms, and the international sector. Use the diagram to explain the effects of a decision by the household sector to increase saving.

10. Suppose there are three countries in the world. Country A exports $11 million worth of goods to country B and $5 million worth of goods to country C; country B exports $3 million worth of goods to country A and $6 million worth of goods to country C; and country C exports $4 million worth of goods to country A and $1 million worth of goods to country B.

    a. What are the net exports of countries A, B, and C?

    b. Which country is running a trade deficit? A trade surplus?

11. Over time, there has been a shift away from outdoor drive in movie theaters to indoor movie theaters. Use supply and demand curves to illustrate and explain how consumers can bring about such change when tastes change.

12. Figure 3 indicates that the youngest and the oldest households have the lowest household incomes. Why should middle-aged households have higher incomes than the youngest and oldest?

13. The chapter provides data indicating that there are many more sole proprietorships than corporations or partnerships. Why are there so many sole proprietorships? Why is the revenue of the average sole proprietorship less than that of the typical corporation?

14. List the four sectors of the economy along with the type of spending associated with each sector. Order the types of spending in terms of magnitude and give an example of each kind of spending.

15. The circular flow diagram of Figure 14 excludes the government sector. Draw a new version of the figure that includes this sector with government spending and taxes added to the diagram. Label your new figure and be sure to include arrows to illustrate the direction of flows.

COOPERATIVE LEARNING EXERCISE

Each student pairs up with his or her neighbor. Each pair uses the circular flow diagram to illustrate the effect of an increase in spending on U.S. goods by residents of foreign nations. Students should think about the following questions. How would the increased spending increase the flow of goods and services and money between the sectors? How would the increased spending be paid for? How would that affect income and output? Student pairs should share ideas.

Turning to the Next Page in Glossy Tastes

Tired of reading about O.J. Simpson? Fed up with the baseball strike? If so, you might be part of an apparent trend among the American magazine-buying public that is turning away from the supermarket tabloids and shunning the inside skinny on on the national pastime.

While nations do not stand still long enough for snapshots, the passing interests of a nation can be seen in the public's reading habits—specifically, the magazines people buy. And, according to the most recent circulation figures from the Schaumburg-based Audit Bureau of Circulations, the traditional tabloids and baseball-related publications suffered significant declines in circulation in the last six months of 1994.

The ABC report is part of the semiannual physical exam that magazines get, focusing on the vital signs of circulation in an industry where only the strong—or the deep-pocketed—survive. The baseball strike was the likely culprit in the plummeting circulation of several baseball-related publications, analysts say: Street & Smith's Baseball slid 12.6 percent; Beckett Baseball Card Monthly fell 22 percent; and Petersen's Pro Baseball plunged 46.4 percent from the year earlier.

Other sports-related magazines saw declines, albeit smaller: Sport magazine fell 5.3 percent, while Sports Illustrated was off 3.1 percent.

Despite the commonly heard lament that Americans are being dragged into the cultural sewer by tabloid news, the standard-bearers of sleaze suffered a continued decline in circulation: The National Enquirer's was down 9.9 percent; the Star's was off 6.9 percent; and the Weekly World News dropped 7.1 percent.

Source: "Turning to the Next Page in Glossy Tastes," Tim Jones, *Chicago Tribune*, Feb. 14, 1995, Section 3, p. 1. © Copyrighted Chicago Tribune Company. All rights reserved. Used with permission.

Chicago Tribune/February 14, 1995

Commentary

Standing in line at the grocery store you notice the headlines on the tabloid, "Aliens take body of Roseanne" and you wonder how anyone could pay for these tabloids. Some people not only wonder about that but, as this article notes, think that these tabloids are "pulling society into the sewer." The article goes on to note that the "standard-bearers of sleaze suffered a continued decline in circulation." Notice the perjorative view of the tabloids by the writer of the article. Who determines whether these newspapers and magazines are appropriate or not? Who defines whether the tabloids are pulling us into the sewer?

In a market system, it is consumers who determine whether the magazines and newspapers exist. If the producers of the newspapers and magazines can not cover their costs with their revenues from sales and advertisements, then the producers will change what they do. They will either alter the coverage or presentation of stories or they will get out of the business altogether.

In a market system, products are provided if they result in a profit to producers. This means the customer must be willing and able to pay for them. If stories about baseball have no interest to readers, then consumers will not purchase magazines that focus on baseball. As a result, magazines will have to alter what they do present in order to attempt to retain their sales. *Sports Illustrated* has to have stories about other sports, swimsuits, and other topics instead of baseball. If sports magazines can not write about baseball because major league baseball does not exist, then those consumers who want to read primarily about baseball will not purchase the magazines.

If people do not want to read tabloids and they are unwilling to purchase the newspapers, then the tabloids will not exist. Only if people are willing and able to pay the price sufficient for the newspaper publishers to make a profit will the newspapers be published. No one is forcing anyone to read the tabloids.

Suppose that the market for tabloids is represented in the demand and supply diagram shown below. Suppose that for some reason, perhaps the live drama of the O.J. Simpson trial, that the willingness to purchase tabloids decreases. This is illustrated by an inward shift of the demand curve, from D_1 to D_2. The magazine and newspaper prices will decline, from P_1 to P_2. In addition, fewer magazines and newspapers are purchased—quantity sold falls from Q_1 to Q_2.

According to the article, the sales of the tabloids has been declining for a few years. The article implies that is a good thing. All it really is, is a change in tastes and preferences and a shift of the demand curve. For some reason, people are not willing and able to purchase as many of the tabloids as they did before. There is no "good" or "bad" to this fact. It is simply a positive statement.

The lesson here is that the consumer does reign supreme in a market system. No profit-maximizing firm will ignore customer desires. Firms may try new cost-reducing approaches or revenue enhancing techniques, but whether the tabloids are published depends on whether customers are willing and able to buy them.

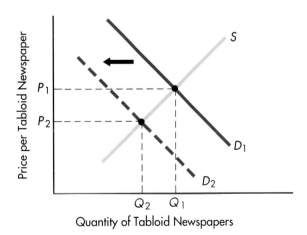

5

The Public Sector

FUNDAMENTAL QUESTIONS

1. How does the government interact with the other sectors of the economy?
2. What is the economic role of government?
3. Why is the public sector such a large part of a market economy?
4. What does the government do?
5. How do the sizes of public sectors in various countries compare?

From conception to death, we are affected by the activities of the government. Many mothers receive prenatal care through government programs. We are born in hospitals that are subsidized or run by the government. We are delivered by doctors who received training in subsidized colleges. Our births are recorded on certificates filed with the government. Ninety percent of us attend public schools. Many of us live in housing that is directly subsidized by the government or whose mortgages are insured by the government. Most of us at one time or another put savings into accounts that are insured by the government. Virtually all of us, at some time in our lives, receive money from the government—from student loan programs, unemployment compensation, disability insurance, social security, or Medicare. Twenty percent of the work force is employed by the government. The prices of wheat, corn, sugar, and dairy products are controlled or strongly influenced by the government. The prices we pay for cigarettes, alcohol, automobiles, utilities, water, gas, and a multitude of other goods are

directly or indirectly influenced by the government. We travel on public roads and publicly subsidized or controlled airlines, airports, trains, and ships. Our legal structure provides a framework in which we all live and act; the national defense ensures our rights of citizenship and protects our private property. By law, the government is responsible for employment and the general health of the economy.

According to virtually any measure, government in the United States has been a growth industry since 1930. The number of people employed by the local, state, and federal governments combined grew from 3 million in 1930 to almost 19 million today; there are now more people employed in government than there are in manufacturing. Annual expenditures by the federal government rose from $3 billion in 1930 to approximately 1.5 trillion today, and total government (federal, state, and local) expenditures now equal about $2 trillion annually. In 1929, government spending constituted less than 2.5 percent of total spending in the economy. Today, it is around 22 percent. The number of rules and regulations created by the government is so large that it is measured by the number of telephone-book-sized pages needed just to list them, and that number is more than 67,000. The cost of all federal rules and regulations is estimated to be somewhere between $4,000 and $17,000 per U.S. household each year, and the number of federal employees required to police these rules is about 125,000.

There is no doubt that the government (often referred to as the *public sector*) is a major player in the United States economy. But in the last few chapters we have been learning about the market system and how well it works. If the market system works so well, why is the public sector such a large part of the economy? In this chapter we discuss the public sector and the role government plays in a market economy.

I. THE CIRCULAR FLOW

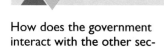

How does the government interact with the other sectors of the economy?

Government in the United States exists at the federal, state, and local levels. Local government includes county, regional, and municipal units. Economic discussions tend to focus on the federal government because national economic policy is set at that level. Nevertheless, each level affects us through its taxing and spending decisions, and laws regulating behavior.

To illustrate how the government sector affects the economy, let's add government to the circular flow model presented in the previous chapter. Government at the federal, state, and local levels interacts with both households and firms. Because the government employs factors of production to produce government services, households receive payments from the government in exchange for the services of the factors of production. The flow of resource services from households to government is illustrated by the blue-green line flowing from the households to government in Figure 1. The flow of money from government to households is shown by the gold line flowing from government to households. We assume that government, like a household, does not trade directly with foreign countries but obtains foreign goods from domestic firms who do trade with the rest of the world.

Households pay taxes to support the provision of government services, such as national defense, education, and police and fire protection. In a sense, then, the household sector is purchasing goods and services from the government as well as from private businesses. The flow of tax payments from households and businesses to government is illustrated by the gold lines flowing from households and businesses to government, and the flow of government services to households and businesses is illustrated by the purple lines flowing from government.

The addition of government brings significant changes to the model. Households have an additional place to sell their resources for income, and businesses have an additional market for goods and services. The value of *private* production no longer equals the value of household income. Households receive income from government in exchange for providing resource services to government. The total value of output in the economy is equal to the total income received, but government is included as a source of income and a producer of services.

RECAP

1. The circular flow diagram illustrates how the main sectors of the economy fit together.

2. Government interacts with both households and firms. Households get government services and pay taxes; they provide resource services and receive income. Firms sell goods and services to government and receive income.

Figure 1
The Circular Flow: Households, Firms, Government, and Foreign Countries
The diagram assumes that households and government are not directly engaged in international trade. Domestic firms trade with firms in foreign countries. The government sector buys resource services from house-holds and goods and services from firms. This government spending represents income for the households and revenue for the firms. The government uses the resource services and goods and services to provide government services for households and firms. Households and firms pay taxes to the government to finance government expenditures.

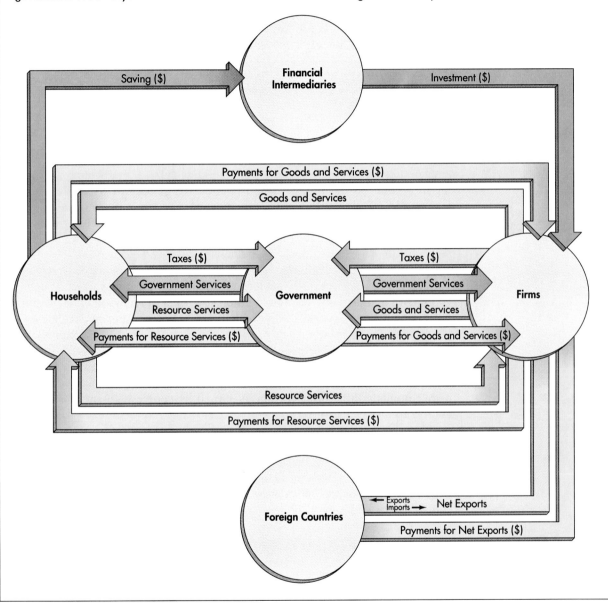

2. THE ROLE OF GOVERNMENT IN THE MARKET SYSTEM

What is the economic role of government?

We have learned that consumers use their limited incomes to buy the goods and services that give them the greatest satisfaction; that resource owners offer the services of their resources to the highest bidder; and that firms produce the goods and services and use the resources that enable them to generate the highest profits. In other words, everyone—consumers, firms, resource suppliers—attempts to get the most benefits for the least cost.

This apparently narrow, self-interested behavior is converted by the market into a social outcome in which no one can be made better off without making someone else worse off. Any resource allocation that could make someone better off and no one any worse off would increase efficiency. When all such allocations have been realized, so that the *only* way to make one person better off would harm someone else, then we have realized the best allocation society can achieve. As Adam Smith noted in 1776, self-interested individuals, wholly unaware of the effects of their actions, act as if driven by an *invisible hand* to produce the greatest social good.

2.a. Government as the Guardian of Efficiency

economic efficiency:
a situation where no one in society can be made better off without making someone else worse off

technical efficiency:
producing at a point on the PPC

Economic efficiency is the name given to the events described by Adam Smith. Efficiency can mean many things to many different people. Even within economics there are different definitions of efficiency. We have already talked about the production possibilities curve and efficiency; operating at a point on the PPC is called **productive** or **technical efficiency**. A firm is said to be operating efficiently when it produces a given quantity and quality of goods at the lowest possible cost. Consumers are said to be efficient when they are getting the greatest bang for the buck, using their scarce resources to get the greatest benefits. *Economic efficiency* encompasses all of these definitions of efficiency. When *one person cannot be made better off without harming someone else*, then we say economic efficiency prevails.

Somewhat amazingly, economic efficiency occurs in a market system simply through the self-interested individual actions of participants in that system. Efficiency is not the result of some despot controlling the economy and telling people what they can and cannot do. The market system results in efficiency because people own their resources and goods and will exchange their goods or resources for others only if the exchange makes them better off. The higher profits go, the more income is earned by people with entrepreneurial ability. In order to earn profits, entrepreneurs have to provide, at the lowest possible cost, the goods and services that consumers want and are able to buy. This means that the least-cost combination of resources is used by each firm, but it also means that resources are employed in their most highly valued uses. Any reallocation of resources results in a situation that is worse—some resources will not be used where they are most highly valued, and some consumers will be less satisfied with the goods and services they can purchase.

As we saw in the Preview, the government plays a significant role in the U.S. economy; governmental influence is even larger in other market economies and is especially large in a socialist economy like Cuba. Why, if the actions of individuals in the market system results in the best social outcome, does the government play such a large role?

Why is the public sector such a large part of a market economy?

There are two justifications given for the government's role in a market economy beyond ensuring private property rights. One is based on cases where the market may not always result in economic efficiency. The second is based on the idea that people who do not like the market outcome use the government to change the outcome. Sections 2.b through 2.f are brief discussions of some cases where the market system may fail to achieve economic efficiency. Section 2.g is a brief discussion of cases where people manipulate the market outcome.

2.b. Information and the Price System

As you learned in Chapters 3 and 4, a market is a place or service that allows buyers and sellers to exchange information on what they know about a product, what buyers are willing and able to pay for a product, and what sellers want to receive in order to produce and sell a product. A market price is a signal indicating when more or less of a good is desired. When the market price rises, buyers know that the quantity demanded at the prior equilibrium price exceeded the quantity supplied.

A market price is only as good an indicator as the information that exists in the market. It takes time for people to gather information about a product. It takes time to go to a market and purchase an item. It takes time for producers to learn what people want and bring together the resources necessary to produce that product. Thus, people are not likely to be perfectly informed, nor will everyone have the same information. This means that not all markets will adjust instantaneously or even at the same speed to a change in demand or supply. It also means that some people may pay higher prices for a product than others pay. Some people may be swindled by a sharp operator, and some firms may fail to collect debts owed them.

market imperfection:
a lack of efficiency that results from imperfect information in the marketplace

When information is not perfect, **market imperfections** may result. As a result of market imperfections, least-cost combinations of resources may not be used, or resources may not be used where they have the highest value. Often in such cases, people have argued for the government to step in with rules and regulations concerning the amount of information that must be provided. The government requires, for example, that specific information be provided on the labels of food products, that warning labels be placed on cigarettes and alcohol products, and that statements about the condition of a used car be made available to buyers. The government also declares certain actions by firms or consumers to be fraudulent or illegal. It also tests and licenses pharmaceuticals and members of many professions—medical doctors, lawyers, beauticians, barbers, nurses, and others.

2.c. Externalities

The market system works efficiently only if the market price reflects the full costs and benefits of producing and consuming a particular good or service. Recall that people make decisions on the basis of their opportunity costs and the market price is a measure of what must be forgone to acquire some good or service. If the market price does not reflect the full costs, then decisions cannot reflect opportunity costs. For instance, when you use air conditioners, you contaminate the ozone layer with Freon but you don't pay the costs of that contamination. When you drive, you don't pay for all of the pollution created by your car. When you have a loud, late-night party, you don't pay for the distractions you impose on your neighbors. When firms dump wastes or create radioactive by-products, they don't pay the costs. When homeowners allow their properties to become rundown, they reduce the value of neighboring properties but they don't pay for the loss of value. When society is educated, it costs less to produce signs, ballots, tax forms, and other information tools. Literacy enables a democracy to function effectively, and higher education may stimulate scientific discoveries that improve the welfare of society. When you acquire an education, however, you do not get a check in the amount of savings your education will create for society. All these side effects—some negative and some positive—which are not covered by the market price are called **externalities**.

externalities:
costs or benefits of a transaction that are borne by someone not directly involved in the transaction

Externalities are the costs or benefits of a market activity borne by someone who is not a direct party to the market transaction. When you drive, you pay only for gasoline and car maintenance. You don't pay for the noise and pollutants that your car emits. You also don't pay for the added congestion and delays that you impose on other drivers. Thus, the *market* price of driving understates the *full* cost of driving to society; as a result, people drive more frequently than they would if they had to pay the full cost.

The government is often called upon to intervene in the market to resolve externality problems. Government agencies, such as the Environmental Protection Agency, are established to set and enforce air quality standards, and taxes are imposed to obtain funds to pay for external costs or subsidize external benefits. Thus, the government provides education to society at below-market prices because the positive externality of education benefits everyone.

2.d. Public Goods

The market system works efficiently only if the benefits derived from consuming a particular good or service are available only to the consumer who buys the good or service. You buy a pizza, and only you receive the benefits of eating that pizza. What would happen if you weren't allowed to enjoy that pizza all by yourself? Suppose your neighbors have the right to come to your home when you have a pizza delivered and share your pizza. How often would you buy a pizza? There is no way to exclude others from enjoying the benefits of some of the goods you purchase. These types of goods are called **public goods**, and they create a problem for the market system.

public goods:
goods whose consumption cannot be limited only to the person who purchased the good

Radio broadcasts are public goods. Everyone who tunes in a station enjoys the benefits. National defense is also a public good. You could buy a missile to protect your house, but your neighbors, as well as you, would benefit from the protection it provided. A pizza, however, is not a public good. If you pay for it, only you get to enjoy the benefits. Thus, you have an incentive to purchase pizza. You don't have that incentive to purchase public goods. If you and I both benefit from the public good, who will buy it? I'd prefer that you buy it so that I receive its benefits at no cost. Conversely, you'd prefer that I buy it. The result may be that no one will buy it.

Fire protection provides a good example of the problem that occurs with public goods. Suppose that as a homeowner you have the choice of subscribing to fire protection services from a private firm or having no fire protection. If you subscribe and your house catches fire, the fire engines will arrive as soon as possible and your house may be saved. If you do not subscribe, your house will burn. Do you choose to subscribe? You might say to yourself that as long as your neighbors subscribe, you need not do so. The fact that your neighbors subscribe means that fires in their houses won't cause a fire in yours, and you do not expect a fire to begin in your house. If many people made decisions in this way, fire protection services would not be available because not enough people would subscribe to make the services profitable.

Government Creates a Market for Fishing Rights

There is no practical way to establish ownership rights of ocean fish stocks. Traditionally, fish have been free for the taking—a common pool resource. Theory teaches that such underpricing leads to overconsumption. In the halibut fisheries off Alaska, fishing fleets caught so many halibut that the survival of the stock was threatened. No single fishing boat had an incentive to harvest fewer fish since the impact on its own future catch would be minimal and others would only increase their take. This is an example of what is known as "the tragedy of the commons."

Officials tried limiting the length of the fishing season. But this effort only encouraged new capital investment such as larger and faster boats with more effective (and expensive) fishing equipment. In order to control the number of fish caught, the season was shortened in some areas from 4 months to 2 days by the early 1990s. Most of the halibut caught had to be frozen rather than marketed fresh, and halibut caught out of season had to be discarded.

In late 1992, the federal government proposed a new approach: assigning each fisherman a permit to catch a certain number of fish. The total number of fish for which permits are issued will reflect scientific estimates of the number of fish that can be caught without endangering the survival of the species. Also, the permits will be transferable—they can be bought and sold. By making the permits transferable, the system in effect creates a market where one did not exist previously. The proposed system will encourage the most profitable and efficient boats to operate at full capacity by buying permits from less successful boats, ensuring a fishing fleet that uses labor and equipment efficiently. Moreover, the transferable permits system establishes a market price for the opportunity to fish—a price that better reflects the true social cost of using this common resource.

Source: *Economic Report of the President,* 1993 (Washington, D.C.: U.S. Government Printing Office, 1993), p. 207.

private property right:
the limitation of ownership to an individual

The problem with a public good is the communal nature of the good. No one has a **private property right** to a public good. If you buy a car, you must pay the seller an acceptable price. Once this price is paid, the car is all yours and no one else can use it without your permission. The car is your private property, and you make the decisions about its use. In other words, you have the private property right to the car. Public goods are available to all because no one individual owns them or has property rights to them.

free ride:
the enjoyment of the benefits of a good by a producer or consumer without having to pay for it

When goods are public, people have an incentive to try to obtain a **free ride**—the enjoyment of the benefits of a good without paying for the good. Your neighbors would free-ride on your purchases of pizza if you didn't have the private property rights to the pizza. People who enjoy public radio and public television stations without donating money to them are getting free rides from those people who do donate to them. People who benefit from the provision of a good whether they pay for it or not have an incentive not to pay for it.

Typically, in the absence of private property rights to a good, people call on the government to claim ownership and provide the good. For instance, governments act as owners of police departments and specify how police services are used. The Economic Insight "Government Creates a Market for Fishing Rights" provides one example of government specifying private property rights.

2.e. Monopoly

monopoly:
a situation where there is only one producer of a good

If only one firm produces a good that is desired by consumers, then that firm might produce a smaller amount of the good in order to charge a higher price. In this case, resources might not be used in their most highly valued manner and consumers might not be able to purchase the goods they desire. A situation where there is only one producer of a good is called a **monopoly**. The existence of a monopoly can imply the lack of economic efficiency. The government is often called on to regulate the behavior of firms that are monopolies or even to run the monopolies as government enterprises.

2.f. Business Cycles

business cycles:
fluctuations in the economy between growth and stagnation

People are made better off by economic growth. Economic growth increases the number of jobs and draws people out of poverty and into the mainstream of economic progress. Economic stagnation, on the other hand, throws the relatively poor out of their jobs and into poverty. These fluctuations in the economy are called **business cycles**. People call on the government to protect them against the periods of economic ill health and to minimize the damaging effects of business cycles. Government agencies are established to control the money supply and other important parts of the economy, and government-financed programs are implemented to offset some of the losses that result during bad economic times. The U.S. Congress requires that the government provide economic growth and minimize unemployment. History has shown that this is easier said than done.

2.g. The Public Choice Theory of Government

The efficiency basis for government intervention in the economy discussed in sections 2.b through 2.f implies that the government is a monolithic unit functioning in much the same way that a benevolent dictator would. This monolith intervenes in the market system only to correct the ills created by the market. Not all economists agree with this view of government. Many claim that the government is not a benevolent dictator looking out for the best interests of society, but is instead merely a collection of individuals who respond to the same economic impulses we all do—that is, the desire to satisfy our own interests.

Economic efficiency does not mean that everyone is as well off as he or she desires. Economic efficiency merely means that someone or some group cannot be made better off without harming some other person or group of people. People always have an incentive to attempt to make themselves better off. If their attempts result in the transfer of benefits to themselves and away from others, however, economic efficiency has not increased. Moreover, the resources devoted to enacting the transfer of benefits are not productive; they do not create new income and benefits but merely transfer income and benefits. Such activity is called **rent seeking**. Rent seeking refers to cases where people devote resources to attempting to create income transfers to themselves. Rent seeking includes the expenditures on lobbyists in Congress, the time and expenses that health-care professionals devote to fighting nationalized health care, the time and expenses farmers devote to improving their subsidies, and millions of other examples.

rent seeking:
the use of resources to transfer income from one sector to another

public choice:
the study of how government actions result from the self-interested behaviors of voters and politicians

A group of economists, referred to as **public choice** economists, argue that government is more the result of rent seeking than it is market failure. The study of public choice focuses on how government actions result from the self-interested behaviors of voters and politicians. Whereas the efficiency justification of government argues that it is only in cases where the market does not work that the government steps in, the public choice theory says that the government may be brought into the market system whenever someone or some group can benefit, even if efficiency is not served.

According to the public choice economists, price ceilings or price floors may be enacted for political gain rather than market failure; government spending or taxing policies may be enacted not to resolve a market failure but instead to implement an income redistribution from one group to another; government agencies such as the Food and Drug Administration may exist not to improve the functioning of the market but to enact a wealth transfer from one group to another. Each such instance of manipulation leads to a larger role for government in a market economy. Moreover, government employees have the incentive to increase their role and importance in the economy and therefore transfer income or other benefits to themselves.

The government sector is far from a trivial part of the market system. Whether the government's role is one of improving economic efficiency or the result of rent seeking is a topic for debate, and in later chapters we discuss this debate in more detail. For now, it is satisfactory just to recognize how important the public sector is in the market system and what the possible reasons for its prevalence are.

RECAP

1. The government's role in the economy may stem from the inefficiencies that exist in a market system.

2. The market system does not result in economic efficiency when there are market imperfections such as imperfect information or when the costs or benefits of the transaction are borne by parties not directly involved in the transaction. Such cases are called externalities. Also, the market system may not be efficient when private ownership rights are not well defined. The government is called upon to resolve these inefficiencies that exist in the market system.

3. The government is asked to minimize the problems that result from business cycles.

4. The public choice school of economics maintains that the government's role in the market system is more the result of rent seeking than of reducing market inefficiencies.

3. OVERVIEW OF THE UNITED STATES GOVERNMENT

What does the government do?

When Americans think of government policies, rules, and regulations, they typically think of Washington, D.C., because their economic lives are regulated and shaped more by policies made there than by policies made at the local and state levels. Who actually is involved in economic policymaking? Important government institutions that shape U.S. economic policy are listed

TABLE 1
U.S. Government Economic Policymakers and Related Agencies

Institution	Role
Fiscal policymakers	
President	Provides leadership in formulating fiscal policy
Congress	Sets government spending and taxes and passes laws related to economic conduct
Monetary policymaker	
Federal Reserve	Controls money supply and credit conditions
Related agencies	
Council of Economic Advisers	Monitors the economy and advises the president
Office of Management and Budget	Prepares and analyzes the federal budget
Treasury Department	Administers the financial affairs of the federal government
Commerce Department	Administers federal policy regulating industry
Justice Department	Enforces legal setting of business
Comptroller of the Currency	Oversees national banks
International Trade Commission	Investigates unfair international trade practices
Federal Trade Commission	Administers laws related to fair business practices and competition

in Table 1. This list is far from inclusive, but it includes the agencies with the broadest powers and greatest influence.

Economic policy involves macroeconomic issues like government spending and control of the money supply and microeconomic issues aimed at providing public goods like police and military protection, correcting externalities like pollution, and maintaining a competitive economy.

3.a. Microeconomic Policy

Government provides public goods to avoid the free-rider problem that would occur if private firms provided the goods.

One reason for government's microeconomic role is the free-rider problem associated with the provision of public goods. If an army makes all citizens safer, then all citizens should pay for it. But even if one person does not pay taxes, the army still protects this citizen from foreign attack. To minimize free riding, the government collects mandatory taxes to finance public goods.

In the United States, the President is a leader in determining the agenda for economic policy. President Bill Clinton is shown presenting the annual Economic Report of the President. Behind him are members of the President's Council of Economic Advisors. In the center is chairperson of the Council, Laura Tyson.

Government taxes or subsidizes some activities that create externalities.

Government regulates industries where free market competition may not exist and polices other industries to promote competition.

Congress and the president determine the level of public goods needed and how to finance them.

Microeconomic policy also deals with externalities. Activities that cause air or water pollution impose costs on everyone. For instance, a steel mill may generate air pollutants that have a negative effect on the surrounding population. A microeconomic function of government is to internalize the externality—that is, to force the steelmaker to bear the full cost to society of producing steel. In addition to assuming the costs of hiring land, labor, and capital, the mill should bear the costs associated with polluting the air. Congress and the president determine which externalities to address and the best way of taxing or subsidizing each activity in order to ensure that the amount of the good produced and its price reflect the true value to society.

Another of government's microeconomic roles is to promote competition. Laws to restrict the ability of business firms to engage in practices that limit competition exist and are monitored by the Justice Department and the Federal Trade Commission. Some firms, such as public utilities, are monopolies and face no competition. The government defines the output, prices, and profits of many monopolies. In some cases, the monopolies are government-run enterprises.

3.b. Macroeconomic Policy

monetary policy:
policy directed toward control of money and credit

Federal Reserve:
the central bank of the United States

The focus of the government's macroeconomic policy is monetary and fiscal policy. **Monetary policy** is policy directed toward control of money and credit. The major player in this policy arena is the Federal Reserve, commonly called "the Fed." The **Federal Reserve** is the central bank of the United States. It serves as a banker for the U.S. government and regulates the U.S. money supply.

The Federal Reserve System is run by a seven-member Board of Governors. The most important member of the Board is the chairman, who is appointed by the president for a term of four years. The Board meets regularly (from ten to twelve times a year) with a group of high-level officials to review the current economic situation and set policy for the growth of U.S. money and credit. The Federal Reserve exercises a great deal of influence on U.S. economic policy.

fiscal policy:
policy directed toward government spending and taxation

Government has the responsibility of minimizing the damage from business cycles.

Fiscal policy, the other area of macroeconomic policy, is policy directed toward government spending and taxation. In the United States, fiscal policy is determined by laws that are passed by Congress and signed by the president. The relative roles of the legislative and executive branches in shaping fiscal policy vary with the political climate, but usually it is the president who initiates major policy changes. Presidents rely on key advisers for fiscal policy information. These advisers include Cabinet officers such as the secretary of the treasury and the secretary of state as well as the director of the Office of Management and Budget. In addition, the president has a Council of Economic Advisers made up of three economists—usually a chair, a macroeconomist, and a microeconomist—who, together with their staff, monitor and interpret economic developments for the president. The degree of influence wielded by these advisers depends on their personal relationship with the president.

3.c. Government Spending

Federal, state, and local government spending for goods and services between 1959 and 1993 is shown in Figure 2. Except during times of war in

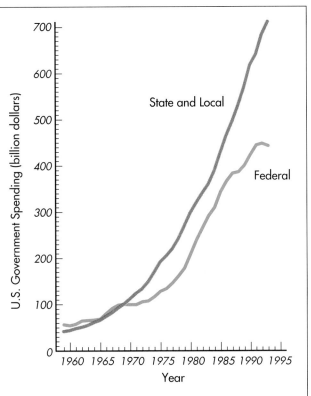

Figure 2
Federal, State, and Local Government Expenditures for Goods and Services, 1959–1993
In the 1950s and early 1960s, federal government spending was above state and local government spending. In 1969, state and local expenditures rose above federal spending and have remained higher ever since.
Source: Data are from the *Economic Report of the President, 1994* (Washington, D.C.: U.S. Government Printing Office, 1994).

the 1940s and 1950s, federal expenditures were roughly similar in size to state and local expenditures until 1969. Since 1969, state and local spending has been growing more rapidly than federal spending.

Combined government spending on goods and services is larger than investment spending but much smaller than consumption. In 1993, combined government spending was $1,157.1 billion, investment spending was $892 billion, and consumption was $4,390.6 billion.

Besides government expenditures on goods and services, government also serves as an intermediary, taking money from taxpayers with higher incomes and transferring this income to those with lower incomes. Such **transfer payments** are a part of total government expenditures, so that the total government budget is much larger than the expenditures on goods and services reported in Figure 2. In 1993, total expenditures of federal, state, and local government for goods and services was $1,157.1 billion. In this same year, transfer payments paid by all levels of government were $904 billion.

The magnitude of federal government spending relative to federal government revenue from taxes has become an important issue in recent years. Figure 3 shows that the federal budget was roughly balanced until the early 1970s. The budget is a measure of spending and revenue. A balanced budget occurs when federal spending is approximately equal to federal revenue. This was the case through the 1950s and 1960s. If federal government spending is less than tax revenue, a **budget surplus** exists. The U.S. government last had a budget surplus in 1969. By the early 1980s, federal government spending was much larger than revenue, so a large **budget deficit** existed. The federal budget deficit grew very rapidly to around $200 billion by the mid-1980s.

transfer payments:
the transfer of money by the government from taxpayers with higher incomes to those with lower incomes

budget surplus:
the excess that results when government spending is less than revenue

budget deficit:
the shortage that results when government spending is greater than revenue

Figure 3
U.S. Federal Budget Deficits, 1959–1993
The budget deficit is equal to the excess of government spending over tax revenue. If taxes are greater than government spending, a budget surplus (shown as a negative deficit) exists. The United States has run a budget deficit for all but two years in the period 1959–1993. Source: Data are from the *Economic Report of the President, 1994* (Washington, D.C.: U.S. Government Printing Office, 1994).

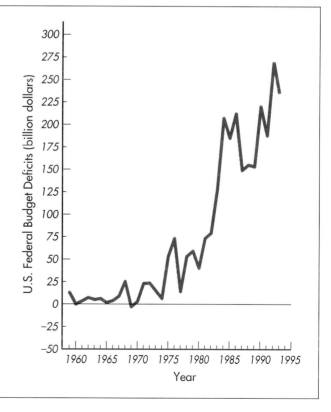

When spending is greater than revenue, the excess spending must be covered by borrowing, and this borrowing can have effects on investment and consumption as well as on economic relationships with other countries.

RECAP

1. The microeconomic functions of government include correcting externalities, redistributing income from high-income groups to lower-income groups, enforcing a competitive economy, and providing public goods.
2. Macroeconomic policy attempts to control the economy through monetary and fiscal policy.
3. The Federal Reserve conducts monetary policy. Congress and the president formulate fiscal policy.
4. Government spending is larger than investment spending but much smaller than consumption spending.
5. When government spending exceeds tax revenue, a budget deficit exists. When government spending is less than tax revenue, a budget surplus exists.

4. GOVERNMENT IN OTHER ECONOMIES

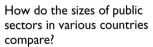

How do the sizes of public sectors in various countries compare?

centrally planned economy: an economic system in which the government determines what goods and services are produced and the prices at which they are sold

The government plays a role in every economy, and in most the public sector is a much larger part of the economy than it is in the United States. In some economies, referred to as **centrally planned**, or nonmarket, economies, the public sector is the principal component of the economy. There are significant differences between the market system and the centrally planned systems. In market economies, people can own businesses, be private owners of land, start new businesses, and purchase what they want as long as they can pay the price. They may see their jobs disappear as business conditions worsen, but they are free to take business risks and to reap the rewards if taking these risks pays off. Under centrally planned systems, people are not free to own property other than a house, a car, and personal belongings. They are not free to start a business. They work as employees of the state. Their jobs are guaranteed regardless of whether their employer is making the right or wrong decisions and regardless of how much effort they expend on the job. Even though they might have money in their pockets, they may not be able to buy many of the things they want. Money prices are often not used to ration goods and services, so people may spend much of their time standing in lines to buy the products available on the shelves of government stores. Waiting in line is a result of charging a money price lower than equilibrium and imposing a quantity limit on how much a person can buy. The time costs, along with the money price required to buy goods, will ration the limited supply.

The Soviet Union implemented a centrally planned economy in the 1920s, following its October 1917 revolution. During, and especially following, World War II, the Soviet system expanded into Eastern Europe, China, North Korea, and Vietnam. At the peak of Soviet influence, about one-third of the world's population lived in countries generally described as having centrally planned economic systems. The 1980s and 1990s ushered in a new world order, however. The Soviet Union's economy failed and ultimately led to the fall of the communist governments in Eastern Europe, the disintegration of the Soviet Union, the end of the Cold War, and the reunification of West and East Germany.

4.a. Overview of Major Market Economies

Figure 4 shows the size of government and the type of economy for several countries. The United States and Canada are representative of nations that are market economies with relatively small public sectors. Cuba is representative of nations that are primarily centrally planned. Although China has some pockets of a market economy, it is more like the centrally planned economy. Germany, Japan, and the United Kingdom are market economies but the public sector plays a larger role than it does in the United States. The nations of the former Soviet Union and those of Eastern Europe are not shown because they currently are in transition from centrally planned to market-oriented systems.

4.a.1. France
The public sector in France is much larger than it is in the United States. France is a market economy in which a national economic plan has been used to influence resource allocation. The French plan, however, does not order firms to do things. The plan is indicative; it offers suggested targets. The state uses its budget and its ownership of firms to attempt to further the implementation of the plan. Government ownership is concentrated in banking, coal, gas and electricity, transportation, and auto and aircraft production. The government-sector share of the economy is quite large; total government expenditures were nearly 50 percent of total output in 1993.

4.a.2. United Kingdom
The role of the public sector in the United Kingdom is significant but not exceptional by European standards. Great Britain is an island economy with a land area slightly greater than that of the state of Minnesota and a population of just over 57 million persons. The resource base of the economy is quite limited, and the British economy is tied very closely

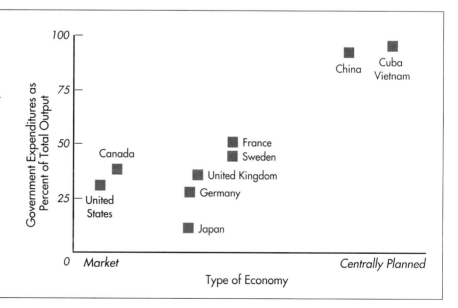

Figure 4
The Economic Systems
The closer a country is to a market economy without a public sector, the closer to the lower-left area of the diagram it is placed. Conversely, the more the country is a centrally planned economy, the closer to the upper-right area of the diagram it is placed.

limits on what firms and consumers can do in certain types of situations. Governments tax externalities or otherwise attempt to make price reflect the full cost of production and consumption. §3.a

8. Governments carry out monetary and fiscal policy to attempt to control business cycles. In the United States, monetary policy is the province of the Federal Reserve, and fiscal policy is up to the Congress and the president. §3.b

▲▼ *How do the sizes of public sectors in various countries compare?*

9. Market systems rely on the decisions of individuals. Centrally planned systems rely on the government to answer economic questions for all individuals. §4

10. The size and influence of the public sector ranges from the market economies of the United States and Canada to the centrally planned economy of Cuba. §4.a

KEY TERMS

economic efficiency §2.a

technical efficiency §2.a

market imperfection §2.b

externalities §2.c

public goods §2.d

private property right §2.d

free ride §2.d

monopoly §2.e

business cycles §2.f

rent seeking §2.g

public choice §2.g

monetary policy §3.b

Federal Reserve §3.b

fiscal policy §3.b

transfer payments §3.c

budget surplus §3.c

budget deficit §3.c

centrally planned economy §4

EXERCISES

1. Illustrate productive or technical efficiency using a production possibilities curve. Can you illustrate economic efficiency? Are you able to show the exact point where economic efficiency would occur?

2. Why would an externality be referred to as a market failure? Explain how your driving on a highway imposes costs on other drivers. Why is this an externality? How might the externality be resolved or internalized?

3. What is the difference between a compact disk recording of a rock concert and a radio broadcast of that rock concert? Why would you spend $12 on the CD but refuse to provide any support to the radio station?

4. "The American buffalo disappeared because they were not privately owned." Evaluate this statement.

5. Which of the following economic policies are the responsibility of the Federal Reserve? Congress and the president?

a. An increase in the rate of growth of the money supply

b. A decrease in the rate of interest

c. An increase in taxes on the richest 2 percent of Americans

d. A reduction in taxes on the middle class

e. An increase in the rate of growth of spending on health care

6. "The Department of Justice plans to file a lawsuit against major airlines, claiming they violated price-fixing laws by sharing plans for fare changes through a computer system, officials said Friday." This statement was reported in newspapers on December 12, 1992. Is this a microeconomic or macroeconomic policy?

7. People sometimes argue that imports should be limited by government policy. Suppose a government quota on the quantity of imports causes net exports to rise. Using the circular flow diagram as a guide, explain why total

expenditures and national output may rise after the quota is imposed. Who is likely to benefit from the quota? Who will be hurt? Explain why the government would become involved in the economy through its imposition of quotas.

8. Most highways are "free" ways: there is no toll charge for using them. What problem does free access create? How would you solve this?

9. Explain why the suggested government action may or may not make sense in each of the following scenarios.

    a. People purchase a VCR with a guarantee provided by its maker, only to find that within a year the company has gone out of business. Consumers demand that the government provide the guarantee.

    b. Korean microchip producers are selling the microchips at a price that is below the cost of making the microchips in the United States. The U.S. government must impose taxes on the Korean microchips imported into the United States.

    c. The economy has slowed down, unemployment has risen, and interest rates are high. The government should provide jobs and force interest rates down.

    d. Fully 15 percent of all United States citizens are without health insurance. The government must provide health care for all Americans.

    e. The rising value of the dollar is making it nearly impossible for U.S. manufacturers to sell their products to other nations. The government must decrease the value of the dollar.

    f. The rich got richer at a faster rate than the poor got richer during the 1980s. The government must increase the tax rate on the rich to equalize the income distribution.

    g. The AIDS epidemic has placed such a state

of emergency on health care that the only solution is to provide some pharmaceutical firm with a monopoly on any drugs or solutions discovered for HIV or AIDS.

10. Many nations of Eastern Europe are undergoing a transition from a centrally planned to a market economic system. An important step in the process is to define private property rights in countries where they did not exist before. What does this mean? Why is it necessary to have private property rights?

11. Using the circular flow diagram, illustrate the effects of an increase in taxes imposed on the household sector.

12. Using the circular flow diagram, explain how the government can continually run budget deficits, that is, spend more than it receives in revenue from taxes.

13. Suppose you believe that government is the problem, not the solution. How would you explain the rapid growth of government during the past few decades?

14. The government intervenes in the private sector by imposing laws that ban smoking in all publicly used buildings. As a result, smoking is illegal in bars, restaurants, hotels, dance clubs, and other establishments. Is such a ban justified by economics?

15. In reference to question 14, we could say that before a ban is imposed, the owners of businesses owned the private property right to the air in their establishments. As owners of this valuable asset they would ensure it is used to earn them the greatest return. Thus, if their customers desired nonsmoking, then they would provide nonsmoking environments. How then does the ban on smoking improve things? Doesn't it merely transfer ownership of the air from the business owners to the nonsmokers?

COOPERATIVE LEARNING EXERCISE

Divide the class into groups of three or four students and assign each group a part of section 2 on the role of government in the market system from which to create a question that may be answered in one sentence. Groups have ten min- *utes to create their questions and then each group should pick another group to answer its question. (In large classes, the instructor should arbitrarily pair groups for questions and answers.)*

Agency Acts to Privatize the Internet; Tricky Transition Has Some Users Worried

Not anymore.

As the 'Net celebrates its silver anniversary this month, the National Science Foundation—which has been spending upward of $10 million a year administering the central "backbone" of the Internet—is preparing to relinquish the world's closest thing to an information highway to the vagaries of the free market.

Many longtime users believe the move is crucial to the growth of the network. People can still find and exchange an enormous amount of data and chat cheaply over thousands of miles, but the Internet is becoming strained by the influx of the curious and the commercial into what was once the preserve of researchers.

But others fear that pieces of the Internet could split apart as profit replaces sharing as the motive to link it all together. As the network of networks becomes central to commerce and begins to touch the lives of ordinary citizens, the stakes in its responsible operation have grown exponentially.

"It's going to be like the Copernican revolution, when people suddenly realized the universe did not have a center," said Bill Washburn, who heads a consortium of smaller networks that is one of the many entities hoping to profit form the new Internet order.

"The Internet is anarchy, it's a form of chaos, and with the disappearance of the NSF network, that chaotic quality will become more immediate and more evident to a lot of people who have been able to ignore it."

Whatever the outcome, the quasi-public network has arrived at a watershed as it begins the first stages of official privatization.

"This is an immense change affecting millions of people, and tens of thousands of individual networks," says Stephen Wolff, National Science Foundation networking chief, who has spearheaded the move. "But the marketplace is there now, and there's no point in having the federal government competing with the private sector."

Indeed, the National Science Foundation's withdrawal is in one sense symbolic, since the network has been de facto open to businesses for years. More than half of the Internet's rapid growth this year is accounted for by commercial traffic, much of which technically conflicts with the agency's rule that it be used for research only.

This "acceptable use" policy, as it is known, had become something of a conundrum for the National Science Foundation—essentially unenforceable, it nonetheless impeded the network's growth by making some firms leery of joining it....

The National Science Foundation plan, set in motion over a year ago, is just beginning to take effect. By the end of this year, if all goes well, each of the 400 billion bytes of data that flow daily over the National Science Foundation's high-speed fiber pathway (each byte is equal to roughly one letter of the alphabet) will have found another, privately owned route to its destination.

Now telephone companies and firms that run regional data networks linking customers to the Internet are rushing to capture the business created by the National Science Foundation's abdication. It promises to be a competitive free-for-all....

Indeed, for the academic world, long addicted to e-mail and the ability to search faraway data bases without leaving campus, the change will likely mean an end to what for most has been unlimited free on-line access.

And that, says Wolff, is part of the point: "The whole idea is to reduce the network to the status of the telephone. The Internet is one of the costs of doing business, and universities will provide for it the same way they provide for desks and chairs and roses in front of the president's house."...

Users who have piggybacked on the government's backbone service may also see connection costs rise. Rural areas and small businesses that must purchase their own connections would likely be hit the hardest.

Source: "Agency Acts to Privatize the Internet; Tricky Transition Has Some Users Worried," Amy Harmon, *Los Angeles Times*, Sept. 6, 1994. Used with permission.

The Los Angeles Times/September 6, 1994

Commentary

The Internet is a world-wide communication system allowing computer users to transmit messages and information. As stated in the article, the Internet was started by the government and has been heavily subsidized by taxpayers since its inception. Now the Internet is being "privatized" or turned over to business firms. There are two questions related to this article that seem particularly relevant in the context of this chapter: 1. Why was the Internet originally started by government rather than private enterprise? and 2. What are the likely implications of privatization for Internet users?

The answer to the first question may be found in several sections of Chapter 5. Section 2.b. informs us that a well-functioning market economy depends on well-informed participants. The lower the cost of information, the more rapidly prices reflect changes in supply and demand and the better decisions firms and households are able to make. The Internet may be thought of as one way in which government has tried to improve the flow of information in the economy. Other ways that government has intervened in the marketplace to improve information includes requiring truthful advertising or labeling ingredients on food products.

Information is only part of the answer in building a case for government provision of the Internet. Section 2.c. discusses the role of government in addressing externalities. The Internet was originally developed to allow researchers in academic institutions and government organizations to more efficiently communicate. Research and development provides beneficial externalities as new technologies are created that offer benefits to the economy at large. The provision of the Internet speeds the transmission of research efforts and allows researchers to accelerate the pace of discovery.

With the reasons just discussed for the government provision of the Internet, why is the Internet now being privatized? Section 2.d. of Chapter 5 discussed the difference between public goods and private goods. If there was no way to exclude potential Internet users from participating in the communication network, then we would consider the Internet a public good. However, it is not difficult to establish private property rights in the computer communication system; it is much like what occurs with the telephone. Given the ease of establishing private property rights and then charging user fees, the existence of a private Internet system is not difficult to establish. The reason why this privatization occurs is to increase the efficiency of the system and improve the quality of service. Service providers will compete for subscribers on the basis of price and quality of service. The end result is expected to be a more user friendly communication system.

The article warns of potential problems of the Internet becoming "a patchwork of private roads." The road analogy is appropriate. In the United States, government has used taxpayer dollars to fund the construction of an interstate highway system along with local freeways and streets. The argument for the government provision of the streets is that everyone benefits from a more efficient transportation network so everyone should pay. A system of privately operated toll roads may not connect as easily and could isolate some would-be travelers. Similarly some skeptics fear that a private Internet could end up with different firms offering different services so that the global connectivity that now exists may disappear. These critics argue that government should continue to operate the Internet as it has continued to operate the interstate highway system.

Only time will tell if privatization yields the benefits of an "information superhighway" that has been much discussed in the mid 1990s. This article serves to remind us that there are few areas of government involvement in economic life that are non controversial.

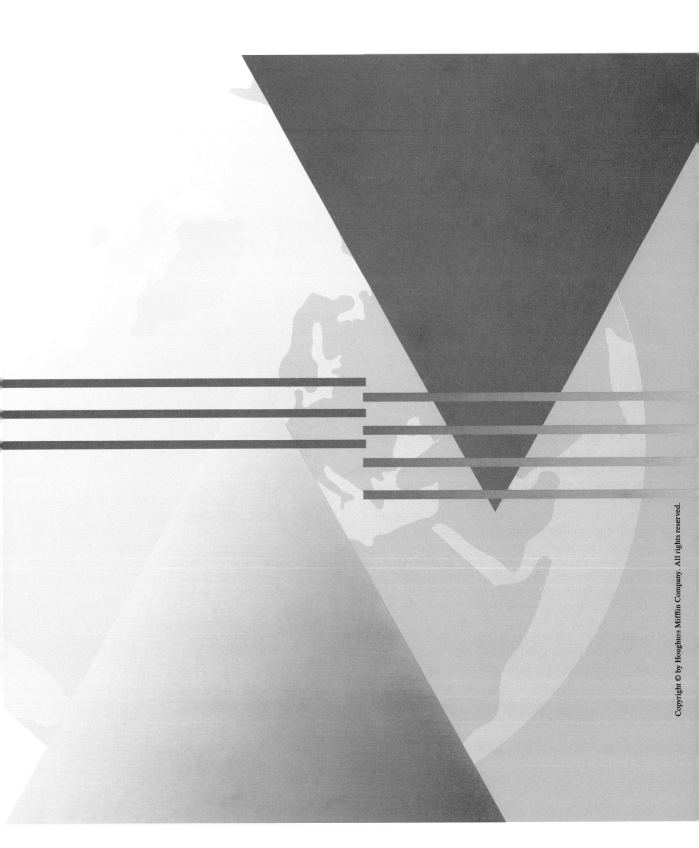

II

Macroeconomic Basics

6

National Income Accounting

FUNDAMENTAL
QUESTIONS

1. How is the total output of an economy measured?
2. Who produces the nation's goods and services?
3. Who purchases the goods and services produced?
4. Who receives the income from the production of goods and services?
5. What is the difference between nominal and real GDP?
6. What is a price index?

T he Korean economy grew at an average rate of 8.4 percent per year from 1970 to 1993. This compares with an average rate of 3.4 percent per year in the United States over the same period. Still, the U.S. economy is much larger than the Korean economy and larger than the economies of the fifty largest developing countries combined. The *size* of an economy cannot be compared across countries without common standards of measurement. National income accounting provides these standards. Economists use this system to evaluate the economic condition of a country and to compare conditions across time and countries.

A national economy is a complex arrangement of many different buyers and sellers—of households, businesses, and government units—and of their interactions with the rest of the world. To assess the economic health of a country or to compare the performance of an economy from year to year, economists must be able to measure national output and real GDP. Without these data, policymakers cannot evaluate their economic policies. For

PREVIEW

instance, real GDP fell in the United States in 1980, 1981, 1982, and again in 1990–1991. This drop in real GDP was accompanied by widespread job loss and a general decline in the economic health of the country. As this information became known, political and economic debate centered on economic policies, on what should be done to stimulate the economy. Without real GDP statistics, policymakers would not have known there were problems, let alone how to go about fixing them.

I. MEASURES OF OUTPUT AND INCOME

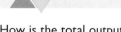

How is the total output of an economy measured?

national income accounting: the framework that summarizes and categorizes productive activity in an economy over a specific period of time, typically a year

In this chapter we discuss gross domestic product, real GDP, and other measures of national productive activity by making use of the **national income accounting** system used by all countries. National income accounting provides a framework for discussing macroeconomics. Figure 1 reproduces the circular flow diagram you saw in Chapter 5. The lines connecting the various sectors of the economy represent flows of goods and services, and money expenditures (income). National income accounting is the process of counting the value of the flows between sectors and then summing them to find the total value of economic activity in an economy. National income accounting fills in the dollar values in the circular flow.

National income accounting measures the output of an entire economy as well as the flows between sectors. It summarizes the level of production in an

Figure 1
The Circular Flow: Households, Firms, Government, and Foreign Countries
The value of national output equals expenditures and income. If the domestic economy has positive net exports (a trade surplus), goods and services flow out of the domestic firms toward the foreign countries and money payments flow from the foreign countries to the domestic firms. If the domestic economy has negative net exports (a trade deficit), just the reverse is true.

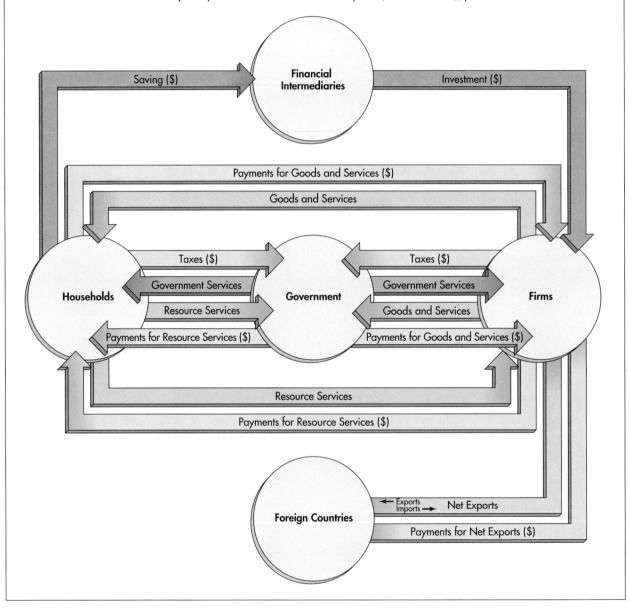

economy over a specific period of time, typically a year. In practice, the process *estimates* the amount of activity that occurs. It is beyond the capability of government officials to count every transaction that takes place in a modern economy. Still, national income accounting generates useful and fairly accurate measures of economic activity in most countries, especially wealthy industrial countries that have comprehensive accounting systems.

1.a. Gross Domestic Product

The most common measure of a nation's output is GDP.

Modern economies produce an amazing variety of goods and services. To measure an economy's total production, economists combine the quantities of oranges, golf balls, automobiles, and all the other goods and services produced, into a single measure of output. Of course, simply adding up the number of things produced—the number of oranges, golf balls, and automobiles—does not reveal the *value* of what is being produced. If a nation produces 1 million more oranges and 1 million fewer automobiles this year than it did last year, the total number of things produced remains the same. But because automobiles are much more valuable than oranges, the value of output has dropped substantially. Prices reflect the value of goods and services in the market, so economists use the money value of things to create a measure of total output, a measure that is more meaningful than the sum of units produced.

The most common measure of a nation's output is gross domestic product. **Gross domestic product (GDP)** is the market value of all final goods and services produced in a year within a country's borders. A closer look at three parts of this definition—*market value*, *final goods and services*, and *produced in a year*—will make clear what the GDP does and does not include.

gross domestic product (GDP):
the market value of all final goods and services produced in a year within a country

Market value The *market value* of final goods and services is their value at market price. The process of determining market value is straightforward where prices are known and transactions are observable. However, there are cases where prices are not known and transactions are not observable. For instance, illegal drug transactions are not reported to the government, which means they are not included in GDP statistics. In fact, almost any activity that is not traded in a market is not included. For example, production that takes place in households, such as homemakers' services (as discussed in the Economic Insight "The Value of Homemaker Services"), is not counted, nor are unreported barter and cash transactions. For instance, if a lawyer has a sick dog and a veterinarian needs some legal advice, by trading services and not reporting the activity to the tax authorities, each can avoid taxation on the income that would have been reported had they sold their services to each other. If the value of a transaction is not recorded as taxable income, it generally does not appear in the GDP. There are some exceptions, however. Contributions toward GDP are estimated for *in-kind wages*, nonmonetary compensation like room and board. GDP values also are assigned to the output consumed by a producer—for example, the home consumption of crops by a farmer.

Final goods and services The second part of the definition of GDP limits the measure to *final goods and services*, the goods and services available to the ultimate consumer. This limitation avoids double-counting. Suppose a retail store sells a shirt to a consumer for $20. The value of the shirt in the GDP is $20. But the shirt is made of cotton that has been grown by a farmer, woven at a mill, and cut and sewn by a manufacturer. What would happen if we counted the value of the shirt at each of these stages of the production process? We would overstate the market value of the shirt.

intermediate good:
a good that is used as an input in the production of final goods and services

Intermediate goods are goods that are used in the production of a final product. For instance, the ingredients for a meal are intermediate goods to a restaurant. Similarly, the cotton and the cloth are intermediate goods in the production of the shirt. The stages of production of the $20 shirt are shown

The Value of Homemaker Services

One way GDP underestimates the total value of a nation's output is by failing to record nonmarket production. A prime example is the work homemakers do. Of course, people are not paid for their work around the house, so it is difficult to measure the value of their output. But notice that we say *difficult*, not impossible. Economists can use several methods to assign value to homemaker services.

One is an opportunity cost approach. This approach measures the value of a homemaker's services by the forgone market salary the homemaker could have earned if he or she worked full time outside the home. The rationale is that society loses the output the homemaker would have produced in the market job in order to gain the output the homemaker produces in the home.

Another alternative is to estimate what it would cost to hire workers to produce the goods and services that the homemaker produces. For example, what would it cost to hire someone to prepare meals, iron, clean, and take care of the household? It has been esti- mated that the average homemaker spends almost 8 hours a day, 7 days a week, on household work. This amounts to over 50 hours a week. At a rate of $10 an hour, the value of the homemaker's services is over $500 a week.

Whichever method we use, two things are clear. The value of homemaker services to the house- hold and the economy is substan- tial. And by failing to account for those services, the GDP substan- tially underestimates the value of the nation's output.

value added:
the difference between the value of output and the value of the intermediate goods used in the production of that output

in Figure 2. The value-of-output axis measures the value of the product at each stage. The cotton produced by the farmer sells for $1. The cloth woven by the textile mill sells for $5. The shirt manufacturer sells the shirt whole- sale to the retail store for $12. The retail store sells the shirt—the final good—to the ultimate consumer for $20.

Remember that GDP is based on the market value of final goods and ser- vices. In our example, the market value of the shirt is $20. That price already includes the value of the intermediate goods that were used to produce the shirt. If we add to it the value of output at every stage of production, we would be counting the value of the intermediate goods twice, and we would be overstating the GDP.

It is possible to compute GDP by computing the **value added** at each stage of production. Value added is the difference between the value of output and the value of the intermediate goods used in the production of that output. In Figure 2, the value added by each stage of production is listed at the right. The farmer adds $1 to the value of the shirt. The mill takes the cotton worth $1 and produces cloth worth $5, adding $4 to the value of the shirt. The manufacturer uses $5 worth of cloth to produce a shirt it sells for $12, so the manufacturer adds $7 to the shirt's value. Finally, the retail store adds $8 to the value of the shirt: it pays the manufacturer $12 for the shirt and sells it to the consumer for $20. The sum of the value added at each stage of produc- tion is $20. The total value added, then, is equal to the market value of the final product.

Economists can compute GDP using two methods: the final goods and ser- vices method uses the market value of the final good or service; the value- added method uses the value added at each stage of production. Both methods count the value of intermediate goods only once. This is an impor- tant distinction: GDP is not based on the market value of *all* goods and ser- vices, but on the market value of all *final* goods and services.

Figure 2
Stages of Production and Value Added in Shirt Manufacturing

A cotton farmer sells cotton to a textile mill for $1, adding $1 to the value of the final shirt. The textile mill sells cloth to a shirt manufacturer for $5, adding $4 to the value of the final shirt. The manufacturer sells the shirt wholesale to the retail store for $12, adding $7 to the value of the final shirt. The retail store sells the final shirt to a consumer for $20, adding $8 to the value of the final shirt. The sum of the prices received at each stage of production equals $38, which is greater than the price of the final shirt. The sum of the value added at each stage of production equals $20, which equals the market value of the shirt.

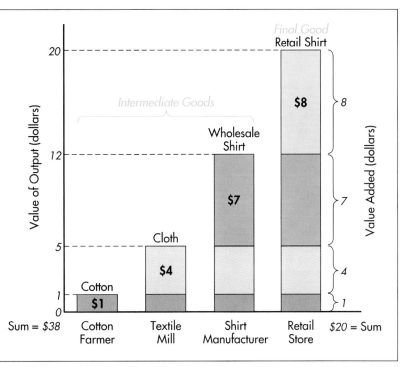

inventory:
the stock of unsold goods held by a firm

Produced in a year   GDP measures the value of output *produced in a year*. The value of goods produced last year is counted in last year's GDP; the value of goods produced this year is counted in this year's GDP. The year of production, not the year of sale, determines allocation to GDP. Although the value of last year's goods is not counted in this year's GDP, the value of services involved in the sale is. This year's GDP does not include the value of a house built last year, but it does include the value of the real estate broker's fee; it does not include the value of a used car, but it does include the income earned by the used-car dealer in the sale of that car.

To determine the value of goods produced in a year but not sold in that year, economists calculate changes in inventory. **Inventory** is a firm's stock of unsold goods. If a shirt that is produced this year remains on the retail store's shelf at the end of the year, it increases the value of the store's inventory. A $20 shirt increases that value by $20. Changes in inventory allow economists to count goods in the year in which they are produced whether or not they are sold.

Changes in inventory can be planned or unplanned. A store may want a cushion above expected sales (*planned inventory changes*), or it may not be able to sell all the goods it expected to sell when it placed the order (*unplanned inventory changes*). For instance, suppose Jeremy owns a surfboard shop, and he always wants to keep 10 surfboards above what he expects to sell. This is done so that in case business is surprisingly good, he does not have to turn away customers to his competitors and lose those sales. At the beginning of the year, Jeremy has 10 surfboards and then builds as many new boards during the year as he expects to sell. Jeremy *plans* on having an inventory at the end of the year of 10 surfboards. Suppose Jeremy expects to sell 100 surfboards during the year, so he builds 100 new boards. If business is surprisingly poor so that Jeremy sells only 80 surfboards, how do we count the 20 new boards that he made but did not sell? We count the change in his inventory. He started the year with 10 surfboards and ends the year with 20 more unsold boards for a year-end inventory of 30. The change in inventory of 20 (equal to the ending inventory of 30 minus the starting inventory of 10) represents output that is counted in GDP. In Jeremy's case, the inventory change is unplanned since he expected to sell the 20 extra surfboards that he has in his shop at the end of the year. But whether the inventory change is planned or unplanned, changes in inventory will count output that is produced but not sold in a given year.

Who produces the nation's goods and services?

GDP is the value of final goods and services produced by domestic households, businesses, and government.

1.a.1. GDP as Output   GDP is a measure of the market value of a nation's total output in a year. Remember that economists divide the economy into four sectors: households, businesses, government, and the international sector. Figure 1 shows how the total value of economic activity equals the sum of the output produced in each sector. Figure 3 indicates where the U.S. GDP was produced in 1993.[1] Since GDP counts the output produced in the United States, U.S. GDP is produced in business firms, households, and government located within the boundaries of the United States.

Not unexpectedly in a capitalist country, privately owned businesses account for the largest percentage of output: in the United States, 85 percent of the GDP is produced by private firms. Government produces 11 percent of the GDP, and households 4 percent.

Figure 3 defines GDP in terms of output: GDP is the value of final goods and services produced by domestic households, businesses, and government units. If some of the firms producing in the United States are foreign-owned, their output produced in the United States is counted in U.S. GDP.

1.a.2. GDP as Expenditures   The circular flow in Figure 1 shows not only the output of goods and services from each sector, but also the payment for goods and services. Here we look at GDP in terms of what each sector pays for the goods and services it purchases.

Who purchases the goods and services produced?

The dollar value of total expenditures—the sum of the amount each sector spends on final goods and services—equals the dollar value of output. In Chapter 4 you learned that household spending is called *consumption*. Households spend their income on goods and services to be consumed. Business spending is called *investment*. Investment is spending on capital goods that will be used to produce other goods and services. The two other components of total spending are *government spending* and *net exports*. Net exports are the value of *exports* (goods and services sold to the rest of the world) minus the value of *imports* (goods and services bought from the rest of the world).

GDP = consumption + investment + government spending + net exports

GDP = C + I + G + X

Or, in the shorter form commonly used by economists,

$$GDP = C + I + G + X$$

where *X* is net exports.

---

[1]Due to rounding, percentages and dollar amounts in the next three figures will not add exactly to the totals given.

Part II/Macroeconomic Basics

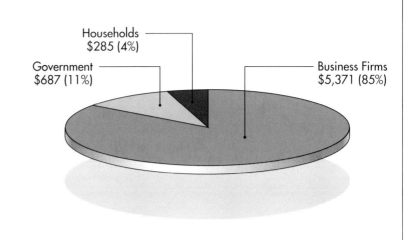

Figure 3
U.S. Gross Domestic Product by Sector, 1993 (billion dollars)
Business firms produce 85 percent of the U.S. GDP. Government produces 11 percent; households, 4 percent. Source: Data from *Economic Report of the President, 1995* (Washington, D.C.: U.S. Government Printing Office, 1995), p. 286.

Households
$285 (4%)

Government
$687 (11%)

Business Firms
$5,371 (85%)

Figure 4 shows the U.S. GDP in terms of total expenditures. Consumption, or household spending, accounts for 69 percent of national expenditures. Government spending represents 18 percent of expenditures, and business investment, 14 percent. Net exports are negative (−1 percent), which means that imports exceeded exports in 1993. To determine total national expenditures on *domestic* output, the value of imports, spending on foreign output, are subtracted from total expenditures.

Who receives the income from the production of goods and services?

1.a.3. GDP as Income The total value of output can be calculated by adding up the expenditures of each sector. And because one sector's expenditures are another's income, the total value of output also can be computed by adding up the income of all sectors.

Business firms use factors of production to produce goods and services. Remember that the income earned by factors of production is classified as wages, interest, rent, and profits. *Wages* are payments to labor, including fringe benefits, social security contributions, and retirement payments. *Interest* is the net interest paid by businesses to households plus the net interest

Figure 4
U.S. Gross Domestic Product as Expenditures, 1993 (billion dollars)
Consumption by households accounts for 69 percent of the GDP, followed by government spending of 18 percent, investment by business firms of 14 percent, and net exports of −1 percent. Source: Data from *Economic Report of the President, 1995* (Washington, D.C.: U.S. Government Printing Office, 1995), pp. 274–275.

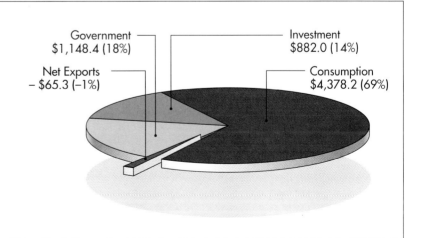

Government
$1,148.4 (18%)

Net Exports
−$65.3 (−1%)

Investment
$882.0 (14%)

Consumption
$4,378.2 (69%)

received from foreigners (the interest they pay us minus the interest we pay them). *Rent* is income earned from selling the use of real property (houses, shops, farms). Finally, *profits* are the sum of corporate profits plus proprietors' income (income from sole proprietorships and partnerships).

Figure 5 shows the U.S. GDP in terms of income. Notice that wages account for 60 percent of the GDP. Interest and profits account for 6 percent and 8 percent of the GDP, respectively. Proprietors' income accounts for 7 percent. Rent (.4 percent) is very small in comparison. *Net factor income from abroad* is income received from U.S.-owned resources located in other countries minus income paid to foreign-owned resources located in the United States. Since U.S. GDP refers only to income earned within U.S. borders, we must deduct this kind of income to arrive at GDP (−.07 percent).

Figure 5 includes two income categories that we have not discussed: capital consumption allowance and indirect business taxes. **Capital consumption allowance** is not a money payment to a factor of production; it is the estimated value of capital goods used up or worn out in production plus the value of accidental damage to capital goods. The value of accidental damage is relatively small, so it is common to hear economists refer to capital consumption allowance as **depreciation**. Machines and other capital goods wear out over time. The reduction in the value of capital stock due to its being used up or worn out over time is called depreciation. A depreciating capital good loses value each year of its useful life until its value is zero.

Even though capital consumption allowance does not represent income received by a factor of production, it must be accounted for in GDP as income. Otherwise the value of GDP measured as output would be higher than the value of the GDP as income. Depreciation is a kind of resource payment, part of the total payment to the owners of capital. All of the income

capital consumption allowance:
the estimated value of depreciation plus the value of accidental damage to capital stock

depreciation:
a reduction in the value of capital goods over time due to their use in production

---

Figure 5
U.S. Gross Domestic Product as Income Received, 1993 (billion dollars)
The largest component of income is wages, at 60 percent of the GDP. Profits represent 8 percent, interest 6 percent, proprietors' income 7 percent, and rent .4 percent. Capital consumption allowance (11 percent) and indirect business taxes (9 percent) are not income received but still must be added; net factor income from abroad must be subtracted (−.07 percent). Source: Data from *Economic Report of the President, 1995* (Washington, D.C.: U.S. Government Printing Office, 1995), pp. 300–301.

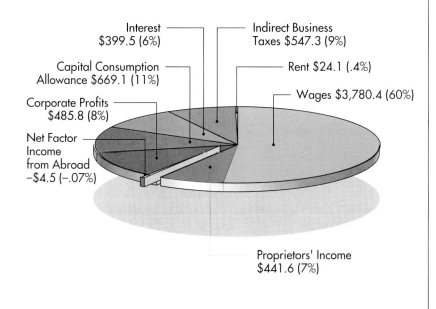

Interest $399.5 (6%)

Indirect Business Taxes $547.3 (9%)

Capital Consumption Allowance $669.1 (11%)

Rent $24.1 (.4%)

Corporate Profits $485.8 (8%)

Wages $3,780.4 (60%)

Net Factor Income from Abroad −$4.5 (−.07%)

Proprietors' Income $441.6 (7%)

categories—wages, interest, rent, profits, and capital consumption allowance—are expenses incurred in the production of output.

indirect business tax:
a tax that is collected by businesses for a government agency

The last item in Figure 5 is indirect business taxes. **Indirect business taxes**, like capital consumption allowances, are not payments to a factor of production. They are taxes collected by businesses that then are turned over to the government. Both excise taxes and sales taxes are forms of indirect business taxes.

For example, suppose a motel room in Florida costs $80 a night. A consumer would be charged $90. Of that $90, the motel receives $80 as the value of the service sold; the other $10 is an excise tax. The motel cannot keep the $10; it must turn it over to the state government. (In effect, the motel is acting as the government's tax collector.) The consumer spends $90; the motel earns $80. To balance expenditures and income, we have to allocate the $10 difference to indirect business taxes.

GDP as income is equal to the sum of wages, interest, rent, profits, less net factor income from abroad, plus capital consumption allowance and indirect business taxes.

To summarize, GDP measured as income includes the four payments to the factors of production: wages, interest, rent, and profits. These income items represent expenses incurred in the production of GDP. To these we must subtract net factor income from abroad in order for the total to sum to GDP. Along with these payments are two nonincome items: capital consumption allowance and indirect business taxes.

GDP = wages + interest + rent + profits – net factor income from abroad + capital consumption allowance + indirect business taxes

GDP is the total value of output produced in a year, the total value of expenditures made to purchase that output, and the total value of income received by the factors of production. Because all three are measures of the same thing—GDP—all must be equal.

1.b. Other Measures of Output and Income

GDP is the most common measure of a nation's output, but it is not the only measure. Economists rely on a number of others in analyzing the performance of components of an economy.

gross national product (GNP):
gross domestic product plus receipts of factor income from the rest of the world minus payments of factor income to the rest of the world

1.b.1. Gross National Product Gross national product (GNP) equals GDP plus receipts of factor income from the rest of the world minus payments of factor income to the rest of the world. If we add to GDP the value of income earned by U.S. residents from factors of production located outside the United States and subtract the value of income earned by foreign residents from factors of production located inside the United States, we have a measure of the value of output produced by U.S.-owned resources—GNP.

Figure 6 shows the national income accounts in the United States in 1993. The figure begins with the GDP and then shows the calculations necessary to obtain the GNP and other measures of national output. In 1993, the U.S. GNP was $6,347.8 billion.

net national product (NNP):
gross national product minus capital consumption allowance

1.b.2. Net National Product Net national product (NNP) equals GNP minus capital consumption allowance. NNP measures the value of goods and services produced in a year less the value of capital goods that became obsolete or were used up during the year. Because NNP includes only net additions to a nation's capital, it is a better measure of the expansion or contraction of current output than is GNP. Remember how we defined GDP in terms of expenditures in section 1.a.2:

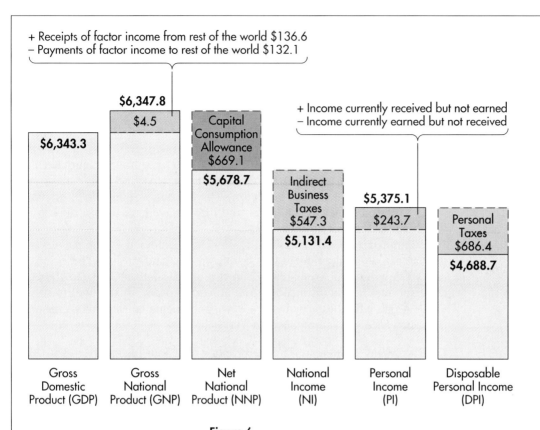

Figure 6
U.S. National Income Accounts, 1993 (billion dollars)
Gross domestic product plus receipts of factor income from the rest of the world minus payments of factor income to the rest of the world equals gross national product. Gross national product minus capital consumption allowance equals net national product. Net national product minus indirect business taxes equals national income. National income plus income currently received but not earned (transfer payments, personal interest, dividend income) minus income currently earned but not received (corporate profits, net interest, social security taxes) equals personal income. Personal income minus personal taxes equals disposable personal income. Source: Data from *Economic Report of the President, 1995* (Washington, D.C.: U.S. Government Printing Office, 1995).

$$GDP = consumption + investment + government\ spending + net\ exports$$

gross investment:
total investment, including investment expenditures required to replace capital goods consumed in current production

net investment:
gross investment minus capital consumption allowance

The investment measure in GDP (and GNP) is called **gross investment**. Gross investment is total investment, which includes investment expenditures required to replace capital goods consumed in current production. NNP does not include investment expenditures required to replace worn-out capital goods; it includes only net investment. **Net investment** is equal to gross investment minus capital consumption allowance. Net investment measures business spending over and above that required to replace worn-out capital goods.

Figure 6 shows that in 1993, the U.S. NNP was $5,678.7 billion. This means that the U.S. economy produced well over $5 trillion worth of goods and services above those required to replace capital stock that had depreciated. Over $669 billion in capital was "worn out" in 1993.

All final goods and services produced in a year are counted in GDP. For instance, the value of a rafting trip down the Colorado River through the Grand Canyon is part of the national output of the United States. The value of the rafting trip would be equal to the amount that travelers would have to pay the guide company in order to take the trip. This price would reflect the value of the personnel, equipment, and food provided by the guide company.

national income (NI):
net national product minus indirect business taxes

1.b.3. National Income National income (NI) equals the NNP minus indirect business taxes, plus or minus a couple of other small adjustments. NI captures the costs of the factors of production used in producing output. Remember that GDP includes two nonincome expense items: capital consumption allowance and indirect business taxes (section 1.a.3). Subtracting both of these items from the GDP leaves the income payments that actually go to resources.

Because the NNP equals the GNP minus capital consumption allowance, we can subtract indirect business taxes from the NNP to find NI, as shown in Figure 6. This measure helps economists analyze how the costs of (or payments received by) resources change.

personal income (PI):
national income plus income currently received but not earned, minus income currently earned but not received

transfer payment:
income transferred from one citizen, who is earning income, to another citizen, who may not be

1.b.4. Personal Income Personal income (PI) is national income adjusted for income that is received but not earned in the current year and income that is earned but not received in the current year. Social security and welfare benefits are examples of income that is received but not earned in the current year. As you learned in Chapter 5, they are called **transfer payments**. Transfer payments represent income transferred from one citizen, who is earning income, to another citizen, who may not be. The government transfers income by taxing one group of citizens and using the tax payments to fund the income for another group. An example of income that is currently earned but not received is profits that are retained by a corporation to finance current needs rather than paid out to stockholders. Another is social security (FICA) taxes, which are deducted from workers' paychecks.

disposable personal income (DPI):
personal income minus personal taxes

1.b.5. Disposable Personal Income Disposable personal income (DPI) equals personal income minus personal taxes—income taxes, excise and real estate taxes on personal property, and other personal taxes. DPI is the income that individuals have at their disposal for spending or saving. The sum of consumption spending plus saving must equal disposable personal income.

RECAP

1. Gross domestic product (GDP) is the market value of all final goods and services produced in an economy in a year.

2. GDP can be calculated by summing the market value of all final goods and services produced in a year, by summing the value added at each stage of production, by adding total expenditures on goods and services (GDP = consumption + investment + government spending + net exports), and by using the total income earned in the production of goods and services (GDP = wages + interest + rent + profits) and subtracting net factor income from abroad, and adding depreciation, and indirect business taxes.

3. Other measures of output and income include gross national product (GNP), net national product (NNP), national income (NI), personal income (PI), and disposable personal income (DPI).

National Income Accounts

GDP = consumption + investment + government spending
        + net exports

GNP = GDP + receipts of factor income from the rest of the world
        − payments of factor income to the rest of the world

NNP = GNP − capital consumption allowance

NI = NNP − indirect business taxes

PI = NI − income earned but not received
        + income received but not earned

DPI = PI − personal taxes

2. NOMINAL AND REAL MEASURES

What is the difference between nominal and real GDP?

GDP is the market value of all final goods and services produced within a country in a year. Value is measured in money terms, so the U.S. GDP is reported in dollars, the German GDP in marks, the Mexican GDP in pesos, and so on. Market value is the product of two elements: the money price and the quantity produced.

2.a. Nominal and Real GDP

nominal GDP:
a measure of national output based on the current prices of goods and services

Nominal GDP measures output in terms of its current dollar value. **Real GDP** is adjusted for changing price levels. In 1980, the U.S. GDP was $2,708 billion; in 1993, it was $6,343.3 billion—an increase of 134 percent. Does this mean that the United States produced 134 percent more goods and services in 1993 than it did in 1980? If the numbers reported are for nominal GDP, we cannot be sure. Nominal GDP cannot tell us whether the economy

Part II/Macroeconomic Basics

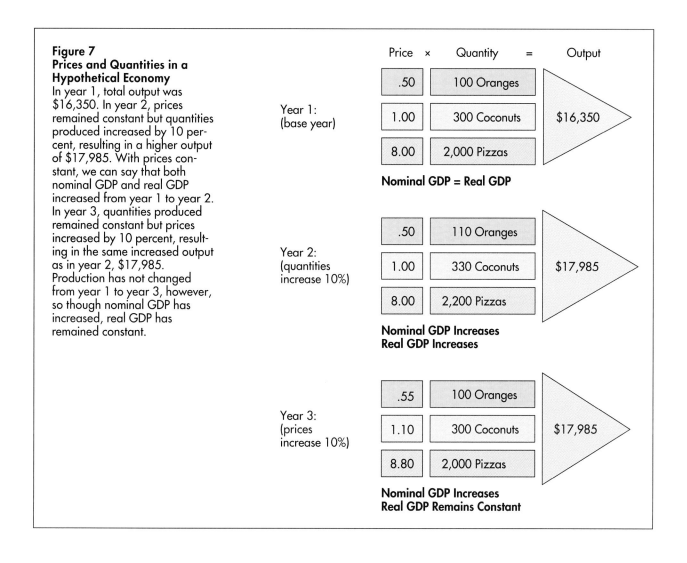

Figure 7
Prices and Quantities in a Hypothetical Economy
In year 1, total output was $16,350. In year 2, prices remained constant but quantities produced increased by 10 percent, resulting in a higher output of $17,985. With prices constant, we can say that both nominal GDP and real GDP increased from year 1 to year 2. In year 3, quantities produced remained constant but prices increased by 10 percent, resulting in the same increased output as in year 2, $17,985. Production has not changed from year 1 to year 3, however, so though nominal GDP has increased, real GDP has remained constant.

real GDP:
a measure of the quantity of final goods and services produced, obtained by eliminating the influence of price changes from the nominal GDP statistics

produced more goods and services, because nominal GDP changes when prices change *and* when quantity changes.

Real GDP measures output in constant prices. This allows economists to identify the changes in actual production of final goods and services: real GDP measures the quantity of goods and services produced after eliminating the influence of price changes contained in nominal GDP. In 1980, real GDP in the United States was $3,776.3 billion; in 1993, it was $5,134.5 billion, an increase of just 36 percent. The 134 percent increase in nominal GDP in large part reflects increased prices, not increased output.

Since we prefer more goods and services to higher prices, it is better to have nominal GDP rise because of higher output than higher prices. We want nominal GDP to increase as a result of an increase in real GDP.

Consider a simple example that illustrates the difference between nominal GDP and real GDP. Suppose a hypothetical economy produces just three goods: oranges, coconuts, and pizzas. The dollar value of output in three different years is listed in the table in Figure 7.

As shown in Figure 7, in year 1, 100 oranges were produced at $.50 per orange, 300 coconuts at $1 per coconut, and 2,000 pizzas at $8 per pizza.

The total dollar value of output in year 1 is $16,350. In year 2, prices are constant at the year 1 values, but the quantity of each good has increased by 10 percent. The dollar value of output in year 2 is $17,985, 10 percent higher than the value of output in year 1. In year 3, the quantity of each good is back at the year 1 level, but prices have increased by 10 percent. Oranges now cost $.55, coconuts $1.10, and pizzas $8.80. The dollar value of output in year 3 is $17,985.

Notice that in years 2 and 3, the dollar value of output ($17,985) is 10 percent higher than it was in year 1. But there is a difference here. In year 2, the increase in output is due entirely to an increase in the production of the three goods. In year 3, the increase is due entirely to an increase in the prices of the goods.

Because prices did not change between years 1 and 2, the increase in nominal GDP is entirely accounted for by an increase in real output, or real GDP. In years 1 and 3, the actual quantities produced did not change, which means that real GDP was constant; only nominal GDP was higher, a product only of higher prices.

2.b. Price Indexes

What is a price index?

price index:
a measure of the average price level in an economy

The total dollar value of output or income is equal to price multiplied by the quantity of goods and services produced:

$$\text{Dollar value of output} = \text{price} \times \text{quantity}$$

By dividing the dollar value of output by price, you can determine the quantity of goods and services produced:

$$\text{Quantity} = \frac{\text{dollar value of output}}{\text{price}}$$

In macroeconomics, a **price index** measures the average level of prices in an economy and shows how prices, on average, have changed. Prices of individual goods can rise and fall relative to one another, but a price index shows the general trend in prices across the economy.

base year:
the year against which other years are measured

The value of the price index in any particular year indicates how prices have changed relative to the base year.

2.b.1. Base Year The example in Figure 7 provides a simple introduction to price indexes. The first step is to pick a **base year**, the year against which other years are measured. Any year can serve as the base year. Suppose we pick year 1 in Figure 7. The value of the price index in year 1, the base year, is defined to be 100. This simply means that prices in year 1 are 100 percent of prices in year 1 (100 percent of 1 is 1). In the example, year 2 prices are equal to year 1 prices, so the price index also is equal to 100 in year 2. In year 3, every price has risen 10 percent relative to the base-year (year 1) prices, so the price index is 10 percent higher in year 3, or 110. The value of the price index in any particular year indicates how prices have changed relative to the base year. A value of 110 indicates that prices are 110 percent of base-year prices, or that the average price level has increased 10 percent.

Price index in any year = 100 + (or −) percentage change in prices from the base year

Beginning in 1995, the U.S. Department of Commerce is calculating the growth of real GDP using a "chain-type" price series instead of the old method of calculating a "constant dollar" real GDP.

The old constant dollar real GDP was calculated by picking a base year and then using prices in the base year to value output in all years. Over time, a constant dollar real GDP will suffer from "substitution bias." This bias occurs because as prices of some goods rise faster than other goods, buyers will substitute away from the higher-priced goods and buy more of the lower priced goods. Such substitutions will cause output to grow faster in the industries with relatively low price increases. Because prices in these industries were relatively high in the base year, their growth will be overstated and constant-dollar real GDP will overestimate the true growth in the economy.

The computer industry provides a good example of substitution bias at work. Prices of computers have fallen about 20 percent since the 1987 base year used for estimating constant-dollar real GDP. By using the 1987 prices of computers in calculating real GDP, the approximate doubling in the output of computer equipment is given too much weight. If evaluated at the falling prices actually occurring, the growth of both the computer industry and the overall economy would be lower.

chain-type real GDP growth: the geometric mean of the growth rates found using beginning and ending year prices

Chain-type indexes of real GDP correct for this bias that is included in constant-dollar real GDP. A chain-type real GDP index utilizes prices in two years to calculate the percentage change in real GDP between the two years. Then an index of real GDP is created based on the estimated percentage growth. Table 1 illustrates the creation of a chain-type real GDP index compared to a constant-dollar index.

Table 1 illustrates a simple economy that only produces two goods: apples and bread. Note that total spending on food is $500 in year 1 and $900 in year 2. How should we compute real GDP to best measure how real output of goods has changed? First, let's see what a constant dollar measure would yield and then compare this to a chain-type index measure as now being used to measure output in the United States. Using Year 1 as the base year, we would construct real GDP in each year using Year 1 prices associated with quantities. Valuing the quantities purchased in each year at Year 1 prices results in a ratio of Year 2 expenditures to Year 1 expenditures of 1.2. This gives us a 20 percent increase in real GDP. Alternatively, we use Year 2 prices to value quantities in each year. Valuing the quantities purchased each year at Year 2 prices results in a ratio of Year 2 expenditures to Year 1 expenditures of 1.06. This gives us a 6 percent increase in real GDP. Moving the base year forward in time has (and actually had) the impact of reducing the estimated growth of constant-dollar real GDP because the goods whose quantities increased the most are those whose prices increased, relatively, the least. So using the old prices gives too much weight to the rapidly growing sectors of the economy where prices are growing relatively slowly.

The chain-type index is calculated by taking an average of the growth rates found with the beginning and ending year prices. The actual average used by the Department of Commerce is a *geometric mean.* The geometric mean is found by multiplying the two expenditures ratios together, taking the square root, and then subtracting 1: $1.2 \times 1.06 = 1.272$, and the square root of 1.272 equals 1.13. So the growth of real GDP measured by the chain-type index is 13 percent. The term "chain-type index" indicates that the growth rate from one year to another is being estimated by "chaining together" the growth rates estimated using both the first and second year prices to value quantities rather than arbitrarily picking one period's prices.

Once the percentage changes in real GDP are estimated, then an index

TABLE I
Constant Dollar and Chain-Type Real GDP Growth

Year 1

	Quantity	Price	Expenditures
Apples	300	$1	$300
Bread	100	2	200
			$500

Year 2

	Quantity	Price	Expenditures
Apples	200	$2	$400
Bread	200	2.50	500
			$900

Constant Dollar Real GDP Growth Using Year 1 as Base Year:

(expenditures in Year 2 using Year 1 prices)/(expenditures in Year 1 using Year 1 prices) − 1 =

$$\frac{(200 \text{ apples} \times \$1) + (200 \text{ bread} \times \$2)}{(300 \text{ apples} \times \$1) + (100 \text{ bread} \times \$2)} = \frac{\$600}{\$500} = \underline{1.2,}$$

$$1.2 - 1.0 = .2 \text{ or } 20\%$$

Constant Dollar Real GDP Growth Using Year 2 as Base Year:

(expenditures in Year 2 using Year 2 prices)/(expenditures in Year 1 using Year 2 prices) − 1 =

$$\frac{(200 \text{ apples} \times \$2) + (200 \text{ bread} \times \$2.50)}{(300 \text{ apples} \times \$2) + (100 \text{ bread} \times \$2.50)} = \frac{\$900}{\$850} = \underline{1.06,}$$

$$1.06 - 1.00 = .06 \text{ or } 6\%$$

Chain-Type Real GDP Growth:

Square root of (expenditures ratio with Year 1 base year × expenditures ratio with Year 2 base year) − 1 =
Square root of (1.2 × 1.06) − 1 = Square root of 1.272 − 1 = 1.13 − 1 = .13 or 13%

number for real GDP is created by picking some arbitrary year to equal 100 (1987 is the year currently used in the United States) and then increasing or decreasing the real GDP index for every other year by the percentage change found from the chain-type measure. We should note that the level of such a real GDP index has no meaning or interpretation apart from the percentage changes from year to year. The value of nominal GDP has a clear interpretation since it is the observable dollar value of expenditures on output. But to say that the level of the chain-type real GDP index equals 116.1 in 1994 gives no meaning other than with comparison to other years. If the real GDP index equals 112.2 in 1993, then we can find the growth rate of real GDP from 1993 to 1994 of 3.5 percent ([116.1/112.2] − 1 = .035 or 3.5%).

The Consumer Price Index

The CPI is calculated by the Department of Labor using price surveys taken in 91 American cities. Although the CPI often is called a *cost of living index*, it is not. The CPI represents the cost of a fixed market basket of goods purchased by a hypothetical household, not a real one.

In fact, no household consumes the market basket used to estimate the CPI. As relative prices change, households alter their spending patterns. But the CPI market basket changes only every 10 years. This is due in part to the high cost of surveying the public to determine spending patterns. Then, too, individual households have different tastes and spend a different portion of their budgets on the various components of household spending (housing, food, clothing, transportation, medical care). Only a household that spends exactly the same portion of its income on each item counted in the CPI would find the CPI representative of its cost of living.

The current CPI market basket is based on spending patterns in the period between 1982 and 1984. The Department of Labor surveys spending in seven major areas. The figure shows the areas

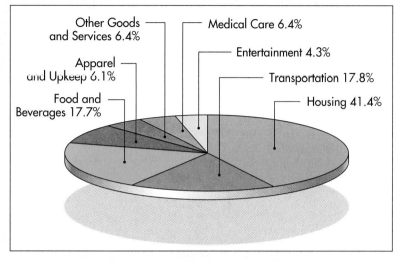

and the percentage of the typical household budget devoted to each area. If you kept track of your spending over the course of several months, you probably would find that you spend much more than the "typical" household on some items and much less on others. In other words, the CPI is not a very good measure of *your* cost of living.

Recently, the CPI has been criticized as overestimating the true inflation rate by about 1 percentage point mainly because it does not take into account the improved quality of many goods and services.

For instance, new automobiles are now more reliable than they were a few years ago, but the CPI does not adjust for this in counting auto prices. If prices rise due to higher-quality goods, then the price increase should not be counted the same as price increases for goods with constant quality. This "bias" in the CPI has provoked much discussion and will probably be addressed in the near future by the Department of Labor.

Source: Data from Bureau of Labor Statistics

2.b.2. Types of Price Indexes The price of a single good is easy to determine. But how do economists determine a single measure of the prices of the millions of goods and services produced in an economy? They have constructed price indexes to measure the price level; there are several different price indexes used to measure the price level in any economy. Not all prices rise or fall at the same time or by the same amount. This is why there are several measures of the price level in an economy.

The price index used to estimate constant dollar real GDP is the **implicit GDP deflator**, a measure of prices across the economy that reflects all of the categories of goods and services included in GDP. The implicit GDP deflator

implicit GDP deflator:
a broad measure of the prices of goods and services included in the gross domestic product

Figure 8
The Implicit GDP Deflator, the CPI, and the PPI
The graph plots the annual percentage change in the implicit GDP deflator, the consumer price index (CPI), and the producer price index (PPI). The implicit GDP deflator is used to construct constant dollar real GDP. The CPI measures the average price of consumer goods and services that a typical household purchases. The PPI measures the average price received by producers; it is the most variable of the three because fluctuations in equilibrium prices of intermediate goods are much greater than for final goods. Source: *Economic Report of the President, 1995* (Washington, D.C.: U.S. Government Printing Office, 1995).

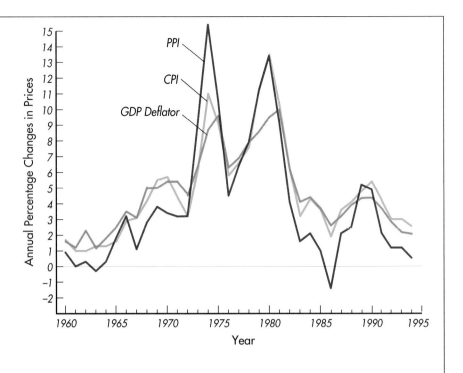

consumer price index (CPI):
a measure of the average price of goods and services purchased by the typical household

cost of living adjustment (COLA):
an increase in wages that is designed to match increases in prices of items purchased by the typical household

producer price index (PPI):
a measure of average prices received by producers

is a very broad measure. Economists use other price indexes to analyze how prices change in more specific categories of goods and services.

Probably the best-known price index is the **consumer price index (CPI)**. The CPI measures the average price of consumer goods and services that a typical household purchases. (See the Economic Insight "The Consumer Price Index.") The CPI is a narrower measure than the implicit GDP deflator because it includes fewer items. However, because of the relevance of consumer prices to the standard of living, news reports on price changes in the economy typically focus on consumer price changes. In addition, labor contracts sometimes include provisions that raise wages as the CPI goes up. Social security payments also are tied to increases in the CPI. These increases are called **cost of living adjustments (COLAs)**, because they are supposed to keep nominal income rising along with the cost of items purchased by the typical household.

The **producer price index (PPI)** measures average prices received by producers. At one time this price index was known as the *wholesale price index (WPI)*. Because the PPI measures price changes at an earlier stage of production than the CPI, it can indicate a coming change in the CPI. If producer input costs are rising, we can expect the price of goods produced to go up as well.

Figure 8 illustrates how the three different measures of prices changed between 1960 and 1991. Notice that the PPI is more volatile than the implicit GDP deflator or the CPI. This is because there are smaller fluctuations in the equilibrium prices of final goods than intermediate goods.

1. Nominal GDP is measured using current dollars.
2. Real GDP measures output with price effects removed.
3. Chain-type real GDP growth equals the geometric mean of the growth rates found with beginning and ending year prices.
4. The implicit GDP deflator, the consumer price index, and the producer price index are all measures of the level of prices in an economy.

3. FLOWS OF INCOME AND EXPENDITURES

GDP is both a measure of total expenditures on final goods and services and a measure of the total income earned in the production of those goods and services. The idea that total expenditures equal total income is clearly illustrated in Figure 1.

The figure links the four sectors of the economy: households, firms, government, and foreign countries. The arrows between the sectors indicate the direction of the flows. Gold arrows with dollar signs represent money flows; blue-green arrows without dollar signs represent flows of real goods and services. The money flows are both income and expenditures. For instance, household expenditures for goods and services from business firms are represented by the gold arrow at the top of the diagram. Household income from firms is represented by the gold arrow flowing from firms to households at the bottom of the diagram. Because one sector's expenditures represent another sector's income, the total expenditures on goods and services must be the same as the total income from selling goods and services, and those must both be equal to the total value of the goods and services produced.

1. Total spending on final goods and services equals the total income received in producing those goods and services.

2. The circular flow model shows that one sector's expenditures represent the income of other sectors.

SUMMARY

▲▼ **How is the total output of an economy measured?**

1. National income accounting is the system economists use to measure both the output of an economy and the flows between sectors of that economy. §1

2. Gross domestic product (GDP) is the market value of all final goods and services produced in a year in a country. §1.a

3. GDP also equals the value added at each stage of production. §1.a

▲▼ Who produces the nation's goods and services?

4. GDP as output equals the sum of the output of households, business firms, and government within the country. Business firms produce 85 percent of the U.S. GDP. §1.a.1

▲▼ Who purchases the goods and services produced?

5. GDP as expenditures equals the sum of consumption plus investment plus government spending plus net exports. In the United States, consumption accounts for roughly two-thirds of total expenditures. §1.a.2

▲▼ Who receives the income from the production of goods and services?

6. GDP as income equals the sum of wages, interest, rent, profits, proprietors' income, capital consumption allowance, and indirect business taxes less net factor income from abroad. Wages account for about 60 percent of the total. §1.a.3

7. Capital consumption allowance is the estimated value of depreciation plus the value of accidental damage to capital stock. §1.a.3

8. Other measures of national output include gross national product (GNP), net national product (NNP), national income (NI), personal income (PI), and disposable personal income (DPI). §1.b

▲▼ What is the difference between nominal and real GDP?

9. Nominal GDP measures output in terms of its current dollar value including the effects of price changes; real GDP measures output after eliminating the effects of price changes. §2.a

▲▼ What is a price index?

10. A price index measures the average level of prices across an economy. §2.b

11. The implicit GDP deflator is a measure of the prices of all the goods and services included in the GDP. §2.b.2

12. The consumer price index (CPI) measures the average price of goods and services consumed by the typical household. §2.b.2

13. The producer price index (PPI) measures average prices received by producers (wholesale prices). §2.b.2

14. Total expenditures on final goods and services equal total income. §3

KEY TERMS

national income accounting §1

gross domestic product (GDP) §1.a

intermediate good §1.a

value added §1.a

inventory §1.a

capital consumption allowance §1.a.3

depreciation §1.a.3

indirect business tax §1.a.3

gross national product (GNP) §1.b.1

net national product (NNP) §1.b.2

gross investment §1.b.2

net investment §1.b.2

national income (NI) §1.b.3

personal income (PI) §1.b.4

transfer payment §1.b.4

disposable personal income (DPI) §1.b.5

nominal GDP §2.a

real GDP §2.a

price index §2.b

base year §2.b.1

chain-type real GDP §2.b.1

implicit GDP deflator §2.b.2

consumer price index (CPI) §2.b.2

cost of living adjustment (COLA) §2.b.2

producer price index (PPI) §2.b.2

EXERCISES

1. The following table lists the stages required in the production of a personal computer. What is the value of the computer in the GDP?

Stage	Value Added
Components manufacture	$ 50
Assembly	250
Wholesaler	500
Retailer	1,500

2. What is the difference between GDP and each of the following?

   a. Gross national product

   b. Net national product

   c. National income

   d. Personal income

   e. Disposable personal income

3.

	Year 1		Year 2	
	Quantity	Price	Quantity	Price
Oranges	100	$3	150	$3
Pears	100	3	75	4

   a. What is the growth rate of constant-dollar real GDP using Year 1 as the base year?

   b. What is the growth rate of constant-dollar real GDP using Year 2 as the base year?

   c. What is the chain-type real GDP growth rate between Years 1 and 2?

4. Why do total expenditures on final goods and services equal total income in the economy?

5. Why don't we measure national output by simply counting the total number of goods and services produced each year?

6. Why isn't the CPI a useful measure of *your* cost of living?

Use the following national income accounting information to answer questions 7–11:

Consumption	$400
Imports	10
Net investment	20
Government purchases	100
Exports	20
Capital consumption allowance	20
Indirect business taxes	5
Receipts of factor income from the rest of the world	12
Payments of factor income to the rest of the world	10

7. What is the GDP for this economy?

8. What is the GNP for this economy?

9. What is the NNP for this economy?

10. What is the national income for this economy?

11. What is the gross investment in this economy?

12. Indirect business taxes and capital consumption allowance are not income, yet they are included in order to find GDP as income received. Why do we add these two non-income components to the other components of income (like wages, rent, interest, profits, and net factor income from abroad) to find GDP?

13. Why has nominal GDP increased faster than real GDP in the United States over time? What would it mean if an economy had real GDP increasing faster than nominal GDP?

14. We usually discuss GDP in terms of what is included in the definition. What is *not* included in GDP? Why are these things excluded?

15. If a surfboard is produced this year but not sold until next year, how is it counted in this year's GDP and not next year's?

COOPERATIVE LEARNING EXERCISE

Divide the class into six groups and assign each group one of the national income accounts defined in sections 1.a and 1.b. The groups are given five minutes to study their account. Then each group in turn states what its account measures. For instance, the first group to speak will tell the class what GDP measures. Each successive group will define its measure and tell how it differs from the prior measure. For example, the second group will state what GNP measures and how GNP differs from GDP, followed by the NNP group, NI group, PI group, and finally the DPI group.

New Report Ties Economic Growth to Environment

The Commerce Department released a report yesterday that tries to determine just how fast the economy is using up the nation's natural resources.

Government economists hope the Green GDP (gross domestic product) report, to be issued annually, will help them determine whether the economy is using natural resources faster than it is finding new reserves or alternative resources.

Such depletion could mean the economic growth rate doesn't reflect the price society will pay if there aren't enough resources to meet future demand.

For example, yesterday's report said the rate of return on capital for the oil and mining industries would have been only 4% to 5% from 1958 to 1991 if depletion costs were included. Existing growth figures estimated the rate of return for the oil and mining industries at 23%.

Economists say it's too soon to say how the Green GDP figures will be used and practically applied. Unlike most traditional economic indicators, such as the regular GDP, which measures the economy's output of goods and services, the Green GDP won't yield a single number that can be compared with previous totals.

Initially, the new report will track oil, gas, coal and minerals, and metals drilled and mined in the United States and its territories.

Over the next few years, the Commerce Department plans to add to the report renewable commodities, such as lumber and farm crops. Later, the government hopes to quantify the cost of air and water pollution.

The new annual report, formally called the Integrated Economic and Environmental Satellite Accounts, also showed:

- Proven oil and mineral reserves would add 3% to 7% to the nation's business assets if included in existing economic growth statistics.

- The value of new reserves discovered over the last three decades has roughly offset the depletion of reserves.

- The value of proven oil and mineral reserves is two to four times greater than existing buildings, equipment and extracted inventories in the oil and mining industries.

Source: "New Report Ties Economic Growth to Environment," by *Bloomberg Business News,* appeared in *The Plain Dealer,* May 11, 1994, p. 3C. Reprinted by permission of *The Bloomberg Times.*

Commentary

In this chapter we learn about different measures of the performance of the economy. The actual compilation of these statistics is a formidable task, especially in a country with an economy as large and complex as that of the United States. The article demonstrates how a "green GDP" may be estimated and provides some insight into the manner in which government economists and statisticians attempt to interpret what is occurring. The impression we are left with is that the collection and reporting of economic data, at least in terms of presenting a picture of recent performance, is somewhat arbitrary and imprecise.

Most macroeconomic data are estimates. It is simply impossible to count every new final good and service produced in a year to measure GDP exactly. Instead, government economists attempt to construct reasonable estimates of GDP by counting small amounts of output in the many different sectors of the economy. For example, veterinary services and pet services provided by pet stores are included in GDP. However, the government does not know the exact number and value of services actually provided by every veterinarian and pet store in a given year. The value of pet services is estimated by the number of purebred dogs reported to be in the United States by the American Kennel Club multiplied by a consumer price index for pet services. As the number of dogs increases, the value of pet services in GDP also increases.

Measuring the value of environmental goods and bads sounds reasonable and desirable, yet it presents a new challenge to government economists charged with gathering national income data. When goods are sold in a market, we observe the price and quantity so that value is fairly easy to estimate. However, placing an annual value on forests or air and water pollution is a much different problem. If such property is not privately owned, we might still assess its "market" value if it were to be sold. However, this would miss the value to society at large in terms of cleaning the air and water. Since no one owns the air and water, it is very difficult to place a monetary value on these benefits to all.

Although there are major practical problems in incorporating environmental costs and benefits in GDP, critics of the current system remind us that not addressing these problems is potentially catastrophic.

7

An Introduction to the Foreign Exchange Market and the Balance of Payments

FUNDAMENTAL QUESTIONS

1. How do individuals of one nation trade money with individuals of another nation?

2. How do changes in exchange rates affect international trade?

3. How do nations record their transactions with the rest of the world?

n Chapter 6, you learned that gross domestic product equals the sum of consumption, investment, government spending, and net exports (GDP $= C + I + G + X$). Net exports (X) are one key measure of a nation's transactions with other countries, a principal link between a nation's GDP and developments in the rest of the world. In this chapter, we extend the macroeconomic accounting framework to include more detail on a nation's international transactions. This extension is known as balance of payments accounting.

International transactions have grown rapidly in recent years as the economies of the world have become increasingly interrelated. Improvements in transportation and communication, and global markets for goods and services, have created a community of world economies. Products made in one country sell in the world market, where they compete against products from other nations. Europeans purchase stocks listed on the New York Stock Exchange; Americans purchase bonds issued in Japan.

PREVIEW

Different countries use different monies. When goods and services are exchanged across international borders, national monies also are traded. To make buying and selling decisions in the global marketplace, people must be able to compare prices across countries, to compare prices quoted in Japanese yen with those quoted in Mexican pesos. This chapter begins with a look at how national monies are priced and traded in the foreign exchange market.

I. THE FOREIGN EXCHANGE MARKET

How do individuals of one nation trade money with individuals of another nation?

foreign exchange:
currency and bank deposits that are denominated in foreign money

foreign exchange market:
a global market in which people trade one currency for another

Foreign exchange is foreign money, including paper money and bank deposits like checking accounts that are denominated in foreign currency. When someone with U.S. dollars wants to trade those dollars for Japanese yen, the trade takes place in the **foreign exchange market**, a global market in which people trade one currency for another. Many financial markets are located in a specific geographic location. For instance, the New York Stock Exchange is a specific location in New York City where stocks are bought and sold. The Commodity Exchange is a specific location in New York City where contracts to deliver agricultural and metal commodities are bought and sold. The foreign exchange market is not in a single geographic location, however. Trading occurs all over the world by telephone. Most of the activity involves large banks in New York, London, and other financial centers. A foreign exchange trader at Morgan Guaranty Bank in New York can buy or sell currencies with a trader at Barclays Bank in London by calling the other trader on the telephone.

Only tourism and a few other transactions in the foreign exchange market involve the actual movement of currency. The great majority of transactions involve the buying and selling of bank deposits denominated in foreign currency. A bank deposit can be a checking account that a firm or individual writes checks against to make payments to others, or it may be an interest-earning savings account with no check-writing privileges. Currency notes, like dollar bills, are used in a relatively small fraction of transactions. When a large corporation or a government buys foreign currency, it buys a bank deposit denominated in the foreign currency. Still, all exchanges in the market require that monies have a price.

1.a. Exchange Rates

exchange rate:
the price of one country's money in terms of another country's money

An **exchange rate** is the price of one country's money in terms of another country's money. Exchange rates are needed to compare prices quoted in two different currencies. Suppose a shirt that has been manufactured in Canada sells for 20 U.S. dollars in Seattle, Washington, and for 25 Canadian dollars in Vancouver, British Columbia. Where would you get the better buy? Unless you know the exchange rate between U.S. and Canadian dollars, you can't tell. The exchange rate allows you to convert the foreign currency price into its domestic currency equivalent, which then can be compared to the domestic price.

Figure 1 reproduces a table of exchange rates that appeared in *The Wall Street Journal*. The table lists exchange rates for two days, Friday, February 17, 1995, and Tuesday, February 21, 1995. (Monday was the President's Day holiday.) The rates are quoted in U.S. dollars per unit of foreign currency in the first two columns, and units of foreign currency per U.S. dollar in the last two columns. For instance, on Tuesday, the Canadian dollar was selling for $.7136, or a little more than 71 U.S. cents. The same day, the U.S. dollar was selling for 1.4014 Canadian dollars (1 U.S. dollar would buy 1.4014 Canadian dollars).

Find the reciprocal of a number by writing it as a fraction and then turning the fraction upside down. In other words, make the numerator the denominator and the denominator the numerator.

If you know the price in U.S. dollars of a currency, you can find the price of the U.S. dollar in that currency by taking the reciprocal. To find the reciprocal of a number, write it as a fraction and then turn the fraction upside down. Let's say that 1 British pound sells for 2 U.S. dollars. In fraction form, 2 is 2/1. The reciprocal of 2/1 is 1/2, or .5. So 1 U.S. dollar sells for .5 British pounds. The figure shows that on Tuesday, the actual dollar price of the pound was 1.5835. The *reciprocal exchange rate*—the number of pounds per dollar—is .6315 (1/1.5835), which was the pound price of 1 dollar that day.

Look at the top of Figure 1. Notice that the exchange rates are the values quoted at a specific time, 3:00 P.M. Eastern time. The time is listed because exchange rates fluctuate throughout the day as the supply of and demand for currencies change. At some other time of day, the exchange rates could have had different values than those listed in the figure. Notice also that the exchange rates quoted are based on large trades ($1 million or more) in what is essentially a wholesale market. The smaller the quantity of foreign currency purchased, the higher the price. A British tourist traveling in the United States would find the pound price of a dollar to be greater than .5184 at the front desk of a hotel.

Figure 1
Exchange Rates
The first two columns list U.S. dollars per foreign currency, or how much one unit of foreign currency is worth in U.S. dollars. On February 21 you could get about 71 American cents for one Canadian dollar. The second two columns list foreign currency per U.S. dollar, or how much one U.S. dollar is worth in foreign currency. On the same day, you could get about 1.40 Canadian dollars for one U.S. dollar. Source: *The Wall Street Journal,* February 22, 1995, p. C15. Reprinted by permission of *The Wall Street Journal,* © 1995 Dow Jones & Company, Inc. All rights reserved worldwide.

EXCHANGE RATES

Tuesday, February 21, 1995
The New York foreign exchange selling rates below apply to trading among banks in amounts of $1 million and more, as quoted at 3 p.m. Eastern time by Bankers Trust Co., Dow Jones Telerate Inc. and other sources. Retail transactions provide fewer units of foreign currency per dollar.

Country	U.S. $ equiv. Tues.	U.S. $ equiv. Fri.	Currency per U.S. $ Tues.	Currency per U.S. $ Fri.
Argentina (Peso)	1.00	1.00	1.00	1.00
Australia (Dollar)	.7430	.7363	1.3460	1.3582
Austria (Schilling)	.09596	.09563	10.42	10.46
Bahrain (Dinar)	2.6524	2.6524	.3770	.3770
Belgium (Franc)	.03285	.03277	30.44	30.52
Brazil (Real)	1.1876485	1.1876485	.84	.84
Britain (Pound)	1.5835	1.5795	.6315	.6331
30-Day Forward	1.5829	1.5789	.6317	.6334
90-Day Forward	1.5817	1.5776	.6323	.6339
180-Day Forward	1.5789	1.5752	.6334	.6349
Canada (Dollar)	.7136	.7126	1.4014	1.4033
30-Day Forward	.7125	.7115	1.4035	1.4055
90-Day Forward	.7103	.7090	1.4079	1.4104
180-Day Forward	.7075	.7063	1.4134	1.4158
Czech. Rep. (Koruna)				
Commercial rate	.0370124	.0368514	27.0180	27.1360
Chile (Peso)	.002413	.002386	414.35	419.15
China (Renminbi)	.118572	.118551	8.4337	8.4352
Colombia (Peso)	.001170	.001174	854.35	851.50
Denmark (Krone)	.1717	.1701	5.8255	5.8793
Ecuador (Sucre)				
Floating rate	.000417	.000416	2400.00	2405.00
Finland (Markka)	.21967	.21713	4.5523	4.6056
France (Franc)	.19444	.19395	5.1430	5.1560
30-Day Forward	.19451	.19403	5.1411	5.1539
90-Day Forward	.19459	.19414	5.1390	5.1509
180-Day Forward	.19463	.19427	5.1379	5.1473
Germany (Mark)	.6786	.6746	1.4735	1.4824
30-Day Forward	.6792	.6752	1.4723	1.4811
90-Day Forward	.6805	.6766	1.4696	1.4780
180-Day Forward	.6825	.6788	1.4652	1.4732
Greece (Drachma)	.004298	.004293	232.65	232.95
Hong Kong (Dollar)	.12936	.12937	7.7303	7.7300
Hungary (Forint)	.0089566	.0089405	111.6500	111.8506
India (Rupee)	.03186	.03188	31.38	31.37
Indonesia (Rupiah)	.0004515	.0004540	2215.00	2202.60
Ireland (Punt)	1.5792	1.5680	.6332	.6378
Israel (Shekel)	.3330	.3339	3.0027	2.9948

Let's go back to comparing the price of the Canadian shirt in Seattle and Vancouver. The symbol for the U.S. dollar is $. The symbol for the Canadian dollar is C$. (Table 1 lists the symbols for a number of currencies.) The shirt sells for $20 in Seattle and C$25 in Vancouver. Suppose the exchange rate between the U.S. dollar and the Canadian dollar is .8. This means that C$1 costs .8 U.S. dollars, or 80 U.S. cents. To find the domestic currency value of a foreign currency price, multiply the foreign currency price by the exchange rate:

$$\text{Domestic currency value} = \text{foreign currency price} \times \text{exchange rate}$$

In our example, the U.S. dollar is the domestic currency:

$$\text{U.S. dollar value} = \text{C\$25} \times .8 = \$20$$

If we multiply the price of the shirt in Canadian dollars (C$25) by the exchange rate (.8), we find the U.S. dollar value ($20). After adjusting for the exchange rate, then, we can see that the shirt sells for the same price when the price is measured in a single currency.

1.b. Exchange Rate Changes and International Trade

Because exchange rates determine the domestic currency value of foreign goods, changes in those rates affect the demand for and supply of goods

TABLE I
International Currency Symbols, Selected Countries

Country	Currency	Symbol
Australia	Dollar	A$
Austria	Schilling	Sch
Belgium	Franc	BF
Canada	Dollar	C$
China	Yuan	Y
Denmark	Krone	DKr
Finland	Markka	FM
France	Franc	FF
Germany	Deutsche mark	DM
Greece	Drachma	Dr
India	Rupee	Rs
Iran	Rial	Rl
Italy	Lira	Lit
Japan	Yen	¥
Kuwait	Dinar	KD
Mexico	Peso	Ps
Netherlands	Guilder	FL
Norway	Krone	NKr
Russia	Ruble	Rub
Saudi Arabia	Riyal	SR
Singapore	Dollar	S$
South Africa	Rand	R
Spain	Peseta	Pts
Sweden	Krona	SKr
Switzerland	Franc	SF
United Kingdom	Pound	£
United States	Dollar	$
Venezuela	Bolivar	B

How do changes in exchange rates affect international trade?

A currency appreciates in value when its value rises in relation to another currency.

A currency depreciates in value when its value falls in relation to another currency.

traded internationally. Suppose the price of the shirt in Seattle and in Vancouver remains the same, but the exchange rate changes from .8 to .9 U.S. dollars per Canadian dollar. What happens? The U.S. dollar price of the shirt in Vancouver increases. At the new rate, the shirt that sells for C$25 in Vancouver costs a U.S. buyer $22.50 (C$25 × .9).

A rise in the value of a currency is called *appreciation*. In our example, as the exchange rate moves from $.8 = C$1 to $.9 = C$1, the Canadian dollar appreciates against the U.S. dollar. As a country's currency appreciates, international demand for its products falls, other things equal.

Suppose the exchange rate in our example moves from $.8 = C$1 to $.7 = C$1. Now the shirt that sells for C$25 in Vancouver costs a U.S. buyer $17.50 (C$25 × .7). In this case the Canadian dollar has *depreciated* in value relative to the U.S. dollar. As a country's currency depreciates, its goods sell for lower prices in other countries and the demand for its products increases, other things equal.

When the Canadian dollar is appreciating against the U.S. dollar, the U.S. dollar must be depreciating against the Canadian dollar. For instance, when

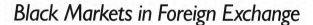
Black Markets in Foreign Exchange

Many developing countries impose restrictions on foreign currency transactions. These restrictions can take the form of government licensing requirements, under which only the government is allowed to exchange foreign currency for domestic currency; quotas on the amount of foreign currency that can be purchased; or even prohibitions on the use of foreign currency by private concerns. One product of these restrictions is illegal markets, or *black markets*, in foreign exchange. In many countries, the black market exists openly with little or no government intervention. In other countries, foreign exchange laws are strictly enforced.

Government policy creates the black market. The demand stems from the legal restrictions on buying foreign exchange; the supply stems from government-mandated exchange rates that offer less than the free market. Ironically, governments cite the need for controls to conserve scarce foreign exchange

for high-priority uses. But controls actually reduce the flow of foreign exchange to the government, as traders turn to the black market instead.

During periods of economic hardship, illegal markets allow normal economic activities to continue through a steady supply of foreign exchange. Some governments unofficially acknowledge the benefits of the black market by allowing the market to exist openly. For instance, Guatemala had an artificially low official exchange rate of 1 quetzal per U.S. dollar for more than three decades. But the government allowed a black market to operate openly in front of the country's main post office. There the exchange rate fluctuated daily with market conditions. In many Latin American countries, the post office is a center for black market trading because relatives living in the United States send millions of dollars in checks and money orders home. This sort of government-tolerated alternative to the official

exchange market often is called a *parallel market* rather than a black market.

Mexico has had a thriving parallel market whenever the official exchange rate between the peso and the U.S. dollar has diverged greatly from the market rate. For example, in August 1982 the Mexican government banned the sale of U.S. dollars by Mexican banks. The parallel market immediately responded. The official exchange rate was 69.5 pesos per 1 U.S. dollar; the rate on the street ranged from 120 to 150. Private currency trades flourished at the Mexico City airport and other public places.

Black markets or parallel markets are common in developing countries where foreign exchange transactions are restricted. In many countries the official exchange rate bears no relation to current economic reality. Economists often look to the black market to see how the supply of and demand for foreign exchange are changing.

the exchange rate between the U.S. dollar and the Canadian dollar moves from $.8 = C$1 to $.9 = C$1, the reciprocal exchange rate—the rate between the Canadian dollar and the U.S. dollar—moves from C$1.25 = $1 (1/.8 = 1.25) to C$1.11 = $1 (1/.9 = 1.11). At the same time that Canadian goods are becoming more expensive to U.S. buyers, U.S. goods are becoming cheaper to Canadian buyers.

In later chapters we look more closely at how changes in exchange rates affect international trade and at how governments use exchange rates to change their net exports. Often when governments restrict trading in the foreign exchange market illegal trading results. An example is given in the Economic Insight "Black Markets in Foreign Exchange".

RECAP

1. The foreign exchange market is a global market in which foreign money, largely bank deposits, is bought and sold.

2. An exchange rate is the price of one money in terms of another.

3. Foreign demand for domestic goods decreases as the domestic currency appreciates and increases as the domestic currency depreciates.

2. THE BALANCE OF PAYMENTS

How do nations record their transactions with the rest of the world?

balance of payments:
a record of a country's trade in goods, services, and financial assets with the rest of the world

The U.S. economy does not operate in a vacuum. It affects and is affected by the economies of other nations. This point was brought home to Americans in the 1980s and 1990s as newspaper headlines announced the latest trade deficit and politicians denounced foreign countries for running trade surpluses against the United States. It seemed as if everywhere there was talk of the balance of payments.

The **balance of payments** is a record of a country's trade in goods, services, and financial assets with the rest of the world. This record is divided into categories, or accounts, that summarize the nation's international economic transactions. For example, one category measures transactions in merchandise; another measures transactions involving financial assets (bank deposits, bonds, stocks, loans). These accounts distinguish between private transactions (by individuals and businesses) and official transactions (by governments). Balance of payments data are reported quarterly for most developed countries.

2.a. Accounting for International Transactions

double-entry bookkeeping:
a system of accounting in which every transaction is recorded in at least two accounts and in which the debit total must equal the credit total for the transaction as a whole

The balance of payments is an accounting statement based on **double-entry bookkeeping**, a system in which every transaction is recorded in at least two accounts. Suppose a U.S. tractor manufacturer sells a $50,000 tractor to a resident of France. The transaction is recorded twice: once as the tractor going from the United States to France, and then again as the payment of $50,000 going from France to the United States.

Double-entry bookkeeping means that for each transaction there is a credit entry and a debit entry. *Credits* record activities that bring payments into a country; *debits* record activities that involve payments to the rest of the world. Table 2 shows the entries in the U.S. balance of payments to record the sale of a $50,000 U.S. tractor to a French importer. The sale of the tractor represents a $50,000 credit entry in the balance of payments because U.S. exports earn foreign exchange for U.S. residents. To complete the record of this trans-

TABLE 2
Balance of Payments Entries for the Sale of a U.S. Tractor to a French Buyer

Activity	Credit	Debit
U.S. firm exports tractor and receives $50,000 from French buyer	$50,000	
French buyer imports tractor and transfers $50,000 from U.S. bank account to U.S. firm		$50,000
	$50,000	$50,000

action, we must know how payment was made for the tractor. Let's assume that the French buyer paid with a $50,000 check drawn on a U.S. bank. Money that is withdrawn from a foreign-owned bank account in the United States is treated as foreign exchange moved out of the country. So we record the payment as a debit entry in the balance of payments. In fact, the money did not leave the country; its ownership was transferred from the French buyer to the U.S. seller.

The tractor sale is recorded on both sides of the balance of payments. There is a credit entry, and there is a debit entry. For every international transaction, there must be both a credit entry and a debit entry. This means that the sum of total credits and the sum of total debits must be equal. Credits always offset, or balance, debits.

The sum of total credits must equal the sum of total debits so that the two columns of the balance of payments always balance.

2.b. Balance of Payments Accounts

current account:
the sum of the merchandise, services, investment income, and unilateral transfers accounts in the balance of payments

surplus:
in a balance of payments account, the amount by which credits exceed debits

deficit:
in a balance of payments account, the amount by which debits exceed credits

balance of trade:
the balance on the merchandise account in a nation's balance of payments

The balance of payments uses several different accounts to classify transactions (Table 3). The **current account** is the sum of the balances in the merchandise, services, investment income, and unilateral transfers accounts.

Merchandise This account records all transactions involving goods. U.S. exports of goods are merchandise credits; U.S. imports of foreign goods are merchandise debits. When exports (or credits) exceed imports (or debits), the merchandise account shows a **surplus**. When imports exceed exports, the account shows a **deficit**. The balance on the merchandise account is frequently referred to as the **balance of trade**.

In 1993, the merchandise account in the U.S. balance of payments showed a deficit of $132,575 million. This means that the merchandise credits of $456,866 million created by U.S. exports were $132,575 million less than the merchandise debits of $589,441 million created by U.S. imports. In other words, the United States bought more goods from other nations than it sold to them.

Services This account measures trade involving services. It includes travel and tourism, royalties, transportation costs, and insurance premiums. In 1993, the balance on the services account was a $56,850 million surplus.

TABLE 3
Simplified U.S. Balance of Payments, 1993 (million dollars)

Account	Credit	Debit	Net Balance
Merchandise	$456,866	$589,441	−$132,575
Services	$184,811	$127,961	$ 56,850
Investment income	$113,856	$109,910	$ 3,946
Unilateral transfers			−$ 32,117
Current account			**−$103,896**
Capital account	**$230,698**	**$147,898**	**$ 82,800**
Statistical discrepancy			$ 21,096

Source: Data from *Economic Report of the President, 1995* (Washington, D.C.: U.S. Government Printing Office, 1995), pp. 394–395.

Every nation uses its own currency: dollars in the United States, pesetas in Spain, kroner in Norway, and pounds in England. Trade between countries must involve buying and selling national currencies. Since U.S. exporters ultimately want U.S. dollars for their products, if they export goods to England, pounds must be exchanged for dollars. The foreign exchange market is where national currencies are bought and sold.

Investment Income The income earned from investments in foreign countries is a credit; the income paid on foreign-owned investments in the United States is a debit. Investment income is the return on a special kind of service: it is the value of services provided by capital in foreign countries. In 1993, there was a surplus of $3,946 million in the investment income account. The United States traditionally shows a surplus in the investment income account because of its large investment in the rest of the world.

Unilateral Transfers In a unilateral transfer, one party gives something but gets nothing in return. Gifts and retirement pensions are forms of unilateral transfers. For instance, if a farmworker in El Centro, California, sends money to his family in Guaymas, Mexico, this is a unilateral transfer from the United States to Mexico. Only the net balance on unilateral transfers is reported. In 1993, that balance was a deficit of $32,117.

The current account is a useful measure of international transactions because it contains all of the activities involving goods and services. The **capital account** is where trade involving financial assets and international investment is recorded. In 1993, the current account showed a deficit of $103,896 million. This means that U.S. imports of merchandise, services, investment income, and unilateral transfers were $103,896 million greater than exports of these items.

If we draw a line in the balance of payments under the current account, then all entries below the line relate to financing the movement of merchandise, services, investment income, and unilateral transfers into and out of the country. In the terminology of the balance of payments, *capital* refers to

capital account:
the record in the balance of payments of the flow of financial assets into and out of a country

financial and investment flows—bank deposits, purchases of stocks and bonds, loans, land purchases, and purchases of business firms—not simply the factories and equipment that are defined as capital in the macroeconomic sense of the word. Credits to the capital account reflect foreign purchases of U.S. financial assets or real property like land and buildings, and debits reflect U.S. purchases of foreign financial assets and real property. In 1993, the U.S. capital account showed a surplus of $82,800 million.

The *statistical discrepancy* account, the last account listed in Table 3, could be called *omissions and errors*. Government cannot accurately measure all transactions that take place. Some international shipments of goods and services go uncounted or are miscounted, as are some international flows of capital. The statistical discrepancy account is used to correct for these omissions and errors. In 1993, measured debits exceeded measured credits, so the statistical discrepancy was $21,096 million.

Over all of the balance of payments accounts, the sum of credits must equal the sum of debits. The bottom line—the *net balance*—must be zero. It cannot show a surplus or a deficit. When people talk about a surplus or a deficit in the balance of payments, they actually are talking about a surplus or a deficit in one of the balance of payments accounts. The balance of payments itself by definition is always in balance, a function of double-entry bookkeeping.

2.c. The Current Account and the Capital Account

The current account reflects the movement of goods and services into and out of a country. The capital account reflects the flow of financial assets into and out of a country. In Table 3, the current account shows a deficit balance of $103,896 million. Remember that the balance of payments must *balance*. If there is a deficit in the current account, there must be a surplus in the capital account that exactly offsets that deficit.

What is important here is not the bookkeeping process, the concept that the balance of payments must balance, but rather the meaning of deficits and surpluses in the current and capital accounts. These deficits and surpluses tell us whether a country is a net borrower from or lender to the rest of the world. A deficit in the current account means that a country is running a net surplus in its capital account. And it signals that a country is a net borrower from the rest of the world. A country that is running a current account deficit must borrow from abroad an amount sufficient to finance that deficit. A capital account surplus is achieved by selling more bonds and other debts of the domestic country to the rest of the world than the country buys from the rest of the world.

Figure 2 shows the current account balance in the United States for each year from 1960 to 1993. The United States experienced large current account deficits in the 1980s and then again in the mid-1990s. Such deficits indicate that the United States consumed more than it produced. This means that the United States sold financial assets and borrowed large amounts of money from foreign residents to finance its current account deficits. This large foreign borrowing made the United States the largest debtor in the world, as discussed in the Economic Insight "The World's Largest Debtor Nation." A *net debtor* owes more to the rest of the world than it is owed; a *net creditor* is owed more than it owes. The United States was an international net creditor from the end of World War I until the mid-1980s. The country financed its

A net debtor owes more to the rest of the world than it is owed; a net creditor is owed more than it owes.

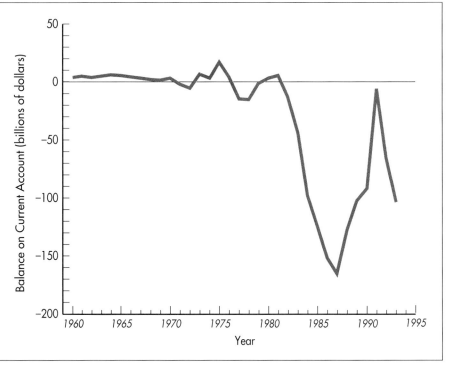

Figure 2
The U.S. Current Account Balance, 1960–1993
The current account of the balance of payments is the sum of the balances in the merchandise, services, investment income, and unilateral transfers accounts. The United States experienced very large current account deficits in the 1980s.
Source: Data from the *Economic Report of the President, 1995.*

large current account deficits in the 1980s by borrowing from the rest of the world. As a result of this accumulated borrowing, in 1985 the United States became an international net debtor for the first time in almost 70 years. Since that time, the net debtor status of the United States has grown steadily.

RECAP

1. The balance of payments is a record of a nation's international transactions.

2. Double-entry bookkeeping requires that every transaction be entered in at least two accounts, so that credits and debits are balanced.

3. In the balance of payments, credits record activities that represent payments into the country, and debits record activities that represent payments out of the country.

4. The current account is the sum of the balances in the merchandise, services, investment income, and unilateral transfers accounts.

5. A surplus exists when credits exceed debits; a deficit exists when credits are less than debits.

6. The capital account is where the transactions necessary to finance the movement of merchandise, services, investment income, and unilateral transfers into and out of the country are recorded.

7. The net balance in the balance of payments must be zero.

8. A deficit in the current account must be offset by a surplus in the capital account. It also indicates that the nation is a net borrower.

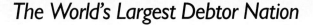
The World's Largest Debtor Nation

On September 16, 1985, the U.S. Department of Commerce announced that the United States was a debtor nation for the first time since World War I. In fact, the size of the deficit in the current account in the mid-1980s made the United States the largest debtor in the world. Its debts now exceed even those of large developing countries like Brazil and Mexico.

The movement from net creditor to debtor followed a decade in which U.S. bank loans abroad had increased the country's net creditor position. In fact, in 1982, with net international investments of $147 billion, the United States was the largest creditor nation in the world. This changed with the current account deficits of the 1980s. In order to consume more at home than it produces (this is what a country does when it is running a current account deficit), a country has to borrow from abroad. In the case of the United States, borrowing was at such a high level that its record net creditor position of 1982 was eliminated in just three years.

The change in the U.S. current account was the product of several economic factors. First, the world debt crisis reduced U.S. foreign lending, as banks tried to lower their exposure to loan defaults by developing countries. Second, record U.S. federal budget deficits forced the U.S. Treasury to borrow huge sums of money. U.S. banks, which had reduced their foreign lending, replaced those loans with relatively high-return loans to the government. Finally, these same high returns, along with the perception of the United States as a safe haven for investment, made U.S. securities more attractive to foreign lenders.

There is nothing wrong with being a net debtor as long as borrowed funds contribute to a more productive economy. Without a large inflow of foreign funds since the late 1980s, U.S. interest rates would have been higher and investment probably would have been lower. If the borrowing increased the rate of production in the United States, then future generations, who share the burden of repaying the debt, will enjoy a higher standard of living. Furthermore, the fact that the United States changed from a net creditor to a net debtor had no perceptible effect on the life of the typical American. Consumers and producers have continued to live life as usual.

Large current account deficits and capital account surpluses will not continue forever. When foreign portfolios reach the point where dollar-denominated assets are no longer needed or wanted, the dollar will tend to depreciate and interest rates will tend to fall. As the capital account surplus falls, the current account deficit falls. Ultimately, the United States could once again become a net lender, and the title "world's largest debtor" could fall to another nation.

SUMMARY

▲▼ *How do individuals of one nation trade money with individuals of another nation?*

1. Foreign exchange is currency and bank deposits that are denominated in foreign currency. §1

2. The foreign exchange market is a global market in which people trade one currency for another. §1

3. Exchange rates, the price of one country's money in terms of another country's money, are necessary to compare prices quoted in different currencies. §1.a

4. The value of a good in a domestic currency equals the foreign currency price times the exchange rate. §1.a

▲▼ *How do changes in exchange rates affect international trade?*

5. When a domestic currency appreciates, domestic goods become more expensive to foreigners and foreign goods become cheaper to domestic residents. §1.b

6. When a domestic currency depreciates, domestic goods become cheaper to foreigners

and foreign goods become more expensive to domestic residents. §1.b

▲▼ *How do nations record their transactions with the rest of the world?*

7. The balance of payments is a record of a nation's transactions with the rest of the world. §2

8. The balance of payments is based on double-entry bookkeeping. §2.a

9. Credits record activities that bring payments into a country; debits record activities that take payments out of a country. §2.a

10. In the balance of payments, the sum of total credits and the sum of total debits must be equal. §2.a

11. The current account is the sum of the balances in the merchandise, services, investment income, and unilateral transfers accounts. §2.b

12. In a balance of payments account, a surplus is the amount by which credits exceed debits, and a deficit is the amount by which debits exceed credits. §2.b

13. The capital account reflects the transactions necessary to finance the movement of merchandise, services, investment income, and unilateral transfers into and out of the country. §2.b

14. The net balance in the balance of payments must be zero. §2.b

15. A deficit in the current account must be offset by a surplus in the capital account. §2.c

16. A country that shows a deficit in its current account (or a surplus in its capital account) is a net borrower. §2.c

KEY TERMS

foreign exchange §1
foreign exchange market §1
exchange rate §1.a
balance of payments §2
double-entry bookkeeping §2.a

current account §2.b
surplus §2.b
deficit §2.b
balance of trade §2.b
capital account §2.b

EXERCISES

1. What is the price of 1 U.S. dollar in terms of each of the following currencies, given the following exchange rates?

   a. 1 Austrian schilling = $.10

   b. 1 Chinese yuan = $.33

   c. 1 Israeli shekel = $.60

   d. 1 Kuwaiti dinar = $4.20

2. A bicycle manufactured in the United States costs $100. Using the exchange rates listed in Figure 1 for Tuesday, what would the bicycle cost in each of the following countries?

   a. Argentina

   b. Brazil

   c. Canada

3. The U.S. dollar price of a Swedish krona changes from $.1572 to $.1730.

   a. Has the dollar depreciated or appreciated against the krona?

   b. Has the krona appreciated or depreciated against the dollar?

   Use the information in the following table on Mexico's 1993 international transactions to answer questions 4–6 (the amounts are the U.S. dollar values in millions):

Merchandise imports	$48,924
Merchandise exports	$30,033
Services exports	$14,766
Services imports	$11,031

Investment income receipts	$ 2,703
Investment income payments	$13,625
Unilateral transfers	$ 2,687

4. What is the balance of trade?

5. What is the current account?

6. Did Mexico become a larger international net debtor during 1993?

7. How reasonable is it for every country to follow policies aimed at increasing net exports?

8. How did the United States become the world's largest debtor nation in the 1980s?

9. Consider *The Wall Street Journal* exchange rate quotes given in Figure 1. What kind of transactions do these quotes apply for? What if you went to a hotel to exchange dollars for foreign currency—how would the price you pay for foreign currency differ from the quotes in *The Wall Street Journal*?

10. If the U.S. dollar appreciated against the German mark, what would you expect to happen to U.S. net exports with Germany?

11. Suppose the U.S. dollar price of a British pound is $1.50; the dollar price of a German mark is $.60; a hotel room in London, England, costs 120 British pounds; and a comparable hotel room in Hanover, Germany, costs 220 German marks.

a. Which hotel room is cheaper to a U.S. tourist?

b. What is the exchange rate between the German mark and the British pound?

12. Many residents of the United States send money to relatives living in other countries. For instance, a Salvadoran farmworker who is temporarily working in San Diego, California, sends money back to his family in El Salvador. How are such transactions recorded in the balance of payments? Are they debits or credits?

13. Suppose the U.S. dollar price of the Canadian dollar is $.75. How many Canadian dollars will it take to buy a set of dishes selling for $60 in Detroit, Michigan?

14. Why is it true that if the dollar depreciates against the yen, the yen must appreciate against the dollar?

15. Why does the balance of payments contain an account called "statistical discrepancy"?

COOPERATIVE LEARNING EXERCISE

Section 2.b discussed how the balance of payments is made up of different accounts. After dividing students into groups of three or four, have each group meet for five minutes to determine how the following transactions would be classified in the current account of the U.S. balance of payments (as either merchandise, services, investment income, or unilateral transfers). In each case, the balancing entry is to the capital account, so students should just find the correct classification for the component of the current account. After the five minutes are over, groups will be called upon to provide their classifications (which account is relevant and whether the transaction is a debit or credit).

1. Telefonos de Mexico pays $5 million to the Bank of America in San Francisco for interest on a loan.

2. Texas Instruments buys $2 million worth of computer chips from a firm in Singapore.

3. The U.S. government gives the government of Egypt $3 million in foreign aid to build a new irrigation system.

4. Lisa from Los Angeles, California, travels to Rome, Italy, and spends $4,000 on hotels and sightseeing.

Yen's Surge Likely to Push Up Japanese Goods' Prices

NEW YORK—Ripples created by the Japanese yen's surge against the dollar are expected to reach U.S. store shelves in the coming months, forcing Americans to pay slightly more for cars, videocassette recorders, cordless phones and other Japanese-made consumer products.

Leading Japanese consumer-electronics makers, including Panasonic and Sony, said Tuesday that prices may rise on selected products by fall, the result of the yen's 10 percent advance in recent months.

The yen's appreciation may mean higher prices for American shoppers, but a strong Japanese currency typically helps the U.S. economy. As the prices of Japanese goods rise, consumers are more likely to buy lower-price American products.

With one round of midyear price increases just ended, automaker American Honda began a new one Monday, raising Honda and Acura prices an average $202 per vehicle. It's unknown when or whether other Japanese automakers will follow, but it's clear that the strength of the yen is affecting all automakers.

However, it takes time for currency fluctuations to show up on price tags.

"The financial markets make instantaneous adjustments, but goods and services take a little longer to adjust" in terms of price, said Marc Chandler, an analyst with IDEA, a New York advisory firm.

It has taken the yen about three months to advance 10 percent to its current level. The dollar ended New York trading Tuesday at 113.40 yen.

Among smaller-ticket items, prices on televisions are unlikely to change, because many Japanese companies assemble their televisions in the United States. But many VCRs, camcorders, telephones and some personal computers are imported from Japan and are likely to be affected. . . .

Japanese manufacturers have ways of holding the line on price increases despite currency fluctuations. When the yen advanced sharply in the late 1980s, Chandler said, Japanese companies put the squeeze on their profit margins to keep prices stable.

"They didn't pass along higher prices to the consumer in order to maintain market share," he said.

But with Japan's economy in recession, it is unlikely that Japanese companies will be willing to crimp profits again. And as the U.S. economy continues to strengthen, Japanese manufacturers are likely to figure that Americans will have more money to spend anyway.

Still, manufacturers are looking for ways to cut costs. Ken Ishihara, a vice president at Toshiba America, said his company is studying ways to increase productivity and possibly shift more production to U.S. factories.

And Mike Kitadeya, a spokesman for Matsushita Electric Corporation of America, a unit of Panasonic Co., noted that his company sets exchange rates for wholesale buyers that remain in effect for up to six months. So some buyers may not see price increases, should they occur, until fall.

"Yen's Surge Likely to Push Up Japanese Goods' Prices," Mariann Caprino, *Arizona Republic*, April 14, 1993, p. A1. Copyright © 1993. Reprinted with permission of The Associated Press.

Commentary

Two components are involved in the determination of the price of an imported good: its price in terms of its home currency and the exchange rate. With constant yen prices of goods in Japan, if the dollar depreciates in value against the yen, Japanese goods will become more expensive to U.S. buyers, as the article emphasizes. However, there is another side to this story—U.S. goods will become cheaper to Japanese buyers. For instance, between March and April of 1993, the yen price of a dollar fell from 118 to 113. The dollar became 5 percent cheaper to Japanese buyers in one month. This is good for U.S. exporters, as the cheaper dollars cause the yen price of U.S. goods to fall.

For instance, suppose Ping Golf Company in Phoenix, Arizona, sells golf clubs to Japanese buyers for $1,000. At an exchange rate of 118 yen per dollar the golf clubs will cost a resident of Japan ¥118,000 (the dollar price of $1,000 times the exchange rate 118). But after the dollar depreciates to 113 yen per dollar, the golf clubs will sell for ¥113,000. The dollar depreciation will tend to increase U.S. exports to Japan due to the lower yen price of U.S. goods.

The article indicates how the depreciating dollar (and appreciating yen) will affect U.S. consumers who buy goods made in Japan. This will mean that even U.S. firms that do not export may have an interest in the exchange rate movements if they produce products that compete against Japanese-made products. As the article states, "as the prices of Japanese goods rise, consumers are more likely to buy lower-price American products." If the yen price of a dollar falls from 118 to 113, the dollar price of a yen rises from $0.0085 (1/118 = .0085) to $0.0088 (1/113 = .0088). Remember, if you know the number of yen per dollar, the number of dollars per yen is found by the reciprocal. The reciprocal of 118 is 1/118 or .0085, so a yen sold for $0.0085 or 85 hundredths of a cent.

If the dollar price of a yen goes from $0.0085 to $0.0088, the dollar price of a Japanese-built Toyota that sells for ¥2,360,000 in Japan will rise from $20,060 to $20,768. This increase in price of more than $700 will tend to reduce the quantity of Japanese-built Toyotas purchased in the United States and increase the quantity of U.S.-built cars demanded. This effect could be mitigated if companies, like Toyota, that export to the United States lower their profit margins by decreasing the yen price of their products in order to stop the dollar price in the U.S. from rising. If Toyota lowered the yen price of the automobile from ¥2,360,000 to ¥2,279,545, then the dollar price to U.S. buyers would be unchanged at $20,060 since the lower yen price just offsets the higher dollar price of a yen. Such behavior is quite common as foreign manufacturers try to protect their U.S. market share by absorbing the effect of currency appreciation through lower profits.

8

Unemployment and Inflation

FUNDAMENTAL QUESTIONS

1. What is a business cycle?
2. How is the unemployment rate defined and measured?
3. What is the cost of unemployed resources?
4. What is inflation?
5. Why is inflation a problem?

I f you were graduating from college today, what would your job prospects be? In 1932, they would have been bleak. A large number of people were out of work (about one in four workers), and a large number of firms had laid off workers or gone out of business. At any time, job opportunities depend not only on the individual's ability and experience, but also on the current state of the economy.

Economies cycles of activity: periods of expansion, where output and employment increase, are followed by periods of contraction, where output and employment decrease. For instance, during the expansionary period of the mid 1990s, only 5.4 percent of U.S. workers had no job by 1995. But during the period of contraction of 1981 1982, 9.5 percent of U.S. workers had no job. When the economy is growing, the demand for goods and services tends to increase. To produce those goods and services, firms hire more workers. Economic expansion also has an impact on inflation. As the demand for goods and services goes up, the prices of those goods and services also

tend to rise. By the mid 1990s, following several years of economic growth, consumer prices in the United States were rising by about 3 percent a year. During periods of contraction, as more people are out of work, demand for goods and services tends to fall and there is less pressure for rising prices. During the period of the Great Depression in the 1930s in the United States, consumer prices fell by more than 5 percent in 1933. Both price increases and the fraction of workers without jobs are affected by business cycles in fairly regular ways. But their effects on individual standards of living, income, and purchasing power are much less predictable.

Why do certain events move in tandem? What are the links between unemployment and inflation? What causes the business cycle to behave as it does? What effect does government activity have on the business cycle—and on unemployment and inflation? Who is harmed by rising unemployment and inflation? Who benefits? Macroeconomics attempts to answer all of these questions.

I. BUSINESS CYCLES

In this chapter we describe the business cycle and examine measures of unemployment and inflation. We talk about the ways in which the business cycle, unemployment, and inflation are related. And we describe their effects on the participants in the economy.

PREVIEW

The most widely used measure of a nation's output is gross domestic product. When we examine the value of real GDP over time, we find periods in which it rises and other periods in which it falls.

1.a. Definitions

What is a business cycle?

business cycle:
pattern of rising real GDP followed by falling real GDP

recession:
a period in which real GDP falls

This pattern—real GDP rising, then falling—is called a **business cycle**. The pattern occurs over and over again, but as Figure 1 shows, the pattern over time is anything but regular. Historically the duration of business cycles and the rate at which real GDP rises or falls (indicated by the steepness of the line in Figure 1) vary considerably.

Looking at Figure 1, it is clear that the U.S. economy has experienced up-and-down swings in the years since 1959. Still, real GDP has grown at an average rate of approximately 3 percent per year. While it is important to recognize that periods of economic growth, or prosperity, are followed by periods of contraction, or **recession**, it is also important to recognize the presence of long-term economic growth—despite the presence of periodic recessions, in the long run the economy produces more goods and services. The long-run growth in the economy depends on the growth in productive resources, like land, labor, capital, and entrepreneurship, along with technological advance. Technological change increases the productivity of resources so that output increases even with a fixed amount of inputs. In recent years there has been concern about the growth rate of U.S. productivity and its effect on the long-run growth potential of the economy.

Figure 2 shows how real GDP behaves over a hypothetical business cycle and identifies the stages of the cycle. The vertical axis on the graph measures the level of real GDP; the horizontal axis measures time in years. In year 1,

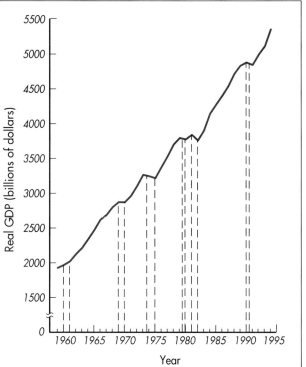

Figure 1
U.S. Real GDP, 1959–1994 (1987 dollars)
The shaded areas represent periods of economic contraction (recession). The table lists the dates of business-cycle peaks and troughs. The peak dates indicate when contractions began; the trough dates, when expansions began. Source: Data from *Economic Report of the President, 1995* (Washington, D.C.: U.S. Government Printing Office, 1995).

Peaks	Troughs
April 1960	February 1961
December 1969	November 1970
November 1973	March 1975
January 1980	July 1980
July 1981	November 1982
July 1990	March 1991

real GDP is growing; the economy is in the *expansion* phase, or *boom* period, of the business cycle. Growth continues until the *peak* is reached, in year 2. Real GDP begins to fall during the *contraction* phase of the cycle, which continues until year 4. The *trough* marks the end of the contraction and the start of a new expansion. Even though the economy is subject to periodic ups and downs, real GDP, the measure of a nation's output, has risen over the long term, as illustrated by the upward-sloping line labeled *trend*.

If an economy is growing over time, why do economists worry about business cycles? Economists try to understand the causes of business cycles so that they can learn to moderate or avoid recessions and their harmful effects on standards of living.

1.b. Historical Record

depression:
a severe, prolonged economic contraction

The official dating of recessions in the United States is the responsibility of the National Bureau of Economic Research (NBER), an independent research organization. The NBER has identified the shaded areas in the graph in Figure 1 as recessions, the unshaded areas as expansions. Recessions are periods between cyclical peaks and the troughs that follow them. Expansions are periods between cyclical troughs and the peaks that follow them. There have been twelve recessions since 1929. The most severe was the Great Depression. Between 1929 and 1933, national output fell by 25 percent; this period is called the Great Depression. A **depression** is a prolonged period of severe economic contraction. The fact that people refer to "the Depression" when speaking about the recession that began in 1929 indicates the severity of that contraction relative to others in recent experience. There was widespread suffering during the Depression. Many people were jobless and homeless, and many firms went bankrupt.

1.c. Indicators

We have been talking about the business cycle in terms of real GDP. There are a number of other variables that move in a fairly regular manner over the business cycle. The Department of Commerce classifies these variables in three categories—leading indicators, coincident indicators, and lagging indicators—depending on whether they move up or down before, at the same time as, or following a change in real GDP (see Table 1).

Figure 2
The Business Cycle
The business cycle contains four phases: the expansion (boom), when real GDP is increasing; the peak, which marks the end of an expansion and the beginning of a contraction; the contraction (recession), when real GDP is falling; and the trough, which marks the end of a contraction and the beginning of an expansion.

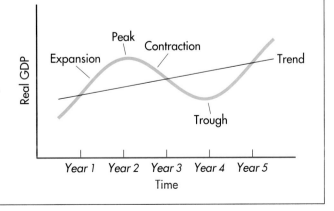

As real income falls, living standards go down. This 1937 photo of a depression-era breadline indicates the paradox of the world's richest nation, as emphasized on the billboard in the background, having to offer public support to feed able-bodied workers who are out of work due to the severity of the business-cycle downturn.

leading indicator:
a variable that changes before real output changes

Leading indicators generally change before real GDP changes. As a result, economists use them to forecast changes in output. Looking at Table 1, it is easy to see how some of these leading indicators could be used to forecast future output. For instance, new building permits signal new construction. If the number of new permits issued goes up, economists can expect the amount of new construction to increase. Similarly, if manufacturers receive more new orders, economists can expect more goods to be produced.

TABLE I
Indicators of the Business Cycle

Leading Indicators

Average workweek	New building permits
Unemployment claims	Delivery times of goods
Manufacturers' new orders	Inventories
New businesses formed	Materials prices
Stock prices	Money supply
New plant and equipment orders	Consumer expectations

Coincident Indicators

Payroll employment
Industrial production
Personal income
Manufacturing and trade sales

Lagging Indicators

Labor cost per unit of output
Inventories to sales ratio
Unemployment duration
Consumer credit to personal income ratio
Outstanding commercial loans
Prime interest rate
Inflation rate for services

Leading indicators are not infallible, however. The link between them and future output can be tenuous. For example, leading indicators may fall one month and then rise the next, while real output rises steadily. Economists want to see several consecutive months of a new direction in the leading indicators before forecasting a change in output. Short-run movements in the indicators can be very misleading.

coincident indicator:
a variable that changes at the same time that real output changes

Coincident indicators are economic variables that tend to change at the same time real output changes. For example, as real output increases, economists expect to see employment and sales rise. The coincident indicators listed in Table 1 have demonstrated a strong tendency over time to change along with changes in real GDP.

lagging indicator:
a variable that changes after real output changes

The final group of variables listed in Table 1, **lagging indicators**, do not change their value until after the value of real GDP has changed. For instance, as output increases, jobs are created and more workers are hired. It makes sense, then, to expect the duration of unemployment (the average time workers are unemployed) to fall. The duration of unemployment is a lagging indicator. Similarly, the inflation rate for services (which measures how prices change for things like dry cleaners, veterinarians, and other services) tends to change after real GDP changes. Lagging indicators are used along with leading and coincident indicators to identify the peaks and troughs in business cycles.

RECAP

1. The business cycle is a recurring pattern of rising and falling real GDP.
2. Although all economies move through periods of expansion and contraction, the duration of expansion and recession varies.
3. Real GDP is not the only variable affected by business cycles; leading, lagging, and coincident indicators also show the effects of economic expansion and contraction.

2. UNEMPLOYMENT

How is the unemployment rate defined and measured?

Recurring periods of prosperity and recession are reflected in the nation's labor markets. In fact, this is what makes understanding the business cycle so important. If business cycles signified only a little more or a little less profit for businesses, governments would not be so anxious to forecast or to control their swings. It is the human costs of lost jobs and incomes—the inability to maintain standards of living—that make an understanding of business cycles and of the factors that affect unemployment so important.

2.a. Definition and Measurement

unemployment rate:
the percentage of the labor force that is not working

The **unemployment rate** is the percentage of the labor force that is not working. The rate is calculated by dividing the number of people who are unemployed by the number of people in the labor force:

$$\text{Unemployment rate} = \frac{\text{number unemployed}}{\text{number in labor force}}$$

This ratio seems simple enough, but there are several subtle issues at work here. First, the unemployment rate does not measure the percentage of the total population that is not working; it measures the percentage of the *labor force* that is not working. Who is in the labor force? Obviously, everybody who is employed is part of the labor force. But only some of those who are not currently employed are counted in the labor force.

The Bureau of Labor Statistics of the Department of Labor compiles labor data each month based on an extensive survey of U.S. households. All U.S. residents are potential members of the labor force. The Labor Department arrives at the size of the actual labor force by using this formula:

You are in the labor force if you are working or actively seeking work.

$$\text{Labor force} = \text{all U.S. residents} - \text{residents under 16 years of age} - \text{institutionalized adults} - \text{adults not looking for work}$$

So the labor force includes those adults (an adult being 16 or older) currently employed or actively seeking work. It is relatively simple to see to it that children and institutionalized adults (for instance, those in prison or long-term care facilities) are not counted in the labor force. It is more difficult to identify and accurately measure adults who are not actively looking for work.

A person is actively seeking work if he or she is available to work, has looked for work in the past four weeks, is waiting for a recall after being laid off, or is starting a job within 30 days. Those who are not working and who meet these criteria are considered unemployed.

2.b. Interpreting the Unemployment Rate

Is the unemployment rate an accurate measure? The fact that the rate does not include those who are not actively looking for work is not necessarily a failing. Many people who are not actively looking for work—homemakers, older citizens, and students, for example—have made a decision to do housework, to retire, or to stay in school. These people rightly are not counted among the unemployed.

But there are people missing from the unemployment statistics who are not working and are not looking for work, yet would take a job if one was offered. **Discouraged workers** have looked for work in the past year but have given up looking for work because they believe that no one will hire them. These individuals are ignored by the official unemployment rate even though they are able to work and may have spent a long time looking for work. Estimates of the number of discouraged workers indicate that in 1994, 1,807,000 people were not counted in the labor force yet claimed that they were available for work. Of this group, 28 percent, or half a million people, were considered to be discouraged workers. It is clear that the reported unemployment rate underestimates the true burden of unemployment in the economy because it ignores discouraged workers.

discouraged workers: workers who have stopped looking for work because they believe no one will offer them a job

Discouraged workers are one source of hidden unemployment; underemployment is another. **Underemployment** is the underutilization of workers—employment in tasks that do not fully utilize their productive potential—including part-time workers who prefer full-time employment. Even if every worker has a job, substantial underemployment leaves the economy producing less than its potential GDP.

underemployment: the employment of workers in jobs that do not utilize their productive potential

The Underground Economy

Official unemployment data, like national income data, do not include activity in the underground economy. Obviously, drug dealers and prostitutes do not report their earnings. Nor do many of the people who supplement their unemployment benefits with part-time jobs. In addition, people like the waiter who reports a small fraction of his actual tips and the house-cleaning person who requests payment in cash in order to avoid reporting taxable income are also part of the underground economy.

Because activity in the underground economy goes unreported, there is no exact way to determine its size. Estimates range from 5 to 33 percent of the gross domestic product. With the GDP at $5 trillion, this places the value of underground activity between $250 billion and $1.33 trillion.

We will never know the true size of the underground economy, but evidence suggests that it is growing. That evidence has to do with cash. The vast majority of people working in the underground economy are paid in cash. One indicator of the growth of that economy, then, is the rise in currency over time relative to checking accounts. Also, per capita

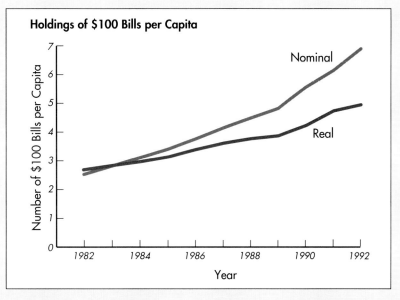

holdings of $100 bills have increased substantially. The graph shows this increase over the 1982 to 1992 period, from 2.5 $100 bills per person in 1982 to 6 bills per person by the early 1990s. Certainly, much of the demand for $100 bills is a product of inflation (as the prices of goods and services go up, it is easier to pay for them in larger-denomination bills). But the lower line in the graph shows a substantial rise in real holdings of $100 bills as well.

The underground economy

forces us to interpret government statistics carefully. We must remember that:

■ Official income statistics understate the true national income.

■ Official unemployment data overestimate true unemployment.

■ When the underground economy grows more rapidly than the rest of the economy, the true rate of growth is higher than reported.

Activity in the underground economy is not included in official statistics.

The effect of discouraged workers and underemployment is an unemployment rate that understates actual unemployment. In contrast, the effect of the *underground economy* is a rate that overstates actual unemployment. A sizable component of the officially unemployed is actually working. The unemployed construction worker who plays in a band at night may not report that activity because he or she wants to avoid paying taxes on his or her earnings as a musician. This person is officially unemployed but has a source of income. Many officially unemployed individuals have an alternate source of income. This means that official statistics overstate the true magnitude of unemployment. The larger the underground economy, the greater this overstatement. (See the Economic Insight "The Underground Economy.")

We have identified two factors, discouraged workers and underemployment, that cause the official unemployment rate to underestimate true unemployment. Another factor, the underground economy, causes the official rate to overestimate the true rate of unemployment. There is no reason to expect these factors to cancel one another out, and there is no way to know for sure which is most important. The point is to remember what the official data on unemployment do and do not measure.

2.c. Types of Unemployment

Economists have identified four basic types of unemployment:

Seasonal unemployment A product of regular, recurring changes in the hiring needs of certain industries on a monthly or seasonal basis.

Frictional unemployment A product of the short-term movement of workers between jobs and of first-time job seekers.

Structural unemployment A product of technological change and other changes in the structure of the economy.

Cyclical unemployment A product of business-cycle fluctuations.

In certain industries, labor needs fluctuate throughout the year. When local crops are harvested, farms need lots of workers; the rest of the year, they do not. (Migrant farmworkers move from one region to another, following the harvests, to avoid seasonal unemployment.) Ski resort towns like Park City, Utah, are booming during the ski season, when employment peaks, but need fewer workers during the rest of the year. In the nation as a whole, the Christmas season is a time of peak employment and low unemployment rates. To avoid confusing seasonal fluctuations in unemployment with other sources of unemployment, unemployment data are seasonally adjusted.

Seasonal unemployment is unemployment that fluctuates with the seasons of the year. For instance, these Santas in training will be employed from fall through Christmas. After Christmas they will be unemployed and must seek new positions. Other examples of seasonal unemployment include farmworkers who migrate to follow the harvest of crops, experiencing unemployment between harvests.

Frictional and structural unemployment are always present in a dynamic economy.

Frictional and structural unemployment exist in any dynamic economy. In terms of individual workers, frictional unemployment is short term in nature. Workers quit one job and soon find another; students graduate and soon find a job. This kind of unemployment cannot be eliminated in a free society. In fact, it is a sign of efficiency in an economy when workers try to increase their income or improve their working conditions by leaving one job for another. Frictional unemployment is often called *search unemployment* because workers take time to search for a job after quitting a job or leaving school.

Frictional unemployment is short term; structural unemployment, on the other hand, can be long term. Workers who are displaced by technological change (assembly line workers who have been replaced by machines, for example) or by a permanent reduction in the demand for an industry's output (cigar makers who have been laid off because of a decrease in demand for tobacco) may not have the necessary skills to maintain their level of income in another industry. Rather than accept a much lower salary, these workers tend to prolong their job search. Eventually they adjust their expectations to the realities of the job market, or they enter the pool of discouraged workers.

Structural unemployment is very difficult for those who are unemployed. But for society as a whole, the technological advances that cause structural unemployment raise living standards by giving consumers a greater variety of goods at lower cost.

Cyclical unemployment is a product of recession.

Cyclical unemployment is a result of the business cycle. As a recession occurs, cyclical unemployment increases, and as growth occurs, cyclical unemployment decreases. It is also a primary focus of macroeconomic policy. Economists believe that a greater understanding of business cycles and their causes may enable them to find ways to smooth out those cycles and swings in unemployment. Much of the analysis in future chapters is related to macroeconomic policy aimed at minimizing business-cycle fluctuations. In addition to macroeconomic policy aimed at moderating cyclical unemployment, other policy measures—for example, job training and counseling—are being used to reduce frictional and structural unemployment.

2.d. Costs of Unemployment

What is the cost of unemployed resources?

potential real GDP:
the output produced at the natural rate of unemployment

natural rate of unemployment:
the unemployment rate that would exist in the absence of cyclical unemployment

The cost of being unemployed is more than the obvious loss of income and status suffered by the individual who is not working. In a broader sense, society as a whole loses when resources are unemployed. Unemployed workers produce no output. So an economy with unemployment will operate inside its production possibilities curve rather than on the curve. Economists measure this lost output in terms of the *GDP gap*:

GDP gap = potential real GDP − actual real GDP

Potential real GDP is the level of output produced when nonlabor resources are fully utilized and unemployment is at its natural rate. The **natural rate of unemployment** is the unemployment rate that would exist in the absence of cyclical unemployment, so it includes seasonal, frictional, and structural unemployment. The natural rate of unemployment is not fixed; it can change over time. For instance, some economists believe that the natural rate of unemployment has risen in recent decades, a product of the influx of baby boomers and women into the labor force. As more workers move into the labor force (begin looking for jobs), frictional unemployment increases, raising the natural rate of unemployment.

Figure 3
The GDP Gap, 1975–1993 (1987 dollars)
The GDP gap is the difference between what the economy can produce at the natural rate of unemployment (potential GDP) and actual output (actual GDP). When the unemployment rate is higher than the natural rate, actual GDP is less than potential GDP. The gap between potential and actual real GDP is a cost associated with unemployment. Recession years are shaded to highlight how the gap widens around recessions.

(a) Potential and Real GDP

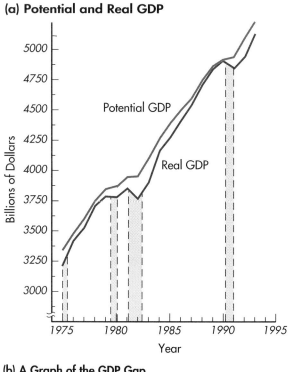

(b) A Graph of the GDP Gap

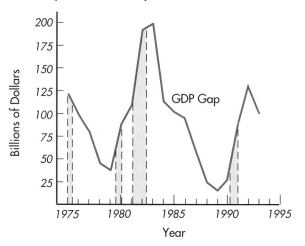

Potential real GDP measures what we are capable of producing at the natural rate of unemployment. If we compute potential real GDP and then subtract actual real GDP, we have a measure of the output lost as a result of unemployment, or the cost of unemployment.

The GDP gap in the United States from 1975 to 1993 is shown in Figure 3(a). The gap widens during recessions and narrows during expansions. As the gap widens (as the output not produced increases), there are fewer goods and services available, and living standards are lower than they would be at the natural rate of unemployment. Figure 3(b) is a graph of the gap between potential and real GDP, taken from Figure 3(a).

Part II/Macroeconomic Basics

Until recently economists used the term *full employment* instead of *natural rate of unemployment.* Today the term *full employment* is rarely used because it may be interpreted as implying a zero unemployment rate. If frictional and structural unemployment are always present, zero unemployment is impossible; there must always be unemployed resources in an economy. *Natural rate of unemployment* describes the labor market when the economy is producing what it realistically can produce in the absence of cyclical unemployment.

What is the value of the natural rate of unemployment in the United States? In the 1950s and 1960s, economists generally agreed on 4 percent. By the 1970s, that agreed-on rate had gone up to 5 percent. In the early 1980s, many economists placed the natural rate of unemployment in the United States at 6 to 7 percent. By the late 1980s, some had revised their thinking, placing the rate back at 5 percent. In fact, economists do not know exactly what the natural rate of unemployment is. Over time it varies within a range from around 4 percent to around 7 percent. It will also vary across countries, as labor markets and macroeconomic policies differ.

2.e. The Record of Unemployment

Unemployment rates in the United States from 1951 to 1994 are listed in Table 2. Over this period, the unemployment rate for all workers reached a low of 2.8 percent in 1953 and a high of 9.5 percent in 1982 and 1983. The table shows some general trends in the incidence of unemployment across different demographic groups:

In most years, the unemployment rate for women is higher than it is for men. Several factors may be at work here. First, during this period, a large number of women entered the labor force for the first time. Second, discrimination against women in the workplace limited job opportunities for them, particularly early in this period. Finally, a large number of women move out of the labor force on temporary maternity leaves.

Teenagers have the highest unemployment rates in the economy. This makes sense because teenagers are the least-skilled segment of the labor force.

Whites have lower unemployment rates than nonwhites. Discrimination plays a role here. To the extent that discrimination extends beyond hiring practices and job opportunities for minority workers to the education that is necessary to prepare students to enter the work force, minority workers will have fewer opportunities for employment. The quality of education provided in many schools with large minority populations may not be as good as that provided in schools with large white populations. Equal opportunity programs and legislation are aimed at rectifying this inequality.

Although exact comparisons across countries are difficult to make because countries measure unemployment in different ways, it is interesting to look at the reported unemployment rates of different countries. Table 3 lists unemployment rates for seven major industrial nations. The rates have been adjusted to match as closely as possible the U.S. definition of unemployment. For instance, the official Italian unemployment data include people who have not looked for work in the past 30 days. The data for Italy in Table 3 have been adjusted to remove these people. If the data had not been adjusted, the Italian unemployment rates would be roughly twice as high as those listed.

Countries not only define unemployment differently, they also use different methods to count the unemployed. All major European countries except

TABLE 2
Unemployment Rates in the United States, 1951–1994

Year	All Civilian Workers	Males	Females	Both Sexes 16–19 Years	White	Black and Other
1951	3.3	2.8	4.4	8.2	3.1	5.3
1953	2.9	2.8	3.3	7.6	2.7	4.5
1955	4.4	4.2	4.9	11.0	3.9	8.7
1957	4.3	4.1	4.7	11.6	3.8	7.9
1959	5.5	5.2	5.9	14.6	4.8	10.7
1961	6.7	6.4	7.2	16.8	6.0	12.4
1963	5.7	5.2	6.5	17.2	5.0	10.8
1965	4.5	4.0	5.5	14.8	4.1	8.1
1966	3.8	3.2	4.8	12.8	3.4	7.3
1967	3.8	3.1	5.2	12.9	3.4	7.4
1968	3.6	2.9	4.8	12.7	3.2	6.7
1969	3.5	2.8	4.7	12.2	3.1	6.4
1970	4.9	4.4	5.9	15.3	4.5	8.2
1971	5.9	5.3	6.9	16.9	5.4	9.9
1972	5.6	5.0	6.6	16.2	5.1	10.0
1973	4.9	4.2	6.0	14.5	4.3	9.0
1974	5.6	4.9	6.7	16.0	5.0	9.9
1975	8.5	7.9	9.3	19.9	7.8	13.8
1976	7.7	7.1	8.6	19.0	7.0	13.1
1977	7.1	6.3	8.2	17.8	6.2	13.1
1978	6.1	5.3	7.2	16.4	5.2	11.9
1979	5.8	5.1	6.8	16.1	5.1	11.3
1980	7.1	6.9	7.4	17.8	6.3	13.1
1981	7.6	7.4	7.9	19.6	6.7	14.2
1982	9.7	9.9	9.4	23.2	8.6	17.3
1983	9.6	9.9	9.2	22.4	8.4	17.8
1984	7.5	7.4	7.6	18.9	6.5	14.4
1985	7.2	7.0	7.4	18.6	6.2	13.7
1986	7.0	6.9	7.1	18.3	6.0	13.1
1987	6.2	6.2	6.2	16.9	5.3	11.6
1988	5.5	5.5	5.6	15.3	4.7	10.4
1989	5.3	5.2	5.4	15.0	4.5	10.0
1990	5.5	5.6	5.4	15.5	4.7	10.1
1991	6.7	7.0	6.3	18.6	6.0	11.1
1992	7.4	7.8	6.9	20.0	6.5	12.7
1993	6.8	7.1	6.5	19.0	6.0	11.7
1994	6.1	6.2	6.0	17.6	5.3	10.5

[1]Unemployed as a percentage of the civilian labor force in the group specified.
Source: *Economic Report of the President, 1995* (Washington, D.C.: U.S. Government Printing Office, 1995), p. 320.

TABLE 3
Unemployment Rates in Major Industrial Countries, 1960–1993

Year	United States	Canada	France	Italy	Japan	United Kingdom	Germany
	Civilian Unemployment Rate (percent)						
1960	5.5	6.5	1.5	3.7	1.7	2.2	1.1
1961	6.7	6.7	1.2	3.2	1.5	2.0	.6
1962	5.5	5.5	1.4	2.8	1.3	2.7	.6
1963	5.7	5.2	1.6	2.4	1.3	3.3	.5
1964	5.2	4.4	1.2	2.7	1.2	2.5	.4
1965	4.5	3.6	1.6	3.5	1.2	2.1	.3
1966	3.8	3.4	1.6	3.7	1.4	2.3	.3
1967	3.8	3.8	2.1	3.4	1.3	3.3	1.3
1968	3.6	4.5	2.7	3.5	1.2	3.2	1.1
1969	3.5	4.4	2.3	3.5	1.1	3.1	.6
1970	4.9	5.7	2.5	3.2	1.2	3.1	.5
1971	5.9	6.2	2.8	3.3	1.3	3.9	.6
1972	5.6	6.2	2.9	3.8	1.4	4.2	.7
1973	4.9	5.5	2.8	3.7	1.3	3.2	.7
1974	5.6	5.3	2.9	3.1	1.4	3.1	1.6
1975	8.5	6.9	4.1	3.4	1.9	4.6	3.4
1976	7.7	7.1	4.5	3.9	2.0	5.9	3.4
1977	7.1	8.1	5.1	4.1	2.0	6.4	3.5
1978	6.1	8.3	5.3	4.1	2.3	6.3	3.3
1979	5.8	7.4	6.0	4.4	2.1	5.4	3.0
1980	7.1	7.5	6.4	4.4	2.0	7.0	2.9
1981	7.6	7.5	7.6	4.9	2.2	10.5	4.1
1982	9.7	11.0	8.3	5.4	2.4	11.2	5.8
1983	9.6	11.8	8.5	5.9	2.7	11.7	7.1
1984	7.5	11.2	10.0	5.9	2.8	11.7	7.4
1985	7.2	10.5	10.4	6.0	2.6	11.2	7.5
1986	7.0	9.5	10.6	7.5	2.8	11.2	6.9
1987	6.2	8.8	10.8	7.9	2.9	10.2	6.4
1988	5.5	7.8	10.4	7.9	2.5	8.3	6.3
1989	5.3	7.5	9.6	7.8	2.3	6.4	5.7
1990	5.5	8.1	9.2	7.0	2.1	6.9	5.0
1991	6.7	10.3	9.4	6.9	2.1	8.8	4.3
1992	7.4	11.3	10.4	7.3	2.2	10.0	4.6
1993	6.8	11.2	11.8	10.5	2.5	10.4	5.8

Source: *Economic Report of the President, 1995* (Washington, D.C.: U.S. Government Printing Office, 1995), p. 401.

Sweden use a national unemployment register to identify the unemployed. Only those people who register for unemployment benefits are considered unemployed. A problem with this method is that it excludes those who have not registered because they are not entitled to benefits and it includes those who receive benefits but would not take a job if one was offered. Other countries—among them the United States, Canada, Sweden, and Japan—conduct monthly surveys of households to estimate the unemployment rate. Surveys allow more comprehensive analysis of unemployment and its causes than does the use of a register. The Organization for Economic Cooperation and Development, an organization created to foster international economic cooperation, compared annual surveys of the labor force in Europe with the official register of unemployment data and found that only 80 to 85 percent of those surveyed as unemployed were registered in Germany, France, and the United Kingdom. In Italy, only 63 percent of those surveyed as unemployed were registered.

Knowing their limitations, we can still identify some important trends from the data in Table 3. Through the 1960s and early 1970s, European unemployment rates generally were lower than U.S. and Canadian rates. Over the next decade, European unemployment rates increased substantially, as did the rates in North America. But in the mid-1980s, while U.S. unemployment began to fall, European unemployment remained high. The issue of high unemployment rates in Europe has become a major topic of discussion at international summit meetings. Japanese unemployment rates, like those in Europe, were much lower than U.S. and Canadian rates in the 1960s and 1970s. However, unlike European rates, Japanese rates remained much lower in the 1980s and 1990s. We will discuss the reasons for Japan's rapid growth and low unemployment in future chapters.

RECAP

1. The unemployment rate is the number of people unemployed as a percentage of the labor force.
2. To be in the labor force, one must either have or be looking for a job.
3. By its failure to include discouraged workers and the output lost because of underemployment, the unemployment rate understates real unemployment in the United States.
4. By its failure to include activity in the underground economy, the U.S. unemployment rate overstates actual unemployment.
5. Unemployment data are adjusted to eliminate seasonal fluctuations.
6. Frictional and structural unemployment are always present in a dynamic economy.
7. Cyclical unemployment is a product of recession; it can be moderated by controlling the period of contraction in the business cycle.
8. Economists measure the cost of unemployment in terms of lost output.
9. Unemployment data show that women generally have higher unemployment rates than men, that teenagers have the highest unemployment rates in the economy, and that blacks and other minority groups have higher unemployment rates than whites.

3. INFLATION

What is inflation?

Inflation is a sustained rise in the average level of prices. Notice the word *sustained*. Inflation does not mean a short-term increase in prices; it means prices are rising over a prolonged period of time. Inflation is measured by the

inflation:
a sustained rise in the average level of prices

percentage change in price level. The inflation rate in the United States was 2.7 percent in 1994. This means that the level of prices increased 2.7 percent over the year.

3.a. Absolute Versus Relative Price Changes

In the modern economy, over any given period, some prices rise faster than others. To evaluate the rate of inflation in a country, then, economists must know what is happening to prices on average. Here it is important to distinguish between *absolute* and *relative* price changes.

Let's look at an example using the prices of fish and beef:

	Year 1	Year 2
1 pound of fish	$1	$2
1 pound of beef	$2	$4

In year 1, beef is twice as expensive as fish. This is the price of beef *relative* to fish. In year 2, beef is still twice as expensive as fish. The relative prices have not changed between years 1 and 2. What has changed? The prices of both beef and fish have doubled. The *absolute* levels of all prices have gone up, but because they have increased by the same percentage, the relative prices are unchanged.

Why is inflation a problem?

Inflation measures changes in absolute prices. In our example, all prices doubled, so the inflation rate is 100 percent. There was a 100 percent increase in the prices of beef and fish. Inflation does not proceed evenly through the economy. Prices of some goods rise faster than others, which means that relative prices are changing at the same time that absolute prices are rising. The measured inflation rate records the *average* change in absolute prices.

3.b. Effects of Inflation

To understand the effects of inflation, you have to understand what happens to the value of money in an inflationary period. The real value of money is what it can buy, its *purchasing power*:

$$\text{Real value of \$1} = \frac{\$1}{\text{price level}}$$

The purchasing power of a dollar is the amount of goods and services it can buy.

The higher the price level, the lower the real value (or *purchasing power*) of the dollar. For instance, suppose an economy had only one good—milk. If a glass of milk sold for $.50, then one dollar would buy two glasses of milk. If the price of milk rose to $1, then a dollar would only buy one glass of milk. The purchasing power, or real value, of money falls as prices rise.

Table 4 lists the real value of the dollar in selected years from 1946 to 1994. The price level in each year is measured relative to the average level of prices over the 1982–1984 period. For instance, the 1946 value, .195, means that prices in 1946 were, on average, only 19.5 percent of prices in the 1982–1984 period. Notice that as prices go up, the purchasing power of the dollar falls. In 1946 a dollar bought five times more than a dollar bought in the early 1980s. The value 5.13 means that one could buy 5.13 times more goods and services with a dollar in 1946 than one could in 1982–1984.

Prices have risen steadily in recent decades. By 1994, they had gone up more than 48 percent above the average level of prices in the 1982–1984 period. Consequently, the purchasing power of a 1994 dollar was lower. In 1994, $1 bought just 67 percent of the goods and services that one could buy with a dollar in 1982–1984.

If prices and nominal income rise by the same percentage, it might seem that inflation is not a problem. It doesn't matter if it takes twice as many dollars now to buy fish and beef than it did before, if we have twice as many dollars in income available to buy the products. Obviously, inflation is very much a problem when a household's nominal income rises at a slower rate than prices. Inflation hurts those households whose income does not keep up with the prices of the goods they buy.

In the 1970s in the United States, the rate of inflation rose to near-record levels. Many workers believed that their incomes were lagging behind the rate of inflation, so they negotiated cost-of-living raises in their wage contracts. The typical cost-of-living raise ties salary to changes in the consumer price index. If the CPI rises 8 percent over a year, workers receive an 8 percent raise plus compensation for experience or productivity increases. As the U.S. rate of inflation fell during the 1980s, concern about cost-of-living raises subsided as well.

It is important to distinguish between expected and unexpected inflation. *Unexpectedly high inflation* redistributes income away from those who receive fixed incomes (like creditors who receive debt repayments of a fixed amount of dollars per month) toward those who make fixed expenditures (like debtors who make fixed debt repayments per month). For example, consider a simple loan agreement:

Maria borrows $100 from Ali, promising to repay the loan in one year at 10 percent interest. In one year, Maria will pay Ali $110—principal of $100 plus interest of $10 (10 percent of $100, or $10).

When Maria and Ali agree to the terms of the loan, they do so with some expected rate of inflation in mind. Suppose they both expect 5 percent inflation over the year. In one year it will take 5 percent more money to buy goods than it does now. Ali will need $105 to buy what $100 buys today. Because Ali will receive $110 for the principal and interest on the loan, he will gain purchasing power. However, if the inflation rate over the year turns out to be surprisingly high—say, 15 percent—then Ali will need $115 to buy what $100 buys today. He will lose purchasing power if he makes a loan at a 10 percent rate of interest.

Economists distinguish between nominal and real interest rates when analyzing economic behavior. The **nominal interest rate** is the observed interest rate in the market and includes the effect of inflation. The **real interest rate** is the nominal interest rate minus the rate of inflation:

$$\text{Real interest rate} = \text{nominal interest rate} - \text{rate of inflation}$$

If Ali charges Maria 10 percent nominal interest and the inflation rate is 5 percent, the real interest rate is 5 percent (10% − 5% = 5%). This means that Ali will earn a positive real return from the loan. However, if the inflation rate is 10 percent, the real return from a nominal interest rate of 10 percent is zero (10% − 10% = 0). The interest Ali will receive from the loan will just compensate him for the rise in prices; he will not realize an increase in purchasing power. If the inflation rate is higher than the nominal interest

Unexpectedly high inflation redistributes income away from those who receive fixed incomes toward those who make fixed expenditures.

nominal interest rate:
the observed interest rate in the market

real interest rate:
the nominal interest rate minus the rate of inflation

TABLE 4
The Real Value of a Dollar, 1946–1994

Year	Average Price Level[1]	Purchasing Power of a Dollar[2]
1946	.195	5.13
1950	.241	4.15
1954	.269	3.72
1958	.289	3.46
1962	.302	3.31
1966	.324	3.09
1970	.388	2.58
1974	.493	2.03
1978	.652	1.53
1982	.965	1.04
1986	1.096	.91
1990	1.307	.77
1991	1.362	.73
1992	1.403	.71
1993	1.445	.69
1994	1.482	.67

[1]Measured by the consumer price index as given in the *Economic Report of the President, 1995* (Washington, D.C.: U.S. Government Printing Office, 1995), p. 341.

[2]Found by taking the reciprocal of the consumer price index (1/CPI).

Real interest rates are lower than expected when inflation is higher than expected.

rate, then the real interest rate is negative—the lender will lose purchasing power by making the loan.

Now you can see how unexpected inflation redistributes income. Borrowers and creditors agree to loan terms based on what they *expect* the rate of inflation to be over the period of the loan. If the *actual* rate of inflation turns out to be different from what was expected, then the real interest rate paid by the borrower and received by the lender will be different from what was expected. If Ali and Maria both expect a 5 percent inflation rate and agree to a 10 percent nominal interest rate for the loan, then they both expect a real interest rate of 5 percent (10% − 5% = 5%) to be paid on the loan. If the actual inflation rate turns out to be greater than 5 percent, then the real interest rate will be less than expected. Maria will get to borrow Ali's money at a lower real cost than she expected, and Ali will earn a lower real return than he expected. Unexpectedly high inflation hurts creditors and benefits borrowers because it lowers real interest rates.

Figure 4 shows the real interest rates on U.S. Treasury bills from 1970 through 1994. You can see a pronounced pattern in the graph. In the late 1970s, there was a period of negative real interest rates, followed by high positive real rates in the 1980s. The evidence suggests that nominal interest rates did not rise fast enough in the 1970s to offset high inflation. This was a time of severe strain on many creditors, including savings and loan associations and banks. These firms had lent funds at fixed nominal rates of interest. When those rates of interest turned out to be lower than the rate of inflation, the financial institutions suffered significant losses. In the early 1980s, the

Figure 4
The Real Interest Rate on U.S. Treasury Bills
The real interest rate is the difference between the nominal rate (the rate actually observed) and the rate of inflation over the life of the bond. The figure shows the real interest rate in June and December for each year. For instance, in the first observation for June 1970, a six-month Treasury bill paid the holder 6.91 percent interest. This is the nominal rate of interest. To find the real rate of interest on the bond, we subtract the rate of inflation that existed over the six months of the bond's life (June to December 1970), which was 5.17 percent. The difference between the nominal interest rate (6.91 percent) and the rate of inflation (5.17 percent) is the real interest rate, 1.74 percent. Notice that real interest rates were negative during most of the 1970s and then turned highly positive (by historical standards) in the early 1980s.

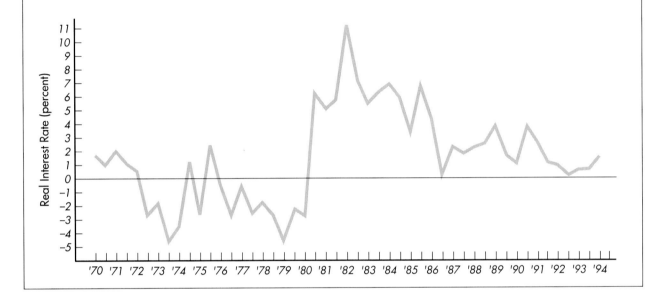

inflation rate dropped sharply. Because nominal interest rates did not drop nearly as fast as the rate of inflation, real interest rates were high. In this period many debtors were hurt by the high costs of borrowing to finance business or household expenditures.

Unexpected inflation affects more than the two parties to a loan. Any contract calling for fixed payments over some long-term period changes in value as the rate of inflation changes. For instance, a long-term contract that provides union members with 5 percent raises each year for five years gives the workers more purchasing power if inflation is low than if it is high. Similarly, a contract that sells a product at a fixed price over a long-term period will change in value as inflation changes. Suppose a lumber company promises to supply a builder with lumber at a fixed price for a two-year period. If the rate of inflation in one year turns out to be higher than expected, the lumber company will end up selling the lumber for less profit than it had planned. Inflation raises costs to the lumber company. Usually the company would raise its prices to compensate for higher costs. Because the company contracted to sell its goods at a fixed price to the builder, however, the builder benefits at the lumber company's expense. Again, unexpectedly high inflation redistributes real income or purchasing power away from those receiving fixed payments to those making fixed payments.

One response to the effects of unexpected inflation is to allow prices, wages, or interest rates to vary with the rate of inflation. Labor sometimes negotiates cost-of-living adjustments as part of new wage contracts. Financial institutions offer variable interest rates on home mortgages to reflect current market conditions. Any contract can be written to adjust dollar amounts over time as the rate of inflation changes.

3.c. Types of Inflation

Economists often classify inflation according to the source of the inflationary pressure. The most straightforward method defines inflation in terms of pressure from the demand side of the market or the supply side of the market:

Demand-pull inflation Increases in total spending that are not offset by increases in the supply of goods and services cause the average level of prices to rise.

Cost-push inflation Increases in production costs cause firms to raise prices to avoid losses.

Sometimes inflation is blamed on "too many dollars chasing too few goods." This is a roundabout way of saying that the inflation stems from demand pressures. Because demand-pull inflation is a product of increased spending, it is more likely to occur in an economy that is producing at maximum capacity. If resources are fully employed, in the short run it may not be possible to increase output to meet increased demand. The result: existing goods and services are rationed by rising prices.

Some economists claim that rising prices in the late 1960s were a product of demand-pull inflation. They believe that increased government spending for the Vietnam War caused the level of U.S. prices to rise.

Cost-push inflation can occur in any economy, whatever its output. If prices go up because the costs of resources are rising, the rate of inflation can go up regardless of demand.

For example, some economists argue that the inflation in the United States in the 1970s was largely due to rising oil prices. This means that decreases in the oil supply (a shift to the left in the supply curve) brought about higher oil prices. Because oil is so important in the production of many goods, higher oil prices led to increases in prices throughout the economy. Cost-push inflation stems from changes in the supply side of the market.

Cost-push inflation is sometimes attributed to profit-push or wage-push pressures. *Profit-push pressures* are created by suppliers who want to increase their profit margins by raising prices faster than their costs increase. *Wage-push pressures* are created by labor unions and workers who are able to increase their wages faster than their productivity. There have been times when "greedy" businesses and unions have been blamed for periods of inflation in the United States. The problem with these "theories" is that people have always wanted to improve their economic status and always will. In this sense, people have always been greedy. But inflation has not always been a problem. Were people less greedy in the early 1980s when inflation was low than they were in the late 1970s when inflation was high? Obviously, we have to look to other reasons to explain inflation. We discuss some of those reasons in later chapters.

3.d. The Inflationary Record

Many of our students, having always lived with inflation, are surprised to learn that inflation is a relatively new problem for the United States. From 1789, when the U.S. Constitution was ratified, until 1940, there was no particular trend in the general price level. At times prices rose, and at times they fell. The average level of prices in 1940 was approximately the same as it was in the late eighteenth century.

Since 1940, prices in the United States have gone up markedly. The price level today is seven times what it was in 1940. But the rate of growth has varied. Figure 5 plots the path of consumer prices in the United States in the post–World War II period. Notice that prices rose rapidly for the first couple of years following the war, and then grew at a relatively slow rate through the 1950s and 1960s. In the early 1970s, the rate of inflation began to accelerate. Prices climbed quickly until the early 1980s, when inflation slowed.

Annual rates of inflation for several industrial and developing nations are shown in Table 5. In 1993, the average rate of inflation across all industrial countries was 2.8 percent; the average across all developing countries was 52.9 percent. Look at the diversity across countries: rates range from 1.3 percent in Japan to 1,987 percent in Zaire.

hyperinflation:
an extremely high rate of inflation

Hyperinflation is an extremely high rate of inflation. In most cases hyperinflation eventually makes a country's currency worthless and leads to the introduction of a new money. Argentina experienced hyperinflation in the 1980s. People had to carry large stacks of currency for small purchases. Cash registers and calculators ran out of digits as prices reached ridiculously high levels. After years of high inflation, Argentina replaced the old peso with the peso Argentino in June 1983. The government set the value of 1 peso

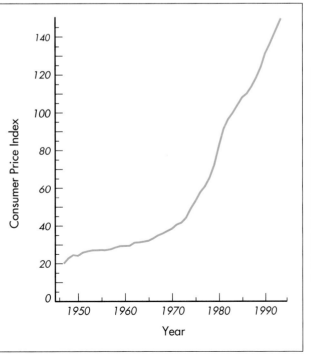

Figure 5
U.S. Consumer Prices, 1946–1994
Prices rose relatively rapidly after World War II, then at a slow rate from the late 1940s until the late 1960s. Prices again rose at a fairly rapid rate through the 1970s. In the early 1980s, price increases moderated.
Source: *Economic Report of the President, 1995* (Washington, D.C.: U.S. Government Printing Office, 1995).

Argentino equal to 10,000 old pesos (striking four zeros from all prices). A product that sold for 10,000 old pesos before the reform sold for 1 new peso after. But Argentina did not follow up its monetary reform with a noninflationary change in economic policy. In 1984 and 1985, the inflation rate exceeded 600 percent each year. As a result, in June 1985, the government again introduced a new currency, the austral, setting its value at 1,000 pesos Argentino. However, the economic policy associated with the introduction of the austral only lowered the inflation rate temporarily. By 1988, the inflation rate was over 300 percent, and in 1989 the inflation rate was over 3,000 percent. The rapid rise in prices associated with the austral resulted in the introduction of yet another currency, again named peso Argentino, in January 1992 with a value equal to 10,000 australes.

The most dramatic hyperinflation in modern times occurred in Europe after World War I. Table 6 shows how the price level rose in Germany between 1914 and 1924 in relation to prices in 1914. For instance, the value in 1915, 126, indicates that prices were 26 percent higher that year than in

TABLE 5
Rates of Inflation for Selected Countries, 1993

Country	Inflation Rate (percent)
All industrial	2.8
All developing	52.9
Selected industrial:	
Canada	1.8
Germany	4.1
Italy	4.5
Japan	1.3
United Kingdom	1.6
United States	3.0
Selected developing:	
Botswana	14
Brazil	2,148
Chile	13
Egypt	12
Hong Kong	9
India	6
Israel	11
Mexico	10
Philippines	8
Poland	37
South Africa	10
Zaire	1,987

Source: International Monetary Fund, *International Financial Statistics* (Washington, D.C.), February 1995.

TABLE 6
German Wholesale Prices, 1914–1924

Year	Price Index
1914	100
1915	126
1916	150
1917	156
1918	204
1919	262
1920	1,260
1921	1,440
1922	3,670
1923	278,500
1924	117,320,000,000,000

Source: J. P. Young, *European Currency and Finance* (Washington, D.C.: U.S. Government Printing Office, 1925).

1914. The value in 1919, 262, indicates that prices were 162 percent higher that year than in 1914. By 1924, German prices were more than 100 trillion times higher than they had been in 1914. At the height of the inflation, the mark was virtually worthless.

In later chapters, we will see how high rates of inflation generally are caused by rapid growth of the money supply. When a central government wants to spend more than it is capable of funding through taxation or borrowing, it simply issues money to finance its budget deficit. As the money supply increases faster than the demand to hold it, spending increases and prices go up.

RECAP

1. Inflation is a sustained rise in the average level of prices.
2. The higher the price level, the lower the real value (purchasing power) of money.
3. Unexpectedly high inflation redistributes income away from those who receive fixed-dollar payments (like creditors) toward those who make fixed-dollar payments (like debtors).
4. The real interest rate is the nominal interest rate minus the rate of inflation.
5. Demand-pull inflation is a product of increased spending; cost-push inflation reflects increased production costs.
6. Hyperinflation is a very high rate of inflation that often results in the introduction of a new currency.

SUMMARY

▲▼ What is a business cycle?

1. Business cycles are recurring changes in real GDP, in which expansion is followed by contraction. §1.a

2. The four stages of the business cycle are expansion (boom), peak, contraction (recession), and trough. §1.a

3. Leading, coincident, and lagging indicators are variables that change in relation to changes in output. §1.c

▲▼ How is the unemployment rate defined and measured?

4. The unemployment rate is the percentage of the labor force that is not working. §2.a

5. To be in the U.S. labor force, an individual must be working or actively seeking work. §2.a

6. Unemployment can be classified as seasonal, frictional, structural, or cyclical. §2.c

7. Frictional and structural unemployment are always present in a dynamic economy; cyclical unemployment is a product of recession. §2.c

▲▼ What is the cost of unemployed resources?

8. The GDP gap measures the output lost because of unemployment. §2.d

▲▼ What is inflation?

9. Inflation is a sustained rise in the average level of prices. §3

10. The higher the level of prices, the lower the purchasing power of money. §3.b

▲▼ Why is inflation a problem?

11. Inflation becomes a problem when income rises at a slower rate than prices. §3.b

12. Unexpectedly high inflation hurts those who receive fixed-dollar payments (like creditors) and benefits those who make fixed-dollar payments (like debtors). §3.b

13. Inflation can stem from demand-pull or cost-push pressures. §3.c

14. Hyperinflation—an extremely high rate of inflation—can force a country to introduce a new currency. §3.d

KEY TERMS

business cycle §1.a

recession §1.a

depression §1.b

leading indicator §1.c

coincident indicator §1.c

lagging indicator §1.c

unemployment rate §2.a

discouraged workers §2.b

underemployment §2.b

potential real GDP §2.d

natural rate of unemployment §2.d

inflation §3

nominal interest rate §3.b

real interest rate §3.b

hyperinflation §3.d

EXERCISES

1. What is the labor force? Do you believe that the U.S. government's definition of the labor force is a good one—that it includes all the people it should include? Explain your answer.

2. List the reasons why the official unemployment rate may not reflect the true social burden of unemployment. Explain whether the official numbers overstate or understate *true* unemployment in light of each reason you discuss.

3. Suppose you are able-bodied and intelligent, but lazy. You'd rather sit home and watch television than work, even though you know you could find an acceptable job if you looked.

   a. Are you officially unemployed?

   b. Are you a discouraged worker?

4. Can government do anything to reduce the number of people in the following categories? If so, what?

   a. Frictionally unemployed

   b. Structurally unemployed

   c. Cyclically unemployed

5. Does the GDP gap measure all of the costs of unemployment? Why or why not?

6. Why do teenagers have the highest unemployment rate in the economy?

7. Suppose you are currently earning $10 an hour. If the inflation rate over the current year is 10% and your firm provides a cost-of-living raise based on the rate of inflation, what would you expect to earn after your raise? If the cost-of-living raise is always granted based on the past year's inflation, is your nominal income really keeping up with the cost of living?

8. Write an equation that defines the real interest rate. Use the equation to explain why unexpectedly high inflation redistributes income from creditors to debtors.

9. Many home mortgages in recent years have been made with variable interest rates. Typically, the interest rate is adjusted once a year based on current interest rates on government bonds. How do variable interest rate loans protect creditors from the effects of unexpected inflation?

10. The word *cycle* suggests a regular, recurring pattern of activity. Is there a regular pattern in the business cycle? Support your answer by examining the duration (number of months) of each expansion and contraction in Figure 1.

11. Using the list of leading indicators in Table 1, write a brief paragraph explaining why each variable changes before real output changes. In other words, provide an economic reason why each indicator is expected to lead the business cycle.

12. Suppose 500 people were surveyed, and of those 500, 450 were working full time. Of the 50 not working, 10 were full-time college students, 20 were retired, 5 were under sixteen years of age, 5 had stopped looking for work because they believed there were no jobs for them, and 10 were actively looking for work.

    a. How many of the 500 surveyed are in the labor force?

    b. What is the unemployment rate among the 500 surveyed people?

13. Consider the following price information:

	Year 1	Year 2
Cup of coffee	$ .50	$1.00
Glass of milk	$1.00	$2.00

   a. Based on the information given, what was the inflation rate between year 1 and year 2?

   b. What happened to the price of coffee relative to that of milk between year 1 and year 2?

14. Use a supply and demand diagram to illustrate:

   a. Cost-push inflation caused by a labor union successfully negotiating for a higher wage.

   b. Demand-pull inflation caused by an increase in demand for domestic products from foreign buyers.

15. During the Bolivian hyperinflation in the 1980s, Bolivians used U.S. dollars as a substitute for the domestic currency (the peso) for many transactions. Explain how the value of money is affected by hyperinflation and the incentives to use a low-inflation currency like the dollar as a substitute for a high-inflation currency like the Bolivian peso.

COOPERATIVE LEARNING EXERCISE

Divide the class into groups of four. Each group is a separate economy. In each group students count off from 1 to 4 and play roles in the following scenarios:

a) 1: full-time worker; 2: full-time student; 3: laid-off worker searching for a new job; 4: full-time worker whose job picking fruit will end in one month.

b) 1: housewife of househusband; 2: recent graduate looking for a job; 3: someone neither working nor looking for work (stays home and watches TV); 4: full-time worker.

c) 1: retired worker; 2: full-time worker; 3: prisoner; 4: full-time worker.

Each group should determine the unemployment rate for each four-person economy in each scenario. (Hint: First determine the size of the labor force and then determine the unemployment

Though Layoffs Make Headlines, Economy Quietly Creates Jobs

To gauge where the economy is headed, just follow Beverly Davidson's mercurial career.

She was laid off by an oil and gas company in 1986 and a bank in 1990. Ms. Davidson found more work—but was laid off again last August. Now the 34-year-old college graduate is working for a small computer firm.

How long that job will last is any economist's guess. "Everybody has to be fast on their feet," said her new boss, Robert Porter of Altai Inc.

Despite a healthy economy and a declining jobless rate, layoffs are still in the news. Last month Halliburton Co. said it would cut 1,200 employees and Delta Airlines said it would slash up to 15,000 jobs.

But Ms. Davidson seems to have a good chance of surviving these uncertain times, especially in Texas. Economists say that many small companies—in industries such as technology, telecommunications and health care—are adding jobs that more than make up for the layoffs.

And some companies are cutting jobs while hiring workers whose technical skills can improve efficiency.

"Either you upgrade your workers or you hire people instead. IBM laid off thousands, but they're still hiring," said Travis Tullos, an analyst with *Texas Perspectives* newsletter.

Mr. Tullos said there is still a lot of restructuring within companies. He cites the high volume of help-wanted ads and the high unemployment claims as evidence that companies are still laying off workers. Jared Hazelton, a Texas A&M economist said: "Most people laid off find other jobs. It's bad for the people involved, but layoffs are a way of becoming more competitive."

At Altai, manufacturing takes place in sleek offices where workers wear jeans and open-necked shirts, sit with their legs propped on desks and invent software that makes computers work more efficiently.

The number of employees at Altai has doubled to 120 in the past four years, said Mr. Porter, vice president of client services.

Recently, he was trying to hire three employees—one to develop new software and two to replace two employees in support services.

Altai's revenue has grown from $4.7 million in 1989 to $12.0 million last year. It is in stiff competition with similar companies, hence the need to add a new software developer. The job typically pays between $35,000 and $60,000 annually, Mr. Porter said.

In Ms. Davidson's case, her new job of assisting clients with technical problems pays less than her other jobs did, but she wanted a career change. Ms. Davidson wouldn't discuss her salary.

In the past year, Altai has hired 10 new employees and has had no layoffs, Mr. Porter said. He said he gets calls from people laid off from other businesses every week and has hired some of them.

Many of the larger computer companies are downsizing, he said, because the efficiency of advanced computer systems is making some jobs obsolete. Although there are many jobs around, Mr. Porter said applicants have to be highly qualified to get one.

"Other companies have data processing layoffs because they're taking advantage of new technologies," Mr. Porter said. "We are creating those new technologies."

"Though Layoffs Make Headlines, Economy Quietly Creates Jobs," Jane Seaberry, *The Dallas Morning News*, June 5, 1994, p. 141. Reprinted with permission of *The Dallas Mornings News*.

Commentary

Structural change in an economy forces difficult adjustments like structural unemployment. Some of the most dramatic examples of this kind of change have occurred in the so-called Rust Belt of the United States—the industrial region of the Northeast and the Midwest, where well-paying factory jobs are disappearing in the face of foreign competition and new production techniques. Many workers in this region who once had jobs in automobile manufacturing and steel production have recently been left with fewer job prospects and uncertain futures.

Many newly unemployed workers have worked for many years and earned higher salaries than they can expect to earn in other jobs. This, of course, is the problem. If they could simply find another job that offers them comparable pay, they would not be so devastated by the prospect of losing their jobs. This raises an interesting question: If someone is highly valued at one firm and paid accordingly, why aren't they as valuable to other companies who could now hire them? In fact, it is often the case that laid-off workers with successful job histories at one firm are unable to meet entry-level requirements at other jobs.

We can better understand the causes of the plight of many laid-off industrial workers if we consider the determinants of people's wages. Economic theory suggests that people's wages are tied to the amount they contribute to their firm, which implies that wages increase with people's skills. We can think of two broad categories of skills: general skills that make people valuable to any firm and more specialized skills that make people valuable to certain firms. Examples of general skills include welding, bookkeeping, and an ability to manage people. Skills that are useful to only one firm are those that are specifically tied to the product or structure of that firm. Specific knowledge of this second type is not transferable to other firms.

People who work in a particular firm for an extended period learn both general skills that make them valuable to any similar company and specific skills that make them valuable to their company only. For example, the article mentions Beverly Davidson, who had been laid off by a bank prior to her current job. The knowledge she acquired while employed by the bank may not be transferable to her current technical support position at the computer firm.

This distinction between general skills and firm-specific skills begins to explain why retraining has not been very successful for individuals who must move to another line of work. To the extent that retraining enhances abilities that new employers value, it will help the workers earn more. But it is difficult to provide workers with firm-specific skills for new jobs. These skills can only be learned on the job.

The distinction between general and firm-specific skills also suggests why workers least likely to benefit from retraining are those within a few years of retirement. Older workers who must undergo on-the-job training will not be able to use their new firm-specific skills for as many years as younger workers. It is not worthwhile for firms to hire and train workers who are near retirement.

Structural change is an integral part of a dynamic, growing economy. Dislocations are probably inevitable when large-scale structural change occurs, and these dislocations benefit some people while hurting others. Although retraining helps mitigate some of the effects of the upheaval that accompanies structural change, unfortunately it cannot solve all the problems that arise. For the economy as a whole, such change is necessary. As Jared Hazelton said in the article: "Most people laid off find other jobs. It's bad for the people involved, but layoffs are a way of becoming more competitive."

9

Macroeconomic Equilibrium: Aggregate Demand and Supply

FUNDAMENTAL
QUESTIONS

1. What factors affect aggregate demand?
2. What causes the aggregate demand curve to shift?
3. What factors affect aggregate supply?
4. Why does the short-run aggregate supply curve become steeper as real GDP increases?
5. Why is the long-run aggregate supply curve vertical?
6. What causes the aggregate supply curve to shift?
7. What determines the equilibrium price level and real GDP?

T otal output and income in the United States have grown over time. Each generation has experienced a higher living standard than the previous generation. Yet, as we learned in Chapter 8, economic growth has not been steady. Economies go through periods of expansion followed by periods of contraction or recession, and such business cycles have major impacts on people's lives, incomes, and living standards.

Economic stagnation and recession throw many, often those who are already relatively poor, out of their jobs and into real poverty. Economic growth increases the number of jobs and draws people out of poverty and into the mainstream of economic progress. To understand why economies grow and why they go through cycles, we must discover why firms decide to produce more or less and why buyers decide to buy more or less. The approach we take is similar to the approach we followed in the first five chapters of the text using demand and supply curves. In Chapters 3, 4, and 5, demand and supply curves were derived and used to examine questions involving the equilibrium price and quantities demanded and supplied of a single good or service. This simple yet powerful microeconomic technique of analysis has a macroeconomic counterpart—aggregate demand and aggregate supply, which are used to determine an equilibrium price level and quantity of goods and services produced for the *entire economy*. In this chapter we shall use aggregate demand and supply curves to illustrate the causes of business cycles and economic growth.

PREVIEW

I. AGGREGATE DEMAND, AGGREGATE SUPPLY, AND BUSINESS CYCLES

What causes economic growth and business cycles? We can provide some answers to this important question using aggregate demand (AD) and aggregate supply (AS) curves. Suppose we represent the economy in a simple demand and supply diagram, as shown in Figure 1. Aggregate demand represents the total spending in the economy at alternative price levels. Aggregate supply represents the total output of the economy at alternative price levels. To understand the causes of business cycles and inflation, we must understand how aggregate demand and supply cause the equilibrium price level and real GDP, the nation's output of goods and services, to change. The intersection between the AD and AS curves defines the equilibrium level of real GDP and level of prices. The equilibrium price level is P_e and the equilibrium level of real GDP is Y_e. This price and output level represents the

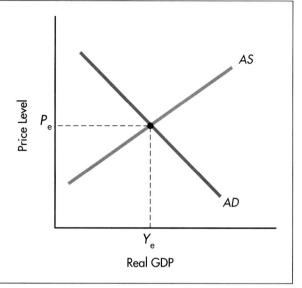

Figure 1
Aggregate Demand and Aggregate Supply Equilibrium
The equilibrium price level and real GDP are determined by the intersection of the *AD* and *AS* curves.

level of prices and output for some particular period of time, say 1995. Once that equilibrium is established, there is no tendency for prices and output to change until changes occur in either the aggregate demand curve or the aggregate supply curve. Let's first consider a change in aggregate demand and then look at a change in aggregate supply.

1.a. Aggregate Demand and Business Cycles

An increase in aggregate demand is illustrated by a shift of the *AD* curve to the right, like the shift from AD_1 to AD_2 in Figure 2. This represents a situation in which buyers are buying more at every price level. The shift causes the equilibrium level of real GDP to rise from Y_{e1} to Y_{e2}, illustrating the expansionary phase of the business cycle. As output rises, unemployment

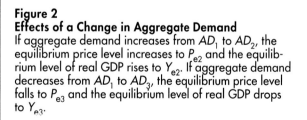

Figure 2
Effects of a Change in Aggregate Demand
If aggregate demand increases from AD_1 to AD_2, the equilibrium price level increases to P_{e2} and the equilibrium level of real GDP rises to Y_{e2}. If aggregate demand decreases from AD_1 to AD_3, the equilibrium price level falls to P_{e3} and the equilibrium level of real GDP drops to Y_{e3}.

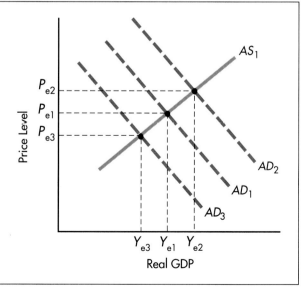

decreases. The increase in aggregate demand also leads to a higher price level, as shown by the change in the price level from P_{e1} to P_{e2}. The increase in the price level represents an example of **demand-pull inflation**, which is inflation caused by increasing demand for output.

demand-pull inflation:
inflation caused by increasing demand for output

If aggregate demand falls, like the shift from AD_1 to AD_3, then there is a lower equilibrium level of real GDP, Y_{e3}. In this case, buyers are buying *less* at every price level. The drop in real GDP caused by lower demand would represent an economic slowdown or a recession, when output falls and unemployment rises.

1.b. Aggregate Supply and Business Cycles

Changes in aggregate supply can also cause business cycles. Figure 3 illustrates what happens when aggregate supply changes. An increase in aggregate supply is illustrated by the shift from AS_1 to AS_2, leading to an increase in the equilibrium level of real GDP from Y_{e1} to Y_{e2}. An increase in aggregate supply comes about when firms produce more at every price level. Such an increase could result from an improvement in technology or a decrease in costs of production.

If aggregate supply decreased, as in the shift from AS_1 to AS_3, then the equilibrium level of real GDP would fall to Y_{e3} and the equilibrium price level would increase from P_{e1} to P_{e3}. A decrease in aggregate supply could be caused by higher production costs that lead producers to raise their prices. This is an example of **cost-push inflation**—where the price level rises due to increased costs of production and the associated decrease in aggregate supply.

cost-push inflation:
inflation caused by rising costs of production

1.c. A Look Ahead

Business cycles result from changes in aggregate demand, from changes in aggregate supply, and from changes in both AD and AS. The degree to which real GDP declines during a recession or increases during an expansion depends on the amount by which the AD and/or AS curves shift. The degree

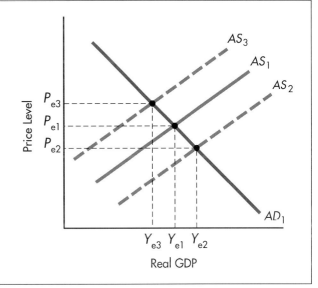

Figure 3
Effects of a Change in Aggregate Supply
If aggregate supply increases from AS_1 to AS_2, the equilibrium price level falls from P_{e1} to P_{e2} and the equilibrium level of real GDP rises to Y_{e2}. If aggregate supply decreases from AS_1 to AS_3, the equilibrium price level rises to P_{e3} and the equilibrium level of real GDP falls to Y_{e3}.

to which an expansion involves output growth or increased inflation depends on the shapes of the *AD* and *AS* curves. We need to consider why the curves have the shapes they do, and what causes them to shift.

The comparison we made earlier, between aggregate demand, aggregate supply, and their microeconomic counterparts, the supply and demand curves, is only superficial. As we examine the aggregate demand and supply curves, you will see that the reasons underlying the shapes and movements of *AD* and *AS* are in fact quite different from those explaining the shapes and movements of the supply and demand curves.

RECAP

1. Aggregate demand (*AD*) represents the total spending in the economy at alternative price levels.
2. Aggregate supply (*AS*) represents the total output of the economy at alternative price levels.
3. The intersection between the *AD* and *AS* curves defines the equilibrium level of real GDP and the level of prices.
4. Business cycles result from changes in *AD* and/or *AS*.

2. FACTORS THAT INFLUENCE AGGREGATE DEMAND

What factors affect aggregate demand?

Aggregate demand is the relation between aggregate expenditures, or total spending, and the price level. Aggregate expenditures are the sum of expenditures of each sector of the economy: households (consumption), business firms (investment), government, and the rest of the world (net exports). Each sector of the economy has different reasons for spending; for instance, household spending depends heavily on household income, while business spending depends on the profits businesses expect to earn. Because each sector of the economy has a different reason for the amount of spending it undertakes, aggregate spending depends on all of these reasons. To understand aggregate demand, therefore, requires that we look at those factors that influence the expenditures of each sector of the economy.

2.a. Consumption

How much households spend depends on their income, wealth, expectations about future prices and incomes, demographics like the age distribution of the population, and taxes.

- Income: If current income rises, households purchase more goods and services.
- Wealth: Wealth is different from income. It is the value of assets owned by a household, including homes, cars, bank deposits, stocks, and bonds. An increase in household wealth will increase consumption.
- Expectations: Expectations regarding future changes in income or wealth can affect consumption today. If households expect a recession and worry about job loss, consumption tends to fall. On the other hand, if

households become more optimistic regarding future increases in income and wealth, consumption rises today.

- Demographics: Demographic change can affect consumption in several different ways. Population growth is generally associated with higher consumption for an economy. Younger households and older households generally consume more and save less than middle-aged households. Therefore, as the age distribution of a nation changes, so will consumption.

- Taxes: Higher taxes will lower the disposable income of households and decrease consumption, while lower taxes will raise disposable income and increase consumption. Government policy may change taxes and thereby bring about a change in consumption.

2.b. Investment

Investment is business spending on capital goods and inventories. In general, investment depends on the expected profitability of such spending, so any factor that could affect the profitability will be a determinant of investment. Factors affecting the expected profitability of business projects include the interest rate, technology, the cost of capital goods, and capacity utilization.

- Interest rate: Investment is negatively related to the interest rate. The interest rate is the cost of borrowed funds. The greater the cost of borrowing, other things being equal, the fewer investment projects that offer sufficient profit to be undertaken. As the interest rate falls, investment is stimulated as the cost of financing the investment is lowered.

- Technology: New production technology stimulates investment spending as firms are forced to adopt new production methods to stay competitive.

- Cost of capital goods: If machines and equipment purchased by firms rise in price, then the higher costs associated with investment will lower profitability and investment will fall.

- Capacity utilization: The more excess capacity (unused capital goods) is available, the more firms can expand production without purchasing new capital goods, and the lower investment is. As firms approach full capacity, more investment spending is required to expand output further.

2.c. Government Spending

Government spending may be set by government authorities independent of current income or other determinants of aggregate expenditures.

2.d. Net Exports

Net exports are equal to exports minus imports. We assume exports are determined by conditions in the rest of the world, like foreign income, tastes, prices, exchange rates, and government policy. Imports are determined by similar domestic factors.

Income   As domestic income rises and consumption rises, some of this consumption includes goods produced in other countries. Therefore, as domestic income rises, imports rise and net exports fall. Similarly, as foreign income rises, foreign residents buy more domestic goods, and net exports rise.

Prices   Other things being equal, higher (lower) foreign prices make domestic goods relatively cheaper (more expensive) and increase (decrease) net exports. Higher (lower) domestic prices make domestic goods relatively more expensive (cheaper) and decrease (increase) net exports.

Exchange rates   Other things being equal, a depreciation of the domestic currency on the foreign exchange market will make domestic goods cheaper to foreign buyers and make foreign goods more expensive to domestic residents so that net exports will rise. An appreciation of the domestic currency will have just the opposite effects.

Government policy   Net exports may fall if foreign governments restrict the entry of domestic goods into their countries, reducing domestic exports. If the domestic government restricts imports into the domestic economy, net exports may rise.

2.e. Aggregate Expenditures

You can see how aggregate expenditures, the sum of all spending on U.S. goods and services, must depend on prices, income, and all of the other determinants discussed in the previous sections. As with the demand curve for a specific good or service, with the aggregate demand curve we want to classify the factors that influence spending into the price and the nonprice determinants for the aggregate demand curves as well. The components of aggregate expenditures that change as the price level changes will lead to movements along the aggregate demand curve—changes in quantity demanded—while changes in aggregate expenditures caused by nonprice effects will cause shifts of the aggregate demand curve—changes in aggregate demand. In the following section we look first at the price effects, or movements along an aggregate demand curve. Following that discussion, we focus on the nonprice determinants of aggregate demand.

RECAP

1. Aggregate expenditures are the sum of consumption, investment, government spending, and net exports.
2. Consumption depends on household income, wealth, expectations, demographics, and taxation.
3. Investment depends on the interest rate, technology, the cost of capital goods, and capacity utilization.
4. Government spending is determined independent of current income.
5. Net exports depend on foreign and domestic incomes, prices, government policies, and exchange rates.

3. THE AGGREGATE DEMAND CURVE

When we examined the demand curves in Chapter 3, we divided our study into two parts: the movement along the curves—changes in quantity demanded—and the shifts of the curve—changes in demand. We take the same approach here in examining aggregate demand. We first look at the movements along the aggregate demand curve caused by changes in the price level. We then turn to the nonprice determinants of aggregate demand that cause shifts in the curve.

3.a. Changes in Aggregate Quantity Demanded: Price-Level Effects

Aggregate demand curves are downward-sloping just like the demand curves for individual goods that were shown in Chapter 3, although for different reasons. Along the demand curve for an individual good, the price of that good changes while the prices of all other goods remain constant. This means that the good in question becomes relatively more or less expensive compared to all other goods in the economy. Consumers tend to substitute a less expensive good for a more expensive good. The effect of this substitution is an inverse relationship between price and quantity demanded. As the price of a good rises, quantity demanded falls. For the economy as a whole, however, it is not a substitution of a less expensive good for a more expensive good that causes the demand curve to slope down. Instead, aggregate quantity demanded, or total spending, will change as the price level changes due to the wealth effect, the interest rate effect, and the international trade effect of a price-level change on aggregate expenditures. We will discuss each of these effects in turn.

3.a.1. The Wealth Effect

Individuals and businesses own money, bonds, and other financial assets. The purchasing power of these assets is the quantity of goods and services the assets can be exchanged for. When the level of prices falls, the purchasing power of these assets increases, allowing households and businesses to purchase more. When prices go up, the purchasing power of financial assets falls, which causes households and businesses to spend less. This is the **wealth effect** (sometimes called the *real-balance effect*) of a price change: a change in the real value of wealth that causes spending to change when the level of prices changes. *Real values* are values that have been adjusted for price-level changes. Here *real value* means "purchasing power." When the price level changes, the purchasing power of financial assets also changes. When prices rise, the real value of assets and wealth falls, and aggregate expenditures tend to fall. When prices fall, the real value of assets and wealth rises, and aggregate expenditures tend to rise.

wealth effect:
a change in the real value of wealth that causes spending to change when the level of prices changes

When the price level changes, the purchasing power of financial assets changes.

3.a.2. The Interest Rate Effect

When the price level rises, the purchasing power of each dollar falls, which means more money is required to buy any particular quantity of goods and services (see Figure 4). Suppose that a family of three needs $100 each week to buy food. If the price level doubles, the same quantity of food costs $200. The household must have twice as much money to buy the same amount of food. Conversely, when prices fall, the family needs less money to buy food because the purchasing power of each dollar is greater.

When prices go up, people need more money. So they sell their other financial assets, like bonds, to get that money. The increase in supply of bonds lowers bond prices and raises interest rates. Since bonds typically pay fixed-dollar interest payments each year, as the price of a bond varies, the interest rate (or yield) will change. For instance, suppose you pay $1,000 for a bond that pays $100 a year in interest. The interest rate on this bond is

Figure 4
The Interest Rate Effect

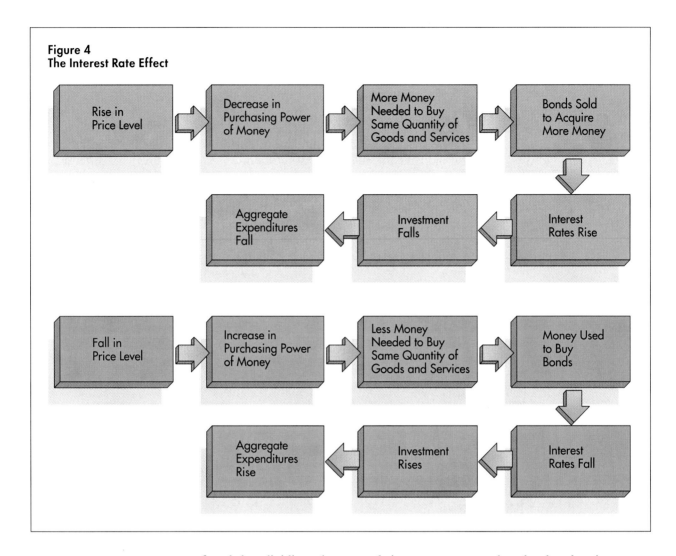

found by dividing the annual interest payment by the bond price, or $100/$1,000 = 10 percent. If the price of the bond falls to $900, then the interest rate is equal to the annual interest payment (which remains fixed at $100 for the life of the bond) divided by the new price of $900: $100/$900 = 11 percent. When bond prices fall, interest rates rise, and when bond prices rise, interest rates fall.

If people want more money and they sell some of their bond holdings to raise the money, bond prices will fall and interest rates will rise. The rise in interest rates is necessary to sell the larger quantity of bonds, but it causes investment expenditures to fall, which causes aggregate expenditures to fall.

When prices fall, people need less money to purchase the same quantity of goods. So they use their money holdings to buy bonds and other financial assets. The increased demand for bonds increases bond prices and causes interest rates to fall. Lower interest rates increase investment expenditures, thereby pushing aggregate expenditures up.

interest rate effect:
a change in interest rates that causes investment and therefore aggregate expenditures to change as the level of prices changes

Figure 4 shows the **interest rate effect**, the relationship among the price level, interest rates, and aggregate expenditures. As the price level rises, interest rates rise and aggregate expenditures fall. As the price level falls, interest rates fall and aggregate expenditures rise.

3.a.3. The International Trade Effect

The International Trade Effect The third channel through which a price-level change affects the quantity of goods and services demanded is called the **international trade effect.** A change in the level of domestic prices can cause net exports to change. If domestic prices rise while foreign prices and the foreign exchange rate remain constant, domestic goods become more expensive in relation to foreign goods.

Suppose the United States sells oranges to Japan. If the oranges sell for $1 per pound and the yen-dollar exchange rate is 100 yen = $1, a pound of U.S. oranges costs a Japanese buyer 100 yen. What happens if the level of prices in the United States goes up 10 percent? All prices, including the price of oranges, increase 10 percent. U.S. oranges sell for $1.10 a pound after the price increase. If the exchange rate is still 100 yen = $1, a pound of oranges now costs the Japanese buyer 110 yen (100 × 1.10). If orange prices in other countries do not change, some Japanese buyers may buy oranges from those countries. The increase in the level of U.S. prices makes U.S. goods more expensive relative to foreign goods and causes U.S. net exports to fall; a decrease in the level of U.S. prices makes U.S. goods cheaper in relation to foreign goods, which increases U.S. net exports.

When the price of domestic goods increases in relation to the price of foreign goods, net exports fall, causing aggregate expenditures to fall. When the price of domestic goods falls in relation to the price of foreign goods, net exports rise, causing aggregate expenditures to rise. The international trade effect of a change in the level of domestic prices causes aggregate expenditures to change in the opposite direction.

3.a.4. The Sum of the Price-Level Effects

The Sum of the Price-Level Effects The **aggregate demand curve** (*AD*) shows how the equilibrium level of expenditures for the economy's output changes as the price level changes. In other words, the curve shows the amount people spend at different price levels.

Figure 5 displays the typical shape of the *AD* curve. The price level is plotted on the vertical axis and real GDP is plotted on the horizontal axis. Suppose that initially the economy is at point *A* with prices at P_0. At this

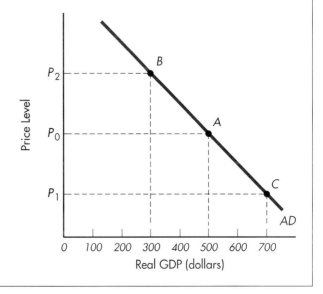

Figure 5
The Aggregate Demand Curve
The aggregate demand curve (*AD*) shows the level of expenditures at different price levels. At price level P_0, expenditures are $500; at P_1, $700; and at P_2, $300.

point, spending equals $500. If prices fall to P_1, expenditures equal $700 and the economy is at point C. If prices rise from P_0 to P_2, expenditures equal $300 at point B.

Because aggregate expenditures increase when the price level decreases, and decrease when the price level increases, the aggregate demand curve slopes down. The aggregate demand curve is drawn with the price level for the *entire economy* on the vertical axis. A price-level change here means that, on average, *all prices in the economy change*; there is no relative price change among domestic goods. The negative slope of the aggregate demand curve is a product of the wealth effect, the interest rate effect, and the international trade effect.

A lower domestic price level increases consumption (the wealth effect), investment (the interest rate effect), and net exports (the international trade effect). As the price level drops, aggregate expenditures rise.

A higher domestic price reduces consumption (the wealth effect), investment (the interest rate effect), and net exports (the international trade effect). As prices rise, aggregate expenditures fall. These price effects are summarized in Figure 6.

3.b. Changes in Aggregate Demand: Nonprice Determinants

What causes the aggregate demand curve to shift?

The aggregate demand curve shows the level of aggregate expenditures at alternative price levels. We draw the curve by varying the price level and finding out what the resulting total expenditures are, holding all other things constant. As those "other things"—the nonprice determinants of aggregate demand—change, the aggregate demand curve shifts. The nonprice determinants of aggregate demand include all of the factors covered in the discussion of the components of expenditures—income, wealth, demographics, expectations, taxes, the interest rate (interest rates can change for reasons other than price-level changes), the cost of capital goods, capacity utilization, foreign income and price levels, exchange rates, and government policy. A change in any one of these can cause the AD curve to shift. In the discussions that follow, we will focus particularly on the effect of expectations, foreign income and price levels, and will also mention government policy, which will be examined in detail in Chapter 12. Figure 7 summarizes these effects, which are discussed next.

3.b.1. Expectations
Consumption and business spending are affected by expectations. Consumption is sensitive to people's expectations of future income, prices, and wealth. For example, when people expect the economy to do well in the future, they increase consumption today at every price level. This is reflected in a shift of the aggregate demand curve to the right, from AD_0 to AD_1, as shown in Figure 8. When aggregate demand increases, aggregate expenditures increase at every price level.

On the other hand, if people expect a recession in the near future, they tend to reduce consumption and increase saving in order to protect themselves against a greater likelihood of losing a job or a forced cutback in hours worked. As consumption drops, aggregate demand decreases. The AD curve shifts to the left, from AD_0 to AD_2. At every price level along AD_2, planned expenditures are less than they are along AD_0.

Expectations also play an important role in investment decisions. Before undertaking a particular project, businesses forecast the likely revenues and

Part II/Macroeconomic Basics

Figure 6
Why the Aggregate Demand Curve Slopes Down
(a) Wealth Effect (b) Interest Rate Effect (c) International Trade Effect

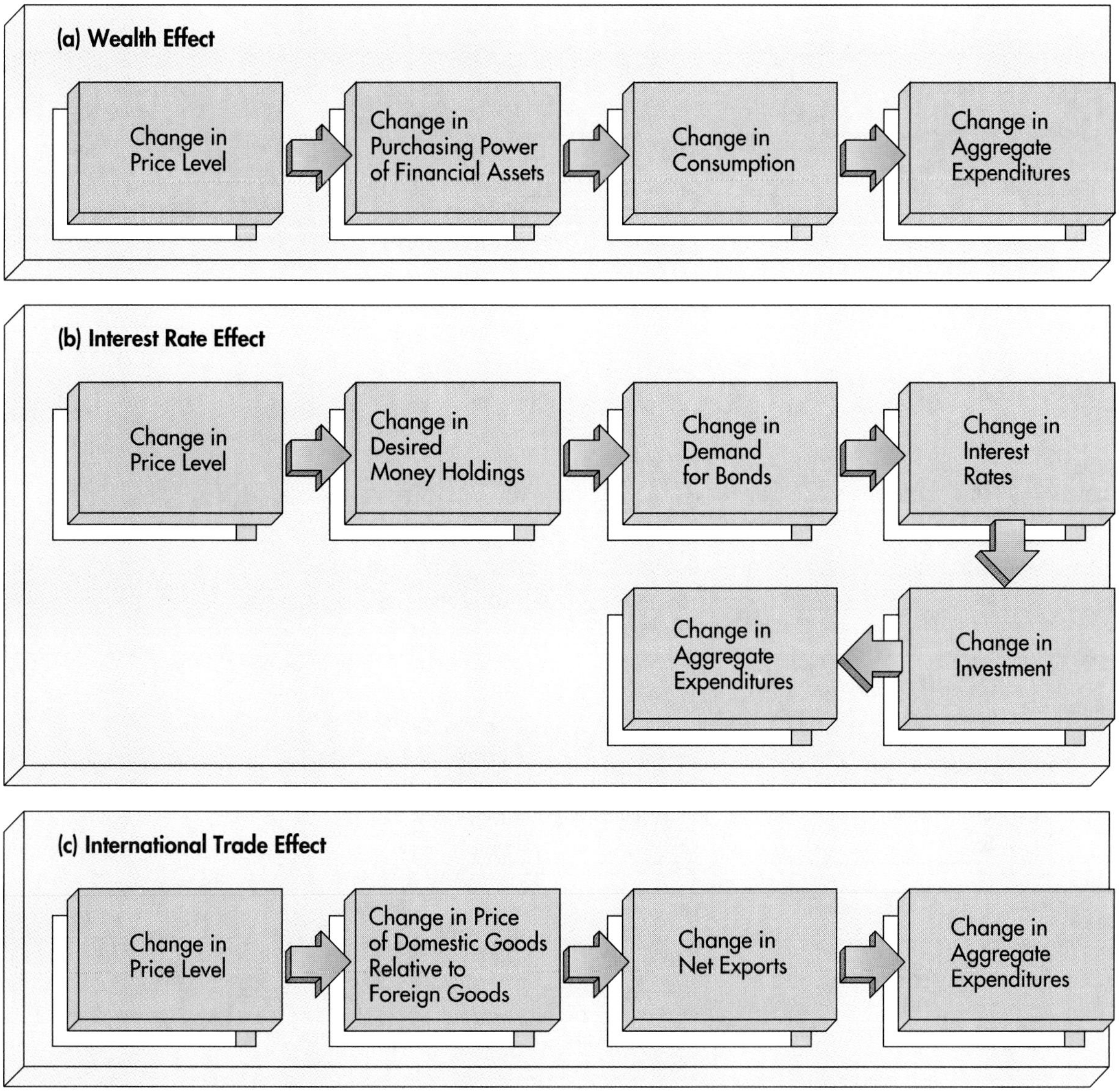

(a) Wealth Effect

Change in Price Level → Change in Purchasing Power of Financial Assets → Change in Consumption → Change in Aggregate Expenditures

(b) Interest Rate Effect

Change in Price Level → Change in Desired Money Holdings → Change in Demand for Bonds → Change in Interest Rates → Change in Investment → Change in Aggregate Expenditures

(c) International Trade Effect

Change in Price Level → Change in Price of Domestic Goods Relative to Foreign Goods → Change in Net Exports → Change in Aggregate Expenditures

costs associated with that project. When the profit outlook is good—say, a tax cut is on the horizon—investment and therefore aggregate demand increase. When profits are expected to fall, investment and aggregate demand decrease.

3.b.2. **Foreign Income and Price Levels**   When foreign income increases, so does foreign spending. Some of this increased spending is for goods produced in the domestic economy. As domestic exports increase, aggregate demand rises. Lower foreign income has just the opposite effect. As foreign

Figure 7
Nonprice Determinants: Changes in Aggregate Demand
(a) Expectations (b) Foreign Income and Price Levels (c) Government Policy

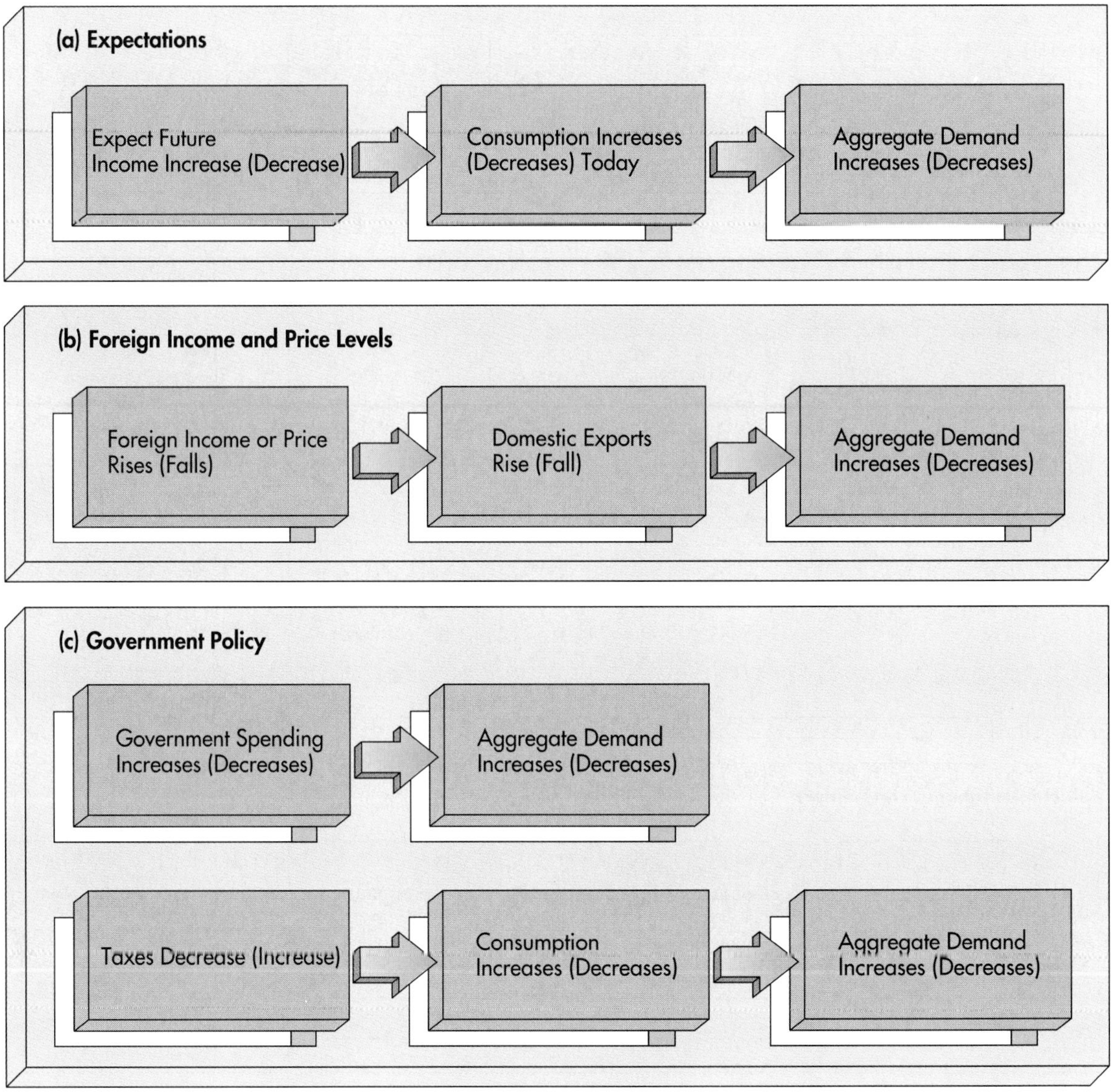

(a) Expectations

Expect Future Income Increase (Decrease) → Consumption Increases (Decreases) Today → Aggregate Demand Increases (Decreases)

(b) Foreign Income and Price Levels

Foreign Income or Price Rises (Falls) → Domestic Exports Rise (Fall) → Aggregate Demand Increases (Decreases)

(c) Government Policy

Government Spending Increases (Decreases) → Aggregate Demand Increases (Decreases)

Taxes Decrease (Increase) → Consumption Increases (Decreases) → Aggregate Demand Increases (Decreases)

Higher foreign income increases net exports and aggregate demand; lower foreign income reduces net exports and aggregate demand.

income falls, foreign spending falls, including foreign spending on the exports of the domestic economy. Lower foreign income, then, causes domestic net exports and domestic aggregate demand to fall.

If foreign prices rise in relation to domestic prices, domestic goods become less expensive relative to foreign goods, and domestic net exports increase. This means that aggregate demand rises, or the aggregate demand curve shifts up, as the level of foreign prices rises. Conversely, when the level

Figure 8
Shifting the Aggregate Demand Curve
As aggregate demand increases, the AD curve shifts to the right, like the shift from AD_0 to AD_1. At every price level, the quantity of output demanded increases. As aggregate demand falls, the AD curve shifts to the left, like the shift from AD_0 to AD_2. At every price level, the quantity of output demanded falls.

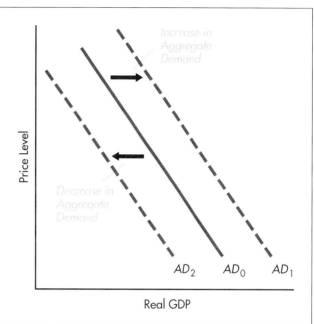

Change in the level of foreign prices changes domestic net exports and aggregate demand in the same direction.

of foreign prices falls, domestic goods become more expensive relative to foreign goods, causing domestic net exports and aggregate demand to fall.

Let's go back to the market for oranges. Suppose U.S. growers compete with Brazilian growers for the Japanese orange market. If the level of prices in Brazil rises while the level of prices in the United States remains stable, the price of Brazilian oranges to the Japanese buyer rises in relation to the price of U.S. oranges. What happens? U.S. exports of oranges to Japan should rise while Brazilian exports of oranges to Japan fall.[1]

3.b.3. Government Policy One of the goals of macroeconomic policy is to achieve economic growth without inflation. For GDP to increase, either AD or AS would have to change. Government economic policy can cause the aggregate demand curve to shift. An increase in government spending or a decrease in taxes will increase aggregate demand; a decrease in government spending or an increase in taxes will decrease aggregate demand. We devote an entire chapter on fiscal policy to an examination of the effect of taxes and government spending on aggregate demand. In another chapter, on monetary policy, we describe how changes in the money supply can cause the aggregate demand curve to shift.

RECAP

1. The aggregate demand curve shows the level of aggregate expenditures at different levels of price.

2. Aggregate expenditures are the sum of consumption, investment, government spending, and net exports.

---

[1]This assumes no change in exchange rates. We consider the link between price levels and exchange rates in the chapter "Macroeconomic Links Between Countries."

3. The wealth effect, the interest rate effect, and the international trade effect are three reasons why aggregate demand slopes down. These effects explain movements along a given *AD* curve.

4. The aggregate demand curve shifts with changes in the nonprice determinants of aggregate demand: expectations, foreign income and price levels, and government policy.

4. AGGREGATE SUPPLY

aggregate supply curve:
a curve that shows the amount of real GDP produced at different price levels

What factors affect aggregate supply?

The **aggregate supply curve** shows the quantity of real GDP produced at different price levels. The aggregate supply curve (*AS*) looks like the supply curve for an individual good, but, as with aggregate demand and the microeconomic demand curve, different factors are at work. The positive relationship between price and quantity supplied of an individual good is based on the price of that good changing in relation to the prices of all other goods. As the price of a single good rises relative to the prices of other goods, sellers are willing to offer more of the good for sale. With aggregate supply, on the other hand, we are analyzing how the amount of all goods and services produced changes as the level of prices changes. The direct relationship between prices and national output is explained by the effect of changing prices on profits, not by relative price changes.

4.a. Changes in Aggregate Quantity Supplied: Price-Level Effects

Along the aggregate supply curve, everything is held fixed except the price level and output. The price level is the price of output. The prices of resources, that is, the costs of production—wages, rent, and interest—are assumed to be constant, at least for a short time following a change in the price level.

If the price level rises while the costs of production remain fixed, business profits go up. As profits rise, firms are willing to produce more output. As the price level rises, then, the quantity of output firms are willing to supply increases. The result is the positively sloped aggregate supply curve shown in Figure 9.

As the price level rises from P_0 to P_1 in Figure 9, real GDP increases from $300 to $500. The higher the price level, the higher are profits, everything else held constant, and the greater is the quantity of output produced in the economy. Conversely, as the price level falls, the quantity of output produced falls.

4.b. Short-Run Versus Long-Run Aggregate Supply

The curve in Figure 9 is a *short-run* aggregate supply curve because the costs of production are held constant. Although production costs may not rise immediately when the price level rises, eventually they will. Labor will demand higher wages to compensate for the higher cost of living; suppliers will charge more for materials. The positive slope of the *AS* curve, then, is a short-run phenomenon. How short is the short run? It is the period of time over which production costs remain constant. (In the long run, all costs change or are variable.) For the economy as a whole, the short run can be months or, at most, a few years.

Figure 9
Aggregate Supply
The aggregate supply curve shows the amount of real GDP produced at different price levels. The AS curve slopes up, indicating that the higher the price level, the greater the quantity of output produced.

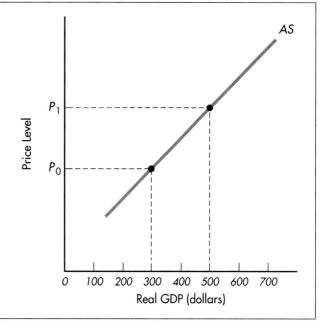

4.b.1. Short-Run Aggregate Supply Curve
Figure 9 represents the general shape of the short-run aggregate supply curve. In Figure 10 you see a more realistic version of the same curve—its steepness varies. The steepness of the aggregate supply curve depends on the ability and willingness of producers to respond to price-level changes in the short run. Figure 10 shows the typical shape of the short-run aggregate supply curve.

Notice that as the level of real GDP increases in Figure 10, the AS curve becomes steeper. This is because each increase in output requires firms to hire more and more resources, until eventually full capacity is reached in

Why does the short-run aggregate supply curve become steeper as real GDP increases?

Figure 10
The Shape of the Short-Run Aggregate Supply Curve
The upward-sloping aggregate supply curve occurs when the price level must rise to induce further increases in output. The curve gets steeper as real GDP increases, since the closer the economy comes to the capacity level of output, the less output will rise in response to higher prices as more and more firms reach their maximum level of output in the short run.

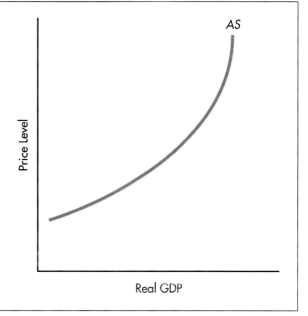

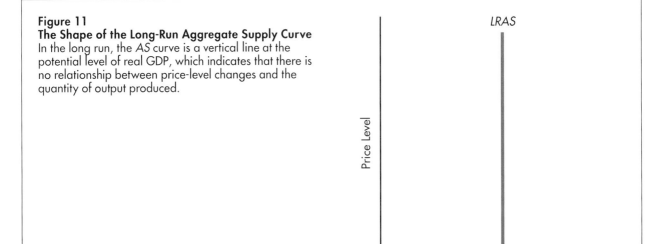

Figure 11
The Shape of the Long-Run Aggregate Supply Curve
In the long run, the *AS* curve is a vertical line at the potential level of real GDP, which indicates that there is no relationship between price-level changes and the quantity of output produced.

some areas of the economy, resources are fully employed, and some firms reach maximum output. At this point, increases in the price level bring about smaller and smaller increases in output from firms as a whole. The short-run aggregate supply curve becomes increasingly steep as the economy approaches maximum output.

4.b.2. Long-Run Aggregate Supply Curve Aggregate supply in the short run is different from aggregate supply in the long run (see Figure 11). That difference stems from the fact that quantities and costs of resources are not fixed in the long run. Over time, contracts expire and wages and other resource costs adjust to current conditions. The increased flexibility of

Technological advance shifts the aggregate supply curve outward and increases output. An example of a technological advance that has increased efficiency in banking is the automated teller machine (or ATM). The photo shows an ATM in Brazil that allows the bank to offer the public a lower-cost way to make withdrawals and deposits than dealing with a bank employee. Such innovations can be important determinants of aggregate supply.

Part II/Macroeconomic Basics

How Lack of Information in the Short Run Affects Wages in the Long Run

Workers do not have perfect information. In other words, they do not know everything that occurs. This lack of information includes information about the price level. If workers form incorrect expectations regarding the price level in the short run, they may be willing to work for a different wage in the short run than in the long run. For example, if workers thought that the inflation rate would be 3 percent over the next year, they would want a smaller wage raise than if they believed that the inflation rate would be 6 percent. If, in fact, they base their wage negotiations on 3 percent inflation and

accept a wage based on that inflation rate, but it turns out that the price level has increased by 6 percent, workers will then seek higher wages. In the long run, wages will reflect price-level changes.

If it cost nothing to obtain information, everyone who was interested would always know the current economic conditions. However, since there are costs of obtaining and understanding information about the economy, people will make mistakes in the short run. Both managers and employees make mistakes due to lack of information. Such mistakes are not due to stupidity but to ignorance—

ignorance of future as well as of current economic conditions. In the long run, mistakes about the price level are realized and wages adjust to the known price level.

We now have two reasons why wages will be more flexible in the long run than in the short run: long-term contracts and lack of information in the short run. The same arguments could be made for other resources as well. Because of these two reasons, the short-run aggregate supply curve is generally upward-sloping due to resource prices being relatively fixed in the short run.

resource costs in the long run has costs rising and falling with the price level and changes the shape of the aggregate supply curve. Lack of information about economic conditions in the short run also contributes to the inflexibility of resource prices as compared to the long run. The Economic Insight "How Lack of Information in the Short Run Affects Wages in the Long Run" shows why this is true for labor, as well as for other resources.

The **long-run aggregate supply curve** (*LRAS*) is viewed by most economists to be a vertical line at the potential level of real GDP or output (Y_p), as shown in Figure 11. Remember that the potential level of real GDP is the income level that is produced in the absence of any cyclical unemployment, or when the natural rate of unemployment exists. In the long run, wages and other resource costs fully adjust to price changes. The short-run *AS* curve slopes up because we assume that the costs of production, particularly wages, do not change to offset changing prices. In the short run, then, higher prices increase producers' profits and stimulate production. In the long run, because the costs of production adjust completely to the change in prices, neither profits nor production increase. What we find here are higher wages and other costs of production to match the higher level of prices.

long-run aggregate supply curve (*LRAS*):
a vertical line at the potential level of national income

Why is the long-run aggregate supply curve vertical?

4.c. Changes in Aggregate Supply: Nonprice Determinants

What causes the aggregate supply curve to shift?

The aggregate supply curve is drawn with everything but the price level and real GDP held constant. There are several things that can change and cause the aggregate supply curve to shift. The shift from AS_0 to AS_1 in Figure 12 represents an increase in aggregate supply. AS_1 lies to the right of AS_0, which means that at every price level, production is higher on AS_1 than on AS_0. The

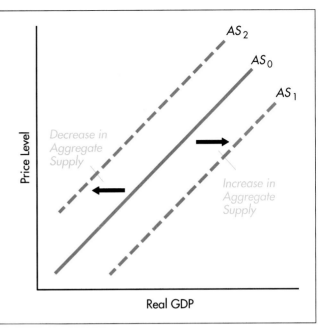

Figure 12
Changes in Aggregate Supply
The aggregate supply curve shifts with changes in resource prices, technology, and expectations. When aggregate supply increases, the curve shifts to the right, like the shift from AS_0 to AS_1, so that at every price level more is being produced. When aggregate supply falls, the curve shifts to the left, like the shift from AS_0 to AS_2, so that at every price level less is being produced.

The aggregate supply curve shifts in response to changes in the price of resources, in technology, and in expectations.

shift from AS_0 to AS_2 represents a decrease in aggregate supply. AS_2 lies to the left of AS_0, which means that at every price level, production along AS_2 is less than along AS_0. The nonprice determinants of aggregate supply are resource prices, technology, and expectations. Figure 13 summarizes the nonprice determinants of aggregate supply, discussed in detail next.

4.c.1. Resource Prices   When the price of output changes, the costs of production do not change immediately. At first, then, a change in profits induces a change in production. Costs eventually change in response to the change in prices and production, and when they do, the aggregate supply curve shifts. When the cost of resources—labor, capital goods, materials—falls, the aggregate supply curve shifts to the right, from AS_0 to AS_1 in Figure 12. This means firms are willing to produce more output at any given price level. When the cost of resources goes up, profits fall and the aggregate supply curve shifts to the left, from AS_0 to AS_2. Here, at any given level of price, firms produce less output.

Remember that the vertical axis of the aggregate supply graph plots the price level for all goods and services produced in the economy. Only those changes in resource prices that raise the costs of production across the economy have an impact on the aggregate supply curve. For example, oil is an important raw material. If a new source of oil is discovered, the price of oil falls and aggregate supply increases. However, if oil-exporting countries restrict oil supplies and the price of oil increases substantially, aggregate supply decreases, a situation that occurred when OPEC reduced the supply of oil in the 1970s (see the Economic Insight "OPEC and Aggregate Supply"). If the price of only one minor resource changed, then aggregate supply would be unlikely to change. For instance, if the price of land increased in Las Cruces, New Mexico, we would not expect the U.S. aggregate supply curve to be affected.

4.c.2. Technology   Technological innovations allow businesses to increase the productivity of their existing resources. As new technology is adopted,

Figure 13
Determinants of Aggregate Supply
(a) Resource Prices (b) Technology (c) Expectations

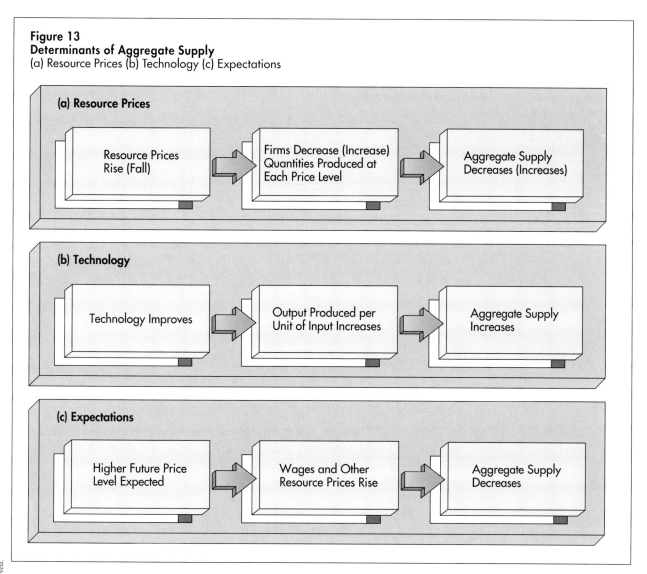

(a) Resource Prices

Resource Prices Rise (Fall) → Firms Decrease (Increase) Quantities Produced at Each Price Level → Aggregate Supply Decreases (Increases)

(b) Technology

Technology Improves → Output Produced per Unit of Input Increases → Aggregate Supply Increases

(c) Expectations

Higher Future Price Level Expected → Wages and Other Resource Prices Rise → Aggregate Supply Decreases

the amount of output that can be produced by each unit of input increases, moving the aggregate supply curve to the right. For example, personal computers and word-processing software have allowed secretaries to produce much more output in a day than typewriters allowed.

4.c.3. **Expectations** To understand how expectations can affect aggregate supply, consider the case of labor contracts. Manufacturing workers typically contract for a nominal wage based on what they and their employers expect the future level of prices to be. Because wages typically are set for at least a year, any unexpected increase in the price level during the year lowers real wages. Firms receive higher prices for their output, but the cost of labor stays the same. So profits and production go up.

If wages rise in anticipation of higher prices but prices do not go up, the cost of labor rises. Higher real wages caused by expectations of higher prices reduce current profits and production, moving the aggregate supply curve to the left. Other things being equal, anticipated higher prices cause aggregate supply to decrease; conversely, anticipated lower prices cause aggregate

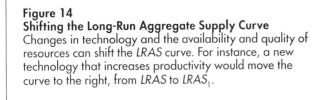

Figure 14
Shifting the Long-Run Aggregate Supply Curve
Changes in technology and the availability and quality of
resources can shift the *LRAS* curve. For instance, a new
technology that increases productivity would move the
curve to the right, from *LRAS* to *LRAS*₁.

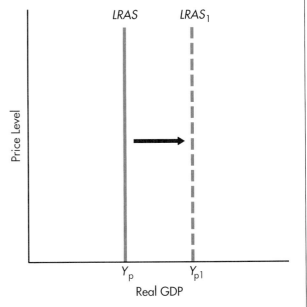

supply to increase. In this sense, expectations of price-level changes that shift
aggregate supply actually bring about price-level changes.

4.c.4. Economic Growth: Long-Run Aggregate Supply Shifts The vertical
long-run aggregate supply curve, as shown in Figure 11, does not mean that
the economy is forever fixed at the current level of potential real gross
domestic product. Over time, as new technologies are developed and the
quantity and quality of resources increase, potential output also increases,
shifting both the short- and long-run aggregate supply curves to the right.
Figure 14 shows long-run economic growth by the shift in the aggregate supply curve from *LRAS* to *LRAS*₁. The movement of the long-run aggregate
supply curve to the right reflects the increase in potential real GDP from Y_p
to Y_{p1}. Even though the price level has no effect on the level of output in the
long run, changes in the determinants of the supply of real output in the
economy do.

RECAP

1. The aggregate supply curve shows the quantity of output (real GDP) pro-
    duced at different price levels.
2. The aggregate supply curve slopes up because, everything else held
    constant, higher prices increase producers' profits, creating an incentive
    to increase output.
3. The aggregate supply curve shifts with changes in resource prices,
    technology, and expectations. These are nonprice determinants of
    aggregate supply.
4. The short-run aggregate supply curve is upward-sloping, showing that
    increases in production are accompanied by higher prices.

OPEC and Aggregate Supply

In 1973 and 1974, and again in 1979 and 1980, the Organization of Petroleum Exporting Countries (OPEC) reduced the supply of oil, driving the price of oil up dramatically. For example, the price of Saudi Arabian crude oil more than tripled between 1973 and 1974, and more than doubled between 1979 and 1980. Researchers estimate that the rapid jump in oil prices reduced output by 17 percent in Japan, by 7 percent in the United States, and by 1.9 percent in Germany.*

Oil is an important resource in many industries. When the price of oil increases due to restricted oil output, aggregate supply falls. You can see this in the graph. When the price of oil goes up, the aggregate supply curve falls from AS_1 to AS_2. When aggregate supply falls, the equilibrium level of real GDP (the intersection of the AS curve and the AD curve) falls from Y_1 to Y_2.

Higher oil prices due to restricted oil output would not only decrease short-run aggregate supply and current equilibrium real GDP, as shown in the figure, but

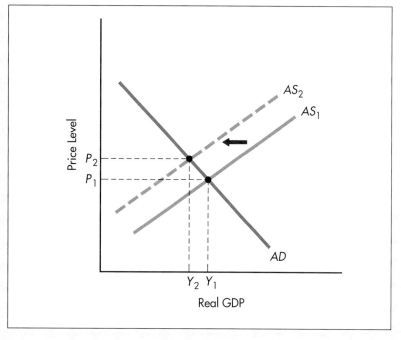

also potential equilibrium income at the natural rate of unemployment. Unless other factors change to contribute to economic growth, the higher resource (oil) price reduces the productive capacity of the economy.

*These estimates were taken from "Energy Price Shocks, Aggregate Supply, and Monetary Policy: The Theory and the International Evidence," Robert H. Rasche and John A. Tatom, in Karl Brunner and Allan H. Meltzer, eds., *Carnegie-Rochester Conference Series on Public Policy* 14 (Spring 1981): pp. 9–93.

5. The long-run aggregate supply curve is vertical at potential real GDP because, eventually, wages and the costs of other resources adjust fully to price-level changes.

5. AGGREGATE DEMAND AND SUPPLY EQUILIBRIUM

What determines the equilibrium price level and real GDP?

Now that we have defined the aggregate demand and aggregate supply curves separately, we can put them together to determine the equilibrium level of price and real GDP.

5.a. Short-Run Equilibrium

Figure 15 shows the level of equilibrium in a hypothetical economy. Initially the economy is in equilibrium at point 1, where AD_1 and AS_1 intersect. At

Figure 15
Aggregate Demand and Supply Equilibrium
The equilibrium level of price and real GDP is at the intersection of the AD and AS curves. Initially equilibrium occurs at point 1, where the AD_1 and AS_1 curves intersect. Here the price level is P_1 and real GDP is $500. If aggregate demand increases, moving from AD_1 to AD_2, in the short run there is a new equilibrium at point 2, where AD_2 intersects AS_1. The price level rises to P_2, and the equilibrium level of real GDP increases to $600. Over time, as the costs of wages and other resources rise in response to higher prices, aggregate supply falls, moving AS_1 to AS_2. Final equilibrium occurs at point 3, where the AS_2 curve intersects the AD_2 curve. The price level rises to P_3, but the equilibrium level of real GDP returns to its initial level, $500. In the long run, there is no relationship between prices and the equilibrium level of real GDP because the costs of resources adjust to changes in the level of prices.

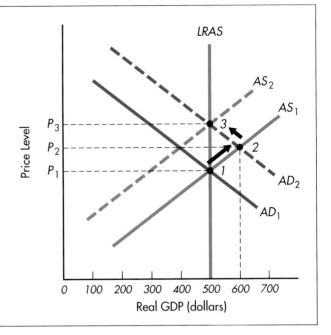

this point, the equilibrium price is P_1 and the equilibrium real GDP is $500. At price P_1, the amount of output demanded is equal to the amount supplied. Suppose aggregate demand increases from AD_1 to AD_2. In the short run, aggregate supply does not change, so the new equilibrium is at the intersection of the new aggregate demand curve, AD_2, and the same aggregate supply curve, AS_1, at point 2. The new equilibrium price is P_2, and the new equilibrium real GDP is $600. Note that in the short run, the equilibrium point on the short-run aggregate supply curve can lie to the right of the long-run aggregate supply curve (*LRAS*). This is because the *LRAS* represents the potential level of real GDP, not the capacity level. It is possible to produce more than the potential level of real GDP in the short run when the unemployment rate falls below the natural rate of unemployment.

5.b. Long-Run Equilibrium

Point 2 is not a permanent equilibrium because aggregate supply decreases to AS_2 once the costs of production rise in response to higher prices. Final equilibrium is at point 3, where the price level is P_3 and real GDP is $500. Notice that equilibrium here is the same as the initial equilibrium at point 1. Points 1 and 3 both lie along the long-run aggregate supply curve (*LRAS*). The initial shock to or change in the economy was an increase in aggregate demand. The change in aggregate expenditures initially led to higher output and higher prices. Over time, however, as resource costs rise and profit falls, output falls back to its original value.

We are not saying that the level of output never changes. The long-run aggregate supply curve shifts as technology changes and new supplies of resources are obtained. But the output change that results from a change in aggregate demand is a temporary, or short-run, phenomenon. The price level eventually adjusts, and output eventually returns to the potential level.

An increase in aggregate demand increases real GDP only temporarily.

RECAP

1. The equilibrium level of price and real GDP is at the point where the aggregate demand and aggregate supply curves intersect.

2. In the short run, a shift in aggregate demand establishes a temporary equilibrium along the short-run aggregate supply curve.

3. In the long run, the short-run aggregate supply curve shifts so that changes in aggregate demand only affect the price level, not the equilibrium level of output or real GDP.

SUMMARY

▲▼ *What factors affect aggregate demand?*

1. Aggregate demand is the relation between aggregate expenditures and the price level. §2

2. Aggregate demand is the sum of consumption, investment, government spending, and net exports at alternative price levels. §2.a, 2.b, 2.c, 2.d

3. Aggregate expenditures change with changes in the price level because of the wealth effect, the interest rate effect, and the international trade effect. These cause a movement along the *AD* curve. §3.a.1, 3.a.2, 3.a.3

▲▼ *What causes the aggregate demand curve to shift?*

4. The aggregate demand (*AD*) curve shows the level of expenditures for real GDP at different price levels. §3.a.4

5. Because expenditures and prices move in opposite directions, the *AD* curve is negatively sloped. §3.a.4

6. The nonprice determinants of aggregate demand include expectations, foreign income and price levels, and government policy. §3.b.1, 3.b.2, 3.b.3

▲▼ *What factors affect aggregate supply?*

7. The aggregate supply curve shows the quantity of real GDP produced at different price levels. §4

▲▼ *Why does the short-run aggregate supply curve become steeper as real GDP increases?*

8. As real GDP rises and the economy pushes closer to capacity output, the level of prices must rise to induce increased production. §4.b.1

▲▼ *Why is the long-run aggregate supply curve vertical?*

9. The long-run aggregate supply curve is a vertical line at the potential level of real GDP. The shape of the curve indicates that there is no effect of higher prices on output when an economy is producing at potential real GDP. §4.b.2

▲▼ *What causes the aggregate supply curve to shift?*

10. The nonprice determinants of aggregate supply are resource prices, technology, and expectations. §4.c.1, 4.c.2, 4.c.3

▲▼ *What determines the equilibrium price level and real GDP?*

11. The equilibrium level of price and real GDP is at the intersection of the aggregate demand and aggregate supply curves. §5.a

12. In the short run, a shift in aggregate demand establishes a new, but temporary, equilibrium along the short-run aggregate supply curve. §5.a

13. In the long run, the short-run aggregate supply curve shifts so that changes in aggregate demand determine the price level, not the equilibrium level of output or real GDP. §5.b

KEY TERMS

demand-pull inflation §1.a
cost-push inflation §1.b
wealth effect §3.a.1
interest rate effect §3.a.2

international trade effect §3.a.3
aggregate demand curve §3.a.4
aggregate supply curve §4
long-run aggregate supply curve (*LRAS*) §4.b.2

EXERCISES

1. How is the aggregate demand curve different from the demand curve for a single good, like hamburgers?

2. Why does the aggregate demand curve slope down? Give real-world examples of the three effects that explain the slope of the curve.

3. How does an increase in foreign income affect domestic aggregate expenditures and demand? Draw a diagram to illustrate your answer.

4. How does a decrease in foreign price levels affect domestic aggregate expenditures and demand? Draw a diagram to illustrate your answer.

5. How is the aggregate supply curve different from the supply curve for a single good, like pizza?

6. There are several determinants of aggregate supply that can cause the aggregate supply curve to shift.

    a. Describe those determinants and give an example of a change in each.

    b. Draw and label an aggregate supply diagram that illustrates the effect of the change in each determinant.

7. Draw a short-run aggregate supply curve that gets steeper as real GDP rises.

    a. Explain why the curve has this shape.

    b. Now draw a long-run aggregate supply curve that intersects a short-run *AS* curve. What is the relationship between short-run *AS* and long-run *AS?*

8. Draw and carefully label an aggregate demand and supply diagram with initial equilibrium at P_0 and Y_0.

    a. Using the diagram, explain what happens when aggregate demand falls.

    b. How is the short run different from the long run?

9. Draw an aggregate demand and supply diagram for Japan. In the diagram, show how each of the following affects aggregate demand and supply.

    a. U.S. gross domestic product falls.

    b. The level of prices in Korea falls.

    c. Labor receives a large wage increase.

    d. Economists predict higher prices next year.

10. If the long-run aggregate supply curve gives the level of potential real GDP, how can the short-run aggregate supply curve ever lie to the right of the long-run aggregate supply curve?

11. What will happen to the equilibrium price level and real GDP if:

    a. aggregate demand and aggregate supply both increase?

    b. aggregate demand increases and aggregate supply decreases?

    c. aggregate demand and aggregate supply both decrease?

    d. aggregate demand decreases and aggregate supply increases?

12. During the Great Depression, the U.S. economy experienced a falling price level and declining real GDP. Using an aggregate demand and aggregate supply diagram, illustrate and explain how this could occur.

13. Suppose aggregate demand increases, causing an increase in real GDP but no change in the price level. Using an aggregate demand and aggregate supply diagram, illustrate and explain how this could occur.

14. Suppose aggregate demand increases, causing an increase in the price level but no change in real GDP. Using an aggregate demand and aggregate supply diagram, illustrate and explain how this could occur.

15. Use an aggregate demand and aggregate supply diagram to illustrate and explain how each of the following will affect the equilibrium price level and real GDP:

    a. Consumers expect a recession.

    b. Foreign income rises.

    c. Foreign price levels fall.

    d. Government spending increases.

    e. Workers expect higher future inflation and negotiate higher wages now.

    f. Technological improvements increase productivity.

COOPERATIVE LEARNING EXERCISE

Divide the class into groups of three or four. Each group has ten minutes to make up a true-false question drawn from the material in this chapter. Call on two groups at a time. One group asks its *question aloud and the other group gives an answer. Then the groups switch roles. After each question, the class has an opportunity for discussion or clarifying questions.*

Confidence Down Now, Up for Future

Peggy Barnett hasn't done any big spending lately.

"I bought a used car about a year ago, but other than that, the most I've spent money on in the past few months has been clothes," said Barnett, as she worked at her part-time job in the Loop—handing out business cards promoting a dentist's office.

Roberta Tello, who was on her lunch break, said she and her husband, Tony, had planned to buy a house this fall but decided to wait.

"We've been trying to save enough for a down payment, but things are just tight right now. We're hoping we can do it," she said.

They are not alone.

According to survey results released Tuesday by the Conference Board, a lot of people are delaying making major purchases—such as homes, cars and appliances—as they wait to see how the economy is going to fare.

The business-research group's report found that for the third straight month, consumers were pretty negative about how they view the country's current economic situation. But they were more optimistic about long-term possibilities.

Consumer confidence in the current economic situation fell in September to 88.4 from a revised index reading of 90.4 in August, 91.3 in July and 92.5 in June.

For 25 years the group has been issuing monthly reports on consumer confidence. The reports are viewed by many in the financial sector as a harbinger of consumer spending patterns.

The survey attempts to guage consumer attitudes on two fronts— how they feel about the current economic situation and whether they expect things to get better, said Conference Board economist Fabian Linden.

"There's been some small increase in concern about the economy in general, but in the area of expectations, optimism is holding up quite well," said Linden.

There's much focus on consumer spending habits because their spending makes up two-thirds of the nation's gross domestic product.

The business-research group said its monthly survey of consumer confidence found that "on balance, optimists continue to outnumber pessimists."

"Although the confidence readings are down . . . the aggregate loss has been relatively moderate," said Linden. And he added, "Historically, when the index readings are between 80 and 90, we've inevitably had a fairly lively economy.

Linden said the Conference Board is not alarmed by the survey results. "In fact," he said, "we're optimistic about how the economy is moving."

Wall Street dismissed the report. It was more concerned with Tuesday's meeting of the Federal Reserve's policy-making committee, the result of which was the Fed left interest rates alone. The Dow Jones industrial average was up 13.80 to 3863.04.

And if other surveys are an indicator, it would seem that while people are putting off major purchases, they are still shopping.

A recent report released by Chicago-based Leo J. Shapiro & Associates found consumer optimism to be quite high—with most of those surveyed saying they planned to spend as much or more than they did last year this holiday season.

The company's president, George Rosenbaum, told *The Wall Street Journal* the survey found "the number of people who are trying to cut back this year is smaller than a year ago."

The Shapiro report was welcomed by the nation's retailers, who saw it as a sign that maybe the holiday season would give them something to cheer about. . . .

Recent signs pointed to a slowing of retail sales after several quarters of record growth—which would definitely be bad news as the all-important holiday season approaches.

While people can delay major purchases, they still have to shop for necessities—such as food and clothing. But it's where they are spending those dollars that has retailers concerned. . . .

Chicago Tribune/September 28, 1994

Commentary

Why would a business firm want to receive reports regarding consumer confidence in the U.S. economy? The answer lies in the role of expectations as a determinant of consumption spending and therefore aggregate demand. If households are confident that incomes will rise and prosperous times are ahead, they are much more likely to spend more than if they expect a recession. By monitoring consumer confidence in the economy, we can better understand consumer spending. Since consumption accounts for about two-thirds of GDP, changes in household spending can play a big role in business-cycle fluctuations.

In terms of aggregate demand and supply analysis, if households are more optimistic about the economy's performance, then the aggregate demand should shift to the right, like the shift from AD_0 to AD_1 in the accompanying figure. This would increase the equilibrium level of real GDP from Y_0 to Y_1. If households are less optimistic about the economy's performance, then the aggregate demand curve should shift to the left, like the shift from AD_0 to AD_2. This would decrease the equilibrium level of real GDP from Y_0 to Y_2.

Because of the implications of shifts in consumer confidence for business-cycle fluctuations, government officials, along with business people, watch the consumer confidence measures to maintain a sense of what is happening in the typical household. The two best-known surveys, the Michigan and Conference Board surveys, ask questions like: "Six months from now do you think business conditions will be better, the same, or worse?" "Would you say that you are better off or worse off financially than you were a year ago?" The answers to these questions and others are used as inputs in constructing an index of consumer confidence, so that the press typically only reports how the overall index changes rather than responses to any particular question.

Although the popular consumer confidence indexes fluctuate up and down every month, researchers have found that the monthly fluctuations are not very useful in predicting consumption or GDP. But major shifts in the indexes or several months of rising or falling indexes may provide an early signal to forthcoming changes in consumption and GDP.

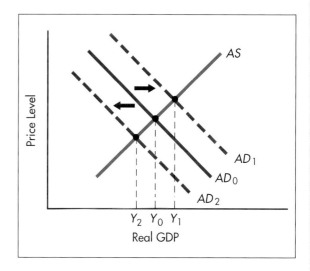

10

Aggregate Expenditures

FUNDAMENTAL QUESTIONS

1. How are consumption and saving related?
2. What are the determinants of consumption?
3. What are the determinants of investment?
4. What are the determinants of government spending?
5. What are the determinants of net exports?
6. What is the aggregate expenditures function?

To understand why real GDP, unemployment, and inflation rise and fall over time, we must know what causes the aggregate demand and aggregate supply curves to shift. We cannot understand why the U.S. economy has experienced ten recessions since 1945 or why the 1980s witnessed the longest peacetime business-cycle expansion in modern times unless we understand why the *AD* and *AS* curves shift. In this chapter, we examine in more detail the demand side of the economy.

Chapter 9 discussed how the price level affects aggregate expenditures through the interest rate, international trade, and wealth effects. This chapter examines in greater detail the nonprice determinants of spending and shifts in aggregate demand and assumes the price level is fixed. This assumption means the aggregate supply curve is a horizontal line at the fixed-price level. This approach was used by John Maynard Keynes, who analyzed the macro economy during the Great Depression. A fixed-price level, as shown in Figure 1, suggests a situation in which unemployment and excess capacity exist. Firms can hire from this pool of unemployed labor and increase their output at no extra cost and without any pressure on the price level. It is not surprising that Keynes would rely on such a model at a time when he was surrounded by mass unemployment. He was more interested in the determination of income and output than in the problem of inflation.

PREVIEW

With a horizontal *AS* curve, as shown in Figure 1, the location of the *AD* curve will determine the equilibrium level of real GDP, Y_e. If we understand what determines aggregate demand—consumption, investment, government spending, and net exports—we will understand what determines real GDP.

We begin our detailed examination of aggregate expenditures by discussing consumption, which accounts for approximately 66 percent of total expenditures in the U.S. economy. We then look at investment (15 percent of total expenditures), government spending (20 percent of total expenditures), and net exports (recently, a small negative percentage of total expenditures).

I. CONSUMPTION AND SAVING

▲

How are consumption and saving related?

Households can do three things with their income. They can spend it for the consumption of goods and services, they can save it, or they can pay taxes. Disposable income is what is left after taxes have been paid. It is the sum of consumption and saving:

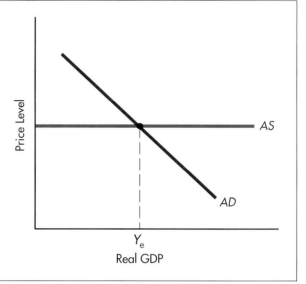

Figure 1
The Fixed-Price Keynesian Model
The Keynesian assumption that the price level is fixed requires a horizontal aggregate supply curve. In this case, aggregate demand will determine the equilibrium level of real GDP.

$$\text{Disposable income} = \text{consumption} + \text{saving}$$

or

$$Yd = C + S$$

Disposable income is the income that households actually have available for spending after taxes. Whatever disposable income is not spent is saved.

Why are we talking about saving, which is not a component of total spending, in a chapter that sets out to discuss the components of total spending? Saving is simply "not consuming"; it is impossible to separate the incentives to save from the incentives to consume.

1.a. Saving and Savings

Saving occurs over a unit of time; it is a flow concept.

Savings are an amount accumulated at a point in time; they are a stock concept.

Before we go on, it is necessary to understand the difference between *saving* and *savings*. *Saving* occurs over a unit of time—a week, a month, a year. For instance, you might save $10 a week or $40 a month. Saving is a *flow* concept. *Savings* are an amount accumulated at a particular point in time—today, December 31, your sixty-fifth birthday. For example, you might have savings of $2,500 on December 31. Savings are a *stock* concept.

Like saving, GDP and its components are flow concepts. They are measured by the year or quarter of the year. Consumption, investment, government spending, and net exports are also flows. Each of them is an amount spent over a period of time.

1.b. The Consumption and Saving Functions

consumption function:
the relationship between disposable income and consumption

The primary determinant of the level of consumption over any given period is the level of disposable income. The higher disposable income, the more households are willing and able to spend. This relationship between disposable income and consumption is called the **consumption function**. To focus on the relationship between income and consumption, we draw a graph, Figure 2, with income on the horizontal axis and consumption on the vertical axis. Figure 2(a) shows a hypothetical consumption function. In this econ-

Figure 2
Consumption and Saving in a Hypothetical Economy

Figure 2(a) shows that consumption is a positive function of disposable income: it goes up as disposable income rises. The line labeled $C = Yd$ forms a 45-degree angle at the origin. It shows all points where consumption equals disposable income. The point at which the consumption function (line C) crosses the 45-degree line—where disposable income measures $100—is the point at which consumption equals disposable income. At lower levels of disposable income, consumption is greater than disposable income; at higher levels, consumption is less than disposable income. Figure 2(b) shows the saving function. Saving equals disposable income minus consumption. When consumption equals disposable income, saving is 0. At higher levels of disposable income, we find positive saving; at lower levels, we find negative saving, or dissaving.

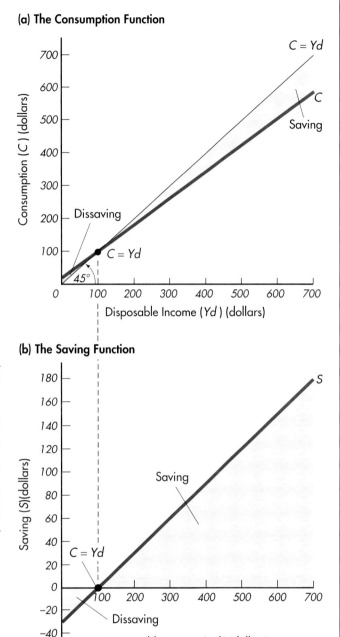

(a) The Consumption Function

(b) The Saving Function

(1) Disposable Income (Yd)	(2) Consumption (C)	(3) Saving (S)
$ 0	$ 30	$−30
100	100	0
200	170	30
300	240	60
400	310	90
500	380	120
600	450	150
700	520	180

omy, when disposable income is zero, consumption is $30. As disposable income rises, consumption rises. For instance, when disposable income is $100, consumption is $100.

We use C to represent consumption and Yd to represent disposable income. The line labeled C in Figure 2(a) is the consumption function: it represents the relationship between disposable income and consumption. The other line in the figure creates a 45-degree angle with either axis. (A 45-degree line makes a graph easier to read because every point on the line represents the

Consumption spending is the largest component of aggregate expenditures. Households in Grenada come to the produce market shown here to purchase food. Their expenditures on food will be counted in the consumption and GDP of Grenada. If the households decide to save less and spend more, then, other things being equal, the higher consumption will raise the GDP of Grenada.

same value on both axes.) In Figure 2(a), the 45-degree line shows all the points where consumption equals disposable income.

The level of disposable income at which all disposable income is being spent occurs at the point where the consumption function (line C) crosses the 45-degree line. In the graph, C equals Yd when disposable income is $100. Consumers save a fraction of any disposable income above $100. You can see this in the graph. Saving occurs at any level of disposable income at which the consumption function lies below the 45-degree line (at which consumption is less than disposable income). The amount of saving is measured by the vertical distance between the 45-degree line and the consumption function. If disposable income is $600, consumption is $450 and saving is $150.

saving function:
the relationship between disposable income and saving

The **saving function** is the relationship between disposable income and saving. Figure 2(b) plots the saving function (S). When the level of disposable income is at $100, consumption equals disposable income, so saving is zero. As disposable income increases beyond $100, saving goes up. In Figure 2(a), saving is the vertical distance between the 45-degree line and the consumption function. In Figure 2(b), we can read the level of saving directly from the saving function.

Notice that at relatively low levels of disposable income, consumption exceeds disposable income. How can consumption be greater than disposable income? When a household spends more than it earns in income, the household must finance the spending above income by borrowing or using savings. This is called **dissaving**. In Figure 2(a), dissaving occurs at levels of disposable income between 0 and $100, where the consumption function lies above the 45-degree line. Dissaving, like saving, is measured by the vertical distance between the 45-degree line and the consumption function, but dissaving occurs when the consumption function lies *above* the 45-degree line. In Figure 2(b), dissaving occurs where the saving function (line S) lies below

dissaving:
spending financed by borrowing or using savings

Part II/Macroeconomic Basics

the disposable income axis, at disposable income levels between zero and $100. For example, when disposable income is $0, dissaving (negative saving) is –$30.

Both the consumption function and the saving function have positive slopes: as disposable income rises, consumption and saving increase. Consumption and saving, then, are positive functions of disposable income. Notice that when disposable income equals zero, consumption is still positive.

There is a level of consumption, called **autonomous consumption**, that does not depend on income. (*Autonomous* here means "independent of income.") In Figure 2(a), consumption equals $30 when disposable income equals zero. This $30 is autonomous consumption; it does not depend on income but will vary with the nonincome determinants of consumption that will soon be introduced. The intercept of the consumption function (the value of *C* when *Yd* equals zero) measures the amount of autonomous consumption. The intercept in Figure 2(a) is $30, which means that autonomous consumption in this example is $30.

1.c. Marginal Propensity to Consume and Save

Total consumption equals autonomous consumption plus the spending that depends on income. As disposable income rises, consumption rises. This relationship between *change* in disposable income and *change* in consumption is the **marginal propensity to consume (*MPC*)**. The *MPC* measures change in consumption as a proportion of the change in disposable income:

$$MPC = \frac{\text{change in consumption}}{\text{change in disposable income}}$$

In Table 1, columns 1 and 2 list the consumption function data used in Figure 2. The marginal propensity to consume is shown in column 4. In our example, each time that disposable income changes by $100, consumption changes by $70. This means that consumers spend 70 percent of any extra income they receive.

TABLE 1
Marginal Propensity to Consume and Save

Disposable Income (Yd)	Consumption (C)	Saving (S)	Marginal Propensity to Consume (MPC)	Marginal Propensity to Save (MPS)
0	$ 30	–$30	—	—
$100	100	0	.70	.30
200	170	30	.70	.30
300	240	60	.70	.30
400	310	90	.70	.30
500	380	120	.70	.30
600	450	150	.70	.30
700	520	180	.70	.30

$$MPC = \frac{\$70}{\$100}$$

$$= .70$$

The *MPC* tells us how much consumption changes when income changes. The **marginal propensity to save (*MPS*)** defines the relationship between change in saving and change in disposable income. It is the change in saving divided by the change in disposable income:

marginal propensity to save (*MPS*):
change in saving as a proportion of the change in disposable income

$$MPS = \frac{\text{change in saving}}{\text{change in disposable income}}$$

The *MPS* in Table 1 is a constant 30 percent at all levels of income. Each time that disposable income changes by $100, saving changes by $30:

$$MPS = \frac{\$30}{\$100}$$

$$= .30$$

The *MPC* and the *MPS* will always be constant at all levels of disposable income in our examples.

Since disposable income will be either consumed or saved, the marginal propensity to consume plus the marginal propensity to save must total 1:

$$MPC + MPS = 1$$

The percentage of additional income that is not consumed must be saved. If consumers spend 70 percent of any extra income, they save 30 percent of that income.

The slope of the consumption function is the same as the MPC; the slope of the saving function is the same as the MPS.

The *MPC* and the *MPS* determine the rate of consumption and saving as disposable income changes. The *MPC* is the slope of the consumption function; the *MPS* is the slope of the saving function. Remember that the slope of a line measures change along the vertical axis that corresponds to change along the horizontal axis; the rise over the run (see the Appendix to Chapter 1). In the case of the consumption function, the slope is the change in consumption (the change on the vertical axis) divided by the change in disposable income (the change on the horizontal axis):

$$\text{Slope of consumption function} = \frac{\text{change in consumption}}{\text{change in disposable income}}$$

$$= MPC$$

The higher the *MPC*, the greater the fraction of any additional disposable income consumers will spend. At .70, consumers spend 70 percent of any change in disposable income; at an *MPC* of .85, consumers want to spend 85 percent of any change in disposable income. The size of the *MPC* shows up graphically as the steepness of the consumption function. The consumption function with an *MPC* of .85 is a steeper line than the one drawn in Figure 2(a). In general, the steeper the consumption function, the larger the *MPC*. If the *MPC* is less than .70, the consumption function would be flatter than the one in the figure.

The slope of the saving function is the *MPS:*

Figure 3
Marginal Propensity to Consume and Save
The *MPC* is the slope of the consumption function. The greater the *MPC*, the steeper the consumption function. The *MPS* is the slope of the saving function. The greater the *MPS*, the steeper the saving function. Because the sum of the *MPC* and the *MPS* is 1, the greater the *MPC*, the smaller the *MPS*. The steeper the consumption function, then, the flatter the saving function.

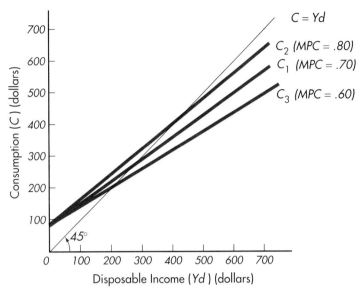

(a) Three Consumption Functions

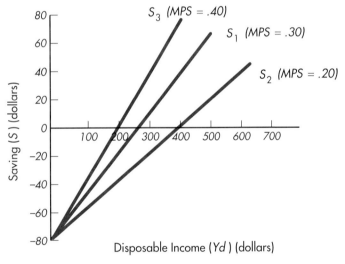

(b) Three Saving Functions

$$\text{Slope of saving function} = \frac{\text{change in saving}}{\text{change in disposable income}}$$

$$= MPS$$

In general, the steeper the saving function, the greater the slope and the greater the *MPS*.

Figure 3(a) shows three consumption functions. Since all three functions have the same intercept, autonomous consumption is the same for all. But each consumption function in Figure 3(a) has a different slope. C_1 has an

MPC of .70. A larger MPC, .80, produces a steeper function (line C_2). A smaller MPC, .60, produces a flatter function (line C_3). The saving functions that correspond to these consumption functions are shown in Figure 3(b). Function S_1, with an MPS of .30, corresponds to consumption function C_1, with an MPC of .70 (remember: $MPS = 1 - MPC$). Function S_2 corresponds to C_2, and S_3 corresponds to C_3. The higher the MPC (the steeper the consumption function), the lower the MPS (the flatter the saving function). If people spend a greater fraction of extra income, they save a smaller fraction.

1.d. Average Propensity to Consume and Save

Suppose our interest is not the proportion of change in disposable income that is consumed or saved, but the proportion of disposable income that is consumed or saved. For this we must know the average propensity to consume and the average propensity to save.

average propensity to consume (APC):
the proportion of disposable income spent for consumption

The **average propensity to consume (APC)** is the proportion of disposable income spent for consumption:

$$APC = \frac{\text{consumption}}{\text{disposable income}}$$

or

$$APC = \frac{C}{Yd}$$

average propensity to save (APS):
the proportion of disposable income saved

The **average propensity to save (APS)** is the proportion of disposable income that is saved:

$$APS = \frac{\text{saving}}{\text{disposable income}}$$

or

$$APS = \frac{S}{Yd}$$

Table 2 uses the consumption and saving data plotted in Figure 2. The APC and APS are shown in columns 4 and 5. When disposable income is

TABLE 2
Average Propensity to Consume and Save

Disposable Income (Yd)	Consumption (C)	Saving (S)	Average Propensity to Consume (APC)	Average Propensity to Save (APS)
0	$ 30	−$30	—	—
$100	100	0	1.00	0
200	170	30	.85	.15
300	240	60	.80	.20
400	310	90	.78	.22
500	380	120	.76	.24
600	450	150	.75	.25
700	520	180	.74	.26

$100, consumption is also $100, so the ratio of consumption to disposable income (*C/Yd*) equals 1 ($100/$100). At this point, saving equals 0, so the ratio of saving to disposable income (*S/Yd*) also equals 0 (0/$100). We really do not have to compute the *APS* because we already know the *APC*. There are only two things to do with disposable income: spend it or save it. The percentage of income spent plus the percentage saved must add up to 100 percent of disposable income. This means that

$$APC + APS = 1$$

If the *APC* equals 1, then the *APS* must equal 0.

When disposable income equals $600, consumption equals $450, so the *APC* equals .75 ($450/$600) and the *APS* equals .25 ($150/$600). As always, the *APC* plus the *APS* equals 1. If households are spending 75 percent of their disposable income, they must be saving 25 percent.

Notice in Table 2 how the *APC* falls as disposable income rises. This is because households spend just a part of any change in income. In Figure 2(a), the consumption function rises more slowly than the 45-degree line. (Remember that consumption equals disposable income along the 45-degree line.) The consumption function tells us, then, that consumption rises as disposable income rises, but not by as much as income rises. Because households spend a smaller fraction of disposable income as that income rises, they must be saving a larger fraction. You can see this in Table 2, where the *APS* rises as disposable income rises. At low levels of income, the *APS* is negative, a product of dissaving (we are dividing negative saving by disposable income). As disposable income rises, saving rises as a percentage of disposable income, which means that the *APS* is increasing.

1.e. Determinants of Consumption

What are the determinants of consumption?

Disposable income is an important determinant of household spending. But disposable income is not the only factor that influences consumption. Wealth, expectations, demographics, and taxation (taxation effects will be considered in Chapter 12) are other determinants of consumption.

1.e.1. Disposable Income
Household income is the primary determinant of consumption, which is why the consumption function is drawn with disposable income on the horizontal axis. Household income usually is measured as current disposable income. By *current* we mean income that is received in the current period—the current period could be today, this month, this year, whatever period we are discussing. Past income and future income certainly can affect household spending, but their effect is through household wealth or expectations, not income. Disposable income is after-tax income.

The two-dimensional graphs we have been using relate consumption only to current disposable income. A change in consumption caused by a change in disposable income is shown by *movement along* the consumption function. The effects of other variables are shown by *shifting* the intercept of the consumption function up and down as the values of these other variables change. All variables *except* disposable income change *autonomous* consumption.

Changes in taxes will affect disposable income. *If we assume that there are no taxes, then* Yd *equals* Y, *and consumption (and other expenditures) may be drawn as a function of real GDP rather than disposable income.* Chapter 12 is devoted to an analysis of government fiscal policy, including taxation. As a result, we put off our discussion of tax effects until then, which allows us to simplify our analysis of aggregate expenditures. The discussion of the components of aggregate expenditures in the remainder of this chapter and in later chapters will be related graphically to pretax real GDP rather than to disposable income.

wealth:
the value of all assets owned by a household

I.e.2. Wealth Wealth is the value of all the assets owned by a household. Wealth is a stock variable; it includes homes, cars, checking and savings accounts, and stocks and bonds, as well as the value of income expected in the future. As household wealth increases, households have more resources available for spending so consumption increases at every level of real GDP. You can see this in Figure 4(a) as a shift of the consumption function from C to C_1. The autonomous increase in consumption shifts the intercept of the

Figure 4
Autonomous Shifts in Consumption and Saving
Autonomous consumption is the amount of consumption that exists when income is 0. It is the intercept of the consumption function. The shift from C to C_1 is an autonomous increase in consumption of $40; it moves the intercept of the consumption function from $60 to $100. The shift from C to C_2 is an autonomous decrease in consumption of $40; it moves the intercept of the consumption function from $60 to $20. Autonomous saving is the amount of saving that exists when real GDP is 0. This is the intercept of the saving function. The shift from S to S_1 is an autonomous decrease in saving of $40; it moves the intercept of the saving function from $-$60 to $-$100. The shift from S to S_2 is an autonomous increase in saving of $40; it moves the intercept of the saving function from $-$60 to $-$20. Because disposable income minus consumption equals saving, an autonomous increase in consumption is associated with an autonomous decrease in saving, and an autonomous decrease in consumption is associated with an autonomous increase in saving.

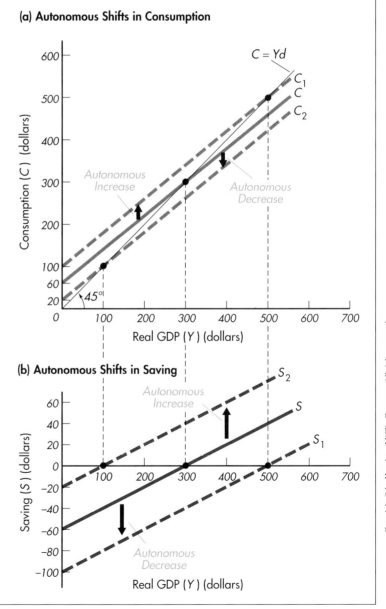

(a) Autonomous Shifts in Consumption

(b) Autonomous Shifts in Saving

consumption function from $60 to $100, so consumption increases by $40 at every level of real GDP. If households spend more of their current income as wealth increases, they save less. You can see this as the downward shift of the saving function in Figure 4(b), from S to S_1. The higher level of wealth has households more willing to dissave at each income level than before. Dissaving now occurs at any level of income below $500.

A decrease in wealth has just the opposite effect. For instance, during the 1990–1991 recession, property values declined in most areas of the United States. Household wealth declined as the value of real estate fell, and spending fell as a result. Here you would see an autonomous drop in consumption, like the shift from C to C_2, and an autonomous increase in saving, like the shift from S to S_2. Now at every level of real GDP, households spend $40 less than before and save $40 more. The intercept of the consumption function is $20, not $60, and the intercept of the saving function is $-$20$, not $-$60$. The new consumption function parallels the old one; the curves are the same vertical distance apart at every level of income. So consumption is $40 lower at every level of income. Similarly, the saving functions are parallel because saving is $40 greater at every level of real GDP along S_2 compared to S.

1.e.3. Expectations   Another important determinant of consumption is consumer expectations about future income, prices, and wealth. When consumers expect a recession, when they are worried about losing jobs or cutbacks in hours worked, they tend to spend less and save more. This means an autonomous decrease in consumption and increase in saving, like the shift from C to C_2 and S to S_2 in Figure 4. Conversely, when consumers are optimistic, we find an autonomous increase in consumption and decrease in saving, like the shift from C to C_1 and S to S_1 in Figure 4.

Expectations are subjective opinions; they are difficult to observe and measure. This creates problems for economists looking to analyze the effect of expectations on consumption. The University of Michigan Survey Research Center surveys households to construct its *Consumer Confidence Index*, a measure of consumer opinion regarding the outlook for the economy. Figure 5 plots this index over time. The shaded areas indicate periods of recession in the U.S. economy.

Notice that the index began to fall in mid-1978, foreshadowing the recession of 1980. And the index fell again just before the recessions in the early 1980s, then rose near the end of the recessions. In retrospect, it seems that consumers were predicting both the recessions and the expansions that followed them. But look at the index over the entire period shown in the figure. Notice the many ups and downs that were not followed by expansion or recession.

Clearly the Consumer Confidence Index is not always a reliable indicator of expansion or recession. Still economists' increasing use of this and other measures to better understand fluctuations in consumption underscores the importance of consumer expectations in the economy (see the Economic Insight "Permanent Income, Life Cycles, and Consumption").

1.e.4. Demographics   Other things being equal, economists expect the level of consumption to rise with increases in population. The focus here is on both the number of people in the economy and the composition of that population. The size of the population affects the position of the consumption function; the age of the population affects the slope of the consumption function. The greater the size of the population, other things equal, the higher the

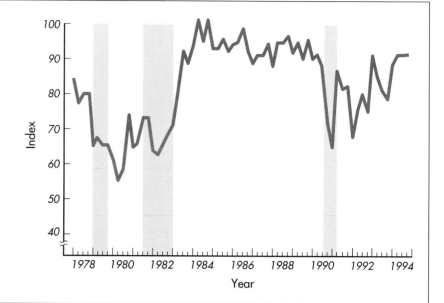

Figure 5
Consumer Confidence Index, 1978–1994
The University of Michigan Survey Research Center uses surveys to produce an index of consumer confidence in the economy. The index increases with consumers' optimism and decreases with their pessimism. The shaded areas represent recessions. These periods are marked by the low points of consumer confidence in the economy. Source: data are from University of Michigan Survey Research Center.

intercept of the consumption function. With regard to the effect of age composition on the economy, young households typically are accumulating durable consumer goods (refrigerators, washing machines, automobiles); they have higher *MPC*s than older households.

RECAP

1. It is impossible to separate the incentives to save from the incentives to consume.
2. Saving is a flow; savings is a stock.
3. Dissaving is spending financed by borrowing or using savings.
4. The marginal propensity to consume measures change in consumption as a proportion of change in disposable income.
5. The marginal propensity to save measures change in saving as a proportion of change in disposable income.
6. The *MPC* plus the *MPS* must equal 1.
7. Change in the *MPC* changes the slope of the consumption function; change in the *MPS* changes the slope of the saving function.
8. The average propensity to consume measures that portion of disposable income spent for consumption.
9. The average propensity to save measures that portion of disposable income saved.
10. The *APC* and the *APS* must equal 1.
11. The determinants of consumption include income, wealth, expectations, demographics, and taxation.
12. A change in consumption caused by a change in disposable income is shown by movement along the consumption function.

Permanent Income, Life Cycles, and Consumption

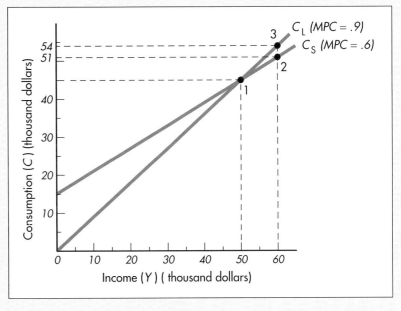

Studies of the consumption function over a long period of time find a function like the one labeled C_L in the graph. This function has a marginal propensity to consume of .90 and an intercept of 0. Consumption functions studied over a shorter period of time have lower *MPC*s and positive intercepts, like function C_S in the graph, with an *MPC* of .60. How do we reconcile these two functions?

Economists offer two related explanations for the difference between long-run and short-run consumption behavior: the permanent income hypothesis and the life-cycle hypothesis. The basic idea is that people consume based on their idea of what their long-run or permanent level of income is. A substantial increase in income this month does not affect consumption much in the short run unless it is perceived as a permanent increase.

Let's use point 1 on the graph as our starting point. Here disposable income is $50,000 and consumption is $45,000. Now suppose household income rises to $60,000. Initially consumption increases by 60 percent, the short-run *MPC*. The household moves from point 1 to point 2 along the short-run consumption function (C_S). The short-run consumption function has a lower *MPC* than the long-run consumption function because households do not completely adjust their spending and saving habits to short-run fluctuations in income. Once the household is convinced that $60,000 is a permanent level of income, it moves from point 2 to point 3 along the long-run consumption function. At point 3, con-

sumption has increased by 90 percent, the long-run *MPC*. In the long run, households adjust fully to changes in income; in the short run, a fluctuation in income does not cause as large a fluctuation in consumption.

When income falls below the permanent income level, the household is willing to dissave or borrow to support its normal level of consumption. When income rises above the permanent income level, the household saves at a higher rate than the long-run *MPS*. The lower *MPC* in the short run works to smooth out consumption in the long run. The household does not adjust current consumption to every up and down movement in household income.

To maintain a steady rate of consumption over time, households follow a pattern of saving over the life cycle. Saving is low

when current income is low relative to permanent income (during school years, periods of unemployment, or retirement). Saving is high when current income is high relative to the lifetime average, typically during middle age.

In the long run, households adjust fully to changes in income. In the short run, in order to smooth consumption over time, they do not. This explains both the difference between the long-run and short-run consumption functions and the stability of consumption over time.

13. Changes in wealth, expectations, or population change autonomous consumption, which is shown as a shift of the consumption function.

2. INVESTMENT

Investment is business spending on capital goods and inventories. It is the most variable component of total spending. In this section we look at the determinants of investment and see why investment changes so much over the business cycle.

2.a. Autonomous Investment

In order to simplify our analysis of real GDP in the next chapter, we assume that investment is autonomous, that it is independent of current real GDP. This does not mean that we assume investment is fixed at a constant amount. There are several factors that cause investment to change, but we assume that current real GDP is not one of them.

As a function of real GDP, autonomous investment is drawn as a horizontal line. This means that investment remains constant as real GDP changes. In Figure 6, the investment function (the horizontal line labeled I) indicates that investment equals $50 at every level of real GDP. As the determinants of investment change, the investment function shifts autonomously. As investment increases, the function shifts upward (for example, from I to I_1); as investment decreases, the function shifts downward (from I to I_2).

2.b. Determinants of Investment

What are the determinants of investment?

Investment is business spending on capital goods and inventories. Capital goods are the buildings and equipment businesses need to produce their products. Inventories are final goods that have not been sold. Inventories can be planned or unplanned. For example, in the fall a retail department store wants to have enough sizes and styles of the new clothing lines to attract customers. Without a good-sized inventory, sales will suffer. The goods it buys are *planned* inventory, based on expected sales. But come February, the store

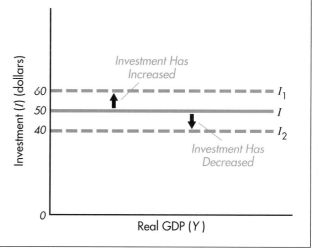

Figure 6
Investment as a Function of Income
Investment is assumed to be autonomous. Because it is independent of current real GDP, it is drawn as a horizontal line. An autonomous increase in investment shifts the function upward, from I to I_1. An increase could be the product of lower interest rates, optimism in business about future sales and revenues, technological change, an investment tax credit that lowers the cost of capital goods, or a need to expand capacity because of a lack of available productive resources. An autonomous decrease in investment moves the function down, from I to I_2. The same factors that cause investment to rise can also cause it to fall as they move in the opposite direction.

wants to have as few fall clothes left unsold as possible. Goods not sold at this stage are *unplanned* inventory. They are a sign that sales were not as good as expected and that too much was produced last year.

Both types of inventories—planned and unplanned—are called investment. But only planned investment—capital purchases plus planned inventories—combine with planned consumer, government, and foreign-sector spending to determine the equilibrium level of aggregate expenditures, as we will see in the next chapter. Unplanned investment and unwanted inventories do not affect the equilibrium. They are simply the leftovers of what has recently gone on in the economy. What economists are interested in are the determinants of planned investment.

2.b.1. The Interest Rate   Business investment is made in the hopes of earning profits. The greater the expected profit, the greater is investment. A primary determinant of whether or not an investment opportunity will be profitable is the rate of interest. The interest rate is the cost of borrowed funds. Much of business spending is financed by borrowing. As the rate of interest goes up, fewer investment projects offer enough profit to warrant their undertaking. In other words, the higher the interest rate, the lower the rate of investment. As the interest rate falls, opportunities for greater profits increase and investment rises.

Let's look at a simple example. A firm can acquire a machine for $100 that will yield $120 in output. Whether or not the firm is willing to undertake the investment depends on whether it will earn a sufficient return on its investment. The return from an investment is the profit from an investment divided by its cost.

If the firm has to borrow $100 for the investment, it will have to pay interest to the lender. Suppose the lender charges 10 percent interest. The firm will have to pay 10 percent of $100, or $10 interest. This raises the cost of the investment to $110, the $100 cost of the machine plus the $10 interest. The firm's return from the investment is 9 percent:

$$\text{Return on investment} = \frac{(\$120 - \$110)}{\$110}$$

$$= .09$$

As the interest rate rises, the firm's cost of borrowing also rises and the return on investment falls. When the interest rate is 20 percent, the firm must pay $20 in interest, so the total cost of the investment is $120. Here the return is 0 ([$120 − $120]/$120). The higher interest rate reduces the return on the investment and discourages investment spending.

As the interest rate falls, the firm's cost of borrowing falls and the return from the investment rises. If the interest rate is 5 percent, the firm must pay $5 in interest. The total cost of the investment is $105, and the return is 14 percent ([$120 − $105]/$105). The lower interest rate increases the return from the investment and encourages investment spending.

2.b.2. Profit Expectations   Firms undertake investment in the expectation of earning a profit. Obviously, they cannot know exactly how much profit they will earn. So they use forecasts of revenues and costs to decide on an appropriate level of investment. It is their *expected* rate of return that actually determines their level of investment.

Many factors affect expectations of profit and, therefore, change the level of investment. Among them are new firms entering the market; political change; new laws, taxes, or subsidies from government; and the overall economic health of the country or world as measured by gross domestic product.

2.b.3. Other Determinants of Investment

Everything that might affect a firm's expected rate of return determines its level of investment. But three factors—technological change, the cost of capital goods, and capacity utilization—warrant special attention.

Technological Change   Technological change is often a driving force behind new investment. New products or processes can be crucial to remaining competitive in an industry. The computer industry, for example, is driven by technological change. As faster and larger-capacity memory chips are developed, computer manufacturers must utilize them in order to stay competitive.

The impact of technology on investment spending is not new. For example, the invention of the cotton gin stimulated investment spending in the early 1800s, and the introduction of the gasoline-powered tractor in 1905 created an agricultural investment boom in the early 1900s. More recently, the development of integrated circuits stimulated investment spending in the electronics industry.

One measure of the importance of technology is commitment to research and development. Data on spending for research and development across U.S. industries and across countries are listed in Table 3. The industries listed in the table are those that rely on innovation and the development of new technologies to remain competitive. Research and development is a multi-billion-dollar commitment for these industries. The data on the four industrial countries indicate that these countries spend roughly the same percentage of GDP on research and development. The most obvious trend is the increase in Japanese spending since the mid-1960s. As Japan has grown to be an industrial giant, the role of technological innovation has become increasingly important there.

Technological progress results from research and development efforts. The photo illustrates the ongoing efforts in the athletic shoe industry to provide technological advances in shoe design through research. In this case, electrodes and reflectors are attached to a subject's leg and foot to allow Reebok researchers to closely monitor the effects of shoe design on running performance. In the event of a major modification of shoe design, competitors would adapt their designs to compete with the innovator. In this manner, research and development expenditures may stimulate investment spending throughout an industry or economy.

244

A commitment to research and development is a sign of the technological progress that marks the industrial nation. The countries listed in Table 3, along with other industrial nations, are the countries where new technology generally originates. New technology developed in any country tends to stimulate investment spending across all nations as firms in similar industries are forced to adopt new production methods to keep up with their competition.

Cost of Capital Goods The cost of capital goods also affects investment spending. As capital goods become more expensive, the rate of return from investment in them drops and the amount of investment falls. One factor that can cause the cost of capital goods to change sharply is government tax policy. The U.S. government has imposed and then removed investment tax credits several times in the past. These credits allow firms to deduct part of the cost of investment from their tax bill. When the cost of investment drops, investment increases. When the cost of investment increases, the level of investment falls.

Capacity Utilization If its existing capital stock is being used heavily, a firm has an incentive to buy more. But if much of its capital stock stands idle,

TABLE 3
Research and Development Expenditures

In Selected U.S. Industries, 1991

Industry	Expenditures (millions of dollars)	Expenditures as Percentage of Sales	Number of Researchers
Aircraft and Missiles	21,692	14.3	116,700
Electrical Equipment	17,279	6.6	141,200
Chemicals and Allied Products	13,183	5.7	80,500

As a Percentage of GDP, Selected Years, 1965–1991

Year	United States	France	Germany	Japan
1965	2.8	2.0	1.7	1.5
1968	2.8	2.1	2.0	1.6
1971	2.4	1.9	2.2	1.9
1974	2.2	1.8	2.1	2.0
1977	2.2	1.8	2.1	1.9
1980	2.3	1.8	2.4	2.2
1983	2.6	2.2	2.5	2.6
1985	2.8	2.3	2.7	2.9
1986	2.7	2.3	2.7	2.8
1987	2.6	2.3	2.8	2.8
1988	2.8	2.3	2.8	2.9
1989	2.7	2.3	2.9	3.0
1990	2.7	2.4	2.7	3.1
1991	2.7	2.4	2.8	3.0

Source: U.S. Bureau of the Census, *Statistical Abstract of the United States, 1994* (Washington, D.C.: U.S. Government Printing Office, 1994).

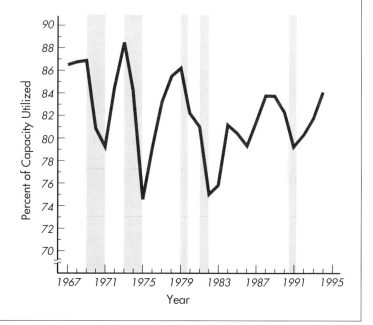

Figure 7
Capacity Utilization Rates for Total U.S. Industry, 1967–1991
The Federal Reserve estimates the rate at which capacity is utilized in U.S. industry. The higher the rate, the greater the pressure for investment to expand productive capacity.

the firm has little incentive to increase that stock. Economists sometimes refer to the productive capacity of the economy as the amount of output that can be produced by businesses. In fact the Federal Reserve constructs a measure of capacity utilization that indicates how close the economy is to capacity output.

Figure 7 plots the rate of capacity utilization in the U.S. economy over the 1967–1994 period. During this time, U.S. industry operated at a high rate of 88.4 percent of capacity in 1973 and at a low rate of 74.6 percent of capacity in the recession year of 1975. We never expect to see 100 percent of capacity utilized for the same reasons that we never expect zero unemployment. There are always capital goods that are temporarily unused, as in the case of frictional unemployment of labor, and there are always capital goods that are obsolete because of technological change, similar to the case of structural unemployment of labor.

When the economy is utilizing its capacity at a high rate, there is pressure to increase the production of capital goods and expand productive capacity. When capacity utilization is low—when factories and machines sit idle—investment tends to fall.

2.c. Volatility

We said that investment is the most variable component of total spending. What role do the determinants of investment play in that volatility?

Figure 8 graphs interest rates on Treasury bills in several industrial countries. Notice that the rates fluctuate widely. They are much more variable than income. Interest rates are a very important determinant of investment. Clearly the fact that they are so variable contributes to the variability of investment.

Expectations are subjective judgments about the future. Expectations can and often do change suddenly with new information. A rumor of a technolog-

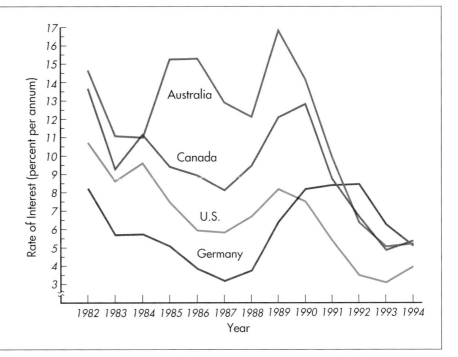

Figure 8
Interest Rates on Treasury Bills, 1982–1994
Treasury bills are government debt. The interest rates on this kind of debt in Australia, Canada, Germany, and the United States over time illustrate how interest rates vary. The variability of interest rates is one reason for the variability of investment. Source: data from International Monetary Fund, *International Financial Statistics*, Washington, D.C., various issues.

ical breakthrough, a speech by the president or a powerful member of Congress, even a revised weather forecast can cause firms to reexamine their thinking about the expected profitability of an investment. In developing economies, the protection of private property rights can have a large impact on investment spending. If a business expects a change in government policy to increase the likelihood of the government's expropriating its property, obviously it is not going to undertake new investments. Conversely, if a firm believes that the government will protect private property and encourage the accumulation of wealth, it will increase its investment spending. The fact that expectations are subject to large and frequent swings contributes to the volatility of investment.

Technological change proceeds very unevenly, making it difficult to forecast. Historically we find large increases in investment when a new technology is first developed and decreases in investment after the new technology is in place. This causes investment to move up and down unevenly through time.

Changes in tax policy occur infrequently, but they can create large incentives to invest or not to invest. U.S. tax laws have swung back and forth on whether or not to offer an investment tax credit. A credit was first introduced in 1962. It was repealed in 1969, then readopted in 1971, and later revised in 1975, 1976, and 1981. In 1986, the investment tax credit was repealed again. Each of these changes had an impact on the cost of capital goods and contributed to the volatility of investment.

Finally, investment generally rises and falls with the rate of capacity utilization over the business cycle. As capacity utilization rises, some firms must add more factories and machines in order to continue increasing output and avoid reaching their maximum output level. As capacity utilization fluctuates, so will investment.

RECAP

1. As a function of real GDP, autonomous investment is drawn as a horizontal line.

2. The primary determinants of investment are the interest rate and profit expectations. Technological change, the cost of capital goods, and the rate of capacity utilization have an enormous impact on those expectations.

3. Investment fluctuates widely over the business cycle because the determinants of investment are so variable.

3. GOVERNMENT SPENDING

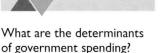

What are the determinants of government spending?

Government spending on goods and services is the second largest component of aggregate expenditures in the United States. In later chapters we examine the behavior of government in detail. Here we focus on how the government sector fits into the aggregate expenditures–income relationship. We assume that government spending is set by government authorities at whatever level they choose, independent of current income. In other words, we assume that government spending, like investment, is autonomous.

Figure 9 depicts government expenditures as a function of real GDP. The function, labeled G, is a horizontal line. If government officials increase government expenditures, the function shifts upward, parallel to the original curve by an amount equal to the increase in expenditures (for example, from G to G_1). If government expenditures are reduced, the function shifts downward by an amount equal to the drop in expenditures (for example, from G to G_2).

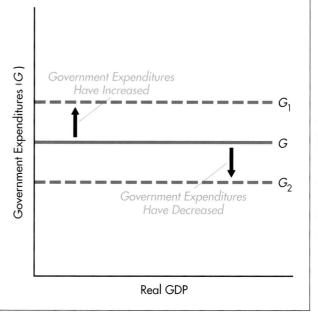

Figure 9
Government Expenditures as a Function of Real GDP
Government spending is assumed to be autonomous and set by government policy. The government spending function is the horizontal line labeled G. Autonomous increases in government spending move the function upward (for example, from G to G_1); decreases move the function downward (for example, from G to G_2).

Part II/Macroeconomic Basics

4. NET EXPORTS

What are the determinants of net exports?

The last component of aggregate expenditures is net exports, spending in the international sector. Net exports equal a country's exports of goods and services (what it sells to the rest of the world) minus its imports of goods and services (what it buys from the rest of the world). When net exports are positive, there is a surplus on the merchandise and services accounts. When net exports are negative, there is a deficit. The United States has had a net exports deficit since 1975. This is a relatively new phenomenon: the country had run surpluses throughout the post–World War II era.

4.a. Exports

We assume that exports are autonomous. There are many factors that determine the actual value of exports, among them foreign income, tastes, prices, government trade restrictions, and exchange rates. But we assume that exports are not affected by current domestic income. You see this in the second column of Table 4, where exports are $50 at each level of real GDP.

As foreign income increases, foreign consumption rises—including consumption of goods produced in other countries—so domestic exports increase at every level of domestic real GDP. Decreases in foreign income lower domestic exports at every level of domestic real GDP. Similarly, changes in tastes or government restrictions on international trade or exchange rates can cause the level of exports to shift autonomously. When tastes favor domestic goods, exports go up. When tastes change, exports go down. When foreign governments impose restrictions on international trade, domestic exports fall. When restrictions are lowered, exports rise. Finally, as discussed in Chapter 7, when the domestic currency depreciates on the foreign exchange market (making domestic goods cheaper in foreign countries), exports rise. When the domestic currency appreciates on the foreign exchange market (making domestic goods more expensive in foreign countries), exports fall.

4.b. Imports

Domestic purchases from the rest of the world (imports) are also determined by tastes, trade restrictions, and exchange rates. Here domestic income plays a role too. The greater domestic real GDP, the greater domestic imports. The

TABLE 4
Hypothetical Export and Import Schedule

Real GDP	Exports	Imports	Net Exports
0	$50	$ 0	$50
$100	50	10	40
200	50	20	30
300	50	30	20
400	50	40	10
500	50	50	0
600	50	60	− 10
700	50	70	− 20

import data in Table 4 show imports increasing with real GDP. When real GDP is 0, autonomous imports equal $0. As real GDP increases, imports increase.

We measure the sensitivity of changes in imports to changes in real GDP by the marginal propensity to import. The **marginal propensity to import** (***MPI***) is the proportion of any extra income spent on imports.

marginal propensity to import (*MPI*):
change in imports as a proportion of change in income

$$MPI = \frac{\text{change in imports}}{\text{change in income}}$$

In Table 4, the *MPI* is .10, or 10 percent. Every time income changes by $100, imports change by $10.

How do other factors—tastes, government trade restrictions, and exchange rates—affect imports? When domestic tastes favor foreign goods, imports rise. When they do not, imports fall. When the domestic government tightens restrictions on international trade, domestic imports fall. When those restrictions are loosened, imports rise. Finally, when the domestic currency depreciates on the foreign exchange market (making foreign goods more expensive to domestic residents), imports fall. And when the domestic currency appreciates on the foreign exchange market (lowering the price of foreign goods), imports rise.

4.c. The Net Export Function

The higher domestic income, the lower net exports.

In our hypothetical economy in Table 4, net exports are listed in the last column. They are the difference between exports and imports. Because imports rise with domestic income, the higher that income, the lower net exports.

The net exports function, labeled *X*, is shown in Figure 10. The downward slope of the function (given by the *MPI*) indicates that net exports fall as real GDP increases. Net exports are the only component of aggregate expenditures that can take on a negative value (saving can be negative, but it is not part of spending). Negative net exports mean that the domestic economy is importing more than it exports. The net exports function shifts with changes in foreign income, prices, tastes, government trade restrictions, and exchange rates. For example, as foreign income increases, domestic exports increase and the net exports function shifts upward.

Recent levels of net exports in the United States are shown in Figure 11. Total U.S. net exports were negative over the years plotted. The figure also shows the net exports of the United States with Canada, Japan, and Western Europe. Clearly the U.S. trade deficit with Japan was a dominant factor in the size of the overall trade deficit.

RECAP

1. Net exports equal a country's exports minus its imports.

2. Exports are determined by foreign income, tastes, government trade restrictions, and exchange rates; they are independent of domestic real GDP.

3. Imports are a positive function of domestic real GDP; they also depend on tastes, domestic government trade restrictions, and exchange rates.

4. The marginal propensity to import measures change in imports as a proportion of the change in domestic income.

5. Net exports fall as domestic real GDP rises.

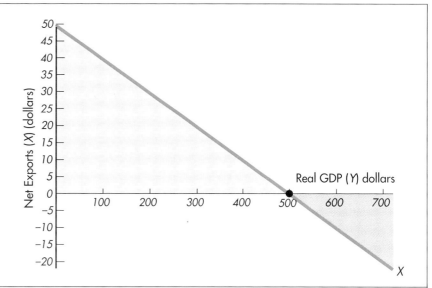

Figure 10
Net Exports as a Function of Real GDP
The net exports function is the downward-sloping line labeled *X*. Because exports are autonomous and imports increase with income, net exports fall as domestic real GDP rises. Notice that net exports can be positive or negative.

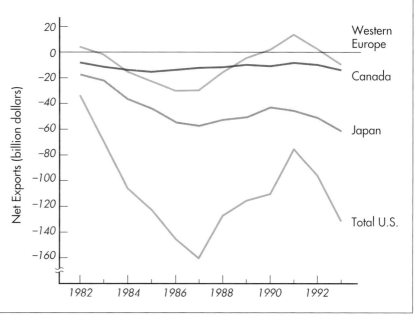

Figure 11
Total U.S. Net Exports and Net Exports with Canada, Japan, and Western Europe, 1985–1993
Total U.S. net exports were negative over the years in the figure, in large part a product of negative net exports with Japan. Net exports with Western European countries were positive in the early 1980s, then turned negative until 1990. Net exports with Canada remained relatively stable over the period. Source: Data from *Economic Report of the President, 1994* (Washington, D.C.: U.S. Government Printing Office, 1994), p. 397.

5. THE AGGREGATE EXPENDITURES FUNCTION

What is the aggregate expenditures function?

The aggregate, or total, expenditures function is the sum of the individual functions for each component of planned spending. Aggregate expenditures (*AE*) equal consumption (*C*), plus investment (*I*), plus government spending (*G*), plus net exports (*X*):

$$AE = C + I + G + X$$

5.a. Aggregate Expenditures Table and Function

The table in Figure 12 lists aggregate expenditures data for a hypothetical economy. Real GDP is in the first column; the individual components of aggregate expenditures are in columns 2 through 5. Aggregate expenditures, listed in column 6, is the sum of the components at each level of income.

The aggregate expenditures function (*AE*) can be derived graphically by summing the individual expenditure functions (Figure 12) in a vertical direction. We begin with the consumption function (*C*) and then add autonomous investment, $50, to the consumption function at every level of income to arrive at the *C + I* function. To this we add constant government spending, $70, at every level of income to find the *C + I + G* function. Finally, we add the net exports function to find *C + I + G + X*, or the *AE* function.

Notice that the *C, C + I,* and *C + I + G* functions are all parallel. They all have the same slope, that determined by the *MPC*. This is because *I* and *G* are autonomous. The *AE* function has a smaller slope than the other functions because the slope of the net exports function is negative. By adding the *X* function to the *C + I + G* function, we are decreasing the slope of the *AE* function; the *C + I + G + X* function has a smaller, flatter slope than the *C + I + G* function.

The *X* function increases spending for levels of real GDP below $500 and decreases spending for levels of real GDP above $500. At $500, net exports equal 0 (see column 5). Because domestic imports increase as domestic income increases, net exports fall as income rises. At incomes above $500, net exports are negative, so aggregate expenditures are less than *C + I + G*.

5.b. The Next Step

Though we have also been using "aggregate demand" to refer to total spending, you can see from Figure 12 that the aggregate expenditures line slopes up while the aggregate demand curve you saw in Figure 1 slopes down. In the next chapter we will explore the formal relationship between these two related concepts, when we go about determining the equilibrium level of real GDP using the *AE* function.

The concept of macroeconomic equilibrium points out the key role aggregate expenditures play in determining output and income. As you will see, the equilibrium level of real GDP is that level toward which the economy automatically tends to move. Once that equilibrium is established, there is no tendency for real GDP to change unless a change in autonomous expenditures occurs. If aggregate expenditures rise, then the equilibrium level of real GDP rises. If aggregate expenditures fall, then the equilibrium level of real GDP falls. Such shifts in the *AE* function are associated with shifts in *C, I, G,* or *X*.

RECAP

1. Aggregate expenditures are the sum of planned consumption, planned investment, planned government spending, and planned net exports at every level of real GDP.

2. Assuming that *I* and *G* are autonomous, the *C, C + I,* and *C + I + G* functions are parallel lines.

3. Net exports increase aggregate expenditures at relatively low levels of domestic real GDP and decrease aggregate expenditures at relatively high levels of domestic real GDP.

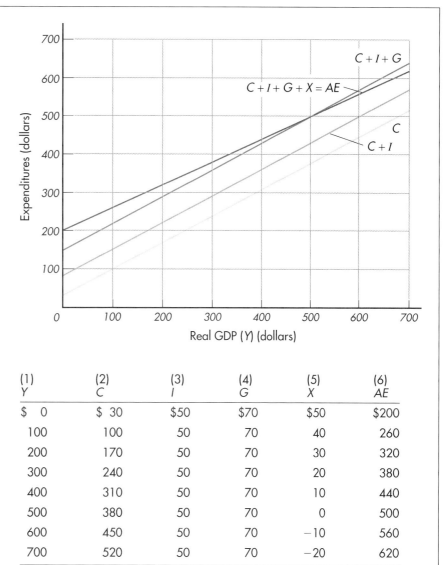

Figure 12
The Aggregate Expenditures Function
To find the aggregate expenditures function, we begin with the consumption function (labeled C) and add the investment function (I), to create the C + I function. We then add the government spending function (G) to find the C + I + G function. Notice that the C, C + I, and C + I + G functions are all parallel. They have the same slope because investment and government spending are assumed to be autonomous. Because I and G do not change with income, the slope of the C + I and C + I + G functions equals the slope of the consumption function (the MPC). Net exports are added to the C + I + G function to find the aggregate expenditures function, C + I + G + X. The aggregate expenditures function has a smaller slope than the other functions because the slope of the net exports function is negative.

(1) Y	(2) C	(3) I	(4) G	(5) X	(6) AE
$ 0	$ 30	$50	$70	$50	$200
100	100	50	70	40	260
200	170	50	70	30	320
300	240	50	70	20	380
400	310	50	70	10	440
500	380	50	70	0	500
600	450	50	70	−10	560
700	520	50	70	−20	620

SUMMARY

▲▼ *How are consumption and saving related?*

1. Consumption and saving are the components of disposable income; they are determined by the same variables. §1

2. Dissaving occurs when consumption exceeds income. §1.b

3. The marginal propensity to consume (*MPC*) is change in consumption divided by change in disposable income; the marginal propensity to save (*MPS*) is change in saving divided by change in disposable income. §1.c

4. The average propensity to consume (*APC*) is consumption divided by disposable income; the average propensity to save (*APS*) is saving divided by disposable income. §1.d

▲▼ *What are the determinants of consumption?*

5. The determinants of consumption are income, wealth, expectations, demographics, and taxation. §1.e.1, 1.e.2, 1.e.3, 1.e.4

▲▼ What are the determinants of investment?

6. Investment is assumed to be autonomous, independent of current income. §2.a

7. The determinants of investment are the interest rate, profit expectations, technological change, the cost of capital goods, and the rate at which capacity is utilized. §2.b.1, 2.b.2, 2.b.3

8. Firms use the expected return on investment to determine the expected profitability of an investment project. §2.b.1

9. Investment is highly variable over the business cycle because the determinants of investment are themselves so variable. §2.c

▲▼ What are the determinants of government spending?

10. Government spending is set by government authorities at whatever level they choose. §3

▲▼ What are the determinants of net exports?

11. Net exports are the difference between what a country exports and what it imports; both exports and imports are a product of foreign or domestic income, tastes, foreign and domestic government trade restrictions, and exchange rates. §4.a, 4.b

12. Because imports rise with domestic income, the higher that income, the lower net exports. §4.c

▲▼ What is the aggregate expenditures function?

13. The aggregate expenditures function is the sum of the individual functions for each component of spending. §5

14. The slope of the aggregate expenditures function is flatter than that of the consumption function because it includes the net exports function, which is negative. §5.a

KEY TERMS

consumption function §1.b

saving function §1.b

dissaving §1.b

autonomous consumption §1.b

marginal propensity to consume (*MPC*) §1.c

marginal propensity to save (*MPS*) §1.c

average propensity to consume (*APC*) §1.d

average propensity to save (*APS*) §1.d

wealth §1.e.2

marginal propensity to import (*MPI*) §4.b

EXERCISES

1. Why do we study the consumption and saving functions together?

2. Explain the difference between a flow and a stock. Classify each of the following as a stock or flow: income, wealth, saving, savings, consumption, investment, government expenditures, net exports, GDP.

3. Fill in the blanks in the following table:

Income	Consumption	Saving	MPC	MPS	APC	APS
$1,000	$ 400	_____			___	.60
2,000	900	$1,100	___		___	___
3,000	1,400	_____	___	.50	___	___
4,000	_____	$2,100	___	___	___	___

4. Why is consumption so much more stable over

the business cycle than investment? In your answer, discuss household behavior as well as business behavior.

5. Assuming investment is autonomous, draw an investment function with income on the horizontal axis. Show how the function shifts if:

   a. The interest rate falls.

   b. An investment tax credit is repealed by Congress.

   c. A new president is expected to be a strong advocate of probusiness policies.

   d. There is a great deal of excess capacity in the economy.

6. Use the following table to answer these questions:

Y	C	I	G	X
$ 500	$500	$10	$20	$60
600	$590	$10	$20	$40
700	$680	$10	$20	$20
800	$770	$10	$20	0
900	$860	$10	$20	−$20
1,000	$950	$10	$20	−$40

a. What is the *MPC*?

b. What is the *MPS*?

c. What is the *MPI*?

d. What is the level of aggregate expenditures at each level of income?

e. Graph the aggregate expenditures function.

7. Based on the table in exercise 6, what is the linear equation for each of the following functions?

a. Consumption

b. Investment

c. Net exports

d. Aggregate expenditures

8. Is the *AE* function the same thing as a demand curve? Why or why not?

9. What is the level of saving if:

a. Disposable income is $500 and consumption is $450?

b. Disposable income is $1,200 and the *APS* is .9?

c. The *MPC* equals .9, disposable income rises from $800 to $900, and saving is originally $120 when income equals $800?

10. What is the marginal propensity to consume if:

a. Consumption increases by $75 when disposable income rises by $100?

b. Consumption falls by $50 when disposable income falls by $100?

c. Saving equals $20 when disposable income equals $100 and saving equals $40 when disposable income equals $300?

11. How can the *APC* fall as income rises if the *MPC* is constant?

12. Why would economies with older populations tend to have greater slopes of the consumption function?

13. Draw a diagram and illustrate the effects of the following on the net exports function for the United States:

a. The French government imposes restrictions on French imports of U.S. goods.

b. U.S. national income rises.

c. Foreign income falls.

d. The dollar depreciates on the foreign exchange market.

14. Why is the slope of the $C + I + G$ function different from the slope of the $C + I + G + X$ function?

15. Suppose the consumption function is $C = \$200 + 0.8Y$.

a. What is the amount of autonomous consumption?

b. What is the marginal propensity to consume?

c. What would consumption equal when real GDP equals $1,000?

COOPERATIVE LEARNING EXERCISE

Divide the class into groups of three or four and give them the following information:

Y	C	I	G	X	AE
$100	___	___	___	$20	___
200	240	___	___	___	___
300	320	___	___	___	___
400	___	20	___	0	$450
500	___	___	___	___	___
600	450	___	___	___	___
700	___	___	___	___	___

*Assume that **I** and **G** are autonomous.*

Each group must fill in the missing values in the table. After ten minutes, groups are called on to give the values for different parts of the table.

U.S. Trade Deficit Balloons 46%

The nation's trade deficit unexpectedly ballooned 46% in February, the Commerce Department said Tuesday, as the vibrant U.S. economy pulled in imports while economic weakness abroad curbed overseas demand for American goods.

The shortfall, covering services such as tourism and finance as well as goods, widened to $9.7 billion in February on a balance-of-payments basis from a revised $6.6 billion deficit in January.

"Consumer sales are sucking in these imports as Americans go out and buy lots of goods," said economist David Wyss of DRI/McGraw Hill.

It was the largest gap in the two years the government has been using a new method to calculate the deficit, and it is expected to dampen economic growth.

"The bottom line is this is a symptom of a stronger U.S. economy, while the rest of the world is doing poorly, and when that happens their sales to us rise faster than our sales to them," Wyss said.

The U.S. Trade gap with Japan was virtually unchanged at $4.63 billion compared with January's $4.62 billion. But China's trade surplus with the United States fell to $1.6 billion from January's $2.1 billion.

Economist Michael Niemira said the gain in imports "obviously reflects domestic economic strength, manifested as it did in more consumer products, automobiles," although industrial goods were well represented.

The trade gap in goods totaled $13.9 billion, partially offset by a $4.2 billion surplus in services. The January trade gap in goods and services was a revised $6.6 billion, with a deficit of $11.3 billion in goods and a surplus of $4.7 billion in services.

Overall exports of goods and services fell 2.6 percent, paced by lower orders for civilian aircraft, semiconductors, pharmaceutical products and other merchandise.

Imports grew 2.7 percent, led by fuel oil and other energy products, autos and other goods.

"We're pulling in imports hand over fist," said Cynthia Latta of DRI/McGraw-Hill Inc.

"Both Europe and Japan are now growing substantially below their potential and, by doing so, create a drag on the U.S. economy," said Commerce Secretary Ron Brown. He called on these nations to take steps to spur their economies.

U.S. Trade Representative Mickey Kantor sought to play down the deficit, saying monthly numbers are volatile.

"Not too much significance should therefore be attached to the data for any single month," he said in a statement.

The United States had a trade deficit in goods with Western Europe of $529 million versus a surplus of $171 million in January.

The deficit with Canada, the United States' single largest trading partner, narrowed slightly, to $1 billion from $1.1 billion in January.

Source: "U.S. trade deficit balloons 46%," *Chicago Tribune*, April 20, 1994, Section 3, p. 1. © Copyrighted Chicago Tribune company. All rights reserved. Used with permission.

Commentary

In this chapter, we saw how net exports contribute to aggregate expenditures. Merchandise exports bring money from the rest of the world, and higher net exports mean greater aggregate expenditures. Merchandise imports involve outflows of money to foreign countries, and lower net exports mean lower aggregate expenditures.

We saw in the chapter that higher domestic real GDP leads to higher imports and lower net exports. This article points out that the U.S. net exports deficit "is a symptom of a stronger U.S. economy." The article also indicates that U.S. exports were not growing like imports because of slow economic growth in the rest of the world. As a result of the effect of net exports on aggregate expenditures, we often hear arguments for policy aimed at increasing exports and decreasing imports. Domestic residents are often resentful of foreign producers and blame foreign competitors for job losses in the home country. However, we must consider the circumstances and then ask if a policy aimed at increasing the national trade surplus (or decreasing the deficit) is really desirable.

Since one country's export is another's import, it is impossible for everyone to have surpluses—on a worldwide basis the total value of exports equals the total value of imports. If someone must always have a trade deficit when others have trade surpluses, is it necessarily true that surpluses are good

and deficits bad so that one country benefits at another's expense? In a sense, imports should be preferred to exports since exports represent goods no longer available for domestic consumption that will be consumed by foreign importers. In later chapters you will learn that the benefits of free international trade include more efficient production and increased consumption. Furthermore, if trade among nations is voluntary, it is difficult to argue that deficit countries are harmed while surplus countries benefit from trade.

In general, it is not obvious whether a country is better or worse off running merchandise surpluses rather than deficits. Consider the following simple example of a world with two countries, R and P. Country R is a rich creditor country that is growing rapidly and has a net exports deficit. Country P is a poor debtor country that is growing slowly and has positive net exports. Should we prefer living conditions in P to R based solely on the knowledge that P has a net exports surplus and R has a net exports deficit? Although this is indeed a simplistic example, there are real-world analogues of rich creditor countries with international trade deficits and poor debtor nations with international trade surpluses. The point is that you cannot analyze the balance of payments apart from other economic considerations. Deficits are not inherently bad, nor are surpluses necessarily good.

10

An Algebraic Model of Aggregate Expenditures

Aggregate expenditures (AE) equal consumption (C) plus investment (I) plus government spending (G) plus net exports (X). If we can develop an equation for each component of spending, we can put them together in a single model.

Consumption The consumption function can be written in general form as

$$C = C^a + c\,Yd$$

where C^a is autonomous consumption and c is the *MPC*. The consumption function for the data in Chapter 10 is

$$C = \$30 + .70\,Yd \text{ as shown in Figure 1.}$$

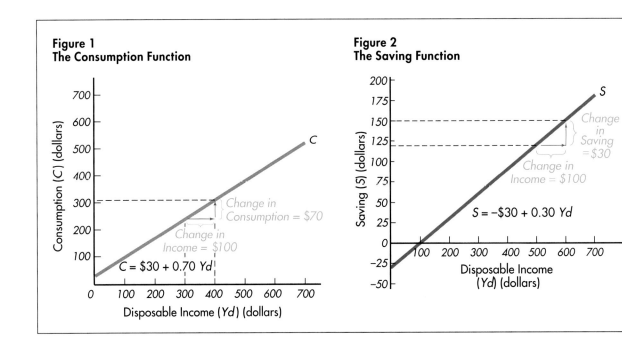

**Figure 1
The Consumption Function**

Consumption (C) (dollars)

Change in
Consumption = $70

Change in
Income = $100

C = $30 + 0.70 Yd

Disposable Income (Yd) (dollars)

**Figure 2
The Saving Function**

Saving (S) (dollars)

Change
in
Saving
= $30

Change in
Income = $100

S = −$30 + 0.30 Yd

Disposable Income
(Yd) (dollars)

Saving The corresponding saving function is

$$S = -\$30 + .30\ Yd \text{ as illustrated in Figure 2.}$$

Investment Investment is autonomous at I^a, which is equal to $50.

Government Spending Government spending is autonomous at G^a, which is equal to $70.

Net Exports Exports are autonomous at EX^a and equal to $50. Imports are given by the function:

$$IM = IM^a + im\ Y$$

where im is the *MPI*. Here, then,

$$IM = \$0 + .10Y$$

Net exports equal exports minus imports, or

$$X = \$50 - \$0 - .10Y$$
$$= \$50 - .10Y$$

as shown in Figure 3.

Aggregate Expenditures Summing the functions for the four components (and ignoring taxes, so that Yd equals Y):

$$AE = C^a + c\ Y + I^a + G^a + EX^a - IM^a - im\ Y$$
$$= \$30 + .70Y + \$50 + \$70 + \$50 - \$0 - .10Y$$
$$= \$200 + .60Y$$

as shown in Figure 4.

In the Appendix to Chapter 11 we use the algebraic model of aggregate expenditures presented here to solve for the equilibrium level of real GDP.

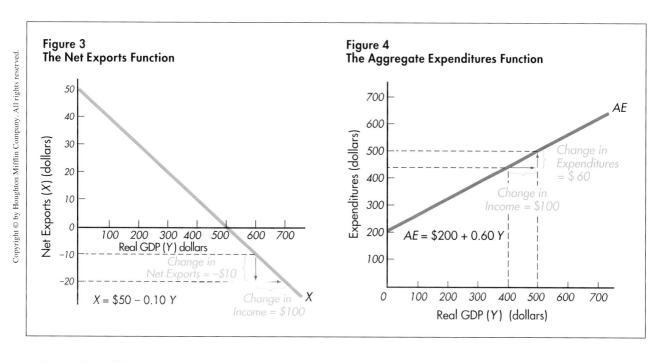

Figure 3
The Net Exports Function

Figure 4
The Aggregate Expenditures Function

11

Income and Expenditures Equilibrium

FUNDAMENTAL QUESTIONS

1. What does equilibrium mean in macroeconomics?

2. How do aggregate expenditures affect income or real GDP?

3. What are the leakages from and injections to spending?

4. Why does equilibrium real GDP change by a multiple of a change in autonomous expenditures?

5. What is the spending multiplier?

6. What is the relationship between the GDP gap and the recessionary gap?

7. How does international trade affect the size of the multiplier?

8. Why does the aggregate expenditures curve shift with changes in the price level?

W hat determines the level of income and expenditures, or real GDP? In Chapter 9 we used aggregate demand and aggregate supply to answer this question. Then in Chapter 10 we developed the components of aggregate expenditures in more detail to provide the foundation for an additional approach to answering the question "What determines the level of real GDP?" If you know the answer to this question, you are well on your way to understanding business cycles. Sometimes real GDP is growing and jobs are relatively easy to find; at other times real GDP is falling and large numbers of people are out of work. Macroeconomists use several models to analyze the causes of business cycles. Underlying all of the models is the concept of macroeconomic equilibrium.

Equilibrium here means what it did when we talked about supply and demand: a point of balance, a point from which there is no tendency to move. In macroeconomics, equilibrium is the level of income and expenditures that the economy tends to move toward and remain at until autonomous spending changes.

PREVIEW

Economists have not always agreed on how an economy reaches equilibrium and on the forces that move an economy from one equilibrium to another. This last issue formed the basis of economic debate during the Great Depression of the 1930s. Before the 1930s, economists generally believed that the economy always was at or moving toward an equilibrium consistent with a high level of employed resources. The British economist John Maynard Keynes did not agree. He believed that an economy could come to rest at a level of real GDP that is too low to provide employment for all those who desired it. He also believed that certain actions are necessary to ensure that the economy rises to a level of real GDP consistent with a high level of employment. In particular, Keynes argued that government must intervene in a big way in the economy (see the Economic Insight "John Maynard Keynes").

To understand the debate that began during the 1930s and continues on various fronts today, it is necessary to understand the Keynesian view of how equilibrium real GDP is determined. This is our focus here. We have seen in Chapter 9 that the aggregate demand and supply model of macroeconomic equilibrium allowed the price level to fluctuate as the equilibrium level of real GDP changed. The Keynesian income-expenditures model assumes that the price level is fixed. It emphasizes aggregate expenditures without explicit consideration of the supply side of the economy. This is why we considered the components of spending in detail in Chapter 10—to provide a foundation for the analysis in this chapter. The Keynesian model may be viewed as a special fixed-price case of the aggregate demand and aggregate

John Maynard Keynes

John Maynard Keynes (pronounced "canes") is considered by many to be the greatest economist of the twentieth century. His major work, *The General Theory of Employment, Interest, and Money*, had a profound impact on macroeconomics, on both thought and policy. Keynes was born in Cambridge, England, on June 5, 1883. He studied economics at Cambridge University, where he became a lecturer in economics in 1908. During World War I, Keynes worked for the British treasury. At the end of the war, he was the treasury's representative at the Versailles Peace Conference. He resigned from the British delegation at the conference to protest the harsh terms being imposed on the defeated countries. His resignation and publication of the *Economic Consequences of the Peace* (1919) made him an international celebrity.

In 1936, Keynes published *The General Theory*. It was a time of world recession (it has been estimated that around one-quarter of the U.S. labor force was unemployed at the height of the Depression), and policymakers were searching for ways to explain the persistent unemployment. In the book, Keynes suggested that an economy could come to equilibrium at less than potential GDP. More important, he argued that government policy could be altered to end recession. His analysis emphasized aggregate expenditures. If private expenditures were not sufficient to create equilibrium at potential GDP, government expenditures could be increased to stimulate income and output. This was a startling concept. Most economists of the time believed that government should not take an active role in the economy. With his *General Theory*, Keynes started a "revolution" in macroeconomics.

supply model. In later chapters we examine the relationship between equilibrium and the level of employed resources, and the effect of government policy on both of these elements.

1. EQUILIBRIUM INCOME AND EXPENDITURES

What does equilibrium mean in macroeconomics?

Equilibrium is a point from which there is no tendency to move. People do not change their behavior when everything is consistent with what they expect. However, when plans and reality do not match, people adjust their behavior to make them match. Determining a nation's equilibrium level of income and expenditures is the process of defining the level of income and expenditures at which plans and reality are the same.

1.a. Expenditures and Income

How do aggregate expenditures affect income or real GDP?

We use the aggregate expenditures function described at the end of Chapter 10 to demonstrate how equilibrium is determined. Keep in mind that the aggregate expenditures function represents *planned* expenditures at different levels of income or real GDP. We focus on planned expenditures because they represent the amount households, firms, government, and the foreign sector expect to spend.

Actual expenditures always equal income and output because they reflect changes in inventories. That is, inventories automatically raise or lower investment expenditures so that actual spending equals income, which equals output, which equals real GDP. However, aggregate expenditures (which are planned spending) may not equal real GDP. What happens when planned spending and real GDP are not equal? When planned spending on goods and services *exceeds* the current value of output, the production of goods and services increases. Because output equals income, the level of real GDP also increases. This is the situation for all income levels below $500 in Figure 1. At these levels, total spending is greater than real GDP, which means that more goods and services are being purchased than are being produced. The only way this can happen is for goods produced in the past to be sold. When planned spending is greater than real GDP, business inventories fall. The change in inventories offsets the excess of planned expenditures over real GDP, so that actual expenditures (including the unplanned change in inventories) equal real GDP. You can see this in column 7 of the table in Figure 1, where the change in inventories offsets the excess of aggregate expenditures over real GDP (the difference between columns 6 and 1).

What happens when inventories fall? As inventories fall, manufacturers increase production to meet the demand for products. The increased production raises the level of real GDP. *When aggregate expenditures exceed real GDP, real GDP rises.*

When aggregate expenditures exceed real GDP, real GDP rises.

At real GDP levels above $500 in the table, aggregate expenditures are less

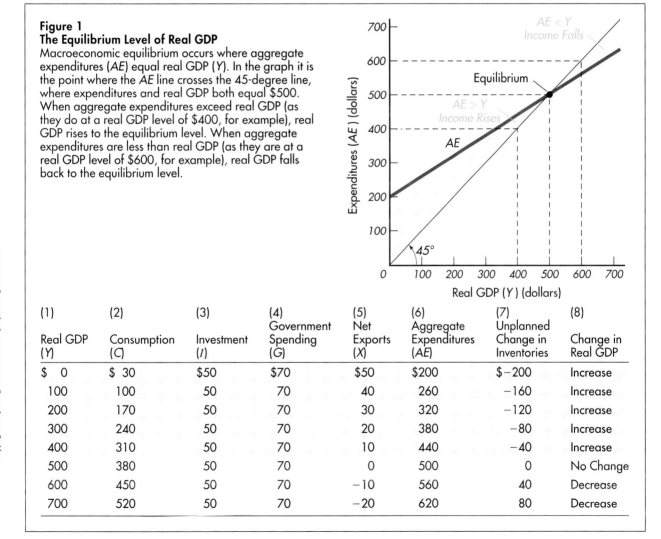

Figure 1
The Equilibrium Level of Real GDP
Macroeconomic equilibrium occurs where aggregate expenditures (*AE*) equal real GDP (*Y*). In the graph it is the point where the *AE* line crosses the 45-degree line, where expenditures and real GDP both equal $500. When aggregate expenditures exceed real GDP (as they do at a real GDP level of $400, for example), real GDP rises to the equilibrium level. When aggregate expenditures are less than real GDP (as they are at a real GDP level of $600, for example), real GDP falls back to the equilibrium level.

(1) Real GDP (*Y*)	(2) Consumption (*C*)	(3) Investment (*I*)	(4) Government Spending (*G*)	(5) Net Exports (*X*)	(6) Aggregate Expenditures (*AE*)	(7) Unplanned Change in Inventories	(8) Change in Real GDP
$ 0	$ 30	$50	$70	$50	$200	$−200	Increase
100	100	50	70	40	260	−160	Increase
200	170	50	70	30	320	−120	Increase
300	240	50	70	20	380	−80	Increase
400	310	50	70	10	440	−40	Increase
500	380	50	70	0	500	0	No Change
600	450	50	70	−10	560	40	Decrease
700	520	50	70	−20	620	80	Decrease

than income. As a result, inventories are accumulating above planned levels—more goods and services are being produced than are being purchased. As inventories rise, businesses begin to reduce the quantity of output they produce. The unplanned increase in inventories is counted as a form of investment spending, so that actual expenditures equal real GDP. For example, when real GDP is $600, aggregate expenditures are only $560. The $40 of produced goods that are not sold are measured as inventory investment. The $560 of aggregate expenditures plus the $40 of unplanned inventories equal $600, the level of real GDP. As inventories increase, firms cut production, which causes real GDP to fall. *When aggregate expenditures are less than real GDP, real GDP falls.*

There is only one level of real GDP in the table in Figure 1 where real GDP does not change. When real GDP is $500, aggregate expenditures equal $500. The equilibrium level of real GDP (or output) is that point at which aggregate expenditures equal real GDP (or output).

When aggregate expenditures equal real GDP, planned spending equals the output produced and the income generated from producing that output. As long as planned spending is consistent with real GDP, real GDP does not change. But if planned spending is higher or lower than real GDP, real GDP does change. Equilibrium is that point at which planned spending and real GDP are equal.

The graph in Figure 1 illustrates equilibrium. The 45-degree line shows all possible points where aggregate expenditures (measured on the vertical axis) equal real GDP (measured on the horizontal axis). The equilibrium level of real GDP, then, is simply the point where the aggregate expenditures line (*AE*) crosses the 45-degree line. In the figure, equilibrium occurs where real GDP and expenditures are $500.

When the *AE* curve lies above the 45-degree line—for example, at a real GDP level of $400—aggregate expenditures are greater than real GDP. What happens? Real GDP rises to the equilibrium level, where it tends to stay. When the *AE* curve lies below the 45-degree line—at a real GDP level of $600, for example—aggregate expenditures are less than real GDP, which pushes real GDP down. Once real GDP falls to the equilibrium level ($500 in our example), it tends to stay there.

1.b. Leakages and Injections

What are the leakages from and injections to spending?

Saving, taxes, and imports are leakages that reduce autonomous aggregate expenditures.

Equilibrium can be determined by using aggregate expenditures and real GDP, which represents income. Another way to determine equilibrium involves leakages from and injections into the income stream, the circular flow of income and expenditures.

Leakages reduce autonomous aggregate expenditures. There are three leakages in the stream from domestic income to spending: saving, taxes, and imports.

■ The more households save, the less they spend. An increase in autonomous saving means a decrease in autonomous consumption, which could cause the equilibrium level of real GDP to fall (see the Economic Insight "The Paradox of Thrift").

■ Taxes are an involuntary reduction in consumption. The government transfers income away from households. Higher taxes lower autonomous consumption, in the process lowering autonomous aggregate expenditures and the equilibrium level of real GDP.

The Paradox of Thrift

People generally believe that saving is good and that more saving is better. However, if every family increased its saving, the result could be less income for the economy as a whole. In fact, increased saving could actually lower savings for all households.

An increase in saving may provide an example of a *paradox of thrift*. A *paradox* is a true proposition that seems to contradict common beliefs. We believe that we will be better off by increased saving, but in the aggregate, increased saving could cause the economy to be worse off. The paradox of thrift is a *fallacy of composition*: the assumption that what is true of a part is true of the whole. It often is unsafe to generalize from what is true at the micro level to what is true at the macro level.

The graph illustrates the effect of higher saving. Initial equilibrium occurs where the $S_1 + T + IM$ curve intersects the $I + G + EX$ curve, at an income of $500. Suppose saving increases by $20 at every level of income. The $S_1 + T + IM$ curve shifts up to the $S_2 + T + IM$ curve. A new equilibrium is

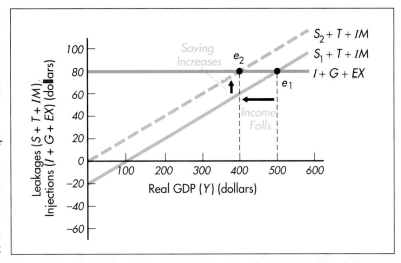

established at an income level of $400. The higher rate of saving causes equilibrium income to fall by $100.

Notice that the graph is drawn with a constant $I + G + EX$ line. If investment increases along with saving, equilibrium income would not necessarily fall. In fact, because saving is necessary before there can be any investment, we would expect a greater demand for investment funds to induce higher

saving. If increased saving is used to fund investment expenditures, the economy should grow over time to higher and higher levels of income. Only if the increased saving is not injected back into the economy is there a paradox of thrift. The fact that governments do not discourage saving suggests that the paradox of thrift generally is not a real-world problem.

Investment, government spending, and exports are injections that increase autonomous aggregate expenditures.

■ Imports are expenditures for foreign goods and services. They reduce expenditures on domestic goods and services. An autonomous increase in imports reduces net exports, causing autonomous aggregate expenditures and the equilibrium level of real GDP to fall.

For equilibrium to occur, these leakages must be offset by corresponding *injections* of spending into the domestic economy, through investment, government spending, and exports.

■ Household saving generates funds that businesses can borrow and spend for investment purposes.

■ The taxes collected by government are used to finance government purchases of goods and services.

■ Exports bring foreign expenditures into the domestic economy.

There is no reason to expect that each injection matches its corresponding leakage—that investment equals saving, that government spending equals taxes, or that exports equal imports. But for equilibrium to occur, total injections must equal total leakages.

Figure 2 shows how leakages and injections determine the equilibrium level of real GDP. Column 5 of the table lists the total leakages from aggregate expenditures: saving (S) plus taxes (T) plus imports (IM). Saving and imports both increase when real GDP increases. We assume that there are no taxes so the total amount of leakages (S + T + IM) increases as real GDP increases.

Column 9 lists the injections at alternative income levels. Because investment (I), government spending (G), and exports (EX) are all autonomous, total injections (I + G + EX) are constant at all levels of real GDP.

To determine the equilibrium level of real GDP, we compare leakages with injections. When injections exceed leakages, planned spending is greater than current income or output, so real GDP rises. In the table in Figure 2, this occurs for levels of real GDP under $500, so real GDP increases if under $500 (see the last column). When leakages exceed injections, planned spending is less than current real GDP, so real GDP falls. In Figure 2, at all levels

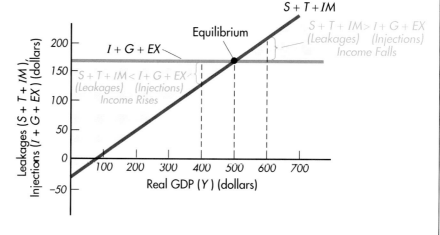

Figure 2
Leakages, Injections, and Equilibrium Income
Leakages equal saving (S), taxes (T), and imports (IM). Injections equal investment (I), government spending (G), and exports (EX). Equilibrium is that point where leakages equal injections. In the graph, equilibrium is the point at which the S + T + IM curve intersects the I + G + EX curve, where real GDP (Y) equals $500. At lower levels of income, injections exceed leakages, so Y rises. At higher levels of income, leakages exceed injections, so Y falls.

(1) Real GDP (Y)	(2) Saving (S)	(3) Taxes (T)	(4) Imports (IM)	(5) Leakages (S + T + IM)	(6) Investment (I)	(7) Government Spending (G)	(8) Exports (EX)	(9) Injections (I + G + EX)	(10) Change in Real GDP
$ 0	$-30	$0	$0	$ 30	$50	$70	$50	$170	Increase
100	0	0	10	10	50	70	50	170	Increase
200	30	0	20	50	50	70	50	170	Increase
300	60	0	30	90	50	70	50	170	Increase
400	90	0	40	130	50	70	50	170	Increase
500	120	0	50	170	50	70	50	170	No Change
600	150	0	60	210	50	70	50	170	Decrease
700	180	0	70	250	50	70	50	170	Decrease

of real GDP above $500, real GDP falls. Only when leakages equal injections is the equilibrium level of real GDP established. When real GDP equals $500, both leakages and injections equal $170, so there is no pressure for real GDP to change. The equilibrium level of real GDP occurs where leakages $(S + T + IM)$ equal injections $(I + G + EX)$.

Figure 2 shows the interaction of leakages and injections graphically. The equilibrium point is where the $S + T + IM$ and $I + G + EX$ curves intersect, at a real GDP level of $500. At higher levels of real GDP, leakages are greater than injections (the $S + T + IM$ curve lies above the $I + G + EX$ curve). When leakages are greater than injections, real GDP falls to the equilibrium point. At lower levels of income, injections are greater than leakages (the $I + G + EX$ curve lies above the $S + T + IM$ curve). Here real GDP rises until it reaches $500. Only at $500 is there no pressure for real GDP to change.

If you compare Figures 1 and 2, you can see that it does not matter whether we use aggregate expenditures or leakages and injections—the equilibrium level of real GDP is the same.

RECAP

1. Equilibrium is a point from which there is no tendency to move.

2. When aggregate expenditures exceed real GDP, real GDP rises.

3. When aggregate expenditures are less than real GDP, real GDP falls.

4. Saving, taxes, and imports are leakages of planned spending from domestic aggregate expenditures.

5. Investment, government spending, and exports are injections of planned spending into domestic aggregate expenditures.

6. Equilibrium occurs at the level of real GDP at which aggregate expenditures equal real GDP, and leakages equal injections.

2. CHANGES IN EQUILIBRIUM INCOME AND EXPENDITURES

Why does equilibrium real GDP change by a multiple of a change in autonomous expenditures?

Equilibrium is a point from which there is no tendency to move. But in fact the equilibrium level of real GDP does move. In the last section we described how aggregate expenditures push real GDP representing the economy's income and output up or down toward their level of equilibrium. Here we examine how changes in autonomous expenditures affect equilibrium. This becomes very important in understanding macroeconomic policy, the kinds of things government can do to control the business cycle.

2.a. The Spending Multiplier

What is the spending multiplier?

Remember that equilibrium is that point where aggregate expenditures equal real GDP. If we increase autonomous expenditures, then we raise the equilibrium level of real GDP. But by how much? It seems logical to expect a 1 to 1 ratio: if autonomous spending increases by a dollar, equilibrium real GDP should increase by a dollar. Actually, equilibrium real GDP increases by *more* than a dollar. The change in autonomous expenditures is *multiplied* into a larger change in the equilibrium level of real GDP.

In Chapter 6 we used a circular flow diagram to show the relationship of expenditures to income. In that diagram we saw how one sector's expenditures become another sector's income. This concept helps explain the effect of a change in autonomous expenditures on the equilibrium level of income or real GDP. If A's autonomous spending increases, then B's income rises. B spends part of that income in the domestic economy (the rest is saved or used to buy foreign goods), generating new income for C. C spends part of that income in the domestic economy, generating new income for D. And the rounds of increased spending and income continue. All of this is the product of A's initial autonomous increase in spending. And each round of increased spending and income affects the equilibrium level of income or real GDP.

Let's look at an example, using Table 1. Suppose government spending goes up $20 to improve public parks. What happens to the equilibrium level of income? The autonomous increase in government spending increases the income of park employees by $20. As their income increases, so does the consumption of park employees. For example, let's say they spend more money on hamburgers. In the process, they are increasing the income of the hamburger producers, who in turn increase their consumption.

Table 1 shows how a single change in spending generates further changes.

TABLE I
The Spending Multiplier Effect

	(1) Change in Income	(2) Change in Domestic Expenditures	(3) Change in Saving	(4) Change in Imports
Round 1	$20	$12	$ 6	$2
Round 2	12	7.20	3.60	1.20
Round 3	7.20	4.32	2.16	0.72
Round 4	4.32	2.59	1.30	0.43
	.	.	.	.
	.	.	.	.
	.	.	.	.
Totals	$50	$30	$15	$5

Column 2 = column 1 $\times$ (MPC $-$ MPI)

Column 3 = column 1 $\times$ MPS

Column 4 = column 1 $\times$ MPI

$$\text{Multiplier} = \frac{1}{MPS + MPI}$$

$$= \frac{1}{.30 + .10}$$

$$= \frac{1}{.40}$$

$$= 2.5$$

Round 1 is the initial increase in government spending to improve public parks. That $20 expenditure increases the income of park employees by $20 (column 1). As income increases, those components of aggregate expenditures that depend on current income—consumption and net exports—also increase by some fraction of the $20.

Consumption changes by the marginal propensity to consume multiplied by the change in income; imports change by the marginal propensity to import multiplied by the change in income. To find the total effect of the initial change in spending, we must know the fraction of any change in income that is spent in the domestic economy. In the hypothetical economy we have been using, the *MPC* is .70 and the *MPI* is .10. This means that for each $1 of new income, consumption rises by $.70 and imports rise by $.10. Spending on *domestic* goods and services, then, rises by $.60. Because consumption is spending on domestic goods and services, and imports are spending on foreign goods and services, the percentage of a change in income that is spent domestically is the difference between the *MPC* and the *MPI*. If the *MPC* equals .70 and the *MPI* equals .10, then 60 percent of any change in domestic income (*MPC* − *MPI* = .60) is spent on domestic goods and services.

In round 1 of Table 1, the initial increase in income of $20 induces an increase in spending on domestic goods and services of $12 (.60 × $20). Out of the $20, $6 is saved because the marginal propensity to save is .30 (1 − *MPC*). The other $2 is spent on imports (*MPI* = .10). The park employees receive $20 more income. They spend $12 on hamburgers at a local restaurant; they save $6; and they spend $2 on imported beer.

Only $12 of the workers' new income is spent on goods produced in the domestic economy, hamburgers. That $12 becomes income to the restaurant's employees and owner. When their income increases by $12, they spend 60 percent of that income ($7.20) on domestic goods (round 2, column 2). The rest of the income is saved and spent on imports.

Each time income increases, expenditures increase. But the increase is smaller and smaller each new round of spending. Why? Because 30 percent of each change in income is saved and another 10 percent is spent on imports. These are leakages out of the income stream. This means just 60 percent of the change in income is spent and passed on to others in the domestic economy as income in the next round.

To find the total effect of the initial change in spending of $20, we could keep on computing the change in income and spending round after round, and then sum the total of all rounds. The change in income and spending never reaches zero, but becomes infinitely small.

Fortunately, we do not have to compute each round-by-round increase in spending to find the total increase. If we know the percentage of additional income that "leaks" from domestic consumption at each round, we can determine the total change in income or real GDP by finding its reciprocal. This measure is called the **spending multiplier**. The leakages are that portion of the change in income that is saved (the *MPS*) and that proportion of the change in income that is spent on imports (the *MPI*).

spending multiplier:
a measure of the change in equilibrium income or real GDP produced by a change in autonomous expenditures

$$\text{Multiplier} = \frac{1}{\text{leakages}}$$

$$= \frac{1}{MPS + MPI}$$

When the *MPS* is .30 and the *MPI* is .10, the multiplier equals 2.5 (1/.4). An initial change in expenditures of $20 results in a total change in real GDP of $50, 2.5 times the original change in expenditures. The greater the leakages, the smaller the multiplier. When the *MPS* equals .35 and the *MPI* equals .15, the multiplier equals 2 (1/.50). The multiplier is smaller here because less new income is being spent in the domestic economy. The more people save, the smaller the expansionary effect on income of a change in spending. And the more people spend on imports, the smaller the expansionary effect on income of a change in spending. Notice that the multiplier would be larger in a *closed economy*, an economy that does not trade with the rest of the world. In that economy, because the *MPI* equals zero, the spending multiplier is simply equal to the reciprocal of the *MPS*.

2.b. The Spending Multiplier and Equilibrium

The spending multiplier is an extremely useful concept. It allows us to calculate how a change in autonomous expenditures affects real GDP. To better understand how changes in spending can bring about changes in equilibrium income or real GDP, let's modify the example we used in Figure 1. In the table in Figure 3 we have increased government spending to $110. The autonomous increase in government spending raises aggregate expenditures by $40 at every level of income. Aggregate expenditures now equal real GDP at $600. The increase in government spending of $40 yields an increase in equilibrium real GDP of $100.

The graph in Figure 3 illustrates the multiplier effect and shows the change in equilibrium income when spending increases by $40. The original aggregate expenditures curve, AE_1, intersects the 45-degree line at a real GDP level of $500. A spending increase of $40 at every level of real GDP creates a new aggregate expenditures curve, AE_2, which lies $40 above the original curve. AE_2 is parallel to AE_1 because the increase is in autonomous spending. The new curve, AE_2, intersects the 45-degree line at an income of $600.

In Chapter 8 we introduced the concept of the natural rate of unemployment—the unemployment rate that exists in the absence of cyclical unemployment. When the economy operates at the natural rate of unemployment, the corresponding level of output (and income) is called potential real GDP. However, equilibrium does not necessarily occur at potential real GDP. Equilibrium is any level of real GDP at which planned expenditures equal real GDP. Suppose that equilibrium real GDP is not at the level of potential real GDP and that government policymakers make the achievement of potential real GDP an important goal. In this case, government policy is addressed to closing the *GDP gap*, the difference between potential real GDP and actual real GDP. The nature of that policy depends on the value of the multiplier.

If we know the size of the GDP gap and we know the size of the spending multiplier, we can determine how much spending needs to change to yield equilibrium at potential real GDP. Remember that the GDP gap equals potential real GDP minus actual real GDP:

$$\text{GDP gap} = \text{potential real GDP} - \text{actual real GDP}$$

What is the relationship between the GDP gap and the recessionary gap?

When real GDP is less than potential real GDP, the GDP gap is the amount the GDP must rise to reach its potential. Suppose potential real GDP is $500, but the economy is in equilibrium at $300. GDP must rise by $200 to reach potential real GDP. How much must spending rise? If we know the size

Figure 3
A Change in Equilibrium Expenditures and Income

A change in aggregate expenditures (AE) causes a change in equilibrium real GDP (Y). Initially equilibrium is $500, the point at which the AE_1 curve intersects the 45-degree line. If autonomous expenditures increase by $40, the aggregate expenditures curve shifts up to AE_2. The new curve intersects the 45-degree line at a new equilibrium level of real GDP, $600. An increase in autonomous expenditures of $40, then, causes equilibrium real GDP to increase by $100.

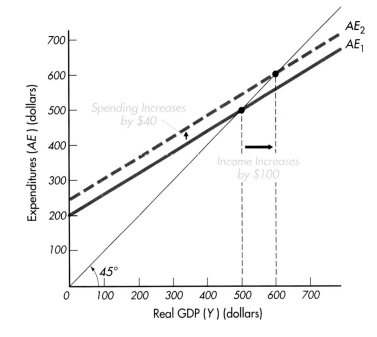

(1) Real GDP (Y)	(2) Consumption (C)	(3) Investment (I)	(4) Government Spending (G)	(5) Net Exports (X)	(6) Aggregate Expenditures (AE)	(7) Unplanned Change in Inventories	(8) Change in Real GDP
$ 0	$ 30	$50	$110	$50	$240	$−240	Increase
100	100	50	110	40	300	−200	Increase
200	170	50	110	30	360	−160	Increase
300	240	50	110	20	440	−120	Increase
400	310	50	110	10	480	−80	Increase
500	380	50	110	0	540	−40	Increase
600	450	50	110	−10	600	0	No Change
700	520	50	110	−20	660	40	Decrease

recessionary gap:
the increase in expenditures required to reach potential GDP

The recessionary gap is the vertical distance between the aggregate expenditures curve and the 45-degree line at the potential level of real GDP.

of the spending multiplier, we simply divide the spending multiplier into the GDP gap to determine how much spending must rise to achieve equilibrium at potential real GDP. This required change in spending is called the **recessionary gap**:

$$\text{Recessionary gap} = \frac{\text{GDP gap}}{\text{spending multiplier}}$$

Figure 4 shows an economy in which equilibrium real GDP (Y_e) is less than potential real GDP (Y_p). The difference between the two—the GDP gap—is $200. It is the *horizontal* distance between equilibrium real GDP and potential real GDP. The amount that spending must rise in order for real GDP to reach a new equilibrium level of $500 is measured by the recessionary gap. The recessionary gap is the *vertical* distance between the aggregate expenditures curve and the 45-degree line at the potential real GDP level.

Figure 4
The GDP Gap and the Recessionary Gap
In the graph, the GDP gap is $200, the difference between potential real GDP (Y_p) of $500 and equilibrium real GDP (Y_e) of $300. The GDP gap tells us that equilibrium real GDP must rise by $200 to reach equilibrium at the potential level of real GDP. The recessionary gap indicates the amount that autonomous expenditures must rise to close the GDP gap. The recessionary gap is the vertical distance between the 45-degree line and the *AE* curve at the potential level of real GDP, or $80. If autonomous expenditures are increased by $80, the *AE* curve moves up, intersecting with the 45-degree line at $500.

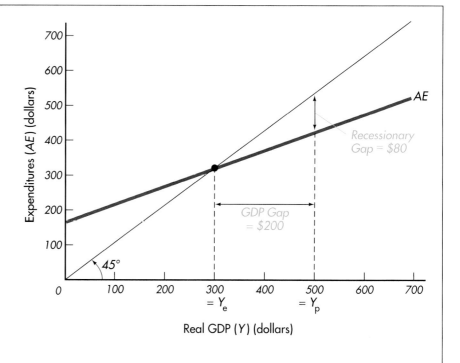

The recessionary gap in Figure 4 is $80:

$$\text{Recessionary gap} = \frac{\$200}{2.5}$$
$$= \$80$$

With a spending multiplier of 2.5, if aggregate expenditures rise by $80, equilibrium income rises by the $200 necessary to close the GDP gap. Government policy may be addressed to closing the gap, as an increase in government expenditures of $80 would move the economy to the potential level of real GDP in this example.

2.c. Real-World Complications

Our definition of the spending multiplier,

$$\frac{1}{MPS + MPI}$$

is a simplification of reality. Often other factors besides the *MPS* and *MPI* determine the actual multiplier in an economy. If prices rise when spending increases, the spending multiplier will not be as large as shown here. Also, taxes (which are ignored until Chapter 12, on fiscal policy) will reduce the size of the multiplier. Another factor is the treatment of imports. We have assumed that whatever is spent on imports is permanently lost to the domestic economy. For a country whose imports are a small fraction of the exports of its trading partners, this is a realistic assumption. But for a country whose imports are very important in determining the volume of exports of the rest of the world, this simple spending multiplier understates the true multiplier effect. To see why, let's examine how U.S. imports affect income in the rest of the world.

How does international trade affect the size of the multiplier?

2.c.1. **Foreign Repercussions of Domestic Imports** When a resident of the United States buys goods from another country, that purchase becomes income to foreign residents. If Mike in Miami buys coral jewelry from Victor in the Dominican Republic, Mike's purchase increases Victor's income. So the import of jewelry into the United States increases income in the Dominican Republic.

Imports purchased by one country can have a large effect on the level of income in other countries. Table 2 shows the importance of U.S. imports to many of its trading partners. Column 4 lists the percentage of total exports from each of the countries listed in column 1 to the United States. Obviously Canada and Mexico are very dependent on sales to the United States, with 81 and 86 percent, respectively, of their exports going to the United States. South Africa, on the other hand, sold just 6 percent of its total exports to U.S. buyers in 1995. If U.S. imports from South Africa doubled, the effect on total South African exports and income would be small. But if imports from Canada or Mexico doubled, the effect on those countries' exports and income would be substantial.

U.S. imports play a key role in determining the real GDP of its major trading partners. This is important because foreign income is a determinant of U.S. exports. As that income rises, U.S. exports rise (see Chapter 10). That

TABLE 2
The Importance of Trade with the United States, 1993 (millions of dollars)

(1) Country	(2) Exports to U.S.	(3) Total Exports	(4) Exports to U.S./ Total Exports (2)/(3)	(5) Imports from U.S.	(6) Total Imports	(7) Imports from U.S./Total Imports (5)/(6)
Australia	3,543	42,592	.08	8,272	43,836	.19
Brazil	8,012	38,783	.21	6,045	25,678	.24
Canada	113,617	140,748	.81	100,177	138,286	.72
Chile	1,702	9,552	.18	2,605	10,977	.24
Germany	29,462	364,277	.08	18,957	329,514	.06
India	4,883	11,964	.41	2,761	22,493	.12
Japan	110,418	362,583	.30	47,950	240,711	.20
Korea	17,780	83,535	.21	14,776	84,338	.18
Mexico	40,745	47,232	.86	41,636	63,878	.65
Philippines	5,176	11,279	.46	3,529	17,965	.14
Saudi Arabia	8,432	47,442	.18	6,066	35,654	.19
South Africa	1,929	31,031	.06	2,197	21,666	.10
Sweden	4,690	49,773	.09	2,354	42,156	.06
Turkey	1,280	16,285	.08	3,434	33,174	.10
U.K.	22,393	180,176	.12	26,376	205,388	.13
Venezuela	8,707	16,926	.51	4,599	13,922	.33

Source: International Monetary Fund, *Direction of Trade Statistics Yearbook,* Washington, D.C., June 1994. Used by permission.

is, foreign imports increase with foreign income, and some of those imports come from the United States. Column 7 of Table 2 shows the percentage of purchases from the United States in the total imports of its trading partners. Canada and Mexico, both of which export in large quantities to the United States, are also important markets for U.S. goods. If the income in these countries goes up, it is likely that their purchases of U.S. goods will rise correspondingly. And, of course, when foreign spending on U.S. goods increases, national income in the United States rises.

The simple spending multiplier understates the true multiplier effects of increases in autonomous expenditures because of the foreign repercussions of domestic spending. Some spending on imports comes back to the domestic economy in the form of exports. This means the chain of spending can be different from that assumed in the simple spending multiplier. Figure 5 illustrates the difference.

Figure 5(a) shows the sequence of spending when there are no foreign repercussions from domestic imports. In this case, domestic spending rises, which causes domestic income or real GDP to rise. Higher domestic real GDP leads to increased spending on imports as well as further increases in domestic spending, which induce further increases in real GDP, and so on, as the multiplier process works itself out. Notice, however, that the imports are simply a leakage from the spending stream.

In Figure 5(b), the sequence of expenditures includes the foreign repercussions of domestic imports. As before, increases in domestic spending cause domestic income or real GDP to rise, which in turn leads to more domestic spending as well as greater domestic imports. Now, however, the greater imports increase foreign income or real GDP, which increases foreign imports of goods produced in the domestic economy. As domestic exports rise, domestic real GDP rises.

The diagrams in Figure 5 show why the multiplier effect is higher with foreign repercussions than without. Rather than complicate the multiplier definition, we continue to use the simple spending multiplier. But remember that (holding prices constant and ignoring taxes) our definition underestimates the true magnitude of the multiplier's effects in open economies. In fact, the foreign repercussions of domestic imports help explain the similarity in business cycles across countries. When the United States is booming, the economies of other countries that depend on exports to the U.S. market also boom. When the United States is in recession, income in these other countries tends to fall.

2.c.2. Multiplier Estimates Many private and public organizations have developed models that are used to analyze current economic developments and to forecast future ones. A large number of these models include foreign repercussions. From these models we get a sense of just how much the simple multiplier underestimates the true multiplier. Table 3 reports multiplier estimates from one well-known model that incorporates foreign repercussions. The numbers listed in the table are the multiplier effects after one year. Because of further rounds of spending in later years, the actual multipliers are larger than those reported in the table.

The first section of the table gives the multiplier effects of an increase in U.S. government spending. The U.S. effect is a multiplier of 2. This means that if autonomous government expenditures increased by $25, U.S. equilibrium national income would be $50 higher after one year.

The income of the other countries in the first part of the table is increased

Figure 5
The Sequence of Expenditures

If there are no foreign repercussions from changes in domestic income or real GDP, the simple spending multiplier holds. Increases in domestic spending increase domestic income or real GDP, which causes domestic spending—including spending on foreign goods—to rise further. Here higher expenditures on domestic imports do not have any effect on domestic exports to foreign countries.

If there are foreign repercussions from changes in domestic real GDP, the simple spending multiplier

underestimates the actual effect of a change in autonomous expenditures on the equilibrium level of real GDP. As part (b) shows, increases in domestic spending increase domestic income or real GDP, which causes domestic spending—including spending on foreign goods—to rise further. Here higher spending on foreign goods causes foreign real GDP to rise, and with it, spending on domestic exports. Higher domestic exports stimulate domestic real GDP further. The actual multiplier effect of an increase in domestic spending, then, is larger than it is when domestic imports have no effect on domestic exports.

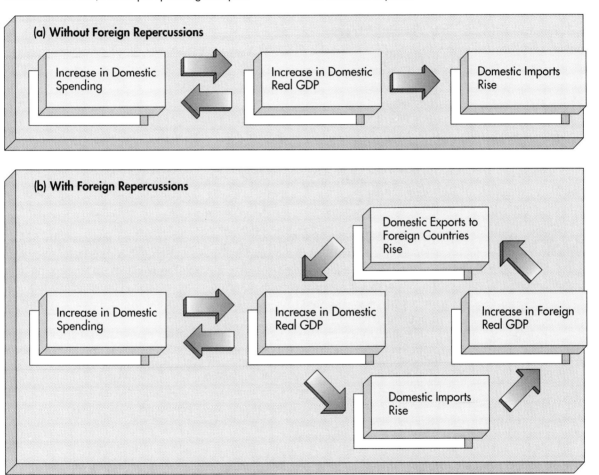

by higher spending in the United States because some of that spending is on imports into the United States. The spending multipliers for these countries range from .7 for Japan to .2 for Germany and the United Kingdom. If U.S. autonomous government expenditures go up $25, U.K. equilibrium national income would be $5 (.2 × $25) higher after one year. Over time, as income in these foreign countries rises, their spending on U.S. goods and services increases. And as U.S. exports increase, so does U.S. income.

The second part of the table shows the sensitivity of U.S. income to changes in foreign government spending. The largest multiplier is only .2, in

TABLE 3
Spending Multiplier Estimates

Multiplier Effects of U.S. Government Spending Increases

Country	Multiplier*
United States	2.0
Canada	.5
Germany	.2
Japan	.7
United Kingdom	.2

Multiplier Effects in the U.S. of Foreign Government
Spending Increases

Country	Multiplier*
Canada	.2
Germany	.1
Japan	.1
United Kingdom	.1

*Based on first year after increase in spending.
Source: Hali J. Edison, Jaime R. Marquez, and Ralph W. Tryon, *The Structure and Properties of the FRB Multicountry Model*, International Finance Discussion Paper, no. 293 (Washington, D.C.: Board of Governors of the Federal Reserve System, 1986).

---

the case of Canada. If autonomous government spending increases by $25 in Canada, U.S. equilibrium national income would be $5 higher after one year. Clearly, U.S. spending increases have a much larger effect on foreign income than foreign spending increases have on U.S. income. The reason for this is the vast size of the domestic market in the United States relative to that in other countries.

The multiplier examples we use in this chapter show autonomous government spending changing. It is important to realize that the multiplier effects apply to any change in autonomous expenditures in any sector of the economy.

RECAP

1. Any change in autonomous expenditures is multiplied into a larger change in the equilibrium level of real GDP.

2. The multiplier measures the change in equilibrium real GDP produced by a change in autonomous spending.

3. The multiplier equals

$$\frac{1}{\text{leakages}} = \frac{1}{MPS + MPI}$$

4. The recessionary gap is the amount spending must increase to achieve equilibrium at potential real GDP; graphically, it is measured by the vertical distance between the 45-degree line and the aggregate expenditures curve at potential real GDP.

5. The true spending multiplier is larger than the simple spending multiplier ($1/[MPS + MPI]$) because of the foreign repercussions of domestic spending. Price changes and taxes cause the simple spending multiplier to overestimate the true multiplier.

3. AGGREGATE EXPENDITURES AND AGGREGATE DEMAND

The approach to macroeconomic equilibrium presented in this chapter focuses on aggregate expenditures and income. It is called the *Keynesian model*. This model of the economy can be very useful in explaining some real-world events, but it suffers from a serious drawback: the model assumes that the supply of goods and services in the economy always adjusts to aggregate expenditures, that there is no need for price changes. The Keynesian model is a *fixed-price model*.

In the real world, we find that shortages of goods and services often are met by rising prices, not just increased production. We also find that when supply increases in the face of relatively constant demand, prices may fall. In other words, prices as well as production adjust to differences between demand and supply. We introduced price as a component of macroeconomic equilibrium in Chapter 9, in the aggregate demand and supply model. You may recall that aggregate expenditures represent demand when the price level is constant. This can be demonstrated by using the income and expenditures approach developed in this chapter to derive the aggregate demand curve that was introduced in Chapter 9.

3.a. Aggregate Expenditures and Changing Price Levels

Why does the aggregate expenditures curve shift with changes in the price level?

As discussed in Chapter 9, the *AE* curve will shift with changes in the price level because of the wealth effect, interest rate effect, and international trade effect. Wealth is one of the nonincome determinants of consumption. Households hold part of their wealth in financial assets like money and bonds. As the price level falls, the purchasing power of money rises and aggregate expenditures increase. As the price level rises, the purchasing power of money falls and aggregate expenditures fall.

The interest rate is a determinant of investment spending. As the price level changes, interest rates may change as households and business firms change their demand for money. The change in interest rates will then affect investment spending. For instance, when the price level rises, more money is needed to buy any given quantity of goods and services. To acquire more money, households and firms sell their nonmonetary financial assets like bonds. The increased supply of bonds will tend to raise interest rates to attract buyers. The higher interest rates will tend to lower investment spending and aggregate expenditures. Conversely, a lower price level will tend to be associated with lower interest rates, greater investment spending, and greater aggregate expenditures.

Net exports may change, causing aggregate expenditures to change, when the domestic price level changes. If domestic prices rise while foreign prices and the exchange rate are constant, then domestic goods become more expensive relative to foreign goods, and net exports and aggregate expenditures tend to fall. If domestic prices fall while foreign prices and the exchange rate are constant, then domestic goods become cheaper relative to foreign goods, and net exports and aggregate expenditures tend to rise.

3.b. Deriving the Aggregate Demand Curve

The aggregate demand curve (AD) shows how the equilibrium level of expenditures changes as the price level changes. In other words, the curve shows the amount people spend at different price levels. Let's use the example of Figure 6 to show how aggregate demand is derived from the shifting aggregate expenditures curve (AE).

The aggregate demand curve is derived from the AE curve. Part (a) of Figure 6 shows three AE curves, each drawn for a different price level. Suppose that the initial equilibrium occurs at point A on curve AE_0 with prices at P_0. At this point, equilibrium real GDP and expenditures are $500.

Figure 6
Aggregate Expenditures and Aggregate Demand
Part (a) shows how changes in the price level cause the AE curve to shift. The initial curve, AE_0, is drawn at the initial level of prices, P_0. On this curve, the equilibrium level of aggregate expenditures (where expenditures equal real GDP) is $500. If the price level falls to P_1, autonomous expenditures increase, shifting the curve up to AE_1 and moving the equilibrium level of aggregate expenditures to $700. If the price level rises to P_2, autonomous expenditures fall, shifting the curve down to AE_2 and moving the equilibrium level of aggregate expenditures to $300.

The aggregate demand curve (AD) in part (b) is derived from the aggregate expenditures curves. The AD curve shows the equilibrium level of aggregate expenditures at different price levels. At price level P_0, equilibrium aggregate expenditures are $500; at P_1, $700; and at P_2, $300.

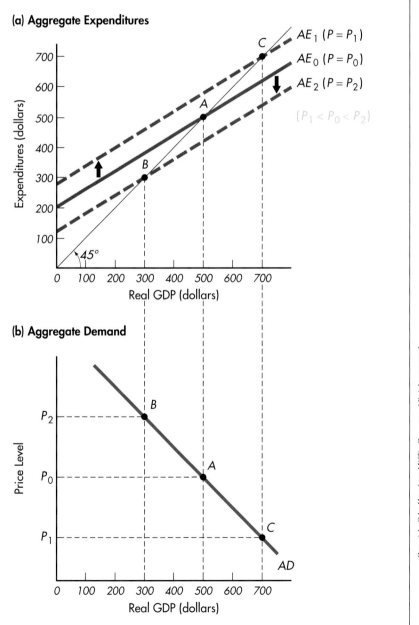

(a) Aggregate Expenditures

(b) Aggregate Demand

If prices fall to P_1, the AE curve shifts up to AE_1. Here equilibrium is at point C, where real GDP equals $700. If prices rise from P_0 to P_2, the AE curve falls to AE_2. Here equilibrium is at point B, where real GDP equals $300.

In part (b) of Figure 6, price level is plotted on the vertical axis and real GDP is plotted on the horizontal axis. A price level change here means that, on average, all prices in the economy change. The negative slope of the aggregate demand curve results from the effect of changing prices on wealth, interest rates, and international trade. If you move vertically down from points A, B, and C in the top figure, you find corresponding points along the aggregate demand curve in the lower figure. The AD curve shows all of the combinations of price levels and corresponding equilibrium levels of real GDP and aggregate expenditures.

3.c. A Fixed-Price AD-AS Model

The Keynesian model is a fixed-price model.

The Keynesian model of fixed-price equilibrium may be considered a special case of the aggregate demand and aggregate supply equilibrium. We can define a horizontal segment of the aggregate supply curve as the Keynesian region of the curve. This represents an economy with substantial unemployment and excess capacity where real GDP and output may be increased without pressure on the price level. Figure 7 illustrates this case.

In Figure 7, the aggregate supply curve is horizontal at price level P_e. Throughout the range of the AS curve, the price level is fixed. Suppose aggregate expenditures increase due to some reason other than a price-level change. For instance, consumers could expect future incomes to rise so they increase consumption now, or business firms expect sales to rise in the future so they increase investment spending now, or government spending rises to improve the national highway system, or foreign prices rise so that net exports increase. If aggregate expenditures rise due to other than a domestic price-level change, then the aggregate demand curve shifts to the right like the shift from AD_1 to AD_2 in Figure 7. This increase in AD causes real GDP to rise to Y_2 yet the price level remains fixed at P_e.

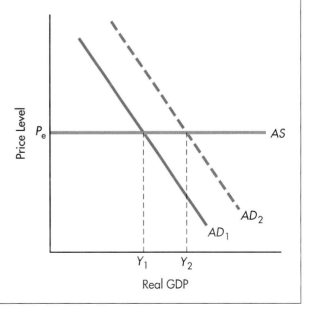

Figure 7
A Fixed-Price AD-AS Model
If the AS curve is horizontal, then shifts in the AD curve will have no effect on the equilibrium level of prices but will change the equilibrium level of real GDP.

Because the fixed-price model of macroeconomic equilibrium requires a horizontal *AS* curve, many economists believe that this model is too restrictive and not representative of the modern economy. As a result, we will generally see the *AD-AS* model using upward-sloping *AS* curves so that price as well as real GDP fluctuates with shifts in aggregate demand.

RECAP

1. As the price level rises (falls), aggregate expenditures fall (rise).
2. Aggregate demand is the equilibrium aggregate expenditures at alternative price levels.
3. The Keynesian fixed-price model is represented by a horizontal aggregate supply curve.

SUMMARY

▲▼ What does equilibrium mean in macro-economics?

1. Macroeconomic equilibrium is that point where aggregate expenditures equal real GDP. §1.a

▲▼ How do aggregate expenditures affect income or real GDP?

2. When aggregate expenditures exceed income or real GDP, real GDP rises; when they are less than real GDP, real GDP falls. §1.a

▲▼ What are the leakages from and injections to spending?

3. Leakages are saving, taxes, and imports; injections are investment, government spending, and exports. §1.b
4. Equilibrium real GDP occurs where leakages equal injections. §1.b

▲▼ Why does equilibrium real GDP change by a multiple of a change in autonomous expenditures?

5. The effect of a change in autonomous spending is multiplied by a spiral of increased spending and income. §2.a

▲▼ What is the spending multiplier?

6. The spending multiplier equals the reciprocal of the sum of the *MPS* and the *MPI*. §2.a

▲▼ What is the relationship between the GDP gap and the recessionary gap?

7. The recessionary gap is the amount autonomous expenditures must change to eliminate the GDP gap and reach potential GDP. §2.b

▲▼ How does international trade affect the size of the spending multiplier?

8. The actual spending multiplier may be larger than the reciprocal of the sum of the *MPS* and the *MPI* because of the foreign repercussions of changes in domestic spending. §2.c.1

▲▼ Why does the aggregate expenditures curve shift with changes in the price level?

9. The *AE* curve shifts with changes in the price level because of the wealth effect, interest rate effect, and international trade effect. §3.a
10. The Keynesian model of fixed-price equilibrium is a special case of the *AD* and *AS* equilibrium. §3.c

KEY TERMS

spending multiplier §2.a

recessionary gap §2.b

EXERCISES

1. Explain the role of inventories in keeping actual expenditures equal to real GDP.

2. Rework Figure 1 assuming a closed economy (net exports equal zero at all levels of income). What is the equilibrium level of real GDP? What is the spending multiplier?

3. Draw a graph representing a hypothetical economy. Carefully label the two axes, the $S + T + IM$ curve, the $I + G + EX$ curve, and the equilibrium level of real GDP. Illustrate the effect of an increase in the level of autonomous saving.

4. Given the following information, what is the spending multiplier in each case?

   a. $MPC = .90$, $MPI = .10$
   b. $MPC = .90$, $MPI = .30$
   c. $MPC = .80$, $MPI = .30$
   d. $MPC = .90$, $MPI = 0$

5. Draw a graph representing a hypothetical economy in a recession. Carefully label the two axes, the 45-degree line, the AE curve, and the equilibrium level of real GDP. Indicate and label the GDP gap and the recessionary gap.

6. Explain the effect of foreign repercussions on the value of the spending multiplier.

7. Suppose the MPC is .80, the MPI is .10, and the income tax rate is 10 percent. What is the multiplier in this economy?

Use the following table information to answer questions 8–15:

Y	C	I	G	X
$100	$120	$20	$30	$10
300	300	20	30	10
500	480	20	30	− 30
700	660	20	30	− 50

8. The MPC equals?

9. The MPI equals?

10. The MPS equals?

11. The multiplier equals?

12. What is the equilibrium level of real GDP?

13. What is the value of autonomous consumption?

14. If government spending increases by $20, what is the new equilibrium level of real GDP?

15. What is the equation for the consumption, net exports, and aggregate expenditures functions?

16. Derive the aggregate demand curve from an aggregate expenditures diagram. Explain how aggregate demand relates to aggregate expenditures.

COOPERATIVE LEARNING EXERCISE

Form the class into pairs of students. Each pair works on the following questions:

1. What is the spending multiplier if the $MPC = .8$ and the $MPI = 0$?

2. Given the multiplier found in question 1, if potential real GDP equals $800 billion and current real GDP equals $700 billion, what is the size of the recessionary gap?

3. How much would investment spending, exports, or government spending have to increase to make current real GDP equal to potential real GDP?

The instructor will call on different pairs of students for their answers.

Economy May Catch Chill

Canada's economic boom could turn to bust next year.

While 1995 may be the economy's best year since 1988, more and more forecasters think that will be reversed abruptly next year as Canada's dominant export market catches a chill.

"A sharp slowdown in the U.S. is likely to have a crushing impact on Canada," said Paul Summerville, chief economist at Richardson Greenshields of Canada Ltd., in his latest forecast.

"A high price will be paid for Canada's overwhelming dependence in this cycle on the above-potential performance of the U.S. economy."

Ted Carmichael, senior economist at Morgan Bank of Canada, added, "Canada has lagged the U.S. recovery, its growth has been driven primarily by exports and business investment, and business investment is largely in the export-oriented industries."

But unlike Canada, the U.S. is growing beyond its capacity. The Federal Reserve Board's determination to change that threatens the underpinnings of Canadian growth, Carmichael said.

Consensus forecasts are for real gross domestic product in Canada to grow by 3.8 percent this year and 3.2 percent in 1996, down from 1994's 4.3 percent increase. But Summerville and Carmichael are more pessimistic, predicting a sharp slowing to about 2 percent in 1996.

This would make the year a "soft landing" or "growth recession," rather than an outright recession, in which GDP actually shrinks.

Having struggled out of recession only two years ago, Canada should by most measures have at least one or two more years of strong, non-inflationary growth ahead. But the current economic expansion differs significantly from its predecessors in its dependence on exports to the U.S., which have risen to 34 percent of GDP from 22 percent in 1990.

Almost one-third of the increase in real output in the past three years has come from our trade surplus. But Carmichael thinks export growth will slide from its blistering 13 percent annual pace of 1993-1995 to just 4 percent next year, reversing the rise in the surplus and making trade a drag on growth.

If U.S. demand for Canadian products drops abruptly, there is little else to take up the slack. Government spending is shrinking, consumer spending remains subdued, construction has been depressed by high mortgage rates, and business investment is closely linked to export sales.

"As the U.S. slows down, which is what the Fed says it will do, and Canadian exports by definition slow down, can Canada make the transition . . . to growing autonomously and independently of the U.S.?" asked Summerville.

"My answer is 'No'."

Forecasters who still see Canada's GDP growing by more than 3 percent next year are generally more optimistic about household consumption picking up.

While a soft landing is not a recession, it means the economy grows less than its long-term potential rate of about 3 percent, below which unemployment tends to rise. Carmichael sees the jobless rate falling to 8.6 percent by the end of this year, but rising to 9 percent over the following nine months.

In fact, economists say such a soft landing is welcome because it contains inflation early enough to give the expansion a second leg.

In postwar history, the U.S. has had nine recessions, but only two soft landings, in 1966 and 1986, said David Wyss, research director at DRI/McGraw Hill in Lexington, Mass. In the 1960s and 1980s, "you had two cycles divided by a growth recession, instead of a real recession."

Ironically, the probability of a real recession rises with the strength of the U.S. economy because this increases the risk the Fed's tightening will overshoot, said Wyss.

"I don't think the Fed has made a mistake yet that will cause a recession, but we're getting nervous," he added. . . .

Source: "Economy May Catch Chill," by Greg IP, *The Financial Post*, Feb. 9, 1995, p. 1. Reprinted with permission.

Commentary

This article re-emphasizes a main point made in Chapter 11: countries are linked internationally, so that aggregate expenditure shifts in one country will have an impact on other nations. When other countries, like Canada, buy goods from the United States, the purchases increase U.S. GDP since net exports is one of the components of GDP. Remembering that net exports increase with a country's GDP, we should expect net exports to vary over the business cycle. Since Canadian imports vary with Canadian GDP, a recession in Canada tends to reduce U.S. exports, leading to lower GDP in the United States. Conversely, when the Canadian economy is booming, U.S. exports to Canada will rise and stimulate GDP growth in the United States.

Table 2 of Chapter 11 indicates that in 1993, the United States bought 81 percent of Canadian exports but only 8 percent of German exports. As a result, we would expect the business cycles of Canada and the United States to be much more similar than that of the United States and Germany. A recession in the United States would be more likely to cause a recession in Canada than Germany.

The United States had a recession in 1990 and 1991. Did the economies of the major trading partners of the United States have recessions around this time? There was a recession in Canada that roughly coincided with the U.S. recession. However, real GDP continued to grow in Germany until the fourth quarter of 1991. These numbers reflect the fact that the Canadian economy is much more integrated with the United States than the economy of Germany.

A look at Table 2 of Chapter 11 suggests that we should expect Mexico to also be greatly affected by U.S. business cycles since 86 percent of Mexican exports go to the United States. Australia, South Africa, Sweden, and Turkey are likely to have business cycles that are more independent of U.S. influences since their exports to the U.S. as a share of total exports range from 6 to 9 percent.

The international links between countries should grow over time as restrictions on international trade are removed and transportation and communication costs continue to fall. The future may be one in which national business cycles are increasingly interdependent and such interdependences will have to be given greater emphasis in national policymaking.

11

An Algebraic Model of Income and Expenditures Equilibrium

Continuing the example we began in the Appendix to Chapter 10, if we know the equations for each component of aggregate expenditures (AE), we can solve for the equilibrium level of real GDP (Y) for the economy represented in Figure 1:

$$C = \$30 + .70Y$$

$$I = \$50$$

$$G = \$70$$

$$X = \$50 - .10Y$$

Summing these components, we can find the aggregate expenditures function:

$$AE = \$30 + .70Y + \$50 + \$70 + \$50 - .10Y$$

$$= \$200 + .60Y$$

Given the AE function, we can solve for the equilibrium level of Y where

$$Y = AE$$

$$\text{or } Y = \$200 + .60Y$$

$$\text{or } Y - .60Y = \$200$$

$$.40Y = \$200$$

$$.40Y/.40 = \$200/.40$$

$$Y = \$500$$

The Spending Multiplier It is also possible to solve for the spending multiplier algebraically. We start by writing the general equations for each function where C^a, I^a, G^a, EX^a, and IM^a represent autonomous consumption, investment, government spending, exports, and imports, respectively, and where c represents the *MPC* and *im* represents the *MPI*:

$$C = C^a + cY$$

$$I = I^a$$

$$G = G^a$$

$$X = EX^a - IM^a - imY$$

Now we sum the individual equations for the components of aggregate expenditures to get the aggregate expenditures function:

$$AE = C + I + G + X$$

$$= C^a + cY + I^a + G^a + EX^a - IM^a - imY$$

$$= (C^a + I^a + G^a + EX^a - IM^a) + cY - imY$$

We know that aggregate expenditures equal income. So

$$Y = (C^a + I^a + G^a + EX^a - IM^a) + cY - imY$$

Solving for Y, we first gather all of the terms involving Y on the left side of the equation:

$$Y[1 - (c - im)] = C^a + I^a + G^a + EX^a - IM^a$$

Next we divide each side of the equation by $[1 - (c - im)]$ to get an equation for Y:

$$Y = \frac{1}{1 - (c - im)}(C^a + I^a + G^a + EX^a - IM^a)$$

A change in autonomous expenditures causes Y to change by

$$\frac{1}{1 - (c - im)}$$

times the change in expenditures. Because c is the *MPC* and *im* is the *MPI*, the multiplier can be written

$$\frac{1}{1 - (MPC - MPI)}$$

or, since $1 - MPC = MPS$, then $1 - (MPC - MPI) = MPS + MPI$, and the multiplier equals:

$$\frac{1}{MPS + MPI}$$

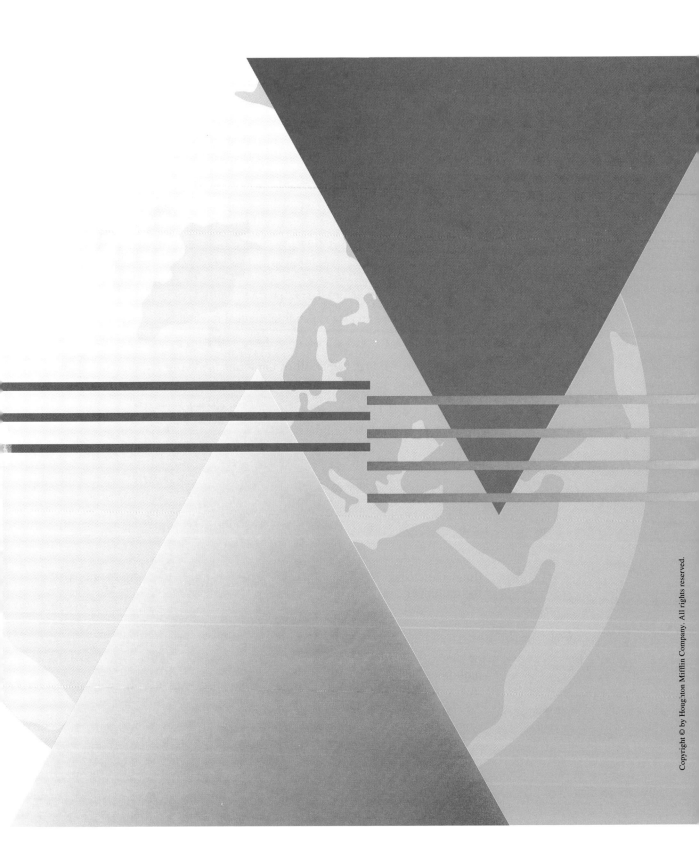

III

Macroeconomic Policy

12

Fiscal Policy

FUNDAMENTAL QUESTIONS

1. How can fiscal policy eliminate a GDP gap?
2. How has U.S. fiscal policy changed over time?
3. What are the effects of budget deficits?
4. How does fiscal policy differ across countries?

Macroeconomics plays a key role in national politics. When Jimmy Carter ran for the presidency against Gerald Ford in 1976, he created a "misery index" to measure the state of the economy. The index was the sum of the inflation rate and the unemployment rate, and Carter showed that it had risen during Ford's term in office. When Ronald Reagan challenged Carter in 1980, he used the misery index to show that inflation and unemployment had gone up during the Carter years. The implication is that presidents are responsible for the condition of the economy. If the inflation rate or the unemployment rate is relatively high coming into an election year, incumbent presidents are open to criticism by their opponents. For instance, many people believe that George Bush was defeated by Bill Clinton in 1992 because of the country's economic conditions. Clinton emphasized the recession that began in 1990—a recession that was not announced as having ended in March 1991 until after the election. As a result, Clinton's campaign made economic growth a focus of its attacks on Bush. This is more than campaign rhetoric, however. By law the government *is* responsible for the macroeconomic health of the nation. The Employment Act of 1946 states:

PREVIEW

"It is the continuing policy and responsibility of the Federal Government to use all practical means consistent with its needs and obligations and other essential considerations of national policy to coordinate and utilize all its plans, functions, and resources for the purpose of creating and maintaining, in a manner calculated to foster and promote free competitive enterprise and the general welfare conditions under which there will be afforded useful employment opportunities, including self-employment for those able, willing, and seeking to work, and to promote maximum employment, production, and purchasing power."

Fiscal policy is one tool that government uses to guide the economy along an expansionary path. In this chapter we examine the role of fiscal policy—government spending and taxation—in determining the equilibrium level of income. Then we review the budget process and the history of fiscal policy in the United States. Finally we describe the difference in fiscal policy between industrial and developing countries.

1. FISCAL POLICY AND AGGREGATE DEMAND

How can fiscal policy eliminate a GDP gap?

As you learned in Chapter 11, the GDP gap is the difference between potential real GDP and the equilibrium level of real GDP. If the government wants to close the GDP gap so that the equilibrium level of real GDP reaches its potential, it must use fiscal policy to alter aggregate expenditures and cause the aggregate demand curve to shift.

Fiscal policy is the government's policy with respect to spending and taxation. Since aggregate demand includes consumption, investment, net exports, and government spending, government spending on goods and services affects the level of aggregate demand directly. Taxes affect aggregate demand indirectly by changing the disposable income of households, which alters consumption.

1.a. Shifting the Aggregate Demand Curve

By varying the level of government spending, policymakers can affect the level of real GDP.

Changes in government spending and taxes shift the aggregate demand curve. Remember that the aggregate demand curve represents combinations of equilibrium aggregate expenditures and alternative price levels. An increase in government spending or a decrease in taxes raises the level of expenditures at every level of prices and moves the aggregate demand curve to the right.

Figure 1 shows an increase in aggregate demand that would result from an increase in government spending or a decrease in taxes. Only if the aggregate supply curve is horizontal do prices remain fixed as aggregate demand increases. In Figure 1(a), equilibrium occurs along the horizontal segment (the Keynesian region) of the AS curve. If government spending increases and the price level remains constant, aggregate demand shifts from AD to AD_1; it increases by the horizontal distance from point A to point B. Once aggregate demand shifts, the AD_1 and AS curves intersect at potential real GDP, Y_p.

But Figure 1(a) is not realistic. The AS curve is not likely to be horizontal all the way to the level of potential real GDP; it should begin sloping up well before Y_p. And once the economy reaches the capacity level of output, the AS curve should become a vertical line, as shown in Figure 1(b).

If the AS curve slopes up before reaching the potential real GDP level, as it does in part (b) of the figure, expenditures have to go up by more than the amount suggested in part (a) for the economy to reach Y_p. Why? Because when prices rise, the effect of spending on real GDP is reduced. This effect is shown in Figure 1(b). To increase the equilibrium level of real GDP from Y_e to Y_p, aggregate demand must shift by the amount from point A to C, a larger increase than that shown in Figure 1(a), where the price level is fixed.

1.b. Multiplier Effects

Changes in government spending may have an effect on real GDP that is a multiple of the original change in government spending; a $1 change in government spending may increase real GDP by more than $1. This is because the original $1 of expenditure is spent over and over again in the economy as it passes from person to person. The government spending multiplier measures the multiple by which an increase in government spending increases real GDP. Similarly, a change in taxes may have an effect on real GDP that is a multiple of the original change in taxes. (The appendix to this chapter provides an algebraic analysis of the government spending and tax multipliers.)

Figure 1
Eliminating the Recessionary Gap: Higher Prices Mean Greater Spending
When aggregate demand increases from AD to AD_1 in Figure 1(a), equilibrium real GDP increases by the full amount of the shift in demand. This is because the aggregate supply curve is horizontal over the area of the shift in aggregate demand. In Figure 1(b), in order for equilibrium real GDP to rise from Y_e to Y_p, aggregate demand must shift by more than it does in part (a). In reality, the aggregate supply curve begins to slope up before potential real GDP (Y_p) is reached, as shown in part (b) of the figure.

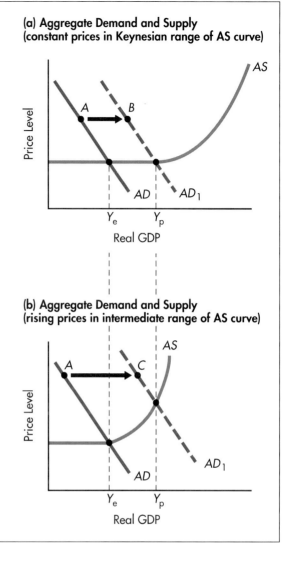

(a) Aggregate Demand and Supply (constant prices in Keynesian range of AS curve)

(b) Aggregate Demand and Supply (rising prices in intermediate range of AS curve)

If the price level rises as real GDP increases, the multiplier effects of any given change in aggregate expenditures are smaller than they would be if the price level remains constant.

If the price level rises as real GDP increases, the multiplier effects of any given change in aggregate demand are smaller than they would be if the price level remains constant. In addition to changes in the price level modifying the effect of government spending and taxes on real GDP, there are other factors that affect how much real GDP will change following a change in government spending. One such factor is how the government pays for, or finances, its spending.

Government spending must be financed by some combination of taxing, borrowing, or creating money:

$$\text{Government spending} = \text{taxes} + \text{change in government debt} + \text{change in government-issued money}$$

In Chapter 14 we discuss the effect of financing government spending by creating money. As you will see, this source of government financing is relied on heavily in some developing countries. Here we talk about the financing problem relevant for industrial countries: how taxes and government debt can modify the expansionary effect of government spending on national income.

1.c. Government Spending Financed by Tax Increases

Suppose that government spending rises by $100 billion and that this expenditure is financed by a tax increase of $100 billion. Such a "balanced-budget" change in fiscal policy will cause equilibrium real GDP to rise. This is because government spending increases aggregate expenditures directly, but higher taxes lower aggregate expenditures indirectly through consumption spending. For instance, if taxes increase $100, consumers will not cut their spending by $100, but by some fraction, say 9/10, of the increase. If consumers spend 90 percent of a change in their disposable income, then a tax increase of $100 would lower consumption by $90. So the net effect of raising government spending and taxes by the same amount is an increase in aggregate demand, illustrated in Figure 2 as the shift from AD to AD_1. However, it may be incorrect to assume that the only thing that changes is aggregate demand. An increase in taxes may also affect aggregate supply.

Aggregate supply measures the output that producers offer for sale at different levels of prices. When taxes go up, workers have less incentive to work because their after-tax income is lower. The cost of taking a day off or extending a vacation for a few extra days is less than it is when taxes are lower and after-tax income is higher. When taxes go up, then, output can fall, causing the aggregate supply curve to shift to the left. Such supply-side effects of taxes have been emphasized by the so-called supply-side economists, as discussed in the Economic Insight "Supply-Side Economics and the Laffer Curve."

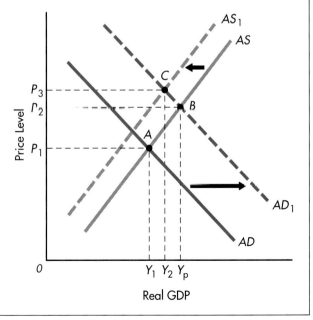

Figure 2
The Effect of Taxation on Aggregate Supply
An increase in government spending shifts the aggregate demand curve from AD to AD_1, moving equilibrium from point A to point B, and equilibrium real GDP from Y_1 to Y_p. If higher taxes reduce the incentive to work, aggregate supply could fall from AS to AS_1, moving equilibrium to point C and equilibrium real GDP to Y_2, a level below potential real GDP.

Much of government expenditures is unrelated to current economic conditions. For instance, the provision of national defense, a legal system, and police and fire protection are all cases where government expenditures would not typically fluctuate with the business cycle. This Canadian mountie serving in Banff National Park in Alberta is employed through booms and recessions in the Canadian economy. Although macroeconomists focus typically on the discretionary elements of fiscal policy that may be altered to combat business cycles, the nondiscretionary elements account for the bulk of governments' budgets.

Figure 2 shows the possible effects of an increase in government spending financed by taxes. The economy is initially in equilibrium at point A, with prices at P_1 and real GDP at Y_1. The increase in government spending shifts the aggregate demand curve from AD to AD_1. If this was the only change, the economy would be in equilibrium at point B. But if the increase in taxes reduces output, the aggregate supply curve moves back from AS to AS_1, and output does not expand all the way to Y_p. The decrease in aggregate supply creates a new equilibrium at point C. Here real GDP is at Y_2 (less than Y_p) and the price level is P_3 (higher than P_2).

The standard analysis of government spending and taxation assumes that aggregate supply is not affected by the change in fiscal policy, leading us to expect a greater change in real GDP than may actually occur. If tax changes do affect aggregate supply, the expansionary effects of government spending financed by tax increases are moderated. The actual magnitude of the effect is the subject of debate among economists. Most argue that the evidence in the United States indicates that tax increases have a fairly small effect on aggregate supply.

l.d. Government Spending Financed by Borrowing

The standard multiplier analysis of government spending does not differentiate among the different methods of financing that spending. Yet you just saw how taxation can offset at least part of the expansionary effect of higher government spending. Borrowing to finance government spending can also limit the increase in aggregate demand.

A government borrows funds by selling bonds to the public. These bonds represent debt that must be repaid at a future date. Debt is, in a way, a kind of substitute for current taxes. Instead of increasing current taxes to finance higher spending, the government borrows the savings of households and

Supply-Side Economics and the Laffer Curve

The large budget deficits incurred by the U.S. government in the 1980s were in part a product of lower tax rates engineered by the Reagan administration. President Reagan's economic team took office in January 1981 apparently believing that lower taxes would stimulate the supply of goods and services to a level that would raise tax revenues even though tax rates as a percentage of income had been cut. These arguments were repeated in 1995 by members of Congress pushing for tax-rate cuts. This emphasis on greater incentives to produce created by lower taxes has come to be known as *supply-side economics*.

The most widely publicized element of supply-side economics was the *Laffer curve*. The curve is drawn with the tax rate on the vertical axis and tax revenue on the horizontal axis. When the rate of taxation is zero, there is no tax revenue. As the tax rate increases, tax revenue increases up to a point. The assumption here is that there is some rate of taxation that is so high that it discourages productive activity. Once this rate is reached, tax revenue begins to fall as the rate of taxation goes up. In the graph, tax revenue is maximized at R_{max} with a tax rate of t

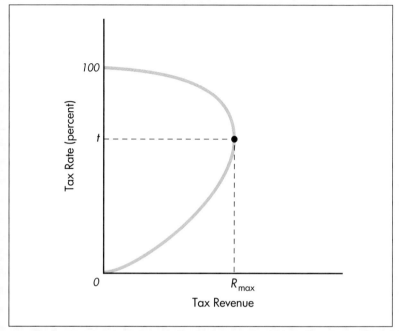

percent. Any increase in the rate of taxation above t percent produces lower tax revenues. In the extreme case—a 100 percent tax rate—no one is willing to work because the government taxes away all income.

Critics of the supply-side tax cuts proposed by the Reagan administration argued that lower taxes would increase the budget deficit. Supply-side advocates insisted that if the United States

was in the backward-bending region of the Laffer curve (above t percent in the graph), tax cuts would actually raise, not lower, tax revenue. The evidence following the tax cuts indicates that the tax cuts did, however, contribute to a larger budget deficit, implying that the U.S. was not on the backward-bending portion of the Laffer curve.

businesses. Of course the debt will mature and have to be repaid. This means that taxes will have to be higher in the future in order to provide the government with the funds to pay off the debt.

Current government borrowing, then, implies higher future taxes. This can limit the expansionary effect of increased government spending. If households and businesses take higher future taxes into account, they tend to save more today so that they will be able to pay those taxes in the future. And as saving today increases, consumption today falls.

The idea that current government borrowing can reduce current non-government expenditures was suggested originally by the early nineteenth-century English economist David Ricardo. Ricardo recognized that government borrowing could function like increased current taxes, reducing current household and business expenditures. *Ricardian equivalence* is the principle that government spending activities financed by taxation or borrowing have the same effect on the economy. If Ricardian equivalence holds, it doesn't matter whether the government raises taxes or borrows more to finance increased spending. The effect is the same: private-sector spending falls by the same amount today, and this drop in private spending will, at least partially, offset the expansionary effect of government spending on real GDP. Just how much private spending drops (and how far to the left the aggregate demand curve shifts) depends on the degree to which current saving increases in response to expected higher taxes. The less that people respond to the future tax liabilities arising from current government debt, the smaller the reduction in private spending.

There is substantial disagreement among economists over the extent to which current government borrowing acts like an increase in taxes. Some argue that it makes no difference whether the government raises current taxes or borrows. Others insist that the public does not base current spending on future tax liabilities. If the first group is correct, we would expect government spending financed by borrowing to have a smaller effect than if the second group is correct. Research on the issue continues, with most economists questioning the relevance of Ricardian equivalence and a small but influential group arguing its importance.

Ricardian equivalence holds if taxation and government borrowing both have the same effect on spending in the private sector.

I.e. **Crowding Out**

crowding out:
a drop in consumption or investment spending caused by government spending

Expansionary fiscal policy can crowd out private-sector spending; that is, an increase in government spending can reduce consumption and investment. **Crowding out** is usually discussed in the context of government spending financed by borrowing rather than by taxing. Though we have just seen how future taxes can cause consumption to fall today, investment can also be affected. Increases in government borrowing drive up interest rates. As interest rates go up, investment falls. This sort of indirect crowding out works through the bond market. The U.S. government borrows by selling Treasury bonds or bills. Because the government is not a profit-making institution, it does not have to earn a return from the money it raises by selling bonds. A corporation does, however. When interest rates rise, fewer corporations offer new bonds to raise investment funds because the cost of repaying the bond debt may exceed the rate of return on the investment.

Crowding out, like Ricardian equivalence, is important in principle, but economists have never demonstrated conclusively that its effects can substantially alter spending in the private sector. Still you should be aware of the possibility to understand the potential shortcomings of changes in government spending and taxation.

RECAP

1. Fiscal policy refers to government spending and taxation.

2. By increasing spending or cutting taxes, a government can close the GDP gap.

3. If government spending and taxes increase by the same amount, equilibrium real GDP rises.

4. If a tax increase affects aggregate supply, then a balanced-budget change in fiscal policy will have a smaller expansionary effect on equilibrium real GDP than otherwise.

5. Current government borrowing reduces current spending in the private sector if people increase current saving in order to pay future tax liabilities.

6. Ricardian equivalence holds when taxation and government borrowing have the same effect on current spending in the private sector.

7. Increased government borrowing can crowd private borrowers out of the bond market so that investment falls.

2. FISCAL POLICY IN THE UNITED STATES

How has U.S. fiscal policy changed over time?

Our discussion of fiscal policy assumes that policy is made at the federal level. In the modern economy this is a reasonable assumption. This was not the case before the 1930s, however. Before the Depression, the federal government limited its activities largely to national defense and foreign policy, and left other areas of government policy to the individual states. With the growth of the importance of the federal government in fiscal policy has come a growth in the role of the federal budget process.

2.a. The Budget Process

Fiscal policy in the United States is the product of a complex process that involves both the executive and legislative branches of government (Figure 3). The fiscal year for the U.S. government begins October 1 of one year and ends September 30 of the next. The budget process begins each spring, when the president directs the federal agencies to prepare their budgets for the fiscal year that starts almost eighteen months later. The agencies submit their budget requests to the Office of Management and Budget (OMB) by early September. The OMB reviews and modifies each agency's request and consolidates all of the proposals into a budget that the president presents to Congress in January.

Once Congress receives the president's budget, the Congressional Budget Office (CBO) studies it and committees modify it before funds are appropriated. The budget is evaluated in Budget Committee hearings in both the House of Representatives and the Senate. In addition, the CBO reports to Congress on the validity of the economic assumptions made in the president's budget. A budget resolution is passed by April 15 that sets out major expenditures and estimated revenues. (Revenues are estimated because future

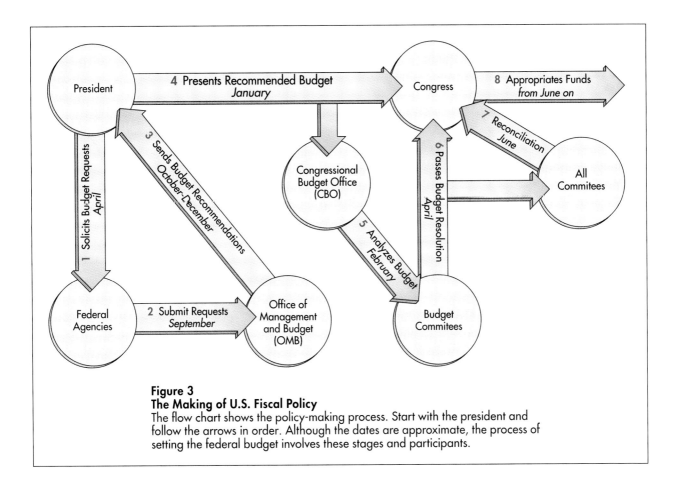

Figure 3
The Making of U.S. Fiscal Policy
The flow chart shows the policy-making process. Start with the president and follow the arrows in order. Although the dates are approximate, the process of setting the federal budget involves these stages and participants.

tax payments can never be known exactly.) The resolution is followed by *reconciliation*, a process in which each committee of Congress must coordinate relevant tax and spending decisions. Once the reconciliation process is completed, funds are appropriated. The process is supposed to end before Congress recesses for the summer, at the end of June. When talking about the federal budget, the monetary amounts of various categories of expenditures are so huge that they are often difficult to comprehend. But if one were to divide up the annual budget by the number of individual taxpayers, you'd come up with an average individual statement that might make more sense, as shown in the Economic Insight "The Taxpayer's Federal Government Credit Card Statement."

The federal budget is determined as much by politics as economics. Politicians respond to different groups of voters by supporting different government programs regardless of the needed fiscal policy. It is the political response to constituents that tends to drive up federal budget deficits (the difference between government expenditures and tax revenues), not the need for expansionary fiscal policy. As a result, deficits have become commonplace.

2.b. The Historical Record

The U.S. government has grown dramatically since the early part of the century. Figure 4 shows federal revenues and expenditures over time. Figure 5

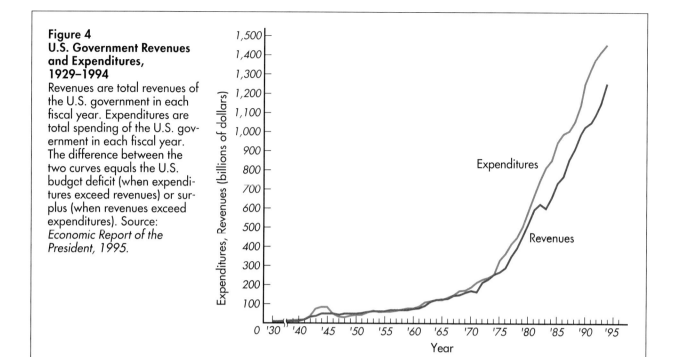

Figure 4
U.S. Government Revenues and Expenditures, 1929–1994
Revenues are total revenues of the U.S. government in each fiscal year. Expenditures are total spending of the U.S. government in each fiscal year. The difference between the two curves equals the U.S. budget deficit (when expenditures exceed revenues) or surplus (when revenues exceed expenditures). Source: *Economic Report of the President, 1995.*

places the growth of government in perspective by plotting U.S. government spending as a percentage of gross domestic product over time. Before the Great Depression, federal spending was approximately 3 percent of the GDP; by the end of the Depression, it had risen to almost 10 percent. The ratio of spending to GDP reached its peak during World War II, when federal spend-

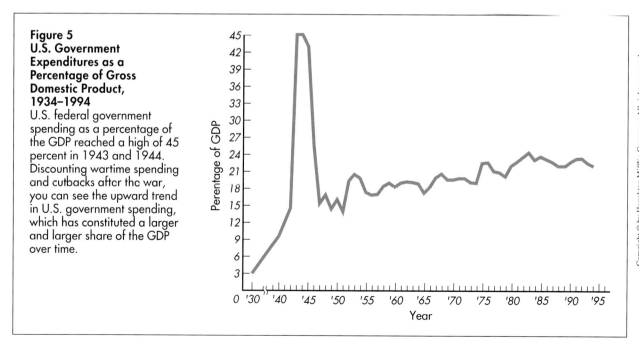

Figure 5
U.S. Government Expenditures as a Percentage of Gross Domestic Product, 1934–1994
U.S. federal government spending as a percentage of the GDP reached a high of 45 percent in 1943 and 1944. Discounting wartime spending and cutbacks after the war, you can see the upward trend in U.S. government spending, which has constituted a larger and larger share of the GDP over time.

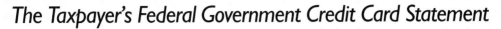

The Taxpayer's Federal Government Credit Card Statement

Suppose the U.S. government's expenditures and revenues were accounted for annually to each individual income tax payer like a credit card statement. For 1994, the statement would look like the following.

Statement for 1994 budget year		
Previous balance (your average taxpayer share of the beginning-of-year national debt)		**$37,106.28**
New purchases during the year (your average taxpayer share)		
Social security	$2,725.06	
National defense	2,401.00	
Income security	1,825.17	
Medicare	1,234.32	
Commerce and housing credit	−28.89	
Health	913.47	
Education, training, and employment	394.88	
Veterans' benefits and services	320.99	
Transportation	325.18	
Natural resources and environment	179.62	
Science, space, and technology	138.37	
International affairs	145.67	
Agriculture	128.94	
Administration of justice	130.09	
General government	96.46	
Community and regional development	89.15	
Energy	44.50	
Payments received—Thank you (your average taxpayer share)		
Individual income taxes		$ 4,630.85
Corporate income taxes		1,197.12
Social security taxes		3,935.18
Other		962.16
Finance charge (your average taxpayer share of net interest on the national debt)	**$1,730.69**	
New balance due (your average taxpayer share of the end-of-year national debt)		**$39,598.79**

ing hit 45 percent of the GDP. After the war, the ratio fell dramatically and then slowly increased to a little more than 20 percent today.

Fiscal policy has two components: discretionary fiscal policy and automatic stabilizers. **Discretionary fiscal policy** refers to changes in government spending and taxation aimed at achieving a policy goal. **Automatic stabilizers** are elements of fiscal policy that automatically change in value as national income changes. Figures 4 and 5 suggest that government spending is dominated by growth over time. But there is no indication here of discretionary changes in fiscal policy, changes in government spending and taxation aimed at meeting specific policy goals. Perhaps a better way to evaluate the fiscal policy record is in terms of the budget deficit. Government expenditures can rise, but the effect on aggregate demand could be offset by a simultaneous increase in taxes, so that there is no expansionary effect on the equilibrium level of national income. By looking at the deficit, we see the combined spending and tax policy results that are missing if only government expenditures are considered.

Figure 6 illustrates the pattern of the U.S. federal deficit and the deficit as a percentage of GDP over time. Part (a) shows that the United States ran close to a balanced budget for much of the 1950s and 1960s. There were large deficits associated with financing World War II, and then large deficits resulting from fiscal policy decisions in the 1970s, 1980s, and 1990s. Figure 6(b) shows that the deficit as a percentage of GDP was much larger during World War II than in recent years.

discretionary fiscal policy:
changes in government spending and taxation aimed at achieving a policy goal

automatic stabilizer:
an element of fiscal policy that changes automatically as income changes

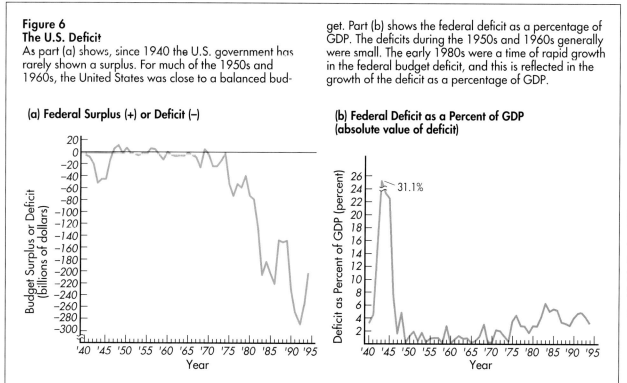

Figure 6
The U.S. Deficit
As part (a) shows, since 1940 the U.S. government has rarely shown a surplus. For much of the 1950s and 1960s, the United States was close to a balanced bud-get. Part (b) shows the federal deficit as a percentage of GDP. The deficits during the 1950s and 1960s generally were small. The early 1980s were a time of rapid growth in the federal budget deficit, and this is reflected in the growth of the deficit as a percentage of GDP.

The deficit increase in the mid-1970s was a product of a recession that cut the growth of tax revenues. Historically, aside from wartime, budget deficits increase the most during recessions. When real GDP falls, tax revenues go down and government spending on unemployment and welfare benefits goes up. These are examples of automatic stabilizers in action. As income falls, taxes fall and personal benefit payments rise to partially offset the effect of the drop in income. The rapid growth of the deficit in the 1980s involved more than the recessions in 1980 and 1982, however. The economy grew rapidly after the 1982 recession ended, but so did the fiscal deficit. The increase in the deficit was the product of a rapid increase in government spending to fund new programs and enlarge existing programs while taxes were held constant.

2.c. Deficits and the National Debt

What are the effects of budget deficits?

The recent increase in the federal deficit has led many observers to question whether a deficit can harm the economy. Figure 6 shows how the fiscal deficit has changed over time. One major implication of a large deficit is the resulting increase in the national debt, the total stock of government bonds outstanding. Table 1 lists data on the debt of the United States. Notice that the total debt doubled between 1981 ($994.8 billion) and 1986 ($2,120.6 billion). Column 3 shows debt as a percentage of GDP. In recent years, the debt has been rising as a percent of GDP. During World War II, the debt was greater than the GDP for five years. Despite the talk of "unprecedented" federal deficits in recent years, clearly the ratio of the debt to GDP was by no means unprecedented.

We have not yet answered the question of whether deficits are bad. To do so, we have to consider their potential effects.

Through their effect on investment, deficits can lower the level of output in the economy.

2.c.1. Deficits, Interest Rates, and Investment Because government deficits mean government borrowing and debt, many economists argue that deficits raise interest rates. Increased government borrowing raises interest rates, which in turn can depress investment. (Remember that as interest rates rise, the rate of return on investment drops, along with the incentive to invest.) What happens when government borrowing crowds out private investment? Lower investment means fewer capital goods in the future. So deficits lower the level of output in the economy both today and in the future. In this sense, deficits are potentially bad.

2.c.2. Deficits and International Trade If government deficits raise real interest rates (the nominal interest rate minus the expected inflation rate), they also may have an effect on international trade. A higher real return on U.S. securities makes those securities more attractive to foreign investors. As the foreign demand for U.S. securities increases, so does the demand for U.S. dollars in exchange for Japanese yen, British pounds, and other foreign currencies. As the demand for dollars increases, the dollar *appreciates* in value on the foreign exchange market. This means that the dollar becomes more expensive to foreigners while foreign currency becomes cheaper to U.S. residents. This kind of change in the exchange rate encourages U.S. residents to buy more foreign goods, and foreign residents to buy fewer U.S. goods.

Ultimately, then, as deficits and government debt increase, U.S. net exports fall. Many economists believe that the growing fiscal deficits of the 1980s were responsible for the record decline in U.S. net exports during that period.

The U.S. federal budget deficit rose from $73.8 billion in 1980 to $212.3 billion in 1985. During this time, the dollar appreciated in value from 1.95 German marks per dollar to 3.32 marks per dollar and from 203 Japanese yen per dollar to 260 yen per dollar. These changes in the dollar exchange rate caused U.S. goods to rise in price to foreign buyers. For instance, a $1,000 IBM personal computer would sell for 1,950 German marks at the exchange rate of 1.95 marks per dollar. But at the rate of 3.32 marks per dollar, the $1,000 computer would sell for 3,320 marks. Furthermore, foreign currencies became cheaper to U.S. residents, making foreign goods cheaper in dollars. In 1980, one German mark sold for $.51. In 1985, one mark sold for $.30. At these prices, a Volkswagen wheel that sells for 100 marks would have changed in dollar price from $51 to $30 as the exchange rate changed. The combination of the dollar price of U.S. imports falling and the foreign currency price of U.S. exports rising caused U.S. net exports to fall dramatically at the same time that the fiscal deficit rose dramatically. Such foreign trade effects are another potentially bad effect of deficits.

2.c.3. Interest Payments on the National Debt The national debt is the stock of government bonds outstanding. It is the product of past and current budget deficits. As the size of the debt increases, the interest that must be paid on the debt tends to rise. Column 4 of Table 1 lists the amount of interest paid on the debt; column 5 lists the interest as a percentage of government expenditures. The numbers in both columns have risen steadily over time. The federal government has been paying a higher dollar amount of interest each year, and this interest has been rising as a percentage of total government expenditures. This means that interest payments have been rising faster than total government spending.

The steady increase in the interest cost of the national debt is an aspect of fiscal deficits that worries some people. However, to the extent that U.S. citizens hold government bonds, we owe the debt to ourselves. The tax liability of funding the interest payments is offset by the interest income bondholders earn. In this case there is no net change in national wealth when the national debt changes.

Of course, we do not owe the national debt just to ourselves. The United States is the world's largest national financial market, and many U.S. securities, including government bonds, are held by foreign residents. In late 1994, foreign holdings of the U.S. national debt amounted to 21 percent of the outstanding debt. Because the tax liability for paying the interest on the debt falls on U.S. taxpayers, the greater the payments made to foreigners, the lower the wealth of U.S. residents, other things being equal.

Other things are not equal, however. To understand the real impact of foreign holdings on the economy, we have to evaluate what the economy would have been like if the debt had not been sold to foreign investors. If the foreign savings placed in U.S. bonds allowed the United States to increase investment and its productive capacity beyond what would have been possible in the absence of foreign lending, then the country could very well be better off for selling government bonds to foreigners. The presence of foreign funds

TABLE 1
Debt of the U.S. Government (dollar amounts in billions)

(1) Year	(2) Total Debt	(3) Debt/GDP (percent)	(4) Net Interest	(5) Interest/Government Spending (percent)
1958	$ 279.7	63	$ 5.6	6.8
1959	287.5	60	5.8	6.3
1960	290.5	57	6.9	7.5
1961	292.6	57	6.7	6.9
1962	302.9	55	6.9	6.5
1963	310.3	53	7.7	6.9
1964	316.1	50	8.2	6.9
1965	322.3	48	8.6	7.3
1966	328.5	44	9.4	7.0
1967	340.4	43	10.3	6.5
1968	368.7	43	11.1	6.2
1969	365.8	40	12.7	6.9
1970	380.9	39	14.4	7.4
1971	408.2	39	14.8	7.0
1972	435.9	38	15.5	6.7
1973	466.3	36	17.3	7.0
1974	483.9	34	21.4	8.0
1975	541.9	36	23.2	7.2
1976	629.0	37	26.7	7.3
1977	706.4	37	29.9	7.5
1978	776.6	36	35.4	7.9
1979	828.9	34	42.6	8.7
1980	909.1	34	52.5	9.1
1981	994.8	34	68.8	10.5
1982	1,137.3	36	85.0	11.6
1983	1,371.7	41	89.8	11.2
1984	1,564.7	42	111.1	13.2
1985	1,817.5	46	129.5	13.6
1986	2,120.6	50	136.0	13.7
1987	2,396.1	53	138.7	13.8
1988	2,601.3	54	151.8	14.3
1989	2,868.0	55	169.3	14.8
1990	3,206.6	59	184.2	14.7
1991	3,598.5	63	194.5	14.7
1992	4,002.1	68	199.4	14.4
1993	4,351.4	70	198.8	14.1
1994	4,643.7	70	203.0	13.9

may keep interest rates lower than they would otherwise be, preventing the substantial crowding out associated with an increase in the national debt.

So while deficits are potentially bad due to the crowding out of investment, larger trade deficits with the rest of the world, and greater interest costs of the debt, we cannot generally say that all deficits are bad. It depends on what benefit the deficit provides. If the deficit spending allowed for greater productivity than would have occurred otherwise, the benefits may outweigh the costs.

2.d. **Automatic Stabilizers**

We have largely been talking about discretionary fiscal policy, the changes in government spending and taxing that policymakers make consciously. *Automatic stabilizers* are the elements of fiscal policy that change automatically as income changes. Automatic stabilizers partially offset changes in income: as income falls, automatic stabilizers increase spending; as income rises, automatic stabilizers decrease spending. Any program that responds to fluctuations in the business cycle in a way that moderates the effect of those fluctuations is an automatic stabilizer. Examples are progressive income taxes and transfer payments.

In our examples of tax changes, we have been using *lump-sum taxes*—taxes that are a flat dollar amount regardless of income. However, income taxes are determined as a percentage of income. In the United States, the federal income tax is a **progressive tax**: as income rises, so does the rate of taxation. A person with a very low income pays no income tax, while a person with a high income can pay more than a third of that income in taxes. Countries use different rates of taxation on income. Taxes can be *regressive* (the tax rate falls as income rises) or *proportional* (the tax rate is constant as income rises). But most countries, including the United States, use a progressive tax, the percentage of income paid as taxes rising with taxable income.

progressive tax:
a tax whose rate rises as income rises

Progressive income taxes act as an automatic stabilizer. As income falls, so does the average tax rate. Suppose a household earning $60,000 must pay 30 percent of its income ($18,000) in taxes, leaving 70 percent of its income ($42,000) for spending. If that household's income drops to $40,000 and the tax rate falls to 25 percent, the household has 75 percent of its income ($30,000) available for spending. But if the tax rate is 30 percent at all levels of income, the household earning $40,000 would have only 70 percent of its income ($28,000) to spend. By allowing a greater percentage of earned income to be spent, progressive taxes help offset the effect of lower income on spending.

transfer payment:
a payment to one person that is funded by taxing others

A **transfer payment** is a payment to one person that is funded by taxing others. Food stamps, welfare benefits, and unemployment benefits are all government transfer payments: current taxpayers provide the funds to pay those who qualify for the programs. Transfer payments that use income to establish eligibility act as automatic stabilizers. In a recession, as income falls, more people qualify for food stamps or welfare benefits, raising the level of transfer payments.

Unemployment insurance is also an automatic stabilizer. As unemployment rises, more workers receive unemployment benefits. Unemployment benefits tend to rise in a recession and fall during an expansion. This countercyclical pattern of benefit payments offsets the effect of business cycle fluctuations on consumption.

1. Fiscal policy in the United States is a product of the budget process.

2. Federal spending in the United States has grown rapidly over time, from just 3 percent of the GDP before the Great Depression to approximately 24 percent of the GDP in the early 1990s.

3. Government budget deficits can hurt the economy through their effect on interest rates and private investment, net exports, and the tax burden on current and future taxpayers.

4. Automatic stabilizers are government programs that are already in place and that respond automatically to fluctuations in the business cycle, moderating the effect of those fluctuations.

3. FISCAL POLICY IN DIFFERENT COUNTRIES

How does fiscal policy differ across countries?

A country's fiscal policy reflects its philosophy toward government spending and taxation. In this section we present comparative data that demonstrate the variety of fiscal policies in the world.

3.a. Government Spending

Government spending has grown over time as a fraction of GNP in all industrial countries.

Our discussion to this point has centered on U.S. fiscal policy. But fiscal policy and the role of government in the economy can be very different across countries. Government has played an increasingly larger role in the major industrial countries over time. Table 2 shows how government spending has gone up as a percentage of output in five industrial nations. In every case, government spending accounted for a larger percentage of output in 1992 than it did 100 years earlier. For instance, in 1880, government spending was

TABLE 2
Share of Government Spending in GNP in Selected Industrial Countries, 1880, 1929, and 1992 (percent)

Year	France	Germany	Sweden	United Kingdom	United States
1880	15	10*	6	10	8
1929	19	31	8	24	10
1992	45	24	48	40	24

*1881

Source: From *World Development Report 1994* by The World Bank. Copyright © 1994 by the International Bank for Reconstruction and Development/The World Bank. Reprinted by permission of Oxford University Press, Inc.

only 10 percent of the GNP in the United Kingdom. By 1929 it had risen to 24 percent; and by 1992, to 40 percent.

Historically in industrial countries, the growth of government spending has been matched by growth in revenues. But in the 1960s, government spending began to grow faster than revenues, creating increasingly larger debtor nations.

Developing countries have not shown the uniform growth in government spending found in industrial countries. In fact, in some developing countries (for instance, Chile, the Dominican Republic, and Peru), government spending was a smaller percentage of GDP in 1992 than it was twenty years earlier. And we find a greater variation in the role of government in developing countries.

One important difference between the typical developed country and the typical developing country is that government plays a larger role in investment spending in the developing country. One reason for this difference is that state-owned enterprises account for a larger percentage of economic activity in developing countries than they do in developed countries. Also, developing countries usually rely more on government than the private sector to build their infrastructure—schools, roads, hospitals—than do developed countries.

How a government spends its money is a function of its income. Here we find differences not only between industrial and developing countries but also among developing countries. Figure 7 divides developing countries into

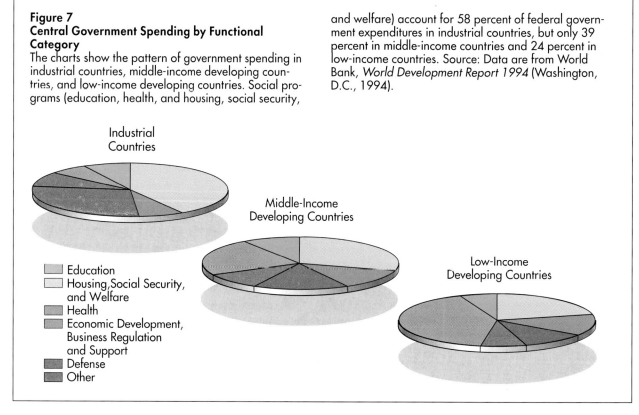

Figure 7
Central Government Spending by Functional Category
The charts show the pattern of government spending in industrial countries, middle-income developing countries, and low-income developing countries. Social programs (education, health, and housing, social security, and welfare) account for 58 percent of federal government expenditures in industrial countries, but only 39 percent in middle-income countries and 24 percent in low-income countries. Source: Data are from World Bank, *World Development Report 1994* (Washington, D.C., 1994).

Industrial Countries

Middle-Income Developing Countries

Low-Income Developing Countries

- Education
- Housing, Social Security, and Welfare
- Health
- Economic Development, Business Regulation and Support
- Defense
- Other

Part III/Macroeconomic Policy

low-income (the poorest) and middle-income (not as poor) groups. It clearly illustrates the relative importance of social welfare spending in industrial and developing countries. Although standards of living are lowest in the poorest countries, these countries do not have the resources to spend on social services (education, health, housing, social security, welfare). The industrial countries, on average, spend 58 percent of their budgets on social programs. Middle-income developing countries spend 39 percent of their budgets on social programs. Low-income countries spend only 24 percent of their budgets on these programs.

The labor forces in industrial countries are much better educated than those in developing countries. Figure 8 shows why. The figure measures the cost of educating a student for a year as a percentage of per capita GDP. On average it costs 49 percent of per capita GDP to educate a college student in an industrial country. It costs 370 percent of per capita GDP to provide a year of college education in the average developing country. In the poorest region of the world, sub-Saharan Africa, a year of college costs 800 percent of per capita GDP. Governments in the poorest countries simply cannot afford to provide a comprehensive system of higher education.

3.b. Taxation

There are two different types of taxes: *direct taxes* (on individuals and firms) and *indirect taxes* (on goods and services). Figure 9 compares the importance of different sources of central government tax revenue across industrial and developing countries. The most obvious difference is that personal income taxes are much more important in industrial countries than in developing countries. Why? Because personal taxes are hard to collect in agricultural

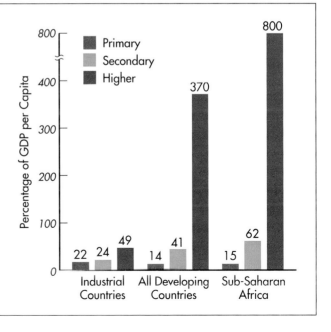

Figure 8
Cost per Student of Public Education as a Percentage of GDP per Capita in Three Country Groups
Industrial countries have much better educated populations than do poor countries. One reason is the higher cost of education in poor countries in terms of percentage of per capita GDP. A year of college education for one student costs an average of 49 percent of per capita GDP in industrial countries; it costs 370 percent on average in developing countries. In the poorest region in the world, sub-Saharan Africa, one year of higher education costs 800 percent of per capita GDP. Source: From *World Development Report 1988* by The World Bank. Copyright © 1988 by the International Bank for Reconstruction and Development/The World Bank. Reprinted by permission of Oxford University Press, Inc.

Figure 9
Central Government Tax Composition by Income Group

When we group countries by income level, the importance of different sources of tax revenue is obvious. Domestic income taxes account for roughly a third of government revenue in industrial and middle-income developing countries and a quarter of government revenue in developing countries. However, personal income taxes are most important in industrial countries, while business income taxes are most important in developing countries. Social security taxes are a major source of government revenue in industrial countries; they are less important in developing countries, which cannot afford social programs. International trade taxes represent just 3 percent of tax revenues in industrial countries; developing countries rely heavily on these taxes. Source: International Monetary Fund, *Government Finance Statistics* (Washington, D.C., 1992).

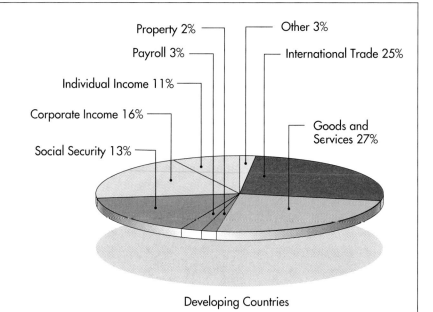

Property 2%
Payroll 3%
Individual Income 11%
Corporate Income 16%
Social Security 13%
Other 3%
International Trade 25%
Goods and Services 27%

Developing Countries

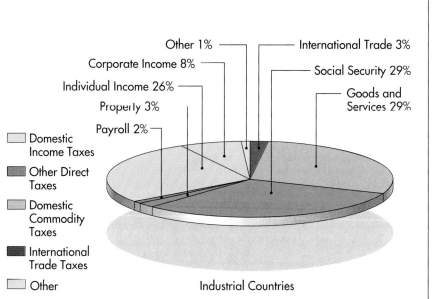

Other 1%
Corporate Income 8%
Individual Income 26%
Property 3%
Payroll 2%
International Trade 3%
Social Security 29%
Goods and Services 29%

Domestic Income Taxes
Other Direct Taxes
Domestic Commodity Taxes
International Trade Taxes
Other

Industrial Countries

nations, where a large percentage of household production is for personal consumption. Taxes on businesses are easier to collect, and thus are more important in developing countries.

That industrial countries are better able to afford social programs is reflected in the great disparity in social security taxes between industrial countries and developing countries. With so many workers living near the subsistence level in the poorest countries, their governments simply cannot tax workers for retirement and health security programs.

Figure 9 also shows that taxes on international trade are very important in developing countries. Because goods arriving or leaving a country must pass through customs inspection, export and import taxes are relatively easy to collect compared to income taxes. In general, developing countries depend more heavily on indirect taxes on goods and services than do developed countries.

Figure 9 lists "goods and services" taxes. Of these, 65 percent are **value-added (VAT) taxes** for industrial countries, while 61 percent of developing country commodity taxes come from value-added taxes. A value-added tax is an indirect tax imposed on each sale at each stage of production. Each seller from the first stage of production on collects the VAT from the buyer, and then deducts any VATs it has paid in buying its inputs. The difference is remitted to the government. From time to time, Congress has debated the merits of a VAT in the United States, but has never approved this kind of tax.

value-added tax (VAT):
a general sales tax collected at each stage of production

RECAP

1. Over time, government spending has become more important in industrial countries.

2. Governments in developing countries typically play a larger role in investment spending in their economies than do the governments of developed countries.

3. Developing countries depend more on indirect taxes on goods and services as a source of revenue than on direct taxes on individuals and businesses.

4. Value-added taxes are general sales taxes that are collected at every stage of production.

SUMMARY

▲▼ *How can fiscal policy eliminate a GDP gap?*

1. A GDP gap can be closed by increasing government spending or by cutting taxes. §1

2. Government spending affects aggregate expenditures directly; taxes affect aggregate expenditures indirectly, through their effect on consumption. §1

3. Aggregate expenditures must rise to bring equilibrium real GDP up to potential real GDP—to eliminate the GDP gap. §1

4. An increase in government spending matched by an increase in taxes raises equilibrium spending and real GDP. §1.c

5. If the public expects to pay higher taxes as a result of government borrowing, then the expansionary effects of government deficits may be reduced. §1.c.

6. Government borrowing can crowd out private spending by raising interest rates and reducing investments. §1.e

▲▼ *How has U.S. fiscal policy changed over time?*

7. Fiscal policy in the United States is a product of the budget process. §2.a

8. Federal government spending in the United States has increased from just 3 percent of the

GDP before the Great Depression to a little more than 20 percent of the GDP today. §2.b

9. Fiscal policy has two components: discretionary fiscal policy and automatic stabilizers. §2.b

▲▼ *What are the effects of budget deficits?*

10. Budget deficits, through their effects on interest rates, international trade, and the national debt, can reduce investment, output, net exports, and national wealth. §2.c.1, 2.c.2, 2.c.3

11. Progressive taxes and transfer payments are automatic stabilizers, elements of fiscal policy

that change automatically as national income changes. §2.d

▲▼ *How does fiscal policy differ across countries?*

12. Industrial countries spend a much larger percentage of their government budget for social programs than do developing countries. §3.a

13. Industrial countries depend more on direct taxes and less on indirect taxes than do developing countries. §3.b

KEY TERMS

crowding out §1.e
discretionary fiscal policy §2.b
automatic stabilizer §2.b

progressive tax §2.d
transfer payment §2.d
value-added tax (VAT) §3.b

EXERCISES

1. What is the role of aggregate demand in eliminating the GDP gap? How does the slope of the *AS* curve affect the fiscal policy actions necessary to eliminate the GDP gap?

2. Briefly describe the process of setting the federal budget in the United States. What is the time lag between the start of the process and the point at which the money is actually spent?

3. In what ways are government deficits harmful to the economy?

4. Define and give three examples of automatic stabilizers.

5. Briefly describe the major differences between fiscal policy in industrial countries and that in developing countries.

6. Why will real GDP tend to rise when government spending and taxes rise by the same amount?

7. How can a larger government fiscal deficit cause a larger international trade deficit?

8. Why do government budget deficits grow during recessions?

9. Taxes can be progressive, regressive, or proportional. Define each, and briefly offer an argument for why income taxes are usually progressive.

The following questions are based on the appendix to this chapter.

Answer questions 10–13 on the basis of the following information. Assume that equilibrium real GDP is $800 billion, potential real GDP is $900 billion, the *MPC* is .80, and the *MPI* is .40.

10. What is the size of the GDP gap?

11. How much must government spending increase to eliminate the GDP gap?

12. How much must taxes fall to eliminate the GDP gap?

13. If government spending and taxes both change by the same amount, how much must they change to eliminate the recessionary gap?

14. Suppose the *MPC* is .90 and the *MPI* is .10. If government expenditures go up $100 billion while taxes fall $10 billion, what happens to the equilibrium level of real GDP?

Use the following equations to answer questions 15–17.

$$C = \$100 + .8Y$$

$$I = \$200$$

$$G = \$250$$

$$X = \$100 - .2Y$$

15. What is the equilibrium level of real GDP?

16. What is the new equilibrium level of real GDP if government spending increases by $100?

17. What is the new equilibrium level of real GDP if government spending and taxes both increase by $100?

COOPERATIVE LEARNING EXERCISE

Split the class into pairs of students. Each pair then uses the information in the chapter to write five answers (one correct and four incorrect choices) to the following multiple-choice question:

A government budget deficit may be harmful because:

a.

b.

c.

d.

e.

The instructor then collects the answers and presents several for the entire class to evaluate.

Think of the Federal Budget as a Little Like Air

CLEVELAND—Think of the federal budget deficit as a little like air.

You can't see it, feel it or hold it in your hand. But it's all around you. And it affects every economic breath you take.

"A deficit has to be covered in one of two ways," explained David Bowers, professor of banking and finance at Case Western Reserve University. "The government either borrows the money from the public or it prints the money. That's the only two choices it has. One gives you higher interest rates. The other gives you higher inflation."

Right now, most economists believe, the deficit's biggest impact is on interest rates. And that determines what we pay for loans. Loans to buy cars or houses. To start or expand businesses.

Frank Clayton feels the pinch. He runs a small, but thriving, wholesale business on Cleveland's southeast side. Like a lot of other entrepreneurs, Clayton occasionally has to go to the bank for a line of credit to keep his operation growing.

And when he does, the frugal, hands-on boss of Central Electric Supply must bid for money against Uncle Sam, that mother of all spendthrifts. Uncle Sam needs to borrow an extra $300 billion or so every year. He also can pay whatever interest is required to get the cash because taxpayers like you pick up the tab.

So Uncle Sam gets what he needs. Frank Clayton and everybody else get what's left—at the prices Uncle Sam set. It's the old law of supply and demand.

"The deficit makes it harder to get the capital because the government competes with you for what's available," Clayton said the other day. "That means the cost of the money just gets higher and higher."

Or at least higher than it ought to be. . . .

Kenneth T. Mayland, senior vice president and chief economist at Society Bank, cautions that hypotheticals about how the economy might look if the budget were balanced tend to ignore the costs of reaching that fiscal promised land.

"Part of the mechanism that results in lower rates puts some people out of work," said Mayland. "Raising taxes $300 billion is going to put some people out of work. Same with cutting government spending. Keep in mind that government spending is somebody's income."

Source: "Think of the Federal Budget as a Little Like Air," Joe Frolik, *Plain Dealer*, Feb. 28, 1993, p. 8A. Reprinted by permission of The Plain Dealer.

Plain Dealer (Cleveland)/February 28, 1993

Commentary

Although the extent, causes, and political impact of the massive budget deficit have been extensively covered by the media, there has been relatively less reporting on the deficit's precise effects on the economy. An implicit message in many reports is that budget deficits are harmful. Other reports suggest that budget deficits are either helpful (at least in moderation) or have no effect. Careful economic reasoning provides us with insight into the consequences of the budget deficit for the U.S. economy.

You may have heard arguments concerning the effects of the budget deficit that proceed by means of an analogy between the government's budget and a family's budget. Just as a family cannot spend more than it earns, so the argument goes, the government cannot follow this practice without bringing itself to ruin. The problem with this analogy is that the government has the ability to raise money through taxes and bond sales, options not open to a family.

A more appropriate analogy is to compare the government's budget to that of a large corporation. Large corporations run persistent deficits that are never paid back. Instead, when corporate debt comes due, the corporations "roll over" their debt by selling new debt. Corporations are able to do this because they use their debt to finance investment that enables them to increase their worth. To the extent that the government is investing in projects like road repairs and building the nation's infrastructure, it is increasing the productive capacity of the economy, which widens the tax base and increases potential future tax receipts.

There are, of course, legitimate problems associated with the budget deficit. The government has two options if it cannot pay for its expenditures with tax receipts. One method of financing the budget deficit is by printing money. This is an unattractive option because it leads to inflation. Another method is to borrow funds by selling government bonds. A problem with this option is that the government must compete for scarce loanable funds and, unless saving increases at the same time, interest rates rise and government borrowing "crowds out" private investment. In the article, the owner of Central Electric Supply in Cleveland complains about how government borrowing makes it harder for him to borrow to finance the growth of his company. If this is a problem throughout the economy, it results in a lower capital stock and diminished prospects for future economic growth.

A balanced federal budget is still many years away. Thus, stories focusing on the budget deficit, which were a mainstay of the economic news of the 1980s, will most likely retain their prominence in the 1990s. Although everyone complains about the harmful effects of the budget deficit, cutting the deficit is politically difficult. As the banker quoted in the article says, "Government spending is somebody's income." Cutting spending means hurting someone, which politicians are hesitant to do. The deficit could also be cut by raising taxes, but that means less private spending and angry taxpayers—not an easy political solution. As a result, it is reasonable to expect tax increases generally to be modest. It may be that the best we can hope for is a reduced growth of government spending coupled with a growing economy. As the economy grows, tax revenue rises and if government spending grows slower than tax revenue, the deficit will fall.

12

An Algebraic Examination of the Balanced-Budget Change in Fiscal Policy

What would happen if government spending and taxes went up by the same amount? We can analyze such a change by expanding the analysis begun in the Appendix to Chapter 11.

The spending multiplier is the simple multiplier defined in Chapter 11:

$$\text{Spending multiplier} = \frac{1}{MPS + MPI}$$

In the Chapter 11 example, because the *MPS* equals .30 and the *MPI* equals .05, the spending multiplier equals 2.5:

$$\text{Spending multiplier} = \frac{1}{MPS + MPI} = \frac{1}{.30 + .10}$$

$$= \frac{1}{.40} = 2.5$$

When government spending increases by $20, the equilibrium level of real GDP increases by 2.5 times $20, or $50.

We also can define a tax multiplier, a measure of the effect of a change in taxes on equilibrium real GDP. Because a percentage of any change in income is saved and spent on imports, we know that a tax cut increases expenditures by less than the amount of the cut. The percentage of the tax cut that actually is spent is the marginal propensity to consume (*MPC*) less the *MPI*. If consumers save 30 percent of any extra income, they spend 70 percent, the *MPC*. But the domestic economy does not realize 70 percent of the extra income because 10 percent of the extra income is spent on imports. The percentage of any extra income that actually is spent at home is the *MPC* minus the *MPI*. In our example, 60 percent (.70 − .10) of any extra income is spent in the domestic economy.

With this information, we can define the tax multiplier like this:

$$\text{Tax multiplier} = -(MPC - MPI)\left[\frac{1}{MPS + MPI}\right]$$

In our example, the tax multiplier is -1.5:

$$\text{Tax multiplier} = -(.70 - .10)\left[\frac{1}{.30 + .10}\right]$$

$$= -(.60)(2.5) = -1.5$$

A tax cut increases equilibrium real GDP by 1.5 times the amount of the cut. Notice that the tax multiplier is always a *negative* number because a change in taxes moves income and expenditures in the opposite direction. Higher taxes lower income and expenditures; lower taxes raise income and expenditures.

Now that we have reviewed the spending and tax multipliers, we can examine the effect of a balanced-budget change in fiscal policy where government spending and taxes change by the same amount. To simplify the analysis, we assume that taxes are lump-sum taxes (taxpayers must pay a certain amount of dollars as tax) rather than income taxes (where the tax rises with income). We can use the algebraic model presented in the Appendix to Chapter 11 to illustrate the effect of a balanced-budget change in government spending. Here are the model equations:

$$C = \$30 + .70Y$$

$$I = \$50$$

$$G = \$70$$

$$X = \$50 - .10Y$$

Solving for the equilibrium level of Y (as we did in the Appendix to Chapter 11), Y equals \$500 where Y equals aggregate expenditures.

Now suppose that G increases by \$10 and that this increase is funded by taxes of \$10. The increase in G changes autonomous government spending to \$80. The increase in taxes affects the autonomous levels of C and X. The new model equations are:

$$C = \$30 + .70(Y - \$10) = \$23 + .70Y$$

$$X = \$50 - .10(Y - \$10) = \$51 - .10Y$$

Using the new G, C, and X functions, we can find the new equilibrium level of real GDP by setting Y equal to AE ($C + I + G + X$):

$$Y = C + I + G + X$$

$$Y = \$23 + .70Y + \$50 + \$80 + \$51 - .10Y$$

$$Y = \$204 + .60Y$$

$$Y - .60Y = \$204$$

$$.40Y = \$204$$

$$Y = \$510$$

Increasing government spending and taxes by \$10 each raises the equilibrium level of real GDP by \$10. A balanced-budget increase in G increases Y by the change in G. If government spending and taxes both fall by the same amount, then real GDP will also fall by an amount equal to the change in government spending and taxes.

13

Money and Banking

FUNDAMENTAL QUESTIONS

1. What is money?
2. How is the U.S. money supply defined?
3. How do countries pay for international transactions?
4. Why are banks considered intermediaries?
5. How does international banking differ from domestic banking?
6. How do banks create money?

U p to this point, we have been talking about aggregate expenditures, aggregate demand and supply, and fiscal policy without explicitly discussing money. Yet money is used by every sector of the economy in all nations and plays a crucial role in every economy. In this chapter we discuss what money is, how the quantity of money is determined, and the role of banks in determining this quantity. In the next chapter, we examine the role of money in the aggregate demand and supply model.

As you will see in the next two chapters, the quantity of money has a major impact on interest rates, inflation, and the amount of spending in the economy. Money is, then, important for macroeconomic policy making, and government officials use both monetary and fiscal policy to influence the equilibrium level of real GDP and prices.

Banks and the banking system also play key roles, both at home and abroad, in the determination of the amount of money in circulation and the movement of money between nations. After we define money and its functions, we look at the banking system. We begin with banking in the United States, and then discuss international banking. Someone once joked that banks follow the rule of 3-6-3. They borrow at 3 percent interest, lend at 6 percent interest, and close at 3 P.M. If those days ever existed, clearly they do not today. The banking industry in the United States and the rest of the world has undergone tremendous change in recent years. New technology and government deregulation are allowing banks to respond to changing economic conditions in ways that were unthinkable only a few years ago, and these changes have had dramatic effects on the economy.

PREVIEW

I. WHAT IS MONEY?

Money is anything that is generally acceptable to sellers in exchange for goods and services. The cash in your wallet can be used to buy groceries or a movie ticket. You simply present your cash to the cashier, who readily accepts it. If you want to use your car to buy groceries or a movie ticket, the exchange is more complicated. You would probably have to sell the car before you could use it to buy other goods and services. Cars are seldom exchanged directly for goods and services (except for other cars). Because cars are not a generally acceptable means of paying for other goods and services, we don't consider them to be money.

What is money?

money:
anything that is generally acceptable to sellers in exchange for goods and services

liquid asset:
an asset that can easily be exchanged for goods and services

Money is the most liquid asset. A **liquid asset** is an asset that can easily be exchanged for goods and services. Cash is a liquid asset; a car is not. How liquid must an asset be before we consider it money? To answer this question, we must first consider the functions of money.

1.a. Functions of Money

Money serves four basic functions: it is a *medium of exchange*, a *unit of account*, a *store of value*, and a *standard of deferred payment*. Not all monies serve all of these functions equally well, as will be apparent in the following discussion. But to be money, an item must perform enough of these functions to induce people to use it.

1.a.1. Medium of Exchange   Money is a medium of exchange; it is used in exchange for goods and services. Sellers willingly accept money in payment for the products and services they produce. Without money, we would have to resort to *barter*, the direct exchange of goods and services for other goods and services.

For a barter system to work, there must be a *double coincidence of wants*. Suppose Bill is a carpenter and Jane is a plumber. In a monetary economy, when Bill needs plumbing repairs in his home, he simply pays Jane for the repairs using money. Because everyone wants money, money is an acceptable means of payment. In a barter economy, Bill must offer his services as a carpenter in exchange for Jane's work. If Jane does not want any carpentry work done, Bill and Jane cannot enter into a mutually beneficial transaction. Bill has to find a person who can do what he wants and also wants what he can do—there must be a double coincidence of wants.

The use of money as a medium of exchange lowers transaction costs.

The example of Bill and Jane illustrates the fact that barter is a lot less efficient than using money. This means that the cost of a transaction in a barter economy is higher than the cost of a transaction in a monetary economy. The use of money as a medium of exchange lowers transaction costs.

The people of Yap Island highly value and thus accept as their medium of exchange giant stones (see the Economic Insight "Yap Island Money"). But in most cultures, money must be portable in order to be an effective medium of exchange—a property the stone money of Yap Island clearly lacks. Another important property of money is *divisibility*. Money must be measurable in both small units (for low-value goods and services) and large units (for high-value goods and services). Yap stone money is not divisible, so it is not a good medium of exchange for the majority of goods bought and sold.

1.a.2. Unit of Account   Money is a unit of account: We price goods and services in terms of money. This common unit of measurement allows us to compare relative values easily. If whole-wheat bread sells for a dollar a loaf and white bread sells for 50 cents, we know that whole-wheat bread is twice as expensive as white bread.

The use of money as a unit of account lowers information costs.

Using money as a unit of account is efficient. It reduces the costs of gathering information on what things are worth. The use of money as a unit of account lowers information costs relative to barter. In a barter economy, people constantly have to evaluate the worth of the goods and services being offered. When money prices are placed on goods and services, their relative value is obvious.

1.a.3. Store of Value   Money functions as a store of value or purchasing power. If you are paid today, you do not have to hurry out to spend your

Yap Island Money

Yap Island is one of the three Federated States of Micronesia. The citizens of Yap Island have been using giant doughnut-shaped stones as money for approximately 1,500 years. Some of the stones are 12 feet in diameter and weigh hundreds of pounds. The ancient Yapese quarried the stones on the island of Palau, over 250 nautical miles from Yap. The stones were towed back to Yap on rafts pulled by canoes. The value of each stone is determined by its history. The larger and more perfect the stone, and the greater the effort to bring the stone to Yap, the higher its value.

The stones lie around the island, propped up along roads and beside houses. The stones do not have to be moved because ownership is transferred by verbal agreement. Each stone is distinct, and the Yapese acknowledge the current and past owners of each stone.

The stones serve as a form of large-denomination money. For instance, a few years ago, the lieutenant governor of the island at the time, Hilary Tacheliol, was quoted as saying, "I recently bought a house that would have cost $12,000 cash. I got it for $2,000 cash and stone money."

Yap stones point out the importance of consumer confidence in determining the value of money. The stones have value because the Yapese believe they are valuable. Norman Angell, in *The Story of Money*, described a Yapese family whose ownership of a very valuable stone was acknowledged by everyone even though no one currently living had ever seen it.* For generations, the stone had been lying at the bottom of the sea. An ancestor was bringing the stone back from Palau when a violent storm forced him to cut his stone-carrying raft loose. When he

arrived back on Yap, the other men who had been on the voyage testified to the great size and perfection of the lost stone. The islanders accepted the value of the stone and the family's increased wealth as though the stone was leaning against the family home. Over time, ownership of the stone lying at the bottom of the ocean passed from person to person by verbal agreement.

A money is acceptable if people believe that it has value. It is not necessary to physically possess the money or for the money to be backed by any promise of redemption in gold or other precious objects. As long as people believe something is money, it functions as money.

*Norman Angell, *The Story of Money* (New York: Garden City Publishing, 1929).

---

money. It will still have value next week or next month. Some monies retain their value better than others. In colonial New England, fish and furs both served as money. But because fish does not store as well as furs, its usefulness as a store of value was limited. An important property of a money is its *durability*, its ability to retain its value over time.

Inflation plays a major role in determining the effectiveness of a money as a store of value. The higher the rate of inflation, the faster the purchasing power of money falls. In high-inflation countries, workers spend their pay as fast as possible because the purchasing power of their money is falling rapidly. It makes no sense to hold on to a money that is quickly losing value. In countries where the domestic money does not serve as a good store of value, it ceases to fulfill this function of money and people begin to use something else as money, like the currency of another nation. For instance, U.S. dollars have long been a favorite store of value in Latin American countries that have experienced high inflation. This phenomenon—**currency substitution**—has been documented in Argentina, Bolivia, Mexico, and other countries during times of high inflation.

currency substitution: the use of foreign money as a substitute for domestic money when the domestic economy has a high rate of inflation

I.a.4. Standard of Deferred Payment Finally, money is a standard of deferred payment. Debt obligations are written in terms of money values. If you have a credit card bill that is due in 90 days, the value you owe is stated in monetary units—for example, dollars in the United States and yen in Japan. We use money values to state amounts of debt and use money to pay our debts.

We should make a distinction here between money and credit. Money is what we use to pay for goods and services. **Credit** is available savings that are lent to borrowers to spend. If you use your Visa or MasterCard to buy a shirt, you are not buying the shirt with your money. You are taking out a loan from the bank that issued the credit card in order to buy the shirt. Credit and money are different. Money is an *asset*, something you own. Credit is *debt*, something you owe.

credit:
available savings that are lent to borrowers to spend

1.b. The U.S. Money Supply

How is the U.S. money supply defined?

The quantity of money available for spending is an important determinant of many key macroeconomic variables, since changes in the money supply affect interest rates, inflation, and other indicators of economic health. When economists measure the money supply, they measure spendable assets. Identifying those assets, however, can be difficult. Although it would seem that *all* bank deposits are money, some bank deposits are held for spending while others are held for saving. In defining the money supply, then, economists must differentiate among assets on the basis of their liquidity and the likelihood of their being used for spending.

The problem of distinguishing among assets has produced several definitions of the money supply: M1, M2, and M3. Economists and policymakers use all three definitions to evaluate the availability of funds for spending. Although economists have tried to identify a single measure that best influences the business cycle and changes in interest rates and inflation, research indicates that different definitions work better to explain changes in macroeconomic variables at different times.

1.b.1. M1 Money Supply The narrowest and most liquid measure of the money supply is the **M1 money supply**, the financial assets that are immediately available for spending. This definition emphasizes the use of money as a medium of exchange. The M1 money supply consists of currency, travelers' checks, demand deposits, and other checkable deposits. Demand and other checkable deposits are **transactions accounts**; they can be used to make direct payments to a third party.

M1 money supply:
financial assets that are the most liquid

transactions account:
a checking account at a bank or other financial institution that can be drawn on to make payments

In 1986 the Federal Reserve Board commissioned a survey to determine how U.S. families pay for their goods and services. It found that families use their main checking account for 39 percent of purchases. (The *main checking account* is the one a household uses most frequently.) Cash transactions account for 34 percent of purchases. Other checking accounts are used for 9 percent of expenditures. Credit cards account for 8 percent, as do savings and money market accounts (part of the M2 money supply). Finally, money orders are used for 2 percent of family expenditures.

If you subtract credit cards, savings and money market accounts, and money orders from total household expenditures, you can see that the components of the M1 money supply are used for 82 percent of family purchases. This is one reason why the M1 money supply may be a useful variable in formulating macroeconomic policy.

Currency Currency includes coins and paper money in circulation (in the hands of the public). In 1995, currency represented 31 percent of the M1 money supply. A common misconception about currency today is that it is backed by gold or silver. This is not true. There is nothing backing the U.S. dollar except the confidence of the public. This kind of monetary system is called a *fiduciary monetary system*. Fiduciary comes from the Latin *fiducia*, which means "trust." Our monetary system is based on trust. As long as we believe that our money is an acceptable form of payment for goods and services, the system works. It is not necessary for money to be backed by any precious object. As long as people believe that a money has value, it will serve as money.

The United States has not always operated under a fiduciary monetary system. At one time the U.S. government issued gold and silver coins and paper money that could be exchanged for silver. In 1967, Congress authorized the U.S. Treasury to stop redeeming "silver certificate" paper money for silver. Coins with an intrinsic value are known as *commodity money*; they have value as a commodity in addition to their face value. The problem with commodity money is that as the value of the commodity increases, the money stops being circulated. People hoard coins when their commodity value exceeds their face value. For example, no one would take an old $20 gold piece to the grocery store to buy $20 worth of groceries because the gold is worth much more than $20 today.

The tendency to hoard money as its commodity value increases is called *Gresham's Law*. Thomas Gresham was a successful businessman and financial adviser to Queen Elizabeth I. He insisted that if two coins have the same face value but different intrinsic values—perhaps one is silver and the other brass—the cheaper coin will be used in exchange while the more expensive coin will be hoarded. People sometimes state Gresham's Law as "bad money drives out good money," meaning that the money with the low commodity value will be used in exchange while the money with the high commodity value will be driven out of hand-to-hand use and be hoarded.[1]

According to Gresham's Law, bad money drives out good money.

Travelers' checks Outstanding U.S. dollar-denominated travelers' checks issued by nonbank institutions are counted as part of the M1 money supply. There are several nonbank issuers, among them American Express and Cook's. (Travelers' checks issued by banks are included in demand deposits. When a bank issues its own travelers' checks, it deposits the amount paid by the purchaser in a special account that is used to redeem the checks. Because this amount is counted as part of demand deposits, it is not counted again as part of outstanding travelers' checks.) Travelers' checks accounted for less than 1 percent of the M1 money supply in 1995.

Demand deposits Demand deposits are checking account deposits at a commercial bank. These deposits pay no interest. They are called *demand deposits* because the bank must pay the amount of the check immediately on the demand of the depositor. Demand deposits accounted for 33 percent of the M1 money supply in 1995.

Other checkable deposits Until the 1980s, demand deposits were the only kind of checking account. Today there are many different kinds of checking accounts, known as *other checkable deposits (OCDs)*. OCDs are accounts at

---

[1]Actually, Gresham was not the first to recognize that bad money drives out good money. A fourteenth-century French theologian, Nicholas Oresme, made the same argument in his book *A Treatise on the Origin, Nature, Law, and Alterations of Money*, written almost 200 years before Gresham was born.

financial institutions that pay interest and give the depositor check-writing privileges. Among the OCDs included in the M1 money supply are the following:

Negotiable orders of withdrawal (NOW) accounts These are interest-bearing checking accounts offered by savings and loan institutions.

Automatic transfer system (ATS) accounts These are accounts at commercial banks that combine an interest-bearing savings account with a non-interest-bearing checking account. The depositor keeps a small balance in the checking account; anytime the checking account balance is overdrawn, funds automatically are transferred from the savings account.

Credit union share draft accounts Credit unions offer their members interest-bearing checking accounts called *share drafts*.

Demand deposits at mutual savings banks Mutual savings banks are non-profit savings and loan organizations. Any profits after operating expenses have been paid may be distributed to depositors.

I.b.2. **M2 Money Supply** The components of the M1 money supply are the most liquid assets, the assets most likely to be used for transactions. M2 is a broader definition of the money supply that includes assets in somewhat less liquid forms. The M2 money supply includes the M1 money supply plus overnight repurchase agreements, overnight Eurodollar deposits, money market deposit accounts, savings and small-denomination time deposits, and balances in individual money market mutual funds.

■ An *overnight repurchase agreement (RP)* is an agreement between a bank and a customer under which the customer buys U.S. government securities from the bank one day and sells them back to the bank the next day at a price that includes the interest earned overnight. Overnight RPs are used by firms that have excess cash one day that may be needed the next.

■ *Overnight Eurodollar deposits* are deposits denominated in dollars but held outside the U.S. domestic bank industry. Overnight Eurodollar deposits mature the day after they are deposited.

■ *Money market deposit accounts* are accounts at commercial banks and savings and loan institutions. They require a minimum balance and place limits on the number of transactions allowed per month.

■ *Savings deposits* are accounts at banks and savings and loan associations that earn interest but offer no check-writing privileges.

■ *Small-denomination time deposits* are often called *certificates of deposit*. Funds in these accounts must be deposited for a specified period of time. (*Small* means less than $100,000.)

■ *Individual money market mutual fund balances* combine the deposits of many individuals and invest them in government Treasury bills and other short-term securities. Many money market mutual funds grant check-writing privileges but limit the size and number of checks.

I.b.3. **M3 Money Supply** The M3 money supply equals the M2 money supply plus *large time deposits* (deposits in amounts of $100,000 or more), *term RPs* and *term Eurodollar deposits* (deposits held by banks for a specified period), and *institution-only money market mutual fund balances* (balances that do not include the balances of individuals). These additional assets are less liquid than those found in the M1 or M2 money supply. Figure 1 summarizes the three definitions of the money supply.

I.c. Global Money

How do countries pay for international transactions?

The currencies of the major developed countries tend to dominate the international medium-of-exchange and unit-of-account functions of money.

international reserve asset: an asset used to settle debts between governments

international reserve currency: a currency held by a government to settle international debts

European currency unit (ECU): a unit of account used by western European nations as their official reserve asset

composite currency: an artificial unit of account that is an average of the values of several national currencies

So far we have discussed the money supply in a domestic context. Just as the United States uses dollars as its domestic money, every nation has its own monetary unit of account. Japan has the yen, Mexico the peso, Canada the Canadian dollar, and so on. Since each nation uses a different money, how do countries pay for transactions that involve residents of other countries? As you saw in Chapter 7, the foreign exchange market links national monies together, so that transactions can be made across national borders. If Sears in the United States buys a home entertainment system from Sony in Japan, Sears can exchange dollars for yen in order to pay Sony in yen. The exchange rate between the dollar and yen determines how many dollars are needed to purchase the required number of yen. For instance, if Sony wants 1,000,000 yen for the component and the exchange rate is ¥100 = $1, Sears needs $10,000 (1,000,000/100) to buy the yen.

Sales contracts between developed countries usually are written (invoiced) in the national currency of the exporter. To complete the transaction, the importer buys the exporter's currency on the foreign exchange market. Trade between developing and developed nations typically is invoiced in the currency of the developed country, whether the developed country is the exporter or importer because the currency of the developed country is usually more stable and more widely traded on the foreign exchange market than the currency of the developing country. As a result, the currencies of the major developed countries tend to dominate the international medium-of-exchange and unit-of-account functions of money.

I.c.1. International Reserve Currencies Governments hold monies as a temporary store of value until money is needed to settle international debts. At one time gold was the primary **international reserve asset**, an asset used to settle debts between governments. Although gold still serves as an international reserve asset, its role is unimportant relative to that of currencies. Today national currencies function as international reserves. The currencies that are held for this purpose are called **international reserve currencies**.

Table 1 shows the importance of the major international reserve currencies over time. In the mid-1970s, the U.S. dollar comprised almost 80 percent of international reserve holdings. By 1990 its share had fallen to less than 50 percent, but the share has risen again recently. One reason for this change was the adoption by the western European nations of a new unit of currency, the ECU, as their official reserve asset.

I.c.2. Composite Currencies The industrial nations of western Europe introduced this new unit of currency, the **European currency unit (ECU)**, in March 1979. These nations use ECUs to settle debts between them. The ECU is a **composite currency**; its value is an average of the values of several different national currencies: the Belgian franc, the Danish krone, the French franc, the German mark, the Greek drachma, the Irish pound, the Luxembourg franc, the Netherlands guilder, the Spanish peseta, and the Portuguese escudo (the Italian lira and the U.K. pound were withdrawn from the system in September 1992). The European Monetary System, an

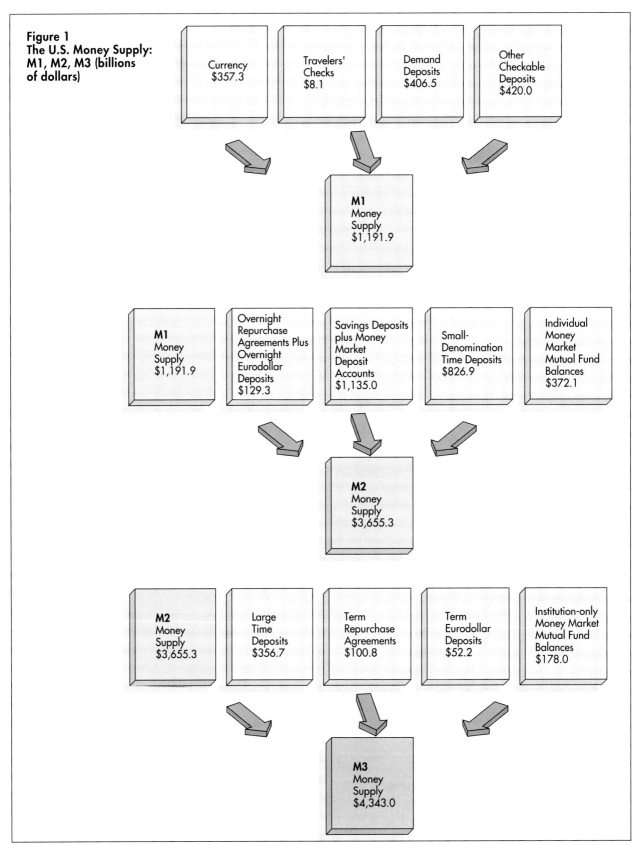

Figure 1
The U.S. Money Supply: M1, M2, M3 (billions of dollars)

Currency $357.3

Travelers' Checks $8.1

Demand Deposits $406.5

Other Checkable Deposits $420.0

M1 Money Supply $1,191.9

M1 Money Supply $1,191.9

Overnight Repurchase Agreements Plus Overnight Eurodollar Deposits $129.3

Savings Deposits plus Money Market Deposit Accounts $1,135.0

Small-Denomination Time Deposits $826.9

Individual Money Market Mutual Fund Balances $372.1

M2 Money Supply $3,655.3

M2 Money Supply $3,655.3

Large Time Deposits $356.7

Term Repurchase Agreements $100.8

Term Eurodollar Deposits $52.2

Institution-only Money Market Mutual Fund Balances $178.0

M3 Money Supply $4,343.0

TABLE 1
International Reserve Currencies (Percentage Shares of National Currencies in Total Official Holdings of Foreign Exchange)

Year	U.S. Dollar	Pound Sterling	Deutsche Mark	French Franc	Japanese Yen	Swiss Franc	Netherlands Guilder	ECUs	Unspecified Currencies
1976	78.8	1.0	8.7	1.5	1.9	2.1	0.8	—	5.2
1980	56.6	2.5	12.8	1.5	3.7	2.8	1.1	16.4	2.7
1984	60.5	2.7	11.3	1.0	5.2	1.9	0.7	11.4	5.3
1990	49.6	3.1	18.7	2.0	8.6	1.5	1.1	8.2	7.2
1993	54.6	3.3	15.5	2.1	8.7	1.4	0.6	7.4	6.3

Source: Data from International Monetary Fund, *Annual Report* (Washington, D.C.), 1994, p. 158. Used by permission.

organization made up of the participating nations, determines the amount of each currency that is used to make up the ECU and regularly publishes its value.

There are no ECU bills or coins in circulation. The ECU is not an actual currency. ECUs are accounting entries; they are transferred between nations by changing the financial statements of the governments that use them. The ultimate goal of the European nations is a common money, and the ECU is a step in that direction. When the ECU was created, the international reserve holdings of western European nations shifted from the dollar to the ECU. (However, the dollar still dominates as an international reserve asset.)

There are bank deposits denominated in ECUs. How do they work? Let's say that on September 25 a firm deposits 1,000,000 French francs in a European bank to open an ECU time deposit. The value of the deposit in ECUs is determined by the franc value of the ECU on that day (Table 2). Suppose the franc value of the ECU on September 25 is 7 (ECU1 = FF7). To convert the francs into ECUs, we divide 7 into 1,000,000. The beginning balance is ECU142,857. To keep things simple, let's assume that the deposit earns no interest. On November 25, the firm wants to withdraw its ECU142,857 from the bank. On that day, the exchange rate is ECU1 = FF7.2. To find the franc value of ECU142,857, we multiply 142,857 by 7.2. ECU142,857 now equals FF1,028,570. This is the amount the firm

TABLE 2
An Example of ECU Transactions

| Date of Transaction | Transaction | | Exchange Rate | ECU Value |
	Bank Deposit	Bank Withdrawal		
September 25	FF1,000,000	—	ECU1 = FF7	ECU142,857
November 25	—	FF1,028,570	ECU1 = FF7.2	ECU142,857

Note: "FF" = French francs

withdraws from the bank. Since the ECU appreciated in value against the French franc, the firm withdraws FF28,570 more francs than were initially deposited.

Notice that the deposit and withdrawal are made in an actual currency. ECUs are simply artificial units of account that change in value as the values of the European currencies that comprise them change. ECUs cannot be spent; they are used to denominate bank deposits and other financial transactions. In our example, the franc value of the ECU increased between the time of the deposit and the time of the withdrawal. There is no guarantee that this will happen, however. Foreign exchange rates change all the time, up and down. But if a firm transacts business in several different European currencies, it may find ECU deposits to be more useful than deposits denominated in any single currency.

special drawing right (SDR): a composite currency whose value is the average of the value of the U.S. dollar, the French franc, the German mark, the Japanese yen, and the U.K. pound

Another composite currency used in international financial transactions is the **special drawing right (SDR)**. The value of the SDR is an average of the values of the currencies of the five major industrial countries: the U.S. dollar, the French franc, the German mark, the Japanese yen, and the U.K. pound. This currency was created in 1970 by the International Monetary Fund, an international organization that oversees the monetary relationships among countries. SDRs, like ECUs, are an international reserve asset; they are used to settle international debts by transferring governments' accounts held at the International Monetary Fund. We discuss the SDR and the role of the International Monetary Fund in later chapters.

RECAP

1. Money is the most liquid asset.
2. Money serves as a medium of exchange, a unit of account, a store of value, and a standard of deferred payment.
3. The use of money lowers transaction and information costs relative to barter.
4. To be used as money, an asset should be portable, divisible, and durable.
5. The M1 money supply is the most liquid definition of money and equals the sum of currency, travelers' checks, demand deposits, and other checkable deposits.
6. The M2 money supply equals the sum of the M1 money supply, overnight repurchase agreements, overnight Eurodollar deposits, money market deposit accounts, savings and small-denomination time deposits, and individual money market mutual fund balances.
7. The M3 money supply equals the sum of the M2 money supply, large time deposits, term repurchase agreements, term Eurodollar deposits, and institution-only money market mutual fund balances.
8. International reserve currencies are held by governments to settle international debts.
9. ECUs and SDRs are composite currencies; their value is an average of the values of several national currencies.

2. BANKING

Commercial banks are financial institutions that offer deposits on which checks can be written. In the United States and most other countries, commercial banks are privately owned. *Thrift institutions* are financial institutions that historically offered just savings accounts, not checking accounts. Savings and loan associations, credit unions, and mutual savings banks are all thrift institutions. Prior to 1980, the differences between commercial banks and thrift institutions were much greater than they are today. For example, only commercial banks could offer checking accounts, and those accounts earned no interest. The law also regulated maximum interest rates. In 1980 Congress passed the Depository Institutions Deregulation and Monetary Control Act, in part to stimulate competition among financial institutions. Now thrift institutions and even brokerage houses offer many of the same services as commercial banks.

2.a. Financial Intermediaries

Why are banks considered intermediaries?

Both commercial banks and thrift institutions are *financial intermediaries*, middlemen between savers and borrowers. Banks accept deposits from individuals and firms, then use those deposits to make loans to individuals and firms. The borrowers are likely to be different individuals or firms from the depositors, although it is not uncommon for a household or business to be both a depositor and a borrower at the same institution. Of course, depositors and borrowers have very different interests. For instance, depositors typically prefer short-term deposits; they don't want to tie their money up for a long time. Borrowers, on the other hand, usually want more time for repayment. Banks typically package short-term deposits into longer-term loans. To function as intermediaries, banks must serve the interests of both depositors and borrowers.

A bank is willing to serve as an intermediary because it hopes to earn a profit from this activity. It pays a lower interest rate on deposits than it charges on loans; the difference is a source of profit for the bank. Islamic banks are prohibited by holy law from charging interest on loans; thus they use a different system for making a profit (see the Economic Insight "Islamic Banking").

2.b. U.S. Banking

2.b.1. Current Structure   Banking in the United States went through many changes in the 1980s. The Depository Institutions Deregulation and Monetary Control Act narrowed the distinction between commercial banks and thrift institutions. The act also narrowed the distinctions among commercial banks. If you add together all the pieces of the pie chart in Figure 2, you see that there were 64,078 banking offices operating in the United States in 1993. Roughly half of these offices were operated by *national banks*, banks chartered by the federal government; the other half, by *state banks*, banks chartered under state laws. Before the deregulation act was passed, the regulations placed on national banks were more stringent than the regulations placed on state banks. The deregulation act made the regulations affecting state and national banks more equal.

Islamic Banking

According to the Muslim holy book, the Koran, Islamic law prohibits interest charges on loans. Banks that operate under Islamic law still act as intermediaries between borrowers and lenders. However, they do not charge interest on loans or pay interest on deposits. Instead they take a predetermined percentage of the borrowing firm's profits until the loan is repaid, then share those profits with depositors.

Since the mid-1970s, over a hundred Islamic banks have opened, most in Arab nations. Deposits in these banks have grown rapidly. In fact, in some banks deposits have grown faster than good loan opportunities, forc-ing the banks to refuse new deposits until their loan portfolio could grow to match available deposits. One bank in Bahrain claimed that over 60 percent of deposits during its first two years in operation were made by people who had never made a bank deposit before.

In addition to profit-sharing deposits, Islamic banks typically offer checking accounts, travelers' checks, and trade-related services on a fee basis. The return on profit-sharing deposits has fluctuated with regional economic conditions. In the late 1970s and early 1980s, when oil prices were high, returns were higher than they were in the mid-1980s, when oil prices were depressed.

Because the growth of deposits has usually exceeded the growth of local investment opportunities, Islamic banks have been lending money to traditional banks, to fund investments that satisfy the moral and commercial needs of both, such as lending to private firms. These funds cannot be used to invest in interest-bearing securities or in firms that deal in alcohol, pork, gambling, or arms. The growth of mutually profitable investment opportunities suggests that Islamic banks are meeting both the dictates of Muslim depositors and the profitability requirements of modern banking.

Another change that has taken place in the U.S. bank market is the growth of interstate banking. Historically, banks were allowed to operate in just one state. In some states, banks could operate in only one location. This is known as *unit banking*. Today there are still many unit banks, but these are typically small community banks. Figure 2 shows that in 1993 less than half of all state banks (3,102) and national banks (1,137) operated as unit banks; the rest operated 25,546 state branch offices and 27,575 national branch offices.

Over time, legal barriers have been reduced so that today almost all states permit entry to banks located out of state. In the future, banking is likely to

Figure 2
U.S. Commercial Banks
In 1993, about half the number of banking offices operating were state banks, and half were national banks. By far the largest number of state and national banks were branch offices. Data from Federal Deposit Insurance Corporation, *Statistics on Banking*, 1993.

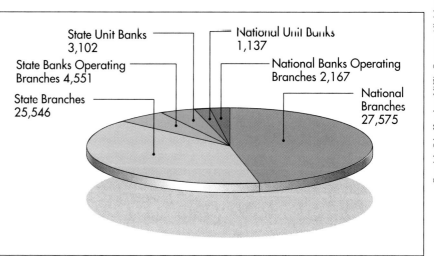

State Unit Banks
3,102

State Banks Operating
Branches 4,551

State Branches
25,546

National Unit Banks
1,137

National Banks Operating
Branches 2,167

National
Branches
27,575

be done on a national rather than a local scale. The growth of automated teller machines (ATMs) is a big step in this direction. ATM networks give bank customers access to services over a much wider geographic area than any single bank's branches cover. These national networks allow a bank customer from Dallas to withdraw cash in Seattle, Boston, or anywhere in the country. Today more than one-fourth of ATM transactions occur at banks that are not the customer's own bank.

2.b.2. Bank Failures Banking in the United States has had a colorful history of booms and panics. Banking is like any other business. Banks that are poorly managed can fail; banks that are properly managed tend to prosper. Regional economic conditions are also very important. In the mid-1980s, hundreds of banks in states with large oil industries, like Texas and Oklahoma, and farming states, like Kansas and Nebraska, could not collect many of their loans due to falling oil and agricultural prices. Table 3 lists the number of banks that failed in the United States between 1985 and 1993.

TABLE 3
Failed Banks by State, 1985–1993

State	Number of Failed Banks	State	Number of Failed Banks
Alabama	4	Missouri	33
Alaska	6	Montana	8
Arizona	16	Nebraska	27
Arkansas	4	New Hampshire	16
California	66	New Jersey	11
Colorado	54	New Mexico	10
Connecticut	30	New York	22
Delaware	1	North Carolina	2
District of Columbia	5	North Dakota	8
Florida	35	Ohio	4
Georgia	2	Oklahoma	107
Hawaii	2	Oregon	4
Idaho	1	Pennsylvania	3
Illinois	11	Rhode Island	2
Indiana	8	South Carolina	1
Iowa	34	South Dakota	4
Kansas	52	Tennessee	8
Kentucky	4	Texas	506
Louisiana	65	Utah	9
Maine	2	Vermont	2
Maryland	2	Virginia	5
Massachusetts	40	Washington	2
Michigan	1	West Virginia	2
Minnesota	31	Wisconsin	2
Mississippi	2	Wyoming	17

Source: Federal Deposit Insurance Corporation, *Annual Report, 1988, 1990, 1993* (Washington, D.C., 1989, 1991, 1993).

Those states that are heavily dependent on the oil industry and farming had significantly more banks fail than did other states. The problem was not so much bad management as it was a matter of unexpectedly bad business conditions. The lesson here is simple: commercial banks, like other profit-making enterprises, are not exempt from failure.

At one time a bank panic could close a bank. A bank panic occurs when depositors, fearing a bank's closing, rush to withdraw their funds. Banks keep only a fraction of their deposits on reserve, so bank panics often result in bank closings as depositors try to withdraw more money than the banks have on a given day. In the United States today, this is no longer true. The **Federal Deposit Insurance Corporation (FDIC)** was created in 1933. The FDIC is a federal agency that insures bank deposits in commercial banks so that depositors do not lose their deposits when a bank fails. Figure 3 shows the number of failed banks and the number without deposit insurance between 1934 and 1990. In the 1930s, many of the banks that failed were not insured by the FDIC. In this environment, it made sense for depositors to worry about losing their money. In the 1980s, the number of bank failures increased dramatically, but none of the failed banks were uninsured. Deposits in those banks were protected by the federal government. Even though large banks have failed in recent times, the depositors have not lost their deposits.

A bank panic occurs when depositors become frightened and rush to withdraw their funds.

Federal Deposit Insurance Corporation (FDIC): a federal agency that insures deposits in commercial banks

2.c. International Banking

How does international banking differ from domestic banking?

Large banks today are truly transnational enterprises. International banks, like domestic banks, act as financial intermediaries, but they operate in a different legal environment. The laws regulating domestic banking in each nation are typically very restrictive, yet many nations allow international banking to operate largely unregulated. Because they are not hampered by regulations, international banks typically can offer depositors and borrowers better terms than could be negotiated at a domestic bank.

2.c.1. Eurocurrency Market Because of the competitive interest rates offered on loans and deposits, there is a large market for deposits and loans at international banks. For instance, a bank in London, Tokyo, or the Bahamas may accept deposits and make loans denominated in U.S. dollars. The inter-

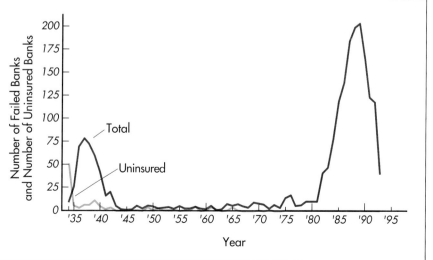

Figure 3
Number of Failed and Uninsured Banks, 1934–1993
The number of banks that went out of business in the 1980s was the highest it had been since the Depression. Unlike the banks that failed in the 1930s, the banks that closed in the 1980s were covered by deposit insurance, so depositors did not lose their money.
Source: Federal Deposit Insurance Corporation, *Annual Report, 1993* (Washington, D.C., 1993), Table A.

Eurocurrency market (offshore banking):
the market for deposits and loans generally denominated in a currency other than the currency of the country in which the transaction occurs

national deposit and loan market often is called the **Eurocurrency market**, or **offshore banking**. In the Eurocurrency market, the currency used in a banking transaction generally is not the domestic currency of the country in which the bank is located. (The prefix *Euro* is misleading here. Although the market originated in Europe, today the market is global and operates with different foreign currencies; it is in no way limited to European currencies or European banks.)

In those countries that allow offshore banking, we find two sets of banking rules: restrictive regulations for banking in the domestic market and little or no regulation of offshore-banking activities. Domestic banks are required to hold reserves against deposits and to carry deposit insurance; and they often face government-mandated credit or interest rate restrictions. The Eurocurrency market operates with few or no costly restrictions, and international banks generally pay lower taxes than domestic banks. Because offshore banks operate with lower costs, they are able to offer better terms to their customers than domestic banks.

Figure 4 compares U.S. domestic deposit and loan rates with Eurodollar deposit and loan rates. (A U.S. dollar-denominated deposit outside the domestic U.S. banking industry is called a *Eurodollar deposit*; a U.S. dollar-denominated loan outside the domestic U.S. banking industry is called a *Eurodollar loan*.)

Offshore banks are able to offer a higher rate on dollar deposits and a lower rate on dollar loans than their domestic competitors. Without these differences, the Eurodollar market probably would not exist because Eurodollar transactions are riskier than domestic transactions in the United States, due to the lack of government regulation and deposit insurance.

There are always risks involved in international banking. Funds are subject to control both by the country in which the bank is located and the country in whose currency the deposit or loan is denominated. Suppose a Canadian firm wants to withdraw funds from a U.S. dollar-denominated bank deposit in Hong Kong. The transaction is subject to control in Hong Kong. For

Figure 4
U.S. and Eurodollar Interest Rate Spreads, Feb. 7, 1995
The U.S. deposit rate is the average rate paid on certificates of deposit by major New York banks. The U.S. loan rate is the *prime rate,* the rate banks charge their best corporate customers. The Eurodollar deposit rate is the rate offered on three-month deposits. The Eurodollar loan rate is the *London interbank offer rate,* the rate London banks charge for interbank deposits. The interest rate for nonbank borrowers will include an additional amount based on the creditworthiness of the borrower.

The *spread* is the difference between the interest rate for a deposit and the interest rate on a loan. Eurodollar spreads are narrower than U.S. spreads. This means that Eurodollar deposits offer a higher interest rate than U.S. bank deposits and that Eurodollar loans charge a lower interest rate than U.S. bank loans. Data from *The Wall Street Journal,* Feb. 7, 1995, p. C12.

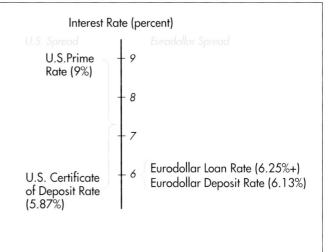

example, the government may not allow foreign exchange to leave the country freely. It is also subject to U.S. control. If the United States reduces its outflow of dollars, for instance, the Hong Kong bank may have difficulty paying the Canadian firm with U.S. dollars.

The Eurocurrency market exists for all of the major international currencies, but the value of activity in Eurodollars dwarfs the rest. Eurodollars account for about 60 percent of deposit and loan activity in the Eurocurrency market. This emphasizes the important role the U.S. dollar plays in global finance. Even deposits and loans that do not involve a U.S. lender or borrower often are denominated in U.S. dollars.

2.c.2. International Banking Facilities The term *offshore banking* is somewhat misleading in the United States today. Prior to December 1981, U.S. banks were forced to process international deposits and loans through their offshore branches. Many of the branches in places like the Cayman Islands and the Bahamas were little more than "shells," small offices with a telephone. Yet these branches allowed U.S. banks to avoid the reserve requirements and interest rate regulations that restricted domestic banking activities.

international banking facility (IBF):
a division of a U.S. bank that is allowed to receive deposits from and make loans to nonresidents of the United States without the restrictions that apply to domestic U.S. banks

In December 1981, the Federal Reserve Board legalized **international banking facilities (IBFs)**, allowing domestic banks to take part in international banking on U.S. soil. IBFs are not a physical entity; they are a bookkeeping system set up in existing bank offices to record international banking transactions. IBFs can receive deposits from and make loans to nonresidents of the United States or other IBFs. These deposits and loans must be kept separate from other transactions because IBFs are not subject to the reserve requirements, interest rate regulations, or FDIC deposit insurance premiums that apply to domestic U.S. banking.

The goal of the IBF plan was to allow banking offices in the United States to compete with offshore banks without having to use offshore banking offices. The location of IBFs reflects the location of banking activity in general. It is not surprising that 47 percent of IBFs are located in New York State, the financial center of the country. New York also receives over 75 percent of IBF deposits.

RECAP

1. The Depository Institutions Deregulation and Monetary Control Act (1980) eliminated many of the differences between commercial banks and thrift institutions.

2. Banks are financial intermediaries.

3. The deregulation act also eliminated many of the differences between national and state banks.

4. Since the FDIC began insuring bank deposits in commercial banks, bank panics are no longer a threat to the banking system.

5. The international deposit and loan market is called the Eurocurrency market, or offshore banking.

6. With the legalization in 1981 of international banking facilities, the Federal Reserve allowed international banking activities on U.S. soil.

How do banks create money?

Banks create money by lending money. They take deposits, then lend a portion of those deposits in order to earn interest income. The portion of deposits that banks keep on hand is a *reserve* to meet the demand for withdrawals. In a **fractional reserve banking system**, banks keep less than 100 percent of their deposits on reserve. If all banks hold 10 percent of their deposits as a reserve, for example, then 90 percent of their deposits are available for loans. When they loan these deposits, money is created.

fractional reserve banking system:
a system in which banks keep less than 100 percent of the deposits available for withdrawal

3.a. Deposits and Loans

Figure 5 shows a simple balance sheet for First National Bank. A *balance sheet* is a financial statement that records a firm's assets (what the firm owns) and liabilities (what the firm owes). The bank has cash assets ($100,000) and loan assets ($900,000). The deposits placed in the bank ($1,000,000) are a liability (they are an asset of the depositors).[2] Total assets always equal total liabilities on a balance sheet.

Banks keep a percentage of their deposits on reserve. In the United States the reserve requirement is set by the Federal Reserve Board (which will be discussed in detail in the next chapter). Banks can keep more than the minimum reserve if they choose. Let's assume that the reserve requirement is set at 10 percent and that banks always hold actual reserves equal to 10 percent of deposits. With deposits of $1,000,000, the bank must keep $100,000 (.10 $\times$ $1,000,000) in cash reserves held in its vault. This $100,000 is the bank's **required reserves**, as the Federal Reserve requires the banks to keep 10 percent of deposits on reserve. This is exactly what First National Bank has on hand in Figure 5. Any cash held in excess of $100,000 would represent **excess reserves**. Excess reserves can be loaned by the bank. A bank is *loaned up* when it has zero excess reserves. Because its total reserves equal its required reserves, First National Bank has no excess reserves and is loaned up.

required reserves:
the cash reserves (a percentage of deposits) a bank must keep on hand

excess reserves:
the cash reserves beyond those required, which can be loaned

---

[2]In our simplified balance sheet, we assume there is no net worth, or owner's equity. Net worth is the value of the owner's claim on the firm (the owner's equity) and is found as the difference between the value of assets and nonequity liabilities.

Figure 5
First National Bank Balance Sheet, Initial Position
The bank has cash totaling $100,000 and loans totaling $900,000, for total assets of $1,000,000. Deposits of $1,000,000 make up its total liabilities. With a reserve requirement of 10 percent, the bank must hold required reserves of 10 percent of its deposits, or $100,000. Because the bank is holding cash of $100,000, its total reserves equal its required reserves. Because it has no excess reserves, the bank cannot make new loans.

First National Bank

Assets		Liabilities	
Cash	$100,000	Deposits	$1,000,000
Loans	900,000		
Total	$1,000,000	Total	$1,000,000

Total reserves = $100,000
Required reserves = 0.1 ($1,000,000) = $100,000
Excess reserves = 0

In our example, the reserve requirement is 10 percent, or .10. So the deposit expansion multiplier equals 1/.10, or 10. An initial increase in deposits of $100,000 expands deposits in the banking system by 10 times $100,000, or $1,000,000. The maximum increase in the money supply is found by multiplying the deposit expansion multiplier by the amount of the new deposit. With no new deposits, the banking system can increase the money supply only by the multiplier times excess reserves:

$$\text{Deposit expansion multiplier} \times \text{excess reserves}$$
$$= \text{maximum increase in money supply}$$

The deposit expansion multiplier indicates the *maximum* possible change in total deposits when a new deposit is made. For the effect to be that large, all excess reserves must be loaned out and all of the money that is deposited must stay in the banking system.

If banks hold more reserves than the minimum required, they lend a smaller fraction of any new deposits, which reduces the effect of the deposit expansion multiplier. For instance, if the reserve requirement is 10 percent, we know that the deposit expansion multiplier is 10. If a bank chooses to hold 20 percent of its deposits on reserve, the deposit expansion multiplier equals 5 (1/.20).

If money (currency and coin) is withdrawn from the banking system and kept as cash, deposits and bank reserves are smaller and less money exists to loan out. This *currency drain*—removal of money—reduces the deposit expansion multiplier. The greater the currency drain, the smaller the multiplier. There is always some currency drain as people carry currency to pay for day-to-day transactions. However, during historical periods of bank panic where people lost confidence in banks, large currency withdrawals contributed to declines in money supply.

Remember that the deposit expansion multiplier measures the *maximum* expansion of the money supply by the banking system. Any single bank can lend only its excess reserves, but the whole banking system can expand the money supply by a multiple of the initial excess reserves. Thus the banking system as a whole can increase the money supply by the deposit expansion multiplier times the excess reserves of the system. The initial bank is limited to its initial loan; the banking system generates loan after loan based on that initial loan. A new deposit can increase the money supply by the deposit expansion multiplier times the new deposit.

In the next chapter we discuss how changes in the reserve requirement affect the money supply and the economy. This area of policy making is controlled by the Federal Reserve.

RECAP

1. The fractional reserve banking system allows banks to expand the money supply by making loans.

2. Banks must keep a fraction of their deposits on reserve; their excess reserves are available for lending.

3. The deposit expansion multiplier measures the maximum increase in the money supply given a new deposit; it is the reciprocal of the reserve requirement.

4. A single bank increases the money supply by lending its excess reserves.

5. The banking system can increase the money supply by the deposit expansion multiplier times the excess reserves in the banking system.

SUMMARY

▲▼ What is money?

1. Money is anything that is generally acceptable to sellers in exchange for goods and services. §1

2. Money serves as a medium of exchange, a unit of account, a store of value, and a standard of deferred payment. §1.a

3. Money, because it is more efficient than barter, lowers transaction costs. §1.a.1

4. Money should be portable, divisible, and durable. §1.a.1, 1.a.3

▲▼ How is the U.S. money supply defined?

5. There are three definitions of money based on its liquidity. §1.b

6. The M1 money supply equals the sum of currency plus travelers' checks plus demand deposits plus other checkable deposits. §1.b.1

7. The M2 money supply equals the sum of the M1 money supply plus overnight repurchase agreements, overnight Eurodollar deposits, money market deposit accounts, savings and small-denomination time deposits, and individual money market mutual fund balances. §1.b.2

8. The M3 money supply equals the M2 money supply plus large time deposits, term repurchase agreements, term Eurodollar deposits, and institution-only money market mutual fund balances. §1.b.3

▲▼ How do countries pay for international transactions?

9. Using the foreign exchange market, governments (along with individuals and firms) are able to convert national currencies to pay for trade. §1.c

10. The U.S. dollar is the world's major international reserve currency. §1.c.1

11. The European currency unit (ECU) is a composite currency whose value is an average of the values of several western European currencies. §1.c.2

▲▼ Why are banks considered intermediaries?

12. Banks serve as middlemen between savers and borrowers. §2.a

▲▼ How does international banking differ from domestic banking?

13. Domestic banking in most nations is strictly regulated; international banking is not. §2.c

14. The Eurocurrency market is the international deposit and loan market. §2.c.1

15. International banking facilities (IBFs) allow U.S. domestic banks to carry on international banking activities on U.S. soil. §2.c.2

▲▼ How do banks create money?

16. Banks can make loans up to the amount of their excess reserves, their total reserves minus their required reserves. §3.a

17. The deposit expansion multiplier is the reciprocal of the reserve requirement. §3.b

18. A single bank expands the money supply by lending its excess reserves. §3.b

19. The banking system can increase the money supply by the deposit expansion multiplier times the excess reserves in the system. §3.b

KEY TERMS

money §1
liquid asset §1
currency substitution §1.a.3

credit §1.a.4
M1 money supply §1.b.1
transactions account §1.b.1

international reserve asset §1.c.1

international reserve currency §1.c.1

European currency unit (ECU) §1.c.2

composite currency §1.c.2

special drawing right (SDR) §1.c.2

Federal Deposit Insurance Corporation (FDIC) §2.b.2

Eurocurrency market (offshore banking) §2.c.1

international banking facility (IBF) §2.c.2

fractional reserve banking system §3

required reserves §3.a

excess reserves §3.a

deposit expansion multiplier §3.b

EXERCISES

1. Describe the four functions of money using the U.S. dollar to provide an example of how dollars serve each function.

2. Discuss how the following would serve the functions of money.

    a. Gold

    b. Yap stone money

    c. Cigarettes

    d. Diamonds

3. What is a financial intermediary? Give an example of how your bank or credit union serves as a financial intermediary between you and the rest of the economy.

4. What is the Eurocurrency market, and how is banking in the Eurocurrency market different from domestic banking?

5. What are IBFs? Why do you think they were legalized?

6. First Bank has cash reserves of $200,000, loans of $800,000, and deposits of $1,000,000.

    a. Prepare a balance sheet for the bank.

    b. If the bank maintains a reserve requirement of 12 percent, what is the largest loan it can make?

    c. What is the maximum amount the money supply can be increased as a result of First Bank's new loan?

7. Yesterday bank A had no excess reserves. Today it received a new deposit of $5,000.

    a. If the bank maintains a reserve requirement of 2 percent, what is the maximum loan bank A can make?

    b. What is the maximum amount the money supply can be increased as a result of bank A's new loan?

8. "M2 is a better definition of the money supply than M1." Agree or disagree with this statement. In your argument, clearly state the criteria on which you are basing your decision.

9. The deposit expansion multiplier measures the maximum possible expansion of the money supply in the banking system. What factors could cause the actual expansion of the money supply to differ from that given by the deposit expansion multiplier?

10. What is liquidity? Rank the following assets in order of their liquidity: $10 bill, personal check for $20, savings account with $400 in it, stereo, car, house, travelers' check.

Use the following table on the components of money in a hypothetical economy to answer questions 11–13.

Money Component	Amount
Travelers' checks	$ 100
Currency	2,000
Small-denomination time deposits	3,500
Term repurchase agreements	2,000
Demand deposits	5,000
Other checkable deposits	9,000
U.S. Treasury bonds	25,000
Large-denomination time deposits	8,000
Individual money market mutual funds	7,500

11. What is the value of M1 in the above table?

12. What is the value of M2 in the above table?

13. What is the value of M3 in the above table?

14. Suppose that on December 1, Bettina deposits DM100,000 (100,000 German marks) in an ECU-denominated bank account. The value of the ECU on December 1 is DM2.5. She with-

draws the marks on February 1, when the value of the ECU is equal to DM3.0.

a. How many ECUs did she originally deposit on December 1?

b. How many marks did she withdraw on February 1?

15. The deposit expansion multiplier has been defined as the reciprocal of the reserve requirement. Suppose that banks must hold 10 percent of their deposits in reserve. However, banks also lose 10 percent of their deposits through cash drains out of the banking system.

a. What would the deposit expansion multiplier be if there was no cash drain?

b. With the cash drain, what is the value of the deposit expansion multiplier?

COOPERATIVE LEARNING EXERCISE

Split the class into groups of four. The students in each group count off 1 through 4. The 1s will be bank 1, the 2s, bank 2, the 3s, bank 3, and the 4s, bank 4. The exercise starts with each bank having zero deposits and zero excess reserves. Assume the reserve requirement is 20 percent. Then bank 1 receives a deposit of $1,000. Each group will simulate the money creation process by having bank 1 make the maximum loan possible, with the loaned money being deposited in bank 2. Then bank 2 makes the maximum loan possible, and the loaned funds go to a deposit in bank 3. Bank 3 makes the maximum loan possible with the funds going to bank 4. Finally, bank 4 makes the maximum loan possible. Including the initial deposit of $1,000, how much money has been created in this exercise by all the banks?

The World Still Loves the Dollar

For the band of traders who peddle souvenirs to tourists taking in the sweeping view of the Russian capital near Moscow State University, there is one preferred currency for doing business: the U.S. dollar. Even the local police like their bribes in greenbacks.

Half a world away in the Cambodian capital, Phnom Penh, foreigners entering the country must pay for an entry visa, a hotel taxi and the hotel itself in a single currency: the U.S. dollar.

In Hamburg, Germany, a local trader buys oil from a Dutch company and ships it to Switzerland. The transaction is completed in a single currency: the U.S. dollar.

"It's the global currency," says Peter Stroink, a spokesman for Royal Dutch Shell in Rotterdam, the Netherlands. "That's the tradition, that's the reality." . . .

- Cash. The U.S. Federal Reserve Board has found a steady increase in demand for cash dollars abroad since the early 1960s. In 1991, the latest year for which the Fed has figures, there were nearly twice as many greenbacks floating around outside the United States as there were within the 50 states.

Seven of every 10 $100 bills in circulation were estimated to be physically outside the United States in 1991, and Fed officials believe the share is higher today. "There's a large potential market out there, with the Russian appetite for dollars unslaked and the Chinese looming over the horizon," said Richard Porter, a Fed economist.

While America's position as the world's leading trading nation certainly helps keep the dollar popular, the American currency is also easy to use.

Like a bottle of Coke or a pair of Levi's, the dollar is instantly recognizable. Unlike those of other major currencies such as the yen, the mark and the Swiss franc, all dollar denominations are the same size, shape and color. What's more, U.S. paper money has not changed in more than half a century. . . .

The Russian language probably has more words for the dollar than for the ruble: baksi (bucks), zely-onyiye (green), kapusta (cabbage), krop (dill), zelon (green herbs) and even just green in accented English.

"There's no currency here more widely accepted than American dollars," said Igor Doronin, chief adviser of the Moscow Interbank Currency Exchange. "Just try to use Swiss francs or Japanese yen here. No one will take them. No one knows what they are."

The story is similar almost everywhere.

In Rio de Janeiro: "When people come from Europe or Asia or other countries, they don't bring their money; they bring dollars because they know they can get a better exchange rate," said Fabio Mame-dio, whose downtown Rio travel agencies have changed money for years. "If they bring yen or francs, I charge them an extra 10% because there's no demand for it." . . .

A standing joke in Warsaw holds that the only similarity between the United States and Communist-era Poland was that a dollar could buy anything in either country, while the Polish zloty was worthless in both.

Although the post-Communist zloty has become a currency of genuine value, the dollar remains king in Poland. Buy a foreign car in Warsaw and the price is in dollars. . . .

In July, Brazil introduced a new currency, the real, and pegged its value to that of the U.S. dollar. That brought inflation down to about 2% in August from the 50% rate in June, the last month of the cruzeiro.

But the public remains understandably jittery. Rosanna Gois, an administrative assistant at a Sao Paulo architectural firm, is just one of many Brazilians who are not quite ready to declare the government's new economic plan a success and give up their caches of dollars.

"These plans come and go," she said. "But I know that the dollar is always going to be there." . . .

Source: "The World Still Loves the Dollar," Tyler Marshall, *Los Angeles Times*, Oct. 9, 1994, p. A1. Reprinted by permission.

Commentary

There is considerable evidence that U.S. dollars are held in large amounts in many developing countries. Residents of these countries hold dollars because their domestic inflation rate is (or has been) very high, and by holding dollars they can avoid the rapid erosion of purchasing power that is associated with holding domestic currency. This "dollarization" of a country begins with people holding dollars as savings rather than domestic currency (the store-of value function of money). But if high inflation continues, dollars, rather than domestic currency, come to be used in day-to-day transactions as the medium of exchange. The article notes that even taxi drivers in Cambodia want dollars. In the late 1980s, as the Polish economy became heavily dollarized, a common joke in Poland was: "What do America and Poland have in common? In America, you can buy everything for dollars and nothing for zlotys [the Polish currency]. In Poland, it is exactly the same."

One implication of the demand for dollars in developing countries is that dollar currency leaves the United States. This currency drain will affect the size of the deposit expansion multiplier. In the chapter, the deposit expansion multiplier was defined as:

$$\text{Deposit expansion multiplier} = \frac{1}{\text{reserve requirement}}$$

This definition was based on the assumption that when a bank receives a deposit, all of the deposit will be loaned except for the fraction the bank is required to keep by the legal reserve requirement set by the Federal Reserve. With a currency drain, some of the deposit is withdrawn from the banking system as cash. As a result, the deposit expansion multiplier is now:

$$\text{Deposit expansion multiplier} = \frac{1}{(\text{reserve requirement} + \text{currency drain})}$$

For instance, if the reserve requirement equals 10 percent, our original definition of the deposit expansion multiplier would have a multiplier equal to $1/.10 = 10$. But if people withdraw 10 percent of their deposits as cash, then the 10 percent currency drain is added to the 10 percent reserve requirement to yield a deposit expansion multiplier of $1/.20 = 5$. So the larger the currency drain, the smaller the money-creating potential of the banking system.

An additional interesting aspect of the foreign demand for dollars is the *seigniorage*, or revenue earned by the government from creating money. If it costs about 7 cents to print a dollar bill but the exchange value is a dollar's worth of goods and services, then the government earns about 93 cents for each dollar put in circulation. If foreigners hold U.S. currency, then the government earns a profit from providing a stable-valued dollar that people want to hold. However, we should not overestimate the value of this in terms of the U.S. government budget. Even if all the new currency issued by the U.S. government flowed out to the rest of the world, the seigniorage earned by the United States over the past decade would have averaged less than 1.7 percent of federal government revenue. This is most certainly an overestimate of the actual seigniorage return to the United States since only a fraction of U.S. currency actually leaves the country. Given the relatively insignificant revenue earned from seigniorage, it is not surprising that U.S. policy with regard to the dollarization of developing countries has largely been one of disinterest.

14

Monetary Policy

FUNDAMENTAL
QUESTIONS

1. What does the Federal Reserve do?
2. How is monetary policy set?
3. What are the tools of monetary policy?
4. What role do central banks play in the foreign exchange market?
5. What are the determinants of the demand for money?
6. How does monetary policy affect the equilibrium level of real GDP?

n the previous chapter, we saw how banks "create" money by making loans. However, that money must get into the system to begin with. Most of us never think about how money enters the economy. All we worry about is having money available when we need it. But there is a government body that controls the U.S. money supply, and in this chapter we will learn about this agency—the Federal Reserve System and the Board of Governors that oversees monetary policy.

The amount of money available for spending by individuals or businesses affects prices, interest rates, foreign exchange rates, and the level of income in the economy. Thus, having control of the money supply gives the Federal Reserve powerful influence over these important economic variables. As we learned in Chapter 12, fiscal policy, or the control of government spending and taxes, is one of two ways by which government can change the equilibrium level of real GDP. Monetary policy as carried out by the Federal Reserve is the other mechanism through which attempts are made to manage the economy. In this chapter we will also explore the tools of monetary policy and see how changes in the money supply affect the equilibrium level of real GDP.

PREVIEW

I. THE FEDERAL RESERVE SYSTEM

The Federal Reserve is the central bank of the United States. A *central bank* performs several functions: accepting deposits from and making loans to commercial banks, acting as a banker for the federal government, and controlling the money supply. We discuss these functions in greater detail below, but first we look at the structure of the Federal Reserve System, or the Fed.

I.a. Structure of the Fed

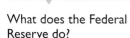

What does the Federal Reserve do?

Congress created the Federal Reserve System in 1913, with the Federal Reserve Act. Bank panics and failures had convinced lawmakers that the United States needed an agency to control the money supply and make loans to commercial banks when those banks found themselves without sufficient reserves. Because Americans tended to distrust large banking interests, Congress called for a decentralized central bank. The Federal Reserve System divides the nation into twelve districts, each with its own Federal Reserve bank (Figure 1).

I.a.I. Board of Governors   Although Congress created a decentralized system so that each district bank would represent the special interests of its own region, in practice the Fed is much more centralized than its creators

Figure 1
The Federal Reserve System
The Federal Reserve System divides the country into twelve districts. Each district has its own Federal Reserve bank, headquarters for Fed operations in that district.

For example, the First District bank is in Boston; the Twelfth is in San Francisco. There are also branch banks in Los Angeles, Miami, and other cities. Source: *Federal Reserve Bulletin* (Washington, D.C.).

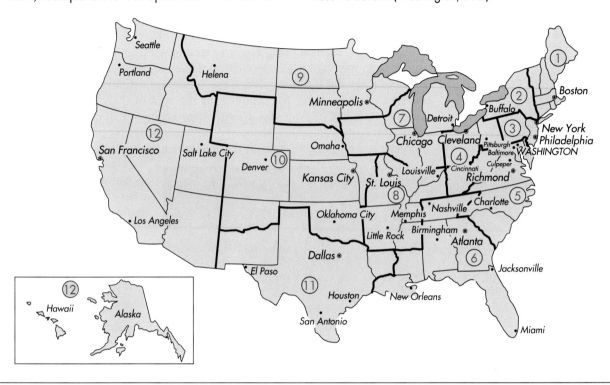

intended. Monetary policy is largely set by the Board of Governors in Washington, D.C. This board is made up of seven members, who are appointed by the president and confirmed by the Senate.

The most visible and powerful member of the board is the chairman. In fact the chairman of the Board of Governors has been called *the second most powerful person in the United States*. This individual serves as a leader and spokesperson for the board, and typically exercises more authority in determining the course of monetary policy than do the other governors.

The chairman is appointed by the president to a four-year term. In recent years most chairmen have been reappointed to an additional term (Table 1). The governors serve fourteen-year terms, the terms staggered so that every two years a new position comes up for appointment. This system allows continuity in the policy-making process and is intended to place the board above politics. Congress created the Fed as an independent agency: monetary policy is supposed to be formulated independent of Congress and the president. Of course, this is impossible in practice because the president appoints and the Senate approves the members of the board. But because the governors serve fourteen-year terms, they outlast the president who appointed them.

1.a.2. **District Banks** Each of the Fed's twelve district banks is formally directed by a nine-person board of directors. Three directors represent com-

TABLE I
Recent Chairmen of the Federal Reserve Board

Name	Age at Appointment	Term Begins	Term Ends	Years of Tenure
William McChesney Martin	44	4/2/51	1/31/70	18.8
Arthur Burns	65	1/31/70	2/1/78	8.0
G. William Miller	52	3/8/78	8/6/79	1.4
Paul Volcker	51	8/6/79	8/5/87	8.0
Alan Greenspan	61	8/11/87		

mercial banks in the district, and three represent nonbanking business interests. These six individuals are elected by the Federal Reserve System member banks in the district. The three remaining directors are appointed by the Fed's Board of Governors. District bank directors are not involved in the day-to-day operations of the district banks, but they meet regularly to oversee bank operations. They also choose the president of the bank. The president, who is in charge of operations, participates in monetary policy making with the Board of Governors in Washington, D.C.

Federal Open Market Committee (FOMC):
the official policy-making body of the Federal Reserve System

1.a.3. The Federal Open Market Committee The **Federal Open Market Committee (FOMC)** is the official policy-making body of the Federal Reserve System. The committee is made up of the seven members of the Board of Governors plus five of the twelve district bank presidents. All of the district bank presidents, except for the president of the Federal Reserve Bank of New York, take turns serving on the FOMC. Because the New York Fed actually carries out monetary policy, that bank's president is always on the committee. In section 2 we talk more about the FOMC's role and the tactics it uses.

1.b. Functions of the Fed

The Federal Reserve System offers banking services to the banking community and the U.S. Treasury, and supervises the nation's banking system. The Fed also regulates the U.S. money supply.

1.b.1. Banking Services and Supervision The Fed provides several basic services to the banking community: it supplies currency to banks, holds their reserves, and clears checks. The Fed supplies U.S. currency (Federal Reserve notes) to the banking community through its twelve district banks. (See the Economic Insight "What's on a Dollar Bill?") Commercial banks in each district also hold reserves in the form of deposits at their district bank. In addition, the Fed makes loans to banks. In this sense, the Fed is a *banker's bank*. And the Fed clears checks, transferring funds to the banks where checks are deposited from the banks on which the checks are drawn.

The Fed also supervises the nation's banks, ensuring that they operate in a sound and prudent manner. And it acts as the banker for the U.S. government, selling U.S. government securities for the U.S. Treasury.

1.b.2. Controlling the Money Supply All of the functions the Federal Reserve carries out are important, but none is more important than managing

What's on a Dollar Bill?

The figure shows both sides of a dollar bill. We've numbered several elements for identification.

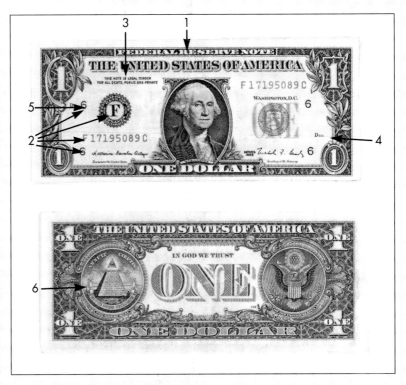

1. Currency is issued by the Federal Reserve System. The top of a dollar bill used to say "SILVER CERTIFICATE" where it now says "FEDERAL RESERVE NOTE." Silver certificates could be exchanged for silver dollars or silver bullion at the U.S. Treasury until 1967, when Congress authorized the Treasury to stop redeeming silver certificates.

2. Every dollar bill indicates which Federal Reserve bank issued it. The stamp with the *F* in the middle reads "FEDERAL RESERVE BANK OF ATLANTA GEORGIA." *F* is the sixth letter of the alphabet, and the Atlanta Fed is headquarters for the sixth Federal Reserve District. Also the serial number begins with an *F*. Finally, there is a number 6 in each corner, again indicating that the bill was issued by the Sixth District bank.

3. The dollar is the legal money of the United States. Debts and tax obligations can be legally discharged with dollars.

4. *D231* is the number of the engraving plate used to print this dollar bill.

5. *D2*, which stands for row D, column 2, is the position on the sheet where this dollar was printed. Money is printed in large sheets, which are then cut to make individual bills.

6. There are several interesting features in the great seal. ANNUIT COEPTIS means "He has favored our undertakings." The eye represents an all-seeing deity. The pyramid stands for strength. NOVUS ORDO SECLORUM means a "new order of the ages." The Roman numerals at the bottom of the pyramid equal 1776.

the nation's money supply. Before 1913 when the Fed was created, the money supply did not change to meet fluctuations in the demand for money. These fluctuations can stem from changes in income or seasonal patterns of demand. For example, every year during the Christmas season, the demand for currency rises because people carry more money to buy gifts. During the holiday season, the Fed increases the supply of currency to meet the demand for cash withdrawals from banks. After the holiday season, the demand for currency drops and the public deposits currency in banks, which then return the currency to the Fed.

The Fed controls the money supply to achieve the policy goals set by the FOMC. It does this largely through its ability to influence bank reserves and the money-creating power of commercial banks that we talked about in Chapter 13.

RECAP

1. As the central bank of the United States, the Federal Reserve accepts deposits from and makes loans to commercial banks, acts as a banker for the federal government, and controls the money supply.
2. The Federal Reserve System is made up of twelve district banks and the Board of Governors in Washington, D.C.
3. The most visible and powerful member of the Board of Governors is the chairman.
4. The governors are appointed by the president and confirmed by the Senate to serve fourteen-year terms.
5. Monetary policy is made by the Federal Open Market Committee, whose members include the seven governors and five district bank presidents.
6. The Fed provides currency, holds reserves, clears checks, and supervises commercial banks.
7. The most important function the Fed performs is controlling the U.S. money supply.

2. IMPLEMENTING MONETARY POLICY

How is monetary policy set?

Changes in the amount of money in an economy affect the inflation rate, the interest rate, and the equilibrium level of national income. Throughout history, monetary policy has made currencies worthless and toppled governments. This is why controlling the money supply is so important.

2.a. Policy Goals

The objective of monetary policy is economic growth with stable prices.

The ultimate goal of monetary policy is much like that of fiscal policy: economic growth with stable prices. *Economic growth* means greater output; *stable prices* means a low, steady rate of inflation.

2.a.1. Intermediate Targets The Fed does not control gross domestic product or the price level directly. Instead it controls the money supply, which in turn affects GDP and the level of prices. The money supply, or the growth of the money supply, is an **intermediate target**, an objective that helps the Fed achieve its ultimate policy objective—economic growth with stable prices.

intermediate target:
an objective used to achieve some ultimate policy goal

Using the growth of the money supply as an intermediate target assumes there is a fairly stable relationship between changes in money and changes in income and prices. The bases for this assumption are the equation of exchange and the quantity theory of money. The **equation of exchange** is a definition that relates the quantity of money to nominal GDP:

equation of exchange:
an equation that relates the quantity of money to nominal GDP

$$MV = PQ$$

where

$$M = \text{the quantity of money}$$

$$V = \text{the velocity of money}$$

The chairman of the Federal Reserve Board of Governors is sometimes referred to as the second most powerful person in the United States. At the time this book was written, Alan Greenspan was the Fed chairman. His leadership of the Fed has important implications for money and credit conditions in the United States.

$$P = \text{the price level}$$

$$Q = \text{the quantity of output, like real income or real GDP}$$

This equation is true by definition: money times the velocity of money will always be equal to nominal GDP.

In Chapter 13 we said there are several definitions of the money supply: M1, M2, and M3. The **velocity of money** is the average number of times each dollar is spent on final goods and services in a year. If P is the price level and Q is real GDP (the quantity of goods and services produced in the economy), then PQ equals nominal GDP. If

velocity of money:
the average number of times each dollar is spent on final goods and services in a year

$$MV = PQ$$

then

$$V = \frac{PQ}{M}$$

Suppose the price level is 2 and real GDP is \$500; PQ, or nominal GDP, is \$1,000. If the money supply is \$200, then velocity is 5 (\$1,000/\$200). A velocity of 5 means that each dollar must be spent an average of 5 times during the year if a money supply of \$200 is going to support the purchase of \$1,000 worth of new goods and services.

quantity theory of money:
with constant velocity, changes in the quantity of money change nominal GDP

The **quantity theory of money** uses the equation of exchange to relate changes in the money supply to changes in prices and output. If the money supply (M) increases and velocity (V) is constant, then nominal GDP (PQ) must increase. If the economy is operating at maximum capacity (producing at the maximum level of Q), an increase in M causes an increase in P. And if there is substantial unemployment so that Q can increase, the increase in M may mean a higher price level (P) as well as higher real GDP (Q).

The Fed attempts to set money growth targets that are consistent with rising output and low inflation. In terms of the quantity theory of money, the Fed wants to increase M at a rate that supports steadily rising Q with slow and steady increases in P. The assumption that there is a reasonably stable

relationship among *M*, *P*, and *Q* is what motivates the Fed to use money supply growth rates as an intermediate target to achieve its ultimate goal—higher
Q with slow increases in *P*.

The FOMC defines upper and lower bounds to describe its intermediate
targets—the range in which it wants the money supply to grow. Figure 2
shows the ranges and the actual growth of the M2 money supply for recent
years. In 1991 and 1992, the targeted growth of the M2 money supply was
between 2.5 and 6.5 percent then it dropped to 2 to 6 percent in 1993 and to
1 to 5 percent in 1994. The upper and lower lines at these growth rates create
a cone that represents the region of growth targeted by the Fed. The upper
part of the cone is the highest growth rate of 5 percent and the lower part of
the cone is the lowest growth rate of 1 percent. The heavy line plots the
actual path of the M2 money supply in each year. If the M2 money supply
grew at a rate of 5 percent over the year 1994, the heavy line would be up at
the top of the cone. If it grew at 1 percent, the heavy line would be at the bottom of the cone—as it was. By specifying a range of growth rather than a single rate of growth, the Fed gives itself more room to maneuver in dealing
with unexpected events that might make managing the money supply
difficult.

From the late 1950s to the mid-1970s, the velocity of the M1 money supply grew at a steady pace, from 3.5 in 1959 to 5.5 in 1975. Knowing that *V*
was growing at a steady pace, the Fed was able to set a target growth rate for
the M1 money supply, confident that it would produce a fairly predictable
growth in nominal GDP. But when velocity is not constant, there can be
problems using money growth rates as an intermediate target. This is exactly
what happened in the late 1970s and early 1980s. Figure 3 plots the velocity

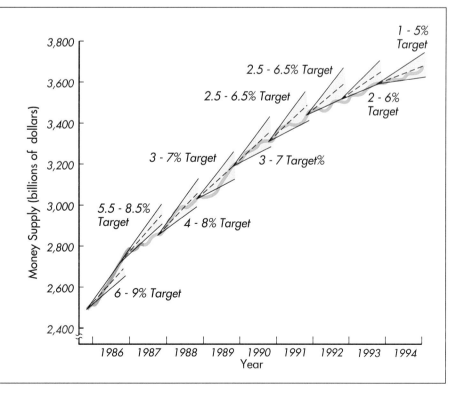

Figure 2
Targeted Versus Actual Growth in the M2 Money Supply
The Fed defines targeted growth in the money supply in terms of upper and lower bounds. These bounds define a region of acceptable growth shaped like a cone. In recent years, the M2 money supply stayed along the bottom of the cone for most of the year. Source: *Economic Report of the President, 1993 and 1995* (Washington D.C.: U.S. Government Printing Office, 1993 and 1995).

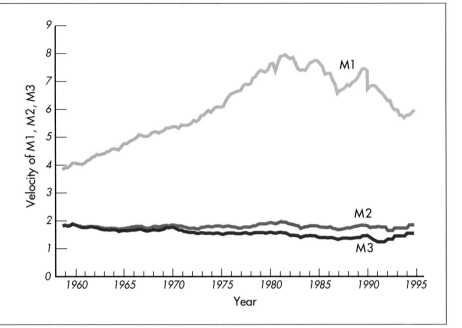

Figure 3
Velocity of the M1, M2, and M3 Money Supplies, 1959–1994
The velocity of money is the ratio of nominal gross domestic product to the money supply. The narrower the definition of money, the higher its velocity. So M1, the narrowest definition, has a higher velocity than M2 or M3. In recent years, the velocity of M1 has been much less stable than the velocity of the broader money definitions.

of the M1, M2, and M3 money supplies from 1959 to 1994. Although the M2 and M3 velocities continued to indicate a stable pattern of growth, M1 velocity behaved erratically. With the breakdown of the relationship between the M1 money supply and GDP, the Fed shifted its emphasis from the M1 money supply, concentrating instead on achieving targeted growth in the M2 and M3 money supplies.

Economists are still debating the reason for the fluctuations in the velocity of the M1 money supply. Some argue that new deposits and innovations in banking led to fluctuations in the money held in traditional demand deposits as bank customers switched to different types of financial assets. These changes would affect the M1 supply because its definition is so narrow. They would not affect the M2 and M3 supplies because their broader definitions include many of the new types of financial products available to the public.

In addition to targeting money growth, the Fed monitors other key variables that are used to indicate the future course of the economy. These include commodity prices, interest rates, and foreign exchange rates. Notice that the Fed simply *monitors* these variables. It does not set formal targets for them, but considers them in setting policy.

2.b. Operating Procedures

The FOMC sets monetary targets and then implements them through the Federal Reserve Bank of New York. The mechanism for translating policy into action is an **FOMC directive**. Each directive outlines the conduct of monetary policy over the six- to eight-week period until the FOMC meets again to adjust monetary targets and specify policy tools.

FOMC directive:
instructions issued by the FOMC to the Federal Reserve Bank of New York to implement monetary policy

2.b.1. Tools of Monetary Policy The Fed controls the money supply by changing bank reserves. There are three tools the Fed can use to change

TABLE 2
Reserve Requirements for U.S. Depository Institutions, January 1995

Type of Deposit	Percent of Deposits
Transaction deposits	
0–$54 million	3
Over $54 million	10
Nonpersonal time deposits	
Mature in less than 1 1/2 years	0
Mature in 1 1/2 years or more	0
Eurocurrency deposits	0

Source: *Federal Reserve Bulletin* (Washington, D.C.), January 1995.

What are the tools of monetary policy?

reserves: the *reserve requirement*, the *discount rate*, and *open market operations*. In the last chapter, you saw that banks can expand the money supply by a multiple of their excess reserves—the deposit expansion multiplier, the reciprocal of the reserve requirement.

Reserve Requirement   The Fed requires banks to hold a fraction of their deposits on reserve. This fraction is the reserve requirement. Table 2 lists the reserve requirements in effect in January 1995. Notice that the requirements are different for different types and sizes of deposits. *Transaction deposits* are checking accounts and other deposits that can be used to pay third parties. Large banks hold a greater percentage of deposits in reserve than do small banks (the reserve requirement increases from 3 to 10 percent for deposits in excess of $54 million). *Nonpersonal time deposits* are deposits held by business firms and are not available for writing checks but are, instead, held for a specific period of time. In January 1995, these deposits had a zero reserve requirement. Finally, Eurocurrency deposits—time deposits offered by U.S. international banking facilities—also had no reserve requirement.

Remember from Chapter 13 that required reserves are the dollar amount of reserves that a bank must hold to meet its reserve requirement. There are two ways in which required reserves may be held: vault cash at the bank or a deposit in the Fed. The sum of a bank's *vault cash* (coin and currency in the bank's vault) and deposit in the Fed is called its **legal reserves**. When legal reserves equal required reserves, the bank has no excess reserves and can make no new loans. When legal reserves exceed required reserves, the bank has excess reserves available for lending.

As bank excess reserves change, the lending and money-creating potential of the banking system changes. One way the Fed can alter excess reserves is by changing the reserve requirement. If it lowers the reserve requirement, a portion of what was previously required reserves becomes excess reserves, which can be used to make loans and expand the money supply. A lower

legal reserves:
the cash a bank holds in its vault plus its deposit in the Fed

TABLE 3

The Effect of a Change in the Reserve Requirement

Balance Sheet of First National Bank			
Assets		**Liabilities**	
Vault cash	$ 100,000	Deposits	$1,000,000
Deposit in Fed	200,000		
Loans	700,000		
Total	$1,000,000	Total	$1,000,000

Legal reserves (*LR*) equal vault cash plus the deposit in the Fed, or $300,000:

$LR = \$100,000 + \$200,000$
$\quad = \$300,000$

Excess reserves (*ER*) equal legal reserves minus required reserves (*RR*):

$ER = LR - RR$

Required reserves equal the reserve requirement (*r*) times deposits (*D*):

$RR = rD$

If the reserve requirement is 10 percent:

$RR = (.10)(\$1,000,000)$
$\quad = \$100,000$

$ER = \$300,000 - \$100,000$
$\quad = \$200,000$

First National Bank can make a maximum loan of $200,000.

The banking system can expand the money supply by the deposit expansion multiplier (1/*r*) times the excess reserves of the bank or $2,000,000:

$(1/.10)(\$200,000) = 10(\$200,000)$
$\qquad\qquad\qquad = \$2,000,000$

If the reserve requirement is 20 percent:

$RR = (.20)(\$1,000,000)$
$\quad = \$200,000$

$ER = \$300,000 - \$200,000$
$\quad = \$100,000$

First National Bank can make a maximum loan of $100,000.

The banking system can expand the money supply by the deposit expansion multiplier (1/*r*) times the excess reserves of the bank or $500,000:

$(1/.20)(\$100,000) = 5(\$100,000)$
$\qquad\qquad\qquad = \$500,000$

reserve requirement also increases the deposit expansion multiplier. By raising the reserve requirement, the Fed reduces the money-creating potential of the banking system and tends to reduce the money supply. A higher reserve requirement also lowers the deposit expansion multiplier.

Consider the example in Table 3. If First National Bank's balance sheet shows vault cash of $100,000 and a deposit in the Fed of $200,000, the bank has legal reserves of $300,000. The amount of money that the bank can lend is determined by its excess reserves. Excess reserves (*ER*) equal legal reserves (*LR*) minus required reserves (*RR*):

$$ER = LR - RR$$

If the reserve requirement (*r*) is 10 percent (.10), the bank must keep 10 percent of its deposits (*D*) as required reserves:

$$RR = rD$$
$$= .10 \ (\$1,000,000)$$
$$= \$100,000$$

In this case, the bank has excess reserves of \$200,000 (\$300,000 − \$100,000). The bank can make a maximum loan of \$200,000. The banking system can expand the money supply by the deposit expansion multiplier (1/*r*) times the excess reserves of the bank, or \$2,000,000 (1/.10 × \$200,000).

If the reserve requirement goes up to 20 percent (.20), required reserves are 20 percent of \$1,000,000, or \$200,000. Excess reserves are now \$100,000, which is the maximum loan the bank can make. The banking system can expand the money supply by \$500,000:

$$\frac{1}{.20} \ (\$100,000) = 5 \ (\$100,000)$$
$$= \$500,000$$

By raising the reserve requirement, the Fed can reduce the money-creating potential of the banking system and the money supply. And by lowering the reserve requirement, the Fed can increase the money-creating potential of the banking system and the money supply.

Discount Rate   If a bank needs more reserves in order to make new loans, it typically borrows from other banks in the federal funds market. The market is called the *federal funds market* because the funds are being loaned from one commercial bank's excess reserves on deposit with the Federal Reserve to another commercial bank's deposit account at the Fed. For instance, if the First National Bank has excess reserves of \$1 million, it can lend the excess to the Second National Bank. When a bank borrows in the federal funds market, it pays a rate of interest called the **federal funds rate**.

At times, however, banks borrow directly from the Fed, although the Fed restricts access to such funds. The **discount rate** is the rate of interest the Fed charges banks. (In other countries, the rate of interest the central bank charges commercial banks is often called the *bank rate*.) Another way the Fed controls the level of bank reserves and the money supply is by changing the discount rate.

When the Fed raises the discount rate, it raises the cost of borrowing reserves, reducing the amount of reserves borrowed. Lower levels of reserves limit bank lending and the expansion of the money supply. When the Fed lowers the discount rate, it lowers the cost of borrowing reserves, increasing the amount of borrowing. As bank reserves increase, so do loans and the money supply.

The discount rate is relatively stable. Although other interest rates can fluctuate daily, the discount rate usually remains fixed for months at a time. Table 4 lists the discount rate over recent years. The most the rate has been changed in a year has been seven times.

federal funds rate:
the interest rate a bank charges when it lends excess reserves to another bank

discount rate:
the interest rate the Fed charges commercial banks when they borrow from it

TABLE 4

Federal Reserve Discount Rates, January 1978–January 1995

Date	Discount Rate (percent)	Date	Discount Rate (percent)
January 9, 1978	6.50	October 12, 1982	9.50
May 11, 1978	7.00	November 22, 1982	9.00
July 3, 1978	7.25	December 15, 1982	8.50
August 21, 1978	7.75	April 9, 1984	9.00
September 22, 1978	8.00	November 21, 1984	8.50
October 16, 1978	8.50	December 24, 1984	8.00
November 1, 1978	9.50	May 20, 1985	7.50
July 20, 1979	10.00	March 7, 1986	7.00
August 17, 1979	10.50	April 21, 1986	6.50
September 19, 1979	11.00	July 11, 1986	6.00
October 8, 1979	12.00	August 21, 1986	5.50
February 15, 1980	13.00	September 4, 1987	6.00
May 30, 1980	12.00	August 9, 1988	6.50
June 13, 1980	11.00	February 24, 1989	7.00
July 28, 1980	10.00	December 19, 1990	6.50
September 26, 1980	11.00	February 1, 1991	6.00
November 17, 1980	12.00	April 30, 1991	5.50
December 5, 1980	13.00	September 13, 1991	5.00
May 5, 1981	14.00	November 6, 1991	4.50
November 2, 1981	13.00	December 20, 1991	3.50
December 4, 1981	12.00	July 2, 1992	3.00
July 20, 1982	11.50	May 17, 1994	3.50
August 2, 1982	11.50	August 16, 1994	4.00
August 16, 1982	10.50	November 15, 1994	4.75
August 27, 1982	10.00		

Source: *Federal Reserve Bulletin* (Washington, D.C.), January 1995.

Open Market Operations   The major tool of monetary policy is the Fed's **open market operations**, the buying and selling of U.S. government bonds. Suppose the FOMC wants to increase bank reserves to stimulate the growth of money. The committee issues a directive to the bond-trading desk at the Federal Reserve Bank of New York to buy bonds. The bonds are purchased from private bond dealers. The dealers are paid with checks drawn on the Federal Reserve, which then are deposited in the dealers' accounts at commercial banks. What happens? As bank deposits and reserves increase, banks are able to make new loans, which in turn expand the money supply through the deposit expansion multiplier process.

If the Fed wants to decrease the money supply, it sells bonds. Private bond dealers pay for the bonds with checks drawn on commercial banks. Commercial bank deposits and reserves drop, and the money supply decreases through the deposit expansion multiplier process.

Its open market operations allow the Fed to control the money supply. To increase the money supply, the Fed buys U.S. government bonds. To

open market operations:
the buying and selling of government bonds by the Fed to control bank reserves and the money supply

To increase the money supply, the Fed buys U.S. government bonds. To decrease the money supply, it sells U.S. government bonds.

decrease the money supply, it sells U.S. government bonds. The effect of selling these bonds, however, varies according to whether or not there are excess reserves in the banking system. If there are excess reserves, the money supply does not necessarily decrease when the Fed sells bonds. The open market sale may simply reduce the level of excess reserves, reducing the rate at which the money supply increases.

Table 5 shows how open market operations change bank reserves and illustrates the money-creating power of the banking system. First National Bank's initial balance sheet shows excess reserves of $100,000 with a 20 percent reserve requirement. Therefore the bank can make a maximum loan of

TABLE 5
The Effect of an Open Market Operation

Balance Sheet of First National Bank			
Assets		**Liabilities**	
Vault cash	$ 100,000	Deposits	$1,000,000
Deposit in Fed	200,000		
Loans	700,000		
Total	$1,000,000	Total	$1,000,000

Initially legal reserves (LR) equal vault cash plus the deposit in the Fed, or $300,000:

$LR = \$100,000 + \$200,000$
$\quad = \$300,000$

If the reserve requirement (r) is 20 percent (.20), required reserves (RR) equal $200,000:

$.20(\$1,000,000) = \$200,000$

Excess reserves (ER), then, equal $100,000 ($300,000 − $200,000). The bank can make a maximum loan of $100,000. The banking system can expand the money supply by the deposit expansion multiplier ($1/r$) times the excess reserves of the bank,
or $500,000:

$(1/.20)(\$100,000) = 5(\$100,000)$
$\qquad\qquad\qquad = \$500,000$

Open market purchase:

The Fed purchases $100,000 worth of bonds from a dealer, who deposits the $100,000 in an account at First National. At this point the bank has legal reserves of $400,000, required reserves of $220,000, and excess reserves of $180,000. It can make a maximum loan of $180,000, which can expand the money supply by $900,000 [(1/.20)($180,000)].

Open market sale:

The Fed sells $100,000 worth of bonds to a dealer, who pays with a check drawn on an account at First National. At this point, the bank has legal reserves of $200,000, required reserves of $180,000 (its deposits now equal $900,000), and excess reserves of $20,000. It can make a maximum loan of $20,000, which can expand the money supply by $100,000 [(1/.20)($20,000)].

$100,000. Based on the bank's reserve position, the banking system can increase the money supply by a maximum of $500,000.

If the Fed purchases $100,000 worth of bonds from a private dealer, who deposits the $100,000 in an account at First National Bank, the excess reserves of First National Bank increase to $180,000. These reserves can generate a maximum increase in the money supply of $900,000. The open market purchase increases the excess reserves of the banking system, stimulating the growth of money and, eventually, nominal GDP.

What happens when an open market sale takes place? If the Fed sells $100,000 worth of bonds to a private bond dealer, the dealer pays for the bonds using a check drawn on First National Bank. First National's deposits drop from $1,000,000 to $900,000, and its legal reserves drop from $300,000 to $200,000. With excess reserves of $20,000, the banking system can increase the money supply by only $100,000. The open market sale reduces the money-creating potential of the banking system from $500,000 initially to $100,000.

2.b.2. **FOMC Directives**   When it sets monetary policy, the FOMC begins with its *ultimate goal*: economic growth at stable prices. It defines that goal in terms of GDP. Then it works backwards to identify its *intermediate target*, the rate at which the money supply must grow to achieve the wanted growth in GDP. Then it must decide how to achieve its intermediate target. In Figure 4, as is usually the case in real life, the Fed uses open market operations. But to know whether it should buy or sell bonds, the FOMC must have some indication of whether the money supply is growing too fast or too slow. The committee relies on a *short-run operating target* for this information. The short-run target indicates how the money supply should change. Both the quantity of excess reserves in the banking system and the federal funds rate can serve as short-run operating targets.

The FOMC carries out its policies through directives to the bond-trading desk at the Federal Reserve Bank of New York. The directives specify a short-run operating target that the trading desk must use in its day-to-day operations. When the FOMC first began setting intermediate monetary targets in 1970, it attempted to prescribe very specific target ranges for the fed-

Figure 4
Monetary Policy: Tools, Targets, and Goals
The Fed primarily uses open market operations to implement monetary policy. The decision to buy or sell bonds is based on a short-run operating target, like the level of reserves held by commercial banks. The short-run operating target is set to achieve an intermediate target, a certain level of money supply. The intermediate target is set to achieve the ultimate goal, a certain level of gross domestic product.

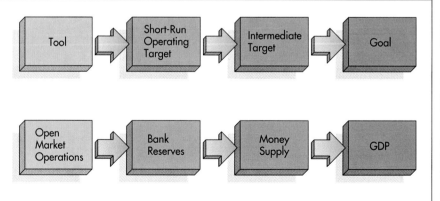

eral funds interest rate. The committee chose the federal funds rate as the short-run target because it believed the rate was the best indicator of the status of reserves. Because the federal funds rate is the interest rate one bank charges another when the second bank borrows reserves from the first, the federal funds rate rises when there are few excess reserves and falls when the banking system has a large amount of excess reserves. The Fed believed that if the federal funds rate rose above the FOMC's target, it would indicate that there were not enough reserves in the banking system, that the money supply was not growing fast enough. The bond-trading desk would then purchase bonds from bond dealers.

In the 1970s, the federal funds rate target worked well to stabilize interest rates. However, the money supply fluctuated a great deal more than the FOMC wanted. For example, when people were spending at a rapid pace and so borrowing increasing amounts of money, the banking system's reserves fell and the federal funds rate rose. The rising rate signaled the trading desk to purchase bonds and increase reserves. These reserves were immediately lent, and the money supply grew more quickly. As long as the federal funds rate continued to go up, new reserves were being pumped into the banking system and the money supply grew faster and faster. Conversely, when people were not spending and excess reserves accumulated, the trading desk sold bonds, the money supply fell and continued to fall as long as the federal funds rate was below the target range. By the fall of 1979, the FOMC had decided that it needed a better indicator of money supply growth for its short-run operating target. The committee chose bank reserves. FOMC directives now phrase their short-run operating targets in terms of the level of bank reserves.

The nature of the Fed's policy regarding reserve targeting has changed over time. In addition, the Fed takes other factors into account. For example, FOMC directives still cite a wanted range for the federal funds rate, but the range is much broader than it was in the days of targeting interest rates. The directives also cite real GDP growth, the rate of inflation, and the foreign exchange value of the dollar, factors that could affect the FOMC-targeted bank reserves. (See the Economic Insight "An FOMC Directive.")

2.c. Foreign Exchange Market Intervention

What role do central banks play in the foreign exchange market?

foreign exchange market intervention:
the buying and selling of foreign exchange by a central bank to move exchange rates up or down to a targeted level

In the mid-1980s, conditions in the foreign exchange market took on a high priority in FOMC directives, which continues to this day. There was concern that the value of the dollar in relation to other currencies was contributing to a large U.S. international trade deficit. Furthermore, the governments of the major industrial countries decided to work together to maintain more stable exchange rates. This meant that the Federal Reserve and the central banks of the other developed countries had to devote more attention to maintaining exchange rates within a certain target band of values, much as the federal funds rate had been targeted in the 1970s.

2.c.1. Mechanics of Intervention Foreign exchange market intervention is the buying and selling of foreign exchange by a central bank in order to move exchange rates up or down. We can use a simple supply and demand diagram to illustrate the role of intervention. Figure 5 shows the U.S. dollar–Japanese yen exchange market. The demand curve is the demand for dollars produced by the demand for U.S. goods and financial assets. The supply curve is the supply of dollars generated by U.S. residents' demand for the

Figure 5
The Dollar-Yen Foreign Exchange Market
The demand is the demand for dollars arising out of the Japanese demand for U.S. goods and services. The supply is the supply of dollars arising out of the U.S. demand for Japanese goods and services. Initially, the equilibrium exchange rate is at the intersection of the demand curve (D_1) and the supply curve (S_1), where the exchange rate is ¥100 = $1. An increase in the U.S. demand for Japanese goods increases S_1 to S_2 and pushes the equilibrium exchange rate down to point B, where ¥90 = $1. If the Fed's target exchange rate is ¥100 = $1, the Fed must intervene, buying dollars in the foreign exchange market. This increases demand to D_2 and raises the equilibrium exchange rate to point C, where ¥100 = $1.

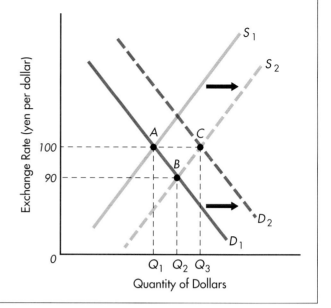

products and financial assets of other countries. Here, the supply of dollars to the dollar-yen market comes from the U.S. demand to buy Japanese products.

The initial equilibrium exchange rate is at point *A*, where the demand curve (D_1) and the supply curve (S_1) intersect. At point *A*, the exchange rate is ¥100 = $1, and Q_1 dollars are exchanged for yen. Suppose that over time, U.S. residents buy more from Japan than Japanese residents buy from the United States. As the supply of dollars increases in relation to the demand for dollars, equilibrium shifts to point *B*. At point *B*, Q_2 dollars are exchanged at a rate of ¥90 = $1. The dollar has *depreciated* against the yen, or, conversely, the yen has *appreciated* against the dollar.

When the dollar depreciates, U.S. goods are cheaper to Japanese buyers (it takes fewer yen to buy each dollar). The depreciated dollar stimulates U.S. exports to Japan. It also raises the price of Japanese goods to U.S. buyers, reducing U.S. imports from Japan. Rather than allow exchange rates to change, with the subsequent changes in trade, central banks often seek to maintain fixed exchange rates because of international agreements or desired trade in goods or financial assets.

Suppose the Fed sets a target range for the dollar at a minimum exchange rate of ¥100 = $1. If the exchange rate falls below the minimum, the Fed must intervene in the foreign exchange market to increase the value of the dollar. In Figure 5, you can see that the only way to increase the dollar's value is to increase the demand for dollars. The Fed intervenes in the foreign exchange market by buying dollars in exchange for yen. It uses its holdings of Japanese yen to purchase $Q_3 - Q_1$ dollars, shifting the demand curve to D_2. Now equilibrium is at point *C*, where Q_3 dollars are exchanged at the rate of ¥100 = $1.

The kind of intervention shown in Figure 5 is only temporary because the Fed has a limited supply of yen. Under another intervention plan, the Bank of Japan would support the ¥100 = $1 exchange rate by using yen to buy dollars. The Bank of Japan could carry on this kind of policy indefinitely

An FOMC Directive

At the conclusion of the FOMC meeting held in November 1994, the following policy directive was issued to the Federal Reserve Bank of New York:

The information reviewed at this meeting suggests that the pace of economic expansion, though perhaps moderating slightly in recent months, remains substantial. Nonfarm payroll employment advanced appreciably further in August, and the civilian unemployment rate was unchanged at 6.1 percent. Reflecting strength in motor vehicles, industrial production rose sharply in August after posting sizable gains in other recent months, and capacity utilization moved up further from already high levels. Retail sales were up considerably in August, boosted by a rebound in sales of durable goods, including motor vehicles. Housing starts rose in August but were unchanged from their second-quarter level. Orders for nondefense capital goods point to a continued strong expansion in spending on business equipment; permits for nonresidential construction remain on a mild uptrend. Inventory accumulation appears to have moderated recently after surging in the second quarter. The nominal deficit on U.S. trade in goods and services widened in July from its second-quarter average. Prices of materials have remained under upward pressure, and increases in broad indexes of consumer and producer prices have been somewhat larger in recent months.

On August 16, 1994, the Board of Governors approved an increase in the discount rate from 3½ to 4 percent, and the Committee agreed that this increase would be allowed to show through completely to interest rates in reserve markets. Most market interest rates are up somewhat on balance since the August meeting. The trade-weighted value of the dollar in terms of the other G-10 currencies depreciated somewhat over the intermeeting period.

M2 and M3 declined in August after expanding moderately in July; for the year through August, M2 and M3 grew at rates slightly above the bottom of their ranges for 1994. Total domestic nonfinancial debt has continued to expand at a moderate rate in recent months.

The Federal Open Market Committee seeks monetary and financial conditions that will foster price stability and promote sustainable growth in output. In furtherance of these objectives, the Committee at its meeting in July reaffirmed the ranges it had established in February for growth of M2 and M3 of 1 to 5 percent and 0 to 4 percent respectively, measured from the fourth quarter of 1993 to the fourth quarter of 1994. The Committee anticipated that developments contributing to unusual velocity increases could persist during the year and that money growth within these ranges would be consistent with its broad policy objectives. The monitoring range for growth of total domestic nonfinancial debt was maintained at 4 to 8 percent for the year. For 1995, the Committee agreed on tentative ranges for monetary growth, measured from the fourth quarter of 1994 to the fourth quarter of 1995, of 1 to 5 percent for M2 and 0 to 4 percent for M3. The Committee provisionally set the associated monitoring range for growth of domestic nonfinancial debt at 3 to 7 percent for 1995. The behavior of the monetary aggregates will continue to be evaluated in the light of progress toward price level stability, movements in their velocities, and developments in the economy and financial markets.

In the implementation of policy for the immediate future, the Committee seeks to maintain the existing degree of pressure on reserve positions. In the context of the Committee's long-run objectives for price stability and sustainable economic growth, and giving careful consideration to economic, financial, and monetary developments, somewhat greater reserve restraint would or slightly lesser reserve restraint might be acceptable in the intermeeting period. The contemplated reserve conditions are expected to be consistent with modest growth in M2 and M3 over the balance of the year.

Source: *Federal Reserve Bulletin* (Washington, D.C.), January 1995, p. 39.

Coordinated intervention involves more than one central bank in attempts to shift the equilibrium exchange rate.

because it has the power to create yen. A third alternative is *coordinated intervention*, in which both the Fed and the Bank of Japan sell yen in exchange for dollars to support the minimum yen-dollar exchange rate.

A famous example of coordinated intervention occurred in September 1985. The "Group of 5," or G-5 countries—the United States, France, Japan, the United Kingdom, and West Germany—issued a joint policy statement aimed at reducing the foreign exchange value of the dollar in the face of mounting concern over the size of the U.S. trade deficit. Even before official sales of the dollar began, the dollar started to depreciate as participants in the foreign exchange market reacted to the announcement. In other words, the free market supply of dollars increased and the free market demand for dollars decreased because traders did not want to be holding dollars when the central banks started selling. The Federal Reserve (along with the U.S. Treasury) sold more than $3 billion during the period of intervention that followed. The central banks of France, Japan, the United Kingdom, and West Germany, combined, sold approximately $5 billion.

2.c.2. Effects of Intervention   Intervention can be used to shift the demand and supply for currency and thereby change the exchange rate. Foreign exchange market intervention also has effects on the money supply. If the Federal Reserve wanted to increase the dollar price of the French franc, it would create dollars to purchase francs. Thus when foreign exchange market intervention involves the use of domestic currency to buy foreign currency, it increases the domestic money supply. The expansionary effect of this intervention can be offset by a domestic open market operation, in a process called **sterilization**. If the Fed creates dollars to buy French francs, for example, it increases the money supply, as we have just seen. To reduce the money supply, the Fed can direct an open market bond sale. The bond sale sterilizes the effect of the intervention on the domestic money supply.

sterilization:
the use of domestic open market operations to offset the effects of a foreign exchange market intervention on the domestic money supply

RECAP

1. The ultimate goal of monetary policy is economic growth with stable prices.

2. The Fed controls GDP indirectly, through its control of the money supply.

3. The equation of exchange ($MV = PQ$) relates the quantity of money to nominal GDP.

4. The quantity theory of money states that with constant velocity, changes in the quantity of money change nominal GDP.

5. Every six to eight weeks, the Federal Open Market Committee issues a directive to the Federal Reserve Bank of New York that defines the FOMC's monetary targets and policy tools.

6. The Fed controls the nation's money supply by changing bank excess reserves.

7. The tools of monetary policy are reserve requirements, the discount rate, and open market operations.

8. The money supply tends to increase (decrease) as the reserve requirement falls (rises), the discount rate falls (rises), and the Fed buys (sells) bonds.

9. Each FOMC directive defines its short-run operating target in terms of bank reserves, but also considers the federal funds rate, the growth of real GDP, the rate of inflation, and the foreign exchange rate of the dollar.

10. Foreign exchange market intervention is the buying and selling of foreign exchange by a central bank to achieve a targeted exchange rate.

11. Sterilization is the use of domestic open market operations to offset the money supply effects of foreign exchange market intervention.

3. MONETARY POLICY AND EQUILIBRIUM INCOME

To see how changes in the money supply affect the equilibrium level of real GDP, we incorporate monetary policy into the aggregate demand and supply model. The first step in understanding monetary policy is understanding the demand for money. If you know what determines money demand, you can see how monetary policy is used to shift aggregate demand and change the equilibrium level of real GDP.

3.a. Money Demand

What are the determinants of the demand for money?

Why do you hold money? What does it do for you? What determines how much money you will hold? These questions are addressed in this section. Wanting to hold more money is not the same as wanting more income. You can decide to carry more cash or keep more dollars in your checking account even though your income has not changed. The quantity of dollars you want to hold is your demand for money. By summing the quantity of money demanded by each individual, we can find the money demand for the entire economy. Once we understand what determines money demand, we can put that demand together with the money supply and examine how money influences the interest rate and the equilibrium level of income.

In Chapter 13 we discussed the functions of money, that is, what money is used for. People use money as a unit of account, a medium of exchange, a store of value, and a standard of deferred payment. These last functions help explain the demand for money.

transactions demand for money:
the demand to hold money to buy goods and services

People use money for transactions, to buy goods and services. The **transactions demand for money** is a demand to hold money in order to spend it on goods and services. Holding money in your pocket or checking account is a demand for money. Spending money is not demanding it; by spending it you are getting rid of it.

If your boss paid you the same instant that you wanted to buy something, the timing of your receipts and expenditures would match perfectly. You would not have to hold money for transactions. But because receipts typically occur much less often than expenditures, money is necessary to cover transactions between paychecks.

precautionary demand for money:
the demand for money to cover unplanned transactions or emergencies

speculative demand for money:
the demand for money created by uncertainty about the value of other assets

People also hold money to take care of emergencies. The **precautionary demand for money** exists because emergencies happen. People never know when an unexpected expense will crop up or when actual expenditures will exceed planned expenditures. So they hold money as a precaution.

Finally, there is a **speculative demand for money**, a demand created by uncertainty about the value of other assets. This demand exists because money is the most liquid store of value. If you want to buy a stock, but you believe the price is going to fall in the next few days, you hold the money until you are ready to buy the stock.

The speculative demand for money is not necessarily tied to a particular use of funds. People hold money because they expect the price of any asset to fall. Holding money is less risky than buying the asset today if the price of the asset seems likely to fall. For example, suppose you buy and sell fine art. The price of art fluctuates over time. You try to buy when prices are low and sell when prices are high. If you expect prices to fall in the short term, you hold money rather than art until the prices do fall. Then you use money to buy art for resale when the prices go up again.

3.a.1. **The Money Demand Function**   If you understand why people hold money, you can understand what changes the amount of money they hold. As you've just seen, people hold money in order to: (1) carry out transactions (transactions demand), (2) be prepared for emergencies (precautionary demand), and (3) speculate on purchases of various assets (speculative demand). The interest rate and nominal income (income measured in current dollars) influence how much money people hold in order to carry out these three activities.

The Interest Rate   There is an inverse relationship between the interest rate and the quantity of money demanded (see Figure 6). The interest rate is the *opportunity cost* of holding money. If you bury a thousand dollar bills in your backyard, that currency is earning no interest—you are forgoing the interest. At a low interest rate, the cost of forgone interest is small. At a higher interest rate, however, the cost of holding wealth in the form of money means giving up more interest. The higher the rate of interest, the greater the interest forgone by holding money, so the less money held. The costs of holding money limit the amount of money held.

The interest rate is the opportunity cost of holding money.

Some components of the money supply pay interest to the depositor. Here the opportunity cost of holding money is the difference between the interest rate on a bond or some other nonmonetary asset and the interest rate on money. If a bond pays 9 percent interest a year and a bank deposit pays 5 percent, the opportunity cost of holding the deposit is 4 percent.

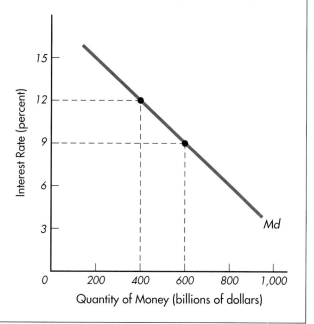

Figure 6
The Money Demand Function
Money demand (*Md*) is a negative function of the rate of interest. The interest rate is the opportunity cost of holding money. The higher the interest rate, the lower the quantity of money demanded. At an interest rate of 9 percent, the quantity of money demanded is $600 billion. At an interest rate of 12 percent, the quantity of money demanded falls to $400 billion.

Figure 7 shows a money demand function where the demand for money depends on the interest rate. The downward slope of the money demand curve (*Md*) shows the inverse relation between the interest rate and the quantity of money demanded. For instance, at an interest rate of 12 percent, the quantity of money demanded is $400 billion. If the interest rate falls to 9 percent, the quantity of money demanded increases to $600 billion.

Nominal Income The demand for money also depends on nominal income. Money demand varies directly with nominal income because as income increases, more transactions are carried out and more money is required for those transactions.

The greater nominal income, the greater the demand for money. This is true whether the increase in nominal income is a product of a higher price level or an increase in real income. Both generate a greater dollar volume of transactions. If the prices of all goods increase, then more money must be used to purchase goods and services. And as real income increases, more goods and services are being produced and sold and living standards rise, which means more money is being demanded to execute the higher level of transactions.

A change in nominal income changes the demand for money at any given interest rate. Figure 7 shows the effect of changes in nominal income on the money demand curve. If income rises from Y_0 to Y_1, money demand increases from *Md* to Md_1. If income falls from Y_0 to Y_2, money demand falls from *Md* to Md_2. When the money demand function shifts from *Md* to Md_1, the quantity of money demanded at an interest rate of 9 percent increases from $600 billion to $800 billion. When the money demand function shifts from *Md* to Md_2, the quantity of money demanded at 9 percent interest falls from $600 billion to $400 billion.

3.a.2. The Money Supply Function The Federal Reserve is responsible for setting the money supply. The fact that the Fed can choose the money supply

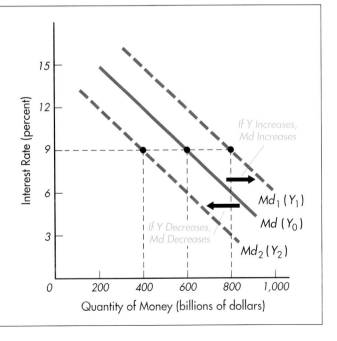

Figure 7
The Effect of a Change in Income on Money Demand
A change in real GDP, whatever the interest rate, shifts the money demand curve. Initially real GDP is Y_0; the money demand curve at that level of income is *Md*. At an interest rate of 9 percent, the quantity of money demanded is $600 billion. If income increases to Y_1, the money demand shifts to Md_1. Here $800 billion is demanded at 9 percent. If income falls to Y_2, the money demand curve falls to Md_2, where $400 billion is demanded at 9 percent.

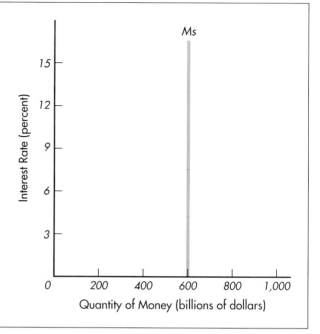

Figure 8
The Money Supply Function
The money supply function is a vertical line. This indicates that the Fed can choose any money supply it wants independent of the interest rate (and real GDP). In the figure, the money supply is set at $600 billion at all interest rates. The Fed can increase or decrease the money supply, shifting the curve to the right or left, but the curve remains vertical.

means that the money supply function is independent of the current interest rate and income. Figure 8 illustrates the money supply function (*Ms*). In the figure, the money supply is $600 billion at all interest rate levels. If the Fed increases the money supply, the vertical money supply function shifts to the right. If the Fed decreases the money supply, the function shifts to the left.

3.a.3. Equilibrium in the Money Market   To find the equilibrium interest rate and quantity of money, we have to combine the money demand and money supply functions in one diagram. Figure 9 graphs equilibrium in the money market. Equilibrium, point *e*, is at the intersection of the money demand and money supply functions. In the figure the equilibrium interest rate is 9 percent and the quantity of money is $600 billion.

What forces work to ensure that the economy tends toward the equilibrium rate of interest? Let's look at Figure 9 again to understand what happens if the interest rate is not at equilibrium. If the interest rate falls below 9 percent, there will be an excess demand for money. People will want more money than the Fed is supplying. But because the supply of money does not change, the demand for more money just forces the interest rate to rise. How? Suppose people try to increase their money holdings by converting bonds and other nonmonetary assets into money. As bonds and other nonmonetary assets are sold for money, the interest rate goes up.

To understand the connection between the rate of interest and buying and selling bonds, you must realize that the current interest rate (yield) on a bond is determined by the bond price:

$$\text{Current interest rate} = \frac{\text{annual interest payment}}{\text{bond price}}$$

The numerator, the annual interest payment, is fixed for the life of the bond. The denominator, the bond price, fluctuates with supply and demand. As the bond price changes, the interest rate changes.

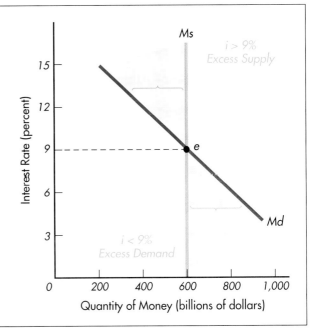

Figure 9
Equilibrium in the Money Market
Equilibrium is at point e, where the money demand and money supply curves intersect. At equilibrium, the interest rate is 9 percent and the money supply is $600 billion. An interest rate above 9 percent would create an excess supply of money because the quantity of money demanded falls as the interest rate rises. An interest rate below 9 percent would create an excess demand for money because the quantity of money demanded rises as the interest rate falls.

Suppose a bond pays $100 a year in interest and sells for $1,000. The interest rate is 10 percent ($100/$1,000). If the supply of bonds increases because people want to convert bonds to money, the price of bonds falls. Suppose the price drops to $800. At that price the interest rate equals 12.5 percent ($100/$800). This is the mechanism by which an excess demand for money changes the interest rate. As the interest rate goes up, the excess demand for money disappears.

Just the opposite occurs at interest rates above equilibrium. In Figure 9, any rate of interest above 9 percent creates an excess supply of money. Now people are holding more of their wealth in the form of money than they would like. What happens? They want to convert some of their money balances into nonmonetary assets, like bonds. As the demand for bonds rises, bond prices increase. And as bond prices go up, interest rates fall. This drop in interest rates restores equilibrium in the money market.

3.b. Money and Equilibrium Income

How does monetary policy affect the equilibrium level of real GDP?

Now we are ready to relate monetary policy to the equilibrium level of real GDP. We use Figure 10 to show how a change in the money supply affects real GDP. In part (a), as the money supply increases from Ms_1 to Ms_2, the equilibrium rate of interest falls from i_1 to i_2.

Remember that investment (business spending on capital goods) declines as the rate of interest increases. The interest rate is the cost of borrowed funds. As the interest rate rises, the return on investment falls and with it the level of investment. As the interest rate falls, the return on investment rises and with it the level of investment. In part (a) of Figure 10, the interest rate falls. In part (b) of the figure you can see the effect of the lower interest rate on investment spending. As the interest rate falls from i_1 to i_2, investment increases from I_1 to I_2.

Figure 10
Monetary Policy and Equilibrium Income
The three diagrams show the sequence of events by which a change in the money supply affects the equilibrium level of Real GDP. In part (a), the money supply increases, lowering the equilibrium interest rate. In part (b), the lower interest rate pushes the equilibrium level of investment up. In part (c), the increase in investment increases aggregate demand and equilibrium Real GDP.

(a) Money Supply Increases and Interest Rate Falls

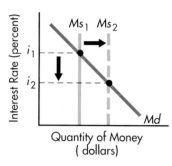

(b) Investment Spending Increases

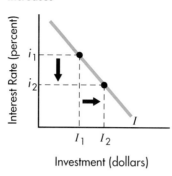

(c) Aggregate Demand and Equilibrium Income Increase

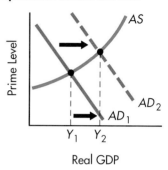

Figure 10(c) is the aggregate demand and supply equilibrium diagram. When investment spending increases, aggregate expenditures are higher at every price level, so the aggregate demand curve shifts to the right, from AD_1 to AD_2. The increase in aggregate demand increases equilibrium income from Y_1 to Y_2.

How does monetary policy affect equilibrium income? As the money supply increases, the equilibrium interest rate falls. As the interest rate falls, the equilibrium level of investment rises. Increased investment increases aggregate demand and equilibrium income. A decrease in the money supply works in reverse: as the interest rate rises, investment falls; as investment falls, aggregate demand and equilibrium income go down.

An excess supply of (demand for) money can increase (decrease) consumption as well as investment.

The mechanism we have just described is an oversimplification because the only element of aggregate expenditures that changes in this model is investment. But an excess demand for or supply of money involves more than simply selling or buying bonds. An excess supply of money probably would be reflected in increased consumption as well. If households are holding more money than they want to hold, they buy not only bonds but also goods and services so that consumption increases. If they are holding less money than they want to hold, they will sell bonds and consume less. So the effect of monetary policy on aggregate demand is a product of a change in both investment and consumption. We discuss this in Chapter 15, where we also examine the important role expected policy changes can play.

RECAP

1. The transactions demand for money is a demand to hold money to buy goods and services.

2. The precautionary demand for money exists because all expenditures cannot be planned.

3. The speculative demand for money is created by uncertainty about the value of other assets.

4. There is an inverse relationship between the interest rate and the quantity of money demanded.

5. The greater nominal income, the greater the demand for money.

6. Because the Federal Reserve sets the money supply, the money supply function is independent of the interest rate and nominal income.

7. The current yield on a bond equals the annual interest payment divided by the price of the bond.

8. An increase in the money supply lowers the interest rate, which raises the level of investment, which in turn increases aggregate demand and equilibrium income. A decrease in the money supply works in reverse.

SUMMARY

▲▼ What does the Federal Reserve do?

1. The Federal Reserve is the central bank of the United States. §1

2. The Federal Reserve System is operated by twelve district banks and a Board of Governors in Washington, D.C. §1.a

3. The Fed services and supervises the banking system, acts as the banker of the U.S. Treasury, and controls the money supply. §1.b

▲▼ How is monetary policy set?

4. The Fed controls nominal GDP indirectly by controlling the quantity of money in the nation's economy. §2.a.1

5. The Fed uses the growth of the money supply as an intermediate target to help it achieve its ultimate goal—economic growth with stable prices. §2.a.1

▲▼ What are the tools of monetary policy?

6. The three tools of monetary policy are the reserve requirement, the discount rate, and open market operations. §2.b.1

7. The Fed buys bonds to increase the money supply and sells bonds to decrease the money supply. §2.b.1

8. The Federal Open Market Committee (FOMC) issues directives to the Federal Reserve Bank of New York outlining the conduct of monetary policy. §2.b.2

▲▼ What role do central banks play in the foreign exchange market?

9. Central banks intervene in the foreign exchange market when it is necessary to maintain a targeted exchange rate. §2.c

▲▼ What are the determinants of the demand for money?

10. The demand for money stems from the need to buy goods and services, to prepare for emergencies, and to retain a store of value. §3.a

11. There is an inverse relationship between the quantity of money demanded and the interest rate. §3.a.1

12. The greater nominal income, the greater the demand for money. §3.a.1

13. Because the Fed sets the money supply, the money supply function is independent of the interest rate and real GDP. §3.a.2

▲▼ How does monetary policy affect the equilibrium level of real GDP?

14. By altering the money supply, the Fed changes the interest rate and the level of investment, shifting aggregate demand and the equilibrium level of real GDP. §3.b

KEY TERMS

Federal Open Market Committee (FOMC) §1.a.3
intermediate target §2.a.1
equation of exchange §2.a.1
velocity of money §2.a.1
quantity theory of money §2.a.1
FOMC directive §2.b
legal reserves §2.b.1
federal funds rate §2.b.1

discount rate §2.b.1
open market operations §2.b.1
foreign exchange market intervention §2.c.1
sterilization §2.c.2
transactions demand for money §3.a
precautionary demand for money §3.a
speculative demand for money §3.a

EXERCISES

1. The Federal Reserve System divides the nation into twelve districts.

   a. List the twelve cities where the district banks are located.

   b. Which Federal Reserve district do you live in?

2. Briefly describe the functions the Fed performs for the banking community. In what sense is the Fed a banker's bank?

3. Draw a graph showing equilibrium in the money market. Carefully label all curves and axes and explain why the curves have the slopes they do.

4. Using the graph you prepared for exercise 3, illustrate and explain what happens when the Fed decreases the money supply.

5. When the Fed decreases the money supply, the equilibrium level of income changes. Illustrate and explain how.

6. Describe the quantity theory of money, defining each variable. Explain how changes in the money supply can affect real GDP and the price level. Under what circumstances could an increase in the money supply have *no* effect on nominal GDP?

7. There are several tools the Fed uses to implement monetary policy.

   a. Briefly describe these tools.

   b. Explain how the Fed would use each tool in order to increase the money supply.

8. First Bank has total deposits of $2,000,000 and legal reserves of $220,000.

   a. If the reserve requirement is 10 percent, what is the maximum loan that First Bank can make, and what is the maximum increase in the money supply based on First Bank's reserve position?

   b. If the reserve requirement is changed to 5 percent, how much can First Bank lend, and how much can the money supply be expanded?

9. Suppose you are a member of the FOMC and the U.S. economy is entering a recession. Write a directive to the New York Fed about the conduct of monetary policy over the next two months. Your directive should address targets for the rate of growth of the M2 and M3 money supplies, the federal funds rate, the rate of inflation, and the foreign exchange value of the dollar versus the Japanese yen and German mark. You may refer to the *Federal Reserve Bulletin* for examples, since this publication reports FOMC directives.

10. Suppose the Fed has a target range for the yen-dollar exchange rate. How would it keep the exchange rate within the target range if free market forces push the exchange rate out of the range? Use a graph to help explain your answer.

11. Why do you demand money? What determines how much money you keep in your pocket, purse, or bank accounts?

12. What is the current yield on a bond? Why do interest rates change when bond prices change?

13. If the Fed increases the money supply, what will happen to each of the following (other things being equal)?

    a. Interest rates

    b. Money demand

    c. Investment spending

    d. Aggregate demand

    e. The equilibrium level of national income

14. It is sometimes said that the Federal Reserve System is a nonpolitical agency. In what sense is this true? Why might you doubt that politics don't affect Fed decisions?

15. Suppose the banking system has vault cash of $1,000, deposits at the Fed of $2,000, and demand deposits of $10,000.

    a. If the reserve requirement is 20 percent, what is the maximum potential increase in the money supply given the banks' reserve position?

    b. If the Fed now purchases $500 worth of government bonds from private bond dealers, what are excess reserves of the banking system? (Assume that the bond dealers deposit the $500 in demand deposits.) How much can the banking system increase the money supply given the new reserve position?

COOPERATIVE LEARNING EXERCISE

Divide the class into groups of three. Each group should construct a "directive" to increase the money supply in order to stimulate the economy. The members of each group will have a particular tool of monetary policy to discuss: one person is assigned the discount rate, another is assigned the reserve requirement, and the other member is assigned open market operations. Each member will announce to the group how his or her tool must be changed and how that change will lead to a greater supply of money.

Economically Speaking

Greenspan and Fed Act Prudently in Raising Rates to Guard Against Inflation

When word hit my computer screen late last week that the Federal Reserve Board had nudged interest rates upward, I promptly reached for a phone to alert one of the most important women in my life.

Because she's a delightful young woman who recently poured her savings into a house with an adjustable rate mortgage, I endeavored to sound sympathetic about the prospect that her house payment would be rising.

I think I succeeded, although it was a stretch. Inwardly, I was applauding the Fed's move to bump short-term interest rates upward in order to dampen potential inflationary pressures. Lordy, I was even thinking benevolent thoughts about Ronald Reagan, of all people, for having the perspicacity to name that old inflation fighter, Alan Greenspan, to the Fed chairmanship. . . .

I spent the late 1960s and all of the '70s covering the inflationary explosion that slashed the value of the dollar by half in less than a dozen years.

I watched as the politicians and the bureaucrats, including the Federal Reserve Board, dithered over escalating prices without having the guts to take decisive action.

I grimaced as retirees on fixed incomes saw their resources chewed into ever-smaller bits.

And I sympathized with small business people hard put to keep up with their escalating costs. . . .

You might logically wonder at these odd reminiscences, particularly since the Consumer Price Index (CPI) rose at a comparatively gentle rate of 2.7 percent in 1993, lowest in seven years. And if you factor out the volatile food and fuel elements of the index, the core inflation rate was running about 1.3 percent.

But anyone with as much gray hair as I'm sporting remembers what made it that way: My thinning mop, at least, began to gray as I watched a fairly moderate inflation rate thunder into double digits almost as fast as you could say John Maynard Keynes.

In 1973, for example, inflation was running at little more than 3 percent. By 1974 it had nearly tripled to 8.7 percent and a year later it blossomed to 12.3 percent. . . .

Despite the absence of serious inflationary pressures, however, Greenspan appropriately cautioned Congress early last week that waiting until the economy starts to overheat would only mean harsher control measures later on.

"By the time inflation pressures are evident, many imbalances that are costly to rectify have already developed, and only harsh monetary therapy can restore the financial stability necessary to sustain growth," Greenspan said in testimony before the Joint Economic Committee. In fact, he noted, there has been some recent upward pressure on a number of industrial materials.

Once again, I offer a bit of history to illustrate his point about how virulent the inflation bug can be, particularly if you mix politics too richly into the economic model.

Consider: Despite the inflationary pressues that remained when he took office, President Jimmy Carter was reluctant to mount a strong anti-inflation program lest it interfere with his commitment to lower the unemployment rate. The result was an inflation-fighting strategy described by Carter's disenchanted Treasury Secretary W. Michael Blumenthal as one that aimed to battle inflation without offending any special interest group "or affecting any natural constituency of the Democratic Party."

The upshot: Carter worked the unemployment rate down from 7.7 percent in 1976 to 5.8 percent in 1979—but at fearful cost on the inflation front. The CPI, which rose 4.9 percent in 1976, soared above 13 percent in 1979 and remained at more than 12 percent in 1980. At that rate, prices will double in little more than five years.

When the Federal Reserve finally got around to taking action in 1980 it required back-to-back recessions—and unemployment rates approaching 10 percent in 1981–82—to damp the inflationary fires. . . .

As history clearly shows us—and as Greenspan obviously knows—a little inflation can easily erupt into both a lot of inflation and much higher unemployment.

Source: "Greenspan and Fed Act Prudently in Raising Rates to Guard Against Inflation," Dick Youngblood, *Minneapolis Star Tribune*, Feb. 9, 1994, p. 2D.

Minneapolis Star Tribune/February 9, 1994

Commentary

The Board of Governors of the Federal Reserve System sets the monetary policy for the country. If the Fed believes that economic growth is too fast and inflation is likely to rise, then it tries to reduce aggregate demand by decreasing money growth. As we learned in Chapter 14, when the Fed decreases the money supply, interest rates rise, aggregate demand falls, and real GDP growth falls.

The article discusses the controversy over Federal Reserve interest rate increases in 1994 that were aimed at fighting inflation. The controversy arose because the inflation rate had been quite low and many people wondered why the Fed was fighting inflation when there was no apparent inflation problem. The reporter reviewed some historical circumstances where he believed that the Fed waited too long to react to rising inflation and, as a result, the contractionary monetary policy needed to end the inflation was much more severe than would have occurred if the Fed had acted sooner to stop the rising inflation.

One problem with such historical analyses is that we can look back and see the mistakes made with the advantage of full information of the circumstances that existed at that time and later. However, the policymakers do not have this same information at the time they must make policy decisions. For instance, the consumer price index is available with a one-month lag, so our knowledge of inflation is always running a month behind the actual economy. GDP is even worse. GDP data are available quarterly and we do not find out about GDP until well after a quarter ends, and even then there are often substantial revisions to the numbers occurring many months after a quarter. The point is simply that the Federal Reserve (and other policymaking institutions) must formulate policy today based on less than complete knowledge of the *current* situation and the policy must be addressed at their best guess of the *future* situation.

For these reasons, policymakers often find themselves the target of critics who dispute the current and future outlook on inflation and other key economic variables. Even though the inflation rate in 1994 was quite low and had been low for several years, the Fed was worried that several indicators of the future course of inflation (like some commodity prices) signaled rising inflation. By acting to reduce the inflationary pressures in the economy before inflation actually rose, the Fed hoped to avoid any significant increase in inflation. Only time will tell if the Fed policy in 1994 was successful in preventing rising inflation.

15

Macroeconomic Policy: Tradeoffs, Expectations, Credibility, and Sources of Business Cycles

FUNDAMENTAL QUESTIONS

1. Is there a tradeoff between inflation and the unemployment rate?
2. How does the tradeoff between inflation and the unemployment rate vary from the short to the long run?
3. What is the relationship between unexpected inflation and the unemployment rate?
4. How are macroeconomic expectations formed?
5. What makes government policies credible?
6. Are business cycles related to political elections?
7. How do real shocks to the economy affect business cycles?
8. How is inflationary monetary policy related to government fiscal policy?

M acroeconomics is a dynamic discipline. Monetary and fiscal policies change over time. And so does our understanding of those policies. Economists debate the nature of business cycles—what causes them and what, if anything, government can do about them. Some economists argue that policies that lower the unemployment rate tend to raise the rate of inflation. Others insist that only unexpected inflation can influence real GDP and employment. If the latter economists are right, does government always have to surprise the public in order to improve economic conditions?

PREVIEW

Some economists claim that politicians manipulate the business cycle to increase their chances of reelection. If they are right, we should expect economic growth just before national elections. But what happens after the elections? What are the long-term effects of political business cycles? Because of these issues, the material in this chapter should be considered somewhat controversial. In Chapter 16 we will examine the controversies in more detail, and it will be more apparent where the sources of controversy lie.

I. THE PHILLIPS CURVE

In 1958 a New Zealand economist, A. W. Phillips, published a study of the relationship between the unemployment rate and the rate of change in wages in England. He found that over the period from 1826 to 1957 there had been an inverse relationship between the unemployment rate and the rate of change in wages: the unemployment rate fell in years when there were relatively large increases in wages and rose in years when wages increased relatively little. Phillips's study started other economists searching for similar relationships in other countries. In those studies, it became common to substitute the rate of inflation for the rate of change in wages.

Early studies in the United States found an inverse relationship between inflation and the unemployment rate. The graph that illustrates this relationship is called a **Phillips curve**. Figure 1 shows a Phillips curve for the United States in the 1960s. Over this period, lower inflation rates were associated with higher unemployment rates, as shown by the downward-sloping curve.

The slope of the curve in Figure 1 depicts an inverse relationship between the rate of inflation and the unemployment rate: As the inflation rate falls, the unemployment rate rises. In 1969 the inflation rate was relatively high, at 5.5 percent, while the unemployment rate was relatively low, at 3.5 percent. In 1967 an inflation rate of 3.1 percent was consistent with an unemployment rate of 3.8 percent; and in 1961, 1 percent inflation occurred with 6.7 percent unemployment.

Phillips curve:
a graph that illustrates the relationship between inflation and the unemployment rate

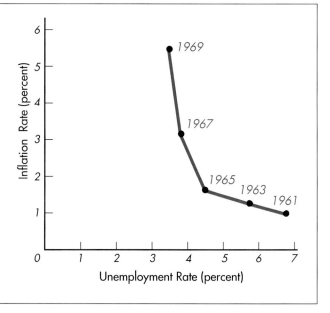

Figure 1
A Phillips Curve, United States, 1961–1969
In the 1960s, as the rate of inflation rose, the unemployment rate fell. This inverse relationship suggests a tradeoff between the rate of inflation and the unemployment rate. Source: Data are from *Economic Report of the President, 1995* (Washington, D.C.: U.S. Government Printing Office, 1995).

The downward-sloping Phillips curve seems to indicate a tradeoff between unemployment and inflation. A country could have a lower unemployment rate by accepting higher inflation, or a lower rate of inflation by accepting higher unemployment. Certainly this was the case in the United States in the 1960s. But is the curve depicted in Figure 1 representative of the tradeoff over long periods of time?

1.a. An Inflation-Unemployment Tradeoff?

Is there a tradeoff between inflation and the unemployment rate?

Figure 2 shows unemployment and inflation rates in the United States for several years from 1955 to 1994. The points in the figure do not lie along a downward-sloping curve like the one shown in Figure 1. For example, in 1955 the unemployment rate was 4.4 percent and the inflation rate was −.4 percent. In 1960 the unemployment rate was 5.5 percent and the inflation rate was 1.7 percent. Both unemployment and inflation rates had increased since 1955. Moving through time, you can see that the inflation rate tended to increase along with the unemployment rate through the 1960s and 1970s. By 1980, the unemployment rate was 7.1 percent and the inflation rate was 13.5 percent.

The scattered points in Figure 2 show no evidence of a tradeoff between unemployment and inflation. A downward-sloping Phillips curve does not seem to exist over the long term.

1.b. Short-Run Versus Long-Run Tradeoffs

How does the tradeoff between inflation and the unemployment rate vary from the short to the long run?

Most economists believe that the downward-sloping Phillips curve and the tradeoff it implies between inflation and unemployment are short-term phenomena. Think of a series of Phillips curves, one for each of the points in Figure 2. From 1955 to 1980, the curves shifted out to the right. In the early 1980s, they shifted in to the left.

Figure 3 shows a series of Phillips curves that could account for the data in Figure 2. At any point in time, a downward-sloping Phillips curve indicates a tradeoff between inflation and unemployment. Many economists

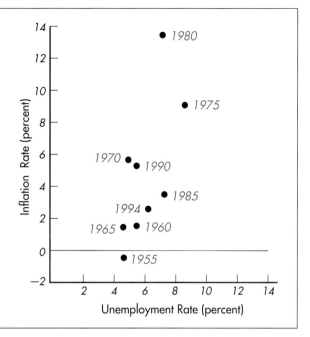

Figure 2
Unemployment and Inflation in the United States, 1955–1994
The data on inflation and unemployment rates in the United States between 1955 and 1994 show no particular relationship between inflation and unemployment over the long run. There is no evidence here of a downward-sloping Phillips curve. Source: Data are from *Economic Report of the President, 1995* (Washington, D.C.: U.S. Government Printing Office, 1995).

The data indicate that the Phillips curve may have shifted out in the 1960s and 1970s and shifted in during the 1980s.

believe that this kind of tradeoff is just a short-term phenomenon. Over time, the Phillips curve shifts so that the short-run tradeoff between inflation and unemployment disappears in the long run.

On the early 1960s curve in Figure 3, 5 percent unemployment is consistent with 2 percent inflation. By the early 1970s, the curve had shifted up. Here 5 percent unemployment is associated with 6 percent inflation. On the late 1970s curve, 5 percent unemployment is consistent with 10 percent inflation. For more than two decades, the tradeoff between inflation and unemployment worsened as the Phillips curves shifted up, so that higher and higher inflation rates were associated with any given level of unemployment. Then in the 1980s, the tradeoff seemed to improve as the Phillips curve shifted down. On the late 1980s curve, 5 percent unemployment is consistent with 4 percent inflation.

The Phillips curves in Figure 3 represent changes that took place over time in the United States. We cannot be sure of the actual shape of a Phillips curve at any time, but an outward shift of the curve in the 1960s and 1970s and an inward shift during the 1980s are consistent with the data. Later in this chapter we describe how changing government policy and the public's expectations about that policy may have shifted aggregate demand and aggregate supply and produced these shifts in the Phillips curves.

1.b.1. In the Short Run Figure 4 uses the aggregate demand and supply analysis we developed in Chapter 9 to explain the Phillips curve. Initially the economy is operating at point 1 in both diagrams. In part (a), the aggregate demand curve (AD_1) and aggregate supply curve (AS_1) intersect at price level P_1 and real GDP level Y_p, the level of potential real GDP. Remember that potential real GDP is the level of income and output generated at the natural rate of unemployment, the unemployment rate that exists in the absence of cyclical unemployment. In part (b), point 1 lies on Phillips curve I, where the inflation rate is 3 percent and the unemployment rate is 5 percent. We assume that the 5 percent unemployment rate at the level of potential real GDP is the

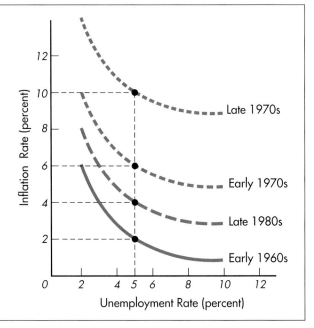

Figure 3
The Shifting Phillips Curve
We can reconcile the long-run data on unemployment and inflation with the downward-sloping Phillips curve by using a series of Phillips curves. (In effect, we treat the long run as a series of short-run curves.) The Phillips curve for the early 1960s shows 5 percent unemployment and 2 percent inflation. Over time, the short-run curve shifted out to the right. The early 1970s curve shows 5 percent unemployment and 6 percent inflation. And the short-run curve for the late 1970s shows 5 percent unemployment and 10 percent inflation. In the early 1980s, the short-run Phillips curve began to shift down toward the origin. By the late 1980s, 5 percent unemployment was consistent with 4 percent inflation.

natural rate of unemployment (U_n). A discussion of the natural rate of unemployment and its determinants is given in the Economic Insight "The Natural Rate of Unemployment."

What happens when aggregate demand goes up from AD_1 to AD_2? A new equilibrium is established along the short-run aggregate supply curve (AS_1) at point 2. Here the price level (P_2) is higher, as is the level of real GDP (Y_2). In part (b), the increase in price and income is reflected in the movement along Phillips curve I to point 2. At point 2, the inflation rate is 6 percent and the unemployment rate is 3 percent. The increase in expenditures raises the inflation rate and lowers the unemployment rate (because national output has surpassed potential output).

Notice that there appears to be a tradeoff between inflation and unemployment on Phillips curve I. The increase in spending increases output and stimulates employment, so that the unemployment rate falls. And the higher spending pushes the rate of inflation up. But this tradeoff is only temporary. Point 2 in both diagrams is only a short-run equilibrium.

I.b.2. In the Long Run As we discussed in Chapter 9, the short-run aggregate supply curve shifts over time as production costs rise in response to higher prices. Once the aggregate supply curve shifts to AS_2, long-run equilibrium occurs at point 3, where AS_2 intersects AD_2. Here, the price level is P_3 and real GDP returns to its potential level, Y_p.

The shift in aggregate supply lowers real GDP. As income falls, the unemployment rate goes up. The decrease in aggregate supply is reflected in the movement from point 2 on Phillips curve I to point 3 on Phillips curve II. As real GDP returns to its potential level (Y_p), unemployment returns to the natural rate (U_n), 5 percent. In the long run, as the economy adjusts to an increase in aggregate demand and expectations adjust to the new inflation rate, there is a period in which real GDP falls and the price level rises.

Over time there is no relationship between the price level and the level of real GDP. You can see this in the aggregate demand and supply diagram. Points 1 and 3 both lie along the long-run aggregate supply curve

Figure 4
Aggregate Demand and Supply and the Phillips Curve

The movement from point 1 to point 2 to point 3 traces the adjustment of the economy to an increase in aggregate demand. Point 1 is initial equilibrium in both diagrams. At this point potential real GDP is Y_p and the price level is P_1 in the aggregate demand and supply diagram, and the inflation rate is 3 percent with an unemployment rate of 5 percent (the natural rate) along short-run curve I in the Phillips curve diagram.

If the aggregate demand curve shifts from AD_1 to AD_2, equilibrium real GDP goes up to Y_2 and the price level rises to P_2 in the aggregate demand and supply diagram. The increase in aggregate demand pushes the inflation rate up to 6 percent and the unemployment

rate down to 3 percent along Phillips curve I. The movement from point 1 to point 2 along the curve indicates a tradeoff between inflation and the unemployment rate.

Over time the AS curve shifts in response to rising production costs at the higher rate of inflation. Along AS_2, equilibrium is at point 3, where real GDP falls back to Y_p and the price level rises to P_3. As we move from point 2 to point 3 in part (b), we shift to short-run Phillips curve II. Here the inflation rate remains high (at 6 percent), while the unemployment rate goes back up to 5 percent, the rate consistent with production at Y_p. In the long run, then, there is no tradeoff between inflation and unemployment. The vertical long-run aggregate supply curve at the potential level of real GDP is associated with the vertical long-run Phillips curve at the natural rate of unemployment.

(a) Aggregate Demand and Supply

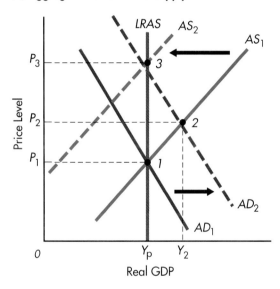

(b) Phillips Curve

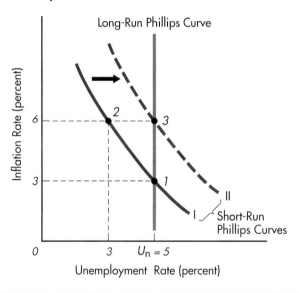

The long-run Phillips curve is a vertical line at the natural rate of unemployment.

(*LRAS*) at potential real GDP. The *LRAS* curve has its analogue in the long-run Phillips curve, a vertical line at the natural rate of unemployment. Points 1 and 3 both lie along this curve.

RECAP

1. The Phillips curve shows an inverse relationship between inflation and unemployment.

2. The downward slope of the Phillips curve indicates a tradeoff between inflation and unemployment.

3. Over the long run that tradeoff disappears.

4. The long-run Phillips curve is a vertical line at the natural rate of unemployment, analogous to the long-run aggregate supply curve at potential real GDP.

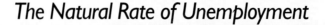
The Natural Rate of Unemployment

The natural rate of unemployment is defined as the unemployment rate that exists in the absence of cyclical unemployment. As we discussed in Chapter 8, the natural rate of unemployment reflects the normal amount of frictional unemployment (people temporarily between jobs), structural unemployment (people who lost jobs because of technological change), and seasonal unemployment (people who lost jobs because the jobs are available only at certain times of the year). What factors determine the normal amount of frictional and structural unemployment?

One of the most important factors is demographic change. As the age, gender, and racial makeup of the labor force changes, the natural rate of unemployment also changes. For instance, when the baby boom generation entered the labor force, the natural rate of unemployment increased because new workers typically have the highest unemployment rates. Between 1956 and 1979, the proportion of young adults (ages sixteen to twenty-four) in the labor force increased, increasing the nat-

ural rate of unemployment. Since 1979, the fraction of young adults in the labor force has fallen, tending to lower the natural rate of unemployment.

In addition to the composition of the labor force, several other factors affect the natural rate of unemployment:

■ In recent years, structural changes in the economy, such as the shift from manufacturing to service jobs and the "downsizing" and restructuring of firms throughout the economy have contributed to a higher natural rate of unemployment. Related to these structural changes is a decline in the demand for low-skilled workers so that rising unemployment is overwhelmingly concentrated among workers with limited education and skills.

■ Increases in the legal minimum wage tend to raise the natural rate of unemployment. When the government mandates that employers pay some workers a higher wage than a freely competitive labor market would pay, fewer workers are employed.

■ The more generous the unemployment benefits, the higher the natural rate of unemployment. Increased benefits reduce the cost of being out of work and allow unemployed workers to take their time finding a new job.

■ Income taxes can also affect the natural rate of unemployment. Higher taxes mean that workers keep less of their earned income and so have less incentive to work.

The effect of these factors on the unemployment rate is complex, so it is difficult to state what the natural rate of unemployment is exactly. But as these factors change over time, the natural rate of unemployment also changes.

One last thing. It is not clear that minimizing the natural rate of unemployment is a universal goal. Minimum wages, unemployment benefits, and taxes have other important implications besides their effect on the natural rate of unemployment. We cannot expect these variables to be set solely in terms of their effect on unemployment.

2. THE ROLE OF EXPECTATIONS

The data and analysis in the previous section indicate that there is no long-run tradeoff between inflation and unemployment. But they do not explain the movement of the Phillips curve in the 1960s, 1970s, and 1980s. To understand why the short-run curve shifts, you must understand the role that unexpected inflation plays in the economy.

2.a. Expected Versus Unexpected Inflation

Figure 5 shows two short-run Phillips curves like those in Figure 4. Each curve is drawn for a particular expected rate of inflation. Curve I shows the tradeoff between inflation and unemployment when the inflation rate is

What is the relationship between unexpected inflation and the unemployment rate?

reservation wage:
the minimum wage a worker is willing to accept

expected to be 3 percent. If the actual rate of inflation (measured along the vertical axis) is 3 percent, the economy is operating at point 1, with an unemployment rate of 5 percent (the natural rate). If the inflation rate unexpectedly increases to 6 percent, the economy moves from point 1 to point 2 along Phillips curve I. Obviously, unexpected inflation can affect the unemployment rate. There are three factors at work here: wage expectations, inventory fluctuations, and wage contracts.

2.a.1. Wage Expectations and Unemployment   Unemployed workers who are looking for a job choose a **reservation wage**, the minimum wage they are willing to accept. They continue to look for work until they receive an offer that equals or exceeds their reservation wage.

Wages are not the only factor that workers take into consideration before accepting a job offer. A firm that offers good working conditions and fringe benefits can pay a lower wage than a firm that does not offer these advantages. But other things being equal, workers choose higher wages over lower wages. We simplify our analysis here by assuming that the only variable that affects the unemployed worker who is looking for a job is the reservation wage.

The link between unexpected inflation and the unemployment rate stems from the fact that wage offers are surprisingly high when the rate of inflation is surprisingly high. An unexpected increase in inflation means that prices are higher than anticipated, as are nominal income and wages. If aggregate demand increases unexpectedly, then, prices, output, employment, and wages go up. Unemployed workers with a constant reservation wage find it easier to obtain a satisfactory wage offer during a period when wages are rising faster than the workers expected. This means that more unemployed workers find jobs, and they find those jobs quicker than they do in a period when the rate of inflation is expected. So the unemployment rate falls during a period of unexpectedly high inflation (Figure 6).

Consider an example. Suppose an accountant named Jason decides that he must find a job that pays at least $105 a day. Jason's reservation wage is

Figure 5
Expectations and the Phillips Curve
Short-run Phillips curve I shows the tradeoff between inflation and the unemployment rate as long as people expect 3 percent inflation. When the actual rate of inflation is 3 percent, the rate of unemployment (U_n) is 5 percent (point 1). Short-run Phillips curve II shows the tradeoff as long as people expect 6 percent inflation. When the actual rate of inflation is 6 percent, the unemployment rate is 5 percent (point 3).

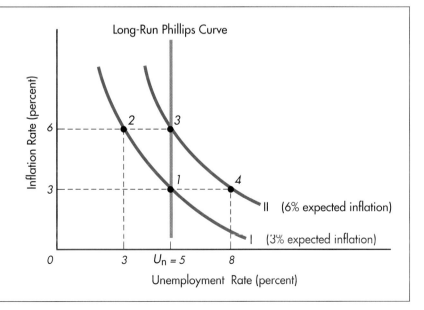

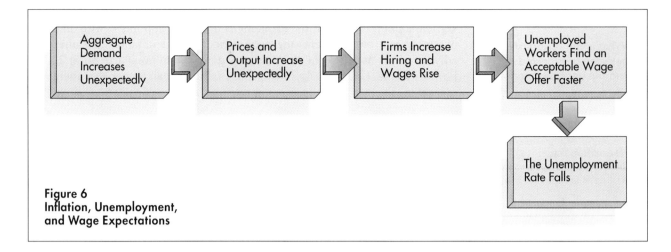

Figure 6
Inflation, Unemployment, and Wage Expectations

$105. Furthermore, Jason expects prices and wages to be fairly stable across the economy; he expects no inflation. Jason looks for a job and finds that the jobs he qualifies for are only offering wages of $100 a day. Because his job offers are all paying less than his reservation wage, he keeps on looking. Let's say that aggregate demand rises unexpectedly. Firms increase production and raise prices. To hire more workers, they increase the wages they offer. Suppose wages go up 5 percent. Now the jobs that Jason qualifies for are offering 5 percent higher wages, $105 a day instead of $100 a day. At this higher wage rate, Jason quickly accepts a job and starts working. This example explains why the move from point 1 to point 2 in Figure 5 occurs.

The short-run Phillips curve assumes a constant *expected* rate of inflation. It also assumes that every unemployed worker who is looking for a job has a constant reservation wage. When inflation rises unexpectedly, then, wages rise faster than expected and the unemployment rate falls. The element of "surprise" is critical here. If the increase in inflation is *expected*, unemployed workers who are looking for a job will revise their reservation wage to match the expected change in the level of prices. If reservation wages go up with the rate of inflation, there is no tradeoff between inflation and the unemployment rate. Higher inflation is associated with the original unemployment rate.

If the reservation wage goes up with the rate of inflation, there is no tradeoff between inflation and the unemployment rate.

Let's go back to Jason, the accountant who wants a job that pays $105 a day. Previously we said that if wages increased to $105 unexpectedly because of an increase in aggregate demand, he would quickly find an acceptable job. However, if Jason knows that the price level is going to go up 5 percent, then he knows that a wage increase from $100 to $105 is not a real wage increase because he needs $105 in order to buy what $100 would buy before. The *nominal wage* is the number of dollars earned; the *real wage* is the purchasing power of those dollars. If the nominal wage increases 5 percent at the same time that prices have gone up 5 percent, it takes 5 percent more money to buy the same goods and services. The real wage has not changed. What happens? Jason revises his reservation wage to account for the higher price level. If he wants a 5 percent higher real wage, his reservation wage goes up to $110.25 (5 percent more than $105). Now if employers offer him $105, he refuses and keeps searching.

In Figure 5, an expected increase in inflation moves us from point 1 on curve I to point 3 on curve II. When increased inflation is expected, the reservation wage reflects the higher rate of inflation and there is no tradeoff between inflation and the unemployment rate. Instead the economy moves along the long-run Phillips curve, with unemployment at its natural rate. The clockwise movement from point 1 to point 2 to point 3 is the pattern that follows an unexpected increase in aggregate demand.

What if the inflation rate is lower than expected? Here we find a reservation wage that reflects higher expected inflation. This means that those people who are looking for jobs are going to have a difficult time finding acceptable wage offers, the number of unemployed workers is going to increase, and the unemployment rate is going to rise. This sequence is shown in Figure 5, as the economy moves from point 3 to point 4. When the actual inflation rate is 6 percent and the expected inflation rate is also 6 percent, the economy is operating at the natural rate of unemployment. When the inflation rate falls to 3 percent but workers still expect 6 percent inflation, the unemployment rate rises (at point 4 along curve II). Eventually, if the inflation rate remains at 3 percent, workers adjust their expectations to the lower rate and the economy moves to point 1 on curve I. The short-run effect of unexpected *disinflation* is rising unemployment. Over time the short-run increase in the unemployment rate is eliminated.

As long as the actual rate of inflation equals the expected rate, the economy operates at the natural rate of unemployment.

As long as the actual rate of inflation equals the expected rate, the economy remains at the natural rate of unemployment. The tradeoff between inflation and the unemployment rate comes from unexpected inflation.

2.a.2. Inventory Fluctuations and Unemployment Businesses hold inventories based on what they expect their sales to be. When aggregate demand is greater than expected, inventories fall below targeted levels. To restore inventories to the levels wanted, production is increased. Increased production leads to increased employment. If aggregate demand is lower than expected, inventories rise above targeted levels. To reduce inventories, production is cut back and workers are laid off from their jobs until sales have lowered unwanted inventories. Once production increases, employment rises again.

When aggregate demand is higher than expected, inventories are lower than expected and prices are higher than expected, so the unemployment rate falls. When aggregate demand is lower than expected, inventories are higher than expected and prices are lower than expected, so the unemployment rate rises.

Inventory, production, and employment all play a part in the Phillips curve analysis (Figure 7). Expected sales and inventory levels are based on an expected level of aggregate demand. If aggregate demand is greater than expected, inventories fall and prices rise on the remaining goods in stock. With the unexpected increase in inflation, the unemployment rate falls as businesses hire more workers to increase output to offset falling inventories. This sequence represents movement along a short-run Phillips curve because there is a tradeoff between inflation and the unemployment rate. We find the same tradeoff if aggregate demand is lower than expected. Here inventories increase and prices are lower than anticipated. With the unexpected decrease

Figure 7
Inflation, Unemployment, and Inventories

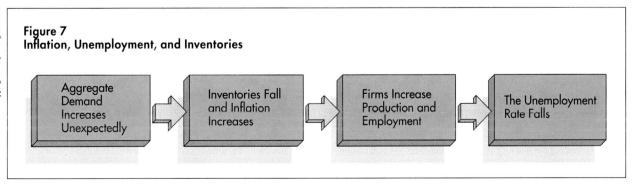

in inflation, the unemployment rate goes up as workers are laid off to reduce output until inventory levels fall.

2.a.3. **Wage Contracts and Unemployment**

Another factor that explains the short-run tradeoff between inflation and unemployment is labor contracts that fix wages for an extended period of time. When an existing contract expires, management must renegotiate with labor. A firm facing lower demand for its products may negotiate lower wages in order to keep as many workers employed as before. If the demand for a firm's products falls while a wage contract is in force, the firm must maintain wages, which means it is going to have to lay off workers.

For example, a pizza restaurant with $1,000 a day in revenues employs 4 workers at $40 a day each. The firm's total labor costs are $160 a day. Suppose revenues fall to $500 a day. If the firm wants to cut its labor costs in half, to $80, it has two choices: it can maintain wages at $40 a day and lay off 2 workers, or it can lower wages to $20 a day and keep all 4 workers. If the restaurant has a contract with the employees that sets wages at $40 a day, it must lay off 2 workers.

If demand increases while a wage contract is in force, a business hires more workers at the fixed wage. Once the contract expires, the firm's workers will negotiate higher wages, to reflect increased demand. For instance, suppose prices in the economy, including the price of pizzas, go up 10 percent. If the pizza restaurant can raise its prices 10 percent and sell as many pizzas as before (because the price of every other food also has gone up 10 percent), its daily revenues increase from $1,000 to $1,100. If the restaurant has a labor contract that fixes wages at $40 a day, its profits are going to go up, reflecting the higher price of pizzas. With its increased profits, the restaurant may be willing to hire more workers. Once the labor contract expires, the workers ask for a 10 percent wage increase to match the price level increase. If wages go up to $44 a day (10 percent higher than $40), the firm cannot hire more workers because wages have gone up in proportion to the increase in prices. If the costs of doing business rise at the same rate as prices, both profits and employment remain the same.

In the national economy, wage contracts are staggered; they expire at different times. Each year only 30 to 40 percent of all contracts expire across the entire economy. As economic conditions change, firms with expiring wage contracts can adjust *wages* to those conditions; firms with existing contracts must adjust *employment* to those conditions.

How do long-term wage contracts tie in with the Phillips curve analysis? The expected rate of inflation is based on expected aggregate demand and reflected in the wage that is agreed on in the contract. When the actual rate of inflation equals the expected rate, businesses retain the same number of workers they had planned on when they signed the contract. For the economy overall, when actual and expected inflation rates are the same, the economy is operating at the natural rate of unemployment. That is, businesses are not hiring new workers because of an unexpected increase in aggregate demand, and they are not laying off workers because of an unexpected decrease in aggregate demand.

When aggregate demand is higher than expected, those firms with unexpired wage contracts hire more workers at the fixed wage, reducing unemployment (Figure 8). Those firms with expiring contracts have to offer higher wages in order to maintain the existing level of employment at the new demand condition. When aggregate demand is lower than expected, those

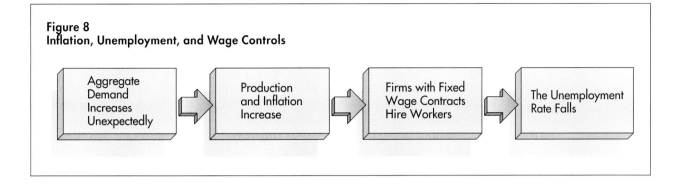

Figure 8
Inflation, Unemployment, and Wage Controls

| Aggregate Demand Increases Unexpectedly | → | Production and Inflation Increase | → | Firms with Fixed Wage Contracts Hire Workers | → | The Unemployment Rate Falls |

firms with unexpired contracts have to lay off workers because they cannot lower the wage, while those firms with expiring contracts negotiate lower wages in order to keep their workers.

If wages were always flexible, unexpected changes in aggregate demand might be reflected largely in *wage* rather than *employment* adjustments. Wage contracts force businesses to adjust employment when aggregate demand changes unexpectedly.

Wage contracts force businesses to adjust employment rather than wages in response to an unexpected change in aggregate demand.

2.b. Forming Expectations

How are macroeconomic expectations formed?

adaptive expectation:
an expectation formed on the basis of information collected in the past

rational expectation:
an expectation that is formed using all available relevant information

Expectations play a key role in explaining the short-run Phillips curve, the tradeoff between inflation and the unemployment rate. How are these expectations formed?

2.b.1. Adaptive Expectations Expectations can be formed solely on the basis of experience. **Adaptive expectations** are expectations that are determined by what has happened in the recent past.

People learn from their experiences. For example, suppose the inflation rate has been 3 percent for the past few years. Based on past experience, then, people expect the inflation rate in the future to remain at 3 percent. If the Federal Reserve increases the growth of the money supply to a rate that produces 6 percent inflation, the public will be surprised by the higher rate of inflation. This unexpected inflation creates a short-run tradeoff between inflation and the unemployment rate along a short-run Phillips curve. Over time, if the inflation rate remains at 6 percent, the public will learn that the 3 percent rate is too low and will adapt its expectations to the actual, higher inflation rate. Once public expectations have adapted to the new rate of inflation, the economy returns to the natural rate of unemployment along the long-run Phillips curve.

2.b.2. Rational Expectations Many economists believe that adaptive expectations are too narrow. If people look only at past information, they are ignoring what could be important information in the current period. **Rational expectations** are based on all available relevant information.

We are not saying that people have to know everything in order to form expectations. Rational expectations require only that people consider the information they believe to be relevant. This information includes their past experience along with what is currently happening and what they expect to happen in the future. For instance, in forming expectations about inflation, people consider rates in the recent past, current policy, and anticipated shifts in aggregate demand and supply that could affect the future rate of inflation.

If the inflation rate has been 3 percent over the past few years, adaptive expectations suggest that the future inflation rate will be 3 percent. No other information is considered. Rational expectations are based on more than the historical rate. Suppose the Fed announces a new policy that everyone believes will increase inflation in the future. With rational expectations the effect of this announcement will be considered. Here, when the actual rate of inflation turns out to be more than 3 percent, there is no short-run tradeoff between inflation and the unemployment rate. The economy moves directly along the long-run Phillips curve to the higher inflation rate, while unemployment remains at the natural rate.

If we believe that people have rational expectations, we do not expect them to make the same mistakes over and over. We expect them to learn and react quickly to new information.

RECAP

1. Wage expectations, inventory fluctuations, and wage contracts help explain the short-run tradeoff between inflation and the unemployment rate.

2. The reservation wage is the minimum wage a worker is willing to accept.

3. Because wage expectations reflect expected inflation, when the inflation rate is surprisingly high, unemployed workers find jobs faster and the unemployment rate falls.

4. Unexpected increases in aggregate demand lower inventories and raise prices. To increase output (to replenish shrinking inventories), businesses hire more workers, which reduces the unemployment rate.

5. When aggregate demand is higher than expected, those businesses with wage contracts hire more workers at the fixed wage, lowering unemployment.

6. If wages were always flexible, unexpected changes in aggregate demand would be reflected in wage adjustments rather than employment adjustments.

7. Adaptive expectations are formed on the basis of information about the past.

8. Rational expectations are formed using all available relevant information.

3. CREDIBILITY AND TIME INCONSISTENCY

The rate of inflation is a product of growth in the money supply. That growth is controlled by the country's central bank. If the Federal Reserve follows a policy of rapidly increasing the money supply, one consequence is rapid inflation. If it follows a policy of slow growth, it keeps inflation down.

To help the public predict the future course of monetary policy, Congress passed the Federal Reserve Reform Act (1977) and the Full Employment and Balanced Growth Act (1978). The Full Employment Act requires that the chairman of the Board of Governors of the Federal Reserve System testify before Congress annually, presenting the Fed's targets for money growth along with other policy plans.

time inconsistent:
a characteristic of a policy or plan that changes over time in response to changing conditions

Of course, the Fed's plans are only plans. There is no requirement that the central bank actually follow the plans announced to Congress. During the course of the year, the Fed may decide that a new policy is necessary in light of economic developments. Changing conditions mean that plans can be **time inconsistent**. A plan is time inconsistent when it is changed over time in response to changed conditions.

3.a. The Policymaker's Problem

Time inconsistency gives the Fed a credibility problem and the public the problem of guessing where monetary policy and the inflation rate are actually heading.

Figure 9 shows an example of how announced monetary policy can turn out to be time inconsistent. The Fed, like all central banks, always announces that it plans to follow a low-money-growth policy to promote a low rate of inflation. (It is unlikely that a central bank would ever state that it intends to follow an inflationary monetary policy.) Yet we know that the world often is characterized by higher rates of inflation. Because the actual inflation rate often ends up being higher than the intended inflation rate, low-inflation plans often are time inconsistent.

In Figure 9, labor contracts are signed following the central bank's announcement. The contracts call for either low wage increases or high wage increases. If everyone believes that the money supply is going to grow at the announced low rate, then the low-wage contracts are signed. However, if there is reason to believe that the announced policy is time inconsistent, the high-wage contracts are signed.

Over time, the central bank either follows the announced low-money-growth policy or implements a high-money-growth policy. If the low-wage contract is in force and the central bank follows the low-money-growth policy, the actual inflation rate will match the low rate that people expected and the unemployment rate will equal the natural rate. If the central bank follows a high-money-growth policy, the rate of inflation will be higher than expected and the unemployment rate will fall below the natural rate.

If the high-wage contract is in force and the low-money-growth policy is followed, the inflation rate will be lower than expected and the unemployment rate will exceed the natural rate. If the high-money-growth policy is followed, the inflation rate will be as expected and the unemployment rate will be at the natural rate.

Look what happens to unemployment. Regardless of which labor contract is signed, if the central bank wants to keep unemployment as low as possible, it must deviate from its announced plan. The plan turns out to be time inconsistent. Because the public knows that unemployment, like the rate of inflation, is a factor in the Fed's policymaking, the central bank's announced plan is not credible.

3.b. Credibility

What makes government policies credible?

If the public does not believe the low-money-growth plans of the central bank, high-wage contracts will always be signed, and the central bank will always have to follow a high-money-growth policy to maintain the natural rate of unemployment. This cycle creates an economy where high inflation persists year after year. If the central bank always followed its announced plan of low money growth and low inflation, the public would believe the

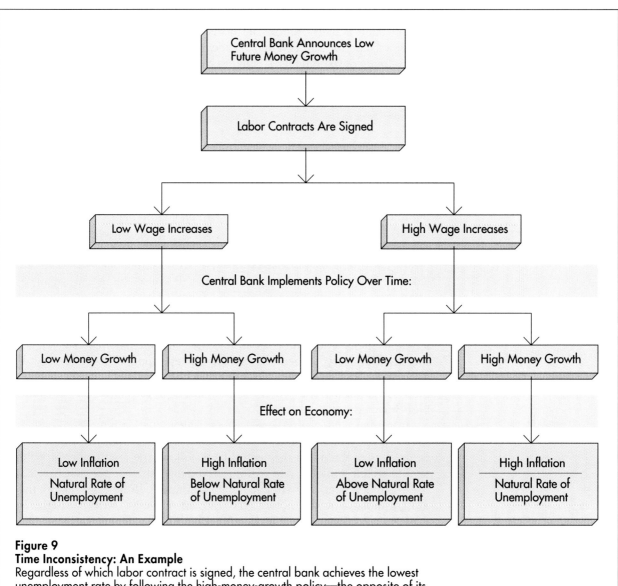

Figure 9
Time Inconsistency: An Example
Regardless of which labor contract is signed, the central bank achieves the lowest unemployment rate by following the high-money-growth policy—the opposite of its announced policy.

plan, low-wage contracts would always be signed, and the natural rate of unemployment would exist at the low rate of inflation. In either case, high or low inflation, if the inflation rate is expected, the unemployment rate does not change. If the central bank eliminates the goal of reducing unemployment below the natural rate, the problem of inflation disappears. However, the public must be convinced that the central bank intends to pursue low money growth in the long run, avoiding the temptation to reduce the unemployment rate in the short run.

How does the central bank achieve credibility? One way is to fix the growth rate of the money supply by law. Congress could pass a law requiring that the Fed maintain a growth rate of, say, 3 to 5 percent a year. There would be problems defining the money supply, but this kind of law would give the Fed's policies credibility.

Another way for the Fed to establish credibility is to create incentives for monetary authorities to take a long-term view of monetary policy. In the long run, the economy is better off if policymakers do not try to exploit the short-run tradeoff between inflation and the unemployment rate. The central bank can achieve a lower rate of inflation at the natural rate of unemployment by avoiding unexpected increases in the rate at which money and inflation grow.

Reputation is a key factor here. If the central bank considers the effects of its actual policy on public expectations, it will find it easier to achieve low inflation by establishing a reputation for low-inflation policies. A central bank with a reputation for time-consistent plans will find labor contracts calling for low wage increases because people believe that the bank is going to follow its announced plans and generate a low rate of inflation. In other words, by maintaining a reputation for following through on announced policy, the Fed can earn the public confidence necessary to produce a low rate of inflation in the long run. An example of a dramatic reduction in inflation with no significant recession is provided in the Economic Insight "Ending Hyperinflation without a Recession." In the cases studied here, the public expected lower inflation so that the fall in inflation had minor effects on real GDP. The central banks were credible in the eyes of the public so that low inflation policies were expected to continue.

RECAP

1. A plan is time inconsistent when it changes over time in response to changing conditions.

2. If the public believes that an announced policy is time inconsistent, policymakers have a credibility problem that can limit the success of their plans.

3. Credibility can be achieved by fixing the growth rate of the money supply by law or by creating incentives for policymakers to follow through on announced plans.

4. SOURCES OF BUSINESS CYCLES

In Chapter 12 we examined the effect of fiscal policy on the equilibrium level of real GDP. Changes in government spending and taxes can expand or contract the economy. In Chapter 14 we described how monetary policy affects the equilibrium level of real GDP. Changes in the money supply also produce booms and recessions. Besides the policy-induced sources of business cycles covered in earlier chapters, there are other sources of economic fluctuations that economists have studied. One is the election campaign of incumbent politicians, and when a business cycle results from this action it is called a *political business cycle*. Macroeconomic policy may be used to promote the reelection of incumbent politicians. We also examine another source of business cycles that is not related to discretionary policy actions, the *real business cycle*.

Those who were around in the 1970s can remember the long lines and shortages at gas stations and the rapid increase in the price of oil that resulted from the oil embargo imposed by the Organization of Petroleum Exporting Countries. There was another effect of the oil price shock—the aggregate supply curve in the United States and other oil-importing nations shifted to the left, lowering the equilibrium level of real GDP while raising the price level. Such "real" sources of business cycles can explain why national output can rise or fall in the absence of any discretionary government macroeconomic policy.

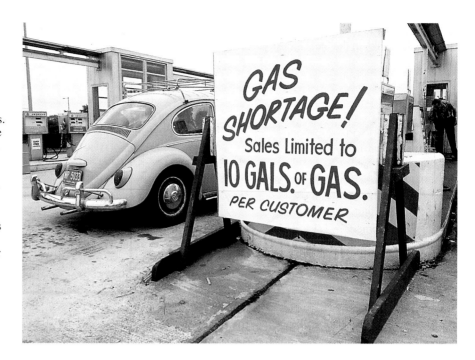

we have talked about monetary policy and fiscal policy individually. Here we consider the relationship between them.

In some countries, monetary and fiscal policies are carried out by a single central authority. Even in the United States, where the Federal Reserve was created as an independent agency, monetary policy and fiscal policy are always related. The actions of the central bank have an impact on the proper role for fiscal policy, and the actions of fiscal policymakers have an impact on the proper role for monetary policy.

For example, suppose the central bank follows a monetary policy that raises interest rates. That policy raises the interest cost of new government debt, in the process increasing government expenditures. On the other hand, a fiscal policy that generates large fiscal deficits could contribute to higher interest rates. If the central bank has targeted an interest rate that lies below the current rate, the central bank could be drawn into an expansionary monetary policy. This interdependence between monetary and fiscal policy is important to policymakers as well as to business people and others who seek to understand current economic developments.

5.a. The Government Budget Constraint

How is inflationary monetary policy related to government fiscal policy?

The *government budget constraint* clarifies the relationship between monetary and fiscal policies:

$$G = T + B + \Delta M$$

where

G = government spending

T = tax revenue

$$B = \text{government borrowing}$$

$$\Delta M = \text{the change in the money supply}[1]$$

The government budget constraint always holds because there are only three ways for the government to finance its spending: by taxing, by borrowing, and by creating money.

We can rewrite the government budget constraint with the change in M on the left-hand side of the equation:

$$\Delta M = (G - T) - B$$

In this form you can see that the change in government-issued money equals the government fiscal deficit $(G - T)$ minus borrowing. This equation is always true. A government that has the ability to borrow at reasonable costs will not have the incentive to create rapid money growth and the consequent inflation that results in order to finance its budget deficit.

5.b. Monetary Reforms

In the United States and other industrial nations, monetary and fiscal policies are conducted by separate, independent agencies. Fiscal authorities (Congress and the president in the U.S.) cannot impose monetary policy on the central bank. But in typical developing countries, monetary and fiscal policies are controlled by a central political authority. Here monetary policy is often an extension of fiscal policy. Fiscal policy can impose an inflationary burden on monetary policy. If a country is running a large fiscal deficit, and much of this deficit cannot be financed by government borrowing, monetary authorities must create money to finance the deficit.

Using money to finance fiscal deficits has produced very rapid rates of inflation in several countries. As prices reach astronomical levels, currency must be issued with very large face values. For instance, when Bolivia faced a sharp drop in the availability of willing lenders in the mid-1980s, the government began to create money to finance its fiscal deficit. As the money supply increased in relation to the output of goods and services, prices rose. In 1985 the government was creating money so fast that the rate of inflation reached 8,170 percent. Lunch in a La Paz hotel could cost 10 million Bolivian pesos. You can imagine the problem of counting money and recording money values with cash registers and calculators. As the rate of inflation increased, Bolivians had to carry stacks of currency to pay for goods and services. Eventually the government issued a 1 million peso note, then 5 million and 10 million peso notes.

This extremely high inflation, or hyperinflation, ended when a new government introduced its economic program in August 1985. The program reduced government spending dramatically, which slowed the growth of the fiscal deficit. At the same time, a monetary reform was introduced. A **monetary reform** is a new monetary policy that includes the introduction of a new monetary unit. The central bank of Bolivia announced that it would restrict money creation and introduced a new currency, the boliviano. It set 1 boliviano equal to 1 million Bolivian pesos.

monetary reform:
a new monetary policy that includes the introduction of a new monetary unit

---

[1]The M in the government budget constraint is government-issued money (usually called *base money*, or *high-powered money*). It is easiest to think of this kind of money as currency, although in practice base money includes more than currency.

Some aspects of the macro-economy are beyond the control of the government. This photo depicts the damage done in Kobe, Japan following an earthquake. Natural disasters, such as earthquakes or bad weather, sometimes play a role in determining the price level and national output in the short run. A major earthquake will lower national output and raise the price level. However, such effects should be important only in the short run as other determinants of the equilibrium price level and real GDP will dominate the forces of nature in normal times.

The introduction of a new monetary unit without a change in fiscal policy has no lasting effect on the rate of inflation.

The new monetary unit, the boliviano, did not lower prices; it lowered the units in which prices were quoted. Lunch now cost 10 bolivianos instead of 10 million pesos. More important, the rate of inflation dropped abruptly.

Did the new unit of currency end the hyperinflation? No. The rate of inflation dropped because the new fiscal policy controls introduced by the government relieved the pressure on the central bank to create money in order to finance government spending. Remember the government budget constraint. The only way to reduce the amount of money being created is to reduce the fiscal deficit $(G - T)$ minus borrowing (B). Once fiscal policy is under control, monetary reform is possible. If a government introduces a new monetary unit without changing its fiscal policy, the monetary unit by itself has no lasting effect on the rate of inflation.

Table 2 lists monetary reforms enacted in recent years. Argentina had a monetary reform in June 1983. Yet by June 1985, another reform was needed. The inflationary problems Argentina faced could not be solved just by issuing a new unit of currency. Fiscal reform also was needed, and none was made. In any circumstances of inflationary monetary policy, monetary reform by itself is not enough. It must be coupled with a reduction in the fiscal deficit or an increase in government borrowing to produce a permanent change in the rate of inflation.

Monetary policy is tied to fiscal policy through the government budget constraint. Although money creation is not an important source of deficit financing in developed countries, it has been and still is a significant source of revenue for developing countries, where taxes are difficult to collect and borrowing is limited.

RECAP

1. The government budget constraint $(G = T + B + \Delta M)$ defines the relationship between fiscal and monetary policies.

2. The implications of fiscal policy for the growth of the money supply

b. how fiscal poli
implement a non

7. Parents, like gove
by seeing to it tha
they outline for t
tent. Analyze the
tency of these rul

a. If you don't ea
30 minutes early

b. If you get any
be allowed to wa
nights!

c. If you don't go
pay for your coll

d. If you marry t
inherit you!

8. Suppose an econ
cent rate of grow
prices over the la
think the public
plan to increase
over the next yea

a. the central bar
meeting its anno

b. the central bar
will do.

9. What are the im
business-cycle fl
business cycles a

COOPERATIVE

**Form pairs of stude
sistency of the follo**

1. Senator Phil Gr
for president of
that if elected h
unless he can ba

2. Alan Greenspar
Congress and st
he sees no need
soon.

TABLE 2
Recent Monetary Reforms

Country	Old Currency	New Currency	Date of Change	Nature of Change
Argentina	Peso	Peso Argentino	June 1983	1 peso argentino = 10,000 pesos
	Peso Argentino	Austral	June 1985	1 austral = 1,000 pesos argentino
	Austral	Peso Argentino	January 1992	1 peso argentino = 10,000 australes
Bolivia	Peso	Boliviano	January 1987	1 boliviano = 1,000,000 pesos
Brazil	Cruzeiro	Cruzado	February 1986	1 cruzado = 1,000 cruzeiros
	Cruzado	New cruzado	January 1989	1 new cruzado = 1,000 cruzados
	New cruzado	Cruzeiro	March 1990	1 cruzeiro = 1 new cruzado
Chile	Peso	Escudo	January 1969	1 escudo = 1,000 pesos
	Escudo	Peso	September 1975	1 peso = 1,000 escudos
Israel	Pound	Shekel	February 1980	1 shekel = 10 pounds
	Old shekel	New shekel	September 1985	1 new shekel = 1,000 old shekels
Mexico	Peso	New peso	January 1993	1 new peso = 1,000 pesos
Peru	Sol	Inti	February 1985	1 inti = 1,000 soles
	Inti	New sol	July 1991	1 new sol = 1,000,000 intis
Poland	Zloty	New zloty	January 1995	1 new zloty = 10,000 zlotys
Uruguay	Old peso	New peso	July 1975	1 new peso = 1,000 old pesos

can be seen by rewriting the government budget constraint this way:
$\Delta M = (G - T) - B$.

3. A monetary reform is a new monetary policy that includes the introduction of a new unit of currency.

4. A government can end an inflationary monetary policy only with a fiscal reform that lowers the fiscal deficit $(G - T)$ minus borrowing (B).

SUMMARY

▲▼ **Is there a tradeoff between inflation and the unemployment rate?**

1. The Phillips curve shows the relationship between inflation and the unemployment rate. §1

▲▼ **How does the tradeoff between inflation and the unemployment rate vary from the short to the long run?**

2. In the long run, there is no tradeoff between inflation and the unemployment rate. §1.b

3. The long-run Phil[...]
the natural rate of [...]

▲▼ **What is the rela[...]**
ed inflation and [...]

4. Unexpected inflati[...]
ment rate through [...]
tory fluctuations, [...]
2.a.1, 2.a.2, 2.a.3 [...]

▲▼ **How are macro[...]**
formed?

5. Adaptive expectat[...]
of past experience[...]
formed on the bas[...]
information. §2.b.[...]

▲▼ **What makes go[...]**

6. A policy is credib[...]
tent. §3.b

KEY TERMS

EXERCISES

1. What is the differe[...]
Phillips curve and [...]
Use an aggregate [...]
to explain why the[...]
them.

2. Give two reasons [...]
tradeoff between [...]
unemployment rat[...]

3. "Unexpected incre[...]
cause clockwise n[...]
curve diagram; un[...]
money supply cau[...]
ments in the Phill[...]
this statement usi[...]
answer.

16

Macroeconomic Viewpoints: New Keynesian, Monetarist, and New Classical

FUNDAMENTAL
QUESTIONS

1. What do Keynesian economists believe about macroeconomic policy?
2. What role do monetarists believe the government should play in the economy?
3. What is new classical economics?
4. How do theories of economics change over time?

E conomists do not all agree on macroeconomic policy. Sometimes disagreements are due to normative differences, or differences in personal values, regarding what the truly pressing needs are that should be addressed. Other disagreements are based on different views of how the economy operates and what determines the equilibrium level of real GDP.

It would be very easy to classify economists, to call them liberals or conservatives, for example. But an economist who believes the government should not intervene in social decisions (abortion, censorship) may favor an active role for government in economic decisions (trade protection, unemployment insurance, welfare benefits). Another economist may support an active role for government in regulating the social behavior of individuals, yet believe that government should allow free markets to operate without interference.

PREVIEW

In this chapter, an overview of important differences among schools of macroeconomic thought is presented. Most economists probably do not align themselves solely with any one theory of macroeconomics, choosing instead pieces of various schools of thought. But the three approaches we discuss in this chapter—Keynesian, monetarist, and new classical—have had enormous impact on macroeconomic thinking and policy.

I. KEYNESIAN ECONOMICS

Keynesian macroeconomics (named after the English economist John Maynard Keynes) dominated the economics profession from the 1940s through the 1960s. Some economists today refer to themselves as "new Keynesians." The common thread that pervades Keynesian economics is an emphasis on the inflexibility of wages and prices. This leads many Keynesians to recommend an activist government macroeconomic policy aimed at achieving a satisfactory rate of economic growth.

What do Keynesian economists believe about macroeconomic policy?

I.a. The Keynesian Model

In Chapter 11 we described the Keynesian model of macroeconomic equilibrium. That simple model assumes that prices are constant and that changes in aggregate expenditures determine equilibrium real GDP. In an aggregate demand and supply analysis, the simple Keynesian model looks like the graph in Figure 1. The aggregate supply curve is a horizontal line at a fixed level of prices, P_1. Changes in aggregate demand, such as from AD_1 to AD_2, cause changes in real GDP with no change in the price level.

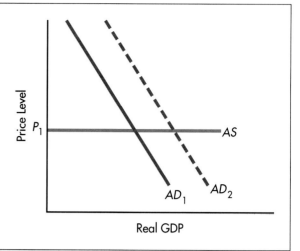

Figure 1
The Fixed-Price Keynesian Model
In the simple Keynesian model, prices are fixed at P_1 by the horizontal aggregate supply curve, so that changes in aggregate demand determine equilibrium real GDP.

Figure 1 reflects the traditional Keynesian emphasis on aggregate demand as a determinant of equilibrium real GDP. But no economist today would argue that the aggregate supply curve is always horizontal at every level of real GDP. More representative of Keynesian economics today is the aggregate supply curve shown in Figure 2. At low levels of real GDP, the curve is flat. In this region (the Keynesian region), increases in aggregate demand are associated with increases in output but not increases in prices. This flat region of the aggregate supply curve reflects the Keynesian belief that inflation is not a problem when unemployment is high. As the level of real GDP increases, and more and more industries reach their capacity level of output, the aggregate supply curve grows steeper.

The economic theories John Maynard Keynes proposed in the 1930s have given way to new theories. Today **Keynesian economics** focuses on the role the government plays in stabilizing the economy by managing aggregate demand. *New Keynesians* believe that wages and prices are not flexible in the short run. They use their analysis of business behavior to explain the

Keynesian economics:
a school of thought that emphasizes the role government plays in stabilizing the economy by managing aggregate demand

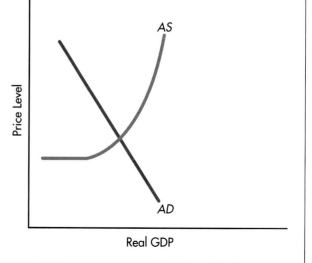

Figure 2
The Modern Keynesian Model
Modern Keynesians typically believe that the aggregate supply curve is horizontal only at relatively low levels of real GDP. As real GDP increases, more and more industries reach their capacity level of output and the aggregate supply curve becomes steeper.

Keynesian region on the aggregate supply curve of Figure 2. They believe that the economy is not always in equilibrium. For instance, if the demand for labor falls, we would expect the equilibrium price of labor (the wage) to fall and, because fewer people want to work at a lower wage, the number of people employed to fall. New Keynesians argue that wages do not tend to fall, because firms choose to lay off workers rather than decrease wages. Businesses retain high wages for their remaining employees in order to maintain morale and productivity. As a result, wages are quite rigid. This wage rigidity is reflected in price rigidity in goods markets according to new Keynesian economics.

I.b. The Policymakers' Role

Keynesians believe the government must take an active role in the economy to restore equilibrium. Traditional Keynesians identified the private sector as an important source of shifts in aggregate demand. For example, they argued that investment is susceptible to sudden changes. If business spending falls, the argument continued, monetary and fiscal policies should be used to stimulate spending and offset the drop in business spending. Government intervention is necessary to offset private-sector shifts in aggregate demand and avoid recession. And if private spending increases, creating inflationary pressure, then monetary and fiscal policies should restrain spending, again to offset private-sector shifts in aggregate demand.

New Keynesian macroeconomics does not focus on fluctuations in aggregate demand as the primary source of the problems facing policymakers. Keynesian economists realize that aggregate supply shocks can be substantial. But whatever the source of the instability—aggregate demand or aggregate supply—they emphasize active government policy to return the economy to equilibrium.

RECAP

1. Keynesian economists today reject the simple fixed-price model in favor of a model in which the aggregate supply curve is relatively flat at low levels of real GDP, sloping upward as real GDP approaches its potential level.

2. Keynesians believe that the tendency for the economy to experience disequilibrium in labor and goods markets forces the government to intervene in the economy.

2. MONETARIST ECONOMICS

The Keynesian view dominated macroeconomics in the 1940s, 1950s, and most of the 1960s. In the late 1960s and the 1970s, Keynesian economics faced a challenge from **monetarist economics**, a school of thought that emphasizes the role changes in the money supply play in determining equilibrium real GDP and prices. The leading monetarist, Milton Friedman, had been developing monetarist theory since the 1940s, but it took several decades before his ideas became popular. In part the shift was a product of the forcefulness of Friedman's arguments, but the relatively poor

monetarist economics: a school of thought that emphasizes the role changes in the money supply play in determining equilibrium real GDP and price level

macroeconomic performance of the United States in the 1970s probably contributed to a growing disenchantment with Keynesian economics, creating an environment ripe for new ideas. The Economic Insight "Milton Friedman" describes how Friedman's monetarist theories became popular.

2.a. The Monetarist Model

Monetarists believe that accelerating inflation is a product of efforts to increase real GDP through expansionary monetary policy.

Monetarists focus on the role of the money supply in determining the equilibrium level of real GDP and prices. In Chapter 14 we discussed monetary policy and equilibrium income. We showed that monetary policy is linked to changes in the equilibrium level of real GDP through changes in investment (and consumption). Keynesians traditionally assumed that monetary policy affects aggregate demand by changing the interest rate and, consequently, investment spending. Monetarists believe that changes in the money supply have broad effects on expenditures through both investment and consumption. An increase in the money supply pushes aggregate demand up by increasing both business and household spending, and raises the equilibrium level of real GDP. A decrease in the money supply does the opposite.

Monetarists believe that changes in monetary policy (or fiscal policy, for that matter) have only a short-term effect on real GDP. In the long run, they expect real GDP to be at a level consistent with the natural rate of unemployment. As a result, the long-run effect of a change in the money supply is fully reflected in a change in the price level. Attempts to exploit the short-run effects of expansionary monetary policy produce an inflationary spiral, in which the level of GDP increases temporarily, then falls back to the potential level while prices rise. This is the rightward shift of the Phillips curve we described in Chapter 15.

2.b. The Policymakers' Role

What role do monetarists believe the government should play in the economy?

Unlike Keynesian economists, monetarists do not believe that the economy is subject to a disequilibrium that must be offset by government action. Most monetarists believe that the economy tends toward equilibrium at the level of potential real GDP. Their faith in the free market (price) system leads them to favor minimal government intervention.

Monetarists often argue that government policy heightens the effects of the business cycle. This is especially true of monetary policy. To prove their point, monetarists link changes in the growth of the money supply to business-cycle fluctuations. Specifically, they suggest that periods of relatively fast money growth are followed by booms and inflation, and that periods of relatively slow money growth are followed by recessions.

Figure 3 shows the rate at which the money supply, consumer prices, and real GDP grew in the United States between 1960 and 1994. The inflation rate (consumer prices) seems to follow changes in the growth rate of the money supply with a lag of one or two years; GDP typically follows a change in the growth rate of the money supply by a year. The links between money growth and inflation, and money growth and GDP, are by no means perfect. Sometimes there seem to be closer relationships than at other times. This makes it difficult to predict the effect of a particular change in monetary policy on prices or real GDP. In addition, a number of other variables influence GDP.

Monetarists favor nonactivist government policy because they believe that the government's attempts to make the economy better off by aiming mone-

Figure 3
The Growth Rate of the Money Supply, Consumer Prices, and Real GDP, United States, 1960–1994
In general, the inflation rate follows the rate at which the money supply grows with a lag of one or two years. Growth in real GDP follows growth in the money supply with a lag of about one year. Data from *Economic Report of the President, 1995.* (Washington, D.C.: U.S. Government Printing Office, 1995).

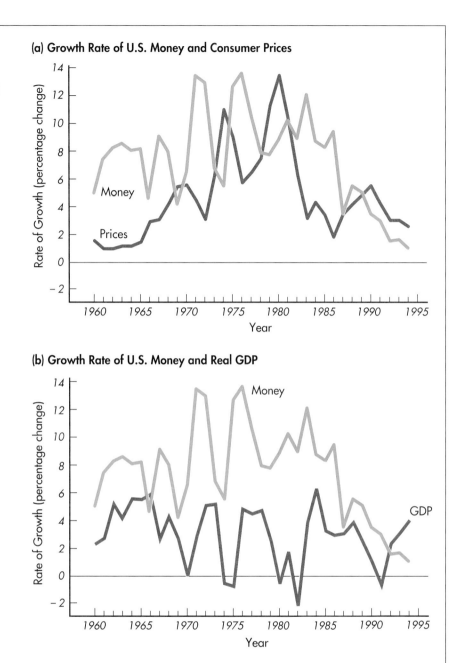

(a) Growth Rate of U.S. Money and Consumer Prices

(b) Growth Rate of U.S. Money and Real GDP

Economic policy operates with a long and variable lag.

tary and fiscal policies at low inflation and low unemployment often make things worse. Why? Because economic policy, which is very powerful, operates with a long and variable lag. First, policymakers have to recognize that a problem exists. This is the *recognition lag.* Then they must formulate an appropriate policy. This is the *reaction lag.* Then the effects of the policy must work through the economy. This is the *effect lag.*

When the Federal Reserve changes the rate of growth of the money supply, real GDP and inflation do not change immediately. In fact, studies show that as much as two years can pass between a change in policy and the effect of that change on real GDP. This means that when policymakers institute a

Milton Friedman

Milton Friedman is widely considered to be the father of monetarism. Born in 1912 in New York City, Friedman has spent most of his career at the University of Chicago. Early in his professional life, he recognized the importance of developing economics as an empirical science—that is, using data to test the applicability of economic theory.

In 1957, Friedman published *A Theory of the Consumption Function.* In the book he discussed the importance of *permanent income,* rather than current income, in understanding consumer spending. His analysis of consumption won widespread acclaim, an acclaim that would be a long time coming for his work relating monetary policy to real output and prices.

In the 1950s, Keynesian theory dominated economics. Most macroeconomists believed that the supply of money in the economy was of little importance. In 1963, with the publication of *A Monetary History of the United States, 1867–1960* (coauthored with Anna Schwartz of the National Bureau of Economic Research), Friedman focused attention on the monetarist argument. Still Keynesian economics dominated scholarly and policy debate.

In the late 1960s and early 1970s, the rate of inflation and unemployment simultaneously increased. This was a situation that Keynesian economics could not explain. The timing was right for a new theory of macroeconomic behavior, and monetarism, with Milton Friedman its most influential advocate, grew in popularity. The new stature of monetarism was clearly visible in 1979, when the Fed adopted a monetarist approach to targeting the money supply.

In 1976, Milton Friedman was awarded the Nobel Prize for economics. By this time he had become a public figure. He wrote a column for *Newsweek* from 1966 to 1984 and in 1980 developed a popular public television series, "Free to Choose," based on his book of the same title. Through the popular media, Friedman became the most effective and well-known supporter of free markets in the United States and much of the rest of the world. Many would argue that only Keynes has had as much influence on scholarly literature and public policy in economics as Milton Friedman.

change targeted at a particular level of real GDP or rate of inflation, the effect of the policy is not felt for a long time. And it is possible that the economy could be facing an entirely different set of problems in a year or two than those policymakers are addressing today. But today's policy will still have effects next year, and those effects may aggravate next year's problems.

Because of the long and variable lag in the effect of fiscal and monetary policies, monetarists argue that policymakers should set policy according to rules that do not change from month to month or even year to year. What kinds of rules? A fiscal policy rule might be to balance the budget annually; a monetary policy rule might be to require that the money supply grow at a fixed rate over time. These kinds of rules restrict policymakers from formulating discretionary policy. Monetarists believe that by reducing discretionary shifts in policy, economic growth is steadier than it is when government consciously sets out to achieve full employment and low inflation.

RECAP

1. Monetarists emphasize the role changes in the money supply play in determining equilibrium real GDP and the level of prices.

2. Monetarists do not believe that the economy is subject to disequilibrium in the labor and goods markets or that government should take an active role in the economy.

3. Because economic policy operates with a long and variable lag, attempts by government to stabilize the economy may, in fact, make matters worse.

4. Monetarists believe that formal rules should govern economic policy-making.

3. NEW CLASSICAL ECONOMICS

In the 1970s an alternative to Keynesian and monetarist economics was developed: new classical economics. But before we discuss the new classical theory, let's look at the old one.

classical economics:
a school of thought that assumes that real GDP is determined by aggregate supply, while the equilibrium price level is determined by aggregate demand

Classical economics is the theory that was popular before Keynes changed the face of economics in the 1930s. According to classical economics, real GDP is determined by aggregate supply, while the equilibrium price level is determined by aggregate demand. Figure 4, the classical aggregate demand and supply diagram, shows the classical economist's view of the world. The vertical aggregate supply curve means that the equilibrium level of output (income) is a product only of the determinants of aggregate supply: the price of resources, technology, and expectations (see Chapter 9).

If the aggregate supply curve is vertical, then changes in aggregate demand, such as from AD_1 to AD_2, change only the price level; they do not affect the equilibrium level of output. Classical economics assumes that prices and wages are perfectly flexible. This rules out contracts that fix prices or wages for periods of time. It also rules out the possibility that people are

Figure 4
The Classical Model
The vertical aggregate supply curve indicates that equilibrium national income is determined strictly by the determinants of aggregate supply.

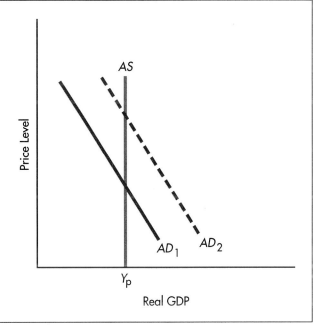

not aware of all prices and wages. They know when prices have gone up and ask for wage increases to compensate.

Keynesians and monetarists would argue that information about the economy, including prices and wages, is not perfect. When workers and businesses negotiate wages, they may not know what current prices are, but they certainly do not know what future prices will be. Furthermore, many labor contracts fix wages for long periods of time. This means that wages are not flexible, that they cannot adjust to new price levels.

3.a. The New Classical Model

new classical economics:
a school of thought that holds that changes in real GDP are a product of unexpected changes in the level of prices

What is new classical economics?

New classical economics was a response to the problems of meeting economic policy goals in the 1970s. New classical economists questioned some of the assumptions on which Keynesian economics was based. For instance, new classical economists believe wages are flexible, while both traditional Keynesian and new Keynesian economists assume wages can be fixed in the short run.

New classical economics does not assume that people know everything that is happening, as the old theory did. People make mistakes because their expectations of prices or some other critical variable are different from the future reality. New classical economists emphasize rational expectations. As defined in Chapter 15, *rational expectations* are based on all available relevant information. This was a new way of thinking about expectations. Earlier theories assumed that people formed adaptive expectations—that their expectations were based only on their past experience. With rational expectations, people learn not only from their past experience but also from any other information that helps them predict the future.

Suppose the chairman of the Federal Reserve Board announces a new monetary policy. Price-level expectations that are formed rationally take this announcement into consideration; those formed adaptively do not. It is much easier for policymakers to make unexpected changes in policy if expectations are formed adaptively rather than rationally.

Another element of new classical economics is the belief that markets are in equilibrium. Keynesian economics argues that disequilibrium in markets demands government intervention. For instance, Keynesian economists define a recession as a disequilibrium in the labor market—a surplus of labor—that requires expansionary government policy. New classical economists believe that because real wages are lower during a recession, people are more willing to substitute nonlabor activities (going back to school, early retirement, work at home, or leisure) for work. As the economy recovers and wages go up, people substitute away from nonlabor activities toward more working hours. The substitution of labor for leisure and leisure for labor, over time, suggests that much of observed unemployment is voluntary in the sense that those who are unemployed choose not to take a job at a wage below their reservation wage (see Chapter 15).

3.b. The Policymakers' Role

New classical economics emphasizes expectations. Its basic tenet is that changes in monetary policy can change the equilibrium level of real GDP only if those changes are *unexpected*. Fiscal policy can change equilibrium real GDP only if it *unexpectedly* changes the level of prices or one of the determinants of aggregate supply.

Figure 5 (which is the same as Figure 4 in Chapter 15) illustrates the new classical view of the effect of an unexpected increase in the money supply. Suppose initially the expected rate of inflation is 3 percent and the actual rate of inflation is also 3 percent. The economy is operating at point 1 in part (b), the Phillips curve diagram, with unemployment at 5 percent, which is assumed to be the natural rate of unemployment. At the natural rate of unemployment, the economy is producing the potential level of real GDP (Y_p), at price level P_1. If the central bank unexpectedly increases the money supply, pushing the inflation rate up from 3 percent to 6 percent, the economy moves from point 1 to point 2 along short-run Phillips curve I, which is based on 3 percent expected inflation. The unemployment rate is now 3 percent, which is less than the natural rate. In part (a), real GDP rises above potential income to Y_2.

Over time, people come to expect 6 percent inflation. They adjust to the higher inflation rate, and the economy moves back to the natural rate of

---

Figure 5
New Classical Economics
New classical economists believe that government-induced shifts in aggregate demand affect real GDP only if they are unexpected. In part (a), the economy initially is operating at point 1, with real GDP at Y_p, the potential level. An unexpected increase in aggregate demand shifts the economy to point 2, where both real GDP (Y_2) and prices (P_2) are higher. Over time, as sellers adjust to higher prices and costs of doing business, aggregate supply shifts from AS_1 to AS_2. This shift moves the economy to point 3. Here GDP is back at the potential level, and prices are even higher. In the long run, an increase in aggregate demand does not increase output. The long-run aggregate supply curve (*LRAS*) is a vertical line at the potential level of real GDP.

In part (b), if the expected rate of inflation is 3 percent and actual inflation is 3 percent, the economy is operating at point 1, at the natural rate of unemployment (U_n). If aggregate demand increases, there is an unexpected increase in inflation from 3 percent to 6 percent. This moves the economy from point 1 to point 2 along short-run Phillips curve I. Here the unemployment rate is 3 percent. As people learn to expect 6 percent inflation, they adjust to the higher rate and the economy moves back to the natural rate of unemployment, at point 3. If the increase in inflation is expected, then the economy moves from point 1 to point 3 directly with no temporary decrease in the unemployment rate.

(a) Aggregate Demand and Supply

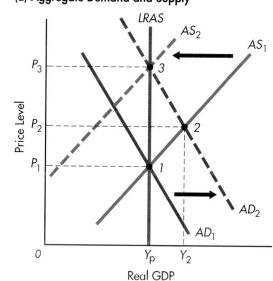

(b) Phillips Curve

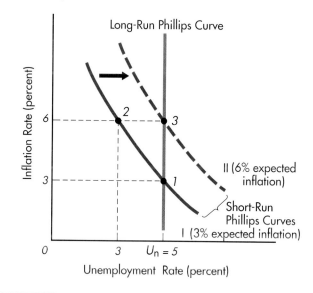

SUM

1.

TABLE I
Major Approaches to Macroeconomic Policy

Approach	Major Source of Problems	Proper Role for Government
New Keynesian	Disequilibrium in private labor and goods markets	Active management of monetary and fiscal policies to restore equilibrium
Monetarist	Government's discretionary policies increase and decrease aggregate demand.	Follow fixed rules for money growth and minimize fiscal policy shocks
New classical	Government policies have effect on real GDP only if unexpected, yet government tries to manipulate aggregate demand.	Follow predictable monetary and fiscal policies for long-run stability

New c
that w
and th
tions r
pected
can aj

should take an active role in stabilizing the economy by managing aggregate demand. §1.a

▲▼ **What role do monetarists believe the government should play in the economy?**

3. Monetarists do not believe that the economy is subject to serious disequilibrium, which means they favor minimal government intervention in the economy. §2.b

4. Monetarists believe that a government that takes an active role in the economy may do more harm than good because economic policy operates with a long and variable lag. §2.b

▲▼ **What is new classical economics?**

5. New classical economics holds that only unexpected changes in policy can influence real GDP, so government policy should target a low, stable rate of inflation. §3.b

▲▼ **How do theories of economics change over time?**

6. New economic theories are a response to changing economic conditions that point out the shortcomings of existing theories. §4

KEY TERMS

Keynesian economics §1.a
monetarist economics §2

classical economics §3
new classical economics §3.a

Hov
ics c

EXERCISES

1. What is the difference between traditional Keynesian and new Keynesian economics?

2. Why does monetary policy operate with a long and variable lag? Give an example to illustrate your explanation.

3. What is the difference between old classical and new classical economics?

4. Draw an aggregate demand and supply diagram for each theory of macroeconomics. Use the diagrams to explain how the government can influence equilibrium real GDP and prices.

5. What, if any, similarities are there among the theories of economics discussed in this chapter regarding the use of fiscal and monetary policies to stimulate real GDP?

6. If unexpected increases in the growth rate of the money supply can increase real GDP, why doesn't the Fed follow a policy of unexpectedly increasing the money supply to increase the growth of real GDP?

7. "The popular macroeconomic theories have evolved over time as economic conditions have changed to reveal shortcomings of existing theory." Evaluate this quote in terms of the emergence of the three theories discussed in this chapter.

For questions 8–15, tell which school of thought would be most likely associated with the following quotes:

8. "Changes in prices and wages are too slow to support the new classical assumption of persistent macroeconomic equilibrium."

9. "The best monetary policy is to keep the money supply growing at a slow and steady rate."

10. "Frictional unemployment is a result of workers voluntarily substituting leisure for labor when wages fall."

11. "A change in the money supply will affect GDP after a long and variable lag, so it is difficult to predict the effects of money on output."

12. "Government policymakers should use fiscal policy to adjust aggregate demand in response to aggregate supply shocks."

13. "The economy is subject to recurring disequilibrium in labor and goods markets, so government can serve a useful function of helping the economy adjust to equilibrium."

14. "Since the aggregate supply curve is horizontal, aggregate demand will determine the equilibrium level of real GDP."

15. "If everyone believed that the monetary authority was going to cut the inflation rate from 6 percent to 3 percent, such a reduction in inflation could be achieved without any significant increase in unemployment."

COOPERATIVE LEARNING EXERCISE

Divide the class into groups of four. Each group is to write one correct and four incorrect answers to the following multiple-choice questions. First each person should write one correct and one incorrect answer on his or her own. Then the group should meet and discuss each answer, making improvements where necessary in order to develop the five final responses to the question.

The groups will take turns calling on other groups to pick the correct answer from their alternatives.

1. Monetarist economists believe that:

2. Keynesian economists believe that:

3. New classical economists believe that:

A Harvard Economist Asks, What's Wrong with Keynes?

[N. Gregory] Mankiw, 36, is a leader of the large group of economists who identify themselves as New Keynesians. They are probably the dominant faction in the profession today. The youngest professor ever to be tenured by Harvard (at 29), Mankiw was also the first Massachusetts Institute of Technology PhD ever to be permanently seated by its far older crosstown rival (five others have been tenured since). . . .

As a graduate student at MIT in the early 1980s he imbibed deeply the Keynesian theory of market failure that had been refined there to the highest degree by the likes of Paul Samuelson, Robert Solow and Franco Modigliani.

This Keynesian theory was, in its fullest sense, a liberal doctrine: It taught that the traditional emphasis on the unfettered marketplace was misplaced, that economic management was virtually always needed, sometimes urgently. "Perhaps the invisible hand guides the economy in normal times," Mankiw wrote in an introduction to a survey of New Keynesian economics (with coauthor David Romer), "but the invisible hand is susceptible to paralysis."

During the 1970s and 1980s there was an outpouring of work on New Keynesian topics, all having to do with scouting out imperfections in the workings of the economy: in the financial markets, where booms and busts get their start; in product markets, where giant corporations contend; in labor markets, where issues of education and training come into play. Unmistakable hopes about the possibility of beneficial government intervention undergirt most of this work; it unabashedly concerned itself with economic engineering.

It unfolded in distinct opposition to the chilly winds of doubt about Keynesian doctrines that blew from Chicago throughout the 1970s. Because the Cambridge aspirations were always couched in terms of being a generous impulse, it was easy to cast the Keynesians as the Good Guys, eager to ameliorate society's ills, and the Chicagoans as the Bad Guys, given over to a faith in the correctness of outcomes produced by market processes bordering at times on the degree of conviction exhibited by rigorous practitioners of Christian Science.

A whole generation of economists made their reputations during the 1970s devising these New Keynesian doctrines of wages, prices and market failures and many of them are now fixtures in the senior councils of the Clinton administration. ...

In a recent paper, Mankiw and co-author Laurence Ball (of Johns Hopkins University) spell out what they see as the key difference between the New Keynesians and everybody else. It has to do with the concept of "sticky prices," meaning prices that do not instantly adjust to changing economic conditions. Sticky prices are at the heart of Keynesian analysis. . . . Those who believe that price stickiness plays a central role in short-term economic fluctuations are traditionalists, Mankiw and Ball say—a group in which they have included David Hume, John Maynard Keynes, Milton Friedman, [Franco] Modigliani, James Tobin. Those who don't see price stickiness being at the heart of the matter they consider heretics.

"A macroeconomist faces no greater decision then whether to be a traditionalist or a heretic," they say, almost as if they were lawyers reaffirming the principle of stare decisis, as the custom of departing as little as possible from precedent is known. But of course economics likes to think of itself as being far more like a science than like the law; it is the function of experiments to help decide when it is appropriate to stick to the conventional wisdom, and when it is necessary to depart.

Source: "A Harvard Economist Asks, What's Wrong with Keynes?" David Warsh, *Boston Globe*, June 5, 1994, p. 75 Copyright © 1994 Globe Newspaper Company. Reprinted courtesy of The *Boston Globe*.

Commentary

Macroeconomics has always been a lively field, filled with controversy over the proper approach to modeling the economy, the correct interpretation of experience, and the role government policy can and should play. Indeed, debate in macroeconomics is as old as the field itself. The views of John Maynard Keynes, the founder of macroeconomics, were challenged by his colleague at Cambridge University, Arthur Pigou. This debate focused on the importance of the "real balance effect," whereby a fall in the price level raises real money balances (or the purchasing power of the money supply), increases wealth, and thus increases consumption. Like most debates in macroeconomics, this was more than an ivory-tower exercise since the real balance effect provides a channel for the economy to bring itself out of a slump without government intervention.

The debate between the Keynesians and the monetarists dominated the macroeconomic discourse of the 1950s and 1960s. During this period, those who identified themselves as Keynesians gave primacy to the role of fiscal policy and to the issue of unemployment; these economists had great faith in the ability of the government to fine-tune the economy through the proper application of policy, thereby ensuring stability and growth. Keynesians of this vintage also believed that changes in the money supply had little effect on the economy. In contrast, monetarists were very concerned about inflation, which they believed to be a purely monetary phenomenon. These economists also doubted that active government intervention could stabilize the economy, for they believed that policy operated only with long and variable lags. Today, you will often hear people refer to Clinton's advisers as "Keynesians." Although none of these economists would necessarily subscribe to the philosophy of John Maynard Keynes, the term is popularly assigned to macroeconomists who emphasize that free markets don't always provide the best solutions, so there is a needed role for government activism to ensure that the economy provides for growth with low inflation.

New Keynesian economists (including Clinton's economic team) take issue with the monetarist and new classical approach to macroeconomics, which is characterized by well-functioning markets, the efficient use of information, and the consequent ineffectiveness of government policy. In criticizing the new classical approach, Keynesian economists consider why prices may be sticky and may not clear markets, why people may not be able to use information efficiently, and thus how government policy affects the economy. Many of the most influential economists who take this "New Keynesian" view are found (or were trained) at universities located in Cambridge, Massachusetts—MIT or Harvard.

Changes in presidential administrations are often associated with changes in economic philosophy. As this article makes clear, President Clinton's advisers were more sympathetic toward the activist government economic policy associated with Keynesian economics.

Although outside observers may view the debate within macroeconomics as evidence of confusion, a more accurate appraisal is that the debate is a healthy intellectual response to a world in which few things are certain and much is unknown—and perhaps unknowable. That there are differences between New Keynesians and other schools of thought masks the fact that there is a great deal of consensus about a number of issues in macroeconomics. This consensus is a product of lessons learned from past debates. In a similar fashion, the controversies of today will yield tomorrow's consensus, and our knowledge of the real workings of the economy will grow.

17

Macroeconomic Links Between Countries

FUNDAMENTAL QUESTIONS

1. How does a change in the exchange rate affect the prices of goods traded between countries?
2. Why don't similar goods sell for the same price all over the world?
3. What is the relationship between inflation and changes in the exchange rate?
4. How do we find the domestic currency return on a foreign bond?
5. What is the relationship between domestic and foreign interest rates and changes in the exchange rate?
6. Why don't similar financial assets yield the same return all over the world?
7. How does fiscal policy affect exchange rates?
8. How does monetary policy affect exchange rates?
9. What can countries gain by coordinating their macroeconomic policies?

n every chapter we have talked about the international aspects of the topics discussed. But we have yet to consider explicitly how individual economies are linked together in a global economy. At a basic level, the economic ties between nations are much like the economic ties between any two markets in different locations. For example, when Mazda introduced the Miata sports car to the United States, there were not enough cars to meet the initial demand. So car dealers began charging thousands of dollars more than the $13,000 sticker price. In some states the cars sold for almost double the sticker price; in others the surcharge was relatively small. In California the price reached approximately $25,000; in Michigan, about $15,000. What happened? Enterprising individuals were buying Miatas in Michigan and reselling them in California. This purchase and resale activity eventually raised the price of the car in Michigan and lowered the price in California until the price in California exceeded the Michigan price only by an amount equal to shipping and other transaction costs.

PREVIEW

The California and Michigan markets were linked by **arbitrage**, the act of buying in a market where the price is low and selling the same product in a market where the price is high to profit from the price differential. Arbitrageurs equalize prices in different markets. When they buy in the low-price market, prices there go up. And when they sell in the high-price market, prices there fall.

We are talking about California and Michigan and the market for sports cars. But we could be talking about Japan and Canada and the market for sulfur, or about Israel and Brazil and the market for diamonds, or about any number of different trading partners and goods. Arbitrage produces similar prices for similar goods and generates similar returns on similar financial assets wherever they are traded. Arbitrage links economies to each other.

In this chapter we discuss the ties among national economies. Our discussion applies to **open economies**, economies that trade goods, services, and financial assets with the rest of the world. Economies that are open will be sensitive to prices and interest rates in other countries and to changes in international economic conditions in general. A closed economy is isolated economically from the rest of the world; it does not trade with other nations. Although no economy is absolutely closed, there are different degrees of openness. Table 1 ranks eighteen countries in order of the value of international trade as a fraction of gross domestic product. We must be careful, however, in considering such measures as indications of how countries differ in terms of their openness. Nations with a large domestic market in relation to

arbitrage:
buying in a market where the price is low and selling the same product in a market where the price is high to profit from the price differential

open economy:
an economy that trades goods, services, and financial assets with the rest of the world

TABLE I
A Sample of Countries Ranked in Order of Importance of International Trade

Country	(Exports + Imports) /GDP	Country	(Exports + Imports) /GDP
Malaysia	1.56	Korea	.61
Jamaica	.99	Sweden	.54
Israel	.81	Paraguay	.52
Austria	.81	Kenya	.51
Thailand	.80	United Kingdom	.48
Egypt	.74	Australia	.35
Germany	.70	Pakistan	.35
Sri Lanka	.67	United States	.21
Philippines	.62	Japan	.19

the value of international trade, like the United States, are generally open to international trade but the size of the domestic economy results in international trade being a relatively small share of GDP. Nations where the value of international trade is large in relation to the size of the domestic market, like Malaysia and Jamaica, will have larger trade shares, as reported in the table.

I. PRICES AND EXCHANGE RATES

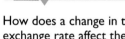

How does a change in the exchange rate affect the prices of goods traded between countries?

An exchange rate, as you learned in Chapters 3 and 7, is the price of one money in terms of another. The exchange rate doesn't enter into the purchase and sale of Miatas in Michigan and California because each state uses the U.S. dollar. But for goods and services traded across national borders, the exchange rate is an important part of the total price. In later chapters we discuss some of the ways nations restrict free trade in their currencies, the ways they "manage" exchange rates. Here we assume that currencies are traded freely for each other and that foreign exchange markets respond to supply and demand without government intervention.

Let's look at an example. A U.S. wine importer purchases 1,000,000 French francs (FF1,000,000) worth of wine from France. The importer demands francs in order to pay the French wine seller. Suppose the initial equilibrium exchange rate is $.15 = FF1. At this rate, the U.S. importer needs 1,000,000 francs at $.15 apiece, or $150,000:

$$\$.15 \times 1,000,000 = \$150,000$$

I.a. Appreciation and Depreciation

When the exchange rate between two currencies changes, we say that one currency *depreciates* while the other *appreciates*. Suppose the exchange rate goes from $.15 = FF1 to $.20 = FF1. The French franc is now worth $.20 instead of $.15. The dollar has *depreciated* in value in relation to the franc; dollars are worth less in terms of francs. At the new equilibrium exchange rate, the U.S. importer needs $200,000 ($.20 × 1,000,000) to buy FF1,000,000 worth of wine.

Instead of saying that the dollar has depreciated against the franc, we can say that the franc has *appreciated* against the dollar. If the dollar is depreciating against the franc, the franc must be appreciating against the dollar. Whichever way we describe the change in the exchange rate, the result is that francs are now worth more in terms of dollars. The price of a franc has gone from $.15 to $.20.

As exchange rates change, the prices of goods and services traded in international markets also change. Suppose the dollar appreciates against the franc. This means that a franc costs fewer dollars; it also means that French goods cost U.S. buyers less. If the exchange rate falls to $.10 = FF1, then FF1,000,000 costs $100,000 ($.10 × 1,000,000). The French wine has become less expensive to the U.S. importer.

- When the domestic (home) currency *depreciates*, foreign goods become *more expensive* to domestic buyers.

- When the domestic currency *appreciates*, foreign goods become *less expensive* to domestic buyers.

Let's look at the problem from the French side. When the dollar price of the franc rises, the franc price of the dollar falls; and when the dollar price of the franc falls, the franc price of the dollar rises. If the dollar price of the franc ($/FF) is originally $.15, the franc price of the dollar (FF/$) is the reciprocal (1/.15), or FF6.67. If the dollar depreciates against the franc to $.20, then the franc appreciates against the dollar to 1/.20, or FF5. As the franc appreciates, U.S. goods become less expensive to French buyers. If the dollar appreciates against the franc to $.10, then the franc depreciates against the dollar to 1/.10, or FF10. As the franc depreciates, U.S. goods become more expensive to French buyers.

- When the domestic currency *depreciates*, domestic goods become *less expensive* to foreign buyers.

- When the domestic currency *appreciates*, domestic goods become *more expensive* to foreign buyers.

The exchange rate is just one determinant of the demand for goods and services. Income, tastes, the prices of substitutes and complements, expectations, and the exchange rate all determine the demand for U.S. wheat, for example. As the dollar depreciates in relation to other currencies, the demand for U.S. wheat increases (along with foreign demand for all other U.S. goods) even if all the other determinants do not change. Conversely, as the dollar appreciates, the demand for U.S. wheat falls (along with foreign demand for all other U.S. goods) even if all the other determinants do not change.

1.b. Purchasing Power Parity

Within a country, where prices are quoted in terms of a single currency, all we need to know is the price in the domestic currency of an item in two different locations to determine where our money buys more. If Joe's bookstore charges $20 for a book and Pete's bookstore charges $40 for the same book, the purchasing power of our money is twice as great at Joe's as it is at Pete's.

International comparisons of prices must be made using exchange rates because different countries use different monies. Once we cross national borders, prices are quoted in different currencies. Suppose Joe's bookstore in New York City charges $20 for a book and Pierre's bookstore in Paris charges FF40. To compare the prices, we must know the exchange rate between dollars and francs.

If we find that goods sell for the same price in different markets, our money has the same purchasing power in those markets, which means that we have **purchasing power parity (PPP)**. PPP reflects a relationship among the domestic price level, the exchange rate, and the foreign price level:

$$P = EP^F$$

where

$$P = \text{the domestic price}$$

$$E = \text{the exchange rate (units of domestic currency per unit of foreign currency)}$$

$$P^F = \text{the foreign price}$$

If the dollar-franc exchange rate is .50 ($.50 = FF1), then a book priced at FF40 in Pierre's store in Paris costs the same as a book priced at $20 in Joe's store in New York:

$$P = EP^F$$
$$= \$.50 \times 40$$
$$= \$20$$

To determine the domestic currency value of a foreign currency price, multiply the exchange rate by the foreign price.

The domestic price (we are assuming that the U.S. dollar is the domestic currency) equals the exchange rate times the foreign price. Because the dollar price of the book in Paris is $20 and the price in the United States is $20, PPP holds. The purchasing power (value) of the dollar is the same in both places.

Realistically, similar goods don't always sell for the same price everywhere. Actually they don't even sell for the same price within a country. If the same textbook is priced differently at different bookstores, it is unrealistic to expect the price of the book to be identical worldwide. There are several reasons why PPP does not hold. The most important are that goods are not identical, that information is costly, that shipping costs affect prices, and that tariffs and legal restrictions on trade affect prices. If these factors did not exist, we would expect that anytime a price was lower in one market than in another, arbitrageurs would buy in the low-price market (pushing prices up) and simultaneously sell in the high-price market (pushing prices down). This arbitrage activity would ensure that PPP holds.

Why don't similar goods sell for the same price all over the world?

Goods are not identical   We would expect PPP to hold for identical goods, but few goods sold around the world are exactly the same in every country. Even goods that are identical and transportable may sell for much different prices in different countries. For instance, a recent survey indicated that a Big Mac hamburger in Paris costs $2.97; a Big Mac in Hong Kong is just $.98. Why? This is where the costs of information, shipping costs, and tariffs and legal restrictions come into play.

Information is costly People do not know everything about everything. To learn about the quality or prices of a product offered by different stores takes time and effort. It is in this sense that information is costly. Goods may thus sell for different prices in different countries in part because of information costs. When we pay $2.97 for a Big Mac in Paris, we may not know that a Big Mac is selling for $.98 in Hong Kong. Furthermore, the price in Hong Kong may be irrelevant to our decision to buy a Big Mac in Paris. The Big Mac is such a small part of our total budget that it would not be worth our time to find out what the item costs in other countries. However, for automobiles and other expensive items, international price differences may determine where goods are bought. When prices are high, the value of information about differences in international prices may be worth the cost of obtaining that information.

Shipping costs alter prices It is costly to ship goods from one country to another. Shipping costs are reflected in price differentials across countries. If prices differ by no more than the costs of shipping, then it is not profitable to buy in the cheap country and sell in the more expensive country. The price difference simply reflects the cost of moving the goods.

Tariffs and legal restrictions on trade affect prices No country permits the free movement of all goods and services across its borders. Nations erect barriers to international trade for different reasons. These barriers may take the form of a *tariff*, a tax on goods that are traded internationally. Prices may differ across countries because of different tariff structures. Other barriers to trade place limits on the quantity of a good that can be bought or sold, or simply prohibit the import of some goods. All of these restrictions on the free movement of goods and services contribute to different prices for the same good in different countries. Big Macs cost more in countries with high tariffs on beef imports than they do in countries that allow beef to move freely into them.

Arbitrage, the act of profiting from international price differences, brings prices closer together. If there were no information costs, shipping costs, or tariffs, PPP would hold for similar goods.

Even though PPP does not hold for most goods, it is a useful concept. It points out an important link between national economies. Exchange rates tend to change as prices change in the direction suggested by PPP. In the next section we describe the impact of purchasing power parity on the relationship between inflation and exchange rates.

1.c. Inflation and Exchange Rate Changes

What is the relationship between inflation and changes in the exchange rate?

The idea of purchasing power parity reflects a tendency for exchange rates to adjust to offset price-level differences in different currencies. Goods tend to sell for equal prices all over the world. Price differences are smaller the more similar the goods being sold in different countries, the easier it is to gather information about prices, the lower the shipping costs, and the less restrictive the government barriers to trade. Even if PPP does not hold exactly, we expect the exchange rate to change in a manner roughly consistent with PPP. Because we measure price-level changes by inflation rates, we can relate changes in exchange rates to inflation differentials between countries.

To see how inflation differences are reflected in exchange rates, let's go back to the book selling for $20 in New York and FF40 in Paris. When the exchange rate is $.50 = FF1, FF40 equals $20, so PPP holds. Now suppose that there is 100 percent inflation in France and zero inflation in the United States. If all prices double in France, the book sells for FF80. With no inflation in the United States, the book still sells for $20 in the United States.

How much must the exchange rate change to maintain PPP? We can find out by rewriting the PPP equation this way:

$$E = \frac{P}{P^F}$$

The exchange rate consistent with PPP equals the ratio of the domestic price to the foreign price. If the book sells for $20 in New York and FF80 in Paris, then the PPP exchange rate is .25 (20/80). Notice what's happened. Because the price level in France doubled while the price level in the United States was constant, the dollar price of the franc was halved. Generally the dollar appreciates against currencies that have a higher inflation rate than the dollar and depreciates against currencies that have a lower inflation rate due to PPP pressures.

Generally the dollar appreciates against currencies that have a higher inflation rate than the dollar and depreciates against currencies with a lower inflation rate.

RECAP

1. When the exchange rate between two currencies changes, one currency depreciates while the other appreciates.

2. Purchasing power parity means that money has the same purchasing power in different markets.

3. Similar goods do not sell for the same price all over the world because goods are not identical, information is costly, shipping costs affect prices, and tariffs and legal restrictions on international trade affect prices.

4. The exchange rate tends to change to offset differences in the rate of inflation between two countries.

2. INTEREST RATES AND EXCHANGE RATES

Exchange rates are used to compare international prices of goods and services. They are also used to compare the return on foreign currency-denominated stocks and bonds to the return on domestic assets. For example, suppose you have a choice of buying a U.S. or a U.K. bond. The U.S. bond is denominated in dollars and pays 15 percent interest; the U.K. bond is denominated in British pounds and pays 10 percent interest. Because you are a U.S. resident and ultimately want dollars for household spending, you must compare the dollar return from holding each bond.

2.a. The Domestic Currency Return from Foreign Bonds

The U.S. bond is denominated in dollars, so the 15 percent interest is a dollar return. The U.K. bond, on the other hand, promises to pay 10 percent in terms of British pounds. If you buy the U.K. bond, you exchange dollars for

When deciding whether to buy a bond denominated in the domestic currency or in a foreign currency, the buyer must take expected changes in the exchange rate into account.

pounds at the time the bond is purchased. When the bond matures, you exchange the principal and interest (the proceeds), trading pounds for dollars. If the exchange rate remains the same, the return on the U.K. bond is 10 percent. But if the exchange rate changes between the time you buy the bond and the time it matures, your return in dollars may be more or less than 10 percent.

Figure 1 shows what happens when a U.S. resident buys a one-year U.K. bond. Suppose the exchange rate is $2 = £1 when the bond is purchased, and the bond sells for £1. The U.S. resident needs $2 to buy the bond. A year later the bond matures. The bondholder receives the principal of £1 plus 10 percent interest (£.10). Now the U.S. resident wants to convert the pounds into dollars. If the exchange rate has gone up from $2 = £1 to $2.10 = £1, the £1.10 proceeds from the bond are converted into dollars at the rate of 2.10 dollars per pound. The *dollar value* of the proceeds is $2.31 (the exchange rate [2.10] multiplied by the pound proceeds [£1.10]). The *dollar return* from the U.K. bond is the percentage difference between the dollar proceeds received after one year, and the initial dollar amount invested, approximately 15 percent:

$$\text{Dollar return} = \frac{\$2.31 - \$2}{\$2}$$

$$= \frac{\$.31}{\$2}$$

$$= .15$$

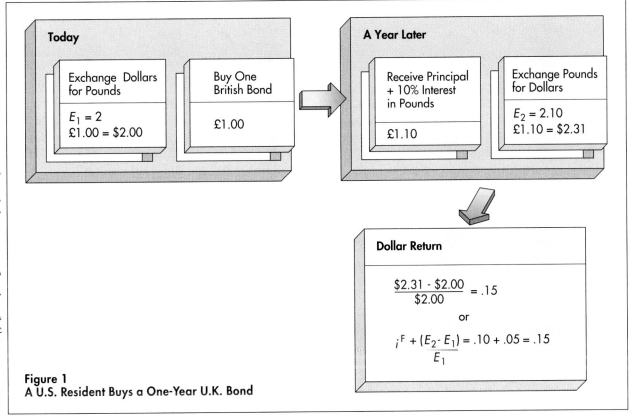

Figure 1
A U.S. Resident Buys a One-Year U.K. Bond

We can also determine the dollar return from the U.K. bond by adding the U.K. interest rate to the percentage change in the exchange rate. The percentage change in the exchange rate is 5 percent:

$$\text{Percentage change in exchange rate} = \frac{\$2.10 - \$2}{\$2}$$

$$= \frac{\$.10}{\$2}$$

$$= .05$$

The dollar return from the U.K. bond equals the 10 percent interest paid in British pounds plus the 5 percent change in the exchange rate, or 15 percent.

In our example, the pound appreciates against the dollar. When the pound increases in value, foreign residents holding pound-denominated bonds earn a higher return on those bonds than the pound interest rate. If the pound depreciates against the dollar, so that the pounds received at maturity are worth less than the pounds originally purchased, then the dollar return from the U.K. bond is lower than the interest rate on the bond. If the pound depreciates 5 percent, the dollar return is just 5 percent (the interest rate [10 percent] *minus* the exchange rate change [5 percent]).

How do we find the domestic currency return on a foreign bond?

We calculate the domestic currency return from a foreign bond by adding the foreign interest rate (i^F) plus the percentage change in the exchange rate ($[E_2 - E_1]/E_1$), where E_2 is the dollar price of a unit of foreign currency next period when the bond matures and E_1 is the exchange rate in the current period when the bond is purchased:

$$\text{Domestic currency return} = \text{foreign interest rate}$$
$$+ \text{percentage change in exchange rate}$$

$$= i^F + \frac{E_2 - E_1}{E_1}$$

2.b. Interest Rate Parity

Because U.S. residents can hold U.S. bonds, U.K. bonds, or the bonds or other securities of any country they choose, they compare the returns from the different alternatives when deciding what assets to buy. Foreign investors do the same thing. One product of the process is a close relationship among international interest rates. Specifically, the return, or interest rate, tends to be the same on similar bonds when returns are measured in terms of the domestic currency. This is called **interest rate parity (IRP)**.

interest rate parity (IRP): the condition under which similar financial assets have the same interest rate when measured in the same currency

Interest rate parity is the financial-asset version of purchasing power parity: Similar financial assets have the same percentage return when that return is computed in terms of one currency. Interest rate parity defines a relationship among the domestic interest rate, the foreign interest rate, and the expected change in the exchange rate:

$$\text{Domestic interest rate} = \text{foreign interest rate}$$
$$+ \text{expected change in exchange rate}$$

What is the relationship between domestic and foreign interest rates and changes in the exchange rate?

In our example, the U.S. bond pays 15 percent interest; the U.K. bond offers 10 percent interest in pounds. If the pound is expected to appreciate 5 percent, the U.K. bond offers U.S. residents an expected dollar return of 15 percent. Interest rate parity holds in this case. The domestic interest rate is 15 percent, which equals the foreign interest rate (10 percent) plus the expected change in the exchange rate (5 percent).

Interest rate parity is the product of arbitrage in financial markets. If U.S. bonds and U.K. bonds are similar in every respect except the currency used to pay the principal and interest, then they should yield similar returns to bondholders. If U.S. investors can earn a higher return from buying U.K. bonds, they are going to buy more U.K. bonds and fewer U.S. bonds. This tends to raise the price of U.K. bonds, pushing U.K. interest rates down. At the same time, the price of U.S. bonds drops, raising U.S. interest rates. The initial higher return on U.K. bonds and resulting greater demand for U.K. bonds increases the demand for pounds, increasing the value of the pound versus the dollar today. As the pound appreciates today, if investors expect the same future exchange rate as they did before the current appreciation, the expected appreciation over the future falls. The change in the exchange rate and interest rates equalizes the expected dollar return from holding a U.S. bond or a U.K. bond. U.K. bonds originally offered a higher return than U.S. bonds, but the increase in demand for U.K. bonds relative to U.S. bonds lowers U.K. interest rates and the expected appreciation of the pound so that the bond returns are equalized.

2.c. Deviations from Interest Rate Parity

Interest rate parity does not hold for all financial assets. Like PPP, which applies only to similar goods, IRP applies only to similar assets. We do not expect the interest rate on a 90-day U.S. Treasury bill to equal the dollar return on a one-year U.K. Treasury bill because the maturity dates are different, 90 days versus a year. Financial assets with different terms to maturity typically pay different interest rates. We also do not expect different kinds of assets to offer the same return. A 90-day Japanese yen bank deposit in a Tokyo bank should not offer the same dollar return as a 90-day U.S. Treasury bill. The bank deposit and the Treasury bill are different assets.

Even with what seem to be similar assets, we can find deviations from interest rate parity. For instance, a 90-day peso certificate of deposit in a Mexico City bank does not offer a U.S. resident the same dollar return as a 90-day certificate of deposit denominated in U.S. dollars in a New York City bank. The reasons for the difference include government controls, political risk, and taxes.

Government controls Certain government controls erect barriers to the free flow of money between countries. These controls can take the form of quotas on the amount of foreign exchange that can be bought or sold, high reserve requirements on foreign-owned bank deposits, or other controls designed to change the pattern in which financial assets flow between countries. These controls are called **capital controls**, where *capital* means "financial capital," not a resource used in producing other goods and services (the usual macroeconomic sense of the word).

Political risk Political risk is the risk associated with holding a financial asset issued in a foreign country. This risk arises from uncertainty. In 1982 the Mexican government imposed capital controls that restricted the flow of foreign exchange out of Mexico. U.S. residents who owned bank deposits or other financial assets in Mexico found that the controls substantially reduced the return on their assets. If U.S. residents believe that a foreign government

Why don't similar financial assets yield the same return all over the world?

capital controls:
quotas or other forms of government-imposed controls on the flow of money between countries

may impose restrictions that reduce the return on assets issued in that country, those foreign-issued assets must offer a higher return than that offered on similar domestic assets. That extra return is called a **risk premium**. A risk premium offsets the higher risk associated with buying a foreign asset.

If political risk exists, IRP does not hold because the return on the foreign asset exceeds the return on the domestic asset by the amount of the risk premium.

Taxes   Taxes also can account for deviations from IRP. Tax rates affect after-tax returns on investments. Different countries have different tax rates, so the same financial asset can yield a different before-tax return for residents of different countries. Because nominal interest rates (the rates observed in the market) are quoted without regard to taxes, some apparent deviations from IRP are only before-tax deviations. After taxes are taken into account, similar assets should yield a similar return in the absence of capital controls and political risk.

If there are no government controls, political risk, or different tax rates, IRP should hold exactly for financial assets that differ only in the currency of denomination. This is evident from the many studies of interest rate parity performed by economists.

RECAP

1. The domestic currency return from a foreign bond equals the foreign interest rate plus the percentage change in the exchange rate.

2. Interest rate parity exists when similar financial assets have the same interest rate when measured in the same currency, or when the domestic interest rate equals the foreign interest rate plus the expected change in the exchange rate.

3. Deviations from interest rate parity are a product of government controls, political risk, and different tax structures.

3. POLICY EFFECTS

The government budget constraint described in Chapter 15 links fiscal and monetary policies. It states that government spending is financed by taxes, borrowing, and changes in the money supply. This means that when government spending exceeds tax revenues, the budget deficit must be financed by borrowing or issuing money. Both methods of financing can affect exchange rates and interest rates. Here we look first at borrowing; then we turn to monetary policy and changes in the money supply.

3.a. Government Borrowing

An increase in government borrowing increases the supply of government bonds. As the supply of bonds increases with a given demand, bond prices fall and interest rates go up. The higher interest rate will induce people to willingly hold the greater bond supply. In Chapter 14 we defined the current interest rate (yield) this way:

$$\text{Current interest rate} = \frac{\text{annual interest payment}}{\text{bond price}}$$

Because the annual interest payment is fixed, only the bond price changes. As the price of a bond increases, the interest rate falls; and as the price falls, the interest rate rises.

Let's continue with our bond example to illustrate the probable effect of financing an increased budget deficit by borrowing. Initially the U.S. bond interest rate is 15 percent, the U.K. bond interest rate is 10 percent, and the expected change in the exchange rate is 5 percent. Remember that when interest rate parity holds, the domestic interest rate equals the foreign interest rate plus the expected change in the exchange rate.

$$i_\$ = i_\pounds + \frac{E_2 - E_1}{E_1}$$

In our example, interest rate parity holds:

$$i_\$ = .10 + \frac{\$2.10 - \$2}{\$2}$$

$$= .10 + \frac{\$.10}{\$2}$$

$$= .10 + .05 = .15$$

How does fiscal policy affect exchange rates?

Suppose that to finance its higher deficit, the government increases the supply of bonds, pushing the interest rate on U.S. bonds up to 20 percent. The higher rate of interest attracts foreign investors, who demand dollars to purchase U.S. bonds. As the demand for dollars increases, the dollar appreciates. Let's say the dollar appreciates today to $1.91 per pound. If the future expected exchange rate is still $2.10 = £1, the expected change in the exchange rate is approximately 10 percent:

$$\frac{E_2 - E_1}{E_1} = \frac{\$2.10 - \$1.91}{\$1.91}$$

$$= \frac{\$.19}{\$1.91} = .10$$

Notice that the interest-rate-parity equation holds true:

$$i_\$ = i_\pounds + \frac{E_2 - E_1}{E_1}$$

$$= .10 + .10 = .20$$

Fiscal policy affects the exchange rate by changing interest rates, which changes the foreign demand for bonds.

Borrowing to finance the higher budget deficit raises the interest rate in the United States and causes the dollar to appreciate against foreign currencies.

The appreciation of the dollar also affects the international trade of goods and services. As the dollar appreciates on the foreign exchange market, U.S. goods become more expensive to foreign buyers and foreign goods become less expensive to U.S. buyers. What happens? U.S. exports decrease and U.S. imports increase. The foreign demand for U.S. bonds created by borrowing to finance the higher budget deficit pushes U.S. net exports down (Figure 2). A change in policy that lowers the budget deficit (reducing government borrowing) has the opposite effect.

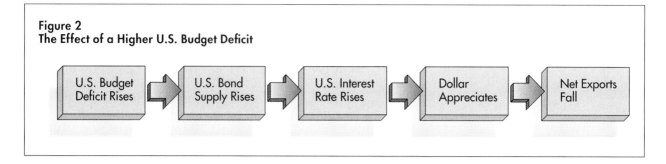

Figure 2
The Effect of a Higher U.S. Budget Deficit

U.S. Budget Deficit Rises → U.S. Bond Supply Rises → U.S. Interest Rate Rises → Dollar Appreciates → Net Exports Fall

3.b. Monetary Policy

In Chapter 8 we said that the actual interest rate observed in the economy, the *nominal interest rate*, has two components: the real interest rate and the rate of inflation. Of course, at the time a bond is purchased, no one knows what the actual rate of inflation is going to be over the life of the bond. This means the expected rate of inflation, not the actual rate of inflation, is reflected in the nominal interest rate:

Nominal interest rate = real interest rate + expected inflation

The greater the rate at which money grows, the greater the expected rate of inflation and the higher the nominal interest rate. So the process of financing government budget deficits by creating money pushes nominal interest rates up.

In the last section we saw that government borrowing to finance budget deficits also raises the nominal interest rate, but there the increase was a product of an increase in the real interest rate. The government must offer higher real interest rates on government bonds to induce domestic and foreign residents to buy the greater quantity of bonds supplied. In the case of monetary policy, higher nominal interest rates are a product of higher expected inflation; the real interest rate does not change.

How does monetary policy affect exchange rates?

As the nominal interest rate on domestic bonds increases, the exchange rate must change in order to maintain IRP. Let's go back to our example, in which the U.S. interest rate is 15 percent, the U.K. interest rate is 10 percent, the expected future exchange rate is $2.10 = £1, and the current exchange rate is $2 = £1. Interest rate parity holds because the dollar interest rate equals the foreign interest rate plus the expected change in the exchange rate:

$$i_\$ = i_£ + \frac{E_2 - E_1}{E_1}$$

$$= .10 + \frac{\$2.10 - \$2}{\$2} = .10 + \frac{\$.10}{\$2}$$

$$= .10 + .05 = .15$$

If one country has a higher rate of money growth than another country, the currency of the country with the higher rate of money growth tends to depreciate against the currency of the country with the lower rate of money growth.

The dollar is expected to depreciate against the pound (or the pound is expected to appreciate against the dollar) by 5 percent, so the U.K. interest rate (10 percent) plus the higher value of U.K. currency (5 percent) equals the U.S. interest rate (15 percent).

Suppose the United States adopts an inflationary monetary policy, pushing the U.S. interest rate up to 20 percent. If the U.K. interest rate is still 10 percent, the dollar must depreciate by 10 percent for the expected return on

International trade links the economies of nations together. Even countries as different as the United States and India will be increasingly interdependent economically as trade between the two nations grows. The photo shows large rolls of textiles from India being off loaded from a barge in Houston, Texas. These textiles will compete with U.S.-produced textiles so that the price of textiles in India has an effect on the prices charged by textile firms in the United States. Trade between nations also links business cycles. For example, a recession in the United States that reduces U.S. imports from India will reduce the real GDP of India.

holding a U.K. bond to equal the return on holding a U.S. bond. The dollar depreciates because the inflation rate in the United States is expected to be higher than that in the United Kingdom.

When a nation is expected to have higher inflation because of some new policy, people want to hold less of that nation's currency. If a new monetary policy raises the expected inflation rate in the United States, the nominal interest rate goes up. The higher expected inflation also has people selling dollars on the foreign exchange market, causing the dollar to depreciate. So higher nominal U.S. interest rates caused by greater expected U.S. inflation are associated with dollar depreciation. Continuing with our example, the U.S. interest rate is now 20 percent, the U.K. interest rate is 10 percent, and the exchange rate is $2.10 = £1. With the higher expected inflation and higher interest rate in the United States, the dollar is expected to depreciate to 2.31 dollars per pound in one year. Interest rate parity still holds:

$$i_\$ = i_£ + \frac{E_2 - E_1}{E_1}$$

$$= .10 + \frac{\$2.31 - \$2.10}{\$2.10} = .10 + \frac{\$.21}{\$2.10}$$

$$= .10 + .10 = .20$$

The depreciation of the dollar has no effect on international trade if the depreciation simply offsets rising prices in the United States. Here purchasing power parity holds: the relative prices of goods in each country stay the same. Even though prices in the United States are rising faster, the depreciation of the dollar lowers the cost of dollars to foreigners, compensating for the higher dollar price of goods. U.S. goods continue to sell for the same foreign currency price they did before the change in monetary policy. So there is no incentive to alter the quantities of goods bought and sold internationally.

If the growth of the money supply slows, other things being equal, the expected inflation rate falls. As a result, the nominal interest rate falls and the domestic currency appreciates. Assuming that appreciation maintains purchasing power parity, the monetary policy has no effect on international trade and investment.

3.c. Linking IRP and PPP

As you have just seen, changes in government policy can affect both the exchange rate and the price level. Both PPP and IRP are relevant to the analysis. In fact now we can link the two together to demonstrate the relationship among inflation differentials between countries, interest rate differentials between countries, and expected changes in exchange rates.

IRP holds when the domestic interest rate equals the foreign interest rate plus the expected change in the exchange rate:

$$i = i_F + \frac{E_2 - E_1}{E_1}$$

We can rewrite the equation with the interest differential (the difference between the domestic and foreign interest rates) equal to the expected change in the exchange rate:

$$\frac{E_2 - E_1}{E_1} = i - i_F$$

PPP holds when the change in the exchange rate equals the inflation differential between countries. Inflation is the percentage change in the price level:

$$\text{Inflation} = \frac{P_2 - P_1}{P_1}$$

So PPP holds when

$$\frac{E_2 - E_1}{E_1} = \frac{P_2 - P_1}{P_1} - \frac{P_2^F - P_1^F}{P_1^F}$$

Let's use the data from our bond example to illustrate the link between IRP and PPP. Initially the U.S. interest rate is 15 percent and the U.K. interest rate is 10 percent. For IRP to hold, the dollar is expected to depreciate against the pound by 5 percent:

$$i_\$ - i_£ = \frac{E_2 - E_1}{E_1}$$

$$.15 - .10 = .05$$

If IRP and PPP hold, the expected change in the exchange rate equals the interest differential between domestic and foreign bonds, which equals the expected inflation differential between the domestic and foreign countries.

For PPP to hold, the expected change in the exchange rate must match the expected inflation differential between the United States and the United Kingdom (assuming the expected U.S. inflation rate is 12 percent and the expected U.K. inflation rate is 7 percent):

$$\frac{E_2 - E_1}{E_1} = \frac{P_2^\$ - P_1^\$}{P_1^\$} - \frac{P_2^£ - P_1^£}{P_1^£}$$

$$.05 = .12 - .07$$

By combining the IRP and PPP conditions, we can see that a change in government policy is reflected in a new interest differential, a new expected change in the exchange rate, and a new expected inflation differential.

RECAP

1. An increase in U.S. government spending financed by borrowing tends to raise the real interest rate in the United States and cause the dollar to appreciate.

2. Changes in the rate of growth of the money supply tend to change the exchange rate but may not affect international trade if PPP holds.

3. If PPP and IRP both hold, then the expected change in the exchange rate equals the interest differential between domestic and foreign bonds, which equals the expected inflation differential between the domestic and foreign countries.

4. INTERNATIONAL POLICY COORDINATION

Economies are linked globally by trade in goods, services, and financial assets. This means the policies of one nation can have important implications for other nations. One way this happens is because of the foreign repercussions of domestic spending. That is, some spending on imports comes back to the domestic economy in the form of exports. An increase in U.S. government expenditures increases U.S. real GDP. As income increases, U.S. imports increase, pushing foreign income up. As foreign income rises, so do foreign imports of goods produced in the United States. Ultimately, then, U.S. income rises by more than it would if based on only the domestic increase in spending. Since one country's economic policy can cause changes that affect other nations, there are potential gains from having economic policy formulated with a view toward the international effects.

Because countries are linked through their trade in goods, services, and financial assets, business cycles tend to follow similar trends across countries. When the U.S. economy is booming, income in countries that depend on exports to the U.S. market increases. When the United States is in a recession, income in other countries tends to fall. Because the nations of the world are linked by their common interests in trade, every country's domestic macroeconomic policy affects more than its domestic economy. And because every country has the potential to affect the economies of other nations, setting macroeconomic policy cooperatively may improve overall macroeconomic performance.

Macroeconomic policy in the United States traditionally has been formulated with little attention to the rest of the world. But in recent years, the potential gains from coordinating economic policies across countries have become increasingly apparent. Large fluctuations in exchange rates and net exports in the 1980s showed the interdependencies among nations. Over time, technological improvements in transportation and communication have created opportunities for substitution in international goods and services markets.

To coordinate economic policies, governments must communicate. Senior economic officials of the leading industrial countries come together regularly at meetings of the International Monetary Fund (IMF) and the Organization for Economic Cooperation and Development (OECD). Since 1975 the leaders of the seven largest industrial nations have held annual economic summit meetings. These seven nations (Canada, France, Germany, Italy, Japan, the

The G7 countries are Canada, France, Germany, Italy, Japan, the United Kingdom, and the United States.

United Kingdom, and the United States), known as the *Group of 7 (G7)* countries, have made a commitment to monitor one another's economic policies. The Economic Insight "The OECD" explains how the OECD operates.

4.a. Potential Gains

What can countries gain by coordinating their macro-economic policies?

Coordination among countries can take several directions. Countries can coordinate their goals, targeting inflation or unemployment, for example. They also can coordinate their information, exchanging forecasts of key macroeconomic variables based on their economic plans. Finally, they can coordinate the policymaking and implementation processes. The potential gains of coordination are a product of the form that coordination takes.

Setting joint goals could induce policy changes that make those goals attainable. For example, let's say that all countries set a goal of reducing the unemployment rate. To meet that goal, the countries would have to set expansionary monetary or fiscal policies. Even if the countries do not explicitly discuss their future policies, the goals they set guide those policies. Of course, this assumes that policymakers target the agreed-on goals when they formulate their domestic economic policy.

The coordination of information regarding the current state of the economy and forecasts of future changes can take place both informally and through formal meetings of key policymakers. Central bank and treasury staff members may regularly talk to compare notes on the world economy.

Coordination of the policymaking process offers the hope of making every country better off. For instance, since the mid-1980s, the United States has experienced a large international trade deficit, while Japan and Germany have had trade surpluses. At several international conferences, leading policymakers have proposed that the United States reduce its fiscal deficit to reduce domestic spending and improve its international balance of trade. Simultaneously, Japan and Germany were going to increase their fiscal deficits to stimulate spending in those countries in order to increase their imports from the United States and to avoid recessions if exports to the United States fell.

The proposed fiscal policy has proven difficult to implement, but future policy actions may very well reflect this kind of multinational decision making. For example, suppose the United States wants to stimulate the domestic economy but is concerned about increasing its international trade deficit (rising income increases imports). If U.S. expansionary policies could be coordinated with expansionary policies in other large countries, so that income rises in all the countries simultaneously, the balance of trade might not change even though all the countries are increasing their real GDP. This is a potential benefit of international cooperation: by acting together, nations can achieve better outcomes than would be possible if they acted individually.

4.b. Obstacles

Obviously, international coordination of macroeconomic policy makes sense. In practice, however, several problems stand in the way of designing and implementing economic policy across countries. First, countries may not agree on goals. Some countries may be willing to exploit the short-run trade-off between inflation and the unemployment rate, while other countries may choose to follow passive policies, refusing to manipulate aggregate demand. In addition, the politicians who are involved in international agreements tend

The OECD

The Organization for Economic Cooperation and Development (OECD) is an association of industrial countries with three goals: to attain the highest sustainable rate of growth while maintaining financial stability, to promote free trade, and to support development in non-OECD countries. The OECD is headquartered in Paris. The secretary general, traditionally a European, is appointed to a five-year term and chairs all meetings of the full council.

The OECD was established in 1961 and now has 25 member countries (see the table). Together they account for one-sixth of the world's population but produce two-thirds of the world's output. As the table shows, the member countries differ greatly in terms of per capita output, population, and area. Given this diversity, it is not surprising that the countries often disagree on economic policy.

The OECD, unlike the IMF and the World Bank, makes no loans and has no authority to make economic policy. It serves as a meeting place where policymakers can discuss problems and points of view. Although the output of meetings is seldom concrete, the process is an important step on the road to international collaboration.

Member Country	GNP per Capita (U.S. dollars)*	Population (millions)	Area (thousands of square kilometers)
Switzerland	36,080	6.9	41
Luxembourg	35,160	0.4	3
Japan	28,190	124.5	378
Sweden	27,010	8.7	450
Denmark	26,000	5.2	43
Norway	25,820	4.3	324
Iceland	23,880	.26	103
United States	23,240	255.4	9,373
Germany	23,030†	80.6	357
Austria	22,380	7.9	84
France	22,260	57.4	552
Finland	21,970	5.0	338
Belgium	20,880	10.0	31
Canada	20,710	27.4	9,976
Netherlands	20,480	15.2	37
Italy	20,460	57.8	301
Britain	17,790	57.8	245
Australia	17,260	17.5	7,687
Spain	13,970	39.1	505
New Zealand	12,300	3.4	271
Ireland	12,210	3.5	70
Portugal	7,450	9.8	92
Greece	7,290	10.3	132
Mexico	3,470	85.0	1,958
Turkey	1,980	58.5	779

*1992 data

†For former West Germany

Source: Organization for Cooperation and Development and World Bank.

to make policies aimed at short-term political gains rather than long-term economic stability.

Second, even if countries can agree on goals, they may disagree on the current economic situation. GDP and other key macroeconomic variables are measured with a lag and are often revised substantially after their values are initially announced. At any point in time, policymakers cannot be sure whether the economy is expanding or contracting. Eventually, as official data are collected, the economic health of the nation is known, but only several months later. This means that the economic policymakers of the major developed countries could disagree on an appropriate course of action because they do not agree on current economic conditions.

Consider an example. In 1994, the Federal Reserve declared that inflation was Public Enemy Number One. So the Fed implemented a restrictive economic policy of raising interest rates aimed at slowing the growth of aggregate demand. As the Fed raised interest rates repeatedly during the year, some economists and politicians in the United States as well as abroad argued that there was no inflation problem and the Fed might create a recession by raising interest rates. Other economists believed that inflationary pressures were building and the Fed was wisely fighting these pressures. We won't know who was "right" until we can look back to see what happened—and even then, as we've seen, what happened may not have been a result of Fed actions. Another example arises out of the dollar depreciation of early 1995. As the dollar fell in value against the yen and mark, Japanese officials argued that the United States should take action to support the dollar while U.S. officials tended to state that while they were surprised at the falling dollar, they did not feel a need to actively change U.S. policy with the aim of increasing the value of the dollar. Such disagreements are commonplace and to be expected in a world where economic policy is made by politicians and is compounded by the fact that good economists often disagree about the proper role of government policy.

Even if countries can agree on goals and current conditions, they still may disagree on appropriate policy because they adhere to different theories of macroeconomics. Some policymakers believe that a new Keynesian fixed-price model (with a horizontal aggregate supply curve) best describes current economic conditions, and that by increasing aggregate demand they can increase output and employment. Others believe that the new classical model (in which the aggregate supply curve is vertical in the presence of expected policy changes) best describes the current economic situation and that increasing aggregate demand in a predictable way has no effect on output and employment but causes the price level to rise. These very basic disagreements make it difficult to reach a consensus on economic policy.

These obstacles may make it impossible to coordinate international economic policy. But at least international economic meetings and discussions help each country understand the views of other nations and the likely course of policy in the rest of the world. This sharing of information allows each nation to formulate its own policy in light of what policy in the rest of the world is likely to be.

RECAP

1. Because every country has the potential to affect the economies of other nations, coordinating macroeconomic policy may improve overall economic performance.

2. Coordination here means setting joint goals, exchanging information, and forming and executing policy cooperatively.

3. Obstacles to the international coordination of economic policy are disagreements over goals, current economic conditions, and macroeconomic theory.

SUMMARY

1. Arbitrage equalizes the prices of similar goods in different markets. § Preview

2. An open economy trades goods, services, and financial assets with the rest of the world. § Preview

▲▼ *How does a change in the exchange rate affect the prices of goods traded between countries?*

3. When the domestic currency depreciates against other currencies, foreign goods become more expensive to domestic buyers and domestic goods become less expensive to foreign buyers. §1.a

4. When the domestic currency appreciates against other currencies, foreign goods become less expensive to domestic buyers and domestic goods become more expensive to foreign buyers. §1.a

5. Purchasing power parity exists when monies have the same value in different markets. §1.b

▲▼ *Why don't similar goods sell for the same price all over the world?*

6. Deviations from PPP arise because goods are not identical in different countries, information is costly, shipping costs affect prices, and tariffs and restrictions on trade affect prices. §1.b

▲▼ *What is the relationship between inflation and changes in the exchange rate?*

7. Exchange rates tend to change to offset inflation differentials between countries. §1.c

▲▼ *How do we find the domestic currency return on a foreign bond?*

8. The domestic currency return from holding a foreign bond equals the foreign interest rate plus the percentage change in the exchange rate. §2.a

▲▼ *What is the relationship between domestic and foreign interest rates and changes in the exchange rate?*

9. Interest rate parity exists when the domestic interest rate equals the foreign interest rate plus the expected change in the exchange rate, so that similar financial assets yield the same return when measured in the same currency. §2.b

▲▼ *Why don't similar financial assets yield the same return all over the world?*

10. Deviations from IRP are a product of government controls, political risk, and taxes. §2.c

▲▼ *How does fiscal policy affect exchange rates?*

11. Financing a government budget deficit by selling bonds (borrowing) tends to raise domestic interest rates, which attracts foreign investors and causes the domestic currency to appreciate. Ultimately, increased government borrowing tends to reduce net exports. §3.a

▲▼ *How does monetary policy affect exchange rates?*

12. Higher expected inflation, a product of increasing the rate at which the money supply grows, tends to increase nominal interest rates. The domestic currency depreciates to offset rising prices but has no effect on net exports. §3.b

13. If IRP and PPP hold, the expected change in the exchange rate equals the interest differential between domestic and foreign bonds, which equals the expected inflation differential between the domestic and foreign economies. §3.c

▲▼ *What can countries gain by coordinating their macroeconomic policies?*

14. By coordinating macroeconomic policies, the goals of those policies become more attainable, nations have greater access to economic information, and the results of those policies are improved. §4.a

15. Obstacles to the international coordination of macroeconomic policy are disagreements over policy goals, the current economic situation, and macroeconomic theory. §4.b

KEY TERMS

arbitrage § Preview

open economy § Preview

purchasing power parity (PPP) §1.b

interest rate parity (IRP) §2.b

capital controls §2.c

risk premium §2.c

EXERCISES

1. Find the U.S. dollar value of each of the following currencies at the given exchange rates:

   a. $1 = C$1.20 (Canadian dollars)

   b. $1 = ¥140 (Japanese yen)

   c. $1 = FL2 (Netherlands guilder)

   d. $1 = SKr6 (Swedish krona)

   e. $1 = SF1.5 (Swiss franc)

2. You are a U.S. importer who buys goods from many different countries. How many U.S. dollars do you need to settle each of the following invoices?

   a. 1,000,000 Australian dollars for wool blankets (exchange rate: A$1 = $.769)

   b. 500,000 British pounds for dishes (exchange rate: £1 = $1.5855)

   c. 100,000 Indian rupees for baskets (exchange rate: Rs1 = $.0602)

   d. 150 million Japanese yen for stereo components (exchange rate: ¥1 = $.0069)

   e. 825,000 German marks for wine (exchange rate: DM1 = $.5515)

3. What is the dollar value of the invoices in exercise 2 if the dollar

   a. depreciates 10 percent against the Australian dollar?

   b. appreciates 10 percent against the British pound?

   c. depreciates 10 percent against the Indian rupee?

   d. appreciates 20 percent against the Japanese yen?

   e. depreciates 100 percent against the German mark?

4. Explain purchasing power parity and why it does not hold perfectly in the real world.

5. Write an equation that describes purchasing power parity and explain the equation.

6. Write an equation that describes interest rate parity and explain the equation.

7. Use the equation in exercise 6 to describe the effects of an increase in domestic government spending financed by

   a. borrowing

   b. money creation

8. If the interest rate on one-year government bonds is 5 percent in Germany and 8 percent in the United States, what do you think is expected to happen to the dollar value of the mark? Explain your answer.

9. Suppose that on January 1 the yen price of the dollar is 100. Over the year, the Japanese inflation rate is 5 percent and the U.S. inflation rate is 10 percent. If the exchange rate is $1 = ¥110 at the end of the year, relative to PPP, does the yen appear to be overvalued, undervalued, or at the PPP level? Explain your answer.

10. In 1960 a U.S. dollar sold for 620 Italian lire. If PPP held in 1960, what would the PPP value of the exchange rate have been in 1987 if Italian prices rose 12 times and U.S. prices rose 4 times between 1960 and 1987?

11. Suppose a personal computer sold for $1,500 in Los Angeles and $1,700 in San Francisco. How would arbitrage operate to keep the prices of the computer in the two cities from moving too far apart?

12. If the U.S. dollar depreciates against the German mark, what will be the economic consequences for U.S. residents?

13. If the price of a pound of salmon is $5 in Seattle, Washington, and the exchange rate between U.S. and Canadian dollars is $.80 =

C$1.00, then what would the Canadian dollar price of salmon have to be in Vancouver, British Columbia, in order for PPP to hold?

14. Suppose at the beginning of the year a best-selling CD sells for FF60 in Paris, France, and DM20 in Hanover, Germany, and PPP holds. Over the year, there is an inflation rate of 33 percent in France and no inflation in Germany. What exchange rate would maintain PPP at the end of the year?

15. Suppose a U.S. investor buys a one-year German bond with a face value of DM10,000 that has a 10 percent annual interest rate. How many dollars will a U.S. investor receive at maturity if the exchange rate is $.40 = DM1.00?

COOPERATIVE LEARNING EXERCISE

The class breaks up into groups of four, and each group is further divided into subgroups of two, A and B. The A subgroups must answer question A below, and the B subgroups must answer question B below. After the subgroups have found the answers, the groups of four come together and the A subgroup explains its answer to the Bs, and the B subgroup explains its answer to the As.

1. Question A: Suppose that today the yen/dollar exchange rate is 100 and purchasing power parity holds. Over the next year there is a 5 percent inflation rate in the United States and a 2 percent inflation rate in Japan. What is the exchange rate after the year that will maintain purchasing power parity?

2. Question B: Suppose a U.S. investor buys a one-year German bond for DM100,000. The German bond pays 10 percent interest over the year. If the exchange rate (dollars per mark) at the time the bond was purchased was $.60 and the exchange rate at the time the bond matures after one year is $.57, what is the dollar return from holding the German bond?

Expats' Currency Conundrum/American Investors Try to Predict Future of the Dollar

Americans living and working in Japan are taking the dollar's tumble against the yen personally.

Foreign-exchange loss has become a big concern among expats, whether they are paid in yen or dollars. "I've been telling my clients to hold onto their yen, but now I would start encouraging people to switch to dollars, says Karen Wenk-Jordan, a former New York resident who runs a financial-services company in Tokyo.

Bob Davis, a management consultant for McKinsey and Co., and a native of Western Springs, Ill., converted a portion of his yen savings two weeks ago at 98 yen, then converted more this week at 94.

"I was doing local certificates of deposits here in Japan that have 1.8% interest, which is all you get. Now I've exchanged everything I had in yen to dollars and have almost no yen," says Davis.

He invested 5% in a U.S. money market fund, 25% in bond mutual funds and the remaining 70% in three different types of stock mutual funds. To move money swiftly, many expats in Japan hold both a yen and foreign-currency account.

Citibank, the only American retail bank in Japan, offers a multi-money account in which clients can hold up to 14 currencies. Transfers can be made instantly over the phone.

"Foreign exchange is our forte," says Susan Nakano, who moved from Hawaii to Tokyo to run the bank's expatriate services. But the multimoney account earns only 0.75% interest, and the yen savings account is even less at 0.25%.

"It's pitiful," says Christine Davis, an English school teacher from Putnam, Conn., who has a yen savings account with Citibank. "The bank charges you $10 a month if you have less than $3,000 in your account."

Banks in Japan offer meager returns on fixed-term deposits as well. "I never recommend holding dollars in Japan because interest rates are so low," says Wenk-Jordan.

"If the person is going home in a couple of years, I suggest keeping dollars in the USA. But expats who plan to be away for a long time should think about moving their money offshore."

Hong Kong is a popular choice. Wenk-Jordan says the Hong Kong Shanghai Bank's multimoney account offers a higher interest rate than banks in Japan and the minimum deposit is only $250.

Other personal investors who want to keep some savings in yen, purchase money management funds—equivalent to money market funds in the USA. Japan's major securities companies sell them in the equivalent of $1,000 units.

But money managers warn that brokerages usually refuse clients who do not read Japanese because of contract liabilities.

Wiring money to a bank account in a home country probably is the easiest investment strategy; Americans paid in yen benefit from both the foreign exchange rate and the high U.S. interest rates.

Finally, expats planning to return to their home country should keep their old bank account and credit card in order to maintain their credit rating.

"Lenders get uncomfortable when they see a dormant period in a person's credit profile," Wenk-Jordan says. "One way to get around this is to occasionally charge up about $500 then pay it off over a period of four or five months. That way you establish a history of payments and reliability."

Source: Nicola Wasson, "Expats' Currency Conundrum/American Investors Try to Predict Future of the Dollar," *USA Today*, March 10, 1995, p. 7A. Copyright 1995, *USA Today*. Used by permission.

Commentary

This article points out the real-world fact of exchange rate uncertainty and the costs it can impose on even thoughtful investors. We are told that Karen Wenk-Jordan, who runs a financial services company in Tokyo, was advising her clients to switch their savings from yen to dollars in the second week of 1995. Bob Davis did just this, converting a portion of his yen savings into dollars at an exchange rate of 98 yen per dollar. Why the switch from yen to dollars? Because the yen interest rate was very low, only 1.8 percent on the yen certificates of deposit (CDs) that Davis held. At this time, dollar CDs in the United States were offering around 6 percent interest. Since 6 percent is greater than 1.8 percent, it seems clear that one should invest in dollar CDs rather than yen.

However, things are not this simple. Only 2 weeks after this article was written, the dollar dropped in value against the yen by a surprisingly large amount. By early April, instead of 98 yen per dollar, the exchange rate was 83 yen per dollar. We can estimate the cost to an investor of switching from yen to dollar CDs prior to the dollar depreciation. For example, suppose Bob Davis has ¥1,000,000 to invest at the beginning of 1995 when the dollar is worth 98 yen. If he buys a yen CD paying 1.8 percent per year in interest, then after 3 months (a quarter of a year) he will have ¥1,004,500. If instead he converts his yen to dollars at the beginning of the year, he will have ¥1,000,000/98 = $10,204 to invest in U.S. CDs. If these CDs earn 6 percent interest, then after a quarter of a year, he will have $10,357. However, when the dollars are converted back into yen at the new exchange rate he ends up with $10,357 × 83 = ¥859,636. Because of the dollar depreciation, he ends up with fewer yen than he started with.

Since international investing involves more than one currency, it is not enough to just compare interest rates. Exchange rate changes will also have an impact on the returns investors earn. The fact that the yen deposits were offering a lower interest rate than dollar deposits, suggests that people believe that the dollar will depreciate against the yen so that the higher dollar interest rate, at least partially, compensates for the falling value of the currency. If investors did not expect the dollar to depreciate, then no one would buy yen deposits offering a lower interest rate as everyone would want the higher interest rate dollar deposits.

The bottom line is that the interest differential between yen and dollar CDs reflects the expected change in the exchange rate. Once expected exchange rate changes are considered, investors will not all agree that the higher interest rate CD is the preferred investment. Since Karen Wenk-Jordan and Bob Davis thought the higher interest rates on U.S. CDs were attractive, they must have expected no significant change in the yen/dollar exchange rate. The surprising (to them) dollar depreciation cost Mr. Davis and Ms. Wenk-Jordan's other clients a substantial loss. The lesson is that both exchange rates and interest rates must be considered when making international investment decisions.

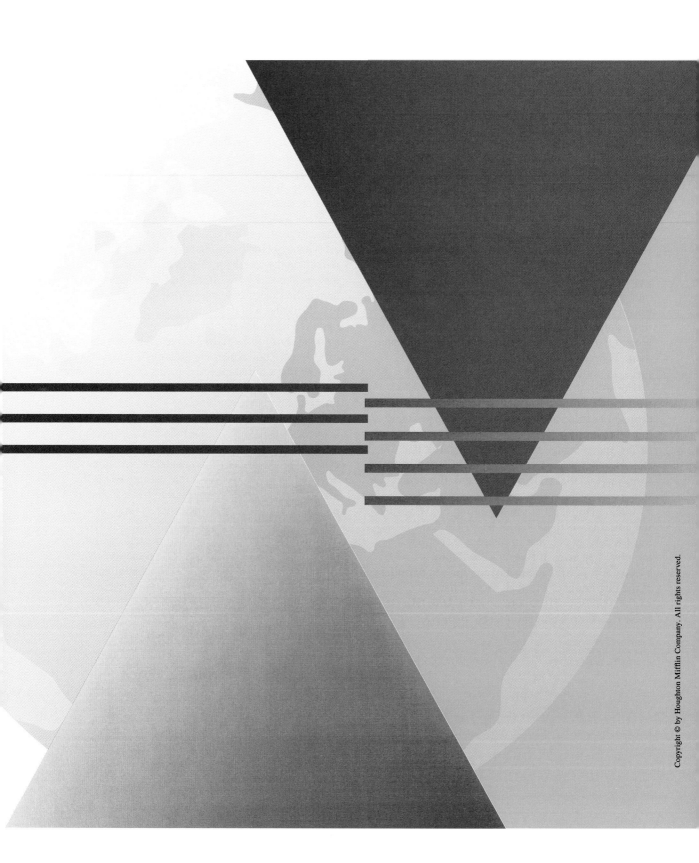

IV

Economic Growth and Development

441

18

Economic Growth

FUNDAMENTAL QUESTIONS

1. What is economic growth?
2. How are economic growth rates determined?
3. What is productivity?
4. Why has U.S. productivity changed?

Between 1970 and 1980, Japanese real GDP grew at an average annual rate of 4.3 percent while U.S. real GDP grew at an average annual rate of only 2.8 percent. Between 1980 and 1992, the Japanese growth rate was 4.1 percent while the U.S. growth rate was 2.7 percent. Why has Japanese real GDP grown at a faster rate in recent decades than U.S. real GDP? Is it because Japanese workers are more diligent or more highly motivated than U.S. workers? Is it because Japanese students study more and so are better educated than U.S. students? Is it because Japanese firms are more concerned with developing new products and new production techniques than U.S. firms? Understanding why and how economic growth happens is a very important part of macroeconomics.

Although much of macroeconomics is aimed at understanding business cycles—recurring periods of prosperity and recession—the fact is that over the long run, most economies do grow wealthier. The long-run trend of real GDP in the United States and most other countries is positive. Yet the rate at

PREVIEW

which real GDP grows is very different across countries. Why? What factors cause economies to grow and living standards to rise?

In this chapter we focus on the long-term picture. We begin by defining economic growth and discussing its importance. Then we examine the determinants of economic growth, to understand what accounts for the different rates of growth across countries.

I. DEFINING ECONOMIC GROWTH

What is economic growth?

What do we mean by economic growth? Economists use two measures of growth—real GDP and per capita real GDP—to compare how economies grow over time.

I.a. Real GDP

economic growth:
an increase in real GDP

Basically, **economic growth** is an increase in real GDP. As more goods and services are produced, the real GDP increases and people are able to consume more.

To calculate the percentage change in real GDP over a year, we simply divide the change in GDP by the value of GDP at the beginning of the year, and then multiply the quotient by 100. For instance, the real GDP of Singapore was approximately 82,281 million Singapore dollars in 1993 and approximately 74,839 million in 1992. So the economy grew 10 percent in 1993:

$$\text{Percentage change in real GDP} = \frac{\text{change over year}}{\text{beginning value}} \times 100$$

$$= \frac{82,281 - 74,839}{74,839} \times 100$$

$$= .10 \times 100$$

$$= 10$$

I.a.1. Compound Growth From 1980 to 1992, the industrial countries of the world showed an average annual growth rate of real GDP of 2.9 percent. Over the same period, the average annual growth rate of real GDP for low-income developing countries was 6.1 percent. The difference between a growth rate of 2.9 percent and one of 6.1 percent may not seem substantial, but in fact it is. Growth is compounded over time. This means that any given rate of growth is applied every year to a growing base of real GDP, so any difference is magnified over time.

Small changes in rates of growth produce big changes in real GDP over a period of many years.

Figure 1 shows the effects of compounding growth rates. The upper line in the figure represents the path of real GDP if the economy grows at a rate of 6.1 percent a year. The lower line shows real GDP growing at a rate of 2.9 percent a year.

Suppose in each case the economy originally is producing a real GDP of $1 billion. After five years, there is not much difference: a GDP of $1.156 billion at 2.9 percent growth versus $1.345 billion at 6.1 percent growth. The effect of compounding becomes more visible over long periods of time. After

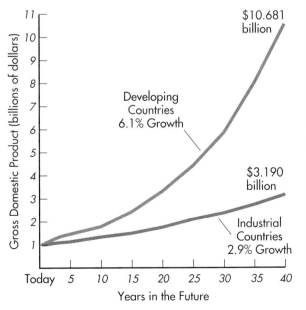

Figure 1
Comparing GDP Growth Rates of 2.9% and 6.1%
Between 1980 and 1992, real GDP in the industrial countries grew at an average annual rate of 2.9 percent, while real GDP in developing countries grew at an average annual rate of 6.1 percent. The difference seems small, but the graph shows how even a small difference is compounded over time, producing a substantial difference in real GDP.

40 years, the difference between 2.9 and 6.1 percent growth, a seemingly small difference, represents a huge difference in output. A 2.9 percent rate of growth yields an output of $3.190 billion; at 6.1 percent, output is $10.681 billion. After 40 years, the level of output is three times as large at the higher growth rate.

1.a.2. **The Rule of 72** Compound growth explains why countries are so concerned about maintaining positive high rates of growth. If growth is maintained at a constant rate, we can estimate the number of years required for output to double by using the **rule of 72**. If we divide 72 by the growth rate, we find the approximate time it takes for any value to double.

Suppose you deposit $100 in a bank account that pays a constant 6 percent annual interest. If you allow the interest to accumulate over time, the amount of money in the account grows at a rate of 6 percent. At this rate of interest, the rule of 72 tells us that your account will have a value of approximately $200 (double its initial value) after 12 years:

$$\frac{72}{6} = 12$$

The interest rate gives the rate of growth of the amount deposited if earned interest is allowed to accumulate in the account. If the interest rate is 3 percent, the amount would double in 24 (72/3) years.

The rule of 72 applies to any value. If real GDP is growing at a rate of 6 percent a year, then real GDP doubles every 12 years. At a 3 percent annual rate, real GDP doubles every 24 years.

Table 1 lists the average annual rate of growth of GDP between 1980 and 1992 and approximate doubling times for ten countries. The countries listed

TABLE 1
GDP Growth Rates and Doubling Times

Country	Average Annual Growth Rate (percent)*	Doubling Time (years)
Korea	9.4	8
India	5.2	14
Bangladesh	4.2	17
Japan	4.1	18
Colombia	3.7	19
Australia	3.1	23
Canada	2.8	26
United States	2.7	27
Germany	2.6	28
Dominican Republic	1.7	42

*Average annual growth rates from 1980 to 1992.

Source: World Bank, *World Development Report* (Washington, D.C., 1994).

range from a high growth rate of 9.4 percent in Korea to a low rate of 1.7 percent in the Dominican Republic. If these growth rates are maintained over time, it would take just 8 years for GDP in Korea to double and 42 years for the GDP in the Dominican Republic to double.

1.b. Per Capita Real GDP

Economic growth is sometimes defined as an increase in per capita real GDP.

per capita real GDP:
real GDP divided by the population

We've defined economic growth as an increase in real GDP. But, if growth is supposed to be associated with higher standards of living, our definition may be misleading. A country could show positive growth in real GDP, but if the population is growing at an even higher rate, output per person can actually fall. Economists, therefore, often adjust the growth rate of output for changes in population. **Per capita real GDP** is real GDP divided by the population. If we define economic growth as rising per capita real GDP, then growth requires a nation's output of goods and services to increase faster than its population.

The World Bank computes per capita GNP for countries as an indicator of economic development. You may recall from Chapter 6 that GNP equals GDP plus net factor income from abroad. From 1980 to 1992, per capita real GNP grew at an average annual rate of 3.9 percent in low-income developing countries and 2.3 percent in industrial countries. The difference in per capita real GNP growth between low-income developing and industrial countries is much smaller than the difference in real GDP. (Remember that real GDP grew at a rate of 6.1 percent in low-income developing countries over the same period, compared to a rate of 2.9 percent in industrial countries.) The difference in growth rates between the level of output and per capita output points out the danger of just looking at real GDP as an indicator of change in the economic well-being of the citizens in developing countries. Population growth rates are considerably higher in developing countries than they are in industrial countries, so real GDP must grow at a faster rate in developing countries than it does in industrial countries just to maintain a similar growth rate in per capita real GDP.

1.c. The Problems with Definitions of Growth

Economic growth is considered to be good because it allows people to have a higher standard of living, to have more material goods. But an increase in real GDP or per capita real GDP does not tell us whether the average citizen is better off. One problem is that these measures say nothing about how income is distributed. The national economy may be growing, yet the poor may be staying poor while the rich get richer.

We thus have to be careful about using per capita real GDP as an indicator of the standard of living. Table 2 shows why. The table lists historical data on the percentage share of household income in Sri Lanka by income groups. In 1969–1970, the poorest 20 percent of households received 7.5 percent of the nation's total income; the next 20 percent received 11.7 percent; the third 20 percent received 15.7 percent; 21.7 percent went to the next group; and, finally, the wealthiest 20 percent of households received 43.4 percent.

Although per capita real GDP did grow in Sri Lanka from 1970 to 1990, we cannot say that all households benefited from that growth. Between 1969–1970 and 1980–1981, the share of household income going to each of the four poorest groups of households in Sri Lanka fell. Only the wealthiest

TABLE 2
Income Distribution, Sri Lanka

	Percentage Share of Household Income Going to				
	Lowest 20 Percent	Second 20 Percent	Third 20 Percent	Fourth 20 Percent	Highest 20 Percent
1969–1970	7.5	11.7	15.7	21.7	43.4
1980–1981	5.8	10.1	14.1	20.3	49.8
1990	8.9	13.1	16.9	21.7	39.3

Source: World Bank, *World Development Report* (Washington, D.C., 1988), p. 272, and 1994, p. 220.

group, which already had a disproportionate share of real GDP, saw that share increase. So from 1970 to 1980, it is not clear that the poorest groups benefited from GDP growth. However, between 1980–1981 and 1990, the share of household income going to the poorest groups increased, so that they were more likely to benefit from GDP growth.

The lesson here is simple. Economic growth may benefit some groups more than others. And it is entirely possible that despite national economic growth, some groups can be worse off than they were before. Clearly, per capita real GDP or real GDP does not accurately measure the standard of living for all of a nation's citizens.

Another reason real GDP or per capita real GDP is misleading is that it says nothing about the quality of life. People have nonmonetary needs—they care about personal freedom, the environment, their leisure time. If a rising per capita GDP goes hand in hand with a repressive political regime or rapidly deteriorating environmental quality, people are not going to feel better off. By the same token, a country could have no economic growth, yet reduce the hours worked each week. More leisure time could make workers feel better off, even though per capita GDP has not changed.

Per capita real GDP is a questionable indicator of the typical citizen's standard of living or quality of life.

Once again, be careful in interpreting per capita GDP. Don't allow it to represent more than it does. Per capita GDP is simply a measure of the output produced divided by the population. It is a useful measure of economic activity in a country, but it is a questionable measure of the typical citizen's standard of living or quality of life.

RECAP

1. Economic growth is an increase in real GDP.

2. Because growth is compounded over time, small differences in rates of growth are magnified over time.

3. For any constant rate of growth, the time required for real GDP to double is 72 divided by the annual growth rate.

4. Per capita real GDP is real GDP divided by the population.

5. Per capita real GDP says nothing about the distribution of income in a country or the nonmonetary quality of life.

2. THE DETERMINANTS OF GROWTH

How are economic growth rates determined?

Economic growth raises the potential level of real GDP, shifting the long-run aggregate supply curve to the right.

The long-run aggregate supply curve is a vertical line at the potential level of real GDP (Y_{p1}). As the economy grows, the potential output of the economy rises. Figure 2 shows the increase in potential output as a rightward shift in the long-run aggregate supply curve. The higher the rate of growth, the farther the aggregate supply curve moves to the right. To illustrate several years' growth, we would show several curves shifting to the right.

To find the determinants of economic growth, we must turn to the determinants of aggregate supply. In Chapter 9, we identified three determinants of aggregate supply: resource prices, technology, and expectations. Changes in expectations can shift the aggregate supply curve, but changing expectations are not a basis for long-run growth in the sense of continuous rightward movements in aggregate supply. The long-run growth of the economy rests on growth in productive resources (labor, capital, land, and entrepreneurial skills) and technological advances.

2.a. Labor

Economic growth depends on the size and quality of the labor force. The size of the labor force is a function of the size of the working-age population (sixteen and older in the United States) and the percentage of that population in the labor force. The labor force typically grows more rapidly in developing countries than in industrial countries because birthrates are higher in developing countries. Figure 3 shows the actual and predicted average annual growth rates of the population for selected developing and industrial countries, as well as average growth rates for all developing countries and all industrial countries. Between 1980 and 1992, the population grew at an average annual rate of 1.9 percent in developing countries and .7 percent in industrial countries. The World Bank forecasts that between 1992 and 2000,

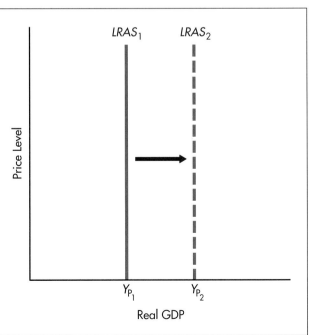

Figure 2
Economic Growth
As the economy grows, the long-run aggregate supply curve shifts to the right. This represents an increase in the potential level of real GDP.

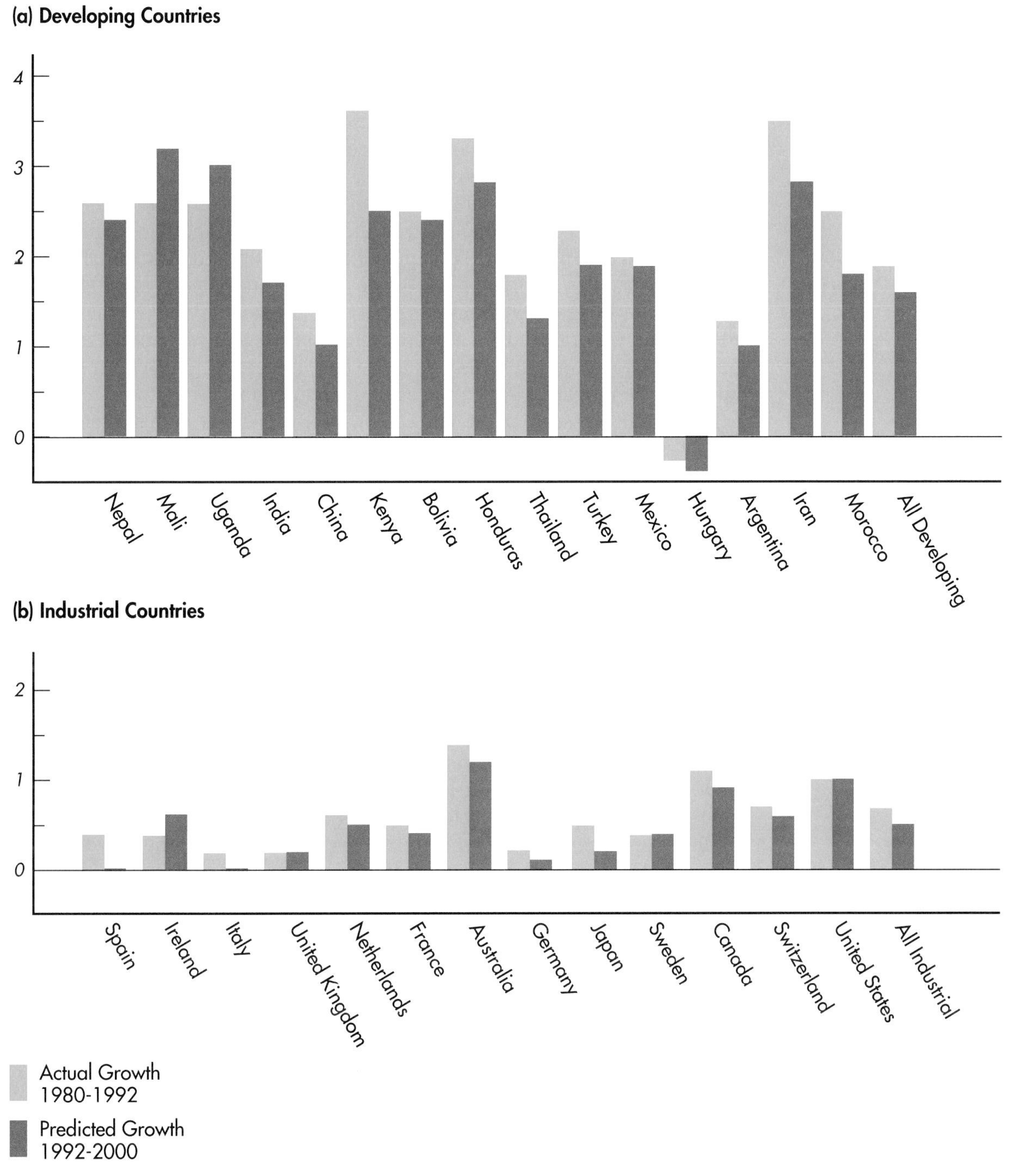

(a) Developing Countries

(b) Industrial Countries

Actual Growth
1980-1992

Predicted Growth
1992-2000

Figure 3
Average Annual Population Growth in Selected Countries (percent)
Population growth rates across countries vary considerably. Generally, population
grows at a much higher rate in developing countries. Source: Data are from World
Bank, *World Development Report* (Washington, D.C., 1994), pp. 210–211.

the population will grow at an average annual rate of 1.6 percent in developing countries and .5 percent in industrial countries.

Based solely on growth in the labor force, it seems that developing countries are growing faster than industrial countries. But the size of the labor force is not all that matters; changes in productivity can compensate for lower growth in the labor force, as we discuss in section 3.

The U.S. labor force has changed considerably in recent decades. The most notable event of the post–World War II period was the baby boom. The children born between the late 1940s and the early 1960s made up more than a third of the total U.S. population in the early 1960s and have significantly altered the age structure of the population. In 1950 the largest percentage of males and females in the population was in the category of young children. By 1970 the largest percentage of the U.S. population was in the five- to twenty-nine-year range. By 1980 this bulge in the age distribution had moved to the twenty- to forty-four-year range, where it remains today. Over time the bulge will be moving to older ranges of the population.

The initial pressure of the baby boom fell on school systems faced with rapidly expanding enrollments. Over time, as these children aged and entered the labor market, they had a large impact on potential output. The U.S. labor force grew at an average rate of about 2.5 percent a year in the 1970s, approximately twice the rate of growth experienced in the 1950s. The growth of the labor force slowed in the 1980s, as the baby boom population moved into its twenties and thirties. Based on the size of the labor force, the 1970s should have been a time of greater economic growth than the 1950s, 1960s, or 1980s. It was not. More important than the size of the labor force is its productivity.

2.b. Capital

Labor is combined with capital to produce goods and services. A rapidly growing labor force by itself is no guarantee of economic growth. Workers need machines, tools, and factories to work. If a country has lots of workers but few machines, then the typical worker cannot be very productive. Capital is a critical resource in growing economies.

The ability of a country to invest in capital goods is tied to its ability to save. A lack of current saving can be offset by borrowing, but the availability of borrowing is limited by the prospects for future saving. Debt incurred today must be repaid by not consuming all output in the future. If lenders believe that a nation is going to consume all of its output in the future, they do not make loans today.

The lower the standard of living in a country, the harder it is to forgo current consumption in order to save. It is difficult for a population living at or near subsistence level to do without current consumption. This in large part explains the low level of saving in the poorest countries.

2.c. Land

Abundant natural resources are not a necessary condition for economic growth.

Land surface, water, forests, minerals, and other natural resources are called *land*. Land can be combined with labor and capital to produce goods and services. Abundant natural resources can contribute to economic growth, but natural resources alone do not generate growth. Several developing countries, like Argentina and Brazil, are relatively rich in natural resources but have not been very successful in exploiting these resources to produce goods and services. Japan, on the other hand, has relatively few natural resources but has shown dramatic economic growth in recent decades. The experience of Japan makes it clear that abundant natural resources are not a necessary condition for economic growth.

2.d. Technology

technology:
ways of combining resources to produce output

Technological advances allow the production of more output from a given amount of resources.

A key determinant of economic growth is **technology**, ways of combining resources to produce goods and services. New management techniques, scientific discoveries, and other innovations improve technology. Technological advances allow the production of more output from a given amount of resources. This means that technological progress accelerates economic growth for any given rate of growth in the labor force and the capital stock.

Technological change depends on the scientific community. The more educated a population, the greater its potential for technological advances. Industrial countries have better-educated populations than do developing countries. Education gives industrial countries a substantial advantage over developing countries in creating and implementing innovations. In addition, the richest industrial countries traditionally have spent 2 to 3 percent of their

It is no longer accurate to consider all developing countries as possessing only large quantities of low-skilled workers. Some countries have produced a significant number of well-trained workers who are employed in modern, high-tech industries. For example, these engineers at Hewlett-Packard's computer plant in Guadalajara, Mexico, have designed components that are manufactured worldwide. Half the employees of this plant have advanced degrees.

GNP on research and development, an investment developing countries cannot afford. The greater the funding for research and development, the greater the likelihood of technological advances.

Impeded by low levels of education and limited funds for research and development, the developing countries lag behind the industrial countries in developing and implementing new technology. Typically these countries follow the lead of the industrial world, adopting new technology developed in that world once it is affordable and feasible, given their capital and labor resources. In the next chapter we discuss the role of foreign aid, including technological assistance, in promoting economic growth in developing countries.

RECAP

1. Economic growth raises the potential level of real GDP, shifting the long-run aggregate supply curve to the right.

2. The long-run growth of the economy is a product of growth in labor, capital, and natural resources, and advances in technology.

3. The size of the labor force is determined by the working-age population and the percentage of that population in the labor force.

4. The post–World War II baby boom has created a bulge in the age distribution of the U.S. population.

5. Growth in capital stock is tied to current and future saving.

6. Abundant natural resources contribute to economic growth but are not essential to that growth.

7. Technology is the way that resources are combined to produce output.

8. Hampered by low levels of education and limited financial resources, developing countries lag behind the industrial nations in developing and implementing new technology.

3. PRODUCTIVITY

What is productivity?

total factor productivity (TFP):
the ratio of the economy's output to its stock of labor and capital

In the last section we described how output depends on resource inputs like labor and capital. One way to assess the contribution a resource makes to output is its productivity. *Productivity* is the ratio of output produced to the amount of input. We could measure the productivity of a single resource— say labor or capital—or the overall productivity of all resources. **Total factor productivity (TFP)** is the term economists use to describe the overall productivity of an economy. It is the ratio of the economy's output to its stock of labor and capital.

3.a. Productivity and Economic Growth

Economic growth depends on both the growth of resources and technological progress. Advances in technology allow resources to be more productive. If the quantity of resources is growing and each resource is more productive, then output grows even faster than the quantity of resources. Economic growth, then, is the sum of the growth rate of total factor productivity and the growth rate of resources:

Economic growth = growth rate of *TFP* + growth rate of resources

The amount that output grows because the labor force is growing depends on how much labor contributes to the production of output. Similarly, the amount that output grows because capital is growing depends on how much capital contributes to the production of output. To relate the growth of labor and capital to the growth of output (we assume no change in natural resources), then, the growth of labor and the growth of capital must be multiplied by their relative contributions to the production of output. The most straightforward way to measure those contributions is to use the share of real GDP received by each resource. For instance, in the United States, labor receives about 70 percent (.70) of real GDP and capital receives about 30 percent (.30). So we can determine the growth of output by using this formula:

$$\%\Delta Y = \%\Delta TFP + .70(\%\Delta L) + .30(\%\Delta K)$$

where

$$\%\Delta = \text{percentage change in}$$
$$Y = \text{real GDP}$$
$$TFP = \text{total factor productivity}$$
$$L = \text{size of the labor force}$$
$$K = \text{capital stock}$$

The equation shows how economic growth depends on changes in productivity ($\%\Delta TFP$) as well as changes in resources ($\%\Delta L$ and $\%\Delta K$). Even if labor (L) and capital stock (K) are constant, technological innovation would generate economic growth through changes in total factor productivity (TFP).

For example, suppose TFP is growing at a rate of 2 percent a year. Then, even with labor and capital stock held constant, the economy grows at a rate of 2 percent a year. If labor and capital stock also grow at a rate of 2 percent a year, output grows by the sum of the growth rates of all three components (TFP, .70 times labor growth, and .30 times the capital stock growth), or 4 percent.

How do we account for differences in growth rates across countries? Because almost all countries have experienced growth in the labor force, percentage increases in labor forces have generally supported economic growth. But growth in the capital stock has been steadier in the industrial countries than in the developing countries, so differences in capital growth rates may explain some of the differences in economic growth across countries. Yet differences in resource growth rates alone cannot explain the major differences we find across countries. In recent years, those differences seem to be related to productivity. In the United States, for example, there is concern that productivity has been growing too slowly. We use the recent history of U.S. productivity growth to illustrate the determinants of total factor productivity and to show how changes in these determinants affect a country's economic growth.

3.b. The U.S. Productivity Slowdown

Why has U.S. productivity changed?

Productivity in the United States became a major topic of discussion in the late 1970s as the growth of total factor productivity fell dramatically. From 1948 to 1965, *TFP* grew at an annual average rate of 2.02 percent. From 1965 to 1973, annual growth slowed to an average of 1.04 percent. And from 1973 to 1987, the growth rate was just .21 percent. If the pre-1965 rate of growth had been maintained, output in the United States would be an estimated 39 percent higher today than it actually is. What happened? What caused this dramatic change in productivity?

Several factors may be at work here. They include a drop in the quality of the U.S. labor force, fewer technological innovations, higher energy prices, and a shift from manufacturing to service industries.

3.b.1. **Labor Quality** Labor productivity is measured as output per hour of labor. Figure 4 shows how the productivity of labor changed in the United States between 1960 and 1993. Although changes in the productivity of labor can stem from technological innovation and changes in the capital stock, we focus here on changes in the quality of labor. These changes may be a product of the level and quality of education in the United States, demographic change, and changing attitudes toward work.

Education level The average level of education in the United States has gone up over time. Table 3 lists three measures of education level. The first, median school years completed, increased from 8.6 years in 1940 to 12.9 years in 1993. In the same period, the percentage of adults with at least a high school education rose from 24.5 to 80.2, and the percentage of those with a college education rose from 4.6 to 21.9. The figures seem to indicate that the level of education is not responsible for the slowdown in U.S. productivity.

Quality of education Some economists argue that it is not the level of education but the quality of education that has declined in the United States. They point to the change in college entrance examination scores to support

---

Figure 4
Percentage Change in Output per Hour of Labor, United States, 1960–1993
Output per labor hour is a measure of productivity. The graph shows the percentage change in productivity. Notice the large fluctuations from one year to the next.
Source: Data taken from *Economic Report of the President* (Washington, D.C., 1995).

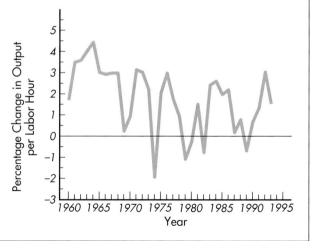

TABLE 3
The Average Level of Education, United States, 1940–1993*

	1940	1950	1960	1970	1980	1990	1993
Median school years completed	8.6	9.3	10.6	12.1	12.5	12.7	12.9
People with at least a high school education (percent)	24.5	34.3	41.1	52.3	66.5	76.9	80.2
People with at least four years of college (percent)	4.6	6.2	7.7	10.7	16.2	21.1	21.9

*People 25 years of age and over.

Source: U.S. Department of Commerce, *Statistical Abstract of the United States, 1994* (Washington, D.C.: U.S. Government Printing Office, 1994), p. 157.

their thinking. For instance, students born in 1945 who took their SATs in 1963 scored an average of 478 on the verbal test and 502 on the math test. Students born in 1962 and tested in 1980 scored an average of 424 on the verbal test and an average of 466 on the math. Figure 5 shows the drop in test scores from the 1960s to the 1990s.

Test scores started to drop in 1967. This decline may have had a significant effect on the productivity of the nation by the early 1970s, as this group of

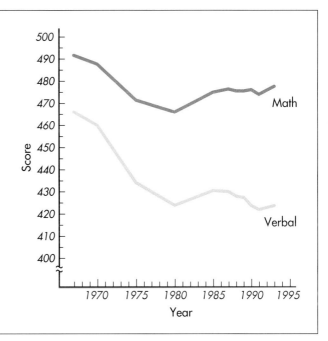

Figure 5
Average Scholastic Aptitude Test (SAT) Scores, 1967–1993
Both the math and verbal scores on the SAT fell between the late 1960s and early 1980s. This trend may have reflected a decline in the average quality of education or of students taking the test. Source: U.S. Department of Commerce, *Statistical Abstract of the United States, 1994* (Washington, D.C.: U.S. Government Printing Office, 1994), p. 174.

Chapter 18 / Economic Growth

students entered the labor market. By the mid-1980s, test scores started to rise again, signaling a turnaround in the quality of education. By the early 1990s, this change is consistent with the increase in the productivity of labor that has occurred.

Demographic change Changes in the size and composition of the population have an impact on the labor market. As the baby boom generation entered the labor force in the late 1960s and early 1970s, a large pool of inexperienced, unskilled workers was created. The average quality of the labor force may have fallen at this time, as reflected in some large drops in output per hour of labor. In the 1980s, the baby boom segment of the labor force had more experience, skills, and education, thus pushing the quality of the labor force up.

Another important demographic change that has affected the quality of the labor force is the participation rates of women. As more and more women entered the labor force in the 1980s, the pool of untrained workers increased, probably reducing the average quality of labor. Over time, as female participation rates stabilize, the average quality of labor should rise as the skills and experience of female workers rise.

Finally, the 1970s and 1980s saw a change in the pattern of U.S. immigration. Although many highly skilled professionals immigrate to the United States as part of the "brain drain" from developing countries, recent immigrants, both legal and illegal, have generally added to the supply of unskilled labor and reduced the average quality of the labor force.

Attitudes toward work Some economists argue that the slowdown in productivity in the United States reflects a loss of traditional values. They assert that education and hard work are not as important to Americans as they once were. As a result, the level of effort in school and on the job has fallen, and so has the quality of labor. One product of this thinking is an interest in Japanese culture. Some observations on Japanese culture are given in the Economic Insight "Culture and Productivity in Japan."

Japan has experienced a dramatic increase in labor productivity since the early 1970s, growing substantially faster than other industrial countries. Many analysts have studied the Japanese economy to understand the source of this growth. One important finding apart from the issue of labor quality is that Japan has a relatively high saving rate, which allows a relatively high rate of growth of capital goods. The popular press in the United States regularly reports on the diligence of Japanese students and the dedication of Japanese workers. Many believe that this effort accounts for the different rates of productivity growth in Japan and the United States. They argue that Americans should rethink their values, focusing on productivity. Unfortunately, things like diligence and dedication are difficult to identify and measure. If in fact a change in attitudes about work has lowered the level of effort U.S. workers are willing to expend, then the quality of labor has fallen.

3.b.2. **Technological Innovation** New technology alters total factor productivity. Innovations increase productivity, so when productivity falls, it is natural to look at technological developments to see whether they are a factor in the change. Like diligence and dedication, the pace of technological innovation is difficult to measure. Expenditures on research and development are

Culture and Productivity in Japan

Japanese culture appears to be more supportive of positive work attitudes than Western cultures are. The degree to which cultural differences contribute to faster productivity growth in Japan is difficult if not impossible to measure. To many observers, however, it seems clear that Japan's social values play an important role in the country's high rate of economic growth.

Japanese workers have a sense of loyalty and duty to their firm and society that is remarkable to Western observers. The Japanese typically consider a job to be a job for life. In addition, cultural traditions encourage people to seek fulfillment by belonging to a group and working toward the success of the group. As a result, labor-management relations are less likely to involve conflict than they are in Western societies. Workers and managers are part of a team that cooperates and works diligently to maximize the sales and profitability of the team. This tendency to put the interests of the group above the interests of the individual has increased productivity in the industrial sector. The typical Japanese worker would face enormous social pressure if he or she asked for a raise. Rather than ask for higher wages, it is more common for workers to accept management's decisions about wages.

Some analysts argue that the selflessness of Japanese workers has its origins in the period from 1600 to the mid-1800s, when the shoguns, or military governors, established a strict social order to preserve their rule. Under the rigid class system they established, status was derived from performing service for one's superior. Workers followed orders from higher authorities without question, and citizens of each region worked for the common good. Many of these attributes can be found in modern Japan. For example, the emphasis on the group, rather than the individual, may account for the fact that Japanese workers and managers typically are paid lower salaries than their Western counterparts. Because salaries are lower, Japanese firms are able to reinvest a larger share of their revenues, to further improve productivity.

The values that exist in Japanese society are not uniquely Japanese. It is the dominance of these values that sets the Japanese apart. Over time, as the country grows wealthier, Japanese attitudes toward work may move closer to those in Western countries. If they do, the quality of labor in Japan is likely to fall.

Sources: Stephen D. Cohen, *Uneasy Partnership* (Cambridge, Mass.: Ballinger, 1985); Kanji Haitani, *The Japanese Economic System* (Lexington, Mass.: Lexington Books, 1976); and Urban C. Lehner, "Japanese May Be Rich, But Are They Satisfied with Quality of Life?" *The Wall Street Journal,* Jan. 9, 1990, p. A1.

related to the discovery of new knowledge, but actual changes in technology do not proceed as evenly as those expenditures. We expect a long lag between funding and operating a laboratory and the discovery of useful technology. Still, a decline in spending on research and development may indicate less of a commitment to increasing productivity.

Figure 6 shows how real expenditures on research and development have changed in the United States over recent decades. Notice that these expenditures grew at a relatively rapid rate in the early 1960s and 1980s, but grew at a relatively slow rate (they actually fell in five separate years) in the late 1960s, early 1970s, late 1980s, and early 1990s. The period of falling expenditures in the 1960s and 1970s may have been a contributing factor in the U.S. productivity slump.

patent:
a legal document that gives an inventor the legal rights to an invention

Some economists look at the record of new patents as an indicator of technological progress. A **paten**t is a document issued by the government that gives an inventor the legal right to develop and profit from an invention.

    457

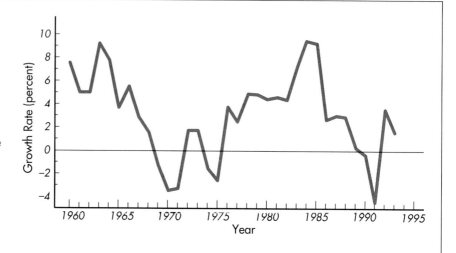

Figure 6
Annual Percentage Change in Real Spending on Research and Development, United States, 1960–1993
Expenditures on research and development reflect a country's commitment to developing new technology. Expenditures in the United States grew rapidly in the early 1960s and 1980s but grew slowly (and in some years fell) in the late 1960s and 1970s.
Source: U.S. Department of Commerce, *Statistical Abstract of the United States, 1994* (Washington, D.C.: U.S. Government Printing Office, 1994), p. 607.

Individuals and business firms seek patents to protect themselves from those who would copy their innovations.

The number of patents issued to U.S. firms serves as a crude measure of technological innovation. Figure 7 shows that the number of patents issued peaked in 1971 and then began to fall. This pattern is consistent with the idea that a decline in technological innovation was responsible for the decline in

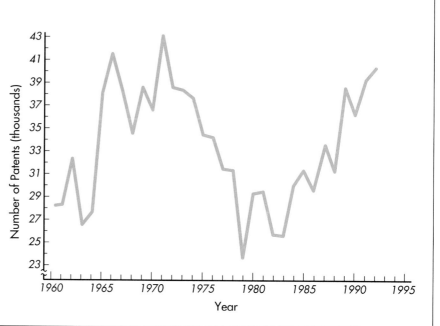

Figure 7
Number of Patents Issued to U.S. Corporations, 1960–1992
The number of patents issued is a rough indicator of technological progress. From a peak in 1971, the number of patents issued in the United States fell. Some economists argue that this decline in patent activity signals a slower rate of technological progress that could be related to the slowdown in U.S. productivity. If so, then the recent resurgence in patents granted could signal greater productivity in the future.
Source: Data are from U.S. Department of Commerce, *Statistical Abstract of the United States, 1989, 1994* (Washington, D.C.: U.S. Government Printing Office, 1989, p. 530, and 1994, p. 552).

U.S. productivity in the 1970s. The recent resurgence in patent activity may indicate increases in productivity in years to come.

3.b.3. **Other Factors**   We have seen how changing labor quality and technological innovation are related to changes in productivity. Other reasons have been offered to explain the decline in the growth of U.S. productivity in the 1970s. We examine two of them: the increased cost of energy and the shift from a manufacturing- to a service-oriented economy.

Energy prices   OPEC succeeded in raising the price of oil substantially in 1973, 1974, and 1979. The timing of the dramatic increase in oil prices coincided with the drop in productivity growth in the United States. A look back at Figure 4 shows that output per labor hour actually fell in 1974 and 1979. Higher energy prices due to restricted oil output should directly decrease aggregate supply because energy is an important input across industries. As the price of energy increases, the costs of production rise and aggregate supply decreases.

Higher energy prices can affect productivity through their impact on the capital stock. As energy prices go up, energy-inefficient capital goods become obsolete. Like any other decline in the value of the capital stock, this change reduces economic growth. Standard measures of capital stock do not account for energy obsolescence, so they suggest that total factor productivity fell in the 1970s. However, if the stock of usable capital actually did go down, it was the growth rate of capital, not TFP, that fell.

Manufacturing versus services   The United States economy has, in recent decades, seen a shift away from manufacturing toward services. Some economists believe that productivity grows more slowly in service industries than

Productivity changes in service industries are difficult to measure. For instance, this café in Paris offers food service to the public. How should we measure the productivity of the café? If the number of meals served per waiter increased, does this mean that productivity has increased? What if the café changed its menu from crepes to multi-course fine dining and the number of meals served per waiter dropped dramatically? This would not signal a drop in productivity but a change in the kind of service provided. Economists still debate the appropriate measurement of productivity in services.

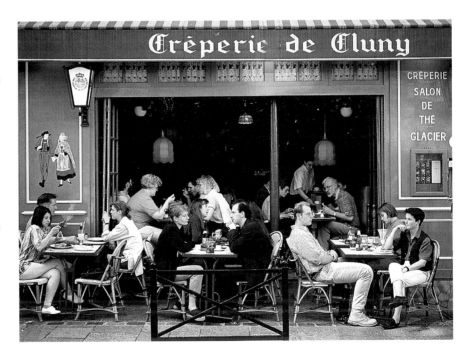

in manufacturing, because of the less capital-intensive nature of providing services. Therefore, the movement into services reduces the overall growth rate of the economy.

Although a greater emphasis on service industries may explain a drop in productivity, we must be careful with this kind of generalization. In fact, labor productivity in communications and some other service industries has grown faster than in manufacturing industries. Also, it is more difficult to measure changes in the quality of services than changes in the quality of goods. If prices in an industry rise with no change in the quantity of output, it makes sense to conclude that the real level of output in the industry has fallen. However, if prices have gone up because the quality of the service has increased, then output actually has changed. Suppose a hotel remodels its rooms. In effect it is improving the quality of its service. Increased prices here would reflect this change in output.

Service industries—fast-food restaurants, airlines, hotels, banks—are not all alike. One way service firms compete is on the basis of the quality of service they provide. Because productivity is measured by the amount of output per unit of input, if we don't adjust for quality changes, we may underestimate the amount of output and so underestimate the productivity of the industry. The issue of productivity measurement in the services industries is an important topic of discussion among economists today.

3.c. Growth and Development

Economic growth depends on the growth of productivity and resources. Productivity grows unevenly, and its rate of growth is reflected in economic growth. Although the labor force seems to grow faster in developing countries than in industrial countries, lower rates of saving have limited the growth of the capital stock in developing countries. Without capital, workers cannot be very productive. This means that the relatively high rate of growth in the labor force in the developing world does not translate into a high rate of economic growth. We use this information on economic growth in Chapter 19 to explain and analyze the strategies used by developing countries to stimulate output and increase standards of living.

RECAP

1. Productivity is the ratio of output produced to the amount of input.

2. Total factor productivity is the nation's real GDP (output) divided by its stock of labor and capital.

3. Economic growth is the sum of the growth of total factor productivity and the growth rate of resources (labor and capital).

4. The decline in U.S. productivity growth may be a product of a drop in the quality of the labor force, fewer technological innovations, higher energy prices, and a shift from manufacturing to service industries.

SUMMARY

▲▼ What is economic growth?

1. Economic growth is an increase in real GDP. §1.a

2. Economic growth is compounded over time. §1.a.1

3. Per capita real GDP is real GDP divided by the population. §1.b

4. The definitions of economic growth are misleading because they do not indicate anything about the distribution of income or the quality of life. §1.c

▲▼ How are economic growth rates determined?

5. The growth of the economy is tied to the growth of productive resources and technological advances. §2

6. Because their populations tend to grow more rapidly, developing countries typically experience faster growth in the labor force than do industrial countries. §2.a

7. The inability to save limits the growth of capital stock in developing countries. §2.b

8. Abundant natural resources are not necessary for rapid economic growth. §2.c

9. Technology defines the ways in which resources can be combined to produce goods and services. §2.d

▲▼ What is productivity?

10. Productivity is the ratio of output produced to the amount of input. §3

11. Total factor productivity is the overall productivity of an economy. §3

12. The percentage change in real GDP equals the percentage change in total factor productivity plus the percentage changes in labor and capital multiplied by the share of GDP taken by labor and capital. §3.a

▲▼ Why has U.S. productivity changed?

13. The slowdown in U.S. productivity growth may be a product of a change in the quality of the labor force, fewer technological innovations, higher energy prices, and a shift away from manufacturing to service industries. §3.b

KEY TERMS

economic growth §1.a
rule of 72 §1.a.2
per capita real GDP §1.b

technology §2.d
total factor productivity (TFP) §3
patent §3.b.2

EXERCISES

1. Why is the growth of per capita real GDP a better measure of economic growth than the growth of real GDP?

2. What is the level of output after four years if initial output equals $1,000 and the economy grows at a rate of 10 percent a year?

3. Use the data in the following table to determine the average annual growth rate for each country in terms of real GDP growth and per capita real GDP growth (real GDP is in millions of units of domestic currency, and population is in millions of people). Which country grew at the fastest rate?

Country (currency)	1990 Real GDP	Population	1992 Real GDP	Population
Ghana (cedi)	2,031,700	15.02	2,222,900	15.96
Nigeria (naira)	260,637	96.15	281,089	102.13
Panama (balboa)	5,009	2.42	5,955	2.51

4. Suppose labor's share of GDP is 70 percent and capital's is 30 percent, real GDP is growing at a rate of 4 percent a year, the labor force is growing at 2 percent, and the capital stock is growing at 3 percent. What is the growth rate of total factor productivity?

5. Suppose labor's share of GDP is 70 percent and capital's is 30 percent, total factor productivity is growing at an annual rate of 2 percent, the labor force is growing at a rate of 1 percent, and the capital stock is growing at a rate of 3 percent. What is the annual growth rate of real GDP?

6. Discuss the possible reasons for the slowdown in U.S. productivity growth and relate each reason to the equation for economic growth. (Does the growth of *TFP* or resources change?)

7. How did the post–World War II baby boom affect the growth of the U.S. labor force? What effect is this baby boom likely to have on the future U.S. labor force?

8. How do developing and industrial countries differ in their use of technological change, labor, capital, and natural resources to produce economic growth? Why do these differences exist?

9. How would an aging population affect economic growth?

10. If real GDP for Spain is 50,000 billion pesetas at the end of 1996 and 52,000 billion pesetas at the end of 1997, what is the annual rate of growth of the Spanish economy?

11. If Kenya's economy grows at a rate of 4 percent during 1998 and real GDP at the beginning of the year is 170,000 shillings, then what is real GDP at the end of the year?

12. Suppose a country has a real GDP equal to $1 billion today. If this economy grows at a rate of 10 percent a year, what will be the value of real GDP after 5 years?

13. Is the following statement true or false? Explain your answer. "Abundant natural resources are a necessary condition for economic growth."

14. What is the difference between total factor productivity and the productivity of labor? Why do you suppose that people often measure a nation's productivity using labor productivity only?

15. How would each of the following affect productivity in the United States?

a. The quality of education increases in high schools.

b. The number of patents issued falls significantly.

c. A cutback in oil production by oil-exporting nations raises oil prices.

d. A large number of unskilled immigrant laborers moves into the country.

COOPERATIVE LEARNING EXERCISE

Divide the class into groups of three or four students. Each group must solve the following problems and have a spokesperson prepared to explain the solution to the rest of the class. A different group will be called upon to explain the answer to each question.*

Part IV/Economic Growth and Development

1. What is the growth rate for an economy where there is no growth of resources but *TFP* grows at a rate of 1 percent per year?

2. What is the growth rate for an economy where *TFP* is constant, labor grows at a rate of 1 percent per year, capital grows at a rate of 2 percent per year, and labor's share of output equals 60 percent, while capital's share equals 40 percent?

3. What is the growth rate for an economy where *TFP* grows at a rate of 3 percent per year, the size of the labor force is unchanged, the capital stock grows at a rate of 2 percent per year, and labor and capital each account for 50 percent of output?

Services: A Future of Low Productivity Growth?

. . . "Is America turning into a nation of hamburger flippers?" The cause for concern is a potentially disturbing pair of trends. First, employment in the United States increasingly has shifted away from manufacturing toward services. In 1963, manufacturing accounted for 30 percent of all jobs, but in 1991 that share had fallen to less than 17 percent.

Second, "real" productivity increases (that is, adjusted for inflation) have been significantly lower in services than in manufacturing. Between 1963 and 1986, real output per worker in manufacturing rose at an annual rate of 2.6 percent, while real output per worker in the services sector rose by only 0.2 percent. Taken together, these trends suggest dire consequences: a sector with negligible productivity gains is rapidly becoming the most important source of new jobs, while the more productive manufacturing sector is losing employment. The inference many observers draw is that America faces stagnation, with most of its labor force engaged in employment that exhibits little productivity growth, and hence, provides little increase in its standard of living.

. . . It appears that the fundamental data on which these dire predictions are made may be misleading. Concern about lack of productivity growth in the service sector emerges from the data released by the U.S. Department of Commerce's Bureau of Economic Analysis (BEA). . . . The difficulty facing BEA in determining changes in real output per worker is daunting. In many cases, output is not directly priced, and often it is difficult or impossible to measure the quantity of the output. . . . Adding to the complexity is the problem of quality changes. With the exception of a few agricultural products, nearly all products change over time, with most embedding improved features. . . .

BEA faces the same conceptual problems in services that it does in manufacturing, but fewer data typically are available for services. Quantity indexes usually are not available—in fact, there often is no physical "good" to count—and prices also are not observed directly. To derive "real output," therefore . . . measures of inputs are used—often the number of employees—to proxy for changes in the level of production.

While this approach is perhaps the only available strategy in some industries, the effects on productivity measurements are predictably biased. When real output is calculated for industries using labor quantities as an important measure of output, then *by definition* the industry will show no productivity growth. Moreover, price indexes based on input costs ignore potential quality improvements—such as higher skilled labor and better capital—and hence, may attribute quality improvements inaccurately to price increases rather than output increases.

. . . One of the central conclusions of economic theory is that . . . changes in compensation should be related to changes in labor's marginal productivity. . . . Compensation growth per worker in an industry, therefore, should be related to the growth in the productivity of its labor force. . . . In contrast to the BEA real output data, compensation data indicate higher gains in services than in manufacturing. Service industry compensation per worker rose at a 1.5 percent annual rate, compared to 1.1 percent for manufacturing (over the 1963–86 period).

. . . While it is clear that compensation growth is not a perfect measure of productivity growth, trends in compensation raise an important question: if productivity growth is so low in some sectors, why are employers willing to pay the workers so much? If market participants are relatively rational, the payment workers receive may be a better indicator of the market's evaluation of their productivity than is the traditional BEA measure. . . .

Source: "Services: A Future of Low Productivity Growth?" Ronald H. Schmidt, *FRBSF Weekly Letter*, Feb. 14, 1992. Used by permission of the Federal Reserve Bank of San Francisco.

Commentary

The accompanying figure illustrates how services (retail and wholesale sales, transportation, communications, finance, insurance, real estate, and health care) have grown as a fraction of GDP since 1960 in the United States. As the figure shows, the shift from the production of goods to services is not new but has continued over recent decades. If services are becoming an increasingly important sector of the U.S. economy, and measurement of productivity in the services sector is subject to large error, it may be that actual productivity in the United States has grown faster than the BEA's figures indicate. In banking, where output is the service provided by tellers and loan officers, productivity has been measured by counting number of employees (on the theory that the busier the bank, the more employees needed). Banking is not alone in this. Other service industries have also estimated output by measuring the quantity of an input. As stated in the article, however, if number of employees is used to measure output of an industry, then productivity will not grow *by definition*. If measured output rises right along with employment, then output per worker cannot change.

The compensation data offer a useful alternative to the measures of output constructed by the BEA. Although wages may rise for reasons other than productivity changes, the large differences between the compensation changes and BEA productivity

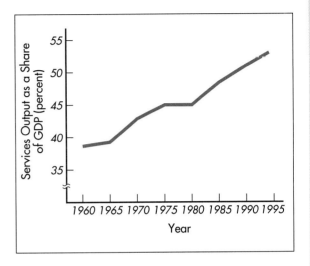

measures should cause us to use great caution with the BEA estimates of productivity. The problem, of course, is that output in the services industry is essentially unmeasurable. As a result, we must resort to looking at related data to try to infer productivity changes. All of this should create a healthy skepticism regarding official productivity figures as services grow in importance. We should also expect to see further refinement in the way productivity is measured in service industries.

19

Development Economics

FUNDAMENTAL QUESTIONS

1. How is poverty measured?
2. Why are some countries poorer than others?
3. What strategies can a nation use to increase its economic growth?
4. How are savings in one nation used to speed development in other nations?

T here is an enormous difference between the standards of living in the poorest and richest countries in the world. In Mozambique the average life expectancy at birth is forty-seven years, almost thirty years less than in the United States. In Burma only an estimated 25 percent of the population has access to safe water. In Burundi only 23 percent of urban houses have electricity. And in Chad only 29 percent of students reach the sixth grade.

The plight of developing countries is our focus in this chapter. We begin by discussing the extent of poverty and how it is measured across countries. Then we turn to the reasons why developing countries are poor and look at strategies for stimulating growth and development. The reasons for poverty are many, and the remedies often are rooted more in politics than economics. Still, economics has much to say about how to improve the living standards of the world's poorest citizens.

PREVIEW

I. THE DEVELOPING WORLD

Three-fourths of the world's population lives in developing countries. These countries are often called *less developed countries (LDCs)* or *Third World countries.* "First World" countries are the industrialized nations of Western Europe and North America, along with Australia, Japan, and New Zealand. Second World countries are (or were) the communist countries of Eastern Europe and the former Soviet Union. The Third World is made up of noncommunist developing countries, although people commonly use the term to refer to all developing countries.

The common link among developing countries is low per capita GNP or GDP, which implies a relatively low standard of living for the typical citizen. Otherwise the LDCs are a diverse group—their cultures, politics, even their geography varying enormously. Although we have used GDP throughout the text as the popular measure of a nation's output, in this chapter we frequently refer to GNP, as this is the measure used by the World Bank in classifying countries in terms of stage of development.

The developing countries are located primarily in South and East Asia, Africa, the Middle East, and Latin America (Figure 1). The total population of developing countries is over 4 billion people. Of this population, 27 percent live in China and 20 percent live in India. The next largest concentration of people is in Indonesia (4 percent), followed by Brazil, Bangladesh,

Figure 1
The World by Stage of Development
This map of the world is colored to show each country's income level. For example, all low-income economies (those with a per capita GNP of $675 or less in 1992) are colored gold. Source: *World Development Report, 1994,* The World Bank. Copyright© 1994 The International Bank for Reconstruction and Development/The World Bank. Reprinted by permission of Oxford University Press, Inc.

Low-income economies ☐
Middle-income economies ▨
High-income economies ▨
Countries where data are not available ▨

Nigeria, and Pakistan. Except for Latin America, where 40 percent of the population lives in cities, most Third World citizens live in rural areas and are largely dependent on agriculture.

I.a. **Measuring Poverty**

How is poverty measured?

Poverty typically is defined in absolute terms.

Poverty is not easy to measure. Typically poverty is defined in an *absolute* sense: a family is poor if its income falls below a certain level. For example, the poverty level for a family of four in the United States in 1993 was an income of $14,763. The government sets the poverty level, basing it on the estimated cost of feeding a family a minimally adequate amount of food. Once the cost of an adequate diet is estimated, it is multiplied by 3 (the assumption is that one-third of income is spent on food) to determine the poverty level income. The World Bank uses per capita GNP of less than $675 as its criterion of a low-income country. The countries in gold in Figure 1 meet this absolute definition of poverty.

Poverty is also a *relative* concept. Family income in relation to other incomes in the country or region is important in determining whether or not a family feels poor. The poverty level in the United States would represent a substantial increase in the living standard of most of the people in the world. Yet a poor family in the United States does not feel less poor because it has more money than the poor in other countries. In a nation where the median income of all families was almost $39,300 in 1993, a family with an income of $14,763 clearly is disadvantaged.

Because poverty is also a relative concept, using a particular level of income to distinguish the poor from the not poor is often controversial. Besides the obvious problem of where to draw the poverty line, there is the more difficult problem of comparing poverty across countries with different currencies, customs, and living arrangements. Also, data are often limited and difficult to obtain because many of the poor in developing countries live in isolated areas. This makes it difficult to draw a comprehensive picture of the typical poor household in the Third World.

I.b. Basic Human Needs

Basic human needs are a minimal level of caloric intake, health care, clothing, and shelter.

Some economists and other social scientists, recognizing the limitations of an absolute definition of poverty (like the per capita GNP measure most commonly used), suggest using indicators of how basic human needs are being met. Although they disagree on an exact definition of *basic human needs*, the general idea is to set minimal levels of caloric intake, health care, clothing, and shelter.

Another alternative to per capita GNP is a physical *quality-of-life index* to evaluate living standards. One approach uses life expectancy, infant mortality, and literacy as indicators—a very narrow definition that ignores elements like justice, personal freedom, environmental quality, and employment opportunities. Nonetheless, these three indicators are, at least in theory, measures of social progress that allow meaningful comparisons across countries whatever their social or political orientation.

A quality-of-life index assigns a value to each indicator in each country according to where it ranks among all countries. A value of zero indicates that a country has the worst performance in one of the indicators; a value of 100 indicates that the country has the best performance in one of the indicators. The values assigned to each country for each indicator are then averaged to arrive at the national quality-of-life index.

Table 1 lists per capita GNP and the indicators of basic human needs for selected countries. The table shows the actual data for the indicators along with the overall index value for each country. The countries are listed by per capita GNP, beginning with the smallest. Generally there is a strong positive relationship between per capita GNP and the quality-of-life index. But there are cases where higher per capita GNP does not mean higher quality of life.

TABLE 1

Quality-of-Life Measures, Selected Countries

Country	Per Capita GNP*	Life Expectancy at Birth (years)	Infant Mortality†	Literacy Rate ‡	Quality Index
Ethiopia	110	49	122	50%	3
Bangladesh	220	55	91	37	8
India	310	61	79	50	20
China	470	69	31	80	48
Philippines	770	65	40	90	48
El Salvador	1,170	66	40	75	40
Turkey	1,980	67	54	82	48
Mexico	3,470	70	35	89	63
Greece	7,290	77	8	94	88
United States	23,240	77	9	99	95

*1992 data measured in terms of U.S. dollars.

†The number of infants who die per 1,000 live births.

‡Percentage of the adult population that is literate.

Data sources: World Bank, *World Development Report, 1994* (Washington, D.C., 1994), various pages, and the *United Nations Human Development Report, 1994* (New York, 1994), various pages.

For instance, El Salvador and Turkey both have a higher per capita GNP than China or the Philippines, but the quality-of-life index is higher in China and the Philippines than it is in El Salvador and is equal to that of Turkey. Remember the limitations of per capita output: it is not a measure of everyone's standard of living in a particular country. However, as the table shows, it is a fairly reliable indicator of differences across countries in living standards. Ethiopia has the lowest per capita GNP and is clearly one of the world's poorest nations. Usually as per capita GNP increases, living standards increase as well.

Per capita GNP and quality-of-life indexes are not the only measures used to determine a country's level of economic development—we could consider the number of households with running water, televisions, or any other good that varies with living standards. Recognizing that there is no perfect measure of economic development, economists and other social scientists often use several indicators to assess economic progress.

RECAP

1. Usually poverty is defined in an absolute sense, as a specific level of family income or per capita GNP.
2. Within a country or region, poverty is a relative concept.
3. Quality-of-life indexes based on indicators of basic human needs are an alternative to per capita GNP for measuring economic development.

2. OBSTACLES TO GROWTH

Why are some countries poorer than others?

Every country is unique. Each nation's history, both political and cultural, helps economists understand why poor nations have not developed and what policies offer the best hope for their development. Generally the factors that impede development are political or social. The political factors include a lack of administrative skills, instability, and the ability of special interest groups to block changes in economic policy. The social obstacles include a lack of entrepreneurs and rapid population growth.

2.a. Political Obstacles

2.a.1. Lack of Administrative Skills Government support is essential to economic development. Whether support means allowing private enterprise to flourish and develop or actively managing the allocation of resources, a poorly organized or corrupt government can present an obstacle to economic growth. Some developing countries have suffered from well-meaning but inept government management. This is most obvious in countries with a long history of colonialization. For example, when Zaire won independence from Belgium, few of its native citizens were college educated. Moreover, Belgians had run most of the important government offices. Independence brought a large group of inexperienced and unskilled workers to important positions of power. And at first there was a period of "learning by doing."

2.a.2. Political Instability and Risk One of the most important functions a government performs in stimulating economic growth is providing a political environment that encourages saving and investment. People do not want to do business in an economy weakened by wars, demonstrations, or uncertainty. For instance, since becoming an independent nation in 1825, Bolivia has had more than 150 changes in government. This kind of instability forces citizens to take a short-run view of the economy. Long-term planning is impossible without knowing the attitudes and policies of the government that is going to be in power next year or even next month.

A country must be able to guarantee the rights of private property if it is going to create an environment that encourages private investment.

The key issue here is *property rights*. A country that guarantees the right of private property encourages private investment and development. Where ownership rights may be changed by revolution or political decree, there is little incentive for private investment and development. People do not start new businesses or build new factories if they believe that a change in government or a change in the political will of the current government could result in the confiscation of their property.

expropriation:
the government seizure of assets, typically without adequate compensation to the owners

This confiscation is called **expropriation**. Countries with a history of expropriating foreign-owned property without compensating the owners (paying them its market value) have difficulty encouraging foreign investment. An example is Uganda. In 1973 a successful revolution by Idi Amin was followed by the expropriation of over 500 foreign-owned (mostly British) firms. Foreign and domestic investment in Uganda fell dramatically as a result.

The loss of foreign investment is particularly important in developing countries. In Chapter 18 we pointed out that developing countries suffer from a lack of saving. If domestic residents are not able to save because they are living at or below subsistence level, foreign saving is a crucial source of investment. Without that investment, the economies of developing countries cannot grow.

2.a.3. Good Economics as Bad Politics   Every Third World politician wants to maximize economic growth, all things being equal. But all things are rarely equal. Political pressures may force a government to work toward more immediate objectives than economic growth.

For example, maximizing growth may mean reducing the size of government in order to lower taxes and increase investment. However, in many developing countries, the strongest supporters of the political leaders are those working for the current government. Obviously it's not good political strategy to fire those workers. So the government stays overstaffed and inefficient, and the potential for economic growth falls. The governments in LDCs often subsidize purchases of food and other basic necessities. Reducing government expenditures and moving toward free market pricing of food, energy, and other items make good economic sense. But the citizens who depend on those subsidies are not going to be happy if they stop.

In 1977 the Egyptian government lowered its food subsidies in order to use those funds for development. What happened? There was widespread rioting that ended only when the government reinstituted the subsidies. In 1989, Venezuela lowered government subsidies on public transportation and petroleum products. Public transit fares went up 30 percent, to the equivalent of 7 U.S. cents, and gasoline prices went from 16 cents to 26 cents a gallon. (One official said that the prices were raised "from the cheapest in the world to the cheapest in the world."[1]) The resulting rioting in Caracas led to 50 deaths,

---

[1]See "Venezuela Rumblings: Riots and Debt Crisis," *New York Times,* March 2, 1989, p. A13.

over 500 injuries, and more than 1,000 arrests. Lowering government expenditures and reducing the role of government in the economy can be politically and physically dangerous.

What we are saying here is that seemingly good economics can make for bad politics. Because some group is going to be hurt in the short run by any change in policy aimed at increasing growth, there always is opposition to change. Often the continued rule of the existing regime depends on not alienating a certain group. Only a government stabilized by military force (a dictatorship), popular support (a democracy), or party support (a communist or socialist country) has the power to implement needed economic change. A government that lacks this power is handicapped by political constraints in its efforts to stimulate economic growth.

2.b. **Social Obstacles**

Cultural traditions and attitudes can work against economic development. In traditional societies, children follow in their parents' footsteps. If your father is a carpenter, there is a good chance that you will be a carpenter. Moreover, production is carried out in the same way generation after generation. For an economy to grow, it must be willing to change.

2.b.1. Lack of Entrepreneurs   A society that answers the questions What to produce? How to produce? and For whom to produce? by doing things as they were done by the previous generation lacks a key ingredient for economic growth: entrepreneurs. Entrepreneurs are risk-takers; they bring innovation and new technology into use. Understanding why some societies are better at producing entrepreneurs than others may help explain why some nations have remained poor while others have grown rapidly.

Entrepreneurs are more likely to develop among minority groups that have been blocked from traditional high-paying jobs.

One theory is that entrepreneurs often come from *blocked minorities*. Some individuals in the traditional society are blocked from holding prestigious jobs or political office because of discrimination. This discrimination can be based on race, religion, or immigrant status. Because discrimination keeps them from the best traditional occupations, these minority groups can achieve wealth and status only through entrepreneurship. The Chinese in Southeast Asia, the Jews in Europe, and the Indians in Africa were all blocked minorities, forced to turn to entrepreneurship to advance themselves.

Immigrants provide a pool of entrepreneurs who have skills and knowledge that often are lacking in the developing country.

In developing countries, entrepreneurship tends to be concentrated among immigrants, who have skills and experience that do not exist in poor countries. Many leaders of industry in Latin America, for example, are Italian, German, Arab, or Basque immigrants or the descendants of immigrants; they are not part of the dominant Spanish or native Indian population. The success of these immigrants is less a product of their being discriminated against than of their expertise in commerce. They know the foreign suppliers of goods. They have business skills that are lacking in developing regions. And they have the traditions—among them, the work ethic—and training instilled in their home country.

Motivation also plays a role in the level of entrepreneurship that exists in developing countries. In some societies, traditional values may be an obstacle to development because they do not encourage high achievement. A good example is provided in the Economic Insight "Development and Cultural Values in Sub-Saharan Africa." Societies in which the culture supports individual achievement produce more entrepreneurs. It is difficult to identify the specific values in a society that account for a lack of motivation. In the past,

Development and Cultural Values in Sub-Saharan Africa

. . . Traditional development projects have erred by focusing unduly on technical prescriptions, ignoring the need to adapt development assistance to the local cultural environment. . . . The lack of success of most traditional approaches to institutional and public sector development in Africa clearly shows the limitations of the technological approach. . . . Western values are not always congruent with traditional incentives and behavioral patterns prevalent in most African countries. Self-reliance and self-interest tend to take a back seat to ethnicity and group loyalty. . . . Generally, the interest of the local and ethnic communities takes precedence over whatever the government may declare as national goals.

Typically, a higher value is placed on interpersonal relations and the timely execution of certain social and religious or mystic activities than on individual achievements. . . . The value of economic acts is measured in terms of their capacity to reinforce the bonds of the group.

Attitudes toward savings and investment

In Sub-Saharan Africa, it might well be said that, in general, the only riches are those shared with—and socially visible to—the community.

There is a social and mystical need for what westerners may call "wastefulness." . . . It is not uncommon for poor, malnourished farmers to give away vast quantities of foods on the occasion of marriages, circumcisions, or burials. . . . Excess income is distributed first to close members of the extended family, then to the neighbors, and then to the ethnic tribe. . . . Economic success in itself does not lead to upward social mobility. In fact, if achieved outside of the group, it may even lead to social ostracism. From the development perspective, the problem is that this tendency—attaching little value to the self-control needed for saving—runs counter to the prerequisites for promoting private investment and African entrepreneurship.

Attitude toward labor

The tendency to value group solidarity and socializing has generally led Africans to attach a high value to leisure and the attendant ability to engage in rituals, ceremonies, and social activities. . . . The high value Africans generally attach to leisure has often been misconstrued by outsiders as "laziness." Simply put, in Africa, these activities serve as a means of reinforcing social bonds, which are the foundation of its society. As a result, farmers tend to adopt innovations

only when the expected return on additional labor, measured in both social and economic terms, is likely to be substantially higher than what they are already receiving from the prevailing combination of leisure and productive activities.

A new vision of management

The reconciliation of these traditional values with the imperatives of economic efficiency and accumulation . . . is, therefore, crucial to economic development. . . . Other societies have successfully modernized without renouncing local customs, culture, or traditional values. Japan, the Republic of Korea, and Taiwan Province of China are examples of economies that have achieved high levels of modern production and advanced technology while maintaining their unique national traits. Their experience proves that acculturation is not a prerequisite to development, that whatever direction the development process may take, its success and sustainability will depend on how well it takes account of the needs and culture of the beneficiaries.

Source: Excerpted from "Development and Cultural Values in Sub-Saharan Africa," Mamadou Dia, *Finance and Development*, Dec. 1991, pp. 10–13. Reprinted with permission.

researchers have pointed to factors that are not always valid across different societies. For instance, at one time many argued that the Protestant work ethic was responsible for the large number of entrepreneurs in the industrial world. According to this argument, some religions are more supportive of the accumulation of wealth than others. Today this argument is difficult to make because we find economic development in nations with vastly different cultures and religions.

2.b.2. **Rapid Population Growth** Remember that per capita real GNP is real GNP divided by the population. Although labor is a factor of production, and labor force growth may increase output, when population rises faster than GNP, the standard of living of the average citizen does not improve. One very real problem for many developing countries is the growth of their population. With the exception of China (where population growth is controlled), population growth in the developing countries is proceeding at a pace that will double the Third World population every 28 years. In large part the rate at which the population of the Third World is growing is a product of lower death rates. Death rates have fallen, but birthrates have not.

Figure 2 shows why birthrates are different in the typical developed country and the typical developing country. The chart illustrates the average age of women at marriage, and at birth of children. There are some fundamental differences here. First, women marry at a much younger age in developing countries, in their late teens versus their early twenties in developed countries. The World Fertility Study found that women in Bangladesh marry at the youngest average age, sixteen years. Other things being equal, the younger women marry, the more children they have. Second, the time between the birth of one child and the conception of another is typically shorter in developing countries. Third, the average family in a developed country is likely to have no more than two children; the average family in a developing country is likely to have seven children.

Social scientists do not all agree on the effects of population growth on development. A growing labor force can serve as an important factor in increasing growth. But those who believe that population growth has a negative effect cite three reasons:

Capital shallowing Rapid population growth may reduce the amount of capital per worker, lowering the productivity of labor.

Age dependency Rapid population growth produces a large number of dependent children, whose consumption requirements lower the ability of the economy to save.

Investment diversion Rapid population growth shifts government expenditures from the country's infrastructure (roads, communication systems) to education and health care.

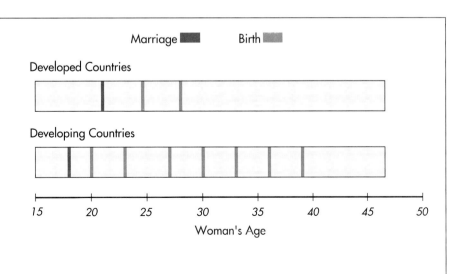

Figure 2
Average Timing of Marriage and Births in Developed and Developing Countries
Women in developing countries tend to marry younger and have more children at a faster rate than do women in developed countries.
Source: From *World Development Report 1984* by The World Bank. Copyright © 1984 by The International Bank for Reconstruction and Development/The World Bank. Reprinted by permission of Oxford University Press, Inc.

Population growth may have had a negative effect on development in many countries, but the magnitude of the effect is difficult to assess. And in some cases, population growth probably has stimulated development. For instance, the fact that children consume goods and services and thus lower the ability of a nation to save ignores the fact that the children grow up and become productive adults. Furthermore, any investment diversion from infrastructure to education and health care is not necessarily a loss, as education and health care will build up the productivity of the labor force. The harmful effect of population growth should be most pronounced in countries where usable land and water are relatively scarce. Although generalizations about acceptable levels of population growth do not fit all circumstances, the World Bank has stated that population growth rates above 2 percent a year act as a brake on economic development.

GNP can grow steadily year after year, but if the population grows at a faster rate, the standard of living of the average individual falls. The simple answer to reducing population growth seems to be education: programs that teach methods of birth control and family planning. But reducing birthrates is not simply a matter of education. People have to choose to limit the size of their families. It must be socially acceptable and economically advantageous for families to use birth control, and for many families it is neither.

Remember that what is good for society as a whole may not be good for the individual. Children are a source of labor in rural families and a support for parents in their old age. How many children are enough? That depends on the expected infant mortality rate. Although infant mortality rates in developing countries have fallen in recent years, they are still quite high relative to the developed countries. Families still tend to follow tradition, to keep having lots of children.

RECAP

1. In some countries, especially those that have been colonies, economic growth has been slow because government officials lack necessary skills.
2. Countries that are unable to protect the rights of private property have difficulty attracting investors.
3. Expropriation is the seizure by government of assets without adequate compensation.
4. Often government officials know the right economic policies to follow but are constrained by political considerations from implementing those policies.
5. Immigrants are often the entrepreneurs in developing countries.
6. Rapid population growth may slow development because of the effects of capital shallowing, age dependency, and investment diversion.

What strategies can a nation use to increase its economic growth?

3. DEVELOPMENT STRATEGIES

Different countries follow different strategies to stimulate economic development. There are two basic types of development strategies: inward oriented and outward oriented.

3.a. Inward-Oriented Strategies

primary product:
a product in the first stage of production, which often serves as an input in the production of another product

The typical developing country has a comparative advantage over other countries in the production of certain primary products. Having a comparative advantage means that a country has the lowest opportunity cost of producing a good. (We talked about comparative advantage in Chapter 2.) A **primary product** is a product in the first stage of production, which often serves as input in the production of some other good. Agricultural produce and minerals are examples of primary products. In the absence of a conscious government policy that directs production, we expect countries to concentrate on the production of that thing in which they have a comparative advantage. For example, we expect Cuba to focus on sugar production, Colombia to focus on coffee production, and the Ivory Coast to focus on cocoa production—each country selling its output of its primary product to the rest of the world.

Today many developing countries have shifted their resources away from producing primary products for export. Inward-oriented development strategies focus on production for the domestic market rather than exports of goods and services. For these countries, development means industrialization. The objective of this kind of inward-oriented strategy is **import substitution**, replacing imported manufactured goods with domestic goods.

import substitution:
the substitution of domestically produced manufactured goods for imported manufactured goods

Import-substitution policies dominate the strategies of the developing world. The basic idea is to identify domestic markets that are being supplied in large part by imports. Those markets that require a level of technology available to the domestic economy are candidates for import substitution. Industrialization goes hand in hand with tariffs or quotas on imports that protect the newly developing domestic industry from its more efficient foreign competition. As a result, production and international trade will not occur solely on the basis of comparative advantages but are affected primarily by these countries' import-substitution policy activities.

Because the domestic industry can survive only with protection from foreign competition, import-substitution policies typically raise the price of the domestically produced goods over the imported goods. In addition, quality may not be as good (at least at first) as the quality of the imported goods. Ideally, as the industry grows and becomes more experienced, price and quality become competitive with foreign goods. Once this happens, the import barriers are no longer needed, and the domestic industry may even become an export industry. Unfortunately, the ideal is seldom realized. The Third World is full of inefficient manufacturing companies that are unlikely ever to improve enough to be able to survive without protection from foreign competitors.

3.b. Outward-Oriented Strategies

The inward-oriented strategy of developing domestic industry to supply domestic markets is the most popular development strategy, but it is not the only one. A small group of countries (notably South Korea, Hong Kong, Singapore, and Taiwan) chose to focus on the growth of exports beginning in the 1960s. These countries follow an outward-oriented strategy, utilizing their most abundant resource to produce those products that they can produce better than others. A more detailed description of this strategy is provided in the Economic Insight "Four Asian Tigers."

The abundant resource in these countries is labor, and the goods they produce are labor-intensive products. This kind of outward-oriented policy is called **export substitution**. The countries use labor to produce manufactured goods for export rather than agricultural products for domestic use.

Outward-oriented development strategies are based on efficient, low-cost production. Their success depends on being able to compete effectively with producers in the rest of the world. Here most governments attempt to stimulate exports. This can mean subsidizing domestic producers to produce goods for export rather than for domestic consumption. International competition is often more intense than the competition at home—producers face stiffer price competition, higher quality standards, and greater marketing expertise in the global marketplace. This means domestic producers may have to be induced to compete internationally. Inducements can take the form of government assistance in international marketing, tax reductions, low-interest-rate loans, or cash payments.

Another inducement of sorts is to make domestic sales less attractive. This means implementing policies that are just the opposite of import substitution.

The Hyundai shipyard in Korea is symbolic of the outward-oriented development strategy of Korea, one of the newly industrialized Asian nations. By emphasizing exports of manufactured products rather than producing substitutes for import goods from the industrial countries, Korea has developed rapidly. Korea is Asia's major shipbuilder and has achieved this success in other industries through aggressive competition in international goods markets.

Four Asian Tigers

Four Asian nations—Hong Kong, Singapore, South Korea, and Taiwan—are now called *NICs*, newly industrialized countries. Their new status is a product of outward-oriented development strategies.

In the 1950s and early 1960s, the governments of the four countries followed the import-substitution strategy that was popular in the Third World. They protected domestic markets from foreign competition to stimulate domestic production for domestic consumption. The resulting lack of incentive to produce efficiently ruled out significant domestic production for export. One problem was that domestic producers utilizing foreign inputs faced restrictions on obtaining those inputs, such as bureaucratic delays in obtaining permission to bring them in. The growth of industry was limited by the growth of domestic demand, and because domestic demand was growing slowly, industrial development lagged.

Taiwan was the first to replace an inward-oriented policy with an outward-oriented policy. The other three countries followed closely behind. The results were soon evident: each country experienced rapid growth in exports and domestic national income.

Hong Kong essentially operates a free market economy, with little restriction on business operations. Korea, Singapore, and Taiwan maintain some restrictions on the domestic economy, but operate with another set of rules for exporting firms. Basically production for export occurs in a free market setting, with no taxes or restrictions on imports of the materials needed to manufacture goods for export. The goal is to rapidly increase exports by allowing domestic producers to seek foreign markets for their output.

Along with revisions in regulations for manufacturers, the governments have developed banking and financial institutions that can finance export production and sales. These nations had a history of severely limited sources of loans for industry, so guaranteeing exporters access to credit has given a big boost to export production.

The experience of Hong Kong, Singapore, South Korea, and Taiwan is often held up as a lesson for other developing countries. But it is important to remember that other countries do not share certain key characteristics with the four NICs. For example, in the four Asian nations, wages basically are set by supply and demand; government seldom intervenes in the labor market. Also, the countries are homogeneous in terms of their culture and have had a history of political stability. Finally, the governments have been willing to incur the political and economic costs of moving from an inward-oriented policy to an outward-oriented policy. This kind of shift hurts those who benefit from protection against foreign competition. In many developing countries, special interests would bring down the government if a policy of import substitution was eliminated. Apparently, learning the lesson and being able to use that knowledge are two very different things.

The government reduces or eliminates domestic tariffs that keep domestic price levels above international levels. As profits from domestic sales fall, domestic industry turns to producing goods for export.

3.c. Comparing Strategies

Import-substitution policies are enacted in countries that believe industrialization is the key to economic development. In the 1950s and 1960s economists argued that specializing in the production and export of primary products does not encourage the rapid growth rates developing countries are looking for. This argument—the *deteriorating-terms-of-trade argument*—was based on the assumption that the real value of primary products would fall over time. If the prices of primary products fall in relation to the prices of manufactured products, then countries that export primary products and import manufactured goods find the cost of manufactured goods rising in terms of the primary products required to buy them. The amount of exports that must be exchanged for some quantity of imports is often called the **terms of trade**.

terms of trade:
the amount of exports that must be exchanged for some amount of imports

The deteriorating-terms-of-trade argument in the 1950s and 1960s led policymakers in developing countries to fear that the terms of trade would become increasingly unfavorable. One product of that fear was the choice of an inward-oriented strategy, a focus on domestic industrialization rather than production for export.

At the root of the pessimism about the export of primary products was the belief that technological change would slow the growth of demand for primary products over time. That theory ignored the fact that if the supply of natural resources is fixed, those resources could become more valuable over time, even if demand grows slowly or not at all. And if the real value of primary products does fall over time, it does not necessarily mean that inward-oriented policy is required. Critics of inward-oriented policies argue that nations should exploit their comparative advantage, that resources should be free to move to their highest-valued use. And they argue that market-driven resource allocation is unlikely to occur in an inward-oriented economy where government has imposed restrictions aimed at maximizing the rate of growth of industrial output.

dual economy:
an economy in which two sectors (typically manufacturing and agriculture) show very different levels of development

Other economists believe that developing countries have unique problems that call for active government intervention and regulation of economic activity. These economists often favor inward-oriented strategies. They focus on the structure of developing countries in terms of uneven industrial development. Some countries have modern manufacturing industries paying relatively high wages that operate alongside traditional agricultural industries paying low wages. A single economy with industries at very different levels of development is called a **dual economy**. Some insist that in a dual economy, the markets for goods and resources do not work well. If resources could move freely between industries, then wages would not differ by the huge amounts observed in certain developing countries. Where markets are not functioning well, these economists support active government direction of the economy, believing that resources are unlikely to move freely to their highest-valued use if free markets are allowed.

The World Bank classifies developing countries according to their trade strategy. The countries are assigned to one of four categories: strongly outward oriented, moderately outward oriented, moderately inward oriented, and strongly inward oriented.

Strongly outward oriented Few or no controls on international trade. Any restrictions on imports that could limit exports are offset by export incentives.

Moderately outward oriented Restrictions biased toward import substitution rather than export promotion. Incentives for exports are more than offset by protection against imports, so the net effect is slightly against export promotion.

Moderately inward oriented Relatively high import-substitution restrictions. There may be some incentives for exports, but they are weakened by inward-oriented policies.

Strongly inward oriented Exports are clearly discouraged by controls to isolate and protect the domestic market.

The growth rates of the outward-oriented economies are significantly higher than the growth rates of the inward-oriented economies.[2] The success of the outward-oriented economies is likely to continue in light of a strong increase in saving in those economies. In 1963, domestic saving as a fraction of GDP was only 13 percent in the strongly outward-oriented economies. After more than two decades of economic growth driven by export-promotion policies, the rate of saving in these countries had increased to 31.4 percent of GDP. This high rate of saving increases investment expenditures, which increase the productivity of labor, further stimulating the growth of per capita real GDP.

Why are outward-oriented strategies more successful than inward-oriented strategies? The primary advantage of an outward orientation is the efficient utilization of resources. Import-substitution policies do not allocate resources on the basis of cost minimization. In addition, an outward-oriented strategy allows the economy to grow beyond the scale of the domestic market. Foreign demand creates additional markets for exports, beyond the domestic market.

RECAP

1. Inward-oriented strategies concentrate on building a domestic industrial sector.
2. Outward-oriented strategies utilize a country's comparative advantage in exporting.
3. The deteriorating-terms-of-trade argument has been used to justify import-substitution policies.
4. Evidence indicates that outward-oriented policies have been more successful than inward-oriented policies at generating economic growth.

4. FOREIGN INVESTMENT AND AID

How are savings in one nation used to speed development in other nations?

Developing countries rely on savings in the rest of the world to finance much of their investment needs. Foreign savings may come from industrial countries in many different ways. In this section we describe the ways that savings are transferred from industrial to developing countries and the benefits of foreign investment and aid to developing countries.

4.a. Foreign Savings Flows

Poor countries that are unable to save enough to invest in capital stock must rely on the savings of other countries to help them develop economically. Foreign savings come from private sources as well as official government sources.

---

[2]Nouriel Roubini and Xavier Sala-i-Martin found that the strongly outward-oriented countries had an annual growth rate 2.5 percentage points higher on average than that of the strongly inward-oriented countries. Source: "Trade Promotes Growth," *NBER Digest*, March 1992.

foreign direct investment:
the purchase of a physical operating unit in a foreign country, or more than 10 percent ownership

portfolio investment:
the purchase of securities

commercial bank loan:
a bank loan at market rates of interest, often involving a bank syndicate

trade credit:
the extension of a period of time before an importer must pay for goods or services purchased

Private sources of foreign savings can take the form of direct investment, portfolio investment, commercial bank loans, and trade credit. **Foreign direct investment** is the purchase of a physical operating unit, like a factory, or an ownership position in a foreign country that gives the domestic firm making the investment ownership of more than 10 percent of the foreign firm. This is different from **portfolio investment**, which is the purchase of securities, like stocks and bonds. In the case of direct investment, the foreign investor may actually operate the business. Portfolio investment helps finance a business, but host-country managers operate the firm; foreign investors simply hold pieces of paper that represent a share of the ownership or the debt of the firm. **Commercial bank loans** are loans made at market rates of interest to either foreign governments or business firms. These loans are often made by a *bank syndicate*, a group of several banks, to share the risk associated with lending to a single country. Finally, exporting firms and commercial banks offer **trade credit**, allowing importers a period of time before payment is due on the goods or services purchased. Extension of trade credit usually involves payment in thirty days (or some other term) after the goods are received.

Direct investment and bank lending have changed over time. In 1970, direct investment in developing countries was greater than bank loans. By the late 1970s and early 1980s, however, bank loans far exceeded direct investment. Bank lending gives the borrowing country greater flexibility in deciding how to use funds. Direct investment carries with it an element of foreign control over domestic resources. Nationalist sentiment combined with the fear of exploitation by foreign owners and managers led many developing countries to pass laws restricting direct investment. By the early 1990s, however, as more nations emphasized the development of free markets, direct investment was again growing in importance as a source of funds for developing countries.

4.b. Benefits of Foreign Investment

Not all developing countries discourage foreign direct investment. In fact many countries have benefited from foreign investment. Those benefits fall into three categories: new jobs, new technology, and foreign exchange earnings.

4.b.1. New Jobs
Foreign investment should stimulate growth and create new jobs in developing countries. But the number of new jobs created directly by foreign investment is often limited by the nature of the industries in which foreign investment is allowed.

Usually foreign investment is invited in capital-intensive industries, like chemicals or mineral extraction. Because capital goods are expensive and often require advanced technology to operate, foreign firms can build a capital-intensive industry faster than the developing country. One product of the emphasis on capital-intensive industries is that foreign investment often has little effect on employment in developing countries. A $.5-billion oil refinery may employ just a few hundred workers; yet the creation of these few hundred jobs, along with other expenditures by the refinery, will stimulate domestic income by raising incomes across the economy, through the multiplier effect.

Developing countries have become a global work force that competes with industrial countries for new firms and expansions of existing firms. The photo shows workers at a 3M plant in Bangalore, India, that makes tapes, chemicals, and electrical parts. Increasingly sophisticated production is being carried out in developing countries as firms in industrial nations tap the talent in low-wage nations. This global competition for jobs should lead to a convergence of wages over time as developing countries' wages rise closer to wages in industrial nations.

4.b.2. Technology Transfer In Chapter 18 we said that economic growth depends on the growth of resources and technological change. Most expenditures on research and development are made in the major industrial countries. These are also the countries that develop most of the innovations that make production more efficient. For the Third World country with limited scientific resources, the industrial nations are a critical source of information, technology, and expertise.

The ability of foreign firms to utilize modern technology in a developing country depends in part on having a supply of engineers and technical personnel in the host country. India and Mexico have a fairly large number of technical personnel, which means new technology can be adapted relatively quickly. Other countries, where a large fraction of the population has less than an elementary-level education, must train workers and then keep those workers from migrating to industrial countries, where their salaries are likely to be much higher.

4.b.3. Foreign Exchange Earnings Developing countries expect foreign investment to improve their balance of payments. The assumption is that the multinational firms located inside the developing country increase exports and thus generate greater foreign currency earnings that can be used for imports or for repaying foreign debt. But this scenario does not unfold if the foreign investment is used to produce goods primarily for domestic consumption. In fact, the presence of a foreign firm can create a larger deficit in the balance of payments if the firm sends profits back to its industrial country headquarters from the developing country and the value of those profits exceeds the value of foreign exchange earned by exports.

4.c. Foreign Aid

foreign aid:
gifts or low-cost loans made to developing countries from official sources

Official foreign savings are usually available as either outright gifts or low-interest-rate loans. These funds are called **foreign aid**. Figure 3 shows the foreign aid commitments of the major developed countries and of some oil-exporting developing countries. The figure shows both the U.S. dollar value of the development assistance and the percentage of each nation's GNP devoted to foreign aid. Large countries, like the United States, provide much more funding in terms of the dollar value of aid than do small countries. However, some small countries—for example, the Netherlands and Norway—commit a much larger percentage of their GNP to foreign aid.

Foreign aid itself can take the form of cash grants or transfers of goods or technology, with nothing given in return by the developing country. Often foreign aid is used to reward political allies, particularly when those allies hold a strategic military location. Examples of this politically inspired aid are the former Soviet support of Cuba and U.S. support of Turkey.

bilateral aid:
foreign aid that flows from one country to another

Foreign aid that flows from one country to another is called **bilateral aid**. Governments typically have an agency that coordinates and plans foreign aid programs and expenditures. The U.S. Agency for International Development (USAID) performs these functions in the United States. Most of the time bilateral aid is project oriented, given to fund a specific project (an educational facility, an irrigation project).

Food makes up a substantial portion of bilateral aid. After a bad harvest or a natural disaster (drought in the Sudan, floods in Bangladesh), major food-producing nations help feed the hungry. Egypt and Bangladesh were the leading recipients of food aid during the late 1980s. In the early 1990s, attention shifted to Somalia. The major recipients of food aid change over time, as nature and political events combine to change the pattern of hunger and need in the world.

The economics of food aid illustrates a major problem with many kinds of charity. Aid is intended to help those who need it without interfering with domestic production. But when food flows into a developing country, food prices tend to fall, pushing farm income down and discouraging local production. Ideally food aid should go to the very poor, who are less likely to have the income necessary to purchase domestic production anyway.

Foreign aid does not flow directly from the donors to the needy. It goes through the government of the recipient country. Here we find another problem: the inefficient and sometimes corrupt bureaucracies in recipient nations. There have been cases where recipient governments have sold products that were intended for free distribution to the poor. In other cases, food aid was not distributed because the recipient government had created the conditions

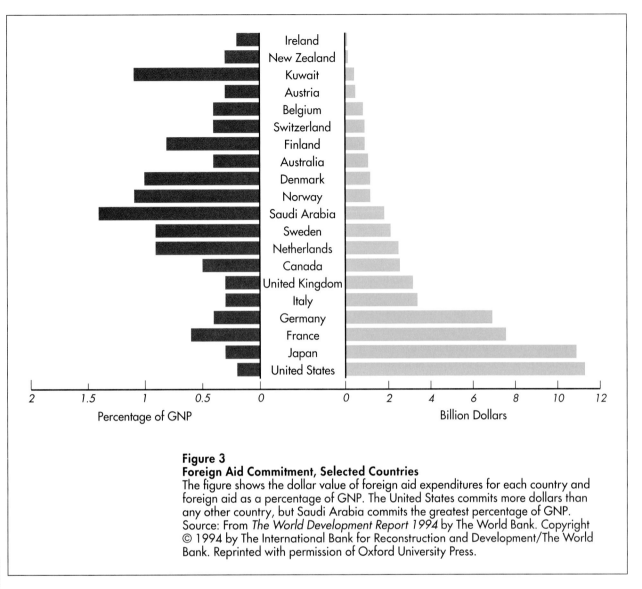

Figure 3
Foreign Aid Commitment, Selected Countries
The figure shows the dollar value of foreign aid expenditures for each country and foreign aid as a percentage of GNP. The United States commits more dollars than any other country, but Saudi Arabia commits the greatest percentage of GNP.
Source: From *The World Development Report 1994* by The World Bank. Copyright © 1994 by The International Bank for Reconstruction and Development/The World Bank. Reprinted with permission of Oxford University Press.

multilateral aid:
aid provided by international organizations supported by many nations

leading to starvation. The U.S. intervention in Somalia in 1993 was aimed at helping food aid reach the starving population. In still other cases, a well-intentioned recipient government simply did not have the resources to distribute the aid, so the products ended up largely going to waste. One response to these problems is to rely on voluntary agencies to distribute aid. Another is to rely on multilateral agencies.

Multilateral aid is provided by international organizations that are supported by many nations. The largest and most important multilateral aid institution is the World Bank. The World Bank makes loans to developing countries at below-market rates of interest and oversees projects it has funded in developing countries. As an international organization, the World Bank is not controlled by any single country. This allows the organization to advise and help developing countries in a nonpolitical way that is usually not possible with bilateral aid.

RECAP

1. Private sources of foreign savings include direct investment, portfolio investment, commercial bank loans, and trade credit.
2. Developing countries can benefit from foreign investment through new jobs, the transfer of technology, and foreign exchange earnings.
3. Foreign aid involves gifts or low-cost loans made available to developing countries by official sources.
4. Foreign aid can be provided bilaterally or multilaterally.

SUMMARY

▲▼ *How is poverty measured?*

1. Poverty usually is defined in an absolute sense as the minimum income needed to purchase a minimal standard of living and is measured by per capita GNP or GDP. §1.a
2. Some economists and social scientists use a quality-of-life index to evaluate standards of living. §1.b

▲▼ *Why are some countries poorer than others?*

3. Both political obstacles (lack of skilled officials, instability, constraints imposed by special interest groups) and social obstacles (cultural attitudes that discourage entrepreneurial activity and encourage rapid population growth) limit economic growth in developing countries. §2.a, 2.b

▲▼ *What strategies can a nation use to increase its economic growth?*

4. Inward-oriented development strategies focus on developing a domestic manufacturing sector to produce goods that can substitute for imported manufactured goods. §3.a

5. Outward-oriented development strategies focus on producing manufactured goods for export. §3.b
6. The growth rates of outward-oriented economies are significantly higher than those of inward-oriented economies. §3.c

▲▼ *How are savings in one nation used to speed development in other nations?*

7. Private sources of foreign savings include direct investment, portfolio investment, commercial bank loans, and trade credit. §4.a
8. Foreign investment in developing countries can increase their economic growth by creating jobs, transferring modern technology, and stimulating exports to increase foreign exchange earnings. §4.b
9. Official gifts or low-cost loans made to developing countries by official sources are called foreign aid. §4.c
10. Foreign aid can be distributed bilaterally or multilaterally. §4.c

KEY TERMS

expropriation §2.a.2
primary product §3.a
import substitution §3.a
export substitution §3.b
terms of trade §3.c

dual economy §3.c
foreign direct investment §4.a
portfolio investment §4.a
commercial bank loan §4.a

trade credit §4.a

foreign aid §4.c

bilateral aid §4.c

multilateral aid §4.c

EXERCISES

1. What are basic human needs? Can you list additional needs besides those considered in the chapter?

2. Per capita GNP is used as an absolute measure of poverty.

   a. What are some criticisms of using per capita GNP as a measure of standard of living?

   b. Do any of these criticisms also apply to a quality-of-life index?

3. In many developing countries there are economists and politicians who were educated in industrial countries. These individuals know the policies that would maximize the growth of their countries, but they do not implement them. Why not?

4. Suppose you are a benevolent dictator who can impose any policy you choose in your country. If your goal is to accelerate economic development, how would you respond to the following problems?

   a. Foreign firms are afraid to invest in your country because your predecessor expropriated many foreign-owned factories.

   b. There are few entrepreneurs in the country.

   c. The dominant domestic religion teaches that the accumulation of wealth is sinful.

   d. It is customary for families to have at least six children.

5. What effect does population growth have on economic development?

6. Why have most developing countries followed inward-oriented development strategies?

7. Why is an outward-oriented development strategy likely to allocate resources more efficiently than an inward-oriented strategy?

8. Who benefits from an import-substitution strategy? Who is harmed?

9. If poverty is a relative concept, why don't we define it in relative terms?

10. "The poor will always be with us." Does this statement have different meanings depending on whether poverty is interpreted as an absolute or relative concept?

11. How do traditional societies answer the questions What to produce? How to produce? and For whom to produce?

12. What are the most important sources of foreign savings for developing countries? Why don't developing countries save more so that they don't have to rely on foreign savings for investment?

13. Private foreign investment and foreign aid are sources of savings to developing countries. Yet each has been controversial at times. What are the potential negative effects of private foreign investment and foreign aid for developing countries?

14. Why do immigrants often play an important role in developing the economies of poor nations?

15. How does a nation go about instituting a policy of import substitution? What is a likely result of such a policy?

COOPERATIVE LEARNING EXERCISE

Students form groups of two. Each group must read the Economically Speaking article at the end of the chapter. The pairs of students then write a one-paragraph memo for aid givers in industrial countries regarding when cash aid *should be preferred to food aid in countries suffering famines. The memo should be addressed to the nations' leaders. Several groups will be called on to read their paragraph to the rest of the class.*

We Need the Will to Feed the Hungry

The world now produces enough food to feed everyone, United Nations experts said recently. Tell that to the 13 million children below age five who die every year of hunger-related causes. Or to the 786 million chronically undernourished people in the developing world. In South Asia, an estimated two out of three children are underweight. And in sub-Saharan Africa, the number of underweight children actually increased during the past 20 years.

Yet the UN Food and Agriculture Organization calculates average food availability in the world rose from 2,290 calories per day per person in 1961 to 2,700 calories in 1990. What's going wrong?

The answer is no great mystery. Harvard economist Amartya Sen, for instance, points out that even the poorest governments can reduce the incidence of hunger if they are committed to the task. Hunger and malnutrition have almost been eradicated in Costa Rica. And since independence India has virtually eliminated the threat of famine.

A government's will to feed its people, however, is intimately linked to the nature of the government. Sen's work suggests that the more dictatorial the regime, the more prone the country is to famine. This is because such governments are unresponsive to the needs of their citizens: political elites are, after all, the last to starve.

Although its record for feeding its people has definitely improved, China experienced one of the worst famines of all time during the Great Leap Forward between 1958 and 1961. An estimated 30 million people died.

While famines often can be blamed on the political and economic failures of dictatorial governments, the rich, democratic nations are not entirely blameless.

The IMF and the World Bank encourage farmers in poor countries to shift from subsistence farming to cash crops worth next to nothing on world markets.

When crises erupt, privileged countries deliver tonnes of food aid from their overstocked shelves. Canada's specialty is wheat. But the beneficiaries of our largesse often have little reason to be grateful.

Sen's research indicates, for example, that famines are not necessarily the result of a decline in food production. During the famines in Bengal in 1943, in Ethiopia in 1973 and in Bangalesh in 1974, those countries produced at least as much food as in previous years. The famines occurred either because incomes fell or because food prices were pushed out of reach by a newly rich group which started demanding more to eat.

In their recent book Hunger and Public Action, Sen and Jean Dreze (formerly of the London School of Economics), observe that where a country's economic system is still functioning it often makes more sense to give people money to buy the local food that is available than to give them food aid. Local traders can deliver food more quickly and efficiently. And domestic agricultural production isn't destroyed.

Somalia, unfortunately, seems beyond such solutions. Famines came and went when dictators ran the country. But neither the government nor the economic system survived the latest crisis.

The Red Cross is now distributing seeds to Somalian farmers in an attempt to circumvent the looters who are after food. Until stability is restored, however, the relief camps are the only hope for thousands of starving people. This is no way to run a world.

Source: "We Need the Will to Feed the Hungry," *The Ottawa Citizen*, Sept. 27, 1992, p. B1. Reprinted by permission.

Commentary

Though efforts to combat famines often take the form of food aid, famines do not necessarily imply a shortage of food. Instead, famines sometimes represent shortfalls in purchasing power of the poorest sectors of society. In many cases, grants of income are a better means of allieviating famines than grants of food.

We can understand this argument using demand and supply analysis. In the following two diagrams we represent the demand for food and the supply of food in a famine-stricken country receiving aid. In each diagram, the demand curve D_1 intersects the supply curve S_1 at an equilibrium quantity of food Q_1, which represents a subsistence level of food consumption. The equilibrium depicted in each graph is one in which, in the absence of aid, a famine would occur.

The first graph illustrates the effects of providing aid in the form of food. The food aid increases the available supply of food, which is shown by an outward shift of the supply curve to S_2. The effect of this aid is to increase the equilibrium quantity of food (Q_2) and lower the equilibrium price (P_2). The lower price of food will adversely affect the income of domestic producers. Domestic producers will thus attempt to grow other crops, or to search for sources of income other than growing food, if they cannot receive enough money for their produce. As the amount of domestic food production falls, a country becomes more dependent upon imports of food.

The second graph illustrates the effect of income aid for the famine-stricken country. The aid is depicted by a shift in the demand curve to D_2. As with food aid, this relief allows consumption to rise to a point above the subsistence level. The effects of this aid on domestic food producers, however, are quite different. The price of food rises, and thus domestic food producers are not hurt by the aid package. As a result, aid in the form of income does not cause disincentives for production. An increase in domestic food production also serves to make a country less dependent upon food imports.

In this analysis we have assumed that markets and food distribution channels work. In Somalia, where civil war has disrupted regular trade paths, we cannot make such assumptions. Starvation there is unlikely to be alleviated by simply sending income aid and not worrying about food distribution. Nevertheless, the importance of recognizing the effects of different types of aids can save lives.

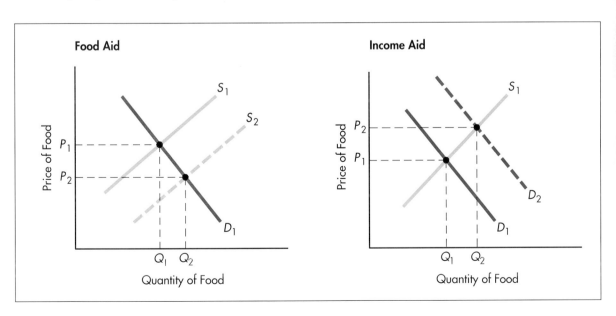

V

Product Market Basics

491

20

Elasticity: Demand and Supply

FUNDAMENTAL QUESTIONS

1. How do we measure how much consumers alter their purchases in response to a price change?

2. Why are measurements of elasticity important?

3. How does a business determine whether to increase or decrease the price of the product it sells in order to increase revenues?

4. Why might senior citizens or children receive price discounts relative to the rest of the population?

5. What determines whether consumers alter their purchases a little or a lot in response to a price change?

6. How do we measure how much income changes, changes in the prices of related goods, or changes in advertising expenditures affect consumer purchases?

7. How do we measure how much producers respond to a price change?

F irms want customers coming back for more. They would prefer to spend a dollar to retain their current and former customers than to attract new customers. Why would a firm care whether it sells a product to a former customer or a new customer; a sale is a sale no matter who the buyer is, isn't it? The answer is "not really." A firm that has created loyalty among its customers can increase the price of its product above the prices of competitive products without having the customers switch their purchases to another firm. Bayer aspirin, Kodak film, Xerox copiers, IBM computers, and hundreds of other products have well-known brand names. These products are typically priced above competitive products that are not as well-recognized. How far can the brand-name product be priced above rival products? The answer depends on how sensitive consumers are to price changes—the subject matter of this chapter.

PREVIEW

Few doubt that consumers *do* respond to price changes. The question is, how large is their response? The answer to this question is vitally important

to businesses and government agencies trying to determine whether and by how much to raise or lower prices. The law of demand tells us that consumers will buy less of a product if the price of that product rises, but the law of demand does not indicate *how much* sales will decline. Economists have devised measures of how much consumers alter their purchases in response to price changes. These measures are called *elasticities*.

Elasticity is a measure of responsiveness. It is used most often to measure the magnitude of consumer responses to price changes, but it can also be used to measure consumer responses to changes in income, advertising, or expectations and to measure seller responses to price changes.

I. THE PRICE ELASTICITY OF DEMAND

How do we measure how much consumers alter their purchases in response to a price change?

Suppose the current price of a personal computer with the latest computer chip, CD-ROM, speakers, fax modem, and other features is $3,000 and that 300,000 computers are sold at that price, shown as point *A* in Figure 1(a). If the price is lowered to $2,000, what will the consumers' response be? If consumers purchase 500,000, then point *B* in Figure 1(b) is relevant; if consumers purchase 700,000, it is point *C* that is relevant. Connecting points *A* and *B* traces out demand curve D_1, while connecting points *A* and *C* traces out the flatter curve D_2 shown in Figure 1(c). Does it matter which curve is correct? It matters to IBM, Compaq, and other computer manufacturers who

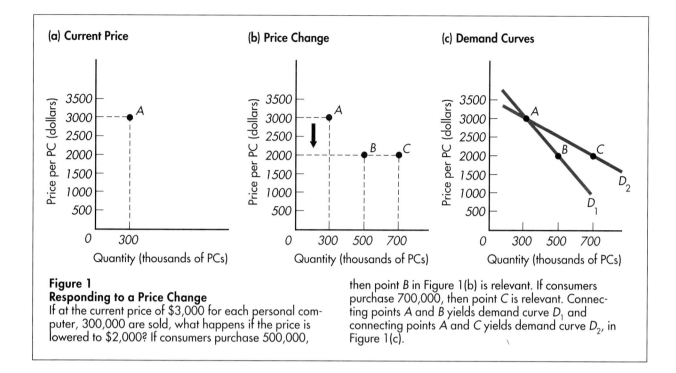

Figure 1
Responding to a Price Change
If at the current price of $3,000 for each personal computer, 300,000 are sold, what happens if the price is lowered to $2,000? If consumers purchase 500,000, then point B in Figure 1(b) is relevant. If consumers purchase 700,000, then point C is relevant. Connecting points A and B yields demand curve D_1 and connecting points A and C yields demand curve D_2, in Figure 1(c).

want to know what the price change will do to their sales and profits. It matters to manufacturers of PC-related products such as Microsoft and LOTUS, who want to know what the increased purchases of computers will mean for the sales of their software. In fact, it is extremely important for businesses to know how the quantity demanded will change when the price changes. The price elasticity of demand provides that information.

The price elasticity of demand is a measure of the magnitude by which consumers alter the quantity of some product they purchase in response to a change in the price of that product. The more price-elastic demand is, the more responsive consumers are to a price change—that is, the more they will adjust their purchases of a product when the price of that product changes. Conversely, the less price-elastic demand is, the less responsive consumers are to a price change.

1.a. The Definition of Price Elasticity

price elasticity of demand:
the percentage change in the quantity demanded of a product divided by the percentage change in the price of that product

The **price elasticity of demand** is the percentage change in the quantity demanded of a product divided by the percentage change in the price of that product:

$$\frac{\%\Delta Q^D}{\%\Delta P}$$

For instance, if the quantity of videotapes that are rented falls by 3 percent whenever the price of a videotape rental rises by 1 percent, the price elasticity of demand for videotape rentals is 3.

According to the law of demand, whenever the price of a good rises, the quantity demanded of that good falls. Thus, the price elasticity of demand is always negative, which can be confusing when referring to a "very high elasticity"—actually, a large negative number—or to a "low elasticity"—a small negative number. To avoid this confusion, economists use the absolute value of the price elasticity of demand and thus ignore the negative sign. Absolute value, denoted as | |, turns the negative number into a positive one. Thus, denoting the price elasticity of demand as e_d, we have:

$$e_d = |-3\%/1\%| = |-3| = 3$$

Demand can be elastic, unit-elastic, or inelastic. When the price elasticity of demand is greater than 1, demand is said to be *elastic*. For instance, the demand for videotape rentals, according to the example of $e_d = 3$, is elastic. When the price elasticity of demand is 1, demand is said to be *unit-elastic*. For example, if the price of private education rises by 1 percent and the quantity of private education purchased falls by about 1 percent, the price elasticity of demand is

$$e_d = |-1\%/1\%| = 1$$

When the price elasticity of demand is less than 1, demand is said to be *inelastic*. In this case, a 1 percent rise in price brings forth a smaller than 1 percent decline in quantity demanded. For example, if the price of gasoline rises by 1 percent and the quantity of gasoline purchased falls by .2 percent, the price elasticity of demand is

$$e_d = |-.2\%/1\%| = .2$$

1.b. Demand Curve Shapes and Elasticity

perfectly elastic demand curve:
a horizontal demand curve indicating that consumers can and will purchase all they want at one price

A **perfectly elastic demand curve** is a horizontal line that shows that consumers can purchase any quantity they want at the single prevailing price. In Figure 2(a), a perfectly elastic demand curve represents the demand for the wheat harvested by a single farmer in Canada. The Canadian farmer is only one small producer of wheat who, because he is just one among many, is unable to charge a price that differs from the price of wheat in the rest of the

Grocery shopping in many nations does not resemble the once-a-week trip to the super-market most households in the United States make. This Indian woman and her child make a daily trip to the stores and shops looking for the best pro-duce and the best bargains. Having more time available to devote to grocery shopping means that the price elasticity of demand for the grocery items is higher. A small price change may induce the woman to make a trip to another store; a small price change for someone without the time to make additional trips to the store will not affect purchases.

Chapter 20 / Elasticity: Demand and Supply

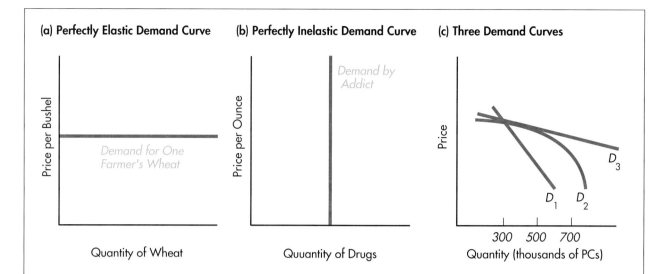

Figure 2
The Price Elasticity of Demand
Figure 2(a), a perfectly elastic demand curve, represents the demand for one farmer's wheat. Because there are so many other suppliers, buyers purchase wheat from the least expensive source. If this farmer's wheat is priced ever so slightly above other farmers' wheat, buyers will switch to another source. Also, because this farmer is just one small producer in a huge market, he can sell everything he wants at the market price. Figure 2(b), a perfectly inelastic demand curve, represents the demand for heroin by a drug addict. A certain quantity is necessary to satisfy the addiction regardless of the price. Figure 2(c) shows two straight-line demand curves, D_1 and D_3, and a "curved" demand curve, D_2. These demand curves are neither perfectly elastic nor perfectly inelastic.

world. If this farmer's wheat is even slightly more expensive than wheat elsewhere, consumers will shift their purchases away from this farmer and buy the wheat produced by other farmers in Canada and the rest of the world. A perfectly elastic demand means that even the smallest price change will cause consumers to change their consumption by a huge amount, in fact, totally switching purchases to the producer with the lowest prices.

A **perfectly inelastic demand curve** is a vertical line illustrating the idea that consumers cannot or will not change the quantity of a good they purchase when the price of the product is changed. Perhaps heroin to an addict is a reasonably vivid example of a good whose demand is perfectly inelastic. The addict will pay almost any price to get the quantity that satisfies the addiction. Of course, this behavior holds only over a certain price range. Eventually, the price rises enough that even the addict will have to decrease the quantity demanded. Figure 2(b) shows a perfectly inelastic demand curve.

In between the two extreme shapes of demand curves are the demand curves for most products. Figure 2(c) shows two downward-sloping straight-line demand curves, D_1 and D_3, and one downward-sloping "curved" demand curve, D_2. Although demand curves can have virtually any shape—curve or straight line—the straight-line shape is used to illustrate the demand for most goods and services.

I.b.I. **Price Elasticity Along a Straight-Line Demand Curve** The price elasticity of demand varies along a straight-line downward-sloping demand curve, declining as we move down the curve. The reason that elasticity

perfectly inelastic demand curve:
a vertical demand curve indicating that there is no change in the quantity demanded as the price changes

The price elasticity of demand declines as we move down a straight-line demand curve.

changes along the straight-line demand curve is due to the way that elasticity is calculated, not to some intuitive economic explanation.

Along a straight-line demand curve, equal changes in price mean equal changes in quantity. For instance, if price changes by $1 in Figure 3, quantity demanded changes by 20 units; as price changes from $1 to $2, quantity demanded falls from 200 to 180; as price changes from $2 to $3, quantity demanded falls from 180 to 160; and so on. Each $1 change in price means a 20-unit change in quantity demanded. But those same amounts (constant amounts of $1 and 20 units) do not translate into constant percentage changes.

A $1 change at the top of the demand curve is a significantly different percentage change from a $1 change at the bottom of the demand curve. A $1 change from $10 is a 10 percent change, but a $1 change from $2 is a 50 percent change. Thus, as we move down the demand curve from higher to lower prices, a given dollar change becomes a larger and larger percentage change in price. The opposite is true of quantity changes. As we move downward along the demand curve, the same change in quantity becomes a smaller and smaller percentage change. A 10-unit change from 20 is a 50 percent change, while a 10-unit change from 200 is a 5 percent change. As we move down the straight-line demand curve, the percentage change in quantity demanded declines while the percentage change in price increases. Because the price elasticity of demand is the ratio of the percentage change in quantity demanded to the percentage change in price, the price elasticity of demand moves close to zero as we move down the straight-line demand curve.

The terms elastic and inelastic refer to a price range, not to the entire demand curve.

The downward-sloping straight-line demand curve is divided into three parts by the price elasticity of demand: the *elastic region*, the *unit-elastic point*, and the *inelastic region*. The demand is elastic from the top of the curve to the unit-elastic point. At all prices below the unit-elastic point, the

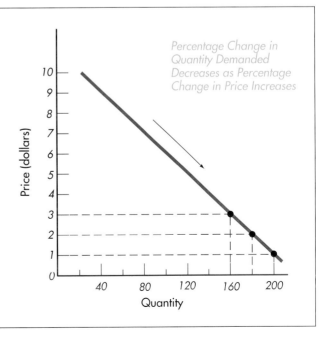

Figure 3
The Price Elasticity of Demand Varies along a Straight-Line Demand Curve
Figure 3 shows that the price elasticity of demand varies along a straight-line demand curve. As we move down the demand curve, the price elasticity varies from elastic to unit-elastic to inelastic.

price elasticity of demand lies between 1 and 0. This is the inelastic portion of the curve.

elastic	$e_d > 1$
unit-elastic	$e_d = 1$
inelastic	$0 < e_d < 1$

I.c. The Price Elasticity of Demand Is Defined in Percentage Terms

Why are measurements of elasticity important?

By measuring the price elasticity of demand in terms of percentage changes, economists are able to compare how consumers respond to changes in the prices of different products. For instance, the impact of a 1 percent increase in the price of gasoline (measured in gallons) can be compared to the impact of a 1 percent change in the price of videotape rentals (measured in number of rentals). Or the impact of a 1 percent increase in the price of college tuition can be compared to the impact of a 1 percent rise in the price of a Big Mac.

Percentage changes ensure that we are comparing apples to apples, not apples to oranges. What sense could be made of a comparison between the effects on quantity demanded of a $1 rise in the price of college tuition, from $5,000 to $5,001, and a $1 rise in the price of Big Macs, from $2 to $3? The dollar change would mean that tuition increases by .02 percent, and the hamburger price increases by 50 percent.

I.d. Average or Arc Elasticity

One of the problems of measuring elasticity is that the value depends on the base, or the starting point. An increase from $5 to $6 is a 20 percent change [($6 − $5)/$5 = 1/5], but a decrease from $6 to $5 is a 16.67 percent change [($5 − $6)/$6 = 1/6]. The result differs according to whether we start from $5 or $6—that is, according to whether the base is $5 or $6. Because the value of the price elasticity of demand varies depending on the base, economists use the average price and average quantity demanded to calculate elasticity. The elasticity obtained when the midpoint, or average, price and quantity are used is often called the **arc elasticity**. The formula used to calculate arc elasticity is

arc elasticity:
the price elasticity of demand measured over a price range using the midpoint, or average, as the base

$$e_d = \frac{|(Q_2 - Q_1)/[(Q_1 + Q_2)/2]|}{|(P_2 - P_1)/[(P_1 + P_2)/2]|}$$

Let's use this formula to calculate an elasticity. At a price of $6 per ticket, the average moviegoer demands 2 tickets per month. At a price of $4 per ticket, the average moviegoer purchases 6 tickets per month. Thus,

$P_1 = \$6$	$Q_1 = 2$
$P_2 = \$4$	$Q_2 = 6$

The *change* in quantity demanded is $Q_2 - Q_1 = 6 - 2 = 4$. The *percentage change* is the change divided by the base. The base is the average, or midpoint between the two quantities, the sum of the two quantities divided by 2: $(Q_1 + Q_2)/2 = (6 + 2)/2 = 4$. With 4 as the base, the percentage change in quantity is 4/4, or 100 percent. We can say that the quantity of movie tickets sold rose by an average of 100 percent as the price of a ticket declined from $6 to $4.

The change in price is $-\$2$, from \$6 to \$4, and the average price is $(P_1 + P_2)/2 = (\$6 + \$4)/2 = \$5$. The percentage change in price is $-\$2/\$5 = -40$ percent.

Because the numerator of the price elasticity of demand is 100 percent and the denominator is -40 percent, the price elasticity is

$$e_d = |100/-40| = 2.5$$

According to these calculations, the price elasticity of demand for movie tickets, over the price range from \$6 to \$4, is 2.5. We can say that demand is elastic over this price range.

RECAP

1. The price elasticity of demand is a measure of the degree to which consumers will alter the quantities of a product they purchase in response to changes in the price of that product.

2. Because the quantity demanded always declines as price rises, the price elasticity of demand is always a negative number. To avoid confusion when discussing price elasticity of demand, we use the absolute value—that is, the negative sign is ignored.

3. The price elasticity of demand is a ratio of the percentage change in the quantity demanded to the corresponding percentage change in the price.

4. When the price elasticity of demand is greater than 1, demand is said to be *elastic*. When the price elasticity of demand is equal to 1, demand is said to be *unit-elastic*. When the price elasticity of demand is less than 1, demand is said to be *inelastic*.

5. The elasticity obtained by using average price and average quantity demanded is called the *arc elasticity*.

2. THE USE OF PRICE ELASTICITY OF DEMAND

The price elasticity of demand may be a manager's best friend. It informs her whether to raise or lower prices, whether to charge different customers different prices, whether to charge different prices at different times of the day, and whether it is better to focus on prices, to advertise, or to carry out business strategies that do not focus on prices.

2.a. Total Revenue and Price Elasticity of Demand

How does a business determine whether to increase or decrease the price of the product it sells in order to increase revenues?

A manager concerned with increasing revenue must know what the current price elasticity of demand is for the firm's product. There is a close relationship between price elasticity of demand and total revenue. **Total revenue (TR)** equals the price of a product multiplied by the quantity sold: $TR = P \times Q$. If P rises by 10 percent and Q falls by more than 10 percent, then total revenue declines as a result of the price rise. If P rises by 10 percent and Q falls by less than 10 percent, then total revenue rises as a result of the price rise. And if P increases by 10 percent and Q falls by 10 percent, total revenue does not change as the price changes. Thus, total revenue increases as price is

total revenue (TR):
$TR = P \times Q$

increased if demand is inelastic, decreases as price is increased if demand is elastic, and does not change as price is increased if demand is unit-elastic.

Whenever the price elasticity of demand for a product is in the elastic region, the product supplier must decrease price in order to increase revenue. For instance, the price elasticity of demand for airline travel has been found to be near 2.4. This means that, over some price range, for each 1 percent increase in the price of an airline ticket, the quantity of tickets demanded will decline by 2.4 percent.

In the spring of 1995, a trip could be made from New York to Los Angeles for $250 each way, if you included a Saturday night stay. If the airlines had increased the fare by 10 percent, to $275 each way, they would have sold 24 percent (2.4 × .10) fewer tickets. As a result, their total revenue would have fallen. The revenue from selling 3,000 tickets per day for the trip between New York and Los Angeles at a fare of $250 was $750,000 per day. At a fare of $275, the quantity of tickets demanded would have declined by 720 to 2,280 per day (3,000 × .24 = 720), and revenue would have fallen to $627,000 per day. As long as the price elasticity of demand exceeds 1, total revenue is decreased if the price is increased.

As long as the price elasticity of demand exceeds 1, total revenue is decreased if the price is increased.

As long as demand is elastic, price must be decreased to increase total revenue. But by how much should the price be lowered? Since the price elasticity of demand declines as the price falls along a straight-line demand curve, eventually price reaches a point where demand becomes unit-elastic. Further price decreases at this stage would cause total revenue to fall. Thus, total revenue can be maximized by setting the price where the demand is unit-elastic.

The table in Figure 4 is a demand schedule for airline tickets listing the price and quantity of tickets sold and the total revenue ($P \times Q$). Figure 4(a) shows a straight-line demand curve representing the demand for air travel. Total revenue is plotted in Figure 4(b), directly below the demand curve. You can see that total revenue rises as price falls in the elastic range of the demand curve, while in the inelastic range of the demand curve, total revenue declines as price falls. *The unit-elastic point is the price at which revenue is at a maximum.* Remember that this is revenue, not profit, we are discussing. A firm may or may not want to maximize revenue, as noted in the Economic Insight "Price, Revenue, and Profit."

To increase revenue:
1) If in elastic range of demand, lower price.
2) If in inelastic range of demand, raise price.

2.b. Price Discrimination

Why might senior citizens or children receive price discounts relative to the rest of the population?

Ads and marquees proudly proclaim that "kids stay free" or that "senior discounts apply," and it is well known that airlines sell vacation travelers tickets for significantly less than the business traveler pays. The price elasticity of demand might explain why firms will not always increase revenue if they lower their prices, but what explains why firms charge different customers different prices for the same product? It is exactly the same principle. When demand is elastic, a price decrease causes total revenue to increase; and when demand is inelastic, a price increase causes total revenue to rise. If different groups of customers have different price elasticities of demand for the same product, and if the groups are easily identifiable and can be kept from trading with each other, then the seller of the product can increase total revenue by

Figure 4
Total Revenue and Price Elasticity
The demand schedule provides data for plotting the straight-line demand curve, Figure 4(a), and the total revenue curve, Figure 4(b). In the elastic region of the demand curve, a price decrease will increase total revenue. At the unit-elastic point, a price decrease will not change total revenue. In the inelastic region of the demand curve, a price decrease will decrease total revenue.

Price per Ticket	Quantity of Tickets Sold per Day	Total Revenue
$1,000	200	$200,000
900	400	360,000
800	600	480,000
700	800	560,000
600	1,000	600,000
500	1,200	600,000
400	1,400	560,000
300	1,600	480,000
200	1,800	360,000
100	2,000	200,000

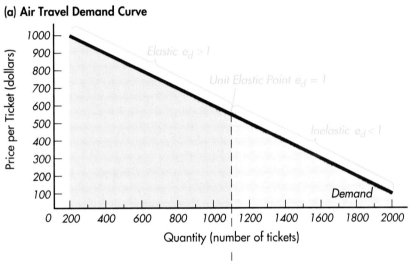

(a) Air Travel Demand Curve

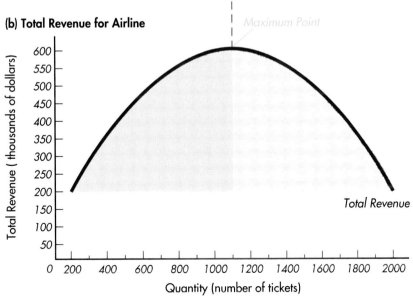

(b) Total Revenue for Airline

Price, Revenue, and Profit

Profit is defined as revenue minus costs. If revenue rises but costs rise more, then profit declines. Whether a price reduction leads to more profits or not depends on how revenue and costs respond to the price change. With the price elasticity of demand we are looking only at the response of revenue to price changes. We do not know what costs are doing and thus we do not know what is happening to profit. (We examine costs in the chapter "Supply: The Costs of Doing Business.")

Many people confuse revenue and profit; and sometimes even businesspeople embark on a strategy of increasing revenue but lose sight of the "bottom line," that is, profit. Stan Shih had a strategy of making his Taiwan-based computer firm, founded in 1983, one of the top five companies by 1995. Shih's firm, known as Acer, entered the United States by purchasing companies in the Silicon Valley. It began producing a low-cost line of PCs known as Acros in 1992. Sales were expected to reach $100 million in the first year. The sales goal was reached, but the company was not particularly pleased. According to Peter A. Janssen, Acer America's marketing vice president, "The revenues are huge. The problem is profitability."[1]

A similar situation befuddled the 3DO Co., a Redwood City video game software and hardware developer. 3DO tripled its revenues but still lost $9.4 million during the last quarter of 1994. The company increased advertising in order to increase revenues, but the advertising expenditures rose more than did revenues.[2]

[1]Statement by Janssen reported in *Business Week*, May 18, 1992, p. 129.

[2]Reported in the *San Francisco Chronicle*, February 10, 1995, p. B2.

price discrimination:
charging different customers different prices for the same product

charging each group a different price. Charging different prices to different customers for the same product is called **price discrimination**. Price discrimination occurs when senior citizens purchase movie tickets at a lower price than younger citizens or when business travelers pay more for airline tickets than vacation travelers.

Senior citizens are frequently offered movie tickets at lower prices than younger people. The reason for the discount is that, on average, older people are more inclined than younger people to respond to a change in the price of admission to a movie.

Suppose everyone pays the same ticket price of $5 and the price elasticity of demand by senior citizens is 2.0, while that by nonsenior citizens is 0.5. Lowering the price of a movie ticket by 10 percent would cause senior citizens to increase their purchases of movie tickets by 20 percent, but nonsenior citizens would increase their purchases by only 5 percent. Total revenue from senior citizens would rise, but that from nonsenior citizens would fall. It would make more sense for the theater to lower the price for senior citizens but not for younger people.

Airline discounts are constructed on the basis of the price elasticity of demand as well. Families planning a vacation know their schedules well in advance and can take advantage of the least expensive means of travel. Business travelers are more constrained. They often do not know their schedules days in advance, and they usually want to travel on Monday through Friday. The airlines recognize that the demand for air travel by vacationers is much more elastic than the demand by business travelers. As a result, airlines offer discounts to travelers who purchase tickets well in advance and stay over a *Saturday night*. For instance, in the spring of 1995, a cross-country round-trip fare was $840 unless the trip included an overnight stay on Saturday. Then the fare dropped to $360. If tickets were purchased two weeks in advance, the fare dropped to $240.

RECAP

1. If the price elasticity of demand is greater than 1, revenue and price changes move in the opposite direction. An increase in price causes a decrease in revenue, and a decrease in price causes an increase in revenue. If the price elasticity of demand is less than 1, revenue and price move in the same direction. If the price elasticity of demand is 1, revenue does not change as price changes.

2. When the price elasticity of demand for one product differs among different groups of easily identified customers, firms can increase revenues by charging each group a different price. The groups with elastic demands will receive lower prices than those with inelastic demands.

3. DETERMINANTS OF THE PRICE ELASTICITY OF DEMAND

What determines whether consumers alter their purchases a little or a lot in response to a price change?

Different groups of consumers—such as senior and nonsenior citizens or business and vacation travelers—may have different price elasticities of demand for the same product. The demand for a product may be elastic or inelastic over a relevant price range, and not all products have the same price elasticity of demand. The degree to which the price elasticity of demand is inelastic or elastic depends on the following factors, which differ among products and among consumers:

■ The existence of substitutes

■ The importance of the product in the consumer's total budget

■ The time period under consideration

3.a. The Existence of Substitutes

Consumers who can switch from one product to another without losing quality or some other attribute associated with the original product will be very sensitive to a price change. Their demand will be elastic. Such consumers will purchase a substitute rather than the original product whenever the relative price of the original product rises.

A senior citizen discount is offered at movie theaters because of the different price elasticities of demand by senior citizens and nonsenior citizens. Why are their elasticities different? More substitutes may be available to senior citizens than to younger folks. Retirees have more time to seek out alternative entertainment activities than do people who are working full time. Retirees can go to movies during the early part of the day or on weekdays when the theater runs a special.

In contrast, drug addicts have few substitutes that satisfy the addiction, and business travelers have few substitutes for the airlines. As a result, their demands are relatively inelastic. The more substitutes there are for a product, the greater the price elasticity of demand.

When there are fewer close substitutes for a product, or the price elasticity of demand for that product is lower. It is for this reason that firms attempt to create brand names and customer loyalty through advertising and other practices. Increasing the brand-name recognition and customer loyalty toward that brand means that fewer close substitutes exist and thus that the price elasticity of demand is lower. A lower price elasticity of demand enables the firm to increase the price without the loss of sales that would occur with a higher price elasticity of demand. It is because of brand-name recognition that Coca-Cola is priced higher than Safeway brand cola and Bayer aspirin is priced higher than Walgreen's aspirin.

The more substitutes there are for a product, the greater the price elasticity of demand.

3.b. The Importance of the Product in the Consumer's Total Budget

Because a new car and a European vacation are quite expensive, even a small percentage change in their prices can take a significant portion of a household's income. As a result, a 1 percent increase in price may cause many households to delay the purchase of a car or vacation. Coffee, on the other hand, accounts for such a small portion of a household's total weekly expenditures that a large percentage increase in the price of coffee will probably have little effect on the quantity of coffee purchased. The demand for vacations is most likely quite a bit more elastic than the demand for coffee. The greater the portion of the consumer's budget a good constitutes, the more elastic is the demand for the good.

The greater the portion of the consumer's budget a good constitutes, the more elastic the demand for the good.

3.c. The Time Period Under Consideration

If we are speaking about a day or an hour, then the demand for most goods and services will have a low price elasticity. If we are referring to a year or to several years, then the demand for most products will be more price-elastic than in a shorter period. For instance, the demand for gasoline is very nearly perfectly inelastic over a period of a month. No good substitutes are available in so brief a period. Over a ten-year period, however, the demand for gasoline is much more elastic. The additional time allows consumers to alter their behavior to make better use of gasoline and to find substitutes for gasoline. The longer the period under consideration, the more elastic is the demand for any product.

The longer the period under consideration, the more elastic the demand for the good.

RECAP

1. The price elasticity of demand depends on how readily and easily consumers can switch their purchases from one product to another.
2. Everything else held constant, the greater the number of close substitutes, the greater is the price elasticity of demand.
3. Everything else held constant, the greater the proportion of a householder's budget a good constitutes, the greater is the householder's price elasticity of demand for that good.
4. Everything else held constant, the longer the time period under consideration, the greater is the price elasticity of demand.

How do we measure how much income changes, changes in the prices of related goods, or changes in advertising expenditures affect consumer purchases?

A price change leads to a movement along the demand curve. When something that affects demand, other than price, changes, the demand curve shifts. How far the demand curve shifts is measured by elasticity—elasticity of the variable whose value changes. As we saw in Chapter 3, "Markets, Demand and Supply, and the Price System," demand is determined by income, prices of related goods, expectations, tastes, number of buyers, and international effects. A change in any one of these will cause the demand curve to shift, and a measure of elasticity exists for each of these demand determinants. The *income elasticity of demand* measures the percentage change in demand caused by a 1 percent change in income; the *cross-price elasticity of demand* measures the percentage change in demand caused by a 1 percent change in the price of a related good; the *advertising elasticity of demand* measures the percentage change in demand caused by a 1 percent change in advertising expenditures (change in tastes); and so on.[1] Each elasticity is calculated by dividing the percentage change in demand by the percentage change in the variable under consideration.

4.a. The Cross-Price Elasticity of Demand

cross-price elasticity of demand:
the percentage change in the quantity demanded for one good divided by the percentage change in the price of a related good, everything else held constant

The **cross-price elasticity of demand** measures the degree to which goods are substitutes or complements (for a discussion of substitutes and complements, see Chapter 3). The cross-price elasticity of demand is defined as the percentage change in the quantity demanded for one good divided by the percentage change in the price of a related good, everything else held constant:

$$\text{Cross-price elasticity of demand} = \frac{\text{percentage change in quantity demanded for good } j}{\text{percentage change in the price of good } k}$$

When the cross-price elasticity of demand is positive, the goods are substitutes; and when the cross-price elasticity of demand is negative, the goods are complements. If a 1 percent *increase* in the price of a movie ticket leads to a 5 percent *increase* in the quantity of videotapes that are rented, movies and videotapes are substitutes. If a 1 percent *rise* in the price of a movie ticket leads to a 5 percent *drop* in the quantity of popcorn consumed, movies and popcorn are complements.

Knowledge of how changes in economic events outside a firm's control affect sales is crucial in order for the firm to respond most effectively to competitors' policies and plan its own best growth strategy. For example, if a firm estimates that the cross-price elasticity of demand for its product with respect to the price of a competitor's product is very high, it will be quick to respond to a competitor's price reduction. If it were not quick, it would lose a great deal of its sales. However, the firm would think twice before being the first to lower its price, for fear of starting a price war. It knows that competitors will respond quickly to a price decrease and offset any advantage that a lower

---

[1]Notice that we define the elasticity as the percentage change in demand rather than percentage change in quantity demanded because it is the entire demand curve that is changing. In calculating the elasticities other than price elasticity of demand, the price is held constant, so that two different quantities are used on two different demand curves. The formula used to calculate the income and price elasticities refers to the change in quantity demanded because the calculation is carried out at one price at a time.

price might yield. If the cross-price elasticity is low, a firm would not care much about whether the other product's price is raised or lowered.

4.b. The Income Elasticity of Demand

income elasticity of demand:
the percentage change in the quantity demanded for a good divided by the percentage change in income, everything else held constant

The income elasticity of demand measures the magnitude of consumer responsiveness to income changes. The **income elasticity of demand** is defined as the percentage change in quantity demanded for a product divided by the percentage change in income, everything else held constant:

$$\text{Income elasticity of demand} = \frac{\text{percentage change in quantity demand for good } j}{\text{percentage change in income}}$$

normal goods:
goods for which the income elasticity of demand is positive

Any good whose income elasticity of demand is greater than zero is a **normal good.** Products often called necessities have lower income elasticities than products known as luxuries. Gas, electricity, health-oriented drugs, and physicians' services might be considered necessities. Their income elasticities are about .4 or .5. On the other hand, people tend to view dental services, automobiles, and private education as luxury goods. Their elasticities are 1.5 to 2.0.

inferior goods:
goods for which the income elasticity of demand is negative

Consumers could have a negative income elasticity of demand for some goods: less of those goods would be consumed as income rose. Such goods are called **inferior goods**. It is difficult to think of examples of inferior goods. Some people claim that potatoes, rice, and hamburger are inferior goods because people who have very low levels of income eat large quantities of these goods but give up those items and begin eating fruit, fish, and higher-quality meats as their incomes rise. The problem with calling these products inferior is that many higher-income households consume large quantities of potatoes, rice, and hamburger.

The income elasticity of demand provides useful information to a firm. If management knows that the income elasticity of the firm's product is very

What used to fill an entire room now can be held on a lap. The laptop, or notebook, computer is capable of carrying out calculations that only twenty years ago required a computer of ten feet by twelve feet. When initially introduced the personal computer and the laptop version appealed primarily to high-income earners—the income elasticity of demand was high. The machine was looked on as an expensive toy. Today, the computer is virtually a necessity and the income elasticity of demand is significantly lower than it was even five years ago. The laptop goes everywhere, even with a marine biologist in a rubber boat off the coast of Fiji who uses the laptop to record and analyze data.

low, it may want to upgrade the quality of its product or move into new product lines for which the income elasticity of demand is higher. The reason is that as incomes rise over time, a firm whose products have a low income elasticity of demand will not experience the sales growth of a firm whose products have a higher income elasticity of demand.

RECAP

1. The cross-price elasticity of demand is the percentage change in the quantity demanded for one product divided by the percentage change in the price of a related product, everything else held constant. If the cross-price elasticity of demand is positive, the goods are substitutes. If the cross-price elasticity of demand is negative, the goods are complements.

2. The income elasticity of demand is the percentage change in the quantity demanded for one product divided by the percentage change in income, everything else held constant. If the income elasticity of a good is greater than zero, the good is called a *normal good*. If the income elasticity of a good is negative, the good is called an *inferior good*.

3. Elasticities can be calculated for any determinant of demand. Although income and related goods elasticities were calculated in the text, other elasticities like international development, service, quality, and expectations could have been calculated.

5. SUPPLY ELASTICITIES

How do we measure how much producers respond to a price change?

Elasticity is a measure of responsiveness. The response of buyers to price changes is measured by the price elasticity of demand. The response of sellers to price changes can also be measured by elasticity. The *price elasticity of supply* is a measure of how sellers adjust the quantity of a good they offer for sale when the price of that good changes.

5.a. The Price Elasticity of Supply

price elasticity of supply:
the percentage change in the quantity supplied divided by the percentage change in price, everything else held constant

The **price elasticity of supply** is the percentage change in the quantity supplied of a good divided by the percentage change in the price of that good, everything else held constant. The price elasticity of supply is usually a positive number because the quantity supplied typically rises when the price rises. Supply is said to be elastic over a price range if the price elasticity of supply is greater than 1 over that price range. It is said to be inelastic over a price range if the price elasticity of supply is less than 1 over that price range.

$$\text{Price elasticity of supply} = \frac{\text{percentage change in the quantity supplied}}{\text{percentage change in the price}}$$

Different shapes the supply curve may take are illustrated in Figure 5. Figure 5(a) is a vertical line, representing a product for which the quantity supplied cannot increase no matter the price. There are some special types of goods for which supply cannot change no matter the length of time allowed for change—land surface, Monet paintings, Beethoven symphonies. For such goods, the price elasticity of supply is zero. Figure 5(b) shows a perfectly

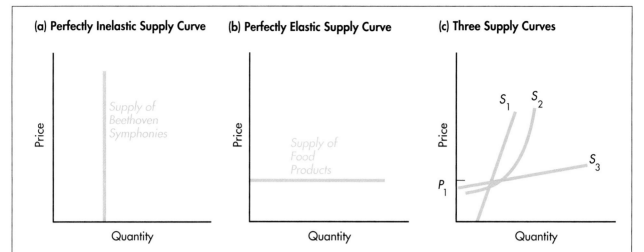

Figure 5
The Price Elasticity of Supply
There are some special types of goods for which supply cannot change no matter the length of time allowed for change. For such goods, the price elasticity of supply is zero and the supply curve is vertical, as shown in Figure 5(a). Figure 5(b) is a perfectly elastic supply curve, a horizontal line. A perfectly elastic supply curve says that the quantity supplied is unlimited at the given price;

a small—infinitesimal—price change would lead to an infinite change in quantity supplied. For most goods, the supply curve lies between the perfectly inelastic and perfectly elastic extremes. In Figure 5(c) three supply curves are drawn. Curve S_1 is steeper than the others but less steep than a perfectly inelastic curve. Curve S_2 is a "curved" supply curve. Curve S_3 is flatter than the others but not as flat as the perfectly elastic curve.

elastic supply curve, a horizontal line. There are some goods for which the quantity supplied at the current price can be whatever anyone wants given sufficient time. The production of food, for instance, has increased tremendously during the past century while the price has remained about the same. For most goods, the supply curve lies between the perfectly inelastic and perfectly elastic extremes. In Figure 5(c), three supply curves are drawn illustrating different shapes the supply curve might have. Curve S_1 is steeper than the others but less steep than a perfectly inelastic curve. Curve S_2 is a "curved" supply curve, and curve S_3 is flatter than the others but not as flat as the perfectly elastic curve.

5.b. **The Long and Short Runs**

short run:
a period of time short enough that the quantities of at least some of the resources cannot be varied

long run:
a period of time just long enough that the quantities of all resources can be varied

The shape of the supply curve depends primarily on the length of time being considered. Economists view time in terms of two distinct periods, the short run and the long run. The **short run** is a period of time long enough for existing firms to change the quantity of output they produce by changing the quantities of *some* of the resources used to produce their output, but not long enough for the firms to change the quantities of *all* of the resources. In the short run, firms are not able to build new factories or retrain workers. The **long run** is a period of time long enough for existing firms to change the quantities of all the resources they use and for new firms to begin producing the product. The chronological time for short and long runs varies from industry to industry. The long run for oil refining may be as long as seven to eight years; for personal computers, perhaps a year; for basket making, probably no longer than a day or two.

Usually, the greater the time period allowed, the more readily firms will increase their quantities supplied. Thus, supply curves applicable to shorter periods of time tend to be more inelastic than supply curves that apply to longer periods of time. If firms have to change their production techniques or switch from the production of one good to another in order to change the quantities they supply, they can respond less in a week to a price change than they could in a year. A baker who can switch from producing cupcakes to muffins within a day has large price elasticities of supply for cupcakes and for muffins; a small increase in the price of muffins relative to cupcakes will cause the bakery to increase significantly the quantity of muffins baked and reduce the quantity of cupcakes baked. An automobile manufacturing plant that requires several months or years to switch from one type of car to another, however, will have a relatively inelastic supply. In response to a large increase in the price of trucks relative to cars in 1994, for example, Japanese auto producers could increase their quantities supplied of trucks only minimally in 1995. Because of the time involved in altering production, it may not be until 1997 that the quantity of trucks supplied by Japanese companies rises to any great extent.

In Figure 5(c), supply curve S_1 represents a shorter-run supply curve. For a given price change, the quantity supplied would change by a small amount, shown by moving along S_1 from point P_1. Curve S_2 represents a firm that is able to increase quantity supplied substantially in the short run if it is currently producing a small amount. But, if it is producing a larger amount, it cannot increase output very much in the short run, perhaps because increased production would require an expansion of the current factory. Curve S_3 represents a longer-run supply curve. The change in output in response to a price change is greater along S_3 than along either of the other curves.

5.c. Price Elasticities of Demand and Supply

Who actually pays a tax levied on some item or some business? Is it the business, or does the consumer ultimately pay? The answer seems straightforward enough: "Clearly, the consumer pays the tax since the consumer takes the item to the checkout counter and forks over the money." Social security is a tax levied one-half on the employer and one-half on the employee. Who pays the social security tax? This too seems straightforward—"They both pay half." The answers are not that easy, however. Who pays the tax depends on the price elasticities of demand *and* supply.

Suppose that the price elasticity of supply for the item being taxed is large and the demand for that item is price-inelastic. In this case, the firm can raise the price without losing sales, which means that the tax can be added to the price and the firm will not lose sales. Moreover, the firm can switch from producing the taxed good to producing a nontaxed good relatively easily. Since the firm will not lose sales as a result of the tax, the firm does not need to worry about lowering the price and thus paying a portion of the tax. Regardless of whether the tax is imposed on the firm or on the consumer, it is the consumer who actually pays the tax. We say that the **tax incidence** falls on the consumer. Consider cigarettes, for example. If smokers will buy the same quantity of cigarettes even if the price rises by 20 percent, then an 8 percent tax levied on cigarettes will not affect sales. Firms would not need to reduce price to keep sales the same.

tax incidence:
a measure of who pays a tax

If, on the other hand, supply is price-inelastic and demand price-elastic, then a price increase means a revenue decrease for the firm. Since the firm cannot raise price without losing sales and cannot readily switch to producing another good, the firm must incorporate the tax in the original price and offer the same total cost to consumers after the tax is levied as before the tax. Hence, the firm will lower the price of the product enough that the price plus the new tax will just about equal the original (before tax) price. In this case, it is the business who pays the tax; the tax incidence falls on the business. If the price elasticity of demand for potato chips was high and the price elasticity of supply low, then an 8 percent tax on potato chips would reduce sales unless the business reduced the price of the chips. Because the business has to lower the price to maintain its sales, it actually pays the tax. The incidence falls on business.

In general, the more elastic the demand and the less elastic the supply, everything else held constant, the more the incidence falls on businesses and the less on consumers.

RECAP

1. The price elasticity of supply is the percentage change in the quantity supplied of one product divided by the percentage change in the price of that product, everything else held constant. The price elasticity of supply increases as the time period under consideration increases.

2. The long run is a period of time just long enough that the quantities of all resources can be varied. The short run is a period of time just short enough that the quantity of at least some of the resources cannot be varied.

3. The interaction of demand and supply determines the price and quantity produced and sold; the relative size of demand and supply price elasticities determines how the market reacts to changes. For instance, the size of supply relative to demand price elasticities determines the incidence of a tax.

SUMMARY

▲▼ *How do we measure how much consumers alter their purchases in response to a price change?*

1. The price elasticity of demand is a measure of the responsiveness of consumers to changes in price. It is defined as the percentage change in the quantity demanded of a good divided by the percentage change in the price of the good. §1.a

2. The price elasticity of demand is always a negative number because price and quantity demanded are inversely related. To avoid confusion about what large or small elasticity means, the price elasticity of demand is calculated as the absolute value of the percentage change in the quantity demanded of a good divided by the percentage change in the price of the good. §1.a

3. As the price is lowered along a straight-line demand curve, the price elasticity of demand declines. §1.b.1

4. The straight-line demand curve consists of three segments: the top part, which is elastic; the unit-elastic region; and the bottom part, which is inelastic. §1.b.1

5. The price elasticity of demand is calculated as the arc, or average, elasticity to avoid the problems created in choosing a starting point, or base. §1.d

▲▼ *Why are measurements of elasticity important?*

6. Comparing the price elasticity of demand for various products/services allows economists to see how consumers respond to price changes. In other words, it can tell us how big a difference price makes in a particular purchasing decision.

▲▼ *How does a business determine whether to increase or decrease the price of the product it sells in order to increase revenues?*

7. If the price elasticity of demand is greater than 1, total revenue and price changes move in opposite directions. An increase in price causes a decrease in total revenue, and a decrease in price causes an increase in total revenue. If demand is inelastic, total revenue and price move in the same direction. §2.a

▲▼ *Why might senior citizens or children receive price discounts relative to the rest of the population?*

8. When the price elasticity of demand for one product differs among different groups of easily identifiable customers, firms can increase total revenue by resorting to price discrimination. The customers with the more elastic demands will receive lower prices than the customers with less elastic demands. §2.b

▲▼ *What determines whether consumers alter their purchases a little or a lot in response to a price change?*

9. Everything else held constant, the greater the number of close substitutes, the greater the price elasticity of demand. §3.a

10. Everything else held constant, the greater the proportion of a household's budget a good constitutes, the greater the household's elasticity of demand for that good. §3.b

11. Everything else held constant, the longer the time period under consideration, the greater the price elasticity of demand. §3.c

▲▼ *How do we measure whether income changes, changes in the prices of related goods, or changes in advertising expenditures affect consumer purchases?*

12. Elasticities can be calculated for any variable that affects demand. §4

13. The cross-price elasticity of demand is defined as the percentage change in the quantity demanded for one good divided by the percentage change in the price of a related good, everything else held constant. §4.a

14. The income elasticity of demand is defined as the percentage change in the quantity demanded of a good divided by the percentage change in income, everything else held constant. §4.b

▲▼ *How do we measure whether producers respond to a price change?*

15. The price elasticity of supply is defined as the percentage change in the quantity supplied of a good divided by the percentage change in the price of that good, everything else held constant. §5.a

16. The short run is a period of time short enough that the quantities of at least some of the resources cannot be varied. The long run is a period of time just long enough that the quantities of all resources can be varied. §5.b

17. The incidence of a tax depends on the price elasticities of demand and supply. In general, the more elastic the demand and the less elastic the supply, everything else held constant, the more the incidence falls on businesses and the less on consumers. §5.c

KEY TERMS

price elasticity of demand §1.a

perfectly elastic demand curve §1.b

perfectly inelastic demand curve §1.b

arc elasticity §1.d

total revenue (TR) §2.a

price discrimination §2.b

cross-price elasticity of demand §4.a

income elasticity of demand §4.b

normal goods §4.b

inferior goods §4.b

price elasticity of supply §5.a

short run §5.b

long run §5.b

tax incidence §5.c

EXERCISES

Use the following hypothetical demand schedule for movies to do exercises 1–4.

Quantity Demanded	Price	Elasticity
100	$ 5	
80	10	
60	15	
40	20	
20	25	
10	30	

1. a. Determine the price elasticity of demand at each quantity demanded using the starting price and quantity as the bases. Next, do the same using the ending price and quantity as the bases; then, use the average price and quantity.

   b. Redo problem 1.a using price changes of $10 rather than $5.

   c. Plot the price and quantity data given in the demand schedule. Indicate the price elasticity value at each quantity demanded using the average price and quantity demanded as the bases. Explain why the elasticity value gets smaller as you move down the demand curve.

2. Below the demand curve plotted in exercise 1, plot the total revenue curve, measuring total revenue on the vertical axis and quantity on the horizontal axis.

3. What would a 10 percent increase in the price of movie tickets mean for the revenue of a movie theater if the price elasticity of demand was .1, .5, 1.0, and 5.0?

4. Using the demand curve plotted in exercise 1, illustrate what would occur if the income elasticity of demand was .05 and income rose by 10 percent. If the income elasticity of demand was 3.0 and income rose by 10 percent, what would occur?

5. Which is easier: to list five substitutes for each of the products listed under the elastic portion of Table 1 or five substitutes for the goods listed under the inelastic portion? Explain.

6. Are the following pairs of goods substitutes or complements? Indicate whether their cross-price elasticities are negative or positive.

   a. Bread and butter

   b. Bread and potatoes

   c. Socks and shoes

   d. Tennis racket and golf clubs

   e. Bicycles and automobiles

   f. Foreign investments and domestic investments

   g. Cars made in Japan and cars made in the United States

7. Suppose the price elasticity of demand for movies by teenagers is .2 and that by adults is 2.0. What policy would the movie theater implement to increase total revenue? Use hypothetical data to demonstrate your answer.

8. Explain how consumers will react to a job loss. What will be the first goods they will do without?

9. Explain why senior citizens can obtain special discounts at movie theaters, drugstores, and other businesses.

10. Calculate the income elasticity of demand from the following data (use the midpoint or average):

Income	Quantity Demanded
$15,000	20,000
20,000	30,000

a. Explain why the value is a positive number.

b. Explain what would happen to a demand curve as income changes if the income elasticity were 2.0. Compare that outcome to the situation that would occur if the income elasticity of demand were .2.

11. The poor tend to have a price elasticity of demand for movie tickets that lies above 1. Why don't you see signs offering "poor people discounts" similar to the signs offering "senior citizen discounts"?

12. Suppose a tax is imposed on a product that has a completely inelastic supply curve. Who pays the tax?

13. During the budget crisis in California, many households called for increasing taxes on businesses. Explain why a 40 percent across-the-board tax on businesses might not benefit the households of California.

14. Explain what must occur for the strategies suggested by the following headlines to be successful.

a. "Ford to go nationwide with plan for one-price selling of Escorts."

b. "P.F. Flyers cut sneaker prices to $20 a pair in a move to triple 1992 sales to 10 million pairs."

c. "Honda plans to launch a less expensive 'value-priced' Accord."

d. "Procter & Gamble cuts prices of Dash detergent 30 to 40 percent."

15. Suppose the demand for cocaine consists of two types of consumers, the addicts and the first-time users. Suppose the price elasticity of demand for the addicts is .01 and that for the first-time users is 4.0. Explain how the government might design an antidrug campaign to reduce cocaine consumption and demand.

COOPERATIVE LEARNING EXERCISE

Students should form themselves into groups of five and then count off from 1 to 5. The number 1s all gather together, number 2s, etc. Each group considers the following problem: Suppose a manager's staff has provided her with the following information about the demand for the firm's product.

Elasticities:		
	advertising	1.4
	cross-price	.9
	income	1.5
	advertising	2.0
	service	3.0

Number 1s are responsible for price elasticity, number 2s for cross-price, number 3s for income elasticity, number 4s for advertising elasticity, and number 5s for service elasticity. Each must explain what the elasticity means and suggest a policy for increasing revenues. Once each numbered group is satisfied, return to original groups and take turns explaining the result to the rest of the group.

Prices Detour Buyers from Dream Cars

Dave DeSmyther figured it was time for a new Jeep Cherokee when the odometer on his 1984 Jeep hit 170,000 miles. But he gasped at the $20,000 price tag. So DeSmyther, self-employed as a photographer's assistant in Chelsea, Mich., decided to buy a Dodge Dakota pickup with an extended cab to stash his gear. Surprise No. 2: He couldn't afford to pay $17,000 for a Dakota.

Finally, DeSmyther settled for a Dakota that cost $13,000 with a regular cab and no frills. His monthly payment: $200 versus $400 for the Cherokee. "Even if I have a slow month, I can handle the payments," DeSmyther says.

Millions of car and truck buyers across the USA are coming to the same painful conclusion: the new models they want cost too much. So they have to settle for what they can afford. Often, that's a used car.

Between December 1984 and last year's third quarter, the average price paid for a new car rose 75 percent to $20,045—first time it's cracked $20,000 and nearly double the rise in consumer prices the same period.

The high cost of new cars threatens to cut short the auto industry's recovery, which started in 1992. Tuesday, Ford Motor confirmed it will shut Escort production in Mexico and Michigan for a week because of slumping sales. In an effort to spur business, Chrysler slapped a $400 rebate for first-time buyers on its Dodge and Plymouth Neon small cars.

The average car on the road is now 7.3 years old, up from 6.7 years in 1991.

Automakers insist they aren't to blame. They point to plants working overtime to crank out models in heated demand, like Chevrolet Blazer, Jeep Grand Cherokee and Ford Mustang. They contend that more than $2,000 of a typical car price goes for safety and emissions equipment, such as dual air bags and anti-lock brakes, that the government requires or buyers demand.

And they have hustled to build cars they think are affordable. GM's Saturn small-car company, launched five years ago to attract budget-conscious buyers posted record sales in 1994.

But they may have to do more. Small cars, such as Neon, Escort and Chevrolet's Cavalier are supposed to appeal to people in their first jobs, college students and people on strict budgets.

But research firm Auto Pacific found the median household income of small-car buyers is $45,000—50 percent higher than the households the automakers have targeted. Midsize cars, such as Ford Taurus and Honda Accord are supposed to appeal to people with household incomes of $35,000 to $45,000. Instead, AutoPacific estimates they're selling to people in households with a median income of $51,000 a year.

Source: "Prices Detour Buyers from Dream Cars" USA Today, January 18, 1995, p. 1B. Copyright 1995, USA Today. Reprinted by permission.

USA Today/January 18, 1995

Commentary

The price elasticity of demand depends on the number of close substitutes and the importance of the item in a consumer's budget, among other things. There are many substitutes for a Jeep Cherokee—other sport utility vehicles, trucks, and sedans. Thus, the price elasticity of demand for the Jeep Cherokee is probably well above 1.0. As the price of the Cherokee rises but the income of consumers does not increase as rapidly, the Cherokee becomes a larger part of the consumer's budget. This increases the price elasticity of demand.

The price elasticity of demand for new automobiles is less than the price elasticity of demand for a specific new vehicle such as the the Jeep Cherokee. There are fewer close substitutes for the new autos than there are for the Jeep Cherokee. However, there are many substitutes for the new automobile. Consumers can hold onto their existing vehicle longer—and this has occurred. In the 1970s the average age of a vehicle on the road was about 4 years; today it is approaching 8 years. Consumers can also purchase used cars rather than new ones. This too is occurring. Recent reports indicate that used car lots are now receiving more attention from car dealers than the new lots. The dealers can make about $300 per vehicle in profit on used cars but only about half that on new vehicles. Consumers are increasingly turning to used cars rather than the new cars.

The income elasticity of demand for new autos has risen during the past two decades. As incomes have risen, fewer new cars are purchased now than two decades ago. It used to be that higher income families would look to purchase a new car every 2 years at the longest; many traded cars annually. The income elasticity of demand for particular models—Chevrolet Cavalier or Ford Taurus—has declined as well. An increase in income from $30,000 to $40,000 used to mean the purchase of a new Taurus or comparable car. It now might mean the purchase of a Neon or subcompact car—or a used car.

The increased price of automobiles and the higher percentage of a family's income the automobile constitutes has altered the price and income elasticities of demand. Automobile executives must figure out how these elasticities have changed and create business strategies for dealing with these changes if they are to be successful.

21

Consumer Choice

FUNDAMENTAL
QUESTIONS

1. Does one more dollar mean less to a millionaire than to a pauper?

2. What does "all you can eat" really mean?

3. How do consumers allocate their limited incomes among the billions of goods and services that exist?

4. Why do Disneyland, Sea World, and other businesses charge an admission fee and then provide the use of the facilities for no extra charge?

5. Does utility maximization really describe consumer behavior?

everal students who had just completed their final exam in economics were joking that any lab animal could be trained to get an A in economics. It would only have to answer "demand and supply" to every question. The students' sarcasm demonstrated both their grasp and lack of understanding of economics. There is no doubt that demand and supply are at the heart of economics, but unless you know *why* demand and supply behave as they do, can you be confident about what they imply? Can firms be sure they will sell more if they lower the price of their product? Should producers confidently assume that when income grows, demand will increase? Can managers rely on a direct relation between price and quantity supplied? To grasp how the economy functions, it is necessary to understand what lies behind demand and supply.

PREVIEW

In this chapter we take a close look at demand. We examine how and why consumers make choices and what factors influence their choices. In the next chapter, "Supply: The Costs of Doing Business," we turn to the supply side and discuss what decisions and factors lie behind the relation between quantities supplied and price.

I. DECISIONS

Do we go to college or get a job? Do we get married or remain single? Do we live in the dorm, a house, or an apartment? "Decisions, decisions, decisions! Don't we ever get a break from the pressure of making choices?" Not unless scarcity disappears will we be freed of having to make choices. Although scarcity and choice are pervasive, how people make decisions is a question that has eluded scientific explanation. Some decisions seem to be based on feelings, or come from the heart, while others seem more calculated. Some are quick and impulsive, while others take months or years of research. Is it the appeal of the book cover that makes you decide to buy one book over another? Does a television commercial affect your decision? Are you more influenced by your spouse, your family, your friends, or your coworkers?

The answers to these questions depend on your values, on your personality, on where you were raised, on how others might react to your decision, and on many other factors. Although the important factors of a decision may vary from person to person, everyone makes decisions in much the same way. People tend to compare perceived costs and benefits of alternatives and select those that they believe give them the greatest relative benefits. This is not to say everyone walks around with a computer into which they continually feed data and out of which comes the answer: "Buy this," or "Do that." Instead, whether the decision is made on the basis of emotion or on the basis of an accountant's balance sheet, people are comparing what they perceive at the time of the decision to be the costs and benefits to them of that decision. To explain how these comparisons are made, philosophers and economists of the nineteenth century developed a concept called *utility*. That concept can help us understand consumer decision-making today.

1.a. Utility

utility:
a measure of the satisfaction received from possessing or consuming goods and services

Individuals behave so as to maximize their utility.

How is success measured in the game of life? It is measured not as the bumper sticker says "The one with the most toys at the end wins" but by happiness—how much fun you have along the way. **Utility** is the term economists and philosophers have used to capture the concept of "happiness." You are nourished by a good meal, entertained by a concert, proud of a fine car, and comforted by a nice home and warm clothing. Whatever feelings are described by *nourishment, entertainment, pride*, and *comfort* are captured in the term *utility*. Utility is another term for *satisfaction* or happiness.

Consumers make choices that give them the greatest satisfaction; they maximize their utility. Whether one item is preferable to another depends on how much utility each provides. If you enjoy a hot fudge sundae more than a piece of angel food cake, you choose the sundae. You select it because it gives you more utility than the angel food cake.

The utility you derive from experiencing some activity or consuming some good depends on your tastes and preferences. You may love opera and intensely dislike country and western music. You may have difficulty understanding how anyone can eat tripe, but you love hot chilies. We shall have little to say about why some people prefer country and western music and others classical music although the issue is interesting; we simply *assume* that tastes and preferences are given and use those given tastes and preferences to describe the process of decision-making.

1.b. Diminishing Marginal Utility

diminishing marginal utility:
the principle that the more of a good that one obtains in a specific period of time, the less is the additional utility yielded by an additional unit of that good

marginal utility:
the extra utility derived from consuming one more unit of a good or service

Utility is used to show why the law of demand is a law. To illustrate how utility maximization can be useful, we must create a hypothetical world where we can measure the satisfaction that people receive from consuming goods and services. Suppose that a consumer named Gabrielle can listen to as much country and western music as she wishes during the course of the day. Assume that Gabrielle is hooked up to a computer that measures satisfaction in units called *utils*. The utils that Gabrielle associates with each hour of listening are presented in Table 1.

Several important concepts associated with consumer choice can be observed in Table 1. First, each *additional* hour of music yields Gabrielle less satisfaction (fewer utils) than the previous hour. According to Table 1, the first hour yields 200 utils, the second 98, the third 50, the fourth 10, and the fifth none. Each additional hour of music, until the fifth hour, adds to total utility; but Gabrielle enjoys each additional hour just a little bit less than she enjoyed the prior hour. This relationship is called **diminishing marginal utility**.

Marginal utility is the change in total utility that occurs because one more unit of the good is consumed or acquired;

$$\text{Marginal utility} = \frac{\text{change in total utility}}{\text{change in quantity}}$$

According to the principle of diminishing marginal utility, the more of a good or service that someone consumes during a particular period of time,

TABLE 1
The Utility of Listening to Country and Western Music

Hours of Listening per Day	Util of Each Hour (marginal utility)	Total Utility
1	200	200
2	98	298
3	50	348
4	10	358
5	0	358
6	−70	288
7	−200	88

disutility:
dissatisfaction

total utility:
a measure of the total satisfaction derived from consuming a quantity of some good or service

the less satisfaction another unit of that good or service provides that individual. Imagine yourself sitting down to a plate piled high with cake. The first piece is delicious, and the second tastes good but not as good as the first. The fourth piece doesn't taste very good at all, and the sixth piece nearly makes you sick. Instead of satisfaction, the sixth piece of cake yields dissatisfaction, or **disutility**.

Notice that we are speaking of diminishing *marginal* utility, not diminishing *total* utility. **Total utility**, the measure of the total satisfaction derived from consuming a quantity of some good or service, climbs until dissatisfaction sets in. For Gabrielle, total utility rises from 200 to 298 to 348 and reaches 358 with the fourth hour of music. From the fifth hour on, total utility declines. Marginal utility, however, is the additional utility gained from listening to another hour of music, and it declines from the first hour on.

To illustrate the relation between marginal and total utility, we have plotted the data from Table 1 in Figure 1(a). The total utility curve rises as quantity rises until the fifth hour of listening. After 5 hours, the total utility curve declines. The reason total utility rises at first is that each additional hour provides a little more utility. The marginal utility of the first hour is 200; the marginal utility of the second hour is 98; of the third, 50; of the fourth, 10; and of the fifth, zero. By the fifth hour, total utility is $200 + 98 + 50 + 10 + 0 = 358$.

We have plotted marginal utility in Figure 1(b), directly below the total utility curve of Figure 1(a). Marginal utility declines with each successive unit, reaches zero, and then turns negative. As long as marginal utility is positive, total utility rises. When marginal utility becomes negative, total utility declines. Marginal utility is zero at the point where total utility is at its maximum (unit 5 in this case).

1.c Diminishing Marginal Utility and Time

The concept of diminishing marginal utility makes sense only if we define the *period of time* during which consumption is occurring. If Gabrielle listened to the music over a period of several days, we would not observe diminishing marginal utility until she had listened more than 5 hours. Usually, the shorter the time period, the more quickly marginal utility diminishes. Once

Figure 1
Total and Marginal Utility

Figure 1(a) shows the total utility obtained from listening to country and western music. Total utility reaches a maximum and then declines as additional listening becomes distasteful. For the first hour, the marginal and total utilities are the same. For the second hour, the marginal utility is the additional utility provided by the second unit. The total utility is the sum of the marginal utilities of the first and second units. The second unit provides less utility than the first unit, the third less than the second, and so on, in accordance with the law of diminishing marginal utility. But total utility, the sum of marginal utilities, rises as long as marginal utility is positive. Figure 1(b) shows marginal utility. When marginal utility is zero, total utility is at its maximum. When marginal utility is negative, total utility declines.

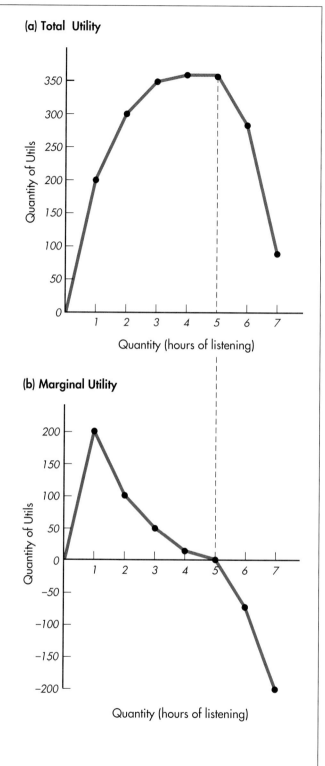

(a) Total Utility

(b) Marginal Utility

the time period has been defined, diminishing marginal utility will apply; it applies to everyone and to every good and service, except perhaps to income itself, as discussed in the Economic Insight "Does Money Buy Happiness?"

1.d. Consumers Are Not Identical

Does one more dollar mean less to a millionaire than to a pauper?

All consumers experience diminishing marginal utility, but the rate at which marginal utility declines is not identical for all consumers. This is where tastes and preferences enter the discussion. The rate at which marginal utility diminishes depends on an individual's tastes and preferences. Gabrielle clearly enjoys country and western music. For a person who dislikes it, the first hour might yield disutility or negative utility.

1.e. An Illustration: "All You Can Eat"

What does "all you can eat" really mean?

The principle of diminishing marginal utility says something about "all you can eat" specials. It says that you will stop eating when marginal utility is zero. At some restaurants consumers who pay a fixed charge may eat as much as they desire. The only restriction is that the restaurant does not allow "doggy bags." Because diminishing marginal utility eventually sets in, all consumers eventually stop eating when their marginal utility is zero. This is the point at which their total utility is at a maximum: one more bite would be distasteful and would decrease utility. The restaurant must determine what fixed price to charge. Knowing that no consumer will eat forever—that each will stop when his or her marginal utility is zero—the restaurant must set a price that yields a profit from the average consumer.

RECAP

1. Utility is a concept used to represent the degree to which goods and services satisfy wants.

2. Total utility is the total satisfaction that a consumer obtains from consuming a particular good or service.

3. Marginal utility is the utility that an additional unit of a good or service yields.

4. Total utility increases until dissatisfaction sets in. When another unit of a good would yield disutility, the consumer has been filled up with the good—more will not bring greater satisfaction.

5. According to the principle of diminishing marginal utility, marginal utility declines with each additional unit of a good or service that the consumer obtains. When marginal utility is zero, total utility is at its maximum.

2. UTILITY AND CHOICE

How do consumers allocate their limited incomes among the billions of goods and services that exist?

Can we simply conclude that people will consume goods until the marginal utility of each good is zero? No, we cannot, for we would be ignoring scarcity and opportunity costs. No one has enough income to purchase everything until the marginal utility of each item is zero. Because incomes

Does Money Buy Happiness?

Diminishing marginal utility affects consumer purchases of every good. Does diminishing marginal utility affect income as well? This question has been a topic of economic debate for years. The case for progressive taxation—the more income you have, the greater the percentage of each additional dollar that you pay in taxes—is based on the idea that the marginal utility of income diminishes. In theory, if each additional dollar brings less utility to a person, the pain associated with giving up a portion of each additional dollar will decline. And as a result of taxing the rich at a higher rate than the poor, the total pain imposed on society from a tax will be less than it would be if the same tax rate were applied to every dollar.

Economists have attempted to confirm or disprove the idea of the diminishing marginal utility of income, but doing so has proved difficult. Experiments have even been carried out on the topic. In one experiment, laboratory rats were trained to work for pay. They had to hit a bar several times to get a piece of food or a drink of water. After a while, after obtaining a certain amount of food and water, the rats reduced their work efforts, choosing leisure instead of more food and water. Thus, the rats did react as if their "income"—food and water—had a diminishing marginal utility.

Economists have also turned to the literature of psychology. Psychologists have carried out many surveys to measure whether people are more or less happy under various circumstances. One survey back in the 1960s asked

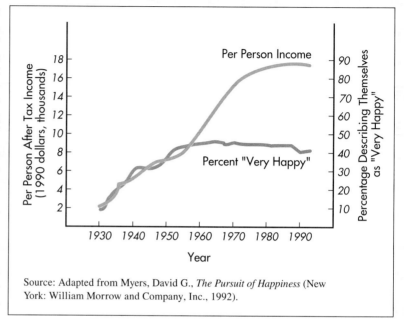

Source: Adapted from Myers, David G., *The Pursuit of Happiness* (New York: William Morrow and Company, Inc., 1992).

people in different income brackets whether they were unhappy, pretty happy, or very happy. The results indicated that the higher income is, the happier people are. A more recent study by David Myers in 1992, however, examined why people are happy and found some results that contradicted the earlier study. Although citizens of the more wealthy nations tend to be happier than citizens of the less wealthy nations, this relationship is not very strong. More important than wealth is the history of democracy; the longer a nation has been democratic, the happier are its citizens. Within any one country, there is only a modest link between well-being and being well-off. "Once we're comfortable, more money therefore provides diminishing returns. The second

helping never tastes as good as the first," says Myers. "The second fifty thousand dollars of income means much less than the first." Myers uses a figure something like the accompanying one to illustrate his findings. Notice how income and percentage who are happy both rise until a 1990 income level of about $7,000 per person after tax is reached. After that income level, as income rises, the percentage who are happy does not change much.

Sources: David G. Myers, *The Pursuit of Happiness* (New York: William Morrow and Company, Inc., 1992); and N. M. Bradburn and D. Caplovitz, *Reports on Happiness* (Chicago: Aldine, 1965), p. 9.

are limited, purchasing one thing means not purchasing other things. Gabrielle, our country and western music fancier, might be able to get more utility by purchasing some other good than by buying more music to listen to.

To illustrate the effect of opportunity costs on consumption, let's turn again to Gabrielle and ask her to allocate a limited income—$10—among three goods: compact disks (CDs), gas for her car, and movies.

2.a. Consumer Choice

Gabrielle has a budget of $10 to spend on CDs, gasoline, and movies. She has found a place selling used CDs. She also goes to a discount gas station and a discount movie theater. We want to know how many units of each she will purchase. The answer is in Table 2.

The price (*P*) of each secondhand CD is $2; the price of each gallon of gas is $1; the price of each movie is $3. The marginal utility (*MU*) provided by each unit and the ratio of the marginal utility to the price (*MU/P*) are presented at the top of the table. In the lower part of the table are the steps involved in allocating income among the three goods.

The first purchase involves a choice among the first unit of each of the three goods. The first CD yields a marginal utility (*MU*) of 200 and costs $2; thus, per dollar of expenditure, the first CD yields 100 utils (*MU/P* = 100). The first gallon of gas yields a marginal utility per dollar of expenditure of 200. The first movie yields a marginal utility per dollar of expenditure of 50; it yields 150 utils and costs $3. Which does Gabrielle choose?

To find the answer, compare the ratios of the marginal utility per dollar of expenditure (*MU/P*), *not* the marginal utility of each good (*MU*). The ratio of marginal utility to price puts the goods on the same basis (utility per dollar) and allows us to make sense of Gabrielle's decisions. Looking only at marginal utilities would not do this. For instance, another diamond might yield 10,000 utils and another apple might yield only 100 utils; but if the diamond costs $100,000 and the apple costs $1, the marginal utility per dollar of expenditure on the apple is greater than the marginal utility per dollar of expenditure on the diamond, and thus a consumer is better off purchasing the apple.

As indicated in Table 2, Gabrielle's first purchase is the gallon of gas. It yields the greatest marginal utility per dollar of expenditure (she needs gas in her car to be able to go anywhere); and because it costs $1, Gabrielle has $9 left to spend.

The second purchase involves a choice among the first CD, the second gallon of gas, and the first movie. The ratios of marginal utility per dollar of expenditure are 100 for the CD, 150 for the gas, and 50 for a movie. Thus, Gabrielle purchases the second gallon of gas and has $8 left.

For the third purchase Gabrielle must decide between the first CD, the first movie, and the third gallon of gas. Because the CD yields a ratio of 100 and both the gas and the movie yield ratios of 50, she purchases the CD. The CD costs $2, so she has $6 left to spend.

A utility-maximizing consumer like Gabrielle always chooses the purchase that yields the greatest marginal utility per dollar of expenditure. If two goods offer the same marginal utility per dollar of expenditure, the consumer will be indifferent between the two—that is, the consumer won't care which is chosen. For example, Table 2 indicates that for the fourth purchase another

TABLE 2
The Logic of Consumer Choice

CD (P = $2)			Gas (P = $1)			Movie (P = $3)		
Units	**MU**	**MU/P**	**Units**	**MU**	**MU/P**	**Units**	**MU**	**MU/P**
1	200	100	1	200	200	1	150	50
2	98	49	2	150	150	2	90	30
3	50	25	3	50	50	3	60	20
4	10	5	4	30	30	4	30	10
5	0	0	5	0	0	5	9	3
6	−70	−35	6	−300	−300	6	0	0
7	−200	−100	7	−700	−700	7	−6	−2

Steps	Choices		Decision	Remaining Budget
1st purchase	1st CD:	$MU/P = 100$	Gas	$10 − $1 = $9
	1st gas:	$MU/P = 200$		
	1st movie:	$MU/P = 50$		
2nd purchase	1st CD:	$MU/P = 100$	Gas	$9 − $1 = $8
	2nd gas:	$MU/P = 150$		
	1st movie:	$MU/P = 50$		
3rd purchase	1st CD:	$MU/P = 100$	CD	$8 − $2 = $6
	3rd gas:	$MU/P = 50$		
	1st movie:	$MU/P = 50$		
4th purchase	2nd CD:	$MU/P = 49$	Gas	$6 − $1 = $5
	3rd gas:	$MU/P = 50$		
	1st movie:	$MU/P = 50$		
5th purchase	2nd CD:	$MU/P = 49$	Movie	$5 − $3 = $2
	4th gas:	$MU/P = 30$		
	1st movie:	$MU/P = 50$		
6th purchase	2nd CD:	$MU/P = 49$	CD	$2 − $2 = 0
	4th gas:	$MU/P = 30$		
	2nd movie:	$MU/P = 30$		

Note: Purchases made with $10: 2 CDs, 3 gallons of gas, and 1 movie ticket.

gallon of gas or a movie would yield 50 utils per dollar. The consumer is completely indifferent between the two and so arbitrarily selects gas. The movie is chosen for the fifth purchase. With the sixth purchase, the total budget is spent. For $10, Gabrielle ends up with 2 CDs, 3 gallons of gas, and 1 movie.

In this example, Gabrielle is portrayed as a methodical, robotlike consumer who calculates how to allocate her scarce income among goods and services in a way that ensures that each additional dollar of expenditure yields the greatest marginal utility. This picture is more than a little farfetched, but it does describe the result if not the process of consumer choice.

People do have to decide which goods and services to purchase with their limited incomes, and people do select the options that give them the greatest utility.

2.b. Consumer Equilibrium

equimarginal principle (consumer equilibrium): to maximize utility, consumers must allocate their scarce incomes among goods so as to equate the marginal utilities per dollar of expenditure on the last unit of each good purchased

With $10, Gabrielle purchases 2 CDs, 3 gallons of gas, and 1 movie ticket. For the second CD, the marginal utility per dollar of expenditure is 49; for the third gallon of gas, it is 50; and for the first movie, it is 50. Is it merely a fluke that the marginal utility per dollar of expenditure ratios are nearly equal? No. *In order to maximize utility, consumers must allocate their limited incomes among goods and services in such a way that the marginal utilities per dollar of expenditure on the last unit of each good purchased will be as nearly equal as possible.* This is called the **equimarginal principle** and also represents **consumer equilibrium**. It is consumer equilibrium because the consumer will not change from this point unless something changes income, marginal utility, or price.

In our example, the ratios are not identical at consumer equilibrium—49, 50, 50—but they are as close to equal as possible because Gabrielle (like all consumers) had to purchase whole portions of the goods. Consumers cannot spend a dollar on any good or service and always get the fractional amount a dollar buys—one-tenth of a tennis lesson, or one-third of a bottle of water. Instead, consumers have to purchase goods and services in whole units—1 piece or 1 ounce or 1 package—and pay the per unit price.

The equimarginal principle is simply common sense. Consumers spend an additional dollar on the good that gives the greatest satisfaction. At the prices given in Table 2, with an income of $10, and with the marginal utilities given, Gabrielle maximizes her utility by purchasing 2 CDs, 3 gallons of gas, and 1 movie ticket. Everything else held constant, no other allocation of the $10 would yield Gabrielle more utility.

Consumers are in equilibrium when they have no incentive to reallocate their limited budget or income. With *MU* standing for marginal utility and *P* for price, the general rule for consumer equilibrium is

$$\frac{MU_{CD}}{P_{CD}} = \frac{MU_{gas}}{P_{gas}} = \frac{MU_{movie}}{P_{movie}} = \cdots = \frac{MU_x}{P_x}$$

MU_x/P_x is the marginal utility per dollar of expenditure on any good other than CDs, gas, or movies. It represents the opportunity cost of spending $1 on CDs, gas, or movies.

RECAP

1. To maximize utility, consumers must allocate their limited incomes in such a way that the marginal utilities per dollar obtained from the last unit consumed are equal among all goods and services; this is the equimarginal principle.

2. As long as the marginal utilities per dollar obtained from the last unit of all products consumed are the same, the consumer is in equilibrium and will not reallocate income.

3. Consumer equilibrium, or utility maximization, is summarized by a formula that equates the marginal utilities per dollar of expenditure on the last item purchased of all goods:

$$MU_a/P_a = MU_b/P_b = MU_c/P_c = MU_x/P_x$$

3. THE DEMAND CURVE AGAIN

We have shown how consumers make choices—by allocating their scarce incomes among goods in order to maximize their utility. The next step is to relate consumer choices to the demand curve.

3.a. The Downward Slope of the Demand Curve

The demand curve or schedule can be derived from consumer equilibrium by altering the price of one good or service.

Recall from Chapter 3 that as the price of a good falls, the quantity demanded of that good rises. This inverse relation between price and quantity demanded arises from diminishing marginal utility and consumer equilibrium.

Consumers allocate their income among goods and services in order to maximize their utility. A consumer is in equilibrium when the total budget is expended and the marginal utilities per dollar of expenditure on the last unit of each good are the same. A change in the price of one good will disturb the consumer's equilibrium; the ratios of marginal utility per dollar of expenditure on the last unit of each good will no longer be equal. The consumer will then reallocate her income among the goods in order to increase total utility.

In the example presented in Table 2, the price of a CD is $2, the price per gallon of gas is $1, and the price of a movie ticket is $3. Now suppose the price of the CD falls to $1 while the prices of gas and movies and Gabrielle's budget of $10 remain the same. Common sense tells us that Gabrielle will probably alter the quantities purchased by buying more CDs. To find out if she does—and whether the equimarginal principle holds—her purchases are traced step by step in Table 3.

Only the *MU/P* ratio for CDs is different from the corresponding figure at the top of Table 2. According to Table 3, at the old consumer equilibrium of 2 CDs, 3 gallons of gas, and 1 movie, the marginal utility per dollar of expenditure (*MU/P*) on each good is:

CD: 98/$1 = 98/$1   Gas: 50/$1 = 50/$1   Movie: 150/$3 = 50/$1

Clearly, the ratios are no longer equal. In order to maximize utility, Gabrielle must reallocate her budget among the goods. Her choices are shown in the lower portion of Table 3.

Gabrielle's first choice now involves the first CD, which yields 200 utils per dollar; the first gallon of gas, which also yields 200 utils per dollar; and the first movie, which yields 50 utils per dollar. She is indifferent between the first CD and the first gallon of gas; we will assume that she chooses a CD. Her remaining budget is $9. For her second purchase, she chooses the gas, and her remaining budget is then $8. When all $10 is spent, Gabrielle finds that she has purchased 3 CDs, 4 gallons of gas, and 1 movie ticket. The lower price of CDs has induced her to purchase an additional CD. Gabrielle's behavior illustrates what you already know: the quantity demanded of CDs increases as the price of the CD decreases.

Part V/Product Market Basics

TABLE 3
A Price Change

CD (P = $1)			Gas (P = $1)			Movie (P = $3)		
Units	**MU**	**MU/P**	**Units**	**MU**	**MU/P**	**Units**	**MU**	**MU/P**
1	200	200	1	200	200	1	150	50
2	98	98	2	150	150	2	90	30
3	50	50	3	50	50	3	60	20
4	10	10	4	30	30	4	30	10
5	0	0	5	0	0	5	9	3
6	−70	−70	6	−300	−300	6	0	0
7	−200	−200	7	−700	−700	7	−6	−2

Steps	Choices			Decision	Remaining Budget
1st purchase	1st CD:	$MU/P =$	200	CD	$10 − $1 = $9
	1st gas:	$MU/P =$	200		
	1st movie:	$MU/P =$	50		
2nd purchase	2nd CD:	$MU/P =$	98	Gas	$9 − $1 = $8
	1st gas:	$MU/P =$	200		
	1st movie:	$MU/P =$	50		
3rd purchase	2nd CD:	$MU/P =$	98	Gas	$8 − $1 = $7
	2nd gas:	$MU/P =$	150		
	1st movie:	$MU/P =$	50		
4th purchase	2nd CD:	$MU/P =$	98	CD	$7 − $1 = $6
	3rd gas:	$MU/P =$	50		
	1st movie:	$MU/P =$	50		
5th purchase	3rd CD:	$MU/P =$	50	Movie	$6 − $3 = $3
	3rd gas:	$MU/P =$	50		
	1st movie:	$MU/P =$	50		
6th purchase	3rd CD:	$MU/P =$	50	CD	$3 − $1 = $2
	3rd gas:	$MU/P =$	50		
	2nd movie:	$MU/P =$	30		
7th purchase	4th CD:	$MU/P =$	10	Gas	$2 − $1 = $1
	3rd gas:	$MU/P =$	50		
	2nd movie:	$MU/P =$	30		
8th purchase	4th CD:	$MU/P =$	10	Gas	$1 − $1 = 0
	4th gas:	$MU/P =$	30		
	2nd movie:	$MU/P =$	30		

Note: Purchases made with $10: 3 CDs, 4 gallons of gas, and 1 movie.

If the price of the CD were increased to $3 and we traced Gabrielle's purchases again, we would find that Gabrielle demands only 1 CD. The three prices for CDs ($1, $2, $3) and the corresponding quantities of CDs purchased give us Gabrielle's demand for CDs, which is shown in Figure 2. At $3 she is willing and able to buy 1 CD; at $2 she is willing and able to buy 2 CDs; and at $1 she is willing and able to buy 3 CDs.

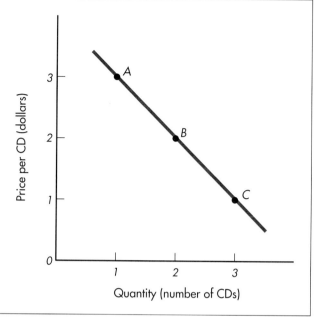

Figure 2
Gabrielle's Demand Curve for CDs
The demand curve shows that Gabrielle purchases 1 CD at a price of $3, 2 CDs at a price of $2, and 3 CDs at a price of $1.

Gabrielle's demand curve is the line connecting points *A*, *B*, and C in Figure 2. The demand curve was derived by changing the price of CDs *while income, tastes and preferences, prices of related goods, the time period over which consumption occurred, and expectations were held constant.*

3.b. Income and Substitution Effects of a Price Change

The substitution effect indicates that following a decrease in the price of a good or service, an individual will purchase more of the now less-expensive good and less of other goods.

The income effect of a price change indicates that an individual's income can buy more of all goods when the price of one good declines, everything else held constant.

When the price of one good falls while everything else is held constant, two things occur: (1) other goods become relatively *more* expensive so consumers buy more of the less expensive good and less of the more expensive goods; and (2) the good purchased prior to the price change now costs less so the consumer can buy more of all goods.

When a good becomes relatively less expensive, it yields more satisfaction per dollar than before, so consumers buy more of it than before as they decrease their expenditures on other goods. This is the *substitution effect* of a price change.

Figure 2 shows that at the price of $2 per CD, Gabrielle spends $4 on CDs. When the price falls to $1, she spends only $2 for those two CDs. As a result, Gabrielle can purchase more of all goods, including the good whose price has fallen. This is the *income effect* of a price change.

3.c. Consumer Surplus

An individual's demand curve measures the value that the individual consumer places on each unit of the good being considered. For example, the value that Gabrielle places on the first CD is the price she would be willing and able to pay for it. The price Gabrielle would be willing to pay for one CD is $3, as shown in Figure 3. At a price of $2, Gabrielle purchases two CDs.

Figure 3
Consumer Surplus and the Demand for CDs
The demand curve shown in Figure 2 is reproduced here. Gabrielle is willing and able to pay $3 for the first CD. She is willing to pay $2 for the second CD. If the market price of CDs is $2, she can buy both the first and the second CDs for $2 each; and she receives a bonus on the first, paying less for it than she is willing and able to pay. This bonus, the consumer surplus, is indicated by the blue area. At a price of $1, the consumer surplus is both the blue and yellow areas.

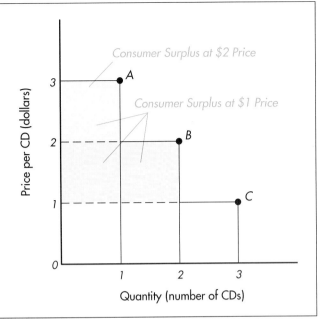

She is willing to pay $3 for the first and $2 for the second, but she gets both for $2 each. She gets a bonus because the value she places on the CD is higher than the price she has to pay for it. This bonus is called *consumer surplus*.

Consumer surplus is a measure of the difference between what a consumer is willing and able to pay and the market price of a good. At a market price of $2, Gabrielle's consumer surplus is equal to ($3 − $2) + ($2 − $2) = $1, shown as the blue area in Figure 3. At a price of $1, Gabrielle is willing and able to purchase 3 CDs, but only the third CD is worth only $1 to her. The first two are worth more than the $1 she has to pay for them. When she purchases the CDs, she gets a bonus of ($3 − $1) + ($2 − $1) + ($1 − $1) = $3, shown as the sum of the yellow and blue areas.

consumer surplus:
the difference between what the consumer is willing to pay for a unit of a good and the price that the consumer actually has to pay

3.d. Disneyland and Consumer Surplus

Why do Disneyland, Sea World, and other businesses charge an admission fee and then provide the use of the facilities for no extra charge?

Consumer surplus provides a basis for explaining aspects of consumer, producer, and government behavior. It can play a part in determining a firm's pricing strategy.

Disneyland has experimented with several different pricing schemes since opening its gates 40 years ago. At one stage patrons paid a small admission fee and could purchase ride or exhibit tickets one by one. Now Disneyland, Disney World, and the Disney Worlds in France and Japan have forgone the pricing of individual rides and exhibits for a larger admission fee. Consumers pay an admission fee that enables them to go on any ride or in any exhibit as many times as desired.

Suppose consumers enjoy the rides at Disneyland according to the utility schedule shown in Table 4. If Disneyland does not charge for rides, consumers who enter the park will want to take in no more than 7 rides, since

TABLE 4
The Utility of Rides at Disneyland

Number of Rides	Marginal Utility	Total Utility
1	100	100
2	90	190
3	70	260
4	50	310
5	25	335
6	10	345
7	0	345
8	−10	335
9	−20	315

the seventh ride provides them zero marginal utility. At a price above zero, consumers will participate in rides until the marginal utility of a ride is equal to the marginal utility of anything else that money could be used for, presumably a number of rides less than 7.

The consumers' demand schedule and demand curve for rides at Disneyland are shown in Figure 4. At $7 per ride, no one wants to ride. At $6

Figure 4
Consumer Surplus and the Demand for Rides at Disneyland

The demand schedule and demand curve for rides at Disneyland are shown. Disneyland wants to set a price that extracts as much of the consumer surplus as possible. The consumer surplus at a zero price per ride is shown as the area bounded by A, E, K. By setting an admission price equal to the consumer surplus and a zero price per ride, Disneyland can extract the full consumer surplus, the area below the demand curve and above the price.

Price per Ride	Quantity Demanded
$7	0
6	1
5	2
4	3
3	4
2	5
1	6
0	7

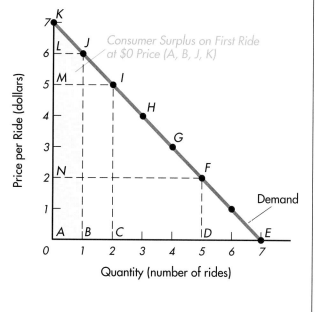

TABLE 5
Consumer Surplus and the Demand
for Rides at Disneyland

Ride	Consumer Surplus
1	$6 − $0 = $ 6
2	5 − 0 = 5
3	4 − 0 = 4
4	3 − 0 = 3
5	2 − 0 = 2
6	1 − 0 = 1
7	0 − 0 = 0
Total	$21

per ride, each consumer purchases 1 ride and Disneyland obtains the total revenue that results when the price listed is multiplied by the quantity. That amount is the area bounded by *A, B, J, L* in the graph in Figure 4. At a price of $5 per ride, each consumer buys 2 rides and Disneyland earns the total revenue in area *A, C, I, M*. At a price of $2 per ride, each consumer buys 5 rides and Disneyland earns the revenue in area *A, D, F, N*. What should Disneyland charge? If Disneyland wants to maximize its total revenue, it must get the consumer to pay an amount equal to the value the consumer places on the rides—that is, Disneyland must collect the entire consumer surplus.

Consumer surplus varies from individual to individual, but let's assume that Figure 4 represents the average individual's demand curve for rides. The consumer surplus is the area that lies below the demand curve and above the per ride price. Figure 4 shows that at $5 per ride, 2 rides are purchased and consumer surplus is the area bounded by *M, I, K*. At $2 per ride, 5 rides are purchased and consumer surplus is the area bounded by *N, F, K*.

If Disneyland charges nothing per ride, total demand is satisfied but Disneyland's revenue is zero. However, by placing an admission charge equal to total consumer surplus, Disneyland is able to collect the entire consumer surplus. At a per ride price of zero, the consumer surplus is about $21. The consumer surplus is calculated in Table 5 by subtracting a zero price from the price the consumer is willing and able to pay for each unit. For instance, the consumer is willing and able to pay $6 for the first ride. Consumer surplus for the first ride, if the price of that ride equals zero, is $6 − $0 = $6. The consumer is willing and able to pay $5 for the second ride; thus, the consumer surplus of that second ride, at a zero price, is $5. Calculating the total consumer surplus at a zero price tells Disneyland that the admission charge has to be about $21 to pick up the entire consumer surplus.

The admission policy is compared to a policy of charging per ride in Table 6. The greatest revenue is obtained when a price of either $3 or $4 is set. There, total revenue is $12. You can see in this example how the per-ride pricing policy generates significantly less revenue than the admission-only pricing policy.

TABLE 6
Pricing Policies

Price per Ride	Rides Taken	Revenue
$7	0	$ 0
6	1	6
5	2	10
4	3	12
3	4	12
2	5	10
1	6	6

3.e. Review of the Determination of Market Demand

Individual demand comes from utility maximization. Individuals allocate their scarce incomes among goods in order to get the greatest utility; this occurs when consumer equilibrium is reached, represented in symbols as $MU_a/P_a = MU_b/P_b = \ldots = MU_x/P_x$. As the price of a good or service is changed, consumer equilibrium is disturbed. In response to the price change, individuals alter their purchases so as to achieve maximum utility. The process of changing the price of one good or service while income, tastes and preferences, and the prices of related goods are held constant, defines the individual's demand for that good or service.

Should income, tastes and preferences, or prices of related goods and services change, then the individual's demand will change. More or less income means more or less goods and services can be purchased. But buying more of everything does not mean you are in equilibrium because the rates of diminishing marginal utility vary from good to good. Thus, a change in income affects the ratios of MU/P and disturbs consumer equilibrium. When the price of a related good changes, the ratio of marginal utility to price for that good changes, thus disturbing consumer equilibrium. And changes in tastes and preferences, represented as changes in the MUs, also alter consumer equilibrium. In each case a new consumer equilibrium point will be reached. Then, based on the new consumer equilibrium, a new demand curve for a good or service can be derived. The new demand curve will lie inside or outside the former demand curve; thus, the demand curve will have shifted.

Consumer equilibrium shows that the nonprice determinants of demand have their effects through the MUs or the prices of other goods and services.

The market demand curve is the sum of all the individual demand curves. This means that anything that affects the individual curves also affects the market curve. In addition, when we combine the individual demand curves into a market demand curve, the number of individuals to be combined determines the position of the market demand curve. Changes in the number of consumers alters the market demand curve. We thus say that the determinants of demand are tastes and preferences, income, prices of related goods, international effects, and number of consumers. Also, recall that diminishing marginal utility is defined for consumption during a specific period of time. Since consumer equilibrium and thus the demand curve depend on diminishing marginal utility, the demand curve is also defined for consumption over a specific period of time. Changes in the time period or changes in expectations will therefore also alter demand.

RECAP

1. The principle of diminishing marginal utility and the equimarginal principle account for the inverse relation between the price of a product and the quantity demanded.

2. A price change triggers the substitution effect and the income effect.

3. The substitution effect occurs because once a good becomes less expensive, it yields more satisfaction per dollar than before and consumers buy more of it than before. They do this by decreasing their purchases of other goods. The income effect of the price change occurs because a lower price raises real income (total utility) and the consumer purchases more of all goods.

4. Consumer surplus is the excess of the amount consumers are willing and able to pay for an item over the price they actually pay.

5. The market demand curve is the summation of all individual demand curves.

6. Economists derive the market demand curve for a good by assuming that individual incomes are fixed, that the prices of all goods except the one in question are constant, that each individual's tastes remain fixed, that expectations do not change, that the number of consumers is constant, and that the time period under consideration remains unchanged. A change in any one of these determinants causes the demand curve to shift.

4. UTILITY MAXIMIZATION AND CONSUMER BEHAVIOR[1]

Does utility maximization really describe consumer behavior?

The theory of utility maximization helps us understand how people behave. Most of us, most of the time, behave in ways that make us feel the happiest. When there is no scarcity, we consume a good or carry out an activity until more will not provide us any satisfaction. And when we must choose among different goods or activities because of the scarcity of our income or time, we allocate our resources so as to get the most "bang for the buck," or most happiness per dollar of expenditure. This and other implications of utility theory do seem to make sense for most of us most of the time.

However, it is silly to think that people are hooked up to a util-measuring machine. People simply do not calculate the utils of each option before making a decision. The model of consumer behavior is just a model—a simplification of reality. Nevertheless, because utility theory appears to be so

---

[1]This section is based on research reported in a series of articles by psychologists and economists. Many are summarized in Richard H. Thaler, *Quasi Rational Economics* (New York: Russell Sage Foundation, 1994).

unrealistic, economics itself is often criticized as being totally unrealistic. This criticism is misplaced. Economists, following the scientific method, narrow a model as much as possible in order to focus on a specific issue, such as individual behavior. But when the model yields implications that do not match reality, economists relax assumptions to generalize the model. This is what must be done with the theory of consumer behavior. In this section we highlight some ways that the theory of consumer behavior must be broadly interpreted to account for actual behavior.

4.a. Evaluating Gains and Losses

According to utility maximization, the satisfaction you get from a gain is equal to the pain (loss of satisfaction) you get from an equal loss. Is this true? Answer the following:

> Who is happier: Person A, who wins the office football pool for $100 on the same day she ruins the carpet in her apartment and must pay the landlord $75, or Person B, who wins the office football pool for $25?

Most people believe Person A is happier even though both A and B end up with the same $25 gain. Consider the same problem with a slight revision.

> Who is happier: Person A, who ruins the carpet in her apartment and must pay the landlord $100, or Person B, who wins the office football pool for $25 but also ruins the carpet in his apartment and must pay the landlord $125?

Most people believe Person B is happier even though A and B must pay the same amount, $100. The implication of these hypothetical questions and answers is that gains and losses are not valued the same. Also, people feel

Consumers have many choices. They can purchase the lowest-priced items, the highest-quality items, items with different colors or shapes, items that cause pollution when they are produced, or items that are biodegradable. Believing that the environment is important to the consumers of the industrial nations, The Body Shop sells only green products. Green refers to environmentally safe products. The British company has branched to several nations with its bodycare products that are environmentally safe and are not animal tested. Although the products are more expensive than many substitute products, enough consumers prefer the green products that The Body Shop has been very successful.

happier when they separate or segregate gains from other gains and from losses. They want the gains to stand out.

Some firms have learned that they can appeal to consumers by providing segregated gains. For instance, auto manufacturers and dealers offer a rebate on "any purchase of" a particular model of car. Similarly, developers often "throw in a swimming pool" if you purchase one of their houses. According to utility theory, firms would never give this type of rebate or provide a "free" good; they would simply lower prices since people would then have more money to spend on any other good.[2] Being able to choose how to spend the savings would yield more utility than having to spend the savings on the car or the swimming pool. For instance, Gabrielle, our hypothetical consumer, faced with a lower price on videos, would use the savings from the now lower-priced videos to purchase additional CDs or gasoline as well as more videos, not just purchase videos.

4.b. Undervaluing Opportunity Cost

All costs are opportunity costs, but some costs are out-of-pocket costs while others are not. Purchasing a bicycle is an out-of-pocket expense. Not going for a bike ride so you can attend class is not an out-of-pocket cost. According to utility theory, it should not matter whether the cost is out-of-pocket or not. A dollar spent is the same as a dollar opportunity forgone. But it seems to matter to people. They tend to value out-of-pocket costs more than they do opportunity costs that are not out-of-pocket. Consider the following hypothetical problem:

> What is the most you would pay for someone to clean your apartment or house? How much would you charge someone else to clean his or her apartment or house?

Are the two values the same? They should be according to utility theory, but for most people they are not the same. You clean your own apartment but could pay someone $25 to do it. This $25 would be an out-of-pocket cost. Yet, you wouldn't clean someone else's house for $50. The $50 is an opportunity cost. Along the same line, consider the following problem:

A. You have been exposed to a disease that causes death. Your probability of getting the disease is .001. How much would you pay for a pill to cure it?

B. Now, suppose that you have a job offer to work where you are exposed to the disease with a .001 chance of getting it—and with no chance of a cure? How much would you demand in pay to accept the job?

Are the answers to A and B the same? For most people the answer given for A is less than that for B. But why? The costs are identical. The difference is

---

[2]A rebate where the customer must mail in a coupon is a form of price discrimination. The price elasticity of demand of those who send in rebates is higher than for those who do not. A general price decrease would not separate customers according to their price elasticities of demand. The rebate discussed in the auto dealer case is one given by the firm without any additional actions on the part of the customers. The rebate is offered to anyone who purchases a car and is not a price-discrimination strategy.

that in purchasing the pill, part A, you face an out-of-pocket cost but in the job case, part B, it is not an out-of-pocket cost.

4.c. Irrelevance of Sunk Costs

sunk cost:
a cost that has occurred and cannot be recovered

You paid your tuition at the beginning of the year or term. The paid tuition is called a **sunk cost**—it has been spent and is gone, no matter whether you attend class or not. A sunk cost is a cost that has occurred and cannot be recovered. Utility theory suggests that sunk costs are irrelevant. Does the tuition ever enter into your decision whether or not to attend classes? For many students it does. Sunk costs arise all the time. Economists say, "Ignore them." But many people find it hard to do that. For instance, many of us must continually decide whether to replace an old car or to repair it.

> Suppose your car is a 1982 Volvo worth at most $1,000. You put $800 into a transmission repair last month. You are now confronted with an additional $300 repair on the brakes. Do you get a new car or repair the current one? Do you count the $800 spent on transmission and figure that that $800 plus the next $300 is more than the car is worth?

Or consider the following problem:

> Suppose you have purchased an advance nonrefundable ticket costing $300 to get you home for the holidays. A few days before the trip you are offered an opportunity to spend the holidays with a friend at a resort. What do you do? Many people say that they must use the $300 ticket.

Is this ignoring sunk costs?

4.d. Evaluating at the Margin

Utility theory tells us that it is the marginal amount that matters, that utility is maximized by spending the last dollar on the good or activity that yields the greatest happiness. Yet people spend that last dollar differently depending on whether they previously had a gain or loss. For instance, when many people gamble, they take more risky bets if they previously had some winnings. They say they are "playing with the house's money." But, of course, a dollar is a dollar whether it comes from the house or from their pocket.

The equimarginal principle, $MU_x/P_x = MU_y/P_y = \ldots$ tells us that the marginal dollar is what is important. People should carry out an activity or purchase a good until the marginal benefits (the additional happiness they get) and marginal costs (additional happiness they forgo by not carrying out other activities or purchasing other goods) are equal. However, people do not always seem to behave this way. Consider the following problem:

> You are at a store shopping for computer software that has a price of $240. Another shopper tells you that the same software is selling for $235 at a store a mile away. Do you go?

Now consider the problem again:

> You are at a store shopping for computer software that has a price of $45. Another shopper tells you that the same software is selling for $40 at a store a mile away. Do you go?

Since the savings are the same in both cases—$5—if you go in one case, you should go in the other. Yet most people go in the case of the $45 software but not in the case of the more expensive software. How many of you have left one gas station to drive to another because the price was a penny or two different per gallon? But consider that even ten cents a gallon difference is only $2 for a 20-gallon tank.

4.e. Weighing Information

What do the situations and results we have discussed in this section imply for how people make decisions? They suggest that:

1. People are motivated by self-interest and want to be as happy as they can be.

2. People are rational; they compare costs and benefits according to the best of their abilities (sometimes referred to as *bounded rationality*).

3. Decision-making abilities, called cognitive abilities, are limited. This means that people make decisions that won't always match a strict interpretation of utility theory.

We've mentioned some common decision-making approaches: segregating gains, overvaluing out-of-pocket costs, and failing to ignore sunk costs. People also tend to be influenced by the information they currently have in mind. They tend to count more recently acquired information more heavily and weigh information heard more often more heavily. For instance, answer the following:

1. In four pages of a novel (about 2000 words) how many words would you expect to find that have the form "----ing" (7 letters that end in "ing")?
   0   1–4   5–9   10–14   14+

2. In four pages of a novel (about 2,000 words) how many words would you expect to find that have the form "-----n-" (7 letters with "n" in the sixth position)?   0   1–4   5–9   10–14   14+

Once you think about it, the answer for question 2 has to be larger than for question 1 since question 2 has more options. Yet most people would say the answer to question 1 is larger because they are more familiar with "ing." Familiarity also comes with hearing something often. Consider the following:

Which is more common in the United States, suicide or murder?

Most people say there are far more murders because they have heard more about the murders. Yet there are about 7,000 more suicides each year than murders.

Understanding individual choices and how people make decisions is a complicated business. In fact, an entire field of study involving psychologists and economists, called behavioral decision research, is devoted to expanding our knowledge of decision-making. Although research is ongoing and although our knowledge is not complete, we do have a general outline of how people behave. That general outline is described adequately by utility theory as long as the utility theory model is flexible enough to include cognitive limitations and the use of rules of thumb.

RECAP

1. Interpreted strictly, utility maximization yields some implications that do not describe the way people actually behave.

2. People are not computers or robots. They have limitations on how much information they can process and what calculations they can make. Individuals often do not know exactly how much happiness a particular decision will yield, and they cannot consider every eventuality.

3. Most people tend to segregate gains, overvalue out-of-pocket costs, fail to ignore sunk costs, weigh information heard more often more heavily, and count more recently acquired information more than information acquired in the past.

SUMMARY

▲▼ Does one more dollar mean less to a millionaire than to a pauper?

1. Utility is a measure of the satisfaction received from possessing or consuming a good. §1.a

2. *Diminishing marginal utility* refers to the decline in utility received from each additional unit of a good that is consumed during a particular period of time. The more of some good a consumer has, the less desirable is another unit of that good. §1.b

▲▼ What does "all you can eat" really mean?

3. Even if a good is free a consumer will eventually reach a point where one more unit of the good would be undesirable or distasteful, and he or she will not consume that additional unit. §1.e

▲▼ How do consumers allocate their limited incomes among the billions of goods and services that exist?

4. *Consumer equilibrium* refers to the utility-maximizing situation in which the consumer has allocated his or her budget among goods and services in such a way that the marginal utilities per dollar of expenditure on the last unit of any good are the same for all goods. It is represented in symbols as: $MU_a/P_a = MU_b/P_b = MU_c/P_c = \ldots = MU_x/P_x$. §2.b

5. The demand curve slopes down because of diminishing marginal utility and consumer equilibrium. §3.a

6. The income and substitution effects of a price change occur because of diminishing marginal utility and the equimarginal principle. When the price of one good falls while all other prices remain the same, it yields more satisfaction per dollar than before, so consumers buy more of it than before. §3.b

▲▼ Why do Disneyland, Sea World, and other businesses charge an admission fee and then provide the use of the facilities for no extra charge?

7. Consumer surplus is the difference between what a consumer is willing and able to pay for a good and what the consumer must pay for the good. §3.c

8. Consumer surplus is the area under the market demand curve and above the price line. The pricing strategy of an admission fee and no charge per ride is an attempt to extract as much of the consumer surplus as possible. §3.d, 4.a

9. Market demand is the summation of individual demands. §4.a

▲▼ Does utility maximization really describe consumer behavior?

10. Due to cognitive limitations, individuals are not able to process every bit of information. As a result, their behavior often does not match the implications of utility theory when strictly interpreted. §4

11. People often tend to segregate gains, overvalue out-of-pocket costs, fail to ignore sunk costs, and place more weight on information acquired more recently or heard more often. §4.a–§4.e

KEY TERMS

utility §1.a

diminishing marginal utility §1.b

marginal utility §1.b

disutility §1.b

total utility §1.b

equimarginal principle §2.b

consumer equilibrium §2.b

consumer surplus §3.c

sunk cost §4.c

EXERCISES

1. Using the following information, calculate total utility and marginal utility.

   a. Plot the total utility curve.

   b. Plot marginal utility directly below total utility.

   c. At what marginal utility value does total utility reach a maximum?

Number of utils for the 1st unit	300
Number of utils for the 2nd unit	250
Number of utils for the 3rd unit	220
Number of utils for the 4th unit	160
Number of utils for the 5th unit	100
Number of utils for the 6th unit	50
Number of utils for the 7th unit	20
Number of utils for the 8th unit	0
Number of utils for the 9th unit	−50

2. Is it possible for marginal utility to be negative and total utility positive? Explain.

3. Suppose Mary is in consumer equilibrium. The marginal utility of good A is 30 and the price of good A is $2.

   a. If the price of good B is $4, the price of good C is $3, the price of good D is $1, and the price of all other goods and services is $5, what is the marginal utility of each of the goods Mary is purchasing?

   b. If Mary has chosen to keep $10 in savings, what is the ratio of MU to P for savings?

4. Using the following utility schedule, derive a demand curve for pizza.
   a. Assume income is $10, the price of each slice of pizza is $1, and the price of each glass of beer is $2. Then change the price of pizza to $2 per slice.
   b. Now change income to $12 and derive a demand curve for pizza.

Slices of Pizza	Total Utility	Glasses of Beer	Total Utility
1	200	1	500
2	380	2	800
3	540	3	900
4	600	4	920
5	630	5	930

5. Using utility explain the following commonly made statements:

   a. I couldn't eat another bite.

   b. I'll never get tired of your cooking.

   c. The last drop tastes as good as the first.

   d. I wouldn't eat broccoli if you paid me.

   e. My kid would eat nothing but junk food if I allowed her.

   f. Any job worth doing is worth doing well.

6. How would guests' behavior likely differ at a BYOB (bring your own bottle) party and one at which the host provides the drinks? Explain your answer.

7. Consider the Disneyland example discussed in section 3.d.

   a. With an admission charge and no charge per ride, we would expect each consumer who enters the park to take more rides than he or she would take if there were a charge per ride. Why?

   b. At Disneyland the typical wintertime wait for a ride on the Star Tours or Matterhorn exhibit is 45 minutes, and that wait can triple during the summer. If the park charged for each ride, would you expect shorter or longer waits?

8. A round of golf on a municipal golf course usually takes about 5 hours. At a private country club golf course a round takes less than 4 hours. What accounts for the difference? Would the time spent playing golf be different if golfers paid only an admission fee (membership fee) and no monthly dues or if they paid only a charge per round and no monthly dues?

9. To increase marginal utility, you must decrease consumption (everything else held constant). This statement is correct even though it sounds strange. Explain why.

10. Suppose that the marginal utility of good A is 4 times the marginal utility of good B, but the price of good A is only 2 times larger than the price of good B. Is this point consumer equilibrium? If not, what will occur?

11. Last Saturday you went to a movie and ate a large box of popcorn and two candy bars and drank a medium soda. This Saturday you went to a movie and ate a medium box of popcorn and one candy bar and drank a large soda. Your tastes and preferences did not change. What could explain the different combinations of goods you purchased?

12. Peer pressure is an important influence on the behavior of youngsters. For instance, many preteens begin smoking because their friends pressure them into being "cool" by smoking. Using utility theory, how would you explain peer pressure?

13. Many people who earn incomes below some level receive food stamps from the government. Economists argue that these people would be better off if the government gave them the cash equivalent of the food stamps rather than the food stamps. What is the basis of the economists' argument?

14. Suppose you are in consumer equilibrium and have chosen to work 10 hours a day, leaving the other 14 hours each day for leisure activities (leisure includes sleeping and anything other than working on the job).

    a. How might you change your behavior if your wage rate per hour rises?

    b. What are the income and substitution effects of the price change?

    c. What would occur if the income effect is larger than the substitution effect?

15. What is the impact on charitable giving of a reduction in the tax rate on income? Will the lower tax rate lead to more or to less charitable giving?

COOPERATIVE LEARNING EXERCISE

The class is divided into groups of four to five people. Each group is to evaluate the following scenarios and then be prepared to explain whether the outcome is consistent with utility maximization.

1. You have joined a tennis club for $100. The club charges $5 per hour and you play 4 hours per week. The club raises its membership fee to $150. How does this affect your behavior?

2. Who is more upset: Mr. A, who received a letter from the IRS saying he made a minor error and owed $100 and who also received a letter from the state saying he owed $50, or Mr. B, who received a letter from the IRS indicating he owed $150?

3. Who is more upset: Person A, who expected and received an A in accounting but who, two days later, received a notice indicating an error had been made and she had actually received a B in accounting, or person B, who expected an A in accounting and when his grades arrived learned that he received a B?

4. When you purchase a gift for someone, do you buy something that person would most like and would purchase for herself, or do you purchase a gift the person would like but would not purchase for herself?

Deplore the Stadium Tax? Don't Buy Cars

As Jerry Colangelo's major league baseball bandwagon rolls on, seemingly unabated, a small pack of stadium-tax foes continues to give chase, yelping like bloodthirsty poodles.

Now, however, one segment of the opposition wants to wage economic warfare.

A group known as Taxpayers Against Corporate Welfare has announced a sales-tax boycott of Maricopa County businesses during the weekend of February 25 and 26.

The group is angry that the Maricopa County Board of Supervisors bypassed the voters in approving a quarter-cent sales tax to raise $238 million for a retractable-roof stadium downtown, then effectively blocked political and legal action aimed at rescinding the tax.

"The only option left to us is to simply take the tax revenue on big-ticket items out of Maricopa County," says Ernest Hancock, treasurer of the taxpayer group and county chair of the Libertarian party.

Hancock says the February 25 and 26 boycott is specifically aimed at car dealers who possess substantial political clout. If car dealers see that they stand to lose business, the Board of Supervisors might be convinced to rethink the sales tax.

Hancock says the tax on a new car makes it worth the consumer's time and money to travel to another county. The sales tax in Phoenix is 6.8 percent, and would got to 7.05 percent if the stadium levy kicks in. By comparison, Flagstaff and Prescott levy 6.5 percent sales taxes, while Tucson charges 7 percent and Casa Grande 7.5 percent. If the stadium levy were in effect today, a buyer would save $137.50 if he purchased a $25,000 vehicle in Flagstaff or Prescott rather than Phoenix.

Mary Jo Heck, a spokeswoman for the Arizona Automobile Dealers Association, says Hancock's group is misguided. If a boycott gains widespread support, vital services that rely on sales taxes—services like police and fire protection—would suffer, she says. Not to mention car dealers and their commissioned sales staffs.

Source: "Deplore the Stadium Tax? Don't Buy Cars," *New Times*, Phoenix, Feb. 16–22, 1995, p. 6. © New Times Inc., Phoenix, AZ. Used by permission.

Commentary

Will consumers boycott purchases in Maricopa County? Will people purchasing a car drive 100 miles to do business in another county in order to save $135? How do people decide how to spend their money?

People allocate their limited incomes among purchases and savings in order to make themselves as happy as they possibly can—that is, to maximize utility. The logic of consumer choice indicates that consumers will allocate their limited incomes among the goods and services and savings they desire until the marginal utility from spending an additional dollar on any good or service is the same. This point is known as consumer equilibrium and is captured by the following formula:

$$MU_a/P_a = MU_b/P_b = MU_c/P_c = \ldots = MU_z/P_z$$

where a, b, c, and z represent all goods, services and savings.

All factors that affect the ratios of marginal utility to price affect consumer choice. For instance, if there are three goods, a, b, and c, and if good "a" represents American goods and goods, b and c are foreign goods, and if American consumers develop a preference for American goods, then the ratio of MU_a/P_a rises because MU_a rises. This means consumers will increase their purchases of "a" and decrease those of b and c until consumer equilibrium is reestablished.

An increase in the price of an item will reduce the ratio of marginal utility to price for that item so that consumers will reduce their purchases of that item and increase those of items whose prices did not rise.

The article indicates that the sales tax will rise for any item purchased in Maricopa County. If a is an item available in Maricopa County and b is identical to a except it is available in another county, then the ratio of marginal utility to price falls for a relative to b when the sales tax is imposed. Everything else the same, consumers will switch their purchases from a to b.

Consumers may not only switch from autos purchased in Maricopa County to autos in another county, they may increase their purchases of other goods or they may increase their savings. Since any item purchased in Maricopa county will face the same .25 percent sales tax increase while savings will face no such increase, the cost of spending in Maricopa County is increased relative to the cost of saving.

How many consumers either switch purchases out of the county or do not purchase autos at all depends on the price elasticity of demand. If the price elasticity of demand for autos is very elastic, then a .25 percent increase in the price will bring about more than a .25 percent reduction in the quantity demanded. Suppose the price elasticity of demand for autos in Maricopa County is 4. Then, of 100,000 autos sold in Maricopa County each year, the sales tax increase of .25 percent would lead to a reduction of 1 percent or 1,000 automobiles purchased.

21

Indifference Analysis

Indifference analysis is an alternative approach to utility theory for explaining consumer choice but does not require us to rely on the concept of utility. Some economists prefer to use indifference analysis instead of utility theory to explain consumer choice, and some prefer to present both approaches. Since both approaches yield the same results, we just briefly discuss indifference analysis.

1. INDIFFERENCE CURVES

In Figure 1, four combinations of CDs and gallons of gasoline are listed in the table and plotted in Figure 1(a). Preferring more to less, the consumer will clearly prefer *C* to the other combinations. Combination *C* is preferred to *B* because *C* offers one more CD and the same amount of gas as *B*. Combination *C* is preferred to *A* because *C* offers 1 more CD and 1 more gallon of gas than *A*. And combination *C* is preferred to *D* because one more CD is obtained with no loss of gas. Combinations *B* and *D* are preferred to *A*; however, it is not obvious whether *B* is preferred to *D* or *D* is preferred to *B*.

Let's assume that the consumer has no preference between *B* and *D*. We thus say that the consumer is **indifferent** between combination *B* (2 CDs and 1 gallon of gas) and combination *D* (1 CD and 2 gallons of gas). Connecting points *B* and *D*, as in Figure 1(b), produces an indifference curve. An **indifference curve** shows all the combinations of two goods that the consumer is indifferent among, or, in other words, an indifference curve shows all the combinations of goods that will give the consumer the same level of total utility.

The quantity of goods increases as the distance from the origin increases. Thus, any combination lying on the indifference curve (like *B* or *D*) is preferred to any combination falling below the curve, or closer to the origin (like *A*). Any combination appearing above the curve, or farther from the origin (like *C*), is preferred to any combination lying on the curve.

indifferent:
lacking any preference

indifference curve:
a curve showing all combinations of two goods that the consumer is indifferent among

1.a. The Shape of Indifference Curves

The most reasonable shape for an indifference curve is a downward slope from left to right, indicating that as less of one good is consumed, more of

Figure 1
Indifference Curve

Four combinations of two goods, CDs and gasoline, are presented to the consumer in Figure 1(a). Preferring more to less, the consumer will clearly prefer *C* to *A*, *B*, and *D*. *B* and *D* are preferred to *A*, but the consumer has no clear preference between *B* and *D*. The consumer is indifferent between *B* and *D*. Figure 1(b) shows that all combinations of goods among which the consumer is indifferent lie along an indifference curve.

Combination	CDs	Gallons of Gasoline
A	1	1
B	2	1
C	2	2
D	1	2

(a) Combinations of CDs and Gasoline **(b) Indifference Curve**

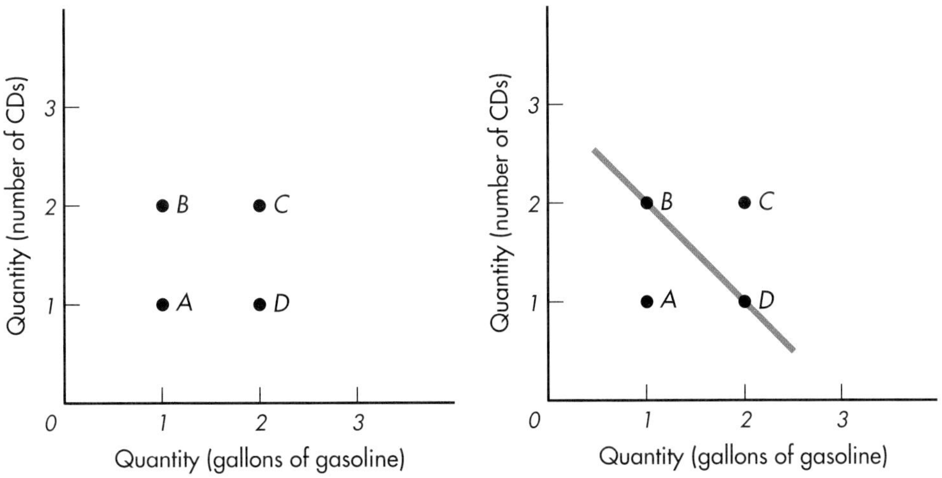

another good is consumed. Indifference curves are not likely to be vertical, horizontal, or upward-sloping. They do not touch the axes, and they do not touch each other.

An indifference curve that is a vertical line, like the one labeled I_v in Figure 2(a), would mean that the consumer is indifferent to combinations *B* and *A*. For most goods this will not be the case because combination *B* provides more of one good with no less of the other good.

Similarly, horizontal indifference curves, such as line I_h in Figure 2(b), are ruled out for most goods. People are not likely to be indifferent between combinations *A* and *B* along the horizontal curve since *B* provides more of one good with no less of the other good than *A*.

An upward-sloping curve, such as I_u in Figure 2(c), would mean that the consumer is indifferent between a combination of goods that provides less of everything and a combination that provides more of everything (compare points *A* and *B*). Rational consumers tend to prefer more to less.

1.b. The Slope of Indifference Curves

The slope, or steepness, of indifference curves is determined by consumer preferences. The amount of one good that a consumer must give up to get an additional unit of the other good and remain equally satisfied changes as the consumer trades off one good for the other. The less a consumer has of a good, the more the consumer values an additional unit of that good. This preference is shown by an indifference curve that bows in toward the origin,

Figure 2
Unlikely Shapes of Indifference Curves

A vertical indifference curve, as in Figure 2(a), would violate the condition that more is preferred to less, as would a horizontal indifference curve, as in Figure 2(b), or an upward-sloping curve, as in Figure 2(c). Thus, indifference curves are not likely to have any of these shapes.

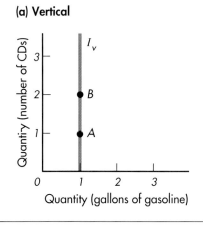
(a) Vertical

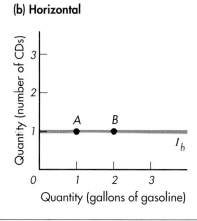
(b) Horizontal

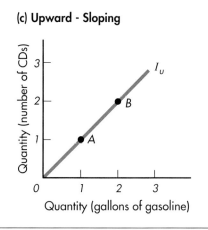
(c) Upward - Sloping

like the curve shown in Figure 3. A consumer who has 4 CDs and 1 gallon of gasoline (point *D*) may be willing to give up 2 CDs for 1 more gallon of gasoline, moving from *D* to *E*. But a consumer who has only 2 CDs may be willing to give up only 1 CD to get that additional gallon of gasoline. This preference is shown as the move from *E* to *F*.

1.c. Indifference Curves Cannot Cross

Indifference curves do not intersect. If the curves crossed, two combinations of goods that are clearly not equally preferred by the consumer would seem to be equally preferred. According to Figure 4, the consumer is indifferent

Figure 3
Bowed-in Indifference Curve

Indifference curves slope down from left to right and bow in toward the origin. They bow in because consumers value a good relatively more if they have less of it, ceteris paribus. At the top of the curve, where a little gasoline and many CDs are represented by point *D*, the consumer is willing to give up 2 CDs to get 1 gallon of gasoline. But lower down on the curve, such as at point *E*, the consumer has more gasoline and fewer CDs than at point *D* and thus is willing to give up fewer CDs to get 1 more gallon of gasoline.

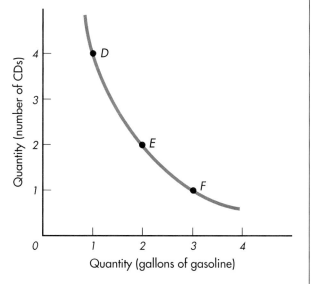

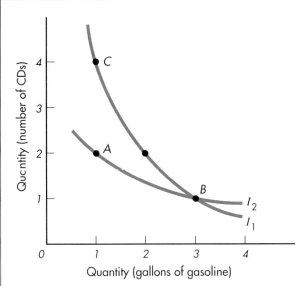

Figure 4
Indifference Curves Do Not Cross
If two indifference curves intersected, such as at point *B*, then the consumer would be indifferent to all points on each curve. But point *C* clearly provides more CDs than point *A* and no less gasoline, so the consumer will prefer *C* to *A*. If the consumer prefers more to less, the indifference curves will not cross.

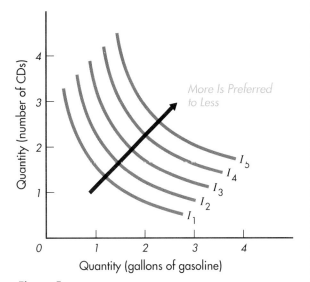

Figure 5
Indifference Map
Indifference curves cover the entire positive quadrant. As we move away from the origin, more is preferred to less: I_5 is preferred to I_4; I_4 is preferred to I_3; and so on.

between *A* and *B* along indifference curve I_2 and indifferent between *B* and *C* along indifference curve I_1. Thus, the consumer appears to be indifferent among *A*, *B*, and *C*. Combination *C*, however, offers more CDs and no less gasoline than combination *A*. Clearly, the consumer, preferring more to less, will prefer *C* to *A*. Thus, indifference curves are not allowed to cross.

1.d. An Indifference Map

indifference map:
a complete set of indifference curves

An **indifference map**, located in the positive quadrant of a graph, indicates the consumer's preferences among all combinations of goods and services. The farther from the origin an indifference curve is, the more the combinations of goods along that curve are preferred. The arrow in Figure 5 indicates the ordering of preferences: I_2 is preferred to I_1; I_3 is preferred to I_2 and I_1; I_4 is preferred to I_3, I_2, and I_1; and so on.

2. BUDGET CONSTRAINT

The indifference map reveals only the combinations of goods and services that a consumer prefers or is indifferent among—what the consumer is *willing* to buy. It does not tell us what the consumer is *able* to buy. Consumers' income levels or budgets limit the amount that they can purchase. Let's suppose a consumer has allocated $6 to spend on gas and CDs. Figure 6 shows the **budget line**, a line giving all the combinations of goods that a budget can buy at given prices.

budget line:
a line showing all the combinations of goods that can be purchased with a given level of income

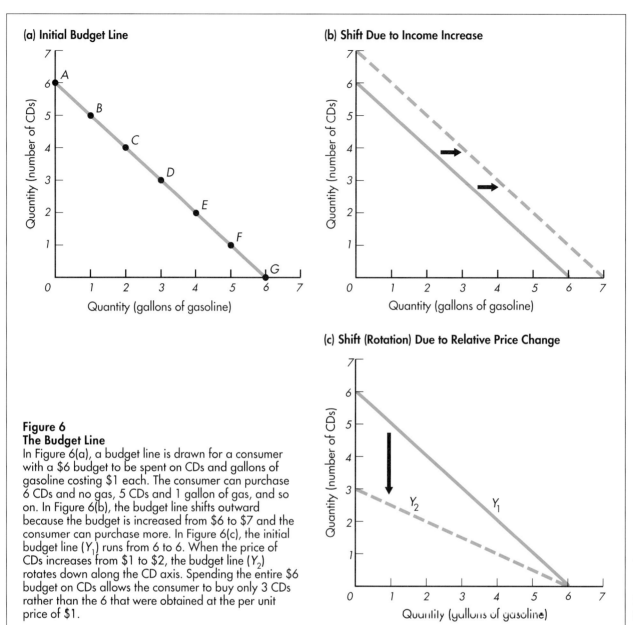

(a) Initial Budget Line

Quantity (number of CDs) vs. Quantity (gallons of gasoline)

(b) Shift Due to Income Increase

Quantity (number of CDs) vs. Quantity (gallons of gasoline)

(c) Shift (Rotation) Due to Relative Price Change

Quantity (number of CDs) vs. Quantity (gallons of gasoline)

Y_2 Y_1

Figure 6
The Budget Line
In Figure 6(a), a budget line is drawn for a consumer with a $6 budget to be spent on CDs and gallons of gasoline costing $1 each. The consumer can purchase 6 CDs and no gas, 5 CDs and 1 gallon of gas, and so on. In Figure 6(b), the budget line shifts outward because the budget is increased from $6 to $7 and the consumer can purchase more. In Figure 6(c), the initial budget line (Y_1) runs from 6 to 6. When the price of CDs increases from $1 to $2, the budget line ($Y_2$) rotates down along the CD axis. Spending the entire $6 budget on CDs allows the consumer to buy only 3 CDs rather than the 6 that were obtained at the per unit price of $1.

Anywhere along the budget line in Figure 6(a), the consumer is spending $6. When the price of CDs is $1 and the price of gas is $1 per gallon, the consumer can choose among several different combinations of CDs and gas that add up to $6. If only CDs are purchased, 6 CDs can be purchased (point *A*). If only gas is purchased, 6 gallons of gas can be purchased (point *G*). At point *B*, 5 CDs and 1 gallon of gas can be purchased. At point *C*, 4 CDs and 2 gallons of gas can be purchased. At point *F*, 1 CD and 5 gallons of gas can be purchased.

An increase in the consumer's income or budget is shown as an outward shift of the budget line. Figure 6(b) shows an increase in income from $6 to

$7. The budget line shifts out to the line running from 7 to 7. A change in income or in the consumer's budget causes a parallel shift of the budget line.

A change in the price of one of the goods causes the budget line to rotate. For example, with a budget of $6 and the prices of both CDs and gas at $1, we have the budget line Y_1 of Figure 6(c). If the price of CDs rises to $2, only 3 CDs can be purchased if the entire budget is spent on CDs. As a result, the budget line (Y_2) is flatter, running from 3 on the vertical axis to 6 on the horizontal axis. Conversely, a rise in the price of gas would cause the budget line to become steeper.

3. CONSUMER EQUILIBRIUM

Putting the budget line on the indifference map allows us to determine the one combination of goods and services that the consumer is both *willing* and *able* to purchase. Any combination of goods that lies on or below the budget line is within the consumer's budget. Which combination will the consumer choose in order to yield the greatest satisfaction (utility)?

The budget line in Figure 7 indicates that most of the combinations along indifference curve I_1 and point C on indifference curve I_2 are attainable. Combinations along indifference curve I_3 are preferred to combinations along I_2, but the consumer is *not able* to buy combinations along I_3 because they cost more than the consumer's budget. Therefore, point C represents the maximum level of satisfaction, or utility, available to the consumer. Point C is the point where the budget line is tangent to (just touches) the indifference curve.

The demand curve for a good can be derived from indifference curves and budget lines by changing the price of one of the goods, leaving everything else the same, and finding the consumer equilibrium points. Budget line Y_1, running from 6 on the vertical axis to 6 on the horizontal axis in Figure 8(a), is the initial budget, in which the price of each CD is $1 and the price of each gallon of gas is $1. We then increase the price of each CD to $2 and draw the

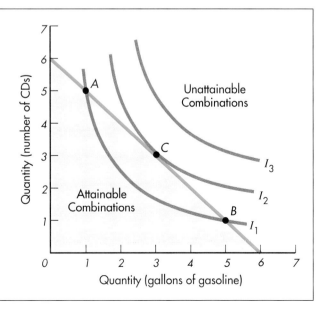

Figure 7
Consumer Equilibrium
The consumer maximizes satisfaction by purchasing the combination of goods that is on the indifference curve farthest from the origin but attainable given the consumer's budget. The combinations along I_1 are attainable, but so are the combinations that lie above I_1. Combinations beyond the budget line, such as those along I_3, cost more than the consumer's budget. Point C, where the indifference curve I_2 just touches, or is tangent to, the budget line, is the chosen combination and the point of consumer equilibrium.

Figure 8
The Demand Curve
By changing the price of one of the goods and leaving everything else the same, we can derive the demand curve. Figure 8(a) shows that as the price of a gallon of gasoline increases from $1 to $2, the budget line rotates in toward the CD axis. Consumer equilibrium occurs at point E instead of at point C. The consumer is purchasing only 2 gallons of gasoline at the $2 per gallon price, whereas the consumer purchased 3 gallons of gasoline at the $1 per gallon price. Plotting the price of gasoline and the number of gallons of gasoline directly below, in Figure 8(b), yields the demand curve for gasoline.

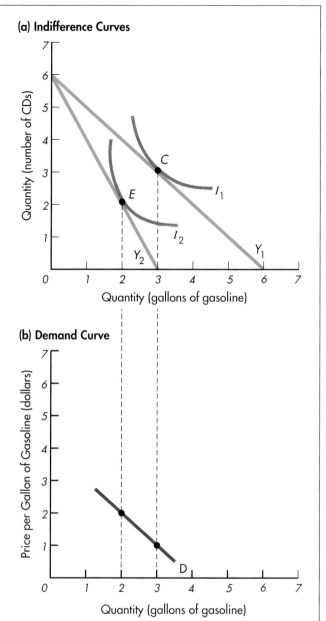

second budget line, Y_2, running from 6 CDs to 3 gallons of gas. For each budget (income) line, we draw the indifference curve that is tangent. For Y_1 it is curve I_1; for Y_2 it is curve I_2. The original consumer equilibrium is point C, the tangency between the initial budget line and curve I_1. The point at which the new budget line is just tangent to an indifference curve is the new consumer equilibrium point. This is point E.

At point C, 3 gallons of gas are purchased; at point E, 2 gallons of gas are purchased. By plotting the combinations of price and quantity demanded below the indifference curves, as in Figure 8(b), we trace out the demand curve for gasoline.

SUMMARY

1. Indifference curves show all combinations of two goods that give the consumer the same level of total utility. §1

2. An indifference map is a complete set of indifference curves filling up the positive quadrant of a graph. §1.d

3. The indifference curve indicates what the consumer is willing to buy. The budget line indicates what the consumer is able to buy. Together they determine the combination of goods the consumer is willing and able to buy. §1, 2

4. Consumer equilibrium occurs at the point where the budget line just touches, or is tangent to, an indifference curve. §3

5. The demand curve can be derived from the indifference curves and budget lines. A change in the relative price causes the budget line to rotate and become tangent to an indifference curve at a different quantity of goods. As the price of one good rises relative to the price of another, the quantity demanded of the higher-priced good falls. §3

KEY TERMS

indifferent §1
indifference curve §1

indifference map §1.d
budget line §2

EXERCISES

1. Use these combinations to answer questions a and b:

Combination	Clothes	Food
A	1 basket	1 pound
B	1 basket	2 pounds
C	1 basket	3 pounds
D	2 baskets	1 pound
E	2 baskets	2 pounds
F	2 baskets	3 pounds
G	3 baskets	1 pound
H	3 baskets	2 pounds
I	3 baskets	3 pounds

a. If more is preferred to less, which combinations are clearly preferred to other combinations? Rank the combinations in the order of preference.

b. Some clothes-food combinations cannot be clearly ranked. Why not?

2. Explain why two indifference curves cannot cross.

3. Using the data that follow, plot two demand curves for cake. Then explain what could have led to the shift of the demand curve.

I. Price of Cake	Quantity of Cake Demanded	II. Price of Cake	Quantity of Cake Demanded
$1	10	$1	14
$2	8	$2	10
$3	4	$3	8
$4	3	$4	6
$5	1	$5	5

22

Supply: The Costs of Doing Business

FUNDAMENTAL QUESTIONS

1. What is the law of diminishing marginal returns?
2. What is the relationship between costs and output in the short run?
3. What is the relationship between costs and output in the long run?

n the previous chapter we discussed demand. In this chapter we begin our analysis of supply. We focus on the firm, for it is firms that supply goods and services. The overriding goal of a firm is to maximize profits. Profits, as you recall, are revenues or sales less costs. Thus, in very simple terms, the manager of a firm must decide how best to increase the difference between revenues and costs. In this chapter we examine costs. In the following chapters we put demand and sales together with costs and discuss business strategies.

The scrap heap of failed businesses is piled high with managers who ignored costs, while the success file is full of managers who understood costs. In 1955, Akio Morita, the founder of Sony Corporation, began selling a small transistor radio in America. "I saw the United States as a natural market," he said. Morita showed the radio to Bulova, a large watch and appliance firm. Bulova offered to purchase a huge amount of radios but with one condition: Sony would have to put Bulova's name on the radio; Sony would be a so-called OEM (original equipment manufacturer) supplier. Morita refused, stating that in a few years the name Sony would be as well known as Bulova.

PREVIEW

Morita soon received another large purchase offer, nearly 100,000 radios, from a chain store. He knew Sony did not have the capacity to produce that many radios. "Our capacity was less than a thousand radios a month." An order of 100,000 would mean hiring and training new employees and expanding facilities even more. Morita sat down and drew a curve that looked something like the lopsided letter "U" shown in Figure 1. The cost for 5,000 would be the beginning of the curve. For 10,000 our costs would fall (and we could offer a lower price), and that was at the bottom of the "U." For 30,000 the cost would begin to climb. For 50,000 the cost per unit would be higher than for 5,000, and for 100,000 units, the cost would be much more per unit than the first 5,000.

Morita explained to the chain store buyer, "If we had to double our production—more labor, more materials, etc.—to complete an order for 100,000 radios and if we could not get a repeat order the following year, we would be in big trouble." The buyer, initially stunned, was eventually persuaded and ended up buying 10,000 radios. That decision was crucial for Sony. Had Morita succumbed to the lure of the larger order and expanded production and costs, it could have led to early failure. Today, however, Sony is one of the world's largest corporations with sales exceeding $30 billion a year.[1]

---

[1]Story paraphrased from Slomo Maital, *Executive Economics* (New York: The Free Press, 1994), pp. 66–75; "The World's Best Brand," *Fortune,* May 31, 1993, p. 31; "Sony Corp.: Globalization," *Harvard Business School Case Study* 391–071, 1990.

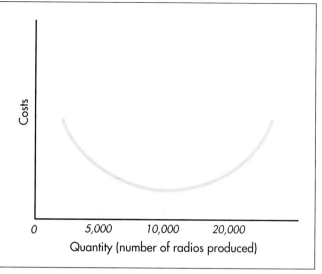

Figure 1
Morita's Cost Curve for Transistor Radios
Visualizing Sony's production capabilities, Akio Morita saw that per unit costs would fall initially and then rise quite rapidly.

Too many managers have ignored costs until their firm was in trouble. In many of the industrial nations, progress and growth in the 1970s and 1980s led to complacency. For instance, in 1992, Germany was an industrial powerhouse with $425 billion in exports annually, second only to the United States. But Germany's hourly manufacturing costs had risen to the highest in the world, $25 an hour compared with $16 in the United States and even less in Japan. As a result of the cost disadvantage German companies found themselves in, many set up manufacturing facilities in nations having lower labor costs. The auto companies, Bavarian Motor Works (BMW) and Daimler-Benz (Mercedes Benz), set up facilities in the United States. Some companies in the United States also found themselves at a serious cost disadvantage relative to firms in other countries and set up facilities in lower labor cost countries. Most companies in the United States cut costs instead of relocating facilities. In the 1990s, downsizing became the most important business policy in the United States. Downsizing meant cutting jobs, particularly jobs at the middle-management level. In 1989, 100,000 jobs were cut, 300,000 more in 1990, and nearly 600,000 per year from 1991 through 1994. The job cutting frenzy peaked in 1994, even though 1994 was a year of very robust economic growth in the United States.

The attention to costs came late to many companies. This is surprising given that profits are simply revenue less costs and that a company must have an understanding of both revenue and costs to be successful. In this chapter we look at the costs of producing and selling goods and services. We examine the relationship between output and costs in both the short run and the long run, beginning with the short run.

I. FIRMS AND PRODUCTION

The terms *company, enterprise,* and *business* are used interchangeably with *firm.* Recall from Chapter 4 that firms can be organized as sole proprietorships, partnerships, or corporations and can be national or multinational companies. In our discussion of the costs of doing business, we use *firm* to refer to all types of business organizations. Thus, we speak of a firm as an institution in which resources—land, labor, capital, and entrepreneurial ability—produce a product or service. The terms *produce* and *production* are also used broadly; they refer not only to manufacturing but also to the retailer who buys goods from a wholesaler and offers the goods to the customers.

1.a. The Relationship Between Output and Resources

The simplest circular flow diagram from Chapter 4 is reproduced here as Figure 2. It shows that money flows from the household sector to the business sector in payment for goods and services. The flow of money from the household sector to the business sector is the firm's total revenue. In turn, money flows from the business sector to households as payment for the use of their resources—land, labor, capital, and entrepreneurial ability. After the owners of land, labor, and capital have been paid, the entrepreneur receives what is left, the profit. Clearly, the amount of profit received by the entrepreneur depends on the output produced by the firm and the quantities and costs of land, labor, and capital used by the firm to produce the output. Entrepreneurs want to produce output at the lowest possible cost. Doing so requires an entrepreneur to compare all combinations of resources (inputs) that can be used to produce output and select the least-cost combination.

Let's use a hypothetical firm, Pacific Western Airlines (PWA), to discuss the relationship between inputs and output. The number of passenger-miles (in thousands) that results when PWA employs alternative combinations of mechanics and airplanes is shown in Table 1. One mechanic can generate 30 (thousand) passenger-miles if PWA has 5 airplanes, 100 (thousand) passenger-miles if PWA has 10 airplanes, 250 (thousand) passenger-miles if PWA has 15 airplanes, and so on. With a second mechanic, output is

Figure 2
The Circular Flow
The flow of goods and services and money between the household and business sectors is pictured. Businesses sell goods and services to households. The money received is total revenue. The difference between total revenue and the payment for land, labor, and capital is profit. The resources —land, labor, capital, and entrepreneurial ability—flow from the household to the business sector. The payment for these resources flows from the business sector to the household sector.

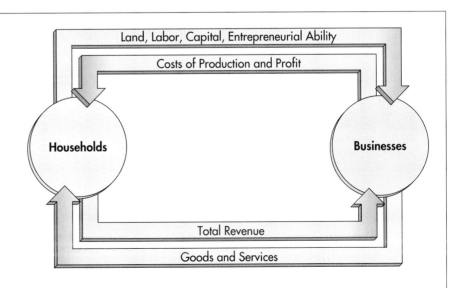

TABLE 1

Alternative Quantities of Output (in thousands) That Can Be Produced by Different Combinations of Resources

Number of Mechanics	Capital (number of airplanes)							
	5	*10*	*15*	*20*	*25*	*30*	*35*	*40*
0	0	0	0	0	0	0	0	0
1	30	100	250	340	410	400	400	390
2	60	250	360	450	520	530	520	500
3	100	360	480	570	610	620	620	610
4	130	440	580	640	690	700	700	690
5	130	500	650	710	760	770	780	770
6	110	540	700	760	800	820	830	840
7	100	550	720	790	820	850	870	890
8	80	540	680	800	830	860	880	900

increased with each quantity of airplanes: 2 mechanics and 5 airplanes now generate 60 (thousand) passenger-miles, and so on.

PWA could produce about the same amount, say 340 to 360 thousand passenger-miles, with several different combinations of mechanics and airplanes—3 mechanics with 10 airplanes, 2 mechanics with 15 airplanes, or 1 mechanic with 20 airplanes. And several other output levels can be produced with a number of different combinations of mechanics and airplanes. Which combination does PWA choose? That depends on whether PWA is making choices for the short run or for the long run. In the long run, or planning period, the firm may consider any and all combinations of resources. In the short run, or production period, the choices open to the firm are limited. Recall that the short run is a period of time just short enough that at least one resource cannot be changed—it is fixed. Suppose that PWA had previously leased or purchased 10 airplanes and cannot change the number of planes for at least a year. In this case, the fixed resource is airplanes. The options open to PWA in the short run thus are only those under the column labeled "10" airplanes shown in Table 1. PWA can vary the number of mechanics but not the number of airplanes in the short run.

total physical product (TPP): the maximum output that can be produced when successive units of a variable resource are added to fixed amounts of other resources

The **total product** (also called total physical product, **TPP**) schedule and curve shows how the quantity of the variable resource (mechanics) and the output produced are related. In Figure 3(a), columns 1 and 3 of Table 1 are reproduced and plotted. With total output measured on the vertical axis and the number of mechanics measured on the horizontal axis, the combinations of output and mechanics trace out the TPP curve. Both the table and the TPP curve in Figure 3(a) show that as additional units of the variable resource are used, total output at first rises, initially quite rapidly and then more slowly, and then declines. As the first units of the variable resource (mechanics) are used, each additional mechanic can provide many passenger-miles for the airline. But after a time, there are "too many chefs stirring one broth" and each additional mechanic adds only a little to total passenger-miles flown and, eventually, actually detracts from the productivity of the other mechanics.

Figure 3
Total, Average, and Marginal Product

The three tables provide plotting data for the graphs to their right. Total, average, and marginal product schedules and curves are shown. The total product schedule, shown in Figure 3(a), is taken from Table 1 by fixing one resource, airplanes, at 10.

Number of Mechanics	Total Output
0	0
1	100
2	250
3	360
4	440
5	500
6	540
7	550
8	540

The average and marginal product schedules are calculated from the total product schedule. Average is total output divided by number of mechanics; marginal is the change in the total output divided by the change in the number of mechanics.

Number of Mechanics	Total Output	Average Product
0	0	–
1	100	100
2	250	125
3	360	120
4	440	110
5	500	100
6	540	90
7	550	78.6
8	540	67.5

Number of Mechanics	Total Output	Average Product	Marginal Product
0	0	–	–
1	100	100	100
2	250	125	150
3	360	120	110
4	440	110	80
5	500	100	60
6	540	90	40
7	550	78.6	10
8	540	67.5	– 10

(a) The Total Product Curve

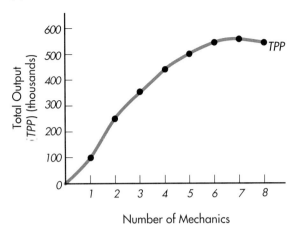

(b) The Average Product Curve

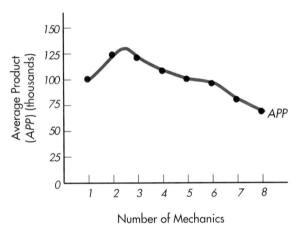

(c) The Marginal Product Curve

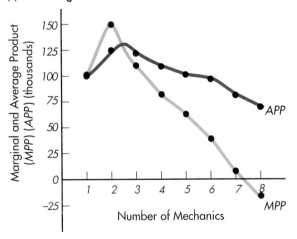

1.b. Diminishing Marginal Returns

law of diminishing marginal returns:
when successive equal amounts of a variable resource are combined with a fixed amount of another resource, marginal increases in output that can be attributed to each additional unit of the variable resource will eventually decline

This relationship between quantities of a variable resource and quantities of output is called the **law of diminishing marginal returns**. According to the law of diminishing marginal returns, when successive equal amounts of a variable resource are combined with a fixed amount of another resource, output will initially accelerate, then decelerate, and eventually will usually decline. Looking at Table 1, you can see the law of diminishing marginal returns at each quantity of airplanes. Just increase the number of mechanics for any given quantity of airplanes and output will rise rapidly at first, but then more slowly. Similarly, if you fix the quantity of mechanics and then vary the number of airplanes, you will also observe the law of diminishing marginal returns. With 1 mechanic, for instance, as the number of airplanes is increased, output rises from 30 to 100 to 250 to 340 and so on. The first increases are large, but the output rises less rapidly and eventually declines as the number of airplanes is increased.

The law of diminishing marginal returns shows up more clearly with the average product (APP) and marginal product (MPP) curves, also called **average physical product (APP)** and **marginal physical product (MPP)** curves. The average product schedule, shown in the third column of the table in Figure 3(b), is calculated by dividing total output by the number of mechanics:

average physical product (APP):
output per unit of resource

marginal physical product (MPP):
the additional quantity that is produced when one additional unit of a resource is used in combination with the same quantities of all other resources

$$APP = \frac{\text{total output}}{\text{number of mechanics}}$$

Plotting APP gives us Figure 3(b), a curve that rises quite rapidly and then slowly declines. The marginal product schedule is the change in total output divided by the change in the quantity of variable resources. In this example, MPP is calculated by dividing the change in total output by the change in the number of mechanics:

$$MPP = \frac{\text{change in output}}{\text{change in number of mechanics}}$$

The MPP schedule is column 4 in the table. The graph of the MPP schedule is shown in Figure 3(c); it is drawn on top of the APP curve so that we can compare MPP and APP. MPP rises initially more rapidly than APP, then falls more rapidly than APP, and eventually reaches zero. When MPP is zero or negative, the additional variable resources are actually detracting from the production of other resources, causing output to decline.

According to the law of diminishing marginal returns, when successive equal amounts of a variable resource are combined with a fixed amount of another resource, output will rise, initially accelerating and then decelerating, and eventually may decline. Diminishing marginal returns are not unique to the airline industry. In every instance where increasing amounts of one resource are combined with fixed amounts of other resources, the additional output that can be produced initially increases but eventually decreases.

For instance, diminishing marginal returns limit the effort to improve passenger safety during collisions by installing air bags in the dashboards of cars. The air bags open on impact to keep the driver and front-seat passengers from hitting the steering wheel and dashboard. The first air bag added to a car increases protection considerably. The second adds an element of safety,

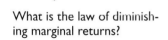

What is the law of diminishing marginal returns?

Entrepreneurs combine quantities of land, labor, and capital to produce goods and services in the most profitable way. Technological improvements help entrepreneurs produce a larger quantity of goods and services at lower cost, thereby increasing profitability. Here, an Egyptian woman supervises several automatic sewing machines. One woman can produce the same quantity with the automatic machines 100 times faster than when the sewing was done by hand. Employing more people may speed up production; eventually, however, employing more people will not speed up production and could actually retard production as the workers interfere with each other's tasks.

particularly for the front-seat passenger. But additional air bags would provide very little additional protection and eventually would lessen protection as they interfered with each other. As successive units of the variable resource, air bags, are placed on the fixed resource, the car, the additional amount of protection provided by the air bags declines.

The law of diminishing marginal returns also applies to studying. On a typical day, during the first hour you study a subject you probably get a great deal of information. During the second hour you may also learn a large amount of new material, but eventually another hour of studying will produce no benefits and could be counterproductive.

Diminishing marginal returns occur because the efficiency of variable resources depends on the quantity of the fixed resources. If the airline mechanics must stand around waiting for tools or for room to work on the jet engines, then an additional mechanic will allow few, if any, additional passenger-miles to be flown. The limited capacity of the fixed resources—the number of planes, tools, and hangar space—causes the efficiency of the variable resource—the mechanics—to decline. Similarly, we often see diminishing marginal returns at restaurants. We walk into a restaurant and see lots of empty tables but are told that there is a 15-minute wait to be seated. The problem is that the number of servers (the fixed resource) is not sufficient to provide quality service to all the tables (the variable resource). The restaurant gives each server one table to serve, then two, then three, and so on, until the quality of the service begins to decline. Without more servers, some tables will have to be left empty.

1.b.1. Average and Marginal Average and marginal relationships behave the same way with respect to each other no matter whether they refer to physical product, cost, utility, grade points, or anything else. For instance, think of the grade point average (GPA) that you get each semester as your *marginal* GPA and your cumulative, or overall, GPA as your *average* GPA. You can see the relation between marginal and average by considering what will happen to your cumulative GPA if this semester's GPA is less than your cumulative

Figure 4
Marginal and Average Physical Product
When the marginal is above the average, the average is rising; when the marginal is below the average, the average is falling. *MPP = APP* at the maximum of the *APP*, between 2 and 3 mechanics.

Number of Mechanics	Total Output	Average Product	Marginal Product
0	0	–	–
1	100	100	100
2	250	125	150
3	360	120	110
4	440	110	80
5	500	100	60
6	540	90	40
7	550	78.6	10
8	540	67.5	–10

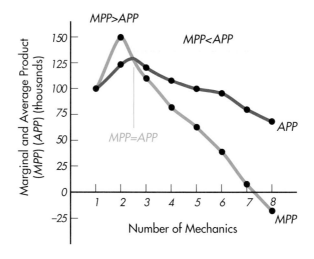

Whenever marginal is less than average, the average is falling, and whenever marginal is greater than average, the average is rising.

GPA. Suppose your GPA this semester is 3.0 for 16 hours of classes and your cumulative GPA, not including this semester, is 3.5 for 48 hours of classes. Your marginal (this semester's) GPA will be less than your average GPA. Thus, when your marginal GPA is added to your average GPA, the average GPA falls, from 3.5 to 3.375. *As long as the marginal is less than the average, the average falls.* If your GPA this semester is 4.0 instead of 3.0, your average GPA will rise from 3.5 to 3.625. *As long as the marginal is greater than the average, the average rises.*

If the average is falling when marginal is below average and rising when marginal is above average, then marginal and average can be the same only when the average is neither rising nor falling. If your GPA this semester is 3.5 and your cumulative GPA up to this semester was 3.5, then your new GPA will be 3.5. Average and marginal are the same when the average is constant. This occurs only when the average curve is at its maximum or minimum point.

In Figure 4 the relationship between average physical product and marginal physical product is illustrated. You can see in both the table and the figure that as long as the MPP is greater than the APP, the APP is rising; whenever the MPP is less than the APP, the APP is falling. Thus, the MPP and APP are equal at the peak or top of the APP curve. This occurs between 2 and 3 mechanics.

RECAP

1. According to the law of diminishing marginal returns, as successive units of a variable resource are added to the fixed resources, the additional output produced will initially rise but will eventually decline.

2. Diminishing marginal returns occur because the efficiency of variable resources depends on the quantity of the fixed resources.

3. As long as the marginal is less than the average, the average falls. As long as the marginal is greater than the average, the average rises.

2. FROM PRODUCTION TO COSTS

Every firm (and every individual and nation as well) is faced with the law of diminishing marginal returns. The law is, in fact, a physical property, not an economic one, but is important to economics because it defines the relationship between costs and output in the short run.

2.a. The Calculation of Costs

The total, average, and marginal physical product schedules and curves show the relationship between quantities of resources (inputs) and quantities of output. To examine the costs of doing business rather than the physical production relationships, we must define the costs of each unit of resources. Suppose, in our airline example, the cost per mechanic, the variable resource, is $1,000 per mechanic, and this is the only cost PWA has. Then, the total costs are those listed in column 3 of the table in Figure 5, calculated by multiplying $1,000 by the number of mechanics necessary to produce the output listed in column 2.

The total cost schedule is plotted on a graph where output is measured on the horizontal axis and total cost on the vertical axis, as shown in Figure 5(a). The total cost curve indicates that as output rises in the short run, costs rise, initially rapidly, then more slowly, and finally more and more rapidly.

Figure 5(b) is the total physical product curve of Figure 3(a) reproduced. You might notice a resemblance between the total cost curve and the total physical product curve. In fact, they are like mirror images, both shaped by the law of diminishing marginal returns.[2]

Since total cost and total physical product have the same shape (except for being mirror images), then average physical product and average cost and marginal physical product and marginal cost should also have the same shapes except for being mirror images. **Average total cost (ATC)** is the per unit cost and is derived by dividing total cost by the quantity of output:

average total cost (ATC): per unit cost

$$ATC = \frac{\text{total cost}}{\text{total output}}$$

---

[2]You might see the resemblance more clearly if the total cost curve is rotated so that output is the vertical axis and cost the horizontal axis.

Figure 5
Total Costs

Figure 5(a) is the total cost curve, columns 2 and 3 of the table. Figure 5(b) is the total product curve, reproduced from Figure 3(a). Both curves illustrate diminishing marginal returns.

Number of Mechanics	Total Output	Total Cost
0	0	0
1	100	1,000
2	250	2,000
3	360	3,000
4	440	4,000
5	500	5,000
6	540	6,000
7	550	7,000
8	540	8,000

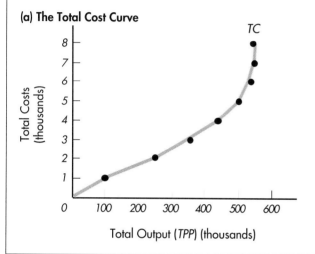

(a) The Total Cost Curve

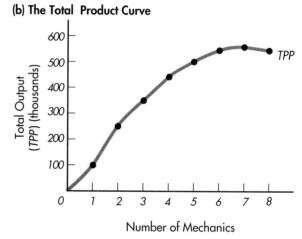

(b) The Total Product Curve

marginal cost (MC):
the additional cost of producing one more unit of output

Marginal cost (MC) is the change in cost caused by a change in output and is derived by dividing the change in total cost by the change in the quantity of output:

$$\text{MC} = \frac{\text{change in total cost}}{\text{change in quantity of output}}$$

The average total cost schedule is listed in column 3 and the marginal cost schedule in column 4 of the table in Figure 6. Notice that these schedules are calculated with respect to output. It is the *relationship* between costs and output produced that is focused on with the cost schedules and curves.

2.b. The U-Shape of Cost Curves

In Figure 6(a) the average cost schedule is plotted next to the *APP* curve of Figure 3(b). In Figure 6(b), the marginal cost schedule is plotted next to the *MPP* curve of Figure 3(c). Can you see the resemblances between the curves? Whereas the *MPP* and *APP* curves might be described as "hump-shaped," the

MC and *ATC* curves can be described as "U-shaped." In Figure 6(c), the *MC* and *ATC* curves are put on the same graph next to the *MPP* and *APP* curves of Figure 4. You can see that the relationship between marginal and average applies to both product and cost curves: whenever the marginal is above the average, the average is rising, and whenever the marginal is below the average, the average is falling; note also that *MPP = APP* at the maximum point of the *APP* curve while *MC = ATC* at the minimum point on the *ATC* curve.

The purpose of comparing the product and cost curves is to emphasize the importance of the law of diminishing marginal returns to short-run costs. Diminishing returns defines the relationship between costs and output in the short run for every firm, no matter whether that firm is a billion-dollar-a-year corporation or a small proprietorship. Obviously, the size or scale of the companies will differ, but the U-shape of the cost curves will not. *Every firm will face a U-shaped cost curve in the short run because of the law of diminishing marginal returns.*

To this point we have used a very simplified situation to describe costs. We placed a cost on the mechanics but on nothing else. Everything has costs. For PWA, the leased airplanes are costs; the buildings, other employees, utilities, and so on are also costs. We now turn to a more in-depth look at costs.

What is the relationship between costs and output in the short run?

RECAP

1. Costs are derived by putting dollar figures on the resources used in production.
2. Average total cost is the cost per unit of output—total cost divided by the number of units of output produced.
3. Marginal cost is the change in costs divided by the change in output.
4. The relationship between costs and output in the short run is defined by the law of diminishing marginal returns.
5. The cost curves (*TC, ATC, MC*) and the product curves (*TPP, APP, MPP*) are like mirror images of each other, all reflecting the law of diminishing marginal returns.
6. The U-shape of the cost curves indicates that as output is increased, a great deal of output can be produced by each additional unit of a variable resource initially. But eventually, the increase in output slows and may decline as more and more units of the variable resource are added.
7. The relationship between marginal and average applies to both product and cost curves. When marginal is above average, average is rising, and when marginal is below average, average is falling. *MPP = APP* at the maximum of *APP; MC = ATC* at the minimum of *ATC*.

3. COST SCHEDULES AND COST CURVES

A firm must pay for the variable resources, such as the mechanics for PWA, but it has other costs as well—it must pay for the fixed resource. In our discussion of costs and production to this point, we have ignored these other costs. Let's now introduce fixed costs and take another look at the cost curves.

Figure 6
Average and Marginal Costs

Figure 6(a) shows the average total cost curve and the *APP* curve. Figure 6(b) shows the marginal cost curve and the *MPP* curve. The cost curves are described as U-shaped, the product curves as hump-shaped. The shapes of the curves are due to the law of diminishing marginal returns. Figure 6(c) shows the relationship between average and marginal curves.

Quantity of Output	Total Cost	Average Cost	Marginal Cost
100	1,000	10	10
250	2,000	8	6.7
360	3,000	8.33	9.1
440	4,000	9	12.5
500	5,000	10	16.7
540	6,000	11.1	25
550	7,000	12.7	100

(a) Compare *APP* with *ATC*

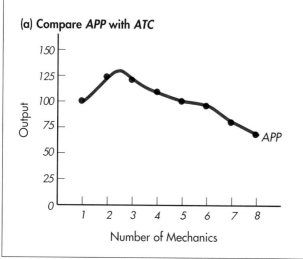

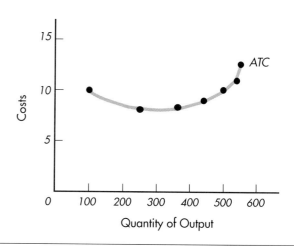

3.a. An Example of Costs

Let's suppose that the costs for PWA of transporting passengers each week are shown in the table in Figure 7. Column 1 lists the total quantity (Q) of output produced (measured in hundred-million passenger-miles). Notice that we have listed the data by equal increments of output, from 1 to 2 to 3 and so on (hundred-millions of passenger-miles) to make it easier to focus on the relationship between output and costs.

Column 2 lists the **total fixed costs (TFC)**, costs that must be paid whether the firm produces or not. Fixed costs are $10,000—this is what must be paid whether 1 or 1 billion passenger-miles are produced. The fixed costs in this example might represent the weekly portion of the annual payment for the planes, which are the resource whose quantity is fixed. Column 3 lists the **total variable costs (TVC)**, costs that rise or fall as production rises or falls. The costs of resources such as employees, fuel, water, and meals rise as output rises. **Total costs (TC)**, the sum of total variable and total fixed costs, are listed in column 4. (Although the distinction between variable and fixed costs is important to economists, many businesspeople focus more on overhead and direct costs. The relation between these concepts is discussed in the

total fixed costs (TFC):
costs that must be paid whether the firm produces or not

total variable costs (TVC):
costs that rise or fall as production rises or falls

total costs (TC):
the sum of total variable and total fixed costs

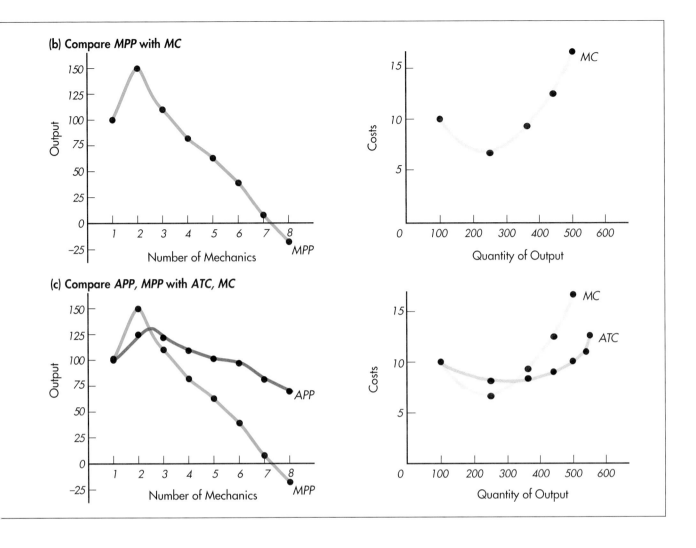

(b) Compare MPP with MC

(c) Compare APP, MPP with ATC, MC

Economic Insight "Overhead.") Overhead is not the same as fixed costs. Overhead refers to costs that are not directly attributable to production, such as administrative costs. Overhead costs may vary, however. For instance, more production may bring with it more paperwork and administration.

Average costs—average total, average fixed, and average variable—are derived by dividing the corresponding total costs by the quantity of output—number of passenger-miles. *Average fixed costs (AFC)* decline as output rises because the total fixed cost, $10,000, is divided by a larger and larger number as output rises. *Average variable costs (AVC)* and *average total costs (ATC)* first decline and then rise, according to the law of diminishing marginal returns. When there are fixed resources and fixed costs, the firm is operating in the short run. For this reason, average total cost is often referred to as the **short-run average total cost (SRATC)**. Marginal costs (MC), the additional costs that come from producing an additional unit of output, are listed in column 8. Marginal costs initially fall and then rise as output rises.

The average and marginal cost schedules are plotted in Figure 7. The *AVC* curve reaches a minimum at the 5 to 6 hundred million passenger-mile level. The *ATC* curve lies above the *AVC* curve by the amount of the average fixed

short-run average total cost (SRATC):
the total cost of production divided by the total quantity of output produced

Figure 7
The Marginal and Average Cost Curves

The table provides plotting data for the figure, which shows the average fixed, average variable, average total, and marginal costs. Average fixed costs (*AFC*) decline steadily from the first unit of output. Average variable costs (*AVC*) initially decline but then rise as output rises. Average total costs (*ATC*), the sum of average fixed and average variable costs, decline and then rise as output rises. The distance between the *ATC* and *AVC* curves is *AFC*. The *MC* curve crosses the *AVC* curve at its minimum point, point *A*, and crosses the *ATC* curve at its minimum, point *B*. (Note: Total output is measured in hundred-million passenger-miles. *TFC*, *TVC*, and *TC* are measured in thousands of dollars. *AFC*, *AVC*, *ATC*, and *MC* are measured in thousands of dollars per hundred-million passenger-miles.

(1) Total Output (Q)	(2) Total Fixed Costs (TFC)	(3) Total Variable Costs (TVC)	(4) Total Costs (TC)	(5) Average Fixed Costs (AFC)	(6) Average Variable Costs (AVC)	(7) Average Total Costs (ATC)	(8) Marginal Costs (MC)	
0	$10	$ 0	$10					
1	10	10	20	$10	$10	$20	$10	
2	10	18	28	5	9	14	8	
3	10	25	35	3.33	8.33	11.6	7	
4	10	30	40	2.5	7.5	10	5	
5	10	35	45	2	7	9	5	
6	10	42	52	1.66	**7**	8.66	**7**	Point A
7	10	50.6	60.6	1.44	7.2	**8.6**	**8.6**	Point B
8	10	60	70	1.25	7.5	8.75	9.4	
9	10	80	90	1.1	8.8	10	20	

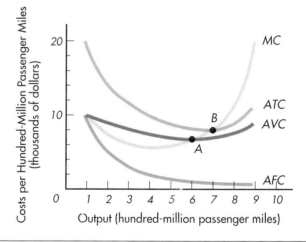

costs. The *ATC* curve declines until the 7 hundred million passenger-mile point and then rises. The *MC* curve begins below the *AVC* and *ATC* curves and declines until the 5 hundred million passenger-mile point, where it begins to climb. The *MC* curve passes through the *AVC* curve at the minimum value of the *AVC* curve and then continues rising until it passes through the *ATC* curve at the minimum point of the *ATC* curve. The marginal cost

Overhead

An article in the May 18, 1992, *Business Week* entitled "Can Corporate America Get Out from Under Its Overhead?" pointed out that throughout the 1980s corporations reduced labor costs by laying off millions of hourly workers. The dollar's fall, on top of cost-cutting, has helped lower U.S. unit labor costs by 42 percent against those of America's major trading partners since 1985. Now, experts say, "The problem is overhead, chiefly plump white-collar bureaucracies." Even though businesses cut middle management in the 1990s, many U.S. companies *still* can't compete with their international rivals because of overhead, which equaled 26 percent of sales for U.S. companies, as opposed to 21 percent for Western European companies and 18 percent for Japanese companies.

Economists classify costs as fixed or variable. Fixed costs do not change as the volume of production changes. Variable costs, on the other hand, depend on the volume of production. In business, costs are often classified into overhead and direct operating costs. Overhead costs are those that are not directly attributable to the production process. They include such items as taxes, insurance premiums, managerial or administrative salaries, paperwork, the cost of electricity not used in the production process, and others. Overhead costs can be either fixed or variable. Insurance premiums, taxes, and managerial salaries are fixed costs. They must be paid regardless of how much is produced. Electricity used to operate the production process is a variable cost, increasing as the quantity of output produced is increased.

Statements like "We need to spread the overhead" sound somewhat like the concept of declining average fixed costs—fixed cost per unit of output declines as output rises. But overhead may also include variable costs. Thus, the need to "spread the overhead" refers to reducing the total costs that are not directly attributable to the production process. The more a firm can keep its overhead costs the same and increase its volume of production, the more that overhead costs look and act like fixed costs. The higher the percentage of overhead costs that are fixed, the more closely related the economists' and the businessperson's classifications will be. But the two are not—and are not meant to be—the same.

The different classifications provide different information. The economist is interested in the decision to produce, how much to produce, and whether to produce at all. This is the information provided by fixed and variable costs. The businessperson is interested in attributing costs to different activities, that is, in determining whether the business is running as cost-efficiently as it can. The classification of costs into direct and overhead provides this information.

The MC curve intersects the AVC curve at the minimum point of the AVC curve; the MC curve intersects the ATC curve at the minimum point of the ATC curve.

curve intersects the average cost curves at the minimum points of the average cost curves.

The role of each of the three types of costs—fixed, variable, and marginal—should be relatively obvious. In the short run, firms can do nothing about fixed costs—they are fixed. It is variable costs that are important in the short run. Firms can alter their variable costs. Average variable costs are the per unit variable costs. Marginal costs play the most important role; they are the incremental costs, the change in costs resulting from a small decline or increase in output. They inform the executive whether the last unit of output produced—the last passenger carried on the plane—increased costs a huge amount, a small amount, or not at all. Thus, the executive can decide whether to produce that last unit. We will see how the costs come into play more clearly in the following chapters.

RECAP

1. Total fixed costs (TFC) are costs that do not vary as the quantity of goods produced varies. An example of a fixed cost is the rent on a building. Rent has to be paid whether or not the firm makes or sells any goods.

2. Total variable costs (TVC) are costs that change as the quantity of goods produced changes. The cost of materials is usually variable. For instance, the cost of leather for making boots or cloth for manufacturing clothing changes as the quantity produced changes. The fuel required to fly planes will increase as more passengers are transported.

3. Total costs (TC) are the sum of fixed and variable costs:

$$TC = TFC + TVC$$

4. Average total costs (ATC) are total costs divided by the total quantity of the good that is produced, Q:

$$ATC = \frac{TC}{Q}$$

5. Average fixed costs (AFC) are total fixed costs divided by the quantity produced:

$$AFC = \frac{TFC}{Q}$$

6. Average variable costs (AVC) are total variable costs divided by the quantity produced:

$$AVC = \frac{TVC}{Q}$$

7. Marginal costs (MC) are the incremental costs that come from producing one more or one less unit of output:

$$MC = \frac{\text{change in } TC}{\text{change in } Q}$$

8. Short-run average total cost (SRATC) is the total cost divided by the total quantity of output.

4. THE LONG RUN

What is the relationship between costs and output in the long run?

A firm can choose to relocate, build a new plant, or purchase additional planes only in the long run, or planning stage. A manager can choose any size of plant or building and any combination of other resources when laying out the firm's plans because all resources are variable in the long run. In essence, during the long run the manager compares all short-run situations.

Table 2, which is based on Table 1, shows the quantities of output that can be produced by alternative combinations of mechanics and airplanes at our hypothetical airline, PWA. You may recall that we specified that PWA had leased 10 airplanes and thus had to constrain itself to producing those combinations under the column labeled "10" in the short run. In the long run, the firm faces no fixed resources—everything is variable. PWA has a choice of how many airplanes to lease and thus has the choice of any combination of resources shown in Table 2.

TABLE 2
The Long Run or Planning Period

Number of Mechanics	Capital (number of airplanes)							
	5	*10*	*15*	*20*	*25*	*30*	*35*	*40*
0	0	0	0	0	0	0	0	0
1	30	100	250	340	410	400	400	390
2	60	250	360	450	520	530	520	500
3	100	360	480	570	610	620	620	610
4	130	440	580	640	690	700	700	690
5	130	500	650	710	760	770	780	770
6	110	540	700	760	800	820	830	840
7	100	550	720	790	820	850	870	890
8	80	540	680	800	830	860	880	900

The law of diminishing marginal returns does not apply when all resources are variable. Diminishing returns applies only when quantities of variable resources are combined with a fixed resource. In the long run everything is variable. Consider the combinations of resources and the resulting output levels colored green in Table 2. A single mechanic combined with 5 airplanes can produce 30 (thousand) passenger-miles. Doubling both mechanics and airplanes (to 2 mechanics and 10 airplanes) means that 250 (thousand) passenger-miles can be produced. Doubling both resources again, to 4 mechanics and 20 airplanes, means that 640 (thousand) passenger-miles can be produced. Doubling the resources once again, to 8 mechanics and 40 airplanes, results in 900 (thousand) passenger-miles being flown. For the first few times the quantities of both resources were doubled, output rose by more than the resources. But eventually, the output increase was less than double as the resources were doubled. This need not have been the case. Output could have continued to rise more rapidly than the resources, or it could have risen at a constant amount, or it could have declined throughout. Unlike the short run, where the relationship between inputs and output is defined by the law of diminishing marginal returns, the long run is not guided by a physical law.

4.a. Economies of Scale and Long-Run Cost Curves

scale:
size; all resources change when scale changes

When all resources are changed, we say that the scale of the firm has changed. **Scale** means size. In the long run, a firm has many sizes to choose from—those given in Table 2 for PWA, for instance. The short run requires that scale be fixed—only a variable resource is changed. For each size or scale, therefore, there is a set of short-run average- and marginal-cost curves. For each quantity of airplanes (each column in Table 2), PWA has a set of average and marginal U-shaped cost curves. Figure 8(a) shows several short-run cost curves along which a firm could produce. Each short-run cost curve is drawn for a particular quantity of the capital resource—that is, a specific column in Table 2. Once the quantity of the capital resource is selected, the firm brings together different combinations of the other resources with the fixed capital resource. If a small quantity of the capital resource is selected, the firm might operate along $SRATC_1$. If the firm selects a slightly larger

Figure 8
The Short-Run and Long-Run Average-Cost Curves
The long-run average-cost curve represents the lowest costs of producing any level of output when all resources are variable. Short-run average-cost curves represent the lowest costs of producing any level of output in the short run, when at least one of the resources is fixed. Figure 8(a) shows the possible *SRATC* curves facing a firm. Figure 8(b) shows the *LRATC* curve, which connects the minimum cost of producing each level of output. Notice that the *SRATC* curves need not indicate the lowest costs of producing in the long run. If the short run is characterized by *SRATC₃*, then quantity Q_4 can be produced at point *A*. But if some of the fixed resources are allowed to change, managers can shift to *SRATC₄* and produce at point *B*.

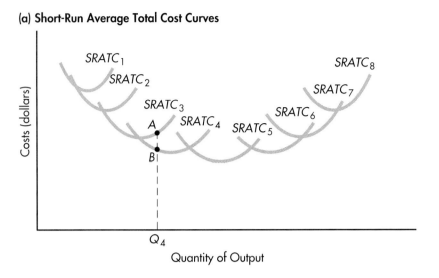

(a) Short-Run Average Total Cost Curves

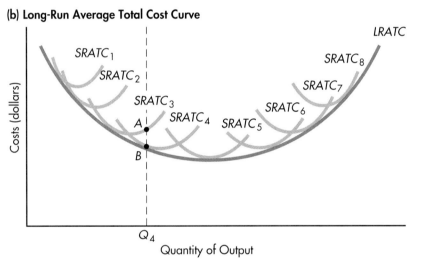

(b) Long-Run Average Total Cost Curve

long-run average total cost (LRATC):
the lowest-cost combination of resources with which each level of output is produced when all resources are variable

quantity of the capital resource, then it will be able to operate anywhere along *SRATC₂*. With a still larger quantity, the firm can operate along *SRATC₃*, *SRATC₄*, *SRATC₅*, or some other short-run average total cost curve.

In the long run, the firm can choose any of the *SRATC* curves. All it needs to do is choose the level of output it wants to produce and then select the least-cost combination of resources with which to reach that level. Least-cost combinations are represented in Figure 8(b) by a curve that just touches each *SRATC* curve. This curve is the **long-run average-total-cost** curve (**LRATC**—the lowest cost per unit of output for every level of output when all resources are variable). If the firm had chosen to acquire or use a quantity of fixed resources indicated by *SRATC₃* in Figure 8(b), then it could produce Q_4 only at point *A*. Only by increasing its quantity of fixed resources could the firm produce at point *B* on *SRATC₄*.

You can see in Figure 8(b) that the long-run average-total-cost curve does *not* connect the minimum points of each of the short-run average-cost curves

($SRATC_1$, $SRATC_2$, etc.). The reason is that the minimum point of a short-run average-total-cost curve is not necessarily the lowest-cost method of producing a given level of output. For instance, point A on $SRATC_3$ is much higher than point B on $SRATC_4$, but output level Q_4 could be produced at either A or B. When the quantities of all resources can be varied, the choices open to the manager are much greater than when only one or a few of the resources are variable.

The long-run average-total-cost curve gets its shape from economies and diseconomies of scale. If producing each unit of output becomes less costly as the amount of output produced rises, there are **economies of scale**—unit costs decrease as the quantity of production increases and all resources are variable. If the cost per unit rises as output rises, there are **diseconomies of scale**—unit costs increase as the quantity of production increases and all resources are variable. Economies of scale account for the downward-sloping portion of the long-run average-cost curve. Diseconomies of scale account for the upward-sloping portion.

If the cost per unit of output is constant as output rises, there are **constant returns to scale**. Figures 9(a), 9(b), and 9(c) show three possible shapes of a long-run average-cost curve. Figure 9(a) is the usual U shape, indicating that economies of scale are followed by constant returns to scale and then diseconomies of scale. Figure 9(b) is a curve indicating only economies of scale. Figure 9(c) is a curve indicating only constant returns to scale. Each of these long-run average-total-cost curves would connect several short-run average-total-cost curves, as shown in Figure 9(d), 9(e), and 9(f).

economies of scale:
per unit costs decline as the quantity of production increases and all resources are variable

diseconomies of scale:
per unit costs rise as the quantity of production increases and all resources are variable

constant returns to scale:
unit costs remain constant as the quantity of production is increased and all resources are variable

4.b. The Reasons for Economies and Diseconomies of Scale

Firms that can specialize more as they grow larger may be able to realize economies of scale. Specialization of marketing, sales, pricing, and research, for example, allows some employees to focus on research while others focus on marketing and still others focus on sales and on pricing.

Economies of scale may also result from the use of large machines, that are more efficient than small ones. Large blast furnaces can produce more than twice as much steel per hour as smaller furnaces, but they do not cost twice as much to build or operate. Large electrical-power generators are more efficient (more output per quantity of resource) than small ones.

Size, however, does not automatically improve efficiency. The specialization that comes with large size often requires the addition of specialized managers. A 10 percent increase in the number of employees may require an increase greater than 10 percent in the number of managers. A manager to supervise the other managers is needed. Paperwork increases. Meetings are held more often. The amount of time and labor that are not devoted to producing output grows. In other words, the overhead increases. In addition, it becomes increasingly difficult for the CEO to coordinate the activities of each division head and for the division heads to communicate with one another. In this way, size can cause diseconomies of scale.

4.c. The Minimum Efficient Scale

The law of diminishing marginal returns applies to every resource, every firm, and every industry. Whether there are economies of scale, diseconomies of scale, constant returns to scale, or some combination of these

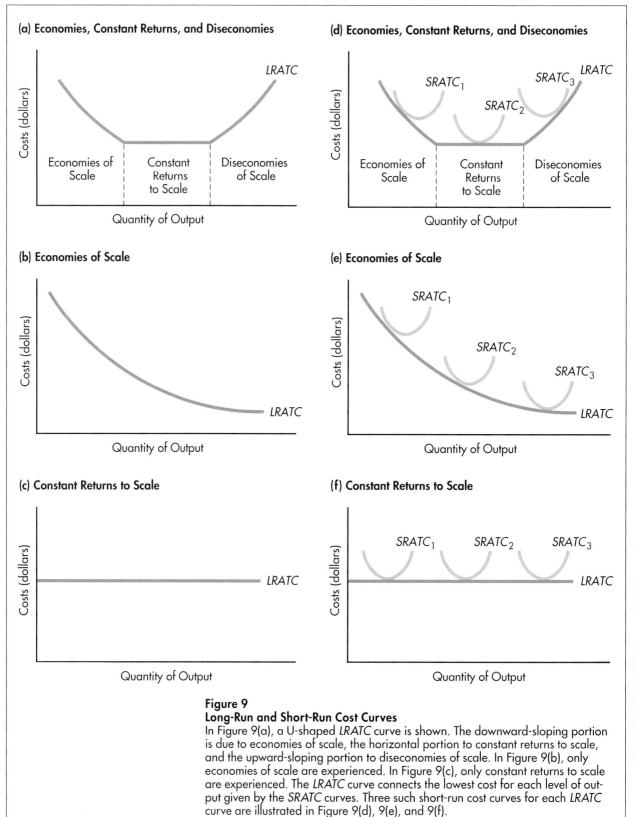

Figure 9
Long-Run and Short-Run Cost Curves
In Figure 9(a), a U-shaped *LRATC* curve is shown. The downward-sloping portion is due to economies of scale, the horizontal portion to constant returns to scale, and the upward-sloping portion to diseconomies of scale. In Figure 9(b), only economies of scale are experienced. In Figure 9(c), only constant returns to scale are experienced. The *LRATC* curve connects the lowest cost for each level of output given by the *SRATC* curves. Three such short-run cost curves for each *LRATC* curve are illustrated in Figure 9(d), 9(e), and 9(f).

depends on the industry under consideration. No law dictates that an industry will have economies of scale eventually followed by diseconomies of scale, although that seems to be the typical pattern. Theoretically, it is possible for an industry to experience only diseconomies of scale, only economies of scale, or only constant returns to scale.

Most industries experience both economies and diseconomies of scale. For example, Mrs. Fields Cookies trains the managers of all Mrs. Fields outlets at its headquarters in Park City, Utah. The training period is referred to as Cookie College. By spreading the cost of Cookie College over more than 700 outlets, Mrs. Fields Cookies is able to achieve economies of scale. However, the company faces some diseconomies because the cookie dough is produced at one location and distributed to the outlets in premixed packages. The dough factory can be large, but the distribution of dough produces diseconomies of scale that worsen as outlets are opened farther and farther away from the factory.

If the long-run average-total-cost curve reaches a minimum, the level of output at which the minimum occurs is called the **minimum efficient scale (MES)**. MES varies from industry to industry; it is significantly smaller, for instance, in the production of shoes than it is in the production of cigarettes. A shoe is made by stretching leather around a mold, sewing the leather, and fitting and attaching the soles and insoles. The process requires one worker to operate just two or three machines at a time. Thus, increasing the quantity of shoes made per hour requires more building space, more workers, more leather, and more machines. The cost per shoe declines for the first few shoes made per hour, but rises thereafter. Cigarettes, on the other hand, can be rolled in a machine that can produce several thousand per hour. Producing 100 cigarettes an hour is more costly per cigarette than producing 100,000 per hour.

4.d. The Planning Horizon

The long run is referred to as a planning horizon because the firm has not committed to a fixed quantity of any resource and has all options available to it. In determining the size or scale to select, the manager must look at expected demand and expected costs of production and then select the size that appears to be the most profitable. Once a scale is selected, the firm is operating in the short run since at least one of the resources is fixed. Sony, for instance, was constrained to a rather small production facility for transistor radios back in the 1950s, as discussed in the Preview. This means that it was operating along a specific short-run average cost curve. To produce 100,000 radios would have meant moving far up the right side of the "U" so that per unit costs would have been extremely high. If Akio Morita had anticipated several more huge purchase orders in future years, he might have committed to produce 100,000 radios and increased the scale of Sony. Expanding the scale of Sony would have meant moving down along the long-run average cost curve, perhaps from the current position of $SRATC_1$ in Figure 10 to $SRATC_5$. Once having committed to the scale of $SRATC_5$, Sony would again be operating in the short run. Increases and decreases in production would be a move along $SRATC_5$. You can see what Morita was worried about. Suppose that production dropped back to the 10,000 radios per year level. Then, being constrained to operate along $SRATC_5$, Sony would have experienced huge per unit costs.

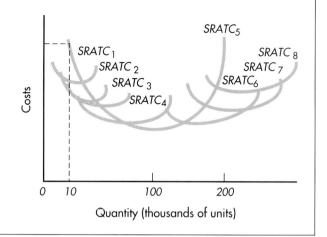

Figure 10
Morita's Problem
Had Sony chosen to produce at $SRATC_5$ it would have been constrained to operate along $SRATC_5$ in the short run. A decrease in production to 10,000 units would have meant rising up the short-run cost curve and producing at very high per unit costs.

RECAP

1. Many industries are characterized by U-shaped long-run average-cost curves, but need not be. There is no law dictating a U-shaped LRATC curve.

2. The long-run average-total-cost curve gets its U shape from economies and diseconomies of scale, unlike the short-run cost curves, which get their U shape from diminishing marginal returns.

3. The minimum efficient scale (MES) is the size of a firm that is at the minimum point of a long-run average-cost curve.

4. The MES varies from industry to industry. Some industries, like the electric-power industry, have large economies of scale and a large MES. Other industries, like the fast-food industry, have a relatively small MES.

5. Economies of scale may result from specialization and technology. Diseconomies of scale may occur because coordination and communication become more difficult as size increases.

SUMMARY

1. A firm is a business organization that brings together land, labor, capital, and entrepreneurial ability to produce a product or service. §1

2. The short run is a period of time just short enough that the quantity of at least one of the resources cannot be altered. §1.a

3. The total-physical-product curve is a picture of the short-run relationship between resources (inputs) and output when one resource is variable. §1.a

▲▼ **What is the law of diminishing marginal returns?**

4. According to the law of diminishing marginal returns, when successive equal amounts of a variable resource are combined with a fixed amount of another resource, there will be a point beyond which the extra or marginal product that can be attributed to each additional unit of the variable resource will decline. §1.a, 1.b

5. The total-cost curve is the mirror image of the *TPP* curve. Similarly, *MC* looks like *MPP* and *AC* looks like *APP,* except for being mirror images. Their shapes are due to the law of diminishing marginal returns. §2.a, 2.b

6. Fixed costs are costs that do not vary as the quantity of goods produced varies. §3.a

7. Variable costs rise as the quantity of goods produced rises. §3.a

8. Total costs are the sum of fixed and variable costs. §3.a

9. Average total costs are the costs per unit of output—total costs divided by the quantity of output produced. §3.a

10. Average costs fall when marginal costs are less than average and rise when marginal costs are greater than average. §3.a.1

11. The U shape of short-run average-total-cost curves is due to the law of diminishing marginal returns. §2.b, 3.b

12. The U shape of long-run average-total-cost curves is due to economies and diseconomies of scale. §4.a

13. Economies of scale result when increases in output lead to decreases in unit costs and the quantities of all resources are variable. §4.a

14. Diseconomies of scale result when increases in output lead to increases in unit costs and the quantities of all resources are variable. §4.a

15. Constant returns to scale occur when increases in output lead to no changes in unit costs and the quantities of all resources are variable. §4.a

16. The minimum efficient scale (MES) occurs at the minimum point of the long-run average-total-cost curve. §4.c

17. The long run is the planning horizon where all resources are variable. Once a size or scale is selected, the firm is operating in the short run. §4.d

KEY TERMS

total physical product (TPP) §1.a

law of diminishing marginal returns §1.a

average physical product (APP) §1.a

marginal physical product (MPP) §1.b

average total costs (ATC) §2.a

marginal costs (MC) §2.a

total fixed costs (TFC) §3.a

total variable costs (TVC) §3.a

total costs (TC) §3.a

average fixed costs (AFC) §3.a

average variable costs (AVC) §3.a

short-run average total cost (SRATC) §3.b

long-run average total cost (LRATC) §4.a

scale §4.a

economies of scale §4.a

diseconomies of scale §4.a

constant returns to scale §4.a

minimum efficient scale (MES) §4.c

EXERCISES

1. Use the following information to list the total fixed costs, total variable costs, average fixed costs, average variable costs, average total costs, and marginal costs.

Output	Costs	TFC	TVC	AFC	AVC	ATC	MC
0	$100						
1	150						
2	225						
3	230						
4	300						
5	400						

2. Use the following table to answer the questions listed below.

Output	Cost	TFC	TVC	AFC	AVC	ATC	MC
0	$ 20						
10	40						
20	60						
30	90						
40	120						
50	180						
60	280						

a. List the total fixed costs, total variable costs, average fixed costs, average variable costs, average total costs, and marginal costs.

b. Plot each of the cost curves.

c. At what quantity of output does marginal cost equal average total cost and average variable cost?

3. Use Table 2 in the chapter to demonstrate the law of diminishing marginal returns. Where does the law apply if there are 20 airplanes in the short run? What occurs if there are only 10 airplanes? Plot the *APP* curve for 20 airplanes and for 10 airplanes.

4. Use Table 2 in the chapter to demonstrate the law of diminishing marginal returns if the fixed resource is mechanics. Plot the *APP* curve for 1 mechanic and for 4 mechanics.

5. Describe some conditions that might cause large firms to experience inefficiencies that small firms would not experience.

6. What is the minimum efficient scale? Why would different industries have different minimum efficient scales?

7. Describe the relation between marginal and average costs. Describe the relation between marginal and average fixed costs and between marginal and average variable costs.

8. Explain why the *APP* curve rises when *MPP* is greater than *APP* and falls when *MPP* is less than *APP*.

9. Explain why the short-run marginal-cost curve must intersect the short-run average-total-cost and average-variable-cost curves at their minimum points. Why doesn't the marginal-cost curve also intersect the average-fixed-cost curve at its minimum point?

10. Explain the relationship between the shapes of the production curves and the cost curves. Specifically, compare the marginal-physical-product curve and the marginal-cost curve, and the average-physical-product curve and the average-total-cost curve.

11. Consider a firm with a fixed-size production facility as described by its existing cost curves.

a. Explain what would happen to those cost curves if a mandatory health insurance program is imposed on all firms.

b. What would happen to the cost curves if the plan required the firm to provide a health insurance program for each employee worth 10 percent of the employee's salary?

c. How would that plan compare to one that requires each firm to provide a $100,000 group program that would cover all employees in the firm no matter the number of employees?

12. Explain the fallacy of the following statement: "You made a real blunder. The $600 you paid for repairs is worth more than the car."

13. Explain the statement "We had to increase our volume to spread the overhead."

14. Three college students are considering operating a tutoring business in economics. This business would require that they give up their current jobs at the student recreation center, which pay $6,000 per year. A fully equipped facility can be leased at a cost of $8,000 per year. Additional costs are $1,000 a year for insurance and $.50 per person per hour for materials and supplies. Their services would be priced at $10 per hour per person.

a. What are fixed costs?

b. What are variable costs?

c. What is the marginal cost?

d. How many students would it take to break even?

15. Express Mail offers overnight delivery to customers. It is attempting to come to some conclusion on whether to expand its facilities or not. Currently its fixed costs are $2 million per month and its variable costs are $2 per package. It charges $12 per package and has a monthly volume of 2 million packages. If it expands, its fixed costs will rise by $1 million and its variable costs will fall to $1.50 per package. Should it expand?

COOPERATIVE LEARNING EXERCISE

Divide the students into groups.

1. Each group is to explain how the law of diminishing marginal returns would show up within the group as group size increases. It must define output and variable and fixed resources for the group.

2. Each group is to explain how it could determine whether the group experienced economies or diseconomies of scale.

Massachusetts-based Raytheon Threatens Relocation to Arizona

Raytheon Co. is citing Arizona as an example of where it could move its defense-manufacturing plants if it doesn't receive a host of economic incentives it is seeking from Massachusetts officials, unions, and utilities.

The company—with a payroll of 19,500, is Massachusetts' biggest private employer—has been pressuring state officials for tax and other financial concessions, saying that it needs to cut its operating costs in the state and if it can't, it will move.

The company has said its electric bill in Massachusetts, which has utility rates that are among the highest in the nation, is about a third more than it would pay in Arizona.

. . . Raytheon has asked the Massachusetts Legislature to approve a bill that would let large defense contractors negotiate directly for cheap power from any generating source and would require utilities to deliver it to their plants for a nominal service charge. Alternately, Raytheon said defense contractors with $5 million or more in annual military sales should get a 40 percent discount on rates.

Raytheon estimates that buying power from low-cost suppliers could cut $5 million a year from its $22 million a year electric bill. A 40 percent discount would save Raytheon about $9.5 million, the company said.

Source: "Massachusetts-based Raytheon Threatens Relocation to Arizona" *The Arizona Republic*, Feb. 21, 1995, p. B4. Used with permission. Permission does not imply endorsement.

Commentary

Raytheon says "it must cut its operating costs in the state and that if it can't, it will move." Operating costs are variable costs—short run costs—while moving is a long run decision—the changing of a fixed resource. Does the Raytheon statement make sense?

In the short run, a firm may reduce variable costs but can not alter location or other fixed inputs. A firm will remain operating in the short run as long as all variable costs are covered by revenues. It will shut down temporarily if all variable costs are not covered by revenues. The firm will shut down permanently if all costs are not covered with the revenues in the long run.

Raytheon is threatening to shut down permanently in Massachusetts if it can not reduce its operating costs. Raytheon estimates that moving to Arizona would reduce its variable costs substantially—between $6 and $9 million. Thus, Raytheon is adding to its accounting costs, the opportunity costs of operating in Arizona. Suppose Raytheon's operating costs are $50 million, and these are its variable costs. If Raytheon operated in Arizona its operating costs would be $44 million, $6 million less than in Massachusetts. This means that Raytheon has an additional opportunity cost of $6 million if it remains in Massachusetts. In order for the company to not shut down in Massachusetts, its revenue must be $56 million, $50 million to cover its variable costs and $6 million to cover the opportunity cost of not operating in Arizona.

Raytheon is deciding where it would be best off locating. This is a planning horizon or long run decision. Once it has made the decision to locate, then it is once again operating in the short run and must then focus on variable costs.

Massachusetts must decide whether to provide benefits to Raytheon that are sufficient to keep it from moving to Arizona. The Massachusetts legislature will look at the benefits of the 19,500 jobs and balance these with the costs of tax breaks, utility discounts and other aspects needed to keep Raytheon in Massachusetts.

VI

Product Markets

23

An Overview of Product Markets and Profit Maximization

FUNDAMENTAL QUESTIONS

1. Why do economists and accountants measure profit differently?
2. How do firms decide how much to supply?
3. What is a market structure?
4. What are price takers?
5. What are price makers?

T here are nearly six million business establishments in the United States alone. And they each face different demands and different costs. As a result, they behave differently. A brewery might spend hundreds of millions of dollars each year to tell you that "This Bud's for you" or that "Not any lite will do." An individual farmer, in contrast, is not likely to spend money to differentiate his or her oats and wheat from other farmers' oats and wheat. Different airlines almost always offer identical fares on the same routes, whereas Kodak sets the prices of its photofinishing chemicals and paper some 15 percent above the prices set by Trebla, Hunt, and Mitsubishi. The price of Bayer aspirin is nearly double the price of generic aspirin. Some firms (such as Sharper Image) offer the first available version of a product at high prices. Other firms (Nordstrom, for instance) offer great service. Still others (like Kmart) don't worry much about service and don't try to be the first to offer a product, but do offer low prices on everything.

PREVIEW

A list of differences among firms could fill many pages. This diversity makes generalization difficult: it is hard to understand why individual firms behave as they do. We know that firms must respond to their customers, that is, to demand. But how firms respond depends on their producing and selling environments: how many competitors or close substitutes there are; how easy it is for them to switch from the production of one product to another; how easy it is for new competitors to start up a business; or, in general, on the factors that influence demand and supply elasticities. Without

some means of simplification, we'd have to consider hundreds of thousands of specific cases every time we wanted to discuss the supply side of a market. The simplification economists have devised is a classification scheme based on producing and selling environments. There are four possible environments, or what are called market structures: *perfect competition*, *monopoly*, *monopolistic competition*, and *oligopoly*. The following three chapters examine these selling environments or market-structure models in detail. In this chapter we introduce the models and look at some of the ways that firms behave.

I. PROFIT MAXIMIZATION

The assumption that consumers behave so as to maximize utility allows economists to describe consumer behavior in a consistent and logical manner. Similarly, the assumption that firms behave so as to maximize profit allows economists to describe firm behavior in a consistent and logical manner. Profit maximization is a simplifying assumption. It does not describe exactly how every firm behaves, but it provides a theory about firm behavior that can be used to examine real-life circumstances.

The profit-maximization assumption does not apply to some firms even in theory. Some firms are explicitly not for profit; they are organized to provide a service, such as education or health care, regardless of whether a profit is made. Public enterprises such as government agencies, public colleges and universities, and some hospitals do not attempt to maximize profits. Objectives other than profit dominate and describe the behavior of these "not-for-profit" firms. Nevertheless, for most firms most of the time, profit maximization appropriately describes their operating behavior.

1.a. Alternative Measures of Profit

Why do economists and accountants measure profit differently?

accounting measure of costs: the direct costs that can be measured

Profit is revenue less costs. Costs are what must be given up to acquire the services of resources. To hire resources a firm must pay the opportunity cost of those resources—what the resources could earn from their best alternative use—otherwise the resources would go to the alternative. For most resources, the payment received for services (salaries, rents, etc.) is a good approximation of opportunity costs and is readily measured. Some resources, however, are not produced in the open market and their costs are not easily measured. For instance, an entrepreneur running her own business puts in a great deal of time and effort and often puts personal funds into the business. How would she determine the cost for her time and effort and personal funds?

The difficulty of measuring the opportunity cost of the entrepreneur's time and funds leads accountants to ignore these aspects of costs. The **accounting measure of costs** includes the direct costs that can be measured. This measure of costs is satisfactory for how it is used. The accountant is interested in reporting, on a consistent basis, the revenues and direct costs of doing business. The accounting measure is not, however, satisfactory for the way economists use costs. Economists want to understand behavior and, as we discussed in Chapters 1 and 2, opportunity costs are a crucial part of decisionmaking. Economists want to understand why someone begins a new business, why an existing corporation expands into a new line of business, or why businesses divest themselves of subsidiaries. These decisions are based on more than direct costs.

Suppose a dentist has a solo practice that generates revenues of $500,000 per year. The expenses for employees, rent on the building, leases on equipment, and supplies run $400,000 per year. According to the accountant, the profit from the business is $100,000 per year. The economist looks differently at this situation. Suppose that the dentist has used $400,000 of her own money to purchase equipment and supplies to get her dental practice started. If she could have earned 10 percent per year on this $400,000, then the best measure of the opportunity cost of the funds she put into the business is $40,000 per year. If, in addition, the dentist could have worked for a health maintenance organization for a salary of $50,000 per year, then that $50,000 is probably the best measure of the opportunity cost of running her own business. Adding these costs on to the accountant's figures indicates that total costs are $490,000. According to the economist's approach, profit from the business is $10,000.

economic costs:
total costs including explicit costs and the full opportunity costs of the resources that the producer does not buy or hire but already owns

Economic costs include the direct costs measured by accountants but also include the opportunity costs of the resources that the producer does not buy or hire but already owns, such as the entrepreneur's time and effort and the personal funds the entrepreneur puts into the business. Sometimes the accountant's measure of costs is called direct costs and the rest of the costs measured by economists are called implicit costs. In this case, economic costs are direct plus implicit costs. The costs economists want to consider are all opportunity costs, not just direct costs.

The cost schedules and curves derived in the previous chapter are economic costs. They measure all opportunity costs: the direct costs plus the opportunity costs of the entrepreneur's time and personal funds put into the business.

economic profit:
total revenue less total direct and implicit costs

accounting profit:
total revenue less total direct costs

Since accountants and economists have different measures of costs, they also have different measures of profit. **Economic profit** is calculated using economic costs. **Accounting profit** takes into consideration only direct costs. The accountant's measure of profit is what you hear about when IBM announces that third-quarter profits are up, Chrysler reports record profits, or Sony announces $167 billion in losses for 1994. Economic profits are never reported but are much more useful for explaining the behavior of firms and individuals. To understand why economic profits are more useful, consider what it means if economic profits are positive or negative.

If a firm is making a positive economic profit, its revenues are sufficient to pay all direct costs and the opportunity costs of an entrepreneur's time and personal funds. In other words, the entrepreneurs, or owners of the firm, could not do better putting their time and funds into another activity. They are doing better than they could in any other activity. What then does a negative economic profit mean? If a firm is earning a negative economic profit, its revenues are not sufficient to pay all direct costs and the opportunity costs of the entrepreneurs' time and personal funds. The entrepreneurs would be better off putting their time and funds into another activity.

Don't accounting profits tell us the same thing? Actually, they don't. A positive accounting profit means that a firm's revenue is greater than its direct costs. However, it is possible that the revenue would not be greater than all opportunity costs. Consider the dentist discussed earlier. Suppose that she could have earned a salary of $60,000 working for another organization. Her accounting profit is $100,000, but she has an economic loss of $10,000. If her opportunity costs are being measured correctly, the dentist would be better off selling her business and joining the health maintenance organization.[1] The accounting profit can't tell us this; only the economic profit can.

zero economic profit (normal profit):
total revenue equals the sum of direct and implicit costs

positive economic profit (above-normal profit):
total revenue exceeds the sum of direct and implicit costs

A **zero economic profit** is called a **normal profit** (or *normal accounting profit*). Zero economic profit means that revenues are just equal to all direct costs plus the opportunity costs of the entrepreneur's time and personal funds put into the business. In other words, the entrepreneur could not do better putting time and personal funds into another activity. A **positive economic profit** is called an **above-normal profit** or *above-normal accounting profit*. A positive economic profit means that the entrepreneur is doing better

_____
[1]It is typically not easy to place a value on an entrepreneur's attitude toward running her own business or being the boss. This value could offset some or all of the opportunity costs.

than she could in any other activity. Moreover, above-normal profits attract new businesses. Another entrepreneur will be likely to begin an identical business.

1.b. Firm Behavior and Price Elasticity of Demand

Profit is revenue less costs. To examine profit we thus look separately at costs and revenue and then put them together. In the short run, all firms must deal with U-shaped average- and marginal-cost curves. Revenue, however, is dependent on demand, and firms do not all have the same-shaped demand curves. The shape of the demand curve depends on the selling environment in which a firm operates.

1.b.1 Total Revenue
Total revenue, as we saw in the chapter "Elasticity: Demand and Supply," is price times quantity sold, $P \times Q$. A demand curve gives price and quantity combinations that are available to a firm. Three demand curves are drawn in Figure 1: a perfectly elastic demand curve in Figure 1(a), the downward-sloping straight-line demand curve in Figure 1(b), and a perfectly inelastic demand curve in Figure 1(c). Below each demand curve is the corresponding total-revenue curve.

With the perfectly elastic demand curve of Figure 1(a), as quantity is increased, total revenue rises. Price is constant at P_1, so $P_1 \times Q$ continues to rise as Q rises. Total revenue is a straight, upward-sloping line starting at the origin.

Along the downward-sloping straight-line demand curve of Figure 1(b), both P and Q change. As we move down a straight-line downward-sloping demand curve, revenue initially rises (in the price-elastic region) and then declines (in the price-inelastic region). This is shown in the lower half of Figure 1(b).

With the perfectly inelastic demand curve, Figure 1(c), quantity is a constant, Q_1, determined by the amount that the buyers must have. Total revenue then depends on what price is, $P \times Q_1$. As price rises, total revenue rises.

Recall from the previous chapter, "Supply: The Costs of Doing Business," that total costs rise relatively slowly at low levels of production but then as diminishing marginal returns set in, total costs rise more and more rapidly. This is shown in Figure 2.

In Figure 3, the total-revenue and total-cost curves are placed together. The firm wants to maximize profit, or find the quantity at which total revenue exceeds total costs by the greatest amount. In Figure 3(a) you can see that profit is maximized at quantity Q^*; in Figure 3(b), profit is maximized at quantity Q^{**}; and in Figure 3(c), profit rises as price rises (until demand no longer exists). Keep in mind that when we say profit, we are referring to economic profit.

Figures 3(a), (b), and (c) give you some idea of the different behaviors we might expect of firms. The firms facing perfectly elastic demand curves have no discretion over price; their goods must have the same price as their competitors' goods. These firms choose how much to produce and, as profit-maximizing firms, produce the quantity where total revenue exceeds total cost by the greatest amount. The firms facing a downward-sloping straight-line demand curve choose both price and quantity. The firms will choose the combination of price and quantity that maximizes profit. Firms facing perfectly inelastic demand select only the price to charge for their products since quantity is defined or determined by how much consumers want (or need). At

Part VI/Product Markets

Figure 1
Demand and Total Revenue

Figure 1(a) shows a perfectly elastic demand curve at price P_1. The total-revenue curve drawn below 1(a) shows that revenue rises as the quantity produced and sold rises, $P_1 \times Q$. Figure 1(b) shows a typical downward-sloping demand curve. Below it is the total-revenue curve. Total revenue rises as price is decreased in the elastic region; total revenue reaches a maximum at the unit-elastic point; total revenue falls as price is decreased in the inelastic region. Figure 1(c) is a perfectly inelastic demand curve. The total revenue is the fixed quantity, Q_1, multiplied by the price. The higher the price, the higher total revenue.

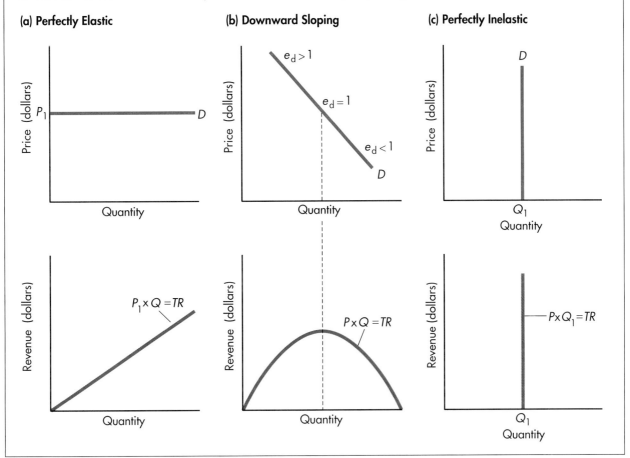

(a) Perfectly Elastic   **(b) Downward Sloping**   **(c) Perfectly Inelastic**

least up to some price where consumers cannot purchase the good, the higher the price the greater the profit.

You can see how firms might prefer to face the most inelastic demand curves possible. Thus, we might expect firms to try to influence the elasticity of demand. How might a firm make the demand for its product more inelastic? Since the price elasticity of demand depends on the availability of substitutes, along with the importance of the product in the buyer's total budget and the period of time under consideration, a firm might attempt to reduce the price elasticity of demand for its product by reducing the availability of substitutes. One strategy some firms take is to differentiate their products from those of competitors. For instance, Procter & Gamble might alter the ingredients of its detergent All to make it different from Tide, or Quaker

Figure 2
Total Costs
Total costs are redrawn from the previous chapter. Total costs rise relatively slowly at first and then, as diminishing marginal returns set in, they rise more and more quickly.

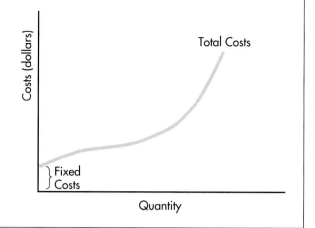

might make sure that the taste or appearance of its raisin bran cereal is different from the raisin bran cereal of General Mills. Anything that successfully distinguishes or differentiates products will reduce the price elasticity of demand because it reduces the number of "close" substitutes.

It may not be possible for a firm to differentiate its product, however. Basic disk drives for personal computers and dynamic random access memory (DRAM) chips are "plain vanilla" commodities that are the same no matter who produces them. Kyrene Scrap Metal is a firm that collects discarded appliances and other metal items and processes them into scrap metal to sell to steel manufacturers. Kyrene Scrap Metal cannot differentiate its scrap from scrap supplied by other scrap metal firms; scrap is scrap to the steel manufacturers. Similarly, it may not be possible for Old MacDonald to differentiate

Figure 3
Total Profit
In Figure 3(a) the total-revenue curve from the perfectly elastic demand curve and the total-cost curve are placed together. In Figure 3(b) the total-revenue curve from the downward-sloping demand curve and the total-cost curve are put together. In Figure 3(c) the total-revenue curve of the perfectly inelastic demand curve is placed together with the total-cost curve.

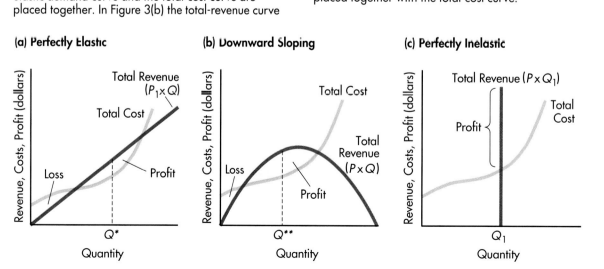

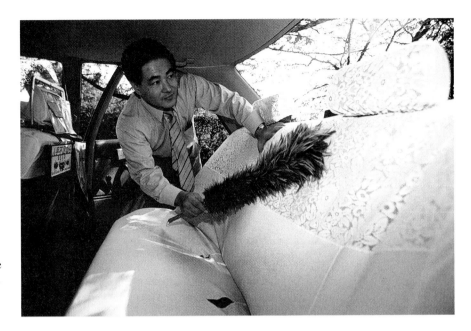

A cab driver in Tokyo dusts the rear seat of his cab prior to picking up passengers. Taxi cabs are tightly regulated in Japan, having to serve specific districts and maintain specified quality standards. A particular company may have a government-created monopoly in a certain part of the city. Nevertheless, each cab company attempts to compete with other cab and limousine companies by providing extra service. Cleanliness and order are emphasized. Many cab drivers wear white gloves; others use feather dusters on the seats before each customer enters the cab; still others provide special music and other services.

his wheat from wheat grown on another farm. The selling environments of the scrap metal company and the individual wheat farm are very different from that of Procter & Gamble.

l.c. Firm Behavior and Price Elasticity of Supply

A firm's producing and selling environment is influenced by the costs of producing and selling. The U-shaped cost curves we derived in the previous chapter represent the cost curves of all firms. However, even though the cost curves are U-shaped, some firms have higher fixed costs than others.

If there are huge fixed costs in a particular line of business, such as automobiles, then entrepreneurs might be reluctant to start up in that business. As a result, existing firms in that business do not have to fear immediate new competition in response to price changes or product differentiation strategies. If existing firms can make above-normal profits, they may be able to keep their above-normal profits for a long period of time because new competition will not immediately arise. Conversely, if fixed costs are very low, such as in desktop publishing, a small profit increase for a firm would induce a multitude of entrepreneurs to start up competing businesses. For these firms, above-normal profits would not last long. Thus, we might expect firms to attempt to increase the fixed costs necessary to begin a new business or to somehow make it difficult for new firms to enter their line of business. In this way, firms might be able to retain above-normal profits for a longer period of time.

Imagine if you were the only producer of a product that consumers really needed (desperately wanted)—say, a life-saving pharmaceutical. Your profit potential would be huge. Thus, we might expect firms to attempt to become the sole suppliers of necessary goods and services. For instance, if a firm could exploit economies of scale and thus be able to produce at a lower average cost than any other firm, it might become the only producer of a good. Or, perhaps a firm could get a law passed that gave it the exclusive rights to supply a good. Being the only producer of a good or service people desperately want could mean above-normal profits for a long time.

RECAP

1. The accounting measure of costs includes direct costs only.

2. The economic measure of costs includes all opportunity costs, the direct accounting costs plus the opportunity costs of resources already owned by the entrepreneur but used in the business, such as the entrepreneur's time and personal funds.

3. Above-normal profit refers to positive economic profit; revenue exceeds all opportunity costs. Below-normal profit refers to negative economic profit; revenue is less than all opportunity costs.

4. Accounting profit can be positive even while economic profit is negative.

5. The assumption that firms behave so as to maximize profit allows economists to describe firm behavior in a consistent, logical way.

6. Profit is maximized at the level of output where total revenue exceeds total costs by the greatest amount.

7. Firm behavior depends on the factors that affect the price elasticities of demand and supply.

2. MARGINAL REVENUE AND MARGINAL COST

A firm's decision to supply a good or service depends on expected profit. An entrepreneur or manager of a firm looks at the demand for the firm's product and at its costs of doing business and determines whether a profit potential exists. To analyze the firm's decisions, we must put the demand for the firm's product together with the firm's costs. We did this in Figure 3. But using total revenue and total cost is not as useful or informative as using the average- and marginal-cost curves along with the demand curve. In this section, we examine firm behavior using the U-shaped cost curves and a demand curve.

2.a. Demand and Cost Curves

How do firms decide how much to supply?

Consider Figure 4, in which the average-total and marginal-cost curves, derived in the previous chapter, are drawn along with a downward-sloping demand curve. The demand curve could also be horizontal or vertical. The shape of the demand curve characterizes the environment in which the firm is selling.

With the downward-sloping demand curve, the firm knows that total revenue first rises and then declines as price is lowered down along the demand curve. Maximum revenue is the point where the price elasticity of demand is 1. But this point is not necessarily the profit-maximizing point. How do we find the profit-maximizing point?

Profit is the difference between total revenue and total costs. Consider the profit the firm shown in Figure 4 earns at price P_1 selling output Q_1. Total revenue is price times quantity, or $P_1 \times Q_1$, the rectangle $ABCD$. At quantity Q_1 total cost is given by $ABEF$, found by determining the average total cost

Figure 4
Revenue, Cost, and Profit

In Figure 4 the demand curve is drawn along with the average-total and marginal-cost curves. A point of output, Q_1, is arbitrarily chosen to illustrate what total costs, total revenue, and total profit would be at that output point. The price, P_1, is given by the demand curve, tracing Q_1 up to the demand curve. Total revenue, $P_1 \times Q_1$, is given by the rectangle labeled $ABCD$. The total costs are given by seeing how much it costs per unit of output to produce Q_1. That quantity, BE, multiplied by the total quantity AB, provides the total cost area, $ABEF$. Total profit is total revenue minus total costs, $ABCD - ABEF = FECD$.

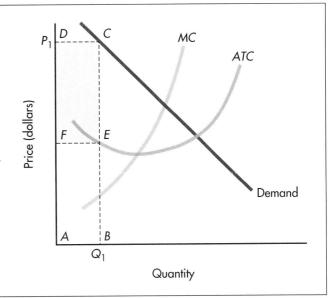

(cost per unit of output) at Q_1 and multiplying that by the price, P_1. Profit at quantity Q_1, then, is the difference between the rectangle $ABCD$ and the rectangle $ABEF$. Profit at Q_1 is given by: $ABCD - ABEF = FECD$.

The profit given by the rectangle $FECD$ in Figure 4 is the profit the firm would earn by producing and selling quantity Q_1. The area $FECD$ is not necessarily the maximum profit—the firm might earn more producing more or less than Q_1. To find the quantity at which profit is maximized, we could compare total revenue and total cost for each output level. There is an easier way, however: to find the quantity of output at which profit is a maximum, simply compare marginal cost and marginal revenue.

Supply rule: produce and offer for sale the quantity at which marginal revenue equals marginal cost (MR = MC).

2.b. Profit Maximum: Marginal Revenue Equals Marginal Cost

Marginal cost is the additional cost of producing one more unit of output. *Marginal revenue* is the additional revenue obtained from selling one more unit of output. If the production of one more unit of output increases costs less than it increases revenue—that is, if marginal cost is less than marginal revenue—then producing (and selling) that unit will increase profit. Conversely, if the production of one more unit costs more than the revenue obtained from the sale of the unit, then producing that unit will decrease profit. When marginal revenue is greater than marginal cost, producing more will increase profit. Conversely, when marginal revenue is less than marginal cost, producing more will lower profit. Thus, *profit is at a maximum when marginal revenue equals marginal cost.*

Profit is maximized at the output level where marginal revenue and marginal cost are equal (MR = MC).

The profit-maximizing rule, $MR = MC$, is illustrated in Table 1, which lists output, total revenue, total cost, marginal revenue, marginal cost, and profit for an individual firm selling custom-made mountain bicycles. The first column is the total quantity (Q) of bikes produced. In column 2 is the total revenue (TR) generated by selling each quantity, and in column 3 is the total cost (TC) of producing each quantity. Fixed costs, the costs the firm encounters even when it produces nothing, amount to $1,000, as listed in column 3,

TABLE I
Profit Maximization

(1) Total Output (Q)	(2) Total Revenue (TR)	(3) Total Cost (TC)	(4) Marginal Revenue (MR)	(5) Marginal Cost (MC)	(6) Profit (TR − TC)
0	$ 0	$1,000			$−1,000
1	1,700	2,000	$1,700	$1,000	− 300
2	3,300	2,800	1,600	800	500
3	4,800	3,500	1,500	700	1,300
4	6,200	4,000	1,400	500	2,200
5	7,500	4,500	1,300	500	3,000
6	8,700	5,200	1,200	700	3,500
7	9,800	6,000	1,100	800	3,800
8	10,800	7,000	1,000	1,000	3,800
9	11,700	9,000	900	2,000	2,700

row 1. Marginal revenue (*MR*), the change in total revenue that comes with the production of an additional bike, is listed in the fourth column. The marginal revenue of the first bike produced is the change in revenue that the firm receives for increasing its production and sales from zero to 1 unit; the marginal revenue of the first bike is listed in the row of bike number 1. The marginal revenue of the second bike produced is the change in revenue that the firm receives for increasing its production and sales from 1 to 2 bikes; the marginal revenue of that second bike is listed in the row of bike number 2. Marginal cost (*MC*), the additional cost of producing an additional bike, is listed in column 5. The marginal cost of the first bike is the additional cost of producing the first bike; the marginal cost of the second bike is the increase in costs that results from increasing production from 1 to 2 bikes. Total profit, the difference between total revenue and total cost (*TR* − *TC*), is listed in the last column.

The first bike costs $2,000 to produce ($1,000 of fixed costs and $1,000 of variable costs); the marginal cost (additional cost) of the first bike is $1,000. When sold, the bike brings in $1,700 in revenue, so the marginal revenue is $1,700. Since marginal revenue is greater than marginal cost, the firm is better off producing that first bike than not producing it.

The second bike costs an additional $800 (column 5) to produce and brings in an additional $1,600 (column 4) in revenue. With the second bike, marginal revenue exceeds marginal cost. Thus the firm is better off producing 2 bikes than none or one.

Profit continues to rise as production rises until the eighth bike is produced. The marginal cost of producing the seventh bike is $800, and the marginal revenue from selling the seventh bike is $1,100. The marginal cost of producing the eighth bike is $1,000, and the marginal revenue from selling that eighth bike is also $1,000. The marginal cost of producing the ninth bike, $2,000, exceeds the marginal revenue obtained from the ninth bike,

$900. Profit declines if the ninth bike is produced. The firm increases profit by producing the seventh bike and reduces profit by producing the ninth bike. Thus, the firm can maximize profit by producing eight bikes, the quantity at which marginal revenue and marginal cost are equal.[2]

2.b.1. The Marginal-Revenue Curve The example of the mountain bikes shows us that the only thing we need to add to Figure 4 to be able to point out the profit-maximizing point is the marginal-revenue curve. Drawing the marginal-revenue curve is really quite simple. The first step is to recognize that the demand curve is also the average-revenue curve; it shows the revenue per unit. Thus, the marginal-revenue curve and the demand curve are related to each other in the same way any average and marginal curves are related. That is, when the average is declining, the marginal is also declining and lies below the average. Thus, when the demand curve is downward-sloping, the marginal-revenue curve is also downward-sloping but lies below the demand curve.

The steeper the demand curve, the steeper the marginal-revenue curve; the marginal-revenue curve for a perfectly inelastic demand curve is the same vertical line as the demand curve. The flatter the demand curve, the flatter the marginal-revenue curve; the marginal-revenue curve for the perfectly elastic demand curve is the same as the demand curve. In between these two extremes, the marginal-revenue curve lies below the demand curve and slopes down.

For the downward-sloping demand curve, we can be more specific in drawing the marginal-revenue curve than to simply note that it slopes down and lies below the demand curve. Recall that the marginal-revenue curve is positive as long as total revenue is rising and is negative as total revenue declines. Since total revenue rises in the price-elastic region of the demand curve, marginal revenue is positive in that region. Total revenue reaches its peak at the unit-elastic point of the demand curve and then turns down; marginal revenue is zero at the unit-elastic point. And total revenue declines in the inelastic region of the demand curve, so marginal revenue must be negative in the inelastic region. Thus, the marginal-revenue curve slopes down and crosses the horizontal axis at the quantity where the demand curve is unit-elastic.

In Figure 5 we have redrawn Figure 4 and added the marginal-revenue curve. Now we can easily find the profit-maximizing point. It is the point at which $MR = MC$. In Figure 5, the profit-maximizing point is given by price P_m and the quantity Q_m, and total profit is given by the rectangle $GHIJ$.

Economists rely heavily on diagrams like Figure 5 to analyze business behavior; the demand curve may be different depending on the price elasticity of demand, or the position of the cost curves might be different depending on cost conditions, but in general, Figure 5 provides a useful and powerful framework of analysis for understanding business behavior.

---

[2]You might notice that profit is at the maximum level for quantities of 7 and 8 bikes. This occurs because we are dealing with integers, 1, 2, 3, etc., when discussing output. There would be a unique quantity for which profit is at its maximum level if we could divide the quantities into small units instead of having to deal with integers. That unique quantity would be where $MR = MC$. Thus, we always choose the quantity at which marginal revenue and marginal cost are the same as the profit-maximizing quantity.

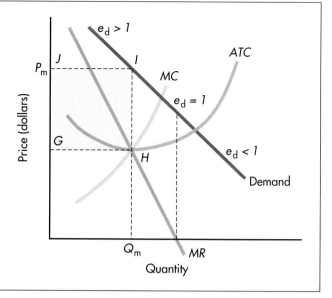

Figure 5
Profit Maximum with MR = MC
The demand, ATC, and MC curves from Figure 4 are redrawn. In addition, the MR curve is added. MR is drawn by recognizing that demand is average revenue, and since average revenue is falling, marginal revenue must also be falling and lie below average. In addition, marginal revenue crosses the horizontal axis at the output level where the price elasticity of demand is unity. Profit is then found where MR = MC. This is quantity Q_m and price P_m. Total profit is the rectangle GHIJ.

RECAP

1. The average- and marginal-cost curves and the demand and marginal-revenue curves together characterize the producing and selling environments of a firm.

2. The demand curve is also the average-revenue curve. Thus, the marginal-revenue and demand curves are related to each other, as are any average and marginal curves. When demand declines, marginal revenue declines and lies below demand.

3. The profit-maximizing rule is to produce where marginal revenue equals marginal cost.

3. SELLING ENVIRONMENTS OR MARKET STRUCTURE

Kyrene Scrap Metal, as mentioned earlier, is a processor of scrap metal; the employees collect used appliances, junked autos, and other scrap metals, and then the metal is processed and offered to steel-manufacturing plants. The demand curve for scrap metal is nearly perfectly elastic; if Kyrene Scrap Metal attempts to increase the price per ton of its metal, the steel-manufacturing plants turn to other scrap collectors. Although Kyrene Scrap Metal has no control over the price of its scrap metal, having to price at whatever all other scrap metals are priced, it does determine the quantity of metal it processes. And the quantity it processes is given by the point where marginal revenue and marginal cost are equal.

Burroughs-Wellcome is the only producer of AZT, for many years the only drug authorized by the FDA to inhibit the emergence of AIDS in those who were found to be HIV positive. Burroughs-Wellcome thus faced an almost perfectly inelastic demand for AZT; buyers had no alternative pharmaceuticals to turn to when the price of AZT rose. Burroughs-Wellcome set a very high price on AZT, approximately $10,000 for a year's supply.

Kyrene Scrap Metal and Burroughs-Wellcome face very different demand curves and thus behave differently. Kyrene Scrap Metal really has no choice over the price to charge for its metal. Burroughs-Wellcome, on the other hand, sets the price of AZT.

In contrast, The Gap clothing firm faces a demand curve that is neither perfectly elastic nor perfectly inelastic. Although it chooses to manufacture a quantity of clothing given by where marginal cost and marginal revenue are equal, The Gap must attempt to convince customers that its clothing is different and better than the lines offered by J. Crew, Limited, Benetton, or others. Neither Kyrene Scrap Metal nor Burroughs-Wellcome has any incentive to advertise, but The Gap devotes considerable resources toward advertising. It wants to convince customers not to switch to the other clothing lines whenever the price of one of the lines is reduced.

Southwest Airlines has been able to differentiate its service from that of other airline companies. But, unlike The Gap, which behaves somewhat independently of all other clothing retailers, anytime Southwest changes fares or alters its service, it has to take into account how America West and other airlines will respond. If Southwest reduces fares and all other airlines follow, Southwest's profits decline. If Southwest introduces a new service and all other airlines follow suit, the new service gains Southwest nothing. Thus, Southwest Airlines is particularly sensitive to the actions its competitors might take.

In just these four firms, we see a wide range of behaviors. Whereas all four firms attempt to maximize profits, and thus operate where $MR = MC$, each differs with respect to its allocation of resources to advertising and its control over the prices of its products. The four differ because they produce and sell in different types of markets.

3.a. Characteristics of the Market Structures

What is a market structure?

Economists analyzing the behavior of firms assume that firms can be classified into one of four market-structure models. Once a market structure is defined, economists can then examine the behavior of firms within it. A market structure is a *model*—a simplification of reality. Few if any industries fit neatly into one market structure or another. Economists use the four models to describe how firms might behave under certain conditions. They can then modify the models to improve their understanding of how firms behave in real life.

The market structure in which a firm produces and sells its product is defined by three characteristics:

- the number of firms that make up the market
- the ease with which new firms may enter the market and begin producing the good or service
- the degree to which the products produced by the firms are different

In some industries, such as agriculture, there are millions of individual firms. In others, such as in the photofinishing supplies industry, there are very few firms. It is relatively easy and inexpensive to enter the desktop publishing business, but it is much more costly and difficult to start a new airline. In some industries entry is strictly prohibited. It is illegal, for example, for any firm other than the U.S. Postal Service to deliver certain classes of mail in the United States.

In some industries, the products offered by each seller are virtually identical; in other industries, each product is slightly different. **Differentiated products** are perceived by consumers as having characteristics that products offered by other sellers do not have. **Standardized or nondifferentiated products** are perceived by consumers as being identical.

3.b. Market-Structure Models

Table 2 summarizes the characteristics of the four market structures discussed in this section. Though it is not stated in the table, it is commonly assumed that consumers and firms have perfect information about prices and other decisions made by a firm. In other words, it is assumed that consumers and firms know the prices, locations, and products of all firms in the market in each market-structure model. Other than this common assumption, the characteristics that define each market structure are listed in the table. The name of the market structure is listed in column 1 of the table. The table lists the number of firms, the entry conditions, and the product type of the firms in each market structure, as well as the kind of price and promotion strategies a firm is likely to follow.

3.b.1. Perfect Competition

Perfect competition is a market structure characterized by a very large number of firms, so large that whatever any *one* firm does has no effect on the market; firms that produce an identical (standardized or nondifferentiated) product; and easy entry. Because of the large number of firms, consumers have many choices of where to purchase the good or service, and there is no cost to the consumer of going to a different store. Because the product is standardized, consumers do not prefer one store to another or one brand to another. In fact, there are no brands—only identical, generic products. For instance, wheat from one farm is no different than wheat from another farm; scrap metal from one firm is no different than scrap metal from another firm; personal computer disk drives from one firm are identical to disk drives from another firm.

TABLE 2
Summary of Market Structures and Predicted Behavior

| Market Structure | Characteristics | | | Behavior | |
	Number of Firms	Entry Condition	Product Type	Price Strategy	Promotion Strategy
Perfect competition	Very large number	Easy	Standardized	Price taker	None
Monopoly	One	No entry possible	Only one product	Price maker	Little
Monopolistic competition	Large number	Easy	Differentiated	Price maker	Large amount
Oligopoly	Few	Impeded	Standardized or differentiated	Interdependent	Little or large amount

Easy entry means a firm cannot earn more than a normal profit. Above-normal profit attracts entrepreneurs who also want to earn more than their opportunity costs. With more firms and more production, the price of the good is driven down and economic profit is reduced. Entry continues until no one is earning more than a normal profit. At this point, firms in the industry cannot do better leaving the industry, and firms outside cannot do better entering. An equilibrium where there is neither entry nor exit is reached at zero economic, or normal, profit.

Perfectly competitive firms sell their goods at the price prevailing in the market. They cannot set a price that is above the market price, and they will not set a lower price because they can sell at the market price *all* they produce. The perfectly competitive firm is just one among very many—for instance, 1 farm among 2 million farms. Thus, a 10 percent or even a 50 percent increase in its output will have no effect on the total quantity produced in the market. About 300 billion tons of oats are grown each year by 2 million farms—each farm produces 150,000 tons. A 66 percent production increase by one farm (a 100,000-ton increase) is only a .03 percent increase in the market supply. It is very unlikely that such a small increase in quantity supplied would affect the market price.

What are price takers?

price taker:
a firm that is unable to set a price that differs from the market price without losing profit

Because each farm is such a small part of the total market, each farmer expects to sell at the *market price* everything produced on his or her farm. A reduction in quantity does not bring a higher price, and an increase in quantity does not require a lower price. For this reason, the perfectly competitive firm is called a **price taker**. It takes the price determined in the market as its price. A firm in perfect competition is the only firm that is a price taker.

The demand curve confronting the individual firm in a perfectly competitive market is perfectly elastic—a horizontal line at the market price. Figure 6(a) shows the market for oats, measured in billions of pounds of oats produced annually in the United States. The price determined by *market* demand and supply is $.50 per pound. Individual producers in a perfectly competitive market know that they could sell all they want to sell at that $.50 per pound price. Each producer is such a small portion of the market, 1 of 2 million farms producing oats, that whether he or she produces a little or a lot will not affect the market supply and thus the market price. In addition, because each is such a small part of the market and the oats produced on one farm are no different from the oats produced on the other 1,999,999 farms, no producer can charge a price that is higher than the market price, as shown in Figure 6(b). Faced with a price increase, buyers (grain silo owners) would immediately purchase from the other farms. Thus, 1 farm among the 2 million that produce oats views demand as a horizontal line at the current market price.

The individual firm in perfect competition does not advertise. By definition the firm can't differentiate its product, and it can't increase the demand for its product independent of the other firms in the market.

3.b.2. Monopoly   Monopoly is a market structure in which there is just one firm and entry by other firms is not possible. Because there is only one firm, consumers have only one place to buy the good, and there are no close substitutes. Because entry is impossible, even if the firm earns above-normal returns, no new firms can compete for those returns. As a result, the firm in a monopoly can earn positive (above-normal) economic profit over a long period of time.

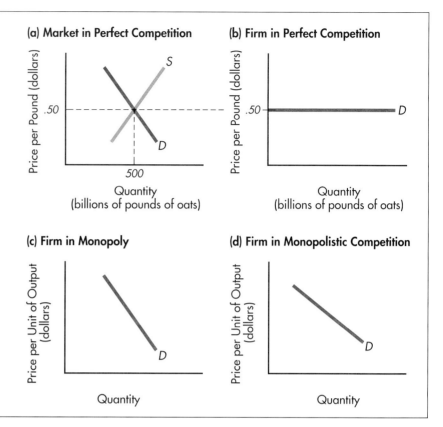

Figure 6
The Demand Curve Facing an Individual Firm
Figure 6(a) shows the market for oats. The price, determined by market demand and supply, defines the demand curve faced by a perfectly competitive firm. The demand curve is a horizontal line at the market price, as shown in Figure 6(b).

Figure 6(c) shows the market demand, which is the demand curve faced by the monopoly firm. The firm is the only supplier and thus faces the entire market demand.

Figure 6(d) shows the downward-sloping demand curve faced by the firm in monopolistic competition. The curve slopes downward because of the differentiated nature of the products in the industry.

natural monopoly:
a monopoly that emerges because of economies of scale

A monopoly may come into existence because of economies of scale: the larger the firm, the lower the cost per unit of output produced by the firm. In the case of economies of scale, a large firm can supply the product at a lower cost per unit than a smaller firm could. As a result, the larger firm can under-price smaller firms and force them out of the market. The large firm then becomes the only supplier. A monopoly that emerges because of economies of scale is called a **natural monopoly**. Electric utilities are often said to be natural monopolies because of the huge economies of scale that exist in the generation of electricity.

A second type of monopoly arises as the result of laws that restrict entry. The U.S. Postal Service is a monopoly supplier of mail delivery. By law, no other firm can provide mail delivery. The Federal Reserve Bank is a monopoly supplier of U.S. currency. By law, no other firm can supply U.S. dollars. In the fifteenth through the seventeenth centuries governments raised revenue by granting monopolies to special interest groups in return for some of their profits. Christopher Columbus was granted a monopoly from Queen Isabella of Spain; the Hudson Bay Company was granted a monopoly by the English monarchy; most of the explorers and trading ships of the time had been granted monopoly charters. Today, patents can provide a government-created monopoly. Burroughs-Wellcome was granted a patent on AZT and thus was, by law, the only supplier of the drug for a period of seventeen years.

For more than a hundred years, it has been argued that a monopoly may result from unfair and anticompetitive practices engaged in by firms, known as the *monopolization of a market*. Many economists argue that no such thing as monopolization occurs, that tactics designed to monopolize a market are simply intense forms of competition. Regardless of the arguments, hundreds of firms have been accused of monopolization and taken to court. A famous case involved the Rockefellers. John D. and William Rockefeller organized Standard of Ohio in 1870 and by 1872 owned all but three or four of the approximately forty-five oil refineries in Cleveland. Standard Oil of Ohio and its successor, Standard Oil of New Jersey, were accused of attempting to create a monopoly in the retail gas market because, by controlling 90 to 95 percent of oil refining, Standard Oil could increase the price of gasoline to competitors and drive them out of business. Another famous case resulted when Alcoa was accused of creating a monopoly because it controlled an ingredient necessary to produce aluminum.[3] And in 1994, Microsoft was accused of monopolization and anticompetitive actions in the computer software business.

People often refer to a business as being a monopoly even though many firms nationwide or worldwide supply the product. Universities, hotels, cable TV companies, newspapers, and electric utilities have all been called monopolies at one time or another. They are not monopolies according to the strict definition of being the only firm providing a good or service, but they may be "local" monopolies. A hotel may be the only supplier within the center of the city, and entry by others is virtually impossible. There may be only one major newspaper in a city, and entry is very difficult. One cable TV company may be the only supplier within a city or a portion of a city, and competition is not allowed by law.

The demand curve facing the single firm in a monopoly is the market demand because the firm is the only supplier in the market. Figure 6(c) shows the demand curve facing the firm in a monopoly. Being the only producer, the firm in a monopoly must carefully consider what price to charge. Unlike a price increase in a perfectly competitive market, a price increase in a monopoly will not drive every customer to another producer. But if the price is too high, revenue will decline as consumers decide to forgo the product supplied by that one firm. A firm operating in any market but perfect competition is not a price taker. Economists have used different names to refer to a firm that is not a price taker, sometimes using **price maker**, other times **price setter**, and still other times **price searcher**. All three terms are meant to imply the same thing: that the firm determines the quantity it produces and the price at which it sells the products.

The firm in a monopoly market structure may advertise in an attempt to increase the market demand (to shift the demand curve out), but advertising and promotion are likely to be low-priority items. For instance, a local electric utility may promote the all-electric home or advertise energy-efficient electric air conditioners or heating systems, but the utility's advertising budget is likely to be a very small portion of its overall budget.

3.b.3. Monopolistic Competition

A monopolistically competitive market structure is characterized by a large number of firms, easy entry, and

What are price makers?

price maker, price setter, price searcher:
a firm that sets the price of the product it sells

---

[3]Stuart B. Bruchey, *The Wealth of the Nation: An Economic History of the United States* (New York: Harper & Row Publishers), 1988, p. 126; Irwin M. Stelzer, *Selected Antitrust Cases: Landmark Decisions* (Homewood, IL: Richard D. Irwin), 1981, pp. 3–90.

differentiated products. Many agricultural products provide good examples of nondifferentiated products—milk is milk and oats are oats. But beer, detergents, cereal, and soft drinks provide examples of differentiated products—Coke is not Pepsi and Cheerios are not Wheaties. Each brand is to some degree different from the others. Sam Adams beer differs from Budweiser, Miller, and Moosehead. Tide detergent differs from All, Clorox, and Fab.

Product differentiation distinguishes a perfectly competitive market from a monopolistically competitive market (in both entry is easy and there are a large number of firms). When a firm enters a perfectly competitive market, it produces an identical product—more scrap metal or more wheat, for example. When a new firm enters a monopolistically competitive market, it produces a slightly different product. For instance, most fast food firms offer several different types of meals, and competition often takes the form of a new line such as a double bacon and cheese burger or chicken fingers.

Even though there are many firms in a monopolistically competitive market structure, the demand curve faced by *any one firm* slopes downward, as in Figure 6(d). Because each product is slightly different from all other products, each firm is like a mini-monopoly—the only producer of that specific product. The downward slope reflects the differentiated nature of the products: the products are not perfect substitutes (identical goods) as in the case of perfect competition. Thus, the firm in monopolistic competition is a price maker. As the price of Big Macs is increased, everything else held constant, consumers switch to Wendy's, Jack-in-the-Box or to other foods at McDonald's. As a result, the quantity demanded of Big Macs falls, but not to zero, as would be the case in perfect competition.

The greater the differentiation among products, the less price-elastic the demand. Thus, a firm in monopolistic competition wants to differentiate its products from its competitors' products as much as possible, and advertising and marketing strategies become very important. One such strategy is discussed in the Economic Insight "Taste Tests."

3.b.4. Oligopoly   In an oligopoly, there are few firms—more than one, but few enough so that each firm alone can affect the market. Auto producers constitute one oligopoly, steelmakers another. Entry into an oligopoly is more difficult than entry into a perfectly competitive or monopolistically competitive market, but in contrast to monopoly, entry can occur. The products offered by the firms in an oligopoly may be differentiated or nondifferentiated. Buicks differ from Fords and Nissans. However, the steel produced by USX is no different from the steel produced by Bethlehem Steel.

Because an oligopoly consists of just a few firms, each firm, or oligopolist, must take the actions of the others into account. Oligopolistic firms are *interdependent*, and this interdependence distinguishes oligopoly from the other market structures. An oligopolist that is trying to decide whether to lower the price of its product must consider whether its competitors will follow suit. If one firm lowers its price and the competitors do follow suit, none of the firms in the oligopoly will be able to increase their sales much. However, if the competitors do not follow suit, the sales of the now lower-priced firm may rise substantially. For instance, as an airline is deciding whether to raise or lower fares, it must consider whether the other airlines will follow suit.

The oligopolist faces a downward-sloping demand curve, but the shape of the curve depends on the behavior of competitors. Oligopoly is the most complicated of the market-structure models to examine because there are so

Taste Tests

If you pay attention to commercials, you may be able to identify some attempts to create differentiated products. Taste tests are a common approach. Suppose consumers strolling through a grocery store are asked whether they prefer Coke or Pepsi. If they say Coke, they are asked to take a taste test. They are given a small white cup with one brand of soft drink in it. Then they are given a second cup containing another brand. They indicate whether they prefer the first or the second. The result, Pepsi might claim, is that more than half of all Coke drinkers preferred Pepsi in a taste test.

At first the results of this test may sound quite convincing. But if most consumers are unable to differentiate between the products in blind taste tests, then it is likely that 50 percent of any group of consumers will choose one of the products and 50 percent the other. Realizing this, the testing company ensures that only the consumers who say they prefer the competitor's product will be asked to participate in the taste test. Coke can, and has, turned the tables by asking those who claim to prefer Pepsi to participate in a test.

In which market structure would such taste tests matter? Clearly not in perfect competition, since products are identical. It is in the market structure of monopolistic competition that we find most efforts to differentiate products.

many behaviors firms might display. Because of its diversity, many economists describe oligopoly as the most realistic of the market-structure models.

3.c. Comparisons of the Market Structures

The characteristics of the four market structures are noted in the left side of Table 2, and the predicted behavior of each of the market structures is summarized in the right side of the table. Possible pricing strategies include being a price taker or a price maker, or, in the case of oligopoly, being interdependent. The promotion strategy refers to whether advertising or marketing is likely to occur. For instance, there would be no advertising or marketing in a perfectly competitive market. The demand curves faced by a firm in each of the market structures (except oligopoly, where the shape of the demand curve varies depending on how firms interact) are shown in Figure 6. The demand curves are all downward-sloping except for the firm in perfect competition, whose demand curve is perfectly elastic. The marginal-revenue curve of all firms but perfect competitors slopes down and lies below the demand curve. For the perfectly competitive firm, the demand and marginal revenue curves are the same.

As you use the market structure models to study the behavior of firms, keep in mind that they are *models*—simplifications of reality—that provide a framework for discussing the behavior of firms in the real world. They do not, themselves, necessarily describe the real world. It is not easy to assign real-life firms and industries to one of the four market structures. An industry is likely to have characteristics of more than one structure. Consider the soft-drink industry. There are many brands (a characteristic of monopolistic competition), yet Pepsi and Coca-Cola account for about 60 percent of the total market (a characteristic of oligopoly). Consider farming. There are millions of farmers (a characteristic of perfect competition), but starting a farming operation can be very expensive (a characteristic of oligopoly).

Figure 7
Opinions Can Vary in Classifying Industries According to Market Structure

The chart shows how twenty economists classified a sampling of industries according to three categories: "effectively competitive," "monopoly," and "oligopoly." In only a few instances was there widespread agreement, such as "Apartment building development," "Hospitals," and "Office building development." The difference of opinion suggests that real-life industries do not often fit any one of the four market-structure categories exactly. Source: John J. Siegfried, "Could a Score of Industrial Organization Economists Agree on Competition?" *Review of Industrial Organization*, vol. 3, no. 4 (Fall 1988), pp. 139–148. Used by permission of the *Review of Industrial Organization*.

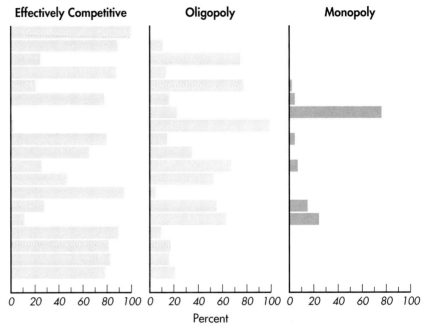

A few years ago, twenty economists were asked to classify several industries into three groups: (1) effectively competitive (perfect or monopolistic competitors), (2) monopoly, and (3) oligopoly. The results are shown in Figure 7. The economists agreed in only a few instances.

RECAP

1. Economists have identified four market structures: perfect competition, monopoly, monopolistic competition, and oligopoly.

2. Perfect competition is a market structure in which many firms are producing a nondifferentiated product and entry is easy.

3. Monopoly is a market structure in which only one firm supplies the product and entry cannot occur.

4. Monopolistic competition is a market structure in which many firms are producing differentiated products and entry is easy.

5. Oligopoly is a market structure in which a few firms are producing either standardized or differentiated products and entry is possible but not easy. The distinguishing characteristic of oligopoly is that the firms are interdependent.

SUMMARY

▲▼ Why do economists and accountants measure profit differently?

1. The basic assumption about the behavior of firms is that firms maximize profit. Although some firms may deviate from profit maximization, the assumption of profit maximization is a useful simplification of reality. §1

2. Accountants measure only the direct costs. Economists measure all opportunity costs. §1.a

3. Normal profit is a zero economic profit. Above-normal profit is positive economic profit. Below-normal profit is a negative economic profit. §1.a

4. Profit is maximized at the output level where total revenue exceeds total costs by the greatest amount. §1.b

5. Firms facing perfectly elastic demand curves have no discretion over price; firms facing perfectly inelastic demand curves select only the price, since quantity is determined by consumers. §1.b

▲▼ How do firms decide how much to supply?

6. The supply rule for all firms is to supply the quantity at which the firm's marginal revenue and marginal cost are equal. §2.b

▲▼ What is a market structure?

7. A market structure is a model of the producing and selling environments in which firms operate. The three characteristics that define market structure are number of firms, the ease of entry, and whether the products are differentiated. §3.a

8. A perfectly competitive market is a market in which a very large number of firms are producing an identical product and entry is easy. §3.b.1

9. A monopoly is a market in which there is only one firm and entry by others cannot occur. §3.b.2

10. A monopolistically competitive market is a market in which a large number of firms are producing differentiated products and entry is easy. §3.b.3

11. The demand curve facing a monopolistically competitive firm is downward-sloping because of the differentiated nature of the products offered by the firm. §3.b.3

12. An oligopoly is a market in which a few firms are producing either differentiated or nondifferentiated products and entry is possible but not easy. The distinguishing characteristic of an oligopoly is that the firms are interdependent. §3.b.4

13. The demand curve facing a firm in an oligopoly is downward-sloping. The elasticity depends on the actions and reactions to price changes by fellow oligopolists in the industry. §3.b.4

▲▼ What are price takers?

14. The demand curve facing a perfectly competitive firm is a horizontal line at the market price. The firm takes the price determined in its market as its price. §3.b.1

▲▼ What are price makers?

15. A firm that determines the quantity it produces and the price at which it sells the products, is a price maker. §3.b.2

16. The marginal-revenue curve for all firms except those in perfect competition is downward-sloping and lies below the demand curve. The marginal-revenue curve for the perfectly competitive firm is the same as the demand curve, a horizontal or perfectly elastic curve. §3.c

KEY TERMS

accounting measure of costs §1.a

economic costs §1.a

implicit costs §1.a

economic profit §1.a

accounting profit §1.a

zero economic profit (normal profit) §1.a

positive economic profit (above-normal profit) §1.a

differentiated products §3.a

standardized or nondifferentiated products §3.a

price taker §3.b.1

natural monopoly §3.b.2

price maker (price setter, price searcher) §3.b.2

EXERCISES

1. Can accounting profit be positive and economic profit negative? Can accounting profit be negative and economic profit positive? Explain.

2. Use the following information to calculate accounting profit and economic profit.

   Sales $100
   Employee expenses $40
   Inventory expenses $20
   Value of owner's labor in any other enterprise $40

3. Why is the assumption of a very large number of firms important to the definition of perfect competition?

4. Which type of market characterizes most businesses operating in the United States today?

5. Since a firm in monopoly has no competitors producing close substitutes, does the monopolist set exorbitantly high prices?

6. Advertising to create brand preferences is most common in what market structures?

7. Draw a perfectly elastic demand curve on top of a standard U-shaped average-total-cost curve. Now add in the marginal-cost and marginal-revenue curves. Find the profit-maximizing point, $MR = MC$. Indicate the firm's total revenues and total cost.

8. Give ten examples of differentiated products. Then list as many nondifferentiated products as you can.

9. Describe profit maximization in terms of marginal revenue and marginal cost.

10. Use the information below to calculate total revenue, marginal revenue, and marginal cost. Indicate the profit-maximizing level of output. If the price was $3 and fixed costs were $5, what would variable costs be? At what level of output would the firm produce?

Output	Price	Total Costs	Total Revenue ($P \times Q$)
1	$5	$10	
2	5	12	
3	5	15	
4	5	19	
5	5	24	
6	5	30	
7	5	45	

11. If agriculture is an example of perfect competition, why are there so many brands of dairy products at the grocery store?

12. Using demand curves, illustrate the effect of product differentiation on the part of haircutters.

13. Why might society prefer perfect competition over monopoly?

14. Try to classify the following firms into one of the four market-structure models. Explain your choice.

   a. Rowena's Gourmet Foods (produces and sells a line of specialty foods)

b. Shasta Pool Company (swimming pool and spa building)

c. Merck (pharmaceutical)

d. America West Airlines

e. UDC Homebuilders

f. Legal Seafoods (restaurant chain)

15. Draw two sets of cost curves. For the first set, assume fixed costs are huge and there are large economies of scale (large MES). For the second set, assume fixed costs are small and the economies of scale are small (small MES). Now, on each set of cost curves place a downward-sloping demand curve. Find the profit-maximizing point in each case.

COOPERATIVE LEARNING EXERCISE

Split the class up into groups of four. The group members choose numbers from 1 to 4. Number 1s get together, number 2s, etc. Each group must solve the associated problem below.

1. Number 1s: "Neither geography nor laboratory technology can restrain the cultivation of illicit drugs. Poppy, coca, and cannabis can be grown almost anywhere and the ability to refine them or to produce synthetic drugs is easily acquired." In which market structure would you classify illicit drugs?

2. Number 2s: "Ben and Jerry's Ice Cream scorns profits. This company cares more about the environment and the health and safety of its employees than it does profit." Explain whether this statement makes sense.

3. Number 3s: "Nearly 75 percent of all new businesses fail within two years. Clearly anyone starting a new business does not understand opportunity costs." Explain whether this statement makes sense.

4. Number 4s: "All costs are opportunity costs." Explain whether this statement is true or false.

After agreeing on a solution, students should return to their original groups. Number 1s explain to all the others the solution to the first problem, then number 2s explain theirs, and so on.

Economically Speaking

Coca Cola to Expand Fruitopia Line with Teas

Coca-Cola Co., looking to grab a bigger share of the fast-growing ready-to-drink tea market, plans to add several teas to its Fruitopia line of juice-based drinks. The teas would complement, rather than replace, the company's current entry, Nestea.

Brandweek magazine reported Monday that bottlers for the Atlanta-based soft drink giant expect to start shipping the new teas this spring under such names as Curious Mango and Peaceable Peach.

Nestea has been plagued by distribution and marketing problems since its launch in 1991, and has consistently trailed Snapple and Lipton, Pepsi-Cola Co.'s joint venture with Thomas J. Lipton Co. Last summer it was bypassed by dark horse AriZona, a product of Ferolito, Vultagio & Sons Inc.

Coca-Cola now markets and distributes Nestea under license from the Swiss food giant Nestle SA.

Industry consultant Tom Pirko said the two-pronged strategy is a "logical solution" to Nestea's disappointing performance.

"The category has reached a point of maturity where it needs to be approached from different angles," he said. Nestea, he said, would target "the real commercial level," with Fruitopia reaching "the whole new mindset of new age and alternative beverages."

Source: "Coca-Cola to Expand Fruitopia Line with Teas," *The Atlanta Journal, The Atlanta Constitution*, Jan. 17, 1995, p. E1. Reprinted with permission from *The Atlanta Journal* and *The Atlanta Constitution*.

Commentary

Ready-to-drink tea is a small fraction of the $52 billion soft drink industry, but it is the fastest growing segment. Sales grew more than 60 percent a year in 1993 and 1994. The ready-to-drink tea segment consists of Nestea with 8.8 percent of sales, AriZona with 11.5 percent, Snapple with 21.6 percent, Lipton with 30.8 percent and all others sharing 27.3 percent of the market. What type of industry is it? What kinds of behavior can we expect? Is Coca-Cola's strategy consistent with economic theory?

Although there are only 4 main firms in the tea segment, there are many close substitutes in the soft drink industry. Yet, even in the soft drink industry, there are a few dominant firms and many small or fringe firms. The industry appears to be an oligopoly although with differentiated products and entry that is not too difficult it has elements of monopolistic competition.

A differentiated oligopoly carries out strategies focusing on product differentiation. Entry takes place with slightly different products. This is exactly what has occurred in the ready to drink tea market. Snapple, AriZona, Nestea, and Lipton all offer slightly different products. Snapple has been packaged in glass bottles while AriZona appears primarily in cans. With the market expanding rapidly, there are above normal profits possible and probably being earned by Snapple and AriZona if not others. For this reason, firms are looking to enter the market and to offer additional lines of existing products. Coca-Cola is offering a new differentiated product—Fruitopia. The company is aiming its new product most closely at Snapple. Yet, it has not forsaken the rest of the market. Its Nestea is closer to AriZona and Lipton.

Economic theory is entirely consistent with the Coca-Cola strategy. Product differentiation is the primary way to compete in the ready-to-drink tea market.

24

Perfect Competition

FUNDAMENTAL QUESTIONS

1. What is perfect competition?
2. What does the demand curve facing the individual firm look like, and why?
3. How does the firm maximize profit in the short run?
4. At what point does a firm decide to suspend operations?
5. When will a firm shut down permanently?
6. What is the break-even price?
7. What is the firm's supply curve in the short run?
8. What is the firm's supply curve in the long run?
9. What is the long-run market supply curve?
10. What are the long-run equilibrium results of a perfectly competitive market?

Agriculture is often used as a real-life example of the perfectly competitive market structure, and indeed, many individual farmers are *price takers*, unable to affect the price of the product. Agriculture is a worldwide industry consisting of hundreds of millions of individual producers. To enter the industry in the low-income developing countries, all one needs is a small plot of land, seed, and access to water and tools. In the developed industrial nations, however, the average farm exceeds 400 acres and relies on combines and tractors costing several hundred thousand dollars, as well as on fertilizers and other materials. Nonetheless, the product is indistinguishable, and each individual firm is a very small part of the entire market. The grain from one farm is indistinguishable from that from another farm, and no single farm is able to increase the price of its grain and still sell the grain. Similarly, many consumer electronics are indistinguishable—the disk drive of a personal computer, the RAM chips, and many other electronic products are vitually identical no matter who manufactures them.

PREVIEW

Another market that closely resembles the model of perfect competition is the market for scrap metal. Scrap metal is junk that is crushed and then melted in open-hearth furnaces to produce new steel. Discarded bicycles, automobiles, refrigerators, and washing machines have value as scrap metal. The metal is essentially nondifferentiated. A scrap-metal processor doesn't care which junk is offered—a ton of scrap is a ton of scrap. It is not particularly difficult to enter the business. If you have a truck and a winch, you can travel around and gather scrap metal to sell to junk dealers or scrap processors. There are nearly 2,000 scrap processors throughout the United States. They collect the scrap and then separate it into grades or types of scrap to sell to steel manufacturers. The steel manufacturers do not care where the Number 1 grade scrap comes from. One seller of Number 1 grade is no different than another seller of Number 1 grade.

Even an industry like oil transport has some of the characteristics of the perfectly competitive model. One supertanker transporting oil is just like another. It is not easy or costless to enter the industry, but it is not too difficult. You must convince an international banker or broker to provide more than $100 million per tanker, but once you have overcome the hurdle of financing, entry is not blocked. Nearly 1,000 firms ranging in size from one supertanker to twenty-five supertankers offer their services to the oil refineries. The oil companies do not care from whom they buy the oil. One shipload is identical to another. Thus, the supertankers are price takers.

The model of perfect competition is not simply an exercise in theory that has no practical basis. Understanding how the firm in a perfectly competitive market structure behaves can provide clues to many real-life situations. In this chapter we use these real-life industries to illustrate many of the concepts and outcomes of the model of a perfectly competitive market. As you read, keep in mind that no industry fits the model perfectly, that it is indeed a *model*.

1. THE PERFECTLY COMPETITIVE FIRM IN THE SHORT RUN

We begin our analysis of perfect competition by taking the viewpoint of an individual farmer who is currently in business, having already procured the necessary land, tools, equipment, and employees to operate a farm. After we discuss how much the individual farmer decides to produce and how the price of the farmer's produce is determined, we discuss the entry and the exit processes. We examine how someone begins a business and how someone leaves or exits the business. We then alter our perspective and look at the market as a whole. Let's start our discussion by reviewing the characteristics of a perfectly competitive market.

1.a. The Definition of Perfect Competition

What is perfect competition?

Perfect competition is a firm behavior when many firms produce identical products and entry is easy.

A market that is perfectly competitive exhibits the following characteristics:

1. There are many sellers. No one firm can have an influence on market price. Each firm is such a minute part of the total market that however much the firm produces—nothing at all, as much as it can, or some amount in between—it will have no effect on the market price.

2. The products sold by the firms in the industry are identical. The product sold by one firm can be substituted perfectly for the product sold by any other firm in the industry. Products are not differentiated by packaging, advertising, or quality.

3. Entry is easy and there are many potential entrants. There are no huge economies of scale relative to the size of the market. Laws do not require producers to obtain licenses or pay for the privilege of producing. Other firms cannot take actions to keep someone from entering the business. Firms can stop producing and can sell or liquidate the business without difficulty.

4. Buyers and sellers have perfect information. Buyers know the price and quantity at each firm. Each firm knows what the other firms are charging and how they are behaving.

1.b. The Demand Curve of the Individual Firm

What does the demand curve facing the individual firm look like, and why?

A firm in a perfectly competitive market structure is said to be a *price taker* because the price of the product is determined by market demand and supply, and the individual firm simply has to accept that price. In 1995 the world market price of corn was about $1 per bushel, and nearly 20 billion bushels worldwide were produced. Approximately 46 percent of all the corn harvested in the world comes from the United States. Nevertheless, the average farm in the United States produces an extremely small percentage of the total quantity harvested each year.

What would occur if one U.S. farmer decided to set the price of corn at $1.20 per bushel when the market price was $1 per bushel? According to the model of a perfectly competitive market, no one would purchase the higher-priced corn because the identical product could be obtained without difficulty elsewhere for $1 per bushel. In this instance, what the model predicts is what actually occurs in the real-world corn market. The grain silo owner who buys the farmers' grain would simply pass on that farm's grain and move to the next truckful of grain at $1 per bushel. By setting a price above the market price, the individual farmer may sell nothing.

Is an individual farmer likely to set a price of $.80 per bushel when the market price is $1 per bushel? Not in a perfectly competitive market. All of the produce from a single farm can be sold at the market price. Why would a farmer sell at $.80 per bushel when he or she can get $1 per bushel? The individual farm is a price taker because it cannot charge more than the market price and it will not charge less.

You could think of price takers as being the sellers in a big auction. The potential buyers bid against each other for the product until a price is determined. The product is then sold at that price. The seller has no control over the price.

Market demand and supply are shown in Figure 1(a). The demand curve of a single firm is shown in Figure 1(b). The horizontal line at the market price is the demand curve faced by an individual firm in a perfectly competitive market structure. It shows that the individual firm is a price taker—that the demand curve is perfectly elastic. The question facing the individual firm in a perfectly competitive industry is how much to produce, not what price to charge.

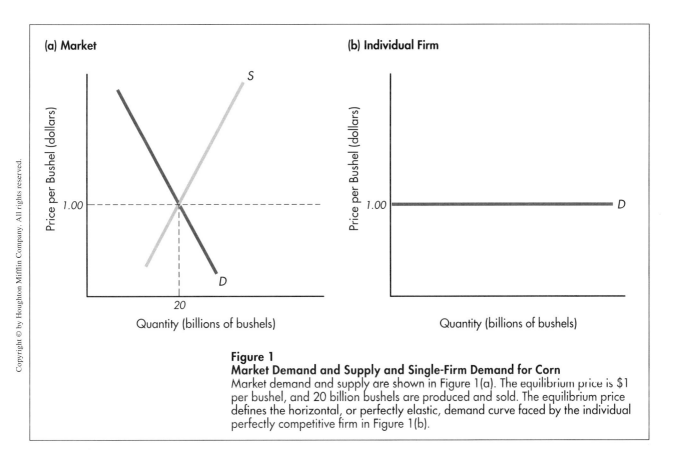

Figure 1
Market Demand and Supply and Single-Firm Demand for Corn
Market demand and supply are shown in Figure 1(a). The equilibrium price is $1 per bushel, and 20 billion bushels are produced and sold. The equilibrium price defines the horizontal, or perfectly elastic, demand curve faced by the individual perfectly competitive firm in Figure 1(b).

I.c. Profit Maximization

How does the firm maximize profit in the short run?

How much should a firm produce? It should produce the quantity at which it will maximize profit. Let's continue to consider an individual corn producer as an example of a perfectly competitive firm maximizing profit. The revenues and costs faced by this farm producing corn in the United States are listed in the table in Figure 2. Total output—number of bushels of corn (Q)—is listed in column 1. The market price (P), $1 per bushel, is listed in the second column. Total revenue (TR) is shown in the third column. Total revenue is equal to price multiplied by total output: $TR = P \times Q$. Total cost (TC) is shown in the fourth column. (You can see that even at a zero output level there is a cost of $1. This is the fixed cost—the land rent and the mortgages on a house and equipment that have to be paid even when no corn is harvested.) Total profit is shown in column 5. It is the difference between total revenue and total costs ($TR - TC$).

As we learned in the last chapter, the profit-maximizing level of output can be determined by comparing marginal revenue (MR), in column 6, to marginal cost (MC), in column 7. *Marginal revenue* is the change in total revenue divided by the change in quantity:

$$MR = \frac{\text{change in total revenue}}{\text{change in quantity of output}} = \frac{\Delta TR}{\Delta Q}$$

Since the demand curve facing the individual firm in perfect competition is perfectly elastic, each additional bushel sells for the same price, in this case, $1. Thus, marginal revenue is a constant $1, the same as price. Recall from the previous chapter that the marginal-revenue curve and the demand curve are the same when demand is perfectly elastic.

Marginal cost is the change in total cost divided by the change in quantity:

$$MC = \frac{\text{change in total cost}}{\text{change in quantity of output}} = \frac{\Delta TC}{\Delta Q}$$

The marginal-cost and marginal-revenue curves are shown in Figure 2. Marginal cost is less than marginal revenue until production reaches 9 bushels. With the tenth and successive bushels, marginal cost exceeds marginal revenue.

Profit maximization occurs at the output level where MR = MC.

We know that profit is maximized when $MR = MC$. Profit rises when the revenue brought in by the sale of one more unit (one more bushel) is greater than the cost of producing that unit. Conversely, if the cost of producing one more unit is greater than the amount of revenue brought in by selling that unit, profit declines with the production of that unit. Only when marginal revenue and marginal cost are the same is profit at a maximum.[1]

---

[1]Marginal revenue and marginal cost could be equal at small levels of production and sales, such as with the first bushel, but profit would definitely not be at its greatest level. The reason is that marginal cost is falling with the first unit of production—the marginal cost of the second unit is less than the marginal cost of the first unit. Since marginal revenue is the same for both the first and second units, profit actually rises as quantity increases. Profit maximization requires that marginal revenue equal marginal cost *and that marginal cost be rising*. Since marginal revenue and marginal cost are the same for the ninth bushel and marginal cost is rising, the ninth bushel is the profit-maximizing level of output.

Figure 2
Profit Maximization

The profit-maximization point for a single firm is shown for a price of $1 per bushel. Marginal revenue and marginal cost are equal at the profit-maximization point, 9 bushels. At quantities less than 9 bushels, marginal revenue exceeds marginal cost, so increased production would raise profits. At quantities greater than 9, marginal revenue is less than marginal cost, so reduced production would increase profits. The point at which profit is maximized is shown by the highlighted row in the table. The profit per unit is the difference between the price line and the average-total-cost curve at the profit-maximizing quantity. Total profit ($1.14) is the rectangle ABCD, an area that is equal to the profit per unit times the number of units.

Total Output (Q)	Price (P)	Total Revenue (TR)	Total Cost (TC)	Total Profit (TR − TC)	Marginal Revenue (MR)	Marginal Cost (MC)	Average Total Cost (ATC)
0	$1	$ 0	$ 1.00	$−1.00			
1	1	1	2.00	−1.00	$1	$1.00	$2.00
2	1	2	2.80	−.80	1	.80	1.40
3	1	3	3.50	−.50	1	.70	1.1667
4	1	4	4.00	0.00	1	.50	1.00
5	1	5	4.50	.50	1	.50	.90
6	1	6	5.20	.80	1	.70	.8667
7	1	7	6.00	1.00	1	.80	.8571
8	1	8	6.86	1.14	1	.86	.8575
9	1	9	7.86	1.14	1	1.00	.8733
10	1	10	9.36	.64	1	1.50	.936
11	1	11	12.00	−1.00	1	2.64	1.09

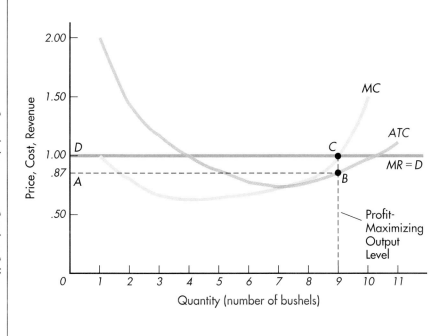

I.d. Short-Run Profits and Losses

At what point does a firm decide to suspend operations?

MR = MC is the profit-maximizing or loss-minimizing output level.

With a price of $1 per bushel, the individual farm maximizes profit by producing 9 bushels. We can illustrate how much profit the individual firm in perfect competition earns, or whether it makes a loss, by calculating total costs at the quantity where $MR = MC$ and comparing that with total revenue.

In Figure 2, the price per bushel of $1 exceeds the cost per bushel (average total cost, $.8733) by the distance BC ($.1267) when 9 bushels are produced. This amount ($.1267) is the profit per bushel. The total profit is the rectangle $ABCD$ (highlighted in the table).

Figure 3 illustrates what occurs to the individual firm in a perfectly competitive market as the market price changes. The only curve in Figure 3 that changes as a result of the price change is the perfectly elastic demand curve (which is also the price line and the marginal-revenue curve). Let's assume that the market price changes to $.70 per bushel so that the individual farm's demand curve shifts down. Whether the firm is making a profit or not is determined by finding the new quantity at which the new marginal-revenue curve, MR_2, equals the marginal-cost curve, at point F, and then tracing a vertical line from point F to the ATC curve at point G. The distance FG is the profit or loss per unit of output. If the demand curve is above the ATC curve at that point, the firm is making a profit. If the ATC curve exceeds the price line, as is the case in Figure 3, the firm is suffering a loss.

A profit cannot be made as long as the price is less than the average-cost curve, because the cost per bushel (ATC) exceeds the revenue per bushel (price). At a price of $.70 per bushel, marginal revenue and marginal cost are equal as the sixth bushel is produced (see Figure 3 and the highlighted bar in the table), but the average total cost is greater than the price. The cost per bushel (ATC) is $.8667, which is higher than the price or revenue per bushel of $.70. Thus, the firm makes a loss, shown as the rectangle $EFGH$ in Figure 3.

Recall that an economic loss means that opportunity costs are not being covered by revenues; that is, the owners could do better in another line of business. An economic loss means that a firm is confronted with the choice of whether to continue producing, shut down temporarily, or shut down permanently. The decision depends on which alternative has the lowest opportunity cost.

I.e. Short-Run Break-Even and Shutdown Prices

When will a firm shut down permanently?

In the short run, certain costs, such as rent on land and equipment, must be paid whether or not any output is produced. These are the firm's fixed costs. If a firm has purchased equipment and buildings but does not produce, the firm still has to pay for the equipment and buildings. Thus, the decision about whether to produce or to temporarily suspend operations depends on which option promises the lesser costs. In order to continue producing in the short run, the firm must earn sufficient revenue to pay all of the *variable* costs (the costs that change as output changes), because then the excess of revenue over variable costs will enable the firm to pay some of its fixed costs. If all of the variable costs cannot be paid for out of revenue, then the firm should suspend operations temporarily because by continuing to produce, the firm must pay its fixed costs as well as those variable costs in excess of revenue.

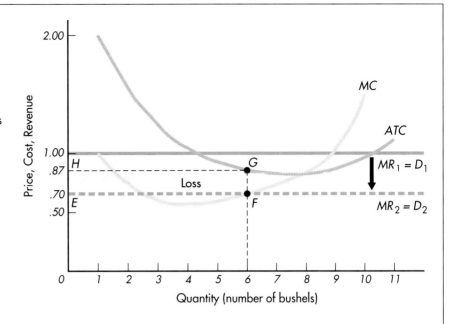

Figure 3
Loss Minimization
In Figure 3 the price changed from $1 per bushel to $.70 per bushel. The profit-maximization, or loss-minimization, point is the level of output where $MR = MC$. If, at this output level, the price is less than the corresponding average-cost curve, the firm makes a loss. At a price of $.70 per bushel, a loss is incurred—the loss-minimizing level of output is 6 bushels, as shown by the highlighted bar in the table. The total loss is the rectangle EFGH.

Total Output (Q)	Price (P)	Total Revenue (TR)	Total Cost (TC)	Total Profit (TR − TC)	Marginal Revenue (MR)	Marginal Cost (MC)	Average Total Cost (ATC)
0	$.70	$0	$1.00	$−1.00			
1	.70	.70	2.00	−1.30	$.70	$1.00	$2.00
2	.70	1.40	2.80	−1.40	.70	.80	1.40
3	.70	2.10	3.50	−1.40	.70	.70	1.1667
4	.70	2.80	4.00	−1.20	.70	.50	1.00
5	.70	3.50	4.50	−1.00	.70	.50	.90
6	.70	4.20	5.20	−1.00	.70	.70	.8667
7	.70	4.90	6.00	−1.10	.70	.80	.8571
8	.70	5.60	6.86	−1.26	.70	.86	.8575
9	.70	6.30	7.86	−1.56	.70	1.00	.8733
10	.70	7.00	9.36	−2.36	.70	1.50	.936
11	.70	7.70	12.00	−4.30	.70	2.64	1.09

Does suspending operations mean quitting the business altogether—shutting down permanently? It may, but it need not. The decision depends on the long-term outlook. If the long-term outlook indicates that revenue will exceed costs, then production is warranted. However, if the outlook is for continued low prices and the inability to cover costs, a firm would be better off quitting the business altogether.

To see how producing at a loss can at times be better than not producing at all, let's return to the individual farm in Figure 4. At a price of $.70 per

Figure 4
Shutdown Price
When the firm is making a loss, it must decide whether to continue producing or suspend operations and not produce. The decision depends on which alternative has higher costs. When the price is equal to or greater than the minimum point of the average-variable-cost curve, $.70, the firm is earning sufficient revenue to pay for all of the variable costs. When the price is less than the minimum point of the average-variable-cost curve, the firm is not covering all of its variable costs. In that case the firm is better off shutting down its operations. For this reason, the minimum point of the AVC curve is called the *shutdown price*. The *break-even price* is the minimum point of the ATC curve because at that point all costs are being paid.

Total Output (Q)	Price (P)	Total Revenue (TR)	Total Cost (TC)	Total Profit (TR − TC)	Marginal Revenue (MR)	Marginal Cost (MC)	Average Total Cost (ATC)	Average Variable Cost (AVC)
0	$.70	$0	$1.00	$−1.00				
1	.70	.70	2.00	−1.30	$.70	$1.00	$2.00	$1.00
2	.70	1.40	2.80	−1.40	.70	.80	1.40	.90
3	.70	2.10	3.50	−1.40	.70	.70	1.1667	.833
4	.70	2.80	4.00	−1.20	.70	.50	1.00	.75
5	.70	3.50	4.50	−1.00	.70	.50	.90	.70
6	.70	4.20	5.20	−1.00	.70	.70	.8667	.70
7	.70	4.90	6.00	−1.10	.70	.80	.8571	.714
8	.70	5.60	6.86	−1.26	.70	.86	.8575	.7325
9	.70	6.30	7.86	−1.56	.70	1.00	.8733	.7622
10	.70	7.00	9.36	−2.36	.70	1.50	.936	.836
11	.70	7.70	12.00	−4.30	.70	2.64	1.09	1.00

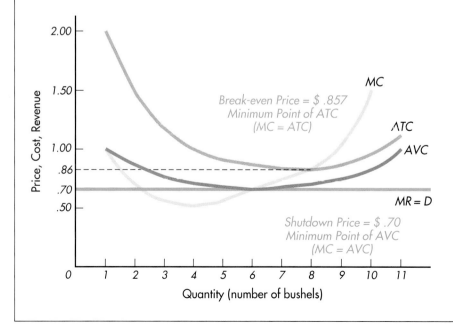

bushel, the output at which $MR = MC$ is 6 bushels, as shown by the highlighted bar in the table. At 6 bushels, total revenue is $4.20 and total cost is $5.20. The farm loses $1 by producing 6 bushels. The question is whether to produce at all. If production is stopped, the fixed cost of $1 must still be paid. Thus, the farmer is indifferent between producing 6 bushels and losing $1 or shutting down and losing $1. Should the price be less than the minimum point of the average-variable-cost curve (*AVC*), as would occur at any price less than $P = \$.70$ per bushel, the farm is not earning enough to cover its variable costs (see Figure 4 and accompanying table). By continuing to produce, the farm will lose more than it would lose if it suspended operations or shut down until the outlook improved. The minimum point of the average-variable-cost curve is the **shutdown price**. If the market price is less than the minimum point of the *AVC* curve, then the firm will incur fewer losses if it does not produce than if it continues to produce in the short run.

At prices above the minimum point of the average-variable-cost curve, the excess of revenue over variable cost means that some fixed costs can be paid. A firm is better off producing than shutting down because by producing it is able to earn enough revenue to pay all the variable costs and some of the fixed costs. If the firm does not produce, it will still have to pay all of the fixed costs. When the price equals the minimum point of the average-total-cost curve, the firm is earning just enough revenue to pay for all of its costs, fixed and variable. This point is called the **break-even price**. At the break-even price, economic profit is zero—all costs are being covered, including opportunity costs. Because costs include the opportunity costs of the resources already owned by the entrepreneur—his or her own labor and capital—zero economic profit means that the entrepreneur could not do better in another activity. Zero economic profit is normal profit, the profit just sufficient to keep the entrepreneur in this line of business.

The shutdown price is the price that is equal to the minimum point of the *AVC* curve. The break-even price is the price that is equal to the minimum point of the *ATC* curve.

In the examples just discussed, the firm continues to operate at a loss because variable costs are being covered and the long-term outlook is favorable. Many firms decide to operate for a while at a loss, then suspend operations temporarily, and finally shut down permanently. A firm will shut down permanently if all costs cannot be covered in the long run. In the long run, the minimum point of the *ATC* curve is the permanent shutdown point. Price must exceed the minimum point of the *ATC* curve in the long run if the firm is to remain in business. Of the 80,000 businesses that shut down permanently in 1992, most went through a period in which they continued to operate even though variable costs were not being covered by revenue.

shutdown price:
the minimum point of the average-variable-cost curve

What is the break-even price?

break-even price:
a price that is equal to the minimum point of the average-total-cost curve

1.f. The Firm's Supply Curve in the Short Run

What is the firm's supply curve in the short run?

As long as revenue equals or exceeds variable costs, an individual firm will produce the quantity at which marginal revenue and marginal cost are equal. This means that the individual firm's supply curve is the portion of the *MC* curve that lies above the *AVC* curve. An individual firm's supply curve shows the quantity that a firm will produce and offer for sale at each price. When the price is less than the minimum point of the *AVC* curve, a firm incurs fewer losses from not producing than from producing. The firm thus produces and supplies nothing, and there is no supply curve. When the price is greater than the minimum point of the *AVC* curve, the firm will produce and offer for sale the quantity yielded at the point where the *MC* curve and the *MR* line intersect for each price. The supply curve is thus the *MC* curve. The portion of the *MC* curve lying above the minimum point of the *AVC* curve is the individual firm's supply curve in the short run.

In our example of an individual farm illustrated in Figure 4, nothing is produced at a price of $.50 per bushel. At $.70 per bushel, the farm produces 6 bushels in the short run; at $1 per bushel, the farm produces 9 bushels. The higher the price, the greater the quantity produced and offered for sale.

A firm may continue to produce and offer its products for sale even if it is earning a negative economic profit, as long as it earns enough revenue to pay its variable costs and expects revenue to grow enough to pay all costs eventually. If the business does not improve and losses continue to pile up, the firm will shut down permanently. In the long run, the firm must be able to earn enough revenue to pay all of its costs. If it does not, the business will not continue to operate. If the firm does earn enough to pay its costs, the firm will produce and offer for sale the quantity of output yielded at the point where *MR* = *MC*. This means that the firm's supply curve is the portion of its *MC* curve that lies above the minimum point of the *ATC* curve.

What is the firm's supply curve in the long run?

RECAP

1. The firm maximizes profit or minimizes losses by producing at the output level at which *MR* and *MC* are equal.

2. In order to remain in business, the firm must earn sufficient revenue to pay for all of its variable costs. The shutdown price is the price that is just equal to the minimum point of the *AVC* curve.

3. The firm's break-even price is the price that is just equal to the minimum point of the *ATC* curve.

4. The portion of the marginal-cost curve lying above the minimum point of the *AVC* curve is the firm's short-run supply curve.

5. The portion of the marginal-cost curve lying above the minimum point of the *ATC* curve is the firm's long-run supply curve.

2. THE LONG RUN

What is the long-run market supply curve?

In the short run, at least one of the resources cannot be altered. This means that new firms cannot be organized and begin producing. Thus the supply of firms in an industry is fixed in the short run. In the long run, of course, all quantities of resources can be changed. Buildings can be built or purchased and machinery accumulated and placed into production. New firms may arise as entrepreneurs not currently in the industry see that they could earn more than they are currently earning and decide to expand into new businesses.

Part VI / Product Markets

Entrepreneurs who were operating in a different line of business put up their own money or organize a group of investors to finance a new business. In 1907, Henry Ford left the Edison Illuminating Company and began the Henry Ford Automobile Company. Steven Jobs and Steve Wozniak gave up positions with Atari and Hewlett-Packard to begin Apple Computer. Estée Lauder gave up acting and began a cosmetics firm. Mary Kay Ash gave up a successful selling job with Stanley Products to begin Mary Kay Cosmetics.

Entry and exit can both occur in the long run. An entrepreneur who is operating a particular business but not covering his or her opportunity costs will quit producing. 3M Corporation gave up the production of photofinishing chemicals and paper. Bricklin quit the automobile business. Eastern, Braniff, and several non-United States airlines got out of the airline business. Drexel Burnham Lambert got out of the stock-trading business.

On average, 4.5 percent of the total number of farms go out of business each year, and more than half of them file for bankruptcy. The numbers leaving the business increased substantially in the 1980s as the costs of doing business rose and agricultural prices fell. On average, 6.5 percent of existing farms left the agricultural industry each year in the 1980s. In the 1990s, the rate declined to about the previous average.

How does exit occur? Entrepreneurs may sell their businesses and move to another industry, or they may use the bankruptcy laws to exit the industry. A sole proprietor or partnership may file Chapter 13 personal bankruptcy; a corporation may file Chapter 7 bankruptcy or a Chapter 11 reorganization; a farmer may file Chapter 12. All of these special sections of the law describe the way creditors are paid off and the firm is dismantled. In the United States nearly 80,000 businesses filed for bankruptcy each year between 1990 and 1992.

Every year, new businesses in all types of industries are begun while others cease to exist. From the mid-1970s to the present, the average birthrate for all industries (the percent of total businesses that begin during a year) has been just over 11.2 percent, and the average death rate (the percent of total businesses that disappear during a year) has been 9.6 percent. The total number of businesses has grown by about 1.6 percent per year since the mid-1970s.

2.a. The Market Supply Curve and Exit and Entry

The short-run *market* supply curve is the horizontal sum of the short-run supply curves of all firms currently operating in a particular business. It is short-run because the quantity of at least one of the inputs—typically the amount of land or the quantity of capital—is fixed. In the long run, however, all inputs are variable. Thus, an existing firm can expand, construct new buildings, purchase new equipment, and hire more workers; an existing firm can also liquidate the business, selling the buildings and equipment and laying off workers. Furthermore, new businesses can spring up.

Recall from Chapter 3 that the market supply curve shifts when the number of suppliers changes. In the corn-producing business, when new farms enter the market, the total quantity of corn supplied at each price increases. In other words, entry causes the market supply curve to shift out to the right.

Conversely, exit means fewer producers and lower quantities supplied at each price and a leftward or inward shift of the market supply curve. Suppose some existing farms are not covering their costs and believe the future is not bright enough to warrant continued production. As a result, they shut down their operations and sell their equipment and land. As the number of farms in the industry declines, everything else held constant, the market supply curve shifts to the left—as long as those remaining in the business produce the same quantity, or less, as they did before the farms exited.

2.b. Normal Profit in the Long Run

One of the principal characteristics of the perfectly competitive market structure is that entry and exit can occur easily. Thus, entry and exit occur whenever firms are earning more or less than a *normal profit* (zero economic profit). When a normal profit is being earned there is no entry or exit. This condition is the long-run equilibrium.

The process of establishing the long-run position is shown in Figure 5. The market demand and supply curves for corn are shown in Figure 5(a), and the cost and revenue curves for a representative firm in the industry are shown in Figure 5(b). Let's assume that the market price is $1. Let's also assume that at $1 per bushel, the demand curve facing the individual farm (the price line) is equal to the minimum point of the *ATC* curve. The quantity produced is 9 bushels. The individual farm and the industry are in equilibrium. There is no

Figure 5
Economic Profit in the Long Run
Market demand and supply determine the price and the demand curve faced by the single perfectly competitive firm. At a price of $1 per bushel, the individual farm is earning normal profit. After an agricultural disaster in

Russia increases the demand for U.S. corn, the price rises to $1.50. At $1.50 per bushel, the single farm makes a profit equal to the yellow rectangle. Above-normal profits induce new farms to begin raising corn and existing farms to increase their production.

(a) Market

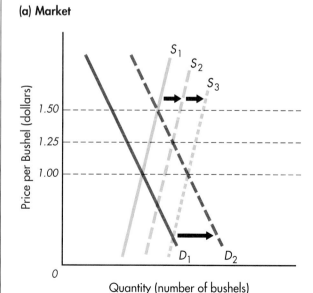

(b) Individual Firm

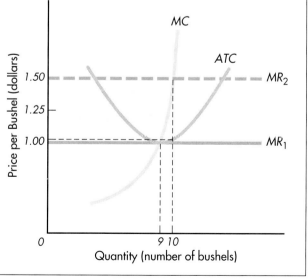

reason for entry or exit to occur, and no reason for individual farms to change their scale of operation.

To illustrate how the process of reaching the long-run equilibrium occurs in the perfectly competitive market structure, let's begin with the market in equilibrium at $S_1 = D_1$. Then let's suppose a major agricultural disaster strikes Russia and Russia turns to the United States to buy agricultural products. As a result of the increased Russian demand, the total demand for U.S. corn increases, as shown by the rightward shift of the demand curve to D_2 in Figure 5(a). In the short run, the market price rises to $1.50 per bushel, where the new market demand curve intersects the initial market supply curve, S_1. This raises the demand curve for the individual farm to the horizontal line at $1.50 per bushel. In the short run, the individual farms in the industry increase production (by adding variable inputs) from 9 bushels to 10 bushels, the point in Figure 5(b) where $MC = MR_2 = 1.50, and earn economic profit of the amount shown by the yellow rectangle.

The above-normal profit attracts others to the farming business. The result of the new entry and expansion is a rightward shift of the market supply curve. How far does the market supply curve shift? It shifts until the market price is low enough that firms in the industry earn normal profit. Let us suppose that the costs of doing business do not rise as the market expands. Then, if the market supply curve shifts to S_2, the new market price, $1.25, is less than the former price of $1.50 but still high enough for firms to earn above-normal profits. These profits are sufficient inducement for more firms to enter, causing the supply curve to shift farther right. The supply curve continues to shift until there is no incentive for additional firms to enter—that is, until firms are earning the normal profit, where price is equal to the minimum ATC, shown as S_3 in Figure 5(a).

Whether the long-run adjustment stops at a price that is above, equal to, or below the original price depends on whether the industry is an increasing-, constant-, or decreasing-cost industry, as discussed in the next section. In any case, when the adjustment stops, firms are just earning the normal profit.

In the long run, perfectly competitive firms earn normal profits.

2.c. Constant-, Increasing-, and Decreasing-Cost Industries

As new operations are begun and as existing firms expand, the quantity of resources—land, labor, water, fuel, equipment, and so on—used in production will rise as well. If the additional use of resources from the expansion and entry into a business does not change the cost of resources, then the industry is said to be a **constant-cost industry**. If the cost of resources increases, then the industry is said to be an **increasing-cost industry**. And if the cost of resources declines due to the expansion of the industry, then the industry is known as a **decreasing-cost industry**. (The Economic Insight "Focus on Terminology" provides a clarification of some of the terms we have used to describe firms and industries.)

The fresh-fish business may be described as a constant-cost industry. Many fish are now farmed rather than caught in natural waters. Trout farms in Idaho provide fresh Idaho trout; catfish farms in Nebraska provide much of the catfish found in restaurants; shrimp farms in Louisiana and Hawaii provide some of the shrimp available in supermarkets; and farms along the U.S. coasts are used to raise shellfish. When the demand for fish rises, new farms

constant-cost industry: an industry that can expand without affecting the prices of the resources it purchases

increasing-cost industry: an industry in which the cost of resources rises when the industry expands

decreasing-cost industry: an industry in which the cost of resources declines as the industry expands

Focus on Terminology

Several terms and concepts used in the last couple of chapters sound sufficiently alike that they could be confused:

■ The law of *diminishing marginal returns*

■ Economies and diseconomies of scale

■ Constant returns to scale

■ Increasing-, decreasing-, and constant-cost industries

Let's take a moment to clarify these terms and concepts.

The *law of diminishing marginal returns* applies only to the short run. It describes the additional output that is produced when additional units of a variable input are combined with a particular quantity of a fixed input.

Economies and diseconomies of scale and *increasing-, constant-, and decreasing-cost industries* are con-

cepts that apply to the long run. Economies and diseconomies of scale refer to an individual firm. Increasing, decreasing, and constant costs refer to an entire industry.

Economies and diseconomies of scale describe what happens to a firm's costs as the firm increases production and no other firms influence it. The shape of the firm's long-run average-cost curve is determined by the extent to which the firm experiences economies and diseconomies of scale.

The concepts of increasing-, constant-, and decreasing-cost industries describe what happens in an entire industry when the industry changes its production quantities. If an entire industry expands, thereby causing resource or input costs to change, the costs to each individual firm change as well. When the costs increase, the industry is called an *increasing-cost*

industry. When the costs decrease, the industry is a *decreasing-cost* industry. When costs do not change, the industry is a *constant-cost* industry. When the input costs change, the individual firm's cost curves shift. Contrast this to the case of economies and diseconomies of scale, where we are talking about a single firm moving up and down one cost curve—the long-run average-total-cost curve. To summarize:

■ Diminishing marginal returns is a short-run concept.

■ Economies and diseconomies of scale and constant returns to scale are long-run concepts applicable to an individual firm.

■ Constant-cost, increasing-cost, and decreasing-cost industries are long-run concepts applicable to an entire industry.

---

start up and existing farms expand their artificial lakes and supply a larger quantity of eggs and feed. The price of the water, feed, and eggs does not increase as a result of the increased demand for fish, because the fish farms use such a small portion of total water and feed that they have almost no impact on the prices of those items.

Let's suppose that the market for fish is in equilibrium at a price of $4 per pound and that the demand for fish increases because of a discovery about the health benefits of eating fish. This is illustrated in Figure 6(a) with the industry demand and supply curves. Because of the increase in demand, existing firms earn an above-normal profit. Entry occurs, causing the market supply curve to shift out. In a constant-cost industry, the short-run market supply curve shifts out until the market price returns to the original level, $4 per pound, but at the larger quantity, point *B*. The long-run market supply curve is obtained by combining the equilibrium points, *A* and *B*; it is the horizontal line, S^{LR}.

When the entry and expansion taking place in an industry raise the prices of resources used, the industry is said to be an *increasing-cost industry*. The

Figure 6
Constant-, Increasing-, and Decreasing-Cost Industries

In Figure 6(a), a constant-cost industry—fish farming—is shown. When firms in the industry are earning above-normal profit, new firms enter. The increased production means that the market supply curve shifts out. Fish farms use just a small amount of the total quantities of water and feed, so the cost of these resources does not change. The combination of equilibrium points—all points where firms are earning normal profits—traces out a horizontal curve, the long-run supply curve, S^{LR}. In

Figure 6(b), an increasing-cost industry—scrap metal— is shown. As expansion of the industry takes place, obtaining a given quantity of scrap becomes increasingly costly. The new equilibrium occurs at a higher price than the original. The combination of equilibrium points traces out an upward-sloping long-run supply curve, S^{LR}. In Figure 6(c), a decreasing-cost industry— consumer electronics (VCRs)—is shown. As expansion of the industry occurs, resource costs decline. The long-run supply curve is the downward-sloping curve, S^{LR}.

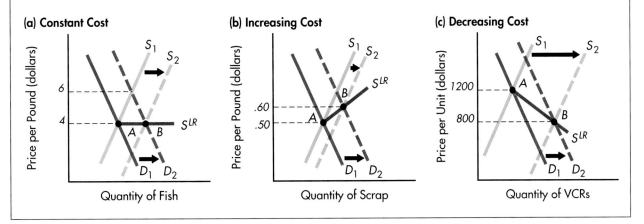

(a) Constant Cost   **(b) Increasing Cost**   **(c) Decreasing Cost**

scrap-metal industry displays the characteristics of a perfectly competitive market structure with increasing costs. Millions of tons of scrap metal are available annually as Americans discard cars, refrigerators, bicycles, and washing machines. Junk and scrap collectors find these discards and take them to processors. When the demand for metal rises, the demand for junk rises. The scrap collectors must travel farther, search harder, and spend more time finding junk. As a result, the costs rise. The increased resource costs mean that each individual firm faces higher costs. Because each firm now has higher costs, each is willing and able to produce and offer for sale a smaller quantity of output at each price than would have occurred had costs not changed. This means that although the expansion and entry cause the market supply curve to shift out, it does not shift as far as it would if the industry were a constant-cost industry. The new long-run equilibrium price for scrap steel rises from $.50 per pound to $.60 per pound, and the long-run market supply curve slopes up, as shown by curve S^{LR}.

When the price of inputs decreases as an industry expands, the industry is said to be a *decreasing-cost industry*. Consumer electronics presents good examples of decreasing-cost industries, although perhaps not perfectly competitive industries. When the first videocassette recorder (VCR) was offered for sale in the 1950s, its price exceeded $1,200. Expansion in the industry led to innovations and efficiencies as well as to additional supplies of the plastics and metals used in VCRs. As a result, the price of the resources used in the production of VCRs actually declined.

In the past decade, U.S. consumers have dramatically switched their consumption from beef to fish. The doubling of the amount of fish consumed has led to an expansion of the fish-producing industry. Most fish consumed are not caught in oceans or rivers but are grown on farms, such as this one in Caldwell, Idaho. As demand rises, prices rise, and existing producers earn above-normal profits. Entry is relatively easy in the industry, so new farms are built and existing farms expand. The expansion and increased demand for fish tanks, pumps, fresh or salt water, and fish food do not drive the prices of these items up because the industry is a constant-cost industry. As a result, the expansion of the industry continues until the price of the fish is the same as it was prior to the demand increase.

The expansion of existing firms and new entry lead to a reduction in resource costs. Even without an increase in the number of firms offering goods, the lower resource costs would cause the market supply curve to shift out. Coupled with new firms and with existing firms producing more is the lower cost of producing. Thus, the market supply curve in a decreasing-cost industry shifts out more in response to the initial demand increase than does the market supply curve in a constant-cost or increasing-cost industry. The result is that the price of the product declines. The long-run market supply curve in the decreasing-cost industry is S^{LR}, a downward-sloping curve shown in Figure 6(c).

In sum, the long-run market supply curve in a perfectly competitive industry can be perfectly horizontal (constant costs), upward-sloping (increasing costs), or downward-sloping (decreasing costs).

2.d. The Predictions of the Model of Perfect Competition

According to the model of perfect competition, whenever above-normal profits are earned by existing firms, entry occurs until a normal profit is earned by all firms. Conversely, whenever economic losses occur, exit takes place until a normal profit is made by all remaining firms.

What are the long-run equilibrium results of a perfectly competitive market?

Perfect competition results in economic efficiency.

economic efficiency:
when the price of a good or service just covers the marginal cost of producing that good or service and people are getting the goods they want

It is so important to keep in mind the distinctions between economic and accounting terms that we repeatedly remind you of them. A *zero economic profit* is a *normal accounting profit*, or just *normal profit*. It is the profit just sufficient to keep an entrepreneur in a particular line of business, the point where revenue exactly equals total opportunity costs. Entrepreneurs earning a normal profit are earning enough to cover their opportunity costs—they could not do better by changing—but are not earning more than their opportunity costs. A *loss* refers to a situation where revenue is not sufficient to pay all of the opportunity costs. A firm can earn a positive accounting profit and yet be experiencing a loss, not earning a normal profit.

The long-run equilibrium position of the perfectly competitive market structure shows firms producing at the minimum point of their long-run average-total-cost curves. If the price is above the minimum point of the *ATC* curve, then firms are earning above-normal profit and entry will occur. If the price is less than the minimum of the *ATC* curve, exit will occur. Only when price equals the minimum point of the *ATC* curve will neither entry nor exit take place.

Producing at the minimum of the *ATC* curve means that firms are producing with the lowest possible costs. They could not alter the way they produce and produce less expensively. They could not alter the resources they use and produce less expensively.

Firms produce at a level where marginal cost and marginal revenue are the same. Since marginal revenue and price are the same in a perfectly competitive market, firms produce where marginal cost equals price. This means that firms are employing resources until the marginal cost to them of producing the last unit of a good just equals the price of the last unit. Moreover, since price is equal to marginal cost, consumers are paying a price that is as low as it can get; the price just covers the marginal cost of producing that good or service. There is no waste—no one could be made better off without making someone else worse off. Economists refer to this result as **economic efficiency**.

2.d.1. Producer Surplus *Efficiency* is the term economists give to the situation where firms are producing with as little cost as they can (minimum point of the *ATC* curve) and consumers are getting the products they desire at a price that is equal to the marginal cost of producing those goods. To say that a competitive market is efficient is to say that all market participants get the greatest benefits possible from market exchange.[2]

How do we measure the benefits of the market? In the chapter on consumer choice, we discussed the concept of consumer surplus, indicating that

---

[2]Economists have classified efficiency into several categories. *Productive* efficiency refers to the firm using the least-cost combination of resources to produce any output level. This output level may not be the goods consumers want, however. *Allocative* efficiency is the term given to the situation where firms are producing the goods consumers most want and consumers are paying a price just equal to the marginal cost of producing the goods. Allocative efficiency may occur when firms are not producing at their most efficient level. Economic efficiency exists when both productive and allocative efficiency occurs.

it is a measure of the difference between what consumers would be willing to pay for a product and the price they actually have to pay to buy the product. Consumer surplus is a measure of the benefits consumers receive from market exchange. A similar measure exists for the firm. It is called **producer surplus**. Producer surplus indicates the difference between the price firms would have been willing to accept for their products and the price they actually receive.

Since the firm is willing to sell the product at the marginal cost, as long as marginal cost is greater than average variable cost, and since the firm receives the market price, the difference between the two is a bonus to the firm, a bonus resulting from market exchange. This bonus is producer surplus.

Consumer surplus = Area above equilibrium price and below the demand curve

Producer surplus = Area below equilibrium price and above the supply curve

Figure 7 illustrates consumer and producer surplus in a competitive market. The sum of producer and consumer surplus represents the total benefits that come from exchange in a market: benefits that accrue to the consumer plus those that accrue to the firm.

The primary result of perfect competition is that things just do not get any better: total consumer and producer surplus is at a maximum. Any interference with the market exchange reduces the total surplus. Consider rent control on apartments, for instance. The market for rental apartments is pictured in Figure 8. As shown in Figure 8, the market solution would yield a monthly rent of $400. The consumer surplus would be the area *ABC*; the producer surplus would be the area *ABD*. Now, suppose the city imposes a rent control at $300 per month. The producer surplus changes to area *EFD* while the con-

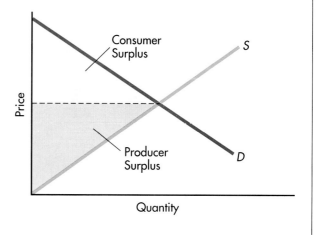

Figure 7
Producer and Consumer Surplus
Since the firm is willing to sell the product at the marginal cost and since the firm receives the market price, the difference between the two is a bonus to the firm, a bonus of market exchange. This bonus is producer surplus. Figure 7 illustrates total producer surplus in a competitive market, the sum of the producer surplus received by each firm in the market. Producer surplus is the area below the price line and above the supply curve. Also pictured is total consumer surplus. Recall that consumer surplus is the difference between what the consumer would be willing to pay for a good, the demand curve, and the price actually paid. The sum of producer and consumer surplus represents the total benefits that come from exchange in a market: benefits that accrue to the consumer plus those that accrue to the firm.

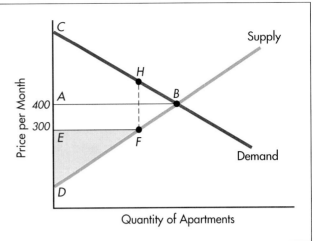

Figure 8
Rent Control and Market Efficiency
The market for rental apartments is pictured in this graph; the market solution would yield a monthly rent of $400. The consumer surplus would be the area *ABC*; the producer surplus would be the area *ABD*. Now, suppose the city imposes rent control at $300 per month. The producer surplus changes to area *EFD* while the consumer surplus changes to *EFHC*. The total surplus has been reduced by the rent control.

sumer surplus changes to *EFHC*. Clearly the total surplus has been reduced. The question policymakers must decide is whether the additional benefits to consumers offset the losses to producers.

RECAP

1. Entry occurs when firms are earning above-normal profit or positive economic profit.

2. A temporary shutdown occurs when firms are not covering their variable costs in the short run. In the long run, exit occurs when firms are not covering all costs.

3. The short-run market supply curve is the horizontal sum of the supply curves of all individual firms in the industry.

4. The long-run market supply curve shows the quantities supplied at each price by all firms in the industry after exit and entry occur.

5. The long-run market supply curve slopes up in increasing-cost industries, down in decreasing-cost industries, and is a horizontal line in constant-cost industries.

6. In a perfectly competitive market, firms produce goods at the least cost, and consumers purchase the goods they most desire at a price that is equal to the marginal cost of producing the good. There is no waste—no one could be made better off without making someone else worse off. Economists refer to this result as economic efficiency.

7. Producer surplus is the benefits the firm receives for engaging in market exchange; it is the difference between the price the firm would be willing to sell its goods for and the price the firm actually receives.

8. Consumer surplus is the area below the demand curve and above the equilibrium price; producer surplus is the area above the supply curve and below the equilibrium price.

SUMMARY

▲▼ **What is perfect competition?**

1. Perfect competition is a market structure in which there are many firms that are producing an identical product and where entry and exit are easy. §1.a

▲▼ **What does the demand curve facing the individual firm look like, and why?**

2. The demand curve of the individual firm is a horizontal line at the market price. Each firm is a price taker. §1.b

▲▼ **How does the firm maximize profit in the short run?**

3. The individual firm maximizes profit by producing at the point where $MR = MC$. §1.c

▲▼ **At what point does a firm decide to suspend operations?**

4. A firm will shut down operations temporarily if price does not exceed the minimum point of the average-variable-cost curve. §1.d

▲▼ **When will a firm shut down permanently?**

5. A firm will shut down operations permanently if price does not exceed the minimum point of the average-total-cost curve in the long run. §1.e

▲▼ **What is the break-even price?**

6. The firm breaks even when revenue and cost are equal—when the demand curve (price) just equals the minimum point of the average-total-cost curve. §1.e

▲▼ **What is the firm's supply curve in the short run?**

7. The firm's short-run supply curve is the portion of its marginal-cost curve that lies above the minimum point of the average-variable-cost curve. §1.f

▲▼ **What is the firm's supply curve in the long run?**

8. The firm produces at the point where marginal cost equals marginal revenue, as long as mar-

ginal revenue exceeds the minimum point of the average-total-cost curve. Thus, the firm's long-run supply curve is the portion of its marginal-cost curve that lies above the minimum point of the average-total-cost curve. §1.f

▲▼ **What is the long-run market supply curve?**

9. The market supply curve is the horizontal sum of the supply curves of the individual firms in an industry. In the long run, if these firms are earning above-normal profit, new firms enter the industry, and the market supply curve shifts to the right. If firms are earning negative economic profit, existing firms exit the industry, and the market supply curve shifts to the left. The movement from one equilibrium position to another traces out the long-run market supply curve. §2.a

10. Entry occurs when firms earn above-normal profit. Exit occurs when a firm's revenues are not sufficient to pay all direct and opportunity costs. An industry is in equilibrium when firms are earning a normal profit. §2.b

11. If resource costs rise as an industry expands, the industry is called an *increasing-cost* industry. If resource costs fall as an industry expands, the industry is a *decreasing-cost* industry. If resource costs do not change as an industry expands, the industry is a *constant-cost* industry. §2.c

12. The long-run market supply curve slopes up in an increasing-cost industry, down in a decreasing-cost industry, and is a horizontal line in a constant-cost industry. §2.c

▲▼ **What are the long-run equilibrium results of a perfectly competitive market?**

13. In the long run, all firms operating in perfect competition will earn a normal profit by producing at the lowest possible cost, and all consumers will buy the goods and services they most want at a price equal to the marginal cost of producing the goods and services. §2.d

14. Economic efficiency is the result of perfect competition. §2.d

15. Producer surplus is the difference between what a firm would be willing to produce and sell a good for and the price the firm actually receives for the good. Consumer surplus is the difference between what an individual would be willing to pay for a good and what the individual actually has to pay. Total consumer and producer surplus is at a maximum in a perfectly competitive market. §2.d.1

KEY TERMS

shutdown price §1.e

break-even price §1.e

constant-cost industry §2.c

increasing-cost industry §2.c

decreasing-cost industry §2.c

economic efficiency §2.d

producer surplus §2.d.1

EXERCISES

1. Cost figures for a hypothetical firm are given in the following table. Use them to answer the questions below. The firm is selling in a perfectly competitive market.

Out- put	Fixed Cost	AFC	Variable Cost	AVC	Total Cost	ATC	MC
1	$50		$ 30				
2	50		50				
3	50		80				
4	50		120				
5	50		170				

a. Fill in the blank columns.

b. What is the minimum price needed by the firm to break even?

c. What is the shutdown price?

d. At a price of $40, what output level would the firm produce? What would its profits be?

2. Label the curves in the following graph.

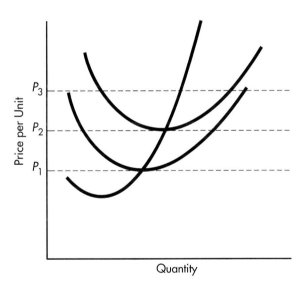

a. At each market price, P_1, P_2, and P_3, what output level would the firm produce?

b. What profit would be earned if the market price was P_1?

c. What are the shutdown and break-even prices?

3. Why might a firm continue to produce in the short run even though the market price is less than its average total cost?

4. Explain why the demand curve facing the individual firm in a perfectly competitive industry is a horizontal line.

5. Explain what occurs in the long run in a constant-cost industry, an increasing-cost industry, and a decreasing-cost industry when the market demand declines (shifts in).

6. What can you expect from an industry in perfect competition in the long run? What will price be? What quantity will be produced? What will be the relation between marginal cost, average cost, and price?

7. Assume that the market for illegal drugs is an example of a perfectly competitive market structure. Describe what the perfectly competitive market model predicts for illegal drugs in the long run. What is likely to be the impact of the U.S. government's war on drugs in the short run? In the long run?

8. If no real-life industry meets the conditions of the perfectly competitive model exactly, why do we study perfect competition? What is the relevance of the model to the decision by Estée Lauder to switch careers? Why might it shed some light on pollution, acid rain, and other social problems?

9. Using the model of perfect competition, explain what it means to say, "Too much electricity is generated," or "Too little education is produced." Would the firm be producing at the bottom of the *ATC* curve if too much or too little was being produced?

10. Private swimming pools can be dangerous. There are serious accidents each year in those areas of the United States where backyard pools are common. Should pools be banned? In other words, should the market for swimming pools be eliminated? Answer this in terms of producer and consumer surplus.

11. Discuss whether the following are examples of perfectly competitive industries.

    a. The U.S. stock market

    b. The automobile industry

    c. The consumer electronics market

    d. The market for college students

12. Macy's was making millions of dollars in profits when it declared bankruptcy. Explain Macy's decision.

13. Entry and exit of firms occur in the long run but not the short run. Why? What is meant by the long run and the short run? Would you say that entry is more or less difficult than exit?

14. Use the following data to answer the questions below.

Price	Quantity Supplied	Quantity Demanded
$20	30	0
18	25	5
16	20	10
14	15	15
12	10	20
10	5	25
8	0	30

a. What is the equilibrium price and quantity?

b. Draw the demand and supply curves. If this represents perfect competition, are the curves individual-firm or market curves? How is the quantity supplied derived?

c. Show the consumer surplus. Show the producer surplus.

d. Suppose that a price ceiling of $12 was imposed. How would this change the consumer and producer surplus? Suppose a price floor of $16 was imposed. How would this change the consumer and producer surplus?

e. Suppose this is an increasing-cost industry and the existing firms are earning above-normal profits. What will occur?

15. Explain the following statement: "The market can better determine the value of polluting than the politicians. Rather than assign an emission fee to a polluting firm, simply allow firms to purchase the rights to pollute."

COOPERATIVE LEARNING EXERCISE

The class is divided into groups of four or five people.

Each group should find the output, profit, and price levels for the firm represented by the data below. Three groups are selected to explain their answer. In addition, one group explains how these data could represent an increasing-cost industry, another group explains how the data could represent a constant-cost industry, and a third group explains how these data could represent a decreasing-cost industry.

Q	TFC (Total Fixed Cost)	TC (Total Cost)	TR (Total Revenue)
0	100	100.00	0
1	100	155.70	110
2	100	205.60	220
3	100	253.90	330
4	100	304.80	440
5	100	362.50	550
6	100	431.20	660
7	100	515.10	770
8	100	618.40	880
9	100	745.30	990
10	100	900.00	1,100

Food Marketers Show a Taste for Video Growth

CHICAGO—Video rental and sales in the supermarket industry have, in the last several years, gone from an afterthought to a major money-maker. That was the consensus of video suppliers, fixturing companies, and manufacturers at the Food Marketing Institute's annual Supermarket Industry Convention, held May 2–6 at McCormick Place here.

"Video is no longer a loss leader in supermarkets," said Stewart Gershenbaum, VP of the Midwest division for JD Store Equipment of Lombard, Ill. "The change has accrued over the last three years. Before, supermarkets weren't marketing video the way they should—all the space they'd devote to video was 20 feet of wall. Now they're operating 5,000-square-foot, and larger, video sections." The St. Louis-based Schnucks supermarket chain, for instance, said Gershenbaum, "has a store-within-a-store setup, and it's the biggest video entity in St. Louis."

"You'll still find grocery stores with the 20-foot wall," he said, "but a relatively large chain will add a video staff and create their own department, headed up by a nonfood video coordinator." . . .

Executives of Selectrak Family Video of Hillside, Ill., which leases video management programs to 200 stores across the country, reported an increase in rental revenues this past year—a testament, they say, to the increasing viability of video in supermarkets. "Unlike the rest of the industry, which reports flat rentals, ours continue to rise," said marketing coordinator Tamara Sokolec.

Selectrak provides fixtures, racking, custom computer setups, and free marketing support to its clients. "Over the last year, we've put a great deal of effort into marketing," said Sokolec, who attributed Selectrak's rental increase to that stepped-up marketing effort.

Selectrak does "target certain titles for sell-through," noted Sokolec, "but rental is still the biggest part of the business. We target three to four sell-through titles a year. Moms with kids are our primary customers." The Selectrak program tends to work best, said Sokolec, in rural areas more so than urban, where there is "less dense competition."

For many supermarkets, video rental vending machines are the way to go. Michael Malet, president of Lakeland, Fla.-based Keyosk Corp. (headquartered in Irvine, Calif.), said 200–300 supermarkets around the country use Keyosk's Video Rental Center vending machines. Typical clients are "stores which don't have the space for a video section, or which don't want to hire extra staff for a video section," he said.

According to Malet, one major California supermarket chain, Hughes Markets, has switched from staffed video centers to Keyosk vending machines over the last year. "The machines are simple to operate and to service," Malet noted. "Our field people don't need to be technicians."

Companies that deal exclusively in sell-through report significant numbers in the supermarket arena, as well as those involved in rental. "We've doubled our supermarket business over the last couple of years," said David Sutton, president of Front Row Entertainment of Edison, N.J., which manufactures and distributes budget sell-through video.

"The programs we offer are lucrative for supermarkets," Sutton continued. "Our titles are $3.99–$8.99, with full exchange privileges, and we offer 30–60-day promotions."

Cabin Fever Entertainment, a video manufacturer based in Greenwich, Conn., made its first FMI appearance this year. "Supermarkets are a growing business for video companies," said national sales director Dick Zima, who said Cabin Fever's 80-title product line has become available in supermarkets just during the past year.

Zima said Cabin Fever has been "utilizing parent company U.S. Tobacco's accounts to expand into supermarkets. There's a huge potential consumer base."

Source: "Food Marketers Show a Taste for Video Growth," Moira McCormick, *Billboard*, May 23, 1992, p. 49. © 1995 BPI Communications, Inc. Used with permission of *Billboard Magazine*.

Billboard/May 23, 1992

Commentary

Video-rental stores have become a staple of the American retail landscape. Their widespread proliferation has increased the number of outlets available to consumers, but owners of these video stores are beginning to realize only meager profits. The rapid growth in the number of video-rental stores suggests an ease of entry that characterizes a perfectly competitive industry. Having video-rental outlets on virtually every corner means there are a large number of sellers. The rising interest in offering video rentals by supermarkets increases the number of sellers even further. And, with the new ways to display videos, the space required to open a video-rental outlet has diminished considerably, allowing even more entry into the industry. All of these facts imply that each video-rental store is a price taker and can be analyzed according to the model of a firm in an industry that is perfectly competitive.

The graph on the left depicts the demand and supply curves for the video-rental market, and the graph on the right illustrates the corresponding cost and marginal-revenue curves for a typical video rental store. The market supply and demand curves

labeled S_1 and D_1 represent the situation a few years ago, when video store owners realized above-normal profit. The rental price of $4 that resulted from the intersection of S_1 and D_1 (at point e_1 in the graph on the left) allowed the typical video store to enjoy a profit (represented by the rectangle $ABCD$ in the graph on the right). This profit occurred because the point at which marginal revenue intersected marginal cost was above the average-total-cost curve.

Everyone wants to get in on a good thing, however, and the presence of above-normal profit led to market entry. New video-rental stores opened and existing supermarkets expanded their video offerings. This led to an outward shift of the market-supply curve to S_2. The new market-supply curve intersects demand at the lower price of $3 per rental (point e_2 in the graph on the left). At this price, the marginal revenue of the typical firm crosses the marginal-cost curve at the bottom of the average-total-cost curve (point F in the graph on the right). The price each firm receives from the video rentals is lower than the initial price, and firms no longer make positive economic profits.

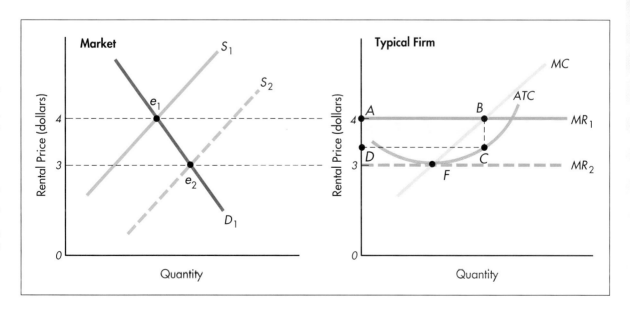

25

Monopoly

FUNDAMENTAL QUESTIONS

1. What is monopoly?
2. How is a monopoly created?
3. What does the demand curve for a monopoly firm look like, and why?
4. Why would someone want to have a monopoly in some business or activity?
5. Under what conditions will a monopolist charge different customers different prices for the same product?
6. How do the predictions of the models of perfect competition and monopoly differ?

I n 1986, Burroughs-Wellcome Company announced the first breakthrough in the treatment of AIDS: the life-prolonging drug AZT. In 1989 the company was accused of "reaping unseemly profits from AIDS patients and federally funded Medicaid by keeping the price of AZT at a level that makes it one of the most expensive drugs ever sold." [1] Many people were outraged by what was referred to as Burroughs-Wellcome's monopolistic practices.

What is a monopoly? Why does the word conjure up dastardly images? If Burroughs-Wellcome is earning an above-normal profit, why won't other pharmaceutical firms enter the business of providing AZT and thus drive the profit down to the normal level? The purpose of this chapter is to answer these questions.

PREVIEW

In the previous chapter, we examined the model of perfect competition. We learned that perfect competition results in consumers getting what they want at the lowest possible prices and firms operating at the lowest cost. The model of monopoly provides a stark contrast: the prediction that comes from it is *inefficiency*. In fact, a comparison of the predictions that come from the models of perfect competition and monopoly provides a set of theoretical bookends to the behavior of all firms. Virtually every real-life action on the part of a firm can be described as a combination of the characteristics of perfect competition and monopoly.

I. THE MARKET STRUCTURE OF MONOPOLY

What is monopoly?

Perhaps the source is the Parker Brothers' board game Monopoly, or maybe there is some other explanation, but there are widespread beliefs about monopoly that demand our attention. One such belief is captured in the Preview regarding the Burroughs-Wellcome Company: that a monopolist can earn unseemly profits by charging outrageously high prices. Another is that a monopolist does not have to respond in any way to customer desires. And a third is that it is impossible for a monopolist to make a loss. We'll discuss these beliefs in this chapter. We begin by defining what a monopolist is.

---

[1]"Burroughs-Wellcome Reaps Profits, Outrage from Its AIDS Drug," Marilyn Chase, *Wall Street Journal,* Sept. 15, 1989, pp. 1, A9.

1.a. Market Definition

Monopoly is a market structure in which there is a single supplier of a product. A **monopoly firm (monopolist)** may be large or small, but whatever its size, it must be the *only supplier* of the product. In addition, a monopoly firm must sell a product for which there are *no close substitutes*. The greater the number of close substitutes for a firm's products, the less likely it is that the firm has a monopoly. Most of us have gone to a movie and purchased popcorn or candy and commented on the excessive prices. Why does popcorn cost so much at the movies? Some people claim that it is because once you are in the theater, you are buying from a monopolist. There are no close substitutes for the popcorn or candy, and a monopoly firm produces a product for which there are no close substitutes. There are, however, substitutes for the movies, so is the popcorn a product sold by a monopolist?

If the movie theater is not a monopolist, what is? You purchase products from monopoly firms every day, perhaps without realizing it. Congress created the U.S. Postal Service to provide first-class mail service. No other firm is allowed to provide that service. (The fax machine, overnight express firms, and the Internet are all substitutes for first-class mail, although perhaps not perfect substitutes.) The currency you use is issued and its quantity is controlled by a government entity known as the Federal Reserve. It is illegal for any organization or individual other than the Federal Reserve to issue currency. When you turn on the lights, the heat, or the air conditioning, you are using electricity produced by a public utility, a monopoly firm. In most instances, either you purchase electricity from that firm or you don't purchase electricity. In cans of coffee, packages of medicine, shoes, and many other goods, you will often find a capsule that looks like a little barrel. This capsule draws moisture out of packages and maintains freshness. For two decades, the capsules contained desiccant clay, a special clay found only in a small mine in New Mexico. The mine was owned by a single family. That family had a monopoly on desiccant clay. All these examples are monopoly firms because they are the sole suppliers of products for which there are no close substitutes.

1.b. The Creation of Monopolies

How is a monopoly created?

Burroughs-Wellcome's profits doubled in the three years following the introduction of AZT. Burroughs-Wellcome was a monopoly supplier of AZT, and it was earning above-normal profits on it. But if a product is valuable and the owners are getting rich from selling it, won't others develop substitutes and also enjoy the fruits of the market? Yes, unless something impedes entry. The name given to that something is **barrier to entry**. There are three general classes of barriers to entry:

- natural barriers, such as economies of scale
- actions on the part of firms that create barriers to entry
- governmentally created barriers

1.b.1. Economies of Scale Economies of scale can be a barrier to entry. There are very large economies of scale in the generation of electricity. The larger the generating plant, the lower the cost per kilowatt-hour of electricity produced. A large generating plant can produce each unit of electricity much less expensively than several small generating plants. Size thus constitutes a barrier to entry since to be able to enter and compete with existing large-scale public utilities, a firm needs to be large so that it can produce each kilowatt-hour as inexpensively as the large-scale plants.

1.b.2. **Actions by Firms**   Entry is barred when one firm owns an essential resource. The owners of the desiccant clay mine in New Mexico had a monopoly position because they owned the essential resource, clay. Inventions and discoveries are essential resources, at least until others come up with close substitutes. The creation of high fixed costs can impede entry. If existing firms can increase the fixed costs for those firms thinking about entering a market, entry will be slowed. Similarly, if existing firms can increase the sunk costs associated with entry, they will have reduced the likelihood new firms will enter the business.

1.b.3. **Government**   Barriers to entry are often created by governments. The U.S. government issues patents, which provide a firm a monopoly on certain products, inventions, or discoveries for a period of seventeen years. Such is the case with the Burroughs-Wellcome monopoly. The company was granted a patent on AZT and thus was, by law, the only supplier of the drug. Domestic government policy also restricts entry into many industries. The federal government issues broadcast licenses for radio and television and grants airlines landing rights at certain airports. City governments limit the number of taxi companies that can operate, the number of cable television companies that can provide service, and the number of garbage collection firms that can provide service. State and local governments issue liquor licenses and restrict the number of electric utility companies. These are just a few of the government-created monopolies in the United States.

1.c. Types of Monopolies

natural monopoly:
a monopoly that arises from economies of scale

The word *monopoly* is often associated with other terms such as *natural monopoly*, *local monopoly*, *regulated monopoly*, and *monopoly power*. A **natural monopoly** is a firm that has become a monopoly because of economies of scale and demand conditions. The adjective *natural* indicates that the monopoly arises from cost and demand conditions, not from government action. If costs decline as the quantity produced rises, only very large producers will be able to stay in business. Their lower costs will enable them to force smaller producers, who have higher costs, out of business. Large producers can underprice smaller producers, as illustrated in Figure 1. The larger firm, operating along ATC_2, can set a price anywhere between P_1 and P_2 and thereby drive the smaller firm, operating along ATC_1, out of business. If the market can support only one producer or if the long-run average-total-cost curve continually slopes downward, the monopoly that results is said to be *natural*. Electric utilities are often considered to be natural monopolies because there are large economies of scale in the generation of electricity. One large power plant can generate electricity at a lower per-kilowatt-hour cost than can several small power plants. The transmission of electricity is different, however. There are diseconomies of scale in the transmission of electricity. The farther that electricity has to be transmitted, the higher are the per-kilowatt-hour costs. Together, generation and transmission imply an

Figure 1
Economies of Scale
A large firm producing along ATC_2 can produce output much less expensively per unit than a small firm operating along ATC_1. The large firm, therefore, can set a price that is below the minimum point of the small firm's average-total-cost curve yet still earn profit. Any price between P_1 and P_2 will provide a profit for the large firm and a loss for the small firm.

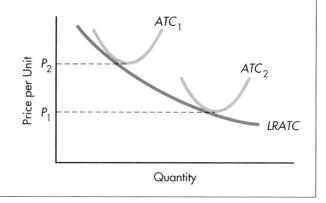

local monopoly:
a monopoly that exists in a limited geographic area

regulated monopoly:
a monopoly firm whose behavior is monitored and prescribed by a government entity

monopoly power:
market power, the ability to set prices

MES that is sufficiently large for a local monopoly but not for a national or international monopoly.

A **local monopoly** is a firm that has a monopoly within a specific geographic area. An electric utility is the sole supplier of electricity in a municipality or local area. A taxicab company may have a monopoly for service to the airport or within a city. Cable TV companies may have monopolies within municipalities. An airline may have a monopoly over some routes.

A **regulated monopoly** is a monopolist whose prices and production rates are controlled by a government entity. Electric utility companies, telephone companies, cable TV companies, and water companies are regulated monopolies. A state corporation or utility commission sets their rates, determines the costs to be allowed in the production of their services, and restricts entry by other firms.

Monopoly power is market power, the ability to set prices. It exists whenever the demand curve facing the producer is downward-sloping. Monopolies exercise monopoly power, but so do all firms except those operating in perfectly competitive markets. A firm that has monopoly power is a price maker rather than a price taker.

RECAP

1. A monopoly firm is the sole supplier of a product for which there are no close substitutes.

2. A monopoly firm remains the sole supplier because of barriers to entry.

3. Barriers to entry may be economic, such as economies of scale, or due to the exclusive ownership of an essential resource, or they may be created by government policy.

4. A natural monopoly is a monopoly that results through economies of scale. A regulated monopoly is a monopoly whose pricing and production are controlled by the government. A local monopoly is a firm that has a monopoly in a specific geographic region.

5. Monopoly power, or market power, is the ability to set prices.

What does the demand curve for a monopoly firm look like, and why?

In any market, the industry demand curve is a downward-sloping line because of the law of demand. Although the industry demand curve is downward-sloping, the demand curve facing an individual firm in a perfectly competitive market is a horizontal line at the market price. This is not the case for the monopoly firm. Because a monopoly firm is the sole producer, it *is* the industry, so its demand curve is the industry demand curve.

2.a. Marginal Revenue

The demand curve facing the monopoly firm is the industry demand curve.

In the early 1990s, a small U.S. company introduced a wireless VCR that could operate from more than one television set and didn't even have to be placed in the same room as the television. For a few years, this company had a monopoly on the wireless VCR. Let's consider the pricing and output decisions of the firm, using hypothetical cost and revenue data.

Suppose a wireless VCR sells for $1,500, and at that price the firm is selling 5 VCRs per day, as shown in Figure 2. If the monopoly firm wants to sell more, it must move down the demand curve. Why? Because of the law of demand. People will do without the wireless VCR rather than pay more than they think it's worth. As the price declines, sales increase. The table in Figure 2 shows that if the monopoly firm lowers the price to $1,350 per unit from $1,400, it will sell 8 VCRs per day instead of 7.

What is the firm's marginal revenue? To find marginal revenue, the total revenue earned at $1,400 per VCR must be compared to the total revenue earned at $1,350 per VCR—the change in total revenue must be calculated. At $1,400 apiece, 7 VCRs are sold each day and total revenue each day is

$$\$1,400 \text{ per VCR} \times 7 \text{ VCRs} = \$9,800$$

Public utilities, such as nuclear power plants, are regulated monopolies in the United States and are government-run enterprises in other parts of the world. With private ownership, it is the stockholders or owners who reap the benefits of profits and could bear the burden of losses. Until the 1990s, the utilities were guaranteed by government regulation not to have losses. Beginning in 1992, government regulation has been relaxed so that utilities must compete or prepare for competition from other electricity generating companies. It is expected that within a decade or more, customers will be able to switch from one electric utility to another, just as they do in purchasing long distance telephone service.

Figure 2
Demand Curve for a Monopolist
As the VCR price is reduced, the quantity demanded increases. But because the price is reduced on all quantities sold, not just on the last unit sold, marginal revenue declines faster than price.

Quantity per Day	Price	Total Revenue	Marginal Revenue
1	$1,700	$ 1,700	$1,700
2	1,650	3,300	1,600
3	1,600	4,800	1,500
4	1,550	6,200	1,400
5	1,500	7,500	1,300
6	1,450	8,700	1,200
7	1,400	9,800	1,100
8	1,350	10,800	1,000
9	1,300	11,700	900

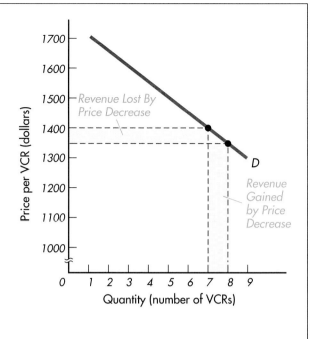

At $1,350 apiece, 8 VCRs are sold and total revenue is

$$\$1,350 \text{ per VCR} \times 8 \text{ VCRs} = \$10,800$$

The difference, change in total revenue, is $1,000. Thus, marginal revenue is

$$\frac{\Delta TR}{\Delta Q} = \frac{\$1,000}{1 \text{ VCR}} = \$1,000$$

The change in revenue is the difference between the increased revenue due to increased quantity sold, the yellow area in Figure 2, and the decreased revenue due to a lower price, the blue area in Figure 2.

The price is $1,350 per VCR, but marginal revenue is $1,000 per VCR. Price and marginal revenue are not the same for a monopoly firm. This is a fundamental difference between a monopoly and a perfect competitor. For a perfect competitor, price and marginal revenue are the same.

Marginal revenue is less than price for a monopoly firm.

Marginal revenue is less than price and declines as output rises because the monopolist must lower the price in order to sell more units. When the price of a VCR is $1,400, the firm sells 7 VCRs. When the price is dropped to $1,350, the firm sells 8 units. The firm does not sell the first 7 VCRs for $1,400 and the eighth one for $1,350. It might lose business if it tried to do that. The customer who purchased the good at $1,350 could sell the product for $1,375 to a customer about to pay $1,400, and the firm would lose the $1,400 sale. Customers who would have paid $1,400 could decide to wait until they too can get the $1,350 price. As long as customers know about the prices paid by other customers and as long as the firm cannot easily distinguish among customers, the monopoly firm is not able to charge a different price for each additional unit. All units are sold at the same price, and in order to sell additional units, the monopolist must lower the price on all units. As a result, marginal revenue and price are not the same.

2.a.1. Marginal and Average Revenue Recall from the chapter "Elasticity: Demand and Supply" that whenever the marginal is greater than the average, the average rises, and whenever the marginal is less than the average, the average falls. Average revenue is calculated by dividing total revenue by the number of units of output sold.

$$AR = \frac{P \times Q}{Q} = P$$

At a price of $1,500 per VCR, average revenue is

$$\frac{\$7,500}{5} = \$1,500$$

Average revenue at a price of $1,450 per VCR is

$$\frac{\$8,700}{6} = \$1,450$$

Average revenue is the same as price; in fact, *the average-revenue curve is the demand curve*. Because of the law of demand, where quantity demanded rises as price falls, average revenue (price) always falls as output rises (the demand curve slopes downward). Because average revenue falls as output rises, marginal revenue must always be less than average revenue. For the monopolist (or any firm facing a downward-sloping demand curve), marginal revenue always declines as output increases, and the marginal-revenue curve always lies below the demand curve.

Also recall from previous chapters that the marginal-revenue curve is positive in the elastic region of the demand curve ($e_d > 1$), is zero at the output level where the demand curve is unit-elastic ($e_d = 1$), and is negative in the inelastic portion of the demand curve ($e_d < 1$).[2] This is illustrated in Figure 3 (repeated from the chapter "Elasticity: Demand and Supply").

RECAP

1. The demand curve facing a monopoly firm is the market demand curve.

2. For the monopoly firm, price is greater than marginal revenue. For the perfectly competitive firm, price and marginal revenue are equal.

3. As price declines, total revenue increases in the elastic portion of the demand curve, reaches a maximum at the unit-elastic point, and declines in the inelastic portion.

4. The marginal-revenue curve of the monopoly firm lies below the demand curve.

5. For both the perfectly competitive firm and the monopoly firm, price = average revenue = demand.

---

[2]The slope of the demand curve is one-half the slope of the marginal-revenue curve. Consider the demand formula $P = a - bQ$; total revenue is $PQ = aQ - bQ^2$, so marginal revenue is $MR = a - 2bQ$.

Figure 3
Downward-Sloping Demand Curve and Revenue

The straight-line downward-sloping demand curve in Figure 3(a) shows that the price elasticity of demand becomes more inelastic as we move down the curve. In the elastic region, revenue increases as price is lowered, as shown in Figure 3(b); in the inelastic region, revenue decreases as price is lowered. The revenue-maximizing point, the top of the curve in Figure 3(b), occurs where the demand curve is unit-elastic, shown in Figure 3(a).

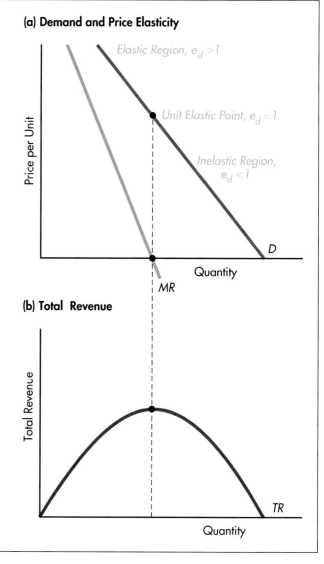

(a) Demand and Price Elasticity

Elastic Region, $e_d > 1$

Unit Elastic Point, $e_d = 1$

Inelastic Region, $e_d < 1$

(b) Total Revenue

3. PROFIT MAXIMIZATION

The objective of the monopoly firm is to maximize profit. Where does the monopolist choose to produce, and what price does it set? Recall from the chapter "An Overview of Product Markets and Profit Maximization," that all profit-maximizing firms produce at the point where marginal revenue equals marginal cost.

3.a. What Price to Charge?

A schedule of revenues and costs for the wireless VCR producer accompanies Figure 4. Total revenue (*TR*) is listed in column 3; total cost (*TC*), in column 4. Total profit (*TR* − *TC*), shown in column 5, is the difference between

Figure 4
Profit Maximization for the VCR Producer
The data listed in the table are plotted in Figure 4(a). The firm produces where $MR = MC$, 8 units; charges a price given by the demand curve directly above the production of 8 units, a price of $1,350 per VCR; and earns a profit (yellow rectangle). In Figure 4(b), the firm is shown to be operating at a loss (blue rectangle). It produces output Q at price P, but the average total cost exceeds the price.

(1) Total Output (Q)	(2) Price (P)	(3) Total Revenue (TR)	(4) Total Cost (TC)	(5) Total Profit (TR − TC)	(6) Marginal Revenue (MR)	(7) Marginal Cost (MC)	(8) Average Total Cost (ATC)
0	$1,750	$ 0	$1,000	$−1,000			
1	1,700	1,700	2,000	−300	$1,700	$1,000	$2,000
2	1,650	3,300	2,800	500	1,600	800	1,400
3	1,600	4,800	3,500	1,300	1,500	700	1,167
4	1,550	6,200	4,000	2,200	1,400	500	1,000
5	1,500	7,500	4,500	3,000	1,300	500	900
6	1,450	8,700	5,200	3,500	1,200	700	867
7	1,400	9,800	6,000	3,800	1,100	800	857
8	1,350	10,800	7,000	3,800	1,000	1,000	875
9	1,300	11,700	9,000	2,700	900	2,000	1,000

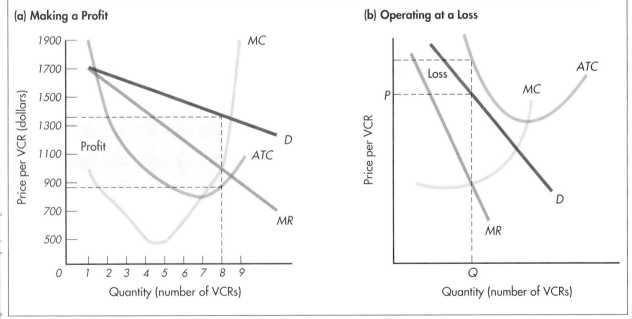

(a) Making a Profit

(b) Operating at a Loss

the entries in column 3 and those in column 4. Marginal revenue (*MR*) is listed in column 6, marginal cost (*MC*) in column 7, and average total cost (*ATC*) in column 8.

The quantity of output to be produced is the quantity that corresponds to the point where $MR = MC$. How high a price will the market bear at that quantity? The market is willing and able to purchase the quantity given by $MR = MC$ at the corresponding price on the demand curve. As shown in Figure 4(a), the price is found by drawing a vertical line from the point where $MR = MC$ up to the demand curve and then extending a horizontal line over to the vertical axis. That price is $1,350 when output is 8.

3.b. Monopoly Profit and Loss

Why would someone want to have a monopoly in some business or activity?

The profit that the monopoly firm generates by selling 8 VCRs at a price of $1,350 is shown in Figure 4(a) as the colored rectangle. The vertical distance between the ATC curve and the demand curve, multiplied by the quantity sold, yields total profit.

Just like any other firm, a monopoly firm could experience a loss. A monopoly supplier of sharpeners for disposable razor blades probably would not be very successful, and the U.S. Postal Service has failed to make a profit in five of the last ten years. Unless price exceeds average costs, the firm loses money. A monopolist producing at a loss is shown in Figure 4(b)—the price is less than the average total cost.

Like a perfectly competitive firm, a monopolist will suspend operations in the short run if its price does not exceed the average variable cost at the quantity the firm produces. And, like a perfectly competitive firm, a monopolist will shut down permanently if revenue is not likely to equal or exceed all costs in the long run (unless the government subsidizes the firm, as it does in the case of the U.S. Postal Service). In contrast, however, if a monopolist makes a profit, barriers to entry will keep other firms out of the industry. As a result, the monopolist can earn above-normal profits in the long run.

A monopolist can earn above-normal profits in the long run.

3.c. Monopoly Myths

There are a few myths about monopoly that we have debunked here. The first myth is that a monopolist can charge any price it wants and will reap unseemly profits by continually increasing the price. We know that a monopolist maximizes profit by producing the quantity that equates marginal revenue and marginal cost. We also know that a monopolist can only price and sell the quantities given by the demand curve. If the demand curve is very inelastic, as would be the case for a lifesaving pharmaceutical, then the price the monopolist would charge will be high. Conversely, if demand is very price-elastic, the monopolist will experience losses by charging exorbitant prices. A second myth is that a monopolist is not sensitive to customers. The monopolist can stay in business only if it earns at least a normal profit. Ignoring customers, producing a good no one will purchase, setting prices that all customers think are exorbitant, and providing terrible service or products customers do not want will not allow a firm to remain in business for long. The monopolist faces a demand curve for its product and must search for a price and quantity that are dictated by that demand curve. The third myth is that the monopolist cannot make a loss. A monopolist is no different than any other firm in that it has costs of doing business and it must earn sufficient revenues to pay those costs. If the monopolist sets too high a price or provides a product few want, revenues may be less than costs and losses may result.

RECAP

1. Profit is maximized at the output level where $MR = MC$.

2. The price charged by the monopoly firm is the point on the demand curve that corresponds to the quantity where $MR = MC$.

3. A monopoly firm can make profits or experience losses. A monopoly firm can earn above-normal profit in the long run.

4. The monopoly firm will shut down in the short run if all variable costs aren't covered. It will shut down in the long run if all costs aren't covered.

4. PRICE DISCRIMINATION

Up to now we have assumed that the monopolist charges all customers the same price. Under certain conditions, a firm operating in markets that are not perfectly competitive can increase profits by charging different customers different prices. This is called *price discrimination*. The objective of the firm is to charge each customer exactly what each is willing to pay and in this way extract the total consumer surplus.

4.a. Necessary Conditions for Price Discrimination

Under what conditions would a monopolist charge different customers different prices for the same product?

You read in section 2.a that the monopoly firm has to sell all of its products at a uniform price; otherwise, one customer could sell to another, thereby reducing the monopoly firm's profits. However, if customers do not come into contact with each other or are somehow separated by the firm, the firm may be able to charge each customer the exact price that he or she is willing to pay. By doing this, the firm is able to collect a great deal more of the consumer surplus than it would receive if it charged all customers the same price. Although a firm does not have to be a monopolist to price-discriminate, the monopolist can more easily separate customers than the oligopolist or monopolistic competitor.

When different customers are charged different prices for the same product or when customers are charged different prices for different quantities of the same product, price discrimination is occurring. Price discrimination occurs when price changes result not from cost changes but from the firm's attempt to extract more of the consumer surplus. Certain conditions are necessary for price discrimination to occur:

- The firm cannot be a price taker (perfect competitor).

- The firm must be able to separate customers according to price elasticities of demand.

- The firm must be able to prevent resale of the product.

4.b. Examples of Price Discrimination

Examples of price discrimination are not hard to find. Senior citizens often pay a lower price than the general population at movie theaters, drugstores, and golf courses. It is relatively easy to identify senior citizens and to ensure that they do not resell their tickets to the general population.

Tuition at state schools is different for in-state and out-of-state residents. It is not difficult to find out where a student resides, and it is very easy to ensure that in-state students do not sell their place to out-of-state students.

Airlines discriminate between business passengers and others. Passengers who do not fly at the busiest times, who purchase tickets in advance, and who can stay at their destination longer than a day pay lower fares than business passengers, who cannot make advance reservations and who must travel during rush hours. It is relatively easy for the airlines to separate business from nonbusiness passengers and to ensure that the latter do not sell their tickets to the former.

Electric utilities practice a form of price discrimination by charging different rates for different quantities of electricity used. The rate declines as the quantity purchased increases. A customer might pay $.07 per kilowatt-hour for the first 100 kilowatt-hours, $.06 for the next 100, and so on. Many utility companies have different rate structures for different classes of customers as well. Businesses pay less per kilowatt-hour than households.

Grocery coupons, mail-in rebates, trading stamps, and other discount strategies are also price-discrimination techniques. Shoppers who are willing to spend time cutting out coupons and presenting them receive a lower price than those not willing to spend that time. Shoppers are separated by the amount of time they are willing to devote to coupon clipping. Is it possible that the popcorn at the movies is also a price-discrimination tactic? If the excess price of the popcorn and other foodstuffs at the movies was simply translated to an admission ticket, the movie theater would lose those customers who do not purchase popcorn. By charging a high price for the popcorn, the movie theater is distinguishing those customers who have a lower price elasticity of demand for the entire package of the movie and the popcorn from those with a higher elasticity of demand.

4.c. The Theory of Price Discrimination

How does price discrimination work? Suppose there are two classes of buyers for movie tickets, senior citizens and everybody else, and each class has a different elasticity of demand. The two classes are shown in Figure 5. Profit is maximized when $MR = MC$. Because the same firm is providing the goods in two submarkets, MC is the same for senior citizens and the general public, but the demand curves differ. Because the demand curves of the two groups differ, there are two MR curves: MR_{sc} for senior citizens, in Figure 5(a), and MR_{gp} for the general population, in Figure 5(b). Profit is maximized when $MR_{sc} = MC$ and when $MR_{gp} = MC$. The price is found by drawing a vertical line from the quantities where $MR = MC$ up to the respective demand curves, D_{sc} and D_{gp}.

Notice that the price to the general population, P_{gp}, is higher than the price to the senior citizens, P_{sc}. The reason is that the senior citizens' demand curve is more elastic than the demand curve of the general population. Senior citizens are more sensitive to price than is the general population, so to attract more of their business, the merchant has to offer them a lower price.

By discriminating, a monopoly firm makes greater profits than it would make by charging both groups the same price. If both groups were charged

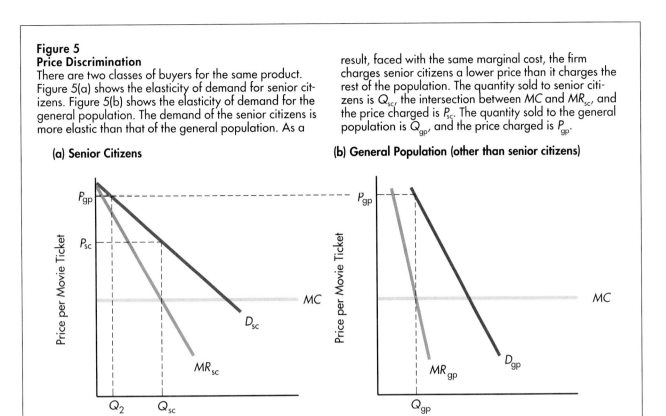

Figure 5
Price Discrimination
There are two classes of buyers for the same product. Figure 5(a) shows the elasticity of demand for senior citizens. Figure 5(b) shows the elasticity of demand for the general population. The demand of the senior citizens is more elastic than that of the general population. As a result, faced with the same marginal cost, the firm charges senior citizens a lower price than it charges the rest of the population. The quantity sold to senior citizens is Q_{sc}, the intersection between MC and MR_{sc}, and the price charged is P_{sc}. The quantity sold to the general population is Q_{gp}, and the price charged is P_{gp}.

(a) Senior Citizens

(b) General Population (other than senior citizens)

the same price, P_{gp}, the monopoly firm would lose sales to senior citizens who found the price too high, Q_{sc} to Q_2. And if both groups were charged P_{sc}, so few additional sales to the general population would be made that revenues would fall.

4.d. Dumping

dumping:
setting a higher price on goods sold domestically than on goods sold in foreign markets

predatory dumping:
dumping to drive competitors out of business

Price discrimination is a strategy used by many firms that sell their products in different countries. A derogatory name for this policy is **dumping**. Dumping occurs when an identical good is sold to foreign buyers for a lower price than is charged to domestic buyers. International dumping is a controversial issue. Producers in a country facing foreign competitors are likely to appeal to their domestic government for protection from the foreign goods being dumped in their market. Typically, the appeal for government assistance is based on the argument that the dumping firms are practicing **predatory dumping**—dumping intended to drive rival firms out of business. A successful predator firm raises prices after the rival is driven from the market.

Canadian electronics manufacturers might accuse Japanese firms of dumping if the Japanese firms are selling electronics in Canada for less than they charge in Japan. The Canadian manufacturers may appeal to the Canadian government, asserting that the Japanese firms are engaged in predatory dumping to drive the Canadian firms out of business and warning that the

Japanese firms will then raise the price of electronics products in Canada without fear of competition by the domestic Canadian firms. Claims of predatory dumping are often emotional and stir up the nationalistic sympathy of the rest of the domestic economy.

The U.S. government frequently responds to charges of dumping brought against foreign firms by U.S. industry. The government has pursued claims of predatory dumping against South African manufacturers of steel plate in 1984; German, Italian, and French winemakers in 1985; Japanese manufacturers of semiconductors in 1985 and 1987; Singapore typewriters in 1993; and nineteen steel-producing nations, also in 1993.

One famous case involved Sony Corporation of Japan. In the United States, Sony was selling Japanese-made TV sets for $180 while charging buyers in Japan $333 for the same model. U.S. television producers claimed that Sony was dumping TV sets in the U.S. market and seriously damaging U.S. television manufacturers. (Although U.S. producers disliked the low price of Japanese competitors, U.S. consumers benefited.) The U.S. government threatened to place high tariffs on Japanese television sets entering the United States unless Japan raised the price of Japanese televisions sold in the United States. The threat worked, and the price of Japanese TVs exported to the United States increased.

Charges of predatory dumping make good news stories, but it is also true that dumping is to be expected when producers with the ability to set prices (as is the case for firms operating in markets that are not perfectly competitive) face segmented markets that have different price elasticities of demand. Conceptually, dumping is no different from what happens when a car dealer charges one buyer a higher price than another for the same car. If both buyers were aware of the range of prices at which the dealer would sell the car, or if both buyers had exactly the same price elasticity of demand, they would pay exactly the same price.

The Japanese electronics manufacturer realizes that the electronics market in Japan is separate from the electronics market in Canada or the United States. If the price elasticity of demand for electronics is different in each country, the Japanese manufacturer will maximize profit by charging a different price in each country.

RECAP

1. Price discrimination occurs when a firm charges different customers different prices for the same product or charges different prices for different quantities of the same product.

2. Three conditions are necessary for price discrimination to occur: (a) the firm must have some market power; (b) the firm must be able to separate customers according to price elasticities of demand; and (c) the firm must be able to prevent resale of the product.

3. Dumping is setting a higher price on goods sold in the domestic market than on goods sold in the foreign market. Dumping is another name for price discrimination in sales to customers that occurs in different countries.

How do the predictions of the models of perfect competition and monopoly differ?

The perfectly competitive market structure results in economic efficiency because price is equal to marginal cost and firms are producing at the bottom of the average-total-cost curve. The monopoly market structure does not yield efficiency.

5.a. Costs of Monopoly: Inefficiency

In the long run, the perfectly competitive firm operates at the minimum point of the long-run average-total-cost curve and the firm's price is equal to its marginal cost. Profit is the normal level. A monopolist does not operate at the minimum point of the average-total-cost curve and does not set price equal to marginal cost. Because entry does not occur, a monopoly firm may earn above-normal profit in the long run.

Figure 6(a) shows a perfectly competitive market. The market demand curve is D; the market supply curve is S. The market price determined by the intersection of D and S is P_{pc}. At P_{pc} the perfectly competitive market produces Q_{pc}. Consumers are able to enjoy the consumer surplus indicated by

---

Figure 6
Monopoly and Perfect Competition Compared
Figure 6(a) shows a perfectly competitive industry; it produces at the point where industry demand, D, and industry supply, S, intersect. The quantity produced by the industry is Q_{pc}; the price charged is P_{pc}. Consumer surplus is the triangle $P_{pc}BA$. Figure 6(b) shows what happens if the industry is monopolized. The single firm faces the industry demand curve, D, and has the marginal-revenue curve MR. The intersection of the

marginal-cost curve and the marginal-revenue curve indicates the quantity that will be produced, Q_m. The price charged for Q_m is P_m. Thus, the monopoly firm produces less and charges more than the perfectly competitive industry. Consumer surplus, shown as the triangle P_mCA, is smaller in the monopoly industry. The area $P_{pc}ECP_m$ is the consumer surplus in perfect competition that is transferred from consumer to producer. The producer surplus is area $OFCP_m$. The deadweight loss is the area CFB.

(a) The Perfectly Competitive Market

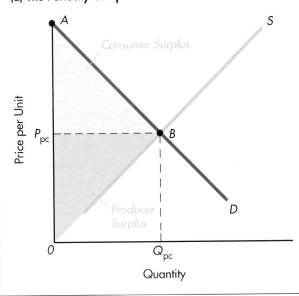

(b) Monopoly

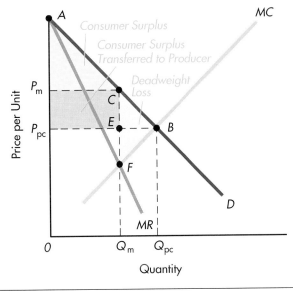

the triangle $P_{pc}BA$, by purchasing the quantity Q_{pc} at the price P_{pc}. Firms receive the producer surplus indicated by triangle OBP_{pc} by producing the quantity Q_{pc} and selling that quantity at price P_{pc}.

Let's assume that all of the firms in a perfectly competitive industry are merged into a single monopoly firm and that the monopolist does not close or alter plants and does not achieve any economies of scale. In other words, what would occur if a perfectly competitive industry is transformed into a monopoly—just one firm determines price and quantity produced? The industry demand curve becomes the monopoly firm's demand curve, and the industry supply curve becomes the monopoly firm's marginal-cost curve. This is illustrated in Figure 6(b).

The monopoly firm restricts quantity produced to Q_m where $MR = MC$, and charges a price P_m as indicated on the demand curve shown in Figure 6(b). *The monopoly firm thus produces a lower quantity than does the perfectly competitive industry, Q_m compared to Q_{pc}, and sells that smaller quantity at a higher price, P_m compared to P_{pc}.* In addition, the consumer surplus in monopoly is the triangle P_mCA, which is smaller than the consumer surplus under perfect competition, $P_{pc}BA$. The rectangle $P_{pc}ECP_m$ is part of consumer surplus in perfect competition. In monopoly, that part of consumer surplus is transferred to the firm. The total producer surplus is area $OFCP_m$.

Thus, firms are better off (more producer surplus) while consumers are worse off (less consumer surplus) under monopoly compared to perfect competition. Consumers are worse off by area $P_{pc}BCP_m$ and firms are better off by area $P_{pc}FCP_m$ less area EFB. The triangle CFB is lost by both consumers and firms and goes to no one. This loss is the reduction in consumer surplus and producer surplus that is not transferred to the monopoly firm or to anyone else; it is called a **deadweight loss**. If a monopoly firm can produce output at the same cost as the perfectly competitive industry, there is a loss to society in going from perfect competition to monopoly; that loss is called deadweight loss. The tradeoff between producers and consumers in perfect competition and monopoly is explored in the Economic Insight "How New York's Taxicab Monopoly Was Broken."

deadweight loss:
the reduction of consumer surplus without a corresponding increase in profit when a perfectly competitive firm is monopolized

5.b. The Deadweight Loss May Be Overstated

The deadweight loss just described may, in reality, be overstated. A monopolist may face the potential of rivals if profit gets too high or may have to worry about government intervention.

5.b.1. Potential Competition
The Intel Corporation has to be concerned that rival firms will take away its virtual monopoly of the computer chip market. As a result, Intel chips such as the P-6 are not priced as high, and more are sold than might be the case if the firm did not fear entry. The lower the price relative to what it could be, the less the deadweight loss. Monopoly firms may keep the price lower and produce more output than is suggested by the theory of monopoly because these firms fear that if their profit is too high, it could bring about entry and competition in the future. The fear of potential entry is called **potential competition**.

potential competition:
possible entry or rivalry capable of forcing existing producers to behave as if the competition actually existed

5.b.2. Government Intervention
Another constant fear for the monopoly firm is that the government will intervene. Since the 1930s, the governments of most of the developed nations have scrutinized business operations in an

How New York's Taxicab Monopoly Was Broken

Many cities require a license, or medallion, to operate a taxi. Under New York City law, for example, anyone who wants to offer taxi service must buy the right to do so from some other operator in the form of a medallion originally issued by the city. Since medallions are limited in number, the holders of the medallion—the yellow taxicabs—have a monopoly.

The number of medallions in New York City remained fixed at 11,787 for nearly half a century. During this time, the value of a medallion—reflecting the profits that can be earned—rose from $10 in 1937 to $105,000 in 1986. These increasingly valuable medallions gave rise to a push to increase the number of medallions in New York City. When the existing medallion holders fought the push, entry

began in other ways. Livery cars, black cars with radio phones that are supposed to respond only when called, have proliferated, for example. While drivers of the yellow medallion cabs cruise the streets and pick up any passengers who hail them, the drivers of the black nonmedallion livery cars have authorization to respond only to customers who have ordered the cabs in advance by phone or other means. The yellow-cab owners, who once had a monopoly by virtue of their 11,787 medallions, complain that the influx of nonmedallion cabs has decreased revenue for them and their drivers. They claim that the nonmedallion cars are illegally picking up passengers on city streets. The taxi industry in New York City now finds itself awash in cabs and is not sure

what to do.

The former monopolists are experiencing a declining profit while passengers are reaping the benefits as more competition is introduced. Customers can negotiate prices with limousines and liveries; corporate customers are negotiating frequent-use discounts with the black cars and limousines. Some neighborhood livery companies are offering special fares to elderly people and to churchgoers on Sundays.

Sources: "Owners Bewail Flood of Cabs in New York," Winston Williams, *New York Times*, April 10, 1989, p. E1; "Taxicab Regulation from Many Directions," Robert O. Boorstin, *New York Times*, Nov. 24, 1986, p. E6; "New York City Looks at Taxi Regulation," *Regulation*, March/April 1982, p. 11.

attempt to discourage the formation of monopolies. Many proposed mergers have been prohibited because of the fear that monopoly might result. The activities of large firms are watched especially closely. This pressure may lessen the deadweight losses of monopoly.

5.b.3. **Economies of Scale**   Underlying the preceding comparison of perfect competition and monopoly is the assumption that cost conditions will not change. However, it seems unrealistic to assume that the acquisition or merger of many firms would not change the cost structure in the industry. If there are economies of scale, the large-scale firm will be able to produce the product at a lower cost per unit than the many smaller firms. As a result, the deadweight losses imposed on society by a monopoly firm may be diminished.

5.c. The Deadweight Losses May Be Understated

The deadweight losses imposed by monopoly firms may be smaller than suggested by the comparison of perfect competition and monopoly, but it is also possible that they could actually be larger than the comparison suggests. The monopoly could operate less efficiently, and resources could be taken away from productive activities and devoted to maintaining a monopoly.

5.c.1. Higher Costs and X-Inefficiency As you have learned, a monopoly firm does not operate at the minimum point on the average-total-cost curve, but a perfectly competitive firm does. Thus, the monopolist not only imposes a deadweight loss but also produces at a higher cost per unit than does the perfectly competitive firm. The high cost may go even higher if the monopolist becomes inefficient because of a lack of competition or potential competition.

Many monopolies are created and maintained by the government. The resulting monopoly firms do not have to worry about potential competition or government intervention. Monopoly firms may not feel the need to operate efficiently because they face no competition from entering firms. Many economists have argued that because monopoly firms have no fear of competition, they operate less efficiently than would competitive firms producing the same output. The inefficiency that occurs in the absence of fear of entry and rivalry is called **X-inefficiency**. X-inefficiency is represented by an upward shift of the average-total-cost curve.

The greater X-inefficiency is, the greater the cost to society when a perfectly competitive industry is monopolized. As the average costs of production rise because of X-inefficiency, consumer surplus falls without a corresponding increase in the monopolist's profit. The additional loss in consumer surplus due to X-inefficiency is an increase in deadweight losses.

X-inefficiency:
the tendency of a firm not faced with competition to become inefficient

5.c.2. Rent Seeking Monopolists devote significant resources to preserving their monopoly positions. Liquor licenses are valuable because they bestow a local monopoly on the recipients. Similarly, radio and television broadcasting rights provide above-normal profits to the holders of those rights. To protect their above-normal profits and ensure political support for their monopoly positions, the owners provide significant amounts of money to lobbyists, lawyers, and political action committees (PACs). Activities that are undertaken simply to create a transfer from one group to another are known as **rent seeking**. Rent-seeking expenditures do not add to productive activity. A lawyer working to take $100 from the consumer and give it to the monopoly firm is giving up some other productive activity. The opportunity cost of the lawyer's time is a deadweight loss to society.

rent seeking:
the use of resources simply to transfer wealth from one group to another without increasing production or total wealth

The potential for rent seeking is indicated in Figure 7 as the above-normal profit, the rectangle *EBCF*. It would be worthwhile for the owners of the monopoly firm to devote resources up to the amount of their profit in order to maintain their monopoly. Any profit that remains in excess of the amount spent on rent seeking would still be above-normal profit to the owners. When profit, *EBCF* in Figure 7, is used to pay for the nonproductive lobbying activities, it becomes part of the deadweight loss.

5.c.3. Innovation If a monopoly firm tends to be more or less innovative than a perfectly competitive firm would be, the costs imposed on society by the monopoly may be smaller or larger than the comparison with perfect competition suggests. If profits that can be obtained with a successful invention are quickly competed away, there might be less incentive to innovate than there would be if above-normal profits could exist for a number of years. This argument forms the basis of patent laws. A patent confers a monopoly on a firm or individual for a certain product or part for seventeen years.

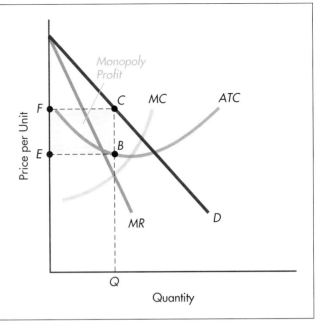

Figure 7
Rent Seeking
A monopoly firm earns an above-normal profit. The managers of the firm are willing to expend all of the profit to retain the monopoly. The amount of the profit used to maintain the monopoly is rent seeking.

The counterargument is that entrepreneurs are always looking for ways to earn additional profit and protect against additional losses. If an entrepreneur is unwilling to spend money for research and development, competitors will quickly put the firm out of business because they will innovate and be able to produce products less expensively or produce better products than the firm that fails to innovate.

5.d. Supply and the Monopoly Firm

For the firm in perfect competition, the supply curve is that portion of the marginal-cost curve that lies above the average-cost curve, and the market supply curve is the sum of all the individual firms' supply curves. The supply curve for the firm selling in any of the other market structures is not as straightforward to derive and, therefore, neither is the market supply curve. The reason is that firms selling in market structures other than perfect competition are price makers rather than price takers. This means that the hypothetical experiment of varying the price of a product and seeing how the firm selling that product reacts makes no sense.

In the case of the monopolist, the firm supplies a quantity determined by setting marginal revenue equal to marginal cost, but it also sets the price to go along with this quantity. Varying the price will not change the decision rule since the firm will choose to produce its profit-maximizing output level and set the price accordingly. There is, therefore, only one quantity and price at which the monopolist will operate. There is a supply point, not a supply curve. Moreover, because the monopolist is the only firm in the market, its supply curve (or supply point) is also the market supply curve (or point).

The complications of the price makers do not alter the supply rule: a firm will produce and offer for sale a quantity that equates marginal revenue and

SUMMARY

▲▼ What is monopoly?

1. Monopoly is a market structure in which there is a single supplier of a product. A monopoly firm, or monopolist, is the only supplier of a product for which there are no close substitutes. §1.a

▲▼ How is a monopoly created?

2. Natural barriers to entry (such as economies of scale), barriers erected by firms in the industry, and barriers erected by government may create monopolies. §1.b, 1.b.1, 1.b.2, 1.b.3

3. The term *monopoly* is often associated with natural monopoly, local monopoly, regulated monopoly, and monopoly power. §1.c

▲▼ What does the demand curve for a monopoly firm look like, and why?

4. Because a monopolist is the only producer of a good or service, the demand curve facing a monopoly firm is the industry demand curve. §2

5. Price and marginal revenue are not the same for a monopoly firm. §2.a

6. The average-revenue curve is the demand curve. §2.a.1

7. A monopoly firm maximizes profit by producing the quantity of output yielded at the point where marginal revenue and marginal cost are equal. §3.a

8. A monopoly firm sets a price that is on the demand curve and that corresponds to the point where marginal revenue and marginal cost are equal. §3.a

▲▼ Why would someone want to have a monopoly in some business or activity?

9. A monopoly firm can make above-normal or normal profit or even a loss. If it makes above-normal profit, entry by other firms does not occur and the monopoly firm can earn above-normal profit in the long run. Exit occurs if the monopoly firm cannot cover costs in the long run. §3.b

▲▼ Under what conditions would a monopolist charge different customers different prices for the same product?

10. Price discrimination occurs when the firm is not a price taker, can separate customers according to their price elasticities of demand for the firm's product, and can prevent resale of the product. §4.a

11. *Dumping* is a derogatory name given to the price discrimination used by firms selling in more than one nation. §4.d

▲▼ How do the predictions of the models of perfect competition and monopoly differ?

12. A comparison of monopoly and perfectly competitive firms implies that monopoly imposes costs on society. These costs include less output being produced and that output being sold at a higher price. §5.a

13. The deadweight losses of monopoly may not be as large as the comparison with perfect competition suggests if (a) monopoly firms are more innovative; (b) the threat of potential competition or of government intervention causes the monopoly firm to lower price and increase quantity; or (c) the monopoly firm operates more efficiently than would a perfectly competitive firm. §5.b

14. The deadweight losses of monopoly may be larger than the comparison with perfect competition suggests if (a) the monopoly firm operates inefficiently because of a lack of competition; (b) rent seeking occurs; or (c) the monopolist is less innovative than the perfect competitor. §5.c

15. Because monopoly is inefficient and perfect competition efficient, governments have attempted to regulate the natural monopolies to make them more like perfect competitors. The huge economies of scale rule out breaking the natural monopolies up into small firms. Instead, price has been set at a fair rate of return, $P = ATC$. §5.e

KEY TERMS

monopoly §1.a

monopoly firm (monopolist) §1.a

barrier to entry §1.b

natural monopoly §1.c

local monopoly §1.c

regulated monopoly §1.c

monopoly power §1.c

dumping §4.d

predatory dumping §4.d

deadweight loss §5.a

potential competition §5.b.1

X-inefficiency §5.c.1

rent seeking §5.c.2

fair rate of return §5.e

EXERCISES

1. About 85 percent of the soup sold in the United States is Campbell's brand. Is Campbell Soup Company a monopoly firm?

2. Price discrimination is practiced by movie theaters, motels, golf courses, drugstores, and universities. Are they monopolies? If not, how can they carry out price discrimination?

3. Why is it necessary for the seller to be able to keep customers from reselling the product in order for price discrimination to occur? There are many products for which you get a discount for purchasing large quantities. For instance, most liquor stores will provide a discount on wine if you purchase a case. Is this price discrimination? If so, what is to keep one customer from purchasing cases of wine and then reselling single bottles at a price above the case price but below the liquor store's single-bottle price?

4. Many people have claimed that there is no good for which substitutes are not available. If so, does this mean there is no such thing as monopoly?

5. Suppose that at a price of $6 per unit, quantity demanded is 12 units. Calculate the quantity demanded when the marginal revenue is $6 per unit. (*Hint*: The price elasticity of demand is unity at the midpoint of the demand curve.)

6. In the following figure, if the monopoly firm faces ATC_1, which rectangle measures total profit? If the monopoly firm faces ATC_2, what is total profit? What information would you need in order to know whether the monopoly firm will shut down or continue producing in the short run? In the long run?

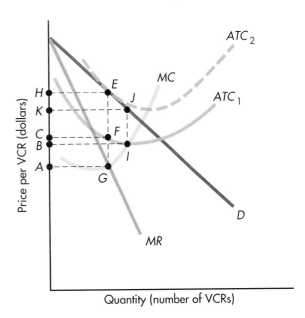

7. In recent years, U.S. car manufacturers have charged lower car prices in western states in an effort to offset the competition by the Japanese cars. This two-tier pricing scheme has upset many car dealers in the eastern states. Many have called it discriminatory and illegal.

a. What conditions are necessary for this pricing scheme to be profitable to the U.S. companies?

b. Is this pricing scheme the same as dumping?

8. Consider the following demand schedule. Does it apply to a perfectly competitive firm? Compute marginal and average revenue.

Price	Quantity
100	1
95	2
88	3
80	4
70	5
55	6
40	7
22	8

9. Suppose the marginal cost of producing the good in question 8 is a constant $10 per unit of output. What quantity of output will the firm produce?

10. Do you agree or disagree with this statement: "A monopoly firm will charge an exorbitant price for its product." Explain your answer.

11. Do you agree or disagree with this statement: "A monopoly firm will run a much less safe business than a perfect competitor." Explain your answer.

12. The pistachio nut growers of California petitioned the U.S. government to restrict the flow of Iranian pistachios because of dumping. Iranian pistachios were being sold in the United States at a price that was lower than it cost to produce the California variety of nuts. If you were an economist with the U.S. government, would you support the petition of the California growers?

13. State colleges and universities have two levels of tuition or fees. The less expensive is for residents of the state, the more expensive for nonresidents. Assume the universities are profit-maximizing monopolists and explain their pricing policy. Now, explain why the colleges and universities give student aid and scholarships.

14. Several electric utilities are providing customers with a choice of billing procedures. Customers can select a "time-of-day" meter that registers electrical usage throughout the day, or they can select a regular meter that registers total usage at the end of the day. With the time-of-day meter, the utility is able to charge customers a much higher rate for peak usage than for nonpeak usage. The regular meter users pay the same rate for electrical usage no matter when it is used. Why would the electrical utility want customers to choose the time-of-day meter?

15. Suppose that a firm has a monopoly on a good with the following demand schedule:

Price	Quantity
$10	0
9	1
8	2
7	3
6	4
5	5
4	6
3	7
2	8
1	9
0	10

a. What price and quantity will the monopolist produce at if the marginal cost is a constant $4?

b. Calculate the deadweight loss from having the monopolist produce, rather than a perfect competitor.

c. What price would the regulatory commission set if it wanted to achieve maximum efficiency?

d. What price would the regulatory commission set if it wanted to allow a normal profit?

COOPERATIVE LEARNING EXERCISE

Students are to count off (1, 2, 3, etc.) and form into groups by number (all the 1s in one group, and so on). The odd-numbered groups are to develop a case for giving firms a monopoly on new drugs. The even-numbered groups are to develop a case against giving firms a monopoly on new drugs. Consider whether one structure or another would foster greater or faster development of new antibiotics.

This is About Money

Last month Houston Industries Chairman Don Jordan sold his company's nine-year-old cable television subsidiary to Time Warner. . . . Getting out of cable means Jordan, 63, can now focus more intensely on Houston Industries' own by no means certain future. Houston Industries is a $3.8 billion (revenues) utility that has long enjoyed monopoly, rights to supply electricity to consumers in the greater Houston area.

But, as in cable television, competition is breathing fire into the electric utility industry. Houston Industries' territory is the refining and petrochemical capital of the world. That means a lot of big industrial customers that could buy their electricity cheaper from other sources if Texas ever opened up its power market. Burdened with excess capacity, many local independent power producers want to sell directly to Houston Industries' customers.

"We will drop rates in Texas," vows Charlie Goff, boss at $727 million (revenues) Destec Energy, a publicly traded independent power producer 73 percent owned by Dow Chemical.

Don Jordan is making life as difficult as possible for Goff and other would-be competitors. Under current law Destec cannot sell power directly to any of Houston Industries' customers but may sell to utilities and to big municipalities that buy their own power. But for that Destec must distribute its power over transmission lines owned by Houston Industries. When Destec tried to sell power to the city of San Antonio last summer, Houston Industries charged transmission rates substantially above what the city might have paid for power bought from a utility.

. . . the threat of competition will only grow. Texas' independent producers will most likely win legislation that insures open access to, and reasonable pricing on, the big utilities' transmission lines. A nastier fight will come over whether the independents can sell directly to big industrial customers, a process known as retail wheeling. Houston Industries and other Texas utilities have proposed a ban—forever—on retail wheeling, arguing that smaller customers' rates will rise if independent producers are allowed to cherry-pick the utilities' best customers. The proposed ban won't pass, but the utilities and their lobbyists will probably keep retail competition at bay for years.

Jordan makes no apologies for his efforts to protect Texans from competition. Thunders he: "One thing you have to remember is that this is not an argument about who can supply power the best or how the customer can benefit. It is purely about money—who's gonna get it, who's gonna pay it."

Source: "This is About Money," *Forbes*, Feb. 27, 1995, p. 52. Reprinted by permission of *Forbes Magazine* © Forbes Inc., 1995.

Commentary

In the chapter we learned that natural monopolies are typically regulated in order to protect the public from monopoly practices of restricting output and raising prices. The electric utility is often cited as an example of a natural monopoly, a firm whose large economies of scale make it the only cost efficient supplier of electricity for a large region. The article noted here suggests that the natural monopoly is not quite so natural and that the industry is using the government to maintain barriers to entry.

If a firm is able to produce at the MES point and that point follows huge economies of scale, then that firm may be the only firm able to supply the market. If so, the firm is a natural monopoly. This is shown in the Figure below, where the Demand curve crosses the ATC curve just beyond the MES point. As a monopolist, the firm would restrict output, relative to a perfectly competitive firm, so that it could increase the price. The resulting monopoly profits would be safe from competition since the economies of scale provide barriers to entry.

Because of the potential of restricting output and raising price, the government is often called on to regulate the monopolist. The regulation may take many forms but typically involves an attempt to make the monopolist look more like a perfectly competitive industry—pricing at marginal cost and/or earning only normal profits.

One problem with the regulation is that it distorts the incentives of the regulated firm's managers.

They have to demonstrate to the regulatory commission that their costs justify increased rates. If they are able to increase costs, they might be able to get increased rates. Often, therefore, the regulated monopolist will have inflated costs relative to a competitive firm. The monopoly profits come not in the form of pure profit but in the form of inflated costs.

Another problem with regulation is that technological advances might not be fully recognized by the regulatory commission. If technology reduces the size of the economies of scale and hence the natural barriers to entry, the regulated monopolist will still have the government as a barrier to entry. And, the monopolist is willing to spend its monopoly profits to ensure that the barrier to entry remains in place. This is what we observe in the article. Houston Industries' executive Don Jordan is fighting to keep the regulation intact. He wants to retain the barriers to entry that he and his company enjoy.

Technological advances enable firms to produce electricity in smaller batches than previously was economical. As a result, many firms generate electricity for their own use and then want to sell their excess. These on-line sellers are severely restricted by most regulatory commissions. Other firms see electrical generation as a new business opportunity. Building new plants and not burdened by the huge costs of nuclear power, new electrical generating firms, like Destec, want to enter the business and compete with the existing regulated utilities.

26

Monopolistic Competition and Oligopoly

FUNDAMENTAL QUESTIONS

1. What is monopolistic competition?
2. What behavior is most common in monopolistic competition?
3. What is oligopoly?
4. In what form does rivalry occur in an oligopoly?
5. Why does cooperation among rivals occur most often in oligopolies?
6. What occurs when the perfect information assumption is relaxed?

How often have you read or heard that some firm is offering a new or different product: McDonald's brings out the McMichael; Volvo introduces passenger-side airbags; Procter & Gamble offers another detergent . . . the list goes on. These are examples of *nonprice competition*. Rather than reducing the price to attract additional customers, the producers use advertising, packaging, color, location, safety features, quality, and size to offer slightly different products. Nonprice competition is a common characteristic of many firms in the real world, but it is not explained by the theory of perfect competition. A monopolist might use nonprice means to discriminate among its customers, but a monopolist is the only producer of a product; clearly breakfast foods, soft drinks, beer, automobiles, and many other industries are not monopolies. To understand much of firm behavior, one or more of the characteristics of perfect competition and monopoly must be altered. These alterations give us the models of monopolistic competition and oligopoly.

PREVIEW

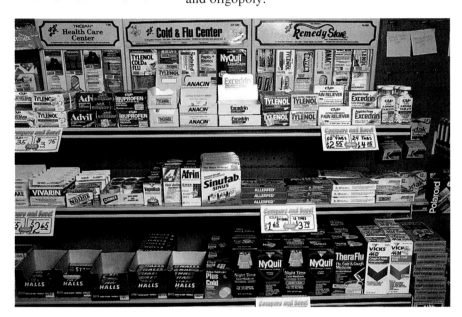

The first model discussed here, *monopolistic competition*, captures many real-world characteristics of competition—brand-name proliferation, product differentiation, advertising, marketing, and packaging—that do not occur in the theory of perfect competition. In a monopolistically competitive market, many firms are producing a slightly different product.

In some industries, however, one large firm dominates. The dominant firm is not a monopoly, but it is not just one among many either. For example, in photofinishing supplies, many agree that Kodak dominates all others. In soup, Campbell Soup Company is a leader. In computer operating systems, Microsoft is dominant. In other industries, such as steel, tobacco, beer, and athletic shoes, two or three firms dominate. In still other industries, such as automobiles and consumer electronics, eight to ten firms account for the lion's share of the market. Oligopoly, like monopolistic competition, allows for nonprice competition but, unlike monopolistic competition, assumes only a few firms have significant market power.

In this chapter we discuss monopolistic competition and oligopoly. We begin with monopolistic competition and then turn to oligopoly in section 2.

I. MONOPOLISTIC COMPETITION

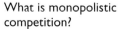

What is monopolistic competition?

Monopolistic competition is a market structure in which (1) there are a large number of firms, (2) the products produced by the firms are differentiated, and (3) entry and exit occur easily. The definitions of *monopolistic competition* and *perfect competition* overlap. In both structures, there are a large number of firms. The difference is that each firm in monopolistic competition produces a product that is slightly different from all other products, whereas in perfect competition the products are standardized. The definition of *monopolistic competition* also overlaps with that of *monopoly*. Because each firm in monopolistic competition produces a unique product, each has a "mini" monopoly over its product. Thus, like a monopolist, the firm in a monopolistically competitive market structure has a downward-sloping demand curve; for a monopolistically competitive firm, marginal revenue is below the demand curve and price is greater than marginal cost. What distinguishes monopolistic competition from monopoly is ease of entry. Anytime firms in monopolistic competition are earning above-normal profit, new firms enter and entry continues until firms are earning normal profit. In monopoly, a firm can earn above-normal profit in the long run. Table 1 summarizes differences among perfect competition, monopoly, and monopolistic competition.

1.a. Profits and Entry

Suppose you are an executive with The Gap clothing stores, and your firm is selling just one type of clothing—adult casual wear. Your firm's product is recognized for its quality and colors, and sales are good, but other firms have introduced several new lines of clothes—more dressy adult clothes and children's clothes. Benetton has expanded its market share by introducing a higher-priced line of clothes, a line of funky clothes, and clothes for kids. The introduction of these clothes has affected the sales of The Gap's clothes; the demand curve for The Gap's clothes has shifted in. How does the firm respond?

You could lower the price of your clothes, and this would increase the quantity demanded. This strategy might attract some of the adults, but it would not attract the kids. You could advertise that The Gap has always

TABLE 1
Summary of Perfect Competition, Monopoly, and Monopolistic Competition

	Perfect Competition	Monopoly	Monopolistic Competition
Number of Firms	Many	One	Many
Type of Product	Undifferentiated	One	Differentiated
Entry Conditions	Easy	Difficult or impossible	Easy
Demand Curve for Firm	Horizontal (perfectly elastic)	Downward-sloping	Downward-sloping
Price and Marginal Cost	$MC = P$	$MC < P$	$MC < P$
Long-run Profit	Zero	Yes	Zero

Monopolistic competitors and some oligopolies offer differentiated products. Cigarettes are differentiated with advertising, size, packaging, and taste. One of the more successful advertising campaigns in recent years has been Joe Camel, the hip, racecar driving, sports-enthusiastic camel shown on the billboard. This particular billboard also shows another aspect of the monopolistically competitive strategy, apppealing to a market segment. Located in a Spanish-speaking area of San Antonio, Texas, this billboard is directed toward the Spanish-speaking citizens. The same billboard, in English, is located a few miles away.

Monopolistically competitive firms produce differentiated products.

offered high quality, but that claim might not be of interest to kids or to those people wanting funky clothes. Your best response is to introduce your own new products: Gap Kids, for instance. In this way you can meet the other retailers head-on. You might even be able to gain market share.

Firms in monopolistic competition tend to use product differentiation more than price to compete. They attempt to provide a product for each market niche. Even though the total market might not be expanding, they divide the market into smaller and smaller segments by introducing variations of products. You can think of a market demand curve for clothes, but within that market there are many niches and many demand curves. In fact, there are separate demand curves for each product—for Gap Kids, The Gap, J. Crew, The Limited, Limited Express, etc. Each individual demand curve is quite price-elastic because of the existence of many close substitutes.

When a new product is introduced, the demand curve for all closely related products shifts in toward the origin because less of the total market is available for each product. What can firms do to offset this effect? Each firm must accept the reduced demand and attempt to increase the demand for its product lines by introducing new products or new variations of existing products. New products are introduced as long as there are above-normal profits.

l.a.l. In the Short Run The demand curve faced by a monopolistically competitive firm is downward-sloping. This means that if a monopolistically competitive firm wants to sell more of one of its products, it must lower the price of that product. Figure 1(a) shows the cost and revenue curves of a monopolistically competitive firm providing a single product in the short run. As with all profit-maximizing firms, production occurs at the quantity where $MR = MC$. The price the firm charges, P_1, is given by the demand curve at the quantity where $MR = MC$. Price P_1 is above average total cost, as indicated by the distance AB. Thus, the firm is earning above-normal profit, shown as the rectangle $CBAP_1$.

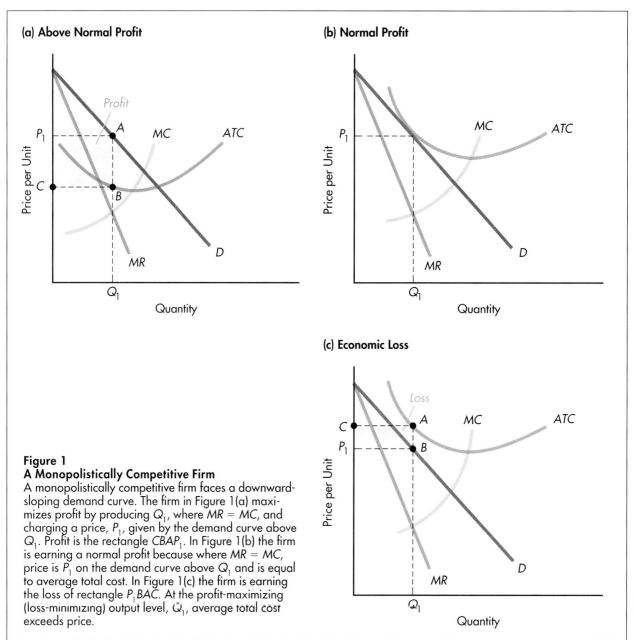

(a) Above Normal Profit

Profit

P_1

C

A

B

MC

ATC

MR

D

Q_1

Price per Unit

Quantity

(b) Normal Profit

P_1

MC

ATC

MR

D

Q_1

Price per Unit

Quantity

(c) Economic Loss

Loss

C

P_1

A

B

MC

ATC

MR

D

Q_1

Price per Unit

Quantity

Figure 1
A Monopolistically Competitive Firm
A monopolistically competitive firm faces a downward-sloping demand curve. The firm in Figure 1(a) maximizes profit by producing Q_1, where $MR = MC$, and charging a price, P_1, given by the demand curve above Q_1. Profit is the rectangle $CBAP_1$. In Figure 1(b) the firm is earning a normal profit because where $MR = MC$, price is P_1 on the demand curve above Q_1 and is equal to average total cost. In Figure 1(c) the firm is earning the loss of rectangle P_1BAC. At the profit-maximizing (loss-minimizing) output level, Q_1, average total cost exceeds price.

If the firms in a monopolistically competitive market are earning normal profit, the marginal-revenue and marginal-cost curves for each firm intersect at quantity Q_1 in Figure 1(b), and the price is P_1. The price is the same as the average total cost at Q_1, so a normal profit is obtained. If the firm is earning a loss, then the average-total-cost curve lies above the demand curve at the quantity produced, as shown in Figure 1(c). At Q_1, the firm is earning a loss, the rectangle P_1BAC. The firm must decide whether to temporarily suspend production of that product or continue producing because the outlook is favorable. The decision depends on whether revenue exceeds variable costs.

I.a.2. In the Long Run Whenever existing firms in a market structure without barriers to entry are earning above-normal profit, new firms enter the business and, in some cases, existing firms expand until all firms are earning the normal profit. In a perfectly competitive industry, the new firms supply a product that is identical to the product being supplied by existing firms. *In a monopolistically competitive industry, entering firms produce a close substitute, not an identical or standardized product.*

As the introduction of new products by new or existing firms occurs, the demand curves for existing products keep shifting in until a normal profit is earned. As each new product is introduced, the demand curves for the existing, slightly differentiated products shift in. For each firm and each product, the demand curve shifts in, as shown in Figure 2, until it just touches the average-total-cost curve at the price charged and output produced, Q_2 and P_2. When profit is at the normal level, expansion and entry cease.

When firms are earning a loss on a product and the long-run outlook is for continued losses, the firms will stop producing that product. Exit means that fewer differentiated products are produced, and the demand curves for the remaining products shift out. This continues until firms are earning normal profits.

I.b. Monopolistic Competition vs. Perfect Competition

Figure 3 shows both a perfectly competitive firm in long-run equilibrium and a monopolistically competitive firm in long-run equilibrium. The perfectly competitive firm, shown as the horizontal demand and marginal-revenue curve, $MR_{pc} = D_{pc}$, produces at the minimum point of the long-run average-total-cost curve at Q_{pc}; and the price, marginal cost, marginal revenue, and average total costs are P_{pc}. The long-run equilibrium for a monopolistically

Figure 2
Entry and Normal Profit
In the long run, the firm in monopolistic competition earns a normal profit. Entry shifts the firm's demand curve in from D_1 to D_2. Entry, which takes the form of a differentiated product, continues to occur as long as above-normal profits exist. When the demand curve just touches the average-total-cost curve, as at P_2 and Q_2, profit is at the normal level.

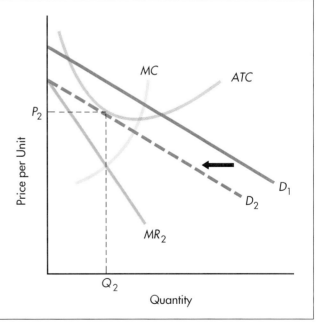

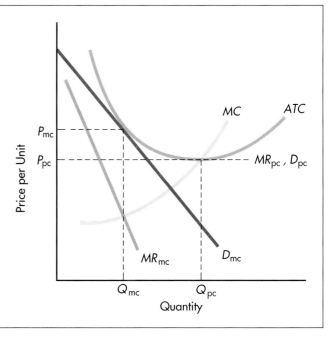

Figure 3
Perfect and Monopolistic Competition Compared
The perfectly competitive firm produces at the point where the price line, the horizontal *MR* curve, intersects the *MC* curve. This is the bottom of the *ATC* curve in the long run, quantity Q_{pc} at price P_{pc}. The monopolistically competitive firm also produces where $MR = MC$. The downward-sloping demand curve faced by the monopolistically competitive firm means that the quantity produced, Q_{mc}, is less than the quantity produced by the perfectly competitive firm, Q_{pc}. The price charged by the monopolistically competitive firm is also higher than that charged by the perfectly competitive firm, P_{mc} versus P_{pc}. In both cases, however, the firms earn only a normal profit.

competitive firm is shown with the demand curve D_{mc} and marginal-revenue curve MR_{mc}. The monopolistically competitive firm produces at Q_{mc}, where $MR_{mc} = MC$, and charges a price determined by drawing a vertical line up from the point where $MR_{mc} = MC$ to the demand curve. That price is just equal to the point where the long-run average-total-cost curve touches the demand curve, P_{mc}. In other words, at Q_{mc} the monopolistically competitive firm is just earning the normal profit.

Monopolistically competitive firms produce less and charge a higher price than perfectly competitive firms.

The difference between a perfectly competitive firm and a monopolistically competitive firm is clear in Figure 3. Because of the downward-sloping demand curve facing the monopolistically competitive firm, the firm does not produce at the minimum point of the long-run average-total-cost curve, Q_{pc}. Instead, it produces a smaller quantity of output, Q_{mc}, at a higher price, P_{mc}. The difference between P_{mc} and P_{pc} is the additional amount consumers pay for the privilege of having differentiated products. If consumers placed no value on product choice—if they desired generic products—they would not pay anything extra for product differentiation, and the monopolistically competitive firm would not exist.

Monopolistic competition does not yield economic efficiency because consumers are willing and able to pay for variety.

Even though price does not equal marginal cost and the monopolistically competitive firm does not operate at the minimum point of the average-total-cost curve, the firm does earn normal profit in the long run. And although the monopolistically competitive firm does not strictly meet the conditions of economic efficiency (since price is not equal to marginal cost), the inefficiency is not due to the firm's ability to restrict quantity and increase price but instead results directly from consumers' desire for variety. It is hard to argue that society is worse off with monopolistic competition than it is with perfect competition since the difference is due solely to consumer desires. Yet, variety is costly and critics of market economies argue that the cost is

Paying for Options

Not everyone is willing to pay for variety, nor has to pay for it. Variety is a luxury good; the income elasticity of demand is greater than 1. This fact is an important element in the pricing strategies of manufacturers. For instance, consider the array of automobiles offered by Toyota, General Motors, Nissan, Honda, Ford, and Chrysler. Toyota has the Camry, the Land Cruiser, the 4Runner, and the Lexus line, among others. Each of these cars incorporates a variety of specialized features that are the result of expensive research and development by the Toyota company.

Some manufacturers place a huge array of options for every automobile, while with others the options are standard features. This strategy seems to be common for the relatively lower-priced automobile lines—those ranging below $25,000. You see this if, for instance, you go to a Jeep dealer; you not only find several models of Jeep, but the combinations of options are remarkable. Moreover, the options are expensive, clearly higher-priced than their marginal costs. This strategy is a means to have those who desire variety pay for the research and development costs. Another strategy is to pro-

vide all options as standard features. This is the approach taken by the Lexus, Acura, Infiniti, and other expensive automobile lines. The approach appears to be a response to price elasticity of demand; consumers of luxury automobiles are less sensitive to price than are consumers of nonluxury automobiles. Several thousand dollars of options on a nonluxury automobile would drive many customers away, but the same options on a luxury automobile will not affect the customer decision. In both cases, the consumer has the choice of whether to purchase the options or not; variety is up to the customer.

not worthwhile. Would the world be a better place if we had a simpler array of products to choose from, if there was a simple generic product—one type of automobile, say—for everyone? Most manufacturers would say no, that they have already developed ways to let the customer who wants variety pay for it, as illustrated in the Economic Insight "Paying for Options."

1.c. Nonprice Competition

What behavior is most common in monopolistic competition?

A firm in a monopolistically competitive market structure attempts to differentiate its product from the products offered by its rivals. Successful product differentiation reduces the price elasticity of demand. The demand curve, shown as the rotation from D_1 to D_2 in Figure 4(a), becomes steeper. McDonald's, for example, has successfully used advertising to differentiate its product. Figure 4(a) shows that a successful differentiation program increases the steepness of the demand curve and may shift it outward, from D_1 to D_2, and successful differentiation could lead to higher profits. Advertising increases costs, however. Suppose McDonald's Corporation spends about 10 cents to advertise each hamburger it sells. If that expenditure rises to 15 cents, then the average-total-cost curve shifts up, as shown in Figure 4(b). Because costs rise and the demand curve becomes steeper and may shift out, the effect on profit depends on the size of changes in the cost and demand curves. A successful advertising campaign is one that causes profit to rise. But costs could increase so much as a result of the advertising

Figure 4
Advertising, Prices, and Profits

A successful differentiation program will reduce the price elasticity of demand, shown as a steeper demand curve, D_2, compared to D_1 in Figure 4(a). The successful differentiation enables the firm to charge a higher price. Advertising is expensive and can cause the cost curves to shift up as well, as shown in Figure 4(b). The combination of higher costs and a more inelastic demand curve can mean greater, the same, or lower profit.

(a) Differentiation Causes Demand Curve to be Less Elastic (at each price)

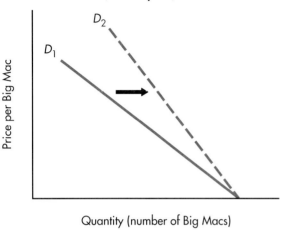

(b) Costs Increase

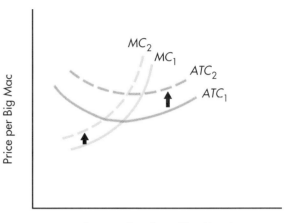

program that profit does not increase. Each firm has to determine the effects of a differentiation program on demand and on costs or, ultimately, on profit.

Numerous characteristics may serve to differentiate products: quality, color, style, safety features, taste, packaging, purchase terms, warranties, and guarantees. A firm might change its hours of operation—for example, a supermarket might offer service 24 hours a day—to call attention to itself. Firms can also use location to differentiate their products. A firm may locate where traffic is heavy and the cost to the consumer of making a trip to the firm is minimal. If location is used for differentiation, however, why do fast-food restaurants tend to group together? Where you find a McDonald's you usually find a Taco Bell or a Wendy's nearby. The model of monopolistic competition explains this behavior. Suppose that five identical consumers— A, B, C, D, and E—are spread out along a line as shown in Figure 5. Consumer C is the median consumer, residing equidistantly from consumers B and D and equidistantly from consumers A and E. Assume that the five consumers care about the costs incurred in getting to a fast-food restaurant and are indifferent between the food offered. McDonald's is the first fast-food provider to open near these five consumers. Where does it locate? It locates as close to consumer C as possible because that location minimizes the total distance of all five consumers from McDonald's.

Taco Bell wants to open in the same area. If it locates near consumer D, then Taco Bell will pull customers D and E from McDonald's but will have no chance to attract A, B, or C. Conversely, if it locates near consumer

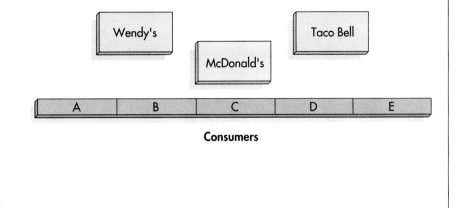

Figure 5
Location Under Monopolistic Competition
Five customers—A, B, C, D, and E—reside along a straight line. C is in the middle, equidistant from B and D and from A and E. McDonald's decides to locate a restaurant at the spot that is closest to all five customers. This is the median position, where consumer C resides. Other fast-food firms locate nearby because any other location will increase the total distance of some consumers from the fast-food restaurant, thereby causing some customers to go elsewhere.

A, only A will go to Taco Bell. Only if Taco Bell locates next door to McDonald's will it have a chance to gather a larger market share than McDonald's. As other fast-food firms enter, they too will locate close to McDonald's.

A prediction that comes from the theory of monopolistic competition is that an innovation or successful differentiation in any area—style, quality, location—leads initially to above-normal profit but eventually brings in copycats that drive profit back down to the normal level. In a monopolistically competitive market structure, innovation and above-normal profit for one firm are followed by entry and normal profit. Differentiation and above-normal profit then occur again. They induce entry, which again drives profit back to the normal level. The cycle continues until product differentiation no longer brings above-normal profit.

RECAP

1. The market structure called *monopolistic competition* is an industry in which many sellers produce a differentiated product and entry is easy.

2. In the short run, a firm in monopolistic competition can earn above-normal profit.

3. In the long run, a firm in a monopolistically competitive market structure will produce at a higher cost and lower output than will a firm in a perfectly competitive market structure. In both market structures, firms earn only a normal profit.

4. Monopolistic competitors may engage more in nonprice competition than in price differentiation.

2. OLIGOPOLY AND INTERDEPENDENCE

What is oligopoly?

Oligopoly is a market structure characterized by (1) few firms, (2) either standardized or differentiated products, and (3) difficult entry. Oligopoly may take many forms. It may consist of one dominant firm coexisting with many smaller firms or a group of giant firms (two or more) that dominate the industry coexisting with other small firms. Whatever the number of firms, the characteristic that describes oligopoly is *interdependence*; an individual firm in an oligopoly does not decide what to do without considering what the other firms in the industry will do. When a large firm in an oligopoly changes its behavior, the demand curves of the other firms are affected significantly.

In monopolistically competitive and perfectly competitive markets, what one firm does affects each of the other firms so slightly that each firm essentially ignores the others. Each firm in an oligopoly, however, must closely watch the actions of the other firms because the action of one can dramatically affect the others. This interdependence among firms leads to actions not found in the other market structures, such as advertising campaigns directed toward a specific rival, cartels and collusion, cost-plus pricing, most-favored-customer pricing, and other behaviors.

2.a. Oligopoly and Strategic Behavior

In what form does rivalry occur in an oligopoly?

Oligopolies are interdependent; each firm in an oligopoly takes into account and reacts to what its rivals are doing. Anything can and does occur under oligopoly. Rivalry is very intense in some cases; in others, means have been devised to live and let live. Because of the great variety of behavior possible under oligopoly, economists have been unable to agree on a single description of how oligopolistic firms behave. The only uniform description of the behavior of oligopolistic firms is *strategic*.

In the United States, the airline industry is best characterized as an oligopoly. There are few firms offering a similar service; each firm must take into account the actions of the other firms when setting fares, routes, and other aspects of the service. In many nations, the airline industry is either a government enterprise or is regulated by the government. For instance, China allows only selected airlines to land in its territory. Dragonair and China Southwest are two airlines serving China. All airlines or airline leasing companies purchase their planes from just a few manufacturers—Boeing, McDonnell Douglas, or the French-British combination known as Airbus. Thus the airline manufacturing industry is also an oligopoly.

strategic behavior:
the behavior that occurs when
what is best for A depends on
what B does, and what is best
for B depends on what A does

game theory:
a description of oligopolistic
behavior as a series of strategic
moves and countermoves

*Game theory can illustrate ways
in which oligopolistic firms interact. Game theory considers each
firm a participant in a game
where the winners are the firms
with the greatest profit.*

Strategic behavior occurs when what is best for A depends on what B does and what is best for B depends on what A does. It is much like a card game—bridge, say—where strategies are designed depending on the cards the players are dealt. Underbidding, overbidding, bluffing, deceit, and other strategies are carried out. In fact, the analogy between games and firm behavior in oligopoly is so strong that economists have applied **game theory** to their analyses of oligopoly. Game theory, developed in the 1940s by John von Neumann and Oskar Morgenstern, describes oligopolistic behavior as a series of strategic moves and countermoves. In this section we briefly discuss some of the theories of oligopolistic behavior.

2.a.1. The Kinked Demand Curve All firms know the law of demand. Thus, they know that sales will rise if price is lowered because people will purchase more of all goods (the income effect) and will substitute away from the more expensive goods to purchase more of the less expensive goods (the substitution effect). But the firms in an oligopoly may not know the shape of the demand curve for their product because the shape depends on how the rivals react to one another. They have to predict how their competitors will respond to a price change in order to know what their demand curve looks like.

Let's consider the auto industry. Suppose General Motors' costs have fallen (its marginal-cost curve has shifted down) and the company is deciding whether to lower the prices on its cars. If GM did not have to consider how the other car companies would respond, it would simply lower the price in order to be sure that the new MC curve intersected the MR curve, as illustrated in Figure 6(a). But GM suspects that the demand and marginal-revenue curves in Figure 6(a) do not represent its true market situation. GM believes that if it lowers the prices on its cars from their current level of P_1, the other auto companies will follow suit. If they also lower the price on their cars, the substitution effect for the GM cars does not occur; sales of GM cars might increase a little but only because of the income effect. In other words, GM does not capture the market as indicated in Figure 6(b) by D_1 but instead finds the quantity demanded increasing along D_2 (below price P_1). GM also suspects that should it increase the price of its cars, none of the other auto companies would raise theirs. In this case, the price increase would mean substantially reduced sales because of both the income and substitution effects. The quantity demanded decreases, as indicated along D_1. Consequently, the demand curve for GM is a combination of D_1 and D_2. It is D_1 above P_1 and D_2 below P_1, a demand curve with a *kink*.

What should GM do? It should price where $MR = MC$. But the resulting marginal-revenue curve is given by a combination of MR_1 and MR_2. MR_1 slopes down gently until reaching the quantity associated with the kink. As we move below the kink, MR_2 becomes the appropriate marginal-revenue curve. Thus, the shaded portions of the two marginal-revenue curves combine to give the firm's marginal-revenue curve. Notice how GM's marginal-cost curves, MC_1 and MC_2, intersect the combined MR curves at the same price and quantity, P_1 and Q_1. Thus, GM's strategy is to do nothing: *not* to change price even though costs have changed.

The firms in an oligopoly might avoid price competition altogether and devote resources to nonprice competition. Even with nonprice competition, however, strategic behavior comes into play, as noted in the next section.

Figure 6
The Kinked Demand Curve

If competitors follow price changes, the demand curve faced by an oligopolistic firm is the curve D_1 in Figures 7(a) and 7(b). If competitors do not follow price changes, the demand curve faced by the firm is D_2 in 7(b). If competitors match price decreases but not price increases, then the firm faces a combination of the two demand curves. If competitors do not follow a price increase, then above the current price, P_1, the relevant demand curve is D_1. If competitors do follow a price decrease, then below price P_1 the relevant demand curve is D_2. The demand curve is the shaded combinations of the two demand curves; it has a kink at the current price. The resulting marginal-revenue curve is also a combination of the two marginal-revenue curves. The marginal-revenue curve is MR_1 to the left of the kink in the demand curve and MR_2 to the right of the kink. Between the two marginal-revenue curves is a gap. The firm produces where $MR = MC$. If the MC curve intersects the MR curve in the gap, the resulting price is P_1 and the resulting quantity produced is Q_1. If costs fall, as represented by a downward shift of MC_1 to MC_2, the price and quantity produced do not change.

(a) Competitors Follow Price Changes

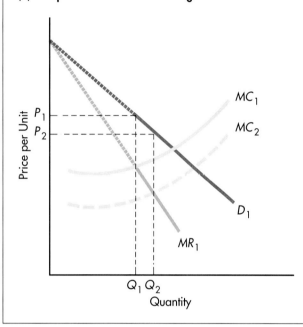

(b) Competitors Do Not Follow Price Changes

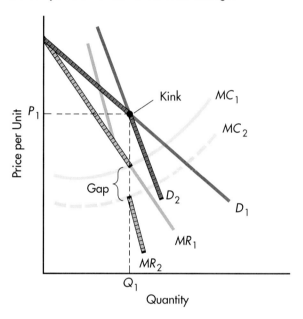

2.a.2. **Dominant Strategy** Consider the situation where firms must decide whether to devote more resources to advertising. When a firm in any given industry advertises its product, its demand increases for two reasons. First, people who had not used that type of product before learn about it, and some will buy it. Second, other people who already consume a different brand of the same product may switch brands. The first effect boosts sales for the industry as a whole, while the second redistributes existing sales within the industry.

Consider the cigarette industry as an example and assume that the matrix in Figure 7 illustrates the possible actions that two firms might undertake and the results of those actions. The top left rectangle represents the payoffs, or results, if both A and B advertise; the bottom left is where A advertises but B does not; the top right is the payoffs when B advertises but A does not; and the bottom right is the payoffs if neither advertises. If firm A can earn higher profits by advertising than by not advertising, whether or not firm B adver-

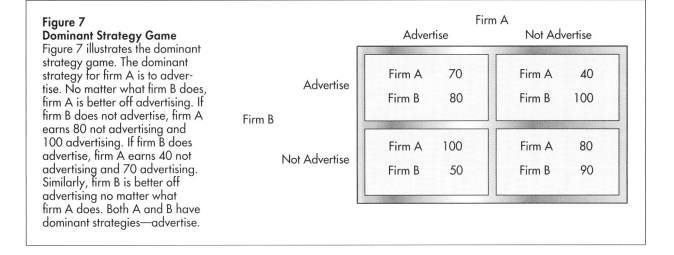

Figure 7
Dominant Strategy Game
Figure 7 illustrates the dominant strategy game. The dominant strategy for firm A is to advertise. No matter what firm B does, firm A is better off advertising. If firm B does not advertise, firm A earns 80 not advertising and 100 advertising. If firm B does advertise, firm A earns 40 not advertising and 70 advertising. Similarly, firm B is better off advertising no matter what firm A does. Both A and B have dominant strategies—advertise.

dominant strategy:
a strategy that produces better results no matter what strategy the opposing firm follows

tises, then firm A will surely advertise. This is referred to as a **dominant strategy**—a strategy that produces the best results no matter what strategy the opposing player follows. Firm A compares the left side of the matrix to the right side and sees that it earns more by advertising no matter what firm B does. If B advertises and A advertises, then A earns 70, but if A does not advertise it earns 40. If B does not advertise, then A earns 100 by advertising and only 80 by not advertising. The dominant strategy for firm A is to advertise. And according to Figure 7, the dominant strategy for firm B also is to advertise. Firm B will earn 80 by advertising and 50 by not advertising if A advertises. Firm B will earn 100 advertising, but only 90 not advertising if A does not advertise. But notice that both firms would be better off if neither advertised; firm A would earn 80 instead of 70, and firm B would earn 90 instead of 80. Yet, the firms cannot afford to *not* advertise because they would lose more if the other firm advertised and they didn't. This situation is known as the prisoner's dilemma; see the Economic Insight "The Prisoner's Dilemma" for a more complete description.

None of the cigarette manufacturers wants to do much advertising, for example. Yet strategic behavior suggests that they must. Firm A advertises, so firm B does also. Each ups the advertising ante. How can this expensive advertising competition be controlled? Each firm alone has no incentive to do it, since unilateral action will mean a significant loss of market share. But if they can ban advertising together, or if the government passes a law banning cigarette advertising, all of the cigarette companies will be better off. In fact, a ban on cigarette advertising on television has been in effect since January 1, 1971. The ban was intended by the government as a means of reducing cigarette smoking—of helping the consumer. Yet who does this ban really benefit?

2.a.3. Nondominant Strategy There are many situations in which not every firm has a dominant strategy. Suppose that the payoffs for the two cigarette firms are such that firm A is better off advertising no matter what firm B does, but firm B is better off advertising only if firm A advertises. Then, in contrast to the prisoner's dilemma, the best strategy for firm B depends on

The Prisoner's Dilemma

Strategic behavior characterizes oligopoly. Perhaps the most well-known example of strategic behavior occurs in what is called the prisoner's dilemma.

Two people have been arrested for a crime, but the evidence against them is weak. The sheriff keeps the prisoners separated and offers each a special deal. If one prisoner confesses, that prisoner can go free as long as only he confesses, and the other prisoner will get ten or more years in prison. If both prisoners confess, each will receive a reduced sentence of two years in jail. The prisoners know that if neither confesses, they will be cleared of all but a minor charge and will serve only two days in jail. The problem is they do not know what deal the other is offered or if the other will take the deal.

The options available to the two prisoners are shown in the four cells of the figure. Prisoner B's options are shown along the horizontal direction and prisoner A's along the vertical direction. In the upper left cell is the result if both

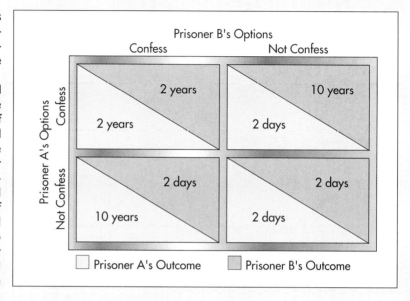

prisoners confess. In the lower left is the result if prisoner A does not confess but prisoner B does; in the upper right cell is the result of A confessing but prisoner B not confessing; and in the lower right cell is the result when neither prisoner confesses. The dominant strategy for both prisoners is to confess and to receive two years of jail time.

If the prisoners had been loyal to each other, each would have received a much smaller penalty. Because both chose to confess, each is worse off than would have been the case if each had known what the other was doing. Yet, in the context of the interdependence of the decisions, each made the best choice.

the particular strategy chosen by firm A. Firm B does not have a dominant strategy.

Suppose the options to both firms are as illustrated in Figure 8 rather than Figure 7. Firm B chooses to advertise if firm A advertises (80 versus 60) and chooses not to advertise if firm A does not advertise (60 versus 50). Even though firm B does not have a dominant strategy, we can indicate what is likely to happen. Firm B is able to predict that firm A will advertise because that is a dominant strategy for firm A. Since firm B knows this, it knows that its own best strategy is also to advertise.

2.a.4. Sequential Games The strategic situations we have considered so far have been ones in which both players must pick their strategies simultaneously. Each player had to choose a strategy knowing only the incentives facing the opponent, not the opponent's actual choice of strategy. But in many

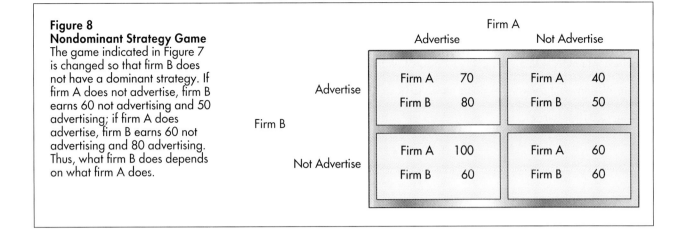

Figure 8
Nondominant Strategy Game
The game indicated in Figure 7 is changed so that firm B does not have a dominant strategy. If firm A does not advertise, firm B earns 60 not advertising and 50 advertising; if firm A does advertise, firm B earns 60 not advertising and 80 advertising. Thus, what firm B does depends on what firm A does.

sequential game:
a situation in which one firm moves first and then the other is able to choose a strategy based on the first firm's choice

situations, one firm moves first, and the other is then able to choose a strategy based on the first firm's choice; this is known as a **sequential game**.

For years Volvo has been known as the safest automobile on the road. This status enables Volvo to command significantly higher prices than otherwise similar automobiles can get. Now suppose that Chrysler is considering whether to build an even safer car. Chrysler knows that the firm known for producing the safest car will be able to earn a large profit but also fears the consequences if Volvo counters by building an even safer car.

Suppose that the situation facing Volvo and Chrysler is as illustrated in Figure 9. Both firms start at point A, where Chrysler must decide whether to enter with a car safer than those Volvo produces. If it does not, Volvo will receive a payoff of 120 and Chrysler a payoff of 0, as noted by point C. If Chrysler enters, however, they move to point B, where Volvo must decide whether to build an even safer car. The payoff to Volvo for building the even safer car is 50, but if Volvo does not build the safer car, its payoff will be 60. Volvo does not want Chrysler to enter, but Chrysler knows the payoffs facing Volvo and can conclude that the best option open to Volvo is not to produce the safer car. Thus, Chrysler builds the safer car and Volvo does not counter.

2.b. Cooperation

Why does cooperation among rivals occur most often in oligopolies?

If the firms in an oligopoly could come to some cooperative agreement, they could all be better off. For instance, Volvo and Chrysler might spend no additional money and agree to share the market; the cigarette companies, discussed with Figures 7 and 8, might agree not to advertise. In each of these cases, the firms would earn greater profits. Cooperation is an integral part of oligopoly because there are only a few firms. The firms can communicate easier than the many firms in a perfectly competitive or monopolistically competitive industry.

2.b.1. **Price-Leadership Oligopoly** One way for firms to communicate is to allow one firm to be the leader in changes in price or advertising activities. Once the leader makes a change, the others duplicate what the leader does.

Figure 9
Sequential Game
The game starts at point A, where Chrysler must decide whether to enter with a safer car. If it does not, Volvo will receive a payoff of 120, Chrysler a payoff of 0. If Chrysler enters, however, the game moves to point B, where Volvo must decide whether to build an even safer car. Suppose that if Volvo builds the safer car, its payoff will be 50 while Chrysler will earn a payoff of −50, and that if Volvo does not build the safer car, its payoff will be 60 while Chrysler will get a payoff of 60. Chrysler knows the payoffs facing Volvo and concludes that the best option open to Volvo is not to produce the safer car.

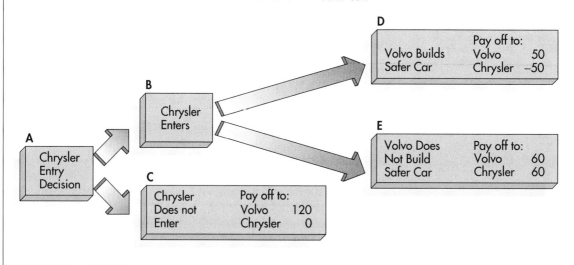

This action enables all firms to know exactly what the rivals will do. It eliminates a kink in the demand curve because both price increases and price decreases will be followed, and it avoids the situation where excessive expenses are made on advertising or other activities. This type of oligopoly is called a *price-leadership oligopoly.*

The steel industry in the 1960s is an example of a dominant-firm price-leadership oligopoly. For many years, steel producers allowed United States Steel to set prices for the entire industry. The cooperation of the steel companies probably led to higher profits than would have occurred with rivalry. However, the absence of rivalry is said to be one reason for the decline of the steel industry in the United States. Price leadership removed the need for the firms to compete by maintaining and upgrading equipment and materials and by developing new technologies. As a result, foreign firms that chose not to behave as price followers emerged as more sophisticated producers of steel than U.S. firms.

For many years airlines also relied on a price leader. In many cases the price leader in the airlines was not the dominant airline, but instead one of the weaker or new airlines. In recent years, airlines have communicated less through a price leader and more through their computerized reservation system, according to the Justice Department.

2.b.2. Collusion, Cartels, and Other Cooperative Mechanisms Acting jointly allows firms to earn more profits than if they act independently or against each other. To avoid the destruction of strategic behavior, the few firms in an oligopoly can collude, or come to some agreement about price and output levels. Typically these agreements provide the members of the oligopoly higher profits and thus raise prices to consumers. Collusion, which leads to secret cooperative agreements, is illegal in the United States, although it is acceptable in many other nations.

A **cartel** is an organization of independent firms whose purpose is to control and limit production and maintain or increase prices and profits. A cartel can result from either formal or informal agreement among members. Like collusion, cartels are illegal in the United States. The cartel most people are familiar with is the Organization of Petroleum Exporting Countries (OPEC), a group of nations rather than a group of independent firms. During the 1970s, OPEC was able to coordinate oil production in such as way that it drove the market price of crude oil from $1.10 a barrel to $32 a barrel. For nearly eight years, each member of OPEC agreed to produce a certain, limited amount of crude oil as designated by the OPEC production committee. Then in the early 1980s, the cartel began to fall apart as individual members began to cheat on the agreement. Members began to produce more than their allocation in an attempt to increase profit. As each member of the cartel did this, the price of oil fell, reaching $12 per barrel in 1988. Oil prices rose again in 1990 when Iraq invaded Kuwait, causing widespread damage to Kuwait's oil fields. But, as repairs have been made to Kuwait's oil wells, it has increased production and oil prices have dropped.

Production quotas are not easy to maintain among different firms or different nations. Most cartels do not last very long because the members chisel on the agreements. If each producer thinks that it can increase its own production, and thus its profits, without affecting what the other producers do, all producers end up producing more than their assigned amounts; the price of the product declines and the cartel falls apart.

Economists have identified certain conditions that make it likely that a cartel will be stable. A cartel is likely to remain in force when

- there are few firms in the industry
- there are significant barriers to entry
- an identical product is produced
- there are few opportunities to keep actions secret
- there are no legal barriers to sharing agreements

The fact that sharing is possible, however, does not mean that successful sharing will occur. The incentive to cheat remains. There must be an ability to punish the cheaters if a cartel is to stick together. Typically a central authority or a dominant member of the cartel will enforce the rules of the cartel. In OPEC, the enforcer has been Saudi Arabia because it has the greatest supply of oil. In other cartels, a governing board acts as the enforcer. Even though cartels are illegal in the United States, a few have been sanctioned by the government. The National Collegiate Athletic Association (NCAA) is a cartel of colleges and universities. It sets rules of behavior and enforces those rules through a governing board. Member schools are placed on probation or their programs are dismantled when they violate the agreement. The citrus cartel, composed of citrus growers in California and Arizona, enforces its actions through its governing board. Sunkist Growers Inc., a cooperative of many growers, represents more than half of the

cartel:
an organization of independent firms whose purpose is to control and limit production and maintain or increase prices and profits

California and Arizona production and also plays an important role in enforcing the rules of the cartel.

2.b.3. Facilitating Practices

Actions by firms can contribute to cooperation and collusion even though the firms do not formally agree to cooperate. Such actions are called **facilitating practices**. Pricing policies can leave the impression that firms are explicitly fixing prices, or cooperating, when in fact they are merely following the same strategies. For instance, the use of **cost-plus/markup pricing** tends to bring about similar if not identical pricing behavior among rival firms. If firms set prices by determining the average cost of an item and adding a 50 percent markup to the cost they would be cost-plus pricing. If all firms face the same cost curves, then all firms will set the same prices. If costs decrease, then all firms will lower prices the same amount and at virtually the same time. Such pricing behavior is common in the grocery business.

Another practice that leads to implicit cooperation is the most-favored-customer policy. Often the time between purchase and delivery of a product is quite long. To avoid the possibility that customer A purchases a product at one price and then learns that customer B purchased the product at a lower price or benefited from product features unavailable to customer A, a producer will guarantee that customer A will receive the lowest price and all features for a certain period of time. Customer A is thus a **most-favored customer (MFC)**.

The most-favored-customer policy actually gives firms an incentive not to lower prices even in the face of reduced demand. A firm that lowers the price of its product must then give rebates to all most-favored customers, which forces all other firms with most-favored-customer policies to do the same. In addition, the MFC allows a firm to collect information on what its rivals are doing. Customers will return products for a rebate when another firm offers the same product for a lower price.

Consider the behavior of firms that produced antiknock additives for gasoline from 1974 to 1979. Lead-based antiknock compounds had been used in the refining of gasoline since the 1920s. From the 1920s until 1948, the Ethyl Corporation was the sole domestic producer of the compounds. In 1948, Du Pont entered the industry. PPG Industries followed in 1961, and Nalco in 1964. Beginning in 1973, the demand for lead-based antiknock compounds decreased dramatically. However, because each company had most-favored-customer clauses, high prices were maintained even as demand for the product declined.

A most-favored-customer policy discourages price decreases because it requires producers to lower prices retroactively with rebates. If all rivals provide all buyers with most-favored-customer clauses, a high price is likely to be stabilized in the industry.

facilitating practices:
actions by oligopolistic firms that can contribute to cooperation and collusion even though the firms do not formally agree to cooperate

cost-plus/markup pricing:
a pricing policy that leads to similar if not identical pricing behavior among rival firms

most-favored customer (MFC):
a customer who receives a guarantee of the lowest price and all product features for a certain period of time

RECAP

1. Oligopoly is a market structure in which there are so few firms that each must take into account what the others do, entry is difficult, and either undifferentiated or differentiated products are produced.

2. Interdependence and strategic behavior characterize an oligopolistic firm.

3. The shape of the demand curve and the marginal-revenue curve facing an oligopolist depends on how rival firms react to changes in price and product.

4. The kinked demand curve is one example of how oligopolistic firms might react to price changes. The kink occurs because rivals follow price cuts but not price increases.

5. Game theory provides a convenient way to describe behavior by oligopolistic firms. Such behavior includes the dominant strategy, as represented by the prisoner's dilemma; the nondominant strategy; and sequential decision-making. In all of these games, the importance of the interdependence of firms is clear.

6. In a price-leadership oligopoly, one firm determines the price and quantity, knowing that all other firms will follow suit. The price leader is usually the dominant firm in the industry.

7. Oligopolistic firms have incentives to cooperate. Collusion, making a secret cooperative agreement, is illegal in the United States. Cartels, also illegal in the United States, rest on explicit cooperation achieved through formal agreement.

8. Facilitating practices implicitly encourage cooperation in an industry.

3. SUMMARY OF MARKET STRUCTURES AND THE INFORMATION ASSUMPTION

We have now discussed in some detail each of the four market structures. Table 2 summarizes the characteristics and the main predictions yielded by each model. The model of perfect competition predicts that firms will produce at a point where price and marginal cost are the same (at the bottom of the average-total-cost curve) and profit will be zero in the long run. The model of monopoly predicts that price will exceed marginal cost and that the firm can earn positive economic profit in the long run. With monopolistic competition, price will exceed marginal cost and the firm will not produce at the bottom point of the average-total-cost curve, but this is due to the consumer's desire for product differentiation. In the long run, the firm in monopolistic competition will earn a normal profit. In oligopoly, a firm may be able to earn above-normal profit for a long time—as long as entry can be restricted. In oligopoly, price exceeds marginal cost, and the firm does not operate at the bottom of the average-total-cost curve.

Under perfect competition, consumers purchase products at the lowest possible price; there is no advertising, no excessive overhead, and no warranties or guarantees. Under monopoly, people purchase a single product and advertising is virtually nonexistent. With monopolistic competition and oligopoly, advertising may occur but it provides information only. Consumers purchase different products because the products are, in fact, physically different, not because of images, feelings, or seeing some famous person endorse the product. Why, then, do we see and hear "image advertising" if the models do not

TABLE 2
Summary of Perfect Competition, Monopoly, Monopolistic Competition, and Oligopoly

	Perfect Competition	*Monopoly*	*Monopolistic Competition*	*Oligopoly*
Number of Firms	Many	One	Many	Few
Type of Product	Undifferentiated	One	Differentiated	Undifferentiated or differentiated
Entry Conditions	Easy	Difficult or impossible	Easy	Difficult
Demand Curve for Firm	Horizontal (perfectly elastic)	Downward-sloping	Downward-sloping	Downward-sloping
Price and Marginal Cost	$MC = P$	$MC < P$	$MC < P$	$MC < P$
Long-run Profit	Zero	Yes	Zero	Depends on whether entry occurs

account for it? Remember that a model is a simplification of reality. A model allows us to focus on one or more real-life aspects without getting bogged down in the details. Then, as we need to consider more or different aspects, we relax some of the assumptions of our model. The assumption we must relax now is the assumption that consumers and firms have perfect information.

Since information is costly to acquire, consumers and firms will not have complete or perfect information. This means that consumers will have to make decisions using incomplete information (as discussed in the chapter on consumer behavior), and firms will have to ensure that consumers have information that will benefit the firms.

3.a. Brand Names

A firm can provide information to consumers by creating brand names. A brand name is a product that consumers associate with a specific firm: Vidal Sassoon hair care products, Guess clothes, Bayer aspirin, McDonald's, and Nike, rather than the names shampoo, jeans, aspirin, fast food, and athletic shoes. If consumers had perfect information, producers would have no incentive to create brand names or to differentiate products other than by actual physical characteristics. Brand names can thus serve as *signals*—indications of the quality of the product or of the firm producing and selling the product.

Consider the case of sidewalk vendors who sell neckties on the streets of any large city. If such a "firm" tells customers that it will guarantee the quality of its ties, customers will certainly question the validity of the guarantee since if the firm decides to go out of business, it can do so with virtually no losses. It has no headquarters, no brand name, no costly capital equipment, no loyal customers to worry about—indeed, no sunk, or unrecoverable, costs of any kind. In short, a firm with no obvious stake in the future has a difficult time persuading potential customers it will make good on its promises.

The incentives are different for a firm that has devoted significant resources to items that have no liquidation value, such as advertising campaigns or specific capital expenditures like McDonald's golden arches. Firms such as these have reputations to protect and want repeat business. And buyers, knowing that, can place greater trust in the promise of a high-quality product.

Businesses, then, purchase advertising time and space on television, on radio, and in the newspapers. They construct elaborate signs, build fancy storefronts, and attempt to locate in places where they are visible and accessible. They also package their products in carefully designed boxes and wrappings. All of these expenditures are intended to convince people that their products, identified by brand names, are quality products.

Consumers are often willing to pay a higher price for a brand-name product than for a similar product without a brand name. Consumers who purchase brand-name pharmaceuticals because they believe the brand name has some value may be right even if a brand-name pharmaceutical and a generic product are chemically identical. Drug companies that spend a great deal of money to create brand names may be less likely to create shoddy or dangerous products than firms that do not offer brand names. In the early 1990s, when President Clinton was describing the cause of high health-care costs, he blamed the drug companies. Supporting his contention, a congressional study pointed out that drug firms spend $10 billion per year on marketing and advertising, $2 billion more than they spend on developing new drugs. But this expenditure may be what is necessary to provide the information consumers want—the sunk costs necessary to provide quality assurance to consumers.[1]

3.b. Guarantees

Another way to inform consumers of the quality of the product is to provide a guarantee against product defects. Guarantees are difficult to fake. A low-quality product would break down frequently, making the guarantee quite costly for the firm. Thus, the higher the quality of the product, the better the guarantee offered by the firm.

Once the highest-quality product appears with its guarantee, consumers have some information about the quality of that product—and also about the quality of all remaining products. They know that products without guarantees are not of the highest quality. Without other information about a product that has no guarantee, consumers might assume the quality of that product to be no better than the average quality of all such products. This places the producer of the second-best product in a difficult position. If it continues to offer no guarantee, consumers will think its product is worse than it really is, but its guarantee cannot match that of the highest-quality product. Thus, the producer of the second-best product must offer a guarantee of its own, but the terms of its guarantee cannot be quite as good as those for the best product.

---

[1]Constance Sommer, "Drug Firms' 'Excess Profit': $2 Billion Yearly," *Los Angeles Times,* Feb. 26, 1993.

With the introduction of the guarantee on the highest-quality product, the competitive process is set in motion and in the end all producers must either offer guarantees or live with the knowledge that consumers rank their products lower in quality. The terms of the guarantees will in general be less liberal the lower a product's quality. Producers clearly do not want to announce their low-quality levels by offering stingy warranty coverage, but failure to offer something makes consumers think the quality level is even lower than it is.

3.c. Adverse Selection

What occurs when the perfect information assumption is relaxed?

adverse selection:
the situation that occurs when higher-quality consumers or producers are driven out of the market because unobservable qualities are misvalued

When you purchase a used car, you are probably unsure of the car's quality. You could hire a mechanic to look at the car before you buy it, but because that procedure is quite expensive, you probably choose to forgo it. Most people assume that cars offered for sale by private individuals are defective in some way, and they are not willing to pay top dollar because they expect that the car will need expensive repairs. As a result, people who do have high-quality used cars for sale cannot obtain the high price they deserve.

Adverse selection occurs when unobservable qualities are misvalued because of a lack of information. The result of adverse selection is that low-quality consumers or producers drive higher-quality consumers or producers out of the market. People with high-quality used cars are most likely to trade their cars in to a dealer, leaving lower-quality used cars for sale by non-dealers.

Adverse selection occurs in many markets. Banks do not always know which people applying for loans will default and which will pay on time. How can a bank distinguish among loan applicants? If the bank increases the interest rate in an attempt to drive high-risk applicants out of the market, adverse selection increases. As the bank raises the interest rate on loans, high-risk applicants continue to apply for loans but high-quality applicants do not. As a result, only high-risk applicants remain in the market.

Adverse selection occurs in insurance markets as well. People purchase automobile or health insurance even if they are excellent drivers and enjoy good health. As the cost of insurance rises, the good drivers and healthy people might reduce their coverage while the poor drivers and unhealthy people maintain their coverage. As a result, high-risk applicants take the place of more desirable low-risk applicants in the market for insurance.

Adverse selection explains why loan companies require down payments, and why insurance companies require copayments or deductibles. Rather than increasing interest rates to eliminate high-risk applicants, a bank requests a higher down payment. Since only people who expect to pay off the loan and who have sufficient wealth or income to pay off the loan are willing to provide the down payment, adverse selection is reduced. Similarly, by requiring that a borrower provide collateral (a house or car or some other asset), a bank can separate high-risk from low-risk applicants. And an insurance company may require a policyholder to carry a deductible—the policyholder agrees to pay the first $300, say, of damage to his or her car. When an insurance company reduces the insurance charge and increases the deductible, good drivers and healthy people are more willing to purchase insurance, and poor drivers and less healthy people are less willing.

3.d. Moral Hazard

moral hazard:
when people alter their behavior from what was anticipated when a transaction was made

When information is costly to obtain, monitoring the behavior of the other party in an exchange may be difficult. When verification of trades or contracts is difficult and when people can change their behavior from what was anticipated when a trade or contract was made, a **moral hazard** exists.

People who discover that they have a serious illness and then purchase health insurance are taking advantage of the insurance company's lack of information and creating a moral hazard. A person who drives much less carefully after obtaining car insurance is creating a moral hazard. A person who takes less care to be healthy after obtaining health insurance is creating a moral hazard.

Sometimes moral hazard can be reduced when the person or firm creating the moral hazard and the person or firm being taken advantage of share in the costs. This is a reason insurance companies require a deductible, so that the company and the customer share in expenses and risks. You are more likely to drive carefully and safeguard your health if you have to pay some of the costs of an accident or illness.

Having seen some of the ways that relaxing the assumption of perfect information might alter firm and consumer behavior, we are now ready to apply our knowledge of product markets to real-world situations. We'll do this in a particular way in the next chapter: we'll take the perspective of the executive attempting to guide the firm to its most profitable activities.

RECAP

1. Brand names, guarantees, and sunk costs are ways firms can provide information to consumers.

2. Adverse selection occurs when low-quality consumers or producers force higher-quality consumers or producers out of the market.

3. Moral hazard exsits when people alter their behavior in an unanticipated way after an agreement or contract has been defined.

SUMMARY

▲▼ *What is monopolistic competition?*

1. Monopolistic competition is a market structure in which many firms are producing a slightly different product and entry is easy. §1

2. Monopolistically competitive firms will earn a normal profit in the long run. §1.a.2

▲▼ *What behavior is most common in monopolistic competition?*

3. Entry occurs in monopolistically competitive industries through the introduction of a slightly different product. §1.a

4. A monopolistically competitive firm will produce less output and charge a higher price than an identical perfectly competitive firm, if demand and costs are assumed to be the same. §1.b

▲▼ *What is oligopoly?*

5. Oligopoly is a market structure in which a few large firms produce identical or slightly different products and entry is difficult but not impossible. §2

▲▼ In what form does rivalry occur in an oligopoly?

6. Strategic behavior characterizes oligopoly. Each oligopolist must watch the actions of other oligopolists in the industry. §2.b

7. The kinked demand curve results when firms follow a price decrease but do not follow a price increase. §2.b.1

8. Strategic behavior can be illustrated using game theory. A dominant strategy is when the strategy that makes the firm best off does not depend on what rivals do. A nondominant strategy occurs when a firm's behavior or strategy varies, depending on what its rivals do. §2.b.2, 2.b.3

9. A sequential game illustrates the situation where one firm selects a strategy before another firm does. §2.b.4

▲▼ Why does cooperation among rivals occur most often in oligopolies?

10. The small number of firms in oligopoly and the interdependence of these firms creates the situation where the firms are better off if they cooperate (as in the prisoner's dilemma). §2.b.2, 2.c

11. Price leadership is another type of strategic behavior. One firm determines price for the entire industry. All other firms follow the leader in increasing and decreasing prices. The dominant firm in the industry is most likely to be the price leader. §2.c.1

12. Practices like collusion and cartels minimize profit-reducing rivalry and ensure cooperation. Both are illegal in the United States but acceptable in many other nations. §2.c.2

13. Cost-plus pricing ensures that firms with the same costs will charge the same prices. The most-favored-customer policy guarantees a customer that the price he or she paid for a product will not be lowered for another customer. Cost-plus pricing and the most-favored-customer policy are facilitating practices. §2.c.3

▲▼ What occurs when the perfect information assumption is relaxed?

14. Firms must ensure that consumers get information about the firm and its products that is beneficial. Brand names, guarantees, and certain (sunk cost) expenditures will indicate product quality. §3.a

15. Adverse selection and moral hazard create problems in situations of imperfect information. §3.c, 3.d

16. Adverse selection occurs when low-quality consumers or producers force higher-quality consumers or producers out of the market. §3.c

17. Moral hazard exists when people alter their behavior in an unanticipated way after an agreement or contract has been defined. §3.d

KEY TERMS

strategic behavior §2.b
game theory §2.b
dominant strategy §2.b.2
sequential game §2.b.4
cartel §2.c.2

facilitating practices §2.c.3
cost-plus/markup pricing §2.c.3
most-favored customer (MFC) §2.c.3
adverse selection §3.c
moral hazard §3.d

EXERCISES

1. Disney, Universal, and MGM, among others, have movie studios in Hollywood. Each of these major studios also has one or several subsidiary studios. Disney, for example, has Touchstone. What market structure best describes these movie production companies? Why would each studio have subsidiary studios? Consider the movies that have come out under Disney and those under Touchstone. Are they different?

2. Suppose that Disney was experiencing above-normal profits for its production of *Beauty and the Beast*, *Aladdin*, and *The Lion King*. If Disney was a member of a monopolistically competitive industry, what would you predict would occur over time to its demand curve (the demand curve for Disney movies)? Suppose that Disney was a member of an oligopoly. How would this change your answer?

3. Why is the monopolistically competitive industry said to be inefficient? Suppose that you counted the higher price the consumer pays for the monopolistically competitive firm's product as part of consumer surplus. Would that change the conclusion regarding the efficiency of monopolistic competition?

4. Why might some people claim that the breakfast cereal industry is monopolistically competitive but the automobile industry is an oligopoly? In both cases, about eight to ten firms dominate the industry.

5. The graph that follows shows an individual firm in long-run equilibrium. What market structure is this firm operating in? Explain. Compare the long-run quantity and price to those of a perfectly competitive firm. What accounts for the difference? Why, or why not? Is the equilibrium price greater than, equal to, or less than marginal cost?

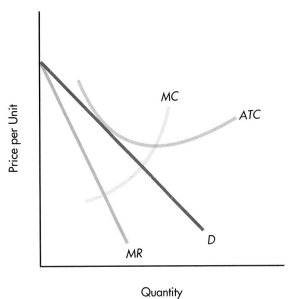

6. Explain what is meant by strategic behavior. How does the kinked demand curve describe strategic behavior?

7. What is the cost to a firm in an oligopoly that fails to take rivals' actions into account? Suppose the firm operates along demand curve D_1, shown below, as if no firms will follow its lead in price cuts or price rises. In fact, however, other firms do follow the price cuts and the true demand curve below price P_1 lies below D_1. If the firm sets a price lower than P_1, what happens?

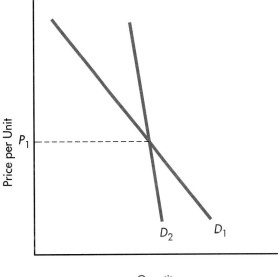

8. Suppose the following demand schedule exists for a firm in monopolistic competition. Suppose the marginal cost is a constant $70. How much will the firm produce? Is this a long- or short-run situation? Suppose the firm is earning above-normal profit. What will occur to this demand schedule?

Price	Quantity
100	1
95	2
88	3
80	4
70	5
55	6
40	7
22	8

9. The cement industry is an example of an undifferentiated oligopoly. The automobile industry is a differentiated oligopoly. Which of these two is most likely to advertise? Why?

10. The South American cocaine industry consists of several "families" who obtain the raw material, refine it, and distribute it to the United States. There are only about three large "families," but there are several small families. What market structure does the industry most closely resemble? What predictions based on the market-structure models can be made about the cocaine business? How do you explain the lack of wars among the families?

11. The NCAA is described as a cartel. In what way is it a cartel? What is the product being produced? How does the cartel stay together?

12. Almost every town has at least one funeral home even if the number of deaths could not possibly keep the funeral home busy. What market structure does the funeral home best exemplify? Use the firm's demand and cost curves and long-run equilibrium position to explain the fact that the funeral home can handle more business than it has. (*Hint*: Is the firm operating at the bottom of the average-total-cost curve?)

13. The payoff matrix below shows the profit two firms earn if both advertise, neither advertises, or one advertises while the other does not. Profits are reported in millions of dollars. Does either firm have a dominant strategy?

	Firm 1	
	Advertise	**Not Advertise**
Advertise	Firm 1 earns profit of 100 Firm 2 earns profit of 20	Firm 1 earns profit of 50 Firm 2 earns profit of 70
Firm 2		
Not Advertise	Firm 1 earns profit of 0 Firm 2 earns profit of 10	Firm 1 earns profit of 20 Firm 2 earns profit of 60

14. Using the payoff matrix below, answer the following questions. The payoff matrix indicates the profit outcome that corresponds to each firm's pricing strategy.

a. Firms A and B are members of an oligopoly.

		Firm A's Price	
		$20	**$15**
Firm B's Price	**$20**	Firm A earns $40 profit Firm B earns $37 profit	Firm A earns $35 profit Firm B earns $39 profit
	$15	Firm A earns $49 profit Firm B earns $30 profit	Firm A earns $38 profit Firm B earns $35 profit

Explain the interdependence that exists in oligopolies using the payoff matrix facing the two firms.

b. Assuming that the firms cooperate, what is the solution to the problem facing the firms?

c. Given your answer to b, explain why cooperation would be mutually beneficial.

d. Given your answer to c, explain why one of the firms might cheat on a cooperative arrangement.

15. What would occur if any maker of aspirin could put a Bayer Aspirin label on its product? Why must a signal between rivals be costly to fake and involve extensive sunk costs?

16. Several studies have shown that when brakes and headlights were first placed on cars, more accidents involving pedestrians occurred. Similarly, the use of seat belts and power-assisted and automatic braking systems have led to an increased incidence of pedestrian-automobile accidents. Explain how this is a moral hazard situation.

COOPERATIVE LEARNING EXERCISE

Part A: Divide the class in half—name one half A and the other half B. Each A is given a certain sum, say a hypothetical $10. Each A must then decide how much of that $10 to offer to a B. The As and the Bs do not know who is matched with whom; all an A knows is that some B will get the offer made by the A. If the offer is accepted, A gets to keep the money, as does the B who accepted the offer. If B rejects the offer, then both participants get zero. Thus, on a piece of paper, the As should indicate their offers. The pieces of paper are distributed one to each B. The Bs are to write on the paper either accept or reject. The offers and responses are then collected.

Part B: Now students are assigned to groups of three to five people. The groups are to count off, 1, 2, 3, etc. The odd-numbered groups are allocated $10. They are to decide how much of that $10 to offer an even-numbered group. The offers (one per group) are written on a piece of paper and passed out to the even-numbered groups. If the offer is accepted, both groups get to retain the money. If the offer is rejected, neither group gets anything.

Have the groups discuss the following:

Is there a difference between the individual behavior and the group behavior? What offers are rejected in each situation? Would it have made any difference if the Bs were completely anonymous—for example, students in another class? Why?

Repeat the exercise with $1,000.

How many of the offers were rejected? What size were the accepted offers? The rejected offers?

Chinese Develop Taste For Brand Names, Says Survey

Deng Xiaoping told fellow Chinese that it doesn't matter whether a cat is black or white as long as it catches mice. But for Chinese consumers, the shampoo should be Head & Shoulders, the television a Hitachi, and the family car a Toyota.

The first foreign-sponsored nation-wide survey of Chinese households, conducted by Gallup China, found that Playboy and Boeing are better known brand names than the British Broadcasting Corporation or American Express.

Gallup China is majority owned by The Gallup Organisation of Princeton, New Jersey, and claims to have been the first research company permitted by the Chinese government to carry out such a survey of consumer attitudes.

Asked to describe their personal philosophy, most respondents expressed a distinctly materialistic outlook, as 68 percent said their philosophy was "to work hard and get rich." By contrast, only 4 percent agreed with the worthy statement: "Never think of yourself, give everything in service to society."

The bicycle is still the most common consumer durable (owned by 81 percent of households) in China, while 54 percent of homes have black-and-white televisions and 40 percent have already bought a colour set. At the other end of the scale, only 9 percent of households have a telephone and 3 percent a car.

The survey highlighted the divide between urban and rural consumers. Nationally, 56 percent of households said they preferred to buy Chinese-made products while only 19 percent said they preferred foreign-made products, but the balance shifted marginally in favour of foreign products among upper-income households in urban areas.

Six of the 10 most highly recognized brands were Japanese, with Hitachi topping the list. Although several U.S. names were among the 20 most recognized brands, with Coca-Cola at number two, only one European company made its way into the top 20: Nestle, the Swiss food group, at number 16.

Source: "Chinese Develop Taste for Brand Names, Says Survey" by Richard Tomkins, *Financial Times*, Feb. 16, 1995, p. 1. Reprinted by permission.

Commentary

Does it matter whether a cat who can catch mice is black or white? Does it matter whether a television set has Hitachi or Mitsubishi on the label? Does it matter whether a soft drink is labeled Coca-Cola or Pepsi? It does. It does in the United States. It does in Europe. And, it does in China.

Brand names are important to consumers. Consumers rely on brand names to provide information about quality, service, taste, smell, color, and other aspects of the product. The Chinese consumers believe the Hitachi name on a television set indicates quality. Consumers know the taste of Coca-Cola and they do not want to be surprised each time they open a can of coke—they don't want it to be Pepsi, Dr. Pepper or 7-Up.

Brand names are important to businesses. A firm that establishes a brand name and brand loyalty has a lower price elasticity of demand than firms without that brand name. As a result, the profit potential is higher because the price can be raised without losing as much revenue as when the elasticity is higher.

Establishing brand names is a differentiation strategy in monopolistic competition and oligopoly. When does product differentiation work and when does it not? How does a firm know whether to focus on price or on product differentiation?

These questions are at the heart of competition within monopolistic competition and oligopoly. Under monopolistic competition, easy entry means many firms competing with close substitutes. The products are differentiated on the basis of marketing, packaging, placement, or even price. The firms would like differentiation to occur so they could reduce the price elasticity of demand. The firms must produce their product at the lowest possible cost and offer the product at the lowest possible price. Otherwise, another firm will enter and take away any above normal profit. When an advertising campaign adds to costs without an increase in revenues and profits, firms in monopolistic competition will give up the advertising campaign. Consumers will dictate whether a brand name is important to them; they will or will not purchase the product having a brand name with a slightly higher price.

Some might have anticipated that brand names would be unimportant for a society dominated by Confucianism—"never think of yourself, give everything in service to society." But, the Gallup poll sets the matter straight. Chinese consumers want to maximize their own happiness and that, for many, means they want certain products identified by brand name.

Under oligopoly, advertising may be used to increase product differentiation and reduce price elasticities of demand but also to create or enhance barriers to entry. An advertising campaign may enhance a brand name but its addition to costs may be desirable from the perspective of the oligopoly firm. Those increased costs may mean that any new entrant would have to spend at least an equal amount simply to begin competing with the existing firm.

The Gallup survey pointed out that the competition for the Chinese consumer has barely begun. Chinese living in rural areas still retained a strong preference for Chinese-made products while those in urban areas preferred foreign-made products. As foreign firms and foreign-made products become more prevalent in the Chinese market place, and Chinese consumers experience the different qualities offered by different products, the nationalistic preferences will decline and preferences for brands will rise. Consumers will not be able to indicate where most products are made.

Firms establishing a strong presence and brand name in China will have a profit advantage. Thus, as the Chinese restrictions on foreign suppliers is relaxed, we should expect a great deal of advertising and other approaches to brand name development. It will be interesting to watch.

27

Product Market Applications

FUNDAMENTAL QUESTIONS

1. How do the different market structures affect what a manager does?
2. What factors affecting a firm can a manager control, and what factors are external to the manager's control?
3. Why would a firm want to raise barriers to entry, and how could it erect barriers?
4. What does it mean to know your business?
5. What does it mean to "know your customer"?
6. Does a firm's strategy depend on cost?
7. Is there an advantage to a firm that is the first to carry out some action?
8. Should a firm care about market share?

A fter having worked their way through the cost curves and the four market structure models, many students ask, "What is the use of this stuff?" Economics professors hope that students will see how the material applies to the students lives and will use the logic of economics to think critically about all issues. But the material has more specific uses as well. In this chapter, we'll discuss how this subject matter—the market structures and costs—is useful to anyone contemplating starting a new business, to anyone planning to work for a major corporation, to a manager or chief executive officer who wishes to ensure that his or her company is profitable, and to the consultant—the management gurus quoted in the media such as Michael Porter (known for such books as *Competitive Advantage*), Tom Peters (known for *In Search of Excellence*), Michael Hammer and James Champy (known for their book *Reengineering the Corporation*), W. Edwards Deming (*Total Quality Management*), Peter Drucker (author of several management books), and C.K. Prahalad and Gary Hamel (known for their work on the

PREVIEW

core competencies of the firm). These consultants base their analyses on economics—and specifically on cost and market structure.

This chapter takes an approach based on **strategic management,** a management process that uses economic information to devise business strategies. The chapter presents the topics of cost and market structure in a way that could be useful to a manager trying to devise successful strategies for his or her firm.

1. MANAGERIAL DECISIONS AND MARKET STRUCTURES

strategic management:
using economics to devise strategies for firms

How do the different market structures affect what a manager does?

A manager of a perfectly competitive firm is at the mercy of the market.

Perhaps the most important aspect of beginning a new business or introducing a new product is to understand what market structure the product will be sold in. The market structure models are summarized in Table 1. As we discussed in the previous chapter, the main characteristics that differentiate the models are number of firms, how much control over price a firm has, whether product differentiation occurs, whether there are barriers to entry, and whether above-normal profit can occur.

We know that in perfect competition, the market structure where there are many firms producing an identical product and no barriers to entry, a firm is a price taker. The firm cannot influence the price at which it sells its product; there is no reason to devote resources to advertising or marketing of any kind. A chief executive officer, or manager, of a firm in this perfectly competitive

TABLE I
Market Structure Models

	Perfect Competition	Monopolistic Competition	Monopoly	Oligopoly
Number of firms	Many	Many	One	Few
Type of product	Undifferentiated	Differentiated	One	Undifferentiated or differentiated
Entry Conditions	Easy	Easy	Impossible	Difficult
Control over Price	None (price taker)	Yes, but limited because there are many substitutes	Total control	Yes, but depends on the actions of rivals
Long-Run Profit	Zero	Zero	Yes	Depends on entry

market is at the mercy of the market. When times are good, the manager experiences the positive aspects associated with increased sales. But when times are bad, the manager has no way to avoid the repercussions. As a manager, you would have to ensure that your costs are not higher than your competitor's costs and then simply respond to the market.

We also know that in an oligopoly, when there are only a few firms producing a single product or similar products, the manager of one of those firms must be concerned with what rival firms are doing. Interdependence is the byword in oligopoly. Each act a manager takes will result in a response by rivals. Lowering price as a competitive strategy is risky because rival firms are likely to match the lower price and induce a price war, causing all firms to lose profits. Raising price is also risky because if other firms don't also raise their price, losses may result. Because price is so important and changes in price virtually ensure strong responses from rivals, firms in oligopoly environments tend to focus on nonprice tactics as a competitive strategy and to behave so that they and their competitors don't get involved in price wars. The manager of a firm in an oligopoly selling environment will use all kinds of nonprice strategies—advertising, marketing, production, warranties, guarantees, and brand-name creation—to be successful.

A manager of an oligopolistic firm will use nonprice strategies to avoid price wars.

A manager of a monopolistically competitive firm focuses primarily on differentiation strategies.

Monopolistically competitive firms also focus on nonprice competition. These firms want to differentiate their product from those of rivals. The greater the differentiation, the fewer the close substitutes, the more freedom a manager has to alter price and increase profits.

In the oligopoly environment, a firm may earn above-normal profit as long as barriers to entry exist. There is no such possibility in the monopolistically competitive environment. Without barriers to entry, any time a firm attains an above-normal profit, others enter the business producing a similar product and drive profits down to the normal level.

If you manage a monopoly, you have no worries about close substitutes and the response of rivals. The only rivals you might have are potential rivals—firms that might arise in the future to offer a related or similar product. Your greatest incentive is to maintain your monopoly. If you are successful, you can earn above-normal profits for a significant period of time. And you would be willing to devote most of that above-normal profit to ensuring that you retained your monopoly.

Which type of firm would you rather manage? The perfectly competitive firm would not be much fun. A monopolistically competitive firm would be better but wouldn't yield the possible profits that oligopoly and monopoly could generate. Perhaps managing a monopoly would be the best; there, you don't have to worry about rivals, and strategies are not as important or potentially disastrous as is the case in an oligopoly. However, as much as we'd all like to be in charge of a monopoly, most businesses are not monopolies. This means that most executives must be concerned with both price and nonprice strategies.

I.a. Strategic Variables

strategic variables:
factors affecting a firm over which the manager has control

A manager of a firm selling in an oligopoly or monopolistically competitive environment has control over many aspects of the business—the price to set, the quantity to produce, and many of the costs. These are called **strategic variables**—they are the factors over which the manager has control. A manager uses these strategic variables to compete with rivals. He or she selects the price, and the demand curve then provides the quantity to produce. The manager also chooses the advertising expenditures and approaches, the packaging, promotions, placement, research and development, location, and the resources to acquire and employ, in order to maximize profits. All this is illustrated by the area in Figure 1 inside the triangle labeled "Rivalry Among Competitors."

I.b. External Factors

What factors affecting a firm can a manager control, and what factors are external to the manager's control?

Although most of a manager's efforts focus on the rivalry among competitors, this is not the only aspect of business with which he or she must be concerned. There are many other things that can influence the firm over which the manager has no control. These other factors are illustrated in Figure 1 by the arrows outside the triangle—economic conditions, the threat of new entrants and substitutes, and the power of customers and suppliers.

I.b.I. Economic Conditions Economic conditions can determine the success or failure of a firm, but they are mainly outside the control of the firm. For instance, in 1995, Louis Gerstner, Jr., the CEO of IBM, was attempting to revive the company just as several economies were struggling with recession and currency problems. Germany and Japan were emerging slowly from recession, and the Mexican peso had collapsed in value, raising the peso price of a dollar. The fall of the peso increased the cost of supplies shipped to Mexico for assembly by IBM subsidiaries. Gerstner had absolutely no way to control these events. Similarly, the booming U.S. economy was not something over which IBM had control. Although these external influences are not strategic variables to the firm, the demand and cost curves are affected by them. Perhaps the booming U.S. economy would shift the IBM demand curve out and/or the slow economies elsewhere would shift the demand curve in. Perhaps the decline of the value of the peso would reduce the profitability of Mexican subsidiaries. In other words, IBM could find its sales and profits rising or falling independent of any actions its management might take.

Economic developments must always be part of the analysis a manager undertakes, but they are not strategic variables. There are *strategic responses*

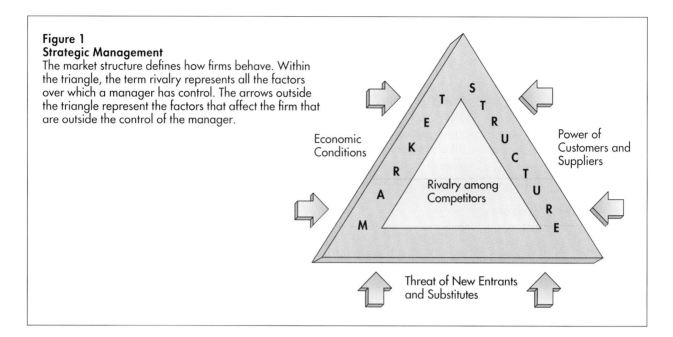

Figure 1
Strategic Management
The market structure defines how firms behave. Within the triangle, the term rivalry represents all the factors over which a manager has control. The arrows outside the triangle represent the factors that affect the firm that are outside the control of the manager.

Economic Conditions

Power of Customers and Suppliers

Rivalry among Competitors

Threat of New Entrants and Substitutes

Exchange rate fluctuations will affect a multinational firm.

to external factors, but the external factors themselves are not strategic variables. For instance, a firm can position its product with respect to income elasticities and can choose to be domestic or multinational, but it cannot control the economic conditions of the nation or nations in which it operates. A firm focusing on a high-income niche of the market would be expected to have a high income elasticity of demand—the demand for the firm's product would be sensitive to changes in income. A high income elasticity of demand means that sales would rise rapidly as the economy prospered but decline significantly during a recession. Many consumer electronics, when first introduced to the market, behave this way. Thus, new consumer electronic equipment might best be introduced when the economy is healthy and growing instead of during a recession. A firm might want to sell two or more products having different income elasticities to even out sales as income rises and falls over the business cycle.

Exchange rate changes can affect costs and sales if a firm sells in, or acquires resources from, other nations or competes with rivals from other nations. Because of the declining value of the dollar relative to the deutsche mark in the 1980s, for example, the German auto producer Mercedes-Benz established factories in the United States. Cars produced in Germany and sold in the United States cost more than cars produced in the United States and sold in the United States because of the rising value of the deutsche mark.

Another example of the effect of economic events on a firm is provided by the experience of the Caterpillar Tractor Company in the 1980s. For decades, Caterpillar was regarded as the leader in the world market for earthmoving equipment. As a result of its brand name and market domination, Caterpillar charged about 15 percent more than its rivals. In the early 1980s, the dollar became very strong relative to the Japanese yen (the dollar price of a yen fell). The result was that Komatsu, a Japanese firm competing with Caterpillar, was able to sell its products in the United States at prices that

Caterpillar found difficult to match. Caterpillar's sales fell by about 29 percent in 1982 as compared to 1981.

I.b.2. Threat of New Entrants and Substitutes The threat of competitors is also a factor that is external to the firm. Managers must constantly be aware of the possibility of new competitors—the threat of new entrants and new substitutes—and devise strategies to deal with them, but they have no direct control over competitors or potential competitors. They can only respond to actions or potential actions by these rivals. Existing airlines often have the prime gates and landing times at major airports reserved. A new airline must use secondary airports or land and take off at times that are not popular. Southwest Airlines entered the business by using destinations that the bigger carriers did not serve. Southwest entered with a no frills and low price package that other carriers have since tried to mimic.

I.b.3. Power of Customers and Suppliers Managers also have to assess and develop strategies to deal with or respond to the power of customers and suppliers. Firms often treat individual customers as price takers but, if the customers have grouped together into a single buyer, such as the American Association of Retired People (AARP), or if a firm is the supplier to another firm, such as software to Nintendo or bearings to automobile manufacturers, then the manager faces something like a monopoly buyer. (We'll discuss this subject in more detail in the chapters on resource markets.) A firm becomes a customer when it purchases supplies. Thus, a manager must be aware of the differences between purchasing from a monopolist or a perfect competitor. (Again, a topic we discuss in the chapters dealing with resource markets.) The manager often must decide whether to have the firm produce the supplies itself (own a supplier) or to purchase the supplies from independent suppliers.

Let's now consider each aspect of Figure 1 in sequence, and then we will consider a specific application to put it all together.

FedEx is the name of the world's largest express transport company. Federal Express, formed in 1971, has been so successful that when people think of overnight delivery they think FedEx. To insure that the term FedEx and the company, Federal Express, were forever linked, the company changed its name to FedEx in 1994. In recent years, FedEx has undertaken several strategies to increase the barriers to entry. It continues to emphasize its brand name through advertising and logos on its trucks and airplanes. It continues to expand worldwide—to more than 175 companies—and domestically. It bought 4,000 new trucks and spent $200 million on surface vehicles and 50 new airplanes in 1994–95. The expansion is an attempt to achieve economies of scale and impose high fixed costs on new entrants. FedEx also continues to computerize every aspect of its business. It placed its tracking scheme on the Internet so that individuals could track their own packages.

RECAP

1. One of the most important pieces of information for anyone contemplating starting a new business or introducing a new product is the market structure in which the new business will operate or the new product will be sold.

2. Strategic variables are those factors under the control of a manager. External factors such as economic conditions affect the firm but cannot be controlled by the firm.

3. Firms can be positioned so that they are not as susceptible to certain economic conditions. For instance, a high income elasticity of demand means that sales will increase significantly when the economy is booming and will drop considerably when the economy is mired in a recession. Thus, a firm might focus on the income elasticity of demand in determining when to introduce a new product or to introduce products with different income elasticities in order to even out sales over the business cycle.

4. Exchange rate changes can affect a firm through costs and sales.

5. New entrants, substitutes, and the power of customers and suppliers also affect a firm's success.

2. BARRIERS TO ENTRY

Why would a firm want to raise barriers to entry, and how could it erect barriers?

One of the crucial defining characteristics of market structure is whether there are barriers to entry. It is very important to assess the barriers to entry to a particular business, whether you are contemplating starting a new business or are a manager of an existing business. If there are only small barriers, then you know that any above-normal profits will be quickly competed away by entry. You also know that one strategy you should consider is to increase the barriers to entry that may exist. Sources of barriers to entry include:

- economies of scale and scope
- product differentiation
- capital requirements
- cost disadvantages independent of size
- access to distribution channels
- unique resources
- government policy

2.a. Economies of Scale and Scope

Economies of scale and scope may be a barrier to entry.

We have seen in previous chapters that the relationship between output and costs in the long run is defined by whether there are economies or diseconomies of scale. If economies of scale exist, a larger firm can produce a product at a lower per unit cost than can a smaller firm. (See the Economic Insight "Does Size Matter?" for a further discussion of this issue.) This means that a new entrant would have to enter as a big firm in order to achieve the economies of scale necessary to compete with existing firms.

In 1882, John D. Rockfeller's Standard Oil Company (the precursor of Exxon) dominated the production of kerosene. Kerosene was at that time the key product refined from crude oil and was by far America's largest nonfarm

Does Size Matter?

Large firms benefit from economies of scale. Small firms benefit from flexibility and speed of decision-making. Which is better, large or small firms? In the 1980s, management consultants believed that it was the small firm. Tom Peters, author of *In Search of Excellence,* argued that the experiences of IBM and General Motors in the early 1980s clearly showed that small firms were better than large ones. Small companies also seemed to be responsible for job creation. In 1984, David Birch, a lecturer at the Massachusetts Institute of Technology, claimed that small businesses created eight out of ten new jobs in the United States.

Recently, the tide has begun to turn for the large firm. IBM and Daimler-Benz may have run into trouble, but Coca-Cola, McDonald's, and Toyota have prospered. Sears Roebuck is losing market share to Wal-Mart, not to the thousands of small firms.

Small businesses are not the job creators they were thought to be. In the United States, plants with more than 100 employees accounted for three-quarters of new jobs created, and firms with more than 500 employees accounted for more than 50 percent.

Large firms are now finding that the flexibility of small firms is something they can copy. Large firms are contracting out many activities, allowing small firms to provide services that are peripheral to the core business of the large firm. Similarly, small firms are finding that they need the economies of scale larger firms have. More and more firms are creating alliances with other companies. In Silicon Valley, tiny software firms have developed partnerships with rivals so they can reap the benefits of economies of scale.

export. Standard Oil made 90 percent of all the kerosene produced in the United States. But when Russia's Caspian Sea oil fields were discovered and kerosene began to be shipped from there to the European market, Standard Oil feared that it would lose its huge domination in Europe. The company had to become more efficient. It did this by closing several small refineries and building three enormous new ones.

The huge scale of production in these new refineries led to impressive cost reductions. In 1880, plants with a 2,000-barrel-a-day capacity made kerosene for 2.5 cents a gallon. In 1885, with the new plants having a 6,000-barrel-a-day capacity, Standard Oil could make kerosene for less than half a penny per gallon. This allowed the company to price its kerosene in Europe below the Russian kerosene even though the American product had much higher shipping costs. As illustrated in Figure 2, with Standard Oil producing at the minimum efficient scale (*MES*), the price it set was below that of potential competitors that would enter at any size other than the *MES,* such as at $SRATC_1$.

In Germany at about the same time, three large chemical companies—Bayer, Hoechst, and BASF—were building huge dye-making factories. Prior to the construction of these large factories, each different dye had been produced in a separate small factory. The new plants were able to produce hundreds of different dyes using the same basic chemical stock. The result was a substantial reduction in costs. This was a case of cost cutting through **economies of scope**. Economies of scope occur when the cost of producing two or more products is less than the cost of producing either one alone. Figure 3 illustrates economies of scope: a lower per unit cost as the number of different products the firm manufactures or offers for sale rises. The *MES*

economies of scope:
a decline in the per unit cost of producing goods as the number of goods produced rises

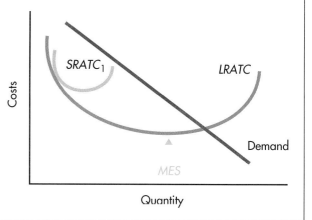

Figure 2
Economies of Scale
A firm that is operating at the *MES* point has a distinct advantage over any firm that attempts to enter the industry at a smaller size, such as at $SRATC_1$. The larger firm can set a price that cannot be matched by the smaller firm.

point in Figure 3 refers to the most efficient diversification point—the least cost per unit of production as the number of products manufactured increases.

In these examples, economies of scale and scope reduced costs dramatically. The cost advantages of scale and scope often give the companies that create them first an almost insurmountable competitive advantage. In some instances, the first company to build a plant of minimum efficient scale remains the industry leader for decades. Such was the case with Standard Oil.

2.b. Product Differentiation

Product differentiation can reduce the price elasticity of demand.

Firms attempt to convince consumers that their product is unique. If they are successful, the price elasticity of demand is reduced, allowing the firm to increase price without losing significant revenues. The more unique consumers perceive a product to be, the greater the price premium they are willing to pay and the less able new firms are to enter and take business away. As mentioned earlier, Caterpillar set its prices about 15 percent above its rivals.

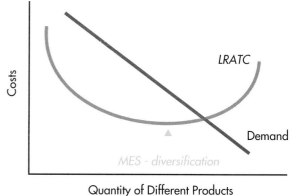

Figure 3
Economies of Scope
When a firm can produce two or more different goods at a lower price per unit than it can produce one good, the firm is experiencing economies of scope. If increasing the number of products produced increases costs per unit then diseconomies of scope occur. If economies of scope is followed by diseconomies of scope then the *LRATC* curve is U-shaped.

Kodak has also set the price of its film and other products about 10 to 15 percent above its rivals. In fact, most successful brands are priced some 10 to 15 percent higher than substitute products.

Mobil Oil embarked on a differentiation strategy to increase sales and profits at the retail level in 1995. Rather than continue with costly price wars at the gas pump, Mobil decided to offer cappuccino, a concierge, and a full convenience store at gas stations. If the company succeeds in creating brand loyalty, it can charge a couple of pennies more per gallon than its competitors. Mobil's decision was based on research showing that only 20 percent of gasoline customers are price shoppers. Some 20 to 30 percent are loyal to a brand, and another 20 percent or so purchase gasoline only if a convenience store is associated with the gas station. Mobil thus decided to focus on increasing brand loyalty by increasing the quality of the purchasing experience and essentially wrote off the 20 percent of customers who are price shoppers.

2.c. Capital Requirements

High sunk costs are a deterrent to entry.

If the capital costs of entering a business are especially high, and if the costs cannot be recouped—that is, if they are sunk costs—then firms are likely to be more reluctant to enter an industry than if they can enter with low capital requirements. To illustrate how firms sometimes increase their capacity in order to deter entry, consider the case of Du Pont, America's largest chemical firm. In the early 1970s, Du Pont accounted for about one-third of the nation's sales of titanium dioxide, a whitener used in paints and other products. Du Pont executives believed the demand for titanium dioxide would grow considerably in the following years and that many new entrants would emerge. The company's managers decided to invest over $300 million to increase the firm's capacity to produce titanium dioxide. The strategy was to install much more capacity than was immediately necessary in order to deter rivals from entering the market.

Another illustration of raising rivals' costs to deter entry can be seen in the response of Maxwell House to a decision by Folgers to move from being a regional coffee retailer to a national one. Maxwell House responded by substantially increasing its advertising and its production facilities. Maxwell House also announced that its advertising budget would be 50 percent more than Folgers' budget. If Folgers increased its advertising, so would Maxwell House. As a result, the cost for Folgers to enter the national market increased significantly.

focused factory:
a factory in which just one product or part of a product is produced

Another way to increase costs to rivals can be seen in the actions of some Japanese companies in the 1960s. These firms altered their production techniques to what was called the **focused factory**. Focused factories specialized in the production of only one specific type of product. For instance, in the ball bearing industry, ball bearings of all sizes and uses were generally produced in a single factory. The Japanese firms entered the ball bearing market by producing only automobile bearings. By specializing, the Japanese firms achieved economies of scale and reduced costs by over 30 percent relative to the factories producing many different types of bearings. The only way that rivals could match the Japanese firms was to construct new factories that were also focused.

2.d. Cost Disadvantages Independent of Size

Even if there are no economies of scale or scope, some firms can gain an advantage over other firms because they have discovered a more efficient way to produce or sell. America's "Big Three" automobile companies—Ford, GM, and Chrysler—lost substantial market share to Japanese competitors in the 1970s and 1980s because they were less efficient and less focused on quality. In 1965, Toyota had a 50 percent higher level of vehicle productivity (cars per worker) than the Big Three, and by 1975, its advantage had grown to 160 percent. The newer, more mechanized factories gave Japanese car manufacturers a major advantage in global markets.

A similar cost disadvantage independent of size occurred in motorcycles. The British motorcycle makers Norton, Villiers, and Triumph found their market share eroding in the late 1960s and early 1970s from competition by the Japanese producers Kawasaki, Yamaha, and Honda. Each Honda worker turned out the equivalent of 200 bikes per year, whereas the British worker rate varied from 10 to 16. These disadvantages had nothing to do with plant size but instead with the way that the products were manufactured. The Japanese factories were much newer and more efficient than the British factories. Harley-Davidson, the United States company, faced a problem similar to the British firms. Harley went to the government for help and received it in the form of trade restrictions. The United States allowed the Japanese to sell only their small motorcycles in this country, which did not compete with the large machines Harley-Davidson produced.

2.e. Access to Distribution Channels

A firm that has an established distribution channel that is not easily replicable has an advantage over potential rivals. The more that established firms can tie up distribution channels, the more difficult entry will be. Many firms set up their own distribution networks. Kodak's distribution network was well established by the time Fuji attempted to enter the film market in the 1970s. Fuji attempted to use Kodak's suppliers, offering to sell them Fuji materials at a fraction of the cost of Kodak products. Kodak responded with ultimatums to distributors that they sell only Kodak or they would not get Kodak products. Most distributors remained with Kodak, at least until the government told Kodak it could not retain exclusivity.

2.f. Unique Resources

If a firm owns a unique resource, it has erected a formidable barrier to entry. De Beers controls about 80 percent of the diamonds outside of Russia. RJR Nabisco owns a significant portion of tobacco growing land. A single family owned the only mine producing desiccant clay, an important ingredient in inhibiting humidity in packaging, until the 1980s. Courtaulds owned a pulp making facility that was situated on a location that gave Courtaulds a big advantage over other producers.

2.g. Government Policy

A company can benefit if it can persuade government officials to create or protect barriers to entry. We mentioned earlier how Harley-Davidson was able to get the government to protect it from competition by Japanese firms. In the 1970s, the government prevented the national brewers—Anheuser-

Busch, Miller, and Schlitz—from acquiring small regional brewers. Heileman, then one of the larger regional brewers, faced no such constraints. It bought out numerous smaller brewers and achieved substantial economies of scale. Heileman's profit rate was higher than the other brewers, and its market share growth was substantial. But by 1982, after Heileman's market share had tripled, the Justice Department blocked further acquisitions. Pressure had been put on Justice Department officials to slow the growth of Heileman. The smaller breweries in conjunction with the larger, national brewers wanted some restrictions on Heileman's activities.

As we mentioned in Chapter 5, and will discuss more in the next chapter, government intervention in markets may be the result of rent seeking. Firms devote resources to securing an advantage through a government-imposed barrier to entry as did both Harley-Davidson and Heileman's competitors. Postal services are another example of rent seeking. Most post offices around the world are owned by government. These monopolies cover all mail below a certain weight or value. Once justified by the need for government to intercept seditious correspondence, today the monopolies are defended as helping to pay for universal service. Universal service means that every address within a country is within reach, usually at a single price. Private deliverers are longing for legislation to curb the monopolists' power but, like any private firm, the private deliverers will decide how to price for delivery depending on demand and cost conditions. It is unlikely that someone living in an isolated part of the wilderness will be charged the same rate for delivery as someone living in New York City. The post offices are not only trying to preserve their monopolies, by lobbying elected officials and with advertising directed toward the general public, they are attempting to move into other areas, such as international express mail, using their government-provided monopoly profits to subsidize the international express mail business. Without their monopolies, these activities would not have taken place. The lobbying and the move into international mail may be wasteful expenditures—rent-seeking costs—because they would not have occurred if the monopoly did not exist.

2.h. Dealing with Change

The one thing all firms face is change.

The threat of entry and the barriers to entry change as conditions change. Patents expire after seventeen years. New technologies change the capital requirements of a business or alter the size of the *MES*. Time often erodes advantages as new technologies arise and break down barriers to entry. Several examples illustrate this point dramatically.

In the early 1970s, the Big Three U.S. auto companies were losing market share to the European cars and their new front-wheel drive. In the spring of 1973, Pete Estes, a top General Motors executive, asked a car expert named David E. Davis to go to Europe and take a look at the new front-wheel-drive cars like the Volkswagen Rabbit that were just coming out. The new cars weighed less and used less fuel without a reduction in performance. They were generating excitement among both customers and engineers. Davis reported to Estes that they were better cars, better engineered and better built than those Detroit was making, and that front-wheel drive was a breakthrough of immense significance. Nevertheless, GM, Ford, and Chrysler remained with rear-wheel drive because none wanted to take the lead and pioneer a new technology. Their decision was costly. In 1992, Ford declared a loss of $7.4 billion, and GM declared a loss of $23.5 billion.

A firm that can differentiate its product and create brand-name loyalty will earn higher profits than a firm that can't do this. But this advantage may disappear over time. In just three years, Nintendo sold 12 million computers in Japan with virtually no competition except for Atari. But while the two companies were battling each other, a more important, and potentially much more deadly, competitor arose from another source—the CD-ROM. The personal computer equipped with a CD-ROM can be used for playing games and for many other activities. The Nintendo and Atari computers can be used *only* for games.

Even a unique resource may not leave barriers to entry standing for long. In the 1960s and 1970s, desiccant clay from New Mexico was about the only product that could be used to inhibit moisture in packaging. The monopoly led to substantial profits for the clay mine and the producers of the moisture-inhibiting packets. The profits induced a search for substitutes, which was successful when a synthetic clay, which had better moisture-reducing properties than the real clay, was developed.

RECAP

1. The barriers to entry depend on economies of scale and scope, product differentiation, capital requirements, cost differences that are not size-dependent, access to distribution channels, unique resources, and government policy.

2. Over time, barriers that occur naturally or are erected by a firm's strategy are likely to be eroded.

3. ALTERNATIVE STRATEGIES

We have discussed the external factors—economic conditions and the threat of new entry and substitutes—illustrated in Figure 1. We then discussed barriers to entry. Now, let's move to the interior of the triangle and discuss strategies used to compete with rivals.

The strategies a firm undertakes as it competes with its rivals depend on both demand conditions (knowing the customer) and cost conditions. The long-run cost structure will help determine whether there are economies of scale or scope and how large a plant, factory, or store should be built; short-run costs will define price and nonprice strategies—whether to devote resources to quality, service, training, or other activities. Let's consider a few strategies firms might undertake.

3.a. Core Competency: Defining Your Business

What does it mean to know your business?

core competency:
the primary business a firm is involved in

The theme of recent management studies is that to be successful a manager should focus on his or her firm's **core competency**. In economic terms, that theme is the familiar adage "specialize according to comparative advantage." One way to find out your core competency or what business you are in is to examine the cross-price elasticity of demand. This is the sensitivity of demand for your product with respect to the prices of related products. High positive cross-price elasticities of demand mean that if your competitors raise their prices and you don't, many of their customers will buy your product. Products related by high cross-price elasticities of demand are good substitutes and may be considered competitors even though at first glance they may seem to be different products. For example, different forms of entertainment, such as movies and professional basketball, are competitors even though they seem to be different products.

If your firm sells more than one product, do you want those products to be substitutes, complements, or unrelated? If the cross-price elasticity across your own products is positive, then your products are substitutes for each other. If the cross-price elasticity is negative, your products are complements. And if the cross-price elasticity is near zero, then your products are not related—at least in the consumer's mind. Either your firm has wandered into several unrelated businesses or it has followed a strategy of **diversification**—your firm produces more than one product because together the products increase profits by reducing costs or by raising revenues. Often a firm diversifies in order to reduce the chance that some single event will lead to disastrous losses.

diversification:
producing more than one product in order to enhance profits or reduce risks of loss

Does a strategy of diversification make sense, or should a firm focus on one product or a few closely related products? The answer depends on the results of comparing marginal revenue and marginal cost. If diversification can reduce costs so that the marginal revenue from the strategy exceeds the marginal cost, then the strategy makes sense. If not, diversification is an incorrect strategy.

Producing or selling a stable of complementary products is the opposite of diversification, since the sales of complementary products are affected by the same events. Sometimes producing complementary products makes sense because the products enhance the overall brand name.

Producing several products that are substitutes for each other could make sense if each was oriented toward a slightly different niche of the marketplace. In fact, this is what a differentiation strategy in monopolistic competition and oligopoly is all about. Coca-Cola markets soft drinks for many different market segments. People who like Coke may be different from those who like Diet Coke and different from those who choose Cherry Coke. Similarly, people who choose Coors may find Coors Light distasteful, and neither group may like Cutter or Killian's Red, both Coors products.

The strategy a firm takes with respect to producing more than one product and whether those products are complements, substitutes, or not related should depend on a comparison of costs and benefits. Often, however, the expansion to more than one product occurs accidentally or without an examination of costs and benefits. An example is provided by Kodak. Although Kodak has the benefit of a powerhouse brand name, the company erred in believing that name would prove beneficial in businesses not related to photography. In the late 1980s, Kodak acquired health-care and other businesses because the photography market had been stagnant for several years. This expansion led to declining profits in the late 1980s and early 1990s. In 1993, the new CEO, George Fisher, decided to focus on digital imaging, a market related to Kodak's core business. He sold off all the businesses not related to imaging.

Sometimes a business can "forget" it has more than one product. In 1994, Ford focused on increasing the sales of its Taurus in order to regain the title of world sales leader from the Honda Accord. Unfortunately, Ford failed to recognize the cross-price elasticity of demand among Ford products. The push on sales of the Taurus cut into sales of the Escort, Thunderbird, and Contour.

3.b. Keeping Up with the Customer: Changing Your Product

What does it mean to "know your customers"?

Demand curves change or shift over time as factors other than price change. Fashions, fads, habits, and other aspects of consumer behavior affect the demand curve. Clothing styles come into and out of favor. People often purchase something simply because others are also purchasing that product. In some consumer markets, demand has a life cycle. Certain products are introduced and demand is small. Demand grows until the market is saturated and an innovation on that product or a new product is then introduced. In Figure 4 you can see the pattern for consumer electronics. Radios yielded to black and white televisions, which in turn gave way to color TVs and then VCRs.

Habits are an important aspect of demand. Activities and products become habits because people have information about these activities and products. Habits are like brand loyalty or store loyalty: the price elasticity of demand is lower than if there is no habit or customer loyalty.

As we know, income influences demand. The greater the income elasticity of demand, the more sensitive demand is to changes in income. Most products are oriented toward a market niche—a certain segment of the population—defined quite often by income level. For example, most new consumer electronics are intended to reach the higher-income population; over time the products are targeted toward the middle- and lower-income groups.

Firms must constantly be measuring price, income, and cross-price elasticities of demand.

3.c. Price vs. Nonprice Strategies

Whether the firm engages in price competition depends on whether it is profitable to do so. A firm in an oligopolistic industry, where rivals will quickly match any price decrease, is less likely to engage in price competition. A firm facing a demand that is inelastic is not going to embark on a price-reduction strategy but will look to price increases. In deciding whether to engage in price strategies, the firm must examine the marginal revenue and marginal

Figure 4
Life Cycle of Products
Managers must deal with change. Products often have a life cycle: they are introduced to the market, grow in popularity, and then begin to lose popularity. A new product or an innovation to the existing product occurs, generating a new period of popularity. *Sources:* Shlomo Maitel, *Executive Economics* (New York: Free Press, 1994); The Ministry of Trade and Industry, "Survey of Consumer Electronics," *The Economist,* April 12, 1991, p. 3; Consumer Electronics Association, Annual Reports.

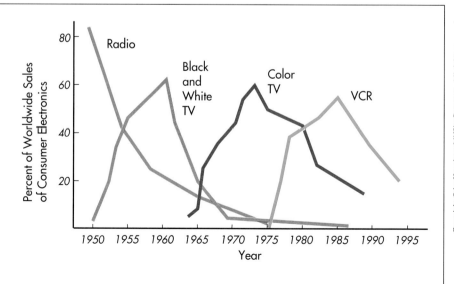

costs of the decision. If the firm gains more than it loses (marginal revenue exceeds marginal cost) from a price change or from a policy of price discrimination, then the firm will undertake the price strategy. Otherwise, the firm must look to nonprice strategies.

Nonprice strategies typically involve marketing. The firm may advertise, offer guarantees or warranties, focus on packaging, or devote resources to ensuring distribution channels.

Another nonprice strategy is the introduction of new or different products. And the new products do not always have to be accompanied by advertising. A few years ago, $150 basketball shoes were in fashion. In 1995 it was the "retro" sneaker: styles from the 1960s and 1970s were the rage—all without the benefit of heavy advertising campaigns.

Other nonprice strategies include focusing on service or quality. A study of 450 firms between 1972 and 1985 concluded that the most important single factor influencing a business's profitability was the quality of its products and services relative to those of rivals.[1] This does not mean that any or all attempts to improve quality will be worthwhile. Only if the marginal cost of devoting more resources to quality enhancement is less than the marginal revenue generated from this change is a strategy of quality improvement beneficial.

3.d. Cost-based Strategies

Does a firm's strategy depend on cost?

In addition to the potential for economies of scale or scope, that is, the long-run cost structure, managers must be aware of the short-run cost conditions. In the short run, a manager does not deal with new entry or changes in scale or scope; these are long-run phenomena. In the short run, the manager focuses on variable and fixed costs and strategies to ensure that revenues exceed variable costs.

Does it matter whether a firm has high fixed costs and small variable costs or vice versa? Remember, a firm must cover all variable costs to remain in business in the short run. But to be profitable, the firm must cover all variable *and* all fixed costs. Managers often ask what sales have to be for revenue to cover costs; in other words, how many units must be sold to break even? This is called **break-even analysis.**

break-even analysis: determining the quantity of units that must be sold to just cover costs

Break-even analysis can help define a cost-based strategy.

Suppose, for illustrative purposes, that a firm's variable and marginal costs are a constant $2 per unit and that its fixed costs are $600,000. How many units of output must be sold for the firm to just break even if the price of the product is $3 per unit? Breakeven is defined as the quantity where total revenue equals total costs: $P \times Q = TFC + AVC \times Q$. Rearranging this equation, we can define the breakeven quantity as: $Q = TFC/(P - AVC)$. As shown in Figure 5(a), the firm would have to sell 600,000 units to break-even; 600,000 units at $3 per unit is $1,800,000. Fixed costs are $600,000 and at 600,000 units, variable costs are $2 \times 600,000 = $1,200,000$, so that total costs are $1,800,000.

If the quantity of sales necessary to break even is very large but the market that a firm can reasonably expect to capture is quite small, then a firm must consider reducing fixed and/or variable costs. Suppose that fixed costs in our

---

[1] R. Buzzell and B. Gale, *The PIMS Principles Linking Strategy to Performance* (New York: Free Press, 1987).

example are reduced by 10 percent, to $540,000. Then the breakeven point is 540,000 units of sales, a reduction of 10 percent. At 540,000 units of sales, the total costs and total revenue are $1,620,000 ($TFC + AVC \times Q = $540,000 + \$2 \times 540,000$). As shown in Figure 5(b), the total-cost curve, labeled TC_1, intersects the total revenue curve at 540,000 units and $1,620,000. Clearly, the smaller the fixed costs, the smaller the break-even point, everything else the same.

Now, what happens if variable costs are reduced by 10 percent? If fixed costs are $600,000 but variable costs are $1.80 per unit, then the break-even point is 500,000 units of sales. As shown in Figure 5(b), the curve labeled TC_2 intersects the total-revenue curve at 500,000 units of output and total costs of $1,500,000. The 10 percent reduction in variable costs leads to a 16.7 percent increase in the necessary sales to break even.

A firm with substantial market share may attempt to increase the costs of rivals so that their breakeven points increase while their ability to increase their market share does not. For instance, by increasing the resources devoted to advertising, a firm will increase the costs of the rivals, who must match the advertising expenditures. But these increased costs may not be recoverable in the short run. If the firm is experiencing losses, particularly if it is not even covering variable costs, it may be forced to shut down production and lose additional market share.

In the 1980s and early 1990s, IBM's costs amounted to one dollar out of every 2.5 sales dollars, while competitors had costs of only one dollar to every 3.3 sales dollars. Obviously, the sales necessary for IBM to reach its break-even point were much higher than other firms, too high for IBM to reach. In 1992, IBM declared a loss of nearly $5 billion. By 1994, IBM had returned to a profitable status primarily by reducing variable costs: personnel costs were cut by $3 billion as 120,000 workers were let go, and decision-making was streamlined.

Sometimes managers fail to realize the difference between marginal and average costs. Many businesses that require a great deal of capital have a cost structure with high fixed costs. For many of these firms, the cost of producing one more unit—the marginal cost—is small. For instance, the cost of one more telephone call or one additional passenger on a flight from New York to Los Angeles is typically very small, while the average total cost of the telephone call or the passenger is quite high. In this situation, a manager must be aware that a strategy to attract that additional passenger or telephone call may involve a price that is less than average cost for that additional passenger or telephone call. Focusing on average costs means focusing on the wrong cost in this case. It is the marginal cost that matters.

3.e. The First Mover Strategy

Is there an advantage to a firm that is the first to carry out some action?

first mover strategy:
being the first firm to carry out some activity

Being first tends to be a very successful business strategy. Typically, the first firm to successfully carry out a differentiation strategy or to bring out a new product is able to sustain an advantage. This is referred to as a **first mover strategy**; first movers typically earn higher returns than the followers for several years. Kodak, Xerox, IBM, Coca-Cola, Microsoft, and Intel are examples of first movers with substantial brand name and market advantages.

The first mover strategy applies to doing business in newly developing economies as well; the first firms to do business in a country often secure long-term advantages. For instance, Coca-Cola is the best known brand name

Figure 5
Breakeven

Figure 5(a) illustrates a breakeven analysis. The breakeven point occurs where total costs and total revenues are equal. At a fixed cost of $600 and a variable cost of $2 per unit, and with the price of $3 per unit, the breakeven point occurs at a quantity of 600. In Figure 5(b), the fixed and variable costs are alternately changed. When fixed costs are reduced by 10 percent, everything else the same, the breakeven quantity of sales is reduced by 10 percent. This is shown by TC_1 crossing the total revenue line. If variable costs are reduced by 10 percent, everything else the same, then the breakeven quantity of sales drops by 16.7 percent, as shown by the line labeled TC_2 intersecting the total revenue line. A firm must consider whether focusing on fixed or variable costs makes more sense.

(a) Break Even

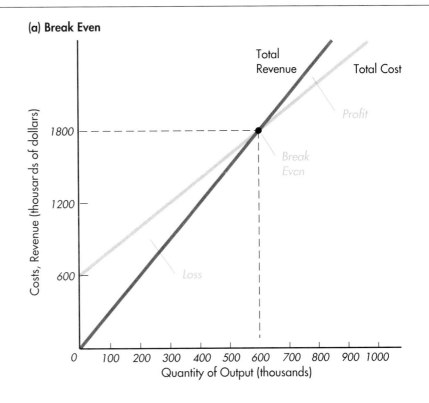

(b) Break Even with Lower Costs

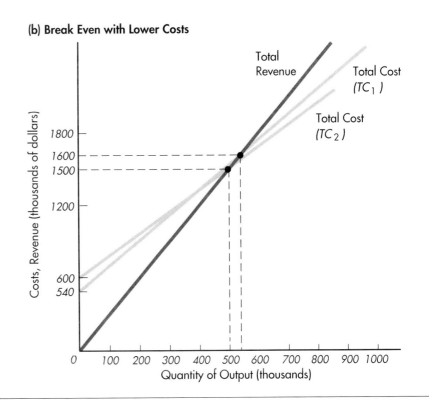

in China. Expecting Vietnam to become another fast growing economy in Asia—one of the "Asian Tigers"—many U.S. firms wanted to ensure that their products were well established. However, until August 1995, the U.S. had imposed a trade embargo on Vietnam. Nevertheless, many U.S. companies used partners from other nations who did not have an embargo on Vietnam to establish their products. PepsiCo, Coca-Cola and Anheuser-Busch, among others, had been selling their products for several years before 1995.

Although the evidence does suggest that first movers gain relative to second or third movers, it is not always the case that to be first is to be most profitable. VF Corporation, a clothing supplier, has made itself a success by moving second. When Sara Lee Corporation introduced its new Wonderbra in the United States in May 1994, VF Corporation watched closely. Once it was clear that American shoppers were buying the new bra, VF offered its own "It Must Be Magic" version. VF's bras were $3 per unit less than the Sara Lee product, and VF's sales exceeded those of Sara Lee. VF's second mover strategy has been successful because the firm is a leader in computerized "market-response systems" that keep close tabs on what shoppers buy and enable them to distribute products more rapidly than any other supplier.

3.f. Market Share as a Strategy

Should a firm care about market share?

First mover and market share strategies have been successful for many firms.

Market share and profitability (accounting profits) are often strongly related. As illustrated in Figure 6, as the market share of a business increases, the rate of return or profit rate tends to increase, although profitability does not increase as much as market share. Why does profitability rise as market share rises? Partly the benefits of increased market share are the result of economies of scale. In addition, brand-name recognition, access to distribution channels, and the resulting reduced price elasticities of demand allow the market leader to charge more than the firms with lesser market share.

There are cases where increased market share has not been beneficial. Yamaha undertook a strategy of taking market share in motorcycles away from Honda in the 1980s. Yamaha cut prices, introduced new models, and increased advertising significantly. Honda responded very aggressively, causing Yamaha to lose sales and experience a decline in profitability.

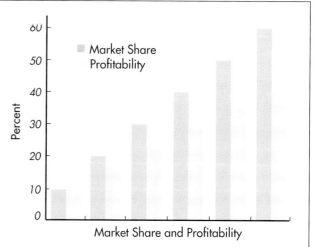

Figure 6: Market Share and Profitability
Research shows that in most industries market share and profitability are positively related. As market share rises, so does profitability. This is due to economies of scale, access to distribution channels, brand-name recognition, and possibly a lower price elasticity of demand.
Source: Adapted with permission of The Free Press, a Division of Simon & Schuster, Inc. from *The Pims Principles: Linking Strategy to Performance* by Robert D. Buzzell and Bradley T. Gale. Copyright © 1987 by The Free Press.

A market share strategy can become a long-run profit-maximizing strategy. When that happens, focusing on short-run profits at the expense of market share could be costly in the long run. Between 1988 and 1990, Apple chose profits over market share, keeping its price higher than those of rival computer firms. Market share dropped from 10 percent to 7 percent but profits rose. The problem with Apple's strategy was that as its market share dropped, more software firms began producing applications only for Microsoft's Windows operating system. Apple then found it harder to sell its computers. Long-run profits declined relative to what would have been the case had Apple increased market share.

When should a manager strive to increase market share and when not? As always, the profit-maximizing rule provides the answer. If the marginal revenue from attempting to increase market share exceeds the marginal cost, the manager should implement strategies to increase market share. If marginal revenue does not exceed marginal cost, then the manager need not focus on market share. (The marginal revenue and marginal cost are calculated using the present value of the revenue and cost streams—that is, the long run impact on revenues and costs. Present value is discussed in the chapter "Capital, Land, and Entrepreneurial Ability.")

RECAP

1. Recent management studies suggest that managers should focus on their business's core competency.

2. The cross-price elasticity of demand provides a measure of how closely products are related in the consumer's mind.

3. Firms must constantly reacquaint themselves with the customer. Knowing the customer means knowing the price, cross-price, and income elasticities of demand.

4. Consumer behavior depends on habits, brand and store loyalty, fads and fashions, and incomes.

5. Firms must decide whether to concentrate on price or nonprice strategies.

6. Short-run cost conditions influence strategy. Breakeven analysis reveals what sales have to be to cover costs.

7. Being first and striving to increase market share are often successful business strategies.

4. A CASE STUDY

As an example of how a manager might devise strategy, we'll consider the disposable diaper industry in the 1970s.[2] Looking back enables us to see the results of decisions made.

[2]Sources include Cynthia A. Montgomery and Michael E. Porter, *Strategy* (Cambridge, MA: Harvard Business School Publications, 1991); Shlomo Maital, *Executive Economics* (New York: The Free Press, 1994); various issues of *Business Week, The Wall Street Journal,* and annual statements from the firms involved. Some of the material, such as actual elasticity numbers, are interpretations by the authors of statements made in the above sources.

4.a. Overview

The disposable diaper industry emerged as one of the largest consumer product industries in the United States in the early 1970s. With sales growth in excess of 25 percent per year, disposable diapers became the single largest brand at Procter & Gamble (P&G). P&G was the industry leader with an estimated 69 percent market share.

P&G had become interested in disposable diapers in the mid-1950s at about the same time it had become interested in the tissue paper market. Both efforts gained momentum with the acquisition of the Charmin Paper Company in 1957. After further development work, P&G began its first test market of disposable diapers in 1962. Its product, priced at 10 cents per diaper, consisted of approximately a dozen layers of tissue paper that had been mechanically embossed to hold them together, backed with a polyethylene plastic outer sheet and a porous rayon facing sheet. Although the new product, Pampers, was highly rated by consumers, it was not widely accepted at that price. Instead, it proved to be a specialty item for use by travelers and high-income buyers.

4.b. What Was the Problem?

The problem was the price and the price and income elasticities of demand. The price elasticity of demand was nearly 2.4 at a price of 10 cents each, and the income elasticity of demand was about 4.0. Pampers cost far more than the 3 to 5 cents per diaper charged by diaper delivery services and the 1 to 2 cents per diaper that it cost to launder cloth diapers at home, even including depreciation of the diapers themselves. Only high-income families used the disposable diapers at home as well as when away from home. Research showed that disposable diapers would have to be priced at 5 to 6 cents apiece to be accepted by the mass market.

4.c. What Should P&G Do?

The formula for success in disposable diapers was a price cut, but the current cost conditions did not allow prices to be cut. As shown in Figure 7, demand was below short-run average total cost ($SRATC_1$) at a price of 5 cents per diaper. A price cut could not occur before a cost reduction without incurring substantial losses. Research suggested that economies of scale were possible, as shown in Figures 7 and 8. Thus, P&G engineers were told to come up with a machine that could assemble diapers at speeds of up to 400 per minute. They did, and the new process allowed P&G to reintroduce *Pampers* at 5.5 cents per diaper in a second major test. P&G was able to move down the *LRATC* to a position given by $SRATC_2$ in Figure 8.

4.d. Rivals

P&G was earning above-normal profits as a result of its cost reductions. Others, therefore, were attracted to the disposable diaper industry. Entry took the form of product differentiation, not price reduction. Kimberly-Clark found that "fluff pulp" was much more absorbent than tissue and was cheaper. It also designed a diaper with built-in adhesive tapes as fasteners and a unique shape to improve fit. It captured approximately a 15 percent

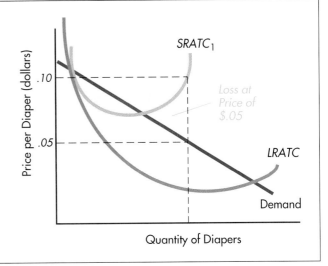

Figure 7
The Loss from a Price Cut
If P&G had reduced its price when it initially introduced the disposable diaper, it would have experienced a significant loss. It had to alter its costs—capture economies of scale—to reduce its costs enough to be able to reduce the price to levels the consumer would accept.

market share. Colgate-Palmolive's Kendall subsidiary marketed an "improved new" disposable diaper. Johnson & Johnson had long been in disposable diapers through its Chicopee subsidiary, but the Chicopee product (Chux and later Chix) was far behind those of the new entrants since Johnson & Johnson's efforts had been concentrated on defending the cloth diaper business. Johnson & Johnson reentered the market with its own brand, using fluff pulp and a unique inner liner sheet. Union Carbide also tested an innovative new disposable diaper. Carbide's product had a patented hydrophobic inner liner made of plastic that allowed liquid to go only one way and thus keep the baby drier than other brands. Scott Paper tested a new disposable diaper to replace its Baby Scott line, which had been discontinued in 1971. International Paper had begun marketing two-piece disposable diapers in the mid-1960s in Canada. It entered the U.S. market in 1968 and constructed a plant in Los Angeles in 1970. Finally, a number of firms, including

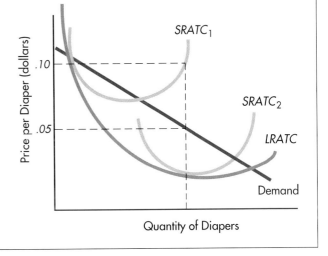

Figure 8
The Gain from Reducing Costs
P&G was able through innovation to reduce its costs. It moved from $SRATC_1$ to $SRATC_2$ and thus reduced price from 10 cents to 5 cents a diaper. At 5 cents per diaper, the company was able to earn a positive profit.

TABLE 2
Firms Producing Disposable Diapers

Branded	Private
P&G	Weyerhaeuser
Kimberly-Clark	IPCO Hospital
Johnson & Johnson	Georgia-Pacific
Kendall/Colgate	
Union Carbide	
Scott Paper	

private label:
the practice of a firm purchasing a product from another firm and putting its own label on the product

Weyerhaeuser and Georgia-Pacific, manufactured, **private label** diapers—they produced the product for sale by other firms, such as JC Penney and Sears, who would put the Penney or Sears' brand on the diapers. All manufacturers offered diapers in three and sometimes five sizes and day and night time versions, and prices were very similar.

The early years of the disposable diaper industry were characterized by monopolistically competitive activity. A great deal of entry and product differentiation occurred. But as costs to enter rose, the industry began to resemble an oligopoly. The firms in the industry in the 1970s are listed in Table 2.

4.e. How Should P&G Respond

New entries, product differentiation, and reduced costs were eroding P&G's market advantage. How should it respond?

4.e.1. Price Strategies Could P&G reduce prices and differentiate its product? The oligopolistic market structure suggested that rivals would respond vigorously to any price cuts unless some cooperation took place. As the largest firm in the market, could P&G serve as a price leader? The answer was no. The other firms were not willing to stay put and accept their current positions. Each of the smaller companies believed it could gain profits by undermining P&G's position. Without cooperation, price wars were an inevitable result of price cutting. Thus, a strategy of brand-name creation and product differentiation appeared to be the better approach.

P&G had to find a way to enhance its brand name. Increasing brand loyalty would reduce the price elasticity of demand and enable P&G to charge a premium over its competitors. P&G's research had shown that the advertising elasticity of demand was greater than 1—thus, a 1 percent increase in advertising expenditures would increase sales by more than 1 percent. In addition, P&G had a cost advantage when it came to advertising since it had a larger volume (larger market share); thus the addition to average costs caused by increased advertising expenditure was less to P&G than to rivals. Since the marginal revenue expected from increasing advertising expenditures exceeded the marginal costs, P&G undertook an expansion in advertising expenditures. P&G also reasoned that brand loyalty could be enhanced if it were to introduce product innovations first. It therefore assumed that the marginal revenue expected from increasing research and development would exceed the marginal costs.

4.e.2. Entry Deterrence P&G considered several possible tactics to deter entry. It could indicate a willingness to carry out activities, or it could actually undertake one or more costly activities.

Signals to Rivals One tactic considered was to inform potential entrants that P&G would defend its position, even to the point of using its larger market share, or "deep pockets," to bear losses in the short run. How could Procter & Gamble signal this information to its rivals? P&G officials could not simply call the rivals on the phone and even if they could, they couldn't be sure that they would reach all potential rivals. P&G could, however, make public statements in press releases and annual reports. The statements would note a "commitment" to remain the leader in the disposable diaper market, to serve the public, etc. These announcements would raise the expected cost of entry because entrants would have to recognize the likely retaliation by P&G.

Another action considered by P&G was rent seeking; it could file a patent suit, claiming that rivals were using P&G innovations. The lawsuit would raise expected costs to anyone thinking about entering.

P&G also considered announcing a planned expansion that would include the most sophisticated manufacturing techniques. This would raise the fixed costs of an entrant because the entrant would have to match P&G's expenditures.

P&G could also announce a new generation of diapers to be introduced in the future, causing all potential rivals to reconsider their product. This would raise the expected cost of entry by forcing entrants to bear product development and changeover costs.

In considering these possible tactics, P&G had to look at the effect on its own costs. If it adopted a tactic that was more costly to itself than to its rivals, that strategy could end up costing P&G more than it would be worth. The objective of a tactic is to raise the cost to a potential entrant, not to cause a loss of profits to P&G.

Capital requirements One strategy to be considered is the cost of capital. The production of disposable diapers involves a highly complex, high-speed continuous process assembly operation using specialized machines. Diaper machines are several hundred feet in length and staffed by four complete crews so that they can be operated twenty-four hours a day and seven days a week. A well-running maching can produce 400 diapers per minute.

Diaper machines can be purchased from outside suppliers, but virtually all the major diaper manufacturers make major and costly proprietary modifications (unique to each firm) to machines in order to achieve competitive machine speeds and to produce their particular variety of diaper. A basic diaper machine costs approximately $300,000 and a complete line, including the building in which it is housed, represents an investment of $2 to $4 million.

The capital requirements are large but not totally restrictive; a larger firm can raise the financing for that capital without difficulty. These capital requirements can, however, impede entry by firms unable to bear large sunk costs. The modifications to equipment mean that much of the capital cost is sunk—the machines cannot be converted to other uses. Thus, firms have to weigh the probability of success against these potential sunk costs.

Distribution channels Another strategy to be considered is access to distribution channels. Supermarket shelves are the marketplace for disposable diapers and supermarkets the distributors. New firms have to take shelf space away from the established brands if they are to gain a foothold in the market. This usually requires a substantial consumer response. Supermarkets typically must forgo some other product if a new one takes shelf space, and they will not do this without strong indications that consumers will purchase the new product. With its large market share and national distribution, P&G was assured of highly visible shelf space in the supermarkets.

4.e.3. Costs

P&G had to compare the marginal revenue and marginal cost of each possible strategy. It also had to focus on both short- and long-run costs. One particularly important cost that was higher for P&G than for its rivals was transportation. Transportation costs amounted to more than 10 percent of the total selling price because diapers are bulky. Only P&G was fully national in 1974, which meant much higher transportation costs. These costs could have been reduced by establishing several factories in various locations around the country and in other countries. However, in doing this, P&G would have lost the economies of scale it achieved by having a central production facility. P&G also could have abandoned its national distribution system to reduce transportation costs. There are several benefits to a national distribution, however. One is that an advertising strategy used throughout the nation means lower costs per unit for advertising. National distribution would mean that P&G had relatively more power for establishing distribution channels and shelf space in the supermarkets. P&G decided that the benefits of national distribution exceeded the costs; it went national believing that economies of scale, access to distribution, and advertising economies outweighed associated costs. In hindsight P&G's decisions appear to have been correct. It has maintained its dominance of the industry.

4.f. The Changing Market

In the 1990s, the market for disposable diapers is changing. The customer is different and the market structure has evolved since the 1970s. In the 1950s and even early 1960s, the baby boom was occurring—the population of babies was growing very rapidly. But, by the 1970s, fewer babies were being born. This meant that families had more income to spend on each child. Disposal diapers have replaced cloth diapers; disposable diapers are used by households almost irrespective of income.

The disposable diaper industry is now an established or mature oligopoly. This suggests several strategies to a manager that may be useful and several that may be disastrous. A firm considering entering the disposable diaper industry today will face a great likelihood of failure. The barriers to entry are considerable, the greatest barrier being the brand names that existing suppliers have. Extensive advertising and product creation would be necessary to gain even a toehold in the market. There are high fixed costs and relatively low marginal costs. This means that it would be difficult for a new firm to price competitively and be profitable. Perhaps a major technological breakthrough on the cost side could change the disposable diaper industry and allow more entry. A firm that develops a fully biodegradable disposable diaper might break into the market quickly. However, odds favor the existing firms for coming up with technological breakthroughs. Procter & Gamble and the other diaper firms are devoting considerable resources to research and development, including the creation of a diaper that is environmentally friendly.

RECAP

1. The case study of disposable diapers illustrates how a manager can use the economic topics of market structure and costs to devise strategies and guide the firm.

2. Procter & Gamble was the first mover in the industry and gained a dominant market share as a result.

3. Procter and Gamble achieved economies of scale based on a national distribution strategy.

SUMMARY

▲▼ **How do the different structures affect what a manager does?**

1. A manager must know the market structure in which a firm operates or intends to operate. §1

▲▼ **What factors affecting a firm can a manager control, and what factors are external to the manager's control?**

2. Strategic variables are those factors under the control of a manager. §1.a

3. External factors such as economic conditions affect the firm but cannot be controlled by the firm. A high income elasticity of demand means that sales will increase significantly when the economy is booming and will drop considerably when the economy is mired in a recession. §1.b

4. Exchange rates are another external factor affecting the firm. Exchange rate changes can affect a firm through costs and sales. A firm may be able to minimize the costs of exchange rate changes by locating subsidiaries in other countries. §1.b

5. New entrants, substitutes, and the power of customers and suppliers are also external factors. §1.b

▲▼ **Why would a firm want to raise barriers to entry, and how could it erect barriers?**

6. The threat of entry depends on economies of scale and scope, product differentiation, capital requirements, cost differences that are not size-dependent, distribution channels, unique resources, and government policy. §2

7. Over time, barriers that occur naturally or are erected by a firm's strategy are likely to be eroded. §2.h

▲▼ **What does it mean to know your business?**

8. Managers may be well-served by focusing on their business's core competency. §3.a

9. The cross-price elasticity of demand provides a measure of how closely products are related. §3.a

10. Whether a firm should diversify depends on whether the marginal revenue from diversification exceeds the marginal cost. §3.a

▲▼ **What does it mean to "know your customer?"**

11. Firms must constantly reacquaint themselves with the customer. Knowing the customer means knowing the price, cross-price, and income elasticities of demand. §3.b

12. Consumer behavior depends on habits or brand and store loyalty, fads and fashions, and incomes. §3.b

▲▼ **Does a firm's strategy depend on cost?**

13. A firm can undertake price and nonprice strategies. Which it chooses depends on which generates the most marginal revenue relative to marginal costs. §3.c

14. The short-run cost conditions influence strategy. The firm must be aware of the cost structure—the fixed, marginal, and variable costs. §3.d

15. First movers often have an advantage over later entrants. Firms that enhance quality and service usually have an advantage over others. §3.e

16. Market share and profitability are often positively related. Thus, a short-run focus on market share may be a good strategy for long-run profitability. A larger market share may lead to greater profitability because of economies of scale, brand-name recognition, distribution channels, and reduced price elasticities of demand. §3.f

KEY TERMS

strategic management § Preview

strategic variables §1.a

economies of scope §2.a

focused factory §2.c

core competency §3.a

diversification §3.a

breakeven analysis §3.d

first mover strategy §3.e

private label §4.c

EXERCISES

1. Mobil Oil is altering its strategy from price cutting to differentiation. In doing so, it is ignoring 20 percent of the market. Why doesn't Mobil price-discriminate, offering lower prices to those customers who are price shoppers and more service and ambience to those who are not price shoppers, and thereby attempt to appeal to the entire market?

2. The Boxite Corporation, a retailer of washing machines, wants to determine how many appliances it will have to sell to earn a profit. The price of each washing machine is $400 and the average variable cost is $200.

   a. What is the required sales volume if fixed costs are $5,000?

   b. What is the required sales volume if fixed costs are $10,000?

   c. If the firm could raise the price of the machines to $450, what would be the answer to part a?

   d. What is the required sales volume if fixed costs are $5,000 and variable costs are $250 per unit?

3. The Carter Company produces 1,000 chairs and 200 tables each year. The total costs are $30,000. If the firm produced just the 1,000 chairs, the total costs would be $15,000. If the firm produced just the 200 tables, the total costs would be $24,000.

   a. Calculate the degree of economies of scope. (Calculate the cost per unit as different products are produced.)

   b. Why might economies of scope exist for the Carter Company?

4. The Benton Company produces automobile bearings and has plants in the United States and Mexico. The executives of the Benton Company have just received word from their managers in Mexico that the peso is likely to fall in value relative to the dollar. What does this mean, and what should the Benton Company do?

5. The HD Company has introduced a television having substantial technological advantages over existing televisions in picture, sound, and programming characteristics. The HD Company has decided to introduce only a few televisions initially at a very high price. It will

then introduce more TVs at a reduced price. What is the basis for this pricing strategy? What conditions are necessary for it to be more successful than merely introducing a huge number of TVs at a lower price?

6. Texas Instruments once announced a price for random access memories that wouldn't be available until two years after the announcement. A few days later, Bowmar announced that it would produce this product and sell it at a lower price than Texas Instruments. A few weeks later, Motorola said it too would produce this product and sell it below the Bowmar price. A few weeks after this, Texas Instruments announced a price that was one-half of Motorola's. The other two firms announced that, after reconsidering their decision, they would not produce the product.

   a. What market structure is described here?

   b. What was Texas Instruments' reason for announcing the price of a product two years before it was actually for sale?

   c. Under what conditions would Motorola not have rescinded its production decision?

7. Explain, using cost curves, how a strategy of increasing expenditures on advertising could deter entry.

8. Under what conditions would a first mover strategy not be beneficial?

9. Suppose you are the manager of a firm that has discovered an innovation that enhances the power of a microchip 1,000 times. What would you do with that unique resource—your innovation? Would you sell the chip to Intel and Motorola and allow them to market the chip under their own brand (a private label)? Would you sell the chip directly to manufacturers like IBM and Macintosh under your own firm's label?

10. Many retailers in monopolistically competitive markets use short-term price cuts to attract customers. These often include "loss leaders," products sold at a loss for a short time. Why would a firm ever sell at a loss? Would a firm in an oligopoly use loss leaders?

COOPERATIVE LEARNING EXERCISE

Divide the class into groups of four to five people. Ask the groups to analyze the following brief case using the framework of Figure 1. Assign each group member to a specific task. Number 1 is the discussion leader, 2 is the recorder (keeps records of the discussion), 3 is the facilitator (keeping the discussion on task), and 4 is the spokesperson. After 15 minutes, the spokespersons present their analyses.

The publishing industry has undergone a decade of shakeout. From an industry of more than thirty companies, there remain about five. Barriers to entry are considerable—huge capital costs and important established distribution channels. Price competition has been virtually nonexistent, but product differentiation is substantial, especially in educational texts. A major technological advance occurred in 1995 with the introduction of Indigo Ltd.'s one-shot-color printing system. This system makes it economi-

cal to print labels and packaging in far smaller lots than before. Some publishers think it might make the breakeven point much smaller. Others think that it might enable educational publishers to customize books, printing several versions of one book, each version designed for a very small market niche. Reto Braun, manager of a major transportation company, is attempting to decide whether it makes sense for his company to enter the publishing business. As a consultant to Braun, what advice would you provide about entering and, if the company enters, what strategies to undertake?

The class can vote on which strategies to pursue.

"Hyper" Business Strategies to Beat Today's Competition

I recently attended the grand finale of the Whittemore Conference on Hypercompetition at Dartmouth's Amos Tuck School of Business. Four messages were delivered with particular force:

- Think disruption.

Tuck's Richard D'Aveni coined the term "hypercompetition." Today's outrageous pace of change, he says, calls for upside-down business approaches.

"Chivalry is dead," D'Aveni writes in "Hypercompetition: Managing the Dynamics of Strategic Maneuvering."

"The new code of conduct is an active strategy of disrupting the status quo to create a series of unsustainable advantages." (That's right, UNsustainable—i.e., hunting for and quickly exploiting competitive edges, then abandoning them before the competition responds.)

"This is not an age of defensive castles, moats and armor," he continues.

"It is rather an age of cunning, speed and surprise. It may be hard for some to hang up the chain mail of sustainable advantage after . . . so many battles. But hypercompetition, a state in which sustainable advantages are no longer possible, is now the only level of competition." . . .

Using scores of compelling examples from hot-sauce wars to computer skirmishes, D'Aveni makes clear that there's no place to hide from this new world order. . . .

The energetic, arm-waving (though academically sound) D'Aveni is a very fresh voice urging managers to "build" enterprises dedicated to perpetual revolution.

- Think service.

How dominant are "services"? Would you believe 96 percent of us ply service trades?

That's Tuck luminary Brian Quinn's estimate. He calculates that 79 percent of us work in the official service sector (transportation, retail, entertainment, etc.), and of the 19 percent still employed in so-called manufacturing, 90 percent do service work (design, engineering, finance, marketing, distribution, etc.).

With capital investment per person in services running above manufacturing, sophisticated sector leaders such as Wal-Mart are now calling the shots—and virtually dictating manufacturers' strategies. The world's two most competitive economies—the United States (No. 1) and Singapore (No. 2)—displaced longtime leader Japan this year, according to the acclaimed World Economic Forum annual survey. A big reason for our high marks: an enormous edge in services productivity.

- Think front line.

Terry Neill, head of Andersen Consulting's worldwide change-management practice, summarized in-house research that pinpoints "death by a thousand initiatives" as the chief reason corporate renewal efforts fail.

TQM on Wednesday, re-engineering on Thursday, a learning organization on Friday.

All these ideas are important, but when fired at employees like Ping-Pong volleys, they overwhelm, confuse—and hopelessly diffuse organizational focus.

Winners, Neill claims, outexecute, rather than outstrategize, their competitors (i.e., it's the front line, dummy!). Neill translates an old French saying, "Change is a door that can only be opened from the inside." Or, as Notre Dame football coach Lou Holtz puts it: "It's not my job to motivate players. They bring extraordinary motivation to our program. It's my job not to DEmotivate them." Genuine empowerment, Neill concludes, is not the things you do to or for people, it's the impediments you take away, leaving room for folks to empower themselves. . . .

Source: " 'Hyper' Strategies to Beat Today's Competition," Tom Peters, *Baltimore Sun*, Oct. 3, 1994, p. 11c.

Commentary

It seems that the latest management technique to be adopted by the gurus is "hypercompetition." The idea being presented is that the pace of change is so rapid in today's business world that businesses must simply strike and run. Be first, take some profits, and then move to another business or take another approach. Just try things—some will work and some won't. The message is one of being ready to deal with constant change or perpetual revolution.

Does this message make sense from an economic standpoint? Part of it does. There is no doubt that successful businesses must be prepared to deal with change. Advantages deteriorate and technology changes, as noted in the chapter, so that if a business is unable or unwilling to change, it will eventually disappear. However, firms must strategize, plan, and execute. They must know what their business is, they must know their customer, and they must understand the market structure in which they operate. In short, they must understand the framework discussed in this chapter. If firms do not have a logical approach to decision-making, they tend to adopt whatever comes along. This leads to confusion among employees, often overwhelming them and causing the firm to lose sight of what its business is.

As the economy shifts from one that is primarily manufacturing to one primarily of services, the barriers to entry change. Perhaps the huge capital costs of the automobile industry give way to the costs of creating brand names in service, such as Wal-Mart, but each is a barrier. Similarly, the speed with which a barrier deteriorates may have increased in certain industries, but it is no easier to gain significant market share from Intel or from Wal-Mart than it was to take market share from GM or Ford. We noted in the chapter how the failure of the Big Three automobile companies to deal with change led to some significant losses in the 1980s.

A manager must strategize how best to generate profits. Honda recently announced that it would produce a clean car in 1997. The other automobile companies claimed that Honda has no advantage here; that they also have clean cars in the works, and Honda simply made the announcement to gain publicity. This was a competitive strategy by Honda. Eli Lilly recently acquired PCS, a pharmaceutical marketing firm, in order to have everything from production to marketing and placement of pharmaceuticals in health-maintenance organizations within one firm. This strategy increases the barriers to entry to the pharmaceutical industry. Starbucks Coffee has expanded from Seattle to New York City, attempting to become a nationwide coffeehouse with some economies of scale and brand-name recognition. Different strategies work for different firms selling in different market structures or environments. A manager must understand which strategies make most sense for which situations. That is what economic thinking will provide. A manager must compare costs and benefits, carry out decisions where marginal revenue exceeds marginal costs, look to economies of scale and economies of scope in the long run, and examine variable and fixed costs in the short run.

Every management technique or approach being offered in the media and pushed by consultants can be considered using the framework presented in this chapter. The successful manager must engage in economic thinking and not simply adopt whatever technique is in vogue.

28

Government Policy Toward Business

FUNDAMENTAL QUESTIONS

1. Why does the government intervene in business activity?
2. Why is antitrust policy subject to political changes?
3. What is the difference between economic regulation and social regulation?
4. Why have governments deregulated and privatized certain lines of business?

I n the 1960s, computers were sold or leased as complete systems, combinations of central processing units and peripherals—tape drives, disk drives, programs, and other components. A Control Data disk drive did not provide direct competition for an IBM disk drive because the Control Data unit would not work with the IBM central processing unit and software. In the late 1960s, however, several companies developed tape and disk drives that were compatible with the IBM units. This allowed the companies to sell these peripherals in direct competition with IBM, forcing IBM to respond to competition on each piece of equipment as well as on the entire system. IBM's ability to control price and output in the peripherals market was reduced, but, because the peripheral companies could not produce a compatible central processing unit, IBM retained the ability to control price and output in the systems market. IBM dropped the price of its peripherals to the point where the other firms could not compete and retained its higher price on the central processing unit. A lawsuit was filed against IBM, charging anticompetitive behavior. The trial concluded that IBM was not acting in an anticompetitive manner.

In February 1986, Coca-Cola Company declared its intention to purchase the Dr Pepper Company and merge the operations of the two companies. Just weeks earlier, Pepsi-Co had announced its intention to purchase the Seven-Up Company, a subsidiary of Philip Morris. These two mergers would have meant the consolidation of the first and fourth and the second and third largest sellers of concentrate for carbonated soft drinks in the United States. Government policymakers determined that these mergers would be anticompetitive and did not allow them.

Cable TV prices rose by nearly twice the rate of inflation in the early 1980s. Complaints that cable TV was a monopoly and acted as such in charging excessively high rates convinced Congress to place cable TV under the control of government policymakers.

In 1994, the Justice Department and the Federal Trade Commission issued guidelines indicating that the United States government could prosecute foreign businesses for actions that attack either American consumers or exporters.

Smoking has been linked to cancer and other diseases for several decades. Recently, secondhand smoke has been tied to cancer in nonsmoking spouses of smokers. All but four states now have laws restricting smoking in public buildings, and the federal government has proposed a smoking ban for any building, except a private residence, in which ten or more people enter a day.

Microsoft, the world's largest software company, has been under U.S. government investigation since 1992 for anticompetitive practices.

These are examples of government intervention in the affairs of business. In this chapter we look at how and why the government intervenes in business activity; we discuss antitrust policy, economic regulation, and social regulation. In the chapters "Market Failure and Environmental Policy" and "Government and Public Choice" we explore government's role in the economy in more detail.

1. GOVERNMENT AND THE PRIVATE SECTOR

The two main approaches the government uses to intervene in the activities of business are *antitrust policy* and *regulation*. Antitrust policy is an attempt to ensure that businesses compete "fairly." Guidelines of behavior and accepted types of behavior are defined, and firms that do not comply are sued. *Economic regulation* involves a more active role for government. It ranges from prescribing the pricing and output behavior of specific industries to the case where the government actually runs and operates the business. *Social regulation*, which applies generally across all businesses, involves health and safety standards for products and the workplace, standards for protecting the environment, and other government restrictions on the behavior of firms and individuals.

1.a. Theories of Why the Government Intervenes in Business Activity

Why does the government intervene in business activity?

public interest theory:
the government intervenes in business activity to benefit the general public

capture theory:
the government intervenes in business activity to transfer wealth from one group to another; to benefit a special interest

Why does the government intervene in the affairs of business? One explanation is that the government's intervention in the economy is for the public good. This is called the **public interest theory** of government intervention. According to this theory, the government carries out antitrust policy, regulates nuclear power, airlines, new pharmaceuticals, workplace safety, product safety, and the environment because the public's well-being depends on the government's actions. Without such intervention, according to this theory, unsafe drugs would be foisted off on an unwary public and unsafe nuclear power plants would be built. It is argued that the government must intervene in agriculture, trucking, airlines, and other industries to protect the public from competition that could destroy these industries. Moreover, the government must prevent large firms from destroying small ones. According to public interest theory, if the government did not intervene, the public would face many more monopolists.

In opposition to the public interest theory of government is the argument that government actions are simply means to transfer wealth from one sector of the economy or one person to another. We might call this the "we don't like the market outcome" theory of government intervention. The market outcome says that those willing and able to pay for a good or service will get the good or service. If we want others to get the good or service, or if we want the good or service to be free or provided at very low cost, we might join together and get the government to intervene in the market. One form of this "we don't like the market outcome" theory is called **capture theory.** According to capture theory, special interests, not the public, receive the benefits of antitrust policy and regulation. For instance, according to capture theory, the antitrust suit against IBM was an attempt to secure benefits for rival firms, not the general public; the group in charge of trucking regulations

Transportation—via air, bus, or truck—is either a nationalized industry (government enterprise) or regulated in most countries. In Mexico City, Mexico, the bus service from the airport is a government enterprise. The quantity demanded for the service often far exceeds the quantity supplied, as waiting passengers stand in line for the next available bus. The shortage of buses during peak hours was further increased by recent regulations limiting the amount of driving people can do with personal automobiles. The inability to use cars meant that more people had to rely on the government bus lines.

is composed of spokesmen from the trucking industry so that the regulations benefit truckers, not the general public; and the agency in charge of regulating nuclear power involves executives from the nuclear power industry, thereby ensuring that the regulations benefit the industry, not necessarily the general public. Capture theory claims that government intervention in business activities is like asking the fox to guard the henhouse.

How could Congress and the regulatory agencies create laws and regulations favorable to a special interest group at the expense of the general public? The primary reason is that as a member of the general public you do not have as much concern over some activity that affects a special interest group as you would as a member of that special interest group. For instance, consider regulation that is favorable toward an industry group and unfavorable toward consumers. As a consumer you do not specialize in hiring moving companies, traveling by bus or air, or studying pharmaceuticals. You merely purchase the products that are offered. The industries concerned do specialize in their business and thus lobby intensely to guide the legislation and regulations that impact the industry. Another factor is that the legislation and regulations do not come with a label spelling out exactly who is benefited or harmed. Laws and rules that end up favoring special interest groups may have been originally intended to benefit, or have been presented as benefiting, the general public. For example, regulation of airport taxis occurred because of the claim that too many consumers were being "ripped off." Thus, the taxi fares were fixed by law. This regulation reduced price competition, restricted entry, and provided stable revenue for the taxi firms—obviously benefiting the taxi firms. Similarly, legislation to increase the safety of new pharmaceuticals through years of testing may benefit the pharmaceutical firms at the expense of consumers, since the process of testing restricts entry and allows above-normal profits for a longer period of time.

With the opposing views of government activity in mind, let's turn to a discussion of antitrust policy and regulation. Antitrust policy began in the late 1800s; the main statutes of antitrust law were passed in 1890 and 1914. Economic regulation came about primarily during the Great Depression; most regulatory agencies were created during the period from 1930 to 1940. Social regulation has come about primarily since 1970.

1.b. Size and Influence

Government policy focuses on the large firm. Government regulations often apply only to large businesses, and antitrust policies are typically directed toward large firms. The basis for the focus on large firms comes from the four market-structure models—perfect competition, monopolistic competition, oligopoly, and monopoly.

When considered as a whole, the four market-structure models suggest that the fewer the number of firms controlling the production in an industry, the greater the chance of collusive activity and other behavior designed to monopolize a market. And under monopoly and oligopoly, it is likely that consumers pay more and firms produce less and earn greater profit than if the firms are small, perfect competitors. To have an idea whether these are serious problems, it is necessary to know how prevalent oligopolies and monopolies are, relative to perfectly competitive markets. Measures of size and influence are intended to provide information about market structures.

1.b.1. Measures of Size and Influence
The most commonly used measure of size and influence is called the **Herfindahl index**. The Herfindahl index is a measure of **concentration**—the degree to which a few firms control the output and pricing decisions in a market.[1] The Herfindahl index of concentration is defined as the sum of the squared market shares of each firm in the industry:

$$\text{Herfindahl index} = (S_1)^2 + (S_2)^2 + \ldots + (S_n)^2$$

where S refers to the market share of the firm, the subscripts refer to the firms, and there are n firms. The higher the Herfindahl index number, the more concentrated the industry.

An industry in which each of five firms has 20 percent of the market would have a Herfindahl index value of 2,000:

$$(20)^2 + (20)^2 + (20)^2 + (20)^2 + (20)^2 = 2,000$$

If the largest firm had 88 percent of the market and each of the others 3 percent, the Herfindahl index value would be 7,780:

$$(88)^2 + (3)^2 + (3)^2 + (3)^2 + (3)^2 - 7,780$$

The higher number indicates a much more concentrated market. As you can see from these examples, the Herfindahl index takes into account the size distribution of the firms in an industry. The idea is that an industry in which there is one dominant firm will be quite different from one in which there are

Herfindahl index:
a measure of concentration calculated as the sum of the squares of the market share of each firm in an industry

concentration:
the degree to which a few firms control the output and pricing decisions in a market

---

[1]The four-firm concentration ratio is another commonly used measured of concentration, but it has come under criticism because it does not account for the size distribution of firms. It merely divides the total output of the four largest firms by the total market output.

TABLE I

Concentration Measures for Selected Industries

Industry	Number of Firms	Herfindahl Index
Aircraft	108	1,358
Soaps and other detergents	642	1,306
Blast furnaces and steel mills	1,787	650
Petroleum refining	282	380
Sawmills	2,430	113
Women's dresses	5,489	24

Source: U.S. Department of Commerce, "Concentration Ratios in Manufacturing," U.S. Bureau of the Census, various years.

several firms of equal size. The Herfindahl indexes for a few industries are shown in Table 1.

In 1982, 1984, and 1992, the Justice Department issued guidelines on market concentration and competition to inform businesses where the government would be especially likely to scrutinize activities. It stated that industries with Herfindahl indexes below 1,000 are considered *highly competitive*; those with indexes between 1,000 and 1,800 are *moderately competitive*; and those with indexes above 1,800 are *highly concentrated*.

I.c. Concentration in the United States

To the extent that concentration reflects oligopolistic or monopolistic behavior, prices and profits in concentrated markets should be higher than in nonconcentrated markets. Many studies of this proposition have been carried out. The evidence does indeed show a positive relationship between prices and concentration levels, higher accounting profit in concentrated than in nonconcentrated industries, and higher profit rates (profit as a percent of assets) for large firms. However, this is not necessarily evidence of the abuse of power or the result of anticompetitive behavior. Those industries in which economies of scale exist may also be higher-cost industries and thus have higher prices without higher profit. Also, recalling the difference between accounting and economic profit, we recognize that higher accounting profit is not necessarily evidence of above-normal profit. Moreover, larger firms may be able to achieve efficiencies and thus earn higher accounting profit than smaller firms. In sum, although evidence supports the notion that large firms are different from small firms and that firms in concentrated markets behave differently from firms in nonconcentrated markets, economists have not been able to demonstrate that concentration means inefficiency, higher costs for consumers, and above-normal profit for firms. Nonetheless, large firms in concentrated markets have long been the focus of government attention.

RECAP

1. Two opposing theories suggest why the government intervenes in business activities, public interest theory and capture theory. According

to public interest theory, intervention occurs to benefit the general public. According to capture theory, intervention occurs to benefit a special interest group.

2. Government policy toward big business involves two areas: antitrust and regulation.

3. The Herfindahl index is a measure of the degree to which a few firms dominate a market. It is the sum of the squares of the sizes of firms in the market.

2. ANTITRUST POLICY

What is antitrust policy?

In this section we describe antitrust policy and discuss its evolution in the United States. **Antitrust policy** is the term used to describe government policies and programs designed to control the growth of monopoly and prevent firms from engaging in undesirable practices.

2.a. Antitrust and Business Activities

antitrust policy:
government policies and programs designed to control the growth of monopoly and enhance competition

As noted in Table 2, three laws define the government's approach to antitrust policy—the Sherman, Clayton, and Federal Trade Commission acts. These antitrust laws are intended to limit the creation and behavior of *trusts*, or combinations of independent firms. Today we refer to the process of combining firms as *mergers* and the resulting firms as large firms, or corporations. Antitrust policy limits what these large firms can do. For instance, the firms cannot together decide to fix prices; they cannot restrict competition; and they cannot combine or become trusts if the resulting firm would have too great an influence in the market.

TABLE 2
Antitrust Acts

> ### Sherman Antitrust Act (1890)
>
> *Section 1* outlaws contracts and conspiracies in restraint of trade.
> *Section 2* forbids monopolization and attempts to monopolize.
>
> ### Clayton Antitrust Act (1914)
>
> *Section 2,* as amended by the Robinson-Patman Act (1936), bans price discrimination that substantially lessens competition or injures particular competitors.
> *Section 3* prohibits certain practices that might keep other firms from entering an industry or competing with an existing firm.
> *Section 7,* as amended by the Celler-Kefauver Act (1950), outlaws mergers that substantially lessen competition.
>
> ### Federal Trade Commission Act (1914)
>
> *Section 5,* as amended by the Wheeler-Lea Act (1938), prohibits unfair methods of competition and unfair or deceptive acts.

2.b. Interpretation

Why is antitrust policy subject to political change?

rule of reason:
to be illegal an action must be unreasonable in a competitive sense, and the anticompetitive effects must be demonstrated

per se rule:
actions that could be anticompetitive are intrinsically illegal

Antitrust policy is the responsibility of two government agencies, the Antitrust Division of the Department of Justice and the Federal Trade Commission. These agencies try to distinguish beneficial from harmful business practices by focusing on *unreasonable* monopolistic activities. What is unreasonable? The answer has varied as the interpretation of the statutes by the courts and government authorities has changed. There have been several distinct phases of antitrust policy in the United States, as illustrated in Figure 1. The first began with passage of the Sherman Antitrust Act in 1890 and lasted until about 1914. In this period, litigation was infrequent. The courts used a **rule of reason** to judge firms' actions: being a monopoly or attempting to monopolize was not in itself illegal; to be illegal, an action had to be unreasonable in a competitive sense, and the anticompetitive effects had to be demonstrated.

The second phase of antitrust policy began in 1914 with the passage of the Clayton Antitrust Act and the Federal Trade Commission Act. Operating under these two acts, the courts used the **per se rule** to judge firms' actions: activities that were potentially monopolizing tactics were illegal; the mere existence of these activities was sufficient evidence to lead to a guilty verdict.

Although the courts define the standard to be applied to antitrust cases, the administration in office appoints judges and defines the degree to which antitrust policy will be enforced. In the 1980s and through the Reagan and Bush administrations, the courts returned to the looser rule-of-reason standard. The only tactic deemed illegal was price fixing—rival firms could not determine prices by agreement; they had to allow prices to be set by demand and supply. Other than that, firms could do just about anything to enhance their profitability. When Clinton became president, an attempt was made to return to the tighter standards. More money was allocated to antitrust enforcement, more lawyers were hired, and more cases were brought. The Department of Justice Antitrust Division received $16 million more per year, allowing it to hire 100 new employees; FTC hired 25 more enforcement personnel. Under Clinton, the Antitrust Division of the Justice Department was

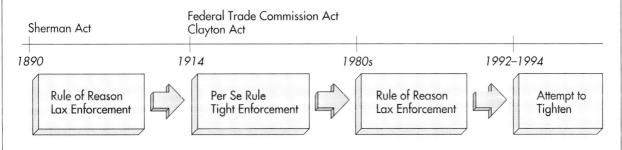

Figure 1
Phases of Antitrust Interpretation
The degree to which antitrust law has been enforced has varied over the years. With the Sherman Act of 1890, the government formally began antitrust policy. But enforcement was lax, based on a rule of reason, until about 1914. Between 1914 and the early 1980s, strict enforcement based on a per se rule was used. With the Reagan and Bush administrations, enforcement was relaxed again to the rule-of-reason standard. President Clinton attempted to enforce antitrust law more strictly but was thwarted in midterm by the Republican majority in Congress.

challenging about 28 mergers per year on average whereas the average number in the Reagan and Bush years was only eight per year. The Justice Department also initiated more than 33 civil antitrust cases compared with an average of ten per year during the Republican predecessors. The FTC under Clinton also doubled the number of enforcement actions it undertook.

The Clinton administration also broadened the province of antitrust actions to foreign firms and to firms involved in innovation. The International Antitrust Enforcement Assistance Act passed by the 1994 Congress and signed by President Clinton allows the Justice Department and the FTC to apply antitrust rules and laws to foreign firms. The Republican administrations of Reagan and Bush had relied on a policy whereby attempts by firms to merge within an industry that had a Herfindahl index greater than 1,800 or a merger that would increase the Herfindahl index by 50 points would be scrutinized. Otherwise, mergers would not be contested. The Clinton administration agencies retained these rules but did say that if a merger involved the "innovation market" that tougher standards would be applied. By the innovation market, the antitrust agencies meant research and development in general and industries that rely heavily on product and technological advancement.

2.c. Procedures

Action against alleged violators of the antitrust statutes may be initiated by the U.S. Department of Justice, by the Federal Trade Commission (FTC), or by private plaintiffs. The Justice Department focuses on the Sherman Antitrust Act. The FTC focuses on the Federal Trade Commission and Clayton Antitrust acts. Private plaintiffs (consumers and businesses) may sue on the basis of any of the statutes except the Federal Trade Commission Act. Since 1941, the FTC and the Justice Department together have filed nearly 2,800 cases, and since 1970, private suits have far outnumbered those filed by the Justice Department and the FTC combined.

2.d. Remedies

Private plaintiffs who prove their injuries can receive compensation up to three times the damages caused by the action. The Justice Department and the FTC do not obtain treble damages but can impose substantial penalties. They can force firms to break up through dissolution or divestiture, and criminal actions can be filed by the Justice Department for violations of the Sherman Act. A guilty finding can result in fines and prison sentences.

2.e. Demonstration of Antitrust Violations

Price fixing is by definition illegal—there is no justification for it. Other aspects of the antitrust statutes are not as clear-cut and are, therefore, difficult to prove. For instance, Section 2 of the Sherman Act outlaws "monopolization" but does not forbid monopolies. Monopoly itself is allowed. *To monopolize* or *to attempt to monopolize* constitutes a violation. If the firm attempts to preserve its monopoly by activities that restrict entry, then the firm may be guilty of a Section 2 violation.

The first step in enforcing an antitrust policy is to define market concentration. Using the Herfindahl index to gauge the extent to which a few firms dominate a market sounds simple, but it is not. Before the concentration of an industry can be calculated, there must be some definition of the market. In a $100 billion market, an $80 billion firm would have an 80 percent market share. But in a $1,000 billion market, an $80 billion firm would have only an 8 percent market share. The Herfindahl index for the former would exceed 2,000, but for the latter it would be less than 1,000. Obviously, antitrust plaintiffs (those accusing a firm of attempting to monopolize a market) would want the market defined as narrowly as possible so that the alleged monopolizer would be seen to have a large market share. Conversely, defendants (those accused of monopolization) would argue for broadly defined markets in order to give the appearance that they possess a very small market share. For example, Coca-Cola, Dr Pepper, PepsiCo, and Seven-Up are usually identified as producers of carbonated soft drinks (CSD). These firms provide bottlers with the concentrate that is used to make the drinks. Would CSD be the appropriate market in which to assess the competitive consequences of a merger, or should the market be more widely defined—perhaps to encompass all potable liquids (fruit juices, milk, coffee, tea, etc.)? In an actual merger case, the market definition was determined through interviews with CSD company executives. The executives indicated that they believed their primary competitors were other CSD producers. Their pricing and marketing strategies were made with other CSD producers in mind—not, as claimed by the defendant, by considering how the sellers of all potable drinks would react. The interviews also revealed that many CSD industry executives thought they could collectively raise the retail prices of carbonated soft drinks by as much as 10 percent with no fear of consumers switching to other beverages. That argument had implications for the definition of the market. If sellers can collectively raise the price by 10 percent without causing consumers to switch to other products, then those sellers represent the lion's share of the market. However, if consumers switch as a result of the price increase, then the market must be more broadly defined to include the substitutes consumers move to.

When the market and market shares have been defined, the next task is to establish intent. The ease or difficulty with which intent can be established depends on whether the per se rule or the rule-of-reason standard is being used. The Economic Insight "The Microsoft Settlement?" illustrates the difficulty of determining intent.

2.f. Concentration and Business Policy from a Global Perspective

Concentration measures and the Justice Department guidelines are often defined for production only within the United States; this can present a misleading picture. For instance, the Herfindahl index in the United States for automobiles is very high, but if it took foreign competition into account, it would be significantly lower. In Sweden, two cars are produced, Volvo and Saab, and the Herfindahl index is greater than 5,000. That figure is also misleading, however, for Volvo and Saab account for only about 30 percent of all automobiles sold in Sweden. An appropriate policy measure must take into account all close substitutes whether domestically produced or not. In addition, it must account for firms producing in more than one nation, the multinationals. The Herfindahl index may not provide a good indication of the competitive situation prevailing in an industry if it does not account for these factors or for the different ways that governments treat their businesses—actions that are legal in one country may be illegal in another, for instance.

The Microsoft Settlement?

For five years Microsoft Corporation had been under the scrutiny of the U.S. Justice Department for practices that were allegedly monopolizing the computer software industry. The MS-DOS operating system and Windows are used on more than 50 million personal computers, some 80 percent of the personal computer market. Rival companies, like Borland International and the Lotus Development Corporation, contended that Microsoft tried to block them from offering other operating systems by using unfair licensing practices. Some companies also said that Microsoft used various dirty tricks, including what is called "vaporware," to leverage its expansion from MS-DOS into almost every kind of software for desktop computers. Vaporware refers to an announcement of an intent to bring out a new product or service in order to keep other firms from entering that business or carrying out research and development on a related product.

In July 1994, the Justice Department reached a settlement with Microsoft whereby Microsoft agreed to drop the practice of licensing MS-DOS to computer manufacturers on the basis of the number of computers they sold. Seven months later, a Federal District Judge refused to approve the consent decree between the Government and Microsoft. The judge wrote that "What the Government fails to show is that the proposed consent decree will open the market and remedy the unfair advantage Microsoft gained in the market through its anti-competitive practices."

The Microsoft case illustrates two difficulties with antitrust actions. One is that an industry seldom remains the same and past actions may no longer be relevant in the current market. The software industry has changed dramatically since 1990 when the Justice Department began investigating Microsoft practices. Then the question was whether the company was using unfair tactics to win market dominance for its personal-computer operating systems. Today, these are history. The Windows operating system now rules the personal computer market and few consumers would choose any other system. The second difficulty is separating monopolizing practices from efficiency. Are consumers better off because Microsoft is large and innovative or are they worse off because Microsoft dominates the industry?

Competitors want the Justice Department to continue investigating Microsoft. But they now want to forgo the examination of licensing practices and have Justice look at the impact of Microsoft in potential markets such as the Internet. Microsoft has announced that it will launch the Microsoft Network, a commercial on-line service along with its Windows, and that it will join forces with Visa, a credit-card company, and other companies, to offer ways to purchase items or pay for purchases safely. Is this "vaporware" or an efficient firm indicating where it sees the industry moving?

Governments also restrict the imports of some goods and services, thereby affecting the number of substitutes available to domestic consumers. The definition of a market did not include worldwide factors until the early 1980s. From then until the early 1990s, market definition could include worldwide factors, but the United States would not apply antitrust sanctions against some action or restrict mergers unless they were deemed to harm American consumers. In 1992, the United States extended its policies to include harm to either American consumers or American firms.

Compared to other countries, the United States is quite restrictive in terms of allowing certain types of business behavior and quite unrestrictive in placing limits on the importation of goods and services. When the per se rule was emerging in the United States during the 1920s and 1930s, most European nations had no antitrust laws at all, and cartels flourished. Today, many nations support cartels and cooperative behavior that is illegal in the United States. Some of these same nations are very restrictive in the importation of goods. Japan, for instance, allows, even supports, systems of cartels domestically while limiting the inflow of foreign-produced goods and services relative to the United States.

At least part of the explanation for the differences among nations lies in the growth and development of the various countries following World War II. The economies of Europe and Japan were severely damaged by the war. As the losers, Germany and Japan were occupied and their laws rewritten by the occupying forces. Thus, their antitrust laws resemble those of the United States. However, because Europe and Japan were not concerned with large business but instead with businesses that were too small to compete in the world markets, the antitrust laws were never enforced. Businesses had to be large enough to achieve economies of scale, and for several decades it seemed that only U.S. firms were of sufficient size. Hence, while the United States was worrying about large businesses becoming too powerful, other countries were attempting to increase the sizes of their businesses. Only since the 1970s have the European countries begun to institute and enforce antitrust laws along the lines the United States has followed since the 1940s. Currently, every Western industrialized nation has some kind of antitrust law.

The differences across nations have led many in the United States to call for a new approach to antitrust activity in the United States, one called **industrial policy**. Industrial policy refers to the government being actively involved in determining the structure of industry. Government would select certain industries to be high-growth areas, would offer low-interest loans or subsidies to these industries, and would provide protection from international competition in order for the industries to mature. Japan's Ministry of International Trade and Industry (MITI) has performed these functions in that country, and many people believe the United States should have a similar industrial policy.

Critics of industrial policy point out that the free market (without government intervention) will determine what people want and will produce what people want in the most efficient manner; a government agency cannot do any better. These critics further point out that Japanese consumers pay higher prices as a result of the industrial policy in Japan. They note that shipbuilding, aluminum smelting, and petrochemicals were industries favored by MITI and these industries have done very poorly. And they point to the huge success of Soichiro Honda, who led his company into the auto industry in defiance of MITI, as proof of the limitations of industrial policy. They argue that an industrial policy simply strengthens the ability of special interests to capture the government for the benefit of these special interests.

industrial policy:
government direction and involvement in defining an economy's industrial structure

Industrial policy looks attractive to policymakers because of Japan's economy. Japan's policy, though, has had failures as well.

RECAP

1. Antitrust policy in the United States is based on the Sherman, Clayton, and Federal Trade Commission acts.

2. The enforcement of antitrust policy has evolved through several phases. The first followed the Sherman Act in 1890 and extended to 1914. During this period, the rule-of-reason standard dictated policy. The second phase started with the Clayton and Federal Trade Commission acts in 1914 and lasted through the 1970s. During this period, the per se rule dictated policy. In the 1980s, most practices were considered to be part

of the competitive process. In the early 1990s, an attempt was made to return to stricter enforcement.

3. Antitrust policy encompasses business actions such as pricing, advertising, restraint of trade, supplier relationships, and mergers.

4. If two or more rivals combine, it is called a merger.

5. Antitrust policy in the United States is stricter than it is in other nations.

6. Industrial policy refers to an industrial structure defined and determined by government actions.

3. REGULATION

What is the difference between economic regulation and social regulation?

economic regulation:
the prescription of price and output for a specific industry

social regulation:
the prescribing of health, safety, performance, and environmental standards that apply across several industries

The intent of antitrust policy is to enhance the competitive environment—to create a "level playing field" on which firms may compete. When the competitive environment cannot be enhanced, such as in the case with a natural monopoly where cost conditions lead to a sole supplier, then regulation is used to ensure that price and output are more beneficial for consumers than the levels the monopolist would set without government influence. Regulation of natural monopolies is far from the only type of government regulation that occurs, however. Regulation of industries that are not natural monopolies is also widespread in the United States. This regulation has a number of different rationales, ranging from the protection of the health and safety of the general public to the health of a particular industry.

There are two categories of regulations, economic and social regulation. **Economic regulation** refers to the prescribing of prices and output levels for both natural monopolies and industries that are not natural monopolies. Economic regulation is specific, applying to a particular industry or line of business. **Social regulation** refers to prescribed performance standards, workplace health and safety standards, emission levels, and a variety of output and job standards that apply across several industries.

3.a. Regulation of Industries That Are Not Natural Monopolies

Let's briefly look at the historical reasons for the regulation of transportation and the airwaves. These industries provide good examples of the rationales for economic regulation. We will then discuss social regulation.

3.a.1. Transportation and Destructive Competition For both railroads and air transport, equipment is extremely expensive and operating costs are relatively quite small—in other words, marginal costs are very low relative to fixed costs. This could mean that firms entering the industry have to set price equal to marginal cost to meet competition, but this is not high enough for them to be able to pay for their total costs—they might be covering their variable costs but not their huge fixed costs. Thus, competition between the firms could lead to the failure of the entire industry. In such cases, the government has often restricted entry, allowing only one firm or a few firms to provide a product. Restricting entry, however, allows existing firms to earn above-normal or monopoly profit. This monopoly profit provides a reason for the government to regulate the firms much as it would a natural monopoly.

The government has been involved in the railroad industry since its inception. Land was provided for construction, loans were provided for development, and transportation rates were defined in many cases. When technological change lowered the costs of some services and brought trucking in as a direct competitor to the railroad, the regulatory net spread from railroads into trucking. Trucking was regulated not because of self-destructive competition or because it was a natural monopoly, but because years of regulation had put railroads at a disadvantage relative to trucking. The Interstate Commerce Commission (ICC) was given jurisdiction over railroads in the last quarter of the nineteenth century. Trucking came under its umbrella in 1935.

Like railroads, the argument for regulating airlines was to create orderly growth and avoid self-destructive competition. From the mid-1930s to the mid-1970s, the Civil Aeronautics Authority and its successor, the Civil Aeronautics Board (CAB), controlled entry into airline markets by establishing boundaries between carriers. Each carrier was further restricted to specific routes. For example, United Air Lines was authorized to serve north-south routes on the West Coast, and Delta and Eastern served such routes on the East Coast.

3.a.2. Airwaves and Private Property Rights

In some cases the resource used to supply a product is available to anyone, so free entry and use could consume the resource and destroy the industry. For instance, if just anyone could broadcast radio or TV signals on any of the airwaves, the main broadcast spectrum could become so crowded that a clear signal could not be obtained. The problem is that there are no clear *private property rights* to the airwaves (no one owns a specific airwave frequency), and in the absence of specific property rights, chaos could result if government did not step in. Limiting entry and assigning airwave frequencies (assigning property rights) may create order, but it also creates a monopoly situation. The existence of the resulting monopoly then lends itself to regulation along the lines of a natural monopoly.

Television and broadcasting rights are granted by the Federal Communications Commission (FCC). Until 1982, the FCC also regulated the telecommunications industry, controlling entry and some prices. The purpose of telecommunication regulation was to make high-quality service available to everyone in the country at reasonable prices and to control the natural monopoly held by AT&T.

3.b. Deregulation and Privatization in the United States

Why have governments deregulated and privatized certain lines of business?

Whether or not the initial rationale justified regulation, sometimes the results were disastrous. Over time it became evident that many regulated companies lacked incentives to keep costs under control and to be responsive to consumer demands. The airlines competed in terms of schedules, movies, food, and size of aircraft because the CAB did not allow price competition. Nonprice competition led to a much more rapid increase in the number of flights and expansion of aircraft capacity than were demanded by passengers. As a result, the load factor (the average percentage of seats filled) fell to less than 50 percent in the early 1970s.

Price competition among truckers was also stifled by regulation. The ICC had a complex rate schedule and restrictions affecting whether trucks could be full or less than full and the routes trucks could take. As a result, by the mid-1970s, 36 percent of all truck-miles were logged by empty trucks.

These problems initiated a change in federal government regulatory policy. In some industries, particularly those in which natural monopolies did not exist, the regulatory apparatus was partially dismantled. Trucking was deregulated in 1980. Trucks can now haul what they want, where they want, at rates set by the trucking companies. In air transportation, deregulation meant the end of government control of entry and prices. Deregulation of route authority and fares was completed by 1982, and the CAB was disbanded.

Much of the telecommunications industry was deregulated in 1982, when an antitrust suit against AT&T, filed by the Department of Justice in 1974, was finally settled. As part of the settlement, AT&T agreed to divest itself of the local portions of the twenty-two Bell operating companies. They were restructured into seven separate regulated monopolies. The seven new operating firms are excluded from long-distance service and from manufacturing terminal equipment. AT&T continues to provide long-distance service and telephone equipment, but other suppliers may compete in both spheres, and customers can choose any supplier they wish.

privatization:
transferring a publicly owned enterprise to private ownership

contracting out:
the process of enlisting private firms to perform certain government functions

Another form of deregulation is privatization. **Privatization** is the term for changing from a government-run business to a privately owned and run business. Advocates of privatization claim that private firms could, in many instances, provide better services at reduced costs. Cities and local governments in the United States have **contracted out** (privatized) many services in recent years. Local governments are now allowing private firms to provide garbage services, water services, and even road building and maintenance. Rural/Metro Co. in Scottsdale, Arizona, has been running a private fire department for several decades. It is now purchasing contracts to run fire departments and emergency medical services throughout Arizona. Corrections Corp. of America in Nashville, Tennessee and California Private Transportation Co. in Anaheim, California, are building prisons and toll roads. Many members of Congress are looking at the U.S. Postal Service and arguing that private firms could deliver mail better and less expensively.

Although regulation leads to problems, not everyone agrees that deregulation is the solution. For instance, many claim that because of deregulation airlines are now less safe.[2] Similar arguments about service and safety apply to other industries that have been deregulated. Cable TV, in fact, was *re*regulated in 1992 because of the public outcry stemming from the price rises during the unregulated period. In short, the move toward deregulation that occurred in several industries during the 1980s has not won unanimous support. Opposing those who want to return to a regulation environment are people who argue that airline safety has indeed improved and that cable TV prices are higher because consumers get more channels and better programming for their money than they did under regulation.

---

[2]See, for example, Richard B. McKenzie and William F. Shughart II, "Deregulation and Air Travel Safety," *Regulation*, nos. 3 and 4, 1987, pp. 42–47; Judith Valente, "Some Airlines Narrow Their Safety Margins Seeking to Cut Costs," *The Wall Street Journal*, Sept. 19, 1988, p. 1; "Happiness Is a Cheap Seat," *The Economist*, Feb. 4, 1989, p. 68; and Nancy L. Rose, "Fear of Flying? Economic Analyses of Airline Safety," *Journal of Economic Perspectives*, Spring 1992, pp. 75–94.

3.c. Social Regulation

Although economists debate the costs and benefits of regulation, the amount of regulation has grown steadily since the Great Depression. Most of this growth has been due to social regulation rather than economic regulation. Although deregulation has occurred in industries faced with economic regulation, social regulation has increased for all industries.

Social regulation is concerned with the conditions under which goods and services are produced and the impact of these goods on the public. The following government agencies are concerned with social regulation:

- The Occupational Safety and Health Administration (OSHA), which is concerned with protecting workers against injuries and illnesses associated with their jobs
- The Consumer Product Safety Commission (CPSC), which specifies minimum standards for safety of products
- The Food and Drug Administration (FDA), which is concerned with the safety and effectiveness of food, drugs, and cosmetics
- The Equal Employment Opportunity Commission (EEOC), which focuses on the hiring, promotion, and discharge of workers
- The Environmental Protection Agency (EPA), which is concerned with air, water, and noise pollution

Social regulation is often applied across all industries. For instance, while the ICC focuses on trucking and railroads, the EPA enforces emission standards related to all businesses.

Social regulation has grown since the early 1970s. The number of rules and regulations and the number of people employed to administer them have increased. The number of rules and regulations imposed by the federal government grew steadily from 1965 until 1980. The number declined until 1984 and then has resumed its growth, as illustrated in Figure 2. Figure 2 shows the number of telephone-book pages in the *Federal Register* required to list the rules and regulations of the federal government.

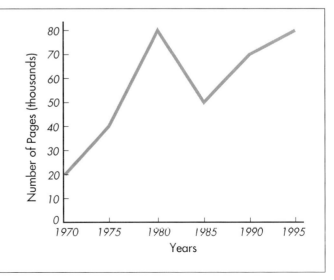

Figure 2
The number of telephone book-sized pages required to list the rules and regulations of the federal government number 80,000. The number of regulations grew until the Reagan years of 1980–1985 and then grew during the Bush and Clinton administrations.

Most of the arguments made in support of social regulation are buttressed by public interest theory. Over 10,000 workers die in job-related accidents in the United States each year. Air pollution is an increasing problem in many cities, leading to cancer and other diseases, which in turn mean increased demands on health-care agencies. Hundreds of children are killed each year as a result of poorly designed toys. Unfair discharges from jobs and discrimination against minorities occur frequently. It is argued that without government regulation, these events would be much more serious and would impose tremendous costs on society.

There are costs to the regulation, however. It is expensive to administer the agencies and enforce the rules and regulations. The annual administrative costs of federal regulatory activities exceed $15 billion. The costs of complying with the rules and regulations, which are imposed on businesses, shift their cost curves up. These costs have been estimated to exceed $300 billion per year. Complying with environmental regulations alone costs business more than $200 billion per year.[3]

Added to the direct costs of regulations are the opportunity costs. For instance, the lengthy FDA process for approving new biotechnology has stymied advances in agriculture. Regulatory restrictions on the telecommunications industry has resulted in the United States lagging behind Japan in the development of fiber optics and high-definition television. The total cost imposed on the U.S. economy from federal government regulations is estimated to be more than $600 billion a year, $6,000 per household.

Whether an action should be undertaken can be determined by comparing the costs of a certain action to the benefits of that action.

There are both enormous costs and enormous benefits to social regulation. Which view is most valid, public interest or capture theory? In other words, does regulation benefit the general public or just special interest groups? To answer this question we need to compare the costs and benefits of the regulations. But this is a difficult proposition. It requires us to answer the question: How much is a life worth? Simply asking the question offends many people. But answering the question is what economists think is necessary for regulation to be restricted from benefiting only special interest groups. To economists, life is worth what people are willing to pay to stay alive. Of course, that differs from person to person, but the values could be used to place limits on what regulations to implement. For instance, using the extra pay that people require to take dangerous jobs, or calculating the total value of expenditures on smoke detectors and safer cars, could provide estimates of how much people value life. Although the estimates vary widely, none exceeds $10 million. Some economists thus argue that any regulation costing more than $10 million per life saved should not be implemented. Rules on unvented space heaters save lives for just $130,000 each; regulations on asbestos removal exceed $100 million per life saved. According to a comparison of costs and benefits, the first rule should be implemented but the second should not.

The cost-benefit test for regulation would limit regulations designed to benefit a very few at the cost of many. However, the cost-benefit test also should include the opportunity costs implied by interfering with the free market, according to many economists. If labeling is desired by the public, won't the public voluntarily pay the higher price for it? Why, then, is regula-

---

[3]William H. Miller, "Make It Rational," *Industry Week,* January 23, 1995, p. 25; and Judi Hasson, "Senate OKs Curbs on Regulations," *USA Today,* March 30, 1995, p. 6A.

tion necessary unless it is to benefit some special interest group? If seat belts and antilock braking systems are desired by the public, won't the public voluntarily pay the price to have these safety systems? Why, if the market would ensure that what the public desires is produced at the lowest possible cost, is it necessary for the government to intervene in the economy and impose regulatory costs of $600 billion or more each year? The debate over social and economic regulation is explored further in the chapters "Market Failure and Environmental Policy" and "Government and Public Choice."

3.d. Regulation and Deregulation in Other Countries

In most European nations, nationalization rather than regulation was the traditional solution to natural monopoly. Nationalization is where the government takes over and operates an industry. Privatization is the opposite of nationalization. Privatization, as discussed earlier, is the transfer of public-sector activities to the private sector. Privatization may take one of three forms: *wholesale privatization*, in which an entire publicly owned firm is transferred to private ownership; *contracting out,* in which a specific aspect of a government operation is carried out by a private firm; and *auctioning*, in which the rights to operate a government enterprise go to the highest private-sector bidder.

While the United States was deregulating, the rest of the world was privatizing. Chile, Argentina, Colombia, and Peru now allow workers to invest their social security payroll deductions into privately managed funds. The Netherlands offered 25 percent of the Dutch postal and telephone system for private ownership in 1994. Britain has privatized its airlines, telephones, steel, and electric and gas utilities. All in all, more than $250 billion in industry has been privatized in the 1990s in Europe.

More than eighty countries have launched ambitious efforts to privatize their state-owned enterprises (SOEs) since 1980. More than 2,000 SOEs have been privatized in developing countries and more than 7,000 worldwide. Most countries carry out privatization because they expect that private firms will outperform SOEs. They fear that employment will decline as firms increase efficiency and cut variable and fixed costs, but they hope that employment will not fall too much.

State-owned enterprises are chronically unprofitable, partly because they are told to increase employment and locate so as to help the local population rather than where efficiency is maximized. Governments provide SOEs with a variety of subsidies, such as reduced prices for resources and guarantees to cover operating losses. Privatization is intended to substitute the single objective of profit maximization for all these other objectives. Subjecting the newly privatized firm to the tests of the market and competition forces the companies to cut costs and increase efficiency or to get out of business altogether. At first glance, this would seem to indicate that the firms will have to cut employment. Interestingly, the experience has been that the privatized firms do perform much more efficiently but that they also increase output and employment relative to the SOEs. Employment in privatized firms has risen by about 10 percent relative to the SOEs.

3.e. Multinationals, International Regulation, and GATT

International regulation occurs at two levels, one in which a specific government regulates the activities of individual firms operating within the country,

GATT:
a trade agreement among over 100 nations that specifies the level of tariffs among the signators

and the other involving several nations. **GATT**, the General Agreement on Tariffs and Trade, is a form of the latter. GATT is the largest international trade deal ever negotiated; it has been signed by more than 120 countries and specifies the levels of tariffs its signators will impose for trade among themselves. GATT is intended to reduce these tariffs and increase trade.

International regulation at the individual firm level arose primarily in response to the growth of *multinationals*, large firms that operate in several different countries. These firms raised concerns over national sovereignty. In cases where the gross domestic product (GDP) of the nation was smaller or not much larger than the sales of the multinational company, the nation feared it would be held hostage to a monopoly firm. A wave of nationalizations and entry restrictions arose in the less-developed countries during the 1960s and 1970s. The conclusion quickly reached by governments was that international action was needed to deal with an international phenomenon such as multinational corporations. The attempt to set up rules of the game, guidelines, standards, and norms of behavior and conduct led to the increased emphasis on regulation at the international level. Because there is no global authority to enforce these rules, and because the interests of countries are so diverse, the international community in most cases settled for something less than regulation. Usually codes containing guidelines are issued as resolutions or declarations of governments rather than as international treaties. They carry moral rather than legal force.

RECAP

1. The stated reason for regulation of industries such as railroads, trucking, and air transport was the potential for self-destructive competition. The stated reason for regulating airwaves was the lack of private property rights.

2. Since the mid-1970s, deregulation has occurred in airlines, trucking, railroads, and communications.

3. Social regulation deals with workplace safety, product safety, the environment, and other aspects of doing business; it applies to all industries.

4. In other countries, nationalization occurred instead of regulation. In those countries, deregulation means privatization.

5. Although deregulation has been the trend since the early 1980s within developed nations, regulation by international agencies and GATT is increasing.

SUMMARY

▲▼ *Why does the government intervene in business activity?*

1. The public interest theory of regulation asserts that regulation is necessary to protect the public interest. The capture theory of regulation claims that regulation benefits only those who are regulated. §1.a

2. The Herfindahl index is used to measure size and influence; industries with a Herfindahl index above 1,800 are considered highly concentrated. §1.b.1

▲▼ *Why is antitrust policy subject to political changes?*

3. Antitrust policy is an attempt to enhance competition by restricting certain activities that could be anticompetitive. §2

4. The antitrust statutes include Sections 1 and 2 of the Sherman Antitrust Act, which forbids conspiracies and monopolization; Sections 2, 3, and 7 of the Clayton Antitrust Act, which prohibits anticompetitive pricing and nonprice restraints; and Section 5 of the Federal Trade Commission Act, which prohibits deceptive and unfair acts. §2.a, Table 2

5. The antitrust statutes have undergone several phases of interpretation. In the early years, a rule of reason prevailed; acts had to be unreasonable to be a violation of the statutes. Between 1914 and 1980, a per se rule applied more often. Under this policy, the mere existence of actions that could be used anticompetitively was a violation. In the early 1980s, the interpretations returned to the rule-of-reason standard. In the early 1990s, another attempt to tighten enforcement was made. §2.b

6. Antitrust laws are more rigorously enforced in the United States than elsewhere. This has led to many calls for a U.S. industrial policy. §2.f

▲▼ *What is the difference between economic regulation and social regulation?*

7. Economic regulation refers to the prescription of price and output for a particular industry. Social regulation refers to the setting of health and safety standards for products and the workplace, and environmental and operating procedures for all industries. §3

8. Some industries are regulated not because they are natural monopolies but because the government wants to limit entry in order to protect an industry from self-destructive competition and from the formation of a monopoly. Examples include airlines and railroads. §3.a

9. Some industries are regulated to prevent chaos because of the lack of private property rights. §3.a.2

▲▼ *Why have governments deregulated and privatized certain lines of business?*

10. By the 1970s, it became apparent that regulation had caused some severe problems. A period of deregulation began in the United States. §3.b

11. Social regulation has increased even as economic regulation has decreased. §3.c

12. Deregulation in other developed countries took the form of privatization: the selling, auctioning, or contracting out of a government enterprise to private interests. §3.d

13. GATT, the General Agreement on Tariffs and Trade, is intended to lower tariffs and increase trade. §3.e

KEY TERMS

public interest theory §1.a

capture theory §1.a

Herfindahl index §1.b.1

concentration §1.b.1

antitrust policy §2

rule of reason §2.b

per se rule §2.b

industrial policy §2.f

economic regulation §3

social regulation §3

privatization §3.b

contracting out §3.b

GATT §3.e

EXERCISES

1. Using demand and cost curves, demonstrate why a typical monopolistically competitive firm might want to create a barrier to entry.

2. Using the demand and cost curves of an individual firm in oligopoly, demonstrate what the effects of each of the following are:

   a. The Clean Air Act

   b. The Nutrition and Labeling Act

   c. A ban on smoking inside the workplace

   d. A sales tax

3. What is self-destructive competition? How does a natural monopoly differ from a firm that has large fixed costs and relatively small marginal costs?

4. Kodak has developed an important brand name through its advertising, innovation, and product quality and service. Suppose Kodak sets up a network of exclusive dealerships, and one of the dealers decides to carry Fuji and Mitsubishi as well as Kodak products. If Kodak terminates the dealership, is it acting in a pro- or anticompetitive manner?

5. Explain why auctioning broadcast licenses might be more efficient than having the FCC assign licenses on some basis designed by the FCC.

6. Which of the three types of government policies—antitrust, social regulation, economic regulation—is the basis for each of the following?

   a. Beautician education standards

   b. Certified Public Accounting requirements

   c. Liquor licensing

   d. Justice Department guidelines

   e. The Clean Air Act

   f. The Nutrition and Labeling Act

7. Provide the arguments for and against each of the rules or regulations listed in question 6 using public interest theory and capture theory.

8. In the chapter "Monopoly," we discussed the Burroughs-Wellcome monopoly on the AIDS drug AZT. As an active member of an AIDS prevention organization, argue that regulation by the FDA has been harmful. As an executive of Burroughs-Wellcome, argue that the FDA regulation has been beneficial.

9. Some airline executives have called for reregulation. Why might an executive of an airline prefer to operate under a regulated environment?

10. Suppose the Herfindahl index for domestic production of televisions is 5,000. Does this imply a very competitive or a noncompetitive environment?

11. Discuss the claim that social regulation is unnecessary. Does the claim depend on whether the industrial structure of an industry is composed primarily of perfect competition or primarily of oligopoly?

12. Suppose a monopolist is practicing price discrimination and a lawsuit against the monopolist forces an end to the practice. Is it possible that the result is a loss in efficiency? Explain.

13. The Justice Department sued several universities for collectively setting the size of scholarships offered. Explain why the alleged price fixing on the part of universities might be harmful to students.

14. Explain the often-heard statement that "There ought to be a law" in terms of public interest theory and capture theory of government intervention in business activity. For instance, suppose a consumer hires Bekins moving company to transfer him from California to Utah and Bekins damages $3,000 worth of furniture and refuses to compensate the consumer. The consumer in frustration says, "There ought to be a law."

15. "The Japanese are beating us at every step. We must act as they do. We must allow and encourage cooperation among firms and we must develop partnerships between business and government. The first place we should begin is with the aerospace industry. Let's use the government to transfer the resources no longer employed in aerospace to nondefense industries such as the environment and health." Evaluate this industrial policy.

COOPERATIVE LEARNING EXERCISE

Divide students equally into four groups, the As, Bs, Cs, and Ds. The topic is the environment. The As are to develop an argument in support of restricting emissions from factories based on public interest theory. The Bs are to develop an argument opposed to that of the As. The Cs are to *develop an argument against government restrictions using capture theory. The Ds are to develop an argument in opposition to that of the Cs. A representative from each group should be chosen to present its argument.*

Kellner suggests PBS Partnership

With the debate over the future of federal funding for the Public Broadcasting System raging in Congress, the president of the nascent WB Network last week suggested in an interview with *Mediaweek* that a public/private partnership with commercial broadcasters could provide a way for PBA to retain quality educational programming in exchange for prime time on its affiliated stations.

"Certainly, we all appreciate that PBS is an important part of the broadcast landscape; I wouldn't want to see it end," said Jamie Kellner, president of the WB. "But I think the way to prevent the ending is to be realistic about what you need and what you need is a revenue stream. You need some way for these stations to be self-supporting in the future, and that could be doing a commercial aspect of their business and that would certainly help us and UPN [the United Paramount Network] and everybody else that's trying to be competitive in the business."

Republicans in Congress, most notably House Speaker Newt Gingrich and Senator Larry Pressler (R-S.D.), are aiming to cut or eliminate funding for the Corporation for Public Broadcasting, the non-profit agency that raises funds that are used to produce the most popular programming on PBS. In a recent appearance on ABC's "Nightline," Pressler said he is going to "introduce legislation to privatize PBS over a three-year basis.

"What I think will happen is that you'll have a relaxation of the rules. You'll have hybrids of commercial/public broadcasters who have certain dayparts that are commercial-free focused on kids' programming, and some of the things that PBS does really well, and other dayparts where they're going to go into business commercially and compete," Kellner suggested. "I can clearly see that day, because then what you can do is you can use the profits generated from the commercial parts of the venture to help build the quality of the programming for the non-commercial part."

The idea of PBS stations giving up two hours of their prime-time schedules for WB Net sitcoms like "Happily Ever After" and "Muscle," as one public television executive who would not speak for attribution put it, would be like "selling out the New York public library system to Waldenbooks. Going from "The Simpsons" to "Shakespeare" or "Masterpiece Theater" on PBS stations wouldn't cut it, either."

Source: "Kellner Suggests PBS Partnership," *Mediaweek*, Jan. 16, 1995, p. 3. © 1995 ASM Communications, Inc. Used with permission from *Mediaweek* Magazine.

Commentary

What does privatization mean? It means that public support (using taxes) to pay for PBS will disappear and the PBS network will have to acquire its own revenues to cover its programming costs. With public support, the PBS stations have been able to avoid commercials, often devoting just a few weeks a year to fundraising. If public support is withdrawn, the PBS stations will have to obtain revenues to pay for the programs like "Sesame Street," "Masterpiece Theater," and "The McNeil-Lehrer Hour." According to Mr. Kellner, the executive of the new network WB, the only way the PBS stations will manage this is to merge with the upstart networks and to offer some commercial television. But, according to a PBS executive, that won't happen—"The Simpsons" and Shakespeare do not match. What is the answer?

Privatization means that the private sector must pay for the PBS programming, that is, that the PBS stations must become either profit maximizing privately owned firms or firms operated on a non-profit basis. The PBS stations will have to sell advertising or use cross-subsidization as suggested by Mr. Kellner. Cross-subsidization would occur if revenue from advertising during commercials of a popular program was used to pay for the "public" oriented program. Firms would then have to decide whether they would pay higher prices to advertise on "The Simpsons" because part of the revenue obtained from the ad would be used to have "Masterpiece Theater" offered without commercial interruption.

An important question is why public broadcasting exists at all. There are two explanations offered. One is that people would not know what quality programming is all about. They would not learn of art, the environment, classical theater, or music, unless the government provides these programs. Once people are exposed to the quality programs, they will learn the value of the programs. But, unless they have developed a taste for the quality programs, they will never try them if they have to put up with commercials like they do for "Married with Children" or other commercial network programs. This is an argument for government intervention in "The Public Interest."

The counterargument is that public broadcasting benefits the wealthy; it is welfare for the wealthy. If the government is used to subsidize the programs that those with high incomes enjoy (and have learned to enjoy because their income allows them to attend arts programs as children, to take music and theater, and to attend elite schools), then the wealthy will not have to pay the full cost. This view of government intervention is capture of special benefits by selected groups.

Resource Markets

29

An Overview of Resource Markets

FUNDAMENTAL QUESTIONS

1. Who are the buyers and sellers of resources?
2. How are resource prices determined?
3. How does a firm allocate its expenditures among the various resources?

F irms are in business to make profits: we have learned how they attempt to differentiate their products, restrict entry, and otherwise behave so as to increase their profits. And we've seen that the type of behavior they undertake depends on the market structure in which they operate. But profit is not just the revenue obtained from selling products. The costs of running the business must be subtracted from that revenue to arrive at the profit figure. Firms attempt to use those combinations of resources that enable them to produce their products at the lowest cost.

Which combinations of resources are most profitable? The answer does not depend solely on what the firms want. It depends also on the resource markets. It is in the resource markets that the demand for and supply of resources determine the prices and the quantities of those resources. Firms are the demanders of resources, and the resource owners are the suppliers. To understand why firms lay off middle managers, use more robotics, provide training for employees, purchase less fuel, locate offices in other nations, or expand

PREVIEW

the size of their buildings, it is necessary to understand how the resource markets function, to know what demand and supply look like and how they interact. This chapter provides an overview of the resource markets.

Since there are four broad categories of resources—land, labor, capital, and entrepreneurial ability—there are four resource markets. The properties that are common to each of these markets and a description of how the markets work are presented. You will see how the prices of resources and the quantities demanded are determined. You will also discover how a firm allocates its spending among different resources in order to maximize profit.

I. BUYERS AND SELLERS OF RESOURCES

Who are the buyers and sellers of resources?

residual claimants:
entrepreneurs who acquire profit, or the revenue remaining after all other resources have been paid

There are four general classes of resources (*factors of production*, or *inputs*) and thus four resource markets: land, labor, capital, and entrepreneurial ability. The price and quantity of each resource are determined in its resource market. Rent and the quantity of land used are determined in the land market. The wage rate and the number of people employed are determined in the labor market. The interest rate and the quantity of capital used are determined in the capital market. Profit is a residual, left from revenue after all costs (including opportunity costs) have been paid. The entrepreneur claims that residual, and for that reason, owners or entrepreneurs are often referred to as **residual claimants**.

l.a. The Resource Markets

To understand the four resource markets, you need to realize that the roles of firms and households are reversed from what they are in the product markets. Figure 1 is the simplest circular flow diagram you saw in Chapter 4. It illustrates the roles of firms and households in the product and resource markets. The product market is represented by the top lines in the figure. Households buy goods and services from firms, as shown by the line going from firms to households; and firms sell goods and services and receive revenue, as shown by the line going from households to firms. The resource market is represented by the bottom half of the diagram in Figure 1. Households are the sellers of resources, and firms are the buyers of resources. Households sell resources, as shown by the line going from households to firms; and firms pay households income, as shown by the line going from firms to households.

Resources are wanted not for themselves but for what they produce. A firm uses resources in order to produce goods and services. Thus, the demand for a resource by a firm depends on the demand for the goods and services that the firm produces. For this reason, the demand for resources is often called a **derived demand**: an automobile manufacturer uses land, labor, capital, and entrepreneurial ability to produce cars; a retail T-shirt store uses land, labor, capital, and entrepreneurial ability to sell T-shirts; a farmer uses land, labor, capital, and entrepreneurial ability to produce agricultural products.

derived demand:
demand stemming from what a resource can produce, not demand for the resource itself

Households supply resources in order to earn income. By offering to work, individuals supply their labor; by purchasing stocks, bonds, and other financial capital, households supply firms with the ability to acquire capital; by offering their land and the minerals, trees, and other natural resources associated with it, households supply land; and by offering to take the risk of business and produce goods and services, households offer their entrepreneurial ability.

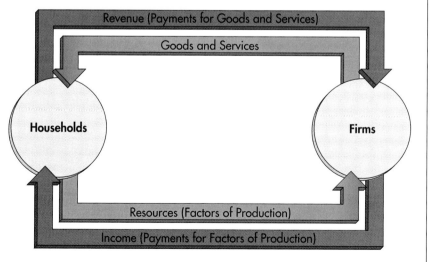

Figure 1
The Market for Resources
The buyers of resources are firms that purchase resources in order to produce goods and services. The sellers of resources are households that supply resources in order to obtain income with which to purchase goods and services.

Revenue (Payments for Goods and Services)

Goods and Services

Households

Firms

Resources (Factors of Production)

Income (Payments for Factors of Production)

1. Resources are classified into four types: land, labor, capital, and entrepreneurial ability.

2. The price of each type of resource—rent, wages, interest, and profits—and the quantity of each resource used are determined in the resource markets.

3. The buyers of resources are firms; the suppliers are households.

2. THE MARKET DEMAND FOR AND SUPPLY OF RESOURCES

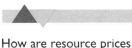

How are resource prices determined?

Firms demand resources and households supply resources. Except for this reversal in buyers and sellers, the supply and demand curves for resource markets look just like the supply and demand curves for product markets. The market demand curve slopes downward and the market supply curve upward. In resource markets, as in product markets, equilibrium defines the price and quantity. Changes in demand or supply cause the equilibrium price and quantity to change.

2.a. Market Demand

A firm chooses inputs in order to maximize profits.

The demand curve for a resource slopes down, as shown in Figure 2, because as the price of the resource falls, everything else held constant, producers are more *willing* and more *able* to use (to purchase or rent) that resource. If the price of the resource falls, that resource becomes relatively less expensive than other resources that the firm could use. Firms will substitute this now relatively less expensive resource for other now relatively more expensive

Figure 2
Resource Market Demand and Market Supply
The demand curve for a resource slopes down, reflecting the inverse relation between the price of the resource and the quantity demanded. The supply curve of a resource slopes up, reflecting the direct relation between the price of the resource and the quantity supplied. Equilibrium occurs where the two curves intersect; the quantities demanded and supplied are the same at the equilibrium price. If the resource price is greater than the equilibrium price, a surplus of the resource arises and drives the price back down to equilibrium. If the resource price is less than the equilibrium price, a shortage occurs and forces the price back up to equilibrium.

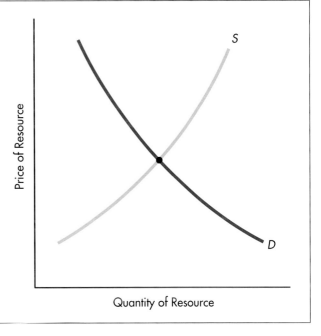

resources. Thus substitution occurs in production just as it does in consumption. Construction firms switch from copper tubing to plastic pipe as copper becomes relatively more expensive than plastic. Firms move from Manhattan to Dallas as land in Manhattan becomes relatively more expensive than land in Dallas. Economists may be hired to teach finance, management, and even accounting classes as the wages of professionals in those other fields rise relative to the wages of economists.

A lower price for a resource also increases a firm's *ability* to hire that resource. At a lower price, everything else held constant, firms can purchase more resources for the same total cost. If the price of a machine drops by 50 percent, the firm can buy two machines at the old cost of one. This means not that the firm will buy two machines but that it is able to buy the second machine. Thus, the demand curve for a resource slopes down because of income and substitution effects just as the demand curve for a product slopes down because of income and substitution effects, as you learned in the chapter on consumer choice.

2.a.1. The Elasticity of Resource Demand   The amount by which firms will alter their use of a resource when the price of that resource changes is measured by the price elasticity of resource demand. The price elasticity of the demand for a resource, e_r, is defined in exactly the same way as the price elasticity of demand—as the percentage change in the quantity demanded of a resource divided by the percentage change in the price of the resource:

$$e_r = \frac{\text{percentage change in quantity demanded of resource } j}{\text{percentage change in price of resource } j}$$

If the price of lumber rises by 10 percent and the quantity demanded falls by 5 percent, the price elasticity of demand for lumber is .5. If the rental rate of office space falls by 5 percent and the quantity demanded increases by 20 percent, the price elasticity of demand for office space is 4. The price elasticity of demand for a resource depends on the

- price elasticity of demand for the product the resource is used to produce
- proportion of total costs constituted by the resource
- number of substitutes for the resource
- time period under consideration

Price elasticity of the product   The price elasticity of demand for a resource depends on the price elasticity of demand for the product the resource is being used to produce. For instance, if the price elasticity of demand for newspapers is very high and the price of newspapers increases, the quantity demanded of newspapers will fall by a "great deal." As a result, a similarly "great deal" fewer resources are needed. Suppose then that the price of one of these resources, ink, rises. If the higher ink cost leads to a rise in the price of newspapers, then the quantity of newspapers demanded will decline by a significant amount and cause the quantity of ink purchased to decline by a significant amount. Everything else the same, we can say that the larger the price elasticity of demand for a product, the larger the price elasticity of demand for resources used to produce that product. The reverse is true as well.

Proportion of total costs   The larger one resource's proportion of the total costs of producing a good, the higher the price elasticity of demand for that resource. If airplanes constitute 60 percent of the total costs of running an airline, the price elasticity of demand for airplanes will be high. A small increase in the price of an airplane will tend to raise the airline's costs significantly, and this is likely to increase the price of tickets. The higher price for tickets will reduce the quantity demanded and thereby reduce the number of airplanes demanded.

Number of substitutes The number of substitutes for a resource affects the price elasticity of demand for a resource. For instance, if copper tubing, plastic tubing, steel tubing, or corrugated aluminum tubing can be used in construction equally well, the price elasticity of demand for any one of these types of tubing will be relatively high. Even a small increase in copper tubing would cause firms to switch immediately to other types of tubing.

Time period The time period is also important in determining the price elasticity of demand. The longer the period of time under consideration, the greater the price elasticity of demand for a resource. A longer period of time enables firms to discover other substitutes and to move relatively immobile resources into or out of use.

The price elasticity of resource demand varies according to the four factors just mentioned. The price elasticity of resource demand also varies along a straight-line resource demand curve, going from elastic to inelastic as we move down the demand curve, just as is the case with a product demand curve (see the chapter on demand and supply elasticities).

2.a.2. Shifts in the Demand for a Resource The demand curve for a resource will shift when one of the *nonprice* determinants of demand changes. Nonprice determinants of demand for a resource include the

- prices of the product the resource is used to produce
- productivity of a resource
- number of buyers of the resource
- prices of related resources
- quantities of other resources

Price of product When the price of copper rises, the demand for copper miners increases—the demand curve shifts out to the right. Mining firms hire more workers at each wage rate in order to produce more copper and earn the higher revenues.

Productivity When a resource becomes more productive—that is, when each unit of the resource can produce more output—the firm will use more of the resource. For instance, if new printing presses are able to produce twice as much in the same amount of time as existing presses, the demand for new printing presses will rise. The demand curve for printing presses will shift out to the right.

Number of buyers When new firms enter an industry, they require resources. The demand curve for resources will shift out to the right. For instance, when Wal-Mart builds a store in a small town, it must hire workers and acquire land, capital, buildings, and other supplies. The demand for workers, for capital, for land, and for the other supplies increases with the entry of Wal-Mart—the demand curves shift out to the right.

Entrepreneurs must combine land, labor, and capital to produce the goods and services they hope to sell for a profit. Leo Lindy's on Broadway in New York City had to spend more on very specific capital, this neon-lighted sign, than if the deli was located off-Broadway since it is competing for the attention of theatergoers. The specific capital provides benefits to the firm in that it provides information to consumers about the stability of the firm and the type of service provided by the firm. Consumers can choose between the deli with the neon sign or a dark bistro down the street.

Substitutes   A change in the price of substitute resources will affect the demand for a resource. For instance, if labor and machines are substitutes in the production of iron ore, then when the price of labor rises, the demand for machines increases—the demand curve for machines shifts out to the right. Conversely, if copper and plastic are substitutes in construction, then when the price of plastic declines, the demand for copper decreases—the demand curve for copper shifts in.

Quantity of other resources   A restaurant using only 10 of its 60 tables requires only one waiter. If the other 50 tables are also used, the restaurant needs more waiters. With a bigger pot and more soil, the quantity of flowers grown with each additional amount of fertilizer applied will be larger than it would be with a smaller pot and less soil. More capital tends to increase the demand for labor; more land tends to increase the demand for tractors. In other words, the demand for a resource depends on how many of the other resources are available.

2.b. Market Supply

A household supplies resources in order to maximize utility.

Individuals act so as to maximize their utility. They receive utility when they consume goods and services, but they need income to purchase the goods and services. To acquire income, households must sell the services of their resources. They must give up some of their leisure time and go to work or offer their other resources in order to acquire income. The quantity of resources that are supplied depends on the wages, rents, interest, and profits offered for those resources. If, while everything else is held constant, people can get higher wages, they will offer to work more hours; if they can obtain more rent for their land, they will offer more of their land for use, and so on. The quantity supplied of a resource rises as the price of the resource rises.

2.b.1. The Elasticity of Resource Supply   The amount by which resource owners alter the quantity they offer for use when the price of the resource

changes is measured by the price elasticity of resource supply, e_r^s. The price elasticity of supply for a resource is defined as the percentage change in the quantity supplied divided by the percentage change in the price of a resource:

$$e_r^s = \frac{\text{percentage change in quantity of resource supplied}}{\text{percentage change in price of resource}}$$

The price elasticity of resource supply depends on the number of substitute uses for a resource and the time period under consideration. Some resources have no substitutes. For instance, there are few if any substitutes for a rocket scientist; as a result, the price elasticity of supply for the rocket scientist is very low. Typically, the longer the period under consideration, the more likely that substitutes for a resource can be discovered. Given a few years, even an economist could be trained to be a rocket scientist. For a month or two, the quantity of oil that can be pulled from the ground is relatively fixed; given a year or so, new wells can be drilled and new supplies discovered. The price elasticity of resource supply increases as the time period increases.

When a resource has a perfectly inelastic supply curve, its pay or earnings is called **economic rent**. If a resource has a perfectly elastic supply curve, its pay or earnings is called **transfer earnings**. For upward-sloping supply curves, resource earnings consist of both transfer earnings and economic rent. Transfer earnings is what a resource could earn in its best alternative use (its opportunity cost). It is the amount that must be paid to get the resource to "transfer" to another use. Economic rent is earnings in excess of transfer earnings. It is the portion of a resource's earnings that is not necessary to keep the resource in its current use. A movie star can earn more than $1 million per movie but probably could not earn that kind of income in another occupation. Thus, the greatest share of the earnings of the movie star is economic rent.

There are two different meanings for the term *rent* in economics. The most common meaning refers to the payment for the use of something, as distinguished from payment for ownership. In this sense, you purchase a house but rent an apartment; you buy a car from Chrysler but rent cars from Avis. The second use of the term *rent* is to mean payment for the use of something that is in fixed—that is, perfectly inelastic—supply. The total quantity of land is fixed; payment to land is economic rent.

2.b.2. Shifts in the Supply of a Resource
The supply of a resource will change—increase or decrease at every price—if

- tastes change
- the number of suppliers changes
- the prices of other uses of the resource change

Suppose it suddenly becomes more prestigious to be a lawyer. The supply of people entering law schools will increase—the supply curve of lawyers will shift up or out to the right. The shift will occur because of a change in tastes (more prestige), not because of a change in the wage rate of lawyers.

An increase in the number of suppliers means that the supply curve shifts out to the right. For instance, discovery of oil in a country that is not currently an oil producer would mean an increase in the supply of oil—at each price a greater quantity of oil would be supplied. Immigration increases

economic rent:
the portion of earnings above transfer earnings

transfer earnings:
the portion of total earnings required to keep a resource in its current use

the supply of labor. More producers of bulldozers increase the supply of bulldozers.

The supply curve of a resource will shift if the price of related resources changes. If the wage rate of professionals in finance rises, economists and others may offer their services in the finance market. The supply curve of finance professionals will shift out. If the rental rate of land used for production of wheat rises, everything else held constant, land currently used to produce alfalfa will be switched over to wheat—the supply curve of land used in the production of wheat will shift out to the right.

2.c. Equilibrium

The intersection between the market demand and supply curves determines the price and quantity of a resource. If the demand curve shifts out, everything else held constant, the price rises; if the supply curve shifts out, everything else held constant, the price decreases. If the price rises above the equilibrium price, then a surplus exists and the price is forced back to equilibrium; if the price falls below the equilibrium level, then a shortage arises and the price is forced back up to equilibrium.

2.c.1. Price Ceilings and Floors
A resource market will move toward its equilibrium price and quantity as long as nothing interferes with the market adjustment. There are many instances where floors or ceilings are placed on the resource price, however. Consider the impact of a price floor in the labor market and a price ceiling in the steel market.

Figure 3(a) shows a labor market, with the quantity of labor in hours along the horizontal axis and the hourly wage rate along the vertical axis. The equilibrium wage determined in the market would be $W_e = \$3.50$. The government has proposed a minimum wage of $5.15 per hour, however, so if the proposed minimum wage is implement that the actual wage paid would be $W_m = \$5.15$, a price floor. At the minimum wage, the quantity of hours that people are willing and able to work is Q_s, while the quantity of hours that firms are willing and able to pay for is Q_d. The difference between Q_s and Q_d is the number of hours that people would like to work but for which there is no work.

A price ceiling works in just the opposite way of the price floor. The price ceiling creates a shortage. For instance, suppose the government requires foreign steel producers to sell their steel to U.S. manufacturers for no more than P_m in Figure 3(b). The quantity of steel demanded rises from Q_s to Q_d, whereas the quantity that the steel suppliers are willing to provide for sale at P_m is Q_s. The difference between Q_d and Q_s represents the shortage of steel.

RECAP

1. Firms purchase resources in such a way that they maximize profits. Households sell resources in order to maximize utility.

2. Transfer earnings is the portion of total earnings required to keep a resource in its current use.

Figure 3
Price Ceilings and Price Floors
Figure 3(a) is a labor market showing the quantity of labor in hours along the horizontal axis and the hourly wage rate along the vertical axis. The equilibrium wage determined in the market would be $W_e = \$3.50$, but because a minimum wage of $5.15 per hour has been imposed, the actual wage paid is $W_m = \$5.15$, a wage floor. At the minimum wage, the quantity of hours that people are willing and able to work is Q_s, while the

quantity of hours that firms are willing and able to pay for is Q_d. The difference between Q_s and Q_d is the number of hours that people would like to work but for which there is no work.

Figure 3(b) represents the market for steel. The equilibrium price is P_e, but because the government has implemented a program whereby foreign steel producers cannot sell their steel for more than P_m, the equilibrium price plays no role. A shortage is created equal to Q_d less Q_s.

(a) Labor Market

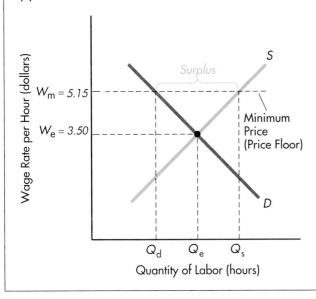

(b) Steel Market

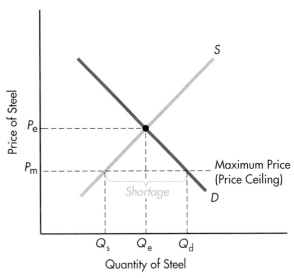

3. Economic rent is earnings in excess of transfer earnings.

4. Equilibrium in a resource market defines the price (wages, rent, interest, profit) of that resource as long as the price and quantity are free to adjust. Price ceilings lead to shortages; price floors lead to surpluses.

3. HOW FIRMS DECIDE WHAT RESOURCES TO BUY

How does a firm allocate its expenditures among the various resources?

The market demand for a resource consists of the demands of each firm willing and able to pay for a resource. An electric utility firm in Iowa demands engineers, as does a construction firm in Minnesota. The market demand for engineers consists of demands of the Iowa utility and the Minnesota construction firm. Each firm's demand depends on separate and distinct factors, however. The electric utility firm hires more engineers to modernize its plant; the construction firm hires more engineers to fulfill its contracts with the state government to build bridges. Yet all firms have the same decision-making process for hiring or acquiring resources.

3.a. Individual Firm Demand: Marginal Revenue Product

How do you decide how much you are willing to pay for something? Don't you decide how much it is worth to you? This is what businesses do when they decide how much to pay a worker or to pay for a machine. A firm uses the quantity of each resource that will enable the firm to maximize profit. Firms maximize profit when they operate at the level where marginal revenue (*MR*) equals marginal cost (*MC*). Thus, firms acquire additional resources until *MR* = *MC*. If the acquisition of a resource will raise the firm's revenues more than it will increase its costs—that is, if *MR* will be greater than *MC*—the firm will hire the resource. Conversely, if the acquisition of a resource will raise costs more than it will raise revenue—that is, if *MR* will be less than *MC*—then the firm will not hire the resource.

A firm will purchase the services of another unit of a resource if that additional unit adds more to the firm's revenue than it costs. Recall from the chapter on the costs of doing business that the additional output an extra unit of a resource produces is called the marginal physical product (*MPP*) of that resource. The *MPP* of tax accountants for a CPA firm is the number of tax returns that additional tax accountant can complete; the *MPP* is listed in column 3 of the table in Figure 4, and the *MPP* curve is drawn in the accompanying graph. The *MPP* curve initially rises and then declines according to the law of diminishing marginal returns.

marginal revenue product (MRP):
the value of the additional output that an extra unit of a resource can produce, $MPP \times MR$; the value to the firm of an additional resource

The value of this additional output to the firm is the additional revenue the output generates—the marginal revenue. Multiplying marginal physical product by marginal revenue yields the value of an additional unit of a resource to the firm, which is called the **marginal revenue product (MRP)**:

$$MRP = MPP \times MR$$

Figure 4
The *MPP* Curve
The value of a resource to a firm depends on the additional output that the resource produces. This additional output is the marginal physical product of the resource. The marginal physical product of accountants measured in number of tax returns per day is listed in the table. The marginal physical product is drawn as a curve in the graph.

(1) Number of Accountants	(2) Number of Tax Returns per Day	(3) MPP
1	6	6
2	19	13
3	25	6
4	29	4
5	31	2
6	32	1
7	32	0

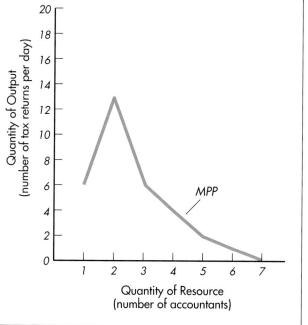

The MRP of a resource, such as labor, is a measure of how much the additional output generated by the last worker is worth to the firm. The marginal-revenue-product curve is drawn in Figure 5. The information from Figure 4 is listed in columns 1–3 of Figure 5. Marginal revenue is calculated in column 6 of the table in Figure 5 and multiplied by the *MPP* to arrive at the *MRP* in column 7. You can see that after rising initially, the *MRP* curve slopes downward.

3.b. Marginal Factor Costs

The *MRP* measures the value of an additional resource to a firm. To determine the quantity of a resource that a firm will hire, the firm must know the cost of each additional unit of the resource. The cost of an additional unit of a resource depends on whether the firm is purchasing resources in a market with many suppliers or in a market with one or only a few suppliers.

(1) Number of Accountants	(2) Number of Tax Returns per Day	(3) MPP	(4) Output Price (per tax return)	(5) Total Revenue	(6) Marginal Revenue	(7) MRP (MPP × MR)
1	6	6	$100	$ 600	$100	$ 600
2	19	13	100	1,900	100	1,300
3	25	6	100	2,500	100	600
4	29	4	100	2,900	100	400
5	31	2	100	3,100	100	200
6	32	1	100	3,200	100	100
7	32	0	100	3,200	0	0

Figure 5
The Marginal Revenue Product
The marginal physical product multiplied by the marginal revenue yields the marginal revenue product. The *MPP* curve from Figure 4 is multiplied by the marginal revenue and plotted in Figure 5 as the *MRP* curve. The information from Figure 4 is listed in columns 1–3 of Figure 5. The output price is listed in column 4, the total revenue, *P* × *Q*, is listed in column 5, and marginal revenue is calculated in column 6. Multiplying column 6 by column 3 yields the *MRP*, listed in column 7.

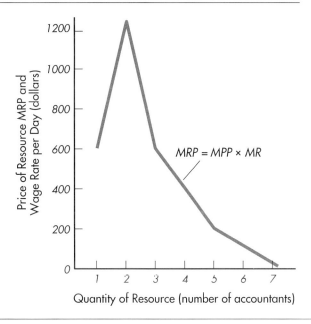

3.b.1. Hiring Resources in a Perfectly Competitive Market

If the firm is purchasing resources in a market where there is a very large number of suppliers of an identical resource—a perfectly competitive resource market—the price of each additional unit of the resource to the firm is constant. Why? Because no seller is large enough to individually change the price. A firm can hire as much of the resource as it wants without affecting either the quantity available or the price of that resource. This situation is shown in Figures 6(a) and 6(b) for the market for accountants. The market wage is defined by the market demand and market supply, as shown in Figure 6(a), and that wage translates to a horizontal supply curve for the individual firm, as shown in Figure 6(b).

Let's assume that the market wage for accountants is $150 per day. The firm can hire as many accountants as it wants at $150 per day without influencing the price. How many accountants will the firm hire? It will hire additional accountants as long as the additional revenue brought in by the last accountant hired is no less than the additional cost of that accountant.

Let's use the information in Figure 7, which combines Figures 5 and 6, to see how many accountants the firm would hire. The first accountant hired has a marginal revenue product of $600 per day and costs $150 per day. It is profitable to hire her. A second accountant, bringing in an additional $1,300 per day and costing $150 per day, is also profitable. The third accountant brings in $600 per day, the fourth $400 per day, the fifth $200 per day, the

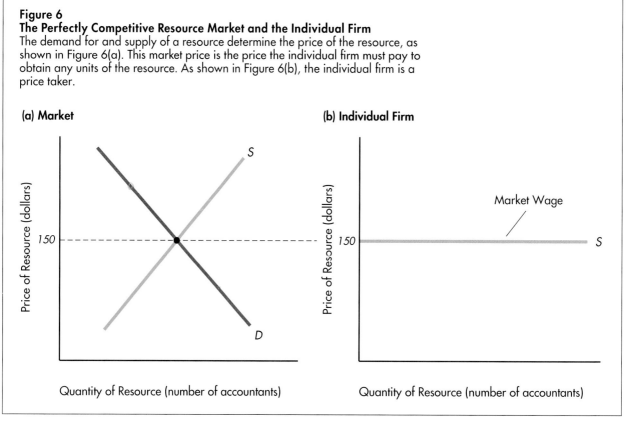

Figure 6
The Perfectly Competitive Resource Market and the Individual Firm
The demand for and supply of a resource determine the price of the resource, as shown in Figure 6(a). This market price is the price the individual firm must pay to obtain any units of the resource. As shown in Figure 6(b), the individual firm is a price taker.

(a) Market

(b) Individual Firm

Figure 7
The Employment of Resources

The marginal revenue product and the marginal factor cost (wage rate) together indicate the number of accountants the individual firm would hire. The *MRP* and the *MFC* for an individual firm are listed in the table. The *MRP* curve and the *MFC* curve are shown in the graph. The marginal revenue product exceeds the marginal factor cost (wage rate) until after the fifth accountant is hired. The firm will not hire more than five, for then the costs would exceed the additional revenue produced by the last accountant hired.

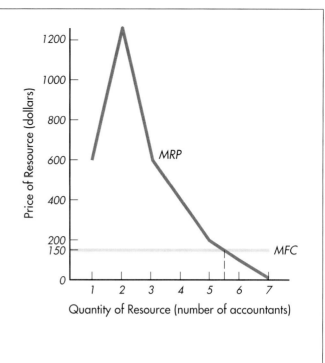

(1) Number of Accountants	(2) MRP	(3) MFC (wage per day)
1	$ 600	$150
2	1,300	150
3	600	150
4	400	150
5	200	150
6	100	150
7	0	150

sixth $100 per day, and the seventh nothing. Thus, the third, fourth, and fifth are profitable, but the sixth and seventh aren't. At $150 per day, the firm hires five accountants. You can see in the graph that the marginal revenue product lies above the wage rate until after the fifth accountant is hired.

The firm hires additional accountants until *MRP* is equal to the cost to the firm of another accountant. Remember, the *MRP* is the value of the additional resource to the firm; thus, the firm wants to be sure that the value of a resource exceeds its costs. The cost of an additional unit of a resource is the **marginal factor cost (MFC)**, also known as the *marginal resource cost* or *marginal input cost*. The marginal factor cost for accountants is listed as column 3 in Figure 7.

The firm hires additional accountants until the marginal revenue product equals the marginal factor cost, *MRP = MFC*. This is a general rule; it holds whether the firm sells its output in a perfectly competitive, monopoly, monopolistically competitive, or oligopoly market; and it holds for all resources, not just accountants.

3.b.2. **Hiring Resources as a Monopoly Buyer**   If only one firm is bidding for a resource or a product, that firm is called a **monopsonist**. In the early days of mining in the United States it was not uncommon for firms to create entire towns in order to attract a readily available supply of labor. The sole provider of jobs in the town was the mining company. Thus, when the company hired labor, it affected the prices of all workers, not just the worker it recently hired. In the 1970s along the Alaskan pipeline, and in the 1980s in

marginal factor cost (MFC): the additional cost of an additional unit of a resource

Resources will be employed up to the point at which MRP = MFC.

monopsonist: a firm that is the only buyer of a resource

The Company Town

Early in his career, Milton Friedman, the Nobel Prize–winning economist, served as an instructor for the navy. His assignment was in Hershey, Pennsylvania, where he stayed at the Hershey Hotel, on the corner of Cocoa Avenue and Chocolate Boulevard, across the street from the Hershey Junior College, down the street from the Hershey Department Store. Friedman describes Hershey as a benevolent company town, but not all company towns that arose in the early 1900s were so benevolent. Workers who were employed in factories or mines located far from large cities were often required to live in company housing and buy their food and other supplies at company stores. The prices many paid at the company store were very high, because the stores were local monopolies.

By the 1940s, most company towns and stores had disappeared, but a few still exist today. Documented and undocumented aliens who work in the agricultural areas of the Southwest often must pay their employers for their sleeping quarters, their food and drinks, and other items. The workers are paid in kind rather than cash and often end up owing more to the company store than they receive in wages.

Sources: Andrew Gulliford, *Boomtown Blues: Colorado Oil Shale, 1885–1985* (Boulder: University Press of Colorado, 1990); Dennis Farney, "Price of Progress," *The Wall Street Journal*, April 3, 1990, pp. 1, A14; Milton Friedman, "The Folly of Buying Health Care at the Company Store," *The Wall Street Journal*, Feb. 3, 1993, p. A14.

foreign countries where U.S. firms were hired to carry out specialized engineering projects or massive construction jobs, small towns dependent on a single U.S. firm were created. There are cases where a monopsony exists even though a company town was not created. For instance, many universities in small communities are monopsonistic employers—they are the primary employer in the town. When these universities hire a mechanic, they affect the wage rates of all mechanics in the town. Other examples of monopsonies are discussed in the Economic Insight "The Company Town."

A monopoly firm will pay resources less than their marginal revenue products. Suppose, for example, that a large semiconductor firm in a small town is the primary employer in the town and that the firm is in the process of hiring accountants. As shown in Figure 8 (see table), at a wage of $25 per day only 1 person is willing and able to work. If the firm pays $50 per day, it can hire 2 accountants. However, the firm isn't able to hire the first at $25 and the second at $50; it must pay both $50. Otherwise, the first will quit and then be rehired at $50 per day (only 2 were willing and able to work for $50). As a result, the total cost (called *total factor cost*) of two accountants is $100, not $75, and the additional, or marginal, factor cost is $75 rather than the $50 wage of the second accountant. If the firm offers $150 per day, it can hire 4 accountants; its total factor cost will be $600 and its marginal factor cost $300. This is shown in columns 8, 9, and 10 of the table. Column 8 is the wage per day, 9 is the total factor cost (column 1 times column 8), and 10 is the marginal factor cost.

The graph in Figure 8 shows the marginal factor cost and the supply curve of accountants in the small town. The *MFC* curve is plotted from data in col-

(1) Number of Accountants	(2) Number of Tax Returns per Day	(3) MPP	(4) Product Price (per tax return)	(5) Total Revenue	(6) MR	(7) MRP	(8) Wage per Day	(9) Total Factor Cost of Accountants	(10) MFC
1	6	6	$100	$ 600	$100	$ 600	$ 25	$ 25	$ 25
2	19	13	100	1,900	100	1,300	50	100	75
3	25	6	100	2,500	100	600	100	300	200
4	29	4	100	2,900	100	400	150	600	300
5	31	2	100	3,100	100	200	200	1,000	400
6	32	1	100	3,200	100	100	250	1,500	500
7	32	0	100	3,200	100	0	300	2,100	600

Note: Marginal revenue is the change in total revenue divided by the change in output. In this case, it is the change in total revenue divided by the change in the number of tax returns produced.

Figure 8
The Monopsonist
When the firm is a monopsonistic buyer of resources, it faces a marginal-factor-cost curve that lies above the supply curve. Each time the firm purchases a unit of the resource, the price of all units of the resource is driven up. As a result, the cost of one additional unit of the resource exceeds the price that must be paid for that additional unit of the resource. This is shown in columns 8 through 10 of the table; columns 8 and 10 are plotted in the graph. The firm hires resources until the marginal revenue product and marginal factor cost are equal. The firm pays resources the price given by the supply curve at the quantity determined by MFC = MRP. Thus, the resource receives less than its marginal revenue product.

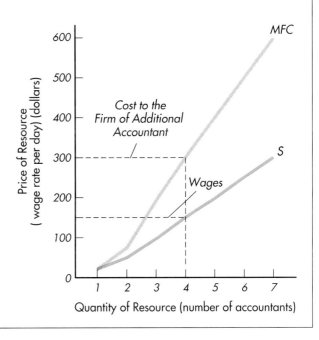

umn 10 of the table, and the supply curve is plotted from data in column 8. For a monopsonist, the *MFC* curve lies above the supply curve. The reason is that the cost of each additional accountant to the firm is the additional accountant's wage *plus* the additional wages paid to all of the other accountants.

The rising marginal factor cost means that the accountants would be paid less than their marginal revenue product. The firm would hire 4 accountants since the fifth accountant costs the firm $400 (*MFC*) but brings in only $200 (*MRP*). The fourth accountant produces $400 of additional revenue for the firm (*MRP*), costs the firm an additional $300 (*MFC*), but is paid only $150.

A firm buying in a perfectly competitive resource market will pay the marginal revenue product; a monopsonistic firm will pay less than the marginal revenue product.

As long as resource services are purchased by other than a monopsonist, they are paid their marginal revenue products. A monopsonist pays less than the marginal revenue product.

3.c. Hiring When There Is More Than One Resource

To this point we've examined the firm's hiring decision for one resource, everything else, including the quantities of all other resources, held constant. However, a firm uses several resources and makes hiring decisions regarding most of them all the time. How does the firm decide what combinations of resources to use? Like the consumer deciding what combinations of goods and services to purchase, the firm will ensure that the benefits of spending one more dollar are the same no matter which resource the firm chooses to spend that dollar on.

You may recall that the consumer maximizes utility when the marginal utility per dollar of expenditure is the same on all goods and services purchased:

$$MU_{CDs}/P_{CDs} = MU_{gas}/P_{gas} = \ldots = MU_n/P_n$$

A similar rule holds for the firm attempting to purchase resource services in order to maximize profit and minimize costs. The firm will be maximizing profit when its marginal revenue product per dollar of expenditure on all resources is the same:

$$MRP_{land}/MFC_{land} = MRP_{labor}/MFC_{labor} = \ldots = MRP_n/MFC_n$$

The last dollar spent on resources must yield the same marginal revenue product no matter which resource the dollar is spent on.

As long as the marginal factor cost of a resource is less than its marginal revenue product, the firm will increase profit by hiring more of the resource. If a dollar spent on labor yields less marginal revenue product than a dollar spent on capital, the firm will increase profit more by purchasing the capital than if it purchases the labor.[1]

If a resource is very expensive relative to other resources, then the expensive resource must generate a significantly larger marginal revenue product than the other resources. For instance, for a firm to remain in Manhattan, it must generate a significantly larger marginal revenue product than could be obtained in Dallas or elsewhere, because rents are so much higher in Manhattan. The price of land in Tokyo is so high that its use requires a very high marginal revenue product.

A firm will streamline its work force when the last dollar of expenditures on labor generates less marginal revenue product than if that dollar were spent on another resource; a firm will streamline by reducing its middle management if the last dollar spent on middle management generates less return (lower *MRP*) than if that dollar were spent on other labor or another resource. During the early 1990s, many U.S. firms decided that their expenditures on middle management particularly, but also on their entire labor force, were not generating the same return that expenditures on other

---

[1]This equimarginal rule can also be written as $MPP_{land}/MFC_{land} = MPP_{labor}/MFC_{labor}$ = . . . since $MRP = MFC$ or $MRP/MFC = 1$ and since $MRP = MPP \times MR$, $MPP/MFC = 1/MR$ for all resources.

resources would yield. As a result, firms reduced their work force; they dismissed many middle-management employees. The media referred to this process as downsizing, but it was part of the ongoing process by firms to ensure that the last dollar of expenditure on each resource generated the same *MRP*.

A firm in equilibrium in terms of allocating its expenditures among resources will alter the allocation only if the cost of one of the resources rises relative to the others. For instance, if government-mandated medical or other benefits mean that labor costs rise while everything else remains constant, then firms will tend to hire less labor and use more of other resources. (This issue is discussed further in the Economic Insight "Labor Regulations and Employment.") Everything else the same, if the costs of doing business in the United States rise, firms will locate offices or plants in other countries.

3.d. Product Market Structures and Resource Demand

Firms purchase the types and quantities of resource services that allow them to maximize profit; each firm equates the *MRP* per dollar of expenditure on all resource services used. The *MRP* depends on the market structure in which the firm sells its output. A perfectly competitive firm produces more output and sells that output at a lower price than a firm operating in any other market, everything else the same. Since the perfectly competitive firm produces more output, it must use more resources. Thus, everything else the same, the demand curve for a resource by a perfectly competitive firm will lie above the demand curve for a resource by a firm selling in monopoly, oligopoly, or monopolistically competitive markets.

For the perfectly competitive firm, price and marginal revenue are the same, $P = MR$. Thus, the marginal revenue product, $MRP = MR \times MPP$, for the perfectly competitive firm can be written as $P \times MPP$. Sometimes this is called the value of the marginal product, *VMP*, to distinguish it from the marginal revenue product.

$$MRP = MR \times MPP$$

$$VMP = P \times MPP$$

The demand for a resource by a single firm is the *MRP* of that resource, no matter whether it sells its goods and services as a monopolist or as a perfect competitor (for the perfectly competitive firm, $VMP = MRP$, so that *MRP* is its resource demand as well). However, since for the firms not selling in a perfectly competitive market, price is greater than marginal revenue, *VMP* would be greater than *MRP*, which indicates that the perfectly competitive firm's demand curve for a resource lies above (or is greater than) the demand curve for a resource by a monopoly firm, oligopoly firm, or monopolistically competitive firm.

3.e. A Look Ahead

In the following chapters, we will examine aspects of the resource markets. In the labor market we discuss why different people receive different wages, why firms treat employees the way they do, the impact of labor laws, and the causes and results of discrimination. In the land market we'll look at problems of the environment and why the government is such a large player in the

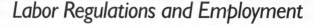
Labor Regulations and Employment

Firms must contribute to workers' compensation programs, which provide medical benefits and cash transfers to workers injured on the job; in some cases, stress is an acceptable basis for providing workers' compensation. The Family Leave Act implemented in 1993 provides for up to a twelve-week period per year for employees to leave their jobs without pay in order to take care of family matters and then to return to their jobs without penalty. How do these rules, regulations, and programs affect the resource market for labor?

If these programs are additional costs of using labor services, then firms will find that the ratios of their marginal revenue product per dollar of expenditure on labor and on all other resources are not equal; the ratio for labor will have been reduced. As a result, firms must find ways to reduce labor costs or use less labor. Firms can reduce labor costs if they find ways to avoid paying workers' compensation or health insurance or allow-

ing workers to take unpaid leaves of absence. Firms have discovered that temporary and part-time workers do not have to be provided these benefits. *The Wall Street Journal* recently reported that temporary employment grew ten times faster than overall employment in the United States between 1982 and 1990, and that temporary and part-time workers now make up about 25 percent of the work force. By turning to temporary agencies, smaller employers may be exempted from providing worker benefits. For instance, the family leave provisions apply only to firms with fifty or more permanent employees. Thus, a firm with sixty permanent employees must provide the benefit of family leave; by making eleven or more of these employees temporary, the firm does not have to provide the benefit of family leave. Moreover, firms do not have to provide workers' compensation or health and medical benefits for temporary employees.[1] Another way that firms can reduce labor costs is to pay the

mandatory benefits but reduce the compensation provided workers. About 85 percent of the costs of workers' compensation are passed on to employees through lower wages.[2] In this sense, the *MFC* of the workers is increased much less than the workers' compensation costs, so the ratio of *MRP/MFC* falls only a little relative to that of other resources. For workers whose wages are near the minimum wage, the costs cannot be shifted to them, so their *MRP/MFC* ratio will decline relatively more. Finally, if labor costs cannot be reduced, employment will fall as firms allocate their expenditures to other resources and away from labor.

[1]Clare Ansberry, "Hired Out," *The Wall Street Journal*, March 11, 1993, p. A1.

[2]Jonathan Gruber and Alan Krueger, "The Incidence of Mandated Employer-Provided Insurance: Lessons from Workers' Compensation Insurance," NBER Working Paper No. 3557, Feb. 1991.

natural resources area. We will discuss the capital market and examine why firms carry out research and development and purchase robotics. Selling resource services creates income, so we'll examine who has income and why. These and other aspects of the resource markets will be examined within the framework discussed in this chapter.

RECAP

1. The *MRP* of a resource is a measure of how much the additional output generated by the last unit of the resource is worth to the firm.

2. Resources are hired up to the point at which *MRP* = *MFC*.

3. In a perfectly competitive resource market, resources are paid an amount equal to their marginal revenue product. In a monopsonistic resource market, resources are paid less than their marginal revenue product.

4. A firm will allocate its budget on resources up to the point that the last dollar spent yields an equal marginal revenue product no matter on which resource the dollar is spent.

5. A perfectly competitive firm will hire and acquire more resources than firms selling in monopoly, oligopoly, or monopolistically competitive product markets, everything else the same.

SUMMARY

▲▼ Who are the buyers and sellers of resources?

1. The term *resource markets* refers to the buyers and sellers of four classes of resources: land, labor, capital, and entrepreneurial ability. §Preview

2. The buyers of resources are firms that purchase resources in order to produce goods and services. §1.a

3. The sellers of resources are households that supply resources in order to obtain income with which to purchase goods and services. §1.a

▲▼ How are resource prices determined?

4. Equilibrium in each resource market defines the rate of pay of the resource and the quantity used. §2

5. The rate of pay of a resource consists of two parts: transfer earnings and economic rent. Transfer earnings is the rate of pay necessary to keep a resource in its current use. Economic rent is the excess of pay above transfer earnings. §2.b.1

6. A single firm's demand for a resource is the downward-sloping portion of the marginal-revenue-product curve for that resource. §3.a

7. A firm purchasing resources in a perfectly competitive resource market will hire resources up to the point that $MRP = MFC$. A firm that is one of only a few buyers or the only buyer of a particular resource (a monopsonist) will face a marginal-factor-cost curve that is above the supply curve for that resource. As a result, the resource is paid less than its marginal revenue product. §3.b.1, 3.b.2

▲▼ How does a firm allocate its expenditures among the various resources?

8. A firm will allocate its budget on resources in such a way that the last dollar spent will yield the same marginal revenue product no matter on which resource the dollar is spent. §3.c

KEY TERMS

residual claimants §1

derived demand §1.a

economic rent §2.b.1

transfer earnings §2.b.1

marginal revenue product (*MRP*) §3.a

marginal factor cost (*MFC*) §3.b.1

monopsonist §3.b.2

EXERCISES

1. What does it mean to say that the demand for resources is a derived demand? Is the demand for all goods and services a derived demand?

2. Using the information in the following table, calculate the marginal revenue product ($MRP = MPP \times MR$).

3. Using the data in question 2, determine how many units of resources the firm will want to acquire.

Units of Resources	Total Output	Output Price	Resource Price
1	10	$5	$10
2	25	5	10
3	35	5	10
4	40	5	10
5	40	5	10

4. Suppose the output price falls from $5 to $4 to $3 to $1 in question 2. How would that change your answers to questions 2 and 3?

5. Using the data in question 2, calculate the marginal factor cost.

6. Suppose the resource price rises from $10 to $12 to $14 to $18 to $20 as resource units go from 1 to 5. How would that change your answer to question 5? How would it change your answer to question 3?

7. Using question 6, calculate the transfer earnings and economic rent of the third unit of the resource when four units of the resource are employed. Do the same calculations when only three units of the resource are employed. How do you account for the different answers?

8. Do resources earn their marginal revenue products? Demonstrate under what conditions the answer is *yes*.

9. What is a monopsonist? How does a monopsonist differ from a monopolist?

10. Supposedly Larry Bird once said that he would play basketball for $10,000 per year. Yet he was paid over $1 million per year. If the quote is correct, how much was Bird's transfer earnings? How much was his economic rent?

11. In 1989 the Japanese spent more than $14 billion to buy 322 foreign companies, half of them in the United States, and $100 billion to buy foreign stocks and bonds. Why was Japanese money flowing so heavily out of Japan and into other parts of the world?

12. Early in her journalistic career, Gloria Steinem posed as a Playboy Bunny to examine the inside of a Playboy Club. Steinem discovered that the Bunnies had to purchase their costumes from the club, pay for the cleaning, purchase their food from the club, and so on. This "company store" exploited the employees (the Bunnies), according to Steinem. Explain what Steinem meant by exploitation.

13. Explain the idea behind the lyrics "You load 16 tons, and what do you get? You get another day older and deeper in debt. Saint Peter, don't you call me, 'cause I can't go. I owe my soul to the company store."

14. The Burroughs-Wellcome Company had a monopoly on AZT, a pharmaceutical that delays the onset of AIDS after someone has become HIV positive. The demand for that pharmaceutical was virtually perfectly price-inelastic. Explain how that might affect the demand for employees by the Burroughs-Wellcome Company.

COOPERATIVE LEARNING EXERCISE

Divide the class into groups of three or four. Have the groups develop four multiple-choice answers (only one correct answer) to the following question:

A firm decides to downsize, or lay off employees, when

a.

b.

c.

d.

Ask two groups to stand. One group reads an answer and the second group says whether the answer is correct or not. Then reverse the roles for the groups. Carry out the procedure with as many groups as desired.

Firms Plan to Keep Hiring, Spending

After a strong 1994, companies this year will again boost spending on equipment and buildings. And they'll again boost hiring. Both trends are good news for the economy and for burned out workers. Unless, many economists warn, companies go too far. The reason spending and hiring will remain healthy: CEOs in a wide variety of industries are very optimistic. Joe Rado is typical. "1994 was a fantastic year—better than I expected—and I'm very optimistic 1995 will be even better," says Rado, CEO of World Electronics, a Morgantown, Pa. based firm that uses robots to assemble computer circuit boards for AT&T and others.

"My friends are CEOs of small companies and they're really opti-

mistic, too," Rado says. "They all say they'll continue to spend, to hire and expand in 1995 because their business outlooks are great. Even a friend who sells sandpaper is doing great."

The story is much the same at businesses across the nation. From giant Motorola—which will spend $4.5 billion on equipment and buildings worldwide this year (up 36 percent from last year—to small companies such as Tray-Pak spending and hiring plans are bullish.

Commentary

The demand for resources—land, labor, capital and entrepreneurial ability—are often referred to as derived demands because these items are not wanted for themselves but for what they produce. When customers are purchasing products such as computers, telephone services, houses and autos, the producers of these goods will provide the products. This means the producers must have the resources needed to produce the products. Capital such as robots, buildings, and computer chips, skilled and unskilled labor, and land that is rented or purchased for constructing new buildings will all be demanded by the producers.

Businesses must forecast what the demand for their products will be in coming weeks, months and years. Since it often takes time to hire resources and increase production, businesses must hire the resources now that will enable the firm to produce the forecasted quantity of goods and services. According to the article, the outlook or forecast at the beginning of 1995 was for another strong year—continued increases in demand for almost all products. As a result, the demand for the resources increased now.

The article also notes that the increased demand for resources will benefit the economy. Why would this be the case? Consider the simple circular flow diagram shown below. As businesses attempt to increase their production, they must hire more resources. Hiring more resources means more money (income) flows from businesses to the household sector. Higher income means that households will have more money with which to purchase goods and services. And, as the circular flow of income and goods and resources speeds up, the value of GDP (Gross Domestic Product) rises.

The article does not say which resources will feel the greatest demand or if some resources will not be affected. But, not all resources are bought and sold in the same type of market. Some resources are unique and the owners of those resources function much like monopolists. Other resources are easily and widely attainable, and their owners are price takers. Some resource owners must sell to only one firm or only a few firms and therefore face monopoly or oligopoly buyers. Other resource owners sell to many different firms. The market structure—the selling and buying environment of the resources—will determine whether prices rise when demand rises and by how much prices rise.

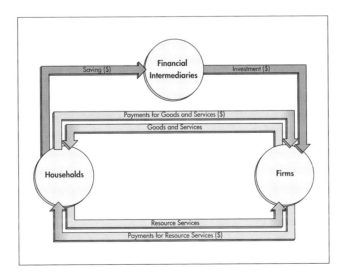

30

The Labor Market: Wage Differentials and Personnel Practices

FUNDAMENTAL QUESTIONS

1. Are people willing to work more hours for higher wages?
2. What are compensating wage differentials?
3. Why might wages be higher for people with more human capital than for those with less human capital?
4. Why do older workers tend to earn more than younger workers?
5. What is the explanation for widespread personnel practices that appear to contradict economic theory?

Older workers tend to earn higher wages than younger workers; males earn more than females; whites earn more than blacks and Hispanics; and unionized workers earn more than nonunionized workers. Yet, as we learned in the previous chapter, a worker will be paid his or her marginal revenue product (except in a monopsonistic firm). Does this mean that older workers are more productive than younger ones, males more productive than females, whites more productive than people of color, and so on, or is there something missing in our theory of the labor market? In this and the next chapter we delve more deeply into the labor market.

I. THE SUPPLY OF LABOR

PREVIEW

The supply of labor comes from individual households. Each member of a household must determine whether to give up a certain number of hours each day to work. That decision is the individual's labor supply decision and is called the *labor-leisure tradeoff*.

I.a. Individual Labor Supply: Labor-Leisure Tradeoff

There are only twenty-four hours in a day, and people have to decide how to allocate this scarce time. They really have only two options: they can spend their time (1) working for pay, or (2) not working. *Any* time spent not working is called *leisure time*. Leisure time includes being a "couch potato," serving as a volunteer coach for your daughter's first-grade soccer team, volunteering to serve food at St. Jude's food bank, or participating in any other activity except working at a paying job. People want leisure time. Although most people enjoy aspects of their jobs, most would rather have more leisure time and less work time. However, people must purchase the desired good, leisure, by forgoing the wages they could earn by working. As wages increase, the cost of leisure time increases, causing people to purchase less leisure. Purchasing less leisure means working more.

The number of hours that people are willing and able to work rises as the wage rate rises, at least until people say, "I have enough income; perhaps I'll enjoy a little more leisure." When the price of leisure increases—in other words, when the wage rate increases—people choose to work more. But, as the wage rate increases, some people choose to enjoy more leisure time. They now have more income with which they can purchase all goods and services, including leisure time. Thus, a wage increase has two opposing effects: one leads to increased hours of work and one leads to decreased hours. This

Are people willing to work more hours for higher wages?

People can allocate their time to work or leisure.

means that the quantity of labor supplied may rise or fall as the wage rate rises.

The labor supply curve shown in Figure 1 is what the labor supply curve for an individual usually looks like. It rises as the wage rate rises until the wage is sufficiently high that people begin to choose more leisure; then the curve begins to turn backward. This is called the **backward-bending labor supply curve**.

backward-bending labor supply curve:
a labor supply curve indicating that a person is willing and able to work more hours as the wage rate increases until, at some sufficiently high wage rate, the person chooses to work fewer hours

1.a.1. **Do People Really Trade Off Labor and Leisure?** As discussed in the Economic Insight "The Overworked American?" not all economists agree with the idea that people trade off work and leisure. There is no doubt that few have the luxury of deciding each minute whether to work or take leisure time. Some might be able to choose between part-time and full-time work, but full-time work usually means eight hours a day, and part-time work typically means lower-quality jobs and much less pay per hour than the full-time job. Most people, then, are unable to choose how much to work on a day-to-day basis depending on their preferences for leisure that day. But over a month, a year, or several years, people do choose to put in more or less time on the job. Some people choose occupations that enable them more flexibility; many prefer to be self-employed in order to be able to choose whether to put in more or less time on the job. People can also *moonlight*, work an additional job or put in extra hours after the full-time job is completed.

1.b. From Individual to Market Supply

labor force participation:
entering the work force

When you enter the labor market, you offer various levels of services at various wage rates. The decision about whether to offer your labor services for employment is a decision about **labor force participation**, joining the work force in the United States. People over the age of sixteen who are actively seeking a job are said to be members of the labor force. These are the people who have chosen to offer their labor services for employment at specific wage

---

Figure 1
The Individual's Labor Supply Curve
As the wage rate rises, people are willing and able to supply more labor, at least up to some high wage rate. A higher wage rate means that the opportunity cost of leisure time increases so that people will purchase less leisure (will work more). Conversely, as the wage rate rises and people's incomes rise, more of all goods are purchased, including leisure time. As a result, fewer hours are supplied for work. Which of these opposing effects is larger determines whether the labor supply curve slopes upward or downward. The most commonly shaped labor supply curve is one that slopes upward until the wage rate reaches some high level and then, as people choose more leisure time, begins to bend backward.

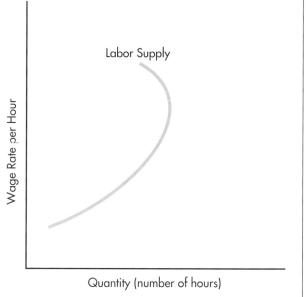

The Overworked American?

The average employed person in America is now on the job an additional 163 hours, or the equivalent of an extra month a year, as compared to 1969.[1] What accounts for the increased hours devoted to work and thus the fewer hours devoted to leisure? The view of most economists is that people choose to work more in order to acquire more income. People trade off leisure for more work and thus more income.

Not all economists agree with the view that people can trade off work and leisure. Many argue that individuals have no choice, that leisure time is simply being squeezed out by the necessity of working and the demands of firms. A group of economists known as *institutionalists* argue that the modern industrial state does not give workers the flexibility economists seem to imply in their labor demand and labor supply model. The institutional economists argue that firms set the hours they require of their employees and employees must accept them or accept significantly lower standards

of living. They point to studies that have asked people about their work habits and found that people did not have a choice of hours; they had a choice of either no job or a job at hours that were not those they would choose.[2] In a popular book, *The Overworked American: The Unexpected Decline of Leisure*, author Juliet Schor argues that consumer-workers become indoctrinated by firms into consuming, which requires more income and thus more hours devoted to work. According to Schor, workers can't really trade off work and leisure but if they could, their indoctrination to consume constrains them; they must work more and more to be able to consume more and more.[3]

The economists opposing the institutionalists' view point out that workers can change occupations or jobs because hours worked vary considerably from occupation to occupation and that workers can also moonlight (work extra jobs or hours) or retire in order to alter their hours.[4] They also point to surveys where it was found that

people preferred their current number of hours and pay to working fewer hours at the same rate of pay or more hours at the same rate of pay.[5] Like most issues in economics, unanimity of opinion over this issue does not exist.

[1]Juliet B. Schor, *The Overworked American: The Unexpected Decline of Leisure* (New York: Basic Books, 1991).
[2]Shulamit Kahn and Kevin Lang, "Constraints on the Choice of Work Hours: Agency vs. Specific-Capital," *National Bureau of Economic Research Working Paper 2238*, May 1987, p. 14; Robert Moffit, "The Tobit Model, Hours of Work, and Institutional Constraints," *Review of Economics and Statistics* 64, August 1982, pp. 510–515.
[3]Schor, op.cit.
[4]Joseph Altonji and Christina H. Paxson, "Labor Supply Preferences, Hours Constraints, and Hour-Wage Tradeoffs," *Journal of Labor Economics* 6, No. 2, 1988, pp. 254–276.
[5]Susan E. Shank, "Preferred Hours of Work and Corresponding Earnings," *Monthly Labor Review* (November 1986), p. 41, table 1.

rates. As the wage rate increases, the number of people participating in the labor force increases.

Figure 2(a) shows the labor *market* supply curve. It consists of the horizontal sum of all individual labor supply curves, such as the sum of the individual labor supply curves shown in Figures 2(b) and 2(c). If the labor supply curve for each individual slopes upward, then the market supply curve, the sum of each individual supply curve, slopes upward. Even if the individual labor supply curve bends backward at some high wage, it is unlikely that all of the curves will bend backward at the same wage. Not everyone has the same tradeoffs between labor and leisure; not all offer to work at the same wage rate; not all want the same kind of job. As the wage rate rises, some people who chose not to participate in the labor market at lower wages are induced to offer their services for employment at a higher wage. You can see in Figure 2(b) that Mary chooses not to enter the labor force at wages below

Figure 2
The Labor Market Supply Curve

Figure 2(a) shows the labor market supply curve obtained by adding the individual labor supply curves of Figures 2(b) and 2(c). Figure 2(a) indicates that as the wage rate rises, the number of hours each person is willing and able to work increases, at least up to some high wage rate, and the number of people willing and able to supply hours of work increases.

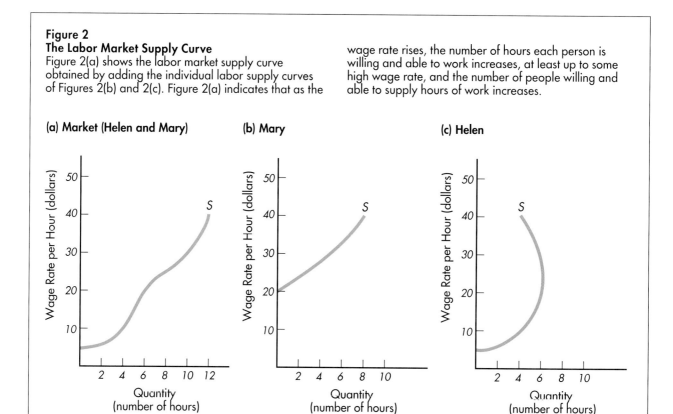

(a) Market (Helen and Mary)   **(b) Mary**   **(c) Helen**

$20 per hour. Helen, in Figure 2(c), enters the labor force for any wage above $5 per hour. Thus, the labor market supply curve slopes up because the number of people willing and able to work rises as the wage rate rises and because the number of hours that each person is willing and able to work rises as the wage rate rises, at least up to some high wage rate.

I.c. Equilibrium

The labor market consists of the labor demand and labor supply curves. We've just discussed labor supply. Labor demand is based on the firms' marginal revenue product curves, as discussed in the previous chapter. The intersection of the labor demand and labor supply curves determines the equilibrium wage, W_e, and the quantity of hours people work at this equilibrium wage, Q_e, as shown in Figure 3.

The labor market pictured in Figure 3 suggests that as long as workers are the same and jobs are the same, there will be one equilibrium wage. In fact, workers are not the same, jobs are not the same, and wages are definitely not the same. College-educated people earn more than people with only a high school education, and people with a high school education earn more than those with only a grammar school education. Older workers earn more than younger workers. Men earn more than women. Whites earn more than nonwhites. Unionized workers tend to earn more than nonunionized workers.

The labor market model also suggests that workers will be paid their marginal revenue products. The more productive a worker is, the higher his or

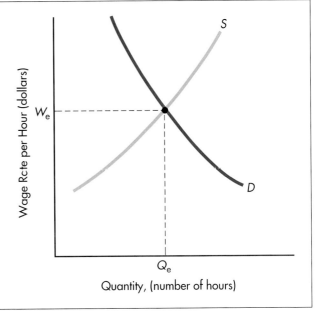

Figure 3
Labor Market Equilibrium
If all workers are identical to firms—that is, if a firm doesn't care whether it hires Bob, Ray, Kate, or Allie—and if all firms and jobs are the same to workers—that is, if a worker doesn't care whether a job is with IBM or Ted's Hot Dog Stand—then one demand curve and one supply curve define the labor market. The intersection of the two curves is the labor market equilibrium at which the wage rate is determined.

her compensation will be, and vice versa. This relationship does not always hold in the real world, however. There are large salary differences for people with similar levels of productivity, and people who are vastly different in terms of productivity are paid the same. Some explanations for these wage differentials are given in the remainder of this chapter.

RECAP

1. An increase in the wage rate causes workers to increase the hours they are willing and able to work and reduce the hours of leisure; at the same time, the wage increase also means that income is higher and more leisure can be purchased. This causes the individual labor supply curve to be backward-bending.

2. The labor market supply curve slopes upward because as the wage rate rises, more people are willing and able to work and people are willing and able to work more hours.

3. Equilibrium in the labor market defines the wage rate and the quantity of hours people work at that wage.

2. WAGE DIFFERENTIALS

If people were identical, if jobs were identical, and if information were perfect, there would be no wage differentials.

If all workers are the same to a firm—that is, if a firm doesn't care whether it hires Bob, Ray, Kate, or Allie—and if all firms and jobs are the same to workers—that is, if IBM is no different from Ted's Hot Dog Stand to individual workers—then the one demand for labor and the one supply of labor define the one equilibrium wage. However, if firms do differentiate among workers and if workers do differentiate among firms and jobs, then there is more than one labor market and more than one equilibrium wage level. In this case, wages may differ from job to job and from person to person. The reasons for wage differences include compensating wage differentials and differences in individual levels of productivity.

2.a. Compensating Wage Differentials

What are compensating wage differentials?

compensating wage differentials:
wage differences that make up for the higher risk or poorer working conditions of one job over another

Some jobs are quite unpleasant because they are located in undesirable locations or are dangerous or unhealthy. In most market economies, enough people voluntarily choose to work in unpleasant jobs that the jobs get filled. People choose to work in unpleasant occupations because of **compensating wage differentials**—wage differences that make up for the high risk or poor working conditions of a job. Workers mine coal, clean sewers, and weld steel beams fifty stories off the ground because, compared to alternative jobs for which they could qualify, these jobs pay well.

Figure 4 illustrates the concept of compensating differentials. There are two labor markets, one for a risky occupation and one for a less risky occupation. At each wage rate, fewer people are willing and able to work in the risky occupation than in the less risky occupation. Thus, if the demand curves were identical, the supply curve of the risky occupation would be above (to the left of) the supply curve of the less risky occupation. As a result, the equilibrium wage rate is higher in the risky occupation ($10) than in the less risky occupation ($5). The difference between the wage in the

Figure 4
Compensating Wage Differentials
Figure 4(a) shows the market for a risky occupation. Figure 4(b) shows the market for a less risky occupation. At each wage rate, fewer people are willing and able to work in the risky occupation than in the less risky occupation. Thus, the supply curve of the risky occupation is higher (supply is less) than the supply curve of the less risky occupation. As a result, the wage in the

risky occupation ($10 per hour) is higher than the wage ($5 per hour) in the less risky occupation. The differential ($10 − $5 = $5) is an equilibrium differential—the amount necessary to induce enough people to fill the jobs. If the differential were any higher, more people would flow to the risky occupation, driving wages there down and wages in the less risky occupation up. If the differential were any lower, shortages would prevail in the risky occupation, driving wages there up.

(a) Risky Occupation

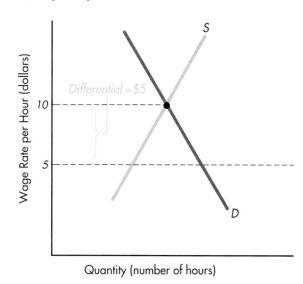

(b) Less Risky Occupation

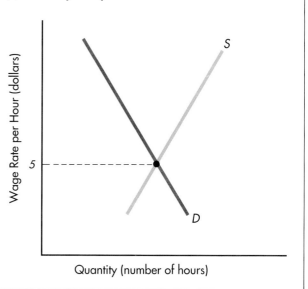

Some jobs are more dangerous than others. Since fewer people are willing to work in the dangerous jobs if they pay the same as less dangerous jobs, it is necessary for the employers to pay more for the dangerous jobs. To induce people to climb tall buildings to wash windows, to construct skyscrapers, or to paint the Golden Gate Bridge, the pay must be increased. Some of the employees undertaking risky jobs earn more in two months than they could in a year undertaking a less risky job.

risky occupation ($10 per hour) and the wage in the less risky occupation ($5 per hour) is an *equilibrium differential*—the compensation a worker receives for undertaking the greater risk.

Commercial deep-sea divers are exposed to the dangers of drowning and several physiological disorders as a result of compression and decompression. They choose this job because they earn about 90 percent more than the average high school graduate. Coal miners in West Virginia or in the United Kingdom are exposed to coal dust, black lung disease, and cave-ins. They choose to work in the mines because the pay is twice what they could earn elsewhere. Wage differentials ensure that deep-sea diving jobs, coal-mining jobs, and other risky occupations are filled.

Any characteristic that distinguishes one job from another may result in a compensating wage differential. A job that requires a great deal of travel and time away from home usually pays more than a comparable job without the travel requirements because most people find extensive travel and time away from home to be costly. If people were indifferent between extensive travel and no travel, there would be no compensating wage differential.

2.b. Human Capital

Why might wages be higher for people with more human capital than for those with less human capital?

People differ with respect to their training and abilities. These differences influence the level of wages for two reasons: (1) skilled workers have higher marginal productivity than unskilled workers, and (2) the supply of skilled workers is smaller than the supply of unskilled workers because it takes time and money to acquire training and education. Because of greater productivity and smaller supply, then, skilled labor will generate higher wages than less skilled labor. For instance, in Figure 5, the skilled-labor market generates a wage of $15 per hour, and the unskilled-labor market generates a wage of $8 per hour. The difference exists because the demand for skilled labor relative to the supply of skilled labor is greater than the demand for unskilled labor relative to the supply of unskilled labor.

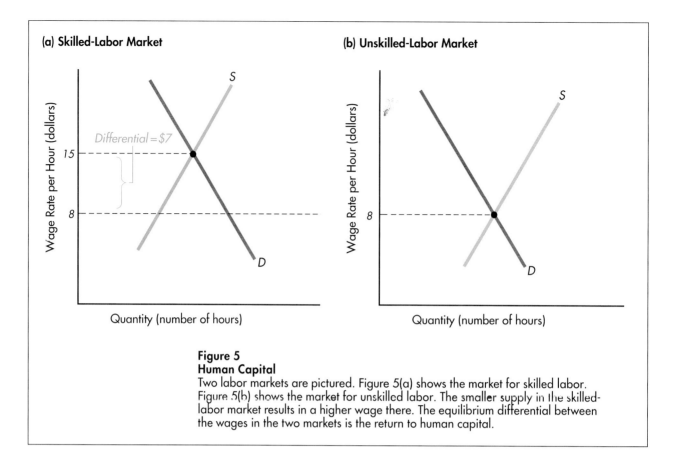

(a) Skilled-Labor Market

Wage Rate per Hour (dollars)

Differential = $7

15

8

Quantity (number of hours)

(b) Unskilled-Labor Market

Wage Rate per Hour (dollars)

8

Quantity (number of hours)

Figure 5
Human Capital
Two labor markets are pictured. Figure 5(a) shows the market for skilled labor. Figure 5(b) shows the market for unskilled labor. The smaller supply in the skilled-labor market results in a higher wage there. The equilibrium differential between the wages in the two markets is the return to human capital.

human capital:
skills and training acquired through education and on-the-job training

The expectation of higher income induces people to acquire **human capital**—skills and training acquired through education and job experience. People go to college or vocational school or enter training programs because they expect the training to increase their future income. When people purchase human capital, they are said to be *investing in human capital*. Like investments in real capital (machines and equipment), education and training are purchased in order to generate output and income in the future.

2.b.1. Investment in Human Capital Individuals who go to college or obtain special training expect the costs of going to college or obtaining the training to be more than offset by the income and other benefits they will obtain in the future. Individuals who acquire human capital reap the rewards of that human capital over time. Figure 6(a) is an example of what the income profiles of workers with college degrees and workers without college degrees might look like. We might expect income of the worker without the degree to increase rapidly from the early working years until the worker gets to be about fifty; then income might rise more slowly, until the worker moves into retirement age. Until around age thirty, the worker without the college degree clearly enjoys more income than the college-educated worker. The shaded areas represent estimated income lost to the college-educated worker while he or she is attending classes and then gaining work experience. It may take several years after entering the labor market for a college-degree recipient to achieve and then surpass the income level of a worker without a degree, but on average a college-educated person does earn more than some-

2.c. W:

Figure 6
Income Profiles and
Educational Level
Income rises rapidly until age fifty, then rises more slowly until retirement. Figure 6 compares the income earned by the worker without a degree with the income earned by a college graduate. Figure 6(a) suggests what the actual pattern looks like. Initially, the college graduate gives up substantial income in the form of direct costs and forgone earnings to go to college. Eventually, however, the income of the college graduate exceeds that of the high school-educated worker. Figure 6(b) illustrates the college income premium, the ratio of median income of college-educated to median income of non–college-educated individuals.
Source: *Statistical Abstract of the United States, 1994; Economic Report of the President, 1995.*

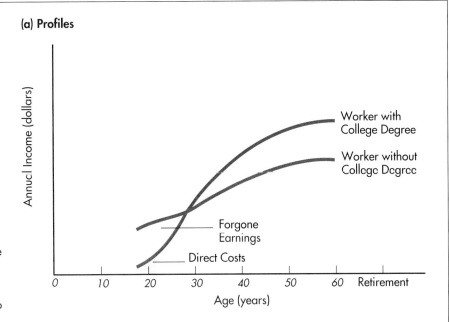

(a) Profiles

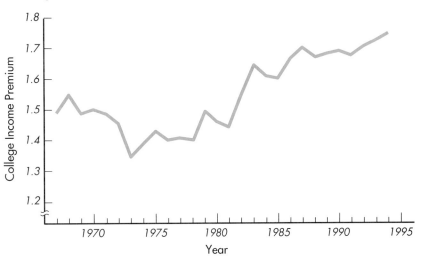

(b) College Income Premium

one without a college education, as shown in Figure 6(b). Figure 6(b) shows the ratios of the median income of college- to high-school-educated workers. This is called the college income premium. As mentioned in Chapter 1, college-educated people earn more over their lifetimes than people without a college degree.

The decision about whether to attend college depends on whether the benefits exceed the costs.[1] Over the course of a lifetime, will the income and

[1]In the chapter "Capital, Land, and Entrepreneurial Ability," we discuss the concept of present value, which is the value today of benefits or costs that occur in the future. A person compares the present value of the benefits of college to the present value of the costs of college in deciding whether to attend college.

personn
a firm's
employe

Chaptei

Different Approaches to Pay and Incentives

The Lincoln Electric Company has had a policy of paying employees for their output since the 1930s. Lincoln's factory workers are paid "piece rates" rather than hourly wages or salaries. The faster an employee works and the more output produced, the higher the employee's pay. Employees are not paid for coffee breaks, lunch breaks, or holidays. They are paid solely on the basis of the output they produce. Over the years pay rates have changed as technology or work methods changed. The workers are also eligible for yearly bonuses that have on average doubled their earnings. The distribution of bonuses is based on merit ratings of the workers on such factors as their dependability, quality, output, ideas, and cooperativeness. The name of the worker who produced a machine is stenciled on the machine. If a quality problem is discovered, the worker responsible must correct it on his or her own time. Also, the worker's bonus is reduced.

Lincoln has a policy of permanent, or lifetime, employment. After two years with the firm, a worker is guaranteed at least 30 hours' work a week. In fact, Lincoln has had no layoffs for over 40 years.

Contrast the Lincoln experience with an experiment at Du Pont.

E.I. Du Pont de Nemours and Company instituted a plan for its 20,000 employees in the fibers division in which employees put some of their annual wage and salary increases in a "pool" that would be at risk of loss or subject to huge gains. Bonuses to the pool were to be paid on how the division performed relative to an earnings target. Just meeting the target would mean the employees got their money back. If earnings exceeded target, employees would get at least twice their money back. If the division achieved only 80 percent of target they would lose the money they had put in the pool. Du Pont was trying to find out whether tying pay to group performance would have any positive effects. In the first year, employees received $19 million more in bonuses than they would have gotten without the pool plan. However, when business slowed in 1990, employees complained about their coworkers, and morale fell so low that the pool plan was rescinded.

As with the Du Pont case, there are instances where a direct tie between pay and performance can be determined. Consider the medical arena, where many health maintenance organizations (HMOs), such as FHP International, Cigna, New York Life Insurance,

and AvMed-Santa Fe, are paying bonuses to doctors on the basis of the patients' sense of quality. Critics do not like the idea, arguing that patients do not really know the quality of a doctor. In addition, some experiments with the idea have made it difficult for the doctors to work together in a collegial way. Dr. Gene Lindsay of the Harvard Community Health Plan said, "We had doctors almost getting into fistfights over what amounted to a $500 bonus." Other HMOs, however, are finding the practice of incentive pay very productive. According to a report in *The Wall Street Journal*, the incentive-pay idea works very well for the HMOs that deal with independent practitioners, as opposed to HMOs that have their own full-time physicians on staff. "That's because pay differentials—even tiny ones—are more likely to heat up rivalries among staff doctors."

Sources: "Here Come Richer, Riskier Pay Plans," *Fortune* (Dec. 19, 1988), pp. 50–58; Paul Milgrom and John Roberts, *Economics, Organization and Management* (Englewood Cliffs, N.J.: Prentice-Hall, 1992), pp. 393, 417; "Du Pont Plan Linking Pay to Fibers Profit Unravels," *The Wall Street Journal*, Oct. 25, 1990, p. B1; George Anders, "More Managed Health-Care Systems Use Incentive Pay to Reward 'Best' Doctors," *The Wall Street Journal*, Feb. 9, 1993, p. B1.

Incentives," some firms link pay directly to marginal revenue product while others seem to have no link between pay and *MRP*. It is common for firms to pay more senior workers more than less senior workers even though the more senior workers are not necessarily more productive. Another widespread practice, until the federal government in 1981 said it was illegal, was mandatory retirement. If older workers are not more productive than younger ones, why pay the older ones more? If they are more productive, then why terminate their employment at some age? A common practice that has come under a great deal of criticism in recent years is to provide chief executive officers (CEOs) with salaries and bonuses that far exceed the salaries and bonuses of the next person in charge. Why pay the CEO such a high salary when many other people could do just as good a job at much less pay? Corporations also spend enormous amounts to relocate middle- and upper-level managers on a fairly regular basis. Why uproot families and sever relationships, causing stress, bad will, and difficulties for those employees the firms most favor? And why not pay more attention to the individuals? Corporations often pay according to job classifications rather than tie the pay to individuals. For instance, a secretary 1 might earn less than a secretary 2 regardless of who the people in those positions are. Let us see if we can discover any reasons for these seemingly irrational behaviors.

3.a. Age Earnings and Age Productivity Profiles

Why do older workers tend to earn more than younger workers?

age-earnings profile:
a representation of the earnings a worker will receive at each age

In the past forty years, the age-earnings profile for any given worker has tended to look like the curve labeled "compensation" in Figure 7. The **age-earnings profile** is a representation of the earnings a worker will receive at each age. The age-earnings profile shown in Figure 7 is upward-sloping because earnings continue to rise throughout most of an individual's work life.

3.a.1. General Human Capital One explanation for the upward-sloping age-earnings profile is that workers acquire on-the-job training. If this training, or human capital, is portable—can be taken by the worker to any job—then the firm is helping the worker by giving him or her the opportunity to acquire on-the-job training. The firm will pay the worker for his or her marginal revenue product, and if that increases over time as the worker acquires more training, then wages will increase over time. In this case, firms and workers are indifferent about job separations; the firm can acquire another

Figure 7
Age-Earnings and Age-Productivity Profiles
The curve labeled "productivity" represents the age-productivity profile of an average worker. Productivity rises until about age forty-five and then declines. The "compensation" curve is the age-earnings profile of an average worker. Earnings continue to increase until late in the worker's life. A comparison of the age-earnings and age-productivity profiles shows that workers can expect to earn less than their current marginal revenue products during the early years of their work lives but more than their current marginal revenue products during their later work lives.

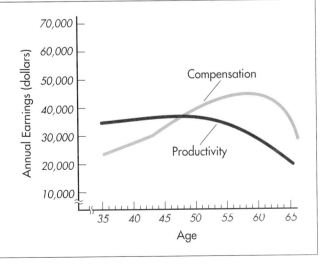

worker and begin the on-the-job training, and the worker can acquire another job and apply his or her human capital to the new job.

3.a.2. Firm-Specific Human Capital Firm-specific training refers to skills that are applicable only on one job or in one firm. Many skills acquired by an employee of Daimler-Benz's automobile manufacturing division can be used only in that division. They are of no use even in other automobile manufacturing firms. If the on-the-job training is firm-specific, the training acquired by the worker is permanently lost if the employment relationship with a given firm is severed. Premature job terminations and separations can be costly to both parties: the firm loses the trained employee, and the worker may find it difficult to transfer skills to another job. To ensure against these losses, both worker and firm are willing to contribute to the payment for the training. The worker contributes by receiving wages that are less than his or her marginal revenue product during the years prior to acquiring the on-the-job training, and the firm contributes by paying the worker more than his or her marginal revenue product after the worker has acquired the on-the-job training.

Whether the on-the-job training is firm-specific or not, in order to explain the upward-sloping age-earnings profile, workers have to become continually more productive over time. The problem is that the facts show that productivity does not continually rise. The curve labeled "productivity" in Figure 7 illustrates the level of productivity of an individual over that individual's work life. The "productivity" curve is called an **age-productivity profile**; productivity rises until the worker is about age forty-five and then declines.

A comparison of the age-earnings and age-productivity profiles shows that workers are paid less than their current marginal revenue products during their early work lives and more than their current marginal revenue products during their later work lives—yet productivity does not continually rise. What are the implications of such a relationship? For one thing, workers are induced to remain with a given firm. A worker who has been paid less than current marginal revenue product in his or her early years will not want to leave the job before recouping the difference between productivity and earnings.

The compensation scheme indicated by Figure 7 can motivate workers to increase productivity over their lifetimes. If a worker is always paid a value equal to his or her current marginal product, there is little cost to quitting or losing a job. The worker can go to another firm at a rate of pay equal to the marginal product. But with a steep age-earnings profile, the closer a worker is to retirement, the greater the cost of losing a job. The worker loses the premium of compensation in excess of current marginal product. Thus, workers have smaller and smaller incentives to slack off or shirk as they get older. Workers know that they will collect an excess above current marginal revenue product if they work to a certain age.

This compensation scheme means that firms could be stuck with workers for a very long time after the workers' productivity levels fall below their compensation levels. How can firms resolve this problem? **Mandatory retirement** was a policy that prevented employees from working after they reached a certain age. Mandatory retirement thus ensured that workers did not remain with a firm too long. Why didn't firms simply terminate workers at the stage when compensation began to exceed productivity? A firm did not

age-productivity profile:
the level of an individual's productivity over his or her work life

Workers are paid less than their marginal revenue products during early years with a firm and more than their MRP during later years.

mandatory retirement:
a policy that prevents employees from working after a certain age

want to be known as an "early terminator" for fear that it would be able to attract only low-productivity employees. Thus, the age-productivity-compensation scheme of Figure 7, coupled with mandatory retirement, seemed to have the result of increasing employee productivity.

Congressional action in 1981 eliminated mandatory retirement. Congress acted in response to pressure from older citizens, who viewed mandatory retirement, which forced them out of their jobs, as a penalty. If mandatory retirement allowed firms to use the age-productivity-compensation scheme of Figure 7 to increase worker productivity over the worker's lifetime, what took the place of mandatory retirement?

The lifting of such rules, while protecting workers' rights to continue at the same job past the age of sixty-five, does not ensure that workers will actually remain on the job. Pension plans exert economic pressure on individuals to leave their jobs or even leave the labor force. A pension that can be taken at a given age provides workers with the option of leaving their jobs and accepting payments at that age. Thus, generous pensions may fulfill the role played by mandatory retirement. In fact, most pension plans are set up to encourage retirement at a particular age; extending work life beyond that age results in incremental decreases in the returns from the pension plans.

3.b. CEO Pay Packages

Chief executive officers (CEOs) commonly earn salaries and bonuses that far exceed the salaries and bonuses of the next person in charge. Steven Ross, the Time Warner boss, gathered $74.8 million in bonuses in 1990 even as *Time* magazine laid off employees. J.F. O'Reilly of H.J. Heinz pulled in $74.8 million in total compensation in 1991 although Heinz had a rather average year. Leon C. Hirsch of U.S. Surgical Corporation collected $169.8 million from stock options as the price of the company's stock rose during 1991. General Motors's former chairman, Roger Smith, receives a $1.2 million annual pension even though GM lost both market share and money during Smith's tenure. In the mid-1970s, CEOs earned about 34 times the pay of the average working person; by the 1990s they earned 110 times that average. Why would competitive firms reward their CEOs so highly?

One answer could be that the market for CEOs has failed. The owners of firms, thousands of shareholders, exert little influence over the day-to-day activities of the manager and have little influence over the manager's pay. As a result, CEOs basically do what they want, including getting paid huge salaries without regard to the desires of the owners. Another possible answer is that CEO pay is the result of a conspiracy involving other CEOs and friends of the CEO who, as members of the compensation board of a firm, fail to listen to investors or look to the firm's performance and simply provide the types of compensation they also want to receive. An alternative explanation to the market failure or conspiracy arguments claims that CEO pay makes sense from an economic efficiency basis. This explanation is built on an analogy with contests or tournaments.

In a tournament, the larger the first prize, and the larger the difference between the first prize and all other prizes, the more productive are the contestants. Thus, if we consider the labor market as a contest where the first prize is the CEO position, a large first prize induces more effort and higher productivity from all contestants. An extremely high pay package for the

High executive salaries could be the result of a tournament where the executive has won first prize; the pay increases the incentive for all employees to work harder and better.

CEO induces that individual, and all employees (current and future), to exert extra efforts during their working lives.

3.c. Frequent Relocation of Managers

Any of you with parents, relatives, or friends employed by a large corporation have probably experienced several geographic moves. Typically the moves bring little in extra compensation but impose large costs on the family in the sense that ties are broken and children uprooted and transplanted. Why would firms expose their employees to such difficult experiences? The tournament view of labor markets provides an answer.

It is possible that the hierarchy within the headquarters location may not provide sufficient "tournaments" to ensure that the best people emerge as winners. The contests are spread geographically in order to provide sufficient opportunities for evaluating workers in various settings. So workers are rotated through various geographic locations to allow more complete evaluations to occur.

An alternative explanation is that geographic moves result in temporary productivity boosts. When a manager has been in a position for a significant length of time, procedures and practices become accepted and commonplace. There is little questioning of the approaches and little examination of whether more efficient or less costly methods are available. Limiting the exposure of teams of workers to the same manager may provide the opportunity for the teams to seek the most efficient means to accomplish the tasks. In addition, long-term relationships tend to provide biases in the relationship between the manager and selected workers. One worker may be a favorite of the manager due to an early experience. That worker may begin to shirk without retribution from the manager. Changing managers on a periodic basis will ensure that such behavior is temporary.

3.d. Team Production, Job Rating, and Firm-Size Effects

Have you ever been assigned a group project in one of your classes—a project that you and several other students working together must complete? For some this is a positive learning experience. For others it is an opportunity to discover firsthand what shirking is. Some team members invariably do not work as hard as others. Yet all members of the group receive the same grade, the grade of the project. Because the teacher is unable to differentiate the contributions of each individual group member, some members can slack off or shirk their responsibility without jeopardizing their rewards as long as other members complete the task.

There are many jobs in which the manager has the same problem of identifying the individual contributions or marginal products of employees. When teams handle a production process, a means of dividing compensation among team members must be determined. The most common approach is through a system of job categories. Job categories define responsibilities and specify compensation. All positions within a firm are ranked according to attributes such as responsibilities, pressure, and time requirements, and each position carries a different compensation level.

For example, suppose that there are three levels of secretarial positions, 1, 2, and 3. Also, suppose that a secretary at level 1 has fewer responsibilities than a secretary at level 2, and that a secretary at level 2 has fewer responsibilities than a secretary at level 3. Finally, suppose that the salary range for the level 1 position is $10,000 to $15,000 per year, the range for the level 2 position is $13,000 to $17,000, and the range for the level 3 position is $15,000 to $21,000.

On average, level 2 secretaries earn more than level 1 secretaries. Also, on average, level 2 secretaries are not as productive as level 3 secretaries but are more productive than level 1 secretaries in the sense that they have fewer or more responsibilities. By assigning compensation to classes and giving classes different responsibilities, compensation based on marginal revenue product is approximated.

Another curious aspect of pay scales in firms is that someone working in a small firm receives less compensation than if that person had the same job and same responsibilities in a large firm. Why should this be if there are no productivity differences? The most credible explanation is that the larger firm has to pay more to offset the fact that monitoring of individual performances is more difficult in a larger firm. By paying more, the larger firm is likely to get the better workers, who are more wary of losing their job and thus shirk less than if they were working with a smaller firm. Thus, in many large firms you will find higher average pay than in smaller firms but a more uniform pay scale based on job categories rather than a pay scale based on merit or productivity.

3.e. The Economics of Superstars

superstar effect:
the situation where people with small differences in abilities or productivity receive vastly different levels of compensation

Sometimes it appears that small differences in ability translate into huge differences in compensation. We saw how this phenomenon occurs in firms at the CEO level. It occurs in other situations as well, particularly in sports enterprises, which gave rise to its name—the **superstar effect**. Consider that the playing ability of the top ten tennis players or golfers is not much better than the playing ability of the players ranked between 40 and 50. Nonetheless, the compensation differences are incredibly large. The average income of the top ten tennis players and golfers is in the millions, while that of the lower-ranked ten players is in the thousands. If their productivity differences are so small, why are their compensation differences so large?

One explanation might be the limited time of those watching tennis or golf tournaments. Since most consumers have limited time, they choose to follow the top players. A tennis match between the 40th and 41st players might be nearly as good as that between the first and second. Yet, given the limited time to allocate between the two, nearly everyone would choose to watch the first and second players. At golf tournaments, huge throngs surround the top players, while lesser-known players play the game without the attention of adoring fans. These differences mean that the demand for the top players is huge relative to the demand for the lesser-ranked players. The sports franchises (the owners of the New York Yankees, for example) or the firms selling tickets to sporting events will be able to earn significantly higher prices if the ranked players are included in the activity; the marginal revenue product of the top-ranked players is thus much higher than that of the lesser-ranked players.

The superstar effect occurs outside of sports. You might, for example, observe two lawyers of relatively equal ability earning significantly different fees, or two economic consultants with apparently similar abilities earning vastly different consulting fees. When there is an "all-or-nothing" result in the market, the superstar effect might occur. Consider, for instance, the economist who offers advice to lawyers in cases involving firm behavior. A lawsuit filed against a firm might mean billions of dollars won or lost. Even if there are very small differences between economists, if the better economist means a win, then the better economist will receive huge compensation relative to the lesser economist. A $40 billion victory means that the marginal revenue product of the better economist is significantly greater than the marginal revenue product of the lesser economist, who has a $40 billion loss.

3.f. The Labor Market Model and Reality

What is the explanation for widespread personnel practices that appear to contradict economic theory?

Personnel practices that seem to be contradictory to the theory of the labor market under perfect information do not seem quite so strange when looked at more closely. These practices ensure that, as much as possible, resources are paid their marginal revenue products. If the practices are successful in one firm, other firms mimic them, thereby eventually leading to similar personnel practices across firms. When we observe widely followed practices that seem to be contradictory to our economic models, we must look closely into the practices to see if they are indeed contradictory. Rather than reject the models or turn to limited explanations, it is likely that we can find explanations for the practices that correspond to the logic of the economic model. Thus, wage scales within firms that are more uniform than productivity levels, huge differences between CEO pay and the pay of others in a firm, geographic moves on a regular basis, and wide differences in compensation accompanying small differences in productivity make sense in the context of the economic model of labor.

RECAP

1. Under perfect information and in perfectly competitive markets, workers are paid their marginal revenue products. In the real world, this often does not occur. Instead, personnel practices arise that replicate the results of the competitive market under perfect information.

2. Personnel practices that appear to contradict economic theory include rising age-earnings profiles relative to age-productivity profiles, mandatory retirement, excessive pay for CEOs, and frequent transfers within a firm.

3. The general explanation for many of the personnel practices that firms engage in rests on the inability to monitor individual actions. To minimize shirking and increase productivity, pay scales tend to benefit the more senior employee. Mandatory retirement plans solved the problem of separation of senior worker and firm in the context of a rising age-earnings profile. CEOs are paid huge amounts because they are the winners of a series of contests or tournaments that are aimed at raising the performance of all employees. Frequent transfers tend to provide many mini-tournaments and induce short-term productivity boosts. And job

categories tend to minimize the problems of assigning marginal products in a setting of team production.

4. Superstar effects occur when there is an all-or-nothing aspect to the market and result in cases where individuals with small productivity differences receive vastly different compensation.

SUMMARY

▲▼ Are people willing to work more hours for higher wages?

1. The individual labor supply curve is backward-bending because at some high wage, people choose to enjoy more leisure rather than to earn additional income. §1.a

▲▼ What are compensating wage differentials?

2. Equilibrium in the labor market defines the wage and quantity of hours worked. If all workers and all jobs were identical, then one wage would prevail. There are differential wages, however, because jobs and workers differ. §1.c

3. A compensating wage differential exists when a higher wage is determined in one labor market than in another due to differences in job characteristics. §2.a

▲▼ Why might wages be higher for people with more human capital than for those with less human capital?

4. Human capital is the training, education, and skills people acquire. Human capital increases productivity. Because acquiring human capital takes time and money, the necessity of obtaining human capital for some jobs reduces the supply of labor to those jobs. §2.b

▲▼ Why do older workers tend to earn more than younger workers?

5. Older workers earn more than younger workers because of on-the-job experience and seniority. Older workers may also earn more than younger workers because firms pay older workers more in order not to lose the training and skills they have invested in these workers. In addition, a firm may use the higher wage for more senior workers to induce younger workers to be more productive. §3.a.1, 3.a.2

▲▼ What is the explanation for widespread personnel practices that appear to contradict economic theory?

6. Firms operating under imperfect information cannot know each employee's marginal product and cannot perfectly monitor the performance of each employee. As a result, personnel practices that tend to mimic the results of the competitive market under perfect information (pay equal to *MRP*) arise. Examples of such practices include rising age-earnings profiles, pension plans, very high executive salaries, frequent transfers within a firm, and compensation tied to job categories. §3

KEY TERMS

backward-bending labor supply curve §1.a
labor force participation §1.b
compensating wage differentials §2.a
human capital §2.b
personnel practices §3

age-earnings profile §3.a
age-productivity profile §3.a.2
mandatory retirement §3.a.2
superstar effect §3.e

EXERCISES

1. What could account for a backward-bending labor supply curve?

2. What is human capital? How does a training program such as Mrs. Fields Cookie College affect human capital? Is a college degree considered to be human capital?

3. Define equilibrium in the labor market. Illustrate equilibrium on a graph. Illustrate the situation in which there are two types of labor, skilled and unskilled.

4. Describe how people choose a major in college. If someone majors in English literature knowing that the starting salary for English literature graduates is much lower than the starting salary for accountants, is the English literature major irrational?

5. Motorola, a U.S. electronics firm, requires that a very extensive process be followed before an employee who has been with the firm for ten years can be terminated or laid off. The division head must discuss the dismissal with the employee; the vice president of the division must discuss the dismissal; and the president of the firm must discuss the dismissal. What is the purpose of such a practice?

6. Explain why a large firm might be expected to have different methods of payment to employees than a smaller firm. Which would be more likely to have the higher pay scales? Which would be more likely to have across-the-board pay raises rather than differential pay raises based on productivity?

7. Explain the following real-world observations: the existence of seniority rules (first in, last out); higher pay than marginal revenue product during later years and lower pay than marginal revenue product during early years; management trainee programs for newly hired college graduates; a willingness on the part of firms to pay more for a college graduate even though the firms readily admit that the classes a student takes in college provide few marketable skills.

8. A study in 1990 indicated that at that time only 13 U.S. firms with more than 1,000 employees had explicit policies never to institute a general layoff: Delta Air Lines, Digital Equipment, Federal Express, IBM, S.C. Johnson, Lincoln Electric, Mazda, Motorola, National Steel, New United Motor, Nissan, Nucor, and Xerox. Why do you think that so few firms have adopted such a policy? After huge losses in 1992, IBM altered its policies and implemented large layoffs. What factors went into IBM's decision?

9. A 1989 study found that workers who were laid off generally received lower wages once they found new jobs. Workers who had been in their previous jobs only a short period of time suffered relatively smaller losses than those who had been with the employer for a longer period. How would you explain this?

10. A 1980 study found that the average worker with forty years' experience with a firm could retire with a pension of $79,000. If the same worker had retired ten years earlier, the pension would have been twice as much, $160,000. What would be the effects of such a policy? Why would firms institute such a policy?

11. In the 1980s and early 1990s, the U.S. airline industry went through a major shakeup. Many airlines went bankrupt and others expanded. Thousands of airline pilots lost their jobs with the bankrupt airlines. The expanding airlines, meanwhile, hired thousands of new pilots. The pilots hired by the expanding airlines, however, were those who had the least experience. The senior pilots from the bankrupt airlines could not get new jobs. Many claimed that this was a wasteful policy, one that the government should stop. How might you defend the practice?

12. The probability of a worker being fired from or quitting a job declines the longer the worker has been with a firm. How would you account for this?

13. It is a common practice in technology-based companies such as Hewlett-Packard, Unisys, and Sun Electronics for employees to experience lateral moves—moves to other locations or other parts of the company that carry no increase in compensation or responsibility. Why would these firms participate in such practices?

14. It is a common practice in the largest multinational companies for employees to experience assignments of three to five years in locations outside the United States. Why would a firm uproot a family and set it down in a new culture and society?

15. Suppose you are in charge of designing employee policies for a firm where failure has huge costs and success only normal benefits. For example, your firm inspects nuclear power plants or ensures the safety of airlines, buses, and trains. How would you recruit, promote, and pay employees?

COOPERATIVE LEARNING EXERCISE

In 1994, when American West Airlines emerged from bankruptcy proceedings, the top officials of the airlines were rewarded with bonuses exceeding $1 million. All other employees, if they kept a job, received a bonus of $1,000.

Divide the class into groups of 4 or 5 people. Then, divide the groups into As and Bs. The A groups are to develop an explanation of why the American West bonus scheme was beneficial to the firm. The B groups are to develop an explanation of why the America West bonus scheme was detrimental to the firm. Call on groups to explain their rationales.

Happy Workers Can Generate High Profits

Are unions good for business? A question such as this would probably have been laughed off the page 10 years ago, dismissed as absurd in its very naivety. Yet, according to an academic who has been no stranger to this column over the years, even the most anti-union companies in the U.S. are no longer able to ignore the successes of competitors which have chosen to accept, and even encourage, collective organization among their employees.

In his latest book, Competitive Advantage Through People, Jeffrey Pfeffer, professor of organizational behavior at Stanford Graduate School of Business, points to the five top performing U.S. companies between 1972 and 1992 in terms of percentage returns on their shares: Southwest Airlines, Wal-Mart, Tyson Foods, Circuit City and Plenum Publishing. All, he writes, have one thing in common: not a strategic position, but in the approach they use to managing their work forces.

Pfeffer was speaking to former students in London last week about potential solutions to the employee malaise that is sweeping the U.S. and manifesting itself in parts of the UK workforce. That there is a deep employee disenchantment in what prides itself as one of the world's most deregulated labor markets was confirmed in a recent survey carried out for President Bill Clinton's commission investigating employer-mission investigating employer-labor relations. It found widespread dissatisfaction with jobs and distrust of management.

Pfeffer was urging managers to consider employment practices which many companies appear to have ignored in the clear-outs of the last few years. Security of employment, union membership, high wages, full-time employees and greater employee share ownership, said Pfeffer, should not be regarded as millstones to competitiveness, but as features that can help define successful companies.

To make his point he offered these 1991 statistics which show that compared to averages for the U.S. airline industry, Southwest Airlines had fewer employees per aircraft (79 against 131) and flew more passengers per employee (2,318 against 848).

In addition to his five top performers, he threw into the pot a few more companies such as Nordstrom, Lincoln Electric and the New United Motor plant of the Toyota-GM joint venture at Fremont, stressing that all had achieved exceptional economic returns in highly competitive and often mundane industries.

Their secret was to pay close attention to the needs of their work forces. A common mistake made my many employers, said Pfeffer, was to confuse labour rates with labour costs. High pay, in both motivating and attracting a more productive workforce, he argued could be a far more cost effective approach to employment than having a low paid unproductive workforce.

Another feature, highlighted and supported by Pfeffer is "wage compression," meaning that team leaders earn little more than other team members. His argument for greater wage compression—creating less of a disparity between the pay of the highest and lowest paid employees—would seem to have lessons in the debate over increasing pay levels for some of the UK's top company chiefs. . . . Where there is no great disparity between lower and higher paid employees, pay is likely to be less emphasized in the reward system and the company culture. . . . people are not constantly worrying about whether they are compensated appropriately and attempting to renegotiate their salaries.

Source: "Happy Workers Can Generate High Profits," Richard Donkin, *Financial Times*, Feb. 10, 1995. Reprinted by permission.

Commentary

Are happy workers productive workers? It would seem to make sense that those workers who really enjoy their jobs would be the most productive, everything else the same. But, what makes workers happy? For some, job stability and security might be the most important factors. For others, "making a difference"—doing something that has an impact on the firm or on society—would be the most important. For still others, the income received would be the most important. And, for some others, power and prestige are most important.

Can a firm ensure that everyone is happy? Probably not. Suppose that power and prestige imply making more money than other employees. Then, creating a situation where you are paid by commission so that the most successful salesperson receives the highest income will make some people very happy. At the same time, commissions may make others very unhappy. They will see that their colleagues are earning double or triple their pay. They may also fear that they will lose their job in the future. Conversely, suppose that you establish a policy guaranteeing everyone a job for life. You will make some people very happy. Others may not be so happy because they will not succeed relative to others; they will earn more but are no more likely to retain the jobs than those who do not perform. Suppose you decree that everyone will earn the same amount—managers, team leaders, and executives will earn only a small amount more than the lowliest worker. You are likely to ensure that the lowliest workers are happy, but perhaps not the executives.

This is what the labor market is all about. It sorts out those people who are happy with a specific personnel policy and those who are not happy with that policy. It sorts out the firms who offer a specific personnel policy and firms who offer different policies.

Why then does the article suggest that unions, wage compression, and egalitarian approaches will make workers the happiest thereby making the firms that use these policies the most successful? The article is providing an incorrect interpretation of facts. Note that the firms offered as evidence of successful personnel policies include Lincoln Electric and Nordstrom's as well as Wal-Mart and Southwest. These firms have very different personnel policies. Lincoln Electric pays their employees by piece-rate; the employee is paid for each unit of output the employee produces. Employees have the choice of taking coffee breaks, lunch breaks, working during holidays, and so on. If they want to take a break or a vacation, they are not paid. If they work and produce, they are paid very well. Nordstrom's pays its employees on a commission basis—a percentage of total sales made. Southwest employees own part of the firm; their pay includes stock ownership. They are paid according to position and the pay scale is quite compressed. Similarly, Wal-Mart employees are paid by position and under a compressed pay scale. People who want to work in sales and want to earn as much as possible would seek a position with Nordstrom's. Those who want a more secure position and not worry about personal selling efforts would choose Wal-Mart. People who want to be compensated for their work and to choose when and where they take breaks and vacations would seek work in Lincoln Electric. If someone who disliked commissions got a position with Nordstrom's, that person would be unhappy and unproductive. Similarly, if someone who wanted to work hard and be paid for their hard work irrespective of what others are doing took a position with Southwest Airlines, they would probably be unhappy.

31

Wage Differentials: Race, Gender, Age, and Unionization

FUNDAMENTAL
QUESTIONS

1. What accounts for earnings disparities between males and females and between whites and nonwhites?
2. Are discrimination and freely functioning markets compatible?
3. What government policies have been implemented to reduce wage differentials?
4. Have unions been able to increase the wages of union members relative to the wages of nonunionized workers?
5. What effects do government policies and programs such as minimum wages and the Family and Medical Leave Act have on the labor market?

I n the United States in 1994, the average black male worker earned only 74 percent of what the average white male worker earned. This ratio was 8 to 10 percentage points higher than it had been in the mid-1960s, when the average black worker earned about 65 percent of what the average white male worker earned. White female weekly wages were about 58 percent of average white male weekly wages in 1976, 59 percent in 1980, and 70 percent in 1994. In 1994, male Hispanics had incomes averaging only 69 percent of those of white males. The average union member earned more than the average nonunion member, somewhere between 30 percent more in 1994.[1]

PREVIEW

The discussion in the previous two chapters suggests that workers receive compensation equal to their marginal revenue products. The economic model of the labor market also suggests that discrimination on the basis of race, sex, or age should not exist. How then do we explain why minorities and women earn significantly less than white males in the U.S. labor market? Moreover, why do union members earn more than nonunion members? These differentials call for a further investigation of the labor market. The purpose of this chapter is to carry out that investigation.

What accounts for earnings disparities between males and females and between whites and nonwhites?

I. DISCRIMINATION

The United States is not alone in having differentials based on race and sex. In fact, there seem to be differentials among certain groups in nearly every country. Studies have found that "colored" workers in Britain earn only about 60 percent of white workers' incomes. There are differentials in Israel between the Oriental-Sephardic Jews and Ashkenazic Jews and in other nations between different groups based on color or religion. And in all countries women earn less than men. The Scandinavian countries, France, Australia, and New Zealand have female-to-male hourly pay ratios of 80 to 90 percent while other countries in Western Europe have pay ratios of 65 to 75 percent.[2]

I.a. Definition of Discrimination

Is discrimination present when there is prejudice or just when prejudice has harmful results? Consider a firm with two branch offices. One office employs only blacks; the other, only whites. Workers in both branches are paid the

---

[1] *Bureau of Labor Statistics*, 1994.

[2] Francine D. Blau and Lawrence M. Kahn, "The Gender Earnings Gap: Some International Evidence," NBER Working Paper No. 4224, December 1992.

same wages and have the same opportunities for advancement. Is discrimination occurring?

Is a firm that provides extensive training to employees discriminating when it prefers to hire young workers who are likely to stay with the firm long enough for it to recoup the training costs? Is an economics department that has no black faculty members guilty of discrimination if black economists constitute only 1 percent of the profession? Would your answer change if the department could show that it advertised job openings widely and made the same offers to blacks and whites? Clearly, discrimination is a difficult subject to define and measure.

From an economist's viewpoint, a worker's value in the labor market depends on the factors affecting the marginal revenue product. When a factor that is unrelated to marginal revenue product acquires a positive or negative value in the labor market, **discrimination** is occurring. In Figure 1, if D_M is the demand for males and D_F is the demand for females, and males and females have identical marginal revenue products, then the resulting wage differences can be attributed to discrimination. Race, gender, age, physical handicaps, religion, sexual preference, and ethnic heritage may be factors that take on positive or negative values in the labor market and yet are unrelated to marginal revenue products.

discrimination:
when factors unrelated to marginal revenue product affect the wages or jobs that are obtained

1.b. Theories of Discrimination

Are discrimination and freely functioning markets compatible?

Wage differentials due to race or gender pose a theoretical problem for economists because the labor market model attributes differences in wages to demand and supply differences that depend on productivity and the labor-leisure tradeoff. How can economists account for different pay scales for men and women, or for one race versus another, in the absence of marginal productivity differences between sexes or races? They identify discrimination as

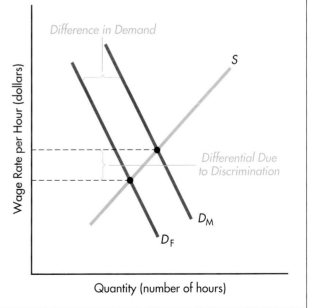

Figure 1
Discrimination
D_M is the demand for males and D_F the demand for females. The two groups of workers are identical except in gender. The greater demand and the higher wage rate for males, even though males and females are equally productive, are due to discrimination.

the cause of the differences even though they find discrimination difficult to rationalize because it is costly to those who discriminate.

In the freely functioning labor market, there is a profit to be made in *not* discriminating; therefore, discrimination should not exist. But, because discrimination does exist, economists have attempted to find plausible explanations for it. They have identified two sources of labor market discrimination. The first is *personal prejudice*: employers, fellow employees, or customers dislike associating with workers of a given race or sex. The second is statistical discrimination: employers project certain perceived group characteristics onto individuals. Economists tend to argue that personal prejudice is not consistent with a market economy, but have acknowledged that statistical discrimination can coexist within a market economy.

1.b.1. Personal Prejudice Certain groups in a society could be precluded from higher-paying jobs or from jobs that provide valuable human capital by personal prejudice on the part of employers, fellow workers, or customers.

Employer prejudice If two workers have identical marginal revenue products and one worker is less expensive than the other, firms will want to hire the lower-cost worker. Otherwise, profits will be lower than they need to be. Suppose white males and others are identically productive, but managers prefer white males. Then the white males will be more expensive than women and minorities, and hiring white males will lower profits.

Under what conditions will lower profits as a result of personal prejudice be acceptable? Perhaps a monopoly firm can forgo some of its monopoly profit in order to satisfy the manager's personal prejudices (see the discussion of X-inefficiency in the chapter on monopoly), or perhaps firms that do not maximize profits can indulge in personal preferences. However, for profit-maximizing firms selling their goods in the market structures of perfect competition, monopolistic competition, or oligopoly, personal prejudice will mean a loss of profit unless all rivals also discriminate. Could firms form a cartel to discriminate? Recall from the discussion of oligopoly that cartels do not last long—there is an incentive to cheat—unless an entity like the government sanctions and enforces the cartel.

In the United States, well-meaning legislation intended to protect women actually created a situation in which women were denied access to training and education and thus were not able to gain the human capital necessary to compete for high-skill, high-paying jobs. Until the 1960s, women were barred from jobs because of legislation that attempted to protect them from heavy labor or injury. In reality, this legislation precluded women from obtaining certain kinds of human capital. Without the human capital, a generation or more of women were unable to obtain many high-paying jobs. For another example, see the Economic Insight "South Africa's Labor Policy."

Worker prejudice Workers may not want to associate with other races or sexes. White males may resist taking orders from females or sharing responsibility with a member of a minority group. White male workers who have these discriminatory preferences will tend to quit employers who employ women or minorities on a nondiscriminatory basis.

The worker prejudice explanation of discrimination assumes that white males are willing to accept lower-paying positions to avoid working with anyone other than a white male. Such discrimination is costly to those who discriminate.

Discrimination might occur as employers attempt to hire only certain kinds of workers, as employees attempt to work only with certain kinds of coworkers, or as customers attempt to purchase goods and services from certain kinds of workers.

Discrimination is costly in that less productive employees or more expensive but not more productive employees are used.

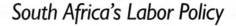
South Africa's Labor Policy

One way to establish barriers is to use government power to serve the interests of special groups at the expense of others. Sometimes the use of government authority is blatantly discriminatory—witness South Africa's Colour Bar Act of 1911, which authorized the establishment of a maximum ratio of African to white employees in that country's mines.

During World War I nonwhites in South Africa were able to make inroads into jobs previously held by whites. Immediately after the war, however, the whites reestablished their dominant positions with government help. The Wage Act of 1925, passed in the name of preventing sweatshops and encouraging industrial efficiency, set up a wage board that had the power to establish wages in various non-union jobs. By setting relatively high wages for the skilled trades in which whites were employed, incumbent white artisans were able to keep nonwhites out of these jobs while appearing to adhere to high-sounding principles. The so-called "civilized labour policy" was built upon the economic reality that social background and inferior educational facilities prevented nonwhites from attaining the skill levels of whites. The only hope nonwhites had of securing jobs held by whites was to offer their services in these occupations at lower wages. The "civilized labour policy" prevented this.

Source: W. H. Hutt, *The Economics of the Colour Bar* (London: Andre Deutsch, 1964).

Consumer prejudice   Customers may prefer to be served by white males in some situations and by minorities or women in others. If their preferences for white males extend to high-paying jobs such as physician and lawyer and their preferences for women and minorities are confined to lower-paying jobs like maid, nurse, and flight attendant, then women and minorities will be forced into occupations that work to their disadvantage.

The consumer prejudice explanation of discrimination assumes that consumers are willing to pay higher prices to be served by white males. In certain circumstances and during certain periods of time, this may be so; but over wide geographic areas or across different nations and over long periods of time, consumer prejudice does not appear to be a very likely explanation of discrimination.

1.b.2. Statistical Discrimination   Discrimination not related to personal prejudices can occur because of a lack of information. Employers must try to predict the potential productivity of job applicants, but rarely do they know what a worker's actual productivity will be. Often, the only information available when they hire someone is information that may be imperfectly related to productivity in general and may not apply to a particular person at all. Reliance on indicators of productivity such as education, experience, age, and test scores may keep some very good people from getting a job and may result in the hiring of some unproductive people. This is called **statistical discrimination.**

statistical discrimination: discrimination that results when an indicator of group performance is incorrectly applied to an individual member of the group

Suppose two types of workers apply for a word-processing job: those who can process 80 words per minute and those who can process only 40 words per minute. The problem is that these actual productivities are unknown to the employer. The employer can observe only the results of a five-minute word-processing test given to all applicants. How can the employer decide who is lucky or unlucky on the test and who can actually process 80 words per minute? Suppose the employer discovers that applicants from a particular vocational college, the DeVat School, are taught to perform well on pre-employment tests but their overall performance as employees is the same as that of the rest of the applicants—some do well and some do not. The employer might decide to reject all applicants from DeVat because the good and bad ones can't be differentiated. Is the employer discriminating against DeVat? The answer is *yes*. The employer is using statistical discrimination.

Let's extend this example to race and gender. Suppose that, on average, minorities with a high school education are discovered to be less productive than white males with a high school education because of differences in the quality of the schools they attend. An employer using this information when making a hiring decision might prefer to hire a white male. Statistical discrimination can cause a systematic preference for one group over another even if some individuals in each group have the same measured characteristics.

1.c. Occupational Segregation

crowding:
forcing a group into certain kinds of occupations

occupational segregation:
the separation of jobs by sex

Statistical discrimination and imperfect information can lead to **crowding**—forcing women and minorities into occupations where they are unable to obtain the human capital necessary to compete for high-paying jobs. Today, even in the industrial nations, some occupations are considered "women's jobs" and different occupations are considered "men's jobs." This separation of jobs by sex is called **occupational segregation**.

There is a substantial amount of occupational segregation in the United States and other industrialized nations.[3] One reason for occupational segregation is differences in the human capital acquired by males and females. Much of the human capital portion of the discrepancy between men and women is due to childbearing. Data suggest that marriage and children handicap women's efforts to earn as much as men. Many women leave the labor market during pregnancy, at childbirth, or when their children are young. These child-related interruptions are damaging to subsequent earnings because three out of four births occur to women before the age of thirty, the period in which men are gaining the training and experience that lead to higher earnings later in life. Second, even when mothers stay in the labor force, responsibility for children frequently constrains their choice of job: they accept lower wages in exchange for shorter or more flexible hours, location near home, limited out-of-town travel, and the like. Third, women have a disproportionate responsibility for child care and often have to make sacrifices that men do not make. For instance, when a young child is present, women are more likely than men to be absent from work, even when the men and women have equal levels of education and wages.

Perhaps most important of all, because most female children are expected to be mothers, they have been less likely than male children to acquire marketable human capital while in school. In the past, this difference was reflected in the choice of a curriculum in primary and secondary schools, in a college major, and in the reluctance of females to pursue graduate school

---

[3]Victor R. Fuchs, "Women's Quest for Economic Equality," *Journal of Economic Perspectives* 3, no. 1 (Winter 1989), pp. 25–42, suggests that about half the occupations in the United States are gender-biased, or "crowded." The ratios vary among the other industrialized nations, some having more and some having less occupational segregation. See Blau and Kahn, op. cit.

training or to undergo the long hours and other rigors characteristic of apprenticeships in medicine, law, business, and other financially rewarding occupations. Females were channeled into languages, typing, and home economics, while males were channeled into mechanical drawing, shop, chemistry, and physics. This situation is changing, but the remnants of the past continue to influence the market. Since the late 1970s, about half of all law school classes and about one-third of medical school classes have been female. Nonetheless, mostly females major in languages, literature, education, and home economics, while mostly males major in physics, mathematics, chemistry, and engineering.

If new female entrants into the labor force have human capital equal to the human capital of new male entrants and thus greater than the human capital of females already in the labor force, then the average human capital and wages of females will rise. But even while the wage gap between males and females is decreasing, a gap will continue to exist because the average male in the labor force has more marketable human capital than the average female. The average rate of pay of males will continue to exceed that of females.

Statistical discrimination has a role in earnings disparities between men and women as well. Childless women earn less than men simply because it is the women who bear children. The human capital (training, education) women acquire will often be different, and less marketable, than that acquired by men. This occurs because many childless women did not know that they would be childless, and the subjects they studied in school as well as the jobs they took upon leaving school did not provide the marketable training that most men received. Also, prospective employers were unlikely to know which young women would have children and which would not, which would leave their jobs and which would not, and this affected the employers' willingness to provide training opportunities or to make other investments in job-related human capital. Because the odds are great that a woman will leave a job for some period of time to have a child, simply being a woman provides a signal to a firm. As a result of this signal, the wage offered a man might be higher than that offered a woman, or the job offered a man might contain better training than the one offered a woman.

Uncertainty about children does not end quickly for women or their employers. Even women who are childless at age thirty have a 1 in 4 chance of having at least one child by the time they are thirty-five. If females came into the world with a sign announcing the number of children that they would ultimately bear, the relationship between women's earnings and their number of children would be much stronger than the one we observe.

1.d. Immigration

While the less marketable human capital that women acquire can account for at least some of the differences between the wages of women and men, immigration accounts for some of the differences between the wages of whites and nonwhites. Immigration increases the supply of labor—causing an outward shift of the labor supply curve, as shown in Figure 2. The equilibrium wage rate is driven down from $10 an hour to $8 an hour. Not all workers are hurt by the immigration, however. If most of the immigrants are unskilled, then the wage rate is driven down only in the unskilled-labor market. The skilled labor does not feel the effects of immigration.

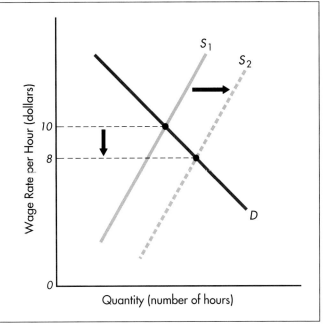

Figure 2
Immigration and the Labor Market
Immigration means an increased supply of labor. The labor supply curve shifts out from S_1 to S_2. The wage rate declines as a result, from $10 to $8, and employment rises.

As can be seen in Figure 3, immigration was quite high in the 1970s and 1980s. It did not exceed the rate between 1900 and 1920, but it was second only to the influx in that twenty-year period. Between 1901 and 1910, 8.8 million immigrants arrived in the United States, the all-time record for a single decade. Between 1911 and 1920, 5.7 million more immigrants came to the United States.

In the early 1900s, immigrants came primarily from Europe. In the 1970s, the flow of people from Europe declined by 0.5 million and the flow from

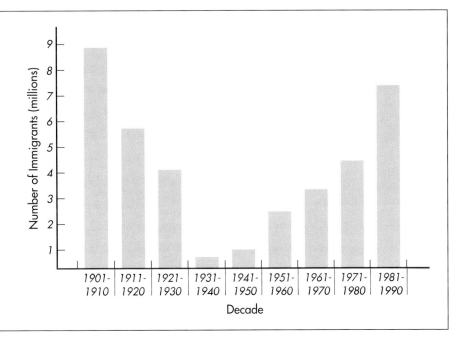

Figure 3
Immigration to the United States, 1901–1990
The total number of immigrants to the United States in each decade is shown. The greatest immigration took place between 1900 and 1920. That period is followed by the decade of the 1980s. Source: U.S. Census Bureau.

Latin America increased sharply. Almost 1.3 million immigrants came from Mexico alone, and another 0.5 million came from the West Indies. Immigration from Asia also increased significantly. In 1980 almost 1.8 million new U.S. residents were from Asia, mostly from the Philippines, South Korea, and Vietnam. Rather than entering the United States along the northern Atlantic seaboard and settling in the eastern and northern states, as European immigrants had done, the new immigrants entered across the southern and western borders and settled in relatively large numbers in the South and West. California alone accounts for more than 25 percent of the foreign-born population in the United States, and California, New York, and Florida have one-half of this population.

As is true of migrants in general, the new immigrants tend to be relatively young, primarily ages twenty to forty-nine. During the late 1960s and early 1970s, many immigrants to the United States were relatively skilled individuals from low-income countries. More than 22 percent of the immigrants had four or more years of college education, whereas in 1980 only 16.2 percent of U.S. residents had attended college for four or more years. Among immigrants twenty-five years old and over, 6.9 percent from Latin America and 37.4 percent from Asia had at least four years of college. Since 1975, skilled immigration to the United States from both low- and high-income countries has remained close to the levels of the early 1970s, but there has been a dramatic growth in the immigration of the unskilled. A large number, 12.8 percent, have less than five years of elementary school education. (The comparable figure for U.S. residents is 3.6 percent.)

This pattern of immigration has had two major effects on the labor market in the United States. First, it has tended to widen the earnings gap between Hispanics and whites, since most of the unskilled immigrants are coming from Latin America and their primary language is Spanish. As a result, Hispanics in the United States must continue to assimilate increasing numbers of the unskilled, who must learn English as well as attempt to acquire marketable skills. As one generation (usually the second) acquires education and training, its average earnings rise. But as new immigrants continue to arrive, average earnings of all Hispanics fall.

The second impact of recent immigration has been to widen the earnings gap between skilled and unskilled workers. More unskilled workers than skilled workers are immigrating to the United States. As a result, the supply of unskilled labor is increasing and wages in the unskilled-labor market are falling without affecting wages in the skilled-labor market. Hence, the wage gap between the two sectors is widening.

RECAP

1. Discrimination occurs when factors unrelated to marginal physical product acquire a positive or negative value in the labor market.

2. Earnings disparities may exist for a number of reasons, including personal prejudice, statistical discrimination, and human capital differentials. Human capital differentials may exist because of occupational choice, statistical discrimination, and unequal opportunities to acquire human capital.

3. There are two general classes of discrimination theories: prejudice theory and statistical theory. Prejudice theories claim that employers, workers, and consumers express their personal prejudices by, respectively, earning lower profits, accepting lower wages, and paying higher prices. Statistical discrimination theory asserts that firms have imperfect information and must rely on general indicators of marginal physical product to pay wages and hire people and that reliance on these general indicators may create a pattern of discrimination.

4. Occupational segregation is the separation of jobs by sex. Some jobs are filled primarily by women, and other jobs are filled primarily by men.

5. In recent years, immigrants to the United States have included increasing numbers of unskilled people from Latin America. The impact of their arrival on the labor market has been to widen the earnings gap between Hispanics and whites and between the skilled and unskilled.

2. WAGE DIFFERENTIALS AND GOVERNMENT POLICIES

What government policies have been implemented to reduce wage differentials?

Not until the 1960s did wage disparities and employment practices become a major public policy issue in the United States. In 1963 the Equal Pay Act outlawed separate pay scales for men and women performing similar jobs, and Title VII of the 1964 Civil Rights Act prohibited all forms of discrimination in employment.

2.a. Antidiscrimination Laws

Since the 1930s, about thirty states have enacted fair employment practice laws prohibiting discrimination in employment on the basis of race, creed, color, or national origin. Under state fair employment practice legislation, it is normally illegal for an organization to refuse employment, to discharge employees, or to discriminate in compensation or other terms of employment because of race.

These state laws did not apply to women, however. In fact, prior to the 1960s, sex discrimination was officially sanctioned by so-called protective labor laws, which limited the total hours that women were allowed to work and prohibited them from working at night, lifting heavy objects, and working during pregnancy.

With the Civil Rights Act of 1964, however, it became unlawful for any employer to discriminate on the basis of race, color, religion, sex, or national origin. Unions also were forbidden from excluding anyone on the basis of those five categories. Historically, it had been very difficult for racial minorities to obtain admission into unions representing workers in the skilled trades. This exclusion prevented minorities from obtaining the human capital necessary to compete for higher-paying jobs.

The Civil Rights Act applied only to actions after the effective date of July 1, 1965. It also permitted exceptions in cases where religion, sex, or national origin is a bona fide occupational qualification reasonably necessary to the normal operation of a business. This qualification might apply to certain jobs in religious organizations, for example. In addition, the act permits an employer to differentiate wages and other employment conditions on the basis of a bona fide seniority system, provided that such differences are not the result of an intention to discriminate. As a result of these exceptions, the Civil Rights Act has had neither as large nor as quick an impact on wage and job differentials as many had anticipated. It has, however, led to a clearer definition of discrimination.

Two standards, or tests, of discrimination have evolved from court cases: disparate treatment and disparate impact. **Disparate treatment** means treating individuals differently because of their race, sex, color, religion, or national origin. The difficulty created by this standard is that personnel policies that appear to be neutral because they ignore race, gender, and so on, may nevertheless continue the effects of past discrimination. For instance, a seniority system that fires first the last person hired will protect those who were historically favored in hiring and training practices. Alternatively, a standard of hiring by word of mouth will perpetuate past discrimination if current employees are primarily of one race or sex.

The concern with perpetuating past discrimination led to the second standard, **disparate impact**. Under this standard it is the result of different treatment, not the motivation, that matters. Thus, statistical discrimination is illegal under the impact standard even though it is not illegal under the treatment standard.

disparate treatment:
treatment of individuals differently because of their race, sex, color, religion, or national origin

disparate impact:
an impact that differs according to race, sex, color, religion, or national origin, regardless of the motivation

2.b. Comparable Worth

comparable worth:
the idea that pay ought to be determined by job characteristics rather than by supply and demand and that jobs with comparable requirements should receive comparable wages

The persistent wage gap between men and women in particular, but also between white males and minorities, has prompted well-meaning reformers to seek a new remedy for eliminating the gap—laws requiring companies to offer equal pay for jobs of comparable worth. **Comparable worth** is a catchword for the idea that pay ought to be determined by job characteristics rather than by supply and demand and that jobs with comparable requirements should receive comparable wages.

To identify jobs of comparable worth, employers would be required to evaluate all of the different jobs in their firms, answering questions such as these: What level of formal education is needed? How much training is necessary? Is previous experience needed? What skills are required? How much supervision is required? Is the work dangerous? Are working conditions unpleasant? By assigning point values to answers, employers could create job classifications based on job characteristics and could pay comparable wages for jobs with comparable "scores." A firm employing secretaries and steelworkers, for example, would determine the wages for these jobs by assessing job characteristics. If the assessment shows secretaries' work to be comparable to that of steelworkers, then the firm would pay secretaries and steelworkers comparable wages.

Proponents of comparable worth claim that market-determined wages are inappropriate because of the market's inability to assess marginal products as a result of statistical discrimination, team production, and personal prejudice. They argue that mandating a comparable worth system would minimize wage differentials that are due to statistical discrimination and occupational segregation, and they charge that a freely functioning market will continue to misallocate pay.

Opponents of comparable worth argue that interference with the functioning of the labor market will lead to shortages in some occupations and excess supplies in others. For instance, Figure 4 shows two markets for university professors, a market for computer science professors and a market for English professors. The supply and demand conditions in each market determine a wage for English professors that is less than the wage for computer science professors. The wage differential exists even though professors in both disciplines are required to have a Ph.D. and have essentially the same responsibilities.

Advocates of comparable worth would say that the two groups of professors should earn the same wage, the wage of the computer science professors, W_{CS}. But at this wage there would be a surplus of English professors, $QE_2 - QE_1$. The higher wage would cause the university to reduce the number of English professors it employs, from QE to QE_1. The net effect of comparable worth would be to reduce the number of English professors employed but to increase the wages of those who are employed. The policy would also have a detrimental effect in the future. The wage would send the incorrect signal to current college students. It would tell students to remain in English instead of forgoing English for computer science.

Comparable worth has not fared well in the U.S. courtroom. On the whole, U.S. federal courts have not accepted the notion that unequal pay for comparable jobs violates existing employment discrimination law. Perhaps not surprisingly, therefore, the concept has made little headway in the private sector. Greater success has occurred in the public sector at the local and state levels.

Figure 4
Comparable Worth
Two markets are shown, a market for computer science professors and a market for English professors. Demand and supply conditions determine that the wages for computer science professors are higher than the wages for English professors. Proponents of comparable worth might argue that the wages of both groups of professors should be equal to the higher wages of computer science professors since the requirements and responsibilities of the two jobs are virtually identical. However, the effect of imposing a higher wage in the market for English professors, W_{CS}, is to create a surplus of English professors, $QE_2 - QE_1$. In addition, the higher wage sends the signal to current college students that majoring in English will generate the same expected income as majoring in computer science. Students who might have studied computer science turn to English. In the future, an excess of English professors remains and even grows while the number of computer science professors shrinks.

(a) Market for Computer Science Professors

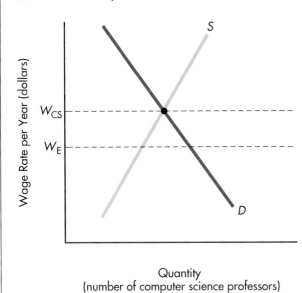

(b) Market for English Professors

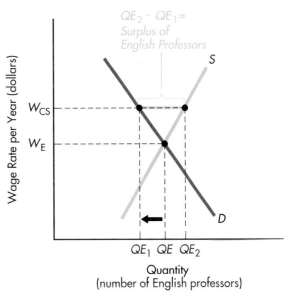

Tom Hanks' first best actor Oscar was for his portrayal of Andy Beckett, a gay attorney who develops AIDS, in the movie *Philadelphia.* Andy was a successful young attorney moving rapidly up the law firm's ladder until the partners discovered he had AIDS. The firm's senior partner terminated Beckett, claiming job malfeasance. The movie focuses on Beckett's attempt to prove in court that the firm discriminated against him and to resolve the case before dying. The scene shown here has Beckett, linked to an IV, listening to and explaining an opera to his attorney, Joe Miller, played by Denzel Washington. The opera scene is one where the singer, like Beckett, realizes that death is imminent.

In Colorado Springs, San Jose, and Los Angeles, and in Iowa, Michigan, New York, and Minnesota, pay adjustments have been made on the basis of comparable worth. More than two-thirds of the state governments have begun studies to determine whether compensation of state workers reflects the worth of their jobs. Why has comparable worth had more success in the government sector? State governments suffer from the problem of team production, and if personal prejudice is to occur, it is more likely to occur in nonprofit organizations such as government where firms do not employ to the profit-maximizing point where $MFC = MRP$. Thus, it is in the state, local, and federal governments that comparable worth can be an effective policy. Comparable worth was adapted nationwide in Australia in the early 1970s and aspects of it have arisen in parts of the United Kingdom.

RECAP

1. The first national antidiscrimination law was the Civil Rights Act of 1964. It forbade firms from discriminating on the basis of sex, race, color, religion, or national origin.

2. Two tests of discrimination have evolved from court cases. According to the disparate treatment standard, it is illegal to intentionally treat individuals differently because of their race, sex, color, religion, or national origin. According to the disparate impact standard, it is the result, not the intention, of actions that is illegal.

3. Comparable worth is the idea that jobs should be evaluated on the basis of a number of characteristics and all jobs receiving the same evaluation should receive the same pay regardless of demand and supply conditions.

Proponents argue that comparable worth is a solution to a market failure problem. Opponents argue that it will create surpluses and shortages in labor markets.

3. UNIONIZATION AND WAGE DIFFERENTIALS

Have unions been able to increase the wages of union members relative to the wages of nonunionized workers?

Unionized sectors of the U.S. economy earn higher wages than nonunionized sectors. Nevertheless, union membership is declining in the private sector of the U.S. economy. In this section we discuss the role of unions in creating wage differentials.

3.a. Monopsony

Many people argue that unions arise under bad management. In other words, unions arise when workers are being exploited or mistreated by mismanagement. According to this viewpoint, a union is a means to offset a monopsony.

A monopsony is a market situation in which there is just one buyer of a resource. A monopsonistic firm hires additional labor as long as labor's value to the firm exceeds its cost. Yet the labor is not paid its value to the firm. It receives a wage rate that is less than its marginal revenue product. Actually, there are not many situations in which just one firm buys a resource. Most monopsonies occur when several firms join together to form a buyers' cartel. Agricultural firms in California might organize a cooperative to bring itinerant labor from Mexico to harvest crops. The cooperative would send workers to farms as needed. Individual public schools do not hire teachers; instead, school districts comprising several schools employ teachers. In some cities, hospitals have formed an organization that hires all nurses and staff other than doctors and then apportions the workers as needed.

Athletics is a particularly fertile area for the formation of monopsony cartels because the government allows, even supports, the cartel even though cartels are illegal in other businesses. One of the most effective is the NCAA, the National Collegiate Athletic Association. Not long after intercollegiate football became a substantial source of income to colleges, the best football players began to receive large money inducements—wages—to attend certain schools. Some college administrators opposed all money payments to amateur athletes. They believed amateurism has some inherent virtue and wanted to maintain the distinction between college athletics and professional sports. That belief, coupled with widespread membership in the NCAA, has resulted in a monopsony situation in which student-athletes are paid substantially less than their marginal revenue products. In fact, student-athletes receive no pay. Universities and colleges are prohibited from offering salaries to athletes, from "making work" for them at the school and paying them relatively high wage rates for a job that usually pays much less (for example, paying athletes $30 an hour to reshelve books in the university library), and from offering cars, clothes, trips, and other inducements to attract athletes.

College is not the only place where athletes have faced a cartel. Players in major league baseball, professional basketball, and professional football have all been subject to such cartels. Players in each sport once worked under a system in which a player could deal only with the team that initially signed him. A reserve clause in most players' contracts made the player the exclusive property of the team that first signed him or the team to which he was traded thereafter. According to the clause, if a player refused to accept the wage of the team whose property he was, he could not play for any other team. People hired by a monopsony are paid wages that are less than their marginal revenue product—in other words, they are exploited.

The monopsonist is said to exploit its employees because of the low compensation level relative to the compensation level offered by a competitive firm. Some have argued that this exploitation also means shoddy working conditions, terrible treatment, and very high levels of injuries. There is no doubt that the monopsonist provides a total compensation package (salary, working conditions, and other job-related factors) that is less than the competitive firm (nonmonopsonist) would offer. However, the composition of that compensation depends on what the workers want. For instance, the coal miners in West Virginia may prefer some compensation in the form of safety equipment or filters in the mines. The coal mining firms would be willing to provide that equipment as part of the compensation package for the employees. The amount of safety would not necessarily be less than a competitive firm would provide, but the total compensation package would be. However, the total compensation has to be sufficient to induce workers to become coal miners. The coal miners, while earning less from a monopsonist than from a competitive firm, nevertheless can earn more than they could doing something other than coal mining.

3.b. Bilateral Monopoly

bilateral monopoly:
a market in which a monopsonistic buyer of resources faces a monopoly seller of resources

When people are paid wages that are less than their marginal revenue products, they have an incentive to find ways to offset this monopsony power. One approach has been for workers to form what we might call a sellers' cartel, a union. Major league baseball players in the 1960s received only about one-fifth of their estimated net marginal revenue products because of the monopsony situation enjoyed by team owners. In the 1970s, the players formed a union. 1976 was the last year of the reserve clause that prohibited players from leaving one team to seek a higher wage with another team.[4] Salaries soared thereafter. The 1977 average salary rose 40 percent from 1976 and by 1994, the average salary exceeded one-half million dollars. Unhappy with the rising salaries, baseball owners decided to place a salary cap on teams; the union refused. A strike ensued, ending the 1994 season prematurely and extending into the 1995 season.

A union can enable workers to speak with one voice—to confront the one buyer with just one seller. The result is a **bilateral monopoly**—a monopsony of buyers facing a monopoly of sellers. Figure 5 shows a monopsonistic labor market. The monopsonistic firm wants to hire a quantity of labor, L_1 (500 hours' worth of labor), given by $MRP = MFC$, and pay a wage rate, $W_1 = \$15$, at which people are willing and able to supply $L_1 = 500$ hours. Instead of accepting this wage, the union demands a higher wage, $W_2 = \$20$, which is equal to the marginal revenue product. The resulting wage rate may be anywhere between W_1 and W_2. Where it ends up depends partly on which side has the stronger bargaining position, partly on the negotiating skills of the parties, and partly on luck.

---

[4]Paul M. Sommers and Noel Quinton, "Pay and Performance in Major League Baseball: The Case of the First Family of Free Agents," *Journal of Human Resources* 17, Summer 1982, p. 227. Also see "Economics of Sport Enterprises," special issue of *Managerial and Decision Finances,* September/October 1994.

Figure 5
The Monopsonistic Labor Market

In a monopsonistic labor market, the firm hires the quantity given by the equilibrium between the marginal revenue product (MRP) and the marginal factor cost (MFC), but the firm pays a wage that is less than the marginal revenue product. The wage rate that is equal to marginal revenue product is W_2 ($20). The wage that the monopsonistic firm pays is W_1 ($15). It is found by dropping a vertical line to the supply curve from the point where $MFC = MRP$.

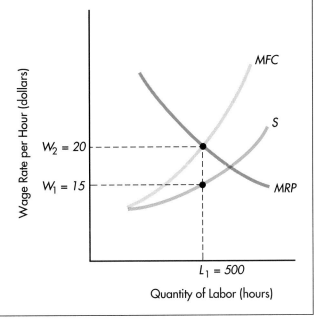

3.b.1. Efficiency Bases for Unions Offsetting the power of the monopsonist is not the only reason for a union. In fact, unions exist in many industries other than monopsonies. A union may serve the purposes of both firms and workers. For instance, a large corporation having many different types of jobs may find negotiating with each and every employee very time consuming and costly. In addition, the firm may have no means to communicate with employees regarding issues such as the performance of the firm and personnel policies the firm is implementing. In such cases, the firm may find it less costly to work with a union. In this way, the firm can communicate with the leaders of the union and allow the union to communicate with workers. The firm can also set wages and working conditions in agreement with the union leaders and have these policies apply to all workers, thus avoiding the costs of negotiating with each employee. Unions may also provide ways that the firm is assured of a supply of skilled labor. The union may require that members have a certain amount of experience or serve an apprenticeship. Also, it and the firm may agree that layoffs occur in a certain order, such as last hired/first fired, and that the callback of employees begins with those employees last laid off. The firm thus does not have to devote resources to attracting new employees and training those employees; a readily available source of employees will exist.

Unions appear able to reduce the firm's costs more in the manufacturing sectors than in the service sectors. At least the manufacturing sectors are more unionized than are the service sectors. However, as manufacturing has become a smaller proportion of total employment in the United States and services have become a larger proportion, the membership in unions has declined. The only area in which union membership has grown in the last 15 years in the United States has been in the public sector—government employees.

Unions may arise as an offset to monopsony or as an institution that benefits both firms and employees.

Chapter 31 / Wage Differentials: Race, Gender, Age, and Unionization

The process by which unions and firms hammer out a compromise regarding wages or working conditions is called **collective bargaining**. Under collective bargaining, union and management meet to negotiate a mutually agreeable contract specifying wages, working conditions, pension benefits, and other aspects of the job. The resulting contract usually extends over two or three years. Most multiyear agreements contain cost-of-living allowances (COLAs). Such allowances allow for periodic changes in money wages during the life of the agreement, based on changes in the purchasing power as measured by inflation. In some cases where a firm is unprofitable, unions have agreed to wage concessions or cuts for a short period of time, depending on the ability of the firm to reach profitability. In recent years, negotiations have focused more on working conditions and fringe benefits than on wages. Health insurance, child care, and retirement benefits are very important issues. While unions and firms carry out collective bargaining in Japan, the approach is very different than in the United States, as noted in the Economic Insight: Unionization in Japan.

3.c. Economic Effects of Unions

Unionized sectors of the U.S. economy earn higher wages than nonunion sectors. In 1991, union wages were on average 30 percent higher than nonunion wages. The union-nonunion differential ranges from no difference in the financial services industry to a 75 percent difference in construction. This wage differential could be the result of union members having jobs that require greater skills than nonunion members and the greater age and experience of union workers. However, even if skill differences are taken into consideration, there is a wage differential of about 10 percent.

A union may have an effect on wages through the demand for and/or the supply of labor. The demand for any resource is its marginal revenue product, $MPP \times MR$; thus, an increase in either MPP or MR causes the demand curve to shift. If the union is able to increase the productivity of labor, to raise MPP, the demand for labor rises. Thus a benefit of unionization for a firm may be increased productivity. By providing workers with a direct means to voice their discontent to management and by basing job rights on seniority, unions may reduce workers' discontent and reduce turnover, or quit, rates. Firms with low quit rates have an incentive to provide training or human capital to employees, and human capital is positively related to productivity. The establishment of a seniority system and of formal grievance procedures may enhance productivity by improving workers' morale, motivation, and effort. Studies analyzing the effects of unions on productivity have shown a great deal of variation. Unions have been shown to have raised the productivity of all U.S. manufacturing by about 20 percent. For specific industries, however, the effects range from a negative 20 percent to a positive 30 percent.[5]

A union may also be able to reduce the wage elasticity of demand for labor. A lower wage elasticity means that any increase in wages will have a smaller effect on the quantity of labor employed. The lower the wage elasticity, the more likely a union is to push for larger wage advances. In addition, a union may be able to increase the demand for union labor or use political

---

[5]See Ronald G. Ehrenberg and Robert S. Smith, *Modern Labor Economics*, 5th ed. (Glenview, Ill.: Scott, Foresman, 1994).

Part VII/Resource Markets

Unionization in Japan

In the United States companies bargain with several unions representing workers with different skills or jobs. For example, airline mechanics, pilots, stewards, and baggage handlers each have their own union. In contrast, unions in Japan are organized on an enterprise (company or plant) basis. All employees in an enterprise are members of the same union. The enterprise-based structure of Japan is consistent with the practice of large Japanese companies to offer lifetime employment. It is not unusual for Japanese workers to spend their entire work life in a single company. In forming unions, then, Japanese workers have been most concerned with factors that affect the well-being of their company or plant.

Unions in Japan seldom mount large-scale offensives against management. Most contracts in Japan are renegotiated annually. Each spring a *shunto*, or spring wage campaign, is organized by the unions. A target for wage demands is set. Each union is allotted one day to strike by a schedule created by the unions and the firms. At the end of the strike, wage and other issues are resolved by the enterprise, and everyone goes back to work at the new wage.

power to influence legislation that benefits the unionized sectors of the economy. In monopsonistic markets a union may affect the supply of labor in order to offset the monopsony power of the resource buyer. In competitive labor markets a union may be able to control the supply of skilled labor.

Suppose Figure 6(a) represents the labor market in the absence of unions. The market demand for and market supply of labor determine a wage rate of $10 and an employment level of L_e. Each individual firm faces a horizontal supply of labor, as shown in Figure 6(b). Now, suppose that a union is able to establish a $20 wage in the industry—$10 more than the current wage. For the individual competitive firm, the higher wage means an upward shift of the marginal-factor-cost curve. This is shown in Figure 6(b) as the shift from $MFC_1 = \$10$ to $MFC_2 = \$20$ and a decline in the quantity of labor employed by the firm. The higher wage means that less labor is employed—L_2 is employed rather than L_1. Since all firms are affected in the same way, the higher wage creates a surplus in the labor market. L_4 workers are willing to work at $20, but only L_3 obtain jobs.

Two questions arise from this analysis. First, how does a union increase wages in a competitive market? Second, what happens to workers who are unable to get union employment?

3.c.1. **How Do Unions Increase Wages?** Unions increase wages by restricting the supply of union labor and by increasing the demand for union labor.

The closed and union shop If a firm could hire only union workers, called a **closed shop**, the union would be able to restrict the supply of labor by restricting union membership. By contrast, in a **union shop**, a workplace in which employees must join the union within a certain amount of time after obtaining a job, a union is unable to effectively control the supply of labor. This difference between union shops and closed shops is why unions opposed the Taft-Hartley Act in 1947, which outlawed closed shops. Since 1947, unions have not been able to restrict the supply of union labor through union membership.

closed shop:
a workplace in which union membership is a condition of employment

union shop:
a workplace in which all employees must join a union within a specific period of time after they are hired

Figure 6
Union Effects on the Labor Market
If the labor market is competitive, as shown in Figure 6(a), an increase in the wage from $10 to $20 per hour increases the quantity of people willing and able to work and decreases the quantity of jobs available that

pay $20 per hour. The result is a labor surplus. Figure 6(b) shows the individual firm's response to an increase in the hourly wage. The higher marginal-factor-cost curve (*MFC₂*) intersects the marginal-revenue-product curve (*MRP*) at a smaller quantity of labor. The firm employs fewer workers.

(a) Labor Market

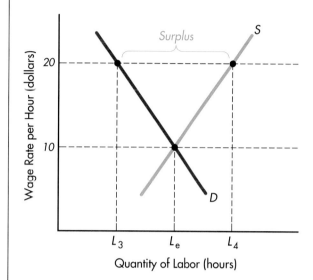

(b) Individual Firm

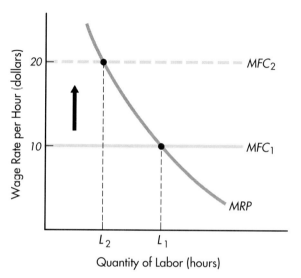

Immigration restrictions Restricting immigration has been a common theme throughout the history of organized labor in the United States. In 1869, the first national convention of labor unions proposed excluding Chinese contract labor. Four months later, the first national convention of black unions likewise voted for exclusion. In 1872, the Working Men's party of California forced passage of a new California constitution that forbade the hiring of Chinese workers by any corporation or public body. In 1882, Congress ended Chinese immigration. Throughout the 1920s and 1930s, the AFL fought to restrict and then to abolish immigration. Unions today strongly oppose the relaxation of immigration restrictions.

Barriers to entering specific occupations To restrict the supply of labor to a particular profession, unions can require lengthy training programs or apprenticeships, and the government can mandate licensing. The entry of electricians, plumbers, beauticians, and others into their professions is limited by the need to acquire a license in order to practice. The ease or difficulty of obtaining a license reflects how high a barrier to entry is desired. High barriers increase the wage rate and reduce the flow of workers from other occupations to the restricted profession.

Increasing demand Unions might try to increase the demand for union labor, causing the demand curve to shift out and become more inelastic. If unions can convince consumers to buy only union-made goods and services, the demand for union labor will rise and the wage elasticity of the demand for union labor will fall. Bumper stickers and advertisements urging support for unions ("Look for the union label") are appeals to consumers to purchase goods made in union shops and thus to stimulate the demand for union workers.

If unions can limit the entry of nonunion firms or restrict the sale of output produced by nonunion labor, the demand for union labor will increase and the wage elasticity of demand for union labor will decrease. For this reason, the United Auto Workers has supported legislation restricting the import of autos, and the textile workers' union has supported tariffs or taxes on imported textiles.

Unions may try to safeguard union jobs by opposing the introduction of new technology and by featherbedding. **Featherbedding** is the requirement that more workers than are actually needed be employed. For several years after diesel engines replaced coal-burning engines and made railroad firemen obsolete, the railway union required firemen on each train. Similarly, airlines were required to carry three pilots even after new planes made the third pilot obsolete. The musicians' union used to require that a certain number of musicians be employed for each performance even if the music did not call for that many.

3.c.2. What Happens to Nonunion Labor? The excess supply of labor forces unions to ration the available jobs among members. One approach is to rely on seniority. Another approach is called *work-spreading*. Under work-spreading, the workweek is shortened so that more people have jobs. Instead of 40 people working 60 hours per week, 60 people work 40 hours per week, for example.

Workers who are rationed out or unable to find union employment look for jobs in the nonunion sector, increasing the supply of labor there and lowering the rate of pay for nonunion workers. Figure 7 shows two labor markets, one for union labor and one for nonunion labor. The same wage initially exists in each market. If the union is able to reduce the supply of union labor, the supply curve in the unionized market shifts in (from S_1 to S_2), driving the union wage up (from W_1 to W_2). Workers unable to obtain employment in the unionized sector ($L_2 - L_1$) move to the nonunion sector (the graph in part [b]). This causes the supply curve in the nonunion sector to shift out (from S_1 to S_2), and the wage rate to be forced down from W_1 to W_2.

RECAP

1. Monopsony exists when there is only one buyer of a resource. Most monopsonies arise because buyers form a cartel.

2. Bilateral monopoly exists when a monopsony faces a single seller of a resource. The outcome of negotiations in a bilateral monopoly depends on the relative strengths of buyer and seller.

3. Collective bargaining is the process of negotiating wage and job contracts.

4. Unions can provide benefits to both employers and employees.

5. Union wages tend to be higher than nonunion wages. The reason for the difference may be the ability of unions to affect the demand for and supply of labor.

featherbedding:
the requirement that more workers than are actually needed be employed

Figure 7
The Economic Effect of Unions
Two labor markets are pictured, one for union labor and one for nonunion labor. Initially the two markets are in equilibrium at the same wage. The union successfully restricts the supply of labor in the unionized mar-

ket, from S_1 to S_2 (part [a]). As a result, the wage rate is driven up. The higher wage means that fewer workers are employed, L_2 instead of L_1. As a result, these workers flow to the nonunion sector (part [b]), increasing supply there from S_1 to S_2 and driving the wage rate down from W_1 to W_2.

(a) Unionized Labor Market

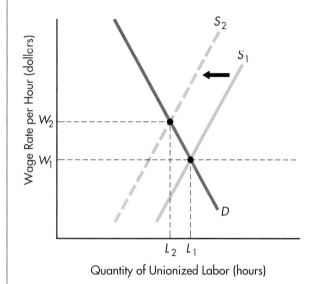

Quantity of Unionized Labor (hours)

(b) Nonunionized Labor Market

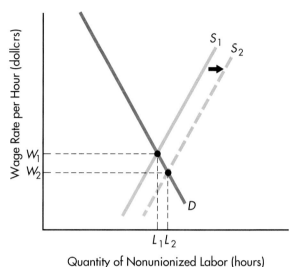

Quantity of Nonunionized Labor (hours)

6. Unions may be able to restrict the supply of labor to the unionized sectors of the economy, thereby driving wages up there and down in the nonunion sectors. The closed shop, now illegal, was one method of reducing the supply of union labor. Restrictions on immigration and barriers to certain occupations may also reduce the supply of labor.

7. Unions may be able to affect the demand for labor by causing it to increase or by reducing the wage elasticity of demand.

4. LABOR MARKET LAWS: MINIMUM WAGES, OCCUPATIONAL SAFETY, AND THE FAMILY AND MEDICAL LEAVE ACT

What effects do government policies and programs such as minimum wages and the Family and Medical Leave Act have on the labor market?

The governments of developed nations have intervened in their labor markets on a regular basis. In most of the European nations, labor market activities are more tightly regulated by the government than they are in the United States. In Germany, for example, all workers are guaranteed thirty days' paid vacation a year. In the United States, minimum wages have been imposed since the late 1930s, rules and regulations regarding job safety have been prescribed by the government since the 1970s, and in 1993, President Clinton enacted the Family and Medical Leave Act, which allows employees in firms of more than fifty workers to take up to twelve weeks of unpaid leave without having their jobs or responsibilities affected. Unions are important advocates of minimum wage laws and health and safety requirements. Why? What impacts do such laws have on the labor market?

4.a. Minimum Wages

A minimum wage is a government policy that requires firms to pay at least a certain wage, the minimum wage. A minimum wage has existed in the United States since 1938 when it was set at $.25 per hour. The minimum wage is currently $4.25 per hour but a proposal to raise it to $5.15 was made in the 1995 Congress. The arguments in favor of the minimum wage are that a worker must earn at least the minimum wage in order to have a decent standard of living. At $5.15 per hour, 40 hours per week, 50 weeks per year, you would earn $10,300 per year. Currently, the government defines the poverty level of income for a family of four to be about $14,765. (See the chapter "Income Distribution, Poverty, and Government Policy" for more on poverty.) Thus, at the minimum wage, a single wage-earner family would be far below the poverty level. The arguments opposed to minimum wages claim that implementation of such minimums will increase unemployment, particularly among those on the bottom of the economic ladder, the unskilled—teenagers, minorities, and women—and lead to worse cases of poverty. Let's discuss the minimum wage policies and their effects on the labor market.

A minimum wage was adopted as part of the Fair Labor Standards Act of 1938. The act set the first minimum wage at $.25 per hour and provided for it to be increased to $.40 by 1945. Over the years, Congress has amended the act in order to increase the minimum wage (see Figure 8). The rate of increase, however, has not kept up with inflation and the rate of increase in the cost of living. In Figure 8, the legal minimum wage, indicated by the solid line, is adjusted for inflation in the dashed line. The dashed line shows

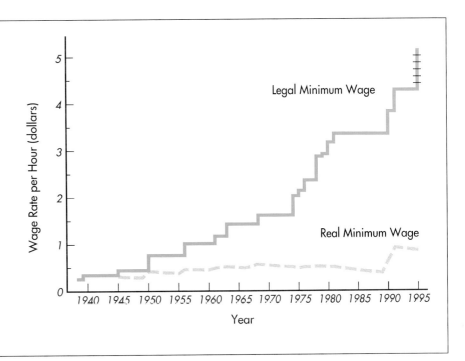

Figure 8
The Pattern of Minimum Wages
The legislated minimum wage is shown as a solid line. In 1995, President Clinton proposed an increase to $5.15. The real minimum wage, the legislated wage adjusted for inflation, is shown as a dashed line. The purchasing power of the real minimum wage has not changed much over time. Sources: *Economic Report of the President, 1995* (Washington, D.C.: U.S. Government Printing Office, 1991–1993); U.S. Bureau of the Census, *Statistical Abstract of the United States, 1994* (Washington, D.C.: U.S. Government Printing Office, 1994).

Figure 9
The Effect of Minimum Wages

In a competitive labor market, a minimum wage above equilibrium causes a surplus—increases unemployment. This is shown in Figure 9(a). In a monopsonistic market, a minimum wage can increase both the wage and employment rates, as shown in Figure 9(b). The wage rises from $W_1 = \$10$ (the wage rate the monopsonistic firm wants to pay) to $W_m = \$15$, the legal minimum wage; and the quantity of labor employed rises from L_1 to L_2.

(a) Competitive Labor Market

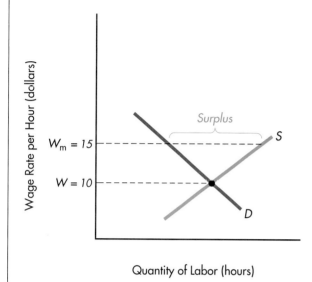

(b) Monopsonistic Labor Market

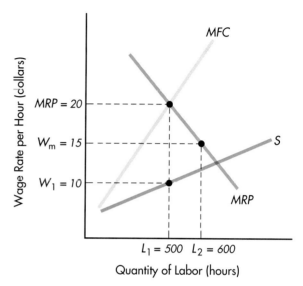

that the purchasing power of the legal minimum wage has in fact changed little since 1938. Not all firms and industries must pay the minimum wage. Some are granted exemptions. Today about 80 percent of all jobs that are not in agriculture are required to pay at least the minimum wage.

In a competitive labor market, a worker's wages are equal to the value of his or her marginal revenue product. A minimum wage set above the equilibrium wage creates a labor surplus (unemployment). If, on the other hand, an employer is a monopsonist, a worker's wage is less than the value of his or her marginal product. In Figure 9(a), setting the minimum wage (W_m) at $15, above the equilibrium wage (W) of $10, creates a labor surplus. Figure 9(b) shows that if an employer is a monopsonist, a worker's wage (W_1) is less than *MRP*. The imposition of a binding minimum wage set at a level that is less than *MRP* but greater than the wage rate that the monopsonistic firm wants to pay may actually increase the level of employment. The minimum wage (W_m) of $15 in Figure 9(b) shows that employment rises from L_1 to L_2.

Thus, in monopsonistic markets a minimum wage benefits all workers, but in nonmonopsonistic markets minimum wages benefit some and harm others. Studies show that the minimum wage adversely affects teenagers and other low-skilled workers, causing increased unemployment among these groups. A 10 percent increase in the minimum wage is estimated to result in a 1 to 3 percent decrease in teenage employment. Allowing a "subminimum" wage for teenagers reduces the job loss. Government policies do allow subminimum wages of about 75 percent of the minimum wage to be paid to teenagers.

Government attempts to reduce wage differentials may be well-intended but may have adverse consequences for the most unskilled sectors of the labor force.

Unions are among the strongest proponents of minimum wages. Why? Considering that the unskilled and those most hurt by minimum wages are not union members, the unemployment effects of minimum wages do not harm the union members. In addition, if firms must pay a minimum wage for an unskilled worker or pay a slightly higher wage for a skilled, union worker, the firm may find it worthwhile to pay for the skilled worker. Unions therefore anticipate that the minimum wage will increase the demand for their members and thus increase the wages of their members.

4.b. Occupational Safety

The minimum wage is far from the only government law that affects the labor market. The government also administers health, safety, and working conditions. The Occupational Safety and Health Act (OSHA), enacted in 1970, requires strict safety standards in the workplace. Its goal is "to insure the highest degree of health and safety protection for the employee." The act would seem to go against the wishes of workers. If a worker is willing to work in a less safe job for additional pay, then by requiring all jobs to have the same safety standards, the act is reducing the income of that worker. Much like the minimum wage, the act increases the costs of doing business to the firm by raising the compensation package offered to employees. This mandated increase will, in competitive markets, reduce employment among the most disadvantaged employees. However, like the minimum wage, the increased safety requirements could theoretically increase employment in the monopsonistic industries in addition to making working conditions better. In this latter case, the question arises as to whether employees would prefer increased pay or increased safety. The act does not allow this choice.

As with minimum wages, unions have been strong proponents of government health and safety requirements based on the belief that the increased costs of employing a worker will shift the demand away from nonunion members toward union members and, as a result, will increase the wages of union members.

Unions have been at the forefront in supporting governmental work-related wages and standards but are not the only proponents. In the case of the Family and Medical Leave Act, unions were generally supportive, but the strongest proponents were women's groups. What is the difference between the effects of the other labor laws and the effect of the Family and Medical Leave Act?

4.c. Family and Medical Leave Act

The Family and Medical Leave Act was the first law enacted after Bill Clinton became president. The act requires firms of more than 50 employees to grant an unpaid leave of absence to any employee for a period of up to twelve weeks a year so that the employee can take care of family matters—to care for a new infant or a sick relative. Approximately one-half of all employees in the United States are affected by the act; they work for firms larger than 50 employees.

The smallest firms were exempted from the act because Congress believed that the act could be a hardship. If a firm has only one employee trained for a specific task, then if that employee takes an unpaid leave, the firm must hire a temporary employee, train that employee, and then terminate the employment of that temporary employee when the permanent employee returns. The firm must either bear the additional expense of cross-training employees, maintain more than one employee trained for a specific task, or undergo the on-the-job training costs of a temporary employee each time a permanent employee requests a leave of absence. Thus, the Family and Medical Leave Act is likely to raise the costs of labor. Congress felt that the large firm could bear those additional costs without a problem while small firms could not and so exempted the small firms.

If labor costs rise, a firm will either hire less labor or attempt to reduce the labor costs. Firms could rely more on temporary employees since temporary employees, those working less than thirty hours a week, are not subject to the act. Bank of America, in fact, announced in February 1993 that from then on it was using only temporary employees for its tellers. Other banks have followed suit. Firms might also lower the wages of employees subject to the leave-of-absence policy, in a sense making the employees pay for at least part of the cost of the Family and Medical Leave Act. This would occur if the demand curve of firms for labor shifted down (the *MRP* declined) as a result of the act.

It is theoretically possible for the Family and Medical Leave Act to improve productivity. If the idea that a leave of absence could be taken in the case of a family emergency without affecting one's future with a firm raises employee morale and makes employees more productive (increases their *MRP*), then the act could have a positive effect on all labor. Or, if the act ensures that less occupational segregation occurs as a result of gender, it may induce firms to employ more women, avoid statistical discrimination, and thus increase the productivity of the labor market overall. If this occurs, the wage gap between males and females would decline over time.

The effects of labor market laws are not necessarily what they would seem to be on the surface. While it might appear that minimum wages, health and safety requirements, and family leave policies are nothing but beneficial for workers, in reality different workers are affected differently. As one of the principles of economics suggests, "there is no free lunch." If such laws raise costs to firms, then firms will respond by reducing employment in general; by reducing the employment of some particular group of workers; or by reducing the wages of its workers. The laws do benefit some groups, however. Minimum wages clearly benefit those who receive the jobs and are paid the minimum wage, when without the law they would receive even lower wages. Minimum wages may also benefit the higher-skilled workers as firms turn more toward the skilled workers and away from the less-skilled workers. Health and safety standards will benefit all employees who retain a job and whose pay does not decline as a result of the standards. And the Family and Medical Leave Act may benefit women who take time off to have a child, or men and women who want to reduce the number of hours they work each year without negatively affecting their jobs.

As we have seen, the U.S. government intervenes in the labor market in a big way. How does the U.S. situation compare to that of other industrial nations? Let's look at some of the other nations' labor market policies.

4.d. Labor Policies in Other Industrial Nations

In general, U.S. policies are less restrictive than those in other industrial nations. The United States was the last Western industrial nation to impose a government-mandated leave at the federal level and that occurred only with the 1993 Family and Medical Leave Act. However, unpaid leaves for child-bearing were provided for about 92 percent of all employees in medium and large firms in the United States prior to the implementation of the act. In Sweden, nearly a year of unpaid parental leave after twelve weeks of paid leave is provided. Australia offers one year of unpaid leave; Italy, five months at 80 percent pay; the United Kingdom forty weeks at about 90 percent pay; and Austria, Germany, Hungary, and Norway provide about 15 weeks of paid leave.[6]

There are significant unionization differences among nations as well. The U.S. unionization rates (percentages of workers that are unionized) of 20.5 percent for male and 12.5 percent for female workers are considerably lower than elsewhere. The unionization rates for men range from 35 percent in Germany to 78 percent in Sweden, and from 18 percent in Germany to 80 percent in Sweden for women. Even these statistics are slightly misleading because the wage-setting process in the U.S. unionized sectors differs considerably from those in other nations. In the United States, collective bargaining is decentralized, with plant-specific or at least firm-specific agreements, while in other nations agreements are nationwide.

The results of these differences are not easy to measure since the composition of the labor forces and the types of industries differ. Nevertheless, there is more wage disparity in the United States than in the other Western industrial nations. There is also less occupational segregation between men and women in the United States than in the other industrial nations. Furthermore, the percentage of employed women in the United States who work part time (less than 35 hours per week) is smaller than in any other country. About 46 percent of Swedish and 53 percent of Norwegian employed women work part time, compared to only 24 percent of U.S. employed women. On the surface, at least, it would appear that the greater involvement of the other nations' government in the labor market might result from higher unionization; that the involvement might lead to more equal wages; and that the involvement might lead to more part-time work and more occupational segregation. Are these laws beneficial? The answer you give to this question depends on where you stand.

RECAP

1. Federal law requires that certain jobs pay no less than the prescribed minimum wage.

2. Minimum wages cause unemployment in competitive markets and increase employment in monopsonistic markets.

3. Job safety rules affect the labor market in much the same way as minimum wages, benefiting some workers and harming others.

4. The Family and Medical Leave Act requires firms with more than fifty employees to grant unpaid leaves of absence to employees for up to twelve weeks a year so they can take care of family emergencies.

---

[6] Blau and Kahn, op. cit.

SUMMARY

▲▼ *What accounts for earnings disparities between males and females and between whites and nonwhites?*

1. Earnings disparities may result from discrimination, occupational choice, human capital differences, educational opportunity differences, age, and immigration. §1.a, 1.c, 1.d

2. Discrimination occurs when some factor not related to marginal revenue product affects the wage rate someone receives. §1.a

▲▼ *Are discrimination and freely functioning markets compatible?*

3. There are two general types of discrimination—personal prejudice and statistical discrimination. §1.b

4. Personal prejudice is costly to those who demonstrate the prejudice and should not last in a market economy. For it to last, some restrictions on the functioning of markets must exist. §1.b.1

5. Statistical discrimination is the result of imperfect information and can occur as long as information is imperfect. §1.b.2

6. Occupational segregation exists when some jobs are held mainly by one group in society and other jobs by other groups. A great deal of occupational segregation exists between males and females in the United States. §1.c

7. High rates of immigration in the 1970s and 1980s, particularly of unskilled workers, has widened the earnings gap between Hispanics and whites and between skilled and unskilled workers. §1.d

▲▼ *What government policies have been implemented to reduce wage differentials ?*

8. Comparable worth is an attempt to resolve the problems of wage differentials, occupational segregation, and discrimination. §2.b

▲▼ *Have unions been able to increase the wages of union members relative to the wages of nonunionized workers?*

9. Bilateral monopoly occurs when a monopoly seller faces a monopsonistic buyer. A monopsonistic firm pays less than the marginal revenue product to resources. §3.b

10. A union attempts to offset the monopsony power of the firm and force the rate of pay up to the marginal revenue product by creating a monopoly of sellers. A union may increase the productivity of the employees. §3.b, 3.c

11. Unionized sectors of the economy tend to have higher wages than nonunion sectors. Reasons for the difference include the impact of unions in monopsonistic markets, restrictions on the supply of union labor, and increases in the demand for union labor. §3.c, 3.c.1, 3.c.2

▲▼ *What effects do government policies and programs such as minimum wages and the Family and Medical Leave Act have on the labor market?*

12. Minimum wages and occupational safety rules benefit some workers and harm others. Low-skilled, new entrants into the labor force are most harmed by minimum wage and occupational safety laws. §4.a, 4.b

KEY TERMS

discrimination §1.a

statistical discrimination §1.b

crowding §1.c

occupational segregation §1.c

disparate treatment §2.a

disparate impact §2.a

comparable worth §2.b

bilateral monopoly §3.b

collective bargaining §3.b.1

closed shop §3.c.1

union shop §3.c.1

featherbedding §3.c.1

EXERCISES

1. What is the effect of immigration on the labor market? Using the production possibilities curve, illustrate what immigration means for society as a whole. Recall that the PPC is based on the existing quantity and quality of resources. (You may want to review Chapter 2.) Immigration is an increase in the quantity of resources; is it an increase in the quality as well?

2. Explain what is meant by discrimination, and explain the difference between personal prejudice and statistical discrimination.

3. Explain why occupational segregation by sex might occur. Can you imagine any society in which you would not expect to find occupational segregation by sex? Explain. Would you expect to find occupational segregation by race in most societies?

4. Why are women's wages only 60 to 80 percent of men's wages, and why has this situation existed for several decades? Now that women are entering college and professional schools in increasing numbers, why doesn't the wage differential disappear?

5. Why do economists say that discrimination is inherently inefficient and therefore will not occur in general?

6. Demonstrate, using two labor markets, what is meant by comparable worth. What problems are created by comparable worth? Under what conditions might comparable worth make economic sense? Explain.

7. Using a perfectly competitive resource market, demonstrate the effect of unionization of the labor force.

8. Using a perfectly competitive resource market, demonstrate the effect of immigration on the labor market.

9. Answer questions 7 and 8 using a monopsonistic labor market.

10. Demonstrate how minimum wages affect the labor market. First use a perfectly competitive labor market, then use a labor market in which the firm is a monopsonist. Do the same for job safety requirements.

11. Why would unions want to limit the number of hours in the workweek?

12. What impact would a mandatory four-week vacation period for all employees have on the economy?

13. There is a great deal of talk in the United States about providing more job flexibility for families. Why is it necessary for the government to provide the flexibility through the Family and Medical Leave Act and other programs? Why doesn't the private market provide this flexibility?

14. Consider the decision of a working woman or man who has young children or elderly relatives to take care of. Explain in terms of the labor supply curve how this person's decision to work is affected by the presence of dependents. What happens to the opportunity cost of working? How is the labor supply curve affected?

COOPERATIVE LEARNING EXERCISE

Divide the class into groups of 4 or 5 students. Then divide the groups into As and Bs. The B group is to develop arguments in favor of increasing the minimum wage. The A group is to devise arguments in favor of eliminating the minimum wage. Choose several students from each group to present their arguments.

Both Sides Wield Same Data in Minimum Wage Debate; Raise Won't Boost Unemployment, Proponents Say

Labor Secretary Robert Reich says minimum-wage working people deserve a raise.

"It is not enough to live on," he says. "The minimum wage is worth about one-third less than what it was just 15 years ago."

About 11 million people earning between $4.25 and $5.15 an hour would benefit by increasing the base wage 90 cents over two years, he says. Full-time minimum-wage workers earn about $8,500 annually.

Mr. Reich argues that inflation already has eaten up 50 percent of the last 90-cent hike in the minimum wage. It was implemented in two 45-cent increments in 1990 and 1991. And Mr. Reich says another increase is critical if lawmakers want to lure people off welfare and into the job market.

"It is vitally important that we make work pay," Mr. Reich says. "And we now have strong evidence from independent academic researchers, and they found that a minimum wage increase caused no job losses."

Mr. Reich points to recent research by the Center on Budget and Policy Priorities concerning job losses and an increased minimum wage. The center reports that a 10 percent increase in the minimum wage would cause the jobless rate for teenagers to climb six-tenths of 1 percent. Earlier research indicated the unemployment rate among youth would rise 1 percentage point.

Kurt Karl, an economist at the WEFA Group, a Bala Cynwyd, Pa., economic consulting firm, says no more than 20,000 workers will lose their jobs if the minimum wage is raised 90 cents.

Analysts say raising the minimum wage has less effect on employment because the number of workers earning the base wage has declined. Many businesses associated with low-paying jobs, such as fast-food outlets, pay more than the minimum wage because they cannot otherwise attract workers.

"It will not have an overall impact on jobs," says Isaac Shapiro, associate director of the center. He says minority workers may reap the biggest benefit, noting, "They are somewhat more likely to have earnings at or near the minimum wage."

For much the same reason, experts say that a wage increase would temporarily raise the inflation rate only 0.1 of a percentage point.

"It turns out that there are so few people on the minimum wage that moving it up 90 cents is not enough to move inflation up," Mr. Karl says.

Proponents say that a wage increase would fit into the White House strategy of trying to raise the living standards of working people. In his Middle Class Bill of Rights, the president proposed a handful of tax cuts to help families with children, those with post-secondary education expenses or those caring for an elderly relative.

Labor officials say they proposed a 90-cent increase because it would not have major effects on employment and inflation. They also note that 90 cents is the same amount that enjoyed wide Republican support the last time Congress increased the rate.

In fact, Mr. Reich is hoping that the president's proposal will not become a partisan issue and will eventually enjoy some Republican support. He notes that conservatives such as Sen. Phil Gramm, R-Texas, and House Speaker Newt Gingrich of Georgia voted for the last increase.

"The Republicans are resistant, but they are the ones who over and over again stress how important it is to reward hard-working people," Mr. Reich says.

Source: "Both Sides Wield Same Data in Minimum Wage Debate; Raise Won't Boost Unemployment, Proponents Say," Robert Dodge, The Dallas Morning News, Feb. 19, 1995. Reprinted with permission of The Dallas Morning News.

Commentary

The federal minimum wage is currently $4.25. Since 1985, the consumer price index has risen 40 percent. This means that in purchasing power terms, $4.25 in 1980 would be equivalent to $2.55 today. It is this reason, primarily, that advocates argue for an increase in the minimum wage. Labor Secretary Robert Reich says "It is not enough to live on." Few would disagree with Reich's statement. The argument over the minimum wage is not its level but rather its effects on those working and those seeking jobs.

The belief among most economists is that minimum wages create unemployment. As we discussed in the text, if a minimum wage is imposed in a monopsonistic industry employment would actually increase. In all other industries, the minimum wage leads to employment losses. But, Secretary Reich referred to a study in which researchers found that a minimum wage increase caused no job losses.

How could a minimum wage not cause job losses? One reason would be if the minimum wage affected few people, that is, if most people earned more than the minimum wage or if the minimum wage affected people who primarily worked at part time jobs. As the article says, "Many businesses associated with low-paying jobs, such as fast-food outlets, pay more than the minimum wage because they cannot otherwise attract workers."

There is no doubt that in other than monopsonistic industries, as the costs of hiring workers rises while everything else does not change, fewer workers will be hired. There also is no doubt that wages reflect a worker's marginal revenue product. Thus, it is the unskilled individual or the person choosing to work at an entry level job or part time job that will earn lower wages. The minimum wage, if it affects anyone, will affect the unskilled and part time workers. How are they affected? It depends on whether they have a job and keep that job or whether they are just entering the labor force looking for a job. While increasing the minimum wage will increase the incomes of those who retain their jobs, it will reduce the number of jobs available. Because fewer minimum wage jobs will exist, those people who are just entering the labor force and have no skills or are looking at part time work to supplement income or provide flexible schedules will have less opportunity of obtaining a position.

32

Capital, Land, and Entrepreneurial Ability

FUNDAMENTAL
QUESTIONS

1. What role does saving play in the economy?
2. What is present value?
3. Does economic rent serve the allocative role that other resource prices serve?
4. What is conservation?
5. Why does the entrepreneur receive profit?
6. How are the resource markets tied together?

D oes a firm spend $100,000 today to acquire a machine that is expected to generate output for ten years? Do we extract more oil from the ground now, or leave it for future generations? Does an individual obtain a college degree, which may provide benefits throughout life, when the cost of a four-year college education exceeds $100,000? The alternatives faced by these decision-makers are similar to those confronting the employees of an aerospace company in suburban Los Angeles who offered to sell their winning California lottery ticket worth $3 million. The employees were willing to take $1.2 million cash. Three million dollars for only $1.2 million—that sounds like a good deal, but it's not as good as it sounds. A $3 million Lotto ticket is not $3 million: it is a promise that if the winner and the lottery survive twenty years, the winner will receive a check for about $150,000 each year before taxes (about $100,000 after taxes). "You're talking about money then versus money now," claimed one of the ticket holders, who figured that lots of undesirable things could happen in the next twenty years:

the lottery fund could go belly-up, the price of a loaf of bread could rise to $10, or nuclear disaster could make the annual payments worthless.

This issue is typical of a great deal of what occurs in the resource markets— comparing values over time. This chapter discusses the role of time in production and consumption as it examines the remaining resource markets—capital, land, and entrepreneurial ability.

I. CAPITAL

Capital is the resource we refer to when we say that a production process is mechanized or when we talk about the capacity of a factory. Capital is buildings and machinery produced for the purpose of producing goods and services. Human capital is the training and education that people acquire in order to increase their productivity.

I.a. Saving

What role does saving play in the economy?

In some less developed countries, farming is done solely by hand; in most nations, however, farming is quite mechanized. No doubt it has occurred to farmers in the less developed countries that they could produce more if they had some capital—for instance, a plow and a horse. Unfortunately, the capital needed to make the switch to a more mechanized operation can be obtained only by sacrificing current consumption. The construction of the plow requires that the farmer spend time away from the planting, care, or harvesting of the crops to build the plow, or she or he can use some of the crops to purchase the plow. Similarly, a horse can be obtained only by accumulating enough crops to purchase the horse; and the care and feeding of the horse, once acquired, would consume some of each year's crops. In order to obtain the capital, the farmer must forgo current consumption of the crops, and this sacrifice could be severe if the farmer's family depends on the crops for sustenance. Nevertheless, if the benefits of the additional production made possible by the plow and horse seem likely to be greater than the forgone consumption, the plow and horse will be acquired.

The process of sacrificing current consumption in order to accumulate capital (plows, horses) with which more output can be produced in the future, and thus more consumption enjoyed in the future, is called roundabout production. It is simply the process of **saving**. With saving, everything produced today is not consumed today. Some output, the amount saved, is used to create more production in the future. If the existing quantities of all resources were used today—if the forests were razed and every bit of timber were used, and if the world's supply of oil were extracted and used—living standards today might be higher but the future would be bleak. Forgoing some current consumption allows households, businesses, and society to obtain capital resources that can be used to increase future production and consumption. Any economy that grows—produces increasing amounts of goods and services and thus generates more income—must save and accumulate significant amounts of capital.

saving:
not consuming all current production

1.b. The Capital Market

The capital market is the channel through which consumers and producers match their future plans with their behavior today. The demand for and supply of capital determine the equilibrium quantity and cost of capital.

1.b.1. Demand for Capital A firm acquires additional capital as long as the marginal revenue product of the additional capital exceeds the marginal factor cost of that additional capital. When a firm rents capital (where *rent* refers to payment for the use of capital), its calculations are identical to the calculations it made when deciding whether to hire another worker. Suppose a rock-crushing firm rents the trucks it uses to haul crushed rock. The firm will rent another truck only if the rental rate is less than the marginal revenue product generated by the rented truck.

Not all capital is rented, however. Firms also purchase capital: they buy buildings and machines that they might use for several years. And, of course, rental or leasing companies must own the capital that they rent to other firms. To decide how much capital to buy, a firm must compare the prices paid for the building or equipment today with the marginal revenue product generated by the capital over the lifetime of the capital.

The firm's problem is identical to the problem faced by the holders of the winning lottery ticket. To know whether a machine should be purchased, or whether the $3 million payoff over twenty years should be purchased for $1.2 million cash today, it is necessary to compare two values: a purchase price today and a return that occurs over several years. To make this comparison, it is necessary to take into account that people prefer to consume today instead of waiting until tomorrow and that there is a risk that future payoffs will not

What is present value?

present value:
the equivalent value today of some amount to be received in the future

future value:
the equivalent value in the future of some amount received today

be made or that money in the future will not purchase as much as it does today. The value today of an amount to be paid or received in the future is called the **present value**. The value at a future date of some amount to be paid or received today is called the **future value**.

How can the future and present values be calculated? If you have $100,000 today, you can deposit that $100,000 into an account that will yield the principal (the original amount, $100,000) plus the interest after some period of time. If the interest rate is 9 percent per year, you will get interest earnings of $9,000 after one year:

$$\$100,000 \times .09 = \$9,000$$

Thus, $109,000 one year in the future is the *future value* of $100,000 today at an interest rate of 9 percent, or $100,000 today is the *present value* of $109,000 one year in the future at a 9 percent interest rate. Let's express "one year in the future" as *FV* (future value) and "today" as *PV* (present value). Then we can write

$$FV = PV(1 + \text{interest rate})$$

If we divide both sides by (1 + interest rate), we have

$$PV = FV/(1 + \text{interest rate})$$

Thus, the present value, *PV*, is $100,000:

$$PV = \$109,000/(1.09) = \$100,000$$

Calculating present and future values is simple when you are looking only one year into the future. The calculations become more complicated when you are looking ahead several years. If there is a stream of values, such as with the Lotto ticket paying $100,000 per year for twenty years, you could calculate the present value of each payment and sum all the values to get the present value of the entire stream. Or you could use tables, such as Table 1, that have been constructed to show what the present value of some future amount is or what the future value of some current amount is.

Let's use Table 1 to see what a Lotto ticket that pays $100,000 per year (after taxes) over twenty years is worth today. To calculate the present value of $100,000 per year for twenty years at a specific rate of interest, find the row for 20 periods and then read across the columns until you reach the appropriate interest rate. For instance, at an 8 percent rate of interest, the number indicated is 9.8181. This number is the present value of payments of $1 per period for 20 periods at 8 percent. To get the present value of a stream of payments of $100,000 per year for twenty years at 8 percent, multiply $100,000 times 9.8181. The result is $981,810. You can see from the table that as the interest rate increases, the present value of the money to be received in the future declines. Look at a 10 percent rate of interest and 20 periods in the table; the value indicated is 8.5136, so $100,000 each year for twenty years is worth $851,360 today at a 10 percent rate of interest.

Now let's put this in the context of a firm that is deciding whether to purchase a unit of capital. Suppose an airline is contemplating the purchase of a new wide-body plane that will yield $100,000 per year for twenty years. As seen in Table 1, the present value of the marginal revenue product from the plane is $981,810 at an 8 percent interest rate. If the price of the plane is $900,000, the firm will buy the plane. As the interest rate rises, the present value of the plane's marginal revenue product declines. At a 10 percent

TABLE 1
Present Value of an Annuity of $1.00 per Period

Period (n)	Interest (Discount) Rate (i)								
	1%	2%	3%	4%	5%	6%	7%	8%	9%
1	0.9901	0.9804	0.9709	0.9615	0.9524	0.9434	0.9346	0.9259	0.9174
2	1.9704	1.9416	1.9135	1.8861	1.8594	1.8334	1.8080	1.7833	1.7591
3	2.9410	2.8839	2.8286	2.7751	2.7232	2.6730	2.6243	2.5771	2.5313
4	3.9020	3.8077	3.7171	3.6299	3.5460	3.4651	3.3872	3.3121	3.2397
5	4.8534	4.7135	4.5797	4.4518	4.3295	4.2124	4.1002	3.9927	3.8897
6	5.7955	5.6014	5.4172	5.2421	5.0757	4.9173	4.7665	4.6229	4.4859
7	6.7282	6.4720	6.2303	6.0021	5.7864	5.5824	5.3893	5.2064	5.0330
8	7.6517	7.3255	7.0197	6.7327	6.4632	6.2098	5.9713	5.7466	5.5348
9	8.5660	8.1622	7.7861	7.4353	7.1078	6.8017	6.5152	6.2469	5.9952
10	9.4713	8.9826	8.5302	8.1109	7.7217	7.3601	7.0236	6.7101	6.4177
11	10.3676	9.7868	9.2526	8.7605	8.3064	7.8869	7.4987	7.1390	6.8052
12	11.2551	10.5753	9.9540	9.3851	8.8633	8.3838	7.9427	7.5361	7.1607
13	12.1337	11.3484	10.6350	9.9856	9.3936	8.8527	8.3577	7.9038	7.4869
14	13.0037	12.1062	11.2961	10.5631	9.8986	9.2950	8.7455	8.2442	7.7862
15	13.8651	12.8493	11.9379	11.1184	10.3797	9.7122	9.1079	8.5595	8.0607
16	14.7179	13.5777	12.5611	11.6523	10.8378	10.1059	9.4466	8.8514	8.3126
17	15.5623	14.2919	13.1661	12.1657	11.2741	10.4773	9.7632	9.1216	8.5436
18	16.3983	14.9920	13.7535	12.6593	11.6896	10.8276	10.0591	9.3719	8.7556
19	17.2260	15.6785	14.3238	13.1339	12.0853	11.1581	10.3356	9.6036	8.9501
20	18.0456	16.3514	14.8775	13.5903	12.4622	11.4699	10.5940	9.8181	9.1285
21	18.8570	17.0112	15.4150	14.0292	12.8212	11.7641	10.8355	10.0168	9.2922
22	19.6604	17.6580	15.9369	14.4511	13.1630	12.0416	11.0612	10.2007	9.4424
23	20.4558	18.2922	16.4436	14.8568	13.4886	12.3034	11.2722	10.3711	9.5802
24	21.2434	18.9139	16.9355	15.2470	13.7986	12.5504	11.4693	10.5288	9.7066
25	22.0232	19.5235	17.4131	15.6221	14.0939	12.7834	11.6536	10.6748	9.8226

interest rate, the present value of the marginal revenue product is $851,360. The airline will not purchase the plane in this case. As the interest rate rises, the quantity of capital purchased declines.

This same relationship holds for households as well. An individual deciding whether to purchase a college education compares the present value of the benefits generated by the degree with the purchase price of the degree. If the purchase price is less than the present value of the benefits, then the person goes to college. At a higher interest rate, the present value of the benefits will not exceed the purchase price. As a result, the human capital will not be purchased.

The market demand for capital is shown in Figure 1(a) as a downward-sloping curve with the quantity of capital measured along the horizontal axis and the price of capital measured along the vertical axis. An increase in the price of capital, say from $80,000 to $100,000 per machine in Figure 1(a), decreases the quantity of capital demanded, from 350,000 to 300,000

Table I (cont.)

Period (n)	Interest (Discount) Rate (i)									
	10%	12%	14%	15%	16%	18%	20%	24%	28%	32%
1	0.9091	0.8929	0.8772	0.8696	0.8621	0.8475	0.8333	0.8065	0.7813	0.7576
2	1.7355	1.6901	1.6467	1.6257	1.6052	1.5656	1.5278	1.4568	1.3916	1.3315
3	2.4869	2.4018	2.3216	2.2832	2.2459	2.1743	2.1065	1.9813	1.8684	1.7663
4	3.1699	3.0373	2.9137	2.8550	2.7982	2.6901	2.5887	2.4043	2.2410	2.0957
5	3.7908	3.6048	3.4331	3.3522	3.2743	3.1272	2.9906	2.7454	2.5320	2.3452
6	4.3553	4.1114	3.8887	3.7845	3.6847	3.4976	3.3255	3.0205	2.7594	2.5342
7	4.8684	4.5638	4.2883	4.1604	4.0386	3.8115	3.6046	3.2423	2.9370	2.6775
8	5.3349	4.9676	4.6389	4.4873	4.3436	4.0776	3.8372	3.4212	3.0758	2.7860
9	5.7590	5.3282	4.9464	4.7716	4.6065	4.3030	4.0310	3.5655	3.1842	2.8681
10	6.1446	5.6502	5.2161	5.0188	4.8332	4.4941	4.1925	3.6819	3.2689	2.9304
11	6.4951	5.9377	5.4527	5.2337	5.0286	4.6560	4.3271	3.7757	3.3351	2.9776
12	6.8137	6.1944	5.6603	5.4206	5.1971	4.7932	4.4392	3.8514	3.3868	3.0133
13	7.1034	6.4235	5.8424	5.5831	5.3423	4.9095	4.5327	3.9124	3.4272	3.0404
14	7.3667	6.6282	6.0021	5.7245	5.4675	5.0081	4.6106	3.9616	3.4587	3.0609
15	7.6061	6.8109	6.1422	5.8474	5.5755	5.0916	4.6755	4.0013	3.4834	3.0764
16	7.8237	6.9740	6.2651	5.9542	5.6685	5.1624	4.7296	4.0333	3.5026	3.0882
17	8.0216	7.1196	6.3729	6.0472	5.7487	5.2223	4.7746	4.0591	3.5177	3.0971
18	8.2014	7.2497	6.4674	6.1280	5.8178	5.2732	4.8122	4.0799	3.5294	3.1039
19	8.3649	7.3658	6.5504	6.1982	5.8775	5.3162	4.8435	4.0967	3.5386	3.1090
20	8.5136	7.4694	6.6231	6.2593	5.9288	5.3527	4.8696	4.1103	3.5458	3.1129
21	8.6487	7.5620	6.6870	6.3125	5.9731	5.3837	4.8913	4.1212	3.5514	3.1158
22	8.7715	7.6446	6.7429	6.3587	6.0113	5.4099	4.9094	4.1300	3.5558	3.1180
23	8.8832	7.7184	6.7921	6.3988	6.0442	5.4321	4.9245	4.1371	3.5592	3.1197
24	8.9847	7.7843	6.8351	6.4338	6.0726	5.4510	4.9371	4.1428	3.5619	3.1210
25	9.0770	7.8431	6.8729	6.4642	6.0971	5.4669	4.9476	4.1474	3.5640	3.1220

machines. This represents the case where, for instance, a farmer will postpone the purchase of a new tractor or buy fewer tractors if the price increases, or an airline will postpone the purchase of a new airplane or purchase fewer airplanes as the price of airplanes increases.

As is the case for any demand curve, the demand curve for capital shifts when one of the nonprice determinants of demand changes. Perhaps the most important nonprice determinant of capital is the interest rate. You have seen how an increase in the interest rate decreases the present value of a future stream of income. In exactly the same manner, a higher interest rate lowers the present value of the marginal revenue product of capital, causing the demand curve for capital to shift in. Each time the interest rate increases, from 10 to 11 to 12 percent, the demand curve for capital shifts in, as shown in Figure 1(b) by the move from $D_1(10\%)$ to $D_2(11\%)$ to $D_3(12\%)$. The number in parentheses next to the demand curves represents the interest rate associated with each demand curve.

Figure 1
The Market Demand for Capital

In Figure 1(a) the demand for capital is shown as a downward-sloping line with the quantity of capital measured on the horizontal axis and the price of capital measured on the vertical axis. As the price of capital changes, say from $80,000 to $100,000 per unit of capital (per machine), the quantity of capital demanded changes, from 350,000 to 300,000 machines. In Figure 1(b) the relationship between the demand for capital and the interest rate is illustrated. As the rate of interest rises, the demand for capital declines—the demand curve shifts in. The interest rate associated with each demand curve is in parentheses beside the curve.

(a) Change in Quantity Demanded

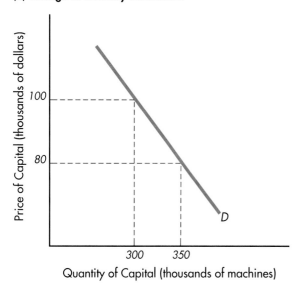

(b) Change in Demand

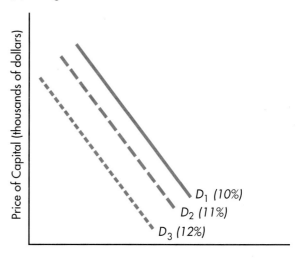

Quantity of Capital (thousands of machines)

The demand curve also shifts when any other determinant of demand changes. For instance, if a technological change increases the marginal physical product of capital, everything else held constant, the demand for capital increases. The invention of jet engines increased the demand for airplanes. The invention of small computers increased the overall demand for computers. Expectations and changes in income will also alter the demand for capital. For example, a business that expects strong demand for its goods purchases more capital now, causing the demand curve for capital to shift out.

1.b.2. Supply of Capital Some firms specialize in producing capital. John Deere supplies farm equipment, Boeing supplies airplanes, IBM produces computers, and so on. The quantity of capital supplied by these producers depends on the price of the capital. As the price of capital rises, the quantity that producers are willing and able to offer for sale rises, as shown in Figure 2 by the upward-sloping curve, S.

1.b.3. Equilibrium The demand for and supply of capital determine the price of capital, as well as the quantity produced and purchased. Changes in demand or supply change the equilibrium price and quantity. For example, changes in the interest rate affect the demand for capital and thus the price of capital. If the interest rate rises, the demand for capital decreases and the

Figure 2
The Interest Rate, the Price of Capital, and the
Rate of Return on Capital

The supply of capital is an upward-sloping curve. The demand for and supply of capital determine the price of capital as well as the quantity of capital produced and purchased. The rate of return on capital is the additional annual revenue generated by additional capital, divided by the purchase price of the capital. As the interest rate rises, the demand for capital declines (the demand curve shifts in) and the price of capital declines. As a result of the lower price, the rate of return rises.

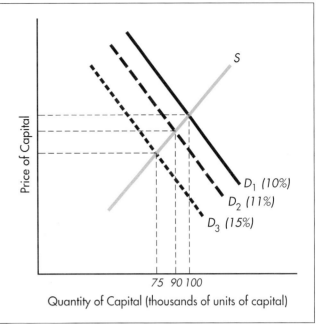

Quantity of Capital (thousands of units of capital)

price of capital falls, shown in Figure 2 in the move from $D_1(10\%)$ to $D_2(11\%)$ to $D_3(15\%)$. At an interest rate of 10 percent, 100,000 units of capital are demanded; at an 11 percent rate of interest, 90,000 units of capital are demanded; and at a 15 percent rate of interest, 75,000 units of capital are demanded. As the demand for capital shifts in, the price of capital falls.

Interest is the payment to the owners of capital for use of the capital services. Figure 2 illustrates the relationship among the price of capital, the interest rate, and the rate of return on capital. The rate of return on capital is the additional revenue generated by the capital each year (in present-value terms) divided by the price of the capital. For instance, if a $100,000 machine generates $10,000 of additional revenue each year (in present-value terms), the rate of return on that machine is 10 percent per year. With a lower price but the same marginal revenue product, the rate of return on the capital increases. The $10,000 per year divided by a $90,909 expenditure is an 11 percent-per-year return. Since the demand curve shifts in and the price of capital decreases each time the interest rate rises, the rate of return on capital must increase each time the interest rate rises. Similarly, the rate of return on capital must decrease each time the interest rate declines.

The interest rate represents the opportunity cost of capital, the annual rate of return available from alternative uses of the funds with which capital is acquired. A firm contemplating a $100,000 expenditure on a piece of equipment has many alternative uses for that $100,000. One alternative is to place the funds in an interest-earning account. Thus, the firm must expect to earn a rate of return on its capital that is at least equal to the interest rate if it is to purchase the capital in the first place. If the interest rate rises above the expected rate of return on capital, the demand for capital declines, the price of capital falls, and the rate of return on capital rises. For example, if the rate of return on a $100,000 piece of equipment is expected to be 10 percent to a firm but the interest rate that can be obtained from other uses of the $100,000 has risen to 11 percent, the firm is better off seeking other uses and not purchasing the piece of equipment. As many firms react this way, the demand for capital declines and the price of capital falls. The price continues to decline until the rate of return equals the interest rate, at a price of $90,909, since $10,000/$90,909 = 11 percent. Conversely, if the rate of return on the $100,000 equipment is expected to be 10 percent per year but the interest rate has fallen to 9 percent, the firm is better off purchasing the equipment. Thus, the demand for capital rises, the price of capital rises, and the rate of return on capital falls. The price will continue to rise until the rate of return equals the interest rate, at a price of $111,111, since $10,000/$111,111 = 9 percent.

The rate of return on capital and the interest rate will be equal in the long run. Any time the two are not equal, the price of capital will change, which in turn causes the rate of return on capital to change.

RECAP

1. Roundabout production is the process of saving and accumulating capital in order to increase production, and thus consumption, in the future.
2. Saving is the act of delaying consumption.
3. The capital market is the channel through which consumers and producers match their plans for the future with their behavior today.
4. Present value is the equivalent value today of some amount to be received in the future. Future value is the equivalent value in the future of some amount received today.
5. The demand for capital is represented by a downward-sloping curve, illustrating that the quantity of capital demanded rises as the price of capital falls.
6. The demand for capital shifts in when the interest rate rises.
7. The supply of capital is represented by an upward-sloping curve, illustrating that the quantity of capital supplied rises as the price of capital rises.
8. The demand for and supply of capital determine the price of capital. An increase in the price of capital lowers the rate of return on capital. Conversely, a decrease in the price of capital raises the rate of return on capital.
9. The rate of interest represents the rate of return on alternative uses of the funds with which capital is purchased. Thus, when the rate of interest rises above the rate of return on capital, the demand for capital declines, the price of capital declines, and the rate of return on capital rises. Conversely, when the rate of interest falls below the rate of return on capital, the demand for capital rises, the price of capital rises, and the rate of return on capital falls.

2. LAND AND NATURAL RESOURCES

Recall from the chapter on resource markets that there are two uses of the term *rent*: payment for the use of something, such as a car or an apartment, and payment for the use of something that is in fixed supply. This latter definition describes the payment to landowners for the use of their land.

2.a. Land Surface and Economic Rent

The aggregate quantity of the land surface—which may have value as a farm, as a pasture, as a city, or in some other use—is fixed. The demand for land depends on the demand for the products and services that the land helps produce, and thus reflects land's marginal revenue product. The demand and supply curves are shown in Figure 3. The demand curve slopes down and the supply curve is perfectly inelastic, the vertical line S, at 2.3 billion acres of land.

The rental rate of land is determined by the point at which the demand curve and the vertical supply curve intersect, $120 per acre in Figure 3. If the demand for land increases, the demand curve shifts out, from MRP_1 to MRP_2, as shown in Figure 3(b), causing the rental rate of land to increase. Because the quantity supplied does not change, the only effect of the demand increase is a rent increase. The rental rate rises from $120 to $200 per acre, and the total payment to landowners rises from $120 per acre times 2.3 billion acres to $200 per acre times 2.3 billion acres. Even with a higher rent, no new land is supplied. The higher rent does not (and cannot) induce owners to increase the quantities of land that are supplied. Pure economic rent does not serve as an incentive to resource owners to increase or decrease quantities supplied.

2.a.1. Different Rents on Different Parcels of Land
The price of land in Tokyo, Japan, is about $1,000 per square foot; land outside of Kearny, Nebraska, sells for about $.02 per square foot. Different parcels of land earn

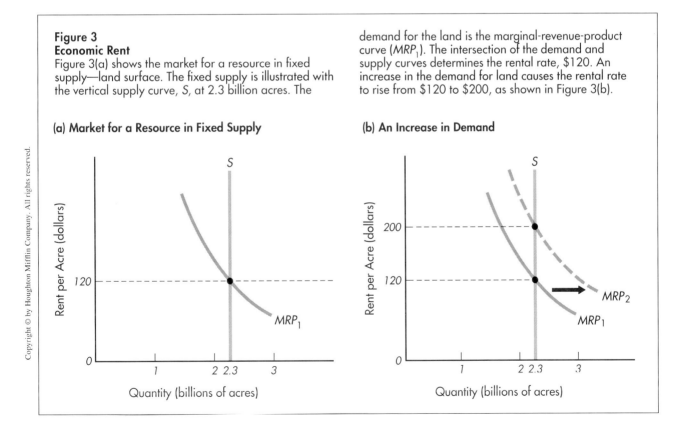

Figure 3
Economic Rent
Figure 3(a) shows the market for a resource in fixed supply—land surface. The fixed supply is illustrated with the vertical supply curve, S, at 2.3 billion acres. The demand for the land is the marginal-revenue-product curve (MRP_1). The intersection of the demand and supply curves determines the rental rate, $120. An increase in the demand for land causes the rental rate to rise from $120 to $200, as shown in Figure 3(b).

(a) Market for a Resource in Fixed Supply

(b) An Increase in Demand

The marginal revenue product of land in Hong Kong is significantly higher than in Montana. A wheat field in Hong Kong would have to generate nearly a million times more revenue than a wheat field in Montana for the land to be converted from its use as a forty-story building site to an agricultural field.

widely varying rents because of differences in demand. Demand for the parcel in Tokyo is substantially higher than demand for the parcel in Kearny. Thus, the rental rate and the total rental income in Tokyo are significantly higher than they are in Kearny.

Why is demand for land in Tokyo greater than demand in Kearny? The marginal revenue product of the land in Tokyo is higher. Location is a major determinant of the marginal revenue product of a particular parcel of land. Suppose you can obtain a McDonald's franchise and place it anywhere you want. All you have to do is pay for the land. You would be willing to pay significantly more for a space in the middle of a city than for one in the country, everything else held constant. The sales that can be generated in the city far exceed the sales that can be made in the country. Hence, the city land offers a much higher marginal revenue product than country land. Physical features of the land, such as fertility and mineral content, and the climate of the area in which the parcel is located also increase the marginal revenue product of land.

Does economic rent serve the allocative role that other resource prices serve?

2.a.2. Rent and the Allocation of Land   Resource prices serve as an allocating mechanism, ensuring that resources flow to their highest-valued uses. You might think that land rent fails to serve as an allocating mechanism because an increase in the rent on land does not increase the quantity of land supplied. Moreover, pure economic rents do not seem to have anything to do with costs because land surface just exists—it is a gift of nature. You might even say that pure economic rents are unearned windfalls to those who happen to own the land.

Despite appearances—that is, despite the fact that the quantity supplied does not change as economic rents change—economic rents do serve the function of allocating parcels of land to their most productive uses. Think of what a typical large city looks like. Tall buildings are clustered in the city center. As the distance from city center increases, the density and the height of the buildings decrease. Let's assume that the land in a city has only two uses, commercial and residential. As the distance from city center increases, the cost of using the land for commercial purposes increases because transportation and communication are more difficult. The aggregate quantity of land is fixed, but the quantity of commercial land is not fixed. Residential land can be used for commercial purposes (businesses can buy and tear down blocks of houses and construct buildings), and commercial land can be used for residential purposes (abandoned warehouses and factories can be converted into apartments).

The market for the commercial use of the land is shown in Figure 4. The supply of commercial land slopes up because as the rental rate rises, more landowners offer their land to the commercial market, everything else held constant. According to Figure 4(a), at a rental rate of $10 per square foot, 5 million square feet of land are used for commercial purposes and the rest of the land is put to residential uses.

Suppose an increased number of businesses move to the city. The demand curve for commercial property shifts out, and the rental rate of existing commercial space rises. This is shown as the move from MRP_1 to MRP_2 in Figure 4(b). As the rental rate rises, from $10 to $15, a certain amount of land that was residential is shifted into commercial uses. This is shown as the shaded area in Figure 4(b). Thus, rent does serve the allocation role that other resource prices serve. As the rental rate changes, the allocation of land among its uses changes. The market for land defines the payments to landowners, and rental rates on different parcels allocate these parcels to their highest-valued use.

Figure 4
The Allocation of Land Among Uses
Figure 4(a) shows the market for commercial uses of land. The supply curve for commercial land rises as the rental rate rises. As the rental rate of commercial land rises, more people take their land currently used for residential purposes and offer it for commercial uses, everything else held constant. The intersection of MRP (the marginal revenue product of land in commercial use) and S (the supply of commercial land) determines the rental rate, $10 per square foot. As the demand for land for commercial uses increases, from MRP_1 to MRP_2 in Figure 4(b), the rental rate rises and more land is used for commercial purposes.

(a) The Market for Commercial Use of Land

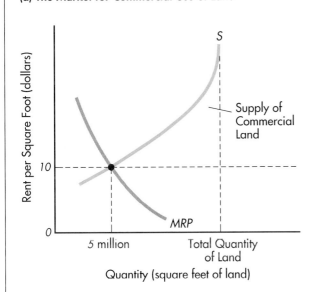

(b) An Increase in Demand for Commercial Use of Land

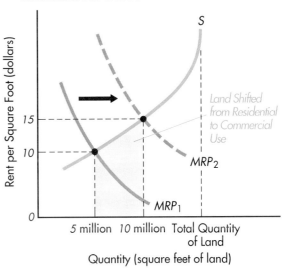

2.b. Natural Resources

**nonrenewable (exhaustible)
natural resources:**
natural resources whose supply
is fixed

**renewable (nonexhaustible)
natural resources:**
natural resources whose supply
can be replenished

The category of resources we call "land" refers not just to land surface but to everything associated with the land—the natural resources. Natural resources are the nonproduced resources with which a society is endowed. **Nonrenewable (exhaustible) natural resources** can be used only once and cannot be replaced. Examples include coal, natural gas, and oil. **Renewable (nonexhaustible) natural resources** can be used repeatedly without depleting the amount available for future use. Examples include the land, sea, rivers, and lakes. Plants and animals are classified as nonexhaustible natural resources because it is possible for them to renew themselves and thus replace those used in production and consumption activities. The prices of natural resources and the quantities used are determined in the market for natural resources.

2.b.1. The Market for Nonrenewable Resources   The market for nonrenewable natural resources consists of the demand for and supply of these resources. Supply depends on the amount of the resource in existence, and the supply curve is perfectly inelastic. Only a fixed amount of oil or coal exists, so the more that is used in any given year, the less that remains for future use. This means that an upward-sloping supply curve exists for a particular period of time, such as a year. The quantity that resource owners are willing to extract and offer for sale during any particular year depends on the price of the resource. The supply curve in Figure 5(a) is upward-sloping to reflect the relationship between the price of the resource today and the amount extracted and offered to users today. Resource owners are willing to extract more of a resource from its natural state and offer it for sale as the price of the resource increases.

As some of the resource is used today, less is available next year. The supply curve of the resource in the future shifts up, as shown in Figure 5(b) by

Figure 5
The Market for Nonrenewable Resources
The demand curve slopes down, and the supply curve slopes up. The intersection of demand and supply determines the quantity used today and the price at which the quantity was sold, as shown in Figure 5(a). As quantities are used today, less remains for the future. Because the available quantities come from increasingly more expensive sources, the supply curve shifts up over time, as shown in Figure 5(b). S_1 represents the quantities supplied in 1890 at $1 per barrel, and S_2 represents the quantities supplied today at $17 per barrel. Figure 5(c) shows the effect on the supply of a resource over time as more of the resource is extracted. If 200 billion barrels of crude oil are extracted this year, then next year the extraction of 200 billion barrels will be more difficult—more expensive— than the extraction of 200 billion barrels was this year. S_1 is the supply in 1990, S_2 the supply in 1991, and so on, as more of the resource is used each year.

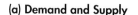

(a) Demand and Supply

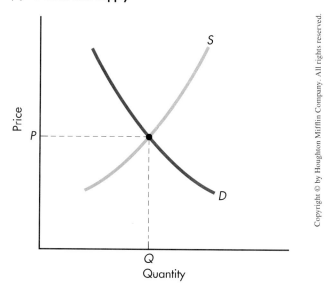

the move from S_1 to S_2. The shift occurs because the cost of extracting any quantity of the resource rises as the amount of the resource in existence falls. The first amounts extracted come from the most accessible sources, and each additional quantity then comes from a less accessible source. For instance, in the late 1800s, oil became an important resource. At first, it was extracted with small pumps that gathered up oil seeping out of the ground. Once that extremely accessible source was gone, wells had to be dug. Over time, wells had to be deeper and be placed in progressively more difficult terrain. From land, to the ocean off California, to the rugged waters off Alaska, to the wicked North Sea, the search for oil has progressed. As more and more is extracted, the marginal cost of extracting any given amount increases, and the supply curve shifts up.

If 200 billion barrels of crude oil are extracted this year, then in the future the extraction of another 200 billion barrels will be more difficult—more expensive—than the extraction of the 200 billion barrels was this year. This increase is illustrated by an upward shift of the supply curve. Figure 5(b) illustrates how the supply of a nonrenewable resource decreases over time as additional amounts of the resource are used. S_1 is the supply in 1990, S_2 in 1991, S_3 in 1992, and so on, as more of the resource is used each year.

The demand for a nonrenewable natural resource is determined in the same way as the demand for any other resource. It is the marginal revenue product of the resource. Thus, anything that affects the *MRP* of the nonrenewable resource will affect the demand for that resource.

Equilibrium occurs in the market for a nonrenewable natural resource when the demand and supply curves intersect, as shown in Figure 6. The equilibrium price, $15, and quantity, 200 billion barrels, represent the price and quantity today. Extracting and selling the equilibrium quantity of 200 billion barrels today reduces the quantity available tomorrow by 200 billion barrels. This means that extracting the resource tomorrow is probably going

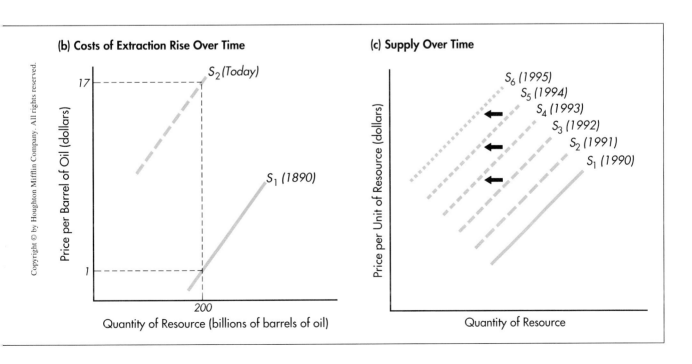

(b) Costs of Extraction Rise Over Time

(c) Supply Over Time

Figure 6
Price Today and in the Future

Equilibrium occurs in the market for an exhaustible natural resource when the demand and supply curves intersect. The equilibrium price, $15, and quantity, 200 billion barrels, represent the price and quantity of the resource used today. Selling the equilibrium quantity of 200 billion barrels today reduces the quantity available tomorrow by 200 billion barrels. With a smaller and probably less accessible quantity, extracting the resource tomorrow is probably going to be more costly than extracting it today. Thus, the supply curve for the resource in the future lies above the supply curve for today, S_2 rather than S_1, if any of the resource is being consumed today. With a higher supply curve, the price is higher, $20 rather than $15. Thus, the price in the future is likely to be higher than the price today.

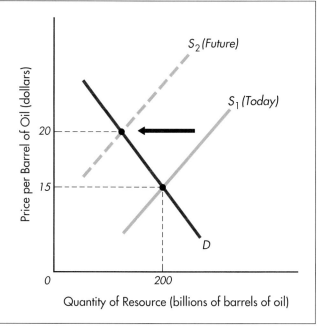

to be more costly than extracting it today. Thus, the supply curve for the resource in the future lies above the supply curve for today, S_2 rather than S_1, if any of the resource is being consumed today. With a higher supply curve and the same demand, the price is higher, $20 rather than $15. Thus, the price in the future is likely to be higher than the price today if some of the resource is extracted and sold today.

The resource owner must decide whether to extract and sell the resource today or leave it in the ground for future use. Suppose that by extracting and selling the oil that lies below someone's land today, the landowner can make a profit of $10 per barrel after all costs of extraction have been paid. With that $10 the owner could buy stocks or bonds or put the money into a savings account or use it to acquire education or marketable skills. If the interest rate is 10 percent, the owner could realize $11 one year from now from the $10 profit obtained today. Should the oil be extracted today? The answer depends on how much profit the resource owner expects to earn on the oil one year from now, and this depends on what the price of oil and the cost of extraction are one year from now. In other words, the answer depends on whether the present value of extracting and selling the resources exceeds the present value of leaving the resource in the ground.

If the owner expects to obtain a profit of $13 a barrel one year from now, the present value of that $13 at a 10 percent rate of interest is $13/1.1 = $11.82. Clearly, the oil should be left in the ground. If the profit on the oil one year from now is expected to be only $10.50, the present value is $10.50/1.1 = $9.55. In this case, the oil should be extracted and the proceeds used to buy stocks, bonds, or savings accounts. If the profit one year from now is $11 a barrel, the present value is $10; the same whether the oil is extracted today or next year.

As discussed in the first section of the chapter, the present value declines as the interest rate rises. Should the interest rate rise from 10 percent to 15 percent, then the present value of $11.50 one year from now is $10. A profit per barrel exceeding $11.50 next year would be necessary to leave the oil in the ground. As the interest rate rises, more is extracted and sold today and less is left for the future.

Because suppliers and potential suppliers continually calculate whether to extract now or in the future and how much to extract, an equilibrium arises where the present value of profit in the future just equals the value today; for this to occur, the year-to-year rate of increase in the price of the resource must equal the rate of interest on alternative uses of the funds. If the rate of interest is 10 percent a year, everything else held constant, the resource price will rise at a rate of about 10 percent a year.

If the present values of extracting and selling the resources now and of leaving them in the ground until a point in the future are to be equal, then the higher the interest rate, the greater the spread between present and future prices of an exhaustible resource must be. Suppose the interest rate rises above the current rate of return on the nonrenewable resource, oil. The higher interest rate means that producers looking to pump the oil out of the ground will pump more today and purchase stocks, bonds, or savings accounts with the money they get from selling the oil. More extraction means that the supply curve today shifts out and today's price falls. At the same time, the supply curve in the future shifts in (since less will be available in the future) and the future price rises. This will occur until the rate of return on leaving the oil in the ground equals the interest rate—that is, until the present value of pumping the oil and selling it is the same as the present value of the oil left in the ground. A higher interest rate implies the use of more resources today. Conversely, a lower interest rate implies the use of fewer resources today.

2.b.2. The Market for Renewable Resources   Renewable resources, unlike exhaustible or nonrenewable resources, can replenish themselves. Forests and wildlife can reproduce and renew their supplies. The role of the market for renewable resources is to determine a price at which the quantity of the resource used is just sufficient to enable the resource to renew itself at a rate that best satisfies society's wants.

Owners of forest lands could harvest all their trees in one year and reap a huge profit. But if they did so, several years would pass before the trees had grown enough to be cut again. The rate at which the trees are harvested depends on the interest rate. A large harvest one year means fewer trees available in the future and a longer time for renewal to occur. This would suggest a lower price today and a higher price in the future. If the interest rate rises, everything else held constant, owners will want to increase harvesting in order to get more money with which to purchase stocks and bonds. This would mean more trees now and fewer in the future, thereby driving up the price of the trees not cut today. If the interest rate falls, owners will want to harvest fewer trees today. This would mean that today's price will rise and the future price will fall. As was the case with the nonrenewable resources, the market adjusts so that the resources are allocated to their highest-valued use now and in the future. The timing of the use of resources depends on the rate of interest.

In summary, the markets for nonrenewable and renewable resources operate to ensure that current and future wants are satisfied in the least costly manner and that resources are used in their highest-valued alternative now and in the future. When a nonrenewable resource is being rapidly depleted, its future price rises and the present value of using the resource in the future rises so that less of the resource is used today. When a renewable resource is being used at a rate that does not allow the resource to replenish itself, the future price rises and the present value of the future use rises so that less of the resource is used today.

What is conservation?

2.b.3. Conservation The term *conservation* is often used to mean that a resource is not used—it is preserved for the future. And conservation in this sense often carries a positive connotation. We are applauded as we use paper bags rather than plastic ones, drive less, use less electricity and less water, avoid ozone-damaging products, and we are called on to help save the rain forest. Is the positive connotation justified? What does *conservation* mean in the context of the markets for natural resources?

Conservation means the *optimal* rate of use, not the *nonuse* of a resource. The optimal use of a resource is one that is determined in the markets for natural resources. It could imply that *more* of a resource is used today, not less. Though this may at first seem contradictory to the way the term *conservation* is normally used, think about what a policy of not using resources at all today in order to save them for future generations means. It means that less income is created today because the costs of production are higher. Less income means that less is available to allocate to capital goods and future production. This, in turn, means that the economy will grow at a slower rate than it otherwise would have grown, which suggests that future generations will have less wealth than they otherwise would have had. If we ignore the markets for resources and simply dictate that a resource cannot be used today, we may be doing a great disservice to future generations. They will face a much more costly world, one in which the combinations of resources necessary to produce goods and services will be less efficient and in which there will be less wealth.

RECAP

1. Pure economic rent is the payment that a resource in fixed supply receives.
2. Rents serve to allocate a resource in fixed supply to its highest-valued use.
3. Nonrenewable natural resources are natural resources whose supply is fixed. Renewable natural resources are natural resources that can be replenished.
4. The gap between the equilibrium price today and the equilibrium price at some point in the future generates a rate of return on nonrenewable resources that is equal to the interest rate on comparable assets. Changes in the interest rate lead to different rates of use of nonrenewable resources.
5. The harvest rate of renewable resources is such that the rate of return on the resources is equal to the interest rate on comparable assets.
6. Conservation refers to the optimal rate of use of natural resources, not to the nonuse of these resources. The optimal rate of use is determined in the markets for natural resources.

3. ENTREPRENEURIAL ABILITY

When Pablo Valdez arrived in Florida penniless in the 1980 Mariel boatlift from Cuba, Miami's Cuban community helped him get a job at a Cuban-run real estate firm. He sold $11 million in property during the first year and now employs Cubans at his own two companies. Julie Pellatt, Paula Chiungus, and Katherine Robinson left the Boston office of stockbroker Kidder Peabody & Co. in the fall of 1987 to begin Beacon Hill Nannies Inc. Just two years later, their Beacon Hill organization had revenues exceeding $500,000 and they were contemplating expansion to Los Angeles. These people are **entrepreneurs**, individuals who recognize an opportunity for earning economic profit, acquire and organize the resources for production, and undertake the risk necessary to obtain this profit. They have **entrepreneurial ability**.

You may hear someone refer to an *intrapreneur*. An intrapreneur is an employee who acts as an entrepreneur within the employee's firm. Unlike an entrepreneur, who starts up a venture, an intrapreneur develops an idea with the full support of the company for which he or she works. William Norris began Control Data in the 1950s, after leaving Sperry-Rand in order to pursue his interest in producing supercomputers. At Control Data, Norris supports the intrapreneurial spirit so that the company does not lose innovative employees to other firms. He formed a separate department dedicated solely to creating the opportunity for existing employees to begin their own businesses within Control Data. Several advances in Control Data have resulted from this encouragement of intrapreneurial ability.

entrepreneur:
someone who recognizes an opportunity for earning economic profit and is able to collect and organize the resources and undertake the risk necessary to obtain this profit

entrepreneurial ability:
someone who has the ability to be an entrepreneur

3.a. Entrepreneurs and Profit

Why does the entrepreneur receive profit?

The owners of labor, land, and capital receive wages, rents, and interest; entrepreneurs receive economic profit. What services performed by entrepreneurs enable them to claim profit? One explanation of why the entrepreneur receives profit is that the entrepreneur is paid for being a trader. Another reason is that profit is the entrepreneur's reward for taking risks. The final explanation is that the entrepreneur is paid for being an innovator.

3.a.1. Trader "Buy low and sell high" is the credo of the successful trader. Many believe that the entrepreneur earns a profit by being a trader—by buying resources low and selling products high. The entrepreneur hires the appropriate combinations of resources, organizes resources, and ensures that production takes place. The entrepreneur receives the residual remaining from revenue after land, labor, and capital are paid. The entrepreneur has an incentive to produce a product in the most cost-effective way and to produce a product and sell it at a price consumers will pay. The better the entrepreneurs do this, the higher their profits.

3.a.2. Risk Bearer At least a portion of the economic profit that entrepreneurs receive is payment for their willingness to bear the risk of offering their time, capital, and abilities in a world of uncertainty. All resource owners bear some risk—they may not be paid for their services. The higher the possibility of not getting paid, the more resource owners will demand for their services. Labor suppliers may demand frequent payments—weekly or biweekly—and lenders may require collateral and down payments before they make loans. These additional restrictions can be considered a return for risk bearing, as can a larger payment or a higher interest rate.

Resource owners also bear the risk that the market value of their resources will fall. Resource owners have to be concerned that their resource will lose value. For instance, homeowners bear the risk that their house will lose market value—that it will sell for less than what they paid for it. Owners of human capital bear such risks as well. If you choose an occupation and acquire human capital only to find after several years of schooling that your occupation is paying substantially less than what you had anticipated, you will have experienced a loss in the value of your human capital. To induce people to undertake an activity in which there are risks, a higher wage, rent, or interest must be paid. Everything else the same, the higher the risk, the greater the payment must be to induce people to undertake the activity. This same idea of reward for risk-taking describes how at least a portion of the return to entrepreneurs is determined. People with entrepreneurial ability bear the risk that a new venture will fail and that their entrepreneurial ability will lose value. Owners of stock, the shareholders of a publicly traded firm, are providing money to the firm in return for dividends and appreciation of the value of the stock. These owners are rewarded for bearing risk as well. Profit is a reward for risk-taking.

3.a.3. Innovator An entrepreneur who can produce a good that consumers are willing and able to buy less expensively than others obtains at least short-run profits. If an entrepreneur invents a new product, above-normal profits will exist until entry and imitation occur.

3.b. Profit and the Supply of Entrepreneurs

Only about seven of every ten new firms succeed, as discussed in the Economic Insight "The Road to Success." What induces people to give up an existing job and undertake the risks of running their own business? In addition to the independence or freedom that comes with "being your own boss," it is the potential income that can be obtained. If someone begins a new business and that business generates a net income of $100,000 per year, then the owner can sell the business for a value that reflects the present value of this earning stream. The entrepreneur may be able to walk away from the business with a lump sum of money. That lump sum is called the **capitalized value** of the firm and is the present value of the future income stream.

capitalized value:
the present value of an expected future income stream

A business generating $1 million in net income each year that is expected to be successful for five to ten more years could have a capitalized value of between $2 million and $5 million. Thus, the entrepreneur could sell the business and walk away with a substantial lump sum of money instead of continuing to manage the business for the next five to ten years. The greater the potential rewards, everything else held constant, the greater the quantity of people willing to undertake the activity.

Profit influences the allocation of resources among alternative uses. It is the expectation of profit that induces firms (or entrepreneurs) to innovate and to make expenditures on new technologies and on research and development. It is the expectation of profit that induces entrepreneurs to leave one activity to carry out another. The production of buggy whips is discarded as the automobile comes along; the production of regular television will be discarded as high-definition television is introduced. It is profit-seeking that leads to the changes: entrepreneurs see the profit potential of the automobile relative to the buggy and the profit potential of high-definition television relative to regular television.

Part VII/Resource Markets

The Road to Success

An estimated 38 percent of the men and nearly half of the women in today's work force want to start their own companies. In 1965 there were 204,000 business start-ups in the United States; in the 1990s, that figure has grown to 700,000. But it is neither easy nor necessarily rewarding to start your own business.

For all industries from 1976 to 1985, the birthrate (the number of new businesses divided by the total number of businesses) averaged 11 percent per year. Over the same period, the death rate (the number of businesses that shut their doors divided by the total number of businesses) averaged nearly 9.5 percent per year. By far the greatest number of new businesses are in the services area. The average birthrate exceeded 13 percent in services and was less than 10 percent in manufacturing. Death rates were highest in retail trade and lowest in wholesale trade.

A survey of 2,994 new businesses by American Express Company and the National Federation of Independent Businesses found that 77 percent of new businesses lived to celebrate their third birthday. This is a higher success rate than had been found in earlier surveys. During the 1970s, fewer than half of all new businesses survived five years.

What determines success or failure? It does not seem to matter whether an entrepreneur has prior managerial experience or not; 75 percent of new entrepreneurs with no prior supervisory experience survived three years, and 77 percent of those with extensive managerial experience also survived three years. It seems that a desire to serve the customer is what counts. Of companies saying that better service was the key to their strategy, 82 percent survived. Among companies that competed mainly on price, the survival rate was 70 percent. In addition, hard work and intimate knowledge of the business are required. Only 9 percent of the business owners surviving three years spent more than a quarter of their time supervising employees. "The typical successful entrepreneur spent more time either selling or working directly with customers than on any other aspect of running a new business," said William J. Dennis, a researcher with the National Federation of Independent Businesses. What has made or broken many of the companies is the ability (or inability) to recognize and react to the completely unpredictable, to use enough managerial sense to plan and anticipate, yet know when things are going wrong and be able to find solutions. In other words, the ability to solve problems may be the most important aspect of success, according to a survey by *Inc.* magazine.

Survival does not necessarily mean huge success or growth. Only 37 percent of the new companies increased the number of employees in their first three years; 15 percent actually reduced the number of employees. Growing companies were more likely than others to have outside investors. In addition, the owners of the growing firms had more formal education and were more likely to be acting on a business idea that occurred to them while they were in a previous job.

The financial rewards of being a manager of a large corporation far exceed the rewards of starting and operating your own business. The average pay of the bosses of the 350 largest firms in the United States exceeds $2 million. The average pay to owners of start-ups was only $25,000.

Sources: Leslie Brokaw, "The Truth About Start-Ups," *Inc.*, April 1991, pp. 52–56; Roger Ricklefs, "Road to Success Becomes Less Littered with Failures," *The Wall Street Journal*, Oct. 10, 1989, p. B2; Diane Cole, "The Entrepreneur," *Psychology Today* (June 1989), p. 60; U.S. Small Business Administration, Office of Advocacy, Small Business Data Base, USELM file, version 6, March 1987; "The Greed and the Glory of Being Boss," *The Economist*, June 17, 1989, p. 17; *Statistical Abstract of the United States*, 1991.

RECAP

1. An entrepreneur is someone who sees an opportunity and acts to take advantage of or make a profit from that opportunity.

2. An intrapreneur serves as an entrepreneur while an employee of a firm.

3. The return to entrepreneurial ability is profits.

4. TYING RESOURCE MARKETS TOGETHER

How are the resource markets tied together?

In this and the previous two chapters, we have been discussing the four broad categories of resources—labor, capital, land, and entrepreneurial ability. We have examined each market somewhat in isolation, but make no mistake about it, the resource markets are linked together; developments in one affect the others. As a general rule, resources flow to their most highly valued use. For instance, if skilled labor is more highly valued than unskilled labor, more resources will flow to the skilled-labor market. If capital used in the service industry provides a greater return than capital used in manufacturing, more capital will flow to the service sector. If high-definition television (HDTV) yields greater profit than regular TV, resources will flow to the HDTV area. As resources flow to their more highly valued use, they flow away from their lower-valued uses.

The value of a use is determined by demand and supply. Businesses demand resource services, allocating their expenditures among resources in order to equate the *MRP* per dollar of expenditure. Households own the resources and earn income by supplying and selling the services of their resources. Households can consume all of their income today, or they can forgo some consumption and enhance the quality of their resources or acquire more resources with which future income can be created—that is, they can save. Households allocate their income across all goods and services, including future goods and services (that is, saving), according to the rule that the marginal utility per dollar of expenditure on each good and service is the same. A change in the *MRP* or *MFC* of a resource will alter the demand for the resource's services; a change in the marginal utility or acquisition price of a resource will alter the supply of resource services.

In each resource market, the demand for resource services (the firm's marginal revenue product) and the supply of resource services offered determine the payment for the use of the resource—the wages, interest, rent, or profit. These payments divided by the purchase price of the resource determine the rate of return of that resource. In present-value terms, a college education costing $100,000 that yields an additional $10,000 per year in salary generates a 10 percent rate of return; a share of stock or a bond that costs $100 and returns $9 per year in interest or dividends generates a 9 percent rate of return; land that has a value of $200,000 and yields a $15,000 profit per year from being farmed has a rate of return of 7.5 percent.

Households can use their savings to enhance the quality of their resource services—to acquire more education or training, for example—or to purchase new or additional resources. Households have a choice of whether to purchase additional education and training, shares of stock or bonds, acres of land or natural resources, or to begin a new business. Which of these households decide to purchase depends on which is expected to yield the greatest rate of return. If college is expected to yield a 10 percent rate of return while all other resources are yielding a 9 percent rate of return and they all have the same risk and generate the same utility, households will purchase more higher education. Their purchases will increase the supply of labor that has a college education and lower the rate of return on the higher education. A college degree that costs $100,000 and generates a return of $10,000 per year has only a 9 percent rate of return if the additional income of the degree falls to $9,000 and the cost of college remains at $100,000.

As households sell assets that are offering lower rates of return and purchase those with higher rates of return, the purchase prices of the assets will change so that the rates of return are equalized. For instance, the rate of return on a college education rose during the 1980s. As a consequence, households reduced their purchases of other resources and spent more on college educations. As a result of more people having acquired college degrees, the return on those degrees will fall, everything else held constant. At the same time, as households reduced their purchases of other resources or sold other resources and spent more on college educations, the rates of return on the other resources rose. All in all, the rates of return on the different resources should equalize over time. When they are not equal, demands and/or supplies will change until they are equal.

RECAP

1. Households own resources and offer them for use to firms. Households choose which resources to own on the basis of expected rate of return.

2. The rate of return is determined by dividing the annual payment for the resource (wages, rent, interest, profit) by the purchase price of the resource. The annual payment is determined in each resource market (labor, land, capital, and entrepreneur) by the demand for and supply of the resource's services.

3. In the long run, rates of return should be equal as households allocate their savings to those resources offering the highest rate of return.

SUMMARY

▲▼ *What role does saving play in the economy?*

1. Saving is the process of using a portion of current production to acquire capital resources so that production can be increased in the future. §1.a

▲▼ *What is present value?*

2. Present value is the equivalent value today of some amount to be received in the future; future value is the equivalent value in the future of some amount received today. §1.b.1

3. The demand for and supply of capital determine the price of capital and the quantity produced and purchased. A change in either demand or supply changes the price and quantity of capital. §1.b.3

4. When the interest rate rises, the demand for capital decreases and the price of capital falls. This, in turn, raises the rate of return on capital. §1.b.3

5. The rate of return on capital and the interest rate tend toward equality. §1.b.3

▲▼ *Does economic rent serve the allocative role that other resource prices serve?*

6. Pure economic rent is payment for the use of a resource that is fixed in supply. §2

7. Rent serves to allocate the fixed resource to its highest-valued use. §2.a.2

▲▼ *What is conservation?*

8. The term *conservation* usually means "not consuming a natural resource to preserve it for the future." §2.b.3

9. The optimal use of natural resources is determined in the markets for renewable and nonrenewable natural resources. The optimal use may not be to save resources for the future and thus may seem contradictory to the customary idea of conservation. §2.b.3

▲▼ Why does the entrepreneur receive profit?

10. An entrepreneur is someone who sees an opportunity to earn a profit and acts to take advantage of that opportunity. §3

11. Entrepreneurs receive profit because they are successful traders, they bear risk, or they are innovators. §3.a

12. The incentive for beginning a new business is profit. §3.b

▲▼ How are the resource markets tied together?

13. The buyers of resource services are firms; the suppliers are the resource owners, households.

Resources flow to their most highly valued uses. As entrepreneurs seek profits, they move resources from unprofitable or less profitable activities to more profitable activities. As households seek to acquire income, they acquire the resources that offer them the greatest income and they offer the resources' services to the areas in which the resources have highest value. §4

14. Rates of return on resources tend to be equal in the long run and will equal the rates of return on alternative uses of household savings, the interest rate. §4

KEY TERMS

saving §1.a
present value §1.b.1
future value §1.b.1
nonrenewable (exhaustible) natural resources §2.b

renewable (nonexhaustible) natural resources §2.b
entrepreneur §3
entrepreneurial ability §3
capitalized value §3.b

EXERCISES

1. What is saving? Would seed be considered the savings of a gardener or farmer? Would expenditures on college be considered part of the savings of a household?

2. Financial capital refers to the stocks, bonds, and other financial instruments businesses use to raise money. What occurs to the present value of financial capital when the interest rate rises, everything else held constant?

3. You purchase a car for $2,000 down and $250 per month for five years. What is your total expenditure on the car? If the sticker price is $12,000, what is your total interest payment?

4. Calculate the present values of the following:
   a. $1,000 one year from today at interest rates of 5, 10, and 15 percent
   b. $1,000 per year for five years at interest rates of 5, 10, and 15 percent

5. Why are banks more willing to lend to a medical student than to a student in a vocational college?

6. Someone who expects to inherit a huge amount of income tends to be a borrower. Could an entire society expect future income to be much greater than current income and therefore borrow? If so, would the interest rate paid by that society tend to be higher or lower than the rate paid by a society that is not expecting future income growth? What would the change in the interest rate mean for capital accumulation?

7. Data appear to tell us that the saving rate in Japan is nearly three times the rate in the United States. If these data are correct, how might this difference affect the two economies?

8. Suppose the interest rate on a one-year bond in the United States is 10 percent and in Japan the rate is 5 percent on an identical bond.

    a. What do you expect would happen?

    b. Suppose that the yen price of a dollar is 250 ($1 can buy 250 yen) but is expected to change to 225 by the end of the year. What impact does this information have on your answer to part a?

9. If the rate of return on capital is higher than the rates of return on all other assets, what will occur? What happens in the other resource markets as a result?

10. What is the basic economic function of the interest rate? What is the difference between the price of an asset (for instance, a resource) and the interest rate?

11. Explain how a government policy to lower interest rates might influence the natural resource markets.

12. You have savings of $20,000. You are deciding what to do with your savings. You have an opportunity to purchase an education that will mean a 10 percent per year higher salary over your lifetime, a stock that will generate 9 percent per year, and a land investment that is promised to return 20 percent per year. Why are these rates of return different? Which use of your savings would you choose?

13. The entrepreneur receives profit. Explain what this means. How does the entrepreneur function in a perfectly competitive world where economic profits are zero? Explain the impact in all resource markets of a tax on profits.

14. The Clinton administration proposed higher taxes on the use of nonrenewable resources. If implemented, what would be the likely impact of these taxes? How would the taxes affect saving? Would future generations be better off as a result of the taxes?

15. Entrepreneurs are profit-seekers. They and thus other resources flow to where the profits are or are expected to be. How, then, will a policy to restrict the flow of foreign-produced goods into the United States affect the functioning of the U.S. economy?

COOPERATIVE LEARNING EXERCISE

Divide the class into groups of 4 people. Have the group members count off from 1 to 4. Have the number 1s get together, the number 2s, and so on. Each set of students is to answer the question with the same number they have (number 1s answer question 1 and so on) and then return to their group to teach the other group members the answers. A representative of each number will be selected to provide and explain the answer.

1. An airline is deciding whether to purchase an additional airplane. It figures that the airplane will generate additional annual revenues of $15,000. The current cost of the airplane is $2 million. The airplane could be financed with a loan at an interest rate of 5 percent per year. Should the airplane be purchased?

2. An airline is deciding whether to purchase an additional airplane. It figures that the airplane will generate additional annual revenues of $15,000. The current cost of the airplane is $2 million. The airplane could be financed with a loan at an interest rate of 8 percent per year. Should the airplane be purchased?

3. A family is deciding whether to send the oldest child to college. The family expects that the college education will mean 1.4 times more income per year than if the child does not go to college. College will cost $100,000 (assume that all costs occur in one year). If the income of someone not going to college is $30,000 per year, how long would it take for the $100,000 investment to be paid back in extra earnings?

4. A family is deciding whether to send the oldest child to college. The family expects that the college education will mean 1.6 times more income per year than if the child does not go to college. College will cost $100,000 (assume that all costs occur in one year). If the income of someone not going to college is $30,000 per year, how long would it take for the $100,000 investment to be paid back in extra earnings?

The New Emperor of Ice Cream

And the winner is . . . a 55 year old MBA and former management consultant who dabbles in writing poetry and loves Cherry Garcia and maple walnut ice cream. After poring over more than 22,000 entries collected in a much-publicized contest, Ben & Jerry's Homemade Inc. yesterday concluded its unconventional search for a new chief executive by naming Robert Holland Jr., a former partner at McKinsey & Co., to succeed cofounder Ben Cohen.

Holland, though, was recruited through a traditional channel: Russell Reynolds Associates, a New York executive recruiter. The appointment marks Ben & Jerry's passage to seasoned business management from the unorthodox, down-home leadership of its founders, Cohen and Jerry Greenfield, two ex-hippies who founded the company in 1978 in an abandoned gas station.

Holland will be charged with bringing the company to a new level of maturity while preserving the company's funky image and socially responsive values. He must do that while facing the business reality of slowing sales of super premium ice cream. Ben & Jerry's has said it expects to report a loss for the fourth quarter, its first quarterly loss ever.

Cohen will step aside from day-to-day management but remain chairman of the board. Ben & Jerry's executives say he will remain as a creative force in the company, while Holland will run daily operations and implement strategy.

"Ben is glad to have help," said Holland. "He's the flavor maven, the new product idea generator. He also is the social conscience of the company. But I'll run the business. There's only one CEO in the company."

Holland will be paid a base salary of $250,000, plus stock options and a bonus of up to $125,000 if he meets certain financial goals.

Overall, analysts say the company needed a seasoned executive to smooth out operations, spearhead new product development, lead the company into foreign markets, such as Europe, and perhaps launch Ben & Jerry's into other types of snack foods.

Source: "The New Emperor of Ice Cream," Maria Shao, *The Boston Globe*, Feb. 2, 1995, p. 35. Reprinted courtesy of *The Boston Globe*.

Commentary

Entrepreneurial ability and management—are they the same? In many small companies, the two are combined in the same person, often the founder of the company. Similarly, in many small companies, the owner and the manager are the same. In the large company, there is typically a separation of ownership and management and the founder and entrepreneur is still another person or persons.

In the text we have discussed the manager or CEO without distinguishing that person from the entrepreneur. A good CEO often has entrepreneurial abilities, able to undertake risk and creatively direct the firm toward increased profitability. But, the CEO is typically not the founder of the company.

There is controversy that has existed since the large corporation emerged in the late 1800s over whether separation of ownership and management affects the behavior of the firm. Many argue that since the owners are a diverse group of shareholders (owners of shares of stock), they exert no power over the CEO in determining the direction the firm takes. The CEO is guided by profits but is most interested in his or her own personal benefits. Thus, the argument goes, a CEO may not make the decisions that best benefit the owners. When the owner and manager are the same person—typically the founder or entrepreneur—there is no separation of ownership and control and the owners' desires are obviously the direction the firm takes.

This article about the co-founder of Ben & Jerry's ice cream, Ben Cohen, giving up the role of CEO to a professional manager, brings up several aspects of the debate over separation of ownership and control. First, Ben and Jerry went public several years ago. In other words, after launching a very successful firm, Ben and Jerry sold their ownership to the general public through stock sales. With the sale, Ben and Jerry acquired a large sum of money—the capitalized value of the firm—and retained a large percentage of ownership for themselves. Thus, we can continue to speak of Ben and Jerry as owners; and clearly, both have entrepreneurial abilities. But, they are not necessarily very good managers. At least the company has not done well in recent years. In 1994, the stock fell from its high of $21 a share to only $12 a share.

The new CEO, Robert Holland, is a traditional manager; he will ". . . smooth out operations, spearhead new product development, lead the company into foreign markets such as Europe, and perhaps launch Ben & Jerry's into other types of snack foods" according to the article. He is to be paid $250,000 a year plus bonuses and incentives to direct the firm back to profitability and growth.

Yes, Ben and Jerry took risks, were efficient traders, and were innovative. These are the traits of the persons with entrepreneurial ability. And Ben and Jerry profited from their abilities. But, like most small firms—eventually the founders, the people with entrepreneurial ability, must realize that their comparative advantage is not in management and that the firm would be better off with someone who specializes in management, someone who has entrepreneurial abilities in terms of managing. But, with the separation of ownership and control comes the possibility that the manager will direct the firm where the owners might not.

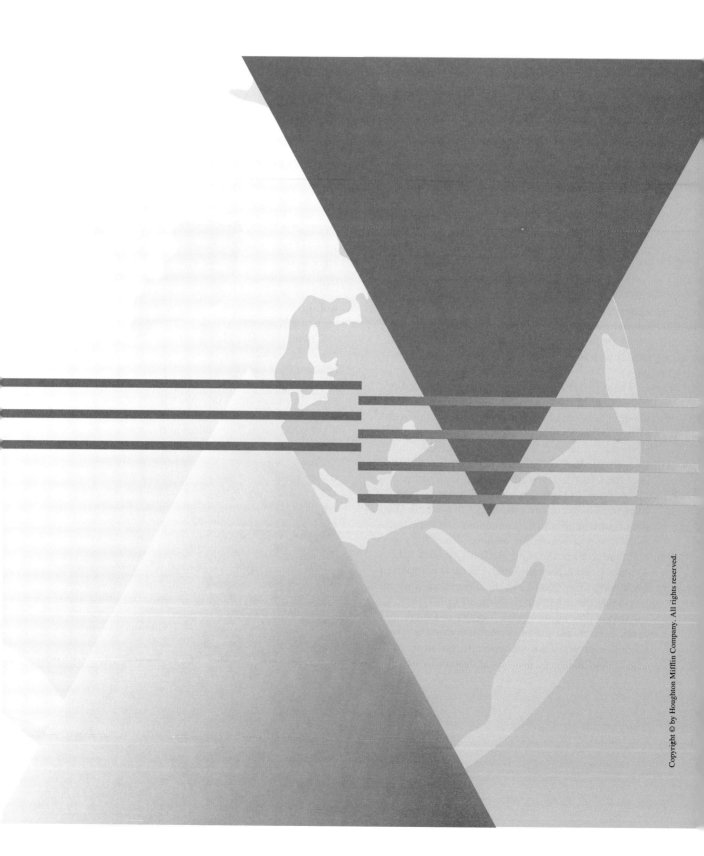

Current Issues Involving the Public Sector and the Market Economy

33

The Economics of Aging and Health Care

FUNDAMENTAL
QUESTIONS

1. What does it mean to say that there is a market for children?
2. Why is the U.S. population aging?
3. Why worry about social security?
4. Why is health care heading the list of U.S. citizens' concerns?

T he population of the United States is aging rapidly. Currently, more than 12 percent of the population is retired—living off pensions, savings, and social security. By the year 2030, 21 percent of the population will be older than sixty-five. The aging of the population is likely to have a dramatic effect on living standards. For instance, the types of goods and services produced will increasingly be influenced by the elderly. In particular, expenditures on health care will continue to rise. Already, people in the United States allocate more than 14 percent of their income to medical care. Is there a limit to how much they are willing to commit? The aging of the population also means that an increasing percentage of people will be retired and a smaller percentage will be producing goods and services and paying taxes. What are the implications for social security and for productivity?

PREVIEW

Why is the population aging? It is a combination of factors: the birthrate has declined and people are living longer than they used to. In the 1950s,

there was 1 birth each year for every 4 people in the population. Today, the rate is 1 birth for every 6 people. Why has the birthrate fallen? In the first section of this chapter we use economic analysis to answer this question. We examine the formation of the family and the decisions to produce children. In the second and third sections we look at the impact of an aging population on retirement and medical care.

I. THE HOUSEHOLD

The average size of the nearly 90 million households in the United States is 2.66 persons. Approximately 63 percent of the population is married, 22 percent single, 7 percent widowed, and 8 percent divorced. Only 28 percent of all households have one income earner; 42 percent have two income earners, and the remaining 30 percent may have none or as many as six income earners.

In 1994 there were nearly 2.4 million marriages, involving 9.1 percent of the population. This rate has declined since 1980 and people are now marrying at an older age. In 1970 the median age of males marrying for the first time was 22.5; of females, 20.6. In 1994 the median age of males marrying for the first time was 25.5; of females, 23.7. Divorce is increasing in frequency. In 1965 the divorce rate was 2.3 percent of the total population. In 1994 it was 5.0 percent. The number of children per family is declining. It is currently less than 1 per household for middle-income households and just over one for all households.[1]

I.a. Children

What does it mean to say that there is a market for children?

In some societies, households consider children as a resource, labor. In others, a child is the only source of pension benefits for the elderly. The extended family—children, parents, and grandparents living together under one roof—is a means of providing retirement benefits for the elderly. In the developed nations of the West, however, children are neither a source of retirement benefits nor a source of labor; they are a source of utility.

The baby's first smile and first step are things of joy to a parent. Like a painting that hangs on the wall, a child provides continual enjoyment. Children are demanded because of the benefits they embody. The demand curve for children slopes down, as shown in Figure 1, indicating that a decrease in the relative "price" of children (an increase in benefits per child) increases the *quantity demanded*.

Supply reflects the marginal cost of each child. The marginal cost of a child includes the cost of the goods and services consumed by the child and the household work provided by family members because of the child. One child increases daily household work by a spouse not employed outside the home by 3 hours, two children by 5 hours, and three by 5.5 hours. Because the opportunity cost of time differs among households, the cost of rearing children differs as well.

The marginal cost of a child may decline for the first few children before it starts to rise. The first child requires baby clothes, cribs, strollers, car seats, and other resources, including the time required to develop child-care skills. Once these items have been obtained for the first child, they may be available at very little extra cost for the second, third, and so on. The second child can wear "hand-me-downs," sleep in the same crib, ride in the same stroller, and use the same car seat as the first.

The greatest cost of children may be the opportunity cost of the time required for their care, but the marginal cost appears to decline because of economies of scale as the number of children increases. Looking after two children may not require twice as much time as looking after one. Cooking for two children may not take any more time than cooking for one. At some point, the older child (children) can assist in caring for the younger child (children). Of course, the age gap between children is an important determinant of the marginal costs of each child. If the gap is too small, the older child cannot help with the younger. If the gap is too wide, many hand-me-downs will not be useful. There is some age difference between children that is optimal in the sense that costs are minimized.

The supply curve of children may decline initially and then rise if the marginal cost of children declines over the first few children and then rises, or the supply curve may rise slowly at first and then more rapidly as the number of children increases, as shown in Figure 1.

The number of children a household has is determined by the demand for and supply of children.

The number of children a household has is determined by the demand for and supply of children. Impacts on this market, such as religious influences or the different requirements of living in an agrarian society versus those of

[1]U.S. Bureau of the Census, *Statistical Abstract of the United States, 1994* (Washington, D.C.: Government Printing Office, 1994).

Figure 1
The Market for Children
The figure shows the initial equilibrium in the market for
children. The number of children, Q_1, and the price per
child, P_1, are determined by the demand for and supply
of children. The demand curve for children slopes down,
reflecting the law of demand. The supply of children is
the marginal cost of each child. The supply curve may
decline initially, but eventually it rises.

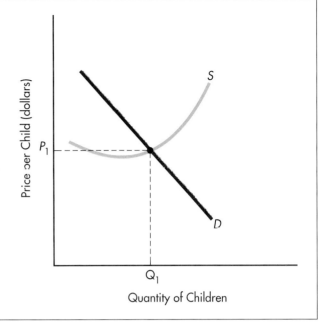

an urbanized society, are reflected in shifts in the demand for or supply of
children. The Second World War had a major impact on the market. By separating men and women, the war virtually destroyed the child market—there
was no demand. At the conclusion of the war, there was a pent-up demand
for children, and a record number were born between 1946 and 1961. The
demand for children that had shifted in from 1940 to 1945 shifted out with a
vengeance in 1946. However, once the marginal cost of another child
exceeded the marginal benefits of another child, couples quit producing children. Because so many children were produced between 1946 and 1961,
there was less demand for additional children after 1961. As a result, a large
number of children were produced between 1946 and 1961 but relatively few
in the years before and after. This increase in the birthrate is known as a
baby boom, and the name given to the population born between 1946 and
1961 is *baby boomers*.

The baby boom generation is contributing to the aging of the U.S. population. The baby boomers, who are now in their thirties and forties, constitute
half of the adult U.S. population. The baby boom, however, is not the only
reason for the aging of the population. A contributing factor is that the number of children being produced has declined.

1.b. Changes in Marriage and the Family

Although the marriage rate has declined only slightly since the mid-1950s,
marriage is changing. Divorce is more prevalent, about double the rate of
thirty years ago, and middle- and upper-income families are having fewer
children. The primary reason for these developments is the revolutionary
change that has taken place in the work force in the last twenty years. More
women work outside the home. More than one-third of the new lawyers,
physicians, and doctoral-degree recipients are women—up from 1 in 16
twenty years ago.

The American family pictured in television shows like "Leave It to Beaver" and "Father Knows Best" comprised four or five people, only one of whom worked outside of the home. Dad went off to his job every morning while Mom and the kids stayed at home. This family was never as common as it was made out to be; even in the 1950s and 1960s, about one-fourth of wives with children held jobs outside of the home. Nevertheless, Mom did have the major responsibilities of caring for the children and homemaking. Within the traditional marriage, specialization has historically meant that the male entered the marketplace and the female remained at home. In the past decade, however, more numbers entered the labor force. As a result, children have become more costly; many women have to leave the labor market during pregnancy, at childbirth, or when their children are young.

As we noted in the chapter "Wage Differentials: Race, Gender, Age, and Unionization," having a child became more costly because the opportunity costs of disrupting careers rose for those women in the labor force. As a result of the higher costs, women are delaying having children, which necessarily means fewer children. Later childbirth, combined with the large baby boom population, means a steadily aging population.

In addition to the baby boom generation and developments in marriage, the length of lifetimes has risen and thus contributed to the aging of the population. In 1930, those who reached age sixty-five could expect to live to age seventy-five. By 1990, someone age sixty-five could expect to live to age eighty-two.

RECAP

1. The number of children a family has depends on the benefits a child produces and on the costs of a child. The benefits include the utility—pleasure—children provide. The costs include the costs of care and feeding and the time involved in raising children.

2. World War II had a major impact on the supply of children—a large number were born in the postwar years.

3. Because it has become increasingly costly for women to have children during the prime years of human-capital acquisition, the decision to have a child has been delayed. This delay, combined with the increased costs imposed on a woman who has a child, has meant a smaller number of children.

4. The aging of the population is due to the aging of the baby boom generation, the decreased birthrates, and the increased life expectancies.

2. AGING AND SOCIAL SECURITY

Why is the U.S. population aging?

The oldest population of the United States, persons sixty-five years or older, numbered 32 million in 1994 and represented more than 12.4 percent of the U.S. population, about one in every eight Americans. The oldest group itself is getting older. In 1994, the sixty-five to seventy-four age group was 8 times larger than in 1900, but the seventy-five to eighty-four group was 12 times larger and the eighty-five-plus group was 22 times larger. The median age in 1850 was 18.9. In 1995 it was 39.

The percentage of the U.S. population over age sixty-five is expected to continue to grow. The most rapid increase ever is expected between the years 2010 and 2030, when the baby boom generation reaches age sixty-five. The pattern of aging is clearly visible in Figure 2, which shows the age of the U.S. population at three points of time, 1970, 1990, and what is anticipated for 2010. The pattern has been described as a python swallowing a pig: the pig represents the baby boom generation working its way up the age scale, the python.

The growth of the older population in the United States has brought several issues to the forefront of political debate. Among them are social security and health care.

2.a. Social Security

Why worry about social security?

An aging population means that the concerns of the aged will dominate national concerns. Retirement and security for the aged is one such concern. Old Age, Survivors, and Disability Insurance (OASDI), also known as social security, had been established in 108 countries by the beginning of 1975. Some of the oldest plans are those of Germany (1889), the United Kingdom (1908), France (1910), Sweden (1913), and Italy (1919). The United States did not enact a national retirement program until 1935.

The social security system in the United States, which covers both old-age, survivors', and disability insurance (commonly referred to as "social

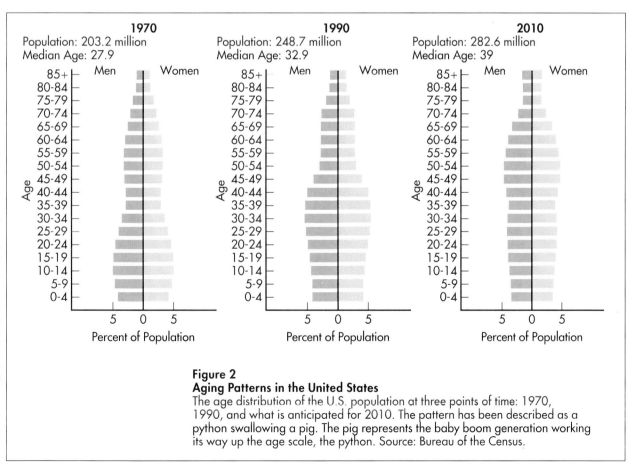

Figure 2
Aging Patterns in the United States
The age distribution of the U.S. population at three points of time: 1970, 1990, and what is anticipated for 2010. The pattern has been described as a python swallowing a pig. The pig represents the baby boom generation working its way up the age scale, the python. Source: Bureau of the Census.

security" and hospital insurance (Medicare), is financed by a payroll tax, FICA, levied in equal portions on the employer and the employee. The initial 1935 tax rate, which covered both social security and Medicare components, was 1 percent of the first $3,000 of wage income paid by both parties. By 1994, this had risen to a tax rate of 7.65 percent (6.2 percent on the first $60,600 of earnings for the social security contribution and 1.45 percent on all earnings for the Medicare contribution).

2.b. The Viability of Social Security

Social security was intended to supplement the retirement funds of individuals.

The social security taxes the working population pays today are used to provide benefits for current retirees. As a result, the financial viability of the system depends on the ratio of those working to those retired. The age distribution of the United States population has affected this viability. The consequence is a change in the ratio of workers to social security beneficiaries, see Figure 3. The ratio has declined from 16.5 in 1950 to about 3 today and is expected to decline to 2 by 2030. The situation in the United States is not any different from that in other parts of the world, as noted in the Economic Insight "The World Is Aging." This trend means that the source of social security benefits is getting relatively smaller. The viability of the system depends on whether the trends of recent years continue. If birthrates remain low and if people continue to live longer, then the obligations to people who will retire in twenty-five years will be large relative to the income of the working population at that time. The Social Security Administration estimates that if everything remains as it currently is, then beginning in the year 2030, social security taxes will be insufficient to fund benefits.

The social security tax has risen more rapidly in the past two decades than any other tax. Social security tax revenues were less than 5 percent of personal income in 1960 and currently exceed 11 percent of personal income. The revenues from the personal income tax were 3.4 percent of personal income in 1940 and rose to the current amount of more than 15 percent in

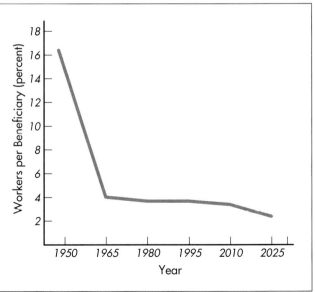

Figure 3
Social Security Viability
The ratio of workers to social security beneficiaries is shown. The ratio has declined from 16.5 in 1950 to about 3 today and is expected to decline to 2 or less by 2030. This trend means that the source of social security benefits is getting relatively smaller. The viability of the system depends on whether the trends of recent years continue. Sources: *Statistical Abstract of the United States, 1994*; Joseph E. Stiglitz, *Economics of the Public Sector* (New York: W.W. Norton, 1986), p. 277; Henry J. Aaron, Barry P. Bosworth, Gary T. Burtless, *Can America Afford to Grow Old?* (Washington, D.C.: Brookings Institution, 1989), p. 38.

The World Is Aging

The United States is not the only country whose population is growing older. Most of the developed nations in the world are experiencing the same aging of their populations. As seen in the accompanying figure, the elderly population constituted about 12 percent in the United States in 1985 but nearly 17 percent in Sweden. Although three-quarters of the world's population resides in developing areas, these areas contain only about 50 percent of the world's elderly. The developed countries are aging because the birthrates in these countries have decreased and life expectancy has increased. Japan's life expectancy of seventy-seven years is the highest among the major countries, but most developed nations approach seventy-five years. In contrast, Bangladesh and some African nations south of the Sahara have life expectancies of forty-nine years.

As longevity has increased and families have had fewer children, the ratio of persons sixty-five and older to persons age twenty to sixty-four has risen in most of the developed countries. These elderly support ratios will rise modestly over the next fifteen years because the large number of people born between 1946 and 1961 will still be in the labor force. But as the large working-age population begins to retire after 2005, the elderly support ratio will rise sharply.

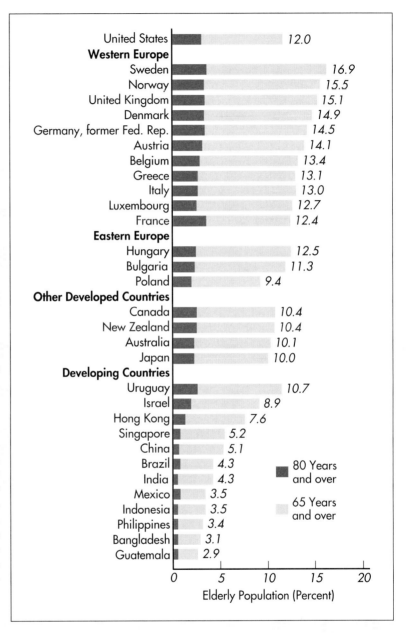

Source: U.S. Department of Commerce, Bureau of the Census, International Population Reports.

the early 1980s. Social security expenditures also have risen more rapidly than any other government program. Social security outlays currently constitute 7 percent of GDP, whereas national defense is less than 5.5 percent, and education and training expenditures are less than 1 percent. From 1979 to 1990, national defense expenditures rose 53.6 percent, education and training expenditures rose 0.8 percent, GDP grew 30.2 percent, and social security grew 70.9 percent, adjusted for inflation.

If the system was funded solely by the revenues collected from the social security tax and if those revenues could be used for no other purpose than to provide benefits to social security recipients, then the worries about the system's viability would be much smaller. However, the social security system is included in the federal government's budget, and its revenues are used to pay for general government expenditures. This means that the excess of social security taxes over social security benefits of $60 billion or so in 1994 was used to pay for other government programs; the funds were not deposited in a trust fund and allowed to accumulate for future years.

If the amount paid into the social security system by an individual was equal, on average, to the amount received by that individual in retirement benefits, the worries about the viability of the system would also be less. But people who retired in the 1980s, after working since the age of twenty-one at the minimum wage level, will recover all social security taxes paid, including employer and employee shares, in less than 4 years; at the maximum taxable amount each year, the employee would have recovered the total contributions in only 5 years. Retirees in the 1990s recover the total contributions and interest earnings in 5 and 7 years. At an age of eighty-two, the average worker who retired at age sixty-five will have received more than twice his and his employer's contributions to social security. Other social security issues are noted in the Economic Insight "Myths About Social Security."

RECAP

1. The U.S. population is aging due to lower birthrates, higher life expectancy, and the impact of the baby boom generation.

2. Social security, otherwise known as Old Age, Survivors, and Disability Insurance, is financed by a tax imposed on employers and employees.

3. Social security is funded by the current working population's contributions being used to provide benefits to the current retirees. As the population ages, the ratio of contributors to beneficiaries declines.

3. HEALTH ECONOMICS

Why is health care heading the list of U.S. citizens' concerns?

3.a. Overview

Spending for health care in the United States exceeds $800 billion. Figure 4 shows that in 1965 health-care expenditures were only 5.9 percent of GDP but were 14 percent by 1994. Per capita spending in 1994 was $3,300. Why have health-care expenditures risen so dramatically?

Figure 5 shows where the nation's health-care dollar is spent and where the money comes from. Figure 5(a) shows that expenditures for hospital services

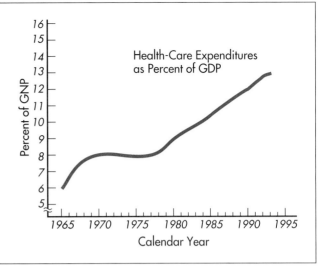

Figure 4
The Growth of U.S. Health-Care Spending
As a percentage of gross domestic product, health-care expenditures have risen from about 6 percent in 1965 to over 12 percent in 1994. Sources: *Health Care Financing Review* (Health Care Financing Administration, 1994); Office of National Health Statistics, Office of the Actuary; *Economic Report of the President, 1995.*

constitute 39 cents of every dollar, or 39 percent of the nation's health-care bill; nursing-home expenditures, 8 percent; spending for physicians' services, 20 percent; and spending for other personal health-care services (dental care, other professional services, drugs and other nondurables, durable medical products, and miscellaneous personal-care services), 21 percent. The remaining 12 percent of national health expenditures goes for medical research, construction of medical facilities, government public health services, and the administration of private health insurance.

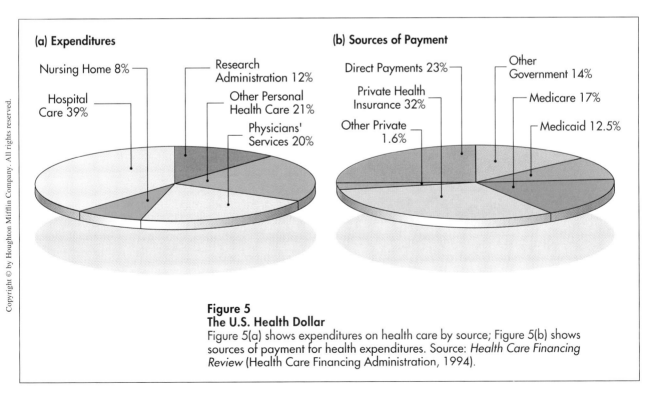

Figure 5
The U.S. Health Dollar
Figure 5(a) shows expenditures on health care by source; Figure 5(b) shows sources of payment for health expenditures. Source: *Health Care Financing Review* (Health Care Financing Administration, 1994).

Myths About Social Security

The first recipient of social security in the United States was Ida Mae Fuller in 1940. Her check was for $22.45. By the time she died, shortly after her one hundredth birthday, she had collected about $20,000 in benefits, a large return considering that she had paid in a total of $22.

"We've contributed to that fund all our lives! It's our money! It's not the government's money!" This is one of the most strongly and widely held myths about the social security system. In fact, the typical retiree collects more than twice the amount represented by employer and employee contributions plus interest.

"The benefits of the system are determined by a scientific formula designed to ensure that the fund remains viable." This is another myth about social security. The system of annually adjusting social security benefits as the cost of living increases dates only from 1975, and it came about as the result of political machinations, not foresight. In 1975, the annual benefits were about $7,000. Attempting to hold the line on federal spending, President Nixon proposed a 5 percent increase in social security benefits and threatened a veto of anything higher. Democrats saw an opportunity to embarrass the president. They decided to pass a 10 percent increase and force Nixon to make an unpopular veto. The 10 percent increase was introduced in the Senate, but then rumors that Nixon would double-cross them and sign the bill anyway began circulating. So Congress increased the benefits to 20 percent, knowing that this huge in- crease would be vetoed. Nixon, however, signed the bill and proudly boasted of how well he had taken care of the elderly. Congress, irritated at being out-flanked, passed the cost-of-living adjustment program to show that it, too, cared about the elderly.

"Social Security ensures that only the elderly poor are cared for." In fact, there are at least a million individu- als currently collecting social secu- rity benefits who also have incomes exceeding $100,000 per year.

Sources: Jack Anderson, "Why Should I Pay for People Who Don't Need It?" *Parade Magazine,* Feb. 21, 1993, p. 4; Eric Blac, "Social Security: Myths, Facts," *Arizona Republic,* Feb. 21, 1993, p. F1.

Medicare:
a federal health care program for the elderly and disabled

Medicaid:
a joint federal-state program that pays for health care for poor families, the neediest elderly, and disabled persons

Figure 5(b) shows the sources of payment for these expenditures. Of the $800 billion spent on health care, 59 percent comes from private sources: private insurance and direct payments. Private health insurance, the single largest payer for health care, accounts for 32 cents of every dollar of national health expenditures, or 32 percent. Private direct payments account for 23 percent. Direct payments consist of out-of-pocket payments made by individ- uals, including copayments and deductibles required by many third-party payers (third-party payers are insurance companies and government).

Government spending on health care constitutes 43.5 percent of the total; the federal government pays about 70 percent of this. **Medicare**, the largest publicly sponsored health-care program, funds health-care services for more than 32 million aged and disabled enrollees. The Medicare program pays for 17 percent of all national health expenditures. **Medicaid**, a jointly funded federal and state program, finances 12.5 percent of all health care covering the costs of medical care for poor families, the neediest elderly, and disabled persons who are eligible for social security disability benefits. Other govern- ment programs pay for 14 percent.

Health-care spending varies tremendously among various groups in the U.S. population. Figure 6 illustrates how health-care expenditures vary across the economy. If each person spent the same amount on health care, the line of perfect equality shown in Figure 6 would describe the distribution of

Figure 6
The Inequality of U.S. Health-Care Spending
High-cost users of health care account for most health-care spending. The top 1 percent account for 30 percent of expenditures, the top 5 percent for 55 percent of expenditures. In contrast, the bottom 70 percent account for only 10 percent of health-care expenditures. Source: Steven A. Garfinkel et al., "High-Cost Users of Medical Care," *Health Care Financing Review* (Health Care Financing Administration, Summer 1988), pp. 41–50.

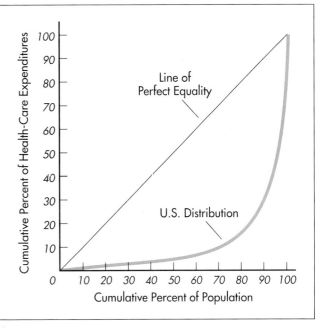

spending. In fact, the distribution of health expenditures is heavily skewed. In 1990, the top 1 percent of persons ranked by health-care expenditures accounted for almost 30 percent of total health expenditures, and the top 5 percent incurred 55 percent of all health expenditures. The bottom 50 percent of the population accounted for only 4 percent of all expenditures, and the bottom 70 percent accounted for only 10 percent of costs.

The high-cost segment of the population is older now than it was twenty years ago. In 1970, 32 percent of the highest 1 percent of users were elderly; the percentage of elderly increased to 43.4 in 1980 and continued to rise during the 1980s. Figure 7 shows that the distribution of spending for hospital care and for nursing homes is heavily dominated by the elderly. The top curve in Figure 7 represents the cumulative percentage of the population in each age group. As the age rises from under five to ten to twenty and so on, there are increasing numbers of people. Eventually 100 percent of the population has been accounted for. The bottom curve represents the cumulative percentage of nursing home expenditures accounted for by people in each age group. Similarly, the middle line represents the cumulative percentage of expenditures on hospitals accounted for by each age group.

3.b. The Market for Medical Care

Health-care costs have risen because the demand for health care has risen relative to supply.

Rising costs or expenditures mean that the demand for medical care has risen relative to supply (Figure 8). The initial demand for medical care is D_1, and the supply of medical care is S_1. The intersection determines the price of medical care, P_1, and the total expenditures, P_1 times Q_1. An increase in demand relative to supply is shown as the outward shift of the demand curve, from D_1 to D_2. As a result, the price of medical care rises, from P_1 to P_2, as do the total expenditures on medical care, from P_1 times Q_1 to P_2 times Q_2. What accounts for the rising demand relative to supply?

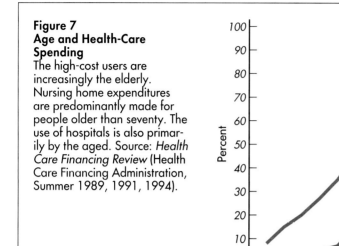

Figure 7
Age and Health-Care Spending
The high-cost users are increasingly the elderly. Nursing home expenditures are predominantly made for people older than seventy. The use of hospitals is also primarily by the aged. Source: *Health Care Financing Review* (Health Care Financing Administration, Summer 1989, 1991, 1994).

3.b.1. Demand Increase: The Aging Population

The aging of the population stimulates the demand for health care. The elderly consume four times as much health care per capita as the rest of the population. About 90 percent of the expenditures for nursing home care are for persons sixty-five or over, a group that constitutes only 12 percent of the population. The aged (sixty-five or older) currently account for 35 percent of hospital expenditures. In contrast, the young, although they constitute 29 percent of the population, con-

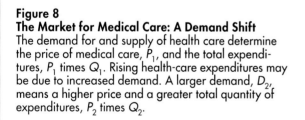

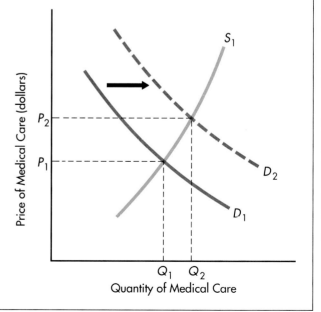

Figure 8
The Market for Medical Care: A Demand Shift
The demand for and supply of health care determine the price of medical care, P_1, and the total expenditures, P_1 times Q_1. Rising health-care expenditures may be due to increased demand. A larger demand, D_2, means a higher price and a greater total quantity of expenditures, P_2 times Q_2.

sume only 11 percent of hospital care. Per capita spending on personal health care for those eighty-five years of age or over is 2.5 times that for people age sixty-five to sixty-nine years. For hospital care, per capita consumption is twice as great for those age eighty-five or over as for those age sixty-five to sixty-nine; for nursing home care, it is 23 times as great.

3.b.2. Demand Increase: The Financing Mechanism

For demand to increase, the aged must be both *willing* to buy medical care and *able* to pay for it. The emergence of Medicare and Medicaid in 1966 gave many elderly the ability. Medicare covers the cost of the first 100 days of hospital or nursing-home care for the elderly and disabled, providing benefits to 32 million people. Like social security, Medicare is funded by payroll taxes and is available on the basis of age (or disability) *not* need. By contrast, Medicaid helps only the neediest people, including many elderly people whose Medicare benefits have run out. As a result, Medicaid is considered the program most associated with long-term health care (such as for people living in nursing homes).

The effect of the Medicare and Medicaid programs has been to increase the demand for services and to decrease the price elasticity of demand because payment to physicians and hospitals is geared to cost. Private sources pay for about 59 percent of personal health care for the general population, and Medicare and Medicaid pick up most of the remainder. Private sources, however, pay for 74 percent of care for people under age sixty-five. For the elderly, the private share of spending is only 15 percent for hospital care, 36 percent for physicians' services, and 58 percent for nursing home care.[2] Medicaid spending for those eighty-five or over is seven times the spending for people age sixty-five to sixty-nine and three times greater than the spending for people age seventy-five to seventy-nine. This difference is attributable to the heavy concentration of Medicaid money in nursing home care, which those eighty-five or over use much more than others. Medicare spending for the oldest group is double that for the sixty-five to sixty-nine group.

3.b.3. Demand Increase: New Technologies

New medical technologies provide the very sick with increased opportunities for survival. Everyone wants the latest technology to be used when their life or the lives of their loved ones are at stake. But because these technologies are cost-increasing innovations and because costs are not paid by the users, the increased technology increases demand.

3.b.4. Supply

Even if the demand curve for medical care was not shifting out rapidly, the cost of medical care could be forced up by an upward shift of the supply curve, as shown in Figure 9. The supply curve, composed of the marginal-cost curves of individual suppliers of medical care, shifts up, from S_1 to S_2, if the cost of producing medical care is rising—that is, if resource prices are rising or if diseconomies of scale are being experienced. The three largest resources in the medical industry in terms of total expenditures are hospitals (39 percent), physicians (20 percent), and nursing homes (8 percent).

Hospitals The original function of hospitals was to provide the poor with a place to die. Not until the twentieth century could wealthy individuals who were sick find more comfort, cleanliness, and service in a hospital than in

---

[2]*Health Care Financing Review,* various issues.

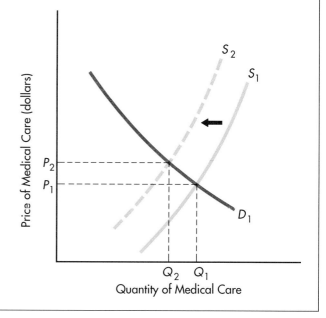

Figure 9
The Market for Medical Care: A Supply Shift
The rising cost of medical care may be caused by an increase in the costs of supplying medical care. The supply curve shifts up, from S_1 to S_2, and the price of medical care rises, from P_1 to P_2.

their own homes. As technological changes in medicine occurred, the function of the hospital changed: the hospital became the doctor's workshop.

The cost of hospital care is attributable in large part to the way current operations and capital purchases are financed. Only a small fraction of the cost of hospital care is paid for directly by patients; the bulk comes from *third parties*, of which the government is the most important. The term *third-party payers* refers to insurance companies and government programs: neither the user (the patient) nor the supplier (the physician or hospital) pays. Until recently, the public-sector, third-party payers made very little effort to question the size of hospital bills. The rate of reimbursement for each hospital was determined primarily by the hospital's costs. Thus, high-cost hospitals were rewarded with higher reimbursement. In 1983, Medicare instituted the prospective payment system, which changed this reimbursement scheme. The **prospective payment system (PPS)** assigns specific reimbursement rates for certain procedures so that high-cost hospitals are reimbursed at the same rate for the same procedure as low-cost hospitals. The result has been to slightly slow the rate of growth of hospital costs and to increase the use of outpatient facilities and at-home care.

Hospital size is typically measured in numbers of beds; efficiency, in expenditures per case or expenditures per patient-day. To make precise determinations of the effect of size on efficiency is difficult because hospitals that differ in size are likely to differ also with respect to location, kind of patient admitted, services provided, and other characteristics. Hospitals that do not provide a large number of complex services need not be very large to be efficient. But if hospitals do provide a large number of services, it is very inefficient for them to be small. A hospital of 200 beds can efficiently provide most of the basic services needed for routine short-term care. If that hospital grows to 600 beds yet still provides only the same basic services, inefficiencies are likely to develop because of increasing difficulties of administrative control. What is more likely to happen, however, is that specialized services

prospective payment system (PPS):
the use of a preassigned reimbursement rate by Medicare to reimburse hospitals and physicians

will be introduced—services that could not have been provided at a reasonable cost when the hospital had only 200 beds.

Hospitals have changed dramatically in the past twenty years. The average number of beds per hospital increased by 50 percent. Inpatient days declined by about 10 percent. Lengths of stay declined by about 10 percent, and occupancy rates declined by nearly 20 percent. The problem that more beds per hospital and shorter stays creates for the hospital is that the present occupancy rate is about 66 percent. The minimum efficient scale (MES) of a hospital occurs with an occupancy rate between 80 and 88 percent.

One problem facing hospital administrators is that many key decisions are made by physicians, who typically have little financial stake in keeping hospital costs down. In fact, many have incentives that run counter to cost control in the hospital. For instance, the use of increased diagnostic testing as a defensive measure against malpractice lawsuits raises the costs of each patient. The role of the physician is particularly important with respect to the cost of care, not just because of physicians' fees but because physicians control the total process of care. Typically, the physician is not an employee of the hospital but is a member of the voluntary staff and is referred to as an attending physician. Although not an employee, the physician has primary influence over what happens. The physician decides who is admitted, what is done to and for the patient, and how long the patient stays.

The delivery of hospital care is typically in the hands of health professionals such as pharmacists, nurses, and technicians, who take their instructions from the physician. Although the pharmacy that fills a prescription is usually an independent business and the pharmacist may be more knowledgeable about drugs than the physician, the pharmacist is legally obliged to fill a prescription exactly as written. In many states a pharmacist cannot substitute one brand of the same drug for another, even if the substitution would result in substantial savings for the patient. Only a physician can prescribe drugs. In addition, all tests and surgery are based solely on the physician's judgment.

Physicians   Physicians affect the cost of medical care not only through their impact on the operation of the hospital but also through their fees. Expenditures on physicians' services rose more rapidly than any other medical-care expenditure category in the 1980s and early 1990s. Is the increased cost of physicians due to a shortage of doctors? The answer is not necessarily "yes." From 1966 to 1990, the supply of physicians increased 100 percent while the American population increased only about 25 percent. As a result, the ratio of active physicians per 100,000 people increased substantially, from 169 in 1975 to 240 in 1994.

The factors that have led to rising physicians' fees include an increase in demand relative to the supply of certain types of physicians, the ability of physicians to restrict price competition, and the payment system. The number of physicians per population has risen in many areas of the country. Yet, because the American Medical Association restricts advertising by physicians, consumers are unable to obtain complete information about prices or professional quality, and physicians are less likely to compete through advertising or lower prices. Moreover, the restrictions on advertising enable established physicians to keep new, entering physicians from competing for their customers by charging lower prices.

The payment system influences physicians' fees and the supply of physicians. Over 31 percent of all physicians' fees are set by the government.

More than 75 percent are set by third-party providers. The physicians are reimbursed on the basis of procedures and according to specialty. A gynecologist would have to examine 275 women a week to achieve the income earned by one cardiac surgeon doing two operations per week. The rates of return from medical education by specialty are shown in Table 1, but most specialists do better than the general practitioner. In fact, more than 60 percent of all physicians in the United States are specialists. You can see that the rate of return varies tremendously among specialties. The payment system has been a windfall (an economic rent) for surgical specialists, anesthesiologists, radiologists, and pathologists and has induced more physicians to specialize in those areas than would have occurred otherwise.

The costs of doing business have risen for physicians. The cost of malpractice insurance, a negligible expense fifteen years ago, has increased about 25 percent a year during the past two decades. Only about 1 percent of healthcare expenditures can be directly attributed to malpractice suits, but there are some implicit costs associated with the fear of malpractice suits. The threat of malpractice suits has caused an increase in both the number of tests ordered by physicians and in the quantity of medical equipment purchased by them.

3.c. Alternatives: HMOs and PPOs

health maintenance organization (HMO):
an organization that provides comprehensive medical care to a voluntarily enrolled consumer population in return for a fixed, prepaid amount of money

The increased costs of medical care and the increased supply of physicians have led to new medical-care delivery systems, the health maintenance organization and the preferred provider organization. A **health maintenance organization (HMO)** provides comprehensive medical care, including preventive, diagnostic, outpatient, and hospital services in return for a fixed, prepaid amount of money from the enrollees.

There are four basic types of HMOs: staff, medical group, independent practice associations (IPAs), and networks. *Staff HMOs,* such as the Group Health Cooperative of Puget Sound in Seattle and ANCHOR Health Plan in

TABLE I
Rates of Return from Medical Education

Specialty	*Rate of Return (percent)*
Pediatrics	9
General practice/family practice	11
Psychiatry	13
Internal medicine	14
Obstetrics-gynecology	16
Pathology	17
Surgery	19
Radiology	20
Anesthesiology	22
Total, all physicians	16

Sources: Steven R. Eastaugh, *Financing Health Care* (Dover, Mass.: Auburn House Publishing Co., 1987), p. 57; *Statistical Abstract of the United States, 1994,* p. 123.

Health-care costs in the United States have risen nearly 300 percent in the past decade. Part of the reason for these costs has been the increasingly sophisticated and expensive equipment used in diagnoses and treatment. This CAT scan provides a picture of the brain; the picture is two-dimensional and can be taken from any angle. Even more sophisticated machines provide virtual reality, showing three-dimensional pictures of the brain.

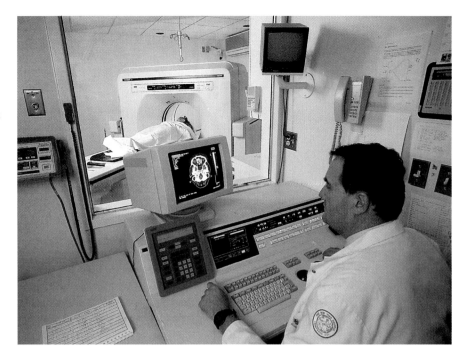

preferred provider organization (PPO):
a group of physicians who contract to provide comprehensive medical services

Chicago, hire physicians as salaried employees. *Group HMOs* function as a medical group practice. Several physicians operating as a partnership or corporation contract with HMO management and an insurance plan to provide services and pool and redistribute income according to a predetermined formula. *Independent practice associations* are separate legal entities that contract with individual physicians practicing in a traditional office setting. *Networks* are organizations that franchise operations, in the same way that McDonald's and Pizza Hut are franchised operations. For instance, Blue Cross/Blue Shield is the main company, and local HMOs are franchises of Blue Cross/Blue Shield.

A **preferred provider organization (PPO)** is a group of physicians who contract with a firm to provide services at a price discount in hopes of increasing their volume of business or a firm that contracts with a group of physicians. A general practitioner serves as a member's primary-care provider and refers patients to specialists as needed. Instead of contacting a specialist directly, a patient must be referred to a specialist by the primary-care provider. Specialists are reimbursed out of the fees paid to the PPO plan by the firms that contract with it. The general practitioners have an incentive to reduce total costs because they split a portion of the fixed fees that remain at the end of the year. As a result, the use of specialists and special tests is lower than in health-care plans that permit patients to select the specialists. Many hospitals are organizing PPOs in hopes of better managing hospital utilization and offsetting declining revenues.

Because HMOs and PPOs provide comprehensive coverage, they alter incentives for the patient. Patients who belong to an HMO or PPO are less likely to seek hospitalization for diagnostic work and other care that can be provided on an outpatient basis than are patients whose health insurance coverage is limited to care provided in the hospital. An HMO also alters incentives for physicians. Because their income is determined by annual payments, they are not likely to provide or order unnecessary care as a way of boosting their incomes.

3.d. National Comparisons

Historically, as per capita national income has risen, the proportion of that income that is spent on health has grown: a 10 percent increase in gross domestic product (GDP) per capita is associated with a 4.4 percent increase in the share of GDP going for health. (*Gross domestic product*, you will recall, is a measure of the total income created in an economy during one year.) Figure 10 shows the health-to-GDP ratios of the twenty-four members of the Organization for Economic Cooperation and Development (OECD). The share of health expenditures in GDP varied from 4.0 percent in Turkey to 13.4 percent in the United States. The average was 2.8 percent.

Per capita expenditures for health range from $142 in Turkey to $2,876 in the United States, as shown in Figure 11. U.S. per capita spending exceeded spending in Canada by 43 percent, France by 86 percent, Germany by 99 percent, and Japan by 124 percent.

Increases in health-care expenditures and the widening gap between the United States and other countries have led to a consideration of how medical care is provided in various countries. The comparison considered most often is between the United States and Canada because the two are neighbors with not too dissimilar economic and political systems and yet very different medical systems.

U.S. and Canadian payment systems differ considerably. In the United States, physicians are paid more for doing more, and the return on their time is higher if they perform a procedure than if they use their cognitive skills. Because procedures often require hospital care, this approach translates into higher expenditures for hospital care. In Canada, by contrast, physicians operate under a system of fee schedules and overall provincial limits on

Figure 10
Total Health Expenditures as a Share of Gross Domestic Product
Total health expenditures are divided by gross domestic product to provide a comparison among countries. The United States allocates a higher percentage of its gross output to medical care than does any other country.
Sources: OECD Health Data 1993, Statistical Abstract of the United States 1994; *Table 1361*; Economic Report of the President, 1994.

Figure 11
Per Capita Health Spending
The per capita expenditures of several countries are shown. U.S. expenditures are the highest. Sources: *Measuring Health Care, 1960–1983* (Paris: Organization for Cooperation and Development, 1985); *OECD Health Data 1991* and *OECD Health Systems: Facts and Trends, 1992; Economic Report of the President, 1994.*

	Per Capita Expenditures		
U.S.	$2,867	Belgium	1,384
Canada	1,917	Netherlands	1,366
Switzerland	1,730	Japan	1,307
Germany	1,663	Norway	1,305
France	1,656	Denmark	1,151
Austria	1,492	New Zealand	1,047
Iceland	1,476	U.K.	1,033
Luxembourg	1,476	Spain	848
Sweden	1,443	Ireland	844
Finland	1,420	Portugal	624
Australia	1,411	Greece	404
Italy	1,408	Turkey	142

health spending, and they have no incentive to increase the number of procedures.

Canadian patients are virtually fully insured. There are no deductibles or copayments. Canadian physicians are mostly reimbursed on a fee-for-service basis. Very little use is made of the prepaid group practices that have grown so rapidly in the United States. Government sanctions cause Canadian physicians to limit their use of tests and other procedures. The biggest difference between the U.S. and Canadian systems is that in Canada most of the funds for health care come from a single source. Because hospital budgets are set in advance by the Canadian government, it is very difficult for hospital administrators, physicians, or patients to spend more than has been budgeted. In addition, Canada has a significantly lower ratio of specialists to general practitioners than the United States has. In the United States, the large number of surgeons and other specialists order a large number of procedures and experience a low average workload.

Canadians receive fewer health services than Americans, yet there is no discernible difference in the infant-mortality and life-expectancy statistics of the two nations. Do Americans enjoy the diversity, the extra services, and the choice that they pay extra for even if there are no discernible differences in measures of health? For instance, the average stay in a hospital is shorter in the United States than it is in Canada, but the tests and procedures are more numerous. Would Canadians pay more for a shorter stay and more tests and procedures if they had the choice? If the answer to these questions is *no*, can we say that the system in the United States is less desirable than the system in Canada?

3.e. Do the Laws of Economics Apply to Health Care?

The explosion of health-care costs and the emergence of health care as a central issue in the administration of Bill Clinton has led many people to claim that, or act as if, health care is different, that the laws of economics do not apply to it.[3] People tend to look at health care as a "right," something everyone is entitled to regardless of costs. You may recall our survey and discussion about allocation mechanisms in Chapter 3; most groups looked on health care as something different from other goods and services. They did not want the market system to determine who got the health care and who didn't. When the Clinton administration was considering health-care reform, it received nearly 100,000 letters from citizens. Most carried the tone of a letter from Mrs. Milford Gray, 72, who described how Medicare and private insurers paid only a portion of the costs for treatment of her husband's irregular heartbeat. Mrs. Gray stated that she and her husband should not have had to pay for any of the treatment and should have received the best treatment available.[4]

Is the product, health care, a scarce good? The answer is a clear *yes*; at a zero price more people want health care than there is health care available, the definition of a scarce good. Scarcity means that choices must be made, that there is an opportunity cost for choosing to purchase the scarce good. The choice is made on the basis of rational self-interest. These principles of economics suggest that health care is an economic good and subject to the laws of economics.

The demand curve for medical care looks like any other demand curve; it slopes down because the higher the price, the lower the quantity demanded. The demand curve is probably quite inelastic, but it does slope downward due to diminishing marginal utility. There also is a standard-looking supply curve. Physicians, hospitals, and medical firms offer an increasing quantity of medical care for sale as the price rises. As shown in Figures 8 and 9 and repeated in Figure 12, the demand and supply curves look no different than the curves representing a market in any other economic good.

In Figure 12, the price for medical care is the level at which the demand and supply curves intersect, the point of equilibrium. At price P_1, the quantity of medical care demanded is equal to the quantity supplied. Those people willing and able to pay price P_1 (all those lying along the demand curve from A to B) get the medical care. Those not willing and able to pay the price (all those lying along the demand curve from B to C) do not get the health care.

The problems that arise in the health-care market are due not to a repeal of the laws of economics but instead to the nature of the product. People believe they and others have an inalienable right to medical care, that it is not right to ignore those people making up the demand curve from B to C. As a result, government programs to provide medical insurance have been created. These programs, along with private insurance programs, mean that most of the payments for medical care are made by third parties, as described earlier in this chapter. The third-party payment system allows many of those who would not be willing and able to purchase the health care, those lying along the demand curve from B to C, to be able to purchase the care. This shifts the

"Repealing the laws of economics" in the case of health care means that the demand for and supply of health care do not determine the price or quantity, and not just those willing and able to pay get the care.

---

[3]David Wessel and Walt Bogdanich, "Laws of Economics Often Don't Apply in Health Care Field," *The Wall Street Journal,* Jan. 22, 1992, p. A1; Nora C. O'Malley, "Age-Based Rationing of Health Care: A Descriptive Study of Professional Attitudes," *Health Care Management Review* 16(1), 1991, pp. 83–93; Horace B. Deets, Executive Director, American Association of Retired Persons, "Health Care Is Not a Commodity," Letters to the Editor, *The Wall Street Journal,* Nov. 23, 1993.

[4]"'Dear Hillary': Letters Clamor for Health Reform," by Les Bowman, Scripps Howard, April 7, 1993, *Arizona Republic,* p. A1.

Figure 12
Do the Laws of Economics Apply to Health Care?
The price of medical care is the level at which the demand and supply curves intersect, the point of equilibrium. At price P_1, the quantity of medical care demanded is equal to the quantity supplied. Those people willing and able to pay price P_1 (all those lying along demand curve D_1 from A to B) get the medical care. Those not willing and able to pay the price (all those lying along the demand curve from B to C) do not get the health care.

The third-party payment system allows many who would not be willing and able to purchase the health care (those lying along the demand curve from B to C) to be able to purchase the care. This shifts the demand curve out, which drives health-care costs up, as shown by the shift in the demand curve from D_1 to D_2.

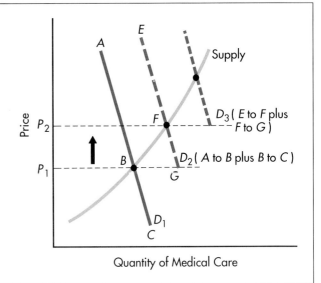

demand curve out, which drives health-care costs up, as shown by the shift from D_1 to D_2 in Figure 12.

The government and private insurance programs thus face ever-rising health-care costs; each new equilibrium means some are unable to afford the care; if their demand is covered, the demand curve shifts out again, to D_3. This continues as long as someone is willing and able to pay the price. That someone has been the government, principally through Medicare, and private employers through employee benefit plans. The result has been double-digit price increases for health care for over a decade.

In the early 1990s, individuals and businesses were demanding that something be done—they did not want to continue using an increasing portion of their income for medical care. Thus, immediately after being elected, President Clinton focused the administration's attention on reforming health care. The Clinton efforts centered on "managed competition."

3.e.1. Managed Care: Changes in the Healthcare Industry Managed **competition** refers to the use of large buying groups to purchase medical care and pharmaceuticals, thereby using monopsony power to force lower prices. The Clinton administration wanted to change the U.S. system to one resembling the Canadian health system. The Canadian system, wherein each province has control over the hospital and medical care budgets, is an example of the monopsony approach of managed competition. The large buyer, the provincial government, purchases services for the citizens in the province. Each citizen alone cannot negotiate lower prices, but all citizens together can. With this market power, the provincial government can demand lower prices.

As the Clinton reform efforts faded, so did the call for managed competition. Reform by the private sector continued to occur, however. The greatest change was the emergence of managed care. **Managed care** refers to the situation where patients purchase membership in a medical firm—the HMO or PPO—that provides physicians, pharmaceuticals, tests, hospitals, and any

managed competition:
government intervention in the health-care market to guide competition so that costs are reduced

managed care:
comprehensive medical care provided within one firm

other medical treatment. As noted in section 3.c., the HMO may contract with pharmaceutical companies, hospitals, and physicians or it may hire the physicians, own the hospitals, and dispense pharmaceuticals itself whereas the PPO contracts with individual physicians, hospitals, and pharmacies.

Enrollment in HMOs rose from 29 million people in 1987 to 45 million people in 1993, while enrollment in PPOs rose from 28 million to more than 90 million. Employers generally pay HMOs and PPOs a flat monthly fee per employee—called a capitation fee. HMOs and PPOs earn revenue only by enrolling members—the more members, the more revenue. Thus, to increase profit, the HMOs and PPOs must control costs. The HMOs must compete for members—either offering lower prices than other HMOs or PPOs or by providing better services. The HMOs also want to reduce the demand for the most costly types of medical services, thereby reducing their costs. Some HMOs and PPOs have provided full coverage for the less costly or routine services and have required co-payments when patients seek specialty services. Having to pay a portion of costs, the patient is less likely to seek the service. The HMOs have also discovered that there are significant economies of scale—many have merged—and their minimum efficient scale (MES) point is becoming increasingly large. Thus, the medical care industry is rapidly changing from one dominated by small firms—the individual physician—to an oligopoly. As the efficient size of an HMO is rising, it is becoming increasingly more difficult to start a new HMO. With very large fixed costs and small marginal costs, entry is restricted. Since the industry is becoming an oligopoly, we should expect to observe the same types of behaviors in the health-care market that we observe in other oligopoly markets.

3.e.2. **What Happened to the Clinton Health Care Reform?** "The ill-fated effort of the Clinton administration to reform our grievously wasteful health-care system is finished. It's death this week was quiet, compared with the fanfare and pageantry of its birth 18 months ago."[5] This type of headline appeared in nearly all newspapers in the fall of 1994. What happened to the reform? According to a poll on election night in November 1994, voters continued to consider their top four priorities for the new Congress as health care, crime, taxes, and the deficit. However, voters wanted small changes, not a government takeover. Part of the reason that voters changed their minds—at first favoring a huge reform and later wanting only small changes—is that the changes in the medical care industry noted above were reducing the rate of cost increase. In 1994, consumer health-care costs rose less than any time in the last decade.

In addition to the changes in the health-care market, the intense debates over health-care reform clarified several issues regarding the government-provided systems of Canada and the European nations and the primarily private system in the United States. Individuals were concerned with the effects of price controls on medical services and of a larger government role. The health-care systems of Canada and Europe and the system proposed by the Clinton administration place a price ceiling in the market for basic medical care and then refuse to provide government payment for the high-technology

---

[5]*USA Today,* September 29, 1994, p. 13A.

medical care. The result is a shortage in the market for basic medical care; quantity demanded exceeds quantity supplied at the price ceiling. With an excess demand and with a restricted price, something other than price must allocate the medical care. Typically, it is waiting times, lines, or delays of weeks or months before getting an appointment that work to ration the scarce good.

Capitalizing on the recognition of possible effects of a government-controlled health-care system, those who stood to lose as a result of government intervention lobbied hard to defeat any reform efforts. Between January 1, 1993 and July 31, 1994, the American Medical Association contributed $1.4 million, the National Association of Life Underwriters $820,000, the American Dental Association $650,000, the American Hospital Association $600,000, and other medical-care associations and insurance associations around $400,000 apiece to lobbying Congress.

RECAP

1. Health care is the fastest-growing portion of total national expenditures. It is rising primarily because of the rising cost of physician services, nursing homes, and hospital services.

2. The demand for medical care has risen at a very rapid rate. One reason for the increase is the introduction of Medicare and Medicaid and private insurance plans that make demand relatively inelastic. The aging of the population has also increased the demand for medical care.

3. The cost of providing medical care has risen because of increases in hospital costs and physicians' fees. Rising hospital costs are partly a result of the reimbursement plans of third-party providers and partly a result of the control of the operation of hospitals by physicians.

4. Physicians' fees have risen even though the supply of physicians has risen. The demand for medical services does not match the supply; reimbursement methods have led to higher rates of return in certain specialties and thus have drawn an increasing number of physicians to those specialties.

5. In some nations, nearly all medical care is provided by the government; in others, most medical care is purchased by patients. In all, the scarce good, health care, must be rationed, either by price or by some other mechanism.

6. The laws of economics do apply to the medical arena. The difficulty is that people do not like the outcome of those laws.

SUMMARY

▲▼ *What does it mean to say that there is a market for children?*

1. Children are demanded either because they provide utility to the parents or because they are a source of labor and pensions. The benefit provided by each additional child declines (the

demand curve slopes down). The cost of supplying children may decrease for the first few children, but it probably rises thereafter so that the supply curve slopes up. The number of children in a family is determined by demand and supply. The number has declined in recent decades as the cost of children has risen. §1.a

▲▼ **Why is the U.S. population aging?**

2. The U.S. population is aging because the number of births has declined while people are living longer than they used to. § 1.b

▲▼ **Why worry about social security?**

3. Social security is a government-mandated pension fund. In the United States it is funded by a tax on employer and employee. The current tax collections are used to provide benefits to current retirees. §2.a

▲▼ **Why is health care heading the list of U.S. citizens' concerns?**

4. The rapidly rising costs of medical care result from increases in demand relative to supply. §3.a

5. The increasing demand results from the aging of the population and from payment systems that decrease the price elasticity of demand. §3.b.1, 3.b.2

6. The reduced supply (higher costs of producing medical care) results from inefficiencies in the allocation of physicians among specialties and inefficiencies in the operation and organization of hospitals. §3.b.4

7. The health industry is changing in response to rapidly rising costs. Alternative methods of providing health care have arisen. HMOs and PPOs provide health care at a lower cost. §3.c

8. The percentage of income allocated to health care varies tremendously from country to country. The United States spends more per capita for health care than any other nation. The United States provides medical care through a combination of government programs (Medicare and Medicaid) and private purchases, insurance, and direct payments. Some nations have primarily government-provided systems; others have primarily private systems. §3.d

KEY TERMS

Medicare §3.a

Medicaid §3.a

prospective payment system (PPS) §3.b.4

health maintenance organization (HMO) §3.c

preferred provider organization (PPO) §3.c

managed competition §3.e

managed care §3.e.1

EXERCISES

1. Describe the market for children. Then answer the following questions.

   a. What is the demand and what is the supply in this market?

   b. What is the price in this market?

   c. What does the intersection of demand and supply mean? Who are the demanders? Who are the suppliers?

2. Explain the result of a law restricting families to only one child (such as exists in China).

3. What is social security? What is Medicare? What is the economic role of these government policies?

4. Why have medical-care expenditures risen more rapidly than expenditures on any other goods and services?

5. Explain how both the supply of physicians and physicians' fees can increase.

6. Why are there more medical specialists and fewer general practitioners in the United States than in Canada?

7. What is the economic logic of increasing social security benefits?

8. What does it mean to say people have a right to a specific good or service? Why do people believe they have a right to medical care but do not believe they have a right to a 3,000-square-foot house?

9. Suppose the objective of government policy is to increase an economy's growth and raise citizens' standards of living. Explain in this context the roles of retirement, social security, Medicare, and mandatory retirement.

10. Explain why the U.S. system of payment for medical procedures leads to higher health costs than a system of payment for physicians' services.

11. Analyze the following solutions to the problem of social security.

    a. The retirement age is increased to seventy.

    b. The FICA tax is increased.

    c. The income plus social security payments cannot exceed the poverty level.

    d. The total amount of social security benefits received cannot exceed the amount paid in by employer and employee plus the interest earnings on those amounts.

12. Oregon proposed a solution to the health costs problem that was widely criticized. The solution would allow the state to pay only for common medical problems. Special and expensive problems would not be covered. Using the market for medical care, analyze the Oregon plan.

13. What would be the impact of a policy that did away with Medicare and Medicaid and instead provided each individual with the amounts they contributed during their working lives to the Medicare program?

14. Why is a third-party payer a problem? Private insurance companies are third-party payers and yet they want to maximize profit. So wouldn't they ensure that the allocation of dollars was efficient?

15. "We must recognize that health care is not a commodity. Those with more resources should not be able to purchase services while those with less do without. Health care is a social good that should be available to every person without regard to his or her resources." Evaluate this statement.

COOPERATIVE LEARNING EXERCISE

Assign students to different population segments. Group A represents those aged 0-18. Group B is the age segment 19-30. Group C is the age segment 31-64. Group D is the age segment 65+. Each group is to propose a way to solve the problem of not enough money to pay social security benefits in the years after 2010. The proposals are to be based on the perspective of the age segment to which each student has been assigned. The class is then to vote on which proposals to support.

Many Travel a Painful Circuit for Their Managed Health Care

Some hobble with injured legs across town for X rays before returning to their doctor, who could have taken the pictures in the first place. Others find themselves pressured to leave one hospital for another, even when their conditions are fragile. And some are referred back to their doctor's office for blood tests, tests that could have been done at the same lab where they had just undergone other screenings. Consumers in the Philadelphia area have discovered that health care under managed care can be a frustrating experience. While some patients are paying less out-of-pocket for well-coordinated care, others are finding unanticipated quirks and limitations that seem to complicate treatment rather than ease it. Managed care is not supposed to be a maze. Its goals include making medical care more accessible for consumers and less expensive for employers by overseeing who receives treatment, how much they get, and where they go for it. Until now, the Philadelphia area has lagged in replacing traditional indemnity plans—patients pick doctors, insurers pay bill—with managed care. But, that's changing,

as employers and consumers alike face rising health-care costs. One estimate indicates that nearly 4 to 10 people in the region belong to a health maintenance organization, one type of managed care. Among them are Sonya and Gus Pappas of Swarthmore, whose experiences under managed care could not have been more different, even though both were treated last year under the same insurance plan.

Gus Pappas, 32, an accountant, said he had been swaddled in the best health care imaginable from the moment he collapsed on his way to his doctor's office last March, through surgery for colon cancer, and nearly a year of follow-up chemotherapy. And he never saw a bill. By contrast, his wife, 28, a fund-raiser, encountered a bureaucratic morass as she sought treatment for infertility. Rather than travel to the lab to which the insurer directed her for tests, she paid hundreds of dollars a month out-of-pocket to use the lab at her doctor's office.

"You feel trapped," said Sonya Pappas, who sees patients as caught in a riptide of change racing through

health care. "It is almost like you don't know what everyone's role is and where they stand."

Some observers say the insurers seem to use their advantage to direct patients to services with low rates, even if they weren't user-friendly. Consequently, doctors and patients complain about inefficiencies, delays, higher costs, and even compromised care. "In searching for the best price, they fragment the system," said Alan Zuckerman, executive vice president in Philadelphia for Chi Systems, a health-care consulting firm.

"Our position is that we have more comprehensive benefits, high-quality delivery systems and better prices," said John Daddis, the Philadelphia insurer's senior vice president for managed care. "There are some trade-offs on choice. But that's inherent in the whole concept."

Source: "Many Travel a Painful Circuit for Their Managed Health Care," by Marian Uhlman, *The Philadelphia Inquirer,* February 1, 1995, p. 1. Reprinted by permission.

Commentary

Rationing of one kind or another is inevitable with a scarce good. For the vast majority of goods people have chosen rationing by price. Many have difficulty with applying that same choice to medical care. Moreover, because of the way that firms have provided medical care benefits to employees, there has been little regard to the price of medical care over the past twenty years. Since patients do not pay directly for care, the patients have no incentive to be price conscious. They encourage doctors to carry out additional tests and to provide the most technologically advanced medical care. This, combined with the government provision of medical care for the elderly, drove the prices of medical care and medical insurance up at accelerating rates during the 1970s and 1980s.

To reduce their costs, firms began to look for alternative ways to provide their employees medical insurance benefits. What evolved is managed care— a firm enlists physicians and all medical experts to provide services to enrollees. Some firms hire the physicians directly while others contract with the physicians to provide services at a certain fee. Most physicians accept the conditions because the demand for their services on a fee-for-service basis is rapidly declining. To reduce costs, the managing firm allocates patients among doctors so that work-loads are about equal. The managing firm also provides only the basic types of medical procedures. Fertility, plastic surgery, and certain high-technology or experimental procedures, like bone-marrow transplants, are not covered by the managed care. If enrollees want to go outside of the firm or network for care, then they must pay out-of-pocket. This is what Sonya Pappas decided to do.

The demand curve for medical care looks like any other demand curve; it slopes down because the higher the price, the lower the quantity of medical care demanded. There also is a standard-looking supply curve; physicians, hospitals, and medical firms offer an increasing quantity of medical care for sale as the price rises. As shown in the diagram below, with demand rising—the demand curve shifting out—the price of medical care rose. Managed care is an attempt to reduce the rate at which the demand curve shifts out—shown as the smaller shifts from D_3 to D_4 to D_5. It also is an attempt to reduce the cost of supplying medical care—causing the supply curve to shift down— shown as the shift from S_1 to S_2. If successful, the managed care approach would lead to an equilibrium at a lower price and higher quantity.

As the article noted, there are tradeoffs involved. If people are willing and able to pay the price, then they can get any medical care they want. If they are not willing or able to pay the price, they must take what is available at the lower price. In other words, rationing the care in some way other than price occurs. In some cases, services are not available— are not supplied. In other cases, it is a first-come, first-served basis; those coming into the office first get served first. Lines and waiting in offices result. In still other cases, the patient is shuffled from place to place and medical facility to medical facility— time and convenience allocate the scarce goods.

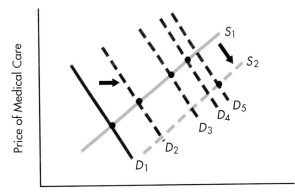

34

Income Distribution, Poverty, and Government Policy

FUNDAMENTAL QUESTIONS

1. Are incomes distributed equally in the United States?
2. How is poverty measured, and does poverty exist in the United States?
3. Who are the poor?
4. What are the determinants of income?
5. How does the government try to reduce poverty?

H alf a million Americans will spend today living on city streets or in temporary shelters, and more than a million will do so over the next year. The trickle of people surviving on city streets a decade ago has become a steady stream—men, women, children, white, black, Hispanic, mentally healthy, mentally ill. "Homeless" used to describe people who were transient, poor, socially isolated, and living in the cheap hotels and flophouses on skid row. They had housing, but they didn't have homes. Today, the homeless are "houseless" too.

Even the poor in this country are better off than the entire populations of other nations, however. In Bolivia, the average life expectancy is only fifty-three years, a full twenty years less than in the United States. In Burma, only about one-fourth of the population has access to safe water. In Burundi, less than one-fourth of the urban houses have electricity. In Chad, less than one-third of the children reach the sixth grade. In Ethiopia, the per capita income is $120, sixty times lower than in the United States.

PREVIEW

What accounts for the inequality among nations and among households within a nation? Who are the poor and the rich? Is the inequality of incomes something that can or should be corrected? These questions are the topic of this chapter. Previous chapters have discussed how the market system works to ensure that resources flow to their highest-valued uses, that output is produced in the least-cost manner, and that people get what they want at the lowest possible price—in other words, the efficiency of the market system. Efficiency and equity do not necessarily go together, however. Efficiency implies that goods and services are allocated to those with the ability to pay, not necessarily to those with needs.

I. INCOME DISTRIBUTION AND POVERTY

Are incomes distributed equally in the United States?

In a market system, incomes are distributed according to the ownership of resources. Those who own the most highly valued resources have the highest incomes. One consequence of a market system, therefore, is that incomes are distributed unequally.

I.a. A Measure of Income Inequality

In the United States, as in every country, there are rich and there are poor. If there were no distinctions between rich and poor—that is, if everyone had the same income—then income would be distributed equally. Incomes are not distributed equally, however, and the degree of inequality varies widely from country to country. In order to compare income distributions, economists need a measure of income inequality. The most widely used measure is the **Lorenz curve**, which provides a picture of how income is distributed among members of a population.

Equal incomes among members of a population can be plotted as a 45-degree line that is equidistant from the axes (see Figure 1). The horizontal axis measures the total population in cumulative percentages. As we move along the horizontal axis, we are counting a larger and larger percentage of the population. The numbers end at 100, which designates 100 percent of the population. The vertical axis measures total real GDP in cumulative percentages. As we move up the vertical axis, the percentage of total real GDP being counted rises to 100 percent. The 45-degree line splitting the distance between the axes is called the *line of income equality*. At each point on the line, the percentage of total population and the percentage of total real GDP are equal. The line of income equality indicates that 10 percent of the population earns 10 percent of the income, 20 percent of the population earns 20 percent of the income, and so on, until we see that 90 percent of the population earns 90 percent of the income and 100 percent of the population earns 100 percent of the income.

Points off the line of income equality indicate an income distribution that is unequal. Figure 1 shows the line of income equality and a curve that bows down below the income-equality line. The bowed curve is a Lorenz curve. The Lorenz curve in Figure 1 is for the United States. The bottom 20 percent of the population receives 3.6 percent of total real GDP income, seen at point *A*. The second 20 percent accounts for another 9.6 percent of real GDP

Lorenz curve:
a curve measuring the degree of inequality of income distribution within a society

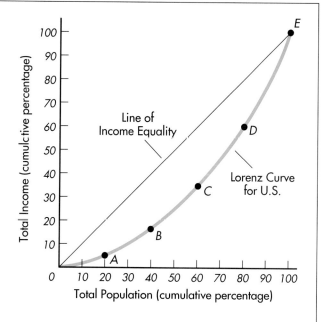

Figure 1
The U.S. Lorenz Curve
The farther a Lorenz curve lies from the line of income equality, the greater the inequality of the income distribution. The bottom 20 percent of the U.S. population receives 4.6 percent of total real GDP income, seen at point *A*. The second 20 percent accounts for another 9.6 percent of real GDP income, shown as point *B*, where the bottom 40 percent of the population has 12.8 percent of the real GDP income (3.6 percent owned by the first 20 percent of the population plus the additional 9.6 percent owned by the second 20 percent). The third 20 percent accounts for another 15.2 percent of real GDP income, so point *C* is plotted at a population of 60 percent and an income of 28.4 percent. The fourth 20 percent accounts for another 23.4 percent of the real GDP income, shown as point *D*, where 80 percent of the population owns 51.8 percent of the income. The richest 20 percent accounts for the remaining 48.2 percent of real GDP income, shown as point *E*. With the last 20 percent of the population and the last 48.2 percent of real GDP income, 100 percent of population and 100 percent of real GDP income are accounted for. Point *E*, therefore, is plotted where both income and population are 100 percent. Source: *Statistical Abstract of the United States*, 1994, Table 708. Bureau of the Census, 1994.

Figure 2
Lorenz Curves for Mexico and the United States
Based on data for the United States and Mexico, the
two Lorenz curves show that total real GDP income in
Mexico is distributed among Mexican citizens much
more unequally than total real GDP income in the
United States is distributed among citizens of the United
States. Source: World Bank, *World Development
Report, 1992* (New York: Oxford University Press),
Table 30.

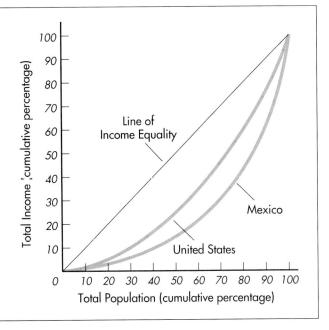

income, shown as point *B*, so the bottom 40 percent of the population has
12.8 percent of the real GDP income (3.6 percent owned by the first 20 percent of the population plus the additional 9.6 percent owned by the second 20
percent). The third 20 percent accounts for another 15.7 percent of real GDP
income, so point *C* is plotted at a population of 60 percent and an income of
28.4 percent. The fourth 20 percent accounts for another 23.4 percent of the
national income, shown as point *D*, where 80 percent of the population
receives 51.8 percent of the income. The richest 20 percent accounts for the
remaining 48.2 percent of real GDP income, shown as point *E*. With the last
20 percent of the population and the last 48.2 percent of real GDP income,
100 percent of population and 100 percent of real GDP income are accounted
for. Point *E*, therefore, is plotted where both income and population are 100
percent.[1]

The farther the Lorenz curve bows down, away from the line of income
equality, the greater the inequality of the distribution of income. In Chapter
4 it was noted that on average, in developed countries, the richest 20 percent
of households receive about 40 percent of household income and the poorest
20 percent receive only about 5 or 6 percent of household income. That distribution, however, is much more equal than the distribution found in less
developed countries. The most unequal distribution of income is found in
less developed countries: the richest 20 percent of the population receives
more than 50 percent of total household income, and the poorest 20 percent
receives less than 4 percent of total household income. Figure 2 shows two
Lorenz curves, one for the United States and one for Mexico. The curve for

---

[1]A Lorenz curve for wealth could also be shown. It would bow down below the Lorenz
curve for income, indicating that wealth is more unequally distributed than income.
Wealth and income are different and should be kept distinct. Wealth is the stock of assets.
Income is the flow of earnings that results from the stock of assets.

Mexico bows down far below the curve for the United States, indicating the greater inequality in Mexico.

I.b. Income Distribution among Nations

Incomes differ greatly from one nation to another as well as within nations. The per capita annual income in Mexico is $2,500, while in the United States it exceeds $23,000. Mexico's income distribution is less equal than in the United States, but income levels in Mexico are also significantly lower than in the United States. Figure 3 shows the per capita incomes of several countries. The figure illustrates how great the differences in per capita income are. The Economic Insight "Economic Development and Happiness" suggests that the feeling of well-being of a population generally depends on the levels of per capita income.

The distribution of total world income among nations is very unequal, as shown in Figure 4. Three-fourths of the world's population lives in developing countries, but the income earned by the people in these countries—the lowest 90 percent of the population in terms of income—is only about 20 percent of the total world income, shown as point *A*. The richest countries, earning nearly 80 percent of total world income, have only 10 percent of the world's population, the difference between *A* and *B*.

I.c. Measuring Poverty

How is poverty measured, and does poverty exist in the United States?

A Lorenz curve does not indicate who the poor are or what their quality of life is. It is a relative measure. On the other hand, an absolute measure such as per capita income does not necessarily indicate how people feel about their income status nor whether they enjoy good health and a decent standard of living. Those who are comfortable in one country could be impoverished in another. The poverty level in the United States would represent a substantial increase in living standards in many other nations. Yet members of a poor family in the United States would probably not feel less poor if they knew that their income level exceeds the median income in other countries.

Figure 3
Per Capita Real Gross National Product
Levels of income vary tremendously among nations; for instance, per capita income in Switzerland is the highest, at $36,080 per year; Ethiopia has the lowest, $110 per year. Source: World Bank, *World Development Report, 1994* (New York: Oxford University Press), Table 1.

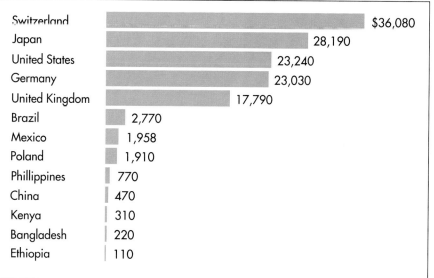

Switzerland	$36,080
Japan	28,190
United States	23,240
Germany	23,030
United Kingdom	17,790
Brazil	2,770
Mexico	1,958
Poland	1,910
Phillippines	770
China	470
Kenya	310
Bangladesh	220
Ethiopia	110

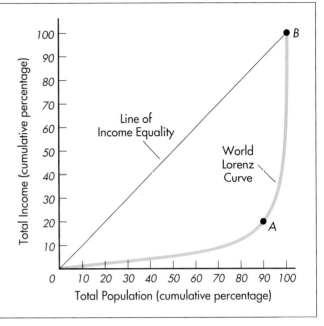

Figure 4
World Lorenz Curve
The Lorenz curve is typically used to illustrate the income distribution within countries. In this figure a Lorenz curve is drawn to compare how world income is distributed across countries. The bottom 90 percent of the world's population, residing in the less developed countries, accounts for 20 percent of the world's income, shown as point A. The richest 10 percent of the population, residing in the developed countries, accounts for 80 percent of total income, shown as point B. Source: World Bank, *World Development Report, 1994* (New York: Oxford University Press).

1.d. The Definition of Poverty

If income or per capita income is to be used as a measure of poverty, then the proper definition of *income* must be used. Economists can measure income before any government intervention affecting the distribution of income, after accounting for government cash transfers, or after accounting for government cash transfers and assistance like food or shelter.

The first of these measurements indicates what people would earn from the market system in the absence of government intervention. To obtain a good measure of this income figure is virtually impossible because the government is such an important part of the economic system in almost all countries, including the United States. The U.S. government transfers over $400 billion annually from taxpayers to various groups.

Poverty statistics published by the federal government are based on incomes that include earnings from cash transfers but often not in-kind transfers. **Cash transfers** are unearned funds given to certain sectors of the population. They include social security retirement benefits, disability pensions, and unemployment compensation to those who are temporarily out of work. **In-kind transfers**, or noncash transfers, are services or products provided to certain sectors of society. They include food purchased with food stamps and medical services provided under Medicaid. Although economists agree that these in-kind transfers increase the economic well-being of those who receive them, there is much debate over how they should be accounted for and the extent to which they should be added to money income for the purpose of defining *poverty*. For example, the official poverty rate measure does not account for in-kind transfers. If it did, the 1990 rate of 13.5 percent of the U.S. population who are in poverty would have been 11.0 percent.[2]

cash transfers:
money allocated away from one group in society to another

in-kind transfers:
the allocation of goods and services from one group in society to another

[2]*Economic Report of the President, 1992*, p. 143.

TABLE 1

Average Income Poverty Cutoffs for a Nonfarm Family of Four in the United States, 1959–1993

Year	Poverty Level	Year	Poverty Level
1959	$2,973	1982	$ 9,862
1960	3,022	1983	10,178
1966	3,317	1984	10,609
1969	3,743	1985	10,989
1970	3,968	1986	11,203
1975	5,500	1987	11,611
1976	5,815	1988	12,090
1977	6,191	1989	12,675
1978	6,662	1990	13,359
1979	7,412	1991	13,924
1980	8,414	1992	13,950
1981	9,287	1993	14,764

Sources: U.S. Bureau of the Census, *Current Population Reports*, series P-60, no. 174 (Washington, D.C.: U.S. Government Printing Office, 1992); *Social Security Bulletin*, Spring 1995.

The U.S. government uses after-transfers income to measure poverty, but does not include all such transfers. It adds market earnings, the cash equivalent of noncash transfers, and cash transfers to calculate family incomes. But it does not include food stamps, aid to families with dependent children (AFDC), or housing subsidies. In sum, the poverty measure is arbitrary. It is an arbitrary level of income, and income is an arbitrary measure of the ability to purchase necessities.

Table 1 lists the average poverty levels of income for a nonfarm family of four since 1959. Families with incomes above the cutoffs would be above the poverty level, in the eyes of the federal government.

Where does the arbitrary poverty income level come from? A 1955 study found that the average family in the United States spent about one-third of its income on food, so when the government decided to begin measuring poverty in the 1960s, it calculated the cost to purchase a meal that met a predetermined nutritional standard and multiplied that cost by 3. That is where it drew the poverty line. Since then, the official poverty-line income has been adjusted for inflation each year. In 1993, a family of four whose income, measured as noted above, fell below $14,764 was defined as being in poverty.

1.e. Poverty Distribution and Economic Trends

How many Americans fall below the poverty line? In 1994, more than 39 million U.S. residents received incomes that were lower than the cutoff. Figure 5 compares the number of people living in poverty and the percentage of the total population living in poverty (the incidence of poverty) for each year from 1960 to 1994. From 1960 to the late 1970s, the incidence of poverty declined rapidly. From the late 1970s until the early 1980s, the incidence of poverty rose; it then began to decline again after 1982. Small upswings in the incidence of poverty occurred in 1968 and 1974, and a large

Figure 5
The Trends of Poverty Incidence
The number of people classified as living in poverty is measured on the left vertical axis. The percentage of the population classified as living in poverty is measured on the right vertical axis. The number and the percentage declined steadily throughout the 1960s, rose during the recessions of 1969, 1974, 1981, and 1990 and fell during the economic growth between 1982 and 1990. Sources: U.S. Bureau of the Census, *Current Population Reports* (Washington, D.C.: U.S. Government Printing Office, 1994); *Economic Report of the President, 1995.*

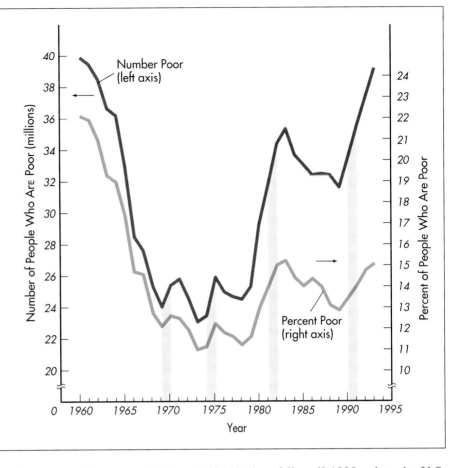

The health of the economy is a primary determinant of the incidence of poverty.

rise occurred between 1978 and 1982. It then fell until 1990, when the U.S. once again dipped into recession. It has continued to rise even as the economy grew in 1993 and 1994.

A major factor accounting for the incidence of poverty is the health of the economy. The economy grew at a fairly sustained rate between 1960 and 1969 and from 1982 through 1990. During both growth periods, the poverty rate fell. But from 1992 to 1994, the rate rose even as the economy improved. This surprised the U.S. Census Bureau officials who said, "This is somewhat surprising." They had expected the rate to fall.[3]

People are generally made better off by economic growth. Economic stagnation and recession throw the relatively poor out of their jobs and into poverty. Economic growth increases the number of jobs and draws people out of poverty and into the mainstream of economic progress.

Four recent recessions have had important impacts on the numbers of people thrown into poverty. The recession of 1969–1970 was relatively mild. Between 1969 and 1971, the unemployment rate rose from 3.4 to 5.8 percent, and the total number of people unemployed rose from 2,832,000 to 5,016,000. This recession halted the decline in poverty rates for two years. When the economy once again began to expand, the poverty rates dropped. The 1974 recession brought on another bout of unemployment that threw

---

[3]"Number of Poor Rises Despite Recession's End," M. L. Usdansky, *USA Today,* October 7, 1994, p. 1A.

Economic Development and Happiness

A nation's standard of living influences the attitudes of the nation's population toward life in general, although it is not the only factor. Year after year, the Danes, Swiss, Irish, and Dutch feel happier and more satisfied with life than do the French, Greeks, Italians, and Germans. Regardless of whether they are German-, French-, or Italian-speaking, the Swiss rank very high on life satisfaction—much higher than their German, French, and Italian neighbors. People in the Scandinavian countries generally are both prosperous and happy. However, the link between national affluence and

well-being isn't consistent. Germans, for instance, average more than double the per capita income of the Irish, but the Irish are happier. Similarly, although the developed nations all had higher per capita incomes than the Mexicans, the Mexicans stated a higher satisfaction with life than the populations of many of the developed nations. The overall pattern does show that wealthier nations tend to show higher levels of life satisfaction than poorer ones, but income and wealth are not the only factors influencing happiness. Related to wealth is the type of government under which citizens

live. The most prosperous nations have enjoyed stable democratic governments, and there is a link between a history of stable democracy and national well-being. The thirteen nations that have maintained democratic institutions continuously since 1920 all enjoy higher life satisfaction levels than do the eleven nations whose democracies developed after World War II.

Sources: Ronald Inglehart, *Culture Shift in Advanced Industrial Society* (Princeton: Princeton University Press, 1990); David G. Myers, *The Pursuit of Happiness* (New York: William Morrow and Company, Inc., 1992).

people into poverty. The 1974 recession was relatively serious, causing the unemployment rate to rise to 8.3 percent by 1975 and the number of unemployed to rise to 7,929,000. Once again, however, the poverty rate declined as the economy picked up after 1975. The recession of 1980–1982 threw the economy off track again. In 1979, the total number of people unemployed was 6,137,000; by 1982, a whopping 10,717,000 were without jobs. As the economy came out of this recession, the poverty rate began to decline, and it continued to decline as the economy grew throughout the 1980s. However, the poverty rate rose as the economy fell into recession in 1990 and struggled into 1992. The poverty rate of 14.2 percent in 1991 was the highest level in nearly three decades; the number of people living in poverty grew to 35.7 million.[4] Somewhat surprising was that the number of people in poverty and the incidence of poverty both grew in 1993 and 1994, years of economic growth. Some people point to this as evidence that the poverty measure is flawed, that it does not give an accurate indication of who and how many do not get proper nutrition and health care. Some argue that the poverty rate is really not nearly as high as these figures indicate; that government transfers and programs are not properly taken into account. Others argue that it is an indication that government programs must be increased, that not enough care is taken to provide for the poor. Still others point to the increase in the number of people working full time who do not earn more than the poverty level. Nearly 18 percent of the nation's full-time workers earned less than $14,000 in 1994 while only 12 percent were less than that figure (in real terms) in

---

[4]U.S. Bureau of the Census, *Statistical Abstract of the United States, 1994* (Washington, D.C.: U.S. Government Printing Office, 1994). *Social Security Bulletin, Annual Statistical Supplement,* 1994.

Incomes are unequally distributed in every nation. In less developed nations, the distinction between rich and poor is greater than in the industrial nations, although the per capita income is significantly less in the LDCs. For instance, although the per capita income in Nigeria is only seven percent of the per capita income in the United States, the wealthy in Lagos, Nigeria live very well, with large houses, servants, expensive clothes, and other accouterments of wealth. During the 1970s, many Nigerians became very wealthy as the price of oil surged and Nigerian oil production rose. Economic crisis and the collapse of oil prices since the late 1970s has led to a decline in Nigeria that wiped out the gains of the previous twenty years.

1980. These numbers indicate how the pay for unskilled jobs has declined over the last decade.

There are many controversies over the poverty measure. The measure makes no distinction between the needs of a three-month-old and a fourteen-year-old or between a rural family in a cold climate and an urban family in the subtropics. It draws no distinction between income and purchasing power. A welfare mom living on $400 a month is treated identically to a graduate student who earns $400 a month at a part-time job and borrows an additional $1,500 from her parents. Nor does it consider the problem of income from the underground economy—the income not reported or measured in income statistics. Nevertheless, the measure is used to determine how federal government money is to be allocated among states and regions and is used to support or not support anti-poverty programs.

RECAP

1. The Lorenz curve shows the degree to which incomes are distributed equally in a society.

2. The Lorenz curve bows down below the line of equality for all nations. It is less bowed for developed nations than for less developed countries, because income is more equally distributed in developed than in less developed nations.

3. There are two ways to measure poverty: with an absolute measure and with a relative measure. The Lorenz curve is a relative measure. Per capita income is an absolute measure.

4. Per capita income after cash and in-kind transfers is used by the U.S. government to define poverty.

5. Recessions increase the incidence of poverty; economic growth reduces the incidence of poverty.

2. THE POOR

Who are the poor?

Poverty is not a condition that randomly strikes women and men and white, black, and Hispanic families equally. Nor does it strike the educated and well trained in the same way it strikes the uneducated. The incidence of poverty itself is unequally distributed among sectors of the society.

2.a. Temporary and Permanent Poverty

If those who are poor at any one time are poor only temporarily, then their plight is only temporary. If people in poverty are able to improve their situation while others slip into poverty temporarily, the problem of poverty for society is not as serious as it is if poverty is a permanent condition once a person has slipped into it.

Studies indicate that approximately 25 percent of all Americans fall below the poverty line at some time in their lives. Many of these spells of poverty are relatively short; nearly 45 percent last less than a year. However, more than 50 percent of those in poverty at a particular time remain in poverty for at least ten years.[5]

One major determinant of an individual's income is age. A young person or a senior citizen has a much greater chance of suffering a low income than a person who is between thirty and sixty years old. Figure 6 shows the percentage of the population below the poverty level by race and age in 1992. The highest incidence of poverty by age occurs among those under eighteen years. The second highest occurs among those between eighteen and twenty-four. The third highest occurs among those twenty-five to thirty-four.

Poverty does not affect races, sexes, or different age groups equally.

Poverty does not affect all racial and all age groups equally. As Figure 7 shows, the percentages of the population of different groups that fall below the poverty level each year are not equal. Blacks and Hispanics carry a much heavier burden of poverty relative to the size of their populations than do whites.

Poverty does not affect males and females equally either. Approximately 35 percent of all families headed by a female have poverty-level incomes. Only 8 percent of all families headed by a male have incomes so low. More than 55 percent of households with a female head and children are living in poverty.

2.b. Causes of Poverty

What are the determinants of income?

The primary characteristic of those who fall below the poverty line is the lack of a job. In 1994, almost half of all such households were headed by people sixty-five years of age and over. Another 12 percent were headed by disabled people. Another 7 percent of such households were headed by women with children under six. Nonworking students constituted 5 percent of the poverty group. Thus, those not working accounted for nearly three-fourths of the poverty group.

The primary characteristic of those who fall below the poverty line is the lack of a job.

People who fall below the poverty line may have jobs but work less than full time, or their jobs may pay so little that their income does not exceed the poverty cutoff. For instance, a job paying $5.15 per hour for 40 hours a week

---

[5]Mary Jo Bane and David T. Ellwood, "Slipping into and out of Poverty," *Journal of Human Resources* 21, no. 1 (Winter 1986), pp. 1–23.

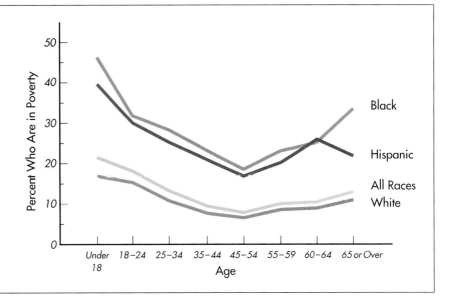

Figure 6
Age, Race, and Poverty
The young and old constitute most of the poverty group: 24 percent of the children under age six live in poverty. And 12.9 percent of people sixty-five or older also live in poverty. The poverty rate among whites is 11.6 percent; among blacks, 33.3 percent; and among Hispanics, 29.3 percent. Source: *Statistical Abstract of the United States, 1994,* Table 730.

and 50 weeks a year yields an income of $10,300, fully $4,000 below the poverty level.

Place of residence also affects a person's ability to earn income. A little over half of the poor live in big cities, where they tend to be concentrated downtown. The remainder live in rural areas.

The less education an individual has, the lower the income that individual earns. The less education an individual has, the greater the chance that individual will experience poverty. A significant percentage of those in poverty have less than eight years of education. Fully 25 percent of the people with less than eight years of education fall below the poverty level of income.

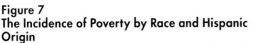

The less education a person has, the greater his or her chance of experiencing poverty.

Figure 7
The Incidence of Poverty by Race and Hispanic Origin
The incidence of poverty is higher for blacks and Hispanics than it is for whites. Good times help whites more than they help other races, and bad times harm whites less than they harm other races. Sources: U.S. Bureau of the Census, *Current Population Reports* (Washington, D.C.: U.S. Government Printing Office, 1988, 1991, 1994); U.S. Department of Commerce, *Statistical Abstract of the United States, 1994.*

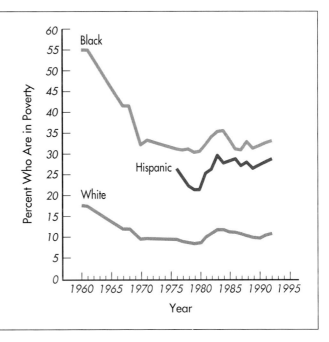

Only 4 percent of those with one year or more of college fall below the poverty cutoff. Lack of education prevents people from securing well-paying jobs. Without the human capital obtained from education or training programs, finding a job that is stable and will not disappear during a recession is very difficult. Even someone who has the desire to work but has no exceptional abilities and has not acquired the skills necessary for a well-paying job is unlikely to escape poverty completely. Minorities and women, the young, the disabled, and the old have disproportionately less education than the rest of the population and as a result have a higher likelihood of falling into poverty.

RECAP

1. Many people experience poverty only temporarily. Nearly 45 percent of the spells of poverty last less than a year. However, nearly 50 percent of those in poverty remain there for at least ten years.

2. The highest incidences of poverty occur among those who are under twenty-one or over sixty-five.

3. The incidence of poverty is much higher among blacks and Hispanics than it is among whites.

4. A poor person may be poor because of age, lack of a job, lack of education, or place of residence.

3. GOVERNMENT ANTIPOVERTY POLICIES

How does the government try to reduce poverty?

Why are economists and others concerned with income inequality and poverty? One reason might be normative. People might have compassion for those who have less than they do, or people might not like to see the squalid living conditions endured by some in poverty. In other words, the existence of poverty may mean lower levels of utility for members of society not in poverty. If increases in poverty mean decreases in utility, then people will want less poverty. They will be willing and able to purchase less poverty by allocating portions of their income or their time to alleviating the problem.

Another reason for concern about income inequality and poverty might be positive, or not dependent on value judgments. Perhaps the inequality is a result of inefficiency, and a correction of the situation that creates the inefficiency will improve the functioning of the economy. For instance, if inequality is partly the result of a market failure (see the next chapter for a full discussion of externalities and market failures), then the economic system will function more efficiently after the market failure is corrected. If education provides benefits for society that are not taken into account in individual decisions to acquire education, for example, then too few people acquire education. People who would have acquired education if the positive benefits for society had been subsidized, but did not, are wasted resources. These people would have earned more income; fewer would have fallen into poverty; and the distribution of income might have been more equal. In this sense, the number of people in poverty and the existence of income inequality provide indications that allocative efficiency has failed to occur.

The government is often called on to resolve market failures. If income inequality and poverty are the result of such failures, then the government plays a role in resolving the failures and thereby decreasing poverty and reducing income inequality. If poverty is distasteful to society, then citizens, by paying taxes and through their votes, may ask the government to reduce poverty. Whatever the rationale, positive or normative, the fact is that the government is involved in antipoverty programs and in the attempt to reduce income inequality. Having accepted this fact, several questions arise. For instance, is the government carrying out its antipoverty programs efficiently? What are the ramifications of the government programs? Have the programs reduced poverty?

Once levels of poverty and degrees of inequality are identified, the first question to be answered is whether to reallocate resources to reduce them. If resources are to be reallocated, the next question is how to reallocate them. Clearly, an important way to decrease poverty is by increasing the rate of growth of real GDP and avoiding recessions. The incidence of poverty typically declines during periods of economic growth and rises during recessionary periods. Government policies designed to stimulate economic growth over the short and long terms may be important weapons against poverty. Whether these policies are effective in reducing poverty, and the policies themselves, are the subject matter of macroeconomics. Another way to approach the poverty problem is through tax and transfer programs.

3.a. Tax Policy

progressive income tax:
a tax whose rate increases as income increases

proportional tax:
a tax whose rate does not change as the tax base changes

regressive tax:
a tax whose rate decreases as the tax base changes

One approach to reducing poverty is to provide people with enough income to bring them above the poverty level. Funds used to supplement the incomes of the poor must come from somewhere. Many societies adopt a Robin Hood approach, taxing the rich to give to the poor. Income taxes can influence income distribution through their impact on after-tax income. Taxes may be progressive, proportional, or regressive.

A **progressive income tax** is a tax that rises as income rises—the marginal tax rate increases as income increases. If someone with an annual income of $20,000 pays $5,000 in taxes while someone else with an annual income of $40,000 pays $12,000 in taxes, the tax rate is progressive. The first person is paying a 25 percent rate, and the second is paying a 30 percent rate.

A **proportional tax** is a tax whose rate does not change as the tax base changes. The rate of a proportional income tax remains the same at every level of income. If the tax rate is 20 percent, then individuals who earn $10,000 or $100,000 pay 20 percent.

A **regressive tax** is a tax whose rate decreases as the tax base changes. The social security tax is regressive; a specified rate is paid on income up to a specified level. On income beyond that level, no social security taxes are paid. In 1994, the cutoff level of income was $60,000 and the tax rate was 7.65 percent. A person earning $300,000 paid no more social security taxes than someone earning $60,000.

A progressive tax rate tends to reduce income inequality; a proportional tax does not affect income distribution; and a regressive tax increases inequality. The progressive tax takes larger percentages of income from high-income members of society than it takes from low-income members. This tends to equalize after-tax incomes. In the United States, the federal income tax is progressive. The tax rate rises from zero to 36 percent as income rises (39 percent for incomes above $1 million).

3.b. Transfers

The main transfer programs are social insurance, cash welfare or public assistance, in-kind transfers, and employment programs. Social security—officially known as Old Age, Survivors, and Disability Insurance (OASDI) and listed as FICA on your paycheck stubs—is the largest social insurance program. It helps a family replace income that is lost when a worker retires in old age, becomes severely disabled, or dies. Coverage is nearly universal, so the total amount of money involved is immense—nearly $200 billion annually. Two-thirds of the aged rely on social security for more than half of their income.

Unemployment insurance provides temporary benefits to regularly employed people who become temporarily unemployed. Funded by a national tax on payrolls levied on firms with eight or more workers, the system is run by state governments. Benefits normally amount to about 50 percent of a worker's usual wage.

Aid to Families with Dependent Children (AFDC) is the largest cash welfare program. The average AFDC family is headed by a mother with two small children and receives about $300 per month. Recipients of AFDC must not have savings of more than $1,000 and must not earn more than about $8,000.

Supplemental Security Income (SSI) ranks second among cash welfare programs. Fully 65 percent of the SSI population is blind or otherwise disabled. The rest are over age sixty-five. Unlike social security recipients, who are *entitled* to receive benefits because they are a certain age or otherwise qualify, recipients of SSI must meet certain disability requirements or be of a certain age and must have incomes below about $4,500 per year.

About 60 percent of all poor households receive in-kind transfers. The largest of these programs is Medicaid (for a discussion of Medicaid and the medical-care industry, see the chapter "The Economics of Aging and Health Care"). Medicaid provides federal funds to states to help them cover the costs of long-term medical and nursing home care. Second in magnitude is the food stamp program, which gives households coupons that are redeemable at grocery stores. The amounts vary with income and household size. Other programs include jobs and training directed toward disadvantaged workers and the Head Start program, an education program available to poor children. Total government outlays for social service (welfare) programs run more than $700 billion annually. As shown in Figure 8, the 1995 federal budget allocated $87.5 billion to Medicaid, and about $20 billion to each of the other welfare programs except for the child nutrition program, which was allocated $7.2 billion. In 1970 there were 2 million families on AFDC; in 1994 there were 5 million.

3.c. The Effectiveness of Welfare Programs

In 1964, President Lyndon Johnson declared "unconditional war on poverty." In 1967, total transfers were about $10 billion. After nearly a quarter-century of increasing outlays to reduce poverty, is the war being won? Unfortunately, there is no easy or straightforward answer to that question. In fact, there is disagreement about whether antipoverty programs have reduced or increased

Figure 8
Welfare Expenditures, 1995
In 1995, government funds allocated to welfare programs included Medicaid, food stamps, Supplemental Security Income, housing assistance, Aid to Families with Dependent Children (AFDC), and child nutrition. The largest expenditure is for Medicaid, nearly four times more than any other welfare program.
Source: 1995 Budget of the U.S. National Vital Statistics System.

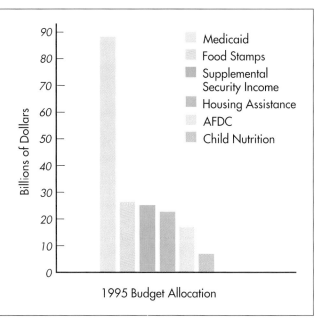

poverty. Some people maintain that without the programs, income inequality and poverty would have been much more severe. Others argue that welfare has been a drag on the economy and may have made poverty and inequality worse than they otherwise would have been.

It is impossible to compare what did happen with what would have happened in the absence of the government's programs. All economists can do is look at what actually occurred. The distribution of money income among families in 1929 and 1992 is shown in Figure 9. The Lorenz curve has

Figure 9
Income Distribution over Time
Income distribution in the United States is more equal now than in 1929. This is shown by the movement of the Lorenz curve in toward the line of income equality.
Sources: World Bank, *World Development Report, 1994* (New York: Oxford University Press); U.S. Bureau of the Census, *Current Population Reports* (Washington, D.C.: U.S. Government Printing Office, 1988, 1992, 1994).

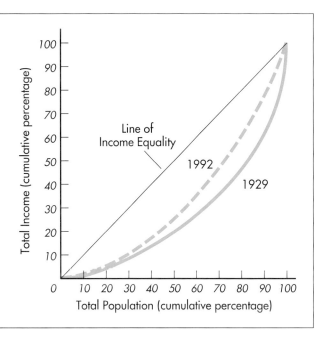

shifted in toward the line of income equality since 1929. In 1929, the lowest 20 percent of the population had 4 percent of the income and the top 5 percent had 30 percent of the income. In 1992, the lowest 20 percent had about 4 percent and the top 5 percent had about 18 percent.

Another measure of income distribution is provided by a **Gini ratio**. The Gini ratio is a measure of the dispersion of income that ranges between 0 and 1. The Gini ratio measures the deviation between the Lorenz curve and the line of perfect equality; it is a measure of the area between the Lorenz curve and the line of perfect equality divided by the total area if one family had all of the income. A lower Gini value indicates less dispersion in the income distribution: a Gini of 0 would occur if every family had the exact same amount of income; a Gini of 1 would occur if all income accrued to only one family. Figure 10 shows that from 1947 to 1968 the dispersion of income fell gradually but has risen slowly since.

Figure 11 shows the annual expenditures on poverty programs along with the incidence of poverty from 1960 to 1990. The incidence-of-poverty curve is taken from Figure 5. During the 1960s, as transfers and spending increased, the incidence of poverty fell. Since the early 1970s, transfers and spending have increased much more rapidly than in the previous decade, but the incidence of poverty has changed little, and in fact, it rose during the recessions of the early 1980s and the early 1990s.

Those who argue that welfare programs are a drag on the economy and may make poverty and income inequality worse typically focus on the disincentives created by the transfers.

3.c.1. **Disincentives Created by the Welfare System**   Incentives for both the rich and the poor to work hard and increase their productivity may be reduced by programs that take from the rich and give to the poor. Those paying taxes may ask themselves, "Why should I work an extra hour every day if all the extra income does is pay additional taxes?" Someone who gets to keep

Gini ratio:
a measure of the dispersion of income ranging between 0 and 1; 0 means all families have the same income; 1 means one family has all of the income

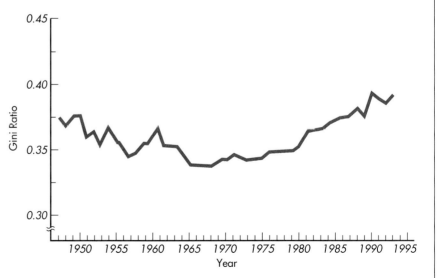

Figure 10
The Gini Ratio
The Gini ratio is a measure of the dispersion of income that ranges between 0 and 1. A lower value indicates less dispersion in the income distribution: a Gini of 0 would occur if every family had the exact same amount of income, while a Gini of 1 would occur if all income accrued to only one family. Figure 10 shows that from 1947 to 1968 the dispersion of income fell gradually. Since then the dispersion has risen slowly.
Source: *Economic Report of the President,* 1994.

Figure 11
Spending and Poverty, 1960–1994
Curves representing total government spending in real (1987) billions of dollars on poverty programs since 1960 and the incidence of poverty since 1960 are shown. Total expenditures on antipoverty programs in equal purchasing power terms (real terms) are measured on the left vertical axis, and the percent of population in poverty is shown on the right vertical axis. During the 1960s, the incidence of poverty decreased as spending increased. Since then, spending has continued to increase, but the incidence of poverty has not declined.
Source: Department of Commerce, *Statistical Abstract of the United States, 1994.*

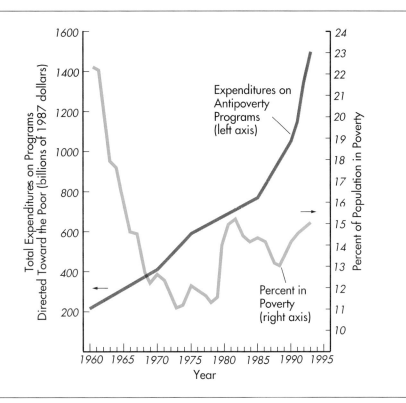

only 60 cents out of the next dollar earned has less incentive to earn that dollar than if he or she got to keep it all.

Those who receive benefits may lose the incentive to change their status. Why should someone take a job paying $6,000 per year when he or she can remain unemployed and receive $8,000? Someone out of work might wonder, "Why should I spend eight hours a day in miserable working conditions when I can relax every day and bring home nearly the same amount of income?" If incentives to work are weak, then the total income created in the economy is less than it otherwise would be. Less income and lower economic growth mean more people in poverty.

3.c.2. Welfare Dependency Some have argued that the welfare system causes welfare dependency—that children who grow up on welfare are likely to become welfare recipients as adults and to have children who eventually become dependent on welfare. Evidence that such a situation occurs is not strong, but the incentives for it to occur do exist. Society tries to provide families with decent living standards but does not want transfers to go to those who do not need them. As a result, transfer programs are designed to provide the greatest benefits to the people with the lowest incomes. As incomes rise, benefits decrease.

Transfer programs are designed much like a progressive income tax. The higher the person's income, the fewer benefits he or she gets. In 1990, a family of four with no earned income could receive about $260 worth of food stamps per month. A family of four with $100 of income per month could receive only about $230 worth of food stamps per month. For earning $100, the second family received food stamps worth $30 less than the stamps received by the nonworking family. This is a 30 percent marginal penalty on working. A family of four with a monthly income of $300 could receive $210 of benefits per month; a family of four with $400 could receive only $130 worth of benefits per month. The additional $100 of income, from $300 to $400 per month, meant a reduction in benefits of $80 per month. This is an 80 percent marginal penalty on working. Eventually, as earned income rises, benefits are reduced dollar for dollar—there is a 100 percent marginal penalty on working.

3.d. Welfare Reform

workfare:
a plan that requires welfare recipients to accept public service jobs or participate in job training

Unhappiness with the results of transfer programs has led to various attempts at welfare reform. Welfare reform has taken two tacks: tying benefits to work and establishing parents' responsibility for children.

Workfare is the name given to plans that require welfare recipients to accept public service jobs or participate in job training. To receive benefits, a person must accept a job provided by the state. To receive AFDC, the head of the household must agree to search for work or obtain training or education. Many states have introduced a work-for-pay component to their welfare programs. In 1988, Congress passed the Family Support Act. This legislation provides federal funding and considerable flexibility to states in designing programs that will encourage work and reduce welfare participation. Under the new legislation, states can make participation in a training or employment program mandatory and can impose penalties on welfare recipients who refuse to accept a job that is offered to them.

The second approach to welfare reform focuses on children and child support. The incidence of poverty among families with children and a female head of household has always been high. More than half of these families are poor, a condition that has changed little since 1930. However, sixty years ago there were fewer such families. Today, as a result of increased divorce rates and more out-of-wedlock childbearing, more than one in five children live in a female-headed family, though in nine out of ten cases these children have a living father. The proportion of all children under age eighteen who are dependent on AFDC rose from around 3 percent in 1960 to 11 percent in 1985. These developments led to an interest in establishing parental financial responsibility for children.

3.e. Equity and Efficiency

Efficiency requires that goods and services go to those willing and able to pay the price. The allocation of goods and services on the basis of equity would provide goods to those who meet the definition of *equity*. For instance, if *equity* means "equality," then all persons would receive the same goods and services whether or not they had the ability to pay. If *equity* means "goods and services go to those with the greatest need," then some definition of *need* must be created. *Equity* requires a definition.

There are two general definitions of *equity*: the means test and the ends test. The *ends test* examines the existing situation, the results of whatever has gone on in the past. For instance, the distribution of income is more equal now than it was fifty years ago. This is an end result of whatever occurred

The top 20 percent of house-hold income earners in the United States earn 44.6 percent of total household income while the bottom 20 percent earn just 4.6 percent. The government provides assistance to the lowest rungs of income recipients through food stamps, Aid to Families with Dependent Children, Medicare, Medicaid, and public housing. In urban areas, public housing known as the projects are multistory buildings housing hundreds of families. In rural areas, the gov-ernment-provided housing often takes the form of wide trailers located on the outskirts of small towns.

during the past fifty years. The *means test* considers the means to achieve the end. If the opportunity to earn income were equally distributed, then accord-ing to the means definition, equity would occur even if the existing distribu-tion of income were unequal.

Policymakers who rely on the ends test tend to support policies directed toward changing the existing distribution of income, such as providing as-sistance to the poor by taking from the rich. A problem with the ends test is that it may be antithetical to efficiency. Policies intended to create a more equal distribution of income can reduce incentives to earn income and thereby reduce the efficiency with which the economy functions.

Policymakers who advocate a means test of equity look not at whether income is distributed equally but instead at whether the opportunity to earn income is distributed equally. To them, *equity* means "equal opportunities to earn, to accumulate wealth, to obtain human capital, and to be an entrepre-neur." There need be no tradeoff between efficiency and equity if the means definition is used. Efficiency is achieved when entry and exit are free and there are no market failures. Once barriers are erected, efficiency is decreased. Thus, policies that tear down the barriers and resolve the market failures increase the efficiency of the market.

3.f. **The Negative Income Tax and Family Allowance Plans**

The solution to the welfare system problems most often proposed by econo-mists is the **negative income tax (NIT)**—a tax system that transfers increas-ing amounts of income to households earning incomes below some specified level. The lower the income, the more that is transferred. As income rises above the specified level, a tax is applied. Economists like the NIT because, at least in theory, it attacks the distribution of income and reduces poverty without reducing efficiency.

Suppose policymakers determine that a family of four is to be guaranteed an income of $10,000. If the family earns nothing, then it will get a transfer of $10,000. If the family earns some income, it will receive $10,000 less a tax on the earned income. If the tax rate is 50 percent, then for each dollar earned, $.50 will be taken out of the $10,000 transfer.

With a 50 percent tax rate, there would always be some incentive to work under the NIT system because each additional dollar of earnings would bring the recipient of the transfer $.50 in additional income. At some income level, the tax taken would be equal to the transfer of $10,000. This level of income is referred to as the *break-even income level*. The break-even income level in the case of a $10,000 guaranteed income and a 50 percent tax rate is $20,000. Once a family of four earns more than $20,000, its taxes exceed the transfer of $10,000.

The break-even level of income is determined by the income floor and the tax rate:

$$\text{Break-even income} = \frac{\text{income floor}}{\text{negative income tax rate}}$$

If the guaranteed income floor is $13,000 and the tax rate is 50 percent, then the break-even income would be $26,000. If the guaranteed income floor is $13,000 but the tax rate is 33 percent, then the break-even income would be $39,000.

In order for the negative income tax to eradicate poverty, the guaranteed level of income has to be equal to the poverty level, $14,764 in 1993. But if the tax rate is less than 100 percent, the break-even income level will be above the poverty level and families who are not officially considered "poor" will also receive benefits. At a guaranteed income level of $14,764 and a 33 percent tax rate, the break-even income level is $44,739. All families of four earning less than $44,739 would receive some income benefits.

For people now covered by welfare programs, the negative income tax would increase the incentive to work, and that is what proponents of the neg-ative income tax like. However, for people who are too well off to receive welfare but would become eligible for NIT payments, the negative income tax might create work disincentives. It provides these families with more income, and they may choose to buy more leisure.

The possibility of disincentive effects worried both social reformers and legislators, so in the late 1960s the government carried out a number of experiments to estimate the effect of the negative income tax on the supply of labor. Families from a number of American cities were offered negative-income-tax payments in return for allowing social scientists to monitor their behavior. A matched set of families, who were not given NIT payments, were also observed. The idea was to compare the behavior of the families receiv-ing NIT payments with that of the families who did not receive them. The experiments lasted about a decade and showed pretty clearly that the net effects of the negative income tax on labor supply were quite small.

Even though disincentive effects did not seem to occur to any great extent, the negative income tax has not gained political acceptability. One reason is the high break-even income level. Politicians are not very supportive of programs that may provide income transfers to a family earning significantly more than the poverty income level. Another reason is the transfer of dollars rather than in-kind benefits (food and medical care). Policymakers do not look favorably on the idea of giving a family cash that the family can use as it pleases.

RECAP

1. Tax policies can affect the distribution of income. A progressive income tax has a rate that increases as income increases. Thus, a progressive tax reduces income inequality. A proportional tax has a rate that is the same no matter the income level. A regressive tax has a rate that declines as income increases.

2. The federal income tax in the United States is slightly progressive, with rates rising from zero to 36 percent as income increases.

3. Spending programs used by the government to fight poverty include social insurance, cash welfare, in-kind transfers, and employment programs.

4. Incomes in the United States have become more equally distributed since 1929.

5. There have been two approaches to welfare reform: workfare and establishing parents' financial responsibility.

6. *Equity* can be defined as an end or as the means to an end. Defined as an end, *equity* means "equal distribution of income." Defined as the means to an end, *equity* means "equal opportunities to earn income."

7. Economists often propose the negative income tax as a way to resolve the welfare issue. It has not gained political acceptability, however.

SUMMARY

▲▼ **Are incomes distributed equally in the United States?**

1. The Lorenz curve illustrates the degree of income inequality. §1.a

2. If the Lorenz curve corresponds with the line of income equality, then incomes are distributed equally. If the Lorenz curve bows down below the line of income equality, then income is distributed in such a way that more people earn low incomes than earn high incomes. §1.a

3. As a rule, incomes are distributed more unequally in less developed countries than in developed countries. §1.b

▲▼ **How is poverty measured, and does poverty exist in the United States?**

4. Poverty is a measure of how well basic human needs are being met. Poverty is both a relative and an absolute concept. §1.c

5. Income consists of resource earnings and transfers. Transfers may be in cash or in kind.

The distribution of income in the United States is more unequal when only market earnings are considered than it is when transfers as well as market earnings are considered. §1.d

6. The incidence of poverty decreases as the economy grows and increases as the economy falls into recession. §1.e

▲▼ **Who are the poor?**

7. Many people fall below the poverty line for a short time only. However, a significant core of people remain in poverty for at least ten years. §2.a

8. The poor are primarily those without jobs (the youngest and oldest members of society), those residing in the centers of large cities and in rural areas, and those without education. §2.b

▲▼ **What are the determinants of income?**

9. Age, a lack of education, and a lack of a full-time or well-paying job are the primary determinants of income. §2.b

▲▼ **How does the government try to reduce poverty?**

10. Tax policies can be used to alter income distribution. A progressive tax takes a higher rate from higher-income groups than from lower-income groups, thus reducing income inequality. §3.a

11. Transfer programs are used to fight poverty. The main transfer programs are social insurance, cash welfare or public assistance, in-kind transfers, and employment programs. §3.b

12. Welfare systems may reduce incentives to work and thereby harm the economy and cause more poverty. §3.c.1

13. Two approaches to welfare reform are tying benefits to work (workfare) and establishing parental financial responsibility. §3.d

14. *Equity* can be defined as an end or as the means to an end. *Equity* defined as an end is judged on the basis of actual income distributions. *Equity* defined as the means to an end is judged on the basis of equal opportunities to earn income, not on the existing income distribution. §3.e

15. The negative income tax is often proposed as a solution to the disincentives created by welfare. The negative income tax would provide income to the lowest-income families. The lower the income, the greater the benefit received by the family. As family income rose, the amount of income transferred to the family would decrease until it reached some break-even level of income. §3.f

KEY TERMS

Lorenz curve §1.a
cash transfers §1.d
in-kind transfers §1.d
progressive income tax §3.a
proportional tax §3.a

regressive tax §3.a
Gini ratio §3.c
workfare §3.d
negative income tax (NIT) §3.f

EXERCISES

1. What is a Lorenz curve? What would the curve look like if income were equally distributed? Could the curve ever bow upward above the line of income equality?

2. Why does the health of the economy affect the number of people living in poverty?

3. What would it mean if the poverty income level of the United States were applied to Mexico?

4. What is the difference between a means and an ends definition of *equity*? What policies in force today would not be used under the means test of equality?

5. What positive arguments can be made for reducing income inequality? What normative arguments are made for reducing income inequality?

6. What does it mean to say that poverty is a luxury good?

7. Are people who are poor today in the United States likely to be poor for the rest of their lives? Under what conditions is generational poverty likely to exist?

8. Use the following information to plot a Lorenz curve.

Percent of Population	Percent of Income
20	5
40	15
60	35
80	65
100	100

9. If the incidence of poverty decreases during periods when the economy is growing and increases during periods when the economy is in recession, what government policies might be used to reduce poverty most effectively?

10. If the arguments for reducing income inequality and poverty are normative, why rely on the government to reduce the inequality? Why doesn't the private market resolve the problem?

11. How could transfer programs (welfare programs) actually increase the number of people in poverty?

12. What is the difference between in-kind and cash transfers? Which might increase the utility of the recipients the most? Why is there political resistance to the negative income tax?

13. Is it possible to eradicate poverty? The government's definition of poverty is a family of four with reported income less than $14,764. According to a recent study by the Heritage Foundation, this figure does not include the housing that 40 percent of those in poverty own or the cars that 62 percent own. Nor does it consider how the poorest 20 percent of households manage to consume twice as much as they earn. Is poverty a relative concept or an absolute concept?

14. Consider the following three solutions offered to get rid of homelessness and discuss whether any would solve the problem. First, provide permanent housing for all who are homeless. Second, provide free hospital care for the one-third of homeless who are mentally ill. Third, provide subsidies for the homeless to purchase homes.

15. What is the relationship between the Gini coefficient and the Lorenz curve? Illustrate your answer using question 8.

COOPERATIVE LEARNING EXERCISE

Divide the class into groups of 4 or 5 people. The groups are then to be classified into As, Bs, Cs, and Ds. Each group is to determine what would occur to the poverty rate (the incidence of poverty) if the event corresponding to their letter occurred. A spokesperson from each group will explain the answer. The groups will need to develop a rationale or basis for their results.

A: The poverty threshold was adjusted for the age of the individuals in a family.

B: The poverty threshold was adjusted for the different costs of living in different parts of the country.

C: The poverty threshold was adjusted for the number of adults in a family of four. (In other words, the threshold would differ if the family was 3 children and an adult rather than 2 adults and 2 children).

D: The poverty threshold was adjusted to reflect whether the head of the household was a female or a male.

Middle Class Grows in Size and Wealth

Moscow—The store shelves are full now, and the splinter-ridden toilet paper and colorless clothes are gone.

Now they're packed with Pop Tarts and Reebok running shoes.

Long bread lines no longer dot Moscow's landscape as in winters past. Instead, there are new 24-hour Tex-Mex restaurants.

And a middle class that can afford what once were luxuries is quickly emerging.

Contrary to the impression of deprivation and product inferiority, residents here say the real story now is how much their country has changed only four years after Western-style economic reforms were introduced.

"The Western caricature of Russia as a destitute country on the verge of collapse could not be more wrong," says Anders Aslund of the Stockholm Institute of East European Economics. It's not falling apart, but coming together. Russia has already become a market economy. Shortages and risks of famine are over."

But experts warn the country is not out of the woods yet.

The average monthly income is still only $100, the ruble is trading at an all-time low of 4,133 to $1,

and inflation is 18% a month and rising quickly.

Worst of all, economists fear, the very success of Russia's reforms, like a market-style economy and privatization of state property, could eventually lead to their demise.

"The gap between the rich and poor is going to grow a social explosion, a revolution, a mass unrest," says Russian Studies fellow Ariel Cohen of the conservative Heritage Foundation.

"Most Russian people are not better off today than they were two years ago."

But at times it sure looks like it.

A recent survey in the popular weekly newspaper *Argumenty I Fakty* shows:

- 30% of Russians now earn 500,000 rubles, or about $125 a month—a new middle class.

- 5% of Russians earn about 1 million rubles, or $250 a month—a new upper middle class.

- 3.5% of Russians earn more than 1 million rubles a month—and they are relatively rich.

"Whether it's a street-level kiosk or a big business, reforms have given

us an opportunity," says Maxim Ignatiev, 33, managing director of Reebok Russia and one of the country's new wealthy and powerful elite. "It has opened up a door."

And there are lots of them, thanks in part to businesses like IBM, 3M and Polaroid, which have been lured here by the reforms and hired thousands of English-speaking Russians. . . .

Nearly everything is available here, but at a price.

Surveys show Moscow is now the world's third most-expensive city after Tokyo and Osaka, Japan. . . .

It's no wonder that many elderly Russians, some so poor they can't afford milk and cheese, equate Western-style reforms with chaos. . . .

"If [the reforms] helped everyone, we would welcome it with open arms," says retired teacher Elena Zaponova, 61. "But we're poorer than ever, with little chance of fitting into the new market. We're being written off."

Source: "Middle Class Grows in Size and Wealth," Jack Kelley, *USA Today*, Feb. 14, 1995, p. 1. Copyright 1995, *USA Today*. Reprinted with permission.

USA Today/February 14, 1995

Commentary

The market system does not guarantee equality of income. Income is earned by selling the use of resources. Thus those who own the most valuable resources receive the highest income. Similarly, the market system does not guarantee everyone will have everything they want or even that everyone will get the same amount of goods and services. Instead, those willing and able to pay the price will receive the goods and services. Those not willing or not able to pay the price will not get the goods and services. It is for these basic reasons that some people do not like the market outcome. The market system ensures that goods that people are willing and able to buy will be offered by suppliers willing and able to produce the goods. As the article notes, everything is available in the new Russia—but at a price.

The transition to a market economy in Russia is resulting in the outcomes expected of a market system. Some people, those with the most valuable resources, are earning high incomes; other people, those with the least valuable resources, are receiving low incomes. Incomes are being distributed unequally.

The question that is facing Russia is whether the market system will benefit sufficient numbers of people to ensure that a counterrevolution does not occur. The have-nots will try to alter the market outcome or to get rid of the market system altogether. Some of the have-nots will be the recently disenfranchised—those who received benefits from the communist or government-allocation economy and do not receive equal benefits in the market system. Some of the have-nots are the people without skills or luck to acquire incomes in the market sys-

tem. For instance, we would expect the uneducated, the unskilled, the elderly, and the infirm to have difficulties in the market system.

Income inequality is a fact of life in a market system. How a society decides to deal with those who are on the lower rungs of income distribution may determine whether a private property and market system continues to exist or whether government ownership will dominate. In the Preview to Chapter 3 we completed a questionnaire on allocation mechanisms. We discovered that even in the United States, citizens preferred government allocation of scarce resources over market allocation in many instances. Why did this preference exist? Perhaps the reason for a preference for government allocation over market allocation arises when people believe that only the rich will get the goods and services and that they might not be among those rich. People do not like unequal distribution of income when they are in the lower part of the income distribution.

As we noted in our discussion in Chapter 3, with scarce goods, someone gets them and someone doesn't. The allocation mechanism determines who receives and who doesn't. Our discussion also pointed out the incentives that arise under the various allocation systems. Only under the market system is it likely that standards of living will improve over time—that technological advances will occur and that everyone will be absolutely better off. Nevertheless, as noted in section 2 of this chapter, people in poverty in the United States will feel poor even though their income level is more than 100 times greater than in many parts of the world. This too is part of the market system.

35

Market Failure and Environmental Policy

FUNDAMENTAL QUESTIONS

1. Why might a market not allocate goods and services efficiently?
2. Why is an externality considered to be a source of market failure?
3. Why don't markets allocate public goods efficiently?
4. Why does the government get involved in environmental issues?
5. How do global environmental problems differ from domestic environmental problems?

How much are Americans willing to pay to make the Blue Ridge Mountains look bluer, to save the brook trout from acid rain, to make living next door to a chemical plant no riskier than smoking a few cigarettes a year, or to ensure that the ozone layer isn't destroyed? To achieve these goals might be expensive. Utility consumers in the Midwest might stagger under double-digit increases in the cost of electricity for several years; thousands of coal-mining jobs in Appalachia could be lost; the cost of a new car could rise by as much as $600 because of new emission standards; and productivity and income growth could slow appreciably. But fears of air-quality deterioration, acid rain, overflowing landfills, and global warming have spurred the public's call for government action.

The government plays an important role in environmental issues. The rationale for government intervention is either to protect the public interest or to change an undesirable market outcome. In the environmental arena, the public interest rationale for government intervention stems from the failure of market-based economies to automatically provide the level of environmental quality that consumers desire. In this chapter we discuss the market failure problem and examine solutions to it.

PREVIEW

1. MARKETS AND EFFICIENCY

We have seen how the market system works. Profit-seeking entrepreneurs undertake those activities in which the profit potential is highest, ensuring that resources flow to their most highly valued uses. In addition, we have seen that entrepreneurs or firms provide what consumers want by using resources efficiently, and consumers get what they want at the lowest possible prices. Markets, demand and supply, and the resulting equilibrium prices allocate goods and services and resources so that no one could be made better off without making someone else worse off. Economists refer to this as economic efficiency.

1.a. Perfect Competition

Economic efficiency results when perfect competition prevails.

We have also learned that if entrepreneurs are free to enter and exit alternative activities in their quest for profit, and if no one producer can affect the market price, then consumers get what they want at a price that equals the marginal cost of production, and resources are paid their marginal revenue products—including entrepreneurs, who earn a normal profit. Thus, the result of perfect competition is economic efficiency.

Figure 1 shows a perfectly competitive market; the equilibrium price and quantity are the economically efficient price and quantity. A different price would mean that consumers are not getting what they want at the lowest possible price or that resources are not being used efficiently. But there is no reason for the price and quantity to be different from that determined in the perfectly competitive market, because a higher price results in a surplus and a movement back to equilibrium, and a lower price leads to a shortage and a movement back to equilibrium. In short, the market works.

1.b. Imperfect Competition

The perfectly competitive market "works" as long as the conditions of perfect competition are met. A firm other than a perfectly competitive firm can set a price that is not equal to marginal cost. And if consumers and producers do not know everything about the market, if information is not perfect, price or quantity can be "too high" or "too low." But how much do these real-world situations cause us to diverge from the economically efficient prices and quantities? The monopolistic competitor produces differentiated goods because that is what consumers want; the oligopolist or monopolist may earn above-normal profit, and the monopsonist may pay resources less than their marginal revenue products as long as entry is restricted. If entry is not restricted or if the potential for entry by profit-seeking entrepreneurs exists whenever above-normal profits are earned (what we earlier referred to as contestable markets), these situations correspond closely to the results of perfect competition. Although we might not achieve the results of our textbook description of perfect competition, we can argue that the markets in the real world tend to move toward economic efficiency. The markets tend to work even if perfect competition does not hold.

Figure 1
The Efficiency of the Market System
In a perfectly competitive market, equilibrium price and quantity are the efficient price and quantity. A different price would mean that consumers are not getting what they want at the lowest possible price or that resources are not being used efficiently. But there is no reason for the price and quantity to be different from that determined in the perfectly competitive market, because a higher price results in a surplus and a movement back to equilibrium, and a lower price leads to a shortage and a movement back to equilibrium. In short, the market works.

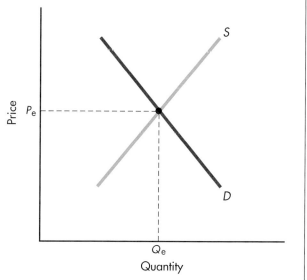

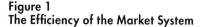

1.c. **Market Failure**

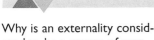

Why might a market not allocate goods and services efficiently?

market failure:
the failure of the market system to achieve economic efficiency

However, even if the conditions of perfect competition hold, there are situations where the market *fails* to allocate goods and services efficiently. If consumers do not have to pay a price that covers the full cost of producing a product or if producers do not have to pay all their costs of production, then "too much" or "too little" might be produced. When this occurs, economists refer to a **market failure**. A market failure occurs when the unrestrained operations of a market (a free market) generate an output level that is different from the economically efficient level.

2. EXTERNALITIES AND PUBLIC GOODS: MARKET FAILURES

Why is an externality considered to be a source of market failure?

In the chapter "Capital, Land, and Entrepreneurial Ability," we discussed the market for natural resources, and you saw how the market functions to ensure that resources are used at a rate that maximizes their value. If the market for natural resources allocates resources to their most highly valued use today and in the future, why do we hear so much about the depletion of the ozone layer, the destruction of the rain forest, the pollution of the oceans and rivers, and the depletion of wildlife? If the market for labor ensures that people acquire skills and education when doing so is valuable, then why are dropout rates so high? Part of the answer may stem from market failures.

Market failures occur when consumers or producers do not have to bear the full costs of transactions they undertake.

Problems may arise in market economies when private individuals and businesses lack incentives to take full account of the consequences of their actions. When consumers or producers do not have to bear the full costs of transactions they undertake, a market failure is said to have occurred. These market failures can be traced to two sources: externalities and public goods.

2.a. **The Definition of Externalities**

private costs:
costs borne by the individual involved in the transaction that created the costs

A business firm knows how much it costs to employ workers, and it knows the costs of purchasing materials or constructing buildings. An individual who buys a new car or pays for a pizza knows exactly what the cost will be. Such costs are **private costs**: They are costs borne solely by the individuals involved in the transaction that created the costs. Many environmental problems arise, however, because the costs of an individual's actions are *not* borne directly by that individual. When a firm pollutes the air or water, or when a tourist leaves trash in a park, the costs of these actions are not easily determined and are not borne by the individual or firm creating them. This situation represents a market failure because the price of the good and the equilibrium quantity produced and consumed do not reflect the full costs of producing or consuming the good. In this sense, "too much" or "too little" is produced.

Consider an oil tanker that runs aground and dumps crude oil into a pristine ocean area teeming with wildlife, or a public beach where people litter, or even your classrooms where people leave their cups, used papers, and food wrappers on the floor. A cost is involved in these actions: the crude oil may kill wildlife and ruin fishing industries, the trash may discourage families from using the beach, and the trash in the classroom may distract from the discussions and lectures. But in none of these cases is the cost of the action solely borne by the individuals who took the action. Instead, the cost is also borne by those who were not participants in the activity. The fishermen, the fish, and other wildlife did not spill the oil, yet they have to bear the cost. The beachgoers who encounter trash and broken bottles were not the litterers, yet they must bear the cost. Many students and professors do not litter and yet must wade through the trash. The cost is external to the activity and is thus called an **externality**, specifically a *negative externality*. When externalities are added to private costs, the result is **social costs**:

externality:
a cost or benefit of an activity that is borne by parties not directly involved in the activity; an external cost or benefit

social costs:
the sum of private costs and externalities

Social costs = private costs + externalities

When private costs differ from social costs, individual decision-makers ignore externalities. The full opportunity cost of using a scarce resource, for example, is borne not by the producer or the consumer but by society. The difference between the private cost and the full opportunity, or social, cost is the externality.

A *positive externality* may result from an activity in which benefits are received by consumers or firms not involved directly in the activity. For instance, inoculations for mumps, measles, and other communicable diseases provide benefits to all of society. The private costs of acquiring the inoculations exceed the social costs by the amount of the externality.

When social and private costs are not the same, then either too much or too little production occurs.

When there is a divergence between social costs and private costs, the result is either too much or too little production and consumption. In either case, resources are not being used in their highest-valued activity, and there is a market failure. For instance, those who pollute do not bear the entire costs of the pollution, and therefore pollute more than they otherwise would.

Consider a gas station selling gasoline with pumps that have no emission control equipment. Each time a consumer pumps gas, a certain quantity of pollutants is released into the air. The consumer demands gasoline at various prices as reflected by the demand curve. The gas station prices the gasoline in order to maximize profit—by equating marginal revenue and marginal cost and setting prices as given by the demand curve at the quantity where marginal revenue and marginal cost are equal, see Figure 2. The actual cost of the gasoline to society—including the private marginal cost and the externality—is given by the marginal social cost curve, *MSC*. Society would like the price to be set at P_{msc} rather than P_{mc} and the quantity to be purchased to be Q_{msc} rather than Q_{mc}. According to society's desires, "too much" gasoline is purchased.

In contrast to negative externalities, private costs exceed social costs when external benefits are created. From society's viewpoint, too few people would be vaccinated from communicable diseases if individuals bore all the costs of inoculations.

In the case of a positive externality, the *MSC* curve would lie below the *MC* curve and "too little" of the good or service would be produced and purchased.

2.b. Private Property Rights and Externalities

private property right:
the right to claim ownership of an item

Market failures may result because of the absence of well-defined **private property rights**. A private property right is the right to claim ownership of an item; it is well-defined if there is a clear owner and if the right is recognized and enforced by society. Suppose you sit next to a person who gets

Figure 2
Externalities

A firm selling a product whose consumption generates a social cost would sell the amount given by $MR = MC$, ignoring the social costs. Society would prefer the price and quantity given by $MR = MSC$ in order to take into account the social costs.

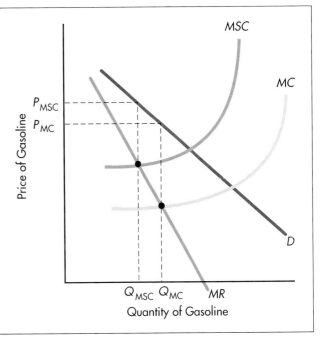

The absence of a well-defined private property right may result in a market failure.

marginal benefits (MB):
the additional benefits of producing or consuming one more unit of a good or service

marginal social costs:
the additional private and external or social costs of producing or consuming one more unit of a good or service

very nervous during exams and as a result coughs, drops pencils, papers, and calculators, and spreads out over the desk, encroaching on your space. The nervous person, Bob, is imposing an externality on you. The problem is that neither you nor Bob owns the space or the noise level. If you did, you could restrict Bob's noise activity or you could charge him for it. If Bob owned it, you could pay him not to make noise. In either case, the externality would no longer be external, it would be part of the private costs.

Figure 3 shows Bob's demand (the marginal revenue product) for the distractions and noise he causes, what we will call his **marginal-benefits (MB)** curve. The marginal-benefits curve measures the additional benefits of consuming one more quantity of something. The first few coughs and the first few dropped pencils provide Bob large benefits. They help him take the exam. But as coughing continues and the dropping of materials increases, Bob gets fewer benefits with each additional cough. The marginal cost (MC) to Bob of his noise and distractions rises as more noise and distractions occur because he has to devote increasing amounts of time to making noise and dropping materials, and this distracts from his taking the examination. The marginal cost Bob faces does not measure the full costs of his actions. The *full costs*, the costs imposed on you and everyone else, are the **marginal social costs**, shown as the upward-sloping curve *MSC*, which lies above the *MC* curve.

Bob chooses the amount of distraction indicated by the intersection of his *MC* and *MB* curves, quantity Q_B. This is an amount greater than is desired by society (you and other students). The amount of activity you would desire is indicated by the intersection of the *MSC* curve and Bob's *MB* curve, quantity Q_S. Thus, "too much" noise is provided because the *MC* curve does not take into account all costs. The market has failed to generate the "right" amount

Figure 3
Externalities

The marginal costs borne by the noisy student, Bob, are shown by the rising curve MC. The costs Bob imposes on others exceed his private costs. As a result, the marginal-social-cost curve, MSC, lies above Bob's marginal-cost curve. Bob's marginal benefits from creating distractions are indicated by the downward-sloping curve, MB. The amount of noise and distraction that Bob creates is given by the point where the MC curve and the MB curve intersect, Q_B. According to society, too much noise and other distractions occur. Society would choose the quantity Q_S, where marginal social costs and marginal benefits are equal. The solution to the externalities problem is to equate private costs and social costs.

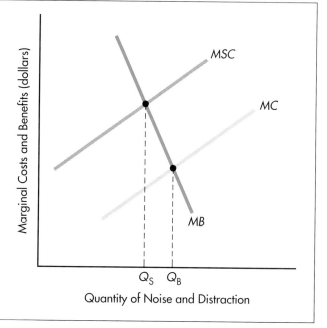

of noise. The reason stems from the fact that no one owns the noise level; that is, no one has a private property right to the noise level.

The lack of private property ownership or rights is a common one in the natural resources area. No one has a private property right to the ocean or air. No one owns the fish in the sea; no one owns the elephants that roam the African plains; and during the past one hundred years no one owned the American buffalo or bald eagle. Because no one owns these natural resources, a "too rapid" rate of use or harvest occurs.

The waters off New England once were among the world's most fertile fishing grounds. Now, fish are severely depleted in the area known as Georges Bank. Overfishing resulting from a lack of private property rights was fueled by the nation's increasing appetite for fish and by technological changes in fishing. A single fishing vessel using radar, sonar, spotter planes, sea-surface observations from satellites, advanced catching gear, onboard processing, and refrigeration can do the job of a hundred older boats and in less time. For some species, the entire fishing season lasts only a few hours. The Economic Insight "The Problems of Common Ownership" discusses some of the results of private and common ownership of resources.

The resource markets would solve the problem of harvesting now or in the future if someone owned the oceans or the fish. As we discussed in the chapter on capital, land, and entrepreneurial ability, the prices would adjust until the present values of harvesting and not harvesting would be the same. Without private ownership, however, no one has the incentive to sell the resources at the profit-maximizing rate. A fishing crew has no incentive to harvest the "right" amount of fish, since leaving fish until the future simply leaves them for other fishing crews today. If someone owned the fish, that resource owner would sell the fish only up to the point that the present value of fish caught in the future would equal the present value of the revenue obtained from the fish caught today.

The Problems of Common Ownership

Lured by the opportunity to earn a year's wages with one squeeze of the trigger, poachers have slaughtered elephants by the tens of thousands. A decade ago, Africa's elephant population was more than a million; it has now fallen to less than half of that. Environmentalists in the United States trying to save the flora and fauna of the ancient forests in the Pacific Northwest are battling local loggers, who see the trees as a means to feed their families. Thousands of acres of Amazon forest are burned each year to provide land for Brazil's ranchers and subsistence farmers, eliminating hundreds of species of plants and animals. The swordfish is being fished to extinction. These and other similar problems result from common ownership. When no one owns the land or the wildlife, no one has an incentive to harvest quantities that ensure reproduction and renewal.

Policies regarding forests illustrate the problem of common ownership. The government of Ontario, Canada, fights with small, private owners of forest lands over how to manage the trees. The Ontario government wants to cut the trees down and sell them, but private owners refuse to clear-cut their private forests (the process of cutting down all the trees in an area). Stories about deforestation and the degradation of Ontario's forest lands make the papers every day in Ontario, but the private sec-

tor, which owns less than 10 percent of the timber, is not to blame. The deforestation is occurring on the government's land.

Sweden has more standing forest today than at any time in its past. Unlike Canada, most of the forest land in Sweden is privately owned. Neighboring Finland also has a huge forest industry and more forest than ever before. It too has mostly privately owned forest lands. In the less developed countries as well, common ownership encourages deforestation. In Brazil's Amazon basin, the government has subsidized the tearing down and burning of a forested area bigger than France. Deforestation has occurred in other regions of Latin America, several Asian nations, and much of Africa. In each case where there is common ownership, there is a problem with the rate of harvest. The difference is that private owners do not cut at a loss and do not cut to maintain employment levels or for other political reasons. They cut at a rate that yields them the greatest return—a rate of return that matches the rates of return earned on alternative assets.

The problems of the African elephant, the swordfish, and other species of plants and animals that are being depleted are no different from the problem of the forests. Proposed solutions typically call for bans on the killing of the species. For example, Kenya, Tanzania, and

several other African nations, with the support of most of the developed nations, are banning the trade of ivory in order to protect African elephants. The elephants' problem may stem partly from the demand for ivory, but it also stems from common ownership of the elephant and the low incomes of the African peoples. To a small farmer in Kenya whose crops are threatened by an elephant, the killing of the elephant means the survival of his family. If the farmer owned the elephants, had enough land to harvest food for them, and could then sell them, the plight of the elephant would change. Once in a while, someone proposes and implements a private ownership system. In South Africa, Zimbabwe, and Botswana, the government gives elephants to certain tribes to be harvested for ivory and for tourism. In those countries, elephants have not declined, and the living standards of the poorest tribes have improved. A ban on ivory in these countries would destroy the industry and lead to the destruction of the animals.

Sources: John H. Cushman, Jr., "World Group to Debate Plan to Protect Species by Numbers," *The New York Times*, Nov. 6, 1994, p. 44; Victoria Butler, "Is This the Way to Save Africa's Wildlife?" *International Wildlife*, March 1995, p. 38.

2.c. Public Goods

Why don't markets allocate public goods more efficiently?

According to the **principle of mutual exclusivity**, the owner of private property is entitled to enjoy the consumption of private property privately. The principle of mutual exclusivity refers to a well-defined private property right. It says that if you own a good, I cannot use it; and if I own a good, you cannot use it. When I purchase a pizza, it is mine to consume as I wish. You have absolutely no right to the pizza unless I provide that right. However, a good or service may also be a **public good**, a good for which the principle of mutual exclusivity does not apply. If you use a public good, I may also. Moreover, a public good is a good or service whose use by one consumer does not diminish the quantity available for other consumers.

The airwaves illustrate the characteristics of a public good quite well. A television station broadcasts on a certain frequency, and anyone can pick up that station. It doesn't matter whether one person or 1 million people tune in to the station, the signal is the same and additional users do not deprive others of any of the public good. If your neighbor tunes in to the channel you are watching, you don't receive a weaker signal.

When goods are public, people have an incentive to be **free riders**—consumers or producers who enjoy a good without paying for it. As an example, suppose that national defense was not provided by the government and paid for with tax money. Suppose that you would not be protected by the armed forces unless you paid a fee. A problem would arise because national defense is a public good; you would be protected whether or not you paid for it as long as others paid. Of course, since each person has an incentive not to pay for it, few voluntarily do and the quantity of the good produced is too small from society's viewpoint. Similarly, clean air and the ozone layer may be public goods. Each person has an incentive to use the good without paying for it, and many people can consume the good simultaneously. As a result, not enough people pay to improve the air quality or to protect the ozone layer, and the resulting environmental quality is lower than society would like.

2.c.1. The Demand for Public Goods   A private good comes in units that can be purchased by individuals, and once the good is purchased, the individual owns it and can decide how to consume it. The market demand curve is the *horizontal* summation of the individual demand curves. A public good, in contrast, is not divisible into units that can be purchased and owned by the buyers. Once the good is produced, the producer is unable to exclude nonpayers from consuming the good. Since they can enjoy the good without paying for it, many individuals will not pay for it. The demand curve for the public good may not exist.

Suppose there are two people in society, Jesse and Rafael, whose demands for a public good are shown in Table 1. The demands show how much each would be *willing* and *able* to pay for the various quantities of the public good. Once the good is produced, however, neither Jesse nor Rafael has any incentive to pay for it. Jesse would be willing and able to pay $5 for one unit of the good, and Rafael would be willing and able to pay $3 for the one unit. But

TABLE I
The Demand for a Public Good

Quantity	Willingness to Pay		Total Willingness to Pay
	Jesse	**Rafael**	
1	$5	$3	$8
2	4	2	6
3	3	1	4
4	2	0	2

neither has an incentive to actually pay anything. The last column in Table 1 shows the total amount society (Jesse and Rafael) would be willing and able to pay for various quantities of the public good. In contrast to the private good, where the market demand is the horizontal summation of the individual demands, the market demand for the public good is the *vertical* summation of the individual demand curves. The market demand for the public good shows how much society would be willing and able to pay for various quantities of a public good. Again, the problem is that the existence of this market demand curve does not mean that people will actually pay for the good; once produced, no one has an incentive to pay for it. There is, therefore, a market failure.

The market demand curve for a public good is derived by summing vertically all individual demand curves.

RECAP

1. Externalities occur when all of the costs of production or consumption are not borne by the private individuals involved in a transaction.

2. Externalities are market failures because the market does not determine the level of a good that society desires. A market failure occurs when social costs and benefits are not equal.

3. A market failure may result when private property rights are not well defined.

4. A public good is a good for which the principle of mutual exclusivity does not hold and thus free riding exists.

5. Free riding occurs when people can enjoy an activity without having to bear any costs for the activity.

6. Market failures may occur in the case of a public good. The demand for the public good may not exist because no one has an incentive to pay for the public good once it is produced.

3. PUBLIC POLICIES

Why does the government get involved in environmental issues?

3.a. Externalities

The government is called on to resolve market failures. It may levy taxes or subsidies, produce public goods, or assign private property rights.

How is a market failure to be resolved? If we call on the government to solve the problem, do we have the government impose regulations, as it does in the case of natural monopolies, or should it impose taxes and subsidies? In this section, we look at some of the approaches the government takes in the case of market failures.

Let's begin with the externality problem. Since the problem is that the marginal social cost (*MSC*) is not equal to the private marginal cost (*MC*), the solution requires that the two be made equal. How can the creators of the externality be required to take the externality into account, to *internalize* the externality? Externalities can be internalized through the imposition of regulations or taxes, the use of subsidies, or the assignment of private property rights.

3.a.1. Regulation Let's consider your noisy classmate Bob again. Suppose your professor owns the property right to the noise level in your class. The professor can regulate the noise, specifying that Bob can cough only *x* times

The Botswana, Zimbabwe, and South African governments allow individuals to own elephants. These elephant "farmers" ensure that the elephants breed and reproduce so that they can be sold for their tusks, for hunting in special hunting parks, or to zoos in developed nations. This privatization has led to a revival of the elephant population in these nations. Most other nations have created national parks in which hunting is forbidden, and the results have not stemmed the tide of extinction of the species. These orphaned elephants are being cared for at a wildlife preserve in Kenya.

emission standard:
a maximum allowable level of pollution from a specific source

per hour. But to ensure that the entire class is made better off, how much noise should the professor allow—5, 10, or 50 coughs per hour? The optimal amount for all of the class would be to restrict Bob's noise to the level where $MSC = MB$.

Environmental regulation is analogous to the regulation of Bob's noise-making. One form of environmental regulation is an **emission standard** that specifies the maximum level of pollution allowed from a specific source. Each automaker, for instance, must create a line of cars that meets fixed emission standards. Emission standards are also applied to steel factories, electric-power plants, and many other industries.

The government defines an emission level and requires firms to meet the standards. Economists argue that the level should be determined by demand and supply—that is, by equating marginal benefits and marginal social costs. Figure 4 shows the market for pollution. (Alternatively, we could show the market for clean air, since the two, clean air and polluted air, add up to 100 percent.) The marginal costs and benefits of pollution are measured on the vertical axis. The horizontal axis measures the quantity of pollution, from perfectly clean air (0 on the graph) to perfectly filthy air (100 on the graph). Moving away from the origin along the horizontal axis, the percentage of polluted air rises (the particles of dirty air increase). When the air is perfectly clean (0 on the graph), the marginal benefit of a particle of pollutants emitted in the air is quite high. As the air becomes dirtier and dirtier, the marginal benefit of a few more polluted particles of air falls, as seen by the downward slope of the marginal-benefit curve, *MB*.

The marginal cost (*MC*) of dirty air rises at an accelerating rate because of diminishing marginal returns. The first 10 percent increase in pollutants occurs easily and is accomplished by not using the very expensive pollution abatement devices installed on automobiles and smokestacks. As the air gets dirtier and dirtier, the benefits a firm or individual might get from some additional pollution are quite small. The difference between the marginal cost and the marginal social cost (*MSC*) is that the marginal cost refers to the

Figure 4
The Optimal Amount of Pollution
The horizontal axis measures the quantity of pollution, from perfectly clean air (0 on the graph) to perfectly filthy air (100 on the graph). Moving away from the origin along the horizonal axis, the percentage of polluted air rises (the particles of dirty air increase). When the air is perfectly clean (0 on the graph), the marginal benefit of a particle of pollutants emitted in the air is quite high. As the air becomes dirtier and dirtier, the marginal benefit of a few more polluted particles of air falls, as seen by the downward slope of the marginal-benefit curve, MB. The optimal amount of pollution is determined by the intersection of the MSC and MB curves: 30 percent dirty air. This is a greater amount of clean air (less pollution) than is determined in the market, where private marginal costs, MC (private), are equal to marginal benefits (MB), or 50 percent dirty air. If a standard greater than 70 percent clean air is set by the government, the demand exceeds the marginal social costs. If a 100 percent clean air standard is set, the marginal benefits exceed the marginal social costs by the distance AC.

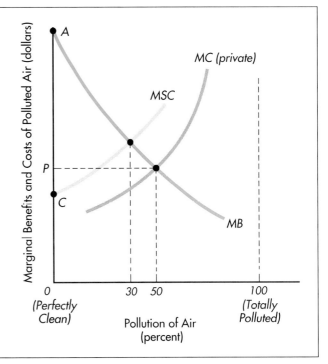

individual's private costs while the marginal social cost refers to society's marginal costs. When I drive my automobile, the costs of the pollution I create are borne by me in the sense that I have to purchase oxygenated fuels and maintain the quality of my car, but costs are also borne by others. Everyone has to breathe the polluted air I create.

The optimal amount of pollution for society is indicated by the intersection of the marginal-social-cost and marginal-benefit curves. This amount—30 percent in this example—is optimal because marginal social costs and marginal benefits are equalized, not because pollution is eliminated (it isn't). At 100 percent cleanliness, the demand for pollution (the marginal benefits) would greatly exceed the marginal costs, by the distance AC.

In reality, the emission level is seldom set at the optimal level. Moreover, the regulations may cause other problems. One hallmark of the standards approach is uniformity: standards apply to all firms and all areas. However, standards appropriate for small firms may be inappropriate for large firms, or standards appropriate for one area might be inappropriate for another. An emission standard for automobiles that is appropriate for Los Angeles would not necessarily be appropriate for Salem, Idaho. An emission standard applied to fishing might restrict the quantity of fish caught per shift. This might be appropriate in the mountain streams of Vermont, but not in Chesapeake Bay.

The regulatory approach also fails to account for private responses that tend to neutralize its impact. For example, a common regulatory practice is to impose standards for new products that are tougher than standards for existing products. This practice induces producers to remain with older products even though they may be environmentally damaging. As a result, the regulation may raise pollution levels higher than they would have been without regulation. Such was the case with the 1990 Clean Air Act. Standards for planned coal plants are tougher than for existing plants. The effect is that firms continue to use old plants even when more efficient or environmentally less damaging plants would be feasible.

Uniform standards can also be problematic if they aid large or existing firms in their attempts to keep smaller or new firms from competing. For instance, the Resource Conservation and Recovery Act, which covers the disposal of more than 450 substances, has 17,000 rulings related to it. These rulings mean that it can cost as much as $1 million and take as long as four years to get approval to operate a business.[1] This is a fixed cost that makes it more difficult for new firms to enter the industry and begin competing with existing firms.

3.a.2. Taxes or Subsidies An alternative to the problems caused by regulatory standards is to levy taxes or provide subsidies to resolve the market failure. Society might want to tax actions that cause a negative externality and subsidize actions that cause a positive externality, by the amount of the externality. In this way, social costs and private costs would be the same. A tax could be placed on automobiles or smokestacks or on products that create litter or damage the ozone layer. The tax would increase the price to the full cost—internal plus external costs—and consumers and producers would have to take the full cost into account in their decision-making.

For instance, instead of mandating that automobile manufacturers install expensive pollution-control equipment on all new cars (the costs of which would be paid by every car buyer nationwide), the government could impose a tax on drivers whose cars exceed federally set emission limits. That way the individual could decide whether or not to drive an old junker that produces a lot of pollution. With the government mandate, new cars become relatively more expensive than the "junkers" and so people drive junkers longer than they otherwise would have.

Disposable diapers are a huge contributor to the solid-waste problem in the United States. They account for 2 percent of the nation's municipal solid waste. In the early 1990s, nearly 20 billion paper and plastic diapers were dumped in landfills in the United States annually—3.6 million tons of waste that researchers believe will take five hundred years to decompose. A tax could be imposed on single-use diapers to pay the costs of their disposal. In this way people could choose whether to use the diapers or not. Under regulation, the diapers would most likely be banned.

A common use of taxes on externalities is the effluent charge—a charge on waste produced or emissions generated. With a tax on emissions, polluters can choose to install pollution-abatement equipment, change production techniques so as to reduce pollution-causing activities, or pay the tax and continue to pollute.

Figure 5 illustrates the demand for and supply of pollution. The amount of pollution that occurs in the absence of a tax is Q_1, at the intersection of S_1 and D_1. An emissions charge levied on waste tends to make pollution more expensive by the amount of the tax. In other words, producers can decide to pollute the same amount and pay the tax or pollute less and pay less tax. The supply curve shifts up to S_2, and the new amount of pollution is Q_2.

---

[1]David Brooks, "Saving the Earth from Its Friends," *National Review*, April 1, 1990, pp. 28–31.

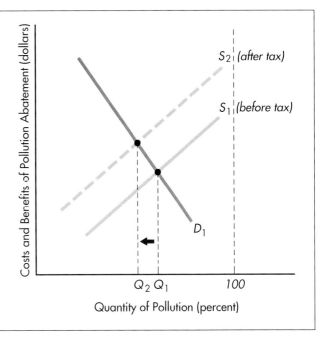

Figure 5
The Effect of an Effluent Charge
The figure illustrates the demand for and supply of pollution. The amount of pollution that occurs in the absence of a tax is Q_1, at the intersection of S_1 and D_1. An emissions charge levied on waste tends to make pollution more expensive by the amount of the tax. In other words, producers can decide to pollute the same amount and pay the tax or pollute less and pay less tax. The supply curve shifts up to S_2, and the new amount of pollution is Q_2.

Although the effluent tax enables individuals to decide whether to pollute and thus relies on self-interest to reduce pollution, the tax can be difficult to administer. A problem with effluent charges is discovering where the supply and demand curves are located and determining what charge is necessary to cover the externality.

3.a.3. The Coase Theorem In cases where the market failure results from a lack of private property rights, the problem can be corrected by the assignment of private property rights rather than by having the government regulate or impose taxes and subsidies. To solve the problem of your classmate Bob imposing an externality on you by being too noisy and distracting, your professor could assign either you or Bob the ownership of the sound level and then allow the two of you to work out the noise pollution problem. If the professor told you that Bob owns the property rights, then you would have to decide how much of his noise and activity you could stand. You would then offer to pay Bob some amount to refrain from any more noise and activity. You would be willing to pay him enough so that your marginal cost just equals the marginal benefits you get from less noise and fewer distractions. Bob would accept a payment that just offsets his marginal cost of not making noise and creating distractions. If the *MSC* curve of Figure 6 represents your marginal-cost curve, and the *MC* curve represents Bob's marginal costs, then you would be willing to pay Bob any amount up to the difference between the *MC* and *MSC* curves because that would induce him to reduce his activity to the level you find best. Bob would be willing to accept any amount equal to or greater than the difference between the *MC* and *MSC* curves to reduce his activity to Q_S.

Conversely, if your professor assigned you the property right, Bob would have to buy some noise and activity level from you. Bob would be willing to

Figure 6
The Assignment of Property Rights

If the *MSC* curve of Figure 6 represents your marginal-cost curve, then you would be willing to pay Bob any amount up to the difference between the *MC* and *MSC* curves because that would induce him to reduce his activity to a level you find acceptable. Bob would be willing to accept any amount equal to or greater than the difference between the *MC* and *MSC* curves to reduce his activity to Q_S.

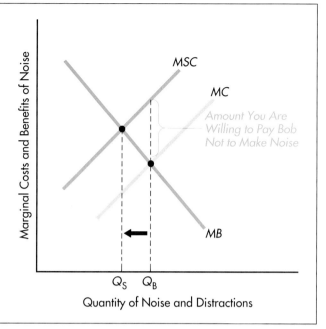

pay up to the difference between the *MC* and *MSC* curves, and you would accept anything equal to or greater than that difference.

Notice that no matter to whom the property rights are assigned, the quantity of noise produced is the same. You and Bob come to an agreement in which the marginal cost to you equals the marginal benefit to Bob and vice versa. The only difference is that one of you provides payments to the other. When bargaining is costless and property rights can be assigned without difficulty, the amount of the externality-creating activity will be the same no matter who has the property right. This is known as the **Coase Theorem**, named after Ronald Coase, the University of Chicago economist and 1991 Nobel Prize winner who discovered the principle.

In some cases where private property rights do not exist, it is not possible for the government to assign private property rights or to enforce them once assigned, and the Coase Theorem does not hold. For instance, society cannot easily assign individual homeowners private rights to air and expect motorists to buy pollution rights from them. It would be virtually impossible for each motorist to speak with each homeowner. In this case the transaction costs are too high. It is possible, in cases where the transaction costs are too high for the Coase Theorem to work, that a market can be created for the property rights and that the market for property rights will reduce the externality problem. The Economic Insight "The Coase Theorem and Smoking Bans" explores the theorem further.

Coase Theorem:
when bargaining is costless and property rights can be assigned without difficulty, the amount of an externality-generating activity will not depend on who is assigned the property rights

3.a.4. A Market for the Property Rights   For the 2,700 southern California plants that account for 85 percent of the region's hydrocarbons and 95 percent of the nitrogen oxides that do not come from automobiles, a new approach is being used to clean up the air. Under the old approach, the amount of pollution allowed from each generator, boiler, baking oven, or other piece of equipment was specified by the smog-control agency. The new approach is to allow a company to choose the least expensive mix of new

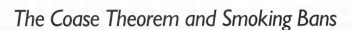
The Coase Theorem and Smoking Bans

Policies to minimize negative externalities must be carefully considered. The policy implemented might not be the best means to reduce the externalities.

Consider recent attempts to deal with the costs smokers impose on nonsmokers. Reports on the established link between secondhand smoke and cancer have stimulated demands for outright bans on smoking in public places. In Italy, France, and an increasing number of cities in the United States, these bans are in fact being imposed. The basis for the bans is the externalities that smokers impose on nonsmokers.

But is the smoke in a privately owned business establishment an externality? Profit-maximizing owners have an incentive to please their customers by catering to their smoking/nonsmoking desires. Whether a business caters solely to smokers or to nonsmokers, or attempts to satisfy both by providing smokers with the right to smoke while at the same time providing nonsmokers with cleaner air through air filtration systems and nonsmoking sections, depends on the extent to which customers want smoking environments and on the marginal costs of one option relative to another. When businesses own the airspace, they will manage that scarce resource so as to promote its long-term value.

The secondhand smoke issue involves people in close proximity to each other interacting over airspace. To the extent that smokers and nonsmokers share the airspace, they must come to some agreement about the allocation of the resource. It is unlikely that these customers will want to bargain with each other over the right to smoke or to have smoke-free air every time they enter a public building, but they can demand that the owner of the restaurant or building accommodate their diverse preferences in mutually advantageous ways. Businesses cater to either smokers or nonsmokers (or some combination) based on which of these two groups values the airspace more.

Regulations that prohibit smoking shift ownership of the airspace within those bars and restaurants. Before a ban, smokers and nonsmokers have equal access to negotiate with business owners over the use of the airspace, and therefore the private market internalizes the negative externalities. Smoking bans, however, eliminate the negotiation process and do not allow the Coase Theorem to work.

emissions offset policy: an environmental policy wherein pollution permits are issued and a market in the permits then develops

controls as long as total pollution does not exceed some assigned level. Each business gets a certificate indicating the amount of pollution it is permitted each year; each is given a property right to that amount of pollution. These permits can then be bought and sold in a market, which is referred to as a "smog" market. A firm easily meeting its standards could sell its excess to a firm having some difficulty meeting its standards. For example, Mobil Corporation purchased the permission to spew out an additional 900 pounds of noxious gas vapors each day, for about $3 million, from the city of South Gate, California. South Gate had acquired the credits from General Motors, which closed a plant there and sold the city the property and the pollution permits that went with the property.[2]

In many regions of the country the Environmental Protection Agency uses an **emissions offset policy**. The EPA owns the air and sells permits to "use" the air. Companies with permits must not produce more pollution than their permits allow. But if they produce less pollution than their permits allow, they can "bank" the difference and use it later, or they can sell it to other

[2]"A Promising New Weapon in the Battle to Clean Up the Air," *Los Angeles Times*, Feb. 16, 1992, p. M4; Jeffrey Taylor, "Smog Swapping," *The Wall Street Journal*, April 14, 1992, p. 1; *Economic Report of the President, 1992*, p. 184.

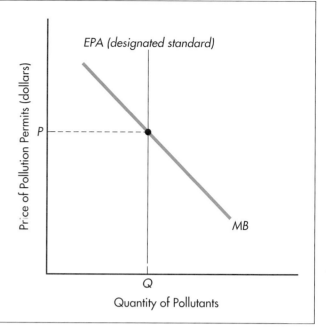

Figure 7
The Value of Pollution Permits
The value of pollution permits depends on the demand for and supply of such permits. The vertical supply curve shows the amount of pollution allowed by EPA standards. The marginal benefits of polluting are shown by the downward-sloping curve, *MB*. With a price for pollution rights determined, firms internalize the externality of polluting by using the price of the pollution rights to define the quantity of pollution they will undertake.

polluters. This, like the approach in southern California, creates a market for the right to pollute.

The amount of pollution wanted by the Environmental Protection Agency is indicated by the vertical supply curve of pollution rights in Figure 7. The demand for permits to pollute is shown by the downward-sloping curve, *MB*. With a price (*P*) for pollution rights determined, firms *internalize* the externality of polluting by using the price of the pollution rights to define the quantity (*Q*) of pollution they will undertake.

How do global environmental problems differ from domestic environmental problems?

3.a.5. Global Problems Global environmental issues arise because of externalities and public goods, and the global problems are complicated by the fact that the individuals involved live in many nations. Sulfur dioxide and nitrogen dioxide emitted by factories in the United States are blown to Canada, where they mix with moisture and fall as acid rain. Manufacturing plants located along the Mexican side of the U.S.-Mexico border emit pollutants that flow across the border into the United States. Because one nation cannot impose its wishes on another, developing and enforcing international policies to resolve market failures is difficult.

The ozone layer poses another international challenge. Many scientists claim that the stratospheric ozone layer has been damaged by several chemical compounds, most notably chlorofluorocarbons and bromofluorocarbons (halons). The appearance of a major hole in the ozone layer over Antarctica, where no emissions originate, indicates the global nature of the externality. The problem is that no one government can claim ownership of the ozone. The standard approach has been to develop a nonbinding policy to which several countries will agree. In 1985, a convention of nations established a framework for international scientific and technical cooperation. In 1987, the Montreal Protocol committed signatories to freeze production levels of chlorofluorocarbons by 1989 and then cut their production in half by 1998. In 1989 in Paris, the world's seven biggest industrial economies agreed to begin major assaults on many environmental problems. The group set a goal of a total ban on chlorofluorocarbon emissions by the year 2000.

The 1985, 1987, 1989, and 1994 meetings seemed to imply that the industrialized nations of the West were in agreement about environmental policy. On November 7, 1989, however, the United States and Japan refused to sign a draft resolution at an international conference on global climate change held in the Netherlands. The resolution called for stabilization of carbon dioxide emissions and the emissions of other greenhouse gases by the year 2000. The United States and Japan made the conference drop all reference to a specific year and to a specific target for carbon dioxide. The reason the United States gave for refusing to sign the draft was that it was unfair to less developed nations. For more than one hundred years, the developed nations have benefited from the use of fossil fuels, which emit carbon dioxide when they are burned. Now, those developed nations, concerned about the environmental impact of carbon dioxide emissions, want to limit the use of fossil fuels by less developed nations. Such a limitation would deprive people in poor countries of the advantages offered by the use of coal and oil in production—advantages enjoyed for years by people in developed countries.

The fairness issue is at the heart of the debate about global warming. The unequal distribution of income among nations (see the chapter on income distribution, poverty, and government policy) creates a sticking point for policies intended to resolve global environmental problems. Environmental quality can be thought of as a normal good or even as a luxury good. The richest nations can better afford the sacrifices needed to improve environmental conditions than the poorest nations. Similarly, within one nation, the richest members of society can better afford environmental improvements than the poorest members. Yet the poor often pay significant costs for improvements to the environment. They usually reside near airports, chemical plants, and other undesirable locations because land values in such places have been driven down. When these areas are improved environmentally and noise is reduced, the value of the land rises and the poor are driven out. The marginal increase in the price of cars due to emission controls or mandatory safety equipment adversely affects the poor more than the wealthy in the sense that the auto purchase is a greater share of their income.

3.b. Government Regulation of Public Goods

Public goods, as you learned earlier, are those goods or services for which the producer is unable to exclude nonpayers so that a free rider problem emerges. Because users have no incentive to pay for the public good, the demand curve for the good will lie far below the demand that would exist if users had to purchase the good. As a result, "too little" of the public good is produced. Since too little is produced, too few resources flow to the production of the public good. How is the public good problem solved?

There have been attempts by private entrepreneurs to convert public goods into private goods. Large stadiums built around baseball or football fields restrict the viewing of the games outside of the stadiums; you have to purchase a ticket to see the contest. The Rural Metro Company of Scottsdale, Arizona, provides private subscription fire protection to residents of Scottsdale and surrounding communities. The company will put out fires at no cost to subscribers but will put out fires for nonsubscribers for a price that equals Rural Metro's average total cost. In general, however, the solution for

"Didn't you see the sign to not pick up hitchhikers?" A grizzly bear in Denali National Park, Alaska, look like it is ready to jump aboard the school bus. The grizzly is protected by the federal government. To preserve the natural lands, the federal government has claimed thousands of acres in the western states and Alaska. The lands cannot be developed nor can animal and plant species be destroyed. Many argue that the national parks are necessary since no one individual would have an incentive to preserve private land—there would be a free-riding problem. Nevertheless, in several locations, private individuals are grouping together to purchase and preserve lands. In Arizona, for instance, desert mountains around Phoenix and Scottsdale have been purchased by citizen committees.

the free rider problems of public goods is to have the government produce the good. National defense, wildlife reserves in Kenya, wilderness areas in the United States, and the park systems in every country would probably not exist if a government did not provide them. Radio and television airwaves, and perhaps police and fire protection, are public goods as well and might not exist unless provided by the government.

How much of a public good should the government provide? The optimal amount is the amount where the market demand curve and the marginal-cost curve (supply curve) of producing the good intersect. If we could measure how much society would actually be willing and able to pay for a public good, we could determine the optimal quantity to produce very readily. For example, we know the marginal cost of producing a missile—all we have to do is equate it to the market demand for the missile to determine the number of missiles to produce. The problem is that we cannot easily determine the market demand. Surveys do not help because people have an incentive not to tell the truth—by indicating they would pay a lot when in reality they know they get it for free, or by indicating they would pay nothing because they know their taxes will be set according to what they say. The only way that the public can register its demand for public goods is through the ballot box. But, as we will discuss in the next chapter, the ballot box does not measure the intensity of consumer preferences, and it too can fail to produce the optimal quantity of the public good.

RECAP

1. The solution to an externality is to ensure that those creating an externality internalize it.

2. Externalities may be internalized through the imposition of regulations or taxes, the use of subsidies, or the assignment of private property rights.

3. The Coase Theorem illustrates the way private individuals can resolve externalities if property rights are assigned. Who has the property right does not matter; what matters is the assigning of the property right.

4. Global environmental issues are particularly difficult to solve because no one government can claim ownership of the property.

5. If a public good cannot be converted to a private good, the solution to providing the right amount of the public good is to have the government provide it.

SUMMARY

▲▼ *Why might a market not allocate goods and services efficiently?*

1. A market failure occurs when the market fails to produce the right amount of output and to allocate the right amount of resources to alternative uses. The right amount refers to the amount that would occur in a world of perfect competition—the economically efficient amount. §1.a, 1.c

▲▼ *Why is an externality considered to be a source of market failure?*

2. When an externality occurs, private costs and benefits differ from social costs. Either too much or too little is consumed or produced relative to the quantities that would occur if all costs and benefits were included. §2.a

3. An externality may result from the lack of private property rights. §2.b

▲▼ *Why don't markets allocate public goods efficiently?*

4. A public good is a good for which the principle of mutual exclusivity does not hold. §2.c

▲▼ *Why does the government get involved in environmental issues?*

5. Possible solutions to externalities include regulations, taxes, subsidies, and the assignment of private property rights. §3.a, 3.a.1, 3.a.2, 3.a.3

6. The most common solution to public goods is for the government to supply the good. §3.b

▲▼ *How do global environmental problems differ from domestic environmental problems?*

7. Global environmental problems are more difficult to resolve than domestic ones because of the lack of property rights. When no one government owns the resource being damaged by an externality, then the externality cannot be resolved by any one government. §3.a.5

KEY TERMS

market failure §1.c
private costs §2.a
externality §2.a
social costs §2.a
private property right §2.b
marginal benefits (*MB*) §2.b

marginal social costs §2.b
principle of mutual exclusivity §2.c
public good §2.c
free rider §2.c
emission standard §3.a.1
Coase Theorem §3.a.3
emissions offset policy §3.a.4

EXERCISES

1. The three following demand schedules constitute the total demand for a particular good.

   a. Determine the market demand schedule for the good if it is a private good.

   b. Determine the market demand schedule for the good if it is a public good.

Bob		Sally		Rafael	
P	Q_d	P	Q_d	P	Q_d
$6	0	$6	0	$6	1
5	1	5	0	5	2
4	2	4	1	4	3
3	3	3	2	3	4
2	4	2	3	2	5
1	5	1	4	1	6

2. Using the public good described in question 1 and the following supply schedule, determine the optimal quantity of the good. Explain how you determined this quantity.

P	Q_s
$10	15
9	11
7	9
6	8
4	7
2	4
1	3

3. Use the following information to answer the questions listed below.

   a. What is the external cost per unit of output?

   b. What level of output will be produced?

   c. What level of output should be produced to achieve economic efficiency?

   d. What is the value to society of correcting the externality?

Quantity	MC	MSC	MB
1	$ 2	$ 4	$12
2	4	6	10
3	6	8	8
4	8	10	6
5	10	12	4

4. What level of tax would be appropriate to internalize the externality in question 3?

5. If, in question 3, the *MC* and *MSC* columns were reversed, you would have an example of what? Would too much or too little of the good be produced? How would the market failure be resolved, by tax or by subsidy?

6. What is meant by the term *overfishing*? What is the fundamental problem associated with overfishing of the oceans? What might lead to *underfishing*?

7. Explain why the optimal amount of pollution is not a zero amount. Use the same explanation to discuss the amount of health and safety that the government should require in the workplace.

8. Suppose the following table describes the marginal costs and marginal benefits of waste (garbage) reduction. What is the optimal amount of garbage? What is the situation if no garbage is allowed to be produced?

Percentage of Waste Eliminated	Marginal Costs (millions of dollars)	Marginal Benefits (millions of dollars)
10%	$ 10	$1,000
20	15	500
30	25	100
40	40	50
50	70	20
60	110	5
70	200	3
80	500	2
90	900	1
100	2,000	0

9. Elephants eat 300 pounds of food per day. They flourished in Africa when they could roam over huge areas of land, eating the vegetation in one area and then moving on so that the vegetation could renew itself. Now, the area over which elephants can roam is declining. Without some action, the elephants will become extinct. What actions might save the elephants? What are the costs and benefits of such actions?

10. What could explain why the value of pollution permits in one area of the country is rising

20 percent per year while in another it is unchanged from year to year? What would you expect to occur as a result of this differential?

11. Smokers impose negative externalities on non-smokers. Suppose the airspace in a restaurant is a resource owned by the restaurant owner.

a. How would the owner respond to the negative externalities of smokers?

b. Suppose that the smokers owned the airspace. How would that change matters?

c. How about if the nonsmokers owned the airspace?

d. Finally, consider what would occur if the government passed a law banning all smoking. How would the outcome compare with the outcomes described above?

12. Discuss the argument that education should be subsidized because it creates a positive externality.

13. If the best solution to solving the positive externality problem of education is to provide a subsidy, explain why education systems in all countries are nationalized, that is, are government entities.

COOPERATIVE LEARNING EXERCISE

Divide the class into groups of four. Each group then counts off, "1, 2, 3, 4."

All the 1s get together and devise a solution to the problem of the destruction of the rain forest based on government intervention. All the 2s get together and devise a solution to the problem of the destruction of the rain forest based on private measures. The 3s develop reasons why the destruction of the rain forest is not a problem. The 4s develop an explanation of why the

destruction of the rain forest is a market failure.

Each 1, 2, 3, and 4 returns to his or her original group and presents the solutions or explanations to the rest of the group.

Boulder Targets Traffic Congestion

What if driving at rush hour cost you lots more money, not just more time? What if parking put such a dent in your pocketbook it made you want to take the bus? Boulder wants to spend $897,000 on a "traffic-congestion pricing study" to get your answers. The aim is to discover new ways to manipulate market demand for car travel and cut driving to and in Boulder. City leaders and federal sponsors say the study may uncover futuristic ways to blunt traffic growth.

"In my opinion, it would be money well spent," said Joe McDonald, who sits on Boulder's transportation advisory board. "Building more highways to fight congestion is like fighting obesity by getting a bigger belt." Councilman Tad Kline isn't sure the study is the wisest use of money. "Y'know, we could deliver a lot of service for that much money," he said. He would prefer another "Hop," Boulder's successful new shuttle between downtown, the University of Colorado campus and Crossroads Mall.

Some of the options for congestion pricing are simple. Others rely on new technology. The ideas include:

A variable toll that would increase at rush hours. The money could be collected electronically, similar to the E-470 toll road, where lasers read windshield bar codes and bills are mailed to car owners.

A mileage tax. Drivers would pay the tax based on their odometer readings when they register their cars.

Hiking parking prices. Charges would be highest during rush hours.

The pricing options are intended to "be in people's faces," said Boulder transit projects manager Debra Baskett, who organized the study. "We want something that's going to modify behavior."

The whole concept makes a lot of sense. The whole premise is that users pay the way. Those who drive more pay more."

Councilman Kline, who said he is undecided but leaning toward the study, is troubled by equity and privacy issues. If driving becomes more expensive, only the more affluent will drive, he said. "And after you get through with the laser readers and the bar codes and the myriad taxing schemes, you get down to the fact that all those things involve a very large data base that is held by the government," Kline said.

Source: "Boulder Targets Traffic Congestion," Mary George, *The Denver Post*, Feb. 5, 1995, p. 1c. Reprinted by permission.

Commentary

Congestion on the roads is a problem plaguing many cities. The source of the problem is that to the individual, the marginal cost of entering the highway or road is less than the social marginal cost the driver imposes. When deciding whether to enter a highway, you consider the time you will spend on the highway versus time spent driving some other way or some other time. If the marginal cost exceeds the marginal benefit, you do not enter the highway or you do not drive. Conversely, if the marginal benefit exceeds the marginal cost you do enter the highway or you do drive. Your calculation of marginal costs does not include the additional congestion you add to the highway.

Suppose there are 50,000 cars on the highway when you are deciding whether to enter the highway or not. You carry out your calculations, determining that entering the highway will save you 10 minutes over taking another approach and will only cost you 15 minutes more of driving time than if you wait an hour until rush hour is over. Thus, you decide to drive now and to drive on the highway.

For you, the decision to enter the highway now made sense. However, your addition to the road causes an additional slowdown of 10 seconds for each of the 50,000 cars or 500,000 seconds total. You have imposed a significant social cost but you did not use that social cost in your calculation. This externality is referred to as a market failure—the additional social costs were not included in your calculation. Since everyone makes the same calculation, the roads become highly congested during rush hours. How can the market failure be corrected?

One approach might be to assign property rights. Suppose that the roadways were privately owned. Then the owners would want to maximize profit. They would do this by raising price when demand rose and by price discriminating according to the price elasticity of demand. Suppose that the price elasticity of demand is lower during rush hour than during off-peak times. Then, by raising the price of entering the highway during rush hour relative to that during off-peak times, total revenue would rise. This would also induce some people to shift their driving to off-peak times. Many of the pricing schemes being considered by the Boulder city council simulate the assignment of property rights and profit maximization.

According to councilman Kline, "If driving becomes more expensive, only the more affluent will drive." This statement indicates the difference between assigning private property rights and having the government act as if it were a private owner. The private owner will behave so as to maximize profits—internalize externalities and operate and price efficiently. The government will not maximize profits. The government will have other objectives—being reelected perhaps, or ensuring a more equitable distribution of the scarce resource. Perhaps the Boulder City Council will decide to tax only those with new cars or those with incomes above a certain level or to exempt older cars or people with incomes below a certain level from the higher price.

Another approach Boulder is considering is to impose a tax on mileage. The tax imposes a penalty on total driving. It does nothing about driving during rush hour. If someone drives many miles each year but always drives off-peak, then that person would pay a higher tax than someone who drives fewer miles but only during rush hour. While reducing total driving, the proposal does nothing for reducing rush hour driving.

36

Government and Public Choice

FUNDAMENTAL QUESTIONS

1. How is collective decision-making different from private decision-making?
2. Individuals maximize utility. What does the government maximize?
3. What is rent seeking?

M any policies and practices are the result of collective rather than individual decisions. Collective decisions are made by groups of people: the members of a union decide whether to accept a contract offered by management; voters decide whether to support a bond issue providing more funds for education; a board of directors of a corporation decides whether the firm should enter new markets; Congress decides whether to support a president's proposals.

Collective decision-making differs from private decision-making. In private decision-making, individuals make the decisions that maximize their utility given the information they have at the time. In a private market, individual decisions are expressed in terms of a willingness and ability to purchase or produce a good or service. Collective decisions are not as straightforward. Individual decisions to maximize utility are expressed as votes. The votes are then combined to reach a collective decision.

PREVIEW

This chapter focuses on the government, or what we call the public sector. As we have seen in previous chapters, the government intervenes in the private market frequently. We will now examine the process that drives the government to take action. We first look at collective decision-making, because it is this mechanism, specifically voting, through which we choose our government officials and make our preferences for government action known.

The study of the public sector and collective decision-making is the study of public choice. **Public choice theory** uses economics to analyze the actions and inner workings of the public sector.

public choice theory:
the use of economics to analyze the actions and inner workings of the public sector

In Chapter 5 we defined public choice as the study of how government actions result from the self-interested behavior of voters and politicians. In this chapter we broaden the definition somewhat to include the role collective decision-making plays in determining the activities of the public sector. As we examine how the government functions, it will become clear that the outcomes of collective decision-making differ from those of individual choice as expressed in the private marketplace. We will also see, as a result, how the government's behavior deviates from the workings of the private marketplace. By the end of this chapter we will have built an explanation for why and how this deviation comes about.

I. COLLECTIVE DECISION-MAKING

If we analyze government in economic terms, we have one large market, where the public's demand for particular actions in the form of votes meets

How is collective decision-making different from private decision-making?

the supply of legislation enacted by politicians. Where is equilibrium? Are the decisions made and actions carried out optimal? As we will see in this section, the process through which the public's votes get translated into government policy is different from the way in which equilibrium is reached in a private market, resulting in different outcomes from collective decision-making than we would expect from the private market at work.

1.a. Differences Between Collective Decision-Making and the Private Marketplace

Unlike individual decision-making in the private marketplace, collective decisions are made by voting, not by consuming or producing goods and services. In collective decision-making, votes replace dollars, bundles of issues or goods are considered rather than one good at a time, and consumers are rationally ignorant.

Dollars versus votes Collective decisions are made on the basis of one vote per person, whereas in the private marketplace, there is one vote per dollar. If you decide to spend a lot of money on a particular good or service, you are expressing the intensity with which you desire that good or service. You vote once in an election no matter what your income is and no matter how intensely you feel about an issue. You cannot express how much you want something with your vote since your vote counts no more than a vote by someone who cares little about the issue being decided.

Full-line supply Voters do not purchase one good at a time as consumers do in the marketplace; instead, they must choose a *full-line supply* of products when they cast their votes. A **full-line supply** is the entire bundle of policies offered by a candidate for office or comprised in an issue. Voters cast a vote for a candidate knowing that the candidate will take stands on many issues. An individual who agrees with a candidate's environmental policies but not with the candidate's support for income redistribution does not vote yes for the environmental policy and no for the income-distribution policy. The voter casts a yes or no vote for the candidate's entire bundle of policies. Similarly, a voter may support a bond issue even though a portion of the funds to be raised with the sale of the bonds is to be used for a baseball field, something the voter does not want, because the remainder of the funds are to be used for community hiking paths, something the voter wants.

full-line supply:
the entire bundle of policies offered by a candidate

Rational ignorance Individuals will compare the marginal costs and marginal benefits of devoting time and income to gathering more information. In the private market, individuals have a greater incentive to gather information than they do in a collective decision-making process because they have to bear the full costs of any mistakes they make in purchasing a good or service. With collective decisions, the entire collectivity bears the costs of any mistakes; one well-informed individual bears the same costs as one ill-informed individual. As a result, no individual has an incentive to become really well informed about each issue.

Knowing all sides of an issue, determining the ramifications of a piece of legislation, knowing all the candidates' stands on issues, and, in general, having perfect information prior to voting would take an inordinate amount of time and money. Because information gathering is costly and because individuals have little incentive to become well informed, we say that voters are rationally ignorant—they choose to make decisions on the basis of limited information. Many voters, in fact, go to the polls without having any knowledge of the issues being voted on.

For all of these reasons, you can see that voting is a much less exact expression of individual preference than the process of purchasing a good or service. In the next section, we look at some of the problems that can result from collective decision-making that do not occur in a private market.

1.b. Problems That Can Arise in Collective Decision-Making

In examining group decision-making we must first acknowledge the set of voting rules used. Under a democratic system the majority is usually favored. The issue or candidate receiving one vote more than one-half of the votes cast wins. There are instances, though, where a clear majority may not emerge and thus where collective decision-making provides no solution.

1.b.1. Voting Cycles

Consider, as an example, a decision of what type of budget to offer to the citizens of the Kyrene School District. The three members of the school board must decide whether to offer a low-budget program, a moderate-budget program, or a high-budget program. Suppose that school board member Melissa High prefers that new schools be built, class sizes be kept small, computers be provided, sports and music be available, and the maintenance of the schools be upgraded. Moreover, if the district does not want to have a high-budget program, Melissa believes most people will enroll their children in private schools. Thus, if she can't have the high-budget program, Melissa would prefer the low budget to the middle budget for the school district. John Middle is not comfortable with the size of tax payments necessary to support the high-quality package Melissa desires. He supports a more moderate budget, but he believes families would be willing to sacrifice to have the high budget if necessary. His least-preferred option is the low budget. Sharon Low prefers a low budget but would go along with a moderate budget if necessary. She is totally opposed to the high-budget program. The three board members must decide which of the programs to offer to the school district.

The choices of the three board members are illustrated in Figure 1. Along the vertical axis are the preferences of each board member ranked from least preferred to most preferred. Along the horizontal axis are the three proposals, low budget, moderate budget, and high budget. Melissa most prefers the high budget and least prefers the moderate budget; her preferences are indicated along the line labeled "Melissa." John most prefers the moderate budget and least prefers the low budget; his preferences are indicated by the line labeled "John." Sharon most prefers the low budget and least the high budget; her preferences are indicated by the line labeled "Sharon."

The board decides to vote on each budget program compared to the other; high budget versus middle budget, then high budget versus low budget, and then middle budget versus low budget. If the board members are asked to choose between the low budget and the moderate budget, the low budget gets the most votes. If they are asked to choose between the low budget and the high budget, the high budget gets the most votes. If they are asked to choose between the moderate budget and the high budget, the moderate budget gets the most votes. There is no clear decision: each alternative wins an election and each loses an election when paired against the other alternatives. A series

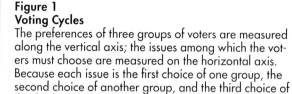

Figure 1
Voting Cycles
The preferences of three groups of voters are measured along the vertical axis; the issues among which the voters must choose are measured on the horizontal axis. Because each issue is the first choice of one group, the second choice of another group, and the third choice of the third group, there is no clear majority supporting any one issue.

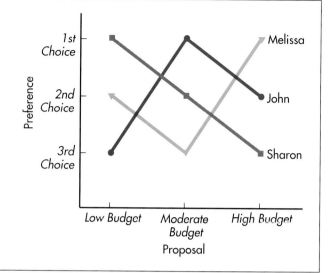

of votes or runoffs to determine the winner would result in an endless cycle. This result of the collective decision-making process is referred to as a **voting cycle**.

Voting cycles are a possible outcome in any election. They are a *failure of collective decision-making*. As a result of the failure, either no decision will be reached or another voting rule or procedure must be used. Often, a two-thirds voting rule is required instead of a simple majority in order to reduce the chance of a voting cycle. In the case we have outlined, a two-thirds voting rule is no different than the majority voting rule, and a change in the rule would not alter the outcome. Unanimity does not work either since there is no compromise position all could agree on. The ultimate outcome in the school board case will depend on whether any one of the three board members can dominate or influence the other members and convince one or both to alter their preferences.

1.b.2. Logrolling   The frustration voters may feel when the collective decision-making process fails may induce them to trade votes. John Middle may agree to support Melissa High's preference on the school budget issue if Melissa will agree to support his preference on some other issue. In this case, the voting cycle will be resolved and the high-budget program will be selected. John traded his vote on the budget issue to Melissa in return for a similar trade from Melissa on some other issue in the future. Vote trading is called **logrolling**.

Vote trading, or logrolling, is common in collective decision-making. It occurs regularly in the U.S. Congress. Suppose voters in Massachusetts want the government to build a large ship in their harbor and voters in Kansas want the government to purchase large quantities of wheat. The senator from Kansas has no reason to support the shipbuilding program in Massachusetts, and the senator from Massachusetts has no incentive to support the wheat-purchase plan. However, if the two senators agree to support each other's program, both can gain. Thus the senator from Kansas will promise to sup-

voting cycle:
the situation where a collective decision process does not reach a conclusion

logrolling:
trading votes or support on one issue in return for votes or support on another issue

port a bill subsidizing the construction of a ship in Boston Harbor in return for the support of the senator from Massachusetts for an increase in the price of wheat. In this way, each senator is able to get something he or she desires. Notice, however, that the outcomes may not be something desired by a majority of voters. As in the school board case, an outcome was determined through vote trading, but no clear majority prevailed.

1.c. The Importance of Brand Names

In private markets brand names provide information about the quality or reliability of products. In collective decision-making, where voters are rationally ignorant, brand names may play even more important roles. For instance, although their policies may seem to differ only slightly from one another, Republicans generally support smaller government, lower taxes, fewer benefits for lower-income citizens, and lower inflation, while Democrats are more likely to favor more government, tax increases, more support for the disadvantaged, and lower unemployment. A voter expects that a vote for a Republican will be a vote in support of a certain type of policy, whereas a vote for a Democrat will be a vote in support of a different type of policy. Political party identification thus provides at least general information to voters.

Incumbency also provides brand-name information; incumbents are better known than newcomers simply because the incumbents have a track record from having been in office. Just as consumers tend to purchase products with brand names, voters tend to support incumbent candidates: since 1980 over 90 percent of incumbents in the U.S. Congress running for reelection have won.

Voters' reliance on the brand names of "Republican" and "Democrat" has made it difficult for members of any other party to be successfully elected to office. Independents seldom enter campaigns for office at the federal or state level and, when they do, seldom win. The fixed costs of the brand name are extremely high: Ross Perot had to outspend George Bush and Bill Clinton in order to run a respectable third place in the 1992 presidential election.

RECAP

1. Collective decisions are reached by a group. The group may be a club or organization, a board of directors, or the citizens of a state or nation.

2. Collective decision-making differs from private decision-making. Collective decisions are made on the basis of one person–one vote; thus, intensity of preference cannot be registered. A full-line supply of issues is voted on rather than a single issue, and, since gathering information about issues is too costly, most voters choose rational ignorance.

3. Collective decision-making may not reach a conclusion or decision; a voting cycle may occur.

4. Logrolling is the trading of votes: One voter agrees to support the preference of another voter on one issue in return for the support of the second voter on an issue preferred by the first voter.

5. Due to rational ignorance, brand names—in this case, identification with a specific political party—may provide the information voters rely on.

2. GOVERNMENT ACTIVITIES AS DETERMINED BY COLLECTIVE DECISION-MAKING

Individuals maximize utility. What does the government maximize?

Although collective decision-making occurs in the private sector—boards of directors, unions, private clubs, and organizations all make collective or group decisions—its most important manifestation is in government: the public's choice with respect to levels of national defense, macroeconomic policy, government intervention in private markets, and other activities is expressed through this process.

2.a. Representative Democracy

In direct democracy, each action is voted on by all of the citizens. In representative democracy, citizens select individuals to represent them, to vote on issues and carry out the day-to-day activities of government. Representative democracy is more common than direct democracy because the transaction costs of direct democracy are too high. Just imagine how difficult it would be to have all of the nearly 200 million eligible voters in the United States vote on every issue confronting the country.

The participants in representative democracy are the voters and the politicians who attempt to become their representatives. Voters are like consumers, demanding the benefits that government can provide, and the representatives are the suppliers, providing the legislation that consumers want. The behavior of voters and representatives thus influences the outcome of the collective decision-making process in representative democracy.

2.b. Representatives Behave in Their Self-Interest

Self-interest characterizes all individuals.

Self-interest characterizes the behavior of every individual. Government representatives are no exception: they act to maximize their own utility. The central objective of any politician is to get elected and then maintain enough support to remain in office. Thus, each candidate running for office and each elected official must behave as his or her constituents want in order to win the election. Yet, each may have personal goals and objectives that do not correspond to what the constituents want. To the extent that the voters cannot monitor the actions of the elected officials, the officials can pursue their own objectives even at the expense of the voters.

Because voters cannot vote directly on every piece of legislation but must instead elect representatives to vote for them, the possibility exists that politicians will allow their own personal interests to enter into their voting decisions.

A great deal of evidence exists to suggest that self-interest characterizes the behavior of elected officials. Consider the difference between senators who are subject to election only once every six years and the members of the House of Representatives, who must compete every other year. Citizens can more easily monitor the behavior of the representatives, while senators have a longer period of time during which entry is barred. We would thus expect senators to act more like monopolists than would representatives. We would expect senators to pursue their own interests rather than their constituents' interests more often than the representatives do. And indeed this is the case. Senators vote their own interests rather than the interests of their constituents much more often than do the representatives.

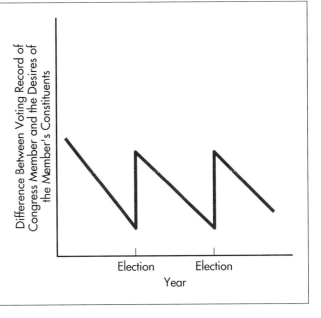

Figure 2
Senatorial Voting Record
Senators face election every six years. As a result, once elected they can vote their own interests for a few years. As an election nears, however, they begin to vote more along the lines desired by their constituents. The jagged curve represents the difference between the voting record of a senator and the voting record desired by the senator's constituents. The difference decreases as an election nears and rises by the greatest amount immediately after an election.

(chart y-axis label) Difference Between Voting Record of Congress Member and the Desires of the Member's Constituents

(chart x-axis) Election   Election
Year

Senators vote their own interests during the first two or three years immediately following an election and then vote as their constituents want in the year or two prior to an election, because the voters forget the earlier actions and focus on the more recent ones when going to the polls. Senators thus have a cyclical voting record relative to the desires of their constituents, as shown in Figure 2. They vote a more conservative line as an election nears if they are from a conservative state, and they vote a more liberal line as an election nears if they are from a liberal state. Once the election is over, they once again vote as their own self-interest dictates. This pattern does not show up in the voting behavior of members of the House of Representatives.

All politicians behave in their own self-interest, and all must appeal to a majority of their constituents at the time of election. Thus policies and programs are offered and implemented in order to ensure election or reelection. A dramatic illustration of this was described by Gore Vidal in his historical novel *Lincoln*. Vidal noted that President Lincoln used troop deployment to ensure his reelection in 1864. Units from states in which his election was in question were moved to the rear or out of the fighting in the hope that they and their friends and families would support Lincoln or at least would not have reason not to support him. Troops from states in which his reelection was virtually either a certainty or an impossibility saw front-line action.[1]

2.c. Public Choice Theory at Work

What results can we expect a system of representative democracy, with its rationally self-interested participants, to yield? In the next sections, we look at four outcomes of our own representative democracy: growth of government; public production of public goods; taxation and spending legislation; and the median voter theorem.

---

[1]Gore Vidal, *Lincoln* (New York: Ballantine Books, 1984). Robert Tollison examined Vidal's thesis and found evidence to support it. See Robert Tollison, "Dead Men Don't Vote," Public Choice Center, George Mason University, 1989.

2.c.1. Agencies and the Growth of Government

Government consists not just of the representatives directly elected by the public but also the bureaucrats appointed by the elected representatives to run the government. This includes the agencies like the Food and Drug Administration, the Federal Communications Commission, the Departments of Labor, State, Health and Human Resources, Treasury, and many others. Although these individuals may be appointed by the president or members of Congress, they have their own objectives.

How does self-interest show up in the bureaucracy? It could mean that a director will attempt to gain visibility and access to power in order to maximize personal income. Books can be written and speeches given after one leaves government service. Not only is the potential of personal wealth enticing, but power and influence alone provide utility. To be the director of a large and powerful agency is better than to be the director of a small, unknown agency. For this reason, it is not at all unusual for an agency to increase its sphere of influence and for the number of employees in an agency to rise over time. In fact, nearly every agency in government has grown, and at a very fast pace, as discussed in the Economic Insight "The Growth of Government." As we learned in Chapter 5, the number of government employees has risen significantly since 1930, and they now constitute about 20 percent of the labor force, at least partly due to the individual self-interest of those involved in the bureaucracy of government.

2.c.2. Private versus Public Production of Public Goods

Although society believes that government should provide public goods, it does not say the government should produce the goods itself. Why doesn't the government have private firms produce the public goods, such as fire protection and police protection, under contract to the government? In this way, the government could rely on the efficiency of the private market to produce high-quality goods at the lowest prices. For instance, the national park service, national postal service, local police and fire protection services, and refuse collection and water supply services could all be run by private firms for the government rather than run and staffed by government employees. Private firms could provide these services for the government at a lower cost in most instances.

One reason that private firms aren't used is that the representatives of government have more control of the public goods if the government produces them than if private firms produce them. If services were provided by the private sector, politicians would have much more difficulty influencing the behavior of the agencies. Not only can politicians influence the behavior of government agencies and bureaus, but they can provide employment in an agency for constituents. It would be more difficult to place an important constituent in a position in a private firm than in a government agency.

Another reason that such a combination of government and private enterprise is problematic is that the private sector may not be able to perform as the public wants. Perhaps a private firm would not produce the quality of goods the public desires. (However, it would be difficult to know how the public felt about the quality of the goods, since the public couldn't switch to another brand; only one would be provided.) Thus, the performance of the private firm would have to be controlled or monitored by some government agency, and it is possible the costs of such monitoring would exceed the efficiencies gained from the private production of the good. While such a system

The Growth of Government

Most federal agencies have grown significantly since the 1970s. Even in the Reagan and Bush administrations, which were purportedly antigovernment, the growth was substantial. The Justice Department increased its staff by 30.4 percent between 1982 and 1988, the Treasury by 23 percent, the Environmental Protection Agency by 11.5 percent, the State Department by 11 percent, and the Department of Defense by about 7 percent. Growth has been pervasive, occurring in virtually every government agency and department.

The desire for growth has implications for the economy. How is it to be paid for? The growth of most agencies is supported by an increase in general government expenditures. The growth of the Federal Reserve System (Fed), however, is covered not by general government revenues but by the Fed's own revenues. The Federal Reserve obtains its funding in a roundabout way from the Treasury: the Fed pays direct expenses and transfers the remainder to the Treasury. The greater the Fed's revenue, the more expenses it is allowed to generate and still be able to transfer profit to the Treasury. How does the Federal Reserve earn revenue? It increases sales of the goods and services it provides—and the primary good it provides is money. In other words, the Federal Reserve increases its revenue by increasing the quantity of money it creates.

The growth of the Federal Reserve has been accompanied by a money-supply growth that has exceeded the rate of growth necessary for a stable, noninflationary economy, and this may explain why inflation has been a problem in the United States for the past four decades. A monetary policy that expands the supply of money and thereby causes inflation may have resulted from the desires of Fed officials to increase their power, prestige, and income by increasing the size of the Federal Reserve rather than through safeguarding the public interest.

might appear to offer a solution to the problem of government inefficiencies, it creates other problems that outweigh the efficiencies.

2.c.3. Taxes versus Spending Representatives want to offer a package of policies that voters believe will improve their well-being. If a representative can ensure that benefits flow to many constituents, the representative can gain more support. Government expenditures create income and provide benefits to constituents. Taxes, in contrast, reduce income and take away benefits from constituents. Thus, politicians favor increasing government spending a lot more than they favor increasing taxes.

The problem for the representatives is that an increase in benefits usually means an increase in costs. An increase in government expenditures must be paid for either through raising taxes or through borrowing. How can a representative increase benefits and support without increasing costs and losing support? One way is to provide benefits to constituents but have everyone, constituents and nonconstituents, pay taxes. In this way, the benefits the constituents receive are substantially more than the costs they pay.

Of course, all representatives are attempting to do the same thing since none want taxes imposed on their constituents. As a result, it is much easier to implement expenditure increases than tax increases. An alternative is to provide benefits to the constituents today but not pay for the benefits until sometime in the future, thereby imposing the costs on future generations. There is a natural bias, then, toward increased government expenditures paid for by borrowing or debt, since debt does not have to be paid until some point in the future.

In schools, children are told to save the *rain forest, recycle, use environmentally safe pesticides,* and *ban anything that destroys the ozone.* The problem with these pronouncements is that they do not take into consideration the costs of the necessary policies. While spectacular for the developed nations' citizens to observe, the rain forests provide only the barest opportunities for the residents to scratch out a substandard living. In contrast, harvesting trees brings with it the employment of many rain forest residents and a much improved standard of living. A ban on harvesting trees enforces substandard living. To preserve the rain forest and provide opportunities for improved living standards, the land could be given to its residents as private ownership. Selling their land for the harvest of trees would provide the residents with a better standard of living. But, rather than having the trees razed, the rain forest residents could sell only portions of the trees and plant new ones each year, ensuring a valuable income stream for years to come.

2.c.4. The Median Voter Theorem

Programs aiming to improve the lot of everyone are prominent features in every representative's policies. The problem for the representative is that there is usually a diversity of opinion on each issue. Some voters favor a large national defense budget; others urge disarmament. Some want a great deal of income redistribution; others urge tax cuts for everyone. Some want large-scale government intervention to protect the environment; others want little government intervention. Faced with this diversity of opinion, it is almost impossible to please everyone. Nevertheless, to attain office, a party must put together a package that attracts a majority of the votes. The search for a majority often results in each candidate offering policies that are very similar to the policies of the other candidates and very similar to the preferences of the median voter.

Suppose all voters are aligned along the continuum of attitudes toward environmental protection shown in Figure 3. The horizontal axis measures the number of voters, and the vertical axis measures the level of government spending on environmental issues supported by each voter. Voter D, labeled *median*, is exactly in the middle: half of the voters support more spending and half support less spending than voter D. Given this range of attitudes, which position will the party stake out?

The greatest support can be gained by selecting a level of spending that corresponds with the level supported by the median voter. The median position differs from the level of spending supported by each other voter by less than any other position. Suppose the party goes along with voter C.

Figure 3
The Median Voter Theorem
Voters are aligned in the order of the amount of government spending on environmental issues they desire. The median voter is the voter whose interests put him or her exactly in the middle of all voters: half want more spending and half want less spending than the median voter. A candidate gains maximum political support by staking out positions that are identical to the positions favored by the median voter.

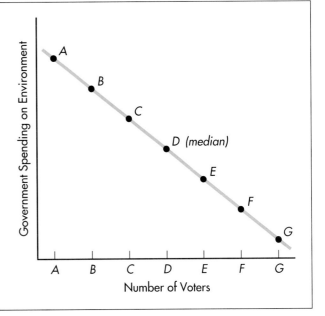

Candidates would pick up more support from voters A and B. Voters D, E, F, and G, however, would decrease their support. The difference between the levels of spending that they favor and the party's chosen position would be larger than it was when the candidate chose to support the median position. Similarly, choosing a position at E would decrease the difference between the spending that F supports and the party's position, but it would increase the differences between the spending levels supported by A, B, and C and by the candidate relative to the median position. By staking out a position that is the median voter position, the party or candidate maximizes support.

The first party stakes out D, the median position. Where should the second party stake out its position? If it chooses point E, it will attract all voters to the right of E and half of the voters between the median position and E; but the first party will obtain the support of all voters between A and the median as well as half of those between the median and E and will win the election. The closer the second party moves to the median voter, the larger the number of votes the second party will receive. Therefore, it too will stake out a position identical to the median voter position. This decision is explained by the **median voter theorem**: parties or candidates select positions on issues that reflect the median voter's position.

The median voter theorem is the result of competition among candidates seeking to maximize votes. The identical result is obtained when profit-maximizing firms look at locations or introduce new products. The median position is the profit-maximizing position—or, in the case of votes, the vote-maximizing position.

Logrolling in collective decision-making can invalidate the median voter theorem and result in voter frustration. Suppose, for example, that voters are deciding on a health-care system. Senior citizens prefer increased spending on health care and want the most lavish system available for preserving lives. The middle-aged citizens prefer a more moderate system, one that will help

median voter theorem:
parties or candidates select positions on issues that reflect the median voter's positions on those issues

them provide for their children's health. Younger citizens prefer no system. The middle-aged citizens are the median voters in this case. But suppose the younger citizens agree to support the lavish health-care system if the seniors will support a system of free education for all college students. In this case, logrolling has led to a decision not favored by the median voter.

RECAP

1. The economic principle of self-interest accounts for the actions of the government.

2. Political outcomes are the result of participants maximizing their self-interest. Political candidates want to be elected to office. Bureaucrats want to acquire income, power, and prestige.

3. According to the median voter theorem, politicians tend to stake out policies and programs that are supported by the median voter.

4. The median voter theorem may not hold because of logrolling in the collective decision-making process.

3. RENT SEEKING

What is rent seeking?

In Chapter 5 we discussed how people attempt to acquire benefits or wealth through government actions rather than through creating goods and services. We referred to this as *rent-seeking activity*. Having discussed collective decision-making in this chapter, we can now see how representative democracy allows rent seeking to occur: people cannot express their intensity of preferences with a single vote; people must find ways to influence others; and representatives pursue their own self-interest as long as constituents cannot closely monitor their actions. These three elements combine to create the conditions for rent seeking.

Representative democracy provides an incentive to citizens to increase their wealth through government regulations, transfers, or direct expenditures without increasing the supply or ownership of resources. If special interest groups want to increase their wealth, are organized and politically powerful, politicians grant benefits that enable these groups to increase their wealth. Such benefits are called rents because, like economic rents, they represent a payment that is larger than necessary for the resource to be supplied. Activities undertaken to obtain special favors (rents) from government are called **rent seeking**; these activities produce zero output but use up resources.

rent seeking:
activities directed toward securing income without increasing the production of output

3.a. Profit Seeking versus Rent Seeking

Rent seeking may increase the efficiency of government.

Throughout the book we have pointed out how profit-seeking resource owners enter industries in which economic profits are positive and exit industries in which economic profits are negative. Profit seeking is an important aspect of competition—it ensures that resources are allocated to their highest-valued uses. Rent seeking, in contrast, simply transfers wealth from one group to another. It does not create wealth or produce goods and services. As a result, it does not ensure that resources flow to their most highly valued use.

3.a.1. An Application of Rent Seeking In the mid-1930s the Agricultural Marketing Agreement was implemented to stop U.S. farmers from ruining each other with too much competition. Since then a number of government

Figure 4
Rent Seeking
The demand for and supply of wheat determine a price of $.80 per bushel and a quantity of 80 million bushels. Farmers, however, are able to convince Congress that $.80 is too low a price, and Congress passes legislation that sets a minimum price for wheat of $1 per bushel. Farmers clearly have an incentive to increase their production at this higher price, to 100 million bushels. To keep the higher price in force, the government must buy all of the surplus. Thus, consumers are paying $1 per bushel instead of $.80 per bushel and the government is paying a direct subsidy to the farmer of $1 per bushel for all wheat not sold to the consumer.

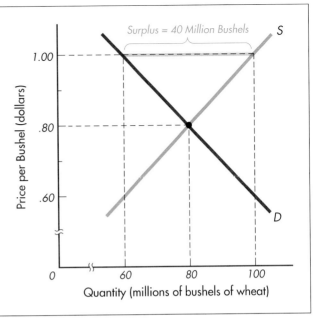

policies have been implemented to benefit farmers. Let's see how rent seeking might explain some of these programs.

Assume the market for wheat is shown in Figure 4. The demand for and supply of wheat determine a price of $.80 per bushel and a quantity of 80 million bushels. This represents a long-run equilibrium in a competitive market so that wheat farmers are earning a normal rate of return. Farmers, however, are able to convince Congress that $.80 is too low a price, and Congress passes legislation that sets a minimum price for wheat of $1 per bushel. Farmers clearly have an incentive to increase production at this higher price. As shown in the figure, the quantity supplied at $1 per bushel is 100 million bushels, but the quantity demanded at this price is only 60 million bushels. A surplus of 40 million bushels is created by the government's program.

With a surplus, the price should fall. However, the government has mandated that the price cannot fall. To keep the higher price in force, the government must buy all of the surplus or must restrict the supply without affecting domestic farmers. By placing quotas on the importing of foreign agriculture, the government causes the total supply of agricultural products in the United States to decline. Thus, consumers are paying a direct subsidy to the farmer (the difference between $.80 per bushel and $1 per bushel), and the government is paying a subsidy to the farmer by purchasing the wheat at $1 per bushel for all wheat not sold to the consumer or by restricting foreign agricultural products.

Each U.S. farmer receives an extra $.20 per bushel over what would have prevailed in the market without government intervention. In addition, the total U.S. farming industry expands. As it expands, the marginal costs of production may rise (if the industry is an increasing-cost industry). As land prices rise, as capital equipment costs rise, as the cost of fertilizer and pesticides rise, the farmer's total operating costs rise. Over the long run, because of the relatively free entry into the wheat-producing business, the farmer ends up earning just a normal rate of return at the higher, subsidized price.

The rent-seeking activity by the farmers has led to deadweight losses—

Rent seeking may benefit few at the expense of many. A government subsidy may benefit those receiving the subsidy, but cost the general public in the form of higher prices and large surpluses. Here we see that a price floor leads to a surplus of blood oranges. The question is how to dispose of the surplus. In many nations the government purchases it. In Sicily, however, the least-cost solution may have been simply to dump the oranges.

higher costs to consumers and no more profits to farmers. Yet the subsidies persist and increase. In 1994, direct subsidies to agriculture from the federal government exceeded $30 billion. Why does rent seeking occur? It occurs because the first group to receive the rewards of rent seeking earns economic rents. Much as the entrepreneur who introduces a new, unique product earns monopoly profit in the short run, special interests who are first to receive a benefit earn economic rents. Since rents are available from special legislation, there is a demand for this legislation. Legislators supply the legislation in return for political support.

3.b. The Costs and Benefits of Rent Seeking

Because profits can be made by a firm or industry that succeeds in acquiring a privilege, firms compete with each other to acquire these privileges. Some of the rents that are created are competed away with resources that could otherwise have been put to productive uses. An industry receiving protection from foreign competition worth $20 million per year is willing to spend up to $20 million a year on lobbyists, campaign committees, and other rent-seeking activities to maintain the special privilege.

The value of rent-seeking activity occurring each year is substantial, ranging upward from about 5 percent of a nation's total output. The amount of rent seeking that occurs depends on the extent to which a government doles out special privileges. The more involved government is in the economy, the greater the extent of rent seeking. The World Bank estimates that rent-seeking activities account for nearly one-fourth of the national income of many developing countries, countries in which the government plays a major role.

Although rent seeking is not considered a productive activity, many economists argue that it may offer some social benefits. Figure 5 shows a firm that has received a government privilege; the firm is earning rents (monopoly profits) of *ABCE*. If the firm were assured of maintaining the privilege—if its costs could rise and it would still earn a profit—it might become lazy and sloppy. However, other firms, seeing the benefits of the privilege, want to

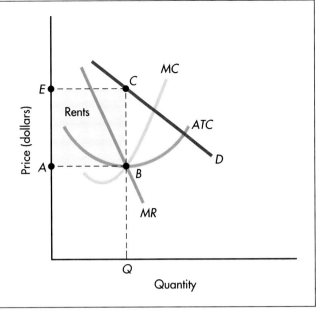

Figure 5
Economic Rents
A firm receives a special privilege from government that enables it to earn rents or monopoly profits of *ABCE*. The firm is willing to devote an amount up to *ABCE* to ensure that it retains those rents. As a result of the competition for the special privilege, the rents are dissipated, used in rent seeking to maintain the rents.

have that special benefit themselves. They lobby politicians and make donations to political campaigns to get politicians to bestow the privilege on them. The firm portrayed in Figure 5 is thus willing to devote some resources to safeguarding its rents. It cannot become lazy and sloppy because if it does it will not have the economic rents to offset its increased costs. The competition for special privileges and the resulting rents tends to dissipate those rents. The most effective rent seekers receive the benefits, but competition for rents forces the firm to be as efficient as a firm without the special privilege.

3.c. Should Government Intervene?

Barriers to entry, above-normal profit, imperfect information, and market failures in the private sector suggest that the government should intervene. If the government were a single entity whose sole purpose was to act in the public interest, there would be little question regarding its intervention. But when the government is understood to be composed of individuals with differing objectives, each a self-interested rational being, then its activities may be the result of rent seeking or the self-interest of bureaucrats or elected officials. In such a case, government actions may *not* be in the best interest of the public. In this chapter we have seen that barriers to entry, imperfect information, and failures occur in the public sector as they do in the private sector. We have seen that collective decision-making may not come to a conclusion. Yet we have provided no definitive answer as to the optimal role of the public sector in an economy. Instead, our discussion has been directed toward creating a healthy skepticism: solving private market problems through the public sector may not always make society better off.

RECAP

1. Rent seeking refers to activities that attempt to secure income without an increase in resource supplies.

2. Rent seeking in a representative democracy may serve to create efficiency within government.

SUMMARY

▲▼ *How is collective decision-making different from private decision-making?*

1. Collective decision-making is the process of reaching a group decision. §Preview

2. Collective decisions differ from private market decisions in that there is one vote per person, a full-line supply of goods is "purchased" (voted on) at one time, and voters are rationally ignorant. §1.a

3. Voting cycles are failures of the collective decision-making process. §1.b.1

4. Logrolling is the process of vote trading. §1.b.2

5. Brand-name recognition (political party identification) plays a key role in collective decision-making. §1.c

▲▼ *Individuals maximize utility. What does the government maximize?*

6. Self-interest characterizes the behavior of individuals involved in collective decision-making. Politicians, representatives, bureaucrats, and citizens behave so as to maximize their own self-interest. §2.b

7. Government grows partly through the growth of agencies and bureaus. §2.c.1

8. There is a bias toward expenditures and away from taxes, and toward expenditures financed by debt, because representatives attempt to maximize their support. §2.c.3

9. According to the median voter theorem, the competition among candidates for votes induces the candidates to stake out similar positions on issues. §2.c.4

10. Logrolling can invalidate the median voter theorem. §2.c.4

▲▼ *What is rent seeking?*

11. Rent-seeking activities are directed toward securing income without increasing the production of output. §3

12. Competition for rents may decrease the amount of inefficiency that results from special legislation. §3.b.

KEY TERMS

public choice theory §Preview
full-line supply §1.a
rationally ignorant voters §1.a
voting cycle §1.b.1

logrolling §1.b.2
median voter theorem §2.c.4
rent seeking §3

EXERCISES

1. Individuals act to maximize their utility. What does the government maximize?

2. Explain why it is easier for the government to spend than to tax. What would occur if the law required the government to spend only what it collected in taxes?

3. Why do political parties exist? What purpose do they serve for voters? What purpose do they serve for candidates?

4. In the Civil War, the Union Army was organized into state regiments. A soldier from Pennsylvania fought with the Pennsylvania

regiment, a soldier from New York fought with the New York regiment, and so on. In the Vietnam War, there were state quotas for draftees, but draftees were assigned to regiments regardless of the state in which they were drafted. Explain how President Lincoln in the Civil War and Presidents Johnson and Nixon in the Vietnam War might have used the armies to enhance their chances for reelection.

5. What is the optimal amount of rent seeking? What could cause this amount to be reduced or increased?

6. Why is voter turnout in the United States usually less than 50 percent of the total eligible voters, while in the former Soviet Union it was 100 percent?

7. U.S. automobile producers are asking Congress to place limits, or quotas, on the number of foreign-made cars and trucks that can be sold in the United States. What would be the outcome of such a policy, if implemented, for consumers and producers? Why would legislators support such a policy?

8. In most national campaigns, the Republican and Democratic platforms are not much different. Other parties, such as the Libertarian party, the Science party, and Up With America, stake out more extreme policies. Why?

9. The U.S. government is in debt to the tune of nearly $5 trillion and the debt keeps growing. Why, when nearly everyone calls the debt bad for the economy and bad for society, does it continue to grow?

10. Evaluate the following statement: "To demonstrate that there are market failures in the private sector is not sufficient to justify government intervention in the private sector."

11. Use the following table to determine whether a voting cycle may occur using majority rule.

Can you think of any other voting rule that would reduce the chance of a voting cycle?

Public Good	Sally	Jesse	Rafael
Park	2nd choice	1st choice	3rd choice
School	3rd choice	2nd choice	1st choice
Bike Path	1st choice	3rd choice	2nd choice

12. Explain what term limits might mean for the political market. (A term limit would allow a senator to serve only two terms of six years and a representative to serve four terms of two years.)

13. Discuss the following three ways to finance political campaigns.

a. Anyone, any firm, or any entity can contribute as much to a politician's campaign as desired.

b. No donation of more $50 can be made.

c. Campaign expenditures are limited to $100,000 for House of Representative campaigns and $300,000 for Senate campaigns.

14. President Clinton forbade his appointees to lobby for a private firm or group for several years following their departure from government service. Explain how this policy might actually reduce the efficiency of government.

15. "Here they go again." This is the statement with which Ronald Reagan defeated Jimmy Carter and which he later used to lament the policies of President Clinton. The statement refers to the tendency of Democrats to increase government involvement in the private sector. Reagan, on the other hand, argues that the government that governs least governs best. How do such apparently opposite views match with the median voter theorem?

COOPERATIVE LEARNING EXERCISE

Divide the students into groups of four. Each group must develop an answer to the following question:

Logrolling explains why government has expanded over the years because . . .

Two groups are called on. One group provides an answer and the other must determine whether the answer is correct or not. Then the roles are reversed.

"Amtrak Routes Must Be Cut, They Agree—'But Not In My State'"

The challenge of reducing Amtrak's nearly $1 billion annual federal subsidy without gorging any oxen came into sharp focus yesterday at a House subcommittee hearing. A parade of 17 members of Congress, Republicans and Democrats alike, from 12 far-flung states, each acknowledged that Amtrak's problems had been years in the making and that it now faced the worst financial crisis since its creation in 1971. Most of the 16 representatives and one senator said some of the passenger railroad's money-losing routes must be cut.

Then, almost every lawmaker testifying before the railroad subcommittee of the House Transportation and Infrastructure Committee made the same plea: The service Amtrak plans to cut from my district is a vital public service and should be saved.

Amtrak in December said it would eliminate or reduce service on 21 percent of its routes, lay off 5,600 employees, and delay overhauls on 40 percent of its car fleet to close an expected $200 million gap in its $1.4 billion operating budget for 1995.

Source: Amtrak Routes Must Be Cut, They Agree—'But Not In My State' by Tom Belden, *The Philadelphia Inquirer*, Feb. 11, 1995, p. D1. Reprinted with permission from the February 11, 1995 issue of *The Philadelphia Inquirer*.

The Philadelphia Inquirer/February 11, 1995

Commentary

Some people argue that railroads, like highways, are a vital part of national defense and because they are a vital part of national defense are a public good. Unless the government provides the public good, too little of it will be produced. How can we identify the correct amount of the public good that should be produced? We could undertake a survey asking each citizen how much he or she would be willing to pay for alternative quantities of the public good. We could then sum the individual demands to get the market demand. The government could then ensure that a quantity was produced such that the marginal cost of producing it and the amount consumers were willing to pay were equal. Then society would get the quantity of the public good for which they were willing and able to pay.

Since such a survey is not feasible, the demand for the public good is usually expressed through the ballot box. Voters choose a president and members of the House and Senate to represent their desires. If, on the whole, the constituents want railroads, they vote for candidates who promise to supply the railroads. There are several problems with this process of expressing public choice. First, individuals do not vote for or against railroads, for or against highways, for or against civil liberties, and on and on. Instead, they vote for a candidate to represent them on every issue. Obviously, representatives will never have interests that align exactly with every voter. Instead, it is the median voter whose interests are represented. Second, a great deal of voting concerns transfers—government programs that tax the nation as a whole to provide benefits to particular areas or segments of society. Votes on transfers typically reflect *NIMBY* or *Not In My Back Yard*. Voters may want new highways constructed but not if the highways go through their neighborhood. Voters may want a new landfill constructed, but not if it is too close to their neighborhood. Voters in Philadelphia may want the railroads to run from Philly to New York but not want the railroads to run from L.A. to San Francisco.

The issue discussed in this article provides insights into why it is so difficult for the public sector to reduce expenditures and why there is a tendency for the public sector to grow. Representatives want to be reelected. To win elections, they need to provide the services their constituents want. Increased government expenditures and transfers provide large benefits to some constituents and impose small costs on all constituents in the form of increased taxes. Reduced expenditures and transfers impose large costs on a few constituents and provide small benefits to many constituents in the form of reduced taxes. Since the large benefits or large costs to a few people will induce those people to act—to protest, to vote, to organize, to raise funds for or against candidates—while the small benefits or small costs to many people will not induce the many to act, the politicians will attempt to cater to the smaller, more active groups. The median voter is more likely to represent the interests of the small active group of constituents.

Thus, all representatives seek to provide large benefits to small groups paid for with taxes on all of society. And all representatives attempt to ensure that there will be no large costs imposed on small groups—in particular their constituents. There is, therefore, almost no constituency for reduced government, reduced taxes, and reduced transfers.

IX

Issues in International Trade and Finance

37

World Trade Equilibrium

FUNDAMENTAL QUESTIONS

1. What are the prevailing patterns of trade between countries? What goods are traded?
2. What determines the goods a nation will export?
3. How are the equilibrium price and the quantity of goods traded determined?
4. What are the sources of comparative advantage?

The United States's once-dominant position as an exporter of color television sets has since been claimed by nations like Japan and Taiwan. What caused this change? Is it because Japan specializes in the export of high-tech equipment? If countries tend to specialize in the export of particular kinds of goods, why does the United States import Heineken beer at the same time it exports Budweiser? This chapter will examine the volume of world trade and the nature of trade linkages between countries. As you saw in Chapter 2, trade occurs because of specialization in production. No single individual or country can produce everything better than others can. The result is specialization of production based on comparative advantage. Remember that comparative advantage is in turn based on relative opportunity costs: a country will specialize in the production of those goods for which its opportunity costs of production are lower than costs in other countries. Nations then trade what they produce in excess of their own consumption to acquire other things they want to consume. In this chapter, we will go a step further to discuss the sources of comparative advantage. We will look at why one country has a comparative advantage in, say, automobile production, while another country has a comparative advantage in wheat production.

The world equilibrium price and quantity traded are derived from individual countries' demand and supply curves. This relationship between the world trade equilibrium and individual country markets will be utilized in Chapter 38 to discuss the ways that countries can interfere with free international trade to achieve their own economic or political goals.

PREVIEW

I. AN OVERVIEW OF WORLD TRADE

Trade occurs because it makes people better off. International trade occurs because it makes people better off than they would be if they could consume only domestically produced products. Who trades with whom, and what sorts of goods are traded? These are the questions we first consider before investigating the underlying reasons for trade.

What are the prevailing patterns of trade between countries? What goods are traded?

I.a. The Direction of Trade

Table 1 shows patterns of trade between two large groups of countries: the industrial countries and the developing countries. The industrial countries include all of Western Europe, Japan, Australia, New Zealand, Canada, and the United States. The developing countries are, essentially, the rest of the

TABLE I
The Direction of Trade
(in billions of dollars and percentages of world trade, 1993)

	Destination: Industrial Countries	Destination: Developing Countries
Origin:		
Industrial Countries	$1,777 48%	$728 20%
Developing Countries	$ 664 18%	$461 13%

Source: International Monetary Fund, *Direction of Trade Statistics Yearbook*, 1994.

Trade between industrial countries accounts for the majority of international trade.

world. The table shows the dollar values and percentages of total trade between these groups of countries. The vertical column at the left lists the origin of exports, and the horizontal row at the top lists the destination of imports.

As Table 1 shows, trade between industrial countries accounts for the bulk of international trade. Trade between industrial countries is a little less than $2 trillion in value and amounts to 48 percent of world trade. Exports from industrial countries to developing countries represent 20 percent of total world trade. Exports from developing countries to industrial countries account for 18 percent of total trade, while exports from the developing countries to other developing countries currently represent only 13 percent of international trade.

Figure 1
Merchandise Trade Flows in North America (billions of dollars)
In 1993, the United States exported $100 billion worth of goods to Canada and imported $113 billion of goods from Canada. The same year, U.S. merchandise exports to Mexico were $42 billion, while merchandise imports from Mexico were $41 billion. Source: International Monetary Fund, *Direction of Trade Statistics Yearbook*, 1994.

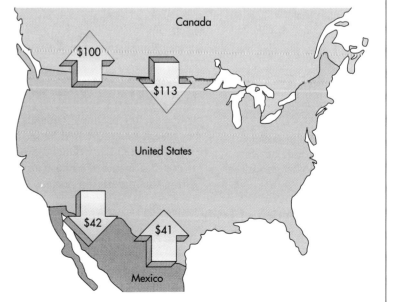

Table 2 lists the major trading partners of selected countries and the percentage of total exports and imports accounted for by each country's top ten trading partners. For instance, 22 percent of U.S. exports went to Canada, and 18 percent of U.S. imports came from Japan. From a glance at the other countries listed in Table 2, it is clear that the United States is a major trading partner for many nations. This is true because of the size of the U.S. economy and the nation's relatively high level of income. It is also apparent that Canada and Mexico are very dependent on trade with the United States: about four-fifths of Canadian exports and 65 percent of its imports, and more than three-fourths of Mexican exports and over 60 percent of its imports involve the United States. The dollar value of trade among the three North American nations is shown in Figure 1.

1.b. What Goods Are Traded?

Because countries differ in their comparative advantages, they will tend to export different goods. Countries also have different tastes and technological needs, and thus tend to differ in what they will import. Some goods are more widely traded than others, as Table 3 shows. Crude petroleum is the most

TABLE 2
Major Trading Partners of Selected Countries

United States				Canada			
Exports		**Imports**		**Exports**		**Imports**	
Canada	22%	Canada	19%	U.S.	81%	U.S.	65%
Japan	10	Japan	18	Japan	5	Japan	6
Mexico	9	Mexico	7	U.K.	2	U.K.	3
U.K.	6	Germany	5	Germany	1	Germany	2
Germany	4	U.K.	4	Korea	1	France	1
Germany				**Mexico**			
Exports		**Imports**		**Exports**		**Imports**	
France	12%	France	11%	U.S.	78%	U.S.	68%
U.K.	8	Netherlands	8	Canada	6	Japan	7
U.S.	8	Italy	8	Japan	2	Germany	4
Italy	7	U.S.	7	Spain	2	Spain	2
Netherlands	7	Belgium	6	Germany	1	France	1
		U.K.	5				
Japan				**United Kingdom**			
Exports		**Imports**		**Exports**		**Imports**	
U.S.	29%	U.S.	23%	U.S.	13%	Germany	13%
Hong Kong	6	China	9	Germany	12	U.S.	12
Germany	5	Australia	5	France	9	France	9
Korea	5	Indonesia	5	Netherlands	6	Netherlands	6
China	5	Korea	5	Belgium-Luxembourg	5	Japan	6

Source: Data for all countries from International Monetary Fund, *Direction of Trade Statistics Yearbook*, 1994.

TABLE 3
The Top Ten Exported Products
(in millions of dollars and percentages of world exports)

Product Category	Value	Percentage of World Trade
Crude petroleum	$180,565	5.67%
Motor vehicles	155,357	4.90
Petroleum products	80,340	2.54
Motor vehicle parts	77,622	2.45
Data processing equipment	64,027	2.02
Special transactions	61,508	1.95
Aircraft	57,818	1.82
Transistors, valves, etc.	57,078	1.80
Telecom equipment, parts	52,973	1.67
Paper and paperboard	46,579	1.47

Source: Data from United Nations Conference on Trade and Development: *Handbook of International Trade and Development Statistics, 1992* (TD/STAT.18), p. 184.

The volume of trade in crude petroleum exceeds that of any other good.

heavily traded good in the world, accounting for 5.67 percent of the total volume of world trade. Crude petroleum is followed by motor vehicles, petroleum products, motor vehicle parts, and automatic data processing equipment. The top ten exported products, however, represent only 25 percent of world trade. The remaining 75 percent is distributed among a great variety of products. The importance of petroleum and motor vehicles in international trade should not obscure the fact that international trade involves all sorts of products from all over the world.

RECAP

1. Trade between industrial countries accounts for the bulk of international trade.
2. The most important trading partners of the United States are Canada and Japan.
3. Crude petroleum is the most heavily traded good in the world, in terms of value of exports.
4. World trade is distributed across a great variety of products.

2. AN EXAMPLE OF INTERNATIONAL TRADE EQUILIBRIUM

The international economy is very complex. Each country has a unique pattern of trade, in terms both of trading partners and of goods traded. Some countries trade a great deal and others trade very little. We already know that countries specialize and trade according to comparative advantage, but what are the fundamental determinants of international trade that explain the pattern of comparative advantage?

The answer to this question will in turn provide a better understanding of some basic questions about how international trade functions: What goods

Comparative advantage is based on what a country can do relatively better than other countries. This photo shows a woman in Sri Lanka picking tea leaves. Sri Lanka is one of the few countries that export a significant amount of tea. Due to favorable growing conditions (a natural resource), these countries have a comparative advantage in tea production.

will be traded? How much will be traded? What prices will prevail for traded goods?

2.a. Comparative Advantage

What determines the goods a nation will export?

Comparative advantage is found by comparing the relative costs of production in each country. We measure the cost of producing a particular good in two countries in terms of opportunity costs—what other goods must be given up in order to produce more of the good in question.

Table 4 presents a hypothetical example of two countries, the United States and India, that both produce two goods, wheat and cloth. The table lists the hours of labor required to produce 1 unit of each good. This example assumes that labor productivity differences alone determine comparative advantage. In the United States, 1 unit of wheat requires 3 hours of labor, and 1 unit of cloth requires 6 hours of labor. In India, 1 unit of wheat requires 6 hours of labor, and 1 unit of cloth requires 8 hours of labor.

absolute advantage:
an advantage derived from one country having a lower absolute input cost of producing a particular good than another country

The United States has an **absolute advantage**—a lower resource cost—in producing both wheat and cloth. Absolute advantage is determined by comparing the absolute cost in different countries of producing each good. Since it requires fewer hours of labor to produce either good in the United States

TABLE 4
An Example of Comparative Advantage

Labor Hours Required to Produce One Unit Each of Two Goods		
	U.S.	**India**
1 unit of wheat	3	6
1 unit of cloth	6	8

than in India, the United States is the more efficient producer of both goods in terms of the domestic labor hours required.

It might seem that since the United States is the more efficient producer of both goods, there would be no need for trade with India. But absolute advantage is not the critical consideration. What matters in determining the benefits of international trade is comparative advantage, as originally discussed in Chapter 2. To find the **comparative advantage**—the lower opportunity cost—we must compare the opportunity cost of producing each good in each country.

The opportunity cost of producing wheat is what must be given up in cloth using the same resources, or number of labor hours. Look again at Table 4 to see the labor hours required for the production of wheat and cloth in the two countries. If the 3 labor hours it takes to produce wheat in the United States are devoted to cloth production, only 1/2 unit of cloth will result, since 6 labor hours are required to produce a full unit of cloth. The opportunity cost of producing wheat equals 3/6, or 1/2 unit of cloth:

$$\frac{\text{No. of labor hours to produce 1 unit of wheat}}{\text{No. of labor hours to produce 1 unit of cloth}} = \begin{array}{l}\text{opportunity cost of} \\ \text{producing 1 unit of wheat} \\ \text{(in terms of cloth given up)}\end{array}$$

$$3/6 = 1/2$$

Applying the same thinking to India, we find that devoting 6 hours of wheat production to the production of cloth yields 6/8, or 3/4 unit of cloth. The opportunity cost of producing 1 unit of wheat in India is 3/4 unit of cloth.

A comparison of the domestic opportunity costs in each country will reveal which one has the comparative advantage in producing each good. The U.S. opportunity cost of producing 1 unit of wheat is 1/2 unit of cloth; the Indian opportunity cost is 3/4 unit of cloth. Because the United States has a lower domestic opportunity cost, it has the comparative advantage in wheat production and will export wheat. Since wheat production costs are lower in the United States, India is better off trading for wheat rather than trying to produce it domestically.

The comparative advantage in cloth is found the same way. A unit of cloth requires 6 hours of labor in the United States. Since a unit of wheat requires 3 hours of labor, producing 1 more unit of cloth costs 2 units of wheat:

$$\frac{\text{No. of labor hours to produce 1 unit of cloth}}{\text{No. of labor hours to produce 1 unit of wheat}} = \begin{array}{l}\text{opportunity cost of} \\ \text{producing 1 unit of cloth} \\ \text{(in terms of wheat given up)}\end{array}$$

$$6/3 = 2$$

In India, 1 unit of cloth requires 8 hours of labor. Since 1 unit of wheat requires 6 hours of labor, shifting 8 hours of labor from wheat production to cloth production means an opportunity cost of 8/6, or 1 1/3 units of wheat for 1 unit of cloth. Comparing the U.S. opportunity cost of 2 units of wheat with the Indian opportunity cost of 1 1/3 units, we see that India has the comparative advantage in cloth production and will therefore export cloth. In this case, the United States is better off trading for cloth than producing it since India's costs of production are lower.

In international trade, as in other areas of economic decision-making, it is opportunity cost that matters—and opportunity costs are reflected in comparative advantage. Absolute advantage is irrelevant, because knowing the absolute number of labor hours required to produce a good does not tell us if we can benefit from trade. We benefit from trade if we are able to obtain a good from a foreign country by giving up less than we would have to give up to obtain the good at home. Because only opportunity cost can allow us to make such comparisons, international trade proceeds on the basis of comparative advantage.

2.b. Terms of Trade

Based on comparative advantage, India will specialize in cloth production and the United States will specialize in wheat production. The two countries will then trade with each other to satisfy the domestic demand for both goods. International trade permits greater consumption than would be possible from domestic production alone. Since countries trade when they can obtain a good more cheaply from a foreign producer than they can at home, international trade allows all traders to consume more. This is evident when we examine the terms of trade.

The **terms of trade** are the amount of an exported good that must be given up to obtain one unit of an imported good. The Economic Insight "The Dutch Disease" provides a popular example of a dramatic shift in the terms of trade. As you saw earlier, comparative advantage dictates that the United States will specialize in wheat production and export wheat to India in exchange for Indian cloth. But the amount of wheat that the United States will exchange for a unit of cloth is limited by the domestic tradeoffs. If a unit of cloth can be obtained domestically for 2 units of wheat, the United States will be willing to trade with India only if the terms of trade are less than 2 units of wheat for a unit of cloth.

India in turn will be willing to trade its cloth for U.S. wheat only if it can receive a better price than its domestic opportunity costs. Since a unit of cloth in India costs 1 1/3 units of wheat, India will gain from trade if it can obtain more than 1 1/3 units of wheat for its cloth.

The limits of the terms of trade are determined by the opportunity costs in each country:

> 1 unit of cloth for more than 1 1/3 but less than 2 units of wheat

Within this range, the actual terms of trade will be decided by the bargaining power of the two countries. The closer the United States can come to giving up only 1 1/3 units of wheat for cloth, the better the terms of trade for the United States. The closer India can come to receiving 2 units of wheat for its cloth, the better the terms of trade for India.

Though each country would like to push the other as close to the limits of the terms of trade as possible, any terms within the limits set by domestic opportunity costs will be mutually beneficial. Both countries benefit because they are able to consume goods at a cost less than their domestic opportunity costs. To illustrate the *gains from trade*, let us assume that the actual terms of trade are 1 unit of cloth for 1 1/2 units of wheat.

Suppose the United States has 60 hours of labor, half of which goes to wheat production and the other half to cloth production. Since a unit of wheat requires 3 labor hours, 10 units of wheat are produced. Cloth requires 6 labor hours, so 5 units of cloth are produced. Without international trade, the United States can produce and consume 10 units of wheat and 5 units of cloth. If the United States, with its comparative advantage in wheat production, chooses to produce only wheat, it can use all 60 labor hours to produce 20 units. If the terms of trade are 1 1/2 units of wheat per unit of cloth, the

The Dutch Disease

The terms of trade are the amount of an export that must be given up for a certain quantity of an import. The price of an import will be equal to its price in the foreign country of origin multiplied by the exchange rate (the domestic-currency price of foreign currency). As the exchange rate changes, the terms of trade will change. This can have important consequences for international trade.

A problem can arise when one export industry in an economy is booming relative to others. In the 1970s, for instance, the Netherlands experienced a boom in its natural gas industry. The dramatic energy price increases of the 1970s resulted in large Dutch exports of natural gas. Increased demand for exports from the Netherlands caused the Dutch currency to appreciate, making Dutch goods more expensive for foreign buyers. This situation caused the terms of trade to worsen for the Netherlands. Although the natural gas sector boomed, Dutch manufacturing was finding it difficult to compete in the world market.

The phenomenon of a boom in one industry causing declines in the rest of the economy is popularly called the Dutch Disease. It is usually associated with dramatic increases in the demand for a primary commodity and can afflict any nation experiencing such a boom. For instance, a rapid rise in the demand for coffee could lead to a Dutch Disease problem for Colombia, where a coffee boom would be accompanied by decline in other sectors of the economy.

United States can keep 10 units of wheat and trade the other 10 for 6 2/3 units of cloth (10 divided by 1 1/2). By trading U.S. wheat for Indian cloth, the United States is able to consume more than it could without trade. With no trade, and half its labor hours devoted to each good, the United States could consume 10 units of wheat and 5 units of cloth. After trade, the United States consumes 10 units of wheat and 6 2/3 units of cloth. By devoting all its labor hours to wheat production and trading wheat for cloth, the United States gains 1 2/3 units of cloth. This is the gain from trade—an increase in consumption, as summarized in Table 5.

The gain from trade is increased consumption.

2.c. Export Supply and Import Demand

The preceding example suggests that countries all benefit from specialization and trade. Realistically, however, countries do not completely specialize. Typically, domestic industries satisfy part of the domestic demand for goods that are also imported. To understand how the quantity of goods traded is determined, we must construct demand and supply curves for each country, and use them to create export supply and import demand curves.

The proportion of domestic demand for a good that is satisfied by domestic production and the proportion that will be satisfied by imports are determined by the domestic supply and demand curves and the international equilibrium price of a good. The international equilibrium price and quantity may be determined once we know the export supply and import demand curves for each country. These curves are derived from the domestic supply and demand in each country. Figure 2 illustrates the derivation of the export supply and import demand curves.

Figure 2(a) shows the domestic supply and demand curves for the U.S. wheat market. The domestic equilibrium price is $6 and the domestic equilibrium quantity is 200 million bushels. (The domestic "no-trade" equilibrium price is the price that exists prior to international trade.) A price above

TABLE 5
Hypothetical Example of U.S. Gains from Specialization and Trade

Without International Trade
30 labor hours in wheat production: produce and consume 10 wheat
30 labor hours in cloth production: produce and consume 5 cloth

With Specialization and Trade
60 labor hours in wheat production: produce 20 wheat and consume 10; trade 10 wheat for 6 2/3 cloth

Before trade: consume 10 wheat and 5 cloth

After trade: consume 10 wheat and 6 2/3 cloth
Gain 1 2/3 cloth by specialization and trade

$6 will yield a U.S. wheat surplus. For instance, at a price of $9, the U.S. surplus will be 200 million bushels. A price below equilibrium will produce a wheat shortage: at a price of $3, the shortage will be 200 million bushels. The key point here is that the world price of a good may be quite different than the domestic "no-trade" equilibrium price. And once international trade occurs, the world price will prevail in the domestic economy.

If the world price of wheat is different than a country's domestic "no-trade" equilibrium price, the country will become an exporter or importer. For instance, if the world price is above the domestic "no-trade" equilibrium price, the domestic surplus can be exported to the rest of the world. Figure 2(b) shows the U.S. **export supply curve**. This curve illustrates the U.S. domestic surplus of wheat for prices above the domestic "no-trade" equilibrium price of $6. At a world price of $9, the United States would supply 200 million bushels of wheat to the rest of the world. The export supply is equal to the domestic surplus. The higher the world price above the domestic "no-trade" equilibrium, the greater the quantity of wheat exported by the United States.

If the world price of wheat is below the domestic "no-trade" equilibrium price, the United States will import wheat. The **import demand curve** is the amount of the U.S. shortage at various prices below the "no-trade" equilibrium. In Figure 2(b), the import demand curve is a downward-sloping line, indicating that the lower the price below the domestic "no-trade" equilibrium of $6, the greater the quantity of wheat imported by the United States. At a price of $3, the United States will import 200 million bushels.

The domestic supply and demand curves and the export supply and import demand curves for India appear as parts (c) and (d) of Figure 2. The domestic "no-trade" equilibrium price in India is $12. At this price, India would neither import nor export any wheat because the domestic demand would be satisfied by domestic supply. The export supply curve for India is shown in Figure 2(d) as an upward-sloping line that measures the amount of the domestic surplus as the price level rises above the domestic "no-trade" equilibrium price of $12. According to Figure 2(c), if the world price of wheat is $15, the domestic surplus in India is equal to 200 million bushels. The corresponding point on the export supply curve indicates that, at a price of $15, 200 million bushels will be exported. The import demand curve for India

export supply curve:
a curve showing the relationship between the world price of a good and the amount that a country will export

import demand curve:
a curve showing the relationship between the world price of a good and the amount that a country will import

Figure 2
The Import Demand and Export Supply Curves

Figures 2(a) and 2(c) show the domestic demand and supply curves for wheat in the United States and India, respectively. The domestic "no-trade" equilibrium price is $6 in the United States and $12 in India. Any price above the domestic "no-trade" equilibrium prices will create domestic surpluses, which are reflected in the export supply curves in Figures 2(b) and (d). Any price below the domestic "no-trade" equilibrium prices will create domestic shortages, which are reflected in the import demand curves in Figures 2(b) and (d).

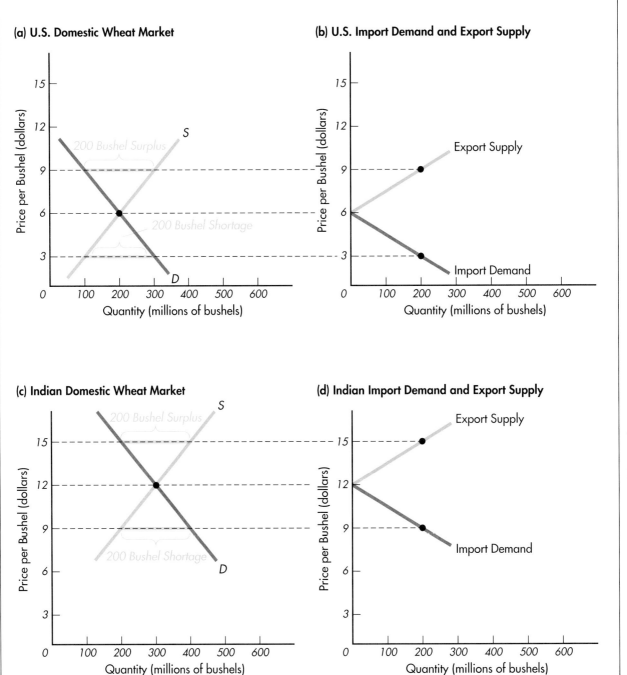

(a) U.S. Domestic Wheat Market

(b) U.S. Import Demand and Export Supply

(c) Indian Domestic Wheat Market

(d) Indian Import Demand and Export Supply

reflects the domestic shortage at a price below the domestic "no-trade" equilibrium price. At $9, the domestic shortage is equal to 200 million bushels: the import demand curve indicates that, at $9, 200 million bushels will be imported.

2.d. The World Equilibrium Price and Quantity Traded

How are the equilibrium price and the quantity of goods traded determined?

International equilibrium occurs at the point where the quantity of imports demanded by one country is equal to the quantity of exports supplied by the other country.

The international equilibrium price of wheat and the quantity of wheat traded are found by combining the import demand and export supply curves for the United States and India, as in Figure 3. International equilibrium occurs if the quantity of imports demanded by one country is equal to the quantity of exports supplied by the other country. In Figure 3, this equilibrium occurs at the point labeled *e*. At this point, the import demand curve for India indicates that India wants to import 200 million bushels at a price of $9. The export supply curve for the United States indicates that the United States wants to export 200 million bushels at a price of $9. Only at $9 will the quantity of wheat demanded by the importing nation equal the quantity of wheat supplied by the exporting nation. So the equilibrium world price of wheat is $9 and the equilibrium quantity of wheat traded is 200 million bushels.

RECAP

1. Comparative advantage is based on the relative opportunity costs of producing goods in different countries.

2. A country has an absolute advantage when it can produce a good for a lower input cost than can other nations.

3. A country has a comparative advantage when the opportunity cost of producing a good, in terms of forgone output of other goods, is lower than that of other nations.

Figure 3
International Equilibrium Price and Quantity
The international equilibrium price is the price at which the export supply curve of the United States intersects with the import demand curve of India. At the equilibrium price of $9, the United States will export 200 million bushels to India.

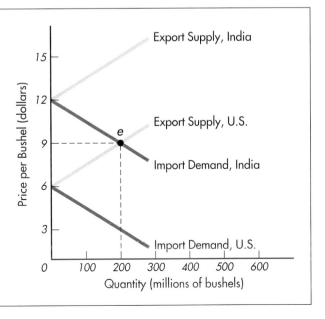

4. The terms of trade are the amount of an export good that must be given up to obtain one unit of an import good.

5. The limits of the terms of trade are determined by the domestic opportunity costs of production in each country.

6. The export supply and import demand curves measure the domestic surplus and shortage, respectively, at different world prices.

7. International equilibrium occurs at the point where one country's import demand curve intersects with the export supply curve of another country.

3. SOURCES OF COMPARATIVE ADVANTAGE

What are the sources of comparative advantage?

We know that countries specialize and trade in accordance with comparative advantage, but what gives a country a comparative advantage? Economists have suggested several theories of the source of comparative advantage. Let us review these theories.

3.a. Productivity Differences

The example of comparative advantage earlier in this chapter showed the United States to have a comparative advantage in wheat production and India to have a comparative advantage in cloth production. Comparative advantage was determined by differences in the labor hours required to produce each good. In this example, differences in the *productivity* of labor accounted for comparative advantage.

Comparative advantage due to productivity differences between countries is often called the Ricardian model of comparative advantage.

For over two hundred years, economists have argued that productivity differences account for comparative advantage. In fact, this theory of comparative advantage is often called the *Ricardian model*, after David Ricardo, a nineteenth-century English economist who explained and analyzed the idea of productivity-based comparative advantage. Variation in the productivity of labor can explain many observed trade patterns in the world.

Although we know that labor productivity differs across countries—and that this can help explain why countries produce the goods they do—there are factors other than labor productivity that determine comparative advantage. Furthermore, even if labor productivity were all that mattered, we would still want to know why some countries have more productive workers than others. The standard interpretation of the Ricardian model is that technological differences between countries account for differences in labor productivity. The countries with the most advanced technology would have a comparative advantage with regard to those goods that can be produced most efficiently with modern technology.

3.b. Factor Abundance

Goods differ in terms of the resources, or factors of production, required for their production. Countries differ in terms of the abundance of different factors of production: land, labor, capital, and entrepreneurial ability. It seems self-evident that countries would have an advantage in producing those goods that use relatively large amounts of their most abundant factor of production.

Certainly countries with a relatively large amount of farmland would have a comparative advantage in agriculture, and countries with a relatively large amount of capital would tend to specialize in the production of manufactured goods.

The idea that comparative advantage is based on the relative abundance of factors of production is sometimes called the *Heckscher-Ohlin model*, after the two Swedish economists, Eli Heckscher and Bertil Ohlin, who developed the original argument. The original model assumed that countries possess only two factors of production: labor and capital. Thus, researchers have examined the labor and capital requirements of various industries to see whether labor-abundant countries export goods whose production is relatively labor-intensive, and capital-abundant countries export goods that are relatively capital-intensive. In many cases, factor abundance has served well as an explanation of observed trade patterns. However, there remain cases in which comparative advantage seems to run counter to the predictions of the factor-abundance theory. In response, economists have suggested other explanations for comparative advantage.

Comparative advantage based on differences in the abundance of factors of production across countries is described in the Heckscher-Ohlin model.

3.c. Other Theories of Comparative Advantage

New theories of comparative advantage have typically come about in an effort to explain the trade pattern in some narrow category of products. They are not intended to serve as general explanations of comparative advantage, as do factor abundance and productivity. These supplementary theories emphasize human skills, product cycles, and preferences.

Human skills This approach emphasizes differences across countries in the availability of skilled and unskilled labor. The basic idea is that countries with a relatively abundant stock of highly skilled labor will have a comparative advantage in producing goods that require relatively large amounts of skilled labor. This theory is similar to the factor-abundance theory, except that here the analysis rests on two segments (skilled and unskilled) of the labor factor.

The human-skills argument is consistent with the observation that most U.S. exports are produced in high-wage (skilled-labor) industries, and most U.S. imports are products produced in relatively low-wage industries. Since the United States has a well-educated labor force, relative to many other countries, we would expect the United States to have a comparative advantage in industries requiring a large amount of skilled labor. Developing countries would be expected to have a comparative advantage in industries requiring a relatively large amount of unskilled labor.

Product life cycles This theory explains how comparative advantage in a specific good can shift over time from one country to another. This occurs because goods experience a *product life cycle*. At the outset, development and testing are required to conceptualize and design the product. For this reason, the early production will be undertaken by an innovative firm. Over time, however, a successful product tends to become standardized, in the sense that many manufacturers can produce it. The mature product may be produced by firms that do little or no research and development, specializing instead in copying successful products invented and developed by others.

Manufactured goods have life cycles. At first they are produced by the firm that invented them. Later, they may be produced by firms in other countries that copy the technology of the innovator.

The product-life-cycle theory is related to international comparative advantage in that a new product will be first produced and exported by the nation in which it was invented. As the product is exported elsewhere and foreign firms become familiar with it, the technology is copied in other countries by foreign firms seeking to produce a competing version. As the product matures, comparative advantage shifts away from the country of origin if other countries have lower manufacturing costs using the now-standardized technology.

The history of color television production shows how comparative advantage can shift over the product life cycle. Color television was invented in the United States, and U.S. firms initially produced and exported color TVs. Over time, as the technology of color television manufacturing became well known, countries like Japan and Taiwan came to dominate the business. Firms in these countries had a comparative advantage over U.S. firms in the manufacture of color televisions. Once the technology is widely available, countries with lower production costs, due to lower wages, can compete effectively against the higher-wage nation that developed the technology.

Preferences The theories of comparative advantage we have looked at so far have all been based on supply factors. It may be, though, that the demand side of the market can explain some of the patterns observed in international trade. Seldom are different producers' goods exactly identical. Consumers may prefer the goods of one firm to those of another firm. Domestic firms usually produce goods to satisfy domestic consumers. But since different consumers have different preferences, some consumers will prefer goods produced by foreign firms. International trade allows consumers to expand their consumption opportunities.

Consumers who live in countries with similar levels of development can be expected to have similar consumption patterns. The consumption patterns of consumers in countries at much different levels of development are much less similar. This would suggest that firms in industrial countries will find a larger market for their goods in other industrial countries than in developing countries.

As you saw earlier in this chapter, industrial countries tend to trade with other industrial countries. This pattern runs counter to the factor-abundance theory of comparative advantage, which would suggest that countries with the most dissimilar endowments of resources would find trade most beneficial. Yet rich countries, with large supplies of capital and skilled labor forces, trade more actively with other rich countries than they do with poor countries. Firms in industrial countries tend to produce goods that relatively wealthy consumers will buy. The key point here is that we do not live in a world based on simple comparative advantage, in which all cloth is identical, regardless of the producer. We inhabit a world of differentiated products, and consumers want choices between different brands or styles of a seemingly similar good.

intraindustry trade:
simultaneous import and export of goods in the same industry by a particular country

Another feature of international trade that may be explained by consumer preference is **intraindustry trade**, a circumstance in which a country both exports and imports goods in the same industry. The fact that the United States exports Budweiser beer and imports Heineken beer is not surprising when preferences are taken into account. Supply-side theories of comparative advantage rarely provide an explanation of intraindustry trade, since they would expect each country to export only those goods produced in industries in which a comparative advantage exists. Yet the real world is characterized by a great deal of intraindustry trade.

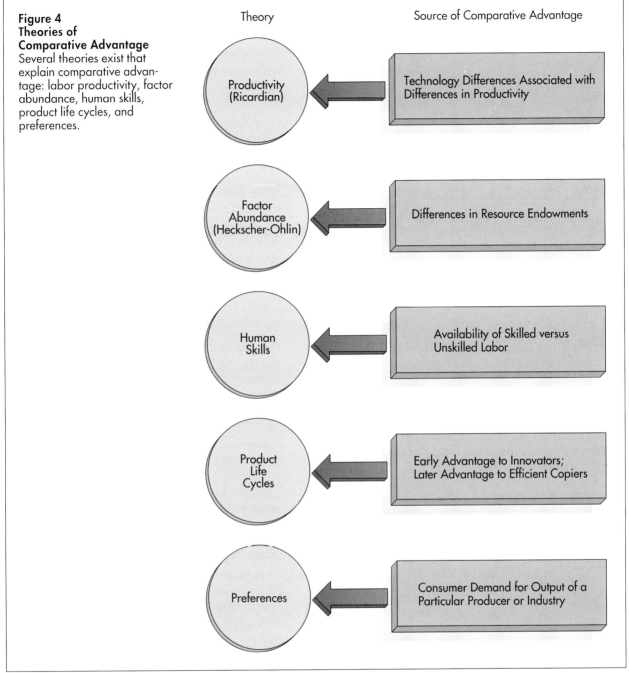

Figure 4
Theories of
Comparative Advantage
Several theories exist that explain comparative advantage: labor productivity, factor abundance, human skills, product life cycles, and preferences.

Theory

Source of Comparative Advantage

Productivity (Ricardian) ← Technology Differences Associated with Differences in Productivity

Factor Abundance (Heckscher-Ohlin) ← Differences in Resource Endowments

Human Skills ← Availability of Skilled versus Unskilled Labor

Product Life Cycles ← Early Advantage to Innovators; Later Advantage to Efficient Copiers

Preferences ← Consumer Demand for Output of a Particular Producer or Industry

We have discussed several potential sources of comparative advantage: labor productivity, factor abundance, human skills, product cycles, and preferences. Each of these theories, summarized in Figure 4, has proven useful in understanding certain trade patterns. Each has also been shown to have limitations as a general theory applicable to all cases. Once again we are reminded that the world is a very complicated place. Theories are simpler than reality. Nevertheless, they help us to understand how comparative advantage arises.

1. Comparative advantage can arise because of differences in labor productivity.

2. Countries differ in their resource endowments, and a given country may enjoy a comparative advantage in products that intensively use its most abundant factor of production.

3. Industrial countries may have a comparative advantage in products requiring a large amount of skilled labor. Developing countries may have a comparative advantage in products requiring a large amount of unskilled labor.

4. Comparative advantage in a new good initially resides in the country that invented the good. Over time, other nations learn the technology and may gain a comparative advantage in producing the good.

5. In some industries, consumer preferences for differentiated goods may explain international trade flows, including intraindustry trade.

SUMMARY

▲▼ *What are the prevailing patterns of trade between countries? What goods are traded?*

1. International trade flows largely between industrial countries. §1.a

2. International trade involves many diverse products, but crude petroleum accounts for more than 5 percent of its total value. §1.b

▲▼ *What determines the goods a nation will export?*

3. Comparative advantage is based on the opportunity costs of production. §2.a

4. Domestic opportunity costs determine the limits of the terms of trade between two countries—that is, the amount of exports that must be given up to obtain imports. §2.b

5. The export supply curve shows the domestic surplus and amount of exports available at alternative world prices. §2.c

6. The import demand curve shows the domestic shortage and amount of imports demanded at alternative world prices. §2.c

▲▼ *How are the equilibrium price and the quantity of goods traded determined?*

7. The international equilibrium price and quantity of a good traded are determined by the intersection of the export supply of one country with the import demand of another country. §2.d

▲▼ *What are the sources of comparative advantage?*

8. The productivity-differences and factor-abundance theories of comparative advantage are general theories that seek to explain patterns of international trade flow. §3.a, 3.b

9. Other theories of comparative advantage aimed at explaining trade in particular kinds of goods focus on human skills, product life cycles, and consumer preferences. §3.c

KEY TERMS

absolute advantage §2.a
comparative advantage §2.a
terms of trade §2.b

export supply curve §2.c
import demand curve §2.c
intraindustry trade §3.c

EXERCISES

1. Why must voluntary trade between two countries be mutually beneficial?

Use the following table to answer questions 2–6.

Labor Hours Required to Produce One Unit of Each Good

	Canada	Japan
Beef	2	4
Computers	6	5

2. Which country has the absolute advantage in beef production?

3. Which country has the absolute advantage in computer production?

4. Which country has the comparative advantage in beef production?

5. Which country has the comparative advantage in computer production?

6. What are the limits of the terms of trade? Specifically, when is Canada willing to trade with Japan, and when is Japan willing to trade with Canada?

7. Use the following supply and demand schedule for two countries to determine the international equilibrium price of shoes. How many shoes will be traded?

Demand and Supply of Shoes (1,000s)

	Mexico		Chile	
Price	Qty. Demanded	Qty. Supplied	Qty. Demanded	Qty. Supplied
$10	40	0	50	0
20	35	20	40	10
30	30	40	30	20
40	25	60	20	30
50	20	80	10	40

8. How would each of the following theories of comparative advantage explain the fact that the United States exports computers?

a. Productivity differences

b. Factor abundance

c. Human skills

d. Product life cycle

e. Preferences

9. Which of the theories of comparative advantage could explain why the United States exports computers to Japan at the same time that it imports computers from Japan? Explain.

10. Developing countries have complained that the terms of trade they face are unfavorable. If they voluntarily engage in international trade, what do you suppose they mean by "unfavorable terms of trade"?

11. If two countries reach equilibrium in their domestic markets at the same price, what can be said about their export supply and import demand curves and about the international trade equilibrium?

COOPERATIVE LEARNING EXERCISE

Divide the class into groups of four. Each group is then further divided into groups of two. In each group, two students are representatives of India, and two students are representatives of China. Using the following table, the representatives of each country must determine what they should export and what they should import. They should also determine the limits to the terms of trade: when they would be willing to trade with the other country. After they determine these

answers, the groups of two then meet in the groups of four to compare their answers. Any inconsistent answer should be reported to the instructor to be discussed by the class.

Labor Hours Required to Produce One Unit of Each Good

	India	China
Cloth	1	2
Sunglasses	4	3

Stop U.S.-Japan Squabbling Over Trade

The United States and Japan stand at the brink of another trade war. If the two governments can't agree by Wednesday on the specifics of an agreement reached in October, the United States could well begin a trade action that would limit Japan's access to the U.S. market.

These sanctions would disrupt Japanese-American trade, increase the price of imported Japanese goods and hurt U.S. consumers. If the agreement is reached, however, it will create more jobs there and help open closed Japanese markets.

At the heart of the dispute is foot-dragging by the Japanese on the import of flat glass from the United States and other countries. Japan is the second-largest flat-glass market in the world, consuming $4.5 billion worth of glass each year in homes, office buildings and autos.

U.S. glass manufacturers are the most efficient in the world and account for 20% to 30% of most markets. In the traditionally closed Japanese market, however, U.S.–based companies account for less than 1%.

That's because three major Japanese glass producers have such close ties with distributors that it is virtually impossible for U.S. manufacturers to bring their product to market. Government-imposed barriers are not the problem. Foreigners are shut out by the government's toleration of anti-competitive practices.

To their credit, the Bush and Clinton administrations have worked diligently to open Japanese markets to our products. The office of U.S. Trade Representative Mickey Kantor has been seeking to erode the effect of these traditional relationships.

While opening the flat-glass market won't erase the $60 billion-per-year U.S.–Japan trade imbalance, it is a step in the right direction.

If Japan imports more glass, our company alone is likely to hire more than 300 additional employees. Our suppliers could add as many as 700 more. Plants from Fullerton and Fresno, Calif., to Corsicana, Texas, Richburg, S.C., and even Thailand will gear up. In return, the Japanese construction industry will get a wider choice of quality products at lower costs.

Some urge Washington to focus instead on broader reforms of the Japanese economy. Rather than push for reforms in sectors such as flat glass, computer chips or telephones, these critics want the United States to demand that Japan take steps in areas such as deregulation and tax policy that would affect its entire economy.

We strongly believe the sector-by-sector approach is working and should be continued. It recognizes the unique complexities of Japan's marketplace and the particular needs of its producers and consumers. Each successful agreement creates new pressure in Japan to open other markets.

If agreement cannot be reached, there will be heavy pressure on the Clinton administration to use U.S. trade laws to take stronger action, possibly retaliating against Japanese imports. This would be a shame in light of the mutual benefits that a more open Japanese market would bring.

Source: "Stop U.S.–Japan Squabbling over Trade," Ralph Gerson, *USA Today*, Dec. 5, 1994, p. 12A. Reprinted by permission of Ralph Gerson, Executive Vice President of Guardian Industries Corp., Auburn Hills, Michigan.

Commentary

There is no lack of stories in the American media on the threat of Japanese economic domination. As this article indicates, many people see the solution coming from more open Japanese markets and point to the large U.S. trade deficit with Japan as evidence that a problem exists.

However, the bilateral trade accounts provide little, if any, information on such issues. Indeed, it is easy to think of an example in which a country has a persistent trade deficit with one of its trading partners but has its overall trade account in balance. Suppose there are three countries that trade among themselves, which we will call countries A, B, and C. The people of each country produce only one type of good and consume only one other type of good. The people of country A produce apples and consume bananas, the people of country B produce bananas and consume cucumbers, and the people of country C produce cucumbers and consume apples. Even when the trade account of each country is balanced, each has a deficit with one of its trading partners and a surplus with the other. Furthermore, a larger trade deficit between countries A and B (with each country retaining balanced trade) implies that the people of country A are better off since they are consuming more. If the government of country A tried to impose a law forcing bilateral trade balance with country B, citizens of country A could not consume as many bananas as before and would be forced to attempt to sell apples to the uninterested citizens of country B.

This simple example demonstrates that the U.S. trade deficit with Japan should not in itself be a cause for concern, especially if the overall trade deficit is shrinking. The United States could have a persistent trade deficit with Japan and yet maintain an overall balanced trade account. In fact, any country would be expected to have a trade deficit with

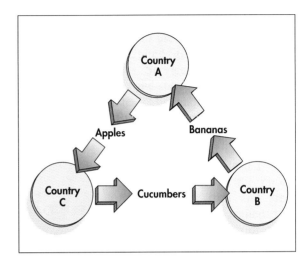

some countries and a trade surplus with others. This reflects comparative advantage. Trade between countries makes both the exporting and the importing countries better off. Rather than point to the U.S. trade deficit with Japan as the problem, it is useful to have anecdotes like the one on the Japanese glass market to establish the existence of a problem. Clearly, U.S. glass producers would benefit from more open access to the Japanese market. Policymakers should be concerned with negotiating the removal of trade barriers rather than bilateral trade deficits.

This is not to say that concern about the *overall* trade deficit is not well founded. An overall trade deficit indicates that a country is consuming more than it is producing. At any particular time, a country may want to run a trade deficit or a trade surplus, depending on the circumstances it faces. But regardless of the overall trade account of a country, we should expect bilateral trade imbalances among trading partners.

TABLE 2
Annual Reduction in U.S. GDP Imposed by U.S. Import Restrictions

Sector	GDP Gain (million dollars)
Simultaneous liberalization of all restraints	18,976
Individual liberalization:	
Textiles and apparel	15,845
Maritime transport (Jones Act)	3,086
Dairy	847
Sugar	657
Peanuts	353
Meat	177
Nonrubber footwear	170
Watches, clocks, and parts	101
Ball and roller bearings, and parts	45
Pressed and blown glass	44
Costume jewelry and costume novelties	42
Machine tools	31
Cyclic organic crudes and intermediates	24
Frozen fruit, fruit juices, and vegetables	13
Ceramic wall and floor tile	12
Personal leather goods	7
Electronic capacitors	5
Leather gloves and mittens	2
China tableware	2

Source: *The Economic Effects of Significant U.S. Imports Restraints* (U.S. International Trade Commission, 1993), p. ix.

1.b. Creation of a "Level Playing Field"

Special interest groups sometimes claim that other nations that export successfully to the home market have unfair advantages over domestic producers. Fairness, however, is often in the eye of the beholder. People who call for creating a "level playing field" believe that the domestic government should take steps to offset the perceived advantage of the foreign firm. They often claim that foreign firms have an unfair advantage because foreign workers are willing to work for very low wages. "Fair trade, not free trade" is the cry that this claim generates. But advocates of fair trade are really claiming that production in accordance with comparative advantage is unfair. This is clearly wrong. A country with relatively low wages is typically a country with an abundance of low-skilled labor. Such a country will have a comparative advantage in products that use low-skilled labor most intensively. To create a "level playing field" by imposing restrictions that eliminate the comparative advantage of foreign firms will make domestic consumers worse off and undermine the basis for specialization and economic efficiency.

Some calls for "fair trade" are based on the notion of reciprocity. If a country imposes import restrictions on goods from a country that does not have similar restrictions, reciprocal tariffs and quotas may be called for in the latter country in order to stimulate a reduction of trade restrictions in the former country. For instance, it has been claimed that U.S. construction firms are discriminated against in Japan, because no U.S. firm has had a major construction project in Japan since the 1960s. Yet Japanese construction firms do billions of dollars' worth of business in the United States each year. Advocates of fair trade could argue that U.S. restrictions should be imposed on Japanese construction firms.

One danger of calls for fairness based on reciprocity is that calls for fair trade may be invoked in cases where, in fact, foreign restrictions on U.S. imports do not exist. For instance, suppose the U.S. auto industry wanted to restrict the entry of imported autos to help stimulate sales of domestically produced cars. One strategy might be to point out that U.S. auto sales abroad had fallen and to claim that this was due to unfair treatment of U.S. auto exports in other countries. Of course, there are many other possible reasons why foreign sales of U.S. autos might have fallen. But blaming foreign trade restrictions might win political support for restricting imports of foreign cars into the United States.

I.c. Government Revenue Creation

Tariffs on trade generate government revenue. Industrial countries, which find income taxes easy to collect, rarely justify tariffs on the basis of the revenue they generate for government spending. But many developing countries find income taxes difficult to levy and collect, while tariffs are easy to collect. Customs agents can be positioned at ports of entry to examine all goods that enter and leave the country. The observability of trade flows makes tariffs a popular tax in developing countries, whose revenue requirements may provide a valid justification for their existence. Table 3 shows that tariffs account for a relatively large fraction of government revenue in many developing countries, and only a small fraction in industrial countries.

I.d. National Defense

It has long been argued that industries crucial to the national defense, like shipbuilding, should be protected from foreign competition. Even though the United States does not have a comparative advantage in shipbuilding, a domestic shipbuilding industry is necessary since foreign-made ships may not be available during war. This is a valid argument as long as the protected industry is genuinely critical to the national defense. In some industries, like copper or other basic metals, it might make more sense to import the crucial products during peacetime and store them for use in the event of war; these products do not require domestic production to be useful. Care must be taken to ensure that the national-defense argument is not used to protect industries other than those truly crucial to the nation's defense.

TABLE 3
Tariffs as a Percentage of Total Government Revenue

Country	Tariffs as Percentage of Government Revenue
United Kingdom	0.1%
Japan	1.3
United States	1.5
Costa Rica	19.7
Bangladesh	28.6
Dominican Republic	40.3
Ghana	44.2
Lesotho	51.8

Source: Data are from World Bank, *World Development Report*, 1994.

I.e. Infant Industries

Countries sometimes justify protecting new industries that need time to become competitive with the rest of the world.

Nations are often inclined to protect new industries on the basis that the protection will give those industries adequate time to develop. New industries need time to establish themselves and to become efficient enough that their costs are no higher than those of their foreign rivals. An alternative to protecting young and/or critical domestic industries with tariffs and quotas is to subsidize them. Subsidies allow such firms to charge lower prices and to compete with more efficient foreign producers, while permitting consumers to pay the world price rather than the higher prices associated with tariffs or quotas on foreign goods.

Protecting an infant industry from foreign competition may make sense, but only until the industry matures. Once the industry achieves sufficient size, protection should be withdrawn, and the industry should be made to compete with its foreign counterparts. Unfortunately, such protection is rarely withdrawn, because the larger and more successful the industry becomes, the more political power it wields. In fact, if an infant industry truly has a good chance to become competitive and produce profitably once it is well established, it is not at all clear that government should even offer protection to reduce short-run losses. New firms typically incur losses, but they are only temporary if the firm is successful.

I.f. Strategic Trade Policy

strategic trade policy:
the use of trade restrictions or subsidies to allow domestic firms with decreasing costs to gain a greater share of the world market

There is another view of international trade that regards as misleading the description of comparative advantage presented in the previous chapter. According to this outlook, called **strategic trade policy,** international trade largely involves firms that pursue economies of scale—that is, firms that achieve lower costs per unit of production the more they produce. In contrast to the constant opportunity costs illustrated in the example of wheat and cloth in Chapter 37, opportunity costs in some industries may fall with

Government can use trade policy as a strategy to stimulate production by a domestic industry capable of achieving increasing returns to scale.

the level of output. Such **increasing-returns-to-scale industries** will tend to concentrate production in the hands of a few very large firms, rather than many competitive firms. Proponents of strategic trade policy contend that government can use tariffs or subsidies to allow domestic firms with decreasing costs an advantage over their foreign rivals.

A monopoly exists when there is only one producer in an industry, and no close substitutes for the product exist. If the average costs of production decline with increases in output, then the larger a firm is, the lower its per unit costs will be. One large producer will be more efficient than many small ones. A simple example of a natural-monopoly industry will indicate how strategic trade policy can make a country better off. Suppose that the production of buses is an industry characterized by increasing returns to scale and that there are only two firms capable of producing buses: Mercedes-Benz in Germany and General Motors in the United States. If both firms produce buses, their costs will be so high that both will experience losses. If only one of the two produces buses, however, it will be able to sell buses at home and abroad, creating a level of output that allows the firm to earn a profit.

Assume further that a monopoly producer will earn $100 million and that if both firms produce, they will each lose $5 million. Obviously, a firm that doesn't produce earns nothing. Which firm will produce? Because of the decreasing-cost nature of the industry, the firm that is the first to produce will realize lower costs and be able to preclude the other firm from entering the market. But strategic trade policy can alter the market in favor of the domestic firm.

Suppose Mercedes-Benz is the world's only producer of buses. General Motors does not produce them. The U.S. government could offer General Motors an $8 million subsidy to produce buses. General Motors would then enter the bus market, since the $8 million subsidy would more than offset the $5 million loss it would suffer by entering the market. Mercedes-Benz would sustain losses of $5 million once General Motors entered. Ultimately, Mercedes-Benz would stop producing buses to avoid the loss, and General Motors would have the entire market and earn $100 million plus the subsidy.

Strategic trade policy is aimed at offsetting the increasing-returns-to-scale advantage enjoyed by foreign producers and at stimulating production in domestic industries capable of realizing decreasing costs. One practical problem for government is the need to understand the technology of different industries and to forecast accurately the subsidy needed to induce domestic firms to produce new products. A second problem is the likelihood of retaliation by the foreign government. If the U.S. government subsidizes General Motors in its attack on the bus market, the German government is likely to subsidize Mercedes-Benz rather than lose the entire bus market to a U.S. producer. As a result, taxpayers in both nations will be subsidizing two firms, each producing too few buses to earn a profit.

RECAP

1. Government restrictions on foreign trade are usually aimed at protecting domestic producers from foreign competition.

2. Import restrictions may save domestic jobs, but the costs to consumers may be greater than the benefits to those who retain their jobs.

3. Advocates of "fair trade," or the creation of a "level playing field," call for import restrictions as a means of lowering foreign restrictions on markets for domestic exports.

4. Tariffs are an important source of revenue in many developing countries.

5. The national-defense argument in favor of trade restrictions is that protection from foreign competition is necessary to ensure that certain key defense-related industries continue to produce.

6. The infant-industries argument in favor of trade restriction is to allow a new industry a period of time in which to become competitive with its foreign counterparts.

7. Strategic trade policy is intended to provide domestic increasing-returns-to-scale industries an advantage over their foreign competitors.

2. TOOLS OF POLICY

How do countries restrict the entry of foreign goods and promote the export of domestic goods?

Commercial policy makes use of several tools, including tariffs, quotas, subsidies, and nontariff barriers like health and safety regulations that restrict the entry of foreign products. Since 1945, barriers to trade have been reduced. Much of the progress toward free trade may be linked to the *General Agreement on Tariffs and Trade*, or *GATT*, that began in 1947. The Economic Insight "The GATT" describes how this document and the continuing negotiations under its auspices have worked to eliminate quotas on manufactured goods and to lower tariffs.

ECONOMIC INSIGHT

The GATT

The General Agreement on Tariffs and Trade, or GATT, is both a document that establishes rules for international trade and an international organization that manages negotiations among nations to lower trade barriers. The basic principles reflected in the GATT document are these:

1. Quotas should be eliminated and other barriers to international trade should be reduced.

2. Barriers to trade should apply equally to all countries, rather than selectively to some.

3. Once tariffs have been lowered, they cannot be increased without compensating trading partners.

4. Disagreements should be settled in consultation, according to the GATT rules.

The World Trade Organization (WTO) oversees the international trading system and provides a forum for periodic meetings of nations to negotiate reduced trade barriers. The WTO was created out of the "Uruguay Round" trade agreement, which took effect on January 1, 1995. In addition to creating the WTO, the Uruguay Round agreement also extended free trade agreements to trade in services and established principles regarding intellectual property rights.

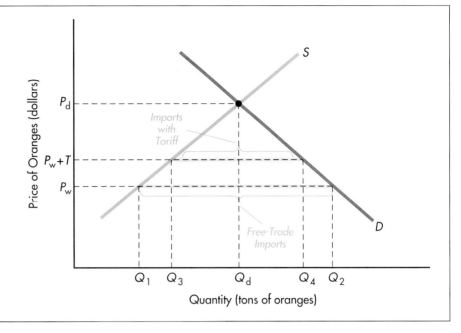

Figure 1
The Effects of a Tariff
The domestic equilibrium price and quantity with no trade are P_d and Q_d, respectively. The world price is P_w. With free trade, therefore, imports will equal $Q_2 - Q_1$. A tariff added to the world price reduces imports to $Q_4 - Q_3$.

2.a. Tariffs

tariff:
a tax on imports or exports

A **tariff** is a tax on imports or exports. Every country imposes tariffs on at least some imports. Some countries also impose tariffs on selected exports as a means of raising government revenue. Brazil, for instance, taxes coffee exports. The United States does not employ export tariffs, which are forbidden by the U.S. Constitution.

Tariffs are frequently imposed in order to protect domestic producers from foreign competition. The dangers of imposing tariffs are well illustrated in the Economic Insight "Smoot-Hawley Tariff." The effect of a tariff is illustrated in Figure 1, which shows the domestic market for oranges. Without international trade, the domestic equilibrium price, P_d, and quantity demanded, Q_d, are determined by the intersection of the domestic demand and supply curves. If the world price of oranges, P_w, is lower than the domestic equilibrium price, this country will import oranges. The quantity imported will be the difference between the quantity Q_1 produced domestically at a price of P_w and the quantity Q_2 demanded domestically at the world price of oranges.

When the world price of the traded good is lower than the domestic equilibrium price without international trade, free trade causes domestic production to fall and domestic consumption to rise. The domestic shortage at the world price is met by imports. Domestic consumers are better off, since they can buy more at a lower price. But domestic producers are worse off, since they now sell fewer oranges and receive a lower price.

Suppose a tariff of T (the dollar value of the tariff) is imposed on orange imports. The price paid by consumers is now $P_w + T$, rather than P_w. At this higher price, domestic producers will produce Q_3 and domestic consumers

Smoot-Hawley Tariff

Many economists believe that the Great Depression of the 1930s was at least partly due to the Smoot-Hawley Tariff Act, signed into law by President Herbert Hoover in 1930. Hoover had promised that, if elected, he would raise tariffs on agricultural products to raise U.S. farm income. Congress began work on the tariff increases in 1928. Congressman Willis Hawley and Senator Reed Smoot conducted the hearings.

In testimony before Congress, manufacturers and other special interest groups also sought protection from foreign competition. The resulting bill increased tariffs on over twelve thousand products. Tariffs reached their highest levels ever, about 60 percent of average import values. Only twice before in U.S. history had tariffs approached the levels of the Smoot-Hawley era.

Before President Hoover signed the bill, thirty-eight foreign governments made formal protests, warning that they would retaliate with high tariffs on U.S. products. A petition signed by 1,028 economists warned of the harmful effects of the bill. Nevertheless, Hoover signed the bill into law.

World trade collapsed as other countries raised their tariffs in response. Between 1930 and 1931, U.S. imports fell 29 percent, but U.S. exports fell 33 percent. By 1933, world trade was about one-third of the 1929 level. As the level of trade fell, so did income and prices. In 1934, in an effort to correct the mistakes of Smoot-Hawley, Congress passed the Reciprocal Trade Agreements Act, which allowed the president to lower U.S. tariffs in return for reductions in foreign tariffs on U.S. goods. This act ushered in the modern era of relatively low tariffs. In the United States today, tariffs are about 5 percent of the average value of imports.

Many economists believe the collapse of world trade and the Depression to be linked by a decrease in real income caused by abandoning production based on comparative advantage. Few economists argue that the Great Depression was caused solely by the Smoot-Hawley tariff, but the experience serves as a lesson to those who support higher tariffs to protect domestic producers.

will purchase Q_4. The tariff has the effect of increasing domestic production and reducing domestic consumption, relative to the free trade equilibrium. Imports fall accordingly, from $Q_2 - Q_1$ to $Q_4 - Q_3$.

Domestic producers are better off, since the tariff has increased their sales of oranges and raised the price they receive. Domestic consumers pay higher prices for fewer oranges than they would with free trade, but they are still better off than they would be without trade. If the tariff had raised the price paid by consumers to P_d, there would be no trade, and the domestic equilibrium quantity, Q_d, would prevail.

The government earns revenue from imports of oranges. If each ton of oranges generates tariff revenue of T, the total tariff revenue to the government is found by multiplying the tariff by the quantity of oranges imported. In Figure 1, this amount is $T \times (Q_4 - Q_3)$. As the tariff changes, so does the quantity of imports and the government revenue.

2.b. Quotas

quantity quota:
a limit on the amount of a good that may be imported

Quotas are limits on the quantity or value of goods imported and exported. A **quantity quota** restricts the physical amount of a good. For instance, through 1994 the United States allowed only 2.5 million tons of sugar to be imported. Even though the United States is not a competitive sugar producer compared to other nations like the Dominican Republic or Cuba, the quota allowed U.S. firms to produce about 6 percent of the world's sugar output. A **value quota** restricts the monetary value of a good that may be traded. Instead of a physical quota on sugar, the United States could have limited the dollar value of sugar imports.

Quotas are used to protect domestic producers from foreign competition. By restricting the amount of a good that may be imported, they increase its price and allow domestic producers to sell more at a higher price than they would with free trade. Figure 2 illustrates the effect of a quota on the domestic orange market. The domestic equilibrium supply and demand curves determine the equilibrium price and quantity without trade to be P_d and 250 tons, respectively. The world price of oranges is P_w. Since P_w lies below P_d, this country will import oranges. The quantity of imports is equal to the amount of the domestic shortage at P_w. The quantity demanded at P_w is 400 tons, and the quantity supplied domestically is 100 tons, so imports will equal 300 tons of oranges. With free trade, domestic producers sell 100 tons at a price of P_w.

But suppose domestic orange growers convince the government to restrict orange imports. The government then imposes a quota of 100 tons on imported oranges. The effect of the quota on consumers is to shift the supply curve to the right by the amount of the quota, 100 tons. Since the quota is less than the quantity of imports with free trade, the quantity of imports will equal the quota. The domestic equilibrium price with the quota occurs at the point where the domestic shortage equals the quota. At price P_q, the domestic

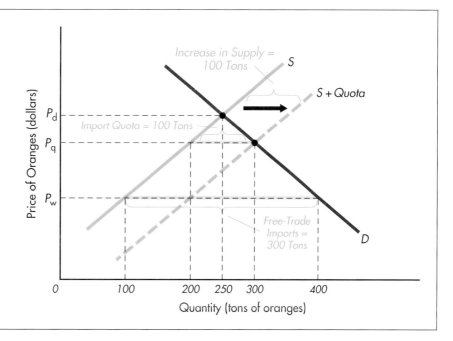

Figure 2
The Effects of a Quota
The domestic equilibrium price with no international trade is P_d. At this price, 250 tons of oranges would be produced and consumed at home. With free trade, the price is P_w and 300 tons will be imported. An import quota of 100 tons will cause the price to be P_q, where the domestic shortage equals the 100 tons allowed by the quota.

quantity demanded (300 tons) is 100 tons more than the domestic quantity supplied (200 tons).

Quotas benefit domestic producers in the same way that tariffs do. Domestic producers receive a higher price (P_q instead of P_w) for a greater quantity (200 instead of 100) than they do under free trade. The effect on domestic consumers is also similar to that of a tariff: they pay a higher price for a smaller quantity than they would with free trade. A tariff generates government tax revenue; quotas do not (unless the government auctioned off the right to import under the quota). Furthermore, a tariff only raises the price of the product in the domestic market. Foreign producers receive the world price, P_w. With a quota, both domestic and foreign producers receive the higher price, P_q, for the goods sold in the domestic market. So foreign producers are hurt by the reduction in the quantity of imports permitted, but they do receive a higher price for the amount they sell.

Voluntary export restraints are a substitute for quotas. They limit the amount exporters ship to an importing country.

In some cases, countries negotiate *voluntary export restraints* rather than imposing quotas. A voluntary export restraint limits the quantity of goods shipped from the exporting country to an importing country, so such restraints have the same practical effect as a quota. For instance, since 1981 the United States has negotiated voluntary export restraints on Japanese auto exports to the United States, limiting such exports to 1.62 million autos in 1981. (U.S. firms produced 1.3 million small cars and 2.6 million large cars that year.) In 1992, the agreement allowed 1.65 million autos ranging from 480,000 Toyotas to 30,000 Suzukis. The Japanese Automobile Manufacturers Association monitors the exports for the Japanese government.

2.c. Other Barriers to Trade

Tariffs and quotas are not the only barriers to the free flow of goods across international borders. There are three additional sources of restrictions on free trade: subsidies, government procurement, and health and safety standards. Though often enacted for reasons other than protection from foreign competition, a careful analysis reveals their import-reducing effect.

Before discussing these three types of barriers, let us note the cultural or institutional barriers to trade that also exist in many countries. Such barriers may exist independently of any conscious government policy. For instance, Japan has frequently been criticized by U.S. officials for informal business practices that discriminate against foreigners. Under the Japanese distribution system, goods typically pass through several layers of middlemen before appearing in a retail store. A foreign firm faces the difficult task of gaining entry to this system to supply goods to the retailer. Furthermore, a foreigner cannot easily open a retail store. Japanese law requires a new retail firm to receive permission from other retailers in the area in order to open a business. A firm that lacks contacts and knowledge of the system cannot penetrate the Japanese market.

In the fall of 1989, the U.S. toy firm Toys "R" Us announced its intent to open several large discount toy stores in Japan. However, local toy stores in each area objected to having a Toys "R" Us store nearby. The U.S. government has argued that the laws favoring existing firms are an important factor in keeping Japan closed to foreign firms that would like to enter the Japanese market. Eventually, Toys "R" Us opened stores in Japan.

2.c.1. Subsidies **Subsidies** are payments by a government to an exporter. Subsidies are paid to stimulate exports by allowing the exporter to charge a lower price. The amount of a subsidy is determined by the international price of a product relative to the domestic price in the absence of trade. Domestic consumers are harmed by subsidies in that their taxes finance the subsidies. Also, since the subsidy diverts resources from the domestic market toward export production, the increase in the supply of export goods could be associated with a decrease in the supply of domestic goods, causing domestic prices to rise.

Subsidies may take forms other than direct cash payments. These include tax reductions, low-interest loans, low-cost insurance, government sponsored research funding, and other devices. The U.S. government subsidizes export activity through the U.S. Export-Import Bank, which provides loans and insurance to help U.S. exporters sell their goods to foreign buyers. Subsidies are more commonplace in Europe than in Japan or the United States.

2.c.2. Government Procurement Governments are often required by law to buy only from local producers. In the United States, a "buy American" act passed in 1933 requires U.S. government agencies to buy U.S. goods and services unless the domestic price is more than 12 percent above the foreign price. This kind of policy allows domestic firms to charge the government a higher price for their products than they charge consumers; the taxpayers bear the burden. The United States is by no means alone in requiring the federal government to purchase domestic goods. Many other nations also use such policies to create larger markets for domestic goods.

2.c.3. Health and Safety Standards Government serves as a guardian of the public health and welfare by requiring that products offered to the public be safe and fulfill the use for which they are intended. Government standards for products sold in the domestic marketplace can have the effect (intentional or not) of protecting domestic producers from foreign competition. These effects should be considered in evaluating the full impact of such standards.

As mentioned in the Preview, the government of Japan once threatened to prohibit foreign-made snow skis from entering the country for reasons of safety. Only Japanese-made skis were determined to be suitable for Japanese snow. Several Western European nations announced that U.S. beef would not be allowed into Europe because hormones approved by the U.S. government are fed to U.S. beef cattle. In the late 1960s, France required tractors sold there to have a maximum speed of 17 miles per hour; in Germany, the permissible speed was 13 mph, and in the Netherlands it was 10 mph. Tractors produced in one country had to be modified to meet the requirements of the other countries. Such modifications raise the price of goods and discourage international trade.

Product standards may not eliminate foreign competition, but standards different from those of the rest of the world do provide an element of protection to domestic firms.

RECAP

1. A tariff is a tax on imports or exports. Tariffs protect domestic firms by raising the prices of foreign goods.

2. Quotas are government-imposed limits on the quantity or value of an imported good. Quotas protect domestic firms by restricting the entry of foreign products to a level less than the quantity demanded.

3. Subsidies are payments by the government to domestic producers. Subsidies lower the price of domestic goods.

4. Governments are often required by law to buy only domestic products.

5. Health and safety standards can also be used to protect domestic firms.

3. PREFERENTIAL TRADE AGREEMENTS

What sorts of agreements do countries enter into to reduce barriers to international trade?

In an effort to stimulate international trade, groups of countries sometimes enter into agreements to abolish most barriers to trade among themselves. Such arrangements between countries are known as preferential trading agreements. The European Union and the North American Free Trade Agreement (NAFTA) are examples of preferential trading agreements.

3.a. Free Trade Areas and Customs Unions

free trade area:
an organization of nations whose members have no trade barriers among themselves but are free to fashion their own trade policies toward nonmembers

Two common forms of preferential trade agreements are **free trade areas** (FTAs) and **customs unions** (CUs). These two approaches differ with regard to treatment of countries outside the agreement. In an FTA, member countries eliminate trade barriers among themselves, but each member country chooses its own trade policies toward nonmember countries. Members of a CU agree to eliminate trade barriers among themselves and to maintain common trade barriers against nonmembers.

The North American Free Trade Agreement will stimulate trade among Mexico, Canada, and the United States. In coming years, there will be more and more container ships from Mexico unloading their cargo at U.S. docks. This ship, *Mexicana,* tied up in Long Beach, California, is a sign of the times ahead for U.S. ports. Similarly, freight from Canada and the United States will increase in volume at Mexican ports as trade barriers among the three nations fall.

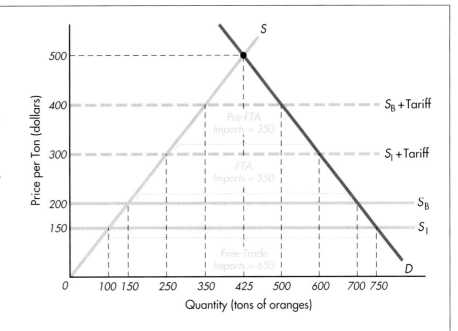

Figure 3
Trade Creation and Trade Diversion with a Free Trade Area

With no trade, the domestic equilibrium price is $500 and the equilibrium quantity is 425 tons. With free trade, the price is $150, and 650 tons would be imported, as indicated by the supply curve for Israel, S_I. A 100 percent tariff on imports would result in imports of 350 tons from Israel, according to the supply curve $S_I + Tariff$. A free trade agreement that eliminates tariffs on Brazilian oranges only would result in a new equilibrium price of $200 and imports of 550 tons from Brazil, according to supply curve S_B.

customs union:
an organization of nations whose members have no trade barriers among themselves but impose common trade barriers on nonmembers

The best-known CU is the European Union (EU), formerly known as the European Economic Community (EEC), created in 1957 by France, West Germany, Italy, Belgium, the Netherlands, and Luxembourg. The United Kingdom, Ireland, and Denmark joined in 1973, followed by Greece in 1981 and Spain and Portugal in 1986. In 1992 the EEC was replaced by the EU with an agreement to create a single market for goods and services in Western Europe. Besides free trade in goods, European financial markets and institutions will eventually be able to operate across national boundaries. For instance, a bank in any EU country will be permitted to operate in any or all other EU countries.

In 1989, the United States and Canada negotiated a free trade area. The United States, Canada, and Mexico negotiated a free trade area in 1992 that became effective on January 1, 1994. Under NAFTA, tariffs are to be lowered on eight thousand different items, and each nation's financial market will be opened to competition from the other two nations. NAFTA will not eliminate all barriers to trade among the three nations but does represent a significant step in that direction.

3.b. Trade Creation and Diversion

Free trade agreements provide for free trade among a group of countries, not worldwide. As a result, a customs union or free trade area may make a nation better off or worse off compared to the free trade equilibrium.

Figure 3 illustrates the effect of a free trade area. With no international trade, the U.S. supply and demand curves for oranges would result in an equilibrium price of $500 per ton and an equilibrium quantity of 425 tons.

KEY TERMS

commercial policy §Preview
strategic trade policy §1.f
increasing-returns-to-scale industry §1.f
tariff §2.a
quantity quota §2.b
value quota §2.b

subsidies §2.c.1
free trade area §3.a
customs union §3.a
trade diversion §3.b
trade creation §3.b

EXERCISES

1. What are the potential benefits and costs of a commercial policy designed to pursue each of the following goals?

   a. Save domestic jobs

   b. Create a level playing field

   c. Increase government revenue

   d. Provide a strong national defense

   e. Protect an infant industry

   f. Stimulate exports of an industry with increasing returns to scale

2. For each of the goals listed in question 1, discuss what the appropriate commercial policy is likely to be (in terms of tariffs, quotas, subsidies, etc.).

3. Tariffs and quotas both raise the price of foreign goods to domestic consumers. What is the difference between the effects of a tariff and the effects of a quota on the following?

   a. The domestic government

   b. Foreign producers

   c. Domestic producers

4. Would trade-diversion and trade-creation effects occur if the whole world became a free trade area? Explain.

5. What is the difference between a customs union and a free trade area?

6. Draw a graph of the U.S. automobile market in which the domestic equilibrium price without trade is P_d and the equilibrium quantity is Q_d. Use this graph to illustrate and explain the effects of a tariff if the United States were an auto importer with free trade. Then use the graph to illustrate and explain the effects of a quota.

7. If commercial policy can benefit U.S. industry, why would any U.S. resident oppose such policies?

8. Suppose you were asked to assess U.S. commercial policy to determine whether the benefits of protection for U.S. industries are worth the costs. Do Tables 1 and 2 provide all the information you need? If not, what else would you want to know?

9. How would the effects of international trade on the domestic orange market change if the world price of oranges were above the domestic equilibrium price? Draw a graph to help explain your answer.

10. Suppose the world price of kiwi fruit is $20 per case and the U.S. equilibrium price with no international trade is $35 per case. If the U.S. government had previously banned the import of kiwi fruit but then imposed a tariff of $5 per case and allowed kiwi imports, what would happen to the equilibrium price and quantity of kiwi fruit consumed in the United States?

COOPERATIVE LEARNING EXERCISE

Students pair off into groups of two. Each group must prepare a graph to illustrate the following:

The domestic auto industry has an equilibrium price of P_d and equilibrium quantity of 5 million autos without international trade. The government now permits a quota of 1 million autos to be imported. After the quota, the domestic price of autos falls to P_q.

The instructor will call on a group to present its graph to the class.

Imports and Competition in Domestic Markets

Foremost among the asserted benefits of reducing trade barriers is competition: firms that operate in an economy with relatively weak domestic competition are supposed to be forced by the onslaught of foreign goods to improve their quality and service and to keep costs and prices down. The benefits of trade liberalization are assumed to be particularly great in developing countries, where a relatively few firms may control a given industry. But while the theoretical benefits of freer trade are well understood, do businesses actually respond in that way? After studying the effects of trade liberalization in Turkey, NBER researcher James Levinsohn concludes that the answer is "yes."

Until 1984, the Turkish economy was highly protected against imports, with tariffs averaging 49 percent and an array of nontariff barriers including quotas, import licenses, and foreign exchange regulations. In 1984, however, tariffs were reduced to an average of 20 percent and restrictions on many types of imports were eliminated. . . . Levinsohn investigated the impact of this sweeping liberalization by using detailed data on individual firms from the Turkish manufacturing census. . . .

Prior to the change in trade policy, Levinsohn finds, firms in six of the eleven industries studied were pricing at marginal cost, indicating a high level of competition. In three industries, companies were pricing above marginal cost, indicating the existence of imperfect competition, while in two industries, including the largely government-owned steel industry, firms were losing money on each unit of output. The 1984 trade liberalization reduced the level of protection enjoyed by nine of the eleven industries. In the three high-margin industries, miscellaneous chemicals, pottery, and electrical machinery, price markups declined as import competition increased. For two of the previously competitive industries, transport equipment and scientific equipment, the trade reform resulted in higher levels of import protection, and price markups in those industries increased. Of the six previously competitive industries that had their protection reduced by the trade reform, three had lower markups and one was unchanged; one of the two industries in that category with higher markups was the steel industry.

Levinsohn warns that the price markups reported by companies to census officials may not be completely accurate. Firms with high profits may be inclined to understate their revenues or overstate costs in case tax officials learn of their reports, while firms with losses may exit the industry and not report. Nonetheless, Levinsohn writes, the Turkish data indicate that imports increase competition and restrict the ability of domestic firms to exercise market power.

Source: From *NBER Digest,* July/August 1991. Used by permission of the National Bureau of Economic Research.

Commentary

Consider the following hypothetical situation: The legislature of the state of Maine considers a tax to support the pineapple farmers of the state. Of course, Maine's climate is not conducive to growing pineapples, but it is possible, at great cost, to grow a few pineapples in greenhouses. The tax on pineapples brought into the state raises the price of Hawaiian pineapples by enough to make pineapples grown in Maine competitive. Thus Maine's pineapple industry is saved from competitors whose price reflects their unfair climatic advantage, though the consumers of the state must pay exorbitant prices for their pineapples.

This scenario, with its absurd distortion of the workings of the market, differs in degree but not in kind from the description of the effects of import competition in the accompanying article. The protectionist measure of imposing quotas or tariffs on imports saves jobs in the domestic import-competing industries, but at a great cost to consumers. It is estimated that the cost of protecting the U.S. domestic textile industry is $238 per family in the United States.

The effect of reducing domestic competition with quotas can be understood using supply and demand analysis. Let's analyze the case of quotas on textile imports into the United States. In the diagram, S_1 is the domestic supply of textiles, S_2 is the sum of the domestic supply and the foreign supply allowed in by the quotas, and D is the demand for textiles. Under the quota system, the price of textiles in the United States is represented by P_q and the quantity of textiles consumed is Q_q. If the quotas were removed, the price of textiles in the United States would equal the world price of P_w, and this lower price would be associated with an increase in the consumption of textiles to Q_w. The quota represents a cost to society in terms of a loss of consumer welfare as well as a loss from the inefficient use of resources in an industry in which this country has no comparative advantage, just as Maine has no comparative advantage in the production of pineapples.

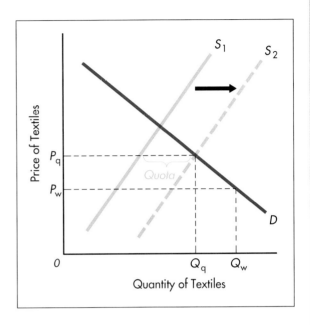

Given the costs to society of these quotas, why is there such strong support for them in Congress? An important political aspect of protectionist policies is that their benefits are concentrated among a relatively small number of people while their costs are diffuse and spread across all consumers. Each individual import-competing producer faces very large losses from free trade while the cost to each consumer of a protectionist policy is less dramatic. It is also easier to organize a relatively small number of manufacturers than to mobilize a vast population of consumers. These factors explain the strong lobby for the protection of industries like textiles and the absence of a legislative lobby that operates specifically in the interest of textile consumers.

It is possible to patch together a case for the protection of the textile or any other industry, just as it is possible to concoct an argument for the protection of the hypothetical Maine pineapple industry. But these arguments should be seen for what they are: an attempt by an industry to increase its profits at the expense of the general public.

39

Exchange-Rate Systems and Practices

1. How does a commodity standard fix exchange rates between countries?

2. What kinds of exchange-rate arrangements exist today?

3. How is equilibrium determined in the foreign exchange market?

4. How do fixed and floating exchange rates differ in their adjustment to shifts in supply and demand for currencies?

5. What are the advantages and disadvantages of fixed and floating exchange rates?

6. What determines the kind of exchange-rate system a country adopts?

E xchange-rate policy is an important element of macroeconomic policy. An exchange rate is the link between two nations' monies. The value of a U.S. dollar in terms of Japanese yen or German marks determines how many dollars a U.S. resident will need to buy goods priced in yen or marks. Thus changes in the exchange rate can have far-reaching implications. Exchange rates may be determined in free markets, or through government intervention in the foreign exchange market, or even by law.

At the beginning of 1995, one U.S. dollar was worth 98 Japanese yen. By April of that year, the dollar was worth 83 yen. Why did the dollar fall in value relative to the yen? What are the effects of such changes? Should governments permit exchange rates to change? What can governments do to discourage changing exchange rates? These are all important questions, which this chapter will help to answer.

PREVIEW

This chapter begins with a review of the history of exchange-rate systems. Then follows an overview of exchange-rate practices in the world today and an analysis of the benefits and costs of alternative exchange-rate arrangements. Along the way, we will introduce terminology and institutions that play a major role in the evolution of exchange rates.

I. PAST AND CURRENT EXCHANGE-RATE ARRANGEMENTS

I.a. The Gold Standard

How does a commodity standard fix exchange rates between countries?

gold standard:
a system whereby national currencies are fixed in terms of their value in gold, thus creating fixed exchange rates between currencies

In ancient times, government-produced monies were made of precious metals like gold. Later, when governments began to issue paper money, it was usually convertible into a fixed amount of gold. Ensuring the convertibility of paper money into gold was a way to maintain confidence in the currency's value, at home and abroad. If a unit of currency was worth a fixed amount of gold, its value could be stated in terms of its gold value. The countries that maintained a constant gold value for their currencies were said to be on a **gold standard**.

Some countries had backed their currencies with gold long before 1880; however, the practice became widespread around 1880, so economists typically date the beginning of the gold standard to this period. From roughly 1880 to 1914, currencies had fixed values in terms of gold. For instance, the

U.S. dollar's value was fixed at $20.67 per ounce of gold. Any other currency that was fixed in terms of gold also had a fixed exchange rate against the dollar. A simple example will illustrate how this works.

Suppose the price of an ounce of gold is $20 in the United States and £4 in the United Kingdom. The pound is worth five times the value of a dollar, since it takes five times as many dollars as pounds to buy one ounce of gold. Because one pound buys five times as much gold as one dollar, the exchange rate is £1 = $5. Since currency values are linked by gold values, as the supply of gold fluctuates, there will be pressure to alter prices of goods and services. The gold standard fixes only the current price of gold. As the stock of gold increases, everything else held constant, the gold and currency prices of goods and services will tend to rise (as would occur when the money supply increases).

A commodity money standard exists when exchange rates are fixed based on the values of different currencies in terms of some commodity.

A gold standard is only one possible *commodity money standard*. Any other highly valued commodity (silver, for instance) could serve as a standard linking monies in a fixed exchange-rate system.

The gold standard ended with the outbreak of World War I. War financing was partially funded by increases in the money supplies of the hostile nations. A gold standard would not permit such a rapid increase in the money supply unless the stock of gold increased dramatically, which it did not. As money supplies grew faster than gold supplies, the link between money and gold had to be broken. During the war years and the Great Depression of the 1930s, and on through World War II, there was no organized system for setting exchange rates. Foreign trade and investment shrunk as a result of the war, obviating the need for a well-functioning method of determining exchange rates.

1.b. The Bretton Woods System

At the end of World War II, there was widespread political support for an exchange-rate system linking all monies in much the same way as the gold standard had. It was believed that a system of fixed exchange rates would promote the growth of world trade. In 1944, delegates from forty-four nations met in Bretton Woods, New Hampshire, to discuss the creation of such a system. The agreement reached at this conference has had a profound impact on the world.

The Bretton Woods agreement established a system of fixed exchange rates.

The exchange-rate arrangement that emerged from the Bretton Woods conference is often called a **gold exchange standard**. Each country was to fix the value of its currency in terms of gold, just as it had under the gold standard. The U.S.-dollar price of gold, for instance, was $35 an ounce. However, there were fundamental differences between this system and the old gold standard. The U.S. dollar, rather than gold, served as the focal point of the system. Instead of buying and selling gold, countries bought and sold U.S. dollars to maintain a fixed exchange rate with the dollar. Since the United States was the major victor nation, its currency was the dominant world currency. The United States had the productive capacity to supply much-needed goods to the rest of the world, and these goods were priced in dollars.

gold exchange standard:
an exchange-rate system in which each nation fixes the value of its currency in terms of gold but buys and sells the U.S. dollar rather than gold to maintain fixed exchange rates

reserve currency:
a currency that is used to settle international debts and is held by governments to use in foreign exchange market interventions

The U.S. dollar was the **reserve currency** of the system. International debts were settled with dollars, and international trade contracts were often denominated in dollars. In effect, the world was on a dollar standard following World War II.

I.c. The International Monetary Fund and the World Bank

International Monetary Fund (IMF):
an international organization that supervises exchange-rate arrangements and lends money to member countries experiencing problems meeting their external financial obligations

Two new organizations also emerged from the Bretton Woods conference: the International Monetary Fund and the World Bank. The **International Monetary Fund**, or **IMF**, was created to supervise the exchange-rate practices of member countries and to encourage the free convertibility of any national money into the monies of other countries. The IMF also lends money to countries that are experiencing problems meeting their international payment obligations. The funds available to the IMF come from the annual membership fees (called *quotas*) of the 178 member countries of the IMF. The U.S. quota, for instance, is almost $23 billion. (The term *quota* has a different meaning in this context than it does in international trade.)

World Bank:
an international organization that makes loans and provides technical expertise to developing countries

The **World Bank** was created to help finance economic development in poor countries. It provides loans to developing countries at more favorable terms than are available from commercial lenders and also offers technical expertise. The World Bank obtains the funds it lends by selling bonds. It is one of the world's major borrowers. See the Economic Insight "The IMF and the World Bank" for an explanation of how these institutions work.

I.d. The Transition Years

foreign exchange market intervention:
buying or selling of currencies by a government or central bank to achieve a specified exchange rate

The Bretton Woods system of fixed exchange rates required countries to actively buy and sell dollars to maintain fixed exchange rates when the *free market equilibrium* in the foreign exchange market differed from the fixed rate. The free market equilibrium exchange rate is the rate that would be established in the absence of government intervention. Governmental buying and selling of currencies to achieve a target exchange rate is called **foreign exchange market intervention**. The effectiveness of such intervention was limited to situations in which free market pressure to deviate from the fixed exchange rate was temporary. For instance, suppose a country has a bad harvest and earns less foreign exchange than usual. This may only be a temporary situation if the next harvest is plentiful and the country resumes its typical export sales. During the period of reduced exports, it will be necessary for the government of this country to intervene to avoid a depreciation of its domestic currency. In the 1960s, however, there were several episodes of permanent rather than temporary changes that called for changes in exchange rates rather than government foreign exchange market intervention. The problems that arise in response to permanent pressures to change the exchange rate will be discussed further in section 2, when we analyze the benefits and costs of alternative exchange-rate systems.

devaluation:
a deliberate decrease in the official value of a currency

The Bretton Woods system officially dissolved in 1971, at a meeting of the finance ministers of the leading world powers at the Smithsonian Institution in Washington, D.C. The Smithsonian agreement changed the exchange rates set during the Bretton Woods era. One result was a **devaluation** of the U.S. dollar. (A currency is said to be devalued when its value is officially lowered.) The official dollar value of gold dropped from $35 an ounce to $38 an ounce.

equilibrium exchange rates:
the exchange rates that are established in the absence of government foreign exchange market intervention

Under the Smithsonian agreement, countries were to maintain fixed exchange rates at newly defined values. It soon became clear, however, that the new exchange rates were not **equilibrium exchange rates** that could be maintained without government intervention, and that government intervention could not maintain the disequilibrium fixed exchange rates forever. The

The IMF and the World Bank

The International Monetary Fund (IMF) and the World Bank were both created at the Bretton Woods conference in 1944. The IMF oversees the international monetary system, promoting stable exchange rates and macroeconomic policies. The World Bank promotes the economic development of the poor nations. Both organizations are owned and directed by their 178 member countries.

The IMF provides loans to nations having trouble repaying their foreign debts. Before the IMF lends any money, however, the borrower must agree to certain conditions. IMF *conditionality* usually requires that the country meet targets for key macroeconomic variables like money-supply growth, inflation, tax collections, and subsidies. The conditions attached to IMF loans are aimed at promoting stable economic growth.

The World Bank assists developing countries by providing long-term financing for development projects and programs. The Bank also provides expertise in many areas in which poor nations lack expert knowledge: agriculture, medicine, construction, and education, as well as economics. The IMF primarily employs economists to carry out its mission.

The diversity of World Bank activities results in the employment of about 6,500 people. The IMF has a staff of approximately 1,700. Both organizations post employees around the world, but most work at the headquarters in Washington, D.C.

World Bank funds are largely acquired by borrowing on the international bond market. The IMF receives its funding from member-country subscription fees, called *quotas*. A member's quota determines its voting power in setting IMF policies. The United States, whose quota accounts for the largest fraction of the total, has the most votes.

U.S. dollar was devalued again in February 1973, when the dollar price of gold was raised to $42.22. This new exchange rate was still not an equilibrium rate, and in March 1973 the major industrial countries abandoned fixed exchange rates.

1.e. Floating Exchange Rates

What kinds of exchange-rate arrangements exist today?

In March 1973, the major industrial countries abandoned fixed exchange rates for floating rates.

managed floating exchange rates:
the system whereby central banks intervene in the floating foreign exchange market to influence exchange rates; also referred to as *dirty float*

When fixed exchange rates were abandoned by the major industrial countries in March 1973, the world did not move to purely free-market-determined floating exchange rates. Under the system in existence since that time, the major industrial countries intervene to keep their currencies within acceptable ranges, while many smaller countries maintain fixed exchange rates.

The world today consists of some countries with fixed exchange rates, whose governments keep the exchange rates between two or more currencies constant over time; other countries with floating exchange rates, which shift on a daily basis according to the forces of supply and demand; and still others whose exchange-rate systems lie somewhere in between. Table 1, which lists the exchange-rate arrangements of over 170 countries, illustrates the diversity of exchange-rate arrangements currently in effect. We will focus here on the differences between fixed and floating exchange rates. All of the other exchange-rate arrangements listed in Table 1 are special versions of these two general exchange-rate systems.

As Table 1 shows, some countries maintain **managed floating exchange rates**, also called a *dirty float*. Although Table 1 lists countries like Japan and the United States as "independently floating," in fact their central banks, such as the Federal Reserve in the United States and the Bank of Japan in

TABLE I
Exchange-Rate Arrangements (As of December 31, 1994)[1]

		Currency Pegged to		
U.S. Dollar	**French Franc**	**Other Currency**	**SDR**	**Other Composite[2]**
Antigua and Barbuda	Benin	Bhutan (Indian rupee)	Libya	Bangladesh
Argentina	Burkina Faso	Eritrea (Ethiopian birr)	Myanmar	Botswana
Bahamas, The	Cameroon	Estonia (deutsche mark)	Rwanda	Burundi
Barbados	C. African Rep.	Kiribati (Australian dollar)	Seychelles	Cape Verde
Belize	Chad	Lesotho (South African rand)		Cyprus
Djibouti	Comoros	Namibia (South African rand)		Czech Republic
Dominica	Congo	San Marino (Italian lira)		Fiji
Grenada	Côte d'Ivoire	Swaziland (South African rand)		Hungary
Iraq	Equatorial Guinea	Tajikistan, Rep. of (Russian ruble)		Iceland
Liberia	Gabon			Jordan
Lithuania	Mali			Kuwait
Marshall Islands	Niger			Malta
Micronesia, Fed. States of	Senegal			Mauritania
Nigeria	Togo			Morocco
Oman				Nepal
Panama				Slovak Republic
St. Kitts and Nevis				Solomon Islands
St. Lucia				Thailand
St. Vincent and the Grenadines				Tonga
Syrian Arab Rep.				Vanuatu
Turkmenistan				Western Samoa
Venezuela				
Yemen, Republic of				

[1]For members with dual or multiple exchange markets, the arrangement shown is that in the major market.
[2]Comprises currencies which are pegged to various "baskets" of currencies of the members' own choice, as distinct from the SDR basket.

(continued on p. 1002)

TABLE I
Exchange-Rate Arrangements (cont.)

Flexibility Limited in Terms of a Single Currency or Group of Currencies		
Single Currency[3]	**Cooperative Arrangements**[4]	**Adjusted According to a Set of Indicators**[5]
Bahrain	Austria	Chile
Qatar	Belgium	Ecuador
Saudi Arabia	Denmark	Nicaragua
United Arab Emirates	France	
	Germany	
	Ireland	
	Luxembourg	
	Netherlands	
	Portugal	
	Spain	

More Flexible

Other Managed Floating		**Independently Floating**			
Algeria	Israel	Afghanistan, Islamic State of	Guinea	Moldova	South Africa
Angola	Korea	Albania	Guyana	Mongolia	Suriname
Belarus	Lao, P.D. Rep. of	Armenia	Haiti	Mozambique	Sweden
Brazil	Malaysia	Australia	India	New Zealand	Switzerland
Cambodia	Maldives	Azerbaijan	Iran, I.R. of	Norway	Tanzania
China, P.R.	Mauritius	Bolivia	Italy	Papua New Guinea	Trinidad and Tobago
Colombia	Pakistan	Bulgaria	Jamaica	Paraguay	Uganda
Croatia	Poland	Canada	Japan	Peru	Ukraine
Dominican Republic	Singapore	Costa Rica	Kazakhstan	Philippines	United Kingdom
Egypt	Slovenia	El Salvador	Kenya	Romania	United States
Georgia	Sri Lanka	Ethiopia	Kyrgyz Rep.	Russia	Zaire
Greece	Sudan	Finland	Latvia	Sao Tome and Principe	Zambia
Guinea-Bissau	Tunisia	Gambia, The	Lebanon	Sierra Leone	Zimbabwe
Honduras	Turkey	Ghana	Macedonia, FYR of	Somalia	
Indonesia	Uruguay	Guatemala	Madagascar		
	Vietnam		Malawi		
			Mexico		

[3]Exchange rates of all currencies have shown limited flexibility in terms of the U.S. dollar.
[4]Refers to the cooperative arrangement maintained under the European Monetary System.
[5]Includes exchange arrangements under which the exchange rate is adjusted at relatively frequent intervals, on the basis of indicators determined by the respective member countries.
Source: International Monetary Fund, *International Financial Statistics*, Washington, D.C., March 1995.

Japan, intervene from time to time in the foreign exchange market. Since exchange-rate variations can alter the prices of goods traded internationally, governments often attempt to push exchange rates to values consistent with some target value of international trade or investment. For example, on April 5, 1995, the U.S. Treasury and the Federal Reserve were concerned that the dollar had fallen in value too much, and investors were becoming concerned about the future stability of the currency. As a result, the Fed bought over $1 billion in exchange for German marks and Japanese yen. This intervention in the foreign exchange market caused the dollar to rise temporarily in value more than private-market pressures would have done.

Some countries, like Antigua, Barbuda and Benin, maintain a fixed value (or peg) relative to a single currency, such as the dollar or French franc. Fixed exchange rates are often called *pegged* exchange rates. Other countries, like Bangladesh, peg to a composite of currencies by setting the value of their currency at the average value of several foreign currencies.

Fixed (pegged) exchange rates are held constant over time.

Some currencies are pegged to the *SDR*, as you learned in the chapter on money and banking. The SDR, which stands for **special drawing right**, is an artificial unit of account. Its value is determined by combining the values of the U.S. dollar, German mark, Japanese yen, French franc, and British pound. A country that pegs to the SDR determines its currency's value in terms of an average of the five currencies that make up the SDR.

special drawing right:
an artificial unit of account created by averaging the values of the U.S. dollar, German mark, Japanese yen, French franc, and British pound

The column entitled "Cooperative Arrangements" in Table 1 lists the countries that belong to the **European Monetary System**, or **EMS**. These countries maintain fixed exchange rates against each other but allow their currencies to float jointly against the rest of the world. In other words, the values of currencies in the EMS all shift together relative to currencies outside the EMS.

European Monetary System (EMS):
an organization composed of Western European nations that maintain fixed exchange rates among themselves and floating exchange rates with the rest of the world

Table 2 lists the end-of-year exchange rates for several currencies versus the U.S. dollar from the 1950s to 1994. For most of the currencies, there was

TABLE 2
Exchange Rates of Selected Countries (currency units per U.S. dollar)

Year	Canadian Dollar	Japanese Yen	French Franc	German Mark	Italian Lira	British Pound
1950	1.06	361	3.50	4.20	625	.36
1955	1.00	361	3.50	4.22	625	.36
1960	1.00	358	4.90	4.17	621	.36
1965	1.08	361	4.90	4.01	625	.36
1970	1.01	358	5.52	3.65	623	.42
1975	1.02	305	4.49	2.62	684	.50
1980	1.19	203	4.52	1.96	931	.42
1985	1.40	201	7.56	2.46	1,679	.69
1990	1.16	134	5.13	1.49	1,130	.52
1994	1.40	100	5.37	1.56	1,624	.64

Source: End-of-year exchange rates from International Monetary Fund, *International Financial Statistics*, Washington, D.C.

little movement in the 1950s and 1960s, the era of the Bretton Woods agreement. In the early 1970s, exchange rates began to fluctuate. More recently, there has been considerable change in the foreign exchange value of a dollar, as Table 2 illustrates.

RECAP

1. Under a gold standard, each currency has a fixed value in terms of gold. This arrangement provides for fixed exchange rates between countries.

2. At the end of World War II, the Bretton Woods agreement established a new system of fixed exchange rates. Two new organizations—the International Monetary Fund (IMF) and the World Bank—also emerged from the Bretton Woods conference.

3. Fixed exchange rates are maintained by government intervention in the foreign exchange market; governments or central banks buy and sell currencies to keep the equilibrium exchange rate steady.

4. The governments of the major industrial countries adopted floating exchange rates in 1973. In fact, the prevailing system is characterized by "managed floating"—that is, by occasional government intervention rather than a pure free-market-determined exchange-rate system.

5. Some countries choose floating exchange rates; others peg their currencies to a single currency or a composite.

6. The European Monetary System maintains fixed exchange rates among several Western European currencies, which then float jointly against the rest of the world.

2. FIXED OR FLOATING EXCHANGE RATES

Is the United States better off today, with floating exchange rates, than it was with the fixed exchange rates of the post–World War II period? The choice of an exchange-rate system has multiple implications for the performance of a nation's economy and, therefore, for the conduct of macroeconomic policy. As is true of many policy issues in economics, economists often disagree about the merits of fixed versus flexible exchange rates. Let us look at the characteristics of the different exchange-rate systems.

2.a. Equilibrium in the Foreign Exchange Market

How is equilibrium determined in the foreign exchange market?

An exchange rate is the price of one money in terms of another. Equilibrium is determined by the supply of and demand for the two currencies in the foreign exchange market. Figure 1 contains two supply and demand diagrams for the U.S. dollar–French franc foreign exchange market. The downward-sloping demand curve indicates that the higher the dollar price of French francs, the fewer francs will be demanded. The upward-sloping supply curve indicates that the higher the dollar price of French francs, the more francs will be supplied.

Part IX/Issues in International Trade and Finance

Figure 1
The Supply of and Demand for Foreign Exchange

This figure represents the foreign exchange market for francs traded for dollars. The demand curve for francs is based on the U.S. demand for French products, and the supply curve of francs is based on the French demand for U.S. products: an increase in demand for French wine causes demand for francs to increase from D_1 to D_2. This shift causes an increase from Q_1 to Q_2 in the equilibrium quantity of francs traded and causes the franc to appreciate to $.18 from the initial equilibrium exchange rate of $.15. A decrease in demand for French wine causes the demand for francs to fall from D_1 to D_3. This shift leads to a fall in the equilibrium quantity traded to Q_3 and a depreciation of the franc to $.12. If the French demand for U.S. tractors falls, fewer francs are supplied for exchange for dollars, as illustrated by the fall in supply from S_1 to S_3. This shift causes the franc to appreciate to $.18 and the equilibrium quantity of francs traded to fall to Q_3. If the French demand for U.S. tractors rises, then more francs are supplied for dollars and the supply curve increases from S_1 to S_2. This causes the franc to depreciate and the equilibrium quantity of francs traded to rise to Q_2.

(a) A Change in the U.S. Demand for French Wine

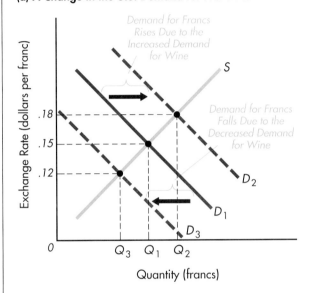

(b) A Change in the French Demand for U.S. Tractors

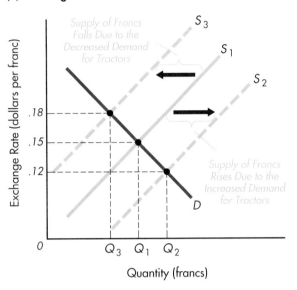

Equilibrium in the foreign exchange market occurs at the point where the foreign exchange demand and supply curves intersect.

In Figure 1(a), the initial equilibrium occurs at the point where the demand curve D_1 intersects the supply curve. At this point, the equilibrium exchange rate is $.15 (1 franc costs $.15) and the quantity of francs bought and sold is Q_1.

Suppose U.S. residents increase their demand for French wine. Because francs are needed to pay for the wine, the greater U.S. demand for French wine generates a greater demand for francs by U.S. citizens, who hold dollars. The demand curve in Figure 1(a) thus shifts from D_1 to D_2. This increased demand for francs causes the franc to appreciate relative to the dollar. The new exchange rate is $.18, and a greater quantity of francs, Q_2, is bought and sold.

If the U.S. demand for French wine falls, the demand for francs also falls, as illustrated by the shift from D_1 to D_3 in Figure 1(a). The decreased demand for francs causes the franc to depreciate relative to the dollar, so that the exchange rate falls to $.12.

So far, we have considered how shifts in the U.S. demand for French goods affect the dollar-franc exchange rate. We can also use the same supply and demand diagram to analyze how changes in the French demand for U.S. goods affect the equilibrium exchange rate. The supply of francs to the foreign exchange market originates with French residents who buy goods from the rest of the world. If a French importer buys a tractor from a U.S. firm, the importer must exchange francs for dollars to pay for the tractor. As French residents' demand for foreign goods and services rises and falls, the supply of francs to the foreign exchange market changes.

Suppose the French demand for U.S. tractors increases. This brings about a shift of the supply curve: as francs are exchanged for dollars to buy the U.S. tractors, the supply of francs increases. In Figure 1(b), the supply of francs curve shifts from S_1 to S_2. The greater supply of francs causes the franc to depreciate relative to the dollar, and the exchange rate falls from $.15 to $.12. If the French demand for U.S. tractors decreases, the supply of francs decreases from S_1 to S_3, and the franc appreciates to $.18.

Foreign exchange supply and demand curves are affected by changes in tastes and technology and by changing government policy. As demand and supply change, the equilibrium exchange rate changes. In fact, continuous shifts in supply and demand cause the exchange rate to change as often as every day, based on free market forces. Now let us consider how fixed exchange rates differ from floating exchange rates.

2.b. Adjustment Mechanisms Under Fixed and Flexible Exchange Rates

How do fixed and floating exchange rates differ in their adjustment to shifts in supply and demand for currencies?

Figure 2 shows the dollar-franc foreign exchange market. The exchange rate is the number of dollars required to buy one franc; the quantity is the quantity of francs bought and sold. Suppose that, initially, the equilibrium is at point A, with quantity Q_1 francs traded at $.15 per franc.

Suppose French wine becomes more popular in the United States, and the demand for francs increases from D_1 to D_2. With flexible exchange rates (as

Figure 2
Foreign Exchange Market Equilibrium
Under Fixed and Flexible Exchange Rates
Initially, equilibrium is at point A; the exchange rate is $.15 and Q_1 francs are traded. An increase in demand for French wine causes the demand for francs to increase from D_1 to D_2. With flexible exchange rates, the franc appreciates in value to $.18 and Q_2 francs are traded; equilibrium is at point B. If the government is committed to maintaining a fixed exchange rate of $.15, the supply of francs must be increased to S_2 so that a new equilibrium can occur at point C. The government must intervene in the foreign exchange market and sell francs to shift the supply curve to S_2.

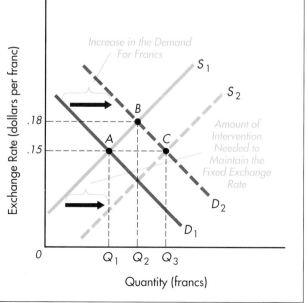

appreciate:
when the value of a currency increases under floating exchange rates—that is, exchange rates determined by supply and demand

depreciate:
when the value of a currency decreases under floating exchange rates

An increase in demand for a currency will cause an appreciation of its exchange rate, unless governments intervene in the foreign exchange market to increase the supply of that currency.

fundamental disequilibrium:
a permanent shift in the foreign-exchange-market supply and demand curves, such that the fixed exchange rate is no longer an equilibrium rate

speculators:
people who seek to profit from an expected shift in an exchange rate by selling the currency expected to depreciate and buying the currency expected to appreciate, then exchanging the appreciated currency for the depreciated currency after the exchange rate adjustment

in Figure 1), a new equilibrium is established at point B. The exchange rate rises to \$.18 per franc, and the quantity of francs bought and sold is Q_2. The increased demand for francs has caused the franc to **appreciate** (rise in value against the dollar) and the dollar to **depreciate** (fall in value against the franc). This is an example of a freely floating exchange rate, determined by the free market forces of supply and demand.

Now suppose the Federal Reserve is committed to maintaining a fixed exchange rate of \$.15 per franc. The increase in demand for francs causes a shortage of francs at the exchange rate of \$.15. According to the new demand curve, D_2, the quantity of francs demanded at \$.15 is Q_3. The quantity supplied is found on the original supply curve S_1, at Q_1. The only way to maintain the exchange rate of \$.15 is for the Federal Reserve to supply francs to meet the shortage of $Q_3 - Q_1$. In other words, the Fed must sell $Q_3 - Q_1$ francs to shift the supply curve to S_2 and thus maintain the fixed exchange rate.

If the increased demand for francs is temporary, the Fed can continue to supply francs for the short time necessary. However, if the increased demand for francs is permanent, the Fed's intervention will eventually end when it runs out of francs. This situation—a permanent change in supply or demand—is referred to as a **fundamental disequilibrium**. The fixed exchange rate is no longer an equilibrium rate. Under the Bretton Woods agreement, a country was supposed to devalue its currency in such cases.

Suppose that the shift to D_2 in Figure 2 is permanent. In this case, the dollar should be devalued. A devaluation to \$.18 per franc would restore equilibrium in the foreign exchange market without requiring further intervention by the government. Sometimes, however, governments try to maintain the old exchange rate (\$.15 per franc, in this case) even though most people believe the shift in demand to be permanent. When this happens, **speculators** buy the currency that is in greater demand (francs, in our example) in anticipation of the eventual devaluation of the other currency (dollars, in Figure 2). A speculator who purchases francs for \$.15 prior to the devaluation and sells them for \$.18 after the devaluation earns \$.03 per franc purchased—a 20 percent profit.

Speculation puts greater devaluation pressure on the dollar: the speculators sell dollars and buy francs, causing the demand for francs to increase even further. Such speculative activity contributed to the breakdown of the Bretton Woods system of fixed exchange rates. Several countries intervened to support exchange rates that were far out of line with free market forces. The longer a devaluation was put off, the more obvious it became that devaluation was forthcoming and the more speculators entered the market. In 1971 and 1973, speculators sold dollars for yen and German marks. They were betting that the dollar would be devalued; both times they were correct. The speculative activity of the early 1970s drew attention to the folly of efforts to maintain fixed exchange rates in the face of a change in the fundamental equilibrium exchange rate.

2.c. Constraints on Economic Policy

Fixed exchange rates can be maintained over time only between countries with similar economic policies and similar underlying economic conditions.

As prices rise within a country, the domestic value of a unit of its currency falls, since the currency buys fewer goods and services. In the foreign exchange market too, the value of a unit of domestic currency falls, since it buys relatively fewer goods and services than the foreign currency does. A fixed exchange rate thus requires that the purchasing power of the two currencies change at roughly the same rate over time. Only if two nations have approximately the same inflation experience will they be able to maintain a fixed exchange rate. This condition was a frequent source of problems in the Bretton Woods era of fixed exchange rates. In the late 1960s, for instance, the U.S. government was following a more expansionary macroeconomic policy than was Germany. U.S. government expenditures on the war in Vietnam and domestic antipoverty initiatives led to inflationary pressures that were not matched in Germany. Between 1965 and 1970, price levels rose by 23.2 percent in the United States but only by 12.8 percent in Germany. Since the purchasing power of a dollar was falling faster than that of the mark, the fixed exchange rate could not be maintained. The dollar had to be devalued.

One of the advantages of floating exchange rates is that countries are free to pursue their own macroeconomic policies without worrying about maintaining an exchange-rate commitment. If U.S. policy produces a higher inflation rate than Japanese policy, the dollar will automatically depreciate in value against the yen. The United States can choose the macroeconomic policy it wants, independent of other nations, and let the exchange rate adjust if its inflation rate differs markedly from that of other nations. If the dollar were fixed in value relative to the yen, the two nations couldn't follow independent policies and expect to maintain the exchange rate.

It became obvious in the late 1960s that many governments considered other issues more important than maintenance of a fixed exchange rate. A nation that puts a high priority on reducing unemployment will typically stimulate the economy to try to increase income and create jobs. This initiative may cause the domestic inflation rate to rise and the domestic currency to depreciate relative to other currencies. If one goal or the other—lower unemployment or a fixed exchange rate—must be given up, it is likely that the exchange-rate goal will be sacrificed.

Floating exchange rates allow countries to formulate their macroeconomic policies independently of other nations. Fixed exchange rates require the economic policies of countries linked by the exchange rate to be similar.

Floating exchange rates allow countries to formulate domestic economic policy solely in response to domestic issues; attention need not be paid to the exchange rate of the rest of the world. For residents of some countries, this freedom may be more of a problem than a benefit. The freedom to choose a rate of inflation and let the exchange rate adjust itself can have undesirable consequences in countries whose politicians, for whatever reason, follow highly inflationary policies. In these countries a fixed-exchange-rate system would impose discipline, since maintenance of the exchange rate would not permit policies that diverged sharply from those of its trading partner.

RECAP

1. Under a fixed-exchange-rate system, governments must intervene in the foreign exchange market to maintain the exchange rate. A fundamental disequilibrium requires a currency devaluation.

2. Fixed exchange rates can be maintained only between countries with similar macroeconomic policies and similar underlying economic conditions.

3. Fixed exchange rates serve as a constraint on inflationary government policies.

3. THE CHOICE OF AN EXCHANGE-RATE SYSTEM

What determines the kind of exchange-rate system a country adopts?

Different countries choose different exchange-rate arrangements. Why does the United States choose floating exchange rates while Barbados adopts a fixed exchange rate? Let us compare the characteristics of countries that choose to float with those of countries that choose to fix their exchange rates.

3.a. Country Characteristics

The choice of an exchange-rate system is an important element of the macro-economic policy of any country. The choice seems to be related to country size, openness, inflation, and diversification of trade.

3.a.1. **Size**   Large countries (measured by economic output or GDP) tend to be both independent and relatively unwilling to forgo domestic policy goals in order to maintain a fixed exchange rate. Because large countries have large domestic markets, international issues are less crucial to everyday business than they are in a small country.

3.a.2. **Openness**   Closely related to size is the relative openness of the economy. By openness, we mean the degree to which the country depends on international trade. Because every country is involved in international trade, openness is very much a matter of degree. An **open economy**, according to economists, is one in which a relatively large fraction of the GDP is devoted to internationally tradable goods. In a closed economy, a relatively small fraction of the GDP is devoted to internationally tradable goods. The more open an economy, the greater the impact of variations in the exchange rate on the domestic economy. The more open the economy, therefore, the greater the tendency to establish fixed exchange rates.

3.a.3. **Inflation**   Countries whose policies produce inflation rates much higher or lower than those of other countries tend to choose floating exchange rates. A fixed exchange rate cannot be maintained when a country experiences inflation much different from that of the rest of the world.

3.a.4. **Trade Diversification**   Countries that trade largely with a single foreign country tend to peg their currencies' value to that of the trading partner. For instance, South Africa accounts for the dominant share of the total trade of Swaziland. By pegging its currency, the lilangeni, to the South African rand, Swaziland enjoys more stable lilangeni prices of goods than it would with floating exchange rates. Trade with South Africa is such a dominant feature of the Swaziland economy that a fluctuating lilangeni price of the rand would be reflected in a fluctuating price level in Swaziland. If the lilangeni depreciated against the rand, the lilangeni prices of imports from South Africa would rise: this would bring about a rise in the Swaziland price level. Exchange-rate depreciation tends to affect the domestic price level in all

open economy:
an economy in which a relatively large fraction of the GDP is devoted to internationally tradable goods

TABLE 3

Characteristics of Countries with Fixed and Floating Exchange Rates

Fixed-Rate Countries	Floating-Rate Countries
Small size	Large size
Open economy	Closed economy
Harmonious inflation rate	Divergent inflation rate
Concentrated trade	Diversified trade

countries, but the effect is magnified if a single foreign country accounts for much of a nation's trade. Countries with diversified trading patterns find fixed exchange rates less desirable, because price stability would prevail only in trade with a single country. With all other trading partners, prices would still fluctuate.

Table 3 summarizes the national characteristics associated with alternative exchange-rate systems. Many countries do not fit into the neat categorization of Table 3, but it is nonetheless useful for understanding the great majority of countries' choices.

3.b. Multiple Exchange Rates

multiple exchange rates:
a system whereby a government fixes different exchange rates for different types of transactions

Most countries conduct all their foreign exchange transactions at a single exchange rate. For instance, if the dollar-pound exchange rate is $1.80, residents of the United States can purchase British pounds at $1.80, no matter what use they make of the pounds. In 1995, however, the eighteen countries listed in Table 4 had **multiple exchange rates**—different exchange rates for different types of transactions. A typical arrangement is a dual exchange-rate system, consisting of a free-market-determined floating exchange rate for financial transactions and a fixed exchange rate that overvalues the domestic currency for transactions in goods and services. Some countries adopt even more elaborate arrangements, with special exchange rates for a variety of different transactions. For example, Venezuela once had a four-tier system. The central bank traded dollars for bolivars (Bs) at the following rates: sell dollars for Bs4.30 for interest payments on foreign debt; sell dollars for Bs6.00 for national petroleum and iron-ore companies; and sell dollars for Bs7.50 for other government agencies. All other transactions took place at the free market floating exchange rate of Bs14.40.

Countries with multiple exchange rates use them as an alternative to taxes and subsidies. Activities that the policymakers want to encourage are subsidized by allowing participants in them to buy foreign exchange at an artificially low price or sell foreign exchange at an artificially high price. Participants in activities that policymakers want to discourage are forced to pay an artificially high price to buy foreign exchange and an artificially low price to sell foreign exchange. For instance, firms that manufacture goods for export, but import some of the resources used in production, may be permitted to buy foreign exchange at an artificially low price. This allows them to

TABLE 4
Countries with Multiple Exchange Rates (as of March 1995)

Afghanistan	El Salvador	Nigeria
The Bahamas	Iran	Somalia
Brazil	Iraq	South Africa
Chile	Kenya	Syrian Arab Republic
Colombia	Lesotho	Uganda
Ecuador	Nicaragua	Zambia

Source: International Monetary Fund, *International Financial Statistics,* Washington, D.C., March 1995.

pay a lower domestic-currency price for their imported resources and consequently to charge a lower price for their output, which increases exports. In Venezuela, as you just saw, petroleum companies could buy dollars from the Central Bank for Bs6.00 even though the free-market rate was Bs14.40. In order to encourage greater production and export of Venezuelan petroleum, the Central Bank subsidized the dollars the petroleum companies needed for imports.

In an effort to discourage imports, developing countries often charge an artificially high price for foreign exchange that will be used to import consumer goods. Such multiple-exchange-rate systems have the same effects as direct government subsidies to exporting manufacturers and taxes on the importation of consumer goods: exports are stimulated and consumer-goods imports are reduced.

The IMF has tried to discourage multiple exchange rates, because they cause the domestic prices of internationally traded goods to differ from the international prices. The result is inefficient resource utilization in consumption and production, since domestic residents respond to the contrived relative prices rather than the true prices set on world markets. Monitoring and administering compliance with multiple exchange rates create additional costs, and people devote resources to avoiding the unfavorable aspects of multiple exchange rates (for example, by getting their transactions classified to the most favorable exchange rate).

3.c. Overvalued Exchange Rates

Developing countries often establish an official exchange rate—the exchange rate set by law—that differs from the equilibrium exchange rate. Figure 3 illustrates an overvalued exchange rate. Assume that a developing country whose currency is called the peso fixes an official peso-dollar exchange rate of 150 pesos per dollar, while the free market equilibrium exchange rate is

Figure 3
Overvalued Exchange Rate
The official exchange rate is 150 pesos per dollar,
while the free market equilibrium exchange rate is
200 pesos per dollar. Since the official peso price of
a dollar is below the equilibrium, the peso is said to
be overvalued.

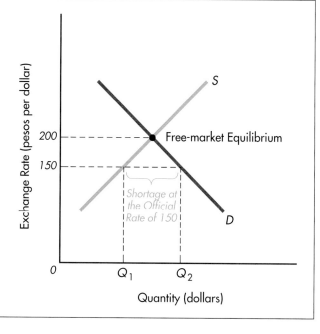

200 pesos per dollar. Since the official rate is less than the equilibrium rate, a dollar shortage results. Q_2 dollars are demanded at 150 pesos per dollar, but only Q_1 are supplied.

When the official peso-dollar rate is less than the free market rate, the peso is overvalued. To support the official rate, the country must impose tariffs or other restrictions on trade to reduce the demand for dollars. Overvaluing the domestic currency subsidizes favored activities or groups: if everyone had access to the official rate, there would be a dollar shortage. In addition to imposing quotas or tariffs on international trade in goods or financial assets, the country can use multiple exchange rates to ensure that only favored groups buy dollars at the official rate. In fact, a typical feature of multiple-exchange-rate regimes is the availability of an overvalued domestic-currency rate for favored transactions. Other residents are forced into the free market, where in this case they pay 200 pesos for their dollars.

Overvalued exchange rates are used to subsidize favored transactions.

RECAP

1. Countries with fixed exchange rates tend to be small, open economies with inflation rates similar to those of their trading partners. Their currencies are typically pegged to that of their main trading partner.
2. Some countries adopt multiple exchange rates for different kinds of transactions.
3. Multiple exchange rates resemble a system of subsidies for favored activities and taxes for activities that are discouraged.

4. An exchange rate is overvalued when the official domestic-currency price of foreign currency is lower than the equilibrium price.

SUMMARY

▲▼ How does a commodity standard fix exchange rates between countries?

1. Between 1880 and 1914, a gold standard provided for fixed exchange rates among countries. §1.a

2. The gold standard ended with World War I, and no established international monetary system replaced it until after World War II, when the Bretton Woods agreement created a fixed-exchange-rate system. §1.b

▲▼ What kinds of exchange-rate arrangements exist today?

3. Today some countries have fixed exchange rates, others have floating exchange rates, and still others have managed floats or other types of systems. §1.e

▲▼ How is equilibrium determined in the foreign exchange market?

4. Foreign-exchange-market equilibrium is determined by the intersection of the demand and supply curves for foreign exchange. §2.a

▲▼ How do fixed and floating exchange rates differ in their adjustment to shifts in supply and demand for currencies?

5. Under fixed exchange rates, central banks must intervene in the foreign exchange market to keep the exchange rate from shifting. §2.b

▲▼ What are the advantages and disadvantages of fixed and floating exchange rates?

6. Floating exchange rates permit countries to pursue independent economic policies. A fixed exchange rate requires a country to adopt policies similar to those of the country whose currency it pegs to. A fixed exchange rate may serve to prevent a country from pursuing inflationary policies. §2.c

▲▼ What determines the kind of exchange-rate system a country adopts?

7. The choice of an exchange-rate system is related to the size and openness of a country, its inflation experience, and the diversification of its international trade. §3.a

8. Multiple exchange rates are used to subsidize favored activities and raise costs for other activities. §3.b

KEY TERMS

gold standard §1.a
gold exchange standard §1.b
reserve currency §1.b
International Monetary Fund (IMF) §1.c
World Bank §1.c
foreign exchange market intervention §1.d
devaluation §1.d
equilibrium exchange rates §1.d
managed floating exchange rates §1.e

special drawing right §1.e
European Monetary System (EMS) §1.e
appreciate §2.b
depreciate §2.b
fundamental disequilibrium §2.b
speculators §2.b
open economy §3.a.2
multiple exchange rates §3.b

EXERCISES

1. Under a gold standard, if the price of an ounce of gold is 400 U.S. dollars and 500 Canadian dollars, what is the exchange rate between U.S. and Canadian dollars?

2. What were the three major results of the Bretton Woods conference?

3. What is the difference between the IMF and the World Bank?

4. How can Mexico fix the value of the peso relative to the dollar when the demand for and supply of dollars and pesos changes continuously? Illustrate your explanation with a graph.

5. Draw a foreign-exchange-market supply and demand diagram to show how the mark-dollar exchange rate is determined. Set the initial equilibrium at a rate of 1.5 marks per dollar.

6. Using the diagram in question 5, illustrate the effect of a change in tastes prompting German residents to buy more goods from the United States. If the exchange rate is floating, what will happen to the foreign-exchange-market equilibrium?

7. Using the diagram in question 5, illustrate the effect of the change in German tastes if exchange rates are fixed. What will happen to the foreign-exchange-market equilibrium?

8. When and why should exchange rates change under a fixed exchange-rate system?

9. Other things being equal, what kind of exchange-rate system would you expect each of the following countries to adopt?

   a. A small country that conducts all of its trade with the United States

   b. A country that has no international trade

   c. A country whose policies have led to a 300 percent annual rate of inflation

   d. A country that wants to offer exporters cheap access to the imported inputs they need but to discourage other domestic residents from importing goods

   e. A large country like the United States or Japan

10. Illustrate and explain the meaning and likely effects of an overvalued exchange rate.

11. The countries listed as pegging to the French franc in Table 1 have a characteristic in common that helps to explain why they maintain fixed exchange rates with the franc. Explain what that characteristic is.

12. Suppose you just returned home from a vacation in Mazatlán, Mexico, where you exchanged U.S. dollars for Mexican pesos. How did your trip to Mexico affect the supply and demand for dollars and the exchange rate (assume that all other things are equal)?

13. What does it mean to say that a currency appreciates or depreciates in value? Give an example of each and briefly mention what might cause such a change.

14. If you were an economic policy czar with total power to choose your country's economic policy, would you want a fixed or floating exchange rate for your currency? Why?

15. How does a currency speculator profit from exchange-rate changes? Give an example of a profitable speculation.

COOPERATIVE LEARNING EXERCISE

Divide the class into groups of four. Ask each group to write a multiple-choice question based on sections 2.a. and 2.b. The question should be written by the group as a whole. Once the question has been written, each individual must independently write one correct and two incorrect responses. Then the group meets and each member reads his or her responses. A critique of each response should be given, after which the group should pick the best correct response and the four best incorrect responses to complete its multiple-choice question.

Each group then meets with another group, and they exchange questions. Each group must determine the correct response to the other group's question and then offer a critique of each incorrect response indicating why it is incorrect.

United We Spend: Europeans to Have Single Currency by '99

Get ready, Europe: A single currency is on the way.

That was the message of a report released last month on the practical problems of introducing a new money for the 15 nations of the European Union.

The group's new Treaty on European Union calls for the nations to create an economic and monetary merger no later than Jan. 1, 1999. A central bank will issue the new currency.

It remains a mystery how the nations will carry out the massive task of trading in the German mark, French franc and other currencies for the new one.

"The changeover to the single currency is a challenge of historical dimensions," said Dutch businessman Cees Maas, chairman of a panel of experts who drew up the EU report.

The bankers and financial experts recommended the switch to the European currency unit, or Ecu, begin as quickly as possible.

They ruled out introducing overnight or over a weekend new Ecu notes and coins and changing savings, checking and other accounts to conform.

Instead, they said that once the European Central Bank is up and running—say, by Jan. 1, 1999—it should take no longer than six months to introduce the Ecu as the union's single currency.

The Ecu, pronounced eh-KOO or eh-CUE, already is used as an accounting unit and for some payments. No notes or coins are in circulation yet.

The Ecu, the German mark and the French franc would initially circulate together—but probably for no more than six months, according to the experts. The report said the new money should be as strong as the mightiest national currency to gain popular support. The mark now is the EU's strongest currency, and there have been misgivings among Germans about turning in their well-known money for the upstart Ecu.

To calm public unease about giving up local currencies, there have been suggestions the new bills carry the EU design on one side and symbols of the old money, whether the mark, the franc or Dutch guilder, on the other side.

Governments and businesses should begin planning for the change immediately, the report said. Maas' group will issue a final report in June.

A monetary union could be formed as early as Jan. 1, 1997, if a majority of nations meet criteria of low inflation and interest rates, stable currencies and healthy public finances. But nearly all the nations have enormous budget deficits.

Source: "United We Spend: Europeans to Have Single Currency by '99," Associated Press, *Rocky Mountain News*, Feb. 5, 1995, p. 14A. Reprinted by permission of Associated Press.

Commentary

A fixed exchange-rate system represents an agreement among countries to convert their individual currencies from one to another at a given rate. The adoption of one money for Europe would be the strongest possible commitment to fixed exchange rates among the EU countries. If every nation used the same currency, then all would be linked to the same inflation rate and there would be no fluctuation of the value of the currency across the EU nations using the currency—just as each state in the United States uses the same money, the U.S. dollar. The adoption of a single currency requires that economic policies be similar across EU countries. This means that individual countries must subjugate their monetary policies to the goals of the European monetary and fiscal authority. If each nation insists on exercising its own monetary and fiscal policy and chooses different interest and inflation rates, there can never be one money.

Today, ten European countries participate in the fixed exchange-rate system of the European Monetary System (EMS). This means that there are only nine independent exchange rates within the system and that one country has the role of "leader" in terms of monetary policy. In fact, much evidence points to the fact that Germany served as the leader of the EU, and other member nations followed its monetary policy. Germany's monetary policy is geared toward keeping inflation low.

A convergence in inflation rates is necessary for the smooth operation of the EMS. Persistent inflation differentials across the members of a fixed exchange-rate system affect the competitiveness of each member's exports in the world market. Though a fixed exchange-rate system maintains stable *nominal exchange rates* (the rate observed in the foreign exchange market), the competitiveness of a currency is represented by the *real exchange rate*. The real exchange rate is the nominal exchange rate adjusted for the price level at home compared to the price level abroad. It is calculated as follows:

$$\text{Real exchange rate} = \frac{(\text{nominal exchange rate} \times \text{foreign price level})}{\text{domestic price level}}$$

The disruptive changes in competitiveness caused by persistent inflation differentials require a realignment of a fixed exchange-rate system that adjusts nominal exchange rates to keep real exchange rates from drifting too far from their correct value. For instance, if the U.S. price level starts to rise faster than foreign prices, U.S. goods will be priced out of the world market unless the dollar depreciates on the foreign exchange market. According to the equation just presented, if the United States is the domestic country and its price level rises, the real exchange rate falls and U.S. goods are, therefore, relatively more expensive unless the nominal exchange rate rises to offset the higher domestic price level. The need for similar inflation rates within a fixed exchange-rate system indicates that a country could successfully join the fixed exchange-rate system or a region with one money only when its inflation rate fell to a level closer to that of other European countries.

Plans have been put forward for the evolution of the EU toward greater exchange-rate convergence, culminating in a single European currency. This plan would force individual countries to abandon completely any control over monetary policy. Proponents of the plan argue that one currency in Europe would facilitate international trade and investment by eliminating exchange-rate fluctuations and the associated uncertainty they add. Opponents of the plan think that the cost of giving up national control over monetary policy is too high relative to the benefits of a single currency. This issue is far from settled, and we can expect to continue to read about the debate over European integration throughout the 1990s.

40

The Transition from Socialism to Capitalism

FUNDAMENTAL QUESTIONS

1. What is socialism, and why did it fail?

2. What microeconomic issues are involved in the transition to capitalism?

3. What macroeconomic issues are involved in the transition to capitalism?

t is becoming more and more clear to all East Europeans, and the Czechs and Slovaks in particular, that the only practical and realistic way to improve their living standards is the total abolition of institutions of central planning, the dismantling of price and wage, exchange rate and foreign trade controls, and the radical transformation of property rights"—Vaclav Klaus, minister of finance for Czechoslovakia at a 1990 conference held by the Federal Reserve Bank of Kansas City.

As the world left the 1980s behind for the 1990s, the economies of the former Soviet Union and its Eastern European satellites were leaving socialism behind and embracing capitalism as the road to future prosperity. The first half of the 1990s indicates that the road is rough—it has proven much more difficult and time-consuming to make the transition from socialism than many thought in 1990. In this chapter, we review the basic institution of socialism and provide an analysis of what went wrong. In a nutshell, the problems were largely related to low productivity and lack of consumption goods—or, as Soviet workers were fond of saying, "We pretend to work and the state pretends to pay us." Next we turn to a discussion of the current problem facing all of the formerly socialist countries: How does a country move from socialism, with widespread government ownership of productive resources and massive government intervention in economic decision-making, to capitalism and its emphasis on private property and private decision-making? The answers are not yet clear, and there is much learning going on as each nation attempts to implement its variant of transition. As a result, we can only suggest certain fundamentals required for a successful transition and then examine the experiences of several countries that are in the process of implementing change to see what lessons may be gained from their experience.

PREVIEW

What is socialism and why did it fail?

I. SOCIALISM

capitalism:
an economic system characterized by private ownership of most resources and the use of markets to allocate goods and services

socialism:
an economic system characterized by government ownership of most resources and centralized decision-making

Socialism and capitalism are types of economic systems. **Capitalism** is characterized by private ownership of most resources and the use of markets to allocate goods and services, while **socialism** is characterized by government ownership of most resources and centralized decision-making or planning to allocate resources. As a specific example of a centrally planned socialist state, let's consider the characteristics of the Soviet Union prior to the era of *perestroika* (the recent reform movement). Of course, today, the Soviet Union has fragmented into independent nations (Russia and the CIS states) and the face of Eastern Europe has been changed, as illustrated by the map in Figure 1.

Figure 1
Republics of the Former U.S.S.R.

Source: *Finance and Development,* September 1992, pp. 24–25. Reprinted with permission.

1.a. Socialism in the Soviet Union

The Soviet Union was characterized by state ownership of all natural resources and almost all of the capital stock. In the late 1980s, state-run enterprises produced more than 88 percent of agricultural output and 98 percent of retail trade, and owned 75 percent of the urban housing space.

The government operation of a large economy spread over a vast geographical space required a huge bureaucracy of government planners and ministries. At the top were the highest authorities of the Communist party. The top party officials held the political power that moved the system and made broad policy decisions. Below the top level, planners were responsible for making party directives operational. Below the planners were agencies (ministries) responsible for specific functions of the economy like construction or agricultural equipment. Each of the agencies supervised a network of lesser agencies and departments under its direction, with the level of responsibility narrowing the further one went down the hierarchy by industrial branch and by region. At the base of the hierarchy were the enterprises and farms that actually carried out the productive activity. In the late 1980s, there were about 47,000 construction enterprises, 46,000 industrial enterprises, and almost 1 million wholesale and retail trade organizations.

The general direction of the economy was defined in five-year plans. More detailed operational plans were specified on an annual basis. The planning process began with goals set by the highest authorities. Government planners would use these goals to determine production priorities and set production targets. As the plans reached the production units through the ministries, enterprises responded with requests for resources needed to achieve the plan. Thus, there was a "give and take" as information flowed down the hierarchy and then back up. The higher authorities sought to maximize the productivity of the producing units by having them increase output with little or no increase in resources, while the producing units sought to lower their goals or quotas of output ordered from above in order to receive more easily attainable tasks. Achievement of tasks meant rewards for managers and workers.

Prices and wages were set by the state authorities and were based on political priorities rather than economic costs or scarcity. Furthermore, prices and wages tended to remain fixed for long periods regardless of actual market supply and demand conditions. Since the state administrators controlled prices of millions of goods and services, there was no practical way to adjust these continuously as supply and demand pressures varied.

1.b. Shortcomings of Socialism

Why did the leaders of the socialist economies of Eastern Europe decide to abandon government ownership and control for private property and individual market-type decision-making? The basic problem with central planning of an economy is that the authorities doing the planning do not possess information regarding the true opportunity costs of their decisions. Since everybody else in the system simply follows the planners' directives, only the top planners have an incentive to consider opportunity costs to maximize efficiency. But there is no possible way that they could monitor all of the relevant costs, even if such information were available.

An additional problem is that those actually carrying out the production have no incentive to use innovative production methods that increase efficiency. The incentives relate to carrying out the plan rather than taking risks in employing new technology. As the Eastern European economies became more developed and complex, the drawbacks to central planning became increasingly obvious. Waste and inefficiency grew, and the achievement of planners' goals were more often than not frustrated. The incentives to produce simply did not create the goods and services that consumers wanted in sufficient quantity and quality. Table 1 provides some comparative information on the demographics and economies of the (formerly) socialist economies of Eastern Europe and of the United States. The data on per capita GDP, cars, and telephones indicate the extent to which the selected Eastern European economies listed lagged behind the United States in terms of production and availability of consumer goods.

The lack of attention to technological advance resulted in a capital stock that became obsolete and uncompetitive internationally. Furthermore, the reliance on old production technologies with steadily growing populations resulted in environmental decay of massive proportions.

An understanding of why socialism has failed is necessary to effectively bring about efficient reforms. Moreover, as the transition from plan to market

Comparative Data on Eastern Europe, the Former U.S.S.R., and the United States prior to Transition

Country	Population (millions)	Population Density (population per square kilometer)	Infant Mortality (per 1,000 births)	Per Capita GDP as Percent of U.S. Per Capita GDP	Cars per 1,000 Persons	Telephones per 1,000 Persons
Bulgaria	8.9	81	12	26%	127	248
Czechoslovakia	15.7	125	11	35	186	246
East Germany	16.3	154	7	43	214	233
Hungary	10.6	114	15	30	156	152
Poland	37.8	124	13	25	112	122
Romania	23.3	101	19	19	na	111
U.S.S.R.	290.9	13	24	31	46	124
United States	250.4	27	10	100	565	789

Source: Selected data taken from tables in Peter Murrell, "Symposium on Economic Transition in the Soviet Union and Eastern Europe," *Journal of Economic Perspectives*, Fall 1991, pp. 5–6.

takes place, reformers must deal with the legacies of the past. The rest of the chapter is devoted to the process of turning a centrally planned economy into a market-oriented system.

RECAP

1. Capitalism is characterized by private ownership of most resources and the use of markets to allocate goods and services.
2. Socialism is characterized by government ownership of most resources and centralized decision-making.
3. Socialist economies are centrally planned: the enterprises carrying out actual production are following orders from higher authorities.
4. The two main shortcomings of socialism were the inability of the planners to take opportunity costs into account and the lack of adequate incentives to increase efficiency and produce the goods and services that consumers wanted.

2. MICROECONOMIC ISSUES

What microeconomic issues are involved in the transition to capitalism?

The transformation of a socialist economy into a capitalist economy requires the creation of markets. Resources that were formerly owned and allocated by government must be **privatized**, or converted from state ownership to private ownership. The state still has a role, since private property rights must be developed, recognized, and protected by government. Privately owned resources will then be allocated by the market system through prices set by supply and demand in a competitive environment with incomes that are based on productivity. Although it is easy to state where an economy should be in terms of free markets rather than central planning, getting there is easier said than done. The issue of privatization is the most obvious case.

2.a. Privatization

Socialist economies are characterized by many state-owned enterprises (SOEs). These enterprises are frequently large, technologically outdated, and unprofitable. The move to a market economy requires that these enterprises be privatized. How should SOEs be sold or otherwise converted to private ownership?

One alternative is to issue shares of ownership (like shares of stock) to existing workers and managers in an enterprise. This method has the advantage of simplicity—the new private owners are easy to identify, and ownership is easy to transfer. The disadvantage is that some SOEs may be uncompetitive in a capitalist environment so that ownership of such a firm is worthless, while other SOEs may be able to compete effectively so that ownership may have considerable value. This privatization system would reward and penalize the working population based on where they were previously assigned to work by the state rather than on the basis of individual investment and risk-taking. Moreover, a simple change of ownership may not change the manner in which the firm operates.

Another alternative is to issue shares of ownership randomly to the public in a kind of lottery. You may have an equal chance of becoming one of the owners of a steel mill, a shoe factory, or a farm. In a truly random assignment of ownership, everyone has an equal chance of receiving a profitable share. This scheme does away with the unfortunate circumstance associated with those who have the misfortune to be employed by the state in an unproductive job when shares are issued only to existing employees of each firm. A problem with this scheme is that those interested in, or knowledgeable about, a particular firm or industry would have no better chance to be involved in that industry than would those who had no interest.

Yet another alternative is to auction ownership of SOEs to the highest bidder. In addition to raising revenue for the state, this method is quite straightforward to carry out. A common argument against this method is that those with enough wealth to make winning bids are likely to be former Communist party leaders or individuals who traded on black markets under the socialist regime. Such people are not favorably viewed by the masses, and as a result, auctions are controversial.

The privatization method chosen by Czechoslovakia (before its split into two nations) was a coupon giveaway to millions of citizens, who then used the coupons to buy stock in SOEs. The goal of this kind of plan was to create a broad-based democratic capitalism with millions of citizens holding ownership positions in productive firms. An advantage of this plan is that the government does not have to find buyers willing to exchange real money for SOEs. Since many SOEs have a questionable initial money value, by granting ownership to a wide group of citizens, the state pushes the burden of managing relatively unproductive firms to the general public.

There is no universal approach to converting SOEs into privately owned firms. Each nation has taken the approach that best seems to fit its particular political and economic system. In all cases, it has been relatively easy to

The transition from socialism to capitalism should create a class of successful entrepreneurs. Here we see Jan Pazdera outside his photo and video store in the Czech Republic. First-wave entrepreneurs like Pazdera should provide useful models for the next generation of risk takers by efficiently providing the goods and services people want. The owners are rewarded with profits not legally obtainable by private citizens under socialism.

privatize small, profitable firms but much more difficult to privatize large, unprofitable firms.

The Russian experience with privatization indicates that once property rights have been reallocated from the government to individuals and firms, other institutions associated with market economies are easier to develop. In the early 1990s, debate over the proper order of events in a privatization scheme included arguments that market-oriented institutions like commercial laws regulating corporate behavior and stock markets needed to be established before property rights were transferred from the government to individuals. The Russian experience shows that the reverse is actually true. Once people have private property, then they are interested in the provision of an infrastructure to protect their rights, and they lobby the government to create appropriate institutions. They have no interest in such institutions prior to the appearance of widespread private property.

The privatization of economies in transition from socialism to capitalism has not been easy, and the work continues today. A brief look at the experiences of Romania and Poland will help to illustrate the way the privatization process has worked.

Romanian authorities have embarked on a massive privatization program that involves selling state-owned enterprises (SOEs). Over the period from 1992 to 1994, 863 SOEs were privatized, of which 750 were small companies, 103 were medium-sized, and 10 were large. The main areas in which privatization has been concentrated are construction, agriculture, retail shops and services, and surface transportation.

In August 1991, the parliament enacted a sweeping privatization law. Vouchers were distributed free of charge to 16.5 million Romanian citizens. These vouchers can be traded for shares in SOEs. In 1994, 670 SOEs were privatized, and the value of the stock issued is estimated to be 450 billion lei (1 U.S. dollar is worth 1,773 lei).

The major problem associated with the privatization effort in Romania thus far is that although the voucher exchange system has been enthusiastically embraced by the population, there has been little interest by either domestic residents or foreigners in buying shares of SOEs with cash. An additional problem exists in some cases where disputes over ownership of land have arisen. This problem has appeared in other countries in transition. The basic problem is that there was once private ownership of many of the parcels of land that were nationalized throughout Eastern Europe in the 1940s. Some of the former owners of this land have made claims that those prior private property rights should be given precedence over any new owners if the land is to be restored to private ownership. Regardless of who is given the property rights, ultimately the title to such land will pass into private ownership.

Poland has been one of the more successful countries in terms of privatization. Between 1990 and 1994, approximately 63 percent of the 8,440 SOEs in existence were privatized. Poland has recently adopted a "Mass Privatization Program" (MPP), which is intended to speed up the privatization process. The MPP has two guiding principles: all adult Polish citizens should have the opportunity for equity ownership at a low cost, and companies should be restructured with the guidance of experienced managers from Poland and the rest of the world. The MPP will operate in the following fashion: Fifteen investment funds will own shares of 444 large and medium-sized companies. Adult Polish citizens will be able to exchange vouchers distributed by the government for ownership shares in the investment funds. The vouchers will cost no more than 10 percent of the average monthly wage. The investment funds may sell their interest in some firms outright to domestic or foreign investors or the funds may retain ownership themselves.

The privatizations have provided a significant revenue source to the Polish government. In 1994, the government netted 860 million zlotys from SOE privatization, and 1995 was expected to provide even greater revenue since some large profitable enterprises were expected to be sold.

As with other countries, the privatization program in Poland is not without problems. A survey of privatized small enterprises revealed two major issues that were thought to hinder further development of the private sector. First, there has been a lack of credit for expansion; and second, frequent changes in regulations have created an environment of legal instability. These problems may be inevitable in periods of such overwhelming change. Time will reveal whether the privatization process will translate into a modern and efficient market-oriented economy.

2.b. Price Reform

Under socialism, prices of goods and services are established by the state. These prices need not reflect economic costs or scarcity. But in a market-oriented economy, prices serve an important signaling role. If consumers want more of a good or service, its price rises, and that induces producers to offer more for sale. If consumer tastes change so that demand for a good or service falls, then the price should fall to induce producers to offer less for sale. If there is an excess supply of a good, its price falls, and that induces consumers to buy more. If there is an excess demand for a good, the price rises to induce consumers to buy less. A major problem with socialism is that prices are not free to serve this role of a signal to producers and consumers. Therefore, an important step in the transition from socialism to capitalism is the freeing of prices so that they may seek their free market levels.

Considering that there were around 25 million goods and services to be priced in the former Soviet Union, it was impossible for government officials to know and then plan a shift from the state-regulated price to the appropriate free market price for each item. However, there is a way to allow the correct prices to be set very quickly. There are prices existing for every good in the rest of the world. By opening the economy to competition from foreign countries, foreign trade will force the domestic prices to be comparable to foreign prices. Of course, the presence of tariffs or quotas on foreign goods will distort the price comparisons, but the lower the restrictions on trade, the more domestic prices will conform to prices in the rest of the world. For goods that are not traded internationally or for many services, foreign trade will not set a domestic price. In this case, the market may be allowed to adjust the price over time to the internal domestic pressures of supply and demand.

The normal response to a freeing of prices from state control is an increase in the availability of goods and services, although initially output may fall. However, the beneficial aspects of price reform require privatization of the economy. Price changes bring about profits and losses that induce profit-seeking producers to provide what buyers want. If production is still controlled by state-owned enterprises that have no profit incentive, then price reform will not have the desired effect of increasing output and efficiency.

It is important to realize that price reform has an initial shock effect on the economy. Prices under socialism are typically well below the true opportunity cost for most items considered to be necessities. Speaking of price reform in Bulgaria, the Bulgarian National Bank's chief economist said, "One no longer has to get up at four or five A.M. to line up for bread and milk. Items that in the past might not even be available when one finally reached the counter now are available, but at ten times higher prices." This is a source of political conflict in taking an economy on the transition path from socialism to capitalism. People have to learn the new rules of the game, and the lessons are often quite harsh to those who have lived under decades of socialism.

2.c. Social Safety Net

Moving from socialism to capitalism will harm many people during the transition period as enterprises are closed and unemployment increases at the same time that prices of many goods and services rise. As a result, it is critical to have a program in place to provide a minimal standard of living for all citizens in order to avoid massive political unrest. Under socialism, the state provided for health care and took care of the disabled, aged, and unemployed. Moreover, many goods such as housing and food were heavily subsidized. Such widespread subsidies were inefficient because they were provided to everyone, even to those who could afford to pay higher prices. It is politically necessary that government subsidies continue, but they should be focused on the most needy groups. Over time, as more and more of the economy is privatized, government programs will have to be financed by explicit taxation of workers and firms. In other cases, user charges will be introduced, a phenomenon much less common under socialism.

The abandonment of socialism was due to populist sentiment in Eastern Europe. The populations of these nations were tired of stagnant or declining standards of living and were ready for change. However, market-oriented economies operate in a democratic framework, and political unrest due to dissatisfaction with the operation of the economy can much more easily be demonstrated in a democratic setting than under the authoritarian rule of the centrally planned economy. A social safety net must be generous enough to buy time for the transition to capitalism to yield benefits for the majority of citizens. Otherwise, the movement toward capitalism may never survive the transition period.

RECAP

1. The transition from socialism to capitalism requires that state-owned enterprises be privatized.
2. A market system requires that prices fluctuate freely to allow producers and consumers to make efficient production and consumption decisions.
3. Since the transition from socialism will create unemployment and lower incomes for many, the government must provide a social safety net.

3. MACROECONOMIC ISSUES

What macroeconomic issues are involved in the transition to capitalism?

Good macroeconomic policy is aimed at providing steady income growth with low inflation. This is true whether we are talking about the United States, Japan, or Russia. Good macroeconomic policy, then, requires limited use of government budget deficits and tight control over monetary and credit growth. Although these features of good macroeconomic policy are

The transition from central planning to a market-based economy is creating opportunities for hard-working, enterprising individuals to earn a standard of living previously only available to high-ranking members of the socialist elite. This woman, Maria Grigoreyeva, is one of Russia's wealthiest. She is a visible result of the opportunities available to new business leaders in Eastern Europe. At the same time, there are large masses of people who have been disenfranchised by the termination of their jobs or income security that existed under socialism. A major problem during the early transition from socialism is providing a safety net to protect the disenfranchised.

universal, there are some macro issues that are unique to the transition from socialism to capitalism.

3.a. Monetary Policy

3.a.1. Monetary Overhang

In many socialist countries, there is believed to be a substantial **monetary overhang**, which is the term used to describe the money that households have accumulated because there was nothing they could buy with it. With limited access to consumer goods, and subsidized housing, food, and health care, the typical household had savings in the form of money building up over time that they would not have had if they had access to more consumer goods. In early 1991, the monetary overhang in the (former) Soviet Union was estimated to be half of household savings deposits.

The potential problem with a large monetary overhang is that inflation could result if goods become available to induce spending of the saved funds. How can the monetary overhang be eliminated? One way is for the state to decontrol prices suddenly and have prices rise sharply, thereby decreasing the purchasing power of the money held by households. The state basically imposes its own inflation tax on the purchasing power of the monetary overhang early in the transition period rather than let the households create their own inflation later in the transition period. This was the approach taken in Poland and Yugoslavia in 1989 and the Soviet Union in 1991. Of course, it is critical that the one-time inflation not turn into a prolonged inflation if the economy is to enjoy long-term prosperity. Unfortunately, the early record suggests that high inflation has been difficult to reduce once allowed to emerge.

An alternative way of reducing the monetary overhang is to privatize—sell state-owned property (like houses or land) to private households. Another alternative is to allow greater access to Western consumer goods so that households spend their excess money balances on such goods. Yet another alternative is to allow interest rates to rise on household savings accounts so that households willingly hold on to their accumulated money.

During the transition from socialism, monetary policy should be aimed at achieving a low and stable inflation rate.

Beyond the issue of monetary overhang, monetary policy will be primarily aimed at controlling inflation during the transition to capitalism. The early lesson of successful transition is that without low inflation, it is impossible to have the growth of saving and investment required for sustainable growth of GDP. By maintaining a steady and low rate of inflation, a nation will also realize stable exchange rates, which will contribute to its speedy integration into trade with the rest of the world.

3.a.2. Currency Convertibility

Closely related to the issue of foreign trade and exchange rates is **currency convertibility**. The currency of the country must be freely convertible into other currencies if domestic prices are to be linked to (and disciplined by) foreign markets. One cannot compare the cost of a tractor in Romania with a tractor in Germany if the currency of Romania cannot be freely traded for the currency of Germany at a market-determined exchange rate.

Socialist countries traditionally did not permit free exchange of their currencies for other currencies. Government controls on foreign exchange trading allowed the government to fix an official exchange-rate value of the domestic currency that was often far from the true market value. As a result, international prices were unable to serve their purpose of increasing production of the goods a country could produce relatively cheaply and increasing imports of those goods that could be produced more cheaply in the rest of the world. For instance, if the true value of a Soviet ruble relative to the U.S. dollar was 30 rubles per dollar, yet the official exchange rate set by the Soviet Union was 3 rubles per dollar, then the ruble was officially overvalued. Suppose a computer monitor produced in the United States sold for $200. At the official exchange rate, the monitor was worth 600 rubles ($200 at 3 rubles per dollar). At the true market value of the currencies, the monitor was worth 6,000 rubles ($200 at 30 rubles per dollar). Since Soviet citizens were unable to buy foreign goods (all foreign trade was in the hands of the state), the official exchange rate was largely irrelevant. However, the absence of free trading in a ruble that was convertible into dollars meant that there was no way to identify which goods the Soviet Union could produce more cheaply than other nations. The absence of such relative cost information made specialization according to comparative advantage a difficult task. If a country cannot determine which goods it can produce more cheaply than others, it will not know which goods it should specialize in.

Under socialism, with central planning of production, the absence of relative price information was not as critical a problem as it is with capitalism. When private decision-makers must decide which goods to produce, they must rely on relative prices to guide them. In international trade, this requires a currency that is convertible into other currencies at market-determined exchange rates.

3.a.3. Money and Credit

In industrial countries with well-developed financial markets, monetary policy is often aimed at changing interest rates in order to change aggregate demand. For instance, when the monetary authorities are concerned that inflation is a problem, money growth is slowed and interest rates tend to rise. The higher interest rates reduce investment and consumption spending and lower (or at least slow the growth of) aggregate demand, or total spending in the economy. In a socialist system just beginning the transformation toward capitalism, financial markets are generally undeveloped, since the state under socialism regulated interest rates and limited the saving and borrowing opportunities for citizens. Changes in the money supply may have little or no effect on interest rates. Therefore, the role of monetary policy in terms of money growth rates should be to maintain a low and steady rate of inflation. Any other effects of money growth on the economy are likely to be of secondary importance until further development of the economy occurs.

Under socialism, credit was often extended to enterprises on the basis of political connections or central planner preferences. A market economy requires that credit occur on the basis of productive potential. Firms that offer good prospects of earning a sufficient profit to repay debts should receive greater credit access than firms that have little hope of competing profitably. The move toward a market economy must include the development of financial institutions like banks that are able to efficiently evaluate creditworthiness and allocate credit accordingly. The experience so far indicates that the development of the banking system requires a low and stable inflation rate. High inflation and uncertainty about future macroeconomic policy make it difficult for banks to evaluate the likely profitability of a firm and discourage lenders (as well as depositors) from committing funds for long periods.

Reform of fiscal policy involves reducing government subsidies and reforming tax policy to avoid large budget deficits. Socialist countries have been characterized by subsidies to enterprises that produced a value of output less than the costs of production. Under a market system, firms that cannot operate at a profit should not be allowed to exist forever by continued subsidies from the government. It is for this reason that, as noted earlier, a safety net is necessary since lower subsidies lead to transitional unemployment.

A socialist government does not rely on explicit or direct taxes on the public since the state controls prices, wages, and production. By paying workers less than the value of their output, the state can extract the revenue needed to operate the government. However, once private ownership and free markets have replaced central planning, the activities of government must be financed by explicit taxes. Reforming countries are implementing income, value-added, and profit taxes to produce revenue for the remaining functions of government. Again, the goal should be to match government revenue and expenditures as closely as possible to avoid a large budget deficit.

The experience of transition economies in terms of implementing successful fiscal policies is quite mixed. Some countries, like Hungary, Poland, Albania, and Slovenia, have had some success in reducing fiscal deficits so that the incentive to finance deficits through money creation has been reduced. This has allowed these economies to free prices without the high inflation experienced by other transition economies. The evidence so far suggests that those countries that have had major political changes have had opportunities to take more aggressive steps in establishing sound fiscal policies than the economies in which many of the remnants of the old socialist regime still linger. If major sectors of the economy are still dependent on government subsidies, or influential politicians cling to their power by offering support to old, inefficient enterprises, then fiscal deficit reduction will be much more difficult than in an environment where the population has clearly rejected the old ways along with the old politicians.

One problem that seems pervasive in the transition economy is collecting taxes. The largest of the old state-owned enterprises typically provided the largest tax revenue for the government. In many cases, these are now declining sectors of the economy and contribute less and less tax revenue. The newly emerging private sector, which should experience the fastest growth, is where tax collection has proved difficult. The problems include political pressures to provide tax exemptions or even ignore evasion of legally required taxes. The issue of tax collection will not be solved quickly, as the economies must computerize tax assessment and collection information to allow efficient monitoring of the system. The development and implementation of effective tax-collection agencies should take place over the next few years.

RECAP

1. Since households could not buy all of the consumer goods they wanted, socialist economies often had a monetary overhang of excess money holdings.

2. The convertibility of the domestic currency into foreign currencies is necessary to link the domestic country with prices in the rest of the world.

3. The transition economy will aim monetary policy at the creation of a low and stable rate of inflation.

4. Credit must be available to firms on the basis of potential profitability rather than political relationships in order to increase productivity.

5. Fiscal policy should be reformed to reduce subsidies from government to firms and also to collect explicit taxes.

4. THE SEQUENCING OF REFORMS

Considering all of the reforms necessary in the transition from socialism to capitalism, how should a country proceed? Are some measures needed before others can be undertaken? How rapidly should the changes be introduced? There are no certain answers to these questions, and there is an ongoing debate regarding the proper order of the reforms, as discussed in the Economic Insight "The Debate on Phasing."

Some economists argue that all reforms should be undertaken simultaneously (or as nearly so as possible). Most tend to agree that macroeconomic stabilization is necessary for any serious conversion of the economy to a

---

ECONOMIC INSIGHT

The Debate on Phasing

Should price reform come before or after enterprise reform?

Before: Enterprise reform and privatization will not succeed if the market cannot judge efficiency and value because prices do not reflect true costs. Budgets cannot be "hardened" before introducing market prices.

After: Freeing prices in the presence of monopolies will lead to excessive prices and profits, undercutting the political consensus for reform. Domestic competition policy should be in place before price liberalization.

Should large-scale privatization be "quick and dirty" or slower and more careful?

Quick: Rapid privatization is of utmost importance. It raises effi-

ciency, speeds restructuring, establishes a constituency for further reforms, and weakens the traditional power centers opposing reform.

Slow: Sales revenues are needed by the government, and preserving fairness in the process is vital for public support. Restructuring should thus precede privatization, and firms should not be given away hastily.

Should trade liberalization come early and fast or later and slowly?

Early: It supports price reform by importing the world price structure and heightens competitive forces.

Later: It shocks the economy in the right direction but with exces-

sive costs and is risky until the economy is stabilized.

Must full-scale financial-sector reform go hand in hand with enterprise reform, or can it come earlier?

Hand in hand: Competitive financial markets require enforceable loan contracts and timely repayment of debt obligations, and enterprise reform and bank portfolio restructuring are best accomplished simultaneously. Cleaning up loan portfolios is futile without enterprise reform.

Earlier: Only independent financial institutions and liberalized financial markets can play the critical role of allocating capital as enterprises are restructured.

---

market system. Inflation must be stabilized at a reasonably low and steady rate, and the fiscal deficit must be brought to a level low enough to support a noninflationary monetary policy (so that the monetary authorities are not creating money to fund the budget deficit). Included in the macroeconomic stabilization is the development of a convertible currency.

Following the macroeconomic reform, micro reforms like privatization may proceed, along with the opening of the economy to foreign trade and competition. Then the foreign prices will guide the deregulation of industry in setting appropriate prices for domestic products. It is generally thought that the micro reforms are intertwined and support one another. In this case, they should be carried out simultaneously. Otherwise, each element will tend to be less effective than it otherwise would be. For instance, privately owned firms need deregulated prices and wages to respond to changing relative prices and produce what consumers want.

RECAP

1. Macroeconomic reform must provide a stable, low-inflation environment for microeconomic reform to succeed.

2. Since microeconomic reforms tend to reinforce one another, they should generally be carried out simultaneously.

SUMMARY

▲▼ *What is socialism, and why did it fail?*

1. Capitalism is characterized by private ownership of most resources and the use of markets to allocate goods and services. §1

2. Socialism is characterized by government ownership of most resources and centralized decision-making. §1

3. Socialism failed because of the planners' inability to consider opportunity costs and because of a lack of incentive to increase efficiency and produce the goods and services consumers wanted. §1.b

▲▼ *What microeconomic issues are involved in the transition to capitalism?*

4. The move toward capitalism requires that state-owned enterprises be privatized. §2.a

5. Prices and incomes must be freed from state control if markets are to work efficiently. §2.b

6. Since many workers may be unemployed and incomes may fall during the transition, there must be a social safety net provided by the government. §2.c

▲▼ *What macroeconomic issues are involved in the transition to capitalism?*

7. There may be a substantial monetary overhang as a result of limited opportunities to exchange money for goods under socialism. §3.a.1

8. Exchange rates can link economies together, but the currency must be freely convertible into other currencies if exchange rates are to indicate accurate price information. §3.a.2

9. Monetary policy should be aimed at providing a low and steady rate of inflation. §3.a.1, 3.a.3

10. Credit must be allocated on the basis of productivity and profitability rather than political connections. §3.a.3

11. Fiscal policy must avoid large deficits and must raise explicit taxes. §3.b

12. Macroeconomic stabilization is generally necessary before microeconomic reforms are implemented. §4

KEY TERMS

capitalism §1   privatize §2   currency convertibility §3.a.2

socialism §1   monetary overhang §3.a.1

EXERCISES

1. Explain the difference between capitalism and socialism and use the key elements of your definitions to explain why socialism failed in the former Soviet Union and Eastern Europe.

2. Why would socialism not be as likely as capitalism to take opportunity costs into account in economic decision-making?

3. Discuss the alternative ways in which state-owned enterprises can be privatized.

4. One problem associated with the transition from socialism to capitalism is deregulating prices of goods and services. How can government officials find the appropriate prices to use when ending the government regulation of prices?

5. What is monetary overhang, and how can government eliminate it?

6. Suppose the official exchange rate is set by the government at 10 rubles per dollar. If the government does not allow its citizens to freely trade rubles for dollars, what is the use of such an exchange rate? How would currency convertibility change things?

7. What is the proper role of monetary policy during the transition from socialism to capitalism?

8. Is there any particular order in which the reforms needed in the transition from social-

ism to capitalism should occur? If so, discuss why.

9. The socialist economies of Eastern Europe had outdated production methods following years of technological stagnation. Why didn't these economies invest in new technology like the industrial countries of Western Europe?

10. The social safety net necessary for easing the transition from socialism will require the government to continue many of its health and public welfare policies to protect the unemployed from creating social and political unrest that threatens the transition. In what sense does the social safety net program also hinder the movement toward a market-based economy?

11. What is the proper role of fiscal policy during the transition from socialism to capitalism?

12. Imagine the United States changing from a market-oriented economy to a socialist economy. If you are appointed chief of economic planning for the nation, how would you go about planning the right amount and kind of output for each firm, the proper prices for goods, and the appropriate incomes for workers? Write a brief essay addressing each of these planning issues and include a discussion of the problems central planners face that are solved by the use of free markets.

COOPERATIVE LEARNING EXERCISE

Split the class into groups of four. Each group is to consider the following scenarios:

1. A major report is due at the end of the term from each group. All members of the group will receive the same grade, regardless of their individual contributions.

2. The group is hired to clean the classroom once a week, and all members will be paid the same wage regardless of their individual effort.

Each group must write answers to the following questions:

1. What do the scenarios described above have to do with the problems that led to the breakup of the socialist economies?

2. How does a market or capitalist system address the problems associated with these scenarios?

Russia Tries Reform—Is It Working?

They lined up for hours in the gloomy cold, stamping their boots in the black slush of Manezh Square. These patient thousands waited not for bread, as they might have two years ago, but to buy shares in a startup automobile factory. In the space of two days in December, they bet a billion rubles on the risky new venture.

Across town, the other side of Russia's economy could be found in the dark and quiet workshops of one of Russia's largest truck makers. The workers of the Zil factory are on month-long furloughs because the plant has been unable to survive without the massive government subsidies of the past.

The two scenes reflect where Russia stands two years into its attempt to convert its economy from Soviet socialism to free-market capitalism. In recent weeks, many here and in the West have concluded that the initiative is in grave, perhaps even fatal, trouble. Reformers have been pushed out of power, and the government of President Boris Yeltsin is now managed by ex-Soviet apparatchiks, eager to slow or reverse the course. Communist and ultranationalist forces are ascendant, riding a wave of public discontent.

But in fact, the situation in Russia today is contradictory and complicated. A rudimentary market economy, crass and corrupt, has burst into life and dramatically changed the face of Russia's cities with billboards and glittery storefronts. Meanwhile, the old Soviet system of massive government subsidies hangs on. Missile factories and muddy collective farms alike seem near collapse and still look to Moscow, and a newly installed conservative cabinet receptive to their appeals, for rescue.

Russia so far has avoided the predicted starvation, mass unrest, and other disasters. Moreover, many Russians have seized on their new freedom to build businesses or spin off private farms with a gusto for personal initiative that many experts had said would be missing for at least a generation. The new entrepreneurs range from human "mules" who cart Turkish leather coats across the steppe to millionaire bankers in bulletproof Mercedes sedans.

At the same time, at least one-quarter of Russians are officially impoverished, unable to afford onions with their nightly potatoes, and an even larger chunk feel themselves worse off than under communism. There is an almost universal sense of exhaustion after two years, and some Russians have begun to ask if their country may be incapable of embracing Western-style capitalism.

There is a widespread feeling that something different must be tried. But there is little agreement on what.

"Russia today is short of political ideas," acknowledged Yegor Gaidar, the architect of Russia's reforms who resigned from the government last month and believes that the solution is to go faster. "All the words have been pronounced. Life has become worse for many people. And a great disappointment has manifested itself."

The mixed results so far mean that it is unlikely, even with a conservative government, that Russia will return to a Soviet-style, state-run economic system. Too much change has occurred, and more will come spontaneously as the new private sector develops on its own. But most economic experts agree that, because so much remains to be done for real capitalism to take hold, a continued policy stalemate could consign Russia to an increasingly chaotic netherworld between socialism and the free market, in which inflation runs rampant and radical political views could flourish. . . .

Source: "Russia Tries Reform—Is It Working?" by Margaret Shapiro and Fred Hiatt, *The Washington Post*, Feb. 20, 1994. © 1994 *The Washington Post*. Reprinted with permission.

Commentary

One of the primary reasons that Eastern European nations abandoned socialism was a desire to achieve living standards comparable to those enjoyed by the industrial nations of Western Europe. However, in the early stages of the transition from socialism to capitalism, output fell substantially in the Eastern European nations as inefficient firms were forced to close. This short-run effect of the transition makes for a difficult political climate to carry out further reforms. The transition process involves more pain than many reformers initially expected. Why has the decline in output occurred, and what should be expected in the future?

The article emphasizes the role of competitive market pressures in forcing the old, inefficient firms that existed under socialism and the attitudes of workers to reform. The Eastern European countries face many other economic shocks during the early stages of the transition process—for instance, major relative price shocks of important goods, like oil, which were provided at artificially low prices under socialism but have now been freed to rise substantially. We would expect such a price shock to have a negative effect on output in the short run as producers and consumers adjust to the new relative prices. Furthermore, these countries face restrictions on the availability of credit from willing lenders, yet such credit would allow the government to ease the transition by providing a more generous social safety net and financing an imbalance in the current account of the balance of payments. Without the more generous availability of funds from foreign creditors, the countries have to substantially reduce domestic consumption to finance imports of goods at now-higher prices.

The international trade effects of the reforms were worsened by the collapse of the CMEA (Council for Mutual Economic Assistance) agreement that tied the socialist countries of Eastern Europe and the U.S.S.R. together to stimulate trade among the group. Over time, each nation will develop new trade relationships with the rest of the world, and trade within the Eastern bloc will become less important. But the short-run costs of moving away from the old relationships include a decrease in the volume of international trade and a consequent drop in output.

If the reforms are allowed sufficient time to work, then producers, consumers, and governments will adjust to the new relative prices and competitive incentives, and the goal of convergence toward the incomes of the West will be achieved. The new reality, however, is that the process of "catching up" to the Western developed nations will take much longer than originally thought. The danger is that the political costs of falling output and the short-run appearance of the failure of reforms to increase living standards will lead to a resurgence of popularity for the old socialist ways and a return to central planning and the inefficiencies of the past. This has been reflected in the recent rise in popularity of the Communist party in several Eastern European nations.

equation of exchange an equation that relates the quantity of money to nominal GNP (14)

equilibrium the point at which quantity demanded and quantity supplied are equal at a particular price (3)

equilibrium exchange rates the exchange rates that are established in the absence of government foreign exchange market intervention (39)

equimarginal principle to maximize utility, consumers must allocate their scarce incomes among goods so as to equate the marginal utilities per dollar of expenditure on the last unit of each good purchased (21)

Eurocurrency market the market for deposits and loans generally denominated in a currency other than the currency of the country in which the transaction occurs; also called offshore banking (13)

European Currency Unit (ECU) a unit of account used by western European nations as their official reserve asset (13)

European Monetary System (EMS) an organization composed of Western European nations that maintain fixed exchange rates among themselves and floating exchange rates with the rest of the world (39)

excess reserves the cash reserves beyond those required, which can be loaned (13)

exchange rate the price of one country's money in terms of another country's money (7)

export substitution the use of labor to produce manufactured products for export rather than agricultural products for the domestic market (19)

export supply curve a curve showing the relationship between the world price of a good and the amount that a country will export (37)

exports products that a country sells to other countries (4)

expropriation the government seizure of assets, typically without adequate compensation to the owners (19)

externalities costs or benefits of a transaction that are borne by someone not directly involved in the transaction (5, 35)

facilitating practices actions by oligopolistic firms that can contribute to cooperation and collusion even though the firms do not formally agree to cooperate (26)

factors of production goods used to produce other goods (1)

fair rate of return a price that allows a monopoly firm to earn a normal profit (25)

fallacy of composition the mistaken assumption that what applies in the case of one applies to the case of many (1)

featherbedding using an inefficient combination of resources in order to preserve union jobs (31)

Federal Deposit Insurance Corporation (FDIC) a federal agency that insures deposits in commercial banks (13)

federal funds rate the interest rate a bank charges when it lends excess reserves to another bank (14)

Federal Open Market Committee (FOMC) the official policy-making body of the Federal Reserve System (14)

Federal Reserve the central bank of the United States (5)

financial intermediaries institutions that accept deposits from savers and make loans to borrowers (4)

first mover strategy being the first firm to carry out some activity (27)

fiscal policy policy directed toward government spending and taxation (5)

focused management a factory in which just one product or part of a product is produced (27)

FOMC directive instructions issued by the FOMC to the Federal Reserve Bank of New York to implement monetary policy (14)

foreign aid gifts or low-cost loans made to developing countries from official sources (19)

foreign direct investment the purchase of a physical operating unit in a foreign country (19)

foreign exchange foreign currency and bank deposits that are denominated in foreign money (7)

foreign exchange market a global market in which people trade one currency for another (7)

foreign exchange market intervention buying or selling of currencies by a government or central bank to achieve a specified exchange rate (14, 39)

foreign exchange risk the threat that future foreign currency payments or receipts will have a different domestic currency value than expected

forward exchange rate the price established today for delivery of a foreign currency at a future date

fractional reserve banking system a system in which banks keep less than 100 percent of the deposits available for withdrawal (13)

free good a good for which there is no scarcity (1)

free ride the enjoyment of the benefits of a good by a producer or consumer without having to pay for it (15)

free rider a consumer or producer who enjoys the benefits of a good without paying for it (35)

free trade area an organization of nations whose members have no trade barriers among themselves but are free to fashion their own trade policies toward non-members (38)

full-line supply the bundle of policies offered by a candidate (36)

fundamental disequilibrium a permanent shift in the foreign-exchange-market supply and demand curves, such that the fixed exchange rate is no longer an equilibrium rate (39)

future value the equivalent value in the future of some amount received today (32)

game theory a description of oligopolistic behavior as a series of strategic moves and countermoves (26)

Gini ratio a measure of the dispersion of income ranging between 0 and 1; 0 means all families have same income; 1 means 1 family has all income (34)

gold exchange standard an exchange-rate system in which each nation fixes the value of its currency in terms of gold, but buys and sells the U.S. dollar rather than gold to maintain fixed exchange rates (39)

gold standard a system whereby national currencies are fixed in terms of their value in gold, thus creating fixed exchange rates between currencies (39)

gross domestic product (GDP) the market value of all final goods and services produced in a year within a country (6)

gross investment total investment, including investment expenditures required to replace capital goods consumed in current production (6)

gross national production (GNP) gross domestic production plus receipts of factor income from the rest of the world minus payments of factor income to the rest of the world (6)

health maintenance organization (HMO) an organization that provides comprehensive medical care to a voluntarily enrolled consumer population in return for a fixed, prepaid amount of money (33)

Herfindahl index a measure of concentration calculated as the sum of the squares of the market share of each firm in an industry (28)

household one or more persons who occupy a unit of housing (4)

human capital skills, training, and personal health acquired through education and on-the-job training (30)

hyperinflation an extremely high rate of inflation (8)

implicit GDP deflator a broad measure of the prices of goods and services included in the gross national product (6)

import demand curve a curve showing the relationship between the world price of a good and the amount that a country will import (37)

import substitution the substitution of domestically produced manufactured goods for imported manufactured goods (19)

imports products that a country buys from other countries (4)

in-kind transfers the allocation of goods and services from one group in society to another (34)

income effect the change in quantity demanded that occurs when the purchasing power of income is altered as a result of a price change (21)

income elasticity of demand the percentage change in the demand for a good divided by the percentage change in income, ceteris paribus (20)

increasing-cost industry an industry in which the costs of resources rise when the industry expands (24)

increasing marginal opportunity cost a rising amount of one good or service that must be given up to obtain one additional unit of any good or service, no matter how many units are being produced (2)

increasing-returns-to-scale industry an industry in which the costs of producing a unit of output fall as more output is produced (38)

independent variable the variable whose value does not depend on the value of other variables (1 App.)

indifference curve a curve showing all combinations of two goods that the consumer is indifferent among (21 App.)

indifference map a complete set of indifference curves (21 App.)

indifferent lacking any preference (21 App.)

indirect business tax a tax that is collected by businesses for a government agency (6)

industrial policy government direction and involvement in defining an economy's industrial structure (28)

inferior goods goods for which the income elasticity of demand is negative (20)

inflation a sustained rise in the average level of prices (8)

inputs goods used to produce other goods (1)

interest rate effect a change in interest rates that causes investment and therefore aggregate expenditures to change as the level of prices changes (9)

interest rate parity (IRP) the condition under which similar financial assets have the same interest rate when measured in the same currency (17)

intermediate good a good that is used as an input in the production of final goods and services (6)

intermediate target an objective used to achieve some ultimate policy goal

international banking facility (IBF) a division of a U.S. bank that is allowed to receive deposits from and make loans to nonresidents of the United States without the restrictions that apply to domestic U.S. banks (13)

International Monetary Fund (IMF) an international organization that supervises exchange-rate arrangements and lends money to member countries experiencing problems meeting their external financial obligations (39)

international reserve asset an asset used to settle debts between governments (13)

international reserve currency a currency held by a government to settle international debts (13)

international trade effect the change in aggregate expenditures resulting from a change in the domestic price level that changes the price of domestic goods in relation to foreign goods (9)

intraindustry trade simultaneous import and export of goods in the same industry by a particular country

inventory the stock of unsold goods held by a firm (6)

inverse or negative relationship the relationship that exists when the values of related variables move in opposite directions (1 App.)

investment spending on capital goods to be used in producing goods and services (4)

Keynesian economics a school of thought that emphasizes the role government plays in stabilizing the economy by managing aggregate demand (16)

Keynesian region the portion of the aggregate supply curve at which prices are fixed because of unemployment and excess capacity (16)

labor the physical and intellectual services of people, including the training, education, and abilities of the individuals in a society (1)

labor force participation entering the work force (30)

lagging indicator a variable that changes after real output changes (8)

land all natural resources, such as minerals, timber, and water, as well as the land itself (1)

law of demand as the price of a good or service rises (falls), the quantity of that good or service that people are willing and able to purchase during a particular period of time falls (rises), ceteris paribus (3)

law of diminishing marginal returns when successive equal amounts of a variable resource are combined with a fixed amount of another resource, marginal increases in output that can be attributed to each additional unit of the variable resource will eventually decline (22)

law of supply as the price of a good or service that producers are willing and able to offer for sale during a particular period of time rises (falls), the quantity of that good or service supplied rises (falls), ceteris paribus (3)

leading indicator a variable that changes before real output changes (8)

legal reserves the cash a bank holds in its vault plus its deposit in the Fed (14)

LIBOR the London interbank offer rate; the interest rate charged for loans between major London banks

liquid asset an asset that can easily be exchanged for goods and services (13)

local monopoly a monopoly that exists in a limited geographic area (25)

logrolling trading votes or support on one issue in return for votes or support on another issue (36)

long run a period of time just long enough that the quantities of all resources can be varied (20)

long-run aggregate supply curve (LRAS) a vertical line at potential level of national income (9)

long-run average total cost curve (LRAC) the lowest-cost combination of resources with which each level of output is produced when all resources are variable (22)

Lorenz curve a curve measuring the degree of inequality of income distribution within a society (34)

M1 money supply financial assets that are most liquid (13)

macroeconomics the study of the economy as a whole (1)

managed care comprehensive medical care provided within one firm (33)

managed competition government intervention in the health-care market to guide competition so that costs are reduced (33)

managed floating exchange rates the system whereby central banks intervene in the floating foreign-exchange market to influence exchange rates; also referred to as dirty float (39)

mandatory retirement a policy that requires workers to retire at a certain age (30)

marginal extra, additional (2)

marginal benefit additional benefit (2, 35)

marginal cost (MC) the additional costs of producing one more unit of output (2, 22)

marginal factor cost (MFC) the additional cost of an additional unit of a resource (29)

marginal opportunity cost the amount of one good or service that must be given up to obtain one additional unit of another good or service (2)

marginal physical product (MPP) the additional quantity that is produced when one additional unit of a resource is used in combination with the same quantities of all other resources (22)

marginal propensity to consume (MPC) change in consumption as a proportion of change in disposable income (10)

marginal propensity to import (MPI) change in imports as a proportion of change in income (10)

marginal propensity to save (MPS) change in saving as a proportion of change in disposable income (10)

marginal revenue the additional revenue obtained by selling an additional unit of output (23)

marginal revenue product (MRP) the value of the additional output that an extra unit of a resource can produce, MPP × MR (29)

marginal social cost the additional social cost that results from a 1-unit increase in production (35)

marginal utility the extra utility derived from consuming one more unit of a good or service (21)

market a place or service that enables buyers and sellers to exchange goods and services (3)

market failure the failure of the market system to achieve economic and technical efficiency (35)

market imperfection a lack of efficiency that results from imperfect information in the market place (5)

median voter theorem candidates or parties select positions on issues that reflect the median voter's positions on those issues (36)

Medicaid a joint federal-state program that pays for health care for poor families, the neediest elderly, and disabled persons (33)

Medicare a federal health care program for poor elderly, and disabled persons (33)

microeconomics the study of economics at the level of the individual (1)

minimum efficient scale (MES) the minimum point of the long-run average cost curve; the output level at which the cost per unit of output is the lowest (22)

model see *theory* (1)

monetarist economics a school of thought that emphasizes the role changes in the money supply play in determining equilibrium national income and price level (16)

monetary overhang money accumulated by households because there was nothing available that they wanted to buy (40)

monetary policy policy directed toward control of the money supply (5)

monetary reform a new monetary policy that includes the introduction of a new monetary unit (15)

money anything that is generally acceptable to sellers in exchange for goods and services (13)

money supply financial assets that are immediately available for spending (13)

monopoly a market structure in which there is a single supplier of a product (25)

monopoly firm (monopolist) a single supplier of a product for which there are no close substitutes (25)

monopoly power market power, the ability to set prices (25)

monopsonist a firm that is the only buyer of a resource (29)

moral hazard the chance that people will alter their behavior in unanticipated ways after an agreement or contract has been defined (26)

most-favored customer (MFC) customer who receives a guarantee of the lowest price and all product features for a certain period of time (26)

multilateral aid aid provided by international organizations supported by many nations (19)

multinational business a firm that owns and operates producing units in foreign countries (4)

multiple exchange rates a system whereby a government fixes different exchange rates for different types of transactions (39)

multiplier a measure of the change in income produced by a change in autonomous expenditures

national income (NI) net national product minus indirect business taxes (6)

national income accounting the process that summarized the level of production in an economy over a specific period of time, typically a year (6)

natural monopoly a monopoly that emerges because of economies of scale (23, 25)

natural rate of unemployment the unemployment rate that would exist in the absence of cyclical unemployment (8)

negative income tax (NIT) a tax system that transfers increasing amounts of income to households earning incomes below some specified level as their income declines (34)

net exports exports minus imports (4)

net investment gross investment minus capital consumption allowance (6)

net national product (NNP) gross national product minus capital consumption allowance (6)

new classical economics a school of thought that holds that changes in real national income are a product of unexpected changes in the level of prices (16)

nominal GDP a measure of national output based on the current prices of goods and services (6)

nominal interest rate the observed interest rate in the market (8)

nonrenewable (exhaustible) natural resources resources that can not be replaced or renewed (32)

normal goods goods for which the income elasticity of demand is positive (20)

normative analysis analysis of what ought to be (1)

occupational segregation the separation of jobs by sex (31)

open economy an economy in which a relatively large fraction of the GDP is devoted to internationally tradable goods (17, 39)

open market operations the buying and selling of government bonds by the Fed to control bank reserves and the money supply (14)

open position the situation of a firm waiting to buy foreign currency at a future spot rate

opportunity costs the highest-valued alternative that must be forgone when a choice is made (2)

partnership a business with two or more owners who share the firm's profits and losses (4)

patent a legal document that gives an inventor the legal rights to an invention (18)

per capita real national income real national income divided by the population (18)

per se rule actions that could be anticompetitive are intrinsically illegal (28)

perfectly elastic demand curve a horizontal demand curve indicating that consumers can and will purchase all they want at one price (20)

perfectly inelastic demand curve a vertical demand curve indicating that there is no change in the quantity demanded as the price changes (20)

personal income (PI) national income plus income currently received but not earned, minus income currently earned but not received (6)

personnel practices a firm's policies toward its employees (30)

Phillips curve a graph that illustrates the relationship between inflation and the unemployment rate (15)

portfolio investment the purchase of securities (19)

positive analysis analysis of what is (1)

positive economic profit (above-normal profit) total revenue equals the sum of direct and opportunity costs (23)

potential competition entry or rivalry capable of forcing existing producers to behave as if the competition actually existed (25)

potential real GDP the output produced at the natural rate of unemployment (8)

precautionary demand for money the demand for money to cover unplanned transactions or emergencies (14)

predatory dumping dumping to drive competitors out of business (25)

preferred provider organization (PPO) group of physicians who contract to provide services at a price discount (33)

present value the equivalent value today of some amount to be received in the future (32)

price ceiling a situation where the price is not allowed to rise above a certain level (3)

price discrimination charging different customers different prices for the same product; charging different prices for different quantities of the same product (20)

price elasticity of demand the percentage change in the quantity demanded of a product divided by the percentage change in the price of that product (20)

price elasticity of supply the percentage change in quantity supplied divided by the percentage change in price ceteris paribus (20)

price floor a situation where the price is not allowed to decrease below a certain level (3)

price index a measure of the average price level in an economy (16)

price maker a firm that sets the price of the product it sells (23)

price taker a firm that is unable to set a price that differs from the market price without losing profit (23)

primary product a product in the first stage of production, which often serves as input in the production of another product (19)

principle of mutual exclusivity the owner of private property is entitled to enjoy the consumption of the property privately (35)

private costs costs borne by the individual in the transaction that created the costs (35)

private label the practice of a firm purchasing a product from another firm and putting its own label on the product (27)

private property right the limitation of ownership to an individual (5, 35)

privatization transferring a publicly owned enterprise to private ownership (28)

producer price index (PPI) a measure of average prices received by producers (6)

producer surplus the difference between the price firms would have been willing to accept for their products and the price they actually receive (24)

production possibilities curve (PPC) a graphical representation showing the maximum quantity of goods and services that can be produced using limited resources to the fullest extent possible (2)

productivity the quantity of output produced per unit of resource (3)

progressive tax a tax whose rate rises as income rises (12, 34)

proportional tax a tax whose rate does not change as the tax base changes (34)

prospective payment system (PPS) the use of a preassigned reimbursement rate by Medicare to reimburse hospitals and physicians (33)

public choice the use of economics to analyze the actions and inner workings of the public sector (5, 36)

public goods goods whose consumption cannot be limited only to the person who purchased the good (5, 35)

public interest theory government actions improve the well-being of the general public (28)

purchasing power the quantity of goods and services that a given quantity of income can buy

purchasing power parity (PPP) the condition under which monies have the same purchasing power in different countries (17)

put the right to sell currency at a certain price

quantity demanded the amount of a product that people are willing and able to purchase at a specific price (3)

quantity quota a limit on the amount of a good that may be imported (38)

quantity supplied the amount sellers are willing and able to offer at a given price, during a given period of time, everything else held constant (3)

quantity theory of money with constant velocity, changes in the quantity of money change nominal GDP (14)

rate of return profit as a percentage of the cost of an investment (10)

rate-of-return regulation definition of a firm's price and profit rate by a regulatory commission

rational expectation an expectation that is formed using all available relevant information (15)

rational self-interest the term economists use to describe how people make choices (1)

rationally ignorant voters voters who do not have perfect information because it is too costly to acquire (36)

real GDP a measure of the quantity of goods and services produced, adjusted for price changes (6)

real interest rate the nominal interest rate minus the rate of inflation (8)

recession a period in which real GDP falls (8)

recessionary gap the increase in expenditures required to reach potential GDP (11)

regressive tax a tax whose rate decreases as the tax base changes (34)

regulated monopoly a monopoly firm whose behavior is monitored and prescribed by a government entity (25)

relative price the price of one good expressed in terms of another good (3)

renewable (nonexhaustible) natural resources resources that can be replaced or renewed (32)

rent seeking the use of resources simply to transfer wealth from one group to another without increasing production or total wealth (5, 25, 36)

required reserves the cash reserves (a percentage of deposits) a bank must keep on hand or on deposit with the Federal Reserve (13)

reservation wage the minimum wage a worker is willing to accept (15)

reserve currency a currency that is used to settle international debts and is held by governments to use in foreign exchange market interventions (39)

residual claimants entrepreneurs who acquire profit or the revenue remaining after all other resources have been paid (29)

resources goods used to produce other goods, i.e., land, labor, capital, entrepreneurial ability (1)

risk premium the extra return required to offset the higher risk associated with investing in a foreign asset (17)

roundabout production the process of saving and accumulating capital in order to increase production in the future (32)

rule of reason to be illegal an action must be unreasonable in a competitive sense and the anticompetitive effects must be demonstrated (28)

rule of 72 the number of years required for an amount to double in value is 72 divided by the annual rate of growth (18)

saving not consuming all current production (32)

saving function the relationship between disposable income and saving (10)

scale size; all resources change when scale changes (22)

scarcity the shortage that exists when less of something is available than is wanted at a zero price (1)

scientific method a manner of analyzing issues that involves five steps: recognition of the problem, assumptions, model building, predictions, tests of model (1)

sequential game a situation in which one firm moves first and then the other firm is able to choose a strategy based on the first firm's choices (26)

shock an unexpected change in a variable (15)

short run a period of time just short enough that the quantities of all resources cannot be varied (20)

short-run average total cost (SRATC) the lowest-cost combination of resources with which each level of output is produced when the quantity of at least one resource is fixed (22)

shortage a quantity supplied that is smaller than the quantity demanded at a given price (3)

shutdown price the minimum point of the average-variable-cost curve (24)

slope the steepness of a curve, measured as the ratio of the rise to the run (1 App.)

social costs the private and external costs of a transaction (35)

socialism an economic system characterized by government ownership of most resources and centralized decision-making (40)

social regulation the prescribing of health, safety, performance, and environmental standards that apply across several industries (28)

sole proprietorship a business owned by one person who receives all the profits and is responsible for all the debts incurred by the business (14)

special drawing right (SDR) an artificial unit of account created by averaging the values of the U.S. dollar, German mark, Japanese yen, French franc, and British pound (13, 39)

speculative demand for money the demand for money created by uncertainty about the value of other assets (14)

speculators people who seek to profit from an expected shift in an exchange rate by selling the currency expected to depreciate and buying the currency expected to appreciate, then exchanging the appreciated currency for the depreciated currency after the rate adjustment (39)

spending multiplier the reciprocal of the sum of the MPS and the MPI (11)

standardized or nondifferentiated products products that consumers perceive to be identical (23)

statistical discrimination discrimination that results when an indicator of group performance is incorrectly applied to an individual member of the group (31)

sterilization the use of domestic open market operations to offset the effects of a foreign exchange market intervention on the domestic money supply (14)

strategic behavior behavior that occurs when what is best for B depends on what A chooses and what A chooses depends on what B is most likely to do (26)

strategic deterrence undertaking an action to prevent certain behavior by rivals (27)

strategic management using economics to devise strategies for firms (27)

strategic variables factors affecting a firm over which the manager has control (27)

subsidies payments made by government to domestic firms to encourage exports (38)

substitute goods goods that can be used in place of each other (as the price of one rises, the demand for the other rises) (3)

substitution effect the tendency of people to purchase less expensive goods that serve the same purpose as a good whose price has risen (21)

sunk cost a cost that has occurred and cannot be recovered (21)

superstar effect the situation where people with small differences in abilities or productivity receive vastly different levels of compensation (30)

supply the amount of a good or service that producers are willing and able to offer for sale at each possible price during a period of time, ceteris paribus (3)

supply curve a graph of a supply schedule that measures price on the vertical axis and quantity supplied on the horizontal axis (3)

supply schedule a list or table of prices and corresponding quantities supplied of a particular good or service (3)

surplus a quantity supplied that is larger than the quantity demanded at a given price (3)

surplus (in a balance of payments account) the amount by which credits exceed debits (7)

tariffs taxes on imports or exports (38)

tax incidence a measure of who pays a tax (20)

tax multiplier a measure of the effect of a change in taxes on the equilibrium level of income

technical efficiency producing at a point on the PPC (5)

technology ways of combining resources to produce output (18)

terms of trade the amount of exports that must be exchanged for some amount of imports (19, 37)

tests trials or measurements used to determine whether a theory is consistent with the facts (1)

theory (or model) a simplified, logical story based on positive analysis that is used to explain an event (1)

time inconsistent a characteristic of a policy or plan that changes over time in response to changing conditions (15)

total costs (TC) the sum of total variable and total fixed costs (22)

total factor productivity (TFP) the ratio of the economy's output to its stock of labor and capital (18)

total fixed costs (TFC) costs that must be paid whether a firm produces or not (22)

total physical product (TPP) the maximum output that can be produced when successive units of a variable resource are added to fixed amounts of other resources (22)

total revenue (TR) TR = P × Q (20)

total utility a measure of the total satisfaction derived from consuming a quantity of some good or service (21)

total variable costs (TVC) costs that rise or fall as production rises or falls (22)

trade creation an effect of a preferential trade agreement, allowing a country to obtain goods at a lower cost than is available at home (38)

trade credit the extension of a period of time before an importer must pay for goods or services purchased (19)

trade diversion an effect of a preferential trade agreement, reducing economic efficiency by shifting production to a higher-cost producer (38)

trade off to give up one good or activity in order to obtain some good or activity (2)

trade surplus (deficit) exists when imports are less than (exceed) exports (4)

transaction costs the costs involved in making an exchange (3)

transactions account a checking account at a bank or other financial institution that can be drawn on to make payments (13)

transactions demand for money the demand to hold money to buy goods and services (14)

transfer earnings the portion of total earnings required to keep a resource in its current use (29)

transfer payment income transferred from one citizen, who is earning income, to another citizen, who may not be (5, 6, 12)

underemployment the employment of workers in jobs that do not utilize their productive potential (8)

underground market unreported exchanges of goods and services (8)

unemployment rate the percentage of the labor force that is not working (8)

union shop a workplace in which all employees must join a union within a specific period of time after they are hired (31)

unlimited wants boundless desires for goods and services (1)

utility a measure of the satisfaction received from possessing or consuming goods and services (21)

value added the difference between the value of output and the value of the intermediate goods used in the production of that output (6)

value-added tax (VAT) a general sales tax collected at each stage of production (12)

value quota a limit on the monetary value of a good that may be imported (38)

velocity of money the average number of times each dollar is spent on final goods and services in a year (14)

venture capital funds provided by a firm or individual that specializes in lending to new, unproven firms (4)

voting cycle the situation where a collective decision process does not reach a decision (36)

wealth the value of all assets owned by a household (10)

wealth effect a change in the real value of wealth that causes spending to change when the price level changes (9)

workfare a plan that requires welfare recipients to accept public service jobs or participate in job training (34)

World Bank an international organization that makes loans and provides technical expertise to developing countries (39)

X-inefficiency the tendency of a firm not faced with competition to become inefficient (25)

zero economic profit (normal profit) total revenue equals the sum of direct and opportunity costs (23)

Credits   *(continued from p. ii)*

International; p. 119 © John Ficara/Sygma; p. 124 © Richemond/The Image Works; p. 131 © Paul Chesley/Tony Stone Images; p. 141 © Mark E. Gibson; p. 155 © Visual Departures, Ltd./Photo Researchers; p. 162 © Jean Pragen/Tony Stone Images; p. 173 © Bob Daemmrich/The Image Works; p. 176 Margaret Bourke-White, Life Magazine © Time Warner; p. 180 © Gilles Mingasson/Gamma-Liaison; p. 201 © F. Carter Smith/Sygma; p. 216 © David R. Frazier Photolibrary; p. 229 © Bob Krist/Tony Stone Images; p. 232 © Richard Bradbury/Tony Stone Images; p. 244 © Richard Pasley/Stock Boston; p. 261 © Larry Mayer/Gamma-Liaison; p. 289 © Wally McNamee/Sygma; p. 293 © Suzanne & Nick Geary/Tony Stone Images; p. 317 © F. Lochon/Gamma-Liaison; p. 343 © Patrick Aventurier/Gamma-Liaison; p. 348 Bettmann Newsphotos; p. 373 © William S. Helsel/Tony Stone Images; p. 391 © Owen Franken/Stock Boston; p. 393 © Patrick Robert/Sygma; p. 401 © Bill Nation/Sygma; p. 417 © Glen Allison/Tony Stone Images; p. 429 © Cameramann International; p. 443 © Alain Le Garsmeur/Tony Stone Images; p. 451 © Alan Levenson; p. 459 © Robert Fried; p. 467 © David R. Frazier Photolibrary; p. 478 © Paul Chesley/Tony Stone Images; p. 483 © Dilip Mehta/Contact Press; p. 493 © Robert Fried; p. 495 © Pablo Bartholomew/Gamma-Liaison; p. 506 © Robert Frerck/Odyssey/Chicago; p. 517 © Robert Fried; p. 534 © Rob Crandall/Stock Boston; p. 553 © James Schnepf/Gamma-Liaison; p. 559 © Schiller/The Image Works; p. 583 © Bob Daemmrich/Stock Boston; p. 589 © Andy Sacks/Tony Stone Images; p. 609 © Robert Frerck/Odyssey/Chicago; p. 624 © David R. Frazier Photolibrary; p. 635 © R. Maiman/Sygma; p. 639 © P. Werner/The Image Works; p. 663 © John Eastcott/YVA Momatiuk/The Image Works; p. 665 © Bob Daemmrich/Tony Stone Images; p. 672 © Kevin H. Stone/Odyssey/Chicago; p. 697 © David R. Frazier Photolibrary; p. 723 © Lisa Quinones/Black Star; p. 725 © Cameramann International; p. 749 © David R. Frazier Photolibrary; p. 754 © Andy Levin/Photo Researchers; p. 773 © Bob Daemmrich; p. 779 © Andy Freeberg; p. 797 © P.F. Bentley/Black Star; p. 808 © Everett Collection; p. 827 © Bob Daemmrich; p. 836 © Keith MacGregor/Tony Stone Images; p. 836 © Buddy Mays/Travel Stock; p. 855 © Jim Harrison/Stock Boston; p. 871 © Mulvehill/The Image Works; p. 883 © Jerry Howard, Positive Images; p. 891 © M. Vertinetti/Photo Researchers; p. 901 © M. Grecco/Stock Boston; p. 909 © Jonathan Nourok/Tony Stone Images; p. 918 © Nicolas Reynard/Gamma-Liaison; p. 926 © Kim Heacox/Tony Stone Images; p. 933 © Bob Daemmrich/Tony Stone Images; p. 942 © Buddy Mays/Travel Stock; p. 946 © Ferdinando Scianna/Magnum Photos; p. 955 © Charles Gupton/Tony Stone Images; p. 959 © Jean-Leo Dugast/Sygma; p. 975 © Fred R. Palmer/Stock Boston; p. 988 © David R. Frazier Photolibrary; p. 997 © Andy Freeberg; p. 1019 © Demetrio Carrasco/Tony Stone Images; p. 1024 © Chris Niedenthal/Black Star; p. 1027 © David Kampfner/Liaison International.

Index

Marginal social costs, 913–914
Marginal utility, 518
    diminishing, see Diminishing marginal
        utility
    utility maximization and, 536–537
Maricopa County Board of Supervisors,
    542
Market(s), 52–53
    barter and money exchanges in, 52
    black (parallel), 159
    capital, see Capital
    definition of, 52
    Eurocurrency, 330–332, 331 (fig.)
    federal funds, 353
    for fishing rights, 115
    foreign exchange, see Exchange rates;
        Foreign exchange entries
    for labor, see Employment; Labor
        demand; Labor market; Labor supply;
        Unemployment; Wage entries
    for medical care, see Health economics
    money, see Money market
    monopolization of, 598–599
    for private property rights, 922–924, 924
        (fig.)
    relative price and, 52–53
    for resources, see Resource(s); specific
        resources, i.e. Capital
Market demand
    determination of, 532–533
    for resources, 751 (fig.), 751–754
Market demand curve, 56, 571
Market failure, 908–927. See also
        Externalities; Pollution; Public goods
    economic efficiency and, 910
Market imperfections, 113
Market share, as strategy, 710 (fig.),
    710–711
Market structures, 594–603, 681–685, 682
    (table). See also Monopolistic compe-
    tition; Monopoly; Oligopoly; Perfect
    competition
    adverse selection and, 684
    brand names and, 682–683
    characteristics of, 595–596
    comparisons of, 601–602, 602 (fig.)
    economic efficiency and, 909–910, 911
        (fig.)
    guarantees and, 683–684
    managerial decisions and, 693–695, 694
        (table)
    as models, 595
    moral hazard and, 685
    resource demand and, 765
Market supply, of labor, 774–776, 776
    (fig.)
Market supply curve, 62–63, 64 (fig.)
    long-run, in perfect competition,
        619–620
Market system, 82–87
    consumer sovereignty and, 82
    flow of resources and, 85
    income determination and, 85–86
    private sectors in, 86, 87–103. See also
        Business firms; Household(s);
        International sector; Private sectors
    public sector in, 108–126. See also
        Government; Public sector

resource allocation and, 82–85, 83 (fig.),
    84 (fig.)
Market value, in gross domestic product,
    133
Marriage, changes in, 855–856, 857–858
Marshall, Tyler, 340
Marubeni, 91 (fig.)
Mary Kay Cosmetics, 619
Matsushita Electric Corporation of
    America, 168
Maxwell House, 701
Mayland, Kenneth T., 312
Mazda, 417
MB (marginal-benefits) curve, externalities
    and, 913–914, 914 (fig.)
MC, see Marginal costs (MC)
Means test, for welfare programs, 901
Median voter theorem, 942–944, 943 (fig.)
Medicaid, 864, 867, 896, 897 (fig.)
Medical care, see Health economics
Medicare, 864, 867
Merchandise, balance of payments and, 161
Mergers, 723, 728. See also Antitrust policy
MES (minimum efficient scale), 571, 573,
    699
Mexico
    black market in foreign exchange in, 159
    per capita real GNP in, 886 (fig.)
    currency of, 158 (table), 695
    debt of, 97
    foreign investment in, 483
    gross national product, population, and
        size of, 433
    immigrants from, 804
    income distribution in, 885 (fig.),
        885–886, 890
    inflation in, 319
    international trade of, 42
    labor force in, 451
    living standard in, 470 (table)
    monetary reforms in, 395 (table)
    NAFTA and, 988, 989
    political risk in, 425
    pollution from, 924
    population growth in, 449 (fig.)
    regulation in, 725
    trade of, 96, 274, 957 (table)
MFC (marginal factor cost), resource
    demand of firm and, 759–764,
    760–762 (fig.)
MFC (most-favored customer) policy, 680
Michel, Kevin, 78
Michigan studies, 227
Microeconomic policy, 118–119
Microeconomics, 13
Microsoft Corporation, 494, 599, 663, 710,
    711, 723, 732
Middle class, in Russia, 905–906
Middle Class Bill of Rights, 824
Milgrom, Paul, 784
Miller, William H., 738n
Miller Brewing, 703
Minimum efficient scale (MES), 571, 573,
    699
Minimum wages, 817 (fig.), 817–819, 818
    (fig.), 824–825
    natural rate of unemployment and, 378
Mining industry, company towns and, 761

Ministry of International Trade and
    Industry (MITI) [Japan], 124, 733
Minorities
    blocked, 473
    discrimination and, see Employment dis-
        crimination
MITI (Ministry of International Trade and
    Industry) [Japan], 124, 733
Mitsubishi, 91 (fig.), 583
Mitsui & Co., 91 (fig.)
M1 money supply, 320–322, 324 (fig.)
    velocity of, 349–350, 350 (fig.)
M2 money supply, 322, 324 (fig.)
    velocity of, 349–350, 350 (fig.)
M3 money supply, 322–323, 324 (fig.)
    velocity of, 349–350, 350 (fig.)
Mobil Oil, 701
Models, 11
    market structures as, 595. See also
        Monopolistic competition; Monopoly;
        Oligopoly; Perfect competition
Modigliani, Franco, 414
Moffett, Matt, 5
Moffit, Robert, 775
Monetarist economics, 403–407
    comparison with other schools,
        410–411, 412 (table)
    model of, 404
    on policymakers' role, 404–406, 405
        (fig.)
A Monetary History of the United States,
    1867-1960 (Friedman and Schwartz),
    406
Monetary overhang, transition to capital-
    ism and, 1028
Monetary policy, 119–120, 342–367,
    370–371. See also Federal Reserve
    System (Fed); Money supply
    Federal Reserve System and, 343–347.
        See also Federal Reserve System (Fed)
    fiscal policy related to, 391–395
    foreign exchange market intervention
        and, 357–360
    goals of, 347–350, 356, 356 (fig.)
    international macroeconomic linkages
        and, 428–430
    monetary reforms and, 393–394, 395
        (table)
    money and equilibrium income and,
        365–366, 366 (fig.)
    money demand and, 361–365
    tools of, 350–356
    transition to capitalism and, 1028–1029
Monetary reforms, 393–394, 395 (table)
Money, 317–326. See also Currencies;
    Exchange rates
    base (high-powered), 394n
    commodity, 321
    demand for, see Money demand
    functions of, 318–320
    hoarding of, 321
    opportunity cost of holding, see Interest
        rate(s)
    quantity theory of, 348–350
    supply of, see Federal Reserve System
        (Fed); Monetary policy; Money supply
    transition to capitalism and, 1029
    velocity of, 348

Selected U.S. Data

Year	Population	Civilian Labor Force	Civilian Labor Force Participation Rate	Civilian Unemployment Rate	Consumer Price Inflation Rate	Interest Rates on Treasury Bills
		Thousands of persons 14 years of age and over				
1940	132,122	55,460	55.7	14.6	.7	.014
1941	133,402	55,910	56.0	9.9	9.9	.103
1942	134,860	56,410	57.2	4.7	9.0	.326
1943	136,739	55,540	58.7	1.9	3.0	.373
1944	138,397	54,630	58.6	1.2	2.3	.375
1945	139,928	53,860	57.2	1.9	2.2	.375
1946	141,389	57,520	55.8	3.9	18.1	.375
1947	144,126	60,168	56.8	3.9	8.8	.594
		Thousands of persons 16 years of age and over				
1947		59,350	58.3	3.9		
1948	146,631	60,621	58.8	3.8	3.0	1.040
1949	149,188	61,286	58.9	5.9	−2.1	1.102
1950	152,271	62,208	59.2	5.3	5.9	1.218
1951	154,878	62,017	59.2	3.3	6.0	1.552
1952	157,553	62,138	59.0	3.0	.8	1.766
1953	160,184	63,015	58.9	2.9	.7	1.931
1954	163,026	63,643	58.8	5.5	−.7	.953
1955	165,931	65,023	59.3	4.4	.4	1.753
1956	168,903	66,552	60.0	4.1	3.0	2.658
1957	171,984	66,929	59.6	4.3	2.9	3.267
1958	174,882	67,639	59.5	6.8	1.8	1.839
1959	177,830	68,369	59.3	5.5	1.7	3.405
1960	180,671	69,628	59.4	5.5	1.4	2.928
1961	183,691	70,459	59.3	6.7	.7	2.378
1962	186,538	70,614	58.8	5.5	1.3	2.778
1963	189,242	71,833	58.7	5.7	1.6	3.157
1964	191,889	73,091	58.7	5.2	1.0	3.549
1965	194,303	74,455	58.9	4.5	1.9	3.954
1966	196,560	75,770	59.2	3.8	3.5	4.881
1967	198,712	77,347	59.6	3.8	3.0	4.321
1968	200,706	78,737	59.6	3.6	4.7	5.339
1969	202,677	80,734	60.1	3.5	6.2	6.677
1970	205,052	82,771	60.4	4.9	5.6	6.458
1971	207,661	84,382	60.2	5.9	3.3	4.348
1972	209,896	87,034	60.4	5.6	3.4	4.071
1973	211,909	89,429	60.8	4.9	8.7	7.041
1974	213,854	91,949	61.3	5.6	12.3	7.886
1975	215,973	93,775	61.2	8.5	6.9	5.838
1976	218,035	96,158	61.6	7.7	4.9	4.989
1977	220,239	99,099	62.3	7.1	6.7	5.265
1978	222,585	102,251	63.2	6.1	9.0	7.221
1979	225,055	104,962	63.7	5.8	13.3	10.041
1980	227,726	106,940	63.8	7.1	12.5	11.506
1981	229,966	108,670	63.9	7.6	8.9	14.029
1982	232,188	110,204	64.0	9.7	3.8	10.686
1983	234,307	111,550	64.0	9.6	3.8	8.63
1984	236,348	113,544	64.4	7.5	3.9	9.58
1985	238,466	115,461	64.8	7.2	3.8	7.48
1986	240,651	117,834	65.3	7.0	1.1	5.98
1987	242,804	119,865	65.6	6.2	4.4	5.82
1988	245,021	121,669	65.9	5.5	4.4	6.69
1989	247,342	123,869	66.5	5.3	4.6	8.12
1990	249,911	124,787	66.4	5.5	6.1	7.51
1991	252,643	125,303	66.0	6.7	3.1	5.42
1992	255,407	126,982	66.3	7.4	2.9	3.45
1993	258,120	128,040	66.2	6.8	2.7	3.02
1994	260,651	131,056	66.6	6.1	2.7	4.29

Source: *Economic Report of the President,* 1995.

U.S. International Transactions

Year	Merchandise			Services		
	Exports	Imports	Net	Net Military Transactions	Net Travel and Transportation Receipts	Other Services, Net
1946	11,764	−5,067	6,697	−424	733	310
1947	16,097	−5,973	10,124	−358	946	145
1948	13,265	−7,557	5,708	−351	374	175
1949	12,213	−6,874	5,339	−410	230	208
1950	10,203	−9,081	1,122	−56	−120	242
1951	14,243	−11,176	3,067	169	298	254
1952	13,449	−10,838	2,611	528	83	309
1953	12,412	−10,975	1,437	1,753	−238	307
1954	12,929	−10,353	2,576	902	−269	305
1955	14,424	−11,527	2,897	−113	−297	299
1956	17,556	−12,803	4,753	−221	−361	447
1957	19,562	−13,291	6,271	−423	−189	482
1958	16,414	−12,952	3,462	−849	−633	486
1959	16,458	−15,310	1,148	−831	−821	573
1960	19,650	−14,758	4,892	−1,057	−964	639
1961	20,108	−14,537	5,571	−1,131	−978	732
1962	20,781	−16,260	4,521	−912	−1,152	912
1963	22,272	−17,048	5,224	−742	−1,309	1,036
1964	25,501	−18,700	6,801	−794	−1,146	1,161
1965	26,461	−21,510	4,951	−487	−1,280	1,480
1966	29,310	−25,493	3,817	−1,043	−1,331	1,497
1967	30,666	−26,866	3,800	−1,187	−1,750	1,742
1968	33,626	−32,991	635	−596	−1,548	1,759
1969	36,414	−35,807	607	−718	−1,763	1,964
1970	42,469	−39,866	2,603	−641	−2,038	2,330
1971	43,319	−45,579	−2,260	653	−2,345	2,649
1972	49,381	−55,797	−6,416	1,072	−3,063	2,965
1973	71,410	−70,499	911	740	−3,158	3,406
1974	98,306	−103,811	−5,505	165	−3,184	4,231
1975	107,088	−98,185	8,903	1,461	−2,812	4,854
1976	114,745	−124,228	−9,483	931	−2,558	5,027
1977	120,816	−151,907	−31,091	1,731	−3,565	5,680
1978	142,075	−176,002	−33,927	857	−3,573	6,879
1979	184,439	−212,007	−27,568	−1,313	−2,935	7,251
1980	224,250	−249,750	−25,500	−1,822	−997	8,912
1981	237,044	−265,067	−28,023	−844	144	12,552
1982	211,157	−247,642	−36,485	112	−992	13,209
1983	201,799	−268,901	−67,102	−563	−4,227	14,095
1984	219,926	−332,418	−112,492	−2,547	−8,438	14,227
1985	215,915	−338,088	−122,173	−4,390	−9,798	14,266
1986	223,344	−368,425	−145,081	−5,181	−7,382	18,855
1987	250,208	−409,765	−159,557	−3,844	−6,481	17,900
1988	320,230	−447,189	−126,959	−6,315	−1,511	19,961
1989	362,116	−477,365	−115,249	−6,726	5,071	26,558
1990	389,303	−498,336	−109,033	−7,567	8,978	28,811
1991	416,913	−490,981	−74,068	−5,485	17,957	33,124
1992	440,361	−536,458	−96,097	−3,034	20,885	37,862
1993	456,866	−589,441	−132,575	−763	20,840	36,773